The Vedic Experience
Mantramañjarī

मन्त्रमञ्जरी

Pūrṇa kumbha

The Vedic Experience
Mantramañjarī

An
Anthology of the Vedas for Modern Man
and Contemporary Celebration

edited and translated with introductions and notes
by

Raimundo Panikkar

with the collaboration of
N. Shanta, M. A. R. Rogers, B. Bäumer, M. Bidoli

UNIVERSITY OF CALIFORNIA PRESS
BERKELEY LOS ANGELES

University of California Press
Berkeley and Los Angeles, California

ISBN: 0-520-02854-6
Library of Congress Catalog Card Number: 74-16714

Printed in the United States of America

शान्तायै समर्पयामि

VEDADĪPA

The World of the Vedas

II: Germination and Growth

III: Blossoming and Fullness

IV: Fall and Decay

V: Death and Dissolution

ABBREVIATIONS

AA	Aitareya Āraṇyaka
AB	Aitareya Brāhmaṇa
AGS	Āśvalāyana Gṛhya Sūtra
ApSS	Āpastambīya Śrauta Sūtra
AU	Aitareya Upaniṣad
AV	Atharva Veda
B	Brāhmaṇa
BG	Bhagavad Gītā
BGS	Baudhāyana Gṛhya Sūtra
BhagPur	Bhāgavata Purāṇa
BrDev	Bṛhad Devatā
BS	Brahma Sūtra
BU	Bṛhadāraṇyaka Upaniṣad
CU	Chāndogya Upaniṣad
GopB	Gopatha Brāhmaṇa
GS	Gṛhya Sūtra
HGS	Hiraṇyakeśi Gṛhya Sūtra
IsU	Īśa Upaniṣad
JabU	Jābāla Upaniṣad
JaimB	Jaiminīya Brāhmaṇa
JaimUB	Jaiminīya Upaniṣad Brāhmaṇa
KaivU	Kaivalya Upaniṣad
KathU	Kaṭha Upanisad
KausB	Kauṣītaki Brāhmaṇa
KausS	Kauśika Sūtra
KausU	Kauṣītaki Upaniṣad

KenU	Kena Upaniṣad
MB	Mahābhārata
MahanarU	Mahānārāyaṇa Upaniṣad
MaitB	Maitrī Brāhmaṇa
MaitS	Maitrāyaṇi Saṁhitā
MaitU	Maitrī Upaniṣad
MandKar	Māṇḍūkya Kārikā
MandU	Māṇḍūkya Upaniṣad
Manu	Mānava Dharmaśāstra (Manu Smṛti)
MundU	Muṇḍaka Upaniṣad
PGS	Pāraskara Gṛhya Sūtra
PaingU	Paiṅgala Upaniṣad
PranagniU	Prāṇāgnihotra Upaniṣad
PrasnU	Praśna Upaniṣad
R	Rāmāyaṇa
RV	Ṛg Veda
S	Saṁhitā
SB	Śatapatha Brāhmaṇa
SGS	Śāṅkhāyana Gṛhya Sūtra
SSS	Śāṅkhāyana Śrauta Sūtra
SuryU	Sūrya Upaniṣad
SU	Śvetāśvatara Upaniṣad
SV	Sāma Veda
TA	Taittirīya Āraṇyaka
TB	Taittirīya Brāhmaṇa
TMB	Tāṇḍya Mahā Brāhmaṇa
TS	Taittirīya Saṁhitā
TU	Taittirīya Upaniṣad
U	Upaniṣad
V	Veda
YS	Yoga Sūtra
YV	Yajur Veda (Vājasaneyi Saṁhitā)
adj.	adjective
caus.	causative
f.	feminine
Gk.	Greek
Lat.	Latin
ll.	lines
lit.	literally
loc.	locative
m.	masculine
n.	neuter
part.	participle
pl.	plural
sg.	singular
v.	verse
vv.	verses

CONTENTS

PREFACE

Vāyu

What would you save from a blazing house? A precious, irreplaceable manuscript containing a message of salvation for mankind, or a little group of people menaced by the same fire? The situation is real and not for this writer alone: How can you be just an "intellectual," concerned with truth, or just a "spiritual," busy with goodness, when Men desperately cry for food and justice? How can you follow a contemplative, philosophical, or even religious path when the world shouts for action, engagement, and politics? And, conversely, how can you agitate for a better world or for the necessary revolution when what is most needed is serene insight and right evaluation? That the burning house is not my private property should be clear to all my neighbors on this earth of ours. But to speak about myself alone: this anthology is the product of an existential overcoming of my concrete situation by denying the ultimate validity of such a dilemma. If I am not ready to save the manuscript from the fire, that is, if I do not take my intellectual vocation seriously, putting it before everything else even at the risk of appearing inhuman, then I am also incapable of helping people in more concrete and proximate ways. Conversely, if I am not alert and ready to save people from a conflagration, that is to say, if I do not take my spiritual calling in all earnestness, sacrificing to it all else, even my own life, then I shall be unable to help in rescuing the manuscript. If I do not involve myself in the concrete issues of my time, and if I do not open my house to all the winds of the world, then anything I may produce from an ivory tower will be barren and cursed. Yet if I do not shut doors and windows in order to concentrate on this work, then I will not be able to offer anything of value to my neighbors.

Indeed, the manuscript may emerge charred and the people may emerge blistered, but the intensity of the one concern has helped me in the other. The dilemma is not whether to choose the Monastery or the Ballroom, Hardwar or Chanakyapuri (Vatican or Quirinal), Tradition or Progress, Politics or Academia, Church or State, Justice or Truth. In a word, reality is not a matter of either-or, spirit or matter, contemplation or action, written message or living people, East or West, theory or praxis or, for that matter, the divine or the human. Indeed, perhaps the fundamental insight of this book is that there is no essence without existence, no existence without an essence.

This study emerges out of an existential struggle between concentrating on the writing of it at the risk of letting people be trapped in the fire, and helping persons out of the house at the price of abandoning the manuscript altogether. The act of faith behind this study is to have denied the inevitability of a choice, not by an act of the will alone or of the mind alone, but by allowing circumstances to guide my intellect, my spirit, and indeed my whole life. Is not the entire Vedic experience based on the life-giving sacrifice.

When, a decade ago, the urgent and long-standing need for a study of this kind pressed on me so hard that it could no longer be resisted, a tantalizing alternative seemed to present itself: either to become a trained mechanic, in Sanskrit and English at least, or else to become a trusty pilot in Vedic and other personal flights. Circumstances again decided for me, and this work has been rendered possible by the unusual team of people collaborating with me. One could hardly have found a more unselfish and devoted group of helpers than the one that has made this anthology possible. One does not fly alone.

First of all, I want to thank the group of collaborators. N. Shanta, to whom this anthology is dedicated, has been decisive in determining the entire gestalt of the book. M. A. R. Rogers has revised the style, especially allowing the texts to reflect the beauty of the original through the genius of the English language. B. Bäumer and M. Bidoli have gone through the Sanskrit texts and contributed creatively to an accurate version of them. Without these collaborators this anthology could not have been completed.

Thanks are also given to a living artist, to a modern scholar, and also to an ancient monk. The entrance *maṇḍala* and the vignettes of the book are original of A. Kunze who, according to tradition, drew them while meditating on the texts. The sanskrit syllables appearing in some of the drawings are *bīja-mantras,* which symbolize, at least partially, the meaning of the corresponding section.

The *devanāgarī* letters illustrating the anthology are reproductions of original xylographs belonging to Sri Lokesh Chandra, Director of the International Academy of Indian Culture, New-Delhi. They are from *Shuji-shu,* a Japanese *"Collection of bījas"* woodprinted by Bhikṣu Chozen in A.D. 1661-1673. They are also *bīja-mantras,* that is, mystical syllables or *akṣara devatās,* each of them symbolizing some Vedic deity as indicated below the reproduction.

Without R. H. Hooker and U. M. Vesci, many a blunder would have remained unchecked; without R. S. Bhattacharya, P. Y. Deshpandey, D. Mumford, and many other friends the book would not have reached its present form. Nor do I forget K. V. C. Subramanyan and A. K. Karmakar, who have typed and retyped the manuscript so many times that they know may of its mantras by heart.

I have also to thank the Vedic Gods and all other spirits who have blessed this venture. I ask them and the reader to pardon the chasm that exists between the real *mantra* an this *mañjarī.* May both Gods and readers by their acceptance of this *mantramañjarī* forgive and forget its compiler so that the silent, Divine Mystery may flow freely through whatever living mantras this anthology may elicit. The feelings of humility, which in many prefaces are somewhat perfunctorily expressed, are in this instance both genuine and overwhelming. How is it possible to touch upon almost all the relevant and central problems of Man, over a time span of at least four millennia, and to dare to present a seed that may germinate elsewhere and a beam capable of setting light to what it touches? If this is so, then even the decade of life and work compressed into this anthology would be no more than a foolish undertaking or an impossible task. How could I venture even to attempt what I have done? I simply wonder at my daring. But, having done something of which I may well repent, I still hope that some readers will not regret that I could not have done otherwise.

R. P.

Varanasi on the Ganges
1964-1976

न वि जानामि यदिवेदमस्मि
निण्यः संनद्धो मनसा चरामि ।
यदा मागन् प्रथमजा ऋतस्या-
दिद् वाचो अश्नुवे भागमस्याः ॥

ऋग्वेदः १.१६४.३७

What thing I am I do not know.
I wander secluded, burdened by my mind.
When the Firstborn of Truth has come to me
I receive a share in that selfsame Word.

RV I, 164, 37

Om

GENERAL INTRODUCTION

The Entrance Maṇḍala shows the wheel of the cosmos, of which the center is the great original and ever-present sacrifice: "this sacrifice is the navel of the world" (RV I, 164, 35), as is written in the inner wheel below the circle containing the 5 beings fit for sacrifice according to old aryan belief. "Man verily is sacrifice" (SB I, 3, 2, 1) and "with desire for heaven may he sacrifice" is written in the upper part of the same 5-spoked wheel "on which all beings stand" (RV I, 164, 13), symbolizing the fivefold world—5 elements, 5 senses, etc. (cf. Upaniṣads). The universe, divided into 6 world spaces (RV I, 164, 6)—3 for sky-heaven, 3 for earth— is surrounded and set in motion by the 12-spoked wheel of time (RV I, 164, 11) which is divided into 12 sections representing the 12 moons of the lunar year, each of which contains two halves, the dark and the bright.

Note: Man, with capital M, stands for the human being (of both sexes) as distinct from the Gods and other living beings. When corresponding to the German *man,* the French *on,* or the English *one,* however, the word has not been capitalized. In the translated texts, except for Part VII, and a few other exceptions, "man" has also not been capitalized. Since the English language has not (yet?) introduced an *utrum,* as an androgynous gender, the pronoun will have to be the morphologically masculine.

A. THE VEDIC EPIPHANY

He who knows not the eternal
syllable of the Veda,
the highest point upon which
all the Gods repose,
what business has he with the Veda?
Only its knowers
sit here in peace and concord.

RV I, 164, 39

One of the most stupendous manifestations of the Spirit is undoubtedly that which has been handed down to us under the generic name of the Vedas. The Vedic Epiphany belongs to the heritage of mankind, and therefore its deepest function is best served, as is that of many of the religious and cultural values of mankind, not by scrupulously preserving it, as if we were zealous guardians of a closed and almost hidden treasure, but by sharing it in a spirit of fellowship with humanity at large. This sharing, however, should be neither a profanation under the pretext of bringing profit to others nor an exploitation under the guise of scholarship and scientific knowledge. Rather, it should be a living communication, or even a communion, but one that is free from any tinge of propaganda or proselytization. It is, then, not mere information that these pages intend to convey; it could be that their message has transforming power.

This anthology aims at presenting the Vedas as a human experience that is still valid and capable of enriching and challenging modern Man, as he seeks to fulfill his responsibility in an age in which, for better or for worse, he is inseparably linked with his fellows and can no longer afford to live in isolation. Experiences cannot be transmitted but they can be described, and they can thus serve as stimuli to trigger our own experiences. An experience, as the word itself suggests, is something we go through, a threshold we cross, an enclosure into which we trespass, a nonrefundable outlay, an irreversible process. This anthology is also an invitation to appropriate for ourselves the basic experience of Vedic Man, not because it is interesting or ancient, but because it is human and thus belongs to us all. Indeed, among the many experiences of mankind, the Vedic experience is one that will evoke a responsive movement in that part of us which is numbed by the heavy pressures of modern life.

We do not claim that what we have termed the *Vedic Experience* is precisely identical to that of Vedic Man. We may not be in a position to appropriate the intimate personal experience of a past generation. Our main concern is to make possible the Vedic experience of modern Man and to describe what modern Man may usefully understand and assimilate by reenacting an experience that, because it is part of the total human experience, has left behind it clues and traces which may be important to follow. Thus it is our own personal Vedic experience that "happens."

The objection to the present Sanskrit title is that according to the strictest tradition the Brāhmaṇas and Upaniṣads are not mantras. For this reason *śrutimañjarī* and *vedamañjarī* were also considered, as well as *āmnāyamañjarī*. The final choice, *mantramañjarī*, is based on two reasons, both of which call for explanation.

As already suggested, it is hoped that this anthology may present the Vedas as a monument of universal religious—and thus deeply human—significance. Yet in so doing we do not want to hurt the feelings or invade the rights of the different religions of the world, especially of those grouped under Hinduism. The Vedas, like the Bible or the Qur'ān, are linked forever to the particular religious sources from which they historically sprang. Eclecticism here would be a damaging procedure. We do not intend to loosen the roots from their historical identity, but we believe that this rootedness does not preclude further growth. We do not dispute the rights of the past but only the freezing of living traditions. In this sense the word "mantra" seems better able to sustain growth than the words *āmnāya, veda,* and *śruti*. By not choosing a more traditional word, we respect the rights of orthodoxy; yet by our choice of the word *mantra* we claim the right to interpret a traditional value in a way that permits precisely what tradition intends, namely, that it be transmitted to subsequent generations in a way that is still relevant and important to them. *Mantra* stands here for the sacred, and *mañjarī* (a word of decidedly profane usage meaning cluster of blossoms) for the secular, dimension of Man. A *mañjarī* (*margarita*) is also a pearl.

The aim and character of this study may perhaps be best explained by commenting on the four concepts contained in the subtitle.

An Anthology

1 You do not pluck flowers, much less arrange them in a bouquet, simply for yourself alone. Similarly you do not collect mantras for selfish purposes, much less compose a *mañjarī* for solipsistic enjoyment. Furthermore, when you decide to arrange a bunch of flowers you do not confine yourself to one single color or one single scent. An anthology is a whole universe. It presents a whole world of objects and of subjects. Moreover, you do not pick the upper portions only, beautiful though they may be; you take hold of the plant deep down near its root, for you may want to put the flowers in water or even in your own garden, so that they may flourish longer and perhaps even blossom again. Nor is this all. The water and the light which are so essential to growth or transplantation both come from outside.

A Vedic anthology seems to be appropriate in our age, when the world is so much in need of serene and balanced wisdom and when the Indian tradition has so powerful an appeal, especially for the younger generation, despite the fact that it is generally known only from secondary or even more remote sources. A Vedic anthology may make direct and fruitful knowledge of the Vedas available to a wider range of people than the small elite of pandits and indologists. The situation of the Vedas today is comparable with that of the Bible in the West a couple of centuries ago, especially in Roman Catholic circles. Theoretically the Bible was central to their entire spirituality, but in actual practice it was almost unknown, and Christian life was fostered mainly from secondary sources. Tradition helped Man to maintain a living contact with "the Word of God," but one of its sources was largely ignored. The Vedas are still too much neglected, not only in the world at large but also in their country of origin.

A bouquet of flowers also has something to do with love and gallantry, because it is usually presented to somebody as a gift symbolizing service, admiration, dedication, and, ultimately, love. This anthology is no different. It is offered to the world at large, to those who have no contact whatsoever with the world of the Vedas as well as to those who, though coming from that same tradition, have lost direct contact with their sources. It is a bouquet of living flowers. Yet a bouquet is not the whole flower-covered valley or the actual field where the flowers grow. It is the sacrificial offering of the meadow which deprives itself of its own ornament in order to offer it to the beloved. An anthology will always remain an anthology. It is plucked from the soil where it grew, from the language in which it was first couched, from the life by which it was sustained, and yet transplants to fresh soil and even grafts onto different plants are possible. What, after all, is the original meaning of "culture"?

Finally, a bouquet is a selection, a representative choice, for if it is to be of special worth all the flowers of the field must be represented in it. It is the same with an authentic anthology, and here lies the crux of the matter: this anthology claims to represent the canon, as one might say, of the whole *śruti* or Indian revelation; it purports to contain the central message of the Vedas, to embody their essence, their *rasa*. Just as a complete bouquet contains all seven colors of the rainbow and all the fragrance of the fields, this anthology seeks to encompass the whole range of the Vedic experience and to convey the main body of the Vedic Revelation.

The criterion of selection obviously cannot be purely sectarian; it must be universally acceptable and it must spring from a simple human experience. The pattern adopted here seems to be the most basic pattern offered by nature, by Man, by life on earth, and by history. It is the pattern that seems to be built into the very core of being itself. It is as much a geological pattern as a historical and cultural one. Significantly enough, it seems to be also the same initiatory pattern that is found almost universally. There is a preparation before a given community comes into the fullness of life; there are growth and decay, and also a way of removal that will facilitate the continuation and survival of the particular group. Yet most peoples and cultures live their lives without much self-reflection of this type. Part VII of this volume, without introductions and without notes, reflects this situation. The seven parts of this anthology follow this pattern:

I. *Dawn and Birth*. Preparation for emergence into existence, the tilling of the ground, or preexistence and bursting into being, into life.

II. *Germination and Growth*. The beginning, the striving, the affirmation of identity, the settling down in the realm of existence.

III. *Blossoming and Fullness*. The acme, the reaching of plenitude, of maturity, the zenith.

IV. *Fall and Decay*. The beginning of the downward path, the discovery that nothing resists the acids of time and that nobody is immune from the corrosion of existence.

V. *Death and Dissolution*. The destiny of all existing things, and the price that must be paid for having been alive and for having been a bearer of existence in time and space.

VI. *New Life and Freedom*. The marvelous mystery of being, the reemergence of life out of the ordeal of death, the disclosure that life is immortal, that being is unfathomable, and that bliss and reality are capable of self-renewal.

VII. *Twilight*. The last part of this anthology, like the ribbon that ties the bouquet, has an altogether different character from the rest. It binds together all that has been explained and integrates all that has been described. It brings back the living unity that the glare of the single aspects may have endangered.

The structure of the parts is not difficult to grasp. Each part is introduced by at least one mantra or antiphon and consists of two or more sections, which in turn have various subsections of several chapters, all of them numbered for easy reference and provided with a double title, English and Sanskrit. The chapters constitute the text proper. The introductions to parts, sections, subsections, and chapters are not intended as commentaries or interpretations of the texts. They are simply designed to introduce the reader to the understanding of the Vedic texts.

There is an inbuilt order in the structure of every part. Some features are easily detectable, such as the chronological order used whenever possible without disturbing the internal unity of the part, section, or chapter. But the function of any structure is to sustain the construct without being unnecessarily conspicuous. We do not feel the need now to spell out the strenuous preliminary work of digging the foundations, selecting the texts, arranging and rearranging them, and changing the presentation according to the findings, for it is not a question of superimposing a scheme but of discovering a pattern.

Clearly the main emphasis is on the texts; they speak for themselves and impart ideas that cannot be included in any introduction. This book, therefore, is neither a commentary nor a treatise on the Vedas, but a version of the Vedas themselves, accompanied by classifications and explanations. In a way the latter are part of the translation itself, and thus the version of the actual text can be more literal and can better convey its complex meaning. Reading the text may not always be easy, and the meaning may not always be apparent at first sight. Thus not only attention and concentration are required, but also what the Vedic tradition requested from the students of Vedic lore: dedication and commitment, not, of course, to a particular view or to a sectarian interpretation but to the truth as one sees it. In other words, this book is not an easy one to be taken lightly; much less is it a mere object of curiosity. It demands prayer, or meditation. It is a book to turn to when one is confronted with an existential personal problem. Since the answers it gives come from the deepest layers of mankind's experience, it does not allow us to be satisfied with the superficial answers that may emerge out of a limited individual memory or from contemporary and collective experiences. It is wise to remember that human memory and experience do not need to be reduced to those of the individual. One's real age is not necessarily to be reckoned by the number of times one's eyes have seen the sun encircle the earth.

The Vedic experience may perhaps refresh a man's memory of his life on earth; it may be a reminder that he himself as well as his ancestors (though not only in and through them) has accumulated the most extraordinary experiences and has reached a depth of vision, feeling, and life which he now urgently needs to rediscover if he is to succeed in breasting the waves of the ocean of technology, science, and other modern devices which threaten his very survival. The Vedic experience may perhaps disclose, not an alternative to the modern view of life and the world, which would probably solve no problem and would certainly prove alienating, but an already existing, although often hidden, dimension of Man himself. It does not simply give "information" about notions of the past, but truly "in-forms" the present by allowing that dimension to appear and actually revealing it as a constituent part of Man's personhood. It is not only my individual past that is present in me; the history of Man too has accumulated in the cave of my heart, to use a Upaniṣadic expression; or, to put the same thought in another way, it is in the dendrites of my nervous system and in the DNA molecules. All these things are far older than my actual chronological age.

Of the Vedas

2 This anthology is not a book on Indian philosophy or even on Hindu spirituality, and much less is it a typical work of Indology, at least in the strict and perhaps nearly obsolete sense of that term. It is not an attempt to scrutinize the past for its own sake. It is rather an account of the Vedic Revelation, understood as an unveiling of depths that still resound in the heart of modern Man, so that he may become more conscious of his own human heritage and thus of the springs of his personal being. Thus the Vedic experience introduces nothing alien to modern Man, but helps him to realize his own life and emphasizes an often neglected aspect of his own being. In this sense the Vedas occupy a privileged position in the crystallized culture of Man. They are neither primitive nor modern. Not being primitive, they present a depth, a critical awareness, and a sophistication not shown by many other ancient cultures. Not being modern, they exhale a fragrance and present an appeal that the merely modern does not possess.

This anthology deals with what is here called Vedic lore, not with the whole of Indian religiousness or exclusively with Brahmanism. Rather it deals with that portion of the human experience which is expressed in condensed form in these amazing documents of the *śruti*, the product of the encounter of two cultures in the second millennium B.C. which gave birth to more than one world view.

Vedic studies have not always been free of ideological and religious enthusiasms of both a positive and a negative kind. This quality imparted liveliness to the study of the Vedas but it has also sometimes resulted in unnecessary religious bias and political overtones. Thus, while some have seen in the Vedas only the product of a "Vedic galimatias" or of a primitive mentality disposed toward magic, others have discovered the supreme manifestation of truth and the final unsurpassable revelation.

This book aims, insofar as possible, at being free of all peculiar preconceptions and particular value judgments. The *śruti* must be rescued from the monopoly of a single group, whether it be a scholarly group of pandits and indologists or an active religiopolitical faction, though of course the Vedas may legitimately be viewed from any of these perspectives. We dare to hope, however, that the vantage point of this anthology is more universal and more central. It sees the Vedas as a revelation, as a disclosure of something that enriches the human experience without elaborating on the nature of that something. We have tried to avoid particular religious or philosophical assumptions without going to the opposite extreme of regarding the Vedas as mere "objective" documents for purely scholarly research.

We do not speculate about the message of one of the most ancient documents of the Indo-European world. Innumerable schools in the East from time immemorial and several generations of scholars in the West have carried on the laborious but rewarding task of Vedic interpretation. No student of the Vedas today can ignore the work done by past generations of sages and indologists of both East and West. As compiler of this anthology, I have had to learn from all schools, ancient and modern, in order to understand what the Vedas say; I have used tools I myself would have been incapable of forging. My chief concern is to give the results of my reading with objective authenticity. Very few people today accept the possibility of an essential objectivity, that is, of a presuppositionless system and an objective world of concepts to which everybody has access. On the other hand, there are people today who would like to learn what the Vedas have to teach them. These people may not care for nor believe in essential objectivity. Yet they have an existential attitude that rejects merely subjective intentions of an apologetic or propagandistic nature; these people want to be confronted with the text itself, not simply because it flatters them or reinforces what they wish to hear, but because they are ready to consider the Vedic Revelation as a living document. Such an attitude relegates to second place what religionists or scholars think about the matter. It does not despise scholarship, but it is a postscholastic attitude.

Let us consider, for example, the nature of the Gods. Many well-known hypotheses about the Gods have been put forward by both Indian and foreign students. Although this book does not stress the idea of the Vedic Gods as cosmic powers, neither does it regard them as mere expressions of Man's psyche. It does not assume that there is one God with sundry little gods acting as his serving spirits or demons; nor does it, by the use of purely historical data, trace the origins of the Gods to certain prehistoric powers acting in history in or through the minds and beliefs of different cultural periods. This, however, does not mean that it views the Gods with a skeptical eye, as if they were merely subjective factors. On the contrary, it assumes that the Gods are real, but it does not elaborate on either the nature or the degree of their reality. Moreover, this anthology aspires to speak a language that makes sense to the "believer" as well as to the "agnostic," to those who give one interpretation to the phenomena as well as to those who give another.

In order to avoid speaking of God in the plural, which monotheism cannot tolerate, it became normal for European languages to write the plural with a small letter, while reserving the capital for the singular, just as we write beings and Being. And indeed the Gods are not the plural of the monotheistic God. We would have preferred to write simply *devas* for Gods, but the problem of the singular would have remained. Is *deva* God or merely a god? Certainly it depends on the context. Even then, where does one draw the dividing line between symbols of the divine representing God or one aspect or one name of him and the minor deities which may even include the sense organs? Because of this difficulty we have decided to keep the ambivalence of the word and write it with a capital letter, except when it clearly refers to a plainly human feature and is thus translated differently.

Contemporary Man tends so much to politicize everything, even though he may do so under the cloak of sociology, that it seems important to stress that this anthology is not to be classified as pro- or anti-Aryan, in favor of or against either Brahmanism or popular forms of religion, in support of or opposed to the idea that India is mainly Vedic India or of the notion that there is such a thing as an Indo-European commonwealth. We have taken no sides on any of these issues. Within the Indian context, for instance, we do not set out to prove that the most important factor in the religiousness of the people of India is the Vedas or that the Vedas constitute Brahmanic wisdom. Yet we do not affirm the reverse. Within the global context we do not insist on the higher value of written tradition or of the so-called greater or major religions; nor do we assert that Indo-European Man has achieved a monument of civilization unparalleled by other cultures. This study simply says what it says without implying anything about what it does not say. To commend one path or to praise one people or to present the positive aspects of one particular religious form is not to denigrate or to minimize other values and other insights. This anthology has only one context—humanity itself. The Vedic Revelation belongs to Man and it is as a document of Man that it is here presented. We know well, however, that human texture is still unfinished and thus our context is also limited. The recognition of this limitation keeps us open and humble but also hopeful and serene.

Two paradoxical and dissimilar ideas may be mentioned here as examples of what we mean. The first is an orthodox and the second a heterodox notion, and yet both seem to tend in the same direction, at least for the purpose of this anthology.

We refer, first, to the traditional notion of the *apauruṣeya* or non-authorship, either human or divine, of the Vedas. This theory has often been ridiculed as a contradiction of common sense and as a denial of causal thinking; or it has been taken as simply holding that the Vedas have no "author" who has written them and no "mind" that has thought them. Without entering into the almost endless subtleties of the Mīmāṁsā, we can simply say that at the core of this conception there is a desire to purify our relationship with the text and to avoid any kind of idolatry. Any one of us is the author of the Vedas when we read, pray, and understand them. Nobody is the author of living words except the one who utters them. The Vedas are living words, and the word is not an instrument of Man but his supreme form of expression. What has no author, according to the *apauruṣeya* insight, is the relation between the word and its meaning or object. The relationship is not an artificial or extrinsic relation caused by somebody. There is no author to posit the type of relationship which exists between the word and its meaning. To do this we would require another relationship and so on ad infinitum. When a word ceases to be a living word, when it ceases to convey meaning, when it is not a word for me, it is not Veda, it does not convey real or saving knowledge.

This conception, paradoxically enough, rescues the Vedas from the grip not only of a certain God functioning as a primal scribe, but also of the Hindu tradition, which cannot be said to be the author of the Vedas. The Vedas without an author cease to be an authoritative book. Only when you become their "author," when through assimilation you are able to utter them, when you yourself are the proper origin, the *auctor* of the text, do the Vedas disclose their authentic "authority." The Vedic Revelation is not the voice of an anthropomorphic Revealer nor the unveiling of the veil that covers reality. In point of fact, the *śruti* is that which is heard (rather than seen), so that the metaphor of unveiling may sometimes be misleading, because it is not by lifting up the veil (and thus seeing the naked reality) that we are going to discover the real, but by realizing that the veil covers and conceals and that the discovery of this fact constitutes the actual revelation. To reveal in this sense is not to unveil, to lift up the veil, but to "reveal" the veil, to make us aware that what we see and all we can see is the veil, and that it is left to us to "guess"—or, as we would say, to "think"—reality, which is made manifest precisely by the veil that covers it. We cannot separate the veil from the thing that is veiled, just as we cannot separate a word from its meaning, or what is heard from what is understood. If I were to lift up the veil of *māyā* I would see nothing. We can see only if we see the veil of *māyā* and recognize it for what it is. The *śruti* is *śruti* when that which is actually heard is not merely the sound but all that there is to be heard, perceived, understood, realized. Our own discovery, our process of discovery, is part of the revelation itself. Only in the spirit are the Vedas Vedas. And now we can understand why for centuries they were neither written down nor expounded to outsiders.

The Vedic Revelation is not primarily a thematic communication of esoteric facts, although a few of its sayings, as, for example, certain passages of the Upaniṣads, disclose some truth that is unknown to the normal range of human experience. But for the and the Brāhmaṇas are reduced to weighty injunctions, the Upaniṣadic part being practically ignored. The Uttara-mīmāṁsā or Vedānta, on the other hand, deals almost exclusively with the Upaniṣads, and even then not as a whole but from a highly specialized perspective, regarding them as embodying saving knowledge which is reduced to the realization of Brahman. Furthermore, the Upaniṣads, which tradition considers part of the *śruti,* incorporate in their structure very little of the four Vedas. It is true that they are supposed to continue them and in point of fact form part of them, but nevertheless their atmosphere is quite different. The Chāndogya Upaniṣad, for instance, one of the most ancient and most important, does not cite a single Vedic mantra; nor do other important Upaniṣads like the Maitrī, Kena, and Māṇḍūkya, though of course there are implicit references. Even the others, when they occasionally do quote the Vedas, adopt the same cryptic and peculiar manner as later tradition does with the Upaniṣads themselves. It is a fact that the Vedas are only partly integrated into later Indian traditions, and yet this very fact gives them a certain universality far beyond the frontiers of Indian culture. They are of Aryan origin but they include undeniably non-Aryan elements; a controversial fact that makes this amazing human document both an imposing monument of cross-cultural interaction and a specific achievement of human vitality.

Yet, when all is said and done, one cannot deny the particular color and character not only of the Indo-European stock but also of the Indian subcontinent. To stress this fact we have followed the usual tradition concerning components of the *śruti,* although, for reasons arising from both external and internal considerations, we have included the Bhagavad Gītā and Gṛhya Sūtras, which certainly do not belong to the traditional *śruti.*

The continuity in Indian tradition is as important as the break we have just mentioned. Yet, just as Hinduism is more an existence than an essence, so too this continuity is not doctrinal but existential. There is a certain physical continuity, an almost bodily belonging, a karmic continuity, which is far more important than doctrinal homogeneity.

An essential feature of any real anthology is that it presents, in the manner of a bouquet, both unity and variety. There is no question about the variety of themes and climates in the Vedic Epiphany, where practically the whole range of human experience is mirrored. Internal unity and harmony, however, are no less important, as emphatically affirmed even in ancient times. The famous fourth aphorism of the Brahma Sūtra (I, 1, 4) says, for example, *tat tu samanvayāt*: "This, indeed, [is] in accordance with the harmony" (of the *śruti*). That is, all passages of the Vedic Revelation have a single purport or ultimate concern, which is (the realization of) Brahman; each text is "in harmony" with the whole. This *samanvaya*, connoting harmony, reconciliation, equanimity, and serenity, is not merely a logical or mental construct, as if the whole *śruti* were a single doctrinal block; nor does it refer simply to unity of intention or purport, for no intention can be totally separated from the ideas it embodies and the aims it intends. The Scriptures do not all teach the same doctrine or possess the same explicit intention, and yet there is a unifying myth, a higher harmony, an existential reconciliation. The bouquet is one, precisely because and not in spite of the fact that it is composed of many flowers.

There are thus both break and continuity in Indian tradition, depending on the angle from which the problem is viewed. In Europe one should avoid confusing Spain with Sweden, but as viewed from India both countries are unmistakably European. The same point could be made about the Vedas and the Indian tradition.

It was only after great hesitation that we decided to omit some texts and to split others up, putting their parts in different places in the book. The use of the notes, however, offers the possibility of a continuous reading, and the notes and the introductions sometimes give the gist of omitted paragraphs. The omissions were not made in order to fit the texts into a Procrustean bed of a preconceived scheme; either the omitted texts are repetitious, or they contribute no substantially new insight, or they are of minor relevance to the overall picture of the Vedic experience. Any gardener knows that if, by mistake, he cuts off parts of a rare plant, in the end the plant will grow stronger and healthier and that the so beautiful landscape will serve as a reminder of his mistake. In rather the same way I am seriously suggesting that this first attempt on our part will be justified only if more competent people plow the field again, turn our efforts upside down, and finally cause them to flourish in a better form.

In order to preserve the identity of the Vedic Revelation and to avoid confusing it with subsequent movements, we avoid direct reference to subsequent developments in the Indian philosophical systems. We eschew above all any comparison with similar or corresponding spiritual movements in other cultures. It has to be confessed that the temptation has been severe and that during the ten years and more that the book has been in preparation an immense amount of material has been gathered which could be of great interest to comparative studies. But I myself have restrained from overstepping the limits of this book, which aims at discovering what the Vedic experience means for modern Man, without forcing him into comparisons and evaluations.

It is perhaps difficult to imagine the intellectual and spiritual asceticism required for such restraint, to understand what it means, for example, to refrain from quoting parallel passages, purposely to disregard the intriguing resemblances to pre-Socratic ideas, to renounce relating the famous maxim of Anaximander, and to let slip the chance of helping to dispel the superficial confrontation between religions by quoting texts and ideas from other sources. To have done otherwise might have been to make a contribution to other fields, but it would have distorted the message of the *śruti* by subordinating it to particular, even if important, problems. The reader may discover for himself some of the hidden threads that constitute, as in the weaving process, the connecting links within the whole fabric of human experience. After all, this work is only a presentation of the texts and does not set out to comment on the meaning of the selected passages. To do that I would need not readers but companions here in Varanasi on the Ganges, so that we might spend together months and years of peaceful fellowship, until such time as dawn might become midday, or midday turn into a moonless night, but always under the stars and above the river.

For Modern Man

3 One may spend much time studying Vedic lore, but our whole enterprise would have little meaning if it was detached from persons and their environment. Our point of reference is modern Man. Yet, as the etymology of the adjective suggests, we do not forget the fleeting and transitory character of what we call modern Man: the contemporary human being in his present though frail mood, Man as he is just now and for the time being: *modo*. Modern Man will soon be modern no longer, and yet we have no key to Man other than modern Man himself; all other "men" are simply

abstractions, for they have already disappeared or have not yet come to be. Even when we come to know our past we do it in terms of modern categories. It is only by accepting the limitations of our concreteness that we can be rooted in truth, and it is only by being true to our own identity that we can become more universal. Thus it is useless to strive after a general validity, which would be artificial and at best limited to the intellectual sphere.

Modern Man may be passing and transient but he is our only real point of reference, because we still live in space and time. He is the gate to the depths of everlasting Man, but the moment we make him into a concept it is this very modern concept that mediates the understanding. Precisely because we think that Man is more than modern Man we try to help him to become aware of some of his roots. Needless to say, not every inhabitant of our planet today is modern Man, cultures are diachronic, and there are many modernities. The modern Man we have in mind is the average reader of a contemporary Western language—a serious, humiliating, but unavoidable limitation. Two settings, among many others that could equally well be emphasized, are here kept in mind when speaking of modern Man: secularism and the transcultural situation.

Modern Man is a secular Man, which does not mean that he is not religious or that he has lost the sense of the sacred. The statement means only that his religiousness and even any sense of sacredness he may possess are both tinged with a secular attitude. "Secular attitude" means a particular temporal awareness that invests time with a positive and real character: the temporal world is seen as important and the temporal play of Man's life and human interactions is taken seriously; the *saeculum,* the *āyus,* is in the foreground. Man can survive on earth, both as a species and as a person, only if he pays careful attention to everything secular. Otherwise he will be swallowed up by the machinery of modern society or the mechanism of cosmic processes. Secular Man is the citizen of a temporal world.

Furthermore, modern Man, owing perhaps to the changes that have taken place in human geography and history, can no longer belong to a homogenous or isolated culture. He is bombarded by ideas, images, and sounds from all four corners of the world. He may have a superficial and even erroneous knowledge of other people, yet cultures mix, ideas intermingle, religions encounter one another, and languages interact and borrow from one another as perhaps never before in human history. The culture of modern Man may not be very stable; in fact he may even be threatened with the loss of all culture, but he is undoubtedly transculturally influenced—and this is true not only for minority groups but for the passive and suffering majority as well.

The fact that we do not comment or explain, much less make comparisons, may allow the Vedic symbols to become living symbols once again and thus to be grafted onto the living growth of modern Man's cultures. Man is in urgent need of developing a global culture. This cannot be done by dialectical methods (useful adjuncts though these may be) but by a rhythmic, natural process. Growth requires assimilation. To assimilate a living symbol is not to interpret it or even to understand it on the merely mental plane. Many traditions refer here to eating the symbol, while other cultures refer to learning and reading, for to read means to select, to gather, not to amass heaps of data, but to collect—and recollect—in that interior center where the assimilation takes place and requires time. Certainly it takes time to read, to pick up, to gather both oneself and others. Our part is to offer a bouquet or, perhaps, a single flower. "The flower is Brahman," says one text (CU III, 5, 1).

How is this offering to be made? Faith is required, but it is not enough to offer the bouquet in the vertical direction. Truth is also needed. There is also a horizon on the horizontal plane. "Faith and Truth are the most sublime pair," says one text (AB VII, 10, or XXXII, 9). In concrete and prosaic words: How is wisdom to be made available? How is it to be made assimilable for those who desire to receive it? Chanting the Vedas to the Gods or reciting them in closed circles may not be enough.

Here we are obliged to take note of a lurking and threatening problem. Instead of elaborating a hermeneutical theory, however, this anthology endeavors to put the theory into practice, to make the "hermeneutical devices" work. We may recall here that Brahman is only one-fourth visible. Within the visible fourth, however, we would like to present some practical and concrete reflections regarding the actual hermeneutical procedure of this anthology: the translation.

The Veda speaks its own new language. Now language is a revelation of the Spirit. Each language has new words and every word represents the disclosure of a new reality. Each language has also a new order in putting words together, and each of these relationships represents a new perspective for looking at reality. Each word is the physical and metaphysical crystallization of centuries of human experience. Through authentic words we can enter into communion with mankind and discover our own links with other people and with the universe. Each texture of words is like fabric on a loom. It has its own color and pattern and through it we share reality with the rest of mankind.

An anthology may be superficially conceived as a mere selection of texts with philological notes added where the translator felt obliged to lay bare his own conscience in regard to the usage of a certain term. But a minimal knowledge of present-day semantics, a certain, even cursory, acquaintance with semantic fields, structures of meaning, morphological senses, etymological limits, semantic shifts, polysemy, and other problems of modern linguistics, some understanding of the issues raised by anthropology and comparative studies in philosophy and religion, and, more especially, a conviction of the symbolic character of every human manifestation, more particularly the linguistic one—in short, an awareness of the impossibility of presenting word-for-word translations or even of achieving the same result by more elaborate paraphrases led the compiler to take the risk, first, of considering the introductions as integral parts of the translation and, second, of treating the criterion of selection as another constituent element of the translation. In this instance philological accuracy consists in human fidelity, and the "correct" version is the outcome of a correct shift of symbols, of such a sort that the reader is brought close to reenacting culturally the Vedic experience for himself.

I am fully aware of the risk, the imperfection, and the limits of such an enterprise. The aim of any translation is not to be a mere transposition of signs. Its purpose is to enable the reader to assimilate the offered material into his or her own life. It aims at making the materials homogenous and so intelligible to the reader. Any translation is provisional in the sense that it is only for the time being, until the moment when illumination comes by itself, the translation is forgotten, and the reader is converted, that is, convinced.

Even so, a certain technique, a particular methodology, and a whole cluster of disciplines are needed. We have used as many forms of interdisciplinary help as possible, but they, like the good ingredients of a tasty dish, remain discreetly in the background, content to enhance the *rasa,* the piquancy, and the flavor; here their function is to promote the understanding of the underlying intuitions. We are not saying that the Vedic fare we offer is predigested or restricted to what we ourselves consider palatable. On the contrary, we present, insofar as possible, the total experience of Vedic Man against the present-day human horizon, in order to make the former intelligible and to enrich, challenge, and perhaps eventually transform the latter. We do not feel a need either to sweeten or otherwise to tamper with the contents of the Vedas, though passages that seem to be less important are given less prominence than other texts.

Furthermore, it is time to give up any claim to a monolithic understanding of cultures and any insistence on the univocal meaning of terms. There is no single word today to convey in another language "Geist," "esprit," and "mind"; much less can we claim that *manas, ṛta,* and *prāṇa* have a single English equivalent each time we come across them. Thus neither a word-for-word nor a paragraph-for-paragraph translation will really satisfy our needs; only the whole *śruti,* the entire Vedic experience, can be conveyed in a meaningful way so that it can enter into our own personal experience. We have to learn another language or another world view, no longer as we used to learn a foreign idiom, but as we learn our own language. Children learning to speak do not refer to an objectified world, nor do they relate the particular word of one language to a corresponding word in another language; they assimilate, they understand, they use a word to express a state of consciousness and eventually a reality which is not disconnected from the word they are using. They learn their own language without a previous term of reference, but in direct connection with the experience conveyed in the word, an experience intimately connected with the voice, the appearance, the sympathy, and the particular relationship that subsists between themselves and the person speaking and, more generally, the world around them from which they learn the expression.

It is also time to overcome the unauthentic hermeneutical device of interpretation by proxy. We mean the pseudo interpretation based on a paradigm of intelligibility which is not one's own, but which one assumes belongs to the "other," the "native," the "primitive." In this way we show generosity and condescension in accepting other people's views because they make sense for them, most part the Vedic Revelation is the discrete illumination of a veil, which was not seen as a veil but as a layer, one might almost say a skin, of Man himself. The Vedic Revelation unfolds the process of Man's "becoming conscious," of discovering himself along with the three worlds and their mutual relationships. It is not the message of another party speaking through a medium, but the very illumination of the "medium," itself the progressive enlightenment of reality. It is not a beam of light coming from a lighthouse or a powerful reflector; it is dawn. It is the revelation of the Word, of the primordial Word, of the Word that is not an instrument, or even a sign, as if it were handling or pointing to something else. It is the revelation of the Word as symbol, as the sound-and-meaning aspect of reality itself. If there were somebody who had spoken the Word first, by what other word could he communicate the meaning of the original to me? I must assume that the Word speaks directly to me, for the Vedas reveal in an emphatic manner the character of reality.

In short, the fact that the Vedas have no author and thus no anterior authority, the fact that they possess only the value contained in the actual existential act of really hearing them, imparts to them a universality that makes them peculiarly relevant today. They dispose us to listen and then we hear what we hear, trusting that it is also what was to be heard.

Second, we refer to a particular example of the universal paradox that by rejecting a value we can in fact enhance it. It is simply a pious exaggeration to say that Hinduism and Indian philosophy are directly nurtured by the Vedas and are a continuation of the Vedic spirit. In hardly any other culture in the world has the fountainhead been paid more lip service but received less real attention. It is a well-known fact, long recognized and now confirmed by recent studies, that Indian philosophical systems, not only the *nāstikas*, that is the so-called heterodox ones, but also the most orthodox ones, have drawn very few of their reflections from the Vedas. Most of the philosophical systems were developed outside the world of Vedic speculation. Even the two Vedāntas make only selective and limited use of Vedic material. Mīmāṁsā deals only with the *karma-kāṇḍa* or active injunctions of the Vedas, and that from a very particular point of view; the mantras are neglected or are reduced to indicative sentences (which later speculation endeavored to interpret by means of hermeneutical rules), though not for us. If we try to report other people's beliefs without in some way sharing in them, we prevent ourselves from expressing what we think is the correct interpretation. Nor can we truly report the interpretation of others, for what they believe to be true we have rejected. In other words, the belief of the believer belongs to the phenomenon itself. Our own interpretation has to face the challenge of meeting both our own convictions and those of the representatives of the document we interpret. Without the former we would not really interpret; we would simply be reporting what for us are nonsensical statements. Without the latter we would not truly interpret; we would be merely expressing our own ideas in the language of a foreign culture. In short, our supreme concern here has been to offer an interpretation of the Vedas which makes sense to modern Man and yet does not distort, but only translates, the insights of Vedic Man. We can make the Vedas understandable to the extent that without distorting them we can make them somewhat acceptable.

There are no fixed and immutable translations; words are much more alive than we tend to think, and all of them have a personal "face." Thus the difficulty is not for us to find out what is the best translation of, say, *ātman,* but to confront the same problem that confronted Vedic Man. The ambivalence of words and concepts constitutes proof that we are dealing with subjects that are still alive. The tragedy of a dead language, as somebody long ago remarked, is that you do not have the luxury of allowing yourself to make innovations, for if you did so nobody would understand you. The beauty of a living language is that you can afford to make mistakes. Not only will somebody point them out to you, but those very mistakes may be incorporated into the treasury of experience conveyed by a particular sentence. No amount of modern semantics—to give one example—can blot out the often "scientifically" incorrect etymologies of Yāska and Sāyaṇa. Yet they belong as much to the meaning and history of the word as do grammatically correct ones. These reflections should not, of course, be taken as an excuse for inaccurate or approximate translations. On the contrary, they should add to our sense of responsibility to find on each occasion the right words, the proper atmosphere.

The problem of translation, however, has another facet. Nearly all Western languages, including English, have been molded by the Jewish-Helleno-Christian tradition against a Gothic, Celtic, or other indigenous background. We may translate *Agni* as "Lord" in order not to mislead the reader, or we may write down "Fire"; in both instances (in spite of the capital letter) the translation is perhaps legitimate, provided that the reader is informed of the original word. But if we translate *gandharva* by "angel" or *apsaras* by "spirit," are we not utilizing equally religion-bound concepts? Are we not saying that the English language is indefectibly bound to one particular tradition? We could speak of "the good fortune of having been invited to a certain *inauguration*," but would it be proper to translate this statement as "we have been summoned by the grace of Lakṣmī to a certain function performed according to śāstric principles laid down by a pandit, after recognition of the maṅgalic moments disclosed by the flying of birds"? Why should the augur, the Roman religious official, and the goddess Fortune be accepted as universalized terms and not the Indian terminology? To reply that nobody will understand the latter sentence deserves only the answer that outside the Western cultural milieu everybody will half understand the former, or else they will reduce it to banality.

We could perhaps put the same problem in terms of the special relationship between proper and common names. Transcultural translations disturb or even destroy the otherwise neatly defined difference between these two types of nouns. Substantives like "grace," "revelation," "democracy," and even "lord" and "god" are undoubtedly common names within a certain cultural area. Yet the moment we speak of Vedic Revelation, the God of Hinduism, the Grace of Viṣṇu, Russian Democracy, the Lord Buddha, and the like, more than one thoughtful person will feel uneasy. He has more or less unconsciously converted those common names into proper names, and he is tied to a particular understanding of them. By "grace" he will understand Christian grace, by "god" and "revelation" the conception of the divinity and its disclosure according to the Semitic religions, while with regard to "democracy" he will have in mind the British model. He will argue further that if we do not delimit in some way the meaning of terms we will fall into an anarchic chaos in which a word can mean anything. The same can be said the other way around. Are the words *agni, karman, dharma, mantra, brahman,* and the like the exclusive property of the Indian religions? When we say "god" or *karman* must we have so orthodox a view as to exclude any other understanding of the term? Words are more than mere labels, and thus we cannot deny the fact that words have their proper orthodoxies. We cannot accept as a criterion of translation the existence of a "thing in itself" apprehended differently by two interpretations of the same word. How do we know that they, in point of fact, refer to the same "thing" (even assuming that such a "thing" was a valid hypothesis)?

It is here that this anthology may make an indirect contribution to modern language—understood as an expression of human consciousness—by introducing into one language the riches of another and thus allowing for a more universal language, without at the same time whittling away the concreteness that all living languages possess. "Grace" may not always necessarily mean what a Christian theology of grace says it means, but there must be something—which, we repeat, is not a thing, and certainly not a "thing" called grace—which makes the use of this word permissible when speaking of Varuṇa, for instance, and meaningless when referring to a certain conception of *karman*. Brahman is undoubtedly not God and yet there is a peculiar homology between these two names, which does not exist between either one of them and the word "banana," for example. The interplay between words and meanings is one of the most exacting and fascinating challenges of our present world situation.

In this regard we should obviously avoid the two extremes of anachronistic and "katachronic" interpretations. The former means to introduce old and obsolete notions into contemporary situations; the latter means to interpret a thing of the past with inadequate categories of the present day. And yet any reading *of* a text is a reading *out* of it as much as *into* it. The connection cannot be a logical one. It has to be an existential or, rather, a mythical connection. But we must stop here lest we overstep our self-imposed discipline by theorizing too explicitly.

For a long time it was forbidden to translate the Vedas or to teach them to the noninitiated. Nowadays, however, there is a universal trend, deeply rooted in the very nature of modern Man, which abhors artificial esoterisms and sectarian separations. Is it simply unfaithfulness to ancient traditions to say that circumcision, baptism by water, and *upanayana* are only signs of the real initiation by the Spirit (to use another debatable word)? So long as the symbolism of the Vedas was alive, so long as it needed no transmythologization in order to be understood and lived, translation amounted to a betrayal; but when Vedic symbolism is no longer alive, survival may well demand emigration, that is, translation.

The process of translation is not only transcultural. It begins within a particular culture. The work of the great *bhāṣyakāras* or commentators consists precisely of such translations, including the translation of the proper names of the tradition itself. When those names cease to stand for a living symbol within a "lived" myth, they are "trans-lated," that is, "shifted," so as to designate henceforward the same "reality" but beyond its proper or native horizon. Uṣas, for example, may no longer be considered the daughter of Prajāpati, the Goddess of the myth, but simply Dawn, or perhaps only dawn. Yet by this very shift Uṣas has arrived where the dawn still dawns but where the daughter of Prajāpati is no longer known or acknowledged and, having traveled to such distant shores, she herself will perhaps help see to it that our dullness of perception is removed and that dawn is reinstated in a more colorful and relevant form, not perhaps as the daughter of Prajāpati but certainly as Dawn, as a symbol of hope, in our contemporary world. Furthermore, the connection between words and meanings is to be sought in the sphere of rite, and that is why Man cannot live without rituals, for he cannot live without words either. For instance, one sūtra says: "May the 'Goddess,' who fashioned this garment . . ." (HGS I, 1, 4, 2); but may not "angel," "woman," "mother," "sister," or even "machine" eventually be a permissible rendering of the word "Goddess" in this text?

After the foregoing remarks about literal translation not being the proper way to render the meaning and message of a text, it may sound somewhat contradictory to say that the utmost care has been taken to provide a faithful translation. In order to offer the Vedic experience in the most truthful manner, we have abstained from flights of fancy and whimsical interpretations and have remained soberly close to the texts, which are sometimes echoed and further translated in the introductions.

A word should be said about the names of the Gods. Through the different hymns and parts of this anthology a certain harmony has been kept in the use of the proper names of the Gods and the common epithets of the divine. Proper names have often been avoided in order to eschew an unnecessarily esoteric flavor. Thus terms like "Lord," "God," "power," and the like have been used to designate proper names like Agni, Indra, and so on. Always, however, the original name is given in the corresponding note so as to prevent confusion. This flexibility may allow for different readings according to the background of the reader or hearers.

At this juncture it may be useful to define the function of the notes. Precisely because this work is an end in itself and not a mere means for further investigation, because the texts are meant to be used for meditation and prayer, and because the Veda deserves the reverence due a human document at least 3,000 years old, we have refrained from distracting the reader with references to the notes, which are therefore not put at the bottom of the page but at the end of the texts. In this way the reader is less influenced by the explanations, however useful they may be, and can incorporate the text into his personal life without unnecessary intermediaries.

It is proper at this moment to thank the many excellent translators who have undertaken a parallel task of giving versions of the Vedas in modern European languages. We have profited from as many as we could lay hands on and from time to time we have adopted their suggestions. It would seem improper to insist on hammering out a slightly different phrase or a more recondite term if some of the known translators have already had a felicitous inspiration. Moreover, we have discovered that this practice has been normal since time immemorial, for there is already an almost universally accepted way of rendering the original of some well-known texts.

And Contemporary Celebration

4 We have been saying that the reader is urged to study the texts in the classical sense of the word "study," which includes not only intellectual effort but also voluntary commitment and human enthusiasm. We would like to suggest that the introductions be studied twice, before the texts as prologues and after the texts as epilogues. The "scriptures" themselves require much more than just reading and attention. They must become real to us by our own act of representation. Much of what we have said so far would be seriously weakened if it were not encouraged by the faith and hope that beyond the theoretical understanding of the Vedas, existential participation in and liturgical reenactment of their message are really possible.

The ultimate aim of this anthology is not to offer merely a new translation of the Vedas. The title expressly says not Vedic translation but "Vedic Experience." It is possible, certainly, to translate a poem by Mīrābāī into a Karnatik melody, a Kathākali dance into a poem, or the Sanskrit Vedas into English idiom. But the intention of this *mantramañjarī* is not 'translation' but representation; that is, its goal is an existential reenactment. It does not desire to turn the symphony into a poem, but to play the music again, even though the instruments are not the same and the skill of the original composer is missing. We do not want to put the music into words or to translate the words into dance. Our aim is to speak the words, to play the music, to perform the dance, to utter the prayers, to sing the songs, to wonder, love, doubt, suffer, hope, and believe along with those documents of human history which we call the Vedas. Even if the instruments are poor and the key is not the same, we may still perceive the original, not by a 'translation' but by a reenactment that allows us both to hear the *śruti* directly and perhaps even to transmit its vibrations, just as it was heard long ago by the ancients and as we may continue to hear it insofar as our ears are open to those same vibrations. The aim of this anthology is to make available to modern Man the riches of the elders and thus to globalize human experience. If there is one thing that characterizes and even distinguishes the Vedic experience, it is its sacrificial character, its overall feature of orthopraxis.

The Vedic experience does not move on a merely theoretical level; it does not carry a doctrinal message, but a universal form of human celebration. Modern Man is inclined today to accept the idea that he is not saved by reason alone or liberated by willpower alone. He seeks an active participation in the overwhelming dynamism of the universe, in which his involvement is possible only if it is actively passive. And this could be said to be the core of the experience of Vedic Man: that he is called upon to perform the sacrifice that makes the world and even the Gods subsist. We do not intend to introduce a new rite, much less to suggest a new religiousness. It is our hope that this anthology will stimulate already existing forms of worship; that it will be at the disposal of those who feel the need to celebrate with friends around them and ancestors behind them in an original and innovative way or else in more traditional forms. No particular form of worship is here favored. It is only assumed that Man is a celebrating being and that sometimes he does not feel it proper to confine himself to solos. For these reasons and others that we are about to explain our style is intended for recitation and liturgical use.

To make a text available for contemporary celebration does not mean that the text is forced to say something it does not really say. We simply surmise, first, that certain of these texts could be relevant and, second, that such an effort is worthwhile. Modern Man, either because he has been isolated by a long process of individualization or because he has been hustled and precipitated into modernity—whatever that may be—urgently needs to celebrate his fellowship with his neighbors and also with the whole of reality. The Vedic Revelation may become a real discovery of new dimensions of life, if it is taken as a celebration of Man.

Celebration does not always mean jumping for joy nor is it always a festival of song and dance. It may include more inward and sober elements. It does, however, invariably contain the awareness that my acts have a deeper, more transcendent, meaning than that which meets the eye, even though I myself may not be able to put this meaning into words. Celebration conveys a sense of cosmic solidarity, of human fellowship, and often of a divine accompaniment by reason of which all our actions are liturgical, meaningful, and expressive, both expressing what now is and creating what is about to be. Celebration is the awareness of the rhythms of life and the festive observance of their frequent recurrence. There is no celebration without recurrence. What happens again and again is the proper subject matter of celebration, as the word *celeber* suggests. We do not need to subscribe to a cyclical or spiral conception of time, but we do need a certain rhythmic consciousness in order truly to celebrate, that is, to transcend the petty routine of daily life which is so easily reduced, if there is no spirit of celebration, to a dispirited and humdrum mediocrity.

Vedic Man is fundamentally a celebrating Man, but he does not celebrate his own victories or even a nature festival in company with his fellowmen; rather, he concelebrates with the whole universe, taking his place in the cosmic sacrifice in which all the Gods are engaged together. Other cultures can boast of better warriors, craftsmen, and adventurers. Vedic Man presents this markedly liturgical attitude to life, this extraordinary power of celebration. Even the frequently irritating minutiae of later periods are nothing but exaggerations of a liturgical and festive consciousness.

Contemporary celebration should be truly contemporary, not a throwback to ancient rites or a mere adaptation of past rituals. It is not a question of imitating olden times. Such imitation would be artificial, self-defeating, and in any event impossible. Contemporary celebration must be spontaneous, creative, and authentic. It can be neither planned nor forced. It simply grows when the time is ripe.

The only thing that stifles Man's power to celebrate is superficiality, which can have several causes but only one main remedy: contemplation, pure love, or, in traditional words, a life of prayer. This anthology is not a book of prayers, but it is an introduction to prayer (*jñāna, dhyāna, anubhava*). It is an invitation to a full human life, a life that is not exhausted either by merely doing or even by being in a two-dimensional spatiotemporal way, but that is fulfilled only by a total becoming of all that one can possibly be.

Yet it is with a certain intention that the subtitle speaks of "contemporary" celebration. This is an indication that the temporal factor cannot be eliminated or neglected, as if Man were a nontemporal being who merely skims the surface of a temporal world. One extreme would not justify the other. The celebration of Vedic Man may be excellent, but it certainly would not satisfy our needs nor would we fulfill our human duty just by going back to the past. This anthology, far from advocating this course, suggests almost the opposite. It takes the past and sets it before us in the future so that we may walk more hopefully with the light step and the ultimate unconcern of the truly liberated Man.

So much for the bouquet. As for the flowers, we simply entrust them to you, reader, with the hope that you may want to make a garland out of them.

"May you delight in these my words"

RV I, 25, 18

B. A NOTE ON VEDIC TRADITION

I ask as a fool
who knows not his own spirit:
Where are the hidden traces
left by the Gods?

RV I, 164, 5ab

The Vedic Literature

1 There are no absolute beginnings in human history. Every historical period has an origin and every culture starts from somewhere outside itself. The *novum* that appeared in the north of the Indian peninsula about, or soon after, 2000 B.C. was the result of an extraordinary and fruitful encounter between the invading Aryans, speaking an Indo-European language, and the indigenous population who are believed to have spoken a language ancestral to the Dravidian languages.

In order to place the Vedic experience in its proper context the following considerations may be useful.

The first oral (and later written) result of this cross-cultural encounter was what we call the Vedas, that is, the entire body of

Vedic literature. It is chanted, spoken, and now also written in the old Indo-Aryan language known as Vedic; Vedic is ancestral to the literary Sanskrit, which was formalized by the grammarian Pāṇini around the middle of the first millennium B.C. Vedic literature is regarded as "revelation" or *śruti* (that which is heard) and gives us the first meaning of the word "Veda." The second meaning of the term is restricted to the four most important parts of that literature, transmitted by four separate schools and often referred to as the four Vedas: Ṛg Veda, Sāma Veda, Yajur Veda, and Atharva Veda. Their age has been a matter of dispute. The most probable dates lie between 1500 and 1200 B.C. for the oldest parts, and down to 600 B.C. for the later. There is still a third and yet more restricted meaning of the word "Veda"; it is used to refer to what is probably the most ancient part of each Veda, the *Saṁhitās* or hymns and prayers that make up the first of the four broad stages into which the Vedas (in the second meaning of the term) are generally divided.

1. The Saṁhitās or mantras are the hymns belonging to the earliest stage. As the word Saṁhitā implies, they represent the basic collection of hymns and as such are the oldest materials in each school. The oldest and most important is the Ṛg Veda Saṁhitā, which contains more than 10,000 verses in the form of a little more than 1,000 hymns. These are written in various meters. Each of the Saṁhitās provides the texts for one of the groups of priests of the Vedic rituals. Thus the Ṛg Veda belonged to the Hotṛ priests and was recited by them at the sacrifices. The Sāma Veda contains chants and melodies (*sāman*), chanted by the priests of that name. With the exception of 75 stanzas, the text is borrowed and rearranged from the Ṛg Veda. The Yajur Veda consists of sacrificial formulas of the Adhvaryu priests, and many of these also are taken from the Ṛg Veda. It has come down to us in several recensions, the Kṛṣṇa or "Black" Yajur Veda whose Saṁhitās are the Taittirīya, the Maitrāyaṇī, and the Kāṭhaka, and the "White" or Śukla Yajur Veda whose Saṁhitā is the Vājasaneyī. The Atharva Veda is somewhat removed from the other three by virtue of the "popular" character of many of the prayers against ills, incantations, and spells which it contains. It also has, however, a number of hymns with an important philosophical content.

2. The Brāhmaṇas form the second broad stage, attached to the various branches of the Saṁhitās. Clearly later works, as their

language reveals, they are written largely in prose and give lengthy explanations and descriptions of the rituals and prayers connected with the sacrifice. They contain more than simple instructions for rituals, and much of the explanatory matter is of a symbolic character.

3. The Āraṇyakas, or "forest treatises," are in a sense continuations of the Brāhmaṇas, dealing with the speculations and spirituality of forest dwellers (*vānaprasthas*), those who have renounced the world. They represent a step toward interiorization, as the hermit in the forest could not perform the elaborate rituals demanded of the householder. Like the Brāhmaṇas, they are attached to the various branches and schools of the Saṁhitās.

4. The Upaniṣads are the fourth or final stage of the process, and are known therefore as the *Vedānta,* or "end of the Veda." They represent the mystical and philosophical culmination of the Vedas. They contain the teachings of the great masters which point toward the path of *mokṣa* or liberation.

With the passing of time a further literature grew up whose main concern was the exegetic study of the Vedas. It is grouped under six headings as Vedāṅgas, or "limbs of the Vedas." The Vedāṅgas include the study of phonetics, and correct pronunciation of the Vedas, of metrics, etymology, grammar, and astronomy, needed to ensure the correct timing of the sacred rites. The sixth Vedāṅga is concerned with *kalpa,* or the correct ways of performing the rituals. The basic texts are written in the form of *sūtras,* brief aphoristic statements phrased with great economy of words. With the further passing of time there were added extended studies, in the form of *śāstras* or treatises. Thus, under the heading of *kalpa* there are several branches of *sūtras* dealing with domestic rituals, including the performance of the *saṁskāras* or sacraments associated with birth, marriage, death, and so on; with the great public sacrifices; and with *dharma* or the rules and laws governing the behavior of the individual in society. From the latter emerged the whole later legal literature known as Dharma-śāstra.

Sanskrit Pronunciation

2 The various Indian scripts in which Sanskrit is written down—nowadays most commonly the Devanāgarī—are, to use the word in its popular sense, phonetic: that is, every sound of the

language has its own unique sign, so that, for example, long and short vowels are distinguished (contrast Latin or Greek) and the written consonants always have the same value (contrast English *get/gentle,* etc.). Conversion of this admirable accuracy into the Roman script requires the use of a number of diacritical marks, which the nonspecialist reader may find troublesome. The present note is intended to provide a rough guide only.

VOWELS

a has the value of the *u* in the English word *but.*
ā has the value of the *a* in the English word *father.*
i has the value of the *i* in the English word *bit.*
ī has the value of the *i* in the English word *machine.*
u has the value of the *u* in the English word *full.*
ū has the value of the *u* in the English word *rule.*
e has the value of the *ay* in the English word *play.*
o has the value of the *o* in the English word *home.*
ai has the value of the *y* in the English word *my.*
au has the value of the *ow* in the English word *how.*
ṛ is not the consonant *r* but a vowel pronounced like the *ri* of *rich.*
ḷ is not the consonant *l* but a vowel pronounced like the *li* of *lick.*

CONSONANTS

The general reader may ignore the distinction between the aspirated and unaspirated forms of consonants. Similarly, the distinction between the dentals *t, d, n, l* and the retroflexes *ṭ, ḍ, ṇ, ḷ* (the Ṛgvedic equivalent of noninitial *ḍ*, not the vowel *ḷ* described above) is best disregarded.

g always has the sound of the *g* in *get,* never that of the *g* in *gentle.*

c is pronounced as the *ch* of *cheese.*

ś and *ṣ* are pronounced as the *sh* of *shudder.*

ṃ at the end of a word and before *p* or *b* is pronounced as *m,* elsewhere as *n.*

The other consonants are pronounced as their English equivalents are.

The Recitation of the Vedas

3 The Vedas are not primarily a written document; they are not even a set of thoughts or a collection of injunctions. They are primordially spoken language, a set of words with meaning, sound, and power. Traditionally the Vedas have to be chanted or recited. Vedic recitation stands for the total and sincere (because also public, or at least audible) participation of the person for whom the Veda is "Veda," that is, knowledge, insight, and ultimately liberation.

The Brāhmaṇa of the Sāma Veda gives us a feeling of the central place of recitation. It consists mainly of detailed instructions regarding fasts and other austerities to be undertaken before and during the recitation of the Sāma Veda, which is, as we have already said, a musical version of parts of the Ṛg Veda for ritual purposes. To prepare oneself by a twelve-day fast, for instance, before the cultic recitation of the sacred text is more than mere superstition, for it implies an integral participation in a total act. The traditional name for this participation is "sacred action" No action is sacred, and thus real and effective, unless it is performed by the whole being and ultimately incorporates the entire reality. Not only Gods, Men, and the world have to take part in it, but the whole Man has to be involved, his body not excluded. Furthermore, the participation of the Gods, the mind, the body, water, and earth, and the like is closely interrelated. The entire universe vibrates at the sound of an authentic prayer. All is interconnected and thus the fasting of the body is related to the cleansing of the mind, for only a clean mind can healthily sustain a bodily fast. Just as there cannot be a good song if the singer does not feel the *rāga*, the emotion of the text, so there cannot be a proper understanding of the prayer if the body is not involved in it equally with the mind.

Modern Man, who reads without pronouncing and often believes he is able to understand without commitment, may find it difficult and even impossible to accept such an interpretation. Whether modern Man is right or wrong is beside the point. Our present concern is to understand the nature of Vedic Revelation. We may now add some more technical remarks.

The Vedic accent which is marked in the Saṁhitās of the four Vedas and also in the Taittirīya and the Śatapatha Brāhmaṇas is a musical accent. The Vedas have been transmitted orally for centuries, and it is owing to the art of memorization and recitation that they have been scrupulously preserved with fewer corruptions that the texts, which have been transmitted in written form. The recitation belongs to the very nature of the Vedic Word which is actualized in the sound vibrations. The sacramental character of the Word is seen in its necessary connection with sound as its physical element. The *śruti,* indeed, needs to be *heard.*

There are three accents corresponding to three different pitches: (1) the *udātta* or raised accent which corresponds to the higher pitch; (2) the *svarita* or sounding accent, the middle pitch, and (3) the *anudātta* or not raised accent, the lower pitch.

There are, however, differences in recitation according to the Veda, the *śākhā* or branch of the Veda, and the particular school. The Sāma Veda has developed, besides the simple recitation, an elaborated musical chant, using five to seven notes. The *chandas* or Vedic meter is measured by the number of syllables. The unit of the meter is the *pada* or foot, that is, a fourth of a *ṛc* or stanza. This *pada* should not be confused with the Greek foot. The quantitative measurement by long and short syllables is another feature of the Vedic meter, but it is not related to the accent. The glossary gives a description of the most important meters (Gāyatrī, Triṣṭubh, Jagatī, Virāj, etc.).

FIRST MANTRA

OM agnim īḷe purohitaṁ
yajñasya devam ṛtvijam
hotāraṁ ratnadhātamam

I magnify God, the Divine Fire,
the Priest, Minister of the sacrifice,
the Offerer of oblation, supreme Giver of treasure.

RV I, 1, 1

We open this anthology with an invocation. To be able to invoke, that is, to call upon, something greater than ourselves and so break our own boundaries is the beginning of wisdom, the source of hope, and the condition of joy. Our first verse is the opening of the whole Vedic Revelation: the invocation to Agni, the mediator par excellence, the sacrificial Fire, who transforms all material and human gifts into spiritual and divine realities, so that they may reach their endless destination. Agni has a priestly role and a threefold composition, his nature being theanthropocosmic (i.e., divine, human, and earthly at one and the same time). Or, in

Magnify: *īḷ-* suggests a call, a request, an entreaty, praise.
The Divine Fire: Agni.
Cf. § III 4 for the entire hymn.

traditional Vedic terms, Agni has a threefold aspect: *ādhidaivika, ādhyātmika,* and *ādhibhautika*. This opening verse contains as in a nutshell the whole of Man's *sanātana dharma* or primordial religiousness: praise, mediation, sacrifice, commerce with the divine, and also remuneration for Man, all caught up in an atmosphere of invocation. We invoke the divine—wherever it may be and however we may conceive it—not because we are lazy or unable to work out by ourselves the contents of our prayers, but because, filled with love, we sense within ourselves a gulf between the finite and the infinite and simply open the sluices that enclose our finitude. The last *sūkta* of the Ṛg Veda is also dedicated to Agni and with its last mantra we close our anthology.

THE GĀYATRĪ

ॐ

tat savitur vareṇyaṁ
bhargo devasya dhīmahi
dhiyo yo naḥ pracodayāt ॐ

RV III, 62, 10

OM

We meditate upon the glorious splendor
of the Vivifier divine.
May he himself illumine our minds!

OM

"There is nothing more exalted than the Gāyatrī."[1] It is the most renowned mantra of the Vedas. It is addressed to the divine life-giver as supreme God, symbolized in Savitṛ, the Sun.[2] For this reason this prayer is also called Sāvitrī. It is recited daily at sunrise and at sunset, usually at the moment of the ritual bath. This mantra derives its name from the meter in which it is written, the *gāyatrī*

1. Manu II, 83.
2. Cf. RV I, 159, 5; V, 82, 1; YV III, 35; XXII, 9; XXX, 2; XXXVI, 3. Usually *bhūr bhuvaḥ svaḥ* is recited before and after the Gāyatrī mantra. Cf. SB XI, 1, 6, 3 (§ VII Introduction); BU V, 5, 4 (§ VI 8).

being a Vedic poetic meter of twenty-four syllables, of which the author according to tradition was the sage Viśvāmitra.

To grasp the relevance of this sacred text we must recall the importance of a mantra, especially in the Vedic period, though the mantra is a primordial human phenomenon to be found in practically all religious traditions. Mantras are not magic formulas, nor are they merely logical sentences; they connect, in a very special way, the objective and subjective aspects of reality. A simple example is often given to illustrate this function. A king asks his minister, who is advanced in the spiritual life and practices *japa* (i.e., the recitation of mantras), to teach him his mantra. The minister declines but the king insists. The minister tells a page who is standing nearby to lay hold on the king, but, despite repeated injunctions, the page does not move. Finally, the enraged king tells his page to lay hold on the minister and the boy does so immediately. The minister bursts out laughing and explains to the king: our orders were the same and so was their recipient; yet in the one case the command was not heeded and in the other it was. In the case of a mantra all depends on the authority and the spiritual preparation of the one who says it. The word "mantra" means that which has been thought or known or that which is privately—or even secretly by initiation (*dīkṣā*)—transmitted and which possesses power to liberate. It is sacred speech, sacrificial formula, efficient counsel.[3] The Bṛhadāraṇyaka Upaniṣad explains how the world came into being by the union of Mind (*manas*) with Word (*vāc*).[4] The mantra is neither a mere sound nor sheer magic. Words have not only a sound but also a meaning, which is not apparent to all those who simply hear the sound. Living words have, furthermore, a power that transcends the purely mental plane. To acquire this energy of the word one has to grasp not only its meaning but also its message, or its vibrations, as they are sometimes called in order to stress the link with the sound itself.[5] Faith, understanding, and physical utterance, as well as physical continuity (the mantra has to be handed down by a master), are essential requisites for an authentic mantra. Every word links us up with the source of all words. The ultimate character of the word, *śabdabrahman*, is a fundamental concept in Indian spirituality.

3. Thus Sanskrit *mantrin*, king's counselor (from *mantra*). The root is obviously *man-*, to think. Cf. *manas*, mind.
4. Cf. AB V, 23 (XXIV, 4); SB VI, 1, 2, 6; BU I, 2, 4 (§ I 14).
5. *Śiva* and *śakti*, or *bindu* and *nāda* in Tantrism, are related to this idea.

Several hymns of the Atharva Veda allude to the privileged position occupied by the Gāyatrī mantra. When the poet is attempting to define the First Principle, the Absolute, and to locate the "Unborn," he says, in order to give us a notion of his inaccessibility, that he is:

> Loftier even than the lofty Gāyatrī,
> beyond the Immortal he strode forth.
> Where was the Unborn then? This even
> the knowers of Vedic lore cannot tell.[6]

In another hymn, composed in honor of Rohita, the Sun, which also extols the grandeur of an earthly king, the poet describes the king's subjects assembled at dawn for the offering of the sacrifice; he depicts them awaiting the appearance of the rising Sun, called in this passage the "tawny Calf," and his "mother" the Dawn, here identified with the Gāyatrī:

> Your people, the offspring of sacred Fervor,
> have come in the wake of the Calf and the Gāyatrī.
> May they enter your presence with intentions of peace,
> preceded by the tawny Calf and his mother![7]

In similar fashion another verse calls the Gāyatrī "Mother of the Vedas."[8]

The Gāyatrī is not necessarily connected with a sacrificial rite; it may be murmured or repeated without the accompaniment of ritual offering. It underwent a process of sublimation or interiorization, but not always successfully.

The Bṛhadāraṇyaka Upaniṣad gives a very elaborate symbolic explanation of the Gāyatrī based on its poetic composition, three feet of eight syllables each: the first foot is made up of the three worlds: the earth, the heavens, and the sky or rather the in-between;[9] the second foot is composed of the threefold knowledge, that is, the wisdom of the three Vedas; the third foot is composed of the three vital forces (*prāṇa*, or in-breath, *apāna* or out-breath, and *vyāna* or diffused breath, which together compose eight syllables). All this is said in order to introduce the fourth foot, which is rendered visible precisely in and through the Gāyatrī,

6. AV X, 8, 41 (§ VII 27).
7. AV XIII, 1, 10.
8. AV XIX, 71, 1.
9. *bhūmi, dyu, antarikṣa*. Cf. BU V, 14, 1.

Savitṛ, the Sun "above the dark skies." Through an interior process effected by reciting the Gāyatrī with insight the whole of reality is reflected and thus also mastered in Man, this mesocosmos, this mirror of total reality.

If he, the knower of the Gāyatrī, receives these three worlds with all their fullness he will be receiving only the first foot of the Gāyatrī. If he receives all that is conferred by the threefold knowledge [of the Vedas], he will be receiving only the second foot. If he receives all that lives and breathes, he will be receiving only the third foot. But that fourth, the foot apparently visible above the dark skies yonder, that [sun] which glows, is not obtainable by anyone at all. How could anyone receive so much? Salutation to the Gāyatrī: O Gāyatrī, you are one-footed, two-footed, three-footed, four-footed. Yet you are footless, because you do not go afoot. Salutation to you, the fourth, the clearly visible foot, above the dark skies![10]

Furthermore, as another important commentary on the Gāyatrī says: "The Gāyatrī, indeed, is this whole universe, all that has come to be. And the Word, indeed, is Gāyatrī, for the Word sings forth and protects this whole universe that has come to be."[11]

The Maitrī Upaniṣad also gives an account of the Gāyatrī, explaining its symbolism verse by verse:

That glorious splendor of Savitṛ: the Sun in the heavens is assuredly Savitṛ. He it is who is to be sought by one desirous of the Self. So it is affirmed by those who disclose the knowledge of Brahman for us.

May we meditate on the Vivifier divine: Savitṛ assuredly is God. Therefore I meditate on that which is called his splendor. So it is affirmed by those who disclose the knowledge of Brahman for us.

May he himself illumine our minds: Mind assuredly is intelligence. May he breathe it into us. So it is affirmed by those who disclose the knowledge of Brahman for us.[12]

The same Upaniṣad introduces us to the Sāvitrī by reciting the following hymn:

> The Swan, the bird of golden color,
> abiding both in the heart and in the Sun,
> the diver-bird of glorious light—
> to him we sacrifice in this fire.[13]

10. BU V, 14, 6-7.
11. CU III, 12, 1.
12. MaitU VI, 7. Those who disclose the knowledge of Brahman: *brahmavādinaḥ*, the expounders of, revealers of, those who make known, instruct . . . *brahman*. Intelligence: *buddhi*, the highest faculty, also understanding, thought, meditation. Cf. § VI 4 for the continuation of this text.
13. MaitU VI, 34; cf. § III 28 for the continuation of this text.

Prayer would be next to nothing or merely the expression of our wishes to a more powerful agency which knows them already, if it did not consist in this assuming, realizing, even becoming the whole of reality; it is a recapitulation, a summing up, of all that there is in the mind and heart, and also in the body of the worshiper. Prayer is participation in the systole and diastole of the whole universe.

What the Gāyatrī is, that indeed the earth is also, for it is on the earth that this whole universe is established; it does not extend beyond it. What the earth is, that indeed the body in man is also, for on it these vital breaths are established; they do not extend beyond it. What the body in man is, that indeed the heart within man is also, for on it these vital breaths are established; they do not extend beyond it. The Gāyatrī has four feet and is sixfold. About this a verse of the Ṛg Veda says: "Such is the measure of his greatness, but greater still is the Man."[14] All beings form a quarter of him, three quarters, the immortal in the sky. What is called Brahman, that indeed the space outside a man is also; what the space outside a man is, that indeed the space within a man is also; what the space within a man is, that indeed the space within the heart is also. That is the *full*, the unchanging. Whoever knows this obtains good fortune, full and unchanging.[15]

One of the traditional words for the fundamental act of prayer is concentration, and we should understand it in the most precise fashion. The man of prayer, in and through his spiritual concentration, really concentrates more and more parts of reality; he condenses, as it were, the less concentrated sparks of the universe floating around him, so as to reduce them to their essence. He can do so because he has found the center of reality which allows him really to concentrate, that is, to center his worlds in one single center. This can be done when the three centers, that of outer reality, that of inner reality, and that of man himself, coincide. The result is harmony and peace. Real prayer is always an act that embraces, all in one, the Divine, the Human, and the Cosmic, that is, the *ādhidaivika*, the *ādhyātmika*, and the *ādhibhautika*. That is what the different texts on the Gāyatrī have been telling us in their different ways.

The Gāyatrī accompanies man not only on his daily round, but also in the most solemn moments of his life. It forms an important part of the initiation ceremony.[16] Henceforward the young man, having received the mantra from his master, will have the right of

14. Cf. RV X, 90, 3 (§ I 5).
15. CU III, 12, 2-9.
16. Cf. § II 14.

uttering it and thus of participating in the spiritual world that links him with all others who praise and worship God through the living words of this cosmic prayer.

Many Sāstras have indicated the way the Gāyatrī has to be recited. Daily, the student of sacred lore should stand at dawn and recite the Sāvitrī (as the Gāyatrī is often called) until he sees the rising sun, and at dusk, seated, recites it until he catches sight of the emerging stars.[17] Another Sāstra adds that while facing the East at the morning twilight and the West in the evening, one may control his breath while reciting the Sāvitrī a hundred times.[18] These and other injunctions tend to harmonize one's heart and mind with the cosmic powers. The chanting of the Gāyatrī at dawn purifies from the sins of the previous night, and the evening prayer of the mantra purifies from the sins committed during that day.[19]

The Gāyatrī is a complete symbol of light. It is certainly much more than the epiphany of light; it is light itself when the recitation is a real prayer, an assimilation to and identification with that which is prayed. Each line emphasizes one aspect of light: the glorious splendor of the Ultimate, his own internal radiance, that is, the uncreatedness of light (line 1); the creating light, the communicative brightness of the uncreated Sun, Savit, the brilliance of the living God who illumines everything (line 2); and, finally, the incidence of this divine light in our beings, and especially in our minds, making us refulgent ourselves and transmitters of the same refulgence and converting us into light: light from light, splendor from splendor, oneness with the source of light, not in a ponderous ontological identity but in a "lightsome" identity of luminosity, totally transparent—*ātman-brahman* (line 3).[18]

17. Cf. Manu II, 101.
18. Cf. Baudhāyana Dharma Sūtra II, 4, 7, 4-14.
19. Cf. Manu II, 102; Baudhāyana Dharma Sūtra II, 4, 7, 18-22. Cf. also KausU II, 7 (§ IV 21). For further codifications cf. Vasiṣṭha Dharma Sūtra XXIII, 35; XXV, 12; XXVII, 18 and Gautama Dharma Sūtra XX, 8; XXIII, 21; XXIV, 11.
20. Cf. MaitU VI, 7 (above); SU IV, 18 (§ 17).

PART I
DAWN AND BIRTH

Agni

Part I deals with the invisible and underlying foundations of reality; *metaontogenesis* could be its academic title. It speaks neither of that which "is" nor of that which "shall be." It uses a past tense, but it does not refer properly to a temporal "was." The origin of time cannot be temporal. The source of being cannot itself be just "being." If this were so, there would be no end: we would then search for the source of the source of being and so on indefinitely. The elements of the world or the elements of life are not just parts of the whole. The primordial Word is not yet spoken, nor is the Lord manifested as sovereign; he is not yet Lord. The topics and heroes of Part I of our anthology are not constituents or, as it were, "bricks" of the universe, as if they were molecules out of which reality is composed. They are rather pre-realities, pre-stages, factors shaping the real, not merely components or parts of it, just as in nuclear physics the elemental "particles" cannot any longer be said to be elements or particles out of which the whole is made. In any event our attention is here directed toward discovering the role of nothingness, or becoming aware of the place of a void which cannot be said to exist but which makes it possible that things can exist by the very act of filling up the void.

The five sections of Part I, though not systematically connected, are deeply related inasmuch as they all try to give expression to God-above-God, the Beginning-before-the-Beginning, the Lord-previous-to-any-Lordship, Life-before-Life, and the Unity underlying all Plurality. We repeat: all that goes on, or rather, in, behind the curtain is not within the range of our experience and thus that Source is neither God, nor Beginning, nor Lord, Life, Light, Unity, Basis, nor even Being or Nonbeing. It is not that I discover what makes Being possible, because it is merely a demand of the mind to find the conditions of possibility for everything. The mind here is by no means outside this very problem. The Prelude is really before the whole play, before all *līlā*, human and divine. It is actually not played. Perhaps the phenomenological mark of "sacred Scriptures," modern or ancient, secular or religious, is that these Scriptures deal with that which cannot be dealt with and speak of the unspeakable, thus positioning themselves beyond the vigilance of the principle of noncontradiction, without, of course, intending or pretending to deny it (for which they would need the help of the same principle). At a later date cosmogonic images were, if not replaced, complemented and in a way overshadowed by metaphysical reflections and, in the course of time, by more religious language and more elaborated cultic performances. Examples of all this are given in Part I. Here our sights are on the invisible, on the origins, on the foundations, on Nonbeing, on the transcendent, but with no intention of stopping there; on the contrary, the whole thrust is on what follows, on what is coming and is being unfolded before our eyes. Liberation lies ahead; there is a long way to go, but the credentials of reality already show that anything is possible with the really real. The Dawn is not the day, nor is Birth really human life, but without them there would be neither day nor our life. The true "be-coming" is an authentic *coming* to *be*; but do not ask where it comes from lest you stop the very becoming. Faith very properly belongs to this section. Without faith nothing takes shape or comes into being. Faith is the beginning of salvation, because it is the very dawn of our true being, the existential openness of our human existence—the very condition of any real, that is, sacred act, the Vedas will say.

A. PRELUDE

Ādi

In the beginning, to be sure, nothing existed,
neither the heaven nor the earth nor space in between.
So Nonbeing, having decided to be, became spirit and
said: "Let me be!"[1] *He warmed himself further and*
from this heating was born fire. He warmed himself
still further and from this heating was born light.

TB II, 2, 9, 1-2

Numerous texts are to be found in the Vedic scriptures, of extraordinary diversity and incomparable richness, which seek unweariedly to penetrate the mystery of the beginnings and to explain the immensity and the amazing harmony of the universe. We find a proliferation of speculations, doubts, and descriptions, an atmosphere charged with solemnity, a sense of life lived to the full—all of which spontaneously bring to mind the landscape of the Himalayas. These texts seem to burst forth impetuously like streams issuing from glaciers. Within this rushing torrent may be discerned a certain life view, deep and basic, an evolving life view that can yet

1. An extremely condensed text: *tad asad eva sanmano 'kuruta syām iti:* "so Nonbeing made a resolve of being: may I be!" *san-manaḥ kṛ*: "make up one's mind [to be]." The text could be read: (*a*) *tad asad eva san, mano 'kuruta*: "so Nonbeing, the only existent [being], decided to be [and] became spirit"; (*b*) *tad asad eva san-mano 'kuruta*: "so Nonbeing decided to be," i.e., "created a resolve to be, or, made up his mind to be." Cf. BU I, 2, 1 (§ 17).

be traced unbroken from the Ṛg Veda, through the Atharva Veda and the Brāhmaṇas, to the Upaniṣads.

What is fascinating about the experience of the Vedic seers is not only that they have dared to explore the outer space of being and existence, piercing the outskirts of reality, exploring the boundaries of the universe, describing being and its universal laws, but that they have also undertaken the risky and intriguing adventure of going beyond and piercing the being barrier so as to float in utter nothingness, so to speak, and discover that Nonbeing is only the outer atmosphere of Being, its protective veil. They plunge thus into a darkness enwrapped by darkness, into the Beyond from which there is no return, into that Prelude of Existence in which there is neither Being nor Nonbeing, neither God nor Gods, nor creature of any type; the traveler himself is volatilized, has disappeared. Creation is the act by which God, or whatever name we may choose to express the Ultimate, affirms himself not only vis-à-vis the world, thus created, but also vis-à-vis himself, for he certainly was neither creator before creation nor God for himself. The Vedic seers make the staggering claim of entering into that enclosure where God is not yet God, where God is thus unknown to himself, and, not being creator, is "nothing." Without this perspective we may fail to grasp the Vedic message regarding the absolute Prelude to everything: *that One, tad ekam* (which is the less imperfect expression), or *this, idam* (which is the other way of saying it). *Idam, this,* that is to say, anything that I can refer to, though it is never exhausted by the reference; *idam, that* which I think, mean, touch, imagine, will, reject, love, hate—anything to which I may be able to point with any means at my disposal, my senses, mind, intuition, emotions, or whatever; *idam, that* which takes as many forms as I am capable of imagining and constantly transcends all of them; *this,* that is, whatever can fall into the range of my experience, *idam,* at the absolute Prelude, was neither Being nor Nonbeing, neither Consciousness nor Ignorance.[2] *This,* in whatever form, is *tad, that*: outside, beyond, transcendent, hidden in its own immanence, absolutely ungraspable and ineffable.[3] Furthermore, this *that* is *ekam,* One, absolute oneness, because all specific generic and ontic differences are included in the *ekam* and it

2. Cf. § VI A a Introduction.
3. Cf. KathU IV, 3 etc. (§ VII 40). "This [is] indeed that": *etad vai tat.*

is precisely this that makes differentiation intrinsically possible. Things can differ only against a background of oneness.

Hiraṇyagarbha, the Golden Germ, appears here as a powerful symbol and Prajāpati is one of the most important mythical names for the carrying out of this process, though he emerges at the very end of it.[4] For a fuller understanding of the myth we may consider it in three stages or moments which are, of course, neither chronological nor perhaps ontological, but which are certainly anthropological (or rather metahistorical) and helpful for our understanding: Solitude, Sacrifice, Integration.

1. SOLITUDE

In the beginning, things undoubtedly began. But what about the beginning itself "before" the actual "beginning"? We cannot say "before" the beginning without falling into contradiction. The beginning is precisely the beginning, because it has no "before," because it is itself beginningless. Thus, if we want to speak about the beginning in itself, we shall have to use a language of opposites and make ample use of paradoxes: in the beginning there was neither Being nor Nonbeing, there was neither space nor the sky beyond, neither death nor nondeath, no distinction between day and night. In the absolute void the One breathed by its own propulsion without breath; shadows were concealed by shadows. The symbol here is utter solitude.

The One enwrapped in the void took birth. Nonbeing made himself *ātman,* and cried: I will be! Let me be! This was the Self in the form of a Person. But the Primal Being is not yet fully born, he is not yet fully "out," for when he is looking around he sees nothing. So he is forced to look upon himself and take cognizance of himself. Only then is he born; only then does he discover properly not only himself but also his total solitude, his helplessness, one could say.

When self-awareness comes to birth it discovers that it is alone and is afraid, "for the one who is alone is afraid," because aloneness is an unnatural state and thus even Being needs to be surrounded and "protected" by Nonbeing. The ontologic anxiety of Being facing Nonbeing is born simultaneously with self-awareness.

4. Cf. also RV III, 38, a cosmogonic hymn in which the primordial Being is conceived in the poet's imagination as appearing in the form of an androgynous Bull.

It looks for an object, for "some-thing" which can be grappled with: anxiety tends to be converted into fear. Now, fear is overcome by a second act of reflection: the discovery that nothing exists to be frightened of. But the cost of this rationalized defense is boredom; there is no joy at all in brooding over oneself. Then arises the desire for another. It is the beginning of the expansion, the breaking of the Self—and thus starts the process of the primordial Sacrifice.

2. SACRIFICE

Prajāpati desires a second but he has no primary matter out of which to create the universe. This dilemma is important. A second identical to him will not satisfy his craving, for it will merge with him; a second inferior to him will obviously not do either, for it will be his puppet, the projection of his own will. It will offer him no resistance, nor will it be a real partner. The Vedic Revelation unveils the mystery by means of the myth of the sacrifice of Prajāpati, who dismembers himself in order to let the world be, and be what it is. Creation is *the* sacrifice, the gift of Prajāpati in an act of self-immolation. There is no other to whom to offer the sacrifice, no other to accept it. Prajāpati is at the same time the sacrificer, the sacrifice (the victim), the one to whom the sacrifice is offered, and even the result of the sacrifice. Even more, as we shall see later on, sacrifice becomes the first Absolute.[5]

Prajāpati, being alone and self-sufficient, can have no external motivation impelling him to create the worlds. The texts, however, mention two factors that are not motives for action but indwelling principles of reality itself: *kāma* and *tapas,* love and ardor. Whether reference is being made to the personalist tradition of Prajāpati or to the nonpersonalist tradition of the One emerging from Nonbeing, it is invariably by means of these two powers that the creative process commences. *Tapas* is the primordial fervor, the original fire, the supreme concentration, the ultimate energy, the creative force that initiates the whole cosmic movement. Order and truth (*ṛta* and *satya*) were born from *tapas*. Furthermore, "desire [*kāma*] was the original development [of the One] which was the first sowing [*retas*] of consciousness [*manas*]."[6] Thus *kāma* enters upon the scene.[7] This

5. Cf. § III B.
6. RV X, 129, 4ab (§ I 1); AV XIX, 52, 1ab (§ II 13). We give here a different translation.
7. For *kâma* cf. § II 12, 13.

love or desire cannot be a yearning toward any object; it is a concentration upon the Self and is related to *tapas*. *Tapas* incited by *kāma* penetrates into the Self to the point of bursting asunder, of dismemberment.

Tapas and *kāma* go together. Love is the fervor that imparts power to create and *tapas* is the energy of love which produces the world. "He desired: Can I multiply myself? Can I engender? He practiced *tapas*, he created the whole world, all that exists."[8] But this world, once in existence, has its own destiny. This is the third act of the drama.

3. INTEGRATION

Whereas the first act of the drama has no actor, properly speaking, and the whole action is played behind the curtain, and whereas the second act has God as the actor, this third part presents Man as the hero. Prajāpati, having created the world out of the self-sacrifice of himself, is exhausted, feeble, drained away, and on the point of death. He is no longer powerful and mighty; the universe has the possibility of escaping the power of God; it stands on its own. "Once engendered, the creatures turned their backs upon him and went away."[9] They try to free themselves from the creator, but fall into chaos and disorder. If the universe has to subsist, God has to come again and penetrate the creatures afresh, entering into them for a second time. This second redeeming act, however, needs the collaboration of the creature. Here is the locus for Man's collaboration with the unique act of Prajāpati which gives consistency and existence to the world. This is Man's place and function in the sacrifice.

This sacrifice is not just a kind of offering to God so that he may release to us what we have earned. On the contrary, it is the action by which we create and procreate along with God and reconstruct his Body. This action gathers the first material for the total *yajña* (sacrifice), not from animals, flowers, or whatever, but from the inmost depth of Man himself. It is the outcome of Man's urge to be in tune with that cosmic dynamism which enables the universe constantly to win over the power of Nonbeing. "That I may become everything!" is the cry that the Śatapatha Brāhmaṇa put not only

8. TU II, 6 (§I 7).
9. TMB XXI, 2, 1.

into the mouth of Prajāpati, but also into the heart of every being.[10] This is the cry that every man will feel in face of the limitations of his own person and the small field of action in which he can operate. When confronted with himself, when beginning to enter into the poised state of contemplation, when at peace with himself and at the threshold of realization, Man has this tremendous desire to be this and that, to become this and that, to be involved in every process and to be present everywhere. It is not so much the hankering for power which drives Man, as some moralists would have us believe, much less a simply hedonistic urge; on the contrary, it is this existential desire to be and thus to be everything and, in the last instance, to Be, not just to share a part or to be present in a corner of the banquet of life and existence, but to be active at the very core of reality, in the divine center itself whence all emerges and is directed. "Let me have a self!" is another refrain. The wise Man, described time and again in the *śruti,* is not the escapist and unfriendly solitary, but the full Man who, having realized his own limitations, knows how to enter into the infinite ocean of *sat, cit,* and *ānanda,* of being, consciousness, and joy.

The Hymn of the Origins *Nāsadīya Sūkta*

1 The vision of this hymn comes out of a profound insight into the mystery of reality. It is the product of a mystical experience that far transcends the limits of logical thinking; it is a religious chant—for only in music or poetry can such a message be conveyed—invoking in splendid verses the Primal Mystery that transcends all categories, both human and divine. This hymn, while trying to plumb the depths of the mystery, formulates no doctrinal system but expresses itself by means of a rich variety of different symbols related to the one single insight. The hymn, in fact, presents an extraordinary consistency, which is patent only to the contemplative mind; in the absence of this latter, however, it is bound to appear either as syncretistic or as agnostic, as has in fact been sometimes asserted.

We are dealing here, in the first place, not with a temporal cosmogonic hymn describing the beginning of creation, or even with an ontological theogony, or with a historical description concerning the formation of the Gods or even of God. It is not the

10. SB XI, 1, 6, 17 (§I 6).

description of a succession of stages through which the world has passed. The starting point of the hymn is not a piece of causal thinking seeking the cause of this world or of God or the Gods, but rather an intuitive vision of the whole. This hymn does not attempt to communicate information but to share a mystical awareness that transcends the sharpest lines of demarcation of which the human mind is capable: the divine and the created, Being and Nonbeing. It seeks to give expression to the insight of the oneness of reality which is experienced as being so totally one that it does not need the horizon of nonreality or the background of a thinking process to appear in its entire actuality. This oneness is so radically one that every distinction is overcome; it is that unutterable and unthinkable process that "sees" all that is and is-not, in its utmost simplicity, which is, of course, not a *jñāna,* a gnosis, but an ignorance, an interrogation. The One is not seen against any horizon or background. All is included. All is pure horizon. There are no limits to the universal or, for that matter, to the concrete.

The first verse brings us straightaway to the heart of the mystery and is composed of a series of questions. Neither an affirmation nor a negation is capable of carrying the weight of the ultimate mystery. Only the openness of an interrogation can embrace what our mere thinking cannot encompass. The Ultimate is neither real nor nonreal, neither being nor nonbeing, and thus neither is nor is-not; the apophatism is total and covers everything, even itself: "darkness was wrapped in darkness."

Being as well as Nonbeing, the Absolute (or Ultimate) as well as the Beginning, are contradictory concepts when applied to the primordial mystery. "Absolute" means unrelatedness, and when we speak or think about it we are negating that character. "Ultimate" points toward the end of a process that has no "after," and "Beginning" toward a point that has no "before." But what is to prevent our thinking a "previous" to the Beginning and a "beyond" to the Ultimate, unless our mind artificially imposes a limit on its thinking or bursts in the effort? If we think "Being" we cannot be prevented from thinking "Nonbeing" also, and so the very concept of an all-including "Being" which does not include "Nonbeing" defeats its own purpose. Indeed, a metaphysician might say that "Nonbeing" *is* a nonentity and an unthinkable concept; yet the fact remains that at least on the level of our thinking the concept of "Being" cannot include its contradiction.

This verse tells us that the primordial mystery cannot be pinpointed to any idea, thing, thought, or being. It is primarily neither the answer to a set of riddles nor the object of current metaphysical speculations concerning the how or the why of creation. It is beyond thinking and Being. The symbol of water is the most pertinent one: the primordial water covers all, supports all, has no form of its own, is visible and invisible, has no limits, pervades everything; it is the first condition of life, the place of the original seed, the fertilizing milieu.

The seer then continues by a series of negatives: there was neither death nor nondeath, nor any distinction between day and night. All the opposites, including the contradictories, are on this side of the curtain. At this point we have not yet reached Being and thus we have not yet the possibility of limiting Being by Nonbeing.[11]

This One is not even a concept. It is not a concept limit like truth, goodness, beauty, and similar concepts when applied to the Absolute; it is rather the limit of a concept, unthinkable in itself and yet present on the other side of the curtain as the necessary condition for the very existence and intelligibility of everything. Whereas the concepts of being, goodness, truth, and the like admit degrees of approximation to the fullness of that to which they refer, the One does not. There are degrees of being, of goodness, of truth. There are no degrees of oneness. The One represents the peak of mystical awareness, which India developed later in her Advaitic philosophy, and the West in Trinitarian theology.

Darkness and emptiness are also symbols of the first moment. This darkness is not, however, the moral or even the ontological darkness of the world, but the primordial darkness of the Origin. The negative as well as the positive aspect of existence belongs to the Ultimate. Evil and good, the positive and the negative, both are embraced in the One that encompasses everything. Now, to cancel darkness by darkness, is it not to let the light shine forth? Furthermore, it is said that desire, love, fervor, were the dynamic forces that brought reality to a temporal process of originating something out of something. Out of nothing nothing can come. Nothingness is not previous to, but coextensive with Being. The source of Being is not another Being or anything that can be considered as *being* an origin out of which things come to be. The process, according to the

11. Cf. §VI A a.

intuition of the Vedic *ṛṣi*, is one of concentration, of condensation, of an emergence by the power of love. This love cannot be a desire toward "something" that does not exist, or even a desire coming out of a nonexisting Being. It is this very concentration that originates the Self which is going to be and have that love. Primordial love is neither a transitive nor an intransitive act; it is neither an act directed toward the other (which in this case does not exist) nor an act directed toward oneself (which in this case is also nonexistent), but it is the constitutive act by which existence comes into being. Without love there is no being, but love does not happen without ardor or *tapas*. It is fervor, *tapas*, that makes the being be; they are not separable. The relation between *kāma*, desire and love, on the one hand, and *tapas*, ardor and heat, on the other, is one of the universal cosmic laws linking Being and the whole realm of beings (vv. 3–4).

The poets, those sages who seek to penetrate the mystery of reality, discover in Nonbeing the gravitational center of Being; only when this is realized can the cord that differentiates them be extended. The rope connecting Being and Nonbeing is the ultimate rope of salvation (v. 5).

The two last stanzas voice several agonized queries and give expression to a deep-rooted unextirpable uncertainty for which no reply is vouchsafed, because reality is still on the move and any definite answer would preclude its constant newness. This insight brings us again to that ultimate level where the One is situated. From that depth the sage expresses the most fundamental question about the essential and existential enigma of the universe: What, he asks, is the origin of this universe, of all this, *idam*? Who, or what, is its purpose, its end, its direction? It cannot be the Gods, for they themselves belong on this side of the curtain. Nobody can know what is the very foundation of knowing, nor can anyone say that it is not known. This latter assumption would amount to being biased in favor of a certain negative theology or philosophy. To say that we do not know can be as assertive as to say that we do know. The last question is not the expression of a renunciation of knowledge or a declaration of agnosticism, which would here amount to a dogmatic affirmation, but the declaration that the problem—and not only the answer—is beyond the subject and object of knowledge itself. Only he who is beyond and above everything may know—or he may not, for how may there be any assurance concerning it? It is not only that we know that we do not know, which would then be mere pretending, but that we really do not know even if it is at all knowable by any possible knowledge. The hymn concludes with this query, this constitutive uncertainty which is of infinite magnitude, because we are all involved in it. To answer the query would amount to killing the very unfolding of reality. It is the openness of this interrogation which allows the universe to emerge and to exist.

Nāsadīya Sūkta

RV X, 129

1. At first was neither Being nor Nonbeing.
   There was not air nor yet sky beyond.
   What was its wrapping? Where? In whose protection?
   Was Water there, unfathomable and deep?

2. There was no death then, nor yet deathlessness;
   of night or day there was not any sign.
   The One breathed without breath, by its own impulse.
   Other than that was nothing else at all.

3. Darkness was there, all wrapped around by darkness,
   and all was Water indiscriminate. Then
   that which was hidden by the Void, that One, emerging,
   stirring, through power of Ardor, came to be.

4. In the beginning Love arose,
   which was the primal germ cell of the mind.
   The Seers, searching in their hearts with wisdom,
   discovered the connection of Being in Nonbeing.

5. A crosswise line cut Being from Nonbeing.
   What was described above it, what below?
   Bearers of seed there were and mighty forces,
   thrust from below and forward move above.

6. Who really knows? Who can presume to tell it?
   Whence was it born? Whence issued this creation?
   Even the Gods came after its emergence.
   Then who can tell from whence it came to be?

7. That out of which creation has arisen,
   whether it held it firm or it did not,
   He who surveys it in the highest heaven,
   He surely knows—or maybe He does not!

1. SB X, 5, 3, 1-2 (§I 13) considers that *manas,* the mind, or rather the spirit, is the one and only thing that fulfills the condition of being neither existent nor nonexistent. The spirit is existent only in things, and things without the spirit are nonexistent.
Cf. §I 14.

Indian tradition has interpreted these first two mantras as voicing all the different perspectives under which the ultimate metaphysical problem can be envisaged. Cf. SU IV, 18 (§ I 7); BG XIII, 12.

2. Own impulse: *svadhā,* the active principle, has been translated as "by its own energy" (Zaehner), "power" (Mascaró, Macdonell, Edgerton), "impulse" (Bose), "of itself" (Misch), "strength" (Raghavan), "will power" (Telang-Chaubey), "élan," "initiative" (Renou), "Eigengesetz" (Geldner), just to give an idea of different readings. Cf. the later idea of *śakti* or the divine power of the Godhead, always represented as the Goddess, spouse of the corresponding God.

The One: *tad ekam.* Cf. §VI 1, and also RV I, 164, 10; X, 82, 2; 6 (§VII 12); AV VIII, 9, 25-26; IX, 9, 7; IsU 4 (§ VII 11).

Cf. other texts in §I 7.

3. For the primordial Waters, cf. §I 15 for further references.

Indiscriminate: *apraketā,* without a recognizable sign, undifferentiated, indistinguishable, unrecognizable, referring to the amorphous chaos, the unformed primordial Waters.

Water: *salila,* flood, surge, waves, the ocean, waters. The Greek word *pelagos* would perhaps render the idea of *salila,* the open sea without shores or boundaries, amorphous water, a kind of chaotic magma.

The Void: *ābhu,* or *ābhū,* the primordial potency, capable of becoming everything.

Ardor: *tapas,* cf. §I 2.

4. Cf. AV XIX, 52, 1 (§II 13), where it is translated somewhat differently.

5. "Bearers of seed" are considered to be the male forces and "mighty forces" the female principle. Cf. *dakṣa* and *aditi* as the masculine and feminine principles, respectively, in RV X, 72, 4 (§ VII 2).

6. Cf. KenU I, 1 (§ VI 3).

Creative Fervor *Tapas*

2 *Tapas* or cosmic ardor, ascetic fire, arduous penance, concentration, which here amounts to an ontic condensation, is said in this last but one hymn of the Ṛg Veda to be the energy giving birth to cosmic order and to truth. The three major concepts of Indian wisdom and of Man's awareness are *tapas, ṛta,* and *satya,* ardor, order, and truth.

In the preceding hymn the universe is said to emerge out of or through ardor.[12] In this hymn (v. 1) the first result of the protocosmic energy is said to be the double principle underlying the whole of reality: on the one hand, order (the structure, the formal principle, the contexture of reality) and on the other, truth (the contents, the substance, the material principle, the concrete and crystallized reality itself). Owing to *ṛta,* this world is not a chaos, but a cosmos, not an anarchic mass, but an ordered and harmonious whole. Owing to *satya,* the world is not a haphazard place, an irresponsible game, or an inconsistent and purely fluid appearance. *Satya* is not primarily an epistemic truth but an ontic truthfulness, an ontological fullness, with content, weight, and reality, namely, being.

The *eka,* the One of the Hymn of the Origins, is still void and devoid of reality. No reality can emerge without these two princi-

12. Cf. RV X, 129, 4 (§ I 1).

ples of order and truthfulness, or, in other words, harmony and self-consistency.

Cosmic ardor gives birth also to that undifferentiated reality which has no better symbol than cosmic night, the night that does not have the day as counterpart, but envelops everything, though in the darkness of the not-yet-manifested.

From this *yoni*, "magma" or "matrix," space and time came to be, that is, the ocean and the year. After space and time, life can appear and thrive; all that "blinks the eye" begins its career through existence. Once life is there, the world can be ordered according to its regular and harmonic forms of existence: sun, moon, heaven, earth, the sidereal spaces and the light, the last-named being the culmination and perfection of the work of fashioning the world—and all by the power of fervor! No wonder that the performance of *tapas* is considered as the reenactment of this primordial and cosmic act by which the universe came to be. The contemplative and meditative saint performing *tapas* is not the Man who sits idle, gazing passively at things or at nothing. He is the most active collaborator in the maintenance of this world and experiences in himself the ardor, fire, energy, and power of concentration which are capable of destroying the world, as later myths will tell us.

Tapas RV X, 190

1. From blazing Ardor Cosmic Order came
   and Truth; from thence was born the obscure night;
   from thence the Ocean with its billowing waves.

2. From Ocean with its waves was born the year
   which marshals the succession of nights and days,
   controlling everything that blinks the eye.

3. Then, as before, did the creator fashion
   the Sun and Moon, the Heaven and the Earth,
   the atmosphere and the domain of light.

1. Blazing Ardor: *tapas* has been translated by "spiritual fire" (Bose), "heat" or "ascetic fervour" (Edgerton), "power of heat" (Macdonell, Zaehner), "fervour" or "warmth" (Griffith), "austerity" (Telang-Chaubey), "chaleur ascétique," "puissance de l'ardeur," "ardeur créatrice" (Renou), "heisser Drang," "heisses Verlangen," "Askese" (Geldner), etc.

Cf. AV X, 7, 1 (§ I 3); BU I, 2, 6 (§ I 14); V, 11; KenU IV, 8; SU I, 15 (§ VI 5); MundU III, 1, 5; MaitU IV, 4. Also cf. AV XI, 8, 2; 6 where it is said that *tapas* is born from *karman*.

Cosmic Order: *ṛta*. Cf. RV IV, 23, 8-10 and § III B Introduction.

Truth: *satya*. Cf. RV X, 85, 1 (§ II 16 Introduction); etc. Cf. also § IV Introduction.

2. Everything that blinks the eye: everything that lives. Cf. MaitS I, 5, 12 for the creation of night by the Gods (§ V 1 Introduction).

3. As before: *yathā-pūrvam*, as previously, suggests a cyclic interpretation, but could equally be considered an expression of a dynamic process: now the world is being created and sustained as before. The creator: *dhātṛ*, or ordainer.

The Cosmic Pillar *Skambha*

3 From time immemorial in many cultures, both archaic and fully developed, *axis mundi*, the center of the world, stands not only for a geographical orientation but also for a historical point of reference and for an ontological foundation. Furthermore, the idea also has a theocosmological meaning: the Godhead is the actual support of the universe. True to type, the *skambha*, the "support," the "pillar," is seen in the Atharva Veda as the frame of creation and, even more, as that invisible and ever transcendent ground on which everything stands and toward which every being tends. The vision is circular and anthropological. Man and the cosmos are not two different creations, each governed by different laws. There is one point, without dimensions, as we would be tempted to word it today, that is, without forming part of the things of which it is the point of reference, which is the support, the ground, of everything. Knowledge of this *skambha* constitutes the full realization of the mystery of existence, the discovery of Brahman and the deciphering of the hidden treasures of the world.

The Cosmic Pillar, the *axis mundi*, is not a sacred place; it is not a particular mountain or shrine, or even a particular event, as many a religious tradition affirms, but a "manifest though hidden" Ground, as another hymn on *skambha* is going to say.[13] It is an ever dynamic pole which stands there not only to offer a static, a sure, foundation of reality, but also to explain the never-ending processes of nature: the wind never tired of blowing, the mind never ceasing to think, the waters—both earthly and celestial—never ceasing to flow (v. 37). *Skambha* holds even opposites together (v. 15); it is a tree whose branches are Being and Nonbeing (v. 21). The whole universe resides in *skambha* and all values that Men acknowledge as authentic are rooted in it; faith (vv. 1, 11), worship (v. 20), sacrifice (v. 16), and all that transcends the empirical level are grounded in it.

The recurrent question of this hymn is: What is *skambha*? Who

13. Cf. AV X, 8, 6 (§ VII 27).

is it? Meditating upon the hymn one discovers the following progression. First, the *skambha* appears as both the epistemic hypothesis and the ontological hypostasis which are needed to make intelligible and to sustain the manifold aspect of reality. There is no intelligibility without a certain reduction to unity. But, second, unity cannot be on the same level as plurality, for that would involve the most blatant contradiction. It must somehow lie deeper. This means, third, that the epistemic plurality does not contradict the ontological unity. But, fourth—and here is the purport of this hymn—the ontological order has to be abandoned no less than the epistemic one. The insight of the Vedas would then seem to be that the *skambha* is the whole of reality deprived not only of its phenomenic character but also of its ontological reality; the *skambha* "is" not, because it stands as the condition and possibility of Being itself. In other words, the *skambha* symbolizes that naked "thatness," *tat-tva,* which renders reality intelligible in its manifold character and also gives a basis to all that is. All lines of thought converge on one single hypothetical point, just as by following the rays of light we would converge on the invisible center of the sun. Now by concentrating on that unthinkable point one reaches a state in which thought is transcended, and that point emerges refulgent and radiant in its unique character, like the sun in the metaphor. It would be a mistake to give any kind of "thinkable" reality to such a point. To be "thought" is to be "born" into reality or into this world, but *skambha* is the unthinkable par excellence; otherwise it would not be *skambha,* the Unborn that is just ready to spring up into the world (v. 31). The intuition regarding this Cosmic Pillar or Support does not consist in seeing it, but in discovering the vestiges of its feet when they have disappeared in order to jump into the real; it is like seeing the vibrations of the springboard a moment after the dive. To know *skambha* is to know the Lord of creatures without his creatures and without his Lordship.

The hymn is traditionally said to be addressed to Skambha or to the *ātman,* the Self of the universe. Underlying the whole symbolism is the idea of the cosmic Man or *puruṣa.*

Skambha AV X, 7

1. In which of his limbs does Fervor dwell?
In which of his limbs is Order set?
In what part of him abides Constancy, Faith?
In which of his limbs is Truth established?

2. From which of his limbs does Fire shine forth?
From which of his limbs issues the Wind?
Which limb does the moon take for measuring rod
when it measures the form of the great Support?

3. In which of his limbs does the earth abide?
In which of his limbs the atmosphere?
In which of his limbs is the sky affixed?
In which of his limbs the great Beyond?

4. Toward whom does the rising Flame aspire?
Toward whom does the Wind eagerly blow?
On whom do all the compass points converge?
Tell me of that Support—who may he be?

5. Where do the half months and months together
proceed in consultation with the year?
Where do the seasons go, in groups or singly?
Tell me of that Support—who may he be?

6. Toward whom run the sisters, day and night,
who look so different yet one summons answer?
Toward whom do the waters with longing flow?
Tell me of that Support—who may he be?

7. The One on whom the Lord of Life
leant for support when he propped up the world—
Tell me of that Support—who may he be?

8. That which of all forms the Lord of Life
created—above, below, and in between—
with how much of himself penetrated the Support?
How long was the portion that did not enter?

9. With how much of himself penetrated the Support
into the past? With how much into the future?
In that single limb whose thousand parts he fashioned
with how much of himself did he enter, that Support?

10. Through whom men know the worlds and what enwraps them,
the waters and Holy Word, the all-powerful
in whom are found both Being and Nonbeing—
Tell me of that Support—who may he be?

11. By whom Creative Fervor waxing powerful
upholds the highest Vow, in whom unite
Cosmic Order and Faith, the waters and the Word—
Tell me of that Support—who may he be?

12. On whom is firmly founded earth and sky
and the air in between; so too the fire,
moon, sun, and wind, each knowing his own place—
Tell me of that Support—who may he be?

13. In whose one limb all the Gods,
three and thirty in number, are affixed—
Tell me of that Support—who may he be?

14. In whom are set firm the firstborn Seers,
the hymns, the songs, and the sacrificial formulas,
in whom is established the Single Seer—
Tell me of that Support—who may he be?

15. In whom, as Man, deathlessness and death
combine, to whom belong the surging ocean
and all the arteries that course within him;
Tell me of that Support—who may he be?

16. Of whom the four cardinal directions
comprise the veins, visibly swollen,
in whom the sacrifice has advanced victorious—
Tell me of that Support—who may he be?

17. Those who know the divine in Man
know the highest Lord; who knows the highest Lord
or the Lord of Life knows the supreme Brahman.
They therefore know the Support also.

18. He whose head is Universal Fire,
who has for his eyes the Aṅgirases
and for his limbs the practitioners of sorcery—
Tell me of that Support—who may he be?

19. He whose mouth, so they say, is Brahman,
whose tongue is a whip steeped in honey,
of whom Virāj is considered the udder—
Tell me of that Support—who may he be?

20. Out of his body were carved the verses,
the formulas being formed from the shavings.
His hairs are the songs, his mouth the hymns
of the Seers Atharvan and Aṅgiras—
Tell me of that Support—who may he be?

21. The branch of Nonbeing which is far-extending
men take to be the highest one of all.
They reckon as inferior those who worship
your other branch, the branch of Being.

22. In whom the Ādityas, Rudras and Vasus,
are held together, in whom are set firm
worlds—that which was and that which shall be—
Tell me of that Support—who may he be?

23. Whose treasure hoard the three and thirty Gods
forever guard—today who knows its contents?
Tell me of that Support—who may he be?

24. In whom the Gods, knowers of Brahman,
acknowledge Brahman as the Supreme—
he who knows the Gods face to face
is truly a Knower, a Vehicle of Brahman.

25. Great are the Gods who were born from Nonbeing,
yet men aver this Nonbeing to be
the single limb of the Support, the great Beyond.

26. The limb in which the Support, when generating,
evolved the Ancient One—who knows this limb
knows too by that same knowledge the Ancient One.

27. It was from his limb that the thirty-three Gods
distributed portions among themselves.
Thus in truth only knowers of Brahman
are also knowers of the thirty-three Gods.

28. Men recognize the Golden Embryo
as the unutterable, the Supreme.
Yet it was the Support who in the beginning
poured forth upon the world that stream of gold.

29. In the Support the worlds consist; in him
Creative Fervor and Order have their ground.
You I have known, O Support, face to face,
in Indra wholly concentrated.

30. In Indra the worlds consist; in Indra
Creative Fervor and Order have their ground.
You I have known, O Indra, face to face,
in the Support wholly established.

31. Before dawn and sunrise man invokes
name after name. This Unborn sprang to birth
already with full sovereignty empowered.
Than he nothing higher ever existed.

32. Homage to him of whom the earth is the model,
the atmosphere his belly, who created the sky
from his head. Homage to this supreme Brahman!

33. Homage to him whose eye is the sun
and the moon which is ever renewed, whose mouth
is the Fire. Homage to this supreme Brahman!

34. Homage to him whose in-breath and out-breath
is the Wind, whose eyes are the Aṅgirases,
whose wisdom consists in the cardinal points.
Homage once again to this supreme Brahman!

35. By the Support are held both heaven and earth,
by the Support the broad domain of space,

by the Support the six divergent directions,
by the Support is this whole world pervaded.

36. Homage to him who, born of labor
and Creative Fervor, has entered all the worlds,
who has taken Soma for his own exclusive
possession. Homage to this Supreme Brahman!

37. How does the wind not cease to blow?
How does the mind take no repose?
Why do the waters, seeking to reach truth,
never at any time cease flowing?

38. A mighty wonder in the midst of creation
moves, thanks to Fervor, on the waters' surface.
To him whatever Gods there are adhere
like branches of a tree around the trunk.

39. To whom the Gods always with hands and feet,
with speech, ear, and eye bring tribute unmeasured
in a well-measured place of sacrifice.
Tell me of that Support—who may he be?

40-41. In him exists no darkness, no evil.
In him are all the lights, including the three
that are in the Lord of Life. The one who knows
the Reed of gold standing up in the water
is truly the mysterious Lord of Life.

1. Fervor: *tapas*.
Order: *ṛta*, eternal Order, Sacred Law.
Faith: *śraddhā*, cf. § I 36.
Truth: *satya*.
2. Support: *skambha*, throughout.
Fire: Agni.
Wind: Mātariśvan, also a form of Agni.
Moon: the yardstick for measuring time.
4. "Whom" could equally well be rendered by "what" here and in all the succeeding verses.
7. Lord of Life: Prajāpati, throughout.
Propped up: the root *stambh-*, to fix, to support, etc., is evidently connected with *skambha* (*stambha* is also a pillar, post, support, cf. RV IV, 13, 5). Skambha is more basic and interior to the universe than its creator, Prajāpati.
8. The penetration of space. The portion that did not enter: i.e., his transcendent part, cf. RV X, 90, 1; 3 (§ I 5).
9. The penetration of time.
10. Holy Word: *brahman*, which here could also be translated by "World-principle." Cf. RV X, 129, 1 (§ I 1).
11. Creative Fervor: *tapas*.
Cosmic Order: *ṛta*.
13. Affixed: *samāhita*, collected, united. The Skambha is the principle that unites all the Vedic Gods. For the number of the Gods, cf. also BU III, 9, 1-9 (§ VI 2).
14. Hymns: the Ṛg Veda.
Songs: the Sāma Veda.
Sacrificial formulas: the Yajur Veda.
Single Seer: *ekarṣi*, often refers to the sun. Cf. the mystical use of this term in the U (IsU 16; § VII 31; MundU III, 2, 10; § I 37), although it also appears as the name of a *ṛṣi* (cf. BU IV, 6, 3).
15. Man: *puruṣa*. The *coincidentia oppositorum*: all meet in Man. Cf. RV X, 121, 2 (§ I 4). Cf. CU III, 19, 2, for the metaphor of the ocean and the arteries.

16. Veins: *nāḍī*. This verse begins the anthropocosmic description which is continued in vv. 18 sq.
17. The divine in Man: *brahman* in *puruṣa*.
Highest Lord: *parameṣṭhin*. There are, so to speak, four aspects of the Absolute; in order of interiority they are: Prajāpati–Parameṣṭhin–Puruṣa–Brahman.
18. Universal Fire: *vaiśvānara*, the sun.
Practitioners of sorcery: *yātavaḥ*, or demons. Evil is part of cosmic reality.
19. Whip steeped in honey: cf. V IX, 1 where the whip symbolizes a cosmological principle.
Virāj: the cosmic Cow, Speech.
20. The four Vedas originate from Skambha.
21. Cf. TU II, 6 (§ I 7). Priority is here given to the ontic apophatism which is developed later in the Indian tradition.
23. For the treasure, cf. AV X, 2, 31-32 (§ III A a Introduction).
24. Face to face: *pratyakṣam*, directly, or else it refers to Brahman, in which case it would mean: "He is a knower of the visible [manifest] Brahman." TU I, 1 (§ VI 10) confirms the latter meaning.
25. The Gods also come out of Nothing.
This "single limb," *ekaṁ tad aṅgam*, of Skambha has sometimes been interpreted as the *liṅga*, the male organ, which is a symbol of the creative principle.
26. The Ancient One: *purāṇa*, the original, primeval principle, in BU IV, 4, 18 (§ VI 11), related to Brahman.
27. Portions: referring to the sacrifice of the *puruṣa* whose parts are distributed (cf. RV X, 90, 7; 11; § I 5).
28. Golden Embryo: *hiraṇyagarbha*, as a manifestation of the nonmanifested Supreme. Skambha is prior even to him. Cf. RV X, 121, 1 (§ I 4); AV IV, 2, 7.
29. Indra is here identified with the supreme God.
Face to face: *pratyakṣam*; here too the other meaning, "visible, manifest," is also possible. It could be understood that Indra is the manifest form of the invisible Skambha.
31. For the birth of the Unborn, cf. RV X, 82, 6 (§ VII 12); BU IV, 4, 20-26 (§§ VI 11; VI 6).
32. Model: *pramā*, it can also mean basis, foundation (i.e., the feet of the cosmic *puruṣa*).
34. Whose wisdom . . . : *prajñā*; one could also translate: who made of the directions his consciousness.
35. Six . . . directions: the four cardinal points together with the above and the below.
37. The waters: a clear reference to the intimate connection between the cosmic and the spiritual elements (*āpaḥ* and *satyam*).
38. An allusion to the cosmic Tree. Cf. RV III, 8 (§ III 19 and Introduction).
40-41. The three lights are probably fire, moon, and sun. Cf. RV VII, 101, 2 (§ VII Bc Antiphon).
Mysterious: *guhya*, secret, hidden.
Reed of gold: a similar idea to that of the Golden Germ, but not referring here to the seed of the *soma*-plant as in RV IV, 58, 5. Three additional stanzas (vv. 42-44) have been omitted here because they are a digression from the theme of the hymn.

The Birth of God *Hiraṇyagarbha*

4 "To the Unknown God," *Deo ignoto*, is the title that, since the days of Max Müller, has usually been given to this solemn hymn of praise and glorification of the Supreme, whose name is kept in suspense until the final and perhaps later interpolated verse.[14] The poem chants the majesty of the cosmos and the glory of its Master whom it is incumbent upon Man to adore. One feels, however, that the *ṛṣi* is tormented as well as enchanted by the splendor of a world so near and tangible, yet so inexplicable and elusive.

Three leading themes concerning the mystery of existence emerge like melodies in a concerto, now sounding together in

14. Prajāpati, who is so familiar a figure in the AV and B, is not mentioned in the RV except in this one passage. On the other hand, if the *śruti* is considered as a whole, it is certainly Prajāpati who comes spontaneously to mind as one reads this hymn.

harmony and counterpoint, now repeated singly or with clashing effect. These three closely connected melodies are all expressed in the first stanza: (*a*) the origin of reality ("In the beginning arose the Golden Germ"); (*b*) the Lordship of God ("He was, as soon as born, the Lord of Being"); (*c*) the human adventure of returning to the primeval state ("What God shall we adore with our oblation?").

a) Verses 1, 7, and 8 explain the divine origin in terms of the cosmic egg, well known to both the Indian and other cosmogonies. Something happened in the womb of the Supreme; it stirred, evolved, it came to be, it manifested itself. Theological thinking will later say that the movement, if any, is seen only from our human point of view, but the Ṛg Veda is not concerned with systematic development and the language is both poetical and mystical, using symbols that disclose themselves only to a meditative gaze, as is suggested here by the symbol of the risen sun, the most powerful symbol for the *hiraṇygarbha,* the Golden Germ. We cannot call this first step a creation: God is not created. Nor can we call it evolution in the usual sense of the word, nor a becoming, as if God first were not and later came to be. Vedic thought here struggles with the primordial problem of the piercing into the very nature of the Godhead and the luminous discovery of its dynamism and life. God as God is only coextensive with beings; God is a relative term, related to the creatures; God is not God to himself; Being appears when the beings are also there. And yet, "previous" to all this there seems to be an internal "divine" life, a disclosure, an explosion, a birth inside the ultimate mystery itself. The idea behind *hiraṇyagarbha* is that there is a production, a process within the "womb" of the Ultimate. Because there is life, there is a birth in and of God. The classical term is sacrifice, as used in verse 8: creation as a sacrifice. But for this the Golden Germ has had to disclose itself and be born. God is born (even to himself). This is the mystery of this hymn. *The Birth of God* is our title.

b) Once born, the Golden Germ becomes the Lord, the Lord of Being itself, in the general and also in the partitive sense: Lord of Being and of beings. He is the only king, and the poet raises his voice in praise and celebration of the lordship, both cosmic and human, of this unknown and nameless God, who, being a Father of all creation, transcends it. It is his lordship that gives unity and harmony to the whole world.

c) Who, what, shall be the object of our worship? To whom shall we direct it? This question encompasses the whole of human destiny: Man's struggle to overcome all existential hazards in order to reach his final goal, which, in a way, is a recovery of his primordial divine state. Two fundamental ideas are contained in this famous line, repeated like a refrain at the end of each verse. The first idea concerns the very name of God; the second, our relation with him.

It is often said that this refrain tells us, certainly, that there is a God, but that he is unknown. Yet this conclusion is not quite in accordance either with the letter of the text or with its spirit. Nor is it in accordance with the main tenor of the Vedas, which are not esoteric texts or agnostic treatises but plain and majestic religious chants to the divine as an integral part, indeed the kernel, of human life. God and the Gods are living realities in the whole Vedic Revelation.

Furthermore, the text does not literally say that the name of God is unknown, for in fact it discloses the name of God; it says only that it is neither a proper name, nor a substantive, nor a substance, nor a "thing," but simply the interrogative pronoun itself. Never has a pronoun been more properly used instead of an unutterable and nonexistent name. His name is simply *ka* (who?) or, to be even more exact, *kasmai* (to whom?).[15] That this is the name of Prajāpati, the Father of all beings, is explicitly affirmed in the following myth, which is reported with slight variations in several texts:

Indra, the last born of Prajāpati, was appointed by his Father Lord of the Gods, but they would not accept him. Indra then asked his Father to give him the splendor that is in the sun, so as to be able to be Lord over the Gods. Prajāpati answered: "If I give it to you, then *who* shall I be?" "You shall be what you say: who? [*ka*], and from then on this was his name."[16] God is an interrogation in the dative, a *to whom?* toward whom all our actions, thoughts, desires, are directed; God is the problematic and interrogative end of all our dynamism. If the proper form of the Greek name for God is the vocative, the Vedic name is a dative: it is not

15. *Kasmai* is the dative singular of the interrogative pronoun *ka* (who?).

16. The text is of an extraordinary immediacy: "Prajāpati to Indra: Come, be the Lord of the *devas*! The *devas* to Indra: Who are you (*kas tvam asi*)? We are better than you. Indra refers it to Prajāpati; . . . Indra to Prajāpati: Give this to me. Then I shall be the Lord of these *devas*. [The "this" refers to *haras:* the same *haras* which is in *āditya*, the sun, is also in Prajāpati; *haras* from the root *hṛ-*, consuming fire, energy, splendor]. Prajāpati: *ko 'ham syām ity abravīt / etat pradāyeti / etat syā ity abravit*. Who am I, he said; he gave the inherent splendor [to Indra] and said: *etat syā:* Be it! Indra: *yad etad bravīsīṭi:* that which you say: *ko ha vai nāma Prajāpatiḥ / ya evaṁ veda*." TB II, 2, 10, 1-2. From now on *ka* is the name of Prajāpati, the Who-by-name is Prajāpati. Cf. also AB III, 21 (XII, 10).

only the term of invocation, it is also the receiver of sacrifice. The contemplative slant will prevail, however, and the name will be the pure nominative: *ka* and ultimately *aham*.[17]

This brings us to our second remark. The *to whom* is not simply a theoretical question; it is the object of our adoration, the term of our worship, the aim of the sacrifice. God cannot be "known" if by knowledge we understand a merely mental consciousness; he can be reached only by sacrifice, by holy action, by orthopraxis, the ultimate concern of all religion. Sacrifice, moreover, needs to know only the interrogative of God. The living God with whom the sacrifice is concerned is not a concept, not a defined and graspable reality, but rather the term of the actual sacrifice which, though constantly running the risk of missing the target, finds in the dynamic *to whom* its justification and its reward. Sacrifice is not a manipulation of the divine, but the existential leap by which Man plunges, as it were, into the not-yet-existent with the cosmic confidence that the very plunge effects the emergence of that reality into which he plunges. The only oblation that the Lord of the Gods, of Men and of the universe, can fittingly accept is the oblation that enables him to go on creating the world by the reenactment of the sacrifice of himself, that sacrifice by which the world is called upon to be.[18] By this act Man shares in the cosmic process by which God creates the world.

The last verse exemplifies a highly characteristic and important feature of the Vedas which we term "cosmotheandric," with reference to a particular union that takes place between the human and the divine, or, as here, between the spiritual and the material, or, in yet another context, between the natural and the supernatural. This life-affirming attitude is far from being a shallow naturalism or a bucolic approach to life; it is a deeply religious and consciously theological attitude. We may substantiate this by simply commenting on the word *rayi*, appearing in the last verse.

The word is commonly translated as "riches."[19] It derives from the root *rā-*, to give, to impart, to bestow.[20] *Rayi* is then a gift, a present, in this instance bestowed on Man by the divine as a reward and as the fruit of a sacrifice offered in integrity of heart. It means

17. Cf. § VI B a.
18. Cf. § I 5.
19. So many translators.
20. Cf. *ratna*, gift (later, jewel), i.e., the thing rejoiced in as well as the joy it produces.

both material prosperity and internal happiness, spiritual wealth. Here it is a gift of grace conferred over and above Man's normal lot. When there remains nothing to be desired, joy is full, and fullness of spiritual wealth is *rayi*, a treasure of riches, the symbols of which in Vedic parlance are cows, horses, chariots, food, sons, gold.[21] It would be "katachronic" to understand this symbolism as evidencing a materialistic outlook, but it would be no less inappropriate to interpret it in a discarnate and spiritualized way, as if it were referring solely to intangible "graces." As we shall see later, the word *rayi* is used in the Upaniṣads to express one of the two factors or elements of the primordial couple which are variously termed Matter and Spirit, Grace and Life, Wealth and Breath.[22]

Hiraṇyagarbha RV X, 121

1. In the beginning arose the Golden Germ:
he was, as soon as born, the Lord of Being,
sustainer of the Earth and of this Heaven.
What God shall we adore with our oblation?

2. He who bestows life-force and hardy vigor,
whose ordinances even the Gods obey,
whose shadow is immortal life—and death—
What God shall we adore with our oblation?

3. Who by his grandeur has emerged sole sovereign
of every living thing that breathes and slumbers,
he who is Lord of man and four-legged creatures—
What God shall we adore with our oblation?

4. To him of right belong, by his own power,
the snow-clad mountains, the world-stream, and the sea.
His arms are the four quarters of the sky.
What God shall we adore with our oblation?

5. Who held secure the mighty Heavens and Earth,
who established light and sky's vast vault above,
who measured out the ether in mid-spheres—
What God shall we adore with our oblation?

6. Toward him, trembling, the embattled forces,
riveted by his glory, direct their gaze.

21. *Rayi* and *ratna* are also semantically connected with *rādha, dhāna, poṣa, vāja, bhaga*, etc., all having a double connotation of wealth and felicity; cf. § VII Introduction.

22. Cf. § II 6.

Through him the risen sun sheds forth its light.
What God shall we adore with our oblation?

7. When came the mighty Waters, bringing with them
the universal Germ, whence sprang the Fire,
thence leapt the God's One Spirit into being.
What God shall we adore with our oblation?

8. This One who in his might surveyed the Waters
pregnant with vital forces, producing sacrifice,
he is the God of Gods and none beside him.
What God shall we adore with our oblation?

9. O Father of the Earth, by fixed laws ruling,
O Father of the Heavens, pray protect us,
O Father of the great and shining Waters!
What God shall we adore with our oblation?

10. O Lord of creatures, Father of all beings,
you alone pervade all that has come to birth.
Grant us our heart's desire for which we pray.
May we become the lords of many treasures!

1. The Golden Germ: *hiraṇyagarbha*, the source of golden light, the Sun-God, the seed of all creation. Cf. RV X, 82, 5-6 (§ VII 12), which tells us of the cosmic egg conceived as a germ by the primeval waters. Cf. AV X, 7, 28 (§ I 3); SB VI, 1, 1, 10-11; XI, 1, 6, 1-2 (§ I 6); CU III, 19; SU III, 4 (§ I 28); IV, 12; also KathU IV, 6 (§ VII 40).

The Lord: lit. the one Lord, *patir eka*.

Sustainer: *dādhāra* from the root *dhṛ-* to hold (whence *dharma*), to support, to sustain (the earth and this heaven). For *ka* cf. SB IV, 5, 6, 4.

2. Obey: *upāsate* from *upa* (near) and the root *ās-* (to sit), to worship, to respect, to honor.

3. Slumbers: *nimiṣataḥ* from *ni* and the root *miṣ-* which may mean either "winking" or "sleeping." Cf. AV IX, 2, 23 (§ II 12); MundU II, 2, 1 (§ VI 3).

Lord: *īśa*, from the root *īś-* to be master.

4. The world-stream (surrounding the earth): *rasā*.

5. Cf. RV II, 12, 2 (§ II 4); also X, 66, 9, to Viśvedevāḥ, where it is said that

> The Holy Ones engendered, according to Laws,
> the heavens, the earth, the waters, plants, and trees.
> As a help to men they filled the world with Light.

6. The embattled forces: *krandasī*, figuratively means Heaven and Earth, though it also suggests two armies helping the Gods in their fight against the demons.

10. Lord of creatures: Prajāpati.

Treasures: *rayi*. Cf. §§ II, 6; II 34; VII Introductions. A literal translation of the last two verses is:

> What we, desiring, offer to you [in sacrifice],
> let that be ours. May we be owners of gifts.

The Primordial Man — *Puruṣa Sūkta*

5 "This Is the Man!" *Ecce homo,* could also serve as title for this hymn, one of the most frequently quoted and most important hymns of the Ṛg Veda. It reveals to us the character of the creation-

sacrifice: its all-embracing function in which the entire universe is involved. It is neither a merely divine affair, nor a purely human endeavor, nor a blind cosmic process; it is human, divine, and cosmic all in one. That is, it is cosmotheandric. God, Man, and the universe are correlates. God without Man is nothing, literally "no-thing." Man without God is exclusively a "thing," not a person, not a really human being, while the world, the cosmos, without Man and God is "any-thing," without consistency and being; it is sheer unexisting chaos. The three are constitutively connected. It is this cosmotheandric communion, described with such inspiration in this unique hymn, which has frightened some commentators and caused them either to minimize its importance or to brand it as simply pantheistic. Nothing separates Man from God. There is neither intermediary nor barrier between them. To discover that nothing separates us from Him is realization, which can often take the form of the discovery of this "nothingness."

The primordial Man is not simply another name for a heteronomous God, nor a mere euphemism for an autonomic individual Man, but the living expression of the ontonomic Man, that total reality of which we are a reflection, a reflection that contains the whole, indeed, but in a rather limited and all too often narrow way. God is not totally other than Man, nor is the world an entity utterly foreign to Man. Man is more than a single individual and more than the sum of all individuals. Without this internal and constitutive link with the whole of reality, any life of contemplation would become sheer egoism or a kind of spiritual narcissism. It would become the ivory tower of a would-be reality, rather than the building of a temple containing all that is. Authentic spiritual life or *dharmic* existence amounts to assimilating in one's self the maximum possible of the *puruṣa* condition of reality. The consecrated expression for this is realization, which means not only to become aware of reality but to become it; that is why many schools will say that to become aware and to be (that which one becomes aware of) are one and the same thing.

Puruṣa is not only the cosmic Man; it is also the personal aspect of the whole of reality. The very concept of person excludes isolation, alienation, and solipsistic solitariness and expresses interconnection and unity. The concept of person involves essentially an internal relationship. Everything that is, is a member of the one and unique *puruṣa*. To have an insight into the working of the cosmic as well as of the historic and divine laws governing this integral biology is to share in the performance of the sacrifice by means of which the body of the *puruṣa* is constantly dismembered and reconstructed. Real time is this process; the rest is only fallacy.

This hymn, of rather late Vedic times, though undoubtedly pre-Upaniṣadic, describes the formation of the world from the body of the primordial Man who is so vast that he covers and even overlaps the earth, not only in space but also in time, for he covers the three ages of the past, the present, and the future. Only one quarter of the cosmic Person is visible and emerges into the sphere of the manifested. Temporal life is only a quarter of the whole Man. We find here the image of the four quarters of reality, which has had a long history in the cosmological conceptions of Man up to the present day. Four is the terrestrial number par excellence and at the same time expresses the mystery of reality, three quarters of which are immortal, concealed, and unspoiled by the shadow of their own external manifestations. On the other hand, nobody can stand for a long time on one single foot, that is, on the external, empirical realm alone. To be conscious of a tree's roots does not imply their conversion into branches.

From the *puruṣa, virāj,* the first divine emanation, proceeded. This uncreated being, whose ontological function is mediatorial in character, ascends and descends into every being and every activity; it is feminine, not only in gender but also in role. Thus the feminine principle is born and from woman henceforth Men are born. With the birth of Men history begins. But history is not all, for the Man overlaps the earth and is related also to the Gods. These Gods stretch out the *puruṣa*'s body, just as threads are stretched on the loom, and offer him as an oblation. He is offered in his entirety according to the prescribed rites and with the use of the proper elements, which are represented by the seasons, ritual butter being springtime, wood for the fire being summertime, and the offering being autumn.

In verses 8 to 14 the *puruṣa* sacrifices himself by dismembering himself and scattering around the necessary number of portions for the completion of the work of creation. He performs an act of self-immolation so that the universe may come into being. From this sacrifice offered completely, that is, from the limbs of the cosmic Man, come all things both animate and inanimate: animals of every type (8, 10); liturgical formulas (9); the four castes of men (12); the cosmic powers (13-14). From his spirit comes the moon, from his eyes the sun, from his mouth Indra and Agni (fire), from his breath the wind, from his navel the air, from his head the sky, from his feet the earth, from the ears the points of the compass—nothing, nobody, is omitted. Verse 15 sums up the idea of the sacrifice and the last stanza repeats the underlying thought of the whole hymn, that the cosmic Man is the total sacrifice. By sacrifice creation reverts to the Man. The sacrifice of the cosmic Man signifies divine transcendence investing humanity. This universal sacrifice possesses a twofold dynamism, for it includes a sacramental downward movement of the All toward the earth and a sacrificial upward movement of the world toward the All; these two aspects are inseparable one from the other precisely because of the unity of the integral sacrifice.

Puruṣa Sūkta

RV X, 90

1. A thousand-headed is the Man
with a thousand eyes, a thousand feet;
encompassing the Earth all sides,
he exceeded it by ten fingers' breadth.

2. The Man, indeed, is this All,
what has been and what is to be,
the Lord of the immortal spheres
which he surpasses by consuming food.

3. Such is the measure of his might,
and greater still than this is Man.
All beings are a fourth of him,
three fourths are the immortal in heaven.

4. Three fourths of Man ascended high,
one fourth took birth again down here.
From this he spread in all directions
into animate and inanimate things.

5. From him the Shining one was born;
from this Shining one Man again took birth.
As soon as born, he extended himself
all over the Earth both behind and before.

6. Using the Man as their oblation,
the Gods performed the sacrifice.
Spring served them for the clarified butter,
Summer for the fuel, and Autumn for the offering.

7. This evolved Man, then first born,
they besprinkled on the sacred grass.
With him the Gods performed the sacrifice,
as did also the heavenly beings and seers.

8. From this sacrifice, full accomplished,
was gathered curd mixed with butter.
Thence came the creatures of the air,
beasts of the forest and the village.

9. From this sacrifice, fully accomplished,
were born the hymns and the melodies;
from this were born the various meters;
from this were born the sacrificial formulas.

10. From this were horses born, all creatures
such as have teeth in either jaw;
from this were born the breeds of cattle;
from this were born sheep and goats.

11. When they divided up the Man,
into how many parts did they divide him?
What did his mouth become: What his arms?
What are his legs called? What his feet?

12. His mouth became the brahmin; his arms
became the warrior-prince, his legs
the common man who plies his trade.
The lowly serf was born from his feet.

13. The Moon was born from his mind; the Sun
came into being from his eye;
from his mouth came Indra and Agni,
while from his breath the Wind was born.

14. From his navel issued the Air;
from his head unfurled the Sky,
the Earth from his feet, from his ear the four directions.
Thus have the worlds been organized.

15. Seven were the sticks of the enclosure,
thrice seven the fuel sticks were made,
when the Gods, performing the sacrifice,
bound the Man as the victim.

16. With the sacrifice the Gods sacrificed to the sacrifice.
Those were the first established rites.
These powers ascended up to heaven
where dwell the ancient Gods and other beings.

1. Cf. AV XIX, 6, where a similar description is given. The word "thousand" stands for innumerable, or even for an infinite number. Cf. also YV XXXI.

For the idea of the primeval sacrifice, cf. RV X, 81, 3 (§ VII 7); X, 130 (§ III 14); TS, VII, 1, 1, 4; TB II, 1, 2, 1; AB II, 18 (VII, 8); VII, 19 (XXXIV, 1); and §§ III 27; 28.

For the *puruṣa* in general, cf. AV X, 2; XI, 8, 4-34; etc., and for the Upaniṣadic idea of the *puruṣa*, cf. § VI 7.

2. The equation without any further qualification of the *idaṁ sarvam*, "all this" (the universe), with the *puruṣa* has caused this hymn to be labeled pantheistic.

The "immortal spheres" is generally understood as the Gods, who are nourished with *amṛta*, the drink of immortality.

At least six different versions have been given of the second part of this *ṛc*—an interesting text for the theology of food.

3. Cf. RV I, 164, 45 (§ I 11); AV II, 1, 2.

5. From him: *tasmāt*, the one quarter of the *puruṣa*.

The Shining one: *virāj*, "the cosmic waters" (Edgerton), "the cosmic egg" (Raghavan), "Mother principle," "*mahat*," "*yoni*" (V. S. Agrawala). It can be understood as a feminine principle, a kind of "primitive *śakti*" (Renou), a cosmic source, a womb fecundated by the *puruṣa*. The union of *virāj* and *puruṣa* gives birth to *virāja* (son of *Virāj*). Cf. RV X, 72, 4-5 (§ VII 2); AV VIII, 10 (the whole hymn is to *virāj*); IX, 2, 5; XI, 8, 30; BU IV, 2, 3.

The theology of *virāj* might offer a fruitful point of encounter between the different notions of the first uncreated emanations of the Supreme which are to be found in more than one religious tradition: *śakti*, *logos*, wisdom, spirit, preexistent Christ, etc. The end of this *ṛc* can be interpreted thus: "He stretched himself further [as Gods, men, etc.], then he created the earth and the astral bodies."

6. Cf. RV X, 81, 1 (§ VII 7). The trinitarian character of the sacrifice has been stressed time and again by scholars of different ages: the three seasons, the three elements, the three offerings, and, more particularly, the trilogy of sacrifice, sacrificed, and sacrificer.

7. A. K. Coomaraswamy renders this freely: "They made the first-born Person their sacrificial victim."

Heavenly beings: *sādhyas*, "a class of semi-divine beings" (Dandekar), "a class of ancient Gods or demi-gods" (Edgerton), "a class of celestial beings, probably ancient divine sacrificers" (Griffith), "an old class of divine beings" (Macdonell), "those who are not spiritually realized" (Renou). Cf. CU III, 10.

Seers: *ṛṣis*, prophets.

To sprinkle is here a cultic, sacrificial act. Man, once born on earth, is being sacrificed again by all the powers of the world.

8. From this sacrifice, fully accomplished: *sarvahut*, the integral sacrifice (*consummatum est!*), the sacrifice of everything without residue, the holocaust. "The sacrifice in which the omniformed *puruṣa* was sacrificed" (Sāyaṇa), "sacrifice completely offered" (Zaehner, Macdonell), "fully offered" (Bose), "offered as whole-offering" (Edgerton), "great general sacrifice" (Griffith), "sacrifice offert en forme totale" (Renou), "vollständig geopfertes Opfer" (Geldner), "from this sacrifice of the Cosmic Being" (Raghavan), etc.

9. Hymns: *ṛcaḥ*.

Melodies: *sāmāni*.

Sacrificial formulas: *yajus*.

12. The first clear mention of the four great social divisions. Common man . . . : *vaiśya*. Lowly serf: *śūdra*.

15. Man as the victim: *puruṣaṁ paśum*, the *puruṣa* as animal for the sacrifice. Important passage for the theory underlying human sacrifice. The *śruti* suggests that it is a degeneration (occurring only when man is likened to an animal). Cf. the legend of Śunaḥśepa (§ III 23).

16. First established rites: *dharmāṇi prathamāni*, "the first ordinance" (Macdonell), "statutes, ordinances" (Griffith), "the first religious rites" (Zaehner), "die ersten Normen (des Opfers)" (Geldner), etc. Cf. RV I, 164, 50; X, 130, 3 (§ III 14); AV VII, 5, 1 (§ III 15); SB X, 2, 2, 1 (§ III 21).

The Sacrifice of God *Devayajña*

6 In the Brāhmaṇas we find on the whole the same basic ideas as in the Vedas regarding the origins, but here the prelude of Being is developed and emphasized along the lines of the cosmic sacrifice and its liturgical meaning. Prajāpati procreates by summoning his creative energy, by performing that burning concentration known as *tapas*. Not having anything out of which to create the world, he

was to resort to himself, dismembering himself, offering himself as a sacrifice, falling into pieces so that life is drained from him. The creatures he has begotten are not only the whole of him, so that, when the creatures are there, there is no longer place for him, but also they abandon him—because he is no longer! It is the function and privilege of Agni, whom we could call the divine Redeemer, to recompose him. The waters, hearing of Prajāpati's situation, run to his aid and offer the *agnihotra* sacrifice and thus Prajāpati recovers his life. Here is a perpetual process of death and resurrection, described in detail by one of the texts that treat this theme: "He reflected upon himself, 'How can I bring these beings into my body again? How can I get them back into my body? How can I become again the body of all these things?'"[23] A vivid description follows as to how Prajāpati made himself a number of bodies in order to win back his creation.

Creation is pictured here as the self-immolation of the Creator. It is only because Prajāpati sacrifices himself fully that he can give to creation his whole Self. It is only by the same sacrifice in the opposite direction, by the same sacrifice in which he has himself been offered as oblation, that Prajāpati is snatched back from death. He has been sacrificed and he lives; he has been dismembered but stays the same because the sacrifice has recomposed him. This almost dialectical situation may explain why in some texts Prajāpati is considered to be half mortal and half immortal. These utterances may be considered as descriptions of that primordial act which, being primordial, transcends time and thus cannot be relegated only to the beginning. It is not possible to express simultaneously in adequate terms the two poles of the event, if we may call an event that act without which no other "happening" has any possibility of happening!

It is unfortunate that certain interpretations of these and similar texts have given the impression that the Brāhmaṇas deal only with empty ritualisms or magic procedures, or even that they do not relate to the present-day form of human consciousness, but mirror a form of mind that might perhaps be called primitive if it were less sophisticated. That there are obsolete parts and metaphors that to a certain type of mind sound odd should not discourage our attempt to understand more deeply the still valid message of the Brāhmanas.

23. SB X, 4, 2, 3.

Devayajña

SB II, 2, 4, 1

i) In the beginning, to be sure, the Lord of creatures was One only. He reflected, "How may I be propagated?" He kindled his own ardor, performing this very act with fervor. He generated the Firstborn from his mouth; and because he generated him from his mouth, therefore the Firstborn is a consumer of food.

SB XI, 1, 6, 1

ii) In the beginning, to be sure, this world was water, nothing but a sea of water. The waters desired, "How can we be propagated?" They kindled their own ardor, performing this very act with fervor. While summoning their creative energy they warmed up and a golden egg was produced. At that time, to be sure, the year was not yet existing. This golden egg floated about for as long as a year.

SB XI, I, 6, 17

iii) The highest Lord said to his father, the Lord of all creatures, "I have found the sacrifice that fulfills wishes: let me do it for you!" "Be it so!" he answered. He accordingly performed it for him. Having sacrificed, he [the Father of creatures] desired: "Would I were everything here!" He became the Breath, for Breath is everything here.

SB XIII, 7, 1, 1

iv) Brahmā, the self-existent, was performing fervid concentration. "In fervid concentration," he reflected, "there is no infinity. Come, let me sacrifice myself in living things and all living things in myself." Then, having sacrificed himself in all living things and all living things in himself, he acquired greatness, self-radiance, and sovereignty.

SB III, 9, 1, 1

v) Now the Lord of creatures, having brought forth living beings, felt himself as it were emptied. The creatures turned away from him; nor did they abide with him for his joy and for his sustenance.

SB X, 4, 2, 2

vi) Having brought forth all things that exist, he felt like one emptied out and was afraid of death.

SB VI, 1, 2, 12-13

vii) When he had procreated all the beings and run through the whole gamut of creation he fell into pieces. . . . When he was fallen into pieces, his breath departed from the midst of him, and when his breath had departed, the Gods abandoned him. He said to Agni, "Put me, I pray you, together again."

TB II, 3, 6, 1

viii) When he had produced the creatures, Prajāpati fell into pieces. Being reduced to a (mere) heart he was lying exhausted. He uttered a cry: "Alas, my life!" The waters heard him. They came to his aid and by means of sacrifice of the Firstborn they restored to him his sovereignty.

■ i) In the beginning: *idam agr'eka evāsa.*
The Lord of creatures: Prajāpati.
May I be propagated: *prajāyeya* (passive of *pra-jan-*; optative to express possibility or probability in the near future), to be born, to be begotten and born again, to be propagated.
He kindled his own ardor, performing this very act with fervor: *tapo 'tapyata,* warmed up his own heat.
The Firstborn: Agni. Cf. SB II, 2, 4, 2: "He thus generated him the first [in the beginning: *agre*] of the Gods; therefore Agni [is he called], for *agni,* it is said, is the same as *agre.*" and in the same text Agni is called again *pūrva,* the First. Cf. also SB II, 5, 1, 1.
■ ii) In the beginning . . . this world was water: lit., water was in the beginning, *āpo ha vā' idam agre.* They desired, "How can we be propagated?": *tā akāmayanta kathaṁnu prajāyemahi.* In SB XI, 1, 1, 1, Prajāpati is identified with *yajña* and this latter with the year (Agni, death, and time). In SB XI, 1, 6, 13, Prajāpati considers the year as a counterpart of himself. The waters are also the result of a sacrifice.
■ iii) The highest Lord: Parameṣṭhin.
The Lord of all creatures: Prajāpati.
Parameṣṭhin has already performed this sacrifice (becoming the waters, SB XI, 1, 6, 16); Prajāpati performs it repeatedly and the whole world of Gods and beings appears (vv. sq.). The procedure is that each time one performs it for another: Parameṣṭhin for Prajāpati, the latter for Indra, his son and Indra for his brothers Agni and Soma; these five deities went on performing this wish-fulfilling sacrifice.
Breath: *prāṇa.*
■ iv) Brahmā, the self-existent, was performing fervid concentration: *brahma vai svayambhu tapo' tapyata.*
No infinity: *na . . . anantyam,* no "un-ending," no limitlessness.
■ v) The exhaustion of Prajāpati is literally an emptying of himself.
■ vi) Afraid of death: *sa mṛtyor bibhayāṁ cakāra.* How can Prajāpati be reintegrated? Is self-oblation going to be the only means? The root *sṛj-* used here means, as in the preceding text, to create, to produce, to bring forth, and also to emanate.
■ vii) He fell into pieces: *vyasraṅsata* from the root *sraṅs-* to fall asunder (as a result of "running through the whole creation").
His breath departed: *visrastāt prāṇaḥ,* i.e., death ensued.
Put me, I pray you, together again: *tvam mā saṁdhehi.* Restoration is achieved by self-oblation, through Agni.
■ viii) Being reduced to a (mere) heart: *sa hṛdayaṃ bhūto 'śayat,* says the text, and the commentary adds: *hṛdayamāvaśeṣaḥ san vyavahartum aśaktaḥ,* lit. "being reduced to the heart, he was unable to manifest [express]." In other words, only the heart of Prajāpati remains, all his other parts having become creation. God is the heart of the world!
Life: *ātman.*

In the Beginning *Agre*

7 In the beginning, that is to say, at every beginning. The Upaniṣadic speculation interiorizes the whole of the Vedic message, but not along temporal lines. The interiorization is within Man certainly, but it is not temporal, for primordial Man is not considered as a historical being. The "beginning" of the cosmological hymns corresponds with the beginning of Man, but it is not only or mainly

a historical beginning or a temporal origin, but rather an ontological principle. The process by which Being springs to "Be" concerns not only the past or the archaeological foundations of the universe or our own temporal origins, but also our profound inmost structure. To know this process means to be involved ontologically in it. One does not reach the "beginning" by riding back on a temporal line but by piercing deep into a Being whose core is not made of time.

The Upaniṣads relate the dawn of human consciousness. Man becomes aware of himself and by this same act becomes aware of his solitude and of the way to break through it. This is not just the desire of another, even of another like him or a part of him; it is a dynamism toward the fullness of the Self, the integration of the Self with the entire universe.

To become aware of the Self does not mean to be conscious of one's own self; on the contrary, it means to have lost any hankering after the small self (*ahaṁkāra*) and, being lost to one's self, to discover, recover, *be*, the Self (*ātman*).

The first experience is the human experience of solitude, of darkness, of anxiety. This experience, endured to its very end, leads to the overcoming of its negative aspect and the overwhelming discovery of the joy of the imperishable. There is certainly a return, though it is not by any means a return with empty hands. But we are still in the prelude of the whole cosmic adventure of all that is.

The selection of texts gives an idea of how the Upaniṣads echo what the Vedas have chanted, and how they orchestrate the tunes of future Indian speculation.[24]

Agre

BU, I, 2, 1

i) 1. In the beginning there was nothing here whatsoever. All this was swathed in Death—in Hunger, for hunger indeed is death. Then he resolved to himself: "Would that I had a self!" So he moved around in worship. While he was worshiping, water was born.

BU I, 4, 1-5; 17

ii) 1. In the beginning this was the Self alone, in the form of a Man. Looking around he saw nothing whatever except himself. He said in the beginning: "I am" and thence arose the name "I." So, even today, when a Man is

24. Cf. also CU VI, 2, 1-3; MaitU VI, 17 (§ VI 2).

addressed, he says in the beginning, "It is I," and then adds any other name he may have. Furthermore, since before the world came to be he had burned up all evils; he is Man. He who knows this also burns up whoever wants to be before him.

2. He was afraid; so, even today, one who is all alone is afraid. He thought to himself: "Since nothing exists except me, of what am I afraid?" Thereupon his fear vanished, for of what should he have been afraid? It is of a second that fear arises.

3. He found no joy; so, even today, one who is all alone finds no joy. He yearned for a second. He became as large as a man and a woman locked in close embrace. This self he split into two; hence arose husband and wife. Therefore, as Yājñavalkya used to observe: "Oneself is like half of a split pea." That is why this void is filled by woman. He was united with her and thence were born human beings.

4. She thought: "How can he unite with me, as he has brought me forth out of himself? Well, I will hide myself." She became a cow, but he became a bull and united with her. Hence cattle arose. She became a mare, he a stallion; she became a she-ass, he a male ass. He united with her and hence single-hoofed animals arose. She became a she-goat, he a he-goat; she became a sheep, he a ram. He united with her and hence goats and sheep arose. In this way be created everything that exists in pairs, down to the ants.

5. He realized: "I indeed am creation, for I produced all this"—for he had become the creation. And he who was this knowledge becomes [a creator] in that same creation.

17. In the beginning there was only the *ātman*, One only. He desired: "May I have a wife in order to have offspring; may I have wealth in order to perform a work!" For desire reaches this far. Even if one wishes, one cannot obtain more than this. Therefore, even nowadays, if a man is alone, he desires: "May I have a wife in order to have offspring; may I have wealth in order to perform a work!" As long as he does not obtain each of these [desires], he thinks himself to be incomplete. His completeness, however, is this: the mind is his Self [*ātman*]; speech is his wife; breath is his offspring; the eye is his human wealth, for he finds it with the eye; the ear is his divine wealth, for he hears it with the ear; the body [*ātman*] is his work, for he works with the body. Fivefold, indeed, is the sacrifice, fivefold is the victim, fivefold is the man. Whatever there is, the whole universe, is fivefold. He attains all this, who knows thus.

AU I, 1, 1-4

iii) 1. In the beginning this was only one, the Self—no other thing that blinks whatever. He thought to himself: "Let me now create the worlds!"

2. He created the worlds of water, rays of light, death, and the waters:
Heaven and beyond is the world of water;
the sky above is the world of light;

this earth of us mortals is the world of death;
what lies below is the world of waters.

3. He thought [again] to himself: "Let me now create the protectors of the worlds." He raised a man from the waters and conferred a form upon him.

4. He brooded over him. Once this was done a mouth broke open, similar to an egg. From the mouth the Word came out and from the Word fire.

TU II, 6-7

iv) 6.

Nonexistent himself does he become
who thinks that Brahman is Nonbeing.
The one who knows that Brahman *is*,
he himself is recognized to *be*.

Next there come the supplementary questions:

Does anyone who does not know Brahman
proceed at death to the other world?
Or is it only the one who knows
who attains, at death, to the other world?

Brahman desired: "Would that I could become many! Let me procreate!" He practiced fervid concentration, he created the whole world, all that exists. Having created it, he penetrated within it. Having penetrated within it, he became both the actual and the beyond, both the manifest and the unmanifest, both the founded and the unfounded, both the conscious and the unconscious, both the real and the nonreal. The real became everything that exists here. That is what men call the real.

7. On this there is the following verse:

In the beginning all this was Nonbeing only.
Therefrom, indeed, was Being born.
That Being made for itself a Self.
Hence this is designated the well-made.

That which is the well made, that is the essence. And [only] he who attains the essence becomes full of bliss. For who could otherwise live and breathe, if there were not this bliss in the atmosphere? It is this [essence] which gives bliss. When man finds absence of fear and a firm ground in that which is invisible, selfless, inexpressible, nonstable, then he attains the state of fearlessness. But when he makes even a fine difference [between the *ātman* and himself], then he has fear, and this is the fear of the one who thinks himself to be wise.

SU IV, 18

v)

There where there is no darkness,
nor night, nor day,
nor Being, nor Nonbeing,

there is the Auspicious one alone,
absolute and eternal;
there is the glorious splendor
of that Light from whom in the beginning
sprang ancient wisdom.

MundU I, 1, 6-7

vi) 6. That which cannot be seen or grasped
is without family and caste, without eyes and ears,
without hands and feet, eternal, omnipresent,
all-pervading, most subtle—that is the Immutable,
regarded by the sages as the source of being.

7. As a spider spins and withdraws its thread,
as plants grow on earth and hair on the head
and body of a living man, so also
out of the Imperishable springs forth this all.

■ i) Death is here cosmic and spiritual, it is *hiraṇyagarbha;* hunger is personal and material. These are two facets of the same entity, i.e., Death. Prajāpati is the eater of food, of all this universe; he eats whatever he has created. Death itself desires an *ātman*. Death is the universal background which envelops everything.

Praise, worship (*arka*), has here a cosmic significance; also a pun is used in order to explain the birth of the waters and of the fire later on (the root *arc-*, to shine, to praise, and *arka,* water or fire).

4-6. Cf. § I 14.

■ ii) 1. Cf. § VI 8 and also MaitU II, 6.

A Man: *puruṣa,* person, the primordial Man, the theandric principle as in RV X, 90 (§ I 5). We have here one of the most powerful accounts of the rise of human self-consciousness: the birth of reflection. The "I" is both the *aham,* unique and One-without-a-second, and also the still-to-be-liberated I which in spite of everything has no name other than "I."

I am: *aham asmi*. This is one of the highest revelations of reality, which should not be hypostatized upon a "He." That is to say, "I am I" is not interchangeable with "He is I" or with "I am He," the first being only a mental projection and the second sheer blasphemy. Cf. KausU I, 6 (§ V 4) for the right place of the *He*: "What you are that am I" (*yas tvam asi so 'ham asmi*). The Sanskrit pun is untranslatable: *pūrva,* before; and *uṣ-*, to burn, give *pur-uṣ-a,* the Man.

2. Real anxiety is only fear of fear and thus a dread of utter nothingness. Our own image is frightening when it reflects its hollowness (cf. CU VIII, 7, 1 sq. § VI 6). A process of "conscientization" can rid us of dread, for confidence in the power of the mind tells us that, if there is nothing to frighten us, we have no reason to be fearful.

3. Again a play upon words: the Self split (*pat-*) into husband (*pati*) and wife (*patnī*). The *ardhanārīśvara* character of man is here symbolized. Man is androgynous as an anthropological reality. The desire for a second is only cathartic when it is a holistic movement toward integration, i.e., when it is not concupiscence but love.

5. To "become a creator" does not necessarily mean to be so substantially but to create along with him, i.e., to be, in the functional sense, creator, i.e., creating, because such a man really creates. No mystic would deny this experience, whatever wording one may use in order to describe it.

8-10. Cf. § VI 9.

16. Cf. § III 27.

17. Perform a work: mainly sacrifice, but secular work may also be understood.

Incomplete: *akṛtsna.* Cf. SB X, 5, 3, 8.

His completeness . . . : i.e., man contains everything within himself, his mind (*manas*), speech (*vāc*), breach (*prāṇa*), eye (*cakṣus*), and ear (*śrotra*) being the five constituents of the human being. Cf. TU I, 7.

Fivefold . . . sacrifice: the *pañcamahāyajña*. Cf. § III 23.

■ iii) 1. The same verb is used throughout: *sṛj-* to create. The operative words are here again: *idam, eka, agre, ātman, loka.*

2. A free translation is given in order to avoid explanations and awkward sentences where the meaning seems to offer no difficulty.

3. The central position of man (*puruṣa*) in creation is hereby stressed. Cf. CU III, 13, 6.

The *ātman* gives a form to man; here the root *mūrch-*, to assume a shape or substance, is used. *Mūrta* is a form already solidified.

4. Cf. CU III, 19, 1.

■ iv) 3-5. Cf. § VI 7.

6. To know is to become the known. Knowledge implies assimilation and to know the nonexistent, therefore, is self-annihilation. Every discourse on anything, even on the Ultimate, belongs to the objective order of the discourse itself. In a way it is not only the subject, but also the object, which sets the level of communication.

7. CU VI, 2, 1-2 (§ VI 2) contradicts the affirmation of Nonbeing as the origin of Being.

Well made: *sukṛta;* just as in AU I, 2, 3, it is said of the *puruṣa* that he is a thing "well done," "well produced," "well created."

Essence: *rasa.* Cf. *brahmarasa* in KausU I, 5 (§ V 4).

Bliss: *ānanda.*

Atmosphere: *ākāśa,* the all-pervading space.

Absence of fear: *abhaya,* fearlessness, peace. Cf. AV VI, 40 (§ II 35) and AV XIX, 15 (§ II 36).

Firm ground: *pratiṣṭhā,* support, foundation.

Nonstable: *anilaya,* lit., homeless, without *nilaya,* resting-place, abode, dwelling.

Thinks himself to be wise: *viduso manvānasya;* there is a variant reading: *viduṣo 'manvānasya,* i.e., wise without thinking.

8-9. Cf. § VI 7.

■ v) Auspicious one: Śiva.

Light: Savitṛ.

Cf. the *tat savitur vareṇyam* of the Gāyatrī mantra.

■ vi). 6. Immutable: *avyaya,* unchangeable.

Source of being: *bhūtayoni,* the womb of existence.

7. For the image of the spider and its thread, cf. BU II, 1, 20 (§ VI 4), SU VI, 10 (§ VI 2), and, with another meaning, MaitU VI, 22 (§ VI 12).

Out of the Imperishable: *aksarāt.* Cf. MundU II, 1, 1 (§ VI 7).

8-9. Cf. § II 11.

The Transcending Immanence *Antaryāmī*

8 The Vedas have described the One as neither Being nor Nonbeing, and the Gītā now closes this section by repeating the same idea, affirming that the One is neither immanent nor transcendent but both at the same time in a unique manner. The Ultimate is the source and origin of all and yet is itself not contained or limited by anything. He transcends all immanence and is immanent in all transcendence. He manifests himself in and through the cosmos; each creature reflects a portion of his glory.

The divine mystery, which is to be seen and contemplated,[25] opens up that unique and thus incomparable knowledge of the divine which is not obtained by abandoning creation but by piercing through it. Transcendence does not mean flight from the world, nor does immanence for the Gītā mean being entangled in the world, in the net of *saṁsāra.* Neither seeing God in creatures nor seeing creatures in God is enough if we are to reach that undivided insight and integrated existence which surpasses all understanding. He is not only the beginning and the end; he is also the in-between, the middle, the very process from one "end" to the other. A new

25. Cf. *paśya:* behold, consider.

human eye is insufficient. The own divine eye is needed.[26] The vision of this eye can no longer be described: the seeing and the seen are one, because the knowing and the known have become the "Light of lights, beyond the darkness," which is nevertheless "abiding in the hearts of all."[27]

Antaryāmī

BG IX, 4-5

i)

4. By me, by my manifested form
   all this world is pervaded.
   All beings subsist in me, but I
   do not subsist in them.

5. Yet beings subsist not in me.
   Consider my sacred mystery.
   My Self is the source and support of all beings,
   yet subsists not in them.

BG X, 2-3; 20; 39-41

ii)

2. The hosts of Gods do not know my origin,
   nor the mighty seers,
   for I am in every respect the beginning
   of both Gods and seers.

3. He who knows me as unborn, beginningless,
   the great Lord of the world,
   he among mortals is undeluded
   and freed from sins.

20. I am the Self seated in the heart
    of every being.
    I of all beings am also the beginning,
    the middle, and the end.

39. Whatever, O man, is the seed of all things,
    that too am I.
    Without me no being, moving or inert,
    is able to exist.

40. There exist no bounds to the diffusion of my glories.
    What here I have disclosed
    illustrates, O strong One, but slightly the extent
    of my infinite glory.

26. Cf. BG XI, 8.
27. Cf. BG XIII, 17 (§ III 7).

41. Whatever is endowed with glory and grace
    and is full of vigor,
  that, you may know, is only a fragment
    of my own splendor.

BG XIII, 15

iii)

15. Outside and within all beings is he;
    he moves and he moves not;
  because of his subtlety, incomprehensible;
    far, but yet near.

■ i) 3. Cf. § I 38.

4. Cf. BG VII, 12.

Unmanifested form: *avyakta-mūrti,* hidden (unmanifest, immanent) form (shape, icon, image).

Subsist in me: *matsthāni,* and dwell: *avasthita,* both contain the root *sthā-* to stand.

5. Sacred mystery: *yogam aiśvaram;* yoga, union, power, means of union, connection.

The word *bhūta,* thing, being, appears four times in this *śloka:* once as subject and the three other times forming part of a compound. The divine is *bhūtabhṛt,* the support of beings, *bhūtabhāvana,* the origin, source, bringer-forth of beings, but is not (*na*) *bhūtastha,* subsisting in them. Cf. "The universal Lord hidden in all beings" (SU IV, 15).

■ ii) 2. Origin: *prabhava.*

Beginning: *ādi,* source.

3. Unborn: *aja.*

Beginningless: *anādi,* with no origin. Cf. BG XIII, 12.

20. The name Guḍākeśa, "the thick-haired," referring to Arjuna, has been omitted here.

The beginning, the middle, and the end: *ādi, madhya, anta,* not only temporally as birth, life, and death, but also ontologically as origin, sustainer, and goal of everything.

39. O man: Arjuna.

Seed: *bīja.* Cf. its importance in the universal symbolism of any agricultural civilization and its use in traditional Indian philosophy.

40. Glory: *vibhūti,* the divine manifestation.

41. A fragment of my own splendor: *tejom'śasaṁbhava,* a product or a part of splendor, a fragment of glory, a portion of refulgence.

■ iii) 15. Incomprehensible: *avijñeya,* unknowable.

Some interpret "far" as "far from the ignorant" and "near" as "near for the wise," but the sentence may also have an ontological meaning.

B. THE WORD

Vāc

The Word, imperishable, is the Firstborn of Truth, mother of the Veda and hub of immortality. May she come to us in happiness in the sacrifice! May she, our protecting Goddess, be easy of entreaty!

TB II, 8, 8, 5

The Person cannot be alone, not merely or mainly on the psychological level but on the constitutive level, that is, the level on which he can be what he is. Being is in fact never alone; it always has its own accompaniment, its shadow, so to speak (really and truly "so to speak"), for this is *vāc*, the Word, the Firstborn. Now, to discover one's own shadow, one's own self, is a terrifying experience; it involves, to begin with, the loss of the original solitude and thus also of the primogenital innocence. The very fact of Being implies Being-with-itself, the principle of reflection, the real beginning: *manas*, the mind, was there at the beginning, the Śatapatha Brāhmaṇa will affirm, qualifying the cryptic verses of the Ṛg Veda. The shadow has been discovered as the (own) image, the icon.

The Vedic Revelation tells us in innumerable texts that *vāc*, the Word is not just a man-made invention or a mere tool of communication, or even simply an expression of what Man is. The Vedic Word is indeed this, but is infinitely more. It is ultimately as important as Brahman and, in a way that has to be properly understood, it is Brahman itself, not as every being "is" ultimately Brahman, but in a special manner: the Word is the first offspring of the Absolute and sprang from it in a peculiar way.[28] In the last analysis God *has* no name because He himself *is* Word.

According to Vedic Revelation, *vāc*, which was at the beginning, cannot be reduced to a single one of its dimensions. To begin with, thought and language are here so intermingled that no separation is possible. *Vāc* is grammatically feminine[29] and this fact has conditioned a great deal of thinking about the Vedic Word. If an ontology of sex has any meaning at all, it would find here a decisive basis. However that may be, *vāc* expresses that total surrender to the source from which it springs which is characteristically found in the archetype of feminine love, the feminine feature of love being that of finding not only fulfillment but being itself in the beloved.

It would be inadequate to describe *vāc* exclusively as the principle of intelligibility of the universe, because she is equally the principle of pure affirmation emerging out of sheer nothingness.[30] *Vāc* is really the total living Word, that is to say, the Word in her entirety, including her material aspects, her cosmic reverberation, her visible form, her sound, her meaning, her message. *Vāc* is more than merely meaning or sound devoid of sense; she is more than just an image or simply a vehicle of certain spiritual truths. She does not contain revelation; she *is* revelation. She was at the beginning. She is the whole of the *śruti*. The *śruti* is *vāc*.

Vāc, indeed, is the primordial mystery combining in herself the three worlds of time: past, present, and future. Everything that is participates in *vāc*; through her everything has come into being and her imprint has been left everywhere. No wonder, then, that every word is sacred and thus powerful. If to throw a stone at a person may be a dangerous activity, to throw a word is much more so. A blessing or a curse does not work by magic; its efficacy depends upon whether you are conveying an empty sound (or an equally

28. Cf. BU I, 3, 21; IV, 1, 2; etc.
29. Cf. JaimUB IV, 22, 11; *vāgiti strī*.
30. Cf. the interpretation of OM in § VI 12.

empty intention or a purely rational idea devoid of power) or rather a full and living reality. Only the Almighty is Lord of the Holy Word; only the Spirit has power over the Word and knows all words. It is not possible here to elaborate the many distinctions Indian speculation has built on the Word, to speak of *śabda* as sound and verbal testimony, of *sphoṭa* as the eternal sound, and so on. We would like, however, to make one comment on the Word as prayer, which is more in tune with the purpose of this anthology.

It is a well-known fact that an epoch-making mutation took place, around the sixth century B.C., in India mainly through the reform movements of Buddha and Mahāvīra and the more orthodox renewal of the early Upaniṣads, and in other countries through parallel movements. The attention (as well as the intention) was now no longer being directed toward external sacrificial actions (*karma-mārga*), but rather toward their interiorized acts. In this development the Word was the link between the religious way of life, based on sacrifice and other actions, and the subsequent spirituality, based on the inner meaning of those same actions and its expression in the words accompanying them. The decisive factor in any religious act was seen no longer in the actual performance of the action but in its intention expressed in the words. Similarly, later, the Word was also the link connecting the path of knowledge, the *jñāna-mārga*, with the path of devotion, the *bhakti-mārga*. The accent here was not so much on the intellectual contents and gnostic power of the Word as on its emotional, sensitive, and concretely efficacious power of moving the will and elevating the whole being to the heights of the Divine.

In the context of the *jñāna-mārga* the mediatory aspect of *vāc* is visible in the *upadeśa* of the *guru*, that is, in his powerful word of instruction, capable of effecting realization in the disciple. In the context of the *bhakti-mārga*, on the other hand, this mediatory character is found in the name of God, as the most powerful means of union with the divine. Here is the place of the *nāma-japa*, or spiritual discipline of the repetition of the name of God.

In each instance the Word is the mediator. The Word, in point of fact, comprises an external action as well as an internal act or movement of the heart; the Word, one might say, has a soul as well as a body and a spirit. Not only are truth and untruth related to the Word, but also love and hate, action and inaction. From the perspective of the Vedic Revelation one would not hesitate to say that the Word is the embodiment of Man as well as of God. In the Word, whose function is both to conceal and to reveal, God and Man meet. It is the cosmotheandric reality par excellence.

The mediatory character of *vāc* is manifested even in post-Vedic times, when the stress is upon the merely anthropological level. From the Upaniṣads onward one could say that the human components are considered to be *prāṇa*, life or the breath of life (often replaced by the body, *kāya*), *vāc*, here the speech or the word at large, and *manas*, the mind.[31] It is significant that *vāc* (standing here for all *indriyas*, sense organs)[32] has in this context a mediatory function between the body and the mind. She shares, in point of fact, in the nature of both, being neither a merely bodily function or a purely spiritual organ. It is owing to this characteristic that *vāc* plays so important a role in the spiritual ascent of Man, and that control and purity of speech are considered essential in almost all spiritualities.

It is also her mediatorial function that explains the importance of the Word in prayer. It is in this sense that the Word is prayer considered as man's most authentic act, that is, as the act by which he reveals himself as he really is, and through which reality is revealed to him. So understood, every authentic word is prayer, and prayer is that act in which and by which man enters into contact with the core of the real. Prayer, furthermore, is both active and passive, a giving and a receiving. Prayer in this sense is inseparable from the Word in the integral meaning given to it by the *śruti*.[33] Every full word is a liturgical act.

Prayer, moreover, is the language of the Gods learned by Men. Yet Men know, as one text of the Brāhmaṇas says,[34] that when Men say "no" (*neti*) the Gods say "yes" (*om iti*), and vice versa. Man cannot cease to be Man, even if he learns the ways of the Gods. What he may do is to integrate both languages, the yes and the no, into his own intuition. When the conflict between the two worlds is too acute he may prefer to keep silent. This silence is not the emptiness of a soundless vacuum, but rather the fullness of having to say complementary and conflicting words at the same time; the *yes* and the *no*, uttered together, produce the full silence of the

31. Cf., e.g., CU VI, 4 sq.
32. Cf. KathU III, 13 (§ III 28), and Śaṅkara's *bhāṣya*.
33. Cf. BS I, 3, 28, and the many commentaries on this important passage dealing with the primacy of the word (here *śabda*).
34. Cf. AB II, 2 (VI, 2).

unspoken word: the total and true word. When man realizes that language, because it is bound by yes and no or by either-or, does not convey adequately his experience, he has to keep silence. Yet *vāc* existed unspoken at the beginning and in the same way she will exist unspoken at the end. It is only in between that the Word speaks. The mediator is not absolute, but without such a mediator there could be no absolute. Out of the silence the Word sprang up[35] and into the silence she will plunge again; meanwhile the world is made by the Word and, moreover, the second silence is not like the first one. Once the Word has become Cosmos, the Word cannot go back to her Source without the Cosmos accompanying her—as the later myths of Yudhiṣṭhira and Hariścandra so beautifully symbolize.

Revelation *Jñāna*

9 After the period of the Brāhmaṇas the whole corpus of the Vedas is often designated by the name *vāc,* the Word, meaning revelation. The Veda is neither "inspired" (having God as its author) nor "the Word of God" (containing or expressing the message of God); it is simply the primordial Word of whom no human being is the author: *apauruṣeya,* according to the doctrine elaborated by the Mīmāṁsā with much scholarly detail and mental acuteness.[36] This Word is *nityā vāc,* the "eternal Word," according to a famous mantra.[37]

The present hymn to the sacred Word, known as a song to holy Wisdom, begins with an address to Bṛhaspati, "the Lord of the Holy Word," the inspirer of sacred poetry. What was the origin of this word? Where does speech come from? From the sages, the seers, who, expressing their own inner experience in words, communicated to mankind all that was best, purest, and most secret in their hearts. They gave a name to each single thing—a lengthy and laborious task. This revelation was motivated by love and achieved by collaboration with one another. Afterward they were able to express their purified thought in adequate words, as meticulous a task as that of sifting flour through a fine sieve (v. 2). The sages, it is said, found a bond of unity and friendship through this sacred work undertaken in common. The Word is here

35. Cf. MaitU VI, 6.
36. Cf. the General Introduction.
37. RV VIII, 75, 6.

represented as the product of mediation, love and a common concern.

The function of name-giving is in the last analysis a divine function and men can do no more than share in it, performing this creative activity on behalf of God. A sacred text tells us: "I know that Great Being who shines like the Sun beyond darkness, who delights in Understanding; who, having created things with their distinct forms and given them names, deals with them through those names that he has given."[38]

To call a thing by its own name is to be capable of discovering its most intimate structure, which is possible only if one participates in the act by which the thing comes into existence. It is for the father to give a name to the child, for the sage to designate an object, for the discoverer to label his discovery, for the lover to apostrophize his beloved, for God to name his creature. When we designate a being by its own name we symbolize the fact that we are dealing with that being through its own freedom, by entering into communication with its inmost structure. We do not command, we call (by name), and only the echo responds. We may note in passing that later philosophical speculation had much to say regarding the function of name-giving, which obviously cannot be equated with the mere act of labeling.

Once expressed, the Word is spread abroad (v. 3); it is the fundamental tool in the performance of sacrifice and it is associated, through sacrifice, with the salvation of Men. There is no salvation without a calling and an answer. The Word, thus, is used in the sacrifice not merely as an accidental instrument, but as a necessary one. It is the Word that, by virtue of its "atoning" function, unites heaven and earth.

Verse 4, continuing the vivid personification of verse 3, speaks of disloyalty to the Word when Men fail to hear and understand her. Yet the Word reveals herself only to certain ones. The others have eyes, indeed, but they have not beheld the Word; they have ears but they have not heard her. The communication of the Word is like the union of man and woman, for the Word comes and offers herself as a bride to her husband, to the one who is worthy to receive her.

The Word is vitally connected with community and communication, and therefore those who are not faithful in friendship are

38. TA III, 12, 7.

excluded from participation in the Word, even if they are Brahmins and hence have a traditional right to "share in the holy Word" (vv. 6, 8). The Word is not a possession to be manipulated at will; on the contrary, one can be worthy of it only by constant attention and by "quickness of mind," degrees of which are here compared to ponds of differing depths (v. 7). Only those who possess a certain depth can really hear the Word; for the others it resembles a tree without flower or fruit (v. 5). This attention, moreover, demands an active collaboration and proper participation in the sacrifice, by means of which the strong thread will be woven that holds together all the threads of the universe (v. 9). Sacred competition forms part of the sacrifice (v. 10), and different roles reflecting the different aspects of the Word are assigned to those who concelebrate in it: the creation of poetry (corresponding to the Ṛg Veda with the *hotṛ* or offerer as priest), the melodious recitation of it bringing out all its inherent sound vibrations (the Sāma Veda with the *udgātṛ* as the singer or celebrant), the exposition of its meaning and of the wisdom contained in it (the Atharva Veda with the *brahman*-priest), and its application in the sacrificial action (the Yajur Veda with the *adhvaryu* as the minister).[39]

Jñāna RV X, 71

1. O Lord of the Holy Word! That was the first
beginning of the Word when the Seers fell to naming each object.
That which was best and purest, deeply hidden
within their hearts, they revealed by the power of their love.

2. The Seers fashioned the Word by means of their mind,
sifting it as with sieves the corn is sifted.
Thus friends may recognize each other's friendship.
An auspicious seal upon their word is set.

3. They followed by sacrifice the path of the Word
and found her entered in among the Seers.
They led her forth and distributed her among many.
In unison the seven Singers chant her.

4. Yet certain ones, though seeing, may not see her,
and other ones, though hearing, may not hear her.
But to some the Word reveals herself quite freely,
like fair-robed bride surrendering to her husband.

39. We have here the four traditional priests required for the performance of the Vedic cult (especially the *agniṣṭoma*) who represent the completion of the sacrifice from all possible angles: cosmic, human, and divine.

5. One man they call morose, unbending in friendship;
him they do not send forward to competitions.
He goes on his way deluded, his endeavors sterile.
Void both of fruit and flowers was the word he heard.

6. No longer does the man who has abandoned
a congenial friend possess a share in the Word.
Vain is his hearing, whatsoever he hears.
He does not recognize the path of goodness.

7. Friends, though endowed alike with sight and hearing,
may yet in quickness of mind be quite unequal.
Some are like ponds that reach to mouth or shoulder,
while others resemble lakes deep enough for bathing.

8. When Brahmins sacrifice together in friendship,
forming within their hearts inspirations of the spirit,
their wise resolves may leave one man behind,
while others, though reckoned as Brahmins, stray away.

9. Those who advance not in this direction or that,
who are not knowers of Brahman or Soma-pressers,
they have obtained the Word in sinful fashion.
Being ignorant, they weave a faulty thread.

10. His comrades all rejoice when their friend returns
covered with glory, proclaimed victor in the assembly.
He frees them from their sin, provides them with food.
Prepared is he, fit for the competition.

11. One man with utmost care creates the verses;
another sings a song in chanted meters.
A third, the Brahmin, tells forth the wisdom of being,
while yet a fourth prescribes the rules of sacrifice.

1. Lord of the Holy Word: Bṛhaspati. Cf. *bṛh-*, *brahman* as utterance. Cf. BU I, 3, 20.

2. Cf. TB II, 8, 8, 5 (§ I B Antiphon), for the idea that the Word is brought forth by the Sages.

3. The seven Singers may refer to the singers who accompany sacrifice with their chanting or perhaps to those same Sages from whom the Word took its origin. Certain commentators, however, see here a reference to the seven well-known Vedic meters, quoted in AV XIX, 21. Others see a reference to the seven stars of the Great Bear. The root *dhā-* with the prefix *vi* may also be translated "to reveal" instead of "to distribute."

4. To hear and understand the Word is not an act of the will or of the intellect alone. The relationship between the Word and the hearer is a much more intimate one; it is a vital assimilation.

5. His endeavors sterile: *adhenu*, lit. without a milch cow.

The word he heard: *vācaṁ śuśruvān*, i.e., the knowledge he received is useless.

6. Share in the Word: cf. also RV I, 164, 37 (§ I 11).

7. In quickness of mind: *manojaveṣu*, in their intuitions.

9. This direction or that: lit. neither forward nor backward.

Faulty thread: *sirīstantra;* a word of doubtful meaning, it could also mean a "thread of water," referring to the useless enterprise of trying to "weave" a tissue out of water (cf. Geldner).

11. One man: the *hotṛ*.

Another: the *udgātṛ*.

Chanted meters: *śakvarī*, a kind of verse or meter.

A third: a Brahmin, a knower of Brahman.

A fourth: the *adhvaryu*.

Prescribes the rules . . . : *yajñasya mātrām*, or "he measures the sacrifice."

The Divine Word *Devī Sūkta*

10 This hymn, though the name *vāc* does not appear in it, is the most magnificent chant to this feminine principle, the *devī* of the supreme power, which later on would be known under the name of *śakti*.

Vāc was before all creation, preexisting before any being came to be. It was she who initiated the creative process. The first two stanzas require a total immersion into the Vedic world in order for their full meaning to be grasped. With a beauty of their own, they say in solemn cadences that the Word is not only the First of the whole Vedic pantheon, but that she has a unique place, for her nature is not to be compared with that of any other being, whether created or uncreated.

The Word is not only an integral part of the sacrifice; she is also the Queen who commands homage in every sphere and who, expressing herself under different forms, remains essentially the unique Word that preserves the unity of all worship. *Vāc* is the life-giving principle within all beings, even if they do not recognize this fact; she is the wind, the breath of life. She is the mother, attentive to the needs of both Gods and Men. She bestows her gifts and favors graciously and freely. She, existing from all eternity, reveals the Father and for the sake of creatures "begets" him who otherwise would remain utterly disconnected and nonexistent.

Devī Sūkta RV X, 125

1. I move with the Rudras and also with the Vasus,
I move with the Ādityas and all the Gods.
I support both Mitra and Varuṇa,
Indra and Agni and the two Aśvins.

2. I uphold Soma the exuberant;
I uphold Tvaṣṭar, Pūṣan, and Bhaga.
I pour wealth on the offerer of oblation,
the worshiper and the pious presser of Soma.

3. I am the ruling Queen, the amasser of treasures,
full of wisdom, first of those worthy of worship.
In various places the divine powers have set me.
I enter many homes and take numerous forms.

4. The man who sees, who breathes, who hears words spoken,
obtains his nourishment through me alone.

Unrecognizing me, he yet dwells in me.
Listen, you who know! What I say is worthy of belief.

5. It is I myself who announce and utter the tidings
that Gods and men alike rejoice to hear.
The man I love I make increase in strength.
I make him a priest, a sage, or a learned seer.

6. It is I who draw the mighty bow of the God,
that an arrow may pierce the hater of the Holy Word.
Among the people I arouse the struggle
and I have permeated Earth and Heaven.

7. At the world's summit I bring forth the Father.
My origin is in the Waters, in the ocean.
Thence I am spread through all existing worlds
and even touch the heaven with my forehead.

8. I breathe out strongly like the wind while clasping
unto myself all worlds, all things that are.
I tower above the earth, above the heavens,
so mighty am I in my power and splendor!

1-2. See glossary for the meanings of the names of the Gods.
3. Cf. RV VIII, 100, 10; VIII, 101, 16.
The Word as the Firstborn has complete primacy over all.
The divine powers: *devāḥ*.
The Word pervades everything and is also expressed in many forms and in many languages, all of which are forms of the one and only unique Word.
4. The power of the Word presupposes consciousness but not self-consciousness. The Word has a power of its own, though not necessarily a magic power.
The literal translation of l. 4 is: "Listen, you who know, I tell you what is to be heard with faith," or "Hear, you that are [yourself] heard [by me]."
5. Priest: *brahman*.
It is the Word that favors men and has the initiative.
6. The God: Rudra.
The third line is conjectural.
Line 4. The whole cosmos is not only a "fruit" of the Word but it is also "steeped" in her.
7. Some would prefer to say in line 1 that the Word "inspires" or "impels," instead of "begets," the cosmic and divine Father. It could also be said that she reveals the Father and declares what He is. The theme of reversible parenthood, on the other hand, is well known in Vedic culture. It is even on occasion the son who saves the father, though this idea may be related to the later conception of *saṁsāra*.
Origin: *yoni*, womb.
For the Waters, cf. RV X, 129, 3 (§ I 1 and notes).
8. Again the theme of the immanence and transcendence of the Word.

Sharing in the Word *Vāco bhāgam*

11 Few texts provide a deeper insight into the cosmic mystery of the Word than the following few stanzas taken from a long poem full of riddles and extraordinary statements. The Word is the central mystery that is situated in the very core of reality; the Word

is the soul, the vital principle of every being, although not every creature can listen and, much less, understand the total sum of words. It is only the Maker of the universe who knows all words: the Word herself. Our field of experience is reduced to one fourth and we realize, as we become more and more aware of this limitation, that even the fourth part is not completely intelligible to us. The Word is not only speech, though constitutively connected with it; it is also intelligibility, the principle of reason, the power of the intellect, the rational structure of reality.

Stanzas 34 and 35 contain the four classic questions found in practically all traditions of the world. In the language of the Vedas these four riddles of the universe are:

> What is the furthest limit of the earth,
> the center of the world,
> the seed of the horse, and
> the highest heaven of the Word?

This symbolic language is investigating:

The boundaries of our existence, its extreme limits; the core of the whole creation, its energy and dynamism; the mystery of life, especially of human life; and the all-encompassing spiritual reality that embraces not only the created world but also transcendent reality, that is, the mystery of the Spirit.

The answers are extremely concise:

The altar of sacrifice is the "limit" of the human condition. Man cannot go further than the altar where all his humanness is concentrated. Any theory about the nature of the altar has to start from this anthropological insight. The "furthest limit" is thus the altar, where the Spirit, Man, and Matter meet, that is, the divine, the human, and the material or *ādhidaivika*, *ādhyātmika*, and *ādhibhautika*.

Sacrifice is the center of the world, its force, that which gives it the strength to be, to be what it is and what it shall be, that which supports the cosmos and maintains it in existence. Sacrifice is not primarily a human affair but a cosmic venture, and God and the Gods are the prime actors in it. Sacrifice is not only the creative act; it is also both the conservational and the actively transforming act of the whole universe. The second question is the cosmological question.

The origin of life resides in Soma, the life-principle. It is the principle of fecundation, of love, and of every form of vital activity. The third question is the psychological or biological question.

The origin and place, the locus, of the Word is prayer, the sacred formula, the *brāhmaṇa* priest or Brahman, the spirit. The Word is not only sound, not only idea and intelligibility; it is also action, spirit, the unique Word permeating everything. This is the right and the deepest theological or philosophical question. Metaphysics and linguistic analysis meet in *vāc*.

We would diminish, however, the power of this enigma if we were to understand it in an abstract and generalized manner. In response to the query of verse 34, the poem affirms that *this* altar is the furthest limit of the earth; *this* sacrifice of ours is the world's center; *this* Soma we offer here and now is the vital seed, the semen of life; *this* word we utter as we make this offering is the highest heaven, the metaphysical location of the Spirit. In each sacrificial act, in each liturgical performance, we are at the very center of space and time, at the navel of the universe, in the very heart of Being. To the centrifugal dispersion of a schizophrenic existence real wisdom, that is to say, the knowledge of the Word, opposes a centripetal dynamism toward the center of all things.

The motto of our anthology, a most astonishing quatrain which has been considered as describing the poetic and divine inspiration of the *ṛṣi* and which can be said to articulate indeed in a profound way the specific human condition with its grandeur and its misery at the same time, is: "What is this that I am, I do not know." Man is a riddle to himself; he is a mystery he cannot decipher. Man is an "I am," he is a spark of being, he is real, but he does not know who he is because the very faculty he is endowed with, the very power he has, his mind, is what reveals to him *that* he is and conceals from him *who* he is. It is by his mind that Man wanders about; it is by his mind that Man recognizes his human condition and that he is free because he knows that he is; but that very mind is for him a burden, almost a prison in which he is secluded. He cannot fly beyond, because it is his own mind that makes the space available and sets the limits to his own incursion into reality; the mind is the organ he has in order to discover reality and even to be real. This is the first distich. Man is because he thinks, and he is because he thinks to be. No pretension is possible here. Thinking and being are not identical, but they are so intrinsically correlated that in Man there is not the one without the other. Man cannot escape the "space" of his own consciousness or transcend the "time" of his own being.

This is perhaps hinted at in the particular Vedic symbolism of this hymn:

> Below the realm above,
> above the realm below
> the Cow has risen,
> leading her calf.
> Where has she turned?
> To which side has she departed?
> Where does she give birth?
> For she is not in the herd.[40]

Here the Cow is the Dawn carrying her rays, all symbolizing the power of human consciousness.

And yet the second distich discloses to us that there is something that does not come from Man as involution, evolution, or development, but falls upon him and hits him as a revolution, revelation, and surprise. It is the mystery of the Word which makes Man aware that he is primarily a spoken rather than a speaking reality, a spoken rather than a speaking Word, a receiver rather than a giver, created rather creator. Man goes around heaven and earth; he wanders in search of what he does not know, of himself, of his Self, of the Self. At a certain moment he meets what was most close to him: the Word; he discovers his world, he realizes that he is in the world, he approaches the Firstborn of Truth, as the parallel text we are commenting upon tells us.[41] He shares then in immortality, in wisdom, in knowledge; he simply picks up the fruit of the tree of life as a bird eats the ripe fruits from the top of an earthly tree.[42]

The Truth, whose Firstborn is the Word, is not a mere static truth or a sheer moral truthfulness; it is the dynamic order of the entire reality, the primordial activity out of which everything comes to be; it is *ṛta*. The first offspring of it is the Word. When the Word overshadows Man, when it dawns upon him, then Man shares in the Word, participates in the speaking structure of the universe, and enters into the dialogical reality; then he can listen, speak, command; he becomes Man when the sounds he emits become words. Man is Word shared, according to this Vedic stanza. Man is by the participation in the Word.[43]

40. RV I, 164, 17.
41. Cf. AV II, 1, 4.
42. Cf. vv. 21-22, which corroborate our interpretation.
43. Cf. § III B Introduction.

The following stanza (v. 38), here omitted, speaks of the sun and/or the spirit marching backward and forward and introduces the thought that the mortal and the immortal, though of the same origin, move in opposite directions, so that he who sees the one does not perceive the other. A Upaniṣadic idea is here insinuated. He who sees the perishable element in the total dynamism of the world is blind to the immortal one and vice versa.

The next text, which is also the Antiphon of the General Introduction, says, first of of all, that without the knowledge of the *akṣara brahman*, the Imperishable, the Spirit, the entire literal cognizance of all the *saṁhitās* is of no avail whatsoever. It formulates the basic hermeneutical principle, that without possessing the key to understanding a text the text remains a dead letter, and it affirms that this key is the eternal, the indestructible Spirit that gives us real understanding of the Scriptures.

In our context, however, this stanza conveys still another, though related, message. It says that the entire gist of the Vedas lies in one syllable, in the unalterable and thus eternal sound. The insight that language is given with consciousness accounts for the conviction that the elements of language, that is, the syllables, are considered the indestructible bricks out of which the intelligible world is made. *Akṣara,* in fact, means both "imperishable" and "syllable." Now, the immutable *ṛc* is here the simplest and the fontal *ṛc* par excellence. It is the syllable contained in all the words; it is the soul of every word, as it were. It is the primal sound which, sounded at the beginning, resounds in every portion of the Vedas, which are nothing but echoes of this syllable. The *praṇava,* or sacred syllable *om,* is not explicitly mentioned, but it is adumbrated.

Our text tells us that only he who has reached this transcending wisdom, which is as simple as a syllable, sits in peace and communion with Gods, Men, and all beings. The knowledge of the true word makes us reach understanding and harmony; it creates the authentic communion with all beings.

The last stanza given here introduces an intuition concerning *vāc* which had far-reaching repercussions in later philosophical and religious schools, specially in Śaivism. It asserts that there is a fourfold division of the Word parallel to the division of *puruṣa,* the primordial Man. In both instances the symbolism of the number four expresses cosmic completeness, though at the same time it is stressed that such fullness is not accessible to Man in his earthbound state. As the verse quoted just before (37) says, even the seer, who has a more than normal insight into reality, obtains only "a share of the Word." Man has a certain consciousness of the Word's totality, but he cannot grasp the whole; he can only grasp a portion of it. This revealed and spoken portion is only one quarter, one foot out of four (the four feet expressing stability and wholeness). Later speculations on the subject say that the first and highest (*parā*) dimension of *vāc* is transcendent and thus inaccessible; the second is illuminated (*paśyantī*, the seeing one) but is still on a transcendental plane; the third, the middle one (*madhyamā*), consists of purely mental articulation; the fourth is the intoned word (*vaikharī*), the external expression of *vāc*, that is, human language in the usual sense.

The four parts of speech have elsewhere been interpreted very differently. The Śatapatha Brāhmaṇa (IV, 1, 3, 16) says: "Only one fourth of the Word shall I speak intelligibly, if they have given me only a fourth each time for my portion. Hence only one fourth of speech, which is that of Men, is intelligible. The fourth that beasts speak is not intelligible. The fourth that birds speak is not intelligible." And the following stanza quotes our particular text. The Taittirīya Upaniṣad I, 5, 1-5 and the Maitrī Upaniṣad VI, 6 also offer speculation on the four utterances.

This text is also related to the *puruṣa* in Ṛg Veda X, 90, 3-4 and belongs to the same fundamental myth that is expressed in the Māṇḍūkya Upaniṣad. The Taittirīya Brāhmaṇa, II, 8, 8, 5 and the Ṛg Veda VIII, 100, 11 are also enlightening in this point.

Vāco bhāgam RV I, 164, 34-35; 37; 39; 45

34. I ask you about the furthest limit of earth;
Where, I ask, is the center of the world?
I ask you about the Stallion's prolific seed;
I ask you about high heaven where abides the Word.

35. The altar is the furthest limit of earth;
this sacrifice of ours is the world's center;
the Soma is the Stallion's prolific seed;
our prayer is the highest heaven where abides the Word.

37. What thing I am I do not know.
I wander secluded, burdened by my mind.
When the Firstborn of Truth has come to me
I receive a share in that selfsame Word.

39. He who knows not the Veda's eternal Syllable,
that highest point on which dwell all the Gods.

What has he to do with the Veda? Only those
who know it sit here in peaceful assembly.

45. The Word is measured in four quarters. The wise
who possess insight know these four divisions.
Three quarters, concealed in secret, cause no movement.
The fourth is the quarter that is spoken by men.

34. Earth: *pṛthivī*.
The center: *nābhi*, lit. the navel.
The world: *bhuvana*, the cosmos, existent things.
The Stallion's seed stands for the essence of virility.
35. Cf. YV XXIII, 62, for the same stanza.
The altar: *vedi*, the place of the sacrifice.
This sacrifice: *yajña*.
Center: *nābhi*, navel. Cf. § III B Antiphon.
The highest heaven: *parama vyoman*, the purest state (of anything).
Cf. also in relation to *vāc* this same hymn (RV I, 164, 41). *Vāc* and *manas* form a divine unity. Cf. AB V, 25 (XXIV, 6); BU I, 2, 4 (§ I 14). *Prāna* and *vāc* also form this same union (*maithuna*). Cf. SB I, 4, 1, 2. After all, *vāc* is the very glory and splendor of Prajāpati; cf. SB II, 2, 4, 4. For the relation between *vāc* and Prajāpati, cf. also SB V, 1, 5, 6; VI, 1, 1, 9; XIII, 4, 1, 15. *Vāc* is also called *parameṣṭhinī vāc* in AV XIX, 9, 3 (§ II 38).
Prayer: lit. *brahman*-priest, though the emphasis here is on the holy utterance.
37. Secluded: *niṇya*, inward, secret, hidden. Perhaps an allusion to the retired life of a forest dweller (*vānaprastha*).
Saṁnaddho manasā means "bound by" and also "bound to" my mind, the mind that is my only instrument and does not give me the clear vision for which I am longing.
39. Eternal Syllable: *akṣara*, imperishable, immutable, and thus the elements of a word, a syllable, and perhaps here the *praṇava* or mystical syllable *om* (cf. § VI 12). Philologists would translate either way; commentators would understand the syllable to be *om*. We have brought the two currents together.
Highest point: *parama vyoman*, highest heaven, place; cf. v. 35.
Vedas: *ṛc*.
Sit here in peaceful assembly: *samāste*, from *sam-ās*, to sit together in assembly, deliberating.
45. The wise: *brāmaṇāh*, the Brahmins, "wise men."
Quarter: *pada*, originally meaning "footprint," is the technical term to designate the fourth part of a Ṛg-Vedic mantra. It means a part that symbolizes the whole.

The Knowledge of the Sacred Word *Brahmavidyā*

12 Brahman, as both word and concept, contains a profound ambiguity which tends to irritate those who approach the Vedas with an exclusively rational curiosity. Brahman is not only everything and nothing; it is also the highest and the lowest and that which lies in between, prayer, the effusion of the Spirit and the Spirit itself, the sacred formula, its meaning, and its ultimate intention. This hymn tries to portray the unity that nevertheless underlies Brahman. This unity constitutes the mystery of *vāc*, the sacred Word.

The first verse recalls the origins of the Word, here Brahman, which is firmly and indissolubly linked with sacrifice and which makes and sustains the world. It says that the Word "was born in the

East," for it is toward the East as the symbol of the origins that the sacrificial rite is performed. The seer, or sage, who discovered the Word penetrated to such an ineffable depth of contemplation that he saw in the Word the matrix of both Being and Nonbeing.

In verse 2 the same Word, now called *vāc*, is seen in its feminine and thus cosmic aspect, the Word that was already in existence at the primordial creation, the all-powerful queen who truly reigns because she dwells within all beings.

In verse 3 the Word is boldly identified with the connecting link that imparts life to all beings and unites them with one another, the metaontic undercurrent that imparts harmony to the entire universe and in the already quoted text[44] is considered to have its ground in Nonbeing rather than in Being. By a sort of two-way relationship the Supreme Principle is said to have drawn forth the Word from the bosom of the Word; the Word is not other than her Source: the Father and the Daughter are one and yet He has begotten Her.

Verse 4 recalls to our minds the support of the universe, the *skambha* who, while dwelling simultaneously in heaven and on earth, upholds them both and keeps them separate. Cosmic Order is neither created nor uncreated. It is not created, for if it were it could not reside in God; nor is it uncreated, for in that event the Supreme and *ṛta* would be identical and there would be no freedom or room for decision in the Ultimate.

Verse 5 contains a profound and enigmatic note: the poet invokes Bṛhaspati, the Lord of the Sacred Word, "born from nothingness but ascended on high," as the supreme and ultimate divinity.

The latter half of this verse and the following two verses extol the power and wisdom of the poet-sage as being so great that he even enhances the lustre of the "ancient God" (the Sun?). He alone among those born on earth is wakeful before the Sun rises (v. 6). Verse 7 shows in a similar way the power of the priest, "friend of the Gods," of whom Atharvan and Bṛhaspati are, respectively, the human and divine prototypes. Through the mediatorship of the priest Man can rise up from his earthly condition and attain divine freedom.

The hymn could be summed up in the following way:

44. Cf. AV X, 7, 10 (§ I 3).

May the Sages, who first discovered the Word, who, after meditating upon it long and silently in their hearts and spirits, were illumined in their own inner beings and succeeded in communicating and pronouncing that same Word to their fellowmen—may they themselves shine with lustrous splendor!

Brahmavidyā AV IV, 1

1. That Sacred Word which was first born in the East
the Seer has revealed from the shining horizon.
He disclosed its varied aspects, high and low,
the womb of both the Existent and the Nonexistent.

2. May this ancestral Queen who dwells among beings
stride forth toward primordial creation!
I have conveyed to her this shining Sunbird.
Let them offer warm milk to the one who is thirsty for worship.

3. The wise who knows from birth this world's hidden thread
discerns the coming to birth of all the Gods.
From the bosom of the Sacred Word he brought forth the Word.
On high, below, he abides in his own laws.

4. Abiding by Cosmic Order, he fixed as his seat
the mighty firmaments of Heaven and Earth.
Mighty from birth, dwelling in earth and heaven,
he fixed those mighty masses, defining their spheres.

5. From birth at depths abysmal the Sacred Word
has passed up to the summit; the cosmic ruler,
the Lord of the Sacred Word, is her divinity.
Just as the luminous day is born from light,
so may the radiant singers shine far and wide!

6. Truly the Poet's wisdom enhances the glory
of the Ordinance decreed by God the powerful, the ancient.
He was born here together with many; they
were found sleeping when the Eastern hemisphere was opened.

7. Whoever you are who approach Atharvan our father
and Bṛhaspati, the friend of the Gods, with reverence,
you shall become the creator of all that is,
a sage, a God, invulnerable, self-dependent.

1. That Sacred Word: *brahman*. Cf. AV X, 2, 21-33; cf. also the two hymns to *skambha*, AV X, 7 and 8 (§§ I 3; VII 27), for this conception of *brahman* as the Holy Utterance.

The Seer: Vena. Cf. AV II, 1, 1 (§ VI 1 Introduction).

Womb: *yoni*.

Existent . . . Nonexistent: *sad* . . . *asat*. Cf. RV X, 129, 1 (§ I 1 and notes).

2. There is a significant transition from *brahman* to *vāc*, who is here regarded as a queen and is the subject of the following verses. Cf., e.g., X, 125, 3 (§ I 10).

Sunbird: *haṁsa*, the mythical bird of Vedic lore.

The boiling (warm) milk is in accordance with a prescribed sacrificial rite.
3. Hidden thread: *bandhu*, connection; cf. AV II, 1, 3; RV X, 129, 4 (§ I 1).
Bosom: *yoni*.
Sacred Word: *brahman*.
4. Cosmic Order: *ṛta*.
5. The Lord of the Sacred Word: Bṛhaspati.
Connecting vv. 1 and 2 with 3 and 4, and recalling the already quoted RV X, 71, 1-2 (§ I 9), we may venture to interpret this obscure text as describing the origin of the Word in the depths of the human spirit. The Word proceeds from an unformed and unconscious state up to one of full manifestation and, finally, to the recognition of Bṛhaspati (Brahmaṇaspati) as her Lord. Cf. BU, I, 3, 20-21.
6. Poet's wisdom: *kāvya*.
Enhances: the root is *hi-*, to further, to increase, to love, to glorify, to praise.
Ordinance: *dhāman*, also abode.
Born . . . together with many: the commentary assumes that sunrays are meant.
7. Atharvan: he is father inasmuch as he was the first priest in ancient times to discover fire.
Friend of the Gods: *devabandhu*.

The Origin of the Word *Vāgvisarga*

13 *Vāc* is truly "the womb of the universe."[45] For "by that Word of his, by that self, he created all this, whatever there is."[46]

The Brāhmaṇas are fascinated, one might almost say obsessed, by the position and function of the Word. They are never far from ascribing to it a magic power and on occasion they virtually do so, but their underlying intuition is of something greater than magic, for they are testifying to the unique character of the Word and its equally unique mediatorial function. The Word belongs to both worlds, the created and the uncreated; the Word is needed for sacrifice, because sacrifice is the Word. *Vāc* and *manas*, Word and mind, go together, though at times not without a certain strain.

A significant tale is told concerning the relative merits of mind and speech. As each claimed superiority they had recourse to Prajāpati, who declared that mind is better than speech because the word or speech can only imitate and follow that which the mind has already conceived (iv).[47] The main themes of Upaniṣadic culture as well as certain characteristics of the Vedāntic world view could be said to stem from this emphasis on the primacy of the spirit over language.

Throughout the Brāhmaṇas we find a certain ambivalence as the texts oscillate between two extremes, sometimes identifying *vāc* with Prajāpati[48] and sometimes considering the Word as a mere

45. AB II, 38 (X, 6).
46. SB X, 6, 5, 5. Cf. BU I, 2, 5 (§ I 14).
47. Cf. TS II, 5, 11, 4.
48. Cf. SB V, 1, 5, 6.

instrument, subordinate not only to *manas* but also to certain other fundamental concepts that constantly reappear in the Brāhmaṇas. The ambiguity is not resolved. There are, however, various texts that introduce us in striking fashion to the power of the Word and its unique character.

The fact that *vāc* is feminine is especially significant in the Brāhmaṇas. She is supreme, but in a very feminine way; she is queen, but she has a king as partner, for she is the consort of Prajāpati, the Creator. She has a feminine characteristic of complementarity, a mediatorial role, and a certain feminine docility and obedience. She needs always to be uttered, by men, by Gods, or by the Creator himself. This element of submission is responsible, however, for her decline. She gradually loses her primordial supremacy until she is defeated by *manas* in the Brāhmaṇas and plays a secondary role in the Upaniṣads.[49]

Vāgvisarga

TMB XX, 14, 2

i) This, [in the beginning], was only the Lord of the universe. His Word was with him. This Word was his second. He contemplated. He said, "I will deliver this Word so that she will produce and bring into being all this world."

TB II, 8, 8, 4

ii) The Word is infinite, immense, beyond all this. . . . All the Gods, the celestial spirits, men and animals, live in the Word. In the Word all the worlds find their support.

SB I, 4, 4, 1

iii) That same fire, then, that one kindles, thinking: in this fire, when kindled, we will sacrifice to the Gods—in this fire, therefore, one first makes two oblations: to Mind and to Word, for Mind and Word, when yoked together, convey the sacrifice to the Gods.

SB I, 4, 5, 8-12

iv) 8. Now once there was a dispute between the Spirit and the Word. "I am excellent," said the Spirit, and the Word said, "I am excellent."

9. The Spirit said: "I am certainly better than you, because you do not utter anything that is not previously understood by me. So, as you just imitate what I am doing and simply follow me, I am certainly better than you."

49. Cf. BU IV, 1, 2 sq.

10. The Word said: "I am certainly better than you, because whatever you know, I make it known, I communicate it."

11. They went to Prajāpati, asking for his decision. Prajāpati spoke in favor of the Spirit, saying [to the Word]: "the Spirit is certainly better, because you only imitate and follow what the Spirit is doing; and he who is imitating and following what another does is undoubtedly inferior."

12. As the Word was thus refuted, she became ashamed and miscarried. The Word spoke to Prajāpati: "I shall never become the carrier of your oblation, I whom you have refuted!" Therefore, whatever in the sacrifice is performed for Prajāpati is done in a low voice, because the Word refused to carry the oblation to Prajāpati.

SB X, 5, 3, 1-5

v) 1. In the beginning this universe was neither Being nor Nonbeing. In the beginning, indeed, this universe existed and did not exist: only Mind was there.

2. . . . This Mind was, so to speak, neither existent nor nonexistent.

3. This Mind, once created, desired to become manifest. . . .

4. That Mind then created the Word. This Word, when created, desired to become manifest, more conspicuous, more physical. It sought after a self. It practiced fervid concentration. It acquired a substance. It was the thirty-six thousand fires of its own self, made of the Word, built up of the Word . . . with the Word they chanted and with the Word they recited. Whatever rite is performed at the sacrifice, whatever sacrificial rite exists, is performed by the Word alone, as a vocal performance, on fires composed of Word, built up by Word. . . .

5. That Word created the Life Breath.

■ i) Cf. similar texts in § I 6.
■ ii) Cf. the continuation of this text in the antiphon of § I B.
■ iii) The indispensable role of both Word and Mind is one of the cornerstones of the concept of worship, from the Vedic sacrifice down to contemporary forms of *pūjā*.
■ iv) Cf. TS II, 5, 11, 4.
8. Spirit: *manas*, mind.
Word: *vāc*, speech.
10. I make it known: *vijñapayāmi*, I reveal it.
12. In a low voice: *upāṁśu*, the "middle way" of recitation at the sacrifice, the other two being *nirukta* (clearly pronounced) and *tūṣṇīm* (silent).
■ v) This text relies on RV X, 129, 1 (§ I 1) and develops the idea of the Word taking its origin from the Mind, the breath from the Word, and thus successively: eye, ear, work, fire.
On *manas*, *vāc*, and *prāṇa* and their homologization with the Vedas cf., e.g., BU I, 5, 5.
4. More conspicuous: *niruktatarā*, more pronounced, explicit.
More physical: *mūrtatarā*, more formed, incarnate. Mind and Word are the two essential elements of worship (cf. the later *nāmarūpa*, etc.).

The Interior Word *Manovāc*

14 The Word, the primordial principle at the origin of everything, has many dimensions, as we have already indicated. Almost all of them are summed up in the liturgical Word as it is understood in the Vedas and Brāhmaṇas. The Upaniṣads add depth to the same vision, but their different language represents also a deep ontological change: the liturgical Word can be called, according to tradition and to etymology, Brahman. The Upaniṣads put emphasis on Brahman and relegate *vāc* to the performance of the other functions of the Word, though without making a clear-cut distinction.

The first cleavage of that which is *one*[50] can be seen in the Ṛg Veda, where in one verse *vāc* is both the subject of speech ("the Word speaks," i.e., "revelation") and the object of speech ("the word is spoken by all kinds of beings," i.e., language). In the first instance she is also the Queen of the Gods; in the second she is produced by the Gods.[51]

The attention of the Upaniṣads is directed more toward the realization of the individual and the interiorization of external actions. In consequence the revelational, liturgical, and cosmological aspect of *vāc* loses momentum. Generally *vāc* is counted among the human organs (*indriya*), and her status varies, although at times her importance is rediscovered, as, for instance, when she is ranked next to *ātman*, which on an interiorized level corresponds to the *puruṣa* or Prajāpati of the Saṁhitās and Brāhmaṇas. As the general tendency of the Upaniṣads, however, is toward the unconditioned knowledge of *ātman* as the knower and not the known, the seer and not the seen, any type of mediation is to be refused—the mediation of the sacrifice and also therefore of the liturgical Word of Revelation. While the Vedic *ṛṣis* were overwhelmed by the power of the Word, the Upaniṣadic sages enquired *whose* is this Word; and so they were directed not only to the speaker, but even beyond him to the Self, which inspires all speech from within, the *antaryāmin*, the Immortal, as one of the texts affirms. Speech cannot know its own source of inspiration, just as the body cannot know its life-

50. Cf. *vāc* as *ekā* in SB VIII, 4, 3, 3.
51. Cf. RV VIII, 100, 10-11.

giving principle, the soul. And yet speech is one of the nearest "bodies," that is, embodiments or manifestations, of the inmost Self, as the same text suggests.

Since the final word of the Upaniṣads is *neti, neti,* "not this, not this,"[52] the Absolute can only be designated as *tad avācyam,* "the unspeakable,"[53] that to which *vāc* cannot be applied and from which any word recoils.[54] Even this world was, at the beginning, unspoken, unuttered, as one Upaniṣad says.[55]

The fact should be kept in mind, nevertheless, that the concept of Brahman arose out of that very horizon of sacred speech and liturgy which we have been describing. Without it the whole religious and mystical fervor of the Upaniṣads could not have come into being; even that which must be transcended, has first to be.

Manovāc

AU Invocation

i) May my word be firmly established in my mind!
May my mind be firmly established in my word!
O Self-manifest one, be manifest to me!
Be for me the cornerstone of Revelation.
May what I have heard not depart from me!
Thus meditating on your wisdom I link nights and days.

I will speak the Right.
I will speak the Truth.
May that protect me!
May it protect my teacher!
Yes, let it protect me
and protect my teacher!
May that protect him!
Om! Peace, peace, peace!

BU I, 2, 4-6

ii) 4. He yearned that a second self might be born to him. He [Death or Hunger] united with the Word by means of the Spirit. In this union the seed became the year, for prior to this there was no year. He bore him for that much time—a year—and after that he brought him forth. When he was born he [Death] opened his mouth to swallow him up. He [the Newborn] cried out *bhāṇ!* And that became the Word.

52. Cf. BU II, 3, 6 (§ VI 7); etc.
53. Cf. MaitU VI, 7 (§ VI 4).
54. Cf. TU II, 4; 9 (§ VI 7): *yato vāco nivartante.*
55. Cf. MaitU VI, 6. The text goes on to say that it was also hidden, i.e., *avyāhṛtam* and *antarhitam.*

5. He pondered by himself: If I destroy him, I shall have less food for myself. Accordingly, with that Word, with that Self, he brought forth this whole universe, everything that exists. . . .

6. He longed to sacrifice again with a still greater sacrifice.

BU III, 7, 17

iii) He who dwells in speech, who is different from and interior to speech, whom speech does not know, whose body is speech, who inspires speech from within, he is the Self, the Inner Inspirer, the Immortal.

BU III, 9, 24-25

iv) 24. "Which is the divinity in the zenith?"
"The divinity Fire."
"In what is this fire established?"
"In speech."
"In what is speech established?"
"In the heart."
"In what is the heart established?"

25. "You absurd man!" said Yājñavalkya, "how can you think that it is anywhere else than in ourselves? If it were to be found in anything else, the dogs might eat it or the birds might tear it to pieces!"

CU III, 18, 3

v) The Word is one quarter of Brahman. It shines and gives warmth with the light of fire. He who knows this shines and gives warmth with glory, with praise, and with Brahman-splendor.

CU VII, 2, 1

vi) The Word verily is greater than name. The Word in fact makes known the Ṛg Veda, the Yajur Veda, the Sāma Veda, the Atharva Veda as the fourth, the Ancient Lore as the fifth [Veda], the Veda of Vedas, the ritual for ancestors, calculus, the augural sciences, the knowledge of the signs of the times, dialectics, ethics, political science, sacred knowledge, theology, knowledge of the spirits, military science, astrology, the science of snakes and of celestial beings. [The Word also makes known] heaven, earth, wind, space, the waters, fire, the Gods, men, animals, birds, grass, and trees, all animals down to worms, insects, and ants. [It also makes known] what is right and wrong, truth and untruth, good and evil, what is pleasing and what is unpleasing. Verily, if there were no Word, there would be knowledge neither of right and wrong, nor of truth and untruth, nor of the pleasing and unpleasing. The Word makes all this known. Meditate on the Word.

■ i) This invocation is traditionally chanted by the student at the beginning of every session of study. It belongs to any Upaniṣad of the Ṛg Veda.

Word: *vāc*; it could also be translated here by "speech."
Firmly established: *pratiṣṭhita*, well fixed, firm.
Mind: *manas*.
O Self-manifest one, be manifest to me: *āvir āvir ma edhi.*
Revelation: *veda*.
The Right: *ṛta* could equally well be rendered here by "the real," as also could *satya*, truth.
Teacher: *vaktṛ*, the speaker or he who instructs.
The first two lines could also read: May my speech rest on my spirit! May my spirit rest on my speech!

■ ii) 4. Cf. SB 1, 4, 4, 1 (§ I 13); X, 6, 5, 5.
The One is called here Hunger and/or Death; cf. § I 7 notes.
Spirit: *manas*.
This union: *maithuna*, i.e., the copulation between *manas* and *vāc*.

■ iii) 1-16. Cf. § VI 5.
Speech: *vāc*, word.
Different from and interior to: *antara*.
Body: *śarīra*, stands here for the external manifestation of the *ātman*, or, in other words, for its symbol. Cf. the other terms in this series, BU III, 7, 3-23 (§ VI 5).
Inner Inspirer: *antaryāmin*, inner controller, inner ruler. Cf. § I C Introduction, note 56.
18-23. Cf. § VI 5.

■ iv) 1-9. Cf. § VI 2.
10-17. Cf. § VI 7.
21. Cf. § I 37.
24. Fire: Agni, here in its aspect as the sun.
Speech: *vāc*. The correspondence between Agni (*devatā*) and *vāc* (sense organ) is common: cf. BU II, 5, 3 (§ VI 6) and CU III, 18, 2, where we find the exact correspondences: speech–fire, breath–air, eye–sun, ear–regions of space.
25. Another instance of asking questions beyond the proper limits of the question (cf. also BU III, 6).
26. Cf. § VI 5.
28. Cf. § VI 3.

■ v) Cf. the fourfold division of the primordial Man, *puruṣa* (I 5). *Vāc* is here one quarter of *brahman* on the individual level, as Agni is on the cosmic level. Again the close correlation between *vāc* and *agni* (or *jyotis*, light in general).

■ vi) The Word is the key to all human knowledge.
Cf. the complete CU VII (§ VI 3) and the corresponding notes regarding the main terms used here.
Fire: *tejas*, light, splendor, glory.
What is right and wrong: *dharmaṁ cādharmaṁ ca.*
Truth and untruth: *satyaṁ cānṛtaṁ ca.*

C. THE ELEMENTS

Mahābhūtāni

May the gleaming Waters
who took Fire as their germ
be for us blessing and joy!

AV I, 33, 1b

The Word has been spoken and has broken the original silence. The cosmic principles are there as fragments of this broken silence. All this is only the beginning. Before the human gaze is directed inward and toward the splendor of the Lord, Man meets the elements of this universe, encounters them, and is gripped at the same time by awe and by admiration. The world is the first manifestation, the primordial revelation to Man. It is not individual things that stir his imagination but the primordial elements of the world. All these elements are at one and the same time both material and spiritual. Indeed, a division between matter and spirit seems to be drawn only at a later date in an artificial way, and only for practical purposes. Nothing solely spiritual or solely material exists in the range of our common experience.

There is one Upaniṣad reflecting the evolution of human consciousness, while it continues at the same time the most authentic Vedic line:

> He who is abiding in the earth, yet different
> from the earth, . . .
> He who is abiding in the water, yet different
> from the water, . . .
> He who is abiding in the wind, yet different
> from the wind. . . .[56]

The very word *antara* used here means both "different from" and "interior to." This total vision of the elements is not concerned with the physical or the scientific alone, or, for that matter, with the merely allegorical or spiritual, but with the integral experience of an undivided though differentiated whole, which has its own role to play and its own constitution to maintain.

He who sees "the waters" only as a colorless material liquid with certain physical properties will surely fail to know what that word has really meant to mankind, nor will he know what water really is. He who, on the other hand, neglects or even despises the internal physical structure of water and does not bother to study its properties will equally miss the point.

Is it possible for the men and women of our times to enjoy so innocent and holistic a view of the elements of the world? The qualified answer, impossible for us to develop here, would be yes, provided we do not look at ourselves at the same time. That is to say, we can still have an ecstatic and integral view of the universe if we cease to claim a privileged and exceptional position for Man, as if he were the goal and the final product of creation. How this second condition can be fulfilled is another problem altogether. It is neither desirable nor possible to go back to a precritical stage, but perhaps there is another step open to our generation, a step that goes beyond the merely outward self-forgetting look and abandons as equally unsatisfactory the claim of Man to be a neutral spectator of this world and king of the whole earth. However that may be, this anthology may help the reader to follow the course of the human pilgrimage by reenacting the past with a present awareness. Doing so does not make us people of the past; on the contrary, it prevents us from being excommunicated from the common human—and cosmic—adventure. Nothing is more barren than to be obsessed with modernity and pretend to forget the past. Roots do not produce flowers, but neither can there be flowers without roots.

56. BU III, 7, 3-7 (§ VI 5): *pṛthivyā antaraḥ . . . eṣa ta ātmāntaryāmy amṛtaḥ,* and the same phrase structure is repeated with the other elements. Thus a possible translation is also: He who dwells in the earth, fire, . . . and is *within* the earth, fire, . . . he is the *antaryāmin,* the inner controller, the immortal.

Yet another word may be required regarding the place and the function of the elements. Any vision or concept of Man needs a horizon against which the vision emerges and the concept is meaningful. This horizon is Man's underlying and more or less conscious picture of the world. Ultimately the intelligible pattern of all human understanding is based on an accepted cosmology. Man cannot get rid of matter, and his material conception of the world is reflected in any of his supposedly spiritual intuitions.

The Vedic cosmology is not our special concern in this anthology, but we need to be acquainted with some of its features in order to understand how the Vedic Revelation viewed the world. Many centuries ago, before the scientific world view, culminating in the splitting of the atom, led to the predominance of the quantit.ve, man had a more qualitative conception of the irreducible factors that underlie all manifest realities. For modern Man Matter and Energy (in spite of their different forms and interchangeability) can be said to form the fundamental elements of the universe. Against this dualistic outlook, Vedic Man was more pluralistic and believed, as was also true of many other ancient cultures, in the existence of certain basic elements of a qualitatively different nature which underlay the constitution of the universe. These elements should not be understood against the background of a rigid atomic theory; they were to a great extent interrelated and were sometimes even interchangeable, so that the Vedic intuition refers, for example, to fire being born out of the waters. The elements are not individual and separated constituents of a whole but, rather, vectors or forces pervading the entire reality. The elements are the real symbols standing for the ultimate constituents of reality; they *are* the primordial "stuff" of the world, but their *being* the cornerstones of reality is a symbolical and not scientific or merely physical being. They stand for the underlying unity behind the manifold appearances of all that they symbolize.

Out of the five classical elements and others that could perhaps have been chosen, we give here texts concerning only three, which we may epitomize thus: water as the reality before creation, earth as the creation par excellence, and wind as the dynamic of the cosmos after creation.[57]

57. Later classifications offer a list of five *mahābhūtāni* or primordial elements, starting from ether or atmosphere (*ākāśa*) and including fire (*tejas* or *agni*). Agni, who will be introduced later (§ III 4) and *ākāśa*, which is a peculiar element pervading everything (*sarvagata*), are here omitted. *Akāśa*, though existing in B and U, does not appear in the RV.

a) Waters

Āpaḥ

In almost all traditions of mankind the waters occupy a special place, being either uncreated or produced in a very peculiar way. In the Śatapatha Brāhmaṇa it is said that they were produced out of *vāc,* the word:[58] the first element out of the first "principle." The waters are the primeval element; everything else rests on them. They belong to the three worlds. The ritual of the Śatapatha Brāhmaṇa states several times that vessels and other utensils must be thrown into the waters after being used in the sacrifice, precisely because these waters are the basis and foundation of the universe. It is still a common practice in everyday life to immerse idols (*mūrtis*), utensils, used things, in the sacred rivers. Moreover, deceased children and holy men are not cremated but are returned either to the earth or to the waters.[59] All this symbolizes the same thing: the return to the origins.

The waters possess an integral reality, and thus they have healing power.[60] Purification is their first anthropocosmic function. The waters possess also a certain intermediate character. They are neither air nor earth; they are on earth but come from heaven; they bring life but they can also be lethal; they purify but they can also be muddy; they flow on the surface but there are also internal rivers of water in the earth, as well as in the individual; they take all forms and have unlimited freedom, but yet they are not supreme.[61] Waters convey divine energy, just as in more modern parlance blood is the conveyor of human life, but they are not the divine principle. What is more powerful, more self-confident, larger, and deeper than the fathomless ocean? What is more mysterious, more needed, more capricious, and more overwhelming than the rains, the vehicles of fertility?[62] What is more vital than the rivers, which, like arteries, vivify the earth and all living beings?[63] What is more

58. Cf. SB VI, 1, 1, 9. The pun that follows is also significant: the waters were set free, they pervaded (*āp-*) everything, and therefore they were called *āpaḥ* (water) and, because they covered (*vṛ-*) everything, they were also called *vāri* (water).
59. Cf. § V A c Introduction.
60. Cf. RV X, 137, 6; AV II, 3, 6; VI, 91, 3; SB III, 6, I, 7 (§ I 15).
61. Cf. CU VII, 10, 1-2 (§ VI 3).
62. Cf. RV V, 83 (§ II 24).
63. Cf., for instance, the many myths and legends about the river Ganges (the Goddess *gaṅgā* is mentioned only twice in the RV: RV VI, 45, 31, and X, 75, 5).

ambivalent than the waters, which on the one hand you cannot live without, while on the other they may unexpectedly flood the land and drown you? No wonder that the Spirit of the waters, the *apāṁ napāt* of the Ṛg Veda,[64] not only has a direct counterpart in certain other traditions (such as the Avestan being of the same name living in the depth of the waters and surrounded by divine spirits) but represents what amounts to an invariant in all ancient cultures of mankind.

> He, the Son of the Waters, of color unfading,
> performs his work within the body of another.[65]

Agni is the "Son of the Waters"; he dwells in the water.[66] Fire and water belong together. At the sight of these waters we find prayer welling within us and in prayer become aware of the marvelous harmony of this universe. "In the Waters, O Lord, is your seat!"[67]

The intermediate character of the waters could be described also from a cosmological point of view: the waters are neither solid like the earth, nor intangible and gaseous like the air or the wind; they possess many of the features of solid matter and many also of the more spiritual elements. It is difficult to conceive of the spirit being unleashed from the earth, while air and ether possess no "earthly" properties at all; the waters, however, occupy an intermediate position and contain both the movement and life of the airy elements and the gravity and consistency of the solid: they are alive.[68] Finally, it is interesting to note the fact that many cosmologies award primordial status to the waters rather than to any of the other elements.

The following is a *stotra* made up of short sentences belonging to longer passages.

The Primordial Waters *Agre āpaḥ*

15

SB III, 6, 1, 7

i) The essence of plant life is Water.

64. Cf. RV II, 35, 9.
65. RV II, 35, 13.
66. Cf. RV X, 45, 1; 3. There are innumerable other places where Agni's connection with the waters is mentioned, specially in RV I.
67. RV VIII, 43, 9. Cf. the same text in SB VI, 8, 2, 4 (iv). The name of the Lord here is Agni: cf. RV X, 121, 7 (§ I 4), where the waters produce Agni.
68. For the primordial waters see the note on *salila*, § I1. Cf. TS V, 7, 5, 3; VII, 1, 5, 1; TB I, 1, 3, 5; II, 2, 9, 3; etc.

SB IV, 4, 3, 15

ii) Water is the elixir of immortality.

SB VI, 8, 2, 3

iii) For from the Waters is this universe produced.

SB VI, 8, 2, 4

iv) In the Waters, O Lord, is your seat, that is, in the Waters, O Lord, is your womb.

SB VII, 4, 1, 6

v) Of this universe, it is in truth the Waters that were made first. Hence when the Waters flow, then everything here, whatsoever exists, is produced.

SB XII, 5, 2, 14

vi) The Waters are the foundation of all this universe.

SB XIV, 3, 2, 13

vii) "Glory to the Waters!" The Waters, to be sure, are a resting place for all the Gods.

TS I, 2, 1

viii) May the Waters, the mothers, purify us.

TS I, 2, 2

ix) Hail to you divine, unfathomable, all-purifying Waters!

■ i) Essence: *rasa*, sap, i.e., the vital juice of plants. Cf. *sapientia*, i.e., the *sapid* science, knowledge through *taste*, personal experience.
■ ii) Elixir of immortality: *amṛta*. Cf. also MaitS IV, 1, 9 (*āpo vāmṛtam*).
■ iv) Lord: Agni.
■ vi) Cf. the same text in SB VI, 8, 2, 2.
Foundation: *pratiṣṭhā*, underlying principle, basis, repository, support, standing place, receptacle.

The Divine Waters *Āpo devīḥ*

16

RV VII, 49

1. Ceaselessly they flow from the depths, pure, never sleeping,
 the Ocean their sponsor,
 following the channels ordained by the Thunderer.
 Now may these great divine Waters quicken me!

2. Waters may pour from heaven or run along channels
   dug out by men;
   or flow clear and pure having the Ocean as their goal.
   Now may these great divine Waters quicken me!

3. In the midst of the Waters is moving the Lord, surveying
   men's truth and men's lies.
   How sweet are the Waters, crystal clear and cleansing!
   Now may these great divine Waters quicken me!

4. From whom King Varuṇa, Soma, and all the Deities drink
   exhilarating strength,
   into whom the Universal Lord has entered,
   now may these great divine Waters quicken me!

1. The Ocean their sponsor: cf. SB XI, 1, 6, 1 (§ I 6).
The Thunderer: Indra.
Divine Waters: *āpo divyāḥ,* celestial waters.
Quicken: the verb of the refrain is *av-*, to drive forward, to animate, to lead (flowing), hence to protect, promote, favor. *Av-* has also the meaning of refreshing, cooling (with water). May these . . . Waters quicken me: *avantu.*
2. All the waters, the celestial as well as those flowing on earth, have the ocean as their goal: *samudrārthāḥ.*
3. The Lord: Varuṇa, who is termed "King Varuṇa."
Sweet: *madhuścutaḥ,* lit. distilling honey. In the next verse the waters are said to be Soma, the elixir of the Gods. Cf. RV II, 35, and RV X, 9, 6 (§ I 17).
4. Universal Lord: Agni *vaiśvānara,* cf. § III 5.

The Waters of Life — *Ūrje dadhātana*

17

RV X, 9

1. O Waters, source of happiness,
   pray give us vigor so that we
   may contemplate the great delight.

2. You like loving mothers are
   who long to give to children dear.
   Give us of your propitious sap.

3. On your behalf we desire, O Waters,
   to assist the one to whose house you send us—
   you, of our life and being the source.

4. These Waters be to us for drink;
   divine are they for aid and joy.
   May they impart to us health and strength!

5. You Waters who rule over precious things
   and have supreme control of men,
   we beg you, give us healing balm.

6. Within the Waters, Soma has told me,
remedies exist of every sort
and Agni who brings blessing to all.

7. O Waters, stored with healing balm
through which my body safe will be,
come, that I long may see the sun.

8. Whatever sin is found in me,
whatever wrong I may have done,
if I have lied or falsely sworn,
Waters, remove it far from me.

9. Now I have come to seek the Waters.
Now we merge, mingling with the sap.
Come to me, Agni, rich in milk!
Come and endow me with your splendor!

1. Vigor: *ūrj*, invigorating and animating sap, nourishment, nourishing juice, hence inspiriting, giving spirit, life. Later commentators say that the great delight is Brahman.

2. Agni is elsewhere called *ūrjas putra*, while here the waters give propitious sap, invigorating nourishment. They are a source of happiness, like mothers giving their milk.

5. For similar texts on the waters cf. AV VI, 23; XIX, 2.

8. Cf. RV I, 23, 22 (§ IV 8).

b) Earth

Pṛthivī

The Vedic attitude toward the earth springs from mankind's primordial experience of being on the one hand a guest, and on the other an offspring, of Earth. The earth is undoubtedly mother, is close to Man, but at the same time she is also alien, other and aloof. The earth is the foundation, the basis out of which emerges all that exists and on which everything rests. The earth is the basis of life and, when considered as a divine being, she always occupies a special place among the Gods.

Man is of the earth and earthly, but the earth is not simply nature, is not merely geographical or material; it is part of Man himself, so that Man can no more live without the earth than he can live without a body. At the same time, though he stands on the earth, he also stands above her. Man is more than earth. The earth is the mother of Man, but Man is also lord over the earth. Man could be said to be like the eldest son of a widowed mother, in the traditional Indian setting.

The tension between Man and earth is conspicuously present, but there is no separation. Vedic Man would find any attempt at dominating or subjugating the earth incomprehensible. The earth is an object of worship and not of exploitation, an object of awe and not of curiosity (or research, as would be said in academic circles). Investigation of the earth is of the same nature as personal introspection. To harm the earth is a masochistic vice. Man is from the earth and part of the earth, yet he surmises more and more that he is not only of the earth, not just an earthly thing.

Worship addressed to the earth is not adoration of a creature as an absolute; that is, it is not idolatory. It is rather the veneration of the highest value in the hierarchy of existence, for "undoubtedly this earth is the firstborn of being."[69] The earth as such is rich and the owner of treasures.[70] Man's work is not to make a shift in ownership, despoiling, as it were, the earth of her possessions and transferring them to the toiler. Man's work is to enjoy the blessings of the earth, because the earth is his home, his own family, his body.

There is only one hymn in the Ṛg Veda addressed to *pṛthivī,* the earth (literally, the broad one), though she is praised in several hymns conjointly with the sky, *dyu.*[71] These two are called father and mother, not only of terrestrial creatures but of the Gods also. In a funeral hymn the earth is described as a gentle mother receiving her dead son into her bosom, preserving him from dissolution.[72] Another hymn sings:

> Who gives us back to Aditi, the great Boundless?
> I wish to see my father and my mother![73]

The second hymn of this section is the famous *Prayer to the Earth,* one of the most beautiful hymns of the Veda. The earth is here called not *pṛthivī* but *bhūmi.* This hymn depicts the universal mother, dispenser of every sort of good. It presents a striking cosmogonic and theanthropological sequence.

The origins of the earth come first. When she was as yet hidden

69. SB XIV, 1, 2, 10.
70. Cf. RV III, 51, 5; SB XI, 5, 6, 3 (§ III 23).
71. Cf. RV I, 185 (§ IV 10); RV I, 160.
72. Cf. RV X, 18, 10-13 (§ V 15).
73. RV I, 24, 1 (the answer in verse 2 is that it is Agni who restores us). Aditi, the unbound (from the root *dā-*, to bind), is a complex figure mentioned also in the Hymn to the Earth (Cf. AV XII, 1, 61; § I 19). "My father and my mother" are interpreted as Heaven and Earth in the light of RV X, 189, 1, where they are thematically invoked as such.

in a fluid state in the bosom of the primeval waters, the seers were already seeking to discern her by means of sacrifice.

A geographical description, or, as we could equally aptly call it, a highly poetical vision of nature, follows. The earth is composed of hills and plains, of snow-clad peaks, of deserts, oceans, and rivers, of lakes and streams, trees and plants, rocks and stones. The seasons appear with unfailing regularity and bring to her their own gradations of climate. Even included is an account of her fragrance, which is described distinctively according to whether it emanates from plants or from water, from the lotus, from animals, from human beings, or even from the Gods. We are also told of her underground treasures of jewels and gold.

Third, earth is the dwelling place of people. It is upon her that in the beginning the first humans were scattered abroad. It is upon her that they sing and dance and find their happiness. It is she who diversifies Men's speech into different languages. It is upon her many paths that men and women pass to and fro and it is her highways that men use for their wagons and chariots.

Further, the earth is protected by the Gods; she is the conveyer of Agni, Universal Fire, and the place where men offer ritual sacrifice. It is upon her breast that men build their altars and construct their tabernacles and shelters and ritual posts. It is she in whose praise priests chant their hymns. The earth points beyond herself by means of the cultic acts of Gods and Men.

She is, furthermore, the dwelling place of all living creatures, mention of whom is not omitted. She is the home of cattle and horses, of the beasts of the forest, of deer and birds, reptiles and two-legged creatures.

She is, finally, a cosmic giant, a cosmic power, the receiver of prayers and the bestower of blessings, the protector and the inscrutable judge. Ecology was a sacred science for Vedic Man.

The Mighty Earth *Pṛthivī mahinī*

18

RV V, 84

1. The mighty burden of the mountains' bulk
   rests, Earth, upon your shoulders; rich in torrents,
   you germinate the seed with quickening power.

2. Our hymns of praise resounding now invoke you,
   O far-flung Earth, the bright one.
   Like a neighing steed you drive abroad your storm clouds.

3. You in your sturdy strength hold fast the forests,
clamping the trees all firmly to the ground,
when rains and lightning issue from your clouds.

1. Earth: *pṛthivī.*
2. Bright one: or lit. "silver-white."

Hymn to the Earth *Bhūmi Sūkta*

19

AV XII, 1

1. High Truth, unyielding Order, Consecration,
Ardor and Prayer and Holy Ritual
uphold the Earth; may she, the ruling Mistress
of what has been and what will come to be,
for us spread wide a limitless domain.

2. Untrammeled in the midst of men, the Earth,
adorned with heights and gentle slopes and plains,
bears plants and herbs of various healing powers.
May she spread wide for us, afford us joy!

3. On whom are ocean, river, and all waters,
on whom have sprung up food and ploughman's crops,
on whom moves all that breathes and stirs abroad—
Earth, may she grant to us the long first draught!

4. To Earth belong the four directions of space.
On her grows food; on her the ploughman toils.
She carries likewise all that breathes and stirs.
Earth, may she grant us cattle and food in plenty!

5. On whom the men of olden days roamed far,
on whom the conquering Gods smote the demons,
the home of cattle, horses, and of birds,
may Earth vouchsafe to us good fortune and glory!

6. Bearer of all things, hoard of treasures rare,
sustaining mother, Earth the golden-breasted
who bears the Sacred Universal Fire,
whose spouse is Indra—may she grant us wealth!

7. Limitless Earth, whom the Gods, never sleeping,
protect forever with unflagging care,
may she exude for us the well-loved honey,
shed upon us her splendor copiously!

8. Earth, who of yore was Water in the oceans,
discerned by the Sages' secret powers,

whose immortal heart, enwrapped in Truth,
abides aloft in the highest firmament,
may she procure for us splendor and power,
according to her highest royal state!

9. On whom the flowing Waters, ever the same,
course without cease or failure night and day,
may she yield milk, this Earth of many streams,
and shed on us her splendor copiously!

10. May Earth, whose measurements the Aśvins marked,
over whose breadth the foot of Viṣṇu strode,
whom Indra, Lord of power, freed from foes,
stream milk for me, as a mother for her son!

11. Your hills, O Earth, your snow-clad mountain peaks,
your forests, may they show us kindliness!
Brown, black, red, multifarious in hue
and solid is this vast Earth, guarded by Indra.
Invincible, unconquered, and unharmed,
I have on her established my abode.

12. Impart to us those vitalizing forces
that come, O Earth, from deep within your body,
your central point, your navel; purify us wholly.
The Earth is mother; I am son of Earth.
The Rain-giver is my father; may he shower on us blessings!

13. The Earth on which they circumscribe the altar,
on which a band of workmen prepare the oblation,
on which the tall bright sacrificial posts
are fixed before the start of the oblation—
may Earth, herself increasing, grant us increase!

14. That man, O Earth, who wills us harm, who fights us,
who by his thoughts or deadly arms opposes,
deliver him to us, forestalling action.

15. All creatures, born from you, move round upon you.
You carry all that has two legs, three, or four.
To you, O Earth, belong the five human races,
those mortals upon whom the rising sun
sheds the immortal splendor of his rays.

16. May the creatures of earth, united together,
let flow for me the honey of speech!
Grant to me this boon, O Earth.

17. Mother of plants and begetter of all things,
firm far-flung Earth, sustained by Heavenly Law,
kindly and pleasant is she. May we ever
dwell on her bosom, passing to and fro!

18. As a vast abode, Earth, you have become great.
Great is your movement, great your trembling, your quaking.
The Lord all-powerful ceaselessly protects you.
O Earth, grant us to shine like burnished gold,
and let no enemy ever wish us ill!

19. Agni resides on earth, within the plants.
The Waters contain Agni; in the stones is he.
Agni abides deep in the hearts of Men.
In cattle and in horses there are Agnis.

20. Agni blazes and flashes from the height of heaven.
To the God Agni belong all airy spaces,
Agni it is whom mortal men enkindle,
conveyer of offerings, lover of the clarified butter.

21. May she who is clothed with Fire, whose knees
are blackened, grant me sharpness of wit
and furnish me with splendor!

22. May Earth on which men offer to the Gods
the sacrifice and decorous oblations,
where dwells the human race on nourishment
proper to the requirements of its nature—
may this great Earth assure us life and breath,
permitting us to come to ripe old age.

23. Instill in me abundantly that fragrance,
O Mother Earth, which emanates from you
and from your plants and waters, that sweet perfume
that all celestial beings are wont to emit,
and let no enemy ever wish us ill!

24. Your fragrance which has entered into the lotus,
wherewith the immortal Gods at the Sun-daughter's wedding
were redolent, O Earth, in times primeval—
instill in me abundantly that fragrance,
and let no enemy ever wish us ill!

25. Your fragrance which adheres to human beings,
the good cheer and the charm of women and men,
that which is found in horses and in warriors,
that which is in wild beasts and in the elephant,
the radiance that shines about a maiden—
O Earth, steep us, too, deeply in that fragrance,
and let no enemy ever wish us ill!

26. Earth is composed of rock, of stone, of dust;
Earth is compactly held, consolidated.
I venerate this mighty Earth, the golden-breasted!

27. Her upon whom the trees, lords of the forest,

stand firm, unshakable, in every place,
this long-enduring Earth we now invoke,
the giver of all manner of delights.

28. Whether we stand upright or sit,
whether we stay quite still or walk,
whether we walk with right foot or left,
never may we stumble upon Earth!

29. O purifying Earth, I you invoke!
O patient Earth, by Sacred Word enhanced,
bearer of nourishment and strength, of food and ghee—
O Earth, we would approach you with due praise!

30. Pure may the Waters flow over our bodies!
That which defiles—I fling it upon our foes!
I cleanse myself, O Earth, as with a filter.

31. Your regions, Earth, to eastward and to northward,
southward and westward, may they receive me kindly,
whenever on their paths I travel. Never,
when standing on your surface, may I totter!

32. Do not thrust us aside from in front or behind,
from above or below! Be gracious, O Earth.
Let us not encounter robbers on our path.
Restrain the deadly weapon!

33. As wide a vista of you as my eye
may scan, O Earth, with the kindly help of Sun,
so widely may my sight be never dimmed
in all the long parade of years to come!

34. Whether, when I repose on you, O Earth,
I turn upon my right side or my left,
or whether, extended flat upon my back,
I meet your pressure from head to foot,
be gentle, Earth! You are the couch of all!

35. Whatever I dig up of you, O Earth,
may you of that have quick replenishment!
O purifying One, may my thrust never
reach right unto your vital points, your heart!

36. Your circling seasons, nights succeeding days,
your summer, O Earth, your splashing rains, your autumn,
your winter and frosty season yielding to spring—
may each and all produce for us their milk!

37. This cleansing Earth, who trembles before the Serpent,
who guards the fires that dwell within the waters,
who castigates the god-insulting demons,

has chosen for her mate Indra, not Vṛtra,
surrendering herself to the powerful one, the potent.

38. On her are erected the platform and the sheds of oblation;
on her is reared the sacrificial post.
On her the brahmins, knowers of the rites,
recite their hymns, intone their melodies.
On her the priests set forth the sacrifice,
that Indra may drink Soma.

39. On her those sages of old, the Seven Seers
who fashioned these worlds, performing the sacrifice
by dint of holy rite and creative Fervor,
sang hymns and lo! the cows came to birth!

40. May Earth afford us all that copious wealth
for which we long! May Bhaga play his part
and Indra go before to show the way!

41. May Earth, the stage where mortals sing and play
with varied shouts and noises, which resounds
with cries of war or beatings of the drum,
drive far my foemen and rid me of all rivals!

42. Earth is the source of food, of rice and barley;
from her derive the five tribes of men.
To rain-steeped Earth, the Rain-giver's wife, be homage!

43. Her castles are built by the Gods, her plains
the arena in which men wage war. The matrix
of all things is Earth. May the Lord of life
dispose for our enjoyment all her regions!

44. May the Goddess Earth, bearer of many a treasure
and of wealth stored up in diverse hidden places,
the generous sharer of riches, impart to us,
in addition to gold and gems, a special portion of her favor!

45. May Earth who bears mankind, each different grouping
maintaining its own customs and its speech,
yield up for me a thousand streams of treasure,
like a placid cow that never resists the hand.

46. The snake and the scorpion which viciously bite,
which, chilled by winter, lie slothfully hidden,
the wriggling worm, all that stirs in the rains—
may it, creeping, not creep on us! Instead,
may you grant us the blessing of all that is wholesome!

47. From your numberless tracks by which mankind may travel,
your roads on which move both chariots and wagons
your paths which are used by the good and the bad,

may we choose a way free from foes and robbers!
May you grant us the blessing of all that is wholesome!

48. She carries in her lap the foolish and also the wise.
She bears the death of the wicked as well as the good.
She lives in friendly collaboration with the boar,
offering herself as sanctuary to the wild pig.

49. The creatures of your forests, dwellers in woods,
lions, tigers, man-eaters that prowl about,
hyena and wolf, misfortune stalking around,
demons both male and female, chase them far!

50. All evil spirits, male and female alike,
drive far from us, O Earth, the ones that grab
and the ones that devour, all vampires and all demons!
Drive each and every one to distant realms!

51. Over the earth the winged bipeds fly,
swans and falcons, eagles, birds of all kinds.
On her the wind comes rushing, Mātariśvan,
raising the dust, causing the trees to tremble
and dragging in his victory train the Fire.

52. May she in whom the bright and also the dark,
the day and the night, associate, though separate,
the far-flung Earth, ofttimes by rain made fertile,
graciously settle each one in his well-loved abode!

53. Heaven and Earth and the space in between
have set me in a wide expanse!
Fire, the Sun, the Waters, the Gods,
have joined to give me inspiration.

54. Behold me now, victorious!
My name is the highest in all the earth.
Ruling in all regions, I subdue all! I conquer!

55. When at the Gods' command, O Goddess,
you unfurled yourself, revealing your grandeur,
then you were imbued with beauty and charm.
You shaped and fashioned the world's four regions.

56. In village or forest, in all the places
where man meets man, in market or forum,
may we always say that which is pleasing to you!

57. Just as a horse scatters dust, so Earth,
when she came into being, scattered the peoples—
Earth, gracious leader and protectress of the world,
who holds in firm grasp both trees and plants.

58. The words that I speak are sweet as honey!
My glances meet with fair glances in return.
Vehement am I, swift and impetuous!
Those who gnash their teeth I utterly vanquish!

59. Peaceful and fragrant, gracious to the touch,
may Earth, swollen with milk, her breasts overflowing,
grant me her blessing together with her milk!

60. The Maker of the world sought her with oblations
when she was shrouded in the depth of the ocean.
A vessel of gladness, long cherished in secret,
the earth was revealed to mankind for their joy.

61. Primeval Mother, disperser of men,
you, far-flung Earth, fulfill all our desires.
Whatever you lack, may the Lord of creatures,
the First-born of Right, supply to you fully!

62. May your dwellings, O Earth, free from sickness and wasting,
flourish for us! Through a long life, watchful,
may we always offer to you our tribute!

63. O Earth, O Mother, dispose my lot
in gracious fashion that I be at ease.
In harmony with all the powers of Heaven
set me, O Poet, in grace and good fortune!

1. Prayer: *brahman* as the sacred liturgical word.

Holy Ritual: *yajña,* sacrifice, the sacramental rite. So we have *satya, ṛta, dīkṣā, tapas, brahman,* and *yajña* as the pillars of the earth as they are of any sacred, i.e., any real activity.

Earth: *bhūmi* throughout.

3. River: *sindhu,* though some have read Indus, the particular river of India. The "stream" here is probably not any specific river but the mythical *rasā* which flows at the ends of the earth. Cf. RV X, 121, 4 (§ I 4).

Ploughman's crops: lit. ploughing furrows.

The long first draught: *pūrvapeya.* The first privilege of Indra, after drinking Soma, was to perform the mighty work of organizing the earth.

5. Gods and demons: *devas* and *asuras.*

Good fortune: *bhaga,* happy lot, luck, what falls to a person by lot, i.e., a person's destiny.

Glory: *varcas,* brilliance, luster, i.e., success owing to good fortune, power of transmitting one's own enlightenment, of fulfilling one's own destiny.

6. Sustaining (mother): *pratiṣṭhā,* support, foundation, basis.

Universal Fire: Agni as *vaiśvānara* (§ III 5). *Vaiśvānara* abides in each *puruṣa,* both on the cosmic plane and in the individual being (SB X, 6, 1). On the human plane Agni *vaiśvānara* is the metabolic fire that eats food and stands for life itself.

Whose spouse is Indra: lit. who mates with the bull Indra or whose bull is Indra. Cf. RV VI, 44, 21.

7. Honey symbolizes both material and spiritual wealth and is often described as "sweet milk" (with which it is often mixed). It stands for *ūrj, rasa,* i.e., *soma.*

Cf. the "vitalizing forces," *ūrjaḥ,* from deep within the body (of the earth) of v. 12; cf. RV, X, 9, 1-2 (§ I 17 and notes).

8. Cf. §§ I 15; 16 on the primordial waters. The "heart" of the earth is transcendent to the earth itself; this is a transcendent immanence.

10. The foot of Viṣṇu: cf. § I 27.

Indra: cf. §§ I 24; II 4.

11. Forests: *araṇya,* woods, and also wilderness.

12. The Rain-giver: Parjanya, the Rain-God. Cf. § II 24.
13. The earth is not only an ecological dwelling place but has also an eschatological and liturgical dimension. Workmen: *viśvakarmaṇaḥ*, a guild of workmen attending the sacrifice, probably the so-called *adhvaryu*.
15. The five human races: may refer to the five tribes. Cf. BU IV, 4, 17 (§ VI 11). Cf. Nirukta III, 8 about *pañcajanāḥ*.
17. Heavenly Law: *dharma*.
18. Lord: Indra.
19. The different forms of fire are mentioned, from the sun (v. 20) down to fire in wood and the "fire" of digestion in living beings.
21. Knees: referring to dark-colored rocks.
22. Human race: *manuṣya*.
23. Celestial beings: Gandharvas and Apsarases. Cf. AV X, 9, 9; etc. Fragrance is their special attribute. They received it as *bhaga*, a special gift, together with invulnerability. Cf. vv. 24-25. Fragrance (*gandha*) is also, in later philosophical systems, the characteristic of the element earth.
24. Reference to the wedding of Sūryā the Sun-maiden with the God Soma. Cf. RV X, 85 (§ II 15).
29. By Sacred Word enhanced: *brahmaṇā vāvṛdhānām. Brahman*, fullness, swelling, enthusiasm of soul in prayer, pious utterance. Cf. the root *bṛh-*, increase, strengthen, and the root *vṛdh-*, increase, grow strong, extend, gladden.
Nourishment: *ūrj*.
Approach you with due praise: *ni ṣīdema*, may we sit down before you with reverence for instruction, approach in homage.
34. Be gentle: lit. do not harm us.
36. On the seasons cf. § VII Introduction.
37. Trembles before the Serpent: obscure expression. Serpent, however, refers to the demon Vṛtra; i.e., in the fight between good and evil the Earth, who is afraid of the dragon, stands at Indra's side.
38. Earth as the stage and support of sacrifice.
39. The Seven Seers: the mythical *ṛṣis*, first sacrificers, mentioned in the RV and to whom names are given in the B. Cf. also BU II, 2, 4.
Holy rite: *yajña*.
Sacrifice: *satra*, the Soma "session."
Creative Fervor: *tapas*.
Sang hymns . . .: *gā udānṛcuḥ*, lit. sang forth the cows. Cows are also a symbol of words or songs.
42. Rain-giver: Parjanya; cf. RV V, 83 (§ II 24).
43. Lord of life: Prajāpati.
44. Wealth stored up: i.e., the mines, which hold the hidden treasures of Earth.
45. Placid: lit. permanent, steady.
48. The wise: *guru*, or the heavy.
Death: *nidhana*, or dwelling (?).
Boar: early reference to the myth of the Boar as an *avatāra* of Viṣṇu.
50. Evil spirits, male and female: Gandharvas and Apsarases; here their negative, demonic aspect is intended, as they are mentioned together with other demons.
53. Gods: lit. All-Gods: *viśvedevāḥ*; cf. RV X, 72 (§ VII 2).
54. The king is speaking.
60. The Maker of the world: *viśvakarman*, cf. RV X, 81; 82 (§§ VII 7; 12).
Mankind: lit. all beings with a mother.
61. Primeval Mother: Aditi, Infinity, begetter and origin of the Gods, a mythical figure of light. Cf. RV I, 136, 3; X, 72, 4-5 (§ VII 2).
Wish-fulfiller: *kāmadughā*, reminds us of *kāmadhenu*, the mythical and miraculous "wish-cow," later colorfully described in the Rāmāyaṇa. In point of fact, in RV I, 153, 3, Aditi is referred to as a cow. In RV I, 72, 9, she is compared to the Earth. She represents the maternal aspect of Earth.
The Lord of creatures: Prajāpati.
Right: *ṛta*.
63. Dispose my lot, etc.: set me down graciously (that I may be) well established.
Poet: *kavi* from the root *kū-*, to see, hence sage or seer.

c) Wind

Vāyu

In the Ṛg Veda the wind is named *vāta* or *vāyu*, the former being used chiefly for the element and the latter chiefly for the God. There is no need to elaborate any particular theory regarding the meaning of the Vedic divinities, for the hymns speak for themselves. They make clear reference to the benefits bestowed by the wind and they pray that such blessings be continued. Particularly striking are the religious tone of the hymns and their invitation to plunge into the cosmogonic origins and to discover the transcendent meaning of natural phenomena.

An ambivalent meaning is suggested by some of the sentences in these two hymns. What is said of the Wind could equally be said of the Spirit. The Wind collects, enraptures, and takes away in his chariot toward the celestial heights those who are caught in his blowing, bringing them together with the same devotion and enthusiasm as that of women congregating for a holy feast or gathering for a marriage. This same Wind is connected with the primordial waters, is called the first-born, and yet is said to be of unknown origin; for nobody knows where it goes and where it comes from: it wanders free, is heard but not seen, is invisible, can only be felt, experienced, sensed, without being comprehended or understood.

The second hymn voices a deep prayer to the Spirit that he may breathe or impart life. There is another, similar text which affirms:

> Breathe, O Wind, your healing breezes.
> Blow away evil. You are the medicine
> of this whole world, the Messenger of the Gods![74]

The Wind holds the gift of eternal life; it is the bestower of the life-principle, the seed of life.[75]

The Glowing of the Spirit *Vāta*

20

RV X, 168

1. Oh, the Wind's chariot, its power and its glory!
   It passes by crashing.
   Out streak the lightnings, dust rises on earth.
   The Wind passes.

2. The hosts of the Wind speed onward after him,
   like women assembling.
   This king of the world lifts them up in his chariot
   through lofty regions.

74. RV X, 137, 3.
75. Cf. also RV I, 134.

3. He speeds on air's pathways, he rests not nor slumbers
   for even a day.
   First-born, the Waters' friend, the righteous, whence came he?
   How was he born?

4. Breath of the Gods and life germ of the universe,
   freely he wanders.
   We bring him our homage, whose voice may be heard
   but whose form is not seen.

1. Wind: *vāta*, breath of the Gods. Cf. AV XI, 4 to *prāṇa* (§ II 5). Its roar is thunder; it reaches the blue sky producing red flashes.
2. The hosts: winds of various kinds or the rains following the wind.
King of the world: lit. the God, king of the whole universe.
3. The righteous: *ṛtāvan*, the holy, the upright, the just, one who goes the right way.
4. Hearing pierces deeper than seeing into the realm of being, though seeing may be clearer than hearing.

The Gifts of the Spirit

Mayas

21

RV X, 186

1. May the Wind breathe healing upon us,
   prolong our life-span,
   and fill our hearts with comfort!

2. You are our father, O Wind,
   our friend and our brother,
   Give us life that we may live.

3. From that immortal treasure, O Lord,
   which is hidden in your abode,
   impart to us that we may live.

1. May the wind breathe: *vāta ā vātu*, both from the same root *vā-*, to blow (cf. Latin *ventus*), with the special meaning here, to inspire, infuse.
Comfort: *mayas* which could be equated with bliss, *ānanda*.
3. Immortal treasure: *amṛtasya nidhiḥ*.
Lord: Vāta.

D. THE LORD

Īśa

The Primal Man is, simply, All:
what is and what shall be.
He is the Lord of Immortality.

AV XIX, 6, 4

The Lord is undoubtedly not a proper name of God; it is not a distinctive name. It is a comprehensive term used not only for the different names of the divinities and of God in different religious traditions, but also for many other forms of preeminence in the human world: the pontiff, the king, the ruler, the judge, the husband, and so on, are called "lords" in many a culture, while in a personified way even the powerful natural phenomena are considered to lord it over human beings. Probably no other name is more universal and more appropriate to denote that mystery greater than ourselves which some traditions have called God. Not every tradition agrees in calling the Supreme either Being or Person or Creator or even God. Further, if we use a proper name, if we say Varuṇa or Śiva or Yahweh, we are not only personifying but also limiting our reference to that one culture where the word is at home. The name of Lord, on the contrary, seems to be universal and capable, at the same time, of taking on a concrete meaning. It betrays, indeed, a certain personalistic bias, but this bias is not essential to it, as we may see not only if we consult the etymology of the many words standing for it, like *bhagavat, īśvara, prabhu,* or, in other traditions, *ba'al, ādōn, kyrios, allāh* (*al-ilāh*), *ahura mazda,* but also and mainly if we consider that the main import of the name Lord (and all its equivalents) is not that of being an individual or even a particular being, but of being the superior term of a relation. The Lord is probably the most universal symbol for that "other term" of the human-cosmic relation which has received so many different names.

On various occasions in the past and also recently it has been affirmed that the Vedas are both magical and pantheistic. It is not the purpose of this anthology to enter into controversy, but in order to facilitate prayer and understanding of the given texts something must be said on these two points.

First, the magical abuse of a text does not mean that the primordial intention and the primary meaning of a text are in fact such. Second, one must add that almost any description or manifestation of something for which one does not possess the clue is bound from an external viewpoint to look like magic; most of the achievements of science and technology would appear so to a Man from another culture, and this applies also to the utterances and descriptions of the Vedas when they are seen with eyes and felt with feelings alien to those of Vedic Man.[76]

Concerning alleged pantheism, one should bear in mind that a process of identification (between worshiper and object of worship), which is bewildering to a rational mind detached from the object of its thought, is an almost obligatory feature of any committed existential attitude. If, when thinking about or desiring one thing or loving one person, we are at the same time thinking about another thing, desiring a different object, and loving a second person, we are bound to say that our acts are far from being perfect, satisfying, and perhaps even authentic. If, when considering one thing, we are being worried by another and are already considering how we are going to integrate this second into a wider picture, our thinking is not only not fully engaged in its primary concern but is already distorting the picture by adopting a double perspective which can only blur the image. When, full of thankfulness for a

76. Cf. § IV A a on the same subject.

benefit, full of joy because of a happening, I have to control my feelings or modify my words in order to reserve place and time for another possible happening, I am already calculating, remembering, manipulating, and in the last analysis I am not fully given to what I am saying or doing. Therefore, there is no need to refer to a particular trend of thinking or an epistemological difference in order to explain the Vedic hymns, though this trend or difference may well be pertinent. We need only recall that each text is a prayer, a hymn, a song, or a commitment and that it does not vault outside itself, so to speak, in order to see its own impact on the reader or its compatibility with what has been said before or will be said afterward. Each ultimate attitude is unique and cannot be compared with another. Any comparison presupposes a neutral or a more general "platform" which makes the comparison possible at the price of robbing the particular attitude of its character of ultimacy.

It is easy to recognize that Light is not the same as Life, or Time Eternity, or Indra Agni, or Savitṛ Vāyu. Yet when we receive properly a divine gift (that is, when we accept the visitation of the Lord), in whatever wrappings that gift may be, there is no room left for anything else. The lordship of the Lord, whatever concrete form it may take, is not only overwhelming; it is also in a way absolute and thus unique. Because of our temporal fragmentation, however, owing to the fact that we cannot live a whole life at one time, a second moment may displace the first one and we may be filled with another equally overpowering experience which will find another unique, and thus incomparable, form of expression. It is only from the outer platform of our memory or from the eyes of an outsider that we can relate the two experiences. Memory is a double-edged sword: it allows for continuity once the real continuity is broken, but because it is a temporal human faculty, memory cannot bear witness to the nontemporal. There is no memory in ecstatic moments or in actual consciousness.

It is tempting, and perhaps it would be rewarding, to take a certain evolutionary perspective and speak of the progressive evolution of the concept of Lord in the Indian scene, but we cannot do so here.

The nouns *īśvara* and *īśa* are not found in the Ṛg Veda, although the verb form is frequently used to express the power of the Gods. Where the terms occur in the Atharva Veda and Brāhmaṇas, they certainly do not have the connotations of later times. Certain Upaniṣads begin to put the concept of the Lord in the foreground and the Śvetāśvatāra Upaniṣad gives it still greater prominence. The personal Lord is finally fully disclosed in the Bhagavad Gitā. On the other hand, if we take into consideration other generic terms such as *pati, prabhu, adhipati,* and so on,[77] we may certainly say that the concept of the Lord does in fact permeate the whole of the Vedas. In addition to the words denoting Lord we can also say that the concept is present in all the hymns, where it is represented each time by one of the Vedic Gods. Thus, if we are considering the omnipotence and majesty of the Godhead, his sovereignty, it is Indra who springs spontaneously to mind. If we reflect upon the great importance of sacrifice or on the incarnate friendly aspect of God—though without in any way diminishing his divinity—it is to Agni that we turn. Indra, Agni, Varuṇa, the Master who surveys Men's deeds, punishes Men, and pities them, Soma, the radiant Lord of Light—each of these will make an appearance according to the place that he has made for himself in the minds and hearts of the Men of the Vedic period.

The different Gods described and worshiped in the Vedas testify to a strong urge in Man toward unity, a longing to arrive at a conception that is both totally divine and totally human. This dynamic process in Man has not yet ceased, and the fascinating evolution discernible in the Indian context from the Vedas through the Bhagavad Gitā to modern times can be paralleled elsewhere. Furthermore, the situation presents in our days a new challenge. Is not the serious thrust of modern atheism a new step toward a deeper theandric unity by which God as Other is dethroned and yet Man as individual does not replace him? Not only does the concept of the Lord undergo an enriching process of inner unification, so that the different Gods and attributes or persons are no longer considered in a polytheistic way, but it also acquires a stronger bond of unity with the world, so that the Lord's relation with the world is no longer considered in either a dualistic or a monistic way: his transcendence does not exclude his immanence or his immanence his transcendence, and thus neither monotheism nor atheism appears satisfactory any longer.

77. When the word "Lord" is used in a hymn to address a particular God, the name of the God is usually given in the notes. When the word "Lord" translates a generic term such as *īśa* or *pati,* however, usually no further explanation is given.

The Vedic Revelation, however, does not need to be interpreted on these lines. Its main message is not to give us a historical picture of the development of human consciousness regarding the divine or to explain to us the evolution of Man's religiousness, but to lead us toward an ever deeper realization of this continuing universal and ever new mystery. The hymns, chants, injunctions, and prayers are not there mainly to foster an intellectual curiosity but to nourish a personal life. The Lord is not only *from* yesterday or only *for* tomorrow; he is also and primarily *in* today's life, as the Scriptures remind us.

The hymns that follow are dedicated to Savitṛ, Agni, Indra, Soma, Varuṇa, and Viṣṇu. Each of them has a proper face and possesses his own symbolic power. But to those who are outside the atmosphere of the traditional religiousness of India, modern Hindus or others, these names may not convey all the riches crystallized in long centuries of fervent prayer and thoughtful meditation; such people may even feel disturbed by these names, interpreting them as mere mythological figures instead of as living symbols. We suggest, therefore, replacing the proper names on occasion with the widely used name of "Lord" and giving to it the broadest possible interpretation: any power superior to the individual. In later sections, where the role of each God is illustrated, there is a descriptive introduction of each, but we purposely introduce the Gods singly in order to allow each unique personality to shine forth clearly and thus to enhance the meditative use of this anthology.

The different texts may give some idea of the wide range of experience undergirding Vedic "theology." No merely naturalistic explanation of the worship of the Gods as natural powers will do justice to the texts or to the sophistication of Vedic culture. No supernaturalistic hypothesis should undermine, on the other hand, the realistic and humanistic approach of the texts. The Gods are intrinsically connected with sacrifice and with the idea of cosmic order; they constitute different expressions of the sacrificial act that maintains universal order. Within the cosmic realm the split that is productive of many Gods is not an ultimate one, just as the parallel split in our consciousness among ourselves, the world, and God is not ultimate either; these three are certainly not one, but neither are they many. The mystery of God is the mystery of Man and the mystery of Reality. The Vedic Revelation does not reveal one God;

it just unveils a little the mystery of life by assuring us that Reality is neither dead nor blind, that there is a Lord of beings—*vaiśvadeva*—residing in the heart of every being as well as in the core of Being itself, and this affirmation is loudly proclaimed in a festive symphony.

Stotra

RV I, 44, 6

i) O most youthful God!

RV I, 44, 9

ii) God of the sacrifice, O Lord, and envoy of men are you.

RV I, 44, 10

iii) O most radiant One, all-visible!

RV I, 45, 9

iv) Good and bountiful, source of vigor!

RV I, 186, 3

v) I sing the Lord, the guest most dearly loved.

RV IV, 17, 17

vi) Friend and Father, most fatherly of fathers!

RV VI, 37, 5

vii) May our songs glorify God, the most mighty!

RV VII, 18, 1

viii) All is with you, O Lord!

RV X, 188, 3

ix) O All-knowing One, may your flames that convey
oblations to the Gods direct our sacrifice!

■ i) Agni. Time does not have a hold on him.
■ ii) Agni.
Envoy: *dūta*, messenger.
■ iii) Agni.
All-visible: *viśvadarśataḥ*, visible to all, conspicuous, revealed in all. This obviously does not refer to philosophical intelligibility.
■ iv) Agni.
Source of vigor: *sahaskṛta*, produced by vigor.
■ v) Agni. Recurrent mystical theme of God's indwelling in the soul.
■ vi) Indra. The relationship of friendship is here added to that of fatherhood. Friendship implies not only a certain equality but also a free choice. Does this suggest nature and grace?

■ vii) Indra. One could say "magnify the mighty" or "glorify the glorious" God, in order to keep the same verbal root as in the original.
■ viii) Indra.
■ ix) Agni.
All-knowing One: *jātavedas*.
Direct: *inv-*, also favor, inspire.

The Refulgent One *Savitṛ*

22 The unique lordship of Savitṛ the resplendent Sun, the vivifier, is so much a part of everyday life that no one will contest his supremacy. We have already seen that the Sun inspired the most sacred Gāyatrī mantra,[78] and later on we encounter him as the dispenser of blessings[79] and, under the name of Sūrya, as the supreme light and dispeller of darkness.[80] The hymn that follows leads us to discover the varied facets of his lordship.

The ocean of golden light in which Savitṛ dwells is much more conducive to an ecstatic than to an analytic approach, but we can descry some of his main features.

The Lord Savitṛ is the giver of life and the origin and end of time.[81] From his rising until his setting everything follows the course of the sun: the life of Men, the functioning of the cosmos, and even the rites of sacrifice. Everything on earth depends on his radiant light and warmth. The actions of Men are regulated according to the hours of the day, each moment of which depends on the sun.[82] The life cycle of both animals and plants is under his surveillance, while the hours of the *agnihotra* sacrifice have been strictly fixed in relation to his appearance;[83] it is in communion with him that, evening and morning, Men pray, meditate, and worship.[84] As the hymn says (v. 5),

> All beings, men and creatures, abide
> forever in the bosom of Savitṛ divine.

It is he, Man's constant companion during the day, who brings him to his rest at night.

Savitṛ, as we have said, is the "golden" Lord. His golden

78. Cf. the Gāyatrī, at the beginning of the anthology.
79. Cf. §§ II 1-3.
80. Cf. §§ III 1-3.
81. On time, cf. §§ II 7-9.
82. Cf. RV II, 38.
83. On the *agnihotra*, cf. § III 16.
84. Cf. § VII Introduction on the subject of *saṁdhyā*.

appearance is frequently mentioned in both descriptive and eulogistic hymns. There is no better adjective to convey simultaneously his shining splendor, his bounty, and his inestimable value for Man. He is "golden-eyed" (v. 8) and "gold-handed" (vv. 9, 10); he appears majestically in a "golden chariot" (v. 2) with "poles of gold" and a "golden shaft" (vv. 4, 5).

The Lord Savitṛ is gracious toward Men. He distributes his favors with magnanimity, repulsing sorrows and dangers (v. 3), conquering sickness (v. 9), and chasing away demons and socerers (v. 10). His realm is the realm of light, of beauty and well-being, and it is to him that Men turn when they are afraid of darkness, whether it be the darkness of night or the darkness of suffering,[85] and when they are longing for light, health, and joy. Their trust in Lord Savitṛ is so strong that they are confident in his power to free them from sin.[86]

Lord Savitṛ abides with us till evening!

Savitṛ

RV I, 35

1. I call first on Agni for our salvation;
on Mitra and Varuṇa, that they may help us,
on Night, who lays the world to rest,
and Savitṛ divine, that he may aid us.

2. God Savitṛ advances in his golden chariot,
wheeling toward us through the pitch-black void,
conducting to their rest both men and Gods,
directing his gaze upon all created beings.

3. Worthy of worship, he pursues his path,
first up, then down, his horses resplendent.
From the ends of the world God Savitṛ comes,
repulsing all sorrow and every danger.

4. The God has now mounted his mighty chariot,
ornate, decked with pearls, with poles of gold.
Resplendent, adorable, he exercises
his powerful thrust, dispelling the darkness.

5. Drawing the chariot with the golden shaft,
his two steeds, white-hoofed, have gazed on mankind.
All beings, men and creatures, abide
forever in the bosom of Savitṛ divine.

85. On sorrow and suffering cf. § IV A.
86. Cf. RV IV, 54, 3 (§ IV 8).

6. Three heavens there are: two in the bosom
of Savitṛ, the third the realm of Yama.
Immortality rests stable as a chariot on its axle.
Let him who understands this now declare it!

7. The Bird in the heavens keeps watchful eye,
the inspired Asura, the perfect guide.
Where now is the sun? Who knows his place?
As far as what heaven has his ray extended?

8. He has surveyed the earth's eight peaks,
its continents three, its tracts, its seven rivers.
Savitṛ, the golden-eyed God, has come,
bringing his worshiper wondrous blessings.

9. Savitṛ, the skillful, gold-handed God
is passing over between Earth and Heaven.
He conquers sickness, directing the sun,
and mounts up to heaven through darksome space.

10. May our gracious God and kind leader, the Asura,
skillful, gold-handed, come now to our aid!
He who chases far both demons and sorcerers,
this God whom we hymn, abides here each evening.

11. Your ancient paths, O Savitr, were dust free
and well established in the vaults of Heaven.
Come to us now by these paths so fair!
Protect us from harm and bless us, O God!

1. Salvation: *svasti.*
3. Sorrow and danger: *durita.*
4. The chariot of the night is meant.
The pearls probably refer to the stars.
6. Three heavens: the two in Savitṛ's bosom are heaven and earth, and the third one is the world beyond, the realm of the dead. For Yama and the world beyond cf. §§ V 2; 7.
7. Bird: *suparṇa,* the Sun.
Asura: the Sun.
Perfect guide: *sunītha.*
8. Wondrous blessings: *ratnā . . . vāryāṇi,* lit. desired treasures.
9. Here it is clear that Savitṛ is not necessarily identical with the sun, but is its impelling force. Cf. RV VII, 45, 2 (§ II 3).

The Friend of Man *Agni*

23 The most appropriate Vedic symbol for the lordship of the Lord is perhaps the figure of Agni, the friend of Man, the mediator, the sacred and sacrificial fire, and at the same time the fire that is in the sun, in burning things, and in the heart of Man,

everywhere the same and yet everywhere different, having varied and even almost contrary effects. The devotion to Agni does not represent nature worship, much less pantheism; it is the recognition of an underlying polymorphic reality that softens wax and honey but hardens mud, dries up plants, may bring life or death, and always transcends all our powers, mental as well as physical.[87]

Agni is acclaimed with praise and veneration both evening and morning at the domestic hearth, when the home is not closed in upon itself but is open to the horizons of the earth and of men. Agni is near to Man, kindly disposed, intimately bound up with his life, the guest of his dwelling, the wise Lord who knows all things, the eternally young, the strong and powerful to whom one offers sacrifice and who is able to shower one with blessings. If modern Man does not follow what has been said, let him wait until winter and evening, kindle the hearth, and simply gaze at the live coals, and he will surely understand that the Lord is he who breaks his isolation without disturbing his solitude.

This hymn, like many of those addressed to Agni, expresses his lordship in terms of wisdom and foreknowledge. He is powerful and yet accessible to Men, full of goodness and mercy, inspiring devotion in such a way that Man approaches him fearlessly as a friend, not as an abstraction or a distant and formidable deity. The lordship of Agni is not seen as the imposition of a divine will, but as an expression of the normal and beautiful order of reality. If nobody knew "the first word and the last," all the other human words in between would be utterly meaningless and could only convey despair. If there were no fire to burn what has already dried up, or what has been done wrongly, no renewal and no hope would subsist on earth for a long time.

Agni RV I, 145

1. Uplift your prayer! He comes! He knows!
   His wisdom is implored.
   In him are counsels, in him requests,
   this Lord of power.

2. Men pray to him, yet he needs no asking;
   his mind has grasped all things. He goes

87. Cf. § III 4 for a further description of Agni; cf. § VII B for several hymns to Agni.

as one who knows the first word and the last,
 with mind composed.

3. To him ascend these hymns, these steed-swift prayers.
He alone hears my words. All-mover, all-conqueror,
conveyer of sacrifice, the Child, ever aiding,
 he assumes great power.

4. What he meets he grasps and, newly born,
advances vehemently, darting with his fellows.
He brings to the weary pleasure and great joy,
 accepting their gifts.

5. He is a being of flood and forest
 who passes aloft.
Knowing the Law, he inspires to right action,
 this wise and true Lord.

1. Counsels and requests: In him are admonitions, advice, instructions, commands; in him are requests, consultations.

Lord of power: *vājasya śavasaḥ śuṣmiṇaspatiḥ*, lit. vigorous Lord of strength and might.

2. His mind has grasped all things: *dhīro manasā*: by means of his own mind he attains to highest insight; having understood by his own mind, he needs no asking.

3. Hymns and steed-swift prayers: lit. ladles and sacrificial mares, being symbols for songs of praise.

All-mover: *puru-praiṣa*, spurring, inciting many.

All-conqueror: *taturi*, overcoming, conquering.

Conveyer of sacrifice: *yajña-sādhana*, perfect accomplisher of sacrifice.

Ever aiding: *acchidra-ūti*, whose protection is unbroken, everlasting; *ūti* may also mean source of joy.

The Child or "Babe ever young" is Agni, the protector of his devotees.

4. Fire is the symbol of Agni; Agni sets fire to whatever he finds. He creeps onward and when he seems to rest, i.e., ceases to burn, he suddenly springs up again vehemently (*sāra*) with his "kin" (i.e., the flames, the yokefellows), ignites, comes nearer, and grasps all those who fall fascinated into his power, enkindling in them the highest joy. There is a triple metaphor running throughout the hymn: the fascination and consuming power of fire; its function in the purification and salvation of man; its use as a lofty symbol for the divine.

5. Passes aloft: lit. has been set in the highest sky. Cf. RV II, 1, 1, for Agni's relationship with the waters. There are both celestial and terrestrial waters.

Lord: Agni. In many texts Agni is said to have taken birth in wood (RV VI, 3, 3; X, 79, 7), to be the embryo of trees (RV I, 70, 4) and of plants. For his birth in the sky as lightning cf. RV I, 143, 2; VI, 8, 2.

The Master of the Universe *Indra*

24 The facet of Indra most celebrated and extolled in the Ṛg Veda is his Lordship, his supreme mastery of men and situations. He is Master of the whole world:[88] "He who is Lord of every world that moves and breathes";[89] "Yourself alone the universal Sovereign."[90] All the hymns dedicated to him contain an element of

88. For further introduction to Indra, cf. § II 4.
89. RV I, 101, 5.
90. RV III, 46, 2.

near ecstasy as they extol his grandeur and his universal dominion. In each hymn he is Master of the universe. He has conquered it, overcoming all foes.[91]

The hymn that follows refers, in the compass of a few concise and beautiful verses, to several of the features of his Lordship: he is Lord of sacrifice (vv. 1, 2, 7) and he is renowned as the drinker of Soma, that energy-giving drink in which he delights. Those who perform the sacrificial rites are at a loss to find words capable of extolling Indra in accordance with his merits. He is always the God-hero, the God of mighty deeds arousing awe and praise. Men are enraptured by the divine display of the Master of the universe.

The second stanza mentions the "two bay steeds" that pull his chariot. The chariot here refers to the Word, that Word whose power is manifested in the performance of the sacrifice. Elsewhere the poet speaks of "his steeds yoked by prayers."[92] Such metaphors refer no doubt to the invocations that summon Indra to the sacrifice.

Lord of the universe (vv. 3, 6), Lord of hosts, all-powerful in battle (vv. 4, 8), Lord and Friend (v. 5), the one who chases away every evil, Indra is full of compassion for his worshipers. His friends are never done to death or overcome by violence.[93]

Indra RV I, 7

1. Indra the singers,
   Indra the reciters,
   Indra the choirs
   have glorified!

2. Indra the golden,
   armed with thunder,
   with his two bay steeds
   and the Word as his chariot!

3. The Sun is his eye,
   raised on high.
   Cloud masses he bursts
   to release the rain.

4. By your dread power,
   Indra, most fearsome,

91. Cf. RV I, 32, etc.
92. RV II, 18, 3.
93. Cf. RV X, 152, 1.

help us in battle
to win ample spoils.

5. Indra we invoke
in all kinds of contests,
our Friend who hurls
at powers of evil his bolts.

6. Burst open for us
yonder cloud in the sky,
ever bounteous Indra,
irresistible hero!

7. Higher, yet higher,
I raise his praises!
I find no words
worthy of him!

8. He drives on his peoples
with strength irresistible,
even as the bull
drives onward the herds.

9. Sole sovereign is Indra
of men and of Gods
and of the fivefold race
of dwellers on earth.

10. Indra we invoke
from all the peoples.
May Indra be for us
and nobody else.

1. Lit. Indra the singers with glory, Indra the reciters with praise (*arka*).
3. Or else: Indra, to see afar, has raised the sun in the sky: *indro dīrghāya cakṣasa ā sūryaṁ rohayad divi.*
4. Fearsome: *ugra,* inspirer of awe, a typical epithet of Indra.
7. Lit. the praises of Indra with the thunderbolt.
I find no words worthy of him: *na vindhe asya suṣṭutim.*
9. The fivefold race: probably the five tribes of the Aryans, with whom Indra was most intimately associated.
10. May Indra be for us and nobody else: *asmākam astu kevalaḥ,* may he be ours alone.

The Heroes of Sundry Exploits *Indra-Soma*

25 Indra and Soma are so closely associated that on most occasions the one is not mentioned without explicit or implicit reference to the other. It is indeed after drinking deeply of Soma that Indra is rendered capable of his heroic tasks.[94] Soma is a God, a

94. For Indra cf. §§ I 24; II 4.

myth, a plant, and the special juice extracted from it, which is utilized in many sacrificial and other rites. In this hymn it is the celestial drink that is invoked.[95]

One of the most important tasks of Indra was the liberation of the world from the dominion of the fearful dragon Vṛtra, who was maintaining the universe in drought and gloom; the dragon was slain, the waters flowed, the shadows were dispelled, the sun rose, and the light shone. Thus Indra is hailed as conquering Lord and as Savior and, because of the work of liberation, achieved in partnership, Indra and Soma are said to give life to the world, for water, light, and sunshine are the necessary conditions for life.

Indra and Soma are thus intimately connected with light because they drive away all shadows, all evil. They cooperate in the task of bringing light to the world, and Soma, the sacrificial drink, the all-purifying (*pavamāna*), is often praised as "Lord of Light." The identification of Soma with light—he is called *indu,* bright drop—derives no doubt from the appearance of the sacred liquid which is of a yellow-golden hue (*hari*). The poets highly praise Soma's luminosity, which may also be connected with his inebriating effect.

Soma, the sacred drink drunk by Indra, not only inspires Indra to perform mighty deeds but is himself a God who performs great cosmic actions: he makes the sun and the dawn shine;[96] he is the Father of Heaven and Earth;[97] it is to please him that the winds blow and the rivers flow.[98] He is even praised as possessing the whole universe, including its five regions.[99] He is also, and independently of Indra, a great and heroic warrior who wins all his battles.[100] No evildoer, no wicked person, can withstand his mighty and luminous power, "for you, Soma purifier, repel all enemies."[101]

Indra-Soma RV VI, 72

1. How great, O Indra and Soma, is your power!
It was you who performed those first and mighty exploits.

95. For Soma cf. § III 17, and §§ VII 5; 10; 15; 20; 25; 30.
96. Cf. RV IX, 28, 5; IX, 37, 4.
97. Cf. RV IX, 90, 1.
98. Cf. RV IX, 31, 3 (§ VII 10).
99. Cf. RV IX, 86, 29 (§ III 17 Introduction).
100. Cf. RV IX, 66, 16-17.
101. RV IX, 94, 5 (§ VII 25).

It was you who subdued the Sun, subdued the Sky,
and chased away all darkness, all the ribald.

2. Indra and Soma, you make the dawn to glow
and cause the Sun to rise in all his splendor.
You have propped up the Sky with a supporting pillar
and spread out Mother Earth in all directions.

3. Indra and Soma, you smote the serpent Vṛtra
who sought to obstruct the waters. To you the heavens
yielded their load; you pierced the river torrents
as with a lance and filled full many a sea.

4. Within the cow's udder, unprepared,
it was you, O Soma and Indra, who placed the milk.
You held the cream-hued unimpeded stream
within the multicolored moving creatures.

5. Great are the riches you grant, O strong Ones,
which free from fear and pass to children's children.
With manly power you invest the sons of men
that they may be victorious in the battle.

2. Supporting pillar: *skambha*, cf. § I 3. In several other passages the same role is attributed to Indra alone. Cf. RV II, 12, 2 (§ II 4); II, 15, 2; II, 21, 4; III, 31, 15; III, 32, 8; III, 49, 4.
3. On the fight with Vṛtra, cf. RV I, 32; etc.
4. Unprepared: lit. the raw belly, in contrast with the warm ("cooked") milk that is prepared in it.

The King of Heaven and Earth — *Varuṇa*

26 Varuṇa, one of the greatest among the Ṛg-Vedic Gods, represents the Lord in his aspect of kingship; he is the supreme Ruler who controls all things, the cosmos as well as the deeds of Men. The sun is the all-seeing eye of Varuṇa; nothing escapes his glance, which sees all, penetrates, surveys, examines, and assesses.[102] In order to symbolize this extraordinary power he is said to have "a thousand eyes."[103] The hymn here given describes the activity of this monarch, thus enhancing our awareness and making us conscious of his presence at all times and in all places. At the beginning of the hymn an invocation implores his mercy after the fashion of nearly all liturgical prayers. He is then depicted as the supreme overseer who has knowledge of all that happens both in heaven and in the ocean.

102. Cf. RV I, 50, 6 (§ III 2); I, 115, 1; VI, 51, 1.
103. Cf. RV VII, 34, 10.

Varuṇa follows attentively the working of the cosmos which has been set in motion by him in accordance with well-defined laws, producing a procession of months. By his wisdom he rules also the "beyond" of time, taking into his purview both past and future. He is close to Men in friendship and consorts with them, watching over their activities. His theophany, that is, the manifestation of his presence, is sometimes so palpable that the worshiper can see him vividly in his mind's eye (v. 18). Men implore this wise Lord, whose gaze they fear, to be well disposed toward them, and they do not ask from him, as they do from other Gods, victory in battle or prosperity, wealth, the gift of children or long life, but to be freed from the fetters of sin and to obtain "true life," exempt from evil.

Varuṇa is also, after Indra, the most anthropomorphic of the Ṛg-Vedic Gods and the most humane of all. It has been said that he acted as a bridge that enabled Men to pass from a so-called polytheistic to a more monotheistic world view.[104]

Varuṇa

RV I, 25, 3-21

3. As a charioteer
   tethers his steed,
   so my songs shall bind
   your heart, O Varuṇa.

4. My desires fly away
   searching for happiness,
   just as birds
   fly to their nest.

5. When shall we move
   Varuṇa to mercy,
   the Lord of glorious might
   whose eye is far-reaching?

6. Common to both
   is the might. Their love
   forsakes not the worshiper
   faithful to Law.

7. He knows the path
   of birds in the heaven;
   as Lord of the sea
   he knows each ship.

104. For further introduction to Varuṇa, cf. § IV B b.

8. True to his Law,
he knows the twelve months
(and the extra month too)
with their offspring the days.

9. The path of the wind—
sweeping, high, powerful—
he knows, and the Gods
who reside in the heavens.

10. He sits among his people,
consistent to Law.
Most wise, he presides
and governs all things.

11. From there, surveying,
he beholds earth's marvels,
both that which has been
and that which shall be.

12. May the wise Āditya
prepare for us always
fair paths to tread,
prolonging our lives!

13. Varuṇa, wearing
a golden mantle,
is clothed in bright garments.
His watchmen sit round him.

14. No men of ill will
or evildoers
or those of wrong intention
wish to harm this God—

15. The One who gives consummate
glory to men,
imparting this glory
to these our own bodies.

16. Yearning for him,
wide-seeing Varuṇa,
my thoughts move onward
as cows to their pasture.

17. Again let us converse!
The nectar has been brought.
You eat, as a priest,
the food that you love.

18. I have seen the One
whom all may behold

and his car passing high!
My songs are accepted!

19. Hear, O Varuṇa!
Show us your favor.
Longing for help,
I have cried to you.

20. Supreme Lord,
ruling the spheres,
hear, O wise God,
as you pass on your way.

21. Free us from fetters
of every sort.
Loosen our bonds
that we may live!

1-2. Cf. § IV 8.
4. Desires: *vimanyavaḥ*, which can also mean "prayers to avert anger" (*manyu*).
5. Mercy: *mṛlīka*.
Of glorious might: *kṣatraśrī*, lit. who brings glory to power (*kṣatra*).
6. Both: Mitra and Varuṇa.
Faithful to Law: *dhṛtavrata* (the same term as in vv. 8, 10), of firm resolve, established in law, is applied both to Varuṇa and to his worshipers.
8. Cosmic as well as moral Order is protected by Mitra and Varuṇa.
12. The wise Āditya: i.e., Varuṇa.
17. The priest (*hotṛ*) is the first to take from the Soma.
21. Cf. RV I, 24, 15 (§ IV 8), where the same thought is expressed.

Measurer of the Three Worlds *Viṣṇu*

27 Viṣṇu, who is so dearly beloved and who has inspired, and indeed still inspires, in his devotees such fervent worship either of his own person or of his earthly manifestations Rāma and Kṛṣṇa, is not a major divinity in the Ṛg Veda.[105] It is the Sāma Veda and Śatapatha Brāhmaṇa, where Viṣṇu is constantly identified with sacrifice, which accord him an important place, while at a later date the prolific literature of the Purāṇas, of which the myths concerning Viṣṇu form the basis, made him immensely popular.[106] This prominence has been maintained and indeed enhanced right up to modern times.

Our hymn mentions the famous strides (*pada*) of Viṣṇu so frequently featured in later iconography and legend. Two of his strides

105. Though his name occurs about a hundred times, only five and a half hymns are dedicated to him.
106. About Viṣṇu, cf. RV VI, 69; SB I, 9, 3, 9-15; TB III, 1, 2, 6.

are visible to Men (those encompassing the earth and the air) and the third is in the heights of heaven (the sky). This third step is like a veil affixed to the sky, the proper abode of Viṣṇu. The sky is his favorite haunt, a place of happiness, where Men go after death and rejoice together with the Gods and where there is to be found a fountain of honey, that is, nectar (hence the allusion to his third step being filled with honey).

His *trivikrama,* or three strides, have also been interpreted in a temporal way, connected with the sun's orbit: the rising, the zenith, and the setting of the sun. In any event Viṣṇu, as the sacrificial rituals remind us, is the deity who encompasses both time and space, that is to say, past, present, and future as well as earth, air, and heaven. The power of Viṣṇu is a disguised one. Time and again he appears as a dwarf, thus hiding his true nature. It is in his dwarf's form that he deceives the *asuras* and makes them accept the challenge described in so many texts.[107]

The story is delightfully told in the Bhāgavata Purāṇa. Bali, king of the *asuras* and grandson of Prahlāda, was performing the *aśvamedha* or horse sacrifice. Present at the sacrifice was Vāmana, that is to say, Viṣṇu in the form of a dwarf, one of his *avatāras.* The king received Vāmana and, though reluctantly and against the advice of his *guru,* adhered to the rules of hospitality to the extent of allowing Vāmana to take for his own "as much land as he could cover with three steps." Thereupon Vāmana assumed his divine form and with just two strides covered all the worlds. This he achieved by virtue of the identification mentioned just now, "Viṣṇu is the sacrifice."[108] Another text affirms in this same connection that "much have they given us, who gave us, that which has the same size as the sacrifice."[109]

Without having recourse to erudite theories that have been put forward regarding the origin and nature of Viṣṇu, we may recall a certain pattern to be found in the later Viṣṇuite myth: Viṣṇu (over against Śiva, who stands for the moon) is related to the Sun and thus he is a deity of daylight and of gold, whereas Śiva is connected with darkness, the night, and silver. Viṣṇu generally is related to the seas (Śiva to the mountains), to life, and to the development of Man in history; thus Viṣṇu, unlike Śiva, has many incarnations.

107. Cf. e.g. AB VI, 15 (XXVIII, 7).
108. SB XIV, 1, 1, 6.
109. SB I, 2, 5, 5.

In the Ṛg Veda the lordship of Viṣṇu seems to follow in the wake of Indra. He is regarded as the close and true friend of Lord Indra,[110] one who shares in his exploits, constantly assists him,[111] particularly in his combat with Vṛtra,[112] and presses for him the Soma of which he is so fond.[113] So close is their association that in one hymn they seem to be identified and addressed as a dual divinity, Indra-Viṣṇu.[114] In fact, the "realms" of verse 6 of this hymn are understood to be the realms of Indra-Viṣṇu. At a later date, whereas Indra's lordship suffers diminishment and he is deprived of certain facets of his supremacy, Viṣṇu develops far more clearly defined features and becomes for generations of worshipers the supreme Lord.

Viṣṇu

RV I, 154

1. I will proclaim the mighty deeds of Viṣṇu
who measured out the earthly regions and propped
the heavens above, accomplishing in his course
three mighty strides.

2. For this his prowess Viṣṇu is acclaimed.
He inhabits the mountains, like a savage beast
wandering at will; in his three mighty paces
are set all worlds.

3. Now may my prayer ascend to the far-striding
Viṣṇu, the Bull, who dwells upon the mountains,
to him who unaided measured with threefold step
these far-flung spheres.

4. The marks of his three strides are filled with honey
imperishable; each is cause of joy.
Alone he supports the three spheres—Earth and Sky
and all things living.

5. May I attain to Viṣṇu's glorious mansion
where the faithful rejoice, where, close beside the Strider,
within his highest footstep springs the well
of purest honey!

110. Cf. RV I, 22, 19.
111. Cf. RV I, 156, 4; VII, 99, 4-5.
112. Cf. RV IV, 18, 11; VI, 20, 2.
113. Cf. RV II, 22, 1.
114. Cf. RV VI, 69.

6. O for your realms where dwell the tireless oxen
   abundantly furnished with horns, whence shine
   from the highest step of the widely striding Hero,
     his multiple splendors!

3. Unaided: *eka,* lit. the One, alone. The same important symbolism of the one and the three (steps and worlds) is found in v. 4.
4. Honey: *madhu,* may refer to Soma. The third step is transcendent and thus is filled with the nectar of immortality (see also v. 5).
5. The Strider: *urukramasya,* "of the far-striding one," one of the oldest epithets of Viṣṇu.
Highest footstep: *pada parama,* later understood as the transcendent abode of Viṣṇu.
6. Tireless oxen: refers to Indra and Viṣṇu.
Multiple splendors: the stars in the sky (the "highest step").

The Supreme Lordship *Sarveśvara*

28 There are three traditional ways, followed by Men and carefully elaborated in the Indian tradition, by which one can reach human fulfillment, or, in religious terms, salvation: the way of works and action, *karma-mārga;* the way of devotion and love, *bhakti-mārga;* and the way of knowledge and contemplation, *jñāna-mārga.* Reflection upon the end and goal of each of the three ways will inevitably yield three different pictures. At the end of the path of action there is a heaven, a bliss, a new and perfect world, for that is what one was striving for in following one's own *dharma* or duty. At the end of the path of devotion there cannot but be a loving person, a personal deity, for love is essentially personal. At the end of the path of knowledge there will be total reality, absolute truth. Every human tradition has given different names to these three goals. Yet in one way or another the three goals, or rather that which stands at the end of the pilgrimage, must be ultimately equivalent: heaven is the vision and enjoyment of God, the love of God is communion with him, and God is only another name for absolute truth and supreme reality. God is here used as a universal symbol. But the unity or oneness of the three goals is only a postulate of our thinking and the fact that they somehow seem to coalesce should not be interpreted in the light of any of the three systems. It is here that the discourse on the Lord becomes relevant and the message of the Upaniṣads important. Let the *karmakāṇḍins,* the men of action—even if the action is the performance of sacred rites and

the offering of sacrifice—assume that the final goal is the building of a perfect world; let the *bhaktas*, the devotees of any kind, aver that there is nothing higher than a personal deity, and let the *jñānins*, the sages of the various schools, claim that God must be transcended in favor of an ineffable Brahman or absolute void. Let them all follow their own paths. At the end they will all find the goal, the aim of their efforts, or of their love, or of their thoughts, the Lord who is not a concept or a reality in the sense in which all other things are such; the Lord is *at the end of* every action, wish, desire, longing, tendency, thought, and will and *is* the end of them all. He is not necessarily a State or a Person or a Being. He cannot be circumscribed, and there is no discussion on this point, because the discussion has meaning only inside a concrete system. But the Upaniṣads, which are at the source of so many systems and schools, cannot be interpreted exclusively in favor of any one of them; the Upaniṣads are the Vedānta, the end of the Vedas, in the double sense of the word: they stand at the end of the Vedas as their culmination but they also represent the end, the surpassing, of them.

If we view the Upaniṣads in this light we may have the clue as to why they seemingly have so many almost contradictory statements. For the Upaniṣads the Lord is not only Brahman, or exclusively a person, or simply a creator. Their standpoint is different. They would be syncretistic if they were attempting an overall synthesis, but they have never purported to offer a complete and coherent philosophical system. It is true that the Upaniṣads, emerging out of the first Vedas and presupposing them, stress the complementary *jñānic* perspective, but this must always be seen against the background of the four Vedas, which emphasize the other two paths. It is not our present task to develop these points further or to give an account of the idea of the Lord in the Upaniṣads. The following points serve as an introduction to our short selection of texts.

By the time of the Śvetāśvatara Upaniṣad the Lord has acquired a more "personal" aspect, or rather a more anthropomorphic character. He is called Rudra, which is not the divine personification of the Ṛg Veda under the same name, but rather Brahman manifesting himself in the One who creates and protects his creatures and who absorbs them at the end of time. He embraces the whole universe, and the Man who recognizes him as sole God is liberated and saved. Salvation is not achieved by human effort alone, nor is it a spontaneous act of divine grace, as later theologies declare, but it is rather a unique act in which "God" and "Man"—for we cannot dispense with these two at this stage—coincide. To recognize the Lord is to be saved, certainly; but, in order to recognize him, not only do I have to be united with him but also he has to disclose himself to me, so that it has little meaning to discuss at this point whence the initiative comes.

This Upaniṣad sees the Lord in everything while carefully differentiating him from nature. Although the universe is ultimately Brahman, Brahman cannot be said without qualifications to be the universe.[115] The Mahānārāyaṇa Upaniṣad, as its name suggests, extols Nārāyaṇa, that is, Viṣṇu, as the universal Lord, distinguishing him from Prajāpati who is mentioned in the cosmogonic context. Nārāyaṇa is the one who penetrates everything, including the human heart; he is the object of our worship. He is invoked in terms recalling the Vedic *puruṣa* and possesses recognizable features of a personal God. He is also the supreme Word, beyond the sound manifested in the Veda (vv. 233–234, 236). Although the weight of tradition is heavy, we should not forget that *Nārāyaṇa* means the Son of Man, of Nara, the original Man.[116] He is the Lord of all things, the knower of all things. He controls the thoughts and the most intimate feelings. He is the matrix of all, for he is both the Origin and the End of all beings. So says the Māṇḍūkya Upaniṣad.

The Upaniṣads constantly remind us that the universe, Men, and the Lord are both united and separate; they are interrelated, but the link, being unique, cannot adequately be expressed by a simile. For the same reason knowledge of Brahman is radically different from any other knowledge. It is truly the only saving realization. The Man eager to learn, the student, the seeker, the one who is humble enough to sit at the feet of the Master, is constantly urged in the Upaniṣads to turn his eyes inward and to make discoveries for himself, to experience a knowledge that is not communicated in the Upaniṣads and is indeed not communicable. The Upaniṣads proffer an invitation to a higher life of contemplation, to the enormous and risky adventure of finding the Lord, who can neither be spoken of nor identified with any objective or subjective reality (which would entail converting him automatically into a deus ex machina or a mere idol).

115. Cf. § VI 3.
116. *Nara*, man. Cf. Greek *anêr* and the Sanskrit *nṛ* with the same meaning of man as hero.

According to the message of the Upaniṣads, both the subjective, or purely immanent, interpretation of the divine and the objective, or merely transcendent, interpretation are inadequate. A mere God within is the product of our heart, our weakness, and our desire for consolation and security; a God who is simply outside is the product of our mind which looks for a support and an end to its speculations. The latter amounts to a logical principle, whereas the former amounts to a psychological one. The Upaniṣads attempt to resolve the dilemma by propounding the way of self-realization, the personal discovery of the hidden treasure. The Lord is within and without, personal and impersonal, moving and unmoving,[117] Being and Nonbeing.[118] He is the Lord precisely because he is not limited by any one pair of opposites.

Sarveśvara

SU III, 3-4

3. On all sides eye, on all sides face,
on all sides arms, on all sides feet,
he, God, the One, creates heaven and earth,
forging them together with arms and wings.

4. He who is source and origin of the Gods,
the Lord of all, Rudra, the mighty sage,
who produced in ancient days the Golden Germ—
may he endow us with purity of mind!

SU V, 13

ii) Without beginning and end is he; in the midst
of chaos he is and brings forth all things. Creator
is he, and sole pervader, of manifold forms.
When a man knows God he is freed from all fetters.

SU VI, 7-9; 16-19

iii) 7. Of lords the Lord Supreme, of kings the King,
of Gods the God, him let us worship—the transcendent,
Lord of all worlds and wholly worthy of worship.

8. In him exists neither action nor organ of action;
no one is found his equal or superior to him.
His supreme power is revealed in manifold forms;
inherent to his nature is the working of his strength and wisdom.

117. Cf. IsU 5 (§ VII 11); KathU II, 21 (§ VI 5).
118. Cf. TU II, 6 (§ I 7).

9. None in this world is his master, none his commander.
He has no distinctive sign; he is the Cause.
Himself unruled, ungenerated, he rules the sense organs.

16. He is the Creator of all, the knower of all things,
the source of the Self, the Knower, the Author of time,
possessor and master of all the qualities, omniscient,
the Lord of both Nature and Spirit, the cause of liberation
from this world's cycle and the bondage of earthly existence.

17. Identical with it, immortal, by nature the Lord,
omnipresent and wise, the guardian and eternal ruler
of the world is he. No other Ground can be found.

18. In him who in days of old created Brahmā
and imparted to him the Veda, in this God, who is illumined
by his own intelligence, I take refuge, longing for liberation,

19. In him who is undivided, inactive, peaceful,
irreproachable, free from blemish, the supreme bridge
to immortality, who resembles a fire whose fuel
is wholly consumed.

MahanarU 233-245

iv) 233. The sound that is uttered in the beginning of the Veda,
the sound that is also established at its end,

234. that which is beyond its absorption in Nature—
that is the supreme Lord.

235. [We adore] the God with a thousand heads,
with an all-seeing eye, who grants peace to all,

236. Nārāyaṇa, universal God,
supreme Word, imperishable,

237. on every side supreme, eternal,
Nārāyaṇa, universal Lord.

238. All this universe exists
vivified by the Person.

239. [We adore] the Master of all, the Lord
of the soul, eternal, benevolent, immobile,

240. Nārāyaṇa, the mighty one to be known,
the Self of all, the supreme goal.

241-242. Nārāyaṇa, Light supreme, the Self,
Nārāyaṇa the Supreme, Nārāyaṇa, supreme
essence of Brahman, Nārāyaṇa, the Supreme!

243. Nārāyaṇa is both the supreme meditator
and meditation itself, Nārāyaṇa, the Supreme.

244. Whatever moves in this universe,
whatever is either seen or heard,

245. whatever is inside or outside—all
is pervaded by the Lord. He is therein established.

MandU 6

v) This is the Lord of all, the Knower of all,
the inner controller. This is the source of all,
the beginning and end of all beings.

■ i) 2. Cf. § V 18.
3. The creator is a smith: cf. RV X, 72, 2 (§ VII 2), X, 81, 3 (§ VII 7); AV XIII, 2, 26; YV XVII, 19.
4. Golden Germ: *hiraṇyagarbha*.
With purity of mind: *buddhyā śubhayā*, lit. with a pure mind, with clear insight.
7-21. Cf. § VI 7.
■ iii) 1-6. Cf. § II 9.
8. His supreme power: *parāsya śaktiḥ*, cf. the Śivaite conception of *śakti*.
The working of his strength and wisdom: *jñāna-bala-kriyā*.
9. Distinctive sign: *liṅga*.
10-13. Cf. § VI 2.
14. The same as KathU V, 15 (§ V 5), and MundU II, 2, 10 (§ III 6).
15. Last two lines the same as SU III, 8 (§ VI 7).
16. Source of the Self: *ātmayoni*, or his own origin.
Lord of both Nature and Spirit: *pradhāna-kṣetrajña-patiḥ*, which in classical Sāṁkhya is *prakṛti* and *puruṣa*.
17. Identical with it: *sa tanmayaḥ*, the same as that, consisting of that, becoming that, being all this.
By nature the Lord: *īśa-saṁsthaḥ*, existing as the Lord, subsistent as the Lord, or established in his own glory.
18. This verse implies a personalistic conception of revelation in contrast with the *apauruṣeya* principle.
19. Supreme bridge to immortality: cf. CU VIII, 4, 1 (§ V 27).
Who resembles a fire . . .: cf. MaitU VI, 34 (§ III 28).
20. Cf. § IV A Antiphon.
■ iv) 233. Sound: *svara*.
234. Absorption in Nature: *prakṛtilīna*.
236. Supreme Word: *paramaṁ padam*, supreme abode.
239. The Lord of the soul: *ātmeśvara*.
242. Supreme essence of Brahman: *brahmatattva*, or the true Being (nature) of Brahman.
■ v) Lord of all: *sarveśvara*. Cf. BU IV, 4, 22 (§ VI 6).
The Knower of all: *sarvajña*, the all-knowing. Cf. MundU I, 1, 9; II, 2, 7 (§§ II 11; VI 5).
The doctrine of the *antaryāmin*, the internal *ātman* or *puruṣa* as inner controller, is of capital importance in Upanisadic spirituality. Cf. BU III, 7 (§§ VI 5; I 14). The dual *prabhava-apyayau* represents the cosmic movement of the coming-forth-into-existence and the absorption-into-the-*avyakta*, the unevolved, unmanifest, the *prakṛti* of certain systems. Cf. its application to yoga in KathU VI, 11 (§ VI 11).
7. Cf. § VI 6.

The Savior *Jagannātha*

29 Perhaps we can summarize the whole message of the Gītā by saying that "this," "he," the "absolute," "Brahman," the

true *ātman,* the *tad,* and the *idam,* that which the Vedic sages sought to clarify and which mankind is constantly seeking, is the Lord, whose subtle and lofty lordship can adopt as many forms as there are types of Men, or even Men, here on earth.

The Bhagavad Gītā does not contradict either the Vedas, the Brāhmaṇas, or the Upaniṣads; it can be understood only against the background of all the previous Scriptures, but it does not elaborate on their past insights; rather, it simplifies all that it has to say, affirming that this mystery, about which any word is improper, is the Lord of all and thus the Savior of mankind as well as of the entire universe. It is not an artificial syncretism that the Bhagavad Gītā preaches. It is, rather, a genial simplification which takes into account the different trends both of Indian tradition and of the human spirit and blends them harmoniously in lofty words, words that are all the more striking by virtue of their simplicity. The Lord is the Master of the universe and, equally, the Master of the human heart and mind. His lordship is not only cosmic, political, ontological, or psychological. When it is said that he saves all that come to him in good faith, this is not a plea for mere subjectivism, but for a deep personalistic attitude, which we could perhaps call existential.

The Bhagavad Gītā truly brings a message of liberation. It reveals, first of all, that there is a Lord, but it adds immediately that this Lord has many names, presents many faces, and performs many functions. Furthermore, it says that nobody can live without a Lord, a master, an ideal, an ambition, a desire, and that it is He, the Lord, the Savior, disguised in accordance with all the variety of the human imagination, who gathers up and vouchsafes the longings of mankind. Nobody escapes his Lordship which acts gently and, many a time, invisibly. Human maturity consists in discovering the face of the Lord and in accepting this growing revelation, for which there are no fixed patterns. All ways lead to him (even the way of wrath),[119] provided they remain ways and do not become final stopping places. Otherwise there is stagnation.

The Bhagavad Gītā uses the same expression, *gati,* to express both the way toward the goal and the goal itself, often called the *paramā gati,* the supreme goal. As the word itself suggests, *gati* (from the root *gam-,* to go, to move) means a going, a movement, motion in general. In the Bhagavad Gītā it has the connotation of

119. It is quite consistent with this spirit that the *saṁrambha-yoga* justifies a way of hostility to God as one possible religious way. Cf. BhagPur III, 16, 30.

the pilgrimage that constitutes human life, a connotation that allows the text to say that he who is on the path has, in a certain sense, already reached the end of it, because the end is not another place outside or after the way itself, but is already contained in it.[120] Like other parts of the Vedic Revelation, this truth can be grasped only by personal experience.[121] The pilgrimage that is life may lead us to its goal, which in the Bhagavad Gītā is described as union with the Lord. The Lord comes down to earth and manifests himself to Man in order to proclaim his message of love and salvation. The Lord is not only the powerful ruler, the mighty God, the just judge, but also the Savior. This is what Kṛṣṇa is telling Arjuna, what the Lord is telling Man.

Jagannātha BG IX, 18; 22; 31-32; 34

18. I am the Way, the supporter; your Lord and your witness,
 home, refuge, and friend,
 origin and dissolution, foundation and treasure-house,
 imperishable seed.

22. On those who meditate on Me and worship
 with undivided heart,
 I confer attainment of what they have not,
 and preserve what they have.

31-32. No devotee of mine is ever lost.
 Taking refuge in Me,
 lowly born, women, artisans, even servants,
 reach the highest goal.

34. Let your mind and your heart, your offerings and worship,
 to Me be devoted.
 With your self thus controlled you shall strive toward Me
 and to Me you shall come.

15-16. Cf. § III 29.
18. Way: *gati*, goal; cf. BG IV, 17; VI, 37; VII, 18; VIII, 26; XII, 5. Cf. CU I, 9, 1, where the question is asked, "What is the *gati* of this world?"
Foundation: *sthāna*, substratum, maintenance.
19. Cf. § V 6.
21. Cf. § V 28.
23-27. Cf. § III 29.
31-32. Devotee: *bhakta*.
Artisans: *vaiśya*.
Servants: *śūdra*.
Highest goal: *paramā gati*, highest way. Cf. BG VI, 45; VIII, 13; XIII, 28; XVI, 22-23.

120. For another slant on this subject, cf. the following text of the MB (*Śāntiparva*): "Truth is the highest way": *satyaṁ hi paramā gatiḥ*. XII, 156, 4.
121. From the latin *ex-perientia*, from the root *per-* (Greek: *peirô*; Sanskrit: *piparti*), to lead, to go through. Cf. English: fare, ferry, etc.

E. EMERGING LIFE

Jīvana

God ever true,
we faint with despair.
Source of all treasure,
grant to us hope
of blessings to come.
Subdue the malevolent
spirits that haunt,
the kindly awaken.
Grant to us hope
of blessings to come.

RV I, 29, 1-2; 4[122]

This final section of Part I is both a conclusion and a beginning. It is a conclusion, for Dawn, Human Birth, and Faith are really at the end of a divine process: the genesis of the Gods. The prelude of the world, the preparation for the emergence of Man, the rising of human consciousness—none of these happen in a single day nor are they the results of spontaneous generation; the way for them has been carefully and painfully prepared. Cosmogony, anthropo-

122. A free translation and selection. "God" stands for Indra, the drinker of Soma; "Source of all treasure," for "O most wealthy One." The refrain literally says: "give us hope of a thousand beautiful horses and cows." "Subdue the malevolent spirits" stands for "may the spirits with the hostile glance [*mithūdṛśā*] sleep."

genesis, and the first intimations of spiritual life do not constitute an absolute beginning but the conclusion of an elaborate preparation, the result of the victory of light over darkness, of the *devas* over the *asuras,* of the spirit over matter. The night has been long, the fight intense, and the tension has almost reached a breaking point, but Life has emerged. Theogenesis has given birth to life.

This section is also a beginning, for Dawn, Human Birth, and Faith are nothing if not ignition sparks, starting points of the real cosmic and human process. Up to now all has happened "behind the curtain." There has been the sacrifice of Prajāpati, the fight of the Gods and the demons, the preparation for human consciousness, the accumulation of conditions favorable to the possibility of human life. Dawn is simply the herald of day, the forerunner of the sun, just as the child is the living hope of growth into a Man and faith the foretaste of things to come and to become.

This process, of course, does not need to be understood in a modern evolutionary way, nor must it be interpreted in a merely temporal manner. The mystery of life goes on under our very eyes day by day, for every day we experience the marvel of dawn and every day we may also experience the reality of faith which comes to us discreetly, invisibly, yet all the more luminously: a light that makes us aware of the ever deepening, the unfathomable, dimension of every spark of reality.

The Vedic Revelation is not a historical record or a document concerning something that took place a long while or even a short while ago. It conveys a transtemporal message, if we are permitted to use this word with reference to the present, in order to make us more aware of the mystery of existence and of life. Dawn, Human Birth, and Faith, from this perspective, belong together. There is no such thing as a purely astronomical dawn. Dawn postulates an eye, or at least a limited and concrete point of reference rooted in the earth. The birds can discover and enjoy the dawn, but a supersonic aircraft traveling around the earth may very well avoid sunrise altogether or may, on the other hand, have it constantly present. In either event it would cease to be dawn. A merely physiological procreation does not constitute a human birth, nor is a simple rationalization of one's situation in the world the emergence of mature human consciousness.

The following texts may succeed in conveying that unified vision in which differences are not overlooked or distinctions ignored, but in which reality is not dissected into small portions, or observations, experiences, and experiments isolated so as to prevent their being integrated into one simple and life-bringing insight. It is not necessarily pantheism to worship dawn, just as it is not always superstition to perform a ceremony of blessing over an infant; nor is it fideism to consider faith a constitutive dimension of the human being, though variable in accordance with a man's individual personality.

Life emerges in and around us, on the cosmic plane and on the human level. We do not need to read any text to become aware of this. The texts we have chosen are an invitation to see reality, not through them, but along with them.

a) Dawn

Uṣas

Uṣas is the Daughter of Heaven who was born in the Sky.[123] She is the Lady of Light, the mistress and wife of the Sun. He follows her as a young man follows a maiden. The Goddess of hope, the elder sister of Night,[124] is mentioned more than 300 times in the Ṛg Veda, in hymns that are among the most beautiful of all the Saṁhitās.

The poetry of these hymns is imbued with intense luminosity. The yearning for light, the deep longing for the sun, and, by contrast, the fear of shadows and of darkness are strongly marked characteristics of the soul-strivings of the Vedic people. It is in keeping with these qualities that in the Ṛg Veda some twenty hymns are addressed to Uṣas and many to the Sun; the name of *dyu*, the sky, is mentioned more than 500 times, but only one hymn is dedicated to Night.[125] The fascination with light bursting forth from the cosmos is heightened in the speculations of the Upaniṣads, where the Spirit is named Light.

It is not difficult to imagine why Uṣas has so prominent a place. The experience of Dawn is one of the simplest and most complete of all human experiences. It unites in itself a vision of nature, an

123. Cf. RV VII, 75, 1 (§ VII 18).
124. Cf. RV I, 124, 8; X, 127, 3 (§§ VII 8; VII 35).
125. Cf. RV X, 127 (§ VII 35).

aesthetic awareness, a fresh opening for Man toward a hopeful future, and a mystical insight into the horizon beyond the rising light from where all good things come. A vision of the Dawn is not an experience of the Sun. You do not see Dawn, but you share in her light; you are not illumined by the Dawn as you are by the Sun; you are enwrapped in her light, you participate in her all-encompassing beauty and sense that nature is more than nature and that God is less than supernatural. In the twilight before sunrise, the union between light and darkness, there are no fixed limits for the senses or the mind. At Dawn you cannot say where the earth begins and where the sky ends, where the light dispels darkness or where the darkness has still the upper hand; you cannot assert what comes from the God or what emerges from the earth. At Dawn you do not mix anything, but you do not separate either; all remains a message, an expectation, a promise. Dawn is the Goddess of hope.[126] Although there are no lines specifically addressed to Hope in the Ṛg Veda, most of the hymns addressed to Dawn could be said to be songs and prayers of hope, mirroring the high optimism and great joy of Vedic culture.

Rather than attempting to describe or to extol the excellences of Dawn, we may compose a hymn of praise by quoting the following:

Stotra

Dawn is "beloved" of Heaven:

RV I, 46, 1

i) Now Dawn with her earliest light shines forth,
beloved of the Sky.

She is closely associated with her lover the Sun:

RV I, 115, 2

ii) Just as a young man follows his beloved,
so does the Sun the Dawn, that shining Goddess.

She becomes his consort:

RV I, 123, 11

iii) Fair as a bride adorned by her mother,
you show your beauty for all to see.

126. Cf. § VII 3; 8; 13; 18; 23; 28, for other hymns addressed to Dawn.

Happy are you, O Dawn. Shine ever more widely,
surpassing every dawn that went before.

Resplendent with light, she drives away darkness:

RV V, 80, 5

iv) Fresh from her toilet, conscious of her beauty,
she emerges visible for all to see.
Dawn, Daughter of Heaven, lends us her luster,
dispersing all shadows of malignity.

RV VI, 64, 3

v) Like a swift warrior she repulses darkness.

RV VII, 75, 1

vi) She drives off wicked spirits and dread darkness.

She awakens living creatures:

RV I, 48, 5

vii) Uṣas comes carefully, fostering all creatures,
stirring to life all winged and creeping things.

RV I, 49, 3

viii) Bright Uṣas, when your rays appear,
all living creatures start to stir,
both four-footed and two.

RV IV, 51, 5

ix) Arousing from deep slumber all that lives,
stirring to motion man and beast and bird.

She is always faithful to the divine order of the universe:

RV I, 123, 9

x) This maiden infringes not the Eternal Law,
day after day coming to the place appointed.

Now Light Has Come

Jyotir āgāt

RV I, 113

30

1. Now there is light, the fairest of all lights.
   Now comes to shining birth a glow of brightness.

Night, sent away before the Sun is rising,
has yielded up to morning her domain.

2. Trailing white offspring the radiant [Dawn] advances
to claim the dwelling by dark [Night] relinquished.
Morning and Night, the immortal sisters, follow
hard on each other's heels with alternate colors.

3. They follow the same pathway, never ending.
Instructed by the Gods they ply their course.
Fair, yet contrasting, following one spirit,
Morning and Night neither collide nor linger.

4. Dawn, the glorious bringer of graces, shines forth
and flings wide open for us her shining doors.
Stirring the whole world she displays her riches,
raising to consciousness all living creatures.

5. She wakes to action all who repose in slumber.
Some rise to labor for wealth, others to worship.
Those who saw little before now see more clearly.
Dawn raises to consciousness all living creatures.

6. One she leads on to power, another to glory;
another she leads on to pursuit of gain;
yet others she directs to varied callings,
raising to consciousness all living creatures.

7. The Daughter of Heaven now appears before us,
a fair young woman clothed in shining garments.
Auspicious Dawn, mistress of earthly treasure,
shine upon us today in queenly splendor.

8. She, first of endless morns to come hereafter,
follows the path of morns that went before.
Dawn at her shining summons forth the living;
the dead she never wakens from their slumbers.

9. O Dawn, you shine forth with the eye of the Sun.
You wake the worshiper and inspire his heart
to kindle the fire and offer sacrifice.
Thus to the Gods you render noble service.

10. How long a time until they meet together,
dawns that have shown and dawns to shine hereafter?
Eagerly she yearns to join her predecessors
and goes forth with the others, gladly shining.

11. Vanished are those who in the days before us
gazed at the rising of the morning Sun.
It is we the living who now behold the Dawn,
and after us her shining others will see.

12. Disperser of our foes, bringer of joys,
born child of Order, to Order ever faithful,
convey our offerings to the Gods, O Dawn,
and shine on us today for wealth and fortune.

13. Never has Goddess Dawn failed to appear.
Again today the generous One has risen.
Ever hereafter will she rise each morning.
She proceeds by her own power, unaging, deathless.

14. On the sky's borders she appears in splendor.
The Goddess has thrown off the robe of darkness.
Her well-yoked chariot of tawny horses
heralds the approach of Dawn and rouses all men.

15. With her she brings all life-sustaining blessings.
Brightly she shines and sheds abroad her radiance.
She is the last of countless vanished mornings.
She is the first of more bright morns to come.

16. Arise! The breath of life again has reached us.
Darkness has fled and light is fast approaching.
She leaves a pathway for the Sun to travel.
We have arrived where life will again continue.

17. With the reins of speech the priest, uttering praises,
drives onward, steering their course, the shining Dawns.
Shine then today, O generous Dawn, for your singer!
Convey to us the gift of life and children!

18. To the mortal who honors them these ascending Dawns
impart both wealth of cattle and hero sons.
May the same accrue to the sacrificer, giver of horses,
when swift as the wind the gifts have been summoned by song!

19. Mother of Gods and brightness of the Godhead,
token of sacrifice, shine forth on high.
Rise up and look upon our prayers with favor.
Bless us among people, Dawn ever desired!

20. Whatever wondrous gift the Dawns convey
as blessing to the offerer who shows himself zealous in worship,
that may Mitra and Varuṇa grant to us,
and Aditi, the Sacred River, Earth, and Heaven!

1. The Sun: Savitṛ.
2. By "white offspring" some understand the white clouds attending the Dawn; lit. a white calf. Uṣas's calf is said to be Agni in RV I, 95, 1, and I, 96, 5, while some commentators affirm it to be the Sun.
3. Following one spirit: *samanasā*, of one and the same mind.
7. Young woman: *yuvati*, maiden.
9. The eye of the Sun: lit. the eye of Sūrya, referring to the sun in heaven. Uṣas causes the fire, Agni, to be kindled, for this takes place at dawn.

11. Allusion to the mystery of life and death, which is only tragic when viewed from an individualistic perspective.

12. Foes: *dveṣāh*, also obstacles, adversities.

Order: *ṛta*. Ll. 2-4 lit.: Born [child] of *ṛta* [truth, Order, divine law], *ṛtejā*, you are the keeper of the divine *ṛta* [*ṛtapā*], [bestow] your favor upon us, let our songs of joy [offerings of praise], resound, [be] propitious, you who transmit the food divine [*deva-vīti*], shine on us today, O Dawn, O you most bright.

14. Cf. RV I, 48, 7, where Uṣas is said to arrive on a hundred chariots drawn by tawny horses (the reddish rays of the morning sun).

The robe of darkness: the night.

15. Lit.: Appearing, she spreads out her bright-colored [glittering, shining] banner.

16. Breath of life: *jīvo asur*.

19. Brightness of the Godhead: *aditer anīkam*, face of Aditi (the Goddess of the infinite, also associated with light). Cf. RV IV 25, 3; VII, 82, 10; AV XII, 1, 61 (§ I 19 and notes).

Dawn ever desired: *viśvavāre* (vocative), lit. O you desired by all.

Daughter of Heaven — *Divo duhitā*

31

RV VII, 81

1. See now, the shining Daughter of Heaven approaches,
dispelling gloom of night that we may see.
The friendly Lady ushers in the light.

2. The ascending Sun, refulgent star of heaven,
co-worker with the Dawn, pours down his beams.
O Dawn, at your arising and the Sun's,
grant us, we pray, our portion in your light.

3. O Dawn, glorious Daughter of high Heaven,
promptly we rise and come to welcome you.
Most generous one, granter of all desires,
to worshipers you give both joy and treasure.

4. O glorious Dawn, you bring the earth to view
and lighten up the lofty vault of heaven.
We yearn to be yours, partaking in your rewards.
Accept our love as that of mother's children.

5. Bring to us, Dawn, your grace most bountiful,
that shall be celebrated far and wide.
Give us what you possess as nourishment for men,
that we may rejoice therein, O Daughter of Heaven.

6. Give to our princes wealth and everlasting fame.
To us grant in the contests herds of kine.
O shining Dawn, you who inspire the generous
and are full of grace, drive from us all our foes.

1. Ushers in: lit. makes light.
2. Pours down his beams: lit. lets out his cows.

Grant us . . . our portion: *saṁ bhaktena gamemahi,* may we obtain (our) share, i.e., may we share in (partake of, enjoy) your light.
5. Grace: *rādhas,* gift, favor.
6. Everlasting: *amṛta,* immortal, deathless.
Contests: refers to the poetical contests well known in the RV.
Full of grace: *sūnṛtāvati* (vocative), graceful, bringer of gladness.

Lady of Light

Hiraṇyavarṇā

RV VII, 77

32

1. Dawn comes shining
like a Lady of Light,
stirring to life all creatures.
Now it is time
to kindle the Fire.
The light of Dawn scatters the shadows.

2. Her face turned toward
this far-flung world,
she rises, enwrapped in bright garments.
Shining with gold,
with rays of light bedecked,
she sends forth the world on its course.

3. Our Lady of Light
brings the Eye of the Gods,
as she rides her white, beautiful steed.
Dawn shines apparent,
bestowing on all men
her store of marvelous treasure.

4. Come with your bounty;
drive away foes.
Grant us secure and lush pastures.
Disperse those who hate us.
O bountiful One,
give to your singer reward.

5. Beam forth your light
to guide and sustain us,
prolonging, O Goddess, our days.
Give to us food,
grant to us joy,
chariots and cattle and horses.

6. Lady nobly born,
   Daughter of Heaven,
worshiped by all the illustrious,
   grant us your blessings,
   riches and wealth.
Now and forever protect us!

1. Fire: Agni.
The light of Dawn . . . : lit. she made the light, chasing away darkness.
2. She sends forth the world on its course: lit. mother of kine (i.e., the rays of light), guide of the days, she shines. Cf. RV IV, 52, 2-3.
3. Our Lady of Light: lit. the shining one, auspicious one, the blessed one.
The Eye of the Gods: the Sun.
She rides . . . : lit. leading her white, beautiful steed.
5. Joy: *rādhas*, gift, favor, or reward.
6. Nobly born: *sujāta*.
Illustrious: Vasiṣṭha, name of the *ṛṣi* who composed the VII *maṇḍala* of the RV, a priestly family. Lit. the most bright.

b) Human Birth

Janman

Man has a peculiar and very special place in the universe. Every origin is sacred and unfathomable, but human birth is a mystery which no amount of rationalization can explain or explain away. To become the father or the mother of a newborn baby dispels any doubt one may have about it. We can speculate and generalize, but when the parents see and feel that the new creature is part and yet more than just a part of them, they cannot be satisfied with any merely scientific or philosophical explanation. No wonder that the danger of exploitation by priestcraft has not always been avoided. The dawn of the human being involves the rising of Life and a new sort of life in the world. The horizon is filled not only with red clouds and auspicious signs, but with the light of a new spark of that universal consciousness in which we are all enwrapped.

The continuation of the universe, of human life, and, more intimately, of the sacred order of things, depends upon the birth of a child and mainly, as far as the continuity of traditional wisdom and sacrifice is concerned, upon the birth of a son. No wonder that the desire for a son is a most holy wish and that the bringing forth of children is a sacred duty. Therefore the mystery of life, from the moment of conception onward through the stages after the birth of a child, is attended by prayers and ritual actions.[127]

127. The first *saṁskāra* after marriage is the *garbhādhāna*, the rite of "placing the embryo."

The dialogue in the Ṛg Veda carried on by the wife of the sacrificer, the sacrificer, and the priest (who assumes the role of Prajāpati or the genius of procreation) shows the delicacy of the relationship between husband and wife and the sacredness of the act of procreation. It is after performing *tapas,* after concentrating energy in an act of restraint, and after deep meditation that the two, husband and wife, meet. The blessing is given by the priest who affirms that all life is produced by Prajāpati, Father of all creatures, who places the seed and brings about new life.

The Atharva Veda contains many prayers for successful conception and childbirth[128] and for the protection of both mother and child against every kind of danger. Various divinities closely connected with fertility are invoked, such as Sarasvatī, Sinīvalī (Goddess of the new moon and of female fertility), the Aśvins (the divine twins),[129] and certain creative divine powers such as Savitṛ, Dhātṛ, Tvaṣṭṛ, and Prajāpati.[130] It is Agni, the life germ of all creatures[131] and the power that fecundates the waters,[132] who bestows children:

> May a son of our flesh be born to us!
> May this your grace come upon us, O Agni![133]

Human birth is both a part and also the culmination of the cosmic birth of all living things. The mother who bears the child is just like mother Earth who patiently carries all beings.

The Gṛhya Sūtras contain a collection of rites and prayers for the celebration of a birth, most of them of *śrautic* origin (i.e., related to the revealed tradition) and for this reason justifiably included in this anthology. Blessings are invoked upon the newborn male child.[134] Some ancient texts stipulate that the ceremony be performed before the cutting of the umbilical cord, though very soon this custom was no longer observed.[135]

The child is fed a little butter and honey, symbols of wisdom, and the protection of Savitṛ, the Goddess Sarasvatī, and the divine Aśvins is entreated. There follows a prayer in the form of a litany

128. Cf. AV III, 23; V, 25; VII, 46.
129. Cf. RV X, 184, 2-3.
130. Cf. RV X, 184, 1.
131. Cf. RV I, 70, 3.
132. Cf. RV X, 21, 8.
133. RV III, 1, 23.
134. Cf. also AV VI, 76 for the blessing of a newborn kṣatriya baby, and VI, 110 for the blessing of a newborn child.
135. It would be out of place here to discuss why this rite (*jātakarman*) was and is administered only to boys.

for the longevity of the child. It is by faithfulness to the distinctive characteristics of the personages invoked that long life is ensured. To conclude the litany, sacrifice and water are mentioned. Next comes a short paean to the Earth, to the particular place on earth where the child has been born. May this plot of earth accord him a long life! A prayer for strength for the newborn child concludes the ceremony. The protection and blessings of Indra, the most powerful of all the Gods, are implored. A short benediction, addressed to the child's mother, asks that she be blessed for having given birth to a son, and in the last petition Water is also implored to grant the mother watchful protection.

When the baby is ten or eleven days old the ceremony called *nāmadheya* or name-giving takes place.[136] The choice of name, based on the caste and the sex of the child, is determined by well-defined rules and is accompanied by offerings. In the sixth month *annaprāśana,* another important ceremony of early infancy, takes place. As an accompaniment to the first morsels of solid food given to the child, some verses of the Ṛg Veda are recited.[137] The symbolism of food is important here.[138] Later on, in about the third year, the ceremony of the first haircut or *cūḍākaraṇa* takes place. Thus the child's first years are hallowed by religious ceremonies marking each stage of its growth.

Desire for a Son — *Putrakāma*

33

RV X, 183

i) [The wife]

1. I saw you as within your mind grew insight,
born from Ardor, strengthened through Ardor.
Bestowing here offspring, bestowing treasure,
produce now, desirous of a son, a progeny!

[The husband]

2. I saw you meditating within your heart,
your body being afflicted at the season.
Rise now to meet me! Be a young woman!
Produce now, desirous of a son, a progeny!

136. Cf. Manu II, 30-32.
137. Cf. also AV VI, 140, for the blessing of a child on the cutting of its first two teeth.
138. Cf. for the U alone: AU I, 3, 1-10; CU I, 11, 9; VII, 9; TU II, 2; III, 2; MaitU VI, 11, all in § II 11, and MaitU VI, 37.

[Prajāpati]

3. It is I who have placed in every plant a seed;
it is I who have placed a seed in all creatures;
it is I who bring forth children on the earth.
I will ever henceforth produce sons in women!

AV VI, 17

ii)

1. Just as the mighty earth bore the seed of all life,
so may you carry the child and bring forth a son!

2. Just as the mighty earth bore the trees of the forest,
so may you carry the child and bring forth a son!

3. Just as the mighty earth bore the mountains and peaks,
so may you carry the child and bring forth a son!

4. Just as the mighty earth bore the whole world's weight,
so may you carry the child and bring forth a son!

■ i) 1. Ardor: *tapas*.
Treasure: *rayi;* the first of all treasures is a son.
Desirous of a son: *putrakāma*.
Meditating within your heart: *manasā dīdhyānām*.
3. Seed: *garbha*, germ, embryo, etc.

The First Birth

Prathamaṁ janma

34

BU VI, 4, 22-24

i) Then he comes to her and says:

22. With a golden fire stick the Aśvins
produce from fire a flame.
Thus we pray for you a seed
that shall come forth in the tenth month.

As the earth bears fire in her womb
and the heaven is pregnant with lightning
and the quarters have wind as their seed,
so I place in you, my wife, this child.

23. As the wind agitates a pond
of lotus from every side,
so may the child stir in you
and come forth together with the afterbirth!

This thunderbolt of Indra is fashioned
with a covering for protection.
Let him come forth, O Indra,
the afterbirth along with the child!

24. In this child I shall prosper a thousandfold,
increasing within my own house.
His fortune, along with his offspring
and cattle, shall never diminish.
Svāhā!

The life-powers that are in me,
I offer them to you in spirit.
Svāhā!

Whatever in my sacred duties
I have done too much or too little—
may Agni, the wise, perfect offerer,
correct and perfect on our behalf!
Svāhā!

AU II, 1-6

ii) 1. In a man this [*ātman*] first becomes a germ, and this semen is his essence taken from all his limbs; in himself, indeed, he carries the Self. When he fecundates a woman, then he causes [a child] to be born. This is his first birth.

2. Then he enters into the very self of a woman, just as a limb of her own. Therefore it does not injure her. She nourishes this self as it has entered into her.

3. As she is the nourisher, she should be nourished. The woman carries it [this self] as an embryo. He [the father] takes care of the boy before the birth and after the birth, and as he takes care of the boy before and after the birth, he takes care of his own self, for the extension of these worlds: for these worlds are thus extended. This is his [a man's] second birth.

4. He [the son] becomes the self of his father for the performance of sacred actions. Then his other self, having accomplished his work and having grown old, departs and, after departing [from this world], is reborn. This is his third birth. Thus it has been said by the seer.

5. "While I was still in the womb I already knew all the generations of the Gods. Though a hundred fortresses of iron guarded me, I came forth with the swiftness of an eagle." Thus spoke Vāmadeva even while he was as yet lying in the womb.

6. He who knows this and rises up [from the body] through the head at the time of separation from the body, having satisfied all his desires in the heavenly world, he becomes immortal, yes, he becomes immortal.

■ i) The entire section is consecrated to the mystery of procreation.

22. The Aśvins are connected with fertility (cf. RV X, 184, 3; AV V, 25, 3). The production of the embryo is compared to the production of fire from the fire sticks.

Seed: *garbha,* embryo.

Heaven: one of the few passages where *dyu* is a Goddess.
Lightning: *indra*.
My wife: lit. so-and-so, i.e., the name of the woman has to be uttered.
23. Cf. RV V, 78, 7-8; PGS I, 14, prayer for successful childbirth.
Thunderbolt of Indra: *indrasya . . . vajraḥ;* the child is compared to Indra's thunderbolt (v. 22 c).
24. I offer them to you in spirit (*manasā*): because the real transmission of the father's life-power into the son takes place at the time of his death (cf. KausU II 15; § V 12).
Sacred duties: *karman*. The father prays that any mistake he has made in performing the sacrifice may not affect his family, i.e., the newborn child.
■ ii) Cf. AV VI, 11, 2.
1. Semen is his essence: cf. BU VI, 4, 1 *puruṣasya retaḥ* (*rasaḥ*).
His first birth: a human being's first birth. For the three human births cf. SB XI, 2, 1, 1 (§ III 23).
3. Nourisher: *bhāvayatrī*.
His own self: *ātman*, body. The son is the continuation of the self of the father; the father is born *as* the son.
For the extension: the verb is *saṁ-tan-*, to spread, to extend, to continue.
Second birth: *dvitīya janman*, not referring here to the conception of the second birth by initiation (cf. *dvija*).
4. Other self: the father.
5. Cf. RV IV, 27, 1. The seer Vāmadeva applies to himself the saying of the eagle in the RV, which refers to an ancient legend where the eagle was detained by demons in a hundred fortresses. The story is here used as an image for liberation.

Ceremony After Birth — *Jātakarman*

35

Prayer for Wisdom

AGS I, 15, 1-2

i) 1. At the birth of a son, the child's father, before anyone else touches him, should feed him (with a golden spoon) a little butter and honey in which a trace of gold (dust) has been mixed and say:

"I feed you with the wisdom of honey,
I feed you with ghee, the gift of God, the beautiful.
May you have long life, protected by the Gods,
may you live in this world a hundred circling years!"

2. Putting his lips close to the child's ears he murmurs:

"May God grant you intelligence,
may his Power grant you intelligence,
may his two divine Messengers, lotus-wreathed,
grant to you intelligence."

Prayer for Vital Power

PGS I, 16, 6

ii) Near the [child's] navel or right ear he says softly:

"The Lord is full of life: through firewood he is full of life.
By this vital power I make you full of life.
The divine Drink is full of life: through herbs
he is full of life.

"By this vital power I make you full of life.
The Brāhman-priest is full of life: through the Brāhmanas
he is full of life.

"By this vital power I make you full of life.
The Gods are full of life: through their nourishment
they are full of life.

"By this vital power I make you full of life.
The sages are full of life: through their observances
they are full of life.

"By this vital power I make you full of life.
The ancestors are full of life: through their offerings
they are full of life.

"By this vital power I make you full of life.
Sacrifice is full of life: through sacrificial fees
it is full of life.

"By this vital power I make you full of life.
The ocean is full of life: through the rivers it is full of life.
By this vital power I make you full of life."

Prayer to the Earth

PGS I, 16, 17

iii) On the spot in which the child was born he prays:

I know your heart, O Earth, that rests in heaven,
in the moon. I know your heart; may it know me!
May we see a hundred circling years,
may we live a hundred circling years,
may we hear [the sounds of] a hundred years!

Prayer for Strength

AGS I, 15, 3

iv) He touches the [child's] shoulders on both sides, saying:

Be a stone, be an ax, be unsurpassed gold.
You in truth are the Veda, called my son.
Live, therefore, a hundred years.
Powerful God, give us the best of treasures.
Grant us your gifts, O bountiful, O swift one.

Infusion of Holy Learning

SGS I, 24, 8

v) *Bhūḥ!*

I instill the Ṛg Veda into you—so and so.

"Bhuvah!

"I instill the Yajur Veda into you—so and so.

"Svaḥ!

"I instill the Sāma Veda into you—so and so.

"Svāhā! Bhūr, bhuvaḥ, svaḥ!

"I instill the Speculations into you,
the History and the Legends into you—*Om;*
all the Vedas I instill into you—so and so.

"Svāhā!

Prayer for the Mother

PGS I, 16, 19; 22

vi) 19. He then prays over the mother:

"You are Iḍā, the daughter of Mitra and Varuṇa.
You, a courageous woman, have borne a vigorous son.
May you be blessed with vigorous children,
you who have blessed us with a vigorous son."

22. He places a jar of water near her head, saying:

"You, O waters, are co-watchers with the Gods.
As co-watchers with the Gods, watch over this mother,
who is now confined, and also her child!"

▪ i) 1. Wisdom: *veda.*
God: Savitṛ.
Years: lit. autumns.
2. He murmurs the *medhā-janana* or "production of intelligence." Ghee, honey, and gold were considered to stimulate the intelligence.
God: Savitṛ.
Power (of God): Sarasvatī.
Two divine Messengers: the Aśvins.

▪ ii) This is the rite for ensuring long life and vital power to the child, called *āyuṣya.* The entire prayer is constructed on the idea of *āyus,* or vital power, health.
Lord: Agni.
Full of life, vitality: *āyuṣmat,* possessed of vital power, health, life. Life-possessing.
Divine Drink: Soma.
The meticulous performance of the *brāhmaṇa* rites ensures long life for Brahmins.
Nourishment (of the Gods): *amṛta.*
Sages: *ṛṣis.*
Offerings: the *svadhā,* the food offered as an oblation for the dead. Cf. RV X, 15, 3.

▪ iii) Prays: *mantrayate*
Years: lit. autumns.

▪ iv) Cf. PGS I, 16, 18, where it is said *ātmā vai putra nāmāsi* "you are the *ātman* called son."
Powerful God: Indra. This line quotes RV II, 21, 6 (§ II A Antiphon). The next line quotes RV III, 36, 10.

▪ v) Speculations: *vākovākya.*
History and Legends: *itihāsapurāṇa.*

▪ vi) 19. Iḍā: cf. the myth of the flood, SB I, 8, 1, 1-10 (§ V 17).
Courageous, vigorous: *vīra,* brave, strong, powerful, generally as male virtues (cf. Latin, *vir*), from which also hero, chief.
20-21. Ceremony of washing the mother's two breasts and giving them to the child.

c) Faith

Śraddhā

Vedic faith is not primarily an intellectual assent, for if it were it would be subservient to the "thing" to which assent is made with the mind. Nor is it a kind of blind trust in certain superhuman beings. We have examples of hymns expressing not only doubt but what some today would call unbelief.[139] Vedic faith is, furthermore, not a result or a product of the will; thus there is no stress on the moral responsibility of the believer. It is rather a quality of the full human being; it is something given to or rather grafted into his being. Man is endowed with faith as he is endowed with other human qualities. For this reason, there are ultimately as many types of faith as there are types of Men, or even as there are human beings.[140]

Vedic faith is previous to thinking and anterior to willing and deciding. It is precisely faith that makes thinking possible, for faith offers the unthought ground out of which thinking can emerge. It is faith that makes moral and other decisions possible, opening to us the horizon against which our actions become meaningful. Any action performed without faith is only an instinctive or automatic movement, without any truly human content; it can hardly be called a truly human action.

You act with faith when you act from such a depth that hesitation is not possible, when you are sure that what you are doing is what you are doing, that is, when you perform an action that springs up from your inmost self and not from a whispered external influence. The Man of doubt perishes; he, in fact, destroys himself. It is not intellectual hesitation we are now talking about, or indecision of the will. It is the main and central thrust of the human being which is our theme here. The word of the Bhagavad Gītā quoted below is self-explanatory: it is the doubt penetrating the very heart of the *ātman* which is lethal. Faith is not made up of those beliefs about which you can entertain intellectual doubt; faith is made of those convictions that are rooted so deeply in your own being that you are not conscious of them; faith is the first emanation

139. Cf. for instance, RV II, 12, 5 (§ II 4); X, 82 7 (§ VII 12).
140. Cf. BG XVII, 3 (§ I 38).

of life, as we shall read in one text; faith is the hidden root of man out of which real human growth proceeds; faith is rooted in the heart and is composed of the heart's intention, the heart being the symbol for the core of Man. This faith is expressed in beliefs and actions which, when they come directly from that inner source, can be called authentic; otherwise they are make-believe, pseudo actions which shoot wide of their mark. Faith is authentic human existence.

A girdle is called "Daughter of Faith" in the Atharva Veda because she is born of *tapas* and seen as its deepest dimension.[141] "Faith wraps the Gods, faith wraps this whole world," says another text,[142] stressing the all-encompassing nature of faith. Without faith the entire universe degenerates into a merely mechanical model; all would be automatic, the result, at best, of a logical syllogism, but with no freedom and with no place for human ambivalence. *Śraddhā,* faith, and *ṛta,* cosmic order, go together.[143] Cosmic order is not to be equated with modern scientific "laws of nature": the faith of the agent is an integral part of the action performed according to *ṛta.* The three groups of texts given here stress different aspects of faith according to the main thrust of the period. The titles given are intended to express this emphasis. Some of the Upaniṣadic texts have to be read in their own context for a better understanding, but even isolated they are meaningful.

The concrete manifestation of faith, according to our first hymn which is representative of the first period, consists in a belief in the meaningfulness and efficacy of the sacrificial action. Indeed, such belief is essential for the man performing the sacrifice, for without it there would be only a mechanical and thus a fruitless action.[144] In the second period, that of the Upaniṣads, faith is represented as the condition for approaching the *guru,* for without such an approach no real knowledge can be transmitted or received. Faith acquires here the form of a concrete personal confidence for the sake of supreme realization. Yet this faith does not depend on our will alone, for, although the germ of faith is given with life itself, an awakening to faith is given as a second grace. The beginning of the story of Naciketas, given here, shows how the Kaṭha Upaniṣad en-

141. Cf. AV VI, 133, 4 (§ II B antiphon).
142. TB II, 8, 8, 8.
143. Cf. TB III, 12, 3, 2.
144. Cf. § III 25 for texts on faith in relation to sacrifice.

visages faith as a grace that takes possession of the young man and gives him the courage to resist his ritualistically minded father, a courage that leads him up to the kingdom of death, guides him throughout his discourse with Death, and leads him finally to attain the highest wisdom.[145] In the Gītā, just to mention our third group of texts, faith is experienced as a loving surrender to the Lord, and here faith is strongly tinged with *bhakti*.

Acting Faith

Śraddhāhaviḥ

RV X, 151

36

1. By Faith is Fire kindled.
   By Faith is offered Sacrifice.
   Sing we now Faith, the pinnacle of joy.

2. Bless Faith, the one who gives.
   Bless him who wills, but has not.
   Bless him who gives his worship unstinting.
   Bless this song I sing.

3. As the Gods evoked Faith
   from the mighty Asuras,
   so may my prayer for the generous worshiper be accepted!

4. The Gods, led by the Spirit,
   honor Faith in their worship.
   Faith is composed of the heart's intention.
   Light comes through Faith.

5. Through Faith men come to prayer,
   Faith in the morning,
   Faith at noon and at the setting of the Sun.
   O Faith, give us Faith!

1. Fire: Agni.
Sing we: lit. we celebrate, *vedayāmasi*.
3. Asuras: cf. RV X, 124, 3; 5.
4. Spirit: Vāyu, in his aspect of uplifter of oblation. This elevation of the heart is also worship and thus the *devas* come near to Faith, inspired by Vāyu.

Thinking Faith

Vijijñāsa

BU III, 9, 21

37

i) "And on what are the offerings to the priests based?
On faith, for when a man has faith, he gives

145. For the dialogue between Naciketas and Yama, cf. § V 5.

offerings to the priests.
Therefore it is on faith that the offerings to
the priests are based.
On what is faith based?
On the heart, for through the heart one knows faith.
In fact, on the heart alone is faith based."

CU I, 1, 10

ii) What one performs with knowledge, with faith, with meditation, that, indeed, becomes more effective.

CU VII, 19-20

iii) 19. "When a man has faith, then he thinks. Nobody thinks
until he has faith. Only by having faith a man thinks.
So you should really desire to understand faith."
"Sir, I do desire to understand faith."

20. "When a man perseveres, then he has faith.
No one has faith without having perseverance.
Only by having perseverance one has faith.
So you should really desire to understand what is
to have perseverance."
"Sir, I do desire to understand perseverance."

TU I, 11, 3

iv) Give with faith; give nothing without faith.

KathU I, I-2

v) Desiring the fruit of the sacrifice, Vājaśravasa gave away all that he possessed. He had a son named Naciketas. As the sacrificial gifts were being led up, faith entered into him, boy though he was.

MundU III, 2, 10

vi) This has been said in a sacred verse:

> Those who perform ritual acts, who know Scripture,
> who are firmly established in the Ultimate,
> who offer themselves with faith to the unique Seer—
> to them should perfect knowledge be declared.

PrasnU I, 2

vii) To them the sage responded: "Dwell with me a year more in fervor, purity, and faith. Ask then all the questions you like and, if we know, we will tell you everything."

PrasnU VI, 4

viii) **He [the Person] emitted life, and from life came faith, then space, wind, light, water, earth, the senses, and the mind. . . .**

Faith: *śraddhā* throughout.
■ i) 10-17. Cf. § VI 7.
21. Based: *pratiṣṭhitā.*
24-25. Cf. § I 14.
■ ii) 1-9. cf. § VI 12.
Knowledge: *vidyā.*
Meditation: *upaniṣad.*
■ iii) For the rest of CU VII and ref. cf. § VI 3 (v. and notes)
20. Perseveres: *nistiṣṭhati,* to endure, tolerate, to be steadfast. The verb *niḥ-ṣṭhā-*, meaning to grow forth. *Niṣṭhā* means the state of being grounded, of resting on such a firm basis that further growth is rendered possible: steadfastness. Thus, used in conjunction with faith it suggests a firm reliance on truth (thus firmly believed): deeply rooted growth. It suggests a steady growth because one is rooted in the ground of one's own being. Faith is not a matter of holding an opinion, but of *being*. The following verse affirms that only by acting can one prove one's own steadfastness. Cf. BG III, 3, where *niṣṭhā* has the meaning of basis, ground, method, and thus law, way of life, perfection.
■ v) The text suggests that faith is a gratuitous gift but that it is linked nevertheless with the generosity of having given everything away.
■ vi) 1-9. Cf. § VI 11.
Firmly established in the Ultimate: *brahmaniṣṭha,* deeply rooted in the ultimate Ground, *brahman,* holy word.
Perfect knowledge: *brahma-vidyā.*
■ vii) 1. Cf. § II 6.
In fervor, purity, and faith: *tapasā brahmacaryeṇā śraddhayā.* Faith is a condition for true wisdom.
3-5. Cf. § II 6.
■ viii) Emitted: from the root *sṛj-*, cause to emanate, send forth.
Life: *prāṇa,* from which faith comes forth because the breath of life is the lord of all living creatures, lord of all that is; cf. PrasnU II, 11 (§ II 6). Faith is the first offering to the Lord of all that lives. Cf. also CU V, 4, 2; VII, 15, 1 (§ VI 3).

Loving Faith — *Bhakti*

38

BG IV, 39-40

i)

39. A man of faith, absorbed in faith,
his senses controlled,
attains knowledge, and, knowledge attained,
quickly finds supreme peace.

40. But the ignorant man, who is without faith,
goes doubting to destruction.
For the doubting self there is neither this world,
nor the next, nor joy.

BG VI, 47

ii)

Who worships Me full of faith, his inmost self
absorbed in Me,
him of all yogis I consider most completely
integrated in Me.

BG IX, 3

iii) Men who, O Arjuna, have no faith
in this Way of Truth
do not attain Me but return to the path
of ever recurring death.

BG XII, 20

iv) But those men of faith who make Me their goal,
adhering to Truth,
exceedingly dear are they to Me,
my loving devotees.

BG XVII, 3; 17; 28

v) 3. The faith of every man, O Arjuna,
accords with his nature.
Man is made up of faith; as is his faith,
so is he.

17. This threefold austerity practiced with faith
by men of balanced mind,
without expectation of any reward,
is said to be "pure."

28. Without faith whatever offering or gift
is made or work done
or penance performed, it is reckoned "not-being"
both now and hereafter.

▪ i) 36-38. Cf § IV 22.
39. Knowledge: *jñāna*.
Supreme peace: *parā śānti,* highest peace.
40. Ignorant: *ajña*.
Without faith: *aśraddadhāna*.
Doubting self: *saṁśayātman*.
▪ iii) Way of Truth: *dharma,* order.
Ever recurring death: *mṛtyu saṁsāra,* cycle of death. Cf. § V 6.
4-5. Cf. § I 8.
▪ iv) Truth: *dharma*.
Devotees: *bhaktāḥ,* partakers, sharers of myself (my love).
▪ v) 3. Accords with his nature: *sattvānurūpa,* according to the fundamental form of being (is the faith of everything: *sarvasya*).
17. The threefold austerity (*tapas*) of action, words, and mind. Cf. the previous *ślokas:* control of the body, of the tongue, and of the mind; but all has to be motivated by faith.
28. Not-being: *asat*.

PART II
GERMINATION AND GROWTH

Indra
Īśāna

Part I of this anthology describes the appearance of Life on earth and in heaven. In Part II we shall watch the growth of Consciousness in Man into self-consciousness. Consciousness is not necessarily self-conscious. In the whole of Part I Man's consciousness was alert and very much alive, but Man had not fully realized that it was he who was conscious; he was not aware of the subject of his own consciousness. Man did not consider himself the real owner but only the enjoyer of consciousness. Now with the discovery of ownership the history of Man begins. In Part II we embark on a path that will lead us to the discovery of Man, and we leave behind that first moment that was primarily cosmological. Man's honeymoon period with a world that encompassed him above and below is over. He will have to come to terms with the Gods, with himself, and with the world. This trilogy is the subject of the three sections of Part II.

Man becomes conscious that he is that pole of the universe which recognizes itself to be something other than the center. He is not the real center, for he discovers that reality evolves and moves around a center that is, by definition, God—whatever this God may be—and not himself; but he is the epistemological pole (which some consider to be the ontological one also), for it is he who recognizes God to be the center of the universe. This discovery gives Man a special and privileged role, even if the role is merely viewed as one of listening and of being open to the real center of everything. Even if we assume the existence of a personal God speaking and revealing himself, the speaking and revealing must of necessity take place with reference to Man and in a way that is intelligible and appropriate to him. Otherwise God's revelation would all be meaningless to him. The initiative may rest with God, but it is up to Man to "tune in," to understand and to accept it.

In other words, Man discovers himself, not as a separate individual, but as a creature that grows toward fulfillment by discovering itself to be that particular pole on which the true center is seen to rotate. God may be the center of the universe and bigger than Man; God is nevertheless God for Man and turns around him like the great and powerful sun that seems to rotate around the tiny earth. Henceforward the dialogue between these two poles will not cease, in spite of the tendency of each pole to overwhelm the other and stifle all dialogue: the total victory of either side (divine or human monism) would amount to the annihilation of both. God without Man is as impossible as Man without God. An idle and solitary God without Man is not only psychologically and epistemologically impossible but is also ontologically untenable—if ontology has to do with more than sheer possibilities. An isolated and single Man without God is also unthinkable, for in order to think "Man" one is bound in the first instance to transcend him in one way or another, and this transcendence is, precisely, God. On the other hand, a total separation (theological or ontological dualism) is tantamount to destroying one of the two, that is to say, to falling again into some type of monism. Only the polarity that does not destroy unity will allow for growth and for the unhampered manifestation of reality. This intuition would seem to point to the work of the Spirit.

However this may be, the movement of the Vedic Revelation is readily discernible. After the Prelude, which sets the stage for the total manifestation of reality, comes the birth of the world, produced by the first disclosure or explosion of the original source: the Word, followed by the existence of the world's elements. Then the Lord, the divine manifestation, appears in splendor in multifarious guises: the Gods of Heaven and Earth. There follows the Emergence of Life in its threefold stage, cosmic, human, and divine (Dawn, Human Birth, and Faith). Now we turn our attention to the germination and subsequent growth of this process.

The three sections are devoted to an exposition of this opening up to reality: first, Man becomes conscious of the existence of the universe as a hierarchical whole consisting of all sorts of gifts: Gods, men, animals, other beings, spirits, souls, the temporal and the timeless. A very special place is occupied by food, that life stuff that is material and spiritual at the same time, human, divine, and even cosmic, for everything in the universe "eats." Furthermore, the law of eating is so central that not only does everything eat, but all things eat one another, eating being the symbol of the solidarity of the whole universe. We all grow together; we all eat one another.

The second section deals with human self-consciousness in its most immediate form, the discovery of love and of the human person, which implies initiation and marriage. There is no human growth without this coming of age. These acts are simultaneously both cosmic and human, but the human aspect patently becomes more and more important; the center of gravity is being shifted from the cosmic to the human.

The third and final section describes that world that is not given, but made, not received, but manufactured, not found, but created: the world of Man, the result of his toil and of his effort. First of all, Man works on the earth, which nourishes him in proportion to his collaboration with the powers of nature. Second, he works in the technical world, by which we do not mean technological in the modern sense, that is, a world where Man becomes subject to his own constructions (which gradually become indispensible for his survival), but a world where Man remains the master of his own creations, embarking on the untried, handling objects of his hands, of his activity, of his work: the world of instruments and utensils. Third and finally, the world of Man does not consist simply in what he does, but in what he enjoys, that is, in everything that contributes toward a harmonious, civilized, and happy life. The first two realms Man employs as means toward an end; the third one is quite different. It is the stuff of human happiness.

A striking feature of the Vedic Revelation is the way in which its secular character in no way undermines the sacredness of life. We may exemplify this by calling attention to one particular point: the power that guides growth, gives direction, and inspires the way, in other words, the power that has sometimes been called the God of the roads, *pathaspati*, "the Lord of the path."[1] Divine Providence is more than just a benign surveillance; it is fundamentally a directing of the growth of all creatures, each according to its nature. Let us quote some passages:

> O God, you are our Providence, our Father.
> We are your brothers, you our Source of life.
>
> You are called Father, caring for the humble;
> supremely wise, you teach the simple wisdom.[2]
>
> The One who is the life spark of the waters,
> of wood, of things both moving and inert,
> who has his dwelling even within the stone,
> immortal God, he cares for all mankind.[3]
>
> He who sees all beings at a glance,
> both separate and united,
> may he be our protector![4]

1. RV VI, 53, 1.
2. RV I, 31, 10; 14. The prayer is addressed to Agni.
3. RV I, 70, 2. God: Agni. Life spark: *garbha*, womb, germ. The text has different versions, some of them rather obscure.
4. RV III, 62, 9. At a glance: from every side, in every direction. Separate and united: lit. discerning all living beings individually and beholding (them) in totality.

The "he" of the last stanza, which immediately precedes the Gāyatrī, is Pūṣan, the divine protector and guard, Vedic providence, the keeper of herds[5] and the surveyor of all, the conductor on the way.[6] He is the Lord of the roads,[7] the one who guards all pathways,[8] and the guardian of hazardous highways.[9] It is Pūṣan's familiarity with the roads which ensures him the privilege of escorting the dead to the abode of the Fathers[10] and has popularized him as a protector and guide in difficult or delicate undertakings, such as travels and marriage. He is the friend of everyone in need.[11]

The Vedic concept of providence seems to emphasize the aspects of protection and nurture (both of which concepts are included in the etymology of the name.).[12] The "providence" of God is not seen here in terms of his attributes of knowledge or wisdom; God is not "provident" because he "foresees" and thus warns, but because he protects and shields, bestows riches and blessings. He is in point of fact "Master of wealth,"[13] "Lord of wealth abundant."[14] The function of God is not primarily to judge, but to protect, to help us to thrive and flourish. The underlying presupposition here is that Man is not burdened with a guilt complex and that he is neither afraid to ask for fulfillment of all his desires nor beset by qualms when he is happy. We are still in the period of germination and growth.

5. Cf. RV VI, 58, 2 where he is called *paśupā*, protector of cattle.
6. Cf. RV X, 17, 5 (§ V 14).
7. Cf. RV VI, 53, 1.
8. Cf. RV VI, 49, 8.
9. Cf. RV I, 42, 1-3, and AV VII, 9 (§§ VII 4; 29). Cf. also RV VI, 53 to 58, all hymns to Pūṣan.
10. Cf. RV X, 17, 3-4 (§ V 14).
11. Cf. RV X, 26, 8.
12. The root *puṣ-* means to cause to thrive, to nourish.
13. RV I, 89, 6.
14. RV VI, 55, 3.

A. THE FIRST BLESSINGS OF THE LORD

Svasti

O God, grant us of boons the best,
a mind to think and a smiling love,
increase of wealth, a healthy body,
speech that is winsome and days that are fair.

RV II, 21 6[15]

The last section of Part I brought to our attention certain tokens of Emerging Life: Uṣas, the cosmic phenomenon of Dawn, *janman*, the biological phenomenon of Birth, and *śraddhā*, the spiritual phenomenon of Faith. The three themes of the next section in Part II are linked in a homologous manner to these phenomena, for the Sun follows Dawn and Breath follows Life, while the discovery of the temporal can be made only against the awareness of the nontemporal[16] which follows the appearance of faith.

The moment that human consciousness becomes conscious of itself, the question of the origin of things arises. Man may not necessarily be investigating the chain of cause and effect, but the moment he becomes conscious of his own existence, he no longer

15. O God: Indra.

16 Cf. the *nityānityavastuviveka* of tradition (discrimination between temporal and nontemporal things). Cf. Śaṅkara's BS *Bhāṣya* I, 1, 1.

takes the existence of the things he sees around him for granted. He begins to question their origin: first he asks "whence" and then "why."

The Vedic Revelation depicts now Man's environment, that is, the little portion of reality man experiences every day, as being a gift of the Gods, the result of divine blessings. It would be katachronic, and thus wrong, to interpret this Vedic awe and wonder at the works of the Gods as simply the primitive attitude of an unscientific mind. The myth of the Gods may be more sophisticated than the myth of science; furthermore, the Vedic Gods are not considered to be extrinsic beings bestowing upon Man their favors according to whim or wisdom. The same cosmic venture in which Gods and Men are engaged is hierarchical rather than democratic, and both perform in their proper way the recreating and restorative sacrifice of time and space and of all that they contain. "Prajāpati [i.e., the total reality] is both Gods and Men."[17]

The texts of Part II urge us to accept reality and, in concrete terms, to recognize human reality as a gift. These texts are only a selection from the vast treasure-house of the *śruti* concerning this world view. It would be naive to interpret the hymns that follow as expressions of an uncritical mind begging the Gods for blessings that could be obtained in no other fashion. The main thrust of this type of mantra is to awaken the consciousness that life itself is a gift, and that all that comes with it or that makes it really alive, and thus worth living, is also a gift, that is, a "coming," something that "happens" to us, in the happening of which we are constitutively involved, though each in a different way. This type of hymn stresses cosmic solidarity in a markedly anthropological way. The world of the Gods overarches that of mortals; the Gods are bridges between Men. Men fight one another, but then they discover that both sides are invoking the same God; Men tend to think of themselves as the center of the universe, and then they realize that the breath of life is common to all living beings; Men are really united when they look in the same direction, contemplating the marvels of the divine. The discovery of time brings with it a realization that it is like a net that not only draws together the different moments of a Man's life but also ties him up with all other temporal creatures. Man may, furthermore, experience a depth in his own being which

17. SB VI, 8, 1, 4.

does not belong to the sphere of temporal reality: all are blessings of the Lord, graces and favors that form the warp and woof of human existence. The fundamental meaning of a blessing is, perhaps, that it communicates life by means of an action, generally embodied in word or gesture. Recognition and acceptance of the fact that there is a blessing at the source of all that we are and have and do are both signs of an already mature spirituality.

Where there are blessings, there may also appear curses. In later periods, and especially in some of the hymns of the Atharva Veda, we find an ample repertoire of curses, but they are then used on another level, on the level of the human word which may be employed either for good or for bad purposes. Indeed, the human word is always powerful, because it is more than just a sound, a wish, or a thought; it is a partial incarnation of the primeval dynamism of the Word. Here, however, we are dealing not with utterances, or with the effort of Man to divert the flow of cosmic energy in one direction or another; we have to do with the very structure of human and divine reality and with the discovery of one of the fundamental "laws" governing the relation between Men and the Gods. This relation is not physical or psychophysical or dialectical; it is specifically religious. Prayer enters at this point and blessing is one of its main categories.

a) Divine Gifts

Maṅgala

Desire for happiness is a basic human urge, but dissatisfaction with every achievement of it is equally human. It seems as if bliss and well-being are ever elusive, never absent and yet never fully grasped. *Maṅgala,* the word summing up this subsection, expresses in itself the ideal of beauty, goodness, and happiness.[18] This felicity, which is elusive or transient in spite of much patient waiting for auspicious moments, is influenced by the conviction that happiness is a divine prerogative, coming to men only as a free gift. In any event true human happiness not only comes from on high, but is also of a "higher" nature.

18. Whatever the root of this word may be, whether *maṅg-* (Monier-Williams), *mañj-* (Grassmann), or whether it is uncertain (Mayrhofer), it signifies this whole cluster of ideas.

Those gifts in the Vedas are simple: Savitṛ, Indra, *prāṇa, kāla.* The Gods and certain "divinized notions" represent the embodiment of human longings, though they are by no means merely subjective projections of unfulfilled desires. The fundamental human values that make life the gift par excellence are, at the same time, the most simple and universal.

This subsection enumerates only a few of these values, of which one of the most precious is the ability to recognize the existence of the ideal, the reality of beauty, the realization of happiness; in short, the sublimity of Savitṛ, one of the most comprehensive divine symbols.

A fundamental human experience is that of being neither alone nor a multitude, but rather of being jointly under the influence of a power that embraces what to us appear to be incompatible. Indra is invoked by those who fight one another. Human enmity is not ultimate, and there is an archway over our heads which links together friends and enemies, and thus also good and evil. There is no ontic excommunication, as it were. Encompassing the whole of the universe there is something greater than Man.

Third, Man is conscious of life throbbing within him; he is aware that he is living and discovers his own vital power. This discovery is not the intellectual discovery of a principle, but the experiential encounter with life itself in its most concrete form: in our lungs, in our organs, in our brains. We observe it ebbing and flowing, increasing and decreasing, and are able to experience its rhythm and even to control its flow: the word for this is *prāṇa*.

Man can be happy here on earth if, finally, he realizes both the reality and the value of his temporal structure and also the nontemporal dimension that accompanies temporal life all the "time." The awareness, not of our historicity, not of the accumulation of time in our lives or in the life of our group or of the whole species, but the awareness of elemental time, of the harmony of our rhythms, of the moments in and through which we really live, the realization of the temporal nature of our being, the experience of the flowing of our own life according to a mysterious pattern which we call time—this is a fundamental human experience. Significantly enough, this experience of the reality of time within ourselves, the realization of our temporal existence, of its passage along the temporal shore, goes hand in hand with the more obscure but no less real intuition of an element incommensurable with time and yet inseparable from it: this is *akāla*, the timeless. None of these gifts can be totally snatched from Man as long as there is life. Living with them he discovers that happiness is neither a mere idea, nor just an ideal, but part and parcel of his life.

His Golden Arms the Godhead Has Extended *Savitṛ*

1 It would be misleading to say that Savitṛ is the divinization of the Sun, that is, the Sun as a personified deity. It would be equally misleading to affirm that they have nothing to do with each other. The angle of vision from which modern Man may be tempted to consider either statement leads him into confusion. Savitṛ is indeed the name of a divinity, celebrated in eleven hymns in the Ṛg Veda alone and mentioned there some one hundred and seventy times; of this divinity the Sun is the symbol, while the reverse is also true, for the Sun, the golden disk in the sky, is itself symbolized by Savitṛ. This interchangeability reflects the fact that by "Sun" is always understood more than just the sun and that by "God" is always understood less than God. The whole reality of the Sun or of God cannot possibly be contained by what we think or imagine, let alone by what we measure or experiment with, in relation to the Sun or to God. The sun in the sky leads us to the supreme Godhead, but this leading is not the leading of one who points out the way and afterward vanishes; God without the creatures is no longer God, because he is, precisely, God of the creatures. To mix God and the creatures would be pantheism; to separate both amounts to idolatry (or atheism if we eliminate the divine). The relation is more intimate than any causal thinking may incline us to suppose. It is not, for instance, that God through the Sun gives us his blessings, warmth, light, and life, as if a higher being were utilizing an instrument. It is rather the awareness that the "Sun" is more than what we may call and think of as the sun, and that God is no stranger to it.[19]

Savitṛ **RV VI, 71**

1. His golden arms the Godhead has extended
   in potent blessing toward the sacrifice.
   Like a grave young priest, he lets the chrism drip
   from his hands onto the airy spaces.

19. Cf. §§ I 22 and VII 22 for further reference to Savitr.

2. May we enjoy the vitalizing force
   of God, the radiant; may he grant us wealth!
   He is the God who sends to rest and wakens
   all life that moves on two feet or on four.

3. With kindly, never failing guardian powers
   protect our house, O Savitṛ, today.
   O gold-tongued God, preserve us in the right path.
   Let no ill-wisher have us in his grasp.

4. God Savitṛ, friend of our homes, gold-handed,
   has risen to meet the evening. With iron cheeks
   and honey-sweet tongue the God, worthy of praise,
   imparts good gifts to every worshiper.

5. Like mediating priest, the God has extended
   his golden arms so lovely to behold.
   The heights of Heaven and Earth he has ascended
   and made each flying monster speed away.

6. Grant favor today, Savitṛ, and tomorrow.
   O you who own an ample treasure store,
   enrich us daily by your life-bringing power.
   May this our song now set us in your grace.

1. Godhead: Savitṛ.
In potent blessing: lit. full of wise efficacy (*sukratu*), toward the libation (*savanāya*).
Grave: *sudakṣa*, skilled liturgically.
Chrism: *ghṛta*, fatness, cream, sacred and consecrating oil.
2. The radiant: Savitṛ.
3. Right path: *suvita*. The meaning could also be: keep us in ever-renewed joy, welfare.
4. Cf. RV I, 35, 10 (§ I 22); II, 38, 1.
Good gifts: *bhūri vāmam*.
5. Lit. like an *upavaktṛ* (cf. Sāyaṇa's commentary), like a mediator, i.e., like a mediator with a priestly function.
Flying monster: *patayat . . . abhvam*; most probably the terror of the night.
6. Favor: *vāma*, wealth, from the root *van-*, to love, to desire, to strive after, to worship. *Vāmabhājaḥ-syāma*, may we share in your grace, favor, reward (by this our song), or, may it impart to us your grace.

Inspirer of Heaven and Earth *Divo dhartā*

2 The verbal root underlying the name of Savitṛ, like that of Sūrya, is *sū-*, meaning to impel, to enliven, and to beget. Savitṛ impels the movement of all beings, arousing and enlivening them; he begets new consciousness, the light of the intellect; Savitṛ illumines not only our physical eyes, but principally our spiritual vision. Savitṛ is the awakener or rather the enlightener, the great stimulator. Our vision, surely, is different once the light of dawn has

given way to the refulgent radiance of the sun. No longer is there "morning" or initial knowledge—matutinal consciousness—but the fullness of light which Savitṛ brings to us—zenithal awareness. This does not come solely from without, of course; our own eyes must be ready and open. Savitṛ must also be in our own eyes, in our own inner beings, so that we may really enjoy the fullness of vision which he bestows.

Savitṛ is obviously connected with truth and cosmic order.[20] He enlightens us according to truth and the dynamic realities of things. Savitṛ himself observes the cosmic laws (v. 4). He is the Lord of all that moves and of all that moves not (v. 6). He has been identified thus with Prajāpati (v. 2) and also with Pūṣan.[21]

This hymn is a wonder of poetry and balance. Nothing has been omitted. Savitṛ is the sustainer of heaven and earth and the arouser of all creatures; he brings life and warmth to everything: following his own course, he comes nigh when the seasons change. Finally the poet expresses the thought that the life of Men must likewise be attuned to that cosmic order of which Savitṛ is both the revealer and the observer.

Divo dhartā RV IV, 53

1. From Savitṛ the God, wise supreme Spirit,
we crave that gift most worthy to be sought,
by which he grants his worshipers protection.
His rays vouchsafe to us the great God's boon.

2. Sustainer of the Heaven, Lord of the cosmos,
this sage puts on his golden-colored mail.
Clear-sighted, far-extending, filling the heavens,
Savitṛ has brought us bliss our lips must praise.

3. Amply he fills the realms of Earth and Heaven;
in tune with his own being he sings the hymn.
The God, with arms outstretched, all creatures fosters,
arousing, lulling all life with his rays.

4. He lights up all things, guards each holy ordinance.
None can deceive him, the great God, the radiant.
He has stretched out his arms to all earth dwellers.
Maintaining his own laws he runs his course.

20. Cf. RV X, 34, 8 (§ IV 12); X, 139, 3.
21. Cf. RV V, 81, 5.

5. With his own greatness Savitṛ has filled
the three domains of space, three worlds, three heavens.
He moves the threefold Heaven and threefold Earth.
With ordinances three he himself protects us.

6. Most gracious God, life-stirrer, bringer of slumber,
controller of all, what moves not and what moves,
may Savitṛ the God vouchsafe us shelter
and security, distress held thrice at bay.

7. God Savitṛ comes nigh with changing seasons.
May he enhance our stock of food and sons!
May he grant strength through days and nights to follow
and may he send us wealth with progeny.

1. Supreme Spirit: Asura. Though Asura is used here as the name of a class of Gods, we have translated it according to the word's etymological meaning: spiritual, incorporeal, divine (from *asu*, spirit, breath, life).
2. Lord of the cosmos: *bhuvanasya prajāpatiḥ*.
3. In tune with his own being or in accordance with his own tune he creates the hymn: *svāya dharmane*.
4. Ordinance: *vrata*, the divine order (also in v. 5).
Maintaining his own laws: *dhṛtavrata*, *vrata* meaning law by personal resolve.
5. Three is here the symbol of fullness and perfection, expressing a quality rather than a quantity.
6. The last line is a metaphor from warding off wild animals.

The Dispenser of Blessings from on High *Vasupati*

3 If human life were lived merely on the horizontal two-dimensional level, not only would forgiveness be impossible (for what has been done, has been done), but also prayers and entreaties would be pointless. Furthermore, the gratuitous blessings that revive life, strengthen Man's hopes, and sustain his expectations would be inconceivable. Of this openness Savitṛ, again, is the living symbol. It is he who bestows blessings,[22] which he can do because he is not entangled in the two-dimensional world, but is on high overseeing both Men and cattle, keeping an eye on every creature, not in order to punish or to judge, but in order to bless, for he is the Lord of all wealth (v. 3). A blessing cannot be something "due," nor can the act of blessing be termed a "duty." A blessing is not an automatic action or the fruit of any kind of regular process. Blessings belong to the realm of spontaneity and freedom. No one has a right to a blessing, for a compulsory blessing would cease to

22. Cf. also RV I, 24, 3; II, 38, 11; etc.

be a blessing. Prayer is an actualization of human freedom, as many a chant of the *śruti* discloses to us. When you pray for a blessing it is not that you try your luck with the Gods on the chance that they may be well disposed toward you; it is rather that you dare to enter and even to interfere in their internal unrestricted sphere and participate in it. Prayer is a joyous and free interplay between Gods and Men, the results of which are always unpredictable. Who is going to win? Will Men make the Gods human or the Gods make Men divine?

Vasupati RV VII, 45

1. May God Savitṛ, chariot-borne, come hither,
filling the heavens, rich in treasure divine,
dispenser of everything that makes man happy,
lulling to sleep, then stirring all that breathes.

2. His arms are far-extended, mighty, golden.
They reach as far as the utmost limits of Heaven.
Now is his greatness highly to be praised.
Even the sun submits its course to him.

3. Now may this God Savitṛ, the strong and mighty,
Lord of all wealth, vouchsafe to us his riches!
May he, extending his far-spreading luster,
bestow on us the food that nourishes men!

4. These songs praise Savitṛ of gentle speech,
whose arms are full, whose hands are beautiful.
Vitality and strength may he afford us!
Preserve us evermore, O Gods, with blessings.

1. Chariot-borne: lit. driven by horses.
2. Limits of Heaven: *divo antān,* the ends of the sky.
Sun: *sūrya.* Here again Savitṛ is not identical with the sun. Cf. RV I, 35, 9 (§ I 22).
Course: *apasyā,* lit. activity.
3. Nourishes: *rāsate,* gives taste to men.
4. Of gentle speech: lit. the honey-tongued one.

The One Invoked by Both Sides in the Battle *Indra*

4 Indra, whose power is praised in more than three hundred hymns in the Ṛg Veda, that is, in more than a quarter of the whole corpus, possesses all human virtues in superlative degree; he is the Hero, the Man-God, of Vedic times. It is natural that it is his

prerogative to bless Men in all their enterprises, for power and guidance lie with him.

The hymn we give here recapitulates nearly all the characteristics of Indra. The text starts with an acclamation of praise to Indra who from the moment of his birth establishes his power and fills the whole universe with his incomparable deeds. Then follows a description of these same deeds and of the characteristics of Indra with a wealth of praise, expressions of awe, and petitions.

Indra organized the whole universe (vv. 2, 7). It is he who has fixed in their places the earth and the mountains, who has measured out space, stretched out the sky, and created both sun and sunrise. The establishment of the universe is one of his functions, for Indra is the Lord especially of space.

He is the hero of sundry exploits (vv. 3, 11-12). The most famous and most frequently recounted is that in which he killed the dragon or "serpent," Vṛtra, who was holding the waters captive. Etymologically *vṛtra* means resister and hence "enemy," "obstacle," "upholder." In the Ṛg Veda Vṛtra is usually interpreted as a demon representing drought, but he has also sometimes been regarded as the personification of darkness. It is by defeating him that Indra imparts light to the whole world. It is not improbable that these struggles with various demons allude to both historical and cosmogonic acts. In myth cosmogony and history converge, and if worship or liturgy is more than sheer magic it is, among other things, because it offers a platform where they can meet. The regeneration of the world is both the cause and the effect of the regeneration of Man.

On another occasion Indra freed the light (called here "cows") that a demon, Vala, had imprisoned in his cavern. In this exploit Indra is called the "powerful bull." The Ṛg Veda says in several passages that it was after liberating the waters that Indra produced the Sun, the Sky, and the Dawn:

> When, Indra, you had slain the chief of dragons
> and overcome the charms of the enchanters,
> then you gave life to Sun and Dawn and Heaven
> and found no single foe to stand against you.[23]

Indra is chief of warriors, endowed with matchless power (vv. 4, 7-9). He was a warrior from birth.[24] As protector of warriors

23. RV I, 32, 4 (the last line is somewhat obscure).
24. Cf. RV III, 51, 8.

and princes he is hailed as commander in chief in the struggle of the invading Aryans against the original inhabitants of the land. Men on all sides, at least among the Aryans, call him to their assistance in battle, for without his help none can be victorious. There could hardly be a better metaphor to express his transcendence. His weapon of war is visible in both east and west: the *vajra* or thunderbolt is the mythical name for lightning. He destroys sinners and all evil (v. 10). His zest in combat is directed toward victory over his foes, and particularly toward victory over all evil demons. He is uncompromising and relentless toward the proud.

Indra is the drinker of Soma, helping and encouraging those who sacrifice (vv. 6, 13, 15). He is famous for his passionate love for the Somajuice and it is thanks to Soma that he can accomplish his extraordinary feats.[25] However we may assess or explain the use of intoxicating agents, one feature may be stressed and pondered here: immortality, strength, and courage come from the outside, that is, from an external agency and through the use of a material substance, not from a merely endogenous procedure.

Our hymn, we may note, makes scant reference to the beauty of Indra, so many aspects of which are acclaimed in other hymns. Here he is, rather, the "terrible," concerning whom Men are seized by fears and doubts. "Where is he?" "Where, he who is the God of all the spaces?" Some may even say that he does not exist. Yet "believe in him," says the text (v. 5) without equivocation, though only at the end is doubt overcome by the experience that he really *is* (v. 15).

The following *stotra* will make the personality of Indra more familiar.

He is everywhere:

RV VI, 47, 18

i) He became the original form of every form;
It is his form that is everywhere to be seen.[26]

He is all-powerful:

RV I, 100, 15

ii) The limits of his power cannot be reached;
neither by Gods, albeit divine, nor mortals,
nor yet the waters.

25. Cf. RV II, 15, 2.

26. This verse, which has here a different and more mythical context (that of Indra adopting many forms) is interpreted in KathU V, 9 (§ VI 2), as referring to the immanence-transcendence of the Absolute *rūpaṁ rūpaṁ pratirūpo babhūva*. Cf. RV III, 53, 8.

RV II, 46, 3

iii) Utterly has he outshone both Heaven and Earth.
This radiant one is greater than all the Gods.

He is full of compassion:

RV I, 165, 9

iv) Before you, O compassionate, all falter;
among the Gods not one is found your equal.

He inspires ardent devotion:

RV III, 53, 2

v) O mighty Indra, with the sweetest songs
I catch your garment's hem as a child his father's.

RV VIII, 1, 5-6

vi) For any price, O Indra, I'll not sell you,
not for a thousand or ten thousand pieces!

O Indra, you are more to me than a father.
I count a brother naught compared to you.
You and a mother, O bountiful, vie with each other
in generous giving and in bestowal of joy.

Indra

RV II, 12

1. He who from birth was chief of the Gods, the wise one,
protecting with his might the other Gods,
before whose energy and mighty exploits
the two worlds tremble: he, Men, is the Lord!
2. Who stilled the quaking of the mighty earth
and set at rest the agitated mountains,
who measured out the middle regions of space
and gave the sky support: he, Men, is the Lord!
3. Who slew the dragon and loosed the seven rivers,
who drove the cattle out of Vala's cavern,
who brought forth fire from between the rocks,
victorious ever: he, Men, is the Lord!
4. Who can, if he so choose, make reel this planet,
who humbled and drove off the inferior race,
who, like a gambler, rakes in all his winnings
from vanquished foeman: he, Men, is the Lord!
5. The Terrible, of whom they ask "Where is he?"
(though sometimes men dare say of him "He is not"),
who, as at dice, sweeps off opposing stakes—
believe in him; for he, Men, is the Lord!

6. Who encourages all, the strong and feeble alike,
   enheartening also the priest who sings his praise;
   the handsome one, who helps the presser of juice
   and him who adjusts the stones: he, Men, is the Lord!

7. In whose control are horses and all chariots,
   all cattle and all habitations of men;
   by whose power Sun and Daybreak come to birth,
   who leads the Waters: he, Men, is the Lord!

8. Who is invoked by both sides in the battle,
   the warriors close by and those far distant,
   entreated differently even by two men mounted
   in the selfsame chariot: he, Men, is the Lord!

9. Without whose aid men never win in battle,
   whose succor they continually implore,
   who proves himself for everyone a match,
   who moves the immovable: he, Men, is the Lord!

10. Who, long before they know it, shoots his darts
    to slay the unnumbered gang of guilty sinners,
    who gives no pardon to the arrogant,
    who slays the demons: he, Men, is the Lord!

11. Who once discovered in the fortieth autumn
    Śambara lurking in the mountain hideouts,
    who slew the demon, confident in his prowess,
    as he lay on the waters: he, Men, is the Lord!

12. The powerful seven-reined bull who freed the seven
    torrents to flow abundantly, the God
    whose thunderbolt caused Rauhiṇa to totter
    as he scaled the heavens: he, Men, is the Lord!

13. Before whom Earth and Heaven both bow down,
    before whose very breath the mountains tremble,
    famed drinker of the Somajuice, the wielder
    of flashing thunderbolt: he, Men, is the Lord!

14. Who with his aid assists all those who press
    the Soma, boiling it, chanting or performing rituals,
    whose soul expands by prayer, by dint of Soma
    or through the gifts they offer: he, Men, is the Lord!

15. You who grant booty seized from fearsome foeman
    to soma presser and cooker, you truly ARE.
    May we be ever well-beloved by you!
    May we with verve intone your ritual praises!

1. He, Men, is the Lord: *sa janā sa indraḥ*. This phrase is repeated at the end of each stanza. We translate Indra by the Lord. About the birth of Indra, cf. RV III, 48; IV 18. In RV X, 90, 13 (§ I 5), it is said that "Indra was born from the mouth of the *puruṣa*."

2. Cf. RV VI, 69, 5 where Indra and Viṣṇu are said to "stretch the spaces for us to live" and to "expand the universe." In several other hymns the great actions of Indra are extolled: RV II, 15, 2; III, 31, 15; III, 49, 4; VIII, 12, 30.

3. Reference to the legends of the release of the waters and of the cows by Indra.

Vala: a mythical cave and a demon who holds back the waters.

4. The inferior race: *dāsaṁ varṇam,* the color of the *dāsa,* probably the darker color of the pre-Aryan clans. *Varṇa,* however, not only refers to color but also connotes a category of beings. Later it refers to the four classes (Brahmin, Kṣatriya, Vaiśya, Śūdra) that form the backbone of the caste system.

5. Cf. RV VIII, 1, 7: "Where are you? Whither are you gone? For in many places is your mind."

10. Demons: *dasyu,* name of a class of demons. The name denotes enemy, barbarian, impious man, stranger, and is related to *dāsa,* slave, demon, infidel, somebody from a foreign land, and later those who are not twice-born (*dvija*). Cf. the name appearing in v. 4.

11. Śambara: name of a demon whom Indra evicts from the mountain where he is hiding himself and terrorizing men.

12. Rauhiṇa: name of another demon, a drought demon.

13. Heaven and Earth: *dyu* and *pṛthivī,* here regarded as two divine beings.

14. With his aid assists: *avati . . . ūtī,* favors.

Whose soul expands by prayer: *yasya brahma vardhanam.*

15. You truly ARE: *sa kilāsi satyaḥ,* you are as such true, or you are truth, truthful, you are real, reality. This is the climax of the hymn.

The Breath of Life *Prāṇa*

5 Wind, Breath, and Life form a triad which modern Man has broken asunder, but which Man some millennia ago still experienced as a whole, for he viewed these three not as identical but as deeply related and belonging together. Movement is a common feature to all three. Movement is not seen here as a metaphysical riddle for our minds, but as a physical datum of our world. The phenomenon of movement may confound our reason (for we may not find a rational explanation for it) but it quickens our being (for without it we would die). Movement is the soul, that is, the life-principle, of every phenomenon in the three worlds. Wind is not just air, but air in movement. Breath is this same movement of the air within living beings. Life is intrinsically movement; it is something that somehow moves without being moved. There is no need to connect this vision with a primitive cosmology or an undeveloped physiology, though the expressions used to describe it may be clothed in the language of the time. The experience takes place at a deeper level of reality, a level where that fatal dichotomy between matter and spirit has not yet occurred. The fear of one extreme should not precipitate us into the other.

Is it possible for contemporary Man to reenact that primordial experience without becoming archaic, primitive, regressive, or even pathological? No amount of intellectual indoctrination, even if it manages to inculcate conviction, will succeed. It is obviously not a question of reverting to an undifferentiated outlook and to an almost animistic level of experience, but rather of viewing things with an integrated and integrating insight which is something more than mere poetic feeling.

Life is an all-pervasive vector in the structure of reality. Something without life is dead, that is, it is nonbeing. The wind reveals to us how alive the earth is, and there was no need to wait until the discovery of the electronic *spin* to discover self-motion. Breath discloses to us the intimate connection between life and matter, and there was likewise no need to wait for psychosomatic medicine or "vital philosophy" in order to come to this conclusion. Life itself is a mere abstraction if there is no living being. But being too is nothing if it is not be-ing, that is, alive. Hell, death, and nonbeing together compose a challenge which is certainly threatening, but which is also evocative of victory and joy as the unfailing concomitants of life.

The hymn given here combines in a masterly way all the different aspects of this world view. The wind gives life to plants and also brings comfort to the animal realm. The plants breathe in and out and perform an ecologically essential purifying function. This Breath of Life, however, is not the wind alone, nor simply the movement of masses of air in one direction or another owing to differences of pressure caused by changes of temperature. This Breath of Life is the symbol of life itself, that is, life as it manifests itself in living beings. For this very reason it is also death and fever, the rain, the sun and the moon, and is not separated from the Father of all beings. Does not life require death in order to assert itself? Would there be Being if there were no Source witnessing its very be-ing, its flow?

A difficult line in the last stanza seems to suggest that the mystery of personal consciousness is bound up with the identification of the person with this same Breath of Life: I am that very Life. I pray that I may clasp to myself this very Breath of Life, so that I may live: "You are indeed I." The conquest of immortality is the realization both that Life is Life, thus that it does not die, and also that I *am* insofar as I realize my own identity with Life. We are here at the threshold of the Upaniṣadic vision.[27]

27. Cf. § VI Introduction.

Prāṇa

AV XI, 4

1. Praise to the Breath of Life!
   He rules this world,
   master of all things,
   on which all things are based.

2. Praise, Breath of Life, to your uproar!
   Praise to your thunder!
   Praise to your lightning!
   Praise, Breath of Life, for your rain!

3. When Breath of Life with his thunder
   roars o'er the plants,
   then, pregnant with pollen,
   the flowers burst forth in abundance.

4. When Breath of Life in due season
   roars o'er the plants,
   all things on earth
   rejoice with great rejoicing.

5. When Breath of Life the broad earth
   with rain bedews,
   the cattle exult:
   "We shall have plenty," they say.

6. The plants converse with this Breath,
   drenched by his moisture:
   "Our life is prolonged,
   for you have made us all fragrant."

7. Praise to you, Breath, when you come
   and praise when you go!
   When you stand up
   and when you sit still, to you praise!

8. Praise to you, Breath of Life, breathing
   both in and out!
   To your turning this side
   and that, to the whole of you, praise!

9. Grant us, O Breath, your dear form
   —and the one dearer still—
   that we may live!
   Give us your healing power!

10. Breath of Life clothes all beings with care
    as a father his son;
    master of all things,
    whether they breathe or breathe not.

11. Breath of Life is death, is fever,
    revered by the Gods.
    In the highest world
 he sets the man who speaks truth.

12. Breath of Life is Queen, is Guide,
    revered by all things;
    he is sun, he is moon;
 he is also the Father of all.

13. The two breaths are rice and barley,
    Breath the ox that pulls.
    In barley resides
 inbreath; out-breath is called rice.

14. A man breathes in, he breathes out,
    within the womb.
    Quickened by you,
 to birth he comes once more.

15. The mighty Wind they call him, or Breeze.
    The future and the past
    exist in him.
 On Breath of Life all things are based.

16. When you, Breath of Life, quicken them,
    then the plants of the Atharvans
    and Angirases,
 of Gods and of Men, come to birth.

17. When Breath has poured down with the rain
    upon the vast earth,
    then plants come forth
 and herbs of every sort.

18. The one who knows you thus, O Breath,
    and that which forms your support,
    to him will all offer
 tribute in yonder highest heaven.

19. Just as all creatures owe tribute
    to you, Breath of Life,
    so may they bring it
 to the one who hears you, O renowned!

20. He moves among the Gods, an inner seed;
    becomes, is, is reborn.
    He has entered the son—
 he, the father, who was, is, and shall be!

21. If the sunbird, rising, extracted
    his foot from the sea,

neither today nor tomorrow
would exist, neither night, day, nor dawn.

22. The eight-wheeled moves on one rim,
to and fro, thousand-syllabled.
With one half it engendered
all creation. Of its other half what sign?

23. Of all that is born is he Lord,
of all that moves.
Of swift bow like the rest,
to you, O Breath of Life, homage!

24. Of all that is born is he Lord,
of all that moves.
Untiring he, steadfast;
may my prayer bring Breath to my aid!

25. Erect he keeps watch among the sleeping.
He falls not prone.
None ever heard
that he among the sleepers should slumber.

26. Breath of Life, do not forsake me.
You are, indeed, I.
Like the Embryo of the Waters
I bind you to me that I may live!

1. Breath of Life: *prāna*, throughout.
12. Queen: *virāj*, the shining One. Cf. RV X, 90, 5 (§ I 5) and the hymn dedicated to her in the AV VIII, 9; cf. also AV XIII, I, 33.
Guide: *deṣṭrī*, an epithet of a Vedic divinity. Lit. she who shows the direction, thus the guide. Father of all: Prajāpati.
13. Even the products of agriculture are related to *prāṇa*.
15. Mighty Wind: Mātariśvan.
Breeze: *vāta*.
16. Of the Atharvans and Aṅgirases: i.e., the herbs used in rites of the AV.
20. Obscure verse. *Prāṇa* appears as the life-principle of even the Gods, and it is he who is born again in every being. He is both the child (embryo, seed: *garbha*) and the father; i.e., he is immanent in all things.
21. Sunbird: *haṁsa*, swan, here referring to the sun. What the sun is in the sky, so breath is in man: time depends upon it. (Translation shortened.)
22. This verse also refers to the sun. The question is about the invisible half of the sun's course. Sign: *ketu*, banner, light, symbol.
23. Of swift bow: *kṣipradhanvan*.
24. Prayer: *brahman*.
26. Allusion to *hiraṇyagarbha*; cf. RV X, 121, 1 (§ I 4).

The Treasure of Life *Prāṇo brahma*

6 *Prāṇa*, the Breath of Life of the preceding pages, has been translated in this section simply as Life, in order to indicate the interiorization and ontologization of the same experience. This

universe is not a dead universe. Life is its most striking feature, while its deepest one is consciousness. The passage from the one to the other is realized in the Upaniṣads by a peculiar transmythization of the Vedic motifs.

From an ecstatic attitude of joy and thankfulness for the gift of life as expressed in the Vedas, the Upaniṣads lead us on to an ecstatic discovery that this life is within us and that we not only enjoy it but also share in it as a treasure—even that we *are* this life. Fullness of life implies a knowledge that I am alive. Life in the four Vedas means the biological fact of movement, growth, and non-reflective consciousness; it is that cosmic life in which all beings, from God down to the particles of earth, share; it is the breath of the universe, breathed also by Men. Life in the Upaniṣads means something more. We enter with them into a new phase, that of self-conscious interiorization. Man ceases to be a mere spectator or even a part of the cosmic play; he becomes the focal point and the very center of operation of the whole of reality. Life is consciousness; consciousness is self-consciousness and self-consciousness is consciousness of the Self.

Two fragmentary examples of the Upaniṣadic adventure are given here. The Praśna Upaniṣad develops a theory of *prāṇa* as the principle of life through six questions (*praśna*) posed by six students to the great master Pippalāda. To the first question, regarding the origin of life, how things in fact came to be, the master replies with some ancient wisdom presented in a new way. He invokes the old myth of Prajāpati but goes on to say that the Father of all creatures brought into existence two principles, Matter and Life, so that they became the origin of all. *Rayi,* which is a common word for wealth in the Vedas,[28] becomes here the stuff, the food, the matter or material principle which enters into the composition of all beings; while *prāṇa,* which is the word used for the vital breath of Men and animals, here possesses an ontological rather than a physiological function. The terms are given a cosmological symbolism: matter is the moon; life is the sun. Matter is the formed and unformed structure of reality. Life is not that which gives form, but that which gives existence.

To the second question, concerning the powers that support a creature and which of these is the foremost, the master replies that

28. Cf. RV I, 73, 1; 169, 4; II, 21, 6 (§ II A Antiphon); III, 1, 19; IV, 2, 7 as well as AV III, 14, 1; VI, 33, 3; VII, 80, 2. Cf. § I 4.

the foremost is life. He gives a proof based on the dependence of every other human faculty on the Breath of Life. If this withdraws, no other power can sustain the body.

To the third question, regarding the origin of this life, the master hesitates to reply. At last he reluctantly proffers his deepest doctrine, saying that life has its origin in the *ātman,* the Self, and that life is as it were the shadow of the *ātman*. It is not the *ātman,* but at the same time it is inseparable from it. It is its first manifestation.[29] The discovery of Life leads to immortality. This sounds like a tautology, and it is precisely the qualification of this statement which is one of the fundamental intentions of the Upaniṣad. As long as we do not know who we are, as long as we walk in darkness or in ignorance, we shall not fulfill our humanness. Once we know it, we are it; or, as our text puts it: "Whatever is one's thinking [*citta*], therewith life comes."[30] If we discover Life, then, in a real way, we are Life, so long as this discovery is not merely an intellectual operation.

The three other questions, which we do not translate here, reveal once again the everlasting desire of Man to penetrate deeper and deeper into the mysteries of life. The fourth question concerns the subject, enjoyer of life in the state of dream and who is the *deva,* the master of the dreams.[31] The fifth query regards the nature of the yonder world which one reaches meditating on *om*.[32] And the final problem deals with the mystery of the *puruṣa,* the complete person (of sixteen parts) which is immortal in spite of the fact that all the parts disappear "like running rivers rushing toward the sea."[33]

The Kauṣītaki Upaniṣad goes a step farther than Pippalāda. Life is Brahman. This is again a statement that needs to be qualified if it is to be understood in its true meaning. Brahman is consciousness, according to one of the great utterances of the Upaniṣads.[34] The main message of the Kauṣītaki Upaniṣad is the affirmation that life is the conscious *ātman*.

These texts should provide a healthy corrective to some merely speculative comments of a certain type of popularized Vedānta. The experience of the Upaniṣads is not only intellectual; it is also vital

29. Cf. PrasnU VI, 4 (§ I 37); MundU II, 1, 3 (§ VI 7).
30. PrasnU III, 10. Cf. BG VIII, 6 (§ V 6) for a similar thought, though the interpretation is not necessarily connected with the popular theory of transmigration.
31. Cf. PrasnU IV.
32. Cf. PrasnU V (§ VI, 12).
33. PrasnU VI, 5.
34. Cf. AU III, 3: *prajñānaṁ brahma*. (§ VI 4).

and, one is tempted to say, primarily existential. Life is to be lived—to the full.

Prāṇo brahma

PrasnU I, 1; 3-5; 8

i) 1. Sukeśa, son of Bharadvāja, Satyakāma, son of Śibi, Gārgya, grandson of Sūrya, Kausalya, son of Aśvalāyana, Bhārgava of Vidarbha and Kabandhi, son of Kātyāyana, all of whom made Brahman their highest goal, were established in Brahman and searching for the supreme Brahman, approached the venerable Pippalāda with fuel in their hands, thinking "He will explain to us everything."

3. Then Kabandhi, son of Kātyāyana, approached him and asked: "Tell me truly, Master, whence have been created all these creatures?"

4. The sage replied: "The creator, out of desire to procreate, devoted himself to concentrated ardor. Whilst thus devoted to concentrated ardor, he produced a couple, Matter and Life, saying to himself, "these two will produce all manner of creatures for me.' "

5. Now Life is the Sun; Matter is the Moon. Matter, indeed, is all this, the formed and the formless. Hence, [whatever has] form is simply matter.

8. All forms has he, the golden one, the all-knowing.
He blazes, final goal and single light.
Emitting a thousand rays, in a hundred movements
proceeding, the Sun arises, the Life of all creatures!

PrasnU II, 1-13

ii) 1. "Tell me, Master, how many powers support a creature? Which of them make him manifest and, again, which is the foremost?"

2. "These powers," he replied, "are space, wind, fire, water, and earth; also speech, mind, sight, and hearing. All these, having made the creature manifest, say, 'It is we who prop up this body and support it!'

3. But the foremost of them, Life, said: 'Do not deceive yourselves. It is I who, dividing myself into five parts, prop up this body and support it.' "

4. They did not believe him. So Life, his pride upset, made as if to leave the body, and when he rose up all the rest of them rose up, and when he settled down they all settled down with him. Just as bees rise up after their queen when she arises, and all of them settle when she settles again, even so do speech, mind, sight, and hearing behave with Life. They, being now satisfied, offer him homage.

5. He is the Fire that burns, he is the Sun.
He is the plenteous Rain, he is the Wind.
He is the Earth and Matter and God,
Being and Nonbeing—he the Immortal.

6. Just as spokes are affixed to the hub of a wheel,
so are all things established in Life,
the Ṛg- and Yajur- and Sāma-Veda,
Sacrifice, the nobility, and also the priesthood.

7. Lord of creatures, you stir in the womb;
it is you yourself that are born again.
To you, Life, creatures bring their offerings,
to you, who dwell in their vital breaths.

8. Chief mediator between Gods and Men
are you, and first offering to the Fathers.
You are the truthful Way of the sages,
the Atharvans and Aṅgirases.

9. You, O Life, by your splendor are Indra.
You are Rudra, being a protector.
In the vault of heaven you move as the sun,
the Lord of all lights.

10. When you send rain upon the earth,
then the creatures breathe and live.
When there is food to their hearts' content,
they dwell in happiness.

11. You are primordial, O Life, the sole Seer,
Lord and consumer of all that is.
We are the givers of your food.
You are our Father, O mighty Wind!

12. That form of yours which resides in speech,
which resides in human hearing and seeing,
which constantly resides in the mind of men—
make it benevolent! Do not depart!

13. This whole universe, whatever exists
in all three heavens, is subject to Life.
Protect us, O Life, as a mother her son,
and grant us happiness and understanding!

PrasnU III

iii) Then Kausalya, son of Aśvalāyana, asked him:

1. "Tell me truly, Master, whence is this Life born?
How does it come into this body?
How does it distribute itself and how does it settle down?
By what means does it go away?
How does it relate to the external world?
How is it related to the internal self?"

2. To him he replied: "You are asking very difficult and lofty questions. However, as you are firmly committed to Brahman, I will therefore tell you.

3. "This Life is born of the *ātman*. As his shadow is to a person, so in this case is Life to the *ātman*. By the action of the mind it comes into the body.

4. "As an earthly ruler commands his subordinates, saying: 'Supervise such and such villages,' even so Life assigns to the vital breaths different functions:

5. "The downward breath is in the organs of excretion and generation, while the life-breath itself is established in the eye, the ear, the mouth, and the nose; the distributive breath is in the middle, and it carries all the food offered in a balanced way. From it arise the seven flames.

6. "In the heart is the *ātman*. Here are the hundred and one arteries to each of which belong a hundred other arteries, and to each of these belong seventy-two thousand small branches: in those moves the diffused breath.

7. "The upward breath rises up through one of these [arteries] and leads [at the time of death] to the world of goodness in consequence of goodness, to the world of evil in consequence of evil, or to the world of men in consequence of both [good and evil].

8. "The sun rises as the external [manifestation of] Life, and it supports the life-breath of the eye. The power that is in the earth supports the downward breath of a person, and that which is in the atmosphere the distributive breath; wind is the diffused breath.

9. "Fire, in truth, is the upward breath. Therefore those whose fire of life is extinguished are reborn with their sense organs merged in their mind.

10. "According to one's thought one enters into life. Life united with fire and accompanid by the *ātman*, leads a man to whatever world his thought has fashioned.

11. "If a man knows Life thus, his offspring will not fail and he will become immortal. On this there is the following verse:

12. When he knows the origin, the mode of entry,
the dwelling place, the fivefold lordship, the dependence
of Life on the *ātman*—whoso knows this,
attains immortality, attains immortality!"

KausU II, 1

iv) "Life is Brahman," said Kauṣītaki. "The messenger of Life, of Brahman, is the mind, its watchman is the eye, its herald is the ear, its servant is speech. . . . To this Life, to Brahman, all the powers bring tribute, even without being asked. So too all beings bring tribute to the one who knows this, even without being asked."

KausU III, 2-3

v) 2. Indra said: "I am Life, the conscious Self. Reverence me as temporal life and also as immortality. Life is temporal life and temporal life is Life. Life is also immortality. For as long as Life remains in the body there is temporal life. By Life man attains immortality in this world and by consciousness true thinking. Whoever reveres me as temporal life and as immortality, lives out in this world his full life span, and attains immortality and indestructibility in the world of heaven.

"On this point people say that the vital breaths merge into a unity, for otherwise nobody would be able to make known a name simply by speech, or a form by the eye, or a sound by the ear, or a thought by the mind, but because the vital breaths have become one, they make known all these [perceptions] one by one. When speech speaks, all the breaths speak along with it; when the eye sees, all the breaths see along with it; when the ear hears, all the breaths hear along with it; when the mind thinks, all the breaths think along with it; when breath breathes, all the breaths breathe along with it. This is how it is," said Indra. "Yet there are degrees of superiority among the vital breaths."

3. One may live without speech, for we sometimes see dumb people. One may live without sight, for we sometimes see blind people. One may live without hearing, for we sometimes see deaf people. One may live without mind, for we sometimes see witless people. One may live with arms or legs cut off, for we sometimes see people without limbs. But it is Life, the conscious Self, which takes hold of this body and makes it stand erect. Therefore one should meditate on this as a praise. By means of Life everything is obtained. Life is consciousness and consciousness is Life. For these two reside together in the body and together they quit. . . .

This is the theory and understanding thereof: when a person is asleep without seeing any dream, then he is absorbed into Life alone. Then speech together with all names is absorbed, the eye together with all forms, the ear together with all sounds, the mind together with all thoughts. Then, when he wakes up, just as sparks spring forth in all directions from a burning fire, similarly from this *ātman* all the vital breaths proceed to their proper places and from there to the senses and from the senses to the sense objects. This Life, consciousness, sizes the body and makes him rise. Therefore one should meditate on this as a praise. By means of Life everything is obtained. Life is consciousness and consciousness is Life. This is the proof and understanding thereof: when a sick person is about to die, having become very weak, he loses consciousness. People say of him: "His mind has departed, he neither hears nor sees nor speaks words nor thinks; then he is absorbed into Life. Then speech together with all names is absorbed, the eye together with all forms, the ear together with all sounds, the mind together with all thoughts. And when he departs from his body, he departs together with all these."

■ i) 1. Pippalāda was a great master of the AV to which this U belongs.

With fuel in their hands: *samitpāṇayaḥ*, a sign of humility in approaching a *guru*, implying the disciple's readiness to serve him.

2. Cf. § I 37.

3. There is a pun here: *kutaḥ*, whence, *prajāḥ*, [these] creatures, *prajāyante*, have been born.

4-5. The "couple" consists of Matter, *rayi*, which has also been interpreted as food and is connected with the Moon as its symbol, and *prāṇa*, energy, the Sun, translated throughout this passage as Life. Tradition has also speculated on the fact that *rayi* is feminine and *prāṇa* masculine. For the description of the Sun, cf. MaitU VI, 8. There is a relation between *prāṇa* (life-force), *āditya* (light-force), and *agni* (the force of the fire).

6-7. Cf. § III 6.

8. He: i.e., the sun.

He blazes: *tapantam*, giving heat, blazing.

■ ii) 1. Powers: *devāḥ*, supporting divinities, or deities presiding over man's activities, i.e., his senses and organs. The question is: which constituent parts or component forces make visible, bring to the light, make manifest, or illumine a creature? Cf. the root *div-*, to shine, from which comes *deva*, divinity, power.

2. Mind: *manas*.

4. Queen (of the bees): lit. "king."

5. Plenteous Rain: Parjanya. The equations of the Upaniṣads are in triads: *prāṇa-agni-sūrya; pṛthivī-rayi-deva; sat-asat-amṛta;* Parjanya-Maghavān (Indra)-Vāyu. There may also be a correlation between the corresponding member of each triad, viz. *pṛthivī-sat; rayi-asat; deva-amṛta*.

6. The nobility: the kṣatriyas.

The priesthood: the *brāhmaṇas*, brahmins.

7. Lord of creatures: Prajāpati. Cf. a similar idea in AV XI, 4, 19 (§ II 5).

8. Chief mediator: *vahnitama*, superlative, "best carrying," "best vehicle." Cf. YV XXXI, 19-20.

Truthful Way: *caritaṁ satyam*, moral conduct.

9. By your splendor: *tejasā*, or sharpness.

Lord of all lights: *jyotiṣāṁ patiḥ*.

10. They dwell in happiness: *ānandarūpās tiṣṭhanti*.

11. Primordial: *vrātya*, a noninitiated person, i.e., one who has not received the sacramental consecration, the *saṁskāras* which make him a full member of the community. Through a so-called *nindāstuti*, a figure of speech in which a word of contrary meaning is used to express what is intended, *vrātya* has been here interpreted as one who does not need ceremonial initiation because he is already totally pure and purified, thus, "ever pure," primordial. Historically speaking the *vrātyas* are thought to have been Aryans living outside the Brahmanical culture. Cf. the whole AV XV dedicated to them.

Lord: *satpatiḥ*, lit. true Lord.

Consumer: lit. eater of all.

Mighty Wind: Mātariśvan.

12. Benevolent: *śiva*, auspicious.

13. Happiness and understanding: *śrī* (success, prosperity) and *prajñā* (intelligence, wisdom).

■ iii) 1. Internal self: *adhyātma*.

3. By the action of the mind: *manokṛtena*, though Deussen reads *mano'kṛtena* and thus translates: "ohne Zutun des (bewussten) Willens."

5. Downward breath: *apāna*.

Distributive breath: *samāna*.

In a balanced way: i.e., the *samāna* distributes the food in the body.

Seven flames: cf. the conception of food as a sacrifice, hence the allusion to the seven flames of Agni (cf. MundU I, 2, 4; § III 27) applied to the "fire of digestion."

6. Artery: *nāḍī*. Cf. CU VIII, 6, 6, and BU II, 1, 9 (§ VI 4).

Diffused breath: *vyāna*.

7. Upward breath: *udāna*.

Goodness: *puṇya*.

Evil: *pāpa*. A reference to the new conception of transmigration (cf. also PrasnU I, 9).

8. The anthropocosmic relations are: sun-eye-*prāna*, earth-*apāna*, *ākāśa-samāna*, *vāyu-vyāna*.

9. Fire: *tejas*, heat or energy.

10. Thought: *citta*, state of mind. Continuation of the idea in v. 8. Cf. CU VIII, 14, 1.

12. Fivefold lordship: the fivefold division of the one breath of life.

■ iv) Cf. BU III, 9, 9 (§ VI 2), for *prāṇa* as *brahman* and also TU III, 3 (§ II 11).

Powers: *devatāḥ*.

5. Cf. § III 28.

■ v) 1. Cf. § IV 21.

2. Life: *prāṇa*.

The conscious Self: *prajñātman*, over against *prajñā* as mere consciousness. Cf. KausU II, 14.

Temporal life: *āyus*, the accent being on fullness of temporal life.

Immortality: *amṛta*. *Āyus* and *amṛta* are often linked together in the B and U.

Correlation: *prāṇa-prajñātman, āyus-amṛta*, on the one hand and *prāṇa-āyus; prajñātman-amṛta*, on the other.

This world: the other world according to recension A.

True thinking: *satya saṁkalpa*, true conception, true desire, purpose, will, the totality of a person's thoughts and feelings in tune with truth. *Satya saṁkalpa* is *prajñā*, or rather, by *prajñā* the *saṁkalpa* becomes *satya*. Cf. CU VII, 4, 3 (§ VI 3).

Vital breaths: *prāṇāḥ*. The plural here has undoubtedly this meaning.

3. Cf. BU VI, 1, 7-14; CU V, 1, 6-15 on the superiority of *prāṇa*.
Makes it stand erect: *utthāpayati.*
Praise: *uktha;* cf. KausU II, 6. Play of words with *utthā(payati),* cf. BU V, 13, 1. For an allegorical interpretation of *uktha* cf. AA II, 1. Cf. also SB X, 6, 2, 8.
Consciousness: *prajñā.*
For these two . . . : omitted in recension B.
Theory: *dṛṣṭi,* seeing, vision.
Senses: *devāḥ,* "gods."
Sense objects: *lokāḥ,* "worlds."
This passage has some variants in the two standard recensions A and B.

Above Time Is Set a Brimful Vessel — *Pūrṇaḥ kumbhaḥ*

7 The poet-sages of the Ṛg Veda do not mention the term "time"[35] nor do they try to elaborate on the nature of time; yet they are not only living in time, but also "living time" and speaking of a most temporal way of existence. They earnestly pray to "live a hundred years," to live "forever," and they are certainly conscious of the temporal nature of existence, that life is ever fleeting and always too short. They wish to halt the march of time by means of cultic acts, but they encourage Men to live in accordance with the rhythm of nature: day and night, the seasons, the year, the human cycle. Hardly ever can one detect an attitude of escapism from time into the timeless. All three worlds are temporal.

The Atharva Veda, which places so much stress on the cosmic rhythms,[36] contains, however, two speculative hymns on the subject of time. In these hymns there is an exaltation of time as that which cannot be transcended and thus must be glorified and divinized. Time is at the beginning and time will be at the end; nothing escapes time, for only in time can beings be.

Hymn XIX, 53, starts with an involved metaphor in which time is pulling a chariot, thought to represent the sun. This vast chariot, whose wheels are composed of all existent creatures, is drawn by time in the shape of a horse. We are thus introduced straightway to an all-inclusive vision that is cosmic in range and metaphysical in tone. The next verses, under the cloak of ascribing honor to time, tend in fact to emphasize the absolute character of temporal relativity. Time created everything, even the Creator himself, not perhaps metaphysically in a timeless ontology, but certainly in our

35. The only exception is the late RV X, 42, 9, where the word is used with reference to the player throwing his dice when his turn comes.
36. Cf. for instance AV X, 8, 23 (§ VII 27).

temporal reality, for lordship over temporal creatures can be meaningful only if it is temporal. Prajāpati, insofar as he is the Father of temporal beings, is temporal in his fatherhood. Time is a concomitant dimension of everything under and above the sun.

There is one enigmatic verse of particular interest in this hymn of incomparable beauty and extraordinary suggestive force: "Above Time is set a brimful vessel." Time is said to replenish itself from a full vessel which, in spite of all efforts, can never be emptied. If from the full one draws away even the full, the full remains, says the famous invocation of the Īśa Upaniṣad. Unlike the Upaniṣads, the Vedas seem to interpret this principle as the inexhaustible reality of time; the vessel set upon time is so full that, however much is drawn from it, time will never empty it. Every text can be twisted and interpreted according to what we read into it, but the clear impression given by the two following hymns is not that of a world-denying spirituality. It is not the timeless, but the "timefull," which wins Vedic approbation.

Pūrṇaḥ kumbhaḥ — AV XIX, 53

1. Time drives like a horse with seven reins,
a thousand-eyed unaging Stallion.
Him the inspired poets mount.
All beings are his chariot wheels.

2. Time draws this chariot with seven wheels.
Seven are the hubs; its axle is nondeath.
At the head of all beings Time proceeds
unceasingly, the first among the Gods.

3. Above Time is set a brimful vessel.
Simultaneously we see Time here, there, everywhere.
Set face to face with all existences,
Time is throned, men say, in the loftiest realm.

4. Time has gathered together all beings that are;
he has passed through all the gathered beings.
He who was father has become their son.
There is no glory higher than his.

5. Time generated the Sky above
and this vast Earth. The passing moments,
present and future, by him set swinging,
are reckoned out in due proportions.

6. Time brought forth fate-filled chance.
In Time the Sun shines and burns.

In Time the eye spies from afar.
In Time all existences are.

7. In Time is consciousness and life,
In Time is concentrated name.
By Time, when he draws close at hand,
all creatures are with gladness filled.

8. In Time is energy, in Time the highest good.
In Time is the Holy Utterance.
Time is the Lord of all that is,
the Father, he, of the Creator.

9. Sent forth by him, from him all this
was born. On him is it established.
So soon as he has become Brahman,
Time supports the highest Deity.

10. Time created the creatures. Time
created in the beginning the Lord of creatures.
From Time comes the Self-Existent.
Energy likewise from Time derives.

1. The image of the horse and the seven reins is taken from the symbolism of the Sun in the RV. Cf. RV I, 164, 2. Cf. AV XIII, 2, 38, where the Sun is homologized to Time. The seven reins may represent a perfect number, or the rainbow, or they may stand for the seven regions of space or, more probably, the seven parts of the year, viz. six double months and one intercalary month. Cf. AV X, 8, 5 (§ VII 27).

Unaging Stallion: or, abundant seed (of which the stallion is the image).

3. A brimful vessel: *pūrṇaḥ kumbhaḥ*, the full jar set upon time. Cf. AV X, 8, 14-15; 29 (§ VII 27). We may relate v. 29 to the often repeated topic of fullness in BU V, 1 (§ VI A Antiphon) or the IsU Invocation (§ VII 6). Cf. also the "golden vessel" covering the face of truth; BU V, 15, 1; IsU 15 (§ VII 31); MaitU VI, 35 (§ VI 8).

Realm: *vyoman*, firmament.

5. Time is here regarded as the axis around which future and past revolve.

Set: *vitiṣṭhate: vi-sthā-* (*kāle ha* stands for *kālena*) means spread (or diffused) over (or through), or inserted at different positions or proportions. In time are set the past and the future in rotation (in a recurrent series).

6. Several readings are put forward: Time created either *bhūta*, i.e., reality, what is, or *bhūmi*, the earth, or *bhūti*, prosperity, auspicious time, chance, in the sense of the Greek word *kairos*, which means propitious or appointed time and is perhaps etymologically connected with *kāla*.

7. Consciousness: *manas*, mind.

Life: *prāṇa* or life-breath.

The name, *nāman*, seems to survive beyond the time of the individual. Cf. BU III, 2, 12 (§ V 12).

8. Energy: *tapas*, also in v. 10.

Highest good: *jyeṣṭha*, *summum bonum*.

Holy Utterance: *brahman*.

Lord: *īśvara*.

Creator: Prajāpati.

Because of AV X, 7, 24; 32-34 (§ I 3), and XI, 5, 5; 23, some relate *jyeṣṭha* to *brahman* and the text would then read: In Time is distilled the All-powerful *brahman*.

9. Sent forth by him: i.e., by Time.

All this: i.e., all that exists, the whole universe.

Brahman: holy word.

The highest Deity: Parameṣṭhin, the Highest, the most exalted One, the Sovereign: a cosmic principle and a personified God, or another epithet for Prajāpati. Cf. AV IX, 3, 11 (§ II 32); IX, 7, 1; X, 2, 20.

10. Self-Existent: Kaśyapa, a sage, sometimes said to be the husband of Aditi (the primordial Goddess) and also identified at times with Prajāpati; Kaśyapa is *svayaṁbhū*, self-existent.

Upon Time All the Worlds Repose *Kāla*

8 Hymn XIX, 54, which originally may have formed a unit with the preceding one, uses the same cosmic imagery and speaks of the sacrifice that time set in motion.[37] It is here that later speculations have seen the first signs of a nontemporal transcendence.[38] Through sacrifice Man overcomes his human condition in order to have access to the divine existence. Now, the problem is whether this superior form of existence is temporal or whether it transcends time. Our hymn seems unequivocally in favor of a rather secular—not profane—interpretation. By means of Brahman, the Holy Word, by means of sacrifice, time conquers this world—not another—and marches on.

A more powerful affirmation of the supremacy of Time would be hard to find. Everything is temporal and time stands at the beginning of everything. These two hymns are endeavoring to stress as emphatically as possible that even the "beginning," to which the more specifically metaphysical Vedic hymns allude, cannot escape the clutches of time, for *agre,* "in the beginning," becomes a temporal concept.[39]

Kāla AV XIX, 54

1. From Time came into being the Waters,
from Time the Holy Word, Energy, and the regions.
By Time [each day] the Sun arises,
in Time he goes to rest again.

2. By Time blows the cleansing Wind,
through Time the vast Earth has her being.
The great Heaven has his post in Time.

3. Their son Time long ago engendered
the things that were and that shall be.
From Time came Scripture into being
and formulas for Sacrifice.

4. By Time was Sacrifice inaugurated,
inexhaustible oblation to the Gods.
In Time live the spirits and the nymphs.
Upon Time all the worlds repose.

37. This idea is frequent in the B. Cf. SB I, 2, 5, 13; I, 7, 3, 3; AB II, 17 (VII, 7); etc.
38. Cf. SV VI, 19 (§ I 28), where God is called *amṛtasya paraṁ setum,* "supreme bridge of immortality!"
39. The difficult etymology of *agra,* summit, beginning, has in any case spatiotemporal connotations: it means "first" either in space (top, peak) or in time (beginning, origin).

5. In Time are set this Aṅgiras
and Atharvan who came from Heaven,
both this world and the world above,
all holy worlds and holy interspaces.

6. Having conquered the worlds by Holy Word,
Time, the God supreme, goes on.

1. Holy Word: *brahman,* also in v. 6.
Energy: *tapas.*
2. There are some variants in the Berlin and Bombay editions.
The cleansing Wind: *vātaḥ pavate,* lit. the Wind cleanses, purifies; this stresses the metaphor of movement.
3. Their son: i.e., Earth and Heaven's.
Scripture: the *ṛc* verses.
Formulas for Sacrifice: *yajus,* sacred prayers.
4. Spirits and nymphs: Gandharvas and Apsarases. Cf. AV XII, 1, 23 (§ I 19).

The Discovery of the Nontemporal *Akāla*

9 There is a *kumbha,* a jar, a vessel that is above time,[40] the Atharva Veda tells us. This pitcher is so full that it is the origin of time inexhaustible. The Upaniṣads attempt to peep into and take possession of the jar in its entirety. The Vedas themselves had suggested the method: breaking the jar by means of sacrifice. The Upaniṣads now assert that this sacrifice must be an internal and spiritual one.

Here is something new and different. Man now is curious; he is concerned to see the jar and not only to enjoy the flow of time that streams from the jar. The jar, that is to say, the container of time, the source of time, cannot also be temporal. We are here approaching one of the most momentous periods of human history: the breaking of "the brimful vessel above time." Perhaps failure will be the outcome of this effort and all that will remain will be the broken pieces of the broken jar, which Man will then have painfully to reconstruct. Maybe the ancient seers had seen our time also.

The adventure of living starts, according to the Upaniṣads, with a twofold discovery, namely, that interiorization is the means of grasping reality, and that nontemporal reality consists of pure transcendence. This epoch-making discovery, while it has led some people to the highest peaks of human experience, has also been the

40. Cf. § II 7.

cause of a strange degeneracy when Man is not capable of living and breathing on such heights. The Upaniṣads begin with a criticism of time. Time is contingent; the earth dissolves; time is folded up. They follow with extolling the intemporal. God alone remains.

The Śvetāśvatara affirms that that which is above time, that in which everything begins and ends, is God. He is the Lord, indeed the very maker of time,[41] for time is also a creature. He it is, the Lord of happiness, that Men should know.

The Maitrī Upaniṣad endeavors to build a bridge and speaks of two kinds of Brahman, of two aspects of ultimate reality, one temporal and the other nontemporal. The former is cosmological; it is thus related to the sun and to the year and belongs to that famous one-fourth of reality which is manifest and graspable. The latter is that which remains when all else falls into ruin, the Brahman without qualities, pure apophatic transcendence.

Later on the Bhagavad Gītā put this into simpler words in the mouth of Lord Kṛṣṇa: "Time am I, world-destroying and mature."[42] Yet Kṛṣṇa had already identified himself with "imperishable time,"[43] so as to stress equally the transcendence and the immanence of the Lord. Never has there been a time, the Bhagavad Gītā also declares, in which creator and creatures did not exist.[44]

Between these two aspects of reality, the temporal and the timeless, oscillate not only the whole of Vedic wisdom but also the universal thinking of mankind. Monodimensional Man, as also monodimensional reality, means death and stagnation. Indeed, the balance is not easy to maintain and a dichotomy is no less harmful than a monistic vision. A subtle form of such a dichotomy, and perhaps one of the most harmful, consists in conferring upon the nontemporal some of the characteristics of temporality; so as to imagine, for instance, that "eternal" life comes "after" this temporal one or that it is "beyond," "behind," or whatever other spatial or temporal word we may use to approach that which by very definition transcends both space and time.

The experience of movement is totally absent in the Upaniṣadic discovery of the nontemporal. Thus it is not an extrapolation in

41. Cf. KathU IV, 13 (§ VII 52): "the Lord of what has been and what is to be." Cf. MandU 1 (§ VI 12) in which OM (*brahman* and *ātman*) transcends time.

42. BG XI, 32.

43. BG X, 33.

44. Cf. BG II, 12. Cf. also II, 20. For other relevant texts of the Gītā on time, cf. BG IV, 2; VII, 26; IX, 7.

either a vertical or a horizontal direction which leads to eternity. You can always go deeper and always beyond; you can always postulate a "fore-beginning" and an "after-end." In this procedure you may be inclined to postulate other worlds, other times, births and rebirths, but you will never reach the nontemporal. The way to it is not the dynamic movement of our mind or the onward thrust of our will, but the static quiet, the acquired rest of our entire being in our inmost depths, the total extinction of desires, thoughts, and movements, both inside and out. Nothing could be more harmful than pretending that we have reached with our mind that which can only be "reached" without mind, or that we have discovered as "something" that which can be neither "attained" nor "desired" nor "thought." To the dialectical question as to how, then, we talk about this ineffable, the only correct answer is that in fact we do not talk about it. "It is not understood by those who understand it; it is understood by those who do not understand it."[45] Is not this also a blessing of the Lord? There is no dynamism leading to the timeless. *Stasis* here "stands" before *dynamis*. This is yoga in a single *sūtra*.

Akāla

SU VI, 1-6

i) 1. Some sages say that inherent nature, others
that time is this world's cause. Both are mistaken.
It is the grandeur of God within this world
by which this wheel of Brahman is made to turn.

2. By whom the universe is ever encompassed, the Knower,
the Author of time, possessor of all qualities, omniscient.
Ruled by him, the world of creation unfolds—
that which is regarded as earth, water, fire, air, and space.

3. When he has performed this work of creation he ceases,
then enters into union with Being by means of his Being,
by one, two, three or eight categories, by time
or the subtle qualities that appertain to the *ātman*.

4. Having begun with works accomplished by the qualities,
he assigns a destiny to all existent beings.
So soon as these cease to be, the work done is destroyed.
At the work's destruction he continues, essentially other.

5. He is the beginning, the cause of this world's cohesion,
to be viewed as transcending the three times—also as partless.

45. KenU II, 3 (§ VI 4).

Worship him first as the Adorable of many forms,
the origin of all existence, in his own thought subsisting.

6. Higher and other is he than all that this world-tree
and time produce. From him this world evolves.
Know him as the bringer of good, the remover of evil,
the Lord of happiness, established within your own *ātman*,
the immortal whose abode is the universe.

MaitU VI, 14-16

ii) 14. It has been said elsewhere that food is the origin of this whole world, that the origin of food is time and, again, that the origin of time is the sun. The form of time is the year, which consists of twelve months and is composed of moments and other measurements of time. Of this one half belongs to Agni (when the sun moves northward) and the other half to Varuṇa (when the sun moves southward). The course from the sign of Magha to half of Śraviṣṭha belongs to Agni, while the course from the sign of Sarpa to half of Śraviṣṭha belongs to the moon. Concerning the year, each of its [parts] consists of nine parts, according to the corresponding course of the sun. Because of the subtlety [of time] this [course of the sun] is a proof, for only by this is time proved to exist, and without proof there is no ascertaining of the thing to be proved. The thing to be proved, however, may be proved because it is distinct and because it reveals itself. About this it has been said: As many divisions of time as there are, in all of these moves yonder sun. From the one who reveres time as Brahman time recedes far away. For thus has it been said:

From time all beings emerge.
From time they advance and grow.
In time, too, they come to rest.
Time is embodied and also bodiless.

15. There are, we aver, two forms of Brahman: time and the timeless. That which is prior to the sun is the timeless; it has no parts. That which begins with the sun, however, is time and this has parts. Now the form of this latter which has parts is the year. From this year, to be sure, are creatures produced; through the year, to be sure, they grow and in the year they disappear. The year, therefore, is assuredly the Lord of creatures, is time, is food, is the abode of Brahman, is the Self; for, as the saying goes:

It is time that cooks all created things
in [the vast cauldron of] his great Self.
In what, however, is this same time cooked?
He who knows this, knows the whole Veda.

16. This embodied time is the royal ocean of creatures. In it stands he who is called Savitṛ, the impeller, from whom the moon, stars, planets, the year, and everything else is begotten. And from them comes the whole

world, as well as whatever is good or evil in this world. Therefore Brahman is the self of the sun. Indeed one should revere the sun under the name of time. Some, in fact, say: "Brahman is the sun." Moreover, it has been said:

> The priest, the enjoyer, the offering, the sacred word,
> the sacrifice itself, Viṣṇu and Prajāpati,
> all these are the Lord, the Witness, the one
> who shines up yonder in the orb of the sun.

■ i) 1. Inherent nature: *svabhāva.*

2. Author of time: *kālakāra.*

Ruled by him: *teneśitam,* cf. the beginning of KenU: *keneṣitam* . . . ("directed by whom . . . ?"), KenU I, 1 (§ VI 3), although the two verbs are from different roots.

The work of creation unfolds: *karma vivartate.* Cf. the later Vedāntic theory of "creation" as *vivarta.*

3. Union: *yoga.* Only the part of reality which corresponds to the Reality of the Creator can be united with him.

Being: *tattva,* "thatness," reality.

Categories: one, i.e., nature; two, i.e., the manifest and unmanifest; three, i.e., the three qualities of nature (*guṇa*); eight, perhaps the five sense organs and three aspects of the "inner organ."

4. *Karman,* consisting of the *guṇas,* shapes the destiny of all beings, yet it is controlled by the Lord.

The work done is destroyed: *kṛta-karma-nāśaḥ,* liberation from *karman* is emancipation. Cf. also MundU II, 2, 9 (§ VI 11).

Essentially other: *tattvato'nyaḥ,* the *puruṣa* who is "the other" by definition (in Sāṁkhya).

5. Traditionally the three times have been interpreted as past, present, and future.

The origin of all existence: *bhavabhūta,* having become all that has become.

In his own thought subsisting: *sva-citta-stha,* established in his own consciousness.

6. World-tree: cf. KathU VI, 1 (§ V 5).

Lord of happiness: *bhageśa.*

Whose abode is the universe: *viśva-dhāma.*

7-9. Cf. § I 28.

10-13. Cf. § VI 2.

■ ii) 10a-13, Cf. § II 11.

14. Cf. AV XIX, 53 and 54 (§§ II 7; 8).

Origin: *yoni,* womb, source.

Belongs to Agni: *āgneya,* because of the heat of summer.

Varuṇa: because of the rainy season (Varuṇa is the God of the waters).

Concerning the year . . . : another translation of this sentence reads: "In this (reckoning) every single (month) of the (year) itself amounts to nine quarters after the fashion of (reckoning) by the progression of lunar mansions" (Van Buitenen). The nine parts are nine quarters, arrived at by the division of the twenty-seven constellations (*nakṣatra*) through the twelve months. Time is embodied and also bodiless: *kālo mūrtir amūrtimān,* i.e., with and without form.

15. Lord of creatures: Prajāpati.

Self: *ātman.* Cf. the saying of the Mokṣadharma: "time matures all beings by itself. But no one here on earth knows him in whom Time is matured" (MB XII, 231, 25; Edgerton's translation).

16. Cf. CU III, 19, 1 for the quotation "Brahman is the sun."

The Lord, the Witness: *prabhuḥ sākṣī,* a reference to the *puruṣa* in the sun.

17. Cf. § VI 2.

b) Food

Anna

Human life, in order to exist, to grow, to develop, depends upon food, Where there is no food there are hunger, famine, and death. Food, indeed, is the source of life. These are simple platitudes, but Vedic man succeeded in elevating them into lofty intuitions without divorcing them from the elemental earthly realities to which they refer. Food is not only a condition for life, so that life must eat in order to live. Food is the very stuff of life. One type of life will require one type of food and another type another, but food will be indispensable for its support all along the way. Do not despise food, say our texts; reverence food, worship food, discover that food is sacrifice and that food is Brahman. Food is our life, says the Rg Veda.[46]

The Soma spirituality, or the theology of Soma, if we prefer, is also a speculation about the mystery of food;[47] nor is there any reflection on the nature of sacrifice without mention of the essential part that food plays in it. The Śatapatha Brāhmaṇa recalls the primordial sacrifice of Prajāpati and addresses Agni, the firstborn of the mouth of Prajāpati, as a consumer of food.[48] It relates how Prajāpati, because there was no other food than himself, had to reproduce himself.[49] "Sacrifice is the food of the Gods," says another text.[50] It is for this reason that food is the highest offering and that, when one offers food to the father, the husband, the family, the guests (whether friends or monks or mendicants), one performs not only a social but also a religious act, for man reenacts the primordial sacrifice and shares in that highest commerce through which the world subsists. This would also be the deeper explanation of a saying that is something more than an exhortation to hygiene: "If your food is pure, your whole nature will be pure."[51] Your being will be pure because your being is made out of and comes from food, not only in a physical but also in an ontological sense: creation is a cosmic metabolic act.

The first text of the subsection is Hymn I, 187, of the Ṛg Veda in which we may be surprised to discover that, unlike later Indian traditions, the act of eating is not only sacred but also social, an expression of communion not only among Men but also between

46. Cf. RV X, 107, 7; VIII, 3, 24, Cf. also RV X, 90, 2 (§ I 5), the hymn of the *puruṣa*, the Primordial Man, which also contains an allusion to food.
47. Cf. RV IX, 108, 13, and the intriguing text of SB III, 9, 4, 22.
48. Cf. SB II, 2, 4, 1 (§ I 6).
49. Cf. SB II, 2, 4, 3-7.
50. SB VIII, 1, 2, 10.
51. CU VII, 26, 2 (§ VI 3). The word *sattva-śuddhi* means purity of mind, of character, of the whole personality and being (*sattva*). The word for food here is *āhāra*: nourishment.

Men and the Gods. We may recall here that "he who eats alone is all sin,"[52] or, as the Bhagavad Gītā says: "Those who prepare food just for themselves are sinful: they eat sin."[53]

Although Soma is mentioned in verse 9, it is not certain that this hymn is addressed to him. Food imparts both physical and spiritual vigor and is appropriate even for the Gods, to whom it is offered in ritual sacrifice (v. 11). Indeed, any real food, that is, any nourishment that strengthens soul and body, is sacrificial food. This hymn has a very elaborate structure with well-planned parallels intended to stress the unifying character of food. Food, it says, keeps the body together and, even more, it keeps Men together in the deep fellowship of a shared table (v. 3). This is not all; food is viewed also as a sacred banquet in which the Gods are brought together to partake with Men. Friendship, human and divine, implies a sharing in that which constitutes our basic and common ground, for through food we assimilate, make our own, what was until now on the periphery of our beings. There is no friendship without a common morsel of food.[54] Eating is a sacred act because food is in itself a holy reality, as is disclosed in the Vedas.

From this text we are led on to the Upaniṣads where there are deep and involved dissertations on the subject of food. The Bṛhadāraṇyaka Upaniṣad takes the student right back to Prajāpati, the Father of creation, who produced for all their proper food, one food common to all beings, food for the Gods, namely the sacrificial fire and the offerings, food for Men and animals, namely milk, and a threefold form of food for himself: mind, life, and word. "For, my dear," says another Upaniṣad, "the mind consists of food, life consists of water, and the word consists of glow."[55] We may remember that this trilogy is the basis of the Upaniṣadic anthropology. Man is a unit of mind, life, and word, or of food, water, and glow.

We could equally well call these seven forms of food the seven elements at the basis of everything; but these elements are not like static bricks out of which the building of creation is made.[56] They

52. RV X, 117, 6.
53. BG III, 13 (§ III 29). Cf. also Manu III, 118.
54. It is precisely because India has taken so seriously the act of taking food together that all the restrictions and regulations (according to caste, etc.) have come to be.
55. CU VI, 7, 6.
56. Cf. MundU II, 1, 8 (§ VI 7).

are, on the contrary, dynamic particles that have to be "eaten," assimilated, transformed, in order that the construction of the world be maintained.

Then an important question arises: since food is always being consumed, assimilated, how does it come about that it does not dwindle? The answer is given here only in a cryptic way. He who knows the imperishableness of food goes to the Gods, and there he shares in the dynamic process of a continuous creation. Food and life go together, affirms the following text. There is an interdependence between them, so that neither alone can be said to be Brahman, but only the two combined.

The Chāndogya Upaniṣad, in a text given later, after reflecting upon the nature of sleep and of the breath of life, inquires into the origin of hunger and thirst. A man becomes hungry because what he consumes is forthwith digested. How then do we explain the fact that life continues? The conclusion is reached: we are a sprout and there is no sprout without a root. "What else could the root be other than food?"[57] From food a connection is traced to water, from water to fire, from fire to being (*sat*), and from there the text introduces us to the knowledge of the *ātman* by means of the famous formula *tat tvam asi*, "that you are."

A proper introduction to the remainder of the texts given here would require a whole treatise on Vedic cosmology and anthropology. We must therefore content ourselves with noting the stupendous crescendo of the texts and their theanthropocosmic connections. All is related and interdependent. The way to Brahman is not like a ladder whose earlier steps we may forget once we have reached a higher one. Brahman is not confined to the top but is in immediate contact with everything, and the mystery of food accompanies us all along the way. There is a process of assimilation, a cosmic metabolism which begins in the lowest strata of reality and continues up to the highest. The culmination is that extraordinary mystical song: "I am food, I am food, I, who am food, eat the eater of food!" There is no deeper unity than that produced by the eating of the other, just as there is no better love than that of being the food of the lover. The tension between *jñāna* and *bhakti*, knowledge and love, is harmoniously solved in the symbol of food. Even more,

57. CU VI, 8, 4 (§ VI 10).

in the eating and preparing of food, human action and divine action are both required; the *karma-mārga,* the way of action, is also integrated into the mystery of food. Matter and spirit are united in the food by which they subsist.

> He consists of mind, is the leader of body and life,
> and reposes on food, directing the heart.[58]

It is again the Bhagavad Gītā which sums it all up with terse simplicity:

> From food all creatures come to be:
> from rain comes food;
> from sacrifice is rain derived
> and sacrifice from works.[59]

A Sacred Meal for Gods and Men

Sadhamāda

RV I, 187

10

1. My song shall be of Food, producer of strength,
   through whom the Keeper of nectar smote the Demon.
2. O savory Food, Food of sweetness, you are our chosen
   for whom we long. Come, be our strong defender!
3. Come to us, Food our delight, bringing pleasurable refreshment.
   Be our friend, source of bliss and brotherhood.
4. Your flavors, O Food, are spread throughout space,
   high like the breezes they are scattered.
5. Those who share your sweetness with others are truly your friends.
   Those who keep your fine taste to themselves are stiff-necked wretches!
6. On you, O Food, is fixed the great Gods' desire.
   Great deeds were done under your sign, the Serpent slain.
7. If you have proceeded on high to the splendor of the mountain,
   even from there, sweet Food, return for our enjoyment.
8. From waters and plants we imbibe the choicest portion.
   Therefore, O Body, thrive; attain full stature.
9. We drink you, Soma, brew of milk and barley.
   Therefore, O Body, thrive; attain full stature.
10. You herbs and wheaten cakes, be wholesome and strengthening.
    Therefore, O Body, thrive; attain full stature.

58. MundU II, 2, 8 (§ VI 5).
59. BG III, 14 (§ III 29). Works: *karman,* as sacrificial actions.

11. We sing your praises, O Food. From you we obtain,
as butter from a cow, our sacrificial offerings,
O you, convivial feast of Gods and men.

1. Food; *pitu,* nurture, including both food and drink.
Keeper of nectar: Trita, a water deity, conqueror of demons, in particular, of Vṛtra (the demon). Cf. RV I, 52, 5; VIII, 7, 24.
3. Source of bliss and brotherhood: Lit. cause of joy, not of repugnance; bringer of enjoyment, free from malevolence.
4. Flavor: *rasā,* juice, essence.
The text has two significant parallel locatives: as in heaven (high), so on earth (spaces, regions).
5. Another parallelism.
6. On you is fixed, etc.: or, in you resides the spirit of the great *devaḥ,* the longing of great souls.
Sign: *ketu,* symbol, ensign.
The Serpent slain: reference either to Indra or to Trita as in v. 1.
7. Mountain: *parvata* which may also mean cloud.
8. O Body: *vātāpe,* vocative of *vātāpi: vātā* plus *āpi,* which may mean friend of Vāta, or wind-swelled, fermenting one (Soma) and, according to Sāyaṇa, the body.
8-10. The triple invocation refers to the two constitutive elements of Soma, one liquid (water, milk, mixture of sap) and one solid (herbs, plants), and it refers also to the ritual, sacramental act of nutrition.
10. Convivial feast: *sadhamāda.*

Food of Eternal Life

Annam brahma

BU I, 5, 1-3

11

i) 1. From the seven kinds of food
which the Father produced by intellect and ardor,
one of his foods was common to all beings,
two he assigned to the Gods,
three he made for his own use,
one he bestowed upon the animals.
On this everything is based:
both that which breathes and that which does not.
How is it then that these foods do not dwindle
when they are constantly eaten up?
He who knows this permanence
eats food with his mouth;
he goes to the Gods,
he lives on power.

[Thus the verses:]

2. "From the seven kinds of food
which the Father produced by intellect and ardor"

—that means that the Father produced it by intellect and ardor.

"One of his foods was common to all beings"

—that means that one of them, that which is eaten here, was common food. He who worships this food is not freed from evil because it is mixed.

"Two he assigned to the Gods"

—that means the fire offerings and the oblations. This is why one offers the fire offerings and the oblations to the Gods. Or else they say, they are the sacrifices of the new and the full moon. Therefore one should not sacrifice in view of any gain.

"One he bestowed upon the animals"

—that is milk, for on milk live men and animals in the beginning. This is why they first feed a newborn child with ghee or give him the breast. They call a newborn calf "One who does not eat grass."

"On this everything is based:
both that which breathes and that which does not"

—this means that on milk everything is based, both that which breathes and that which does not. There is a saying that he who for a year makes oblations with milk will escape recurring death. One should not understand this to be the case. For he who knows this, on the very day he makes the oblation he overcomes recurring death, because he offers all food to the Gods.

"How is it then that these foods do not dwindle
when they are constantly eaten up?"

—this means that the person is permanent, for it is he who again and again produces food.

"He who knows this permanence"

—this means that the person is permanent, for he produces food by constant meditation and sacred works. Food would be exhausted if he did not do this.

"Eats food with his mouth"

—this means that the mouth is the face, and he eats with his mouth.

"He goes to the Gods,
he lives on power"

—this is the praise.

3. "Three he made for himself"

—this means mind, word, and vital breath, which he made for himself. There is a saying: "I had the mind elsewhere, I did not see; I had the mind elsewhere, I did not hear." It is indeed by the mind that one sees, by the mind that one hears. Desire, conception, doubt, faith, unbelief, endurance, weakness, shyness, meditation, fear—all these indeed belong to the mind. This is why even if one is patted from behind one knows it through one's mind.

All that is sound is word. The word is by its intention, but is not in itself.

The in-breath, the out-breath, the sustained breath, the up-breath, the middle-breath—all this is vital breath. Indeed the *ātman* is made of word, mind, and vital breath.

BU V, 12, 1

ii) Some say that Brahman is food. This is not so, however, for food decays without the vital force. Others say that Brahman is the vital force. This is not so either, for the vital force fades away without food. Only when these deities unite together do they reach the highest state.

CU I, 11, 8-9

iii) Which is that deity?

"Food," he (Uṣasti Cākrāyaṇa) said, "for all beings on earth live by absorbing food. That is the deity referred to by your part of the recitation, and if you had chanted it without knowing this, despite my telling you, your head would have fallen off."

CU VII, 9, 1-2

iv) 1. Food, most certainly, is greater than energy. For if a man were to abstain from food for ten days, even though he might still be alive, he would not be able to see, hear, think, be aware of anything, act, or understand. Once he resumes eating, however, he will again be able to see, hear, think, be aware, act, and understand. Meditate then on food.

2. He who meditates on food as Brahman attains the worlds of food and drink. His freedom will extend to the limits of the realm of food, he who meditates on food as Brahman.

"Is there anything greater than food, sir?"
"Yes, there is something greater than food."
"Then please, sir, tell me about it!"

AU I, 3, 1-10

v) 1. He considered: "Here are the worlds and the guardians of the worlds. Let me create food for them."

2. He brooded over the waters and from the waters, thus brooded over, there emerged a form. That which was produced as that form is, indeed, food.

3. Having been so created, it wished to flee away. He sought to grasp it by

speech. He could not grasp it by speech. If indeed he had laid hold of it by speech, merely by talking [about food] one would have been satisfied.

4. Next he sought to grasp it by breath. He could not do so. If indeed he had laid hold of it by breath, merely by breathing [over food] one would have been satisfied.

5. Next he sought to grasp it by sight. He could not do so. If indeed he had laid hold of it by sight, merely by seeing food one would have been satisfied.

6. Next he sought to grasp it by hearing. He could not do so. If indeed he had laid hold of it by hearing, merely by hearing [about food] one would have been satisfied.

7. Next he sought to grasp it by the skin. He could not do so. If indeed he had laid hold of it by the skin, merely by touching food one would have been satisfied.

8. Next he sought to grasp it by the mind. He could not do so. If indeed he had laid hold of it by the mind, merely by thinking [about food] one would have been satisfied.

9. Next he sought to grasp it by the generative organ. He could not do so. If indeed he had laid hold of it by the generative organ, merely by emitting food one would have been satisfied.

10. Then he sought to grasp it by the out-breath. He grasped it. The grasper of food is what wind is. The one living on food is in truth what wind is.

TU II, 2

vi)

From food, indeed, are creatures born.
All living things that dwell on the earth,
by food in truth do they live
and into it they finally pass.
For truly food is the first of all beings
and therefore it is called the universal remedy.
Those who worship Brahman as food
assuredly obtain all the food they need.
For truly food is the first of all beings
and therefore it is called the universal remedy.
From food are all things born,
by food, when born, do they grow and develop.
Food is eaten by beings and itself eats beings.
Because of that its name is food.

TU III, 1-2; 6-10

vii) 1. Bhṛgu, the son of Varuṇa, approached his father Varuṇa and said: "Sir, instruct me about Brahman." He explained to him, saying: "Food, breath, sight, hearing, mind, word."

He said further: "That from which truly all beings are born, by which when born they live and into which finally they all return, that seek to understand; that is Brahman."

He disciplined himself and, having disciplined himself,

2. he realized that Brahman is food; for from food assuredly all beings are born, by food when born do they live and into food finally they all return.

6. He realized that Brahman is joy, for from joy assuredly all beings are born, from joy when born do they live and into joy they finally return.

This is the wisdom of Bhṛgu, son of Varuṇa, which was firmly based in the highest heaven and he who knows this has himself this same firm basis [in Brahman]. He becomes a possessor of food, a consumer of food. He becomes great in offspring and cattle, in the splendor of sacred knowledge and in renown.

7. Do not disparage food. That is a sound precept. Breath, assuredly, is food; the body consumes food and is itself based on breath, while breath is likewise based on the body. So food is based on food. He who knows that food is based on food, has himself a firm basis [in Brahman]. He becomes a possessor of food, a consumer of food. He becomes great in offspring and cattle, in the splendor of sacred knowledge and in renown.

8. Do not despise food. That is a sound precept. The waters, assuredly, are food. Light consumes food and is itself based on the waters, while the waters are likewise based on light. So food is based on food. He who knows that food is based on food, has himself a firm basis [in Brahman]. He becomes a possessor of food, a consumer of food. He becomes great in offspring and cattle, in the splendor of sacred knowledge and in renown.

9. One should produce abundant food. That is a sound pecept. The earth, assuredly, is food. Space consumes food and is itself based on the earth while the earth is likewise based on space. He who knows that food is based on food, has himself a firm basis [in Brahman]. He becomes a possessor of food, a consumer of food. He becomes great in offspring and cattle, in the splendor of sacred knowledge and in renown.

10, 1. Let a man not deny hospitality to anyone. That is a sound precept. Let him therefore lay in a large store of food in whatever way he can. Of such a man people will say: "Food just seems to accrue to him." If this food is prepared in an excellent way for others, it is prepared in an excellent way for him who gives. If it is prepared in a mediocre way, then it is prepared in a mediocre way for him. If it is prepared in in a miserable way for others, then it is prepared in a miserable way for him.

10, 5.
He who knows this,
having quit this world,
having come to the self that consists of food,
having come to the self that consists of mind,

having come to the self that consists of breath,
having come to the self that consists of understanding,
having come to the self that consists of pure joy,
wanders through these worlds
eating food to his fancy,
assuming forms to his fancy;
he stays still and sings the mystic chant:
Oh marvel, Oh marvel, Oh marvel!

10, 6. I am food, I am food, I am food!
I am an eater, I am an eater, I am an eater!
I am a poet, I am a poet, I am a poet!
I am the Firstborn of Cosmic Order,
before the Gods were, from the womb of eternity.
He who gives me to another, he alone preserves me.
I, who am food, eat the eater of food!
I have overcome the whole wide world.
He who knows this has golden radiance within.
Such is the hidden doctrine!

MundU I, 1, 8-9

viii) 8. By the power of ascetic fervor Brahman
expands and thence is food produced.
From food comes life, from life mind, thence truth,
the worlds and the immortality of works.

9. The one who is all-knowing and all-wise,
whose ascetic fervor is his wisdom,
from him this Brahman comes to birth,
composed of name and form and food.

MaitU VI, 10a-13

ix) 10a. Now there is still more to be known. There is a further modification of this sacrifice to the Self, namely, that which concerns food and the eater. This is the further explanation: the conscious Person is in the midst of matter. He is an enjoyer, for he enjoys the food of nature. Even this physical self is food for him, its agent being matter. Therefore that which is to be enjoyed has three qualities and the enjoyer is the person who resides within. The observation [of our senses] is a clear proof of this. Since animals spring from a seed and as seed is food, by this is explained the fact that matter is what is to be enjoyed. Residing within it, he enjoys. The food derived from matter by means of that transforming process owing to the distinction of the three qualities, from the intellect down to the separate elements, is the sign. By this, furthermore, the fourteenfold course is explained. This world called pleasure, pain, and delusion is made up of food. Now there is no apprehension of the type of a seed [cause] unless there is an offshoot [effect]. And even in its three states it [i.e., the seed] has the nature of food, that is, in childhood, youth, and old age. It has the nature of food owing to transformation. When matter becomes manifest, it can be perceived. In order to apprehend this manifestation, intelligence and other faculties such as determination, imagination, and ego sense develop, and in order to apprehend objects the five sense organs and the actions of the motor organs arise. Thus the manifest is food and the unmanifest is food. The enjoyer is free from qualities, but inasmuch as he is an enjoyer, it is evident that he possesses consciousness. Just as Fire is the eater of food among the Gods, and Soma is their food, so he who knows this eats food by fire. The physical self is called Soma. He who has the Unmanifest as his mouth is called Fire, because of the saying: "The person, indeed, with the Unmanifest as his mouth, enjoys the three qualities."

11. The highest form of Self is certainly this: namely food, for the breath of life is made of food. If a man does not eat, he becomes a nonthinker, a nonhearer, a nonfeeler, a nonseer, a nonspeaker, a nonsmeller, a nontaster, and he loses his breath of life. If, on the contrary, he eats, he becomes full of life-breath, he becomes a thinker, a hearer, a feeler, a speaker, a taster, a smeller, a seer. Because of this it has been said:

> From food, indeed, are creatures produced,
> all living things that dwell on the earth.
> Moreover by food, in truth, do they live
> and into it they finally pass.

12. Now it has been said elsewhere: all creatures here set to busily every day out of eager desire for food. The sun absorbs food through his rays and thereby diffuses heat. When supplied with food, living creatures digest it and it is by consuming food that fire also burns. Out of a desire for food Brahman fashioned this universe. Therefore a man should reverence food as the Self. For thus it has been said:

> From food created things are born;
> by food, once born, do they grow and develop.
> Food is eaten by beings and itself eats beings.
> Because of that its name is Food.

13. Now it has elsewhere been said: that form of the blessed Lord which is called "the Supporter of all things" is nothing other than food. For the breath of life is the essence of food, mind of life, the understanding of mind, and bliss of the understanding. The man who recognizes this will come to possess food, life, mind, understanding, and bliss. Recognizing this, he will eat the food of as many creatures here on earth as eat food, for he will abide in them.

For food, assuredly, prevents decay;
food is worshipful, so they declare.
Food is the life of animals, supreme;
food is a healer, so they say.

■ i) 1. Father: *pitā.*

Power: *ūrjas,* nourishment, strength, fullness. Cf. YV I, 1.

2. Worships: *upāste.*

Is not freed from evil: because the sacrificial food is not the one eaten by all, for this latter is polluted, mixed. Only sacred food is a protection against evil and sin.

In view of any gain: *iṣṭa,* an offering made with the desire of obtaining something.

Recurring death: *punarmṛtyu.*

Person: *puruṣa.*

Permanent: *a-kṣiti,* imperishable, undecaying.

Praise: *praśaṁsā.*

3. Mind, word, and vital breath: *manas, vāc, prāṇa.*

Intention: *anta,* end. The word differs from the sound by its intention or contents.

Not in itself: *eṣā hi na,* it (the word) is not. This is a cryptic sentence. Unlike a mere sound, the word cannot be separated from what it "words" or expresses.

■ ii) Vital force: *prāṇa,* breath of life.

Deities: *devatā,* superhuman powers.

■ iii) Note the play on words. Absorbing: *pratiharamāṇāni.*

Recitation: *pratihāra,* a part of the Sāma recitation. A spiritual interpretation is generally given to the last part of this text, viz., that without knowledge the ritual is dead.

■ iv) For the rest of CU VII and all the ref., cf. § VI 3 (v) and notes.

■ v) 2. Form: *mūrti.*

3. Speech: *vāc.*

4. Breath: *prāṇa.*

10. Out-breath: *apāna,* digestive breath.

Wind: *vāyu.*

One living on food: *annāyu.*

■ vi) Food is called *anna,* eatable, "eater," because beings both eat it and are eaten by it.

3-5. Cf. § VI 7.

6-7. Cf. § I 7.

8-9. Cf. § VI 7.

■ vii) 1. Cf. § VI A b Introduction.

2-5. The rest of 2 and following relate to *tapas, manas, vijñāna* and *ānanda* in a similar way.

6. Firmly based: *pratiṣṭhita.*

Sacred knowledge: *brahman.*

7. Sound precept: *vrata.*

Based on the body (and similar expressions): *pratiṣṭhita.*

10,1. Excellent way, mediocre, and miserable: lit. beginning, middle, and end.

10,2-10,4. Omitted.

10,6. Lit. I, food, eat the eater of food.

Hidden doctrine: *upaniṣad.*

■ viii) 8. Ascetic fervor: *tapas.*

Life: *prāṇa.*

9. Name-and-form: *nāma-rūpa,* i.e., individuals.

■ ix) 9. Cf. § III 28.

10a. This text is not only difficult, but is also corrupted (cf. van Buitenen's Vulgate).

Matter: *pradhāna,* lit. that which is put forward, hence, important or chief thing, but also chaos, unevolved nature, matter in this sense.

Nature: *prakṛti.*

The conscious Person: *puruṣa.*

Physical self: *bhūtātman.*

Even this physical self is food for him: i.e., the body is the "material" for the spirit.

Three qualities: *triguṇa,* in Sāṁkhya philosophy the constituents of *prakṛti* (nature), namely *sattva* (purity), *rajas* (activity), *tamas* (inertness, darkness).

The enjoyer: again according to Sāṁkhya, the *puruṣa* as the spiritual principle essentially different from nature.

Agent: *kartṛ,* maker.

Enjoyer is the eater and the enjoyed that which is eaten.

Sign: *liṅga,* here in the logical meaning of an effect that leads to a cause (cf. also KathU VI, 8; § VI 11).

Fourteenfold course: the five sense organs, the five motor organs, and the four aspects of the "inner organ."

Pleasure, pain, and delusion: *sukha, duḥkha, moha.*

Ego sense: *abhimāna* (here not *ahaṁkāra,* which is the usual term).

Just as Fire . . . : here the new (Sāṁkhya) anthropology is related to Vedic theology, and the following correspondences arise: Gods (conscious enjoyers), Agni (mediator, consumer of the oblations), Soma (food of the Gods), and, on the other side: the enjoyer (i.e., the conscious *puruṣa*), fire (the medium of transformation from matter to spirit), and food (the enjoyed, nature, matter).

Unmanifest: *avyakta,* i.e., matter (*pradhāna*).

10b. Cf. § III 28.

11. Highest form of Self: *paraṁ vā etad ātmano rūpam.*

The lines quoted are from TU II, 2 (*vi*).

12. Digest it: lit. cook it.

The lines quoted are also from TU II, 2 (*vi*).

13. Blessed Lord: Viṣṇu.

Food, life, mind, understanding, and bliss: *anna, prāṇa, manas, vijñāna, ānanda.*

B. AWAKENING AND COMING OF AGE

Manuṣyatā

The divine Power who has bound this girdle round us,
who tied us together and yoked us in one,
the divine Power under whose direction we progress,
may he lead us to the other shore and free us!

Daughter of Faith, born out of Fervor,
sister of the sages who mold the world,
grant to us, Girdle, powers of thought and wisdom,
grant to us ardor and manly vigor.

AV VI, 133, 1; 4[60]

The girdle extolled in this hymn is a powerful symbol of human maturity, power, and restraint, that is to say, of a disciplined freedom (for one is bound by one's own freedom); it possesses a material concreteness, but represents also a spiritual reality.[61] The girdle is what the three highest *varṇas* of tradition are accustomed to wear as a sign of their second birth, that is, of having undergone the initiation that makes them *dvija,* "born again." At the time of

60. The rite of the girdle refers to binding together master and disciple. The second line of the first verse: *yaḥ saṁ-nanāha ya u no yuyoja,* could be freely rendered: who equipped us for our work and set us to it. Divine Power: *deva.* Ardor and manly vigor: *tapas.*
61. Cf. § I E c Introduction.

initiation the girdle is a symbol of chastity and obedience and thus it represents the condition of the *brahmacārin*, the student, who is bent on gaining wisdom and progressing on the spiritual path.

The rise of human consciousness is undoubtedly the most important phenomenon that has yet happened in the evolution of the whole universe. One of the most exhilarating features of the Vedic Revelation is that it bears witness to this Awakening, even daring to speculate on it with that same almost unique unselfconscious consciousness with which the problem of reality is investigated, a reality that is at once both objective and subjective, thought and thinking, known and knower.

The ecstatic moment prevalent in Part I has to come to an end, or at least it simply happens that it comes to an end, by the self-discovery of the subject that is having the experience. In the course of time, Life, the Sun, and the Gods become partners in a dialogue that is still cosmic but now includes also the human. Man stands at the other pole of this relationship, and the fact that he now looks at his own end blurs his vision of the other. Man begins to suspect that it may well be that his desire for the Gods in fact constitutes them, at least partly, and that his own sense of beauty may also belong to the Sun as it really is; in that event neither the Gods nor the Sun may be considered simply as something objectively given and totally independent of Man's consciousness.

From now on, the horizontal vision, the evaluation of "things" around Man, will contain a reflection on Man himself: he will discover himself and his own projection in the outside world. That was not true of the vertical vision, when Man was not looking around but up to the heavens. The road to humanness is now open, and the vision is presented to us of a realistic humanness in which every value has a countervalue and every concept is ambivalent. Vedic Man begins to be aware of his own involvement in the universe. We are present here at Man's discovery of himself after he has discovered the Gods. "Man is the nearest to Prajāpati."[62]

The discovery of Man, moreover, like Man's encounter with God, is not an abstract or merely a mental process. In this discovery Man discovers that he has to be really born into personhood, that he has to establish a relationship with the other and also admit him into manhood (initiation), while the other for his part has to assume

62. SB II, 5, 1, 1.

Man to his own self (marriage and children).[63] Furthermore, in this discovery Man recognizes that these two steps are finite and not ultimate. This is the threshold of real life.

Each day Dawn, Uṣas, brings a renewal of hope; the Sun, Savitṛ, brings Earth to life with the warmth of his rays and she, the great Mother, bestows upon Men liberally the blessings of crops and herds. Upon this earth a child grows and develops, entrusted from birth to the care of the Gods, to Savitṛ, Indra, Sarasvatī. Now the young man is on the threshold of manhood, startled at the discovery of himself and of his own special relation to the world around him. Knowledge and love burgeon. Both must be developed. *Upanayana* and *vivāha,* initiation and marriage, are the two starting points. Both are initiatory rites. You do not know your bride; you do not possess knowledge, just as you do not possess love. Both will come and grow, like a plant, if the right seed and a good soil are there, and if the field is properly watered and tended.

What does Vedic Man see when he comes of age? He sees the three worlds: the other shore, his own bank, and the river in between; the heavens, the earth, and the atmosphere (or sky, as the *antarikṣa,* the "in-between," is sometimes translated). It is obvious that the picture of these three worlds has evolved considerably through the ages and that mythical literature has described them in rather different terms from the more philosophical speculations, which speak of knowledge and ignorance and the crossing over from the one to the other.

We may sum up this process of awakening to full human life by saying that we have here the process by which the human being becomes a person. The individual is biologically a single specimen of the human species. He is simply a part of the whole and, even when he acquires consciousness of the surrounding world and a certain awareness of himself as a different and peculiar element in the whole, he is not yet a person. He can perhaps function as a human being if society takes care of him and he conforms to the given pattern. In other words, the individual can act and behave as a human being as long as there is a superior instance, a higher "person," of which he is a part and on behalf of which he performs the acts he is required to do. This superior person can be the family, the tribe, the sect, the religious community, the region, the nation, or any other group that encompasses the whole of human existence.

63. When we say Man we mean the human being, though it has to be said, alas, that ancient civilizations mainly meant the male.

The individual becomes a person when he discovers that he is an unrepeatable complex of relations, a unique knot in a net of relationships; he becomes a person when his individual consciousness becomes aware of being neither a subject looking out upon an objective world nor an object being looked upon, and also looked after, by a superior authority (God, father, chief, husband, etc.), but when he discovers that he himself is subject and object at the same time, that he himself is the whole insofar as the whole is mirrored in him and passes through him.[64]

The Upaniṣads, as the end and crown of the Vedas, complement and refine the merely *karmakāṇḍic* or ritualistic view of human growth. They do so by developing the idea of that internal growth into truly mature human life which takes place only with the discovery of the *ātman*. Man reaches manhood when he discovers the existence of himself and of the world as two distinct but inseparable entities. Human maturity is reached the very moment we make the threefold discovery of ourselves, of others, and of the mysterious link that binds us together: (*a*) Initiation, (*b*) Love, and (*c*) Union.

a) Initiation into Human Life

Mānuṣyaprāpti

Unlike many other traditions, the Vedic Revelation does not stress human initiation as a particular act that men have to perform. Initiation certainly belongs to human growth and development; it takes place alike in the body and mind of the human being, just as it takes place also in the whole evolutionary process of the cosmos. When the right time comes, maturity appears. You do not kill yourself in order to be born anew, and yet a new birth occurs when the previous one is no longer sufficient, no longer "living."

In congruity with this spirit the transition from an undeveloped human life to full manhood is recognized and heralded, but it is not produced or brought about by a particular rite. The Vedic rite witnesses and sanctions rather than produces and effects. No Man, and much less Vedic Man, can live totally without rites. From olden times *rites de passage* have developed and some of them are given

64. Cf. § VI C a Introduction.

here. Initiation, however, would have no meaning or would have to be interpreted in an almost magical way, if Man had not already awakened to the mystery of human life, that is, to the personal discovery of love, though still without an object. This accounts for the two groups of texts of this subsection.

In fact, the first sign of coming of age is not a biological change but a psychological realization: the discovery of the other as a mysterious part of oneself; the realization that he or she is neither oneself nor an "other" and much less another self. The first initiation is not accomplished by a rite, but by a growth, by a personal discovery; the discovery that makes a human being a person. It is the discovery of the relationship of love, in which the other is not an instrument (to be manipulated according to one's own wishes) or a "thing," an obstacle or an enemy, but the beloved, the thou, and—ultimately—the I. The other is still one's own projection. Innocence has not yet been lost.

Loftier Than the Gods *Kāma*

12 Later speculations within the Indian tradition, as is true of other cultures also, have somewhat blurred the powerful, sober, and transparent conception of *kāma,* love, desire, which appears in the Vedic Revelation. It would be of little avail and merely retrograde to revert to a cosmic conception of love or to the unearthing of old myths; but, equally, we would be falsifying and impoverishing human experience if we were to ignore that area of human existence which is powerfully indicated in the texts of the Vedic Revelation. Here we have perhaps some of the deepest sayings regarding that fundamental human archetype.

Kāma, as we have already seen,[65] is considered to be the first principle of activity,[66] the creative and procreative force leading the supreme Being out of the closed circle of its own existence. It is a cosmic force, but not to be understood as a kind of blind energy or impersonal urge. On the contrary, the personal is so much included in the transpersonal element that *kāma* is said to be the first seed of mind, the firstborn of the Absolute and thereafter the loftiest characteristic of all created beings, and more particularly of human beings. *Kāma* is the driving force in any enterprise, the highest of all human qualities. There is one and the same urge stimulating the

65. Cf. RV X, 129, 4 (§ I 1).
66. Cf. BG III, 37, where *kāma* is said to originate from *rajoguṇa,* the principle of activity.

entire range of reality, one and the same energy pushing the universe to expand—and it is *kāma*. Without it there would be only death; time would shrink and reality would collapse. *Kāma* is not a hankering after what is lacking in the individual; it is not an imperfection and thus a cause of suffering. *Kāma* is not the proof that we have not yet arrived, that we are imperfect and enmeshed in unfulfilled longings and unsatisfied urges. *Kāma* is, on the contrary, the perfection of expansion, the quality of creativity, the positive dynamism to be more, to reach higher, to overcome what still stands in front of us, because the adventure of existence is not yet finished, although this unfinished character is just the opposite of the imperfect. A "finished" universe would be in fact finished, limited, finite, deadly, and not divine. *Kāma* proves not that we are poor pilgrims, still on the way, displaced persons in search of a paradise lost, but that we are divine sparks full of creative energy with our own part to play in the structuring of the world. Sharing in this power is indeed the first sign of awakening and coming of age. The adolescent is afraid to love to the extent that he is afraid to be.

Our hymn starts by addressing *kāma* as a powerful ally whose aid a man seeks to secure in his struggle against enemies of all sorts (vv. 1-19). This part consists of a long series of imprecations. Some have seen only magic practices in them, though their interpretation would appear somewhat more complex.

The last part of the hymn is devoted to an address to *kāma*, extolling him above all else. He has the primacy over all things, people, and Gods. He who has *kāma* has all; all goods come with him. Where *kāma* is, there no thoughts of evil intrude.

Kāma

AV IX, 2, 19-21; 23-25

19. Love is the firstborn, loftier than the Gods,
    the Fathers and men.
    You, O Love, are the eldest of all,
    altogether mighty.
    To you we pay homage!

20. Greater than the breadth of Earth and Heaven
    or of Waters and Fire,
    you, O Love, are the eldest of all,
    altogether mighty.
    To you we pay homage!

21. Greater than the quarters and directions, the expanses
 and vistas of the sky,
you, O Love, are the eldest of all,
 altogether mighty.
To you we pay homage!

23. Greater than all things moving and inert,
 than the Ocean, O Passion,
you, O Love, are the eldest of all,
 altogether mighty.
To you we pay homage!

24. Beyond the reach of Wind or Fire,
 the Sun or the Moon,
you, O Love, are the eldest of all,
 altogether mighty.
To you we pay homage!

25. In many a form of goodness, O Love,
 you show your face.
Grant that these forms may penetrate
 within our hearts.
Send elsewhere all malice!

19. Cf. RV X, 129, 4 (§ I 1), from which the idea and its expression are borrowed, though they are developed here in a more prominent way. We here use "we," instead of "I," "Fathers" for "ancestors," and "eldest" for "superior" (because born first).

20. The cosmic waters and Agni are meant here.

22. This verse (omitted) contains obscure names of insects and reptiles.

23. Moving and inert: lit. all that blinks and stands erect (*tiṣṭhati*), i.e., what moves and what does not, the animate and the inanimate.

Passion: *kāma manyo*, O Love (and) fury. *Manyu*, zeal, anger, wrath.

25. Malice stands for evil thoughts or prayers or other devices.

The First Seed of Mind — *Manaso retaḥ*

13 *Kāma* is not here seen, as in later speculation, as a psychological desire, much less as a mere desire for individual pleasure; desire has here no pejorative connotation. Desire is the dynamism inherent in the whole creation, in whatever way we may like to explain it. If it were not for this striving that we call love, the whole universe would be not only cold, but dead, and would not exist at all.

This hymn recalls that *kāma* existed from the beginning and was the first seed of mind. It then proceeds to express a rather subtle identification of and differentiation between the cosmic and primeval *kāma* and that of the individual. Sacrifice is here again the clue. There is an internal and almost inaudible dialogue going on in this hymn, from Love to love, from Desire to desire, from Heart to heart. Without *kāma* it is not possible to achieve anything whatsoever; but *kāma,* unlike other values, is the most universal gift bestowed upon the whole of creation.

Manaso retaḥ — AV XIX, 52

1. In the beginning was Desire,
the first seed of mind.
O desire, twin of Desire,
grant wealth to me!

2. Powerful, unshakable,
shining, companionable,
formidable victor,
grant power to me!

3. He who longed from afar
to furnish a pledge
in response to the eternal
was heeded by the regions.
By means of Desire
they generated light.

4. From Desire springs desire,
leaps from Heart to heart.
The mind of my people,
let that mind be mine!

5. Now prosper, Desire,
the desires of our hearts,
that we may succeed.
Accept this oblation!

1. Desire: *kāma,* translated as Love in the preceding hymn. Cf. also RV X, 129, 4 (§ I 1) for the source of this idea and also its expression in words.
Twin: as being of one origin.
Grant wealth: i.e., wealth and power for the sacrificer; cf. v. 2.
2. Companionable: i.e., a friend or companion to the person who seeks one.
3. Obscure verse. Cf. TA III, 15, 1.
To furnish a pledge: *pratipāṇāya,* lit. for the counterpledge, counterstake (meaning not clear).
Light: *svar,* heaven. It is longing desire and ardent prayer that create light and life.
4. The capital and small letters are intended to stress the anthropocosmic meaning of the verse.
5. Accept: lit. eat.

The Ritual *Upanayana*

14 Human life, like cosmic existence and divine reality, implies a decision, a taking in charge, the following of a direction, the shaping of events, and later the acceptance of what has been so shaped. In the human cycle the process means a coming-of-age so as to take one's life into one's own hands—except that the "one" is not necessarily always the individual. There is a period in human life, however, in which living implies more than sheer passivity. Both biologically and also intellectually and spiritually, creative force appears at a certain age. Man enters into life by living, that is, by overcoming death, setting limits for himself, and following his own path. Initiation is the relatively modern technical word for the *rite de passage* implied in reaching human maturity.[67]

We are not going to enter here into the peculiarities of the *dvija* or twice-born and the philosophy of the Hindu *saṁskāras* or sacraments. It is enough to remark that initiation in one way or another is a natural and universal phenomenon and that the elaborate texts we are giving belong to a post-Upaniṣadic period, though their roots are Vedic.

Since one feature of our times is the loss of proper and meaningful rites, the following rituals, though from another epoch, may well be a source of inspiration. We summarize and simplify by reducing to its essentials a ceremony that is still performed today in various ways. It may be divided into the following stages:

The presentation by the *ācārya* (teacher) to the boy of a *new garment*, symbolizing the new period of his life. Prayer is offered to the Goddess who wove the piece of cloth.

The presentation of the *girdle*, which represents the Goddess of the spirit of austerity (*tapas*) and both physical and mental vigor.

The presentation of the *sacred thread* (or sacrificial cord), which henceforth gives the initiate the right, or rather the power, to take part in the offering of the ritual sacrifice.

The presentation of the *deerskin*, followed by prayers beseeching the Gods to aid the student in his knowledge of the wisdom embodied in the Vedas.

The presentation of the *staff*, accompanied by a prayer in which the student is entrusted to the divine hierarchy.

67. *Upanayana* (from the verb *upa-nī-*, to lead near, to guide, etc.) lit. means the "leading near," "bringing close," i.e., of the disciple to the guru, and hence the act or rite of introduction to the guru and to sacred knowledge.

Having entrusted the student to the vigilant protection of the Gods, the *ācārya* accepts him as a disciple. The unity that has to exist between master and pupil is expressed in prayer and in the touching of the heart.[68]

The Sāvitrī mantra, by which the *dvitīya janman* or second birth is achieved, is now taught to the student.

Next follows the ceremony of the *Fire,* which sets a seal upon the unity of life which is to exist within the student.

The second section, the ceremony of the *departure,* consists of a *ritual bath* taken by the student at the end of his stay (which is generally of several years) with his master.

Before the bath the young man lights the ritual fire. The prayers during the bath, unlike those of the initiation ceremony which contain a note of austerity and renunciation, are full of joy and rejoicing in the good things of life.

Then, putting to one side his ascetic garb, the young man arrays himself in fine new clothing, bedecks himself with flowers, puts on a turban, earrings and new shoewear. He takes an umbrella in his hand and a bamboo staff.

He is now ready to live to the full his adult life, a life that will take its inspiration from the wisdom of the Scriptures.

Upanayana

New Garment

HGS I, 1, 4, 2

i) After the boy has removed his old attire the teacher clothes him in a new garment that has not yet been washed, saying:

"May the Goddess who spun, who wove, who measured and fashioned this garment, clothe you with long life! Put on this garment, endowed with life and strength.

"Clothe him! By this garment may he attain a life span of a hundred years. Lengthen his days. Bṛhaspati gave this garment to King Soma to put on.

"May you live to old age! Put on this garment. Be a protector of mankind against menacing speeches. Live a hundred years, full of vigor. Clothe yourself in ever increasing wealth."

68. We shall see the same ceremony in the celebration of a marriage; cf. § II 17 (vii).

PGS II, 2, 7

ii) "As Bṛhaspati clothed Indra in the garment of immortality, even so I clothe you, with prayer for long life, a good old age, strength, and splendor."

HGS I, 1, 4, 3

iii) Thus clothed [the boy], the following prayers [are said by the teacher]:

"For your own well-being you have put on this garment. You have become a protector of your friends against the curses of men. Live a hundred long years. May you be noble, blessed with fullness of life, sharing generously your wealth."

The Girdle

SGS II, 1, 28-29

iv) 28. After the teacher has offered sacrifice, they both stand behind the fire, the teacher facing East, the other facing West.

29. He should initiate him standing.

II, 2, 1

He ties the girdle from left to right [around the waist of the boy] three times, saying:

"Here has come to us this blessed girdle, friendly Goddess for our defense against evil words and for the purification of our family, investing us with strength by inhalation and exhalation."

The Sacred Thread

SGS II, 2, 3-12

v) 3. He fixes the sacred thread (saying):

"You are the sacred thread. With the sacred thread of sacrifice I initiate you."

4. He takes water in the hollow of his joined hands, the student also joining his hands, and says:

"What is your name?"

5. "I am so-and-so, Sir," replies the student.

6. "Descending from the same patriarchal sages?" asks the teacher.
7. "Descending from the same patriarchal sages," says the student.
8. "Declare yourself as a student."
9. "I am a student, Sir."
10. Then he sprinkles water three times with his joined hands on the joined hands of the student, saying: *"bhūr, bhuvaḥ, svaḥ!"*
11. Then, grasping the student's hands, with right hand uppermost, he says:
12. "By the vivifying power of God Savitṛ, with the strength of the two Aśvins and with Pūṣan's aid, I initiate you, so-and-so."

The Deerskin

HGS I, 1, 4, 6

vi) He then puts on him a deerskin as an outer covering and says:

"Put on this skin, noble so-and-so; may the firm strong eye of Mitra, his glorious splendor, powerful and shining, be a token of swiftness and self-control. Let Aditi gird your loins that you may know the Vedas, that you may acquire insight and faith, and, keeping what you have learned, that you may be endowed with goodness and shining purity."

The Staff

PGS II, 2, 11-12

vii) 11. The teacher hands him the staff.

12. The student accepts it saying:

"This staff which is falling from the sky upon the earth I now take up again, with prayer for life, fullness of spirit, and the splendor of Brahman."

The Dedication

SGS II, 3, 1-5

viii) 1. The teacher then says:

"Bhaga has grasped your hand,
Savitṛ has grasped your hand,
Pūṣan has grasped your hand,

Aryaman has grasped your hand,
Mitra are you now by law,
Agni has become now your master,
along with myself, so-and-so.
Agni, I entrust this student to you,
Indra, I entrust this student to you,
Āditya, I entrust this student to you,
All Gods, I entrust this student to you,
that he may have long life, a blessed posterity,
strength, frequent increase of riches, authority
in all the Vedas, high renown, and happiness."

3. The teacher touches the student's heart saying: "May your pure heart ever hold me dear."
4. He then turns, silently, from right to left.
5. And then, putting his hand with the palm up on the student's heart, he prays in a low voice.

SGS II, 4, 1; 5

ix) 1. "Under my direction I place your heart.
Your mind will follow my mind.
In my word you will rejoice with all your spirit.
May Bṛhaspati unite you with me.

5. "You are a student. Tend the fire. Drink only water.
Perform your service. Do not sleep in the daytime.
Keep silence till the lighting of the fire."

The Sāvitrī Mantra

SGS II, 5, 1-3; 8-12

x) 1. After a year the teacher recites the Sāvitrī mantra (to the student),
2. or, after three nights,
3. or, immediately.
8. They sit to the north side of the fire.
9. the teacher turning towards the East, the student toward the West.
10. Then the student says: "Recite, Sir!"
11. The teacher, after uttering the syllable OM, invites the student to say the mantra: "Recite the Sāvitrī, Sir."
12. Then he recites for him the Sāvitrī, that verse, "That glorious Sāvitrī," at first verse by verse, then line by line, and finally the whole at one stretch.

The Sacred Fire

PGS II, 4, 2-3; 8

xi) 2. The student heaps up the fire with his hand, speaking these words:

"O Lord, the glorious one, make me glorious,
as you, glorious Lord, yourself are glorious.
As you, Lord, are custodian of sacrifice for the Gods,
even so may I be custodian of Sacred Knowledge for men."

3. Having sprinkled water around the fire from left to right, he places some wood on the fire and says, standing:

"To the Lord, the great Seer, I have brought some wood.
As you, O Lord, are set ablaze by wood,
so may I be set ablaze by life, intelligence, and vigor,
by means of offspring, cattle, and divine glory.

May my teacher be one whose sons are living.
May I be capable of insight, not obstructive.
May I increase in honor and divine glory.
May I integrate everything into the cosmic dynamism
of the sacrifice. Svāhā!"

8. He warms his hands at the fire and puts them to his mouth and says:

"You, Lord, are the protector of bodies, Protect my body.
You, Lord, are the giver of life. Grant life to me.
You, Lord, are the giver of vigor. Impart vigor to me.
What is imperfect, Lord, in my body, that restore to fullness.

May the God Savitṛ give me wisdom,
may the Goddess Sarasvatī give me wisdom,
may the two divine Aśvins, wreathed with lotus,
give me wisdom."

The End of Student Life

PGS II, 6, 25-26; 29-31

xii) 25. He puts a turban on his head, reciting:

"A young man, well-dressed."

26. He puts on the two earrings, saying:

"An ornament are you. May I have more!"

29. He takes an umbrella in his hand and says:

"You are the protection of Bṛhaspati;
protect me, then, from evil,
but do not protect me from splendor and renown!"

30. Next he puts on the pair of sandals:

"You are my defense. Defend me from every side."

31. He takes, finally, a bamboo staff, reciting:

"From all destructive powers preserve me on all sides."

■ i) Bṛhaspati is here a house priest, a priest of Soma. Cf. SB IV, 1, 2, 4. The new garment is the *kaupīna* to cover the private parts of the boy who is shortly going to become an adult.
■ ii) Long life and a good old age: (vitality) *āyus* and *āyutva: āyuṣe dīrghāyutvāya balāya varcasa iti.* An expression recurrent throughout.
■ iv) Girdle: *mekhalā,* to hold in position the *kaupīna* made of different fabric according to the family or *varṇa.* On the girdle cf. AV VI, 133 (§ II B Antiphon). Cf. also RV III, 8, 4 (§ III 19).
Friendly Goddess: *sakhā devī.*
Inhalation and exhalation: *prāṇa* and *apāna.*
■ v) 3. Sacred thread: *yajñopavīta.*
I initiate you: *upanayāmi.*
6. Patriarchal sages: *ṛṣis.*
12. Vivifying power: *prasava,* inspiration, impulse. Cf. also the word of the *ācārya* (teacher) in PGS II, 2, 21.
■ vi) Deerskin: *ajina,* generally an antelope skin, though it denotes the skin of any animal. Cf. SB III, 9, 1, 12 for the clothing with skins. Probably used first as an upper garment and afterward to sit on. It may symbolize the putting on of the virtues of a *ṛṣi* and the taking of a vow to strive toward that ideal. The Veda here could meaningfully be rendered by "wisdom."
■ vii) 12. This mantra concerning the staff represents the reintegration of the newly initiated young man into the cosmic order. The *daṇḍa,* the staff, descending from the air upon the ground, symbolizes the *axis mundi,* the pivot on which the earth revolves (perhaps also lightning).
■ viii) 1. The last concepts are traditional and have more than a mere moral meaning: *dīrghāyutvāya, suprajāstvāya, suvīryāya, rāyasposāya, sarveṣām vedānām adhipatyāya, suślokyāya, svastaye.*
3-5. The *ācārya* takes the student in charge, but he dedicates him to the different Gods so as to integrate him into the world of the spirit.
■ ix) 1. The touching of the heart symbolizes the dedication of the student to the sacred world of learning. There is a crescendo in the words of the master: heart (*hṛdaya*), mind (*citta*), spirit (*manas*), you (*tvā*):

mama vrate hṛdayaṁ te dadhāmi
mama cittam anu cittaṁ te astu
mama vācam ekamanā juṣasva
bṛhaspatiṣ ṭvā niyunaktu mahyam (iti).

Direction: *vrata,* lit. that which is chosen, from the root *vṛ-,* to choose, meaning generally a vow, i.e., a firm purpose, the following of a vocation, and thus will and also law, rule, obedience, manner of life, direction. Cf. SB XI, 5, 4.
■ x) 1. For the Sāvitrī mantra, called also Gāyatrī, cf. RV III, 62, 10 at the beginning of this anthology.
12. Verse: *pāda* is the fourth part of a stanza. Two verses form a line or hemistich and four verses the stanza.
■ xi) Lord: Agni throughout.
3. The great Seer: *jātavedas,* he who knows beings.
May I be set ablaze: *samindhe,* may I be inflamed, as you are, O Agni, by *āyus* (life, vital power, vitality, duration of life), *medhā* (wisdom, mental power, intelligence), *varcas* (vigor, energy, activity). Cf. the illuminating power of fire: splendor, dynamic force.
May I . . . : in the Sanskrit the verb is in the imperative form, indicating a firm resolve.
Not obstructive: *anirākariṣṇu,* not hindering, not warding off anyone or, as the Commentary adds, not forgetful of what has been taught.
May I integrate everything . . . : *annāda,* lit. eater or enjoyer of food, implying the vital assimilation, i.e., the integration of everything into a new body, which is only possible thanks to the Fire of the divine sacrifice. Therefore the prayer ends with *svāhā*!
■ xii) 25. Turban: *uṣṇīṣa,* diadem.
All this is done after the student has taken the ritual bath with the permission of the guru at whose feet he has been seated for a number of years. Asceticism is never an end in itself. The preceding texts of the same GS speak of his putting on new garments and of placing flowers on his head.

b) Growing into One

Ekībhāva

The awakening of human consciousness, like the awakening into life, is a process of sifting and discrimination. Growth implies and requires differentiation, separation, a self-affirmation by a negation of the other, a looking into oneself, and a concern with what is happening within one's self, all concentrated in the internal process of finding the self that exists precisely because it has been set apart from other selves and thus from the totality.

Initiation has triggered off the process of growth and development. But the very moment one comes of age, the very moment one gets perspective by differentiation and self-identity by separation, the opposite process starts: that of unification, of integration, of re-acquiring that unity of which one begins to be aware only when one has lost it. The uphill movement of adult human life begins.

The basic experience here is double: the discovery on the one hand that one is separated from the Ground of Existence, which we can still call God, and, on the other hand the discovery that one is separated from the rest of the world, especially from other human beings. In this latter part of the experience a factor of primary importance is the awareness of sex, through which one is aware that in oneself one is not the totality of the human species, or even a complete specimen, for there is another half which has somehow to be integrated.[69] Love is born in this moment—the first seed of mind, as the text has said, or the first 'sprout' of mind discovering its own incompleteness and tending toward the integration of its being by uniting itself with a representative of the other half of mankind.

The young man may begin by having a vague and undiscriminated love, but very soon this same love takes shape and form and is even given a name, the name of the partner in life. No initiation is complete until marriage is performed. In a way marriage is the initiation into absolute life, as has been remarked. Individualization was a necessary process, but he who stays there is dead and will not

69. Cf. BU I, 4, 3 (§ I 7).

reach human maturity. Human life is relationship, but there is no real relationship unless the related parts have really become parts of a whole, that is, unless the relationship has been somehow fused into a fuller integrated human being.

May All the Divine Powers Join Our Two Hearts in One

Sūryā-vivāha

15 This famous hymn describes the marriage of Sūryā, daughter of the Sun (Sūrya), with Soma, who here personifies the Moon. This cosmic event is the model and image of every human marriage. The text has two clear-cut parts. The first introduces us to Soma and the second describes practically all the ceremonies of the marriage.

After the stanzas (1-19) describing the marriage of Soma the Moon with Sūryā the Sun-maiden they are proclaimed an inseparable couple, and the second part of the hymn celebrates the human part of the wedding ceremony. The verses that follow are put into the mouths of the different persons taking part: the priest, the bride, the bridegroom, and so on. The bride is taken solemnly from her father's house to the dwelling of her future husband. The Gandharva is sent away, while those who have arranged the marriage are given a blessing for their journey and enterprises. Then the bride is brought into her new home, where, on her arrival, the marriage is performed. The ceremony of the bridal robe, that of the taking of her hand, the circumambulation of the sacred fire, and the settling into the new home are among the rites described in the second part of this hymn.

Sūryā-vivāha RV X, 85, 20-47

20. Mount, O Sūryā, this gold-hued chariot,
fashioned from many-shaped planks of Kiṁśuka
and Śalmali wood, strong-wheeled, smooth-rolling.
Forth to the world immortal! Prepare
for your husband a happy bridal journey!

21. "This woman has a husband. Go, seek another,
a girl in her father's home ripe for marriage"
—I thus addressed Viśvāvasu in song—
"and thus fulfill the task assigned you."

22. Get up from here, Viśvāvasu!
We entreat you now with due respect.
Seek another willing girl
and leave the wife alone with her husband.

23. Straight be the paths and thornless on which
our friends will travel to present our suit!
May Aryaman and Bhaga lead us together!
May heaven grant us a stable marriage!

24. I free you now from the fetter of Varuṇa
with which the kindly Savitṛ secured you.
Unharmed within the bosom of Order I set you,
along with your husband, in the world of goodness.

25. I free her from this knot, not from that other
in which I have now well and truly bound her,
in such a way that, mothering fine sons,
she may dwell in happiness, O generous Indra!

26. May the Provident One lead you, holding your hand!
May the two Aśvins transport you on their chariot!
Enter your house as that household's mistress.
May authority in speech ever be yours!

27. May happiness await you with your children!
Watch o'er this house as mistress of the home.
Unite yourself wholly with your husband. Thus
authority in speech till old age will be yours.

28. Dark blue and red is the magic sign
which clings so closely. The kinsmen of the bride
prosper; the husband is bound with bonds.

29. Cast away the dirty robe!
Distribute the treasure among the priests!
This magic sign, assuming feet,
approaches the husband in guise of a wife!

30. Ugly his body, of lurid hue,
if with evil intent the husband
covers his member with the robe of his bride.

31. The diseases that belong to her own people
and follow in the wake of the bridal procession—
these may the worshipful Gods despatch
hence to the place from which they came!

32. May those who lurk to bar the pathway
not find the bridal couple as they go!

May they escape by pleasant paths all harm!
Let all the ill-wishers flee away!

33. Signs of good fortune attend the bride.
Congregate, one and all, to see her!
Wish her joy and return to your homes!

34. It is pungent in odor, sharp, full of barbs.
It resembles poison unfit for eating.
Only he who knows the Sūryā hymn
is worthy to take the bridal robe.

35. Now it is cut, severed, and divided!
See the beautiful colors of Sūryā!
Only the priest can purify these.

36. I take your hand in mine for happiness,
that you may reach old age with me as husband.
Bhaga, Savitṛ, Aryaman, Purandhi,
have given you to be my household's mistress.

37. Rouse her, O Provident One, this bride of many charms,
in whom as in a field men sow the seed.
Let her, desirous, open her thighs,
that we, desirous, may insert the member.

38. To you they bring, first, in bridal procession
this Sūryā, guiding her steps in circles.
Return her now, O Agni, to her husband
as rightful wife, and grant to her children.

39. Agni has now returned the bride
endowed with splendors and length of life.
May she live a lengthy span of days
and may her husband live a hundred autumns!

40. This woman was first acquired by Soma.
Next the Gandharva was her guardian.
To Agni, third, was she presented in marriage.
Her fourth husband is born of a woman.

41. Thus Soma passed her on to the Gandarva
and he in turn presented her to Agni.
Agni has given to me wealth and sons;
it is he who has given me this my wife.

42. Dwell in this home; never be parted!
Enjoy the full duration of your days,
with sons and grandsons playing to the end,
rejoicing in your home to your heart's content.

43. May Prajāpati grant to us an issue,
Aryaman keep us till death in holy marriage!
Free from ill omens, enter the home
of your husband. Bring blessing to both humans and cattle.

44. Not evil-eyed nor harmful to your husband,
kind to dumb beasts, radiant, gentle-hearted;
pleasing, beloved by the Gods, bring forth heroes.
To menfolk and beasts alike bring blessing.

45. Bless now this bride, O bounteous Lord,
cheering her heart with the gift of brave sons.
Grant her ten sons; her husband make the eleventh!

46. Act like a queen to your husband's father,
to your husband's mother likewise, and his sister.
To all your husband's brothers be queen.

47. May all the divine Powers together with the Waters
join our two hearts in one! May the Messenger,
the Creator, and Holy Obedience unite us!

1. Cf. § II 16 Introduction.

2-19. Independent part of the hymn describing the relations between Sūryā and Soma, generally taken as a cosmic marriage.

20. Cf. AV XIV, 1 and XIV, 2, wedding hymns where several verses of RV X, 85 have been incorporated with some variations.

Kiṁśuka and Śalmali: two kinds of wood.

21. Viśvāvasu, a Gandharva, is the spirit who "possesses" the girl before her marriage and who has to be sent away in order to give place to the husband.

24. Within the bosom of Order: *ṛtasya yonau.*

In the world of goodness: *sukṛtasya loke,* world of noble conduct.

26. The Provident One: Pūṣan, nourisher of all beings, protector, from *puṣ-*, to nourish. cf. v. 37.

Aśvins: one could render: may the two Angels . . .

May authority in speech, etc.: *vaśinī tvaṁ vidatham ā vadāsi: vidatha,* knowledge given to others, instruction. Power to address the assembly, freedom of speech, right to "take the floor." Cf. the same expression in v. 27 *vidatham ā vad-:* to impart knowledge, give instruction (in a community or congregation, especially during the observance of festal or religious rites).

27. Lit. closely unite your body.

28. Dark blue and red: a reference to the blood of menstruation (see also v. 29).

The husband is bound . . . : *patir bandheṣu badhyate.* This may mean that the "spell" of the bride's "impurity" is now transferred from her parents to her husband, or else it is a general reference to the marital bond (see also v. 29).

29. Distribute . . . : the gifts for the priests performing the ceremony.

30. The last stanzas seem to refer to different magical practices.

31. All the dangers are prayed away.

33. Signs of good fortune: *sumaṅgalī,* to see a bride is auspicious (just as, even today, it is "inauspicious" to see a widow).

Joy: *saubhāgya,* good luck.

34 and 35 again refer to the bridal robe, which has some magical property.

35. Sūryā: i.e., the bride. The colors may again refer to the dirty robe of v. 28 which is to be ritually purified.

37. The metaphor is interesting: the bride is likened to the field (*kṣetra*), and the act of placing the seed is thus generalized.

40. Born of a woman: one of human birth. As the marriage between Sūryā and Soma is the archetype of any marriage, Soma is the first husband of every bride. The Gandharva is the guardian of virginity and is

connected with female fertility, and Agni is the presiding deity of every marriage ceremony. The human bridegroom receives his bride therefore from these Gods.

43. Prajāpati is invoked for offspring. Aryaman is the God of friendship whose task is to take constant care of the unity of the married couple.

45. Lord: Indra.

47. Divine Powers: *viśvedevāḥ*.

Messenger: Mātariśvan.

Creator: Dhātṛ, supporter, establisher (sometimes an epithet of Indra).

Holy Obedience: Deṣṭrī. Cf. Sāyaṇa on PGS I, 4, 14 who calls Deṣṭrī: *dātrī phalānām* (giver of fruits).

I Am He, You Are She *Amo 'ham asmi sā tvam*

16 It is significant that two long and very important hymns on the subject of human marriage should both begin with a stanza that uses cosmic and metaphysical terms to indicate the central place in the entire economy of the universe accorded to the man-woman union:

> By Truth is the Earth supported,
> by the Sun is the Heaven supported;
> by Cosmic Order the Ādityas stand
> and Soma is set upon the Sky.[70]

Man and woman are the symbol of all cosmic polarities and an example of the same polarity. Man and woman do not belong to only one of the two poles; they represent cosmic polarity in toto.

Marriage is here not seen as a more or less free legal contract between two adults. Marriage is the human counterpart of or, more precisely, one of the ways of human participation in the creative tension of dualities (and also the overcoming of them) which constitutes the pattern of the whole of reality. Marriage is a sacrifice.[71] Thus a happy marriage will presumably not be one that takes into account two perhaps unpredictable psychological characters and studies their possible matching together, but one that is in accordance with the cosmic harmony of the universe. What is done in the darkness of night is witnessed by the stars as onlookers and guardians of universal order. Heaven and Earth can meet only at the horizon, light and darkness only in the twilight of morning or of evening; there is no song without its corresponding verse and no

70. RV X, 85, 1, and AV XIV, 1, 1: *satyenottabhitā bhūmiḥ* . . .

71. Cf. TB II, 2, 2, 6.

verse without its proper tune. Man alone, or woman alone, is not yet a person; nor, however, are man and woman mere individuals. They are halves only, each of them representative of the existential split in the existing order of the world and of the desire to overcome that split by a confidence not so much in the individual goodwill of the partner as in the unvarying well-structured pattern of the universe. Cosmic faith is required for the leap into married life. It is all a question of discovering it by tuning into that cosmic harmony, though there is no reason, of course, why psychological laws should not be taken into consideration also. There is more joy among the stars because of a well-performed human wedding than for a thousand other harmonies of the heavenly spheres. The selection that follows is taken from the actual performance of the rite.

Amo 'ham asmi sā tvam

AV VII, 36-37

i) 36. Sweet be the glances we exchange,
our faces showing true concord.
Enshrine me in your heart and let
one spirit dwell within us.

37. I wrap around you this my robe
which came to me from Manu,
so that you may be wholly mine
and never seek another.

AV XIV, 1, 17; 42

ii) 17. We offer praise to the Friend,
the kindly marriage arranger.
Like one who plucks a cucumber
I release you from here, not from yonder.

42. Love, children, happiness, and wealth
will come to answer your hopes.
Devoted to your husband's needs,
be girded for immortality!

AV XIV, 2, 64; 71

iii) 64. Unite, O Lord, this couple like
a pair of Cakravākas.
May they surrounded by children be,
living both long and happily.

71. I am He, you are She,
I am Song, you are Verse,
I am Heaven, you are Earth.
We two shall here together dwell,
becoming parents of children.

■ i) 36. Lit. our eyes be of honey-aspect.
37. The garment given by Manu may be the bride's hair, according to some interpreters. Cf. RV X, 85, 30 (§ II 15).
■ ii) 17. The Friend: Aryaman, a minor Vedic divinity (one of the eight sons of Aditi according to TB I, 1, 9, 1), though he is mentioned about a hundred times, sometimes in the sense of comrade, groomsman, friend.
42. Devoted to: *anuvrata,* adapting yourself or following (your husband's) vocation, vows; obedient or faithful to . . . *vrata,* vow.
■ iii) 64. Cakravākas: birds famous for their faithful love; they are a symbol for an ideal married life (cf. also later Sanskrit literature).
71. I am He, you are She: *amo 'ham asmi sā tvam.* Lit. This I am, that you are. This text is also given in BU VI, 4, 20. Cf. for the same idea similarly expressed, AB VIII, 27 (XL, 4); SB, XIV, 1, 4, 16; TB III, 7, 1, 9; HGS I, 6, 20, 2; PGS I, 6, 3; AGS I, 7, 6; SGS I, 13, 4; etc.

The Rite *Vivāha*

17 Among the *saṁskāras* or sacraments of Vedic origin marriage is undoubtedly the most fully elaborated and also the most important. We give here only a selection from the Gṛhya Sūtras. The Gṛhya Sūtras continue and elaborate the Vedic tradition, following perhaps the earlier Mantra Brāhmaṇa which gives a marriage rite in its entirety.

The young man, after finishing his period of formation, returns to his family. Now is the time when, with the concurrence of his parents and relatives, guided by their common sense as well as by ritualistic tradition, he will marry a wife, settle down, and hope for a long life and many stalwart sons.

Our first short texts begin by describing the ceremony of the holding of the hand of the bride by the bridegroom as a symbol of protection. The bridegroom next requests the bride to tread upon a stone, which symbolizes steadfastness, stability, strength of character—all virtues that the bride as well as the bridegroom should show. Then, generally, comes the lighting of Agni, the sacred Fire, when the appropriate offerings are made to him, accompanied by prayers.

Then the bride scatters parched grain with a prayer for the long life of her husband and her family, while after further prayers the bridegroom in his turn pours the grain into the hands of the girl and then offers it to the fire. After the offering of parched grain the couple goes around the fire while the husband prays to Agni; the rite of the fried grain is repeated and husband and wife go around the fire three times.

An impressive part of the ceremony, though found first only in the Mahābhārata, is the seven steps taken by the bride, each of them representing a virtue and a blessing.

The bridegroom now touches the heart of the bride, saying: "Let your heart become my heart and your mind my mind."[72] Then after still more prayers the wedded couple, followed by parents and guests, set out for the new home, the nuptial fire being carried in a receptacle and not allowed to go out. Once arrived at their new abode, the couple fulfill certain rites and then keep silence until nightfall. When night has fallen they go out under the open sky to gaze upon the polestar which they proceed to worship. The husband extols the polestar, pointing it out to the wife as a model of stability.

As to the social status of women in Vedic times, we may remark that, although the present-day form of theoretical equality between men and women was inconceivable, woman's position was by no means one of slavish submission to masculine tyranny. A deterioration took place later through an exaggeration of the Vedic view that to serve the husband was to serve God according to the custom of the *patideva,* that is, of considering *pati,* the husband, as the God, *deva,* for his wife.

Vivāha

The Grasping of the Hand

HGS I, 6, 20, 1

i) Himself facing the East while she faces the West [or vice versa], the bridegroom takes the bride's hand . . .

> "O Sarasvatī, gracious one, rich in offspring,
> you whom we hymn first of all the Gods,
> may you prosper this marriage."
> "I seize your hand."

72. BGS I, 4, 1 (a different text from that given in the selection). Cf. § II 14 (viii) for the same ceremony.

The Treading on the Stone

SGS I, 13, 11-12

ii) 11. The bridegroom says the words while she stands up:

"Come, beautiful one!"

12. And lets her put the tip of the right foot on the stone, saying:

"Come, step on the stone; be strong like a stone.
Resist the enemies; overcome those who attack you."

The Oblation of Parched Grain

HGS I, 6, 20, 3-4

iii) 3. The bridegroom pours some parched grain into the bride's joined palms:

"This grain I spill.
May it bring to me well-being
and unite you to me.
May Agni hear us."

4. He then causes the bride to spill the grain into the fire, saying:

"This woman, scattering grain into the fire, prays:
Blessings on my husband.
May my relatives be prosperous. *Svāhā*!"

The Circumambulation of the Fire

PGS I, 7, 3-6

iv) 3. Then they walk around [the fire], the bridegroom repeating:

"First now they bring to you in bridal procession
this Sūryā, guiding her steps in circular motion.
Return her now, O Agni, to her husband
as rightful wife, with hope of children to come."

4. Then [the entire rite is repeated] twice more, beginning with [the rite of] the fried grain.

5. At the fourth round she pours [into the fire] all the fried grain from the mouth of the winnowing basket saying:

"To Bhaga *svāhā*!"

6. After the three rounds are performed, and having sacrificed the oblation to Prajāpati [follows the next rite].

The Seven Steps

SGS I, 14, 5-6

v) While the bride takes seven steps to the Northeast [the bridegroom sings the following verses]:

"One Step for Vigor,
Two Steps for Vitality,
Three Steps for Prosperity,
Four Steps for Happiness,
Five Steps for Cattle,
Six Steps for Seasons,
Seven Steps for Friendship.
To me be devoted."

HGS I, 6, 21, 2

vi) After the seventh step he makes her remain where she is and says:

"With seven steps we become friends.
Let me reach your friendship.
Let me not be severed from your friendship.
Let your friendship not be severed from me."

Touching the Heart

PGS I, 8, 8

vii) He then over her right shoulder touches her heart saying:

"I hold your heart in serving fellowship,
your mind follows my mind.
In my word you rejoice with all your heart.
You are joined to me by the Lord of all creatures."

The Departure

HGS I, 7, 22, 1-3; 6; 10

viii) 1. She then abandons her father's house; they let her depart or be taken away from it.

2. They carry behind [the couple] the sacred fire, having put it [into a vessel].

3. They should keep the fire constantly alight.

6. When [she] reaches his house, he says:

"Enter with your right foot.
Do not remain outside."

10. They sit in silence until the stars are visible.

Looking at the Polestar

PGS I, 8, 19

ix) After sunset he lets her look at the polar star, [saying]:

"You are firm and I see you.
Be firm with me, O flourishing one!
Bṛhaspati has given you to me,
so live with me a hundred years
bearing children by me, your husband."

■ i) The grasping of the hand: *pāṇi-grahaṇa.* The ceremony generally commences after the lighting of the sacrificial fire. The so-called promise of marriage follows and the recitation of RV X, 85 (cf. v. 36 § II, 15). Cf. also RV X, 18, 8 (§ V 15) for the grasping of the hand. The husband is sometimes called a *hastagrābha,* the one who holds the hand.
■ ii) The treading on the stone: *aśmārohaṇa.* Cf. HGS I, 6, 19, 8; etc.
■ iii) The oblation of parched grain: *lājāhoma.* Cf. SGS I, 14, 1; etc.
■ iv) Walk around: *parikram-,* the circumambulation of the Fire: *agnipradakṣiṇā.* Cf. HGS I, 6, 20, 5, etc.; SGS I, 13, 13.
3. The verse is taken from RV X, 85, 38 (§ II 15).
5. Mouth of the winnowing basket: *śurpa-kuṣṭaya.*
6. After . . . : now follow the seven steps, *saptapadī.*
■ v) The seven steps: *saptapadī.* The last line is to be found only in PGS I, 8, 1, which is the same as the given text plus this last line. The root of "friendship," *sac-,* implies equality rather than submission. The last line undoubtedly reflects male preeminence. The literal words for the seven steps are: sap, juice, wealth, comfort, cattle, seasons, friend. HGS I, 6, 21, 1 has a little more elaborated version, adding after each step: "May Viṣṇu go after you." The seven steps rite is followed by the *mūrdhābhiṣeka* or the sprinkling of water on the heads of the bridegroom and the bride (AGS I, 7, 20; SGS I, 14, 9) or on the head of the bride only (PGS I, 8, 5).
■ vii) Touching the heart: *hṛdayasparśa.*
Serving fellowship: *vrata,* service, obedience, will, in this context, whereas in the RV it means ordinance, law, rule. It has later the meaning of vow (promise, resolution).
Your mind . . . : *cittam anucittaṁ.*
Lord of all creatures: Prajāpati. Cf. BGS I, 4, 1, given in the Introduction.
■ ix) Looking at the polestar: *dhruvadarśana.*

Husband and Wife *Daṁpatī*

18 Marriage is a cosmic act that involves the whole universe and reflects the mode of operation of the entire world. Yet the Cosmic Revelation does not forget to stress time and again that it is

also the daily common life of a couple within the simple framework of a village household.

Many hymns scattered here and there, as we shall have an opportunity to observe, describe the household life of a married couple, where a rather striking equality between husband and wife is emphasized. To complete our picture of marriage, we adduce a simple, brief example. The very title of this hymn by its use of the dual form of *daṁpatī* (householder, lord of the house) suggests a certain equality between husband and wife.

Daṁpatī

RV VIII, 31, 5-9

5. Husband and wife in sweet accord
give milk oblations to the Gods
and press and strain the Soma.

6. They acquire a plenteous store of food.
they come united to the altar.
Their rewards never lessen.

7. They do not wander from the Gods
or seek to hide their favors granted.
Thus they acquire great glory.

8. With sons and daughters at their side
they live a good long span of years,
both decked with precious gold.

9. Devoted to sacrifice, gathering wealth,
they serve the Immortal and honor the Gods,
united in mutual love.

1-4. Speak about the effect of the sacrifice.

5. Husband and wife in sweet accord: *yā daṁpatī samanasā,* lit. these lords of the household as with one mind.

Gods: *devāḥ*.

6. Altar: lit. sacred grass.

The last line could also be rendered, "Their strength never fails." There is a sacrificial tone in the whole stanza.

10-18. Invoke various deities but are not related to married life.

C. THE WORLD OF MAN

Manuṣyaloka

The seers in the beginning, desiring the excellent and searching the heavens, embarked upon fervor and consecration.
Thence were born energy, force, and kingship.
Let the Gods bestow them upon this man!

AV XIX, 41, 1

Man is not an individual but a person; in other words, he is not an isolated being but a constitutive relationship. This relatedness exists not only between Man and God but also between Man and his fellowman. To *manuṣyatā,* humanity, *manuṣyaloka,* the human world, is both a complement and often a supplement. There is no human life, no true humanness, in disjunction from the world of Man. Man is Man *in* and *with* his environment, and this environment is composed not only of the world of humans. It is also the world of things, the universe that surrounds him and in and with which he toils. Man is not reduced to nakedness in his dealings with his fellowmen. He is "clothed" with a whole world of utensils and instruments, for human relationships involve an exchange of human worlds. There is no man without a house, no woman without a dowry, and no citizen without weapons or utensils, be they ploughs, needles, or pen and parchment. All this, however, is not "given"; it is made, fabricated, conquered, and even created. The tissue of Man's life is no longer nature but culture.

Our antiphon gives magnificent expression to the integrated human experience. The first two lines affirm that this ideal of perfect bliss and human well-being has haunted Man since the beginning, though only the poet-sages whose minds and hearts were directed heavenward toward the light have been able to articulate it. The two key words for this aspiration are *tapas*, concentration, fervor, ardor, austerity, penance, and *dīkṣā*, consecration, initiation, religious preparation, dedication. Freedom and sovereignty, that is, mastery over nature, are reached primarily by means of these two activities: *tapas* and *dīkṣā*. We are encountering here a fundamental human attitude toward the world. Man is here on earth not to "work" on nature, to conquer it, and thus to reign over it, but to consecrate it, to "concentrate" it, and thus to attain strength and sovereignty.

Tapas and *dīkṣā* often appear together in the *śruti*[73] and the latter is even said to be the womb of the former.[74] In the womb of consecration, that is, in the act of offering and sanctifying, takes place the transformation of reality, which is the function of *tapas*. The activity of *tapas* effects an increase in ontic reality, a concentration in the density of the real. By means of Man's integral effort reality is changed; it is no longer diluted and amorphous, but it acquires shape, weight, and relevance. Moreover, by this act "things" become, are incorporated into, Man's world. The attitude of Vedic Man toward the universe is a fundamentally religious attitude, or rather an attitude of communion and consecration. In fact, *dīkṣā* does not refer only to the ceremony of consecrating an altar or a temple, or to the preparatory rite for a sacrifice; it means primarily that act by which the "thing" is converted into a bit of "world," or rather into "human world," into a living relationship with, and indeed part and parcel of, Man. Consecration transforms a thing into "person"; it personifies. A consecrated thing is no longer an excommunicated lifeless "object" but it is incorporated; that is, it is made one body together with the rest of the living community of real persons. It is by *tapas* and *dīkṣā* that Man enters into relationship with, or rather constructs, his world. The religious ceremonies

73. Cf. AV XII, 1, 1 (§ I 19).
74. Cf. ApSS X, 6, 5.

connected with all human activities by no means distract Man from dedicating himself to these activities; on the contrary, they allow him to assimilate them in such a way as to build a higher unity, which integrates "individual" and "thing" into a living person.

The whole congregation of Gods, say the two last lines of our verse, will readily yield to the man practicing *tapas* after his *dīkṣā*. He dominates nature not by sheer power but by harmonious collaboration with the lords of nature, who, having witnessed within him this process of dedication and concentration, incline themselves favorably toward him.

This is the prevailing mood of the following text, and other similar texts. The attention they give to the particular subjects of human activity does not detract from their general attitude, which regards human activities as being undertaken with only one ultimate aim, namely, that of making Man's world the habitat of the Gods, also of converting the three worlds into one.

a) Knowing the Earth

Bhūmi mātṛ

Food is given by God and possesses deep symbolic meaning, as we have seen in an earlier section. Food comes, certainly, from nature, and the trees seem almost to drop their fruits into our laps, but Man's relation both with the Divine and with the Earth is not one of pure passivity. Man has a very concrete and terrestrial way of collaborating both with God and with the world, and this is his involvement in the process of producing food. Man is learning to work with nature, to till the earth, and to grow his own food: he is learning to *know* the Earth as well as to know God.

The relationship between Man and nature is not a technical one, in either a technocratic or a scientific sense; it is not a relationship of dominion or of exploitation, as if nature were itself devoid of anything human and were there only to furnish Man with the possibility of increasing his standard and quality of life. It is rather a relationship of partnership and collaboration. Just as a cow is thankful if human hands relieve her of the burden of her extra milk, so the earth is happy to be worked by Man. To give a more complete picture of the situation, we should broaden this simile so as to include the gratitude of the bull for the "work" done on the cow. To till the earth is not only to help her to produce more and to reach her own plenitude; it is also to collaborate with the Gods in the overall action of sacrifice, to help promote the dynamism of the world and the continuance of life. It is to participate actively in that "commerce," that cosmic and divine exchange, of which the mystery of food has already provided us with an insight.[75]

Every knowledge has its sacred aspect, but the knowledge of the earth—because of its integral character—has a special sacredness of its own, perhaps because in regard to the earth the different dimensions of knowledge cannot be separated one from another, nor can there exist a merely theoretical knowledge divorced from the practical and existential one. There is no need to elaborate here on fertility cults or on religious practices connected with the relationship of Man with nature, such as found expression mainly in the agricultural golden age of human civilization.

Our first hymn is addressed to the Lord of the field, *kṣetrapati*. *Kṣetra* is a word that later acquires a long history in a more philosophical and moral sense, as for example in the very beginning of the Gītā.[76] This hymn begs the Lord of the field to watch over the ploughman's toil and to cause the earth to produce bountifully. It concludes with an invocation to the God of rain: "May Parjanya bedew the earth with honey and water!" Here the whole of human life is seen placed under divine protection. The text from the Atharva Veda (AV III, 17) which follows is no less explicit, and shows man's relation with the riches of nature. It is a prayer that the ploughing and the sowing of seed may be blessed with an ample harvest. Mention is made of corn (the crop most cultivated at that time) and of the horse, the symbol of wealth.

When the tilling of the soil is over, then comes the Harvest Song and the prayer for a bountiful Harvest (AV III, 24; AV VI, 142). Men pray for an abundance, even for a superfluity, of corn which is compared with a spring gushing forth in a thousand streams and yet remaining inexhaustible. The last verse of Atharva Veda III, 24 mentions Reaping and Garnering as the two distributors or attendants of Prajāpati, the Lord of creation, while the second verse powerfully personifies the deity of Reaping.

A rather intriguing symbolism of numbers is apparent in this

75. Cf. § II A b.
76. Cf. BG I, 1 (*dharmakṣetre* . . .); cf. also BG XIII, 1-3.

hymn. Verse 1 mentions one thousand as signifying infinity, verse 3 plays on the number five, whereas verses 4 and 5 use again one hundred and one thousand. Verse 6 speaks of three and four, which perhaps could mean 3/12 and 4/12 (or smaller portions) so as to allow for the "amplest" part of the corn to be given, probably, to the owner of the field.

To pray for a good harvest and corn in plenty would be meaningless if there was not a place, a home, or granary, where the product of the harvest could be kept and from which Man could obtain his daily bread. But even in a well-kept home the corn may be damaged by a violent storm. Therefore, the prayer for security and prosperity (AV VI, 79) is addressed to the Lord of the clouds; he is asked, with utter confidence, not only to protect the stores of the house but also to grant abundance to the family.

The hymn addressed to Rain (RV V, 83) has a beauty of its own and expresses most forcefully the type of relationship we try to describe at the beginning of this introduction. Once Man has done everything in order that the earth may yield its fruit, what is still lacking? The blessings of God, says almost every agricultural civilization. Thus it is Parjanya, the personification of rain, the God of the waters from heaven, who is here invoked. This divinity is likened to a bull whose vitalizing activity will fertilize the earth and its plants.

The marvelous descriptions of the rain contain a wealth of human-cosmic warmth which we today may call poetic imagery: banked-up clouds, rumblings of thunder, the overcast sky, the roaring wind, lightning flashes, Oh joy! the welcome rain, which spills over from the chariot of Parjanya on the earth wide open to receive it, into the pools where the cattle come to quench their thirst. Parjanya, the bringer of fertility, life, and growth is often called "Father." The rain, however, must not be too heavy and too prolonged or there will be risk of flooding. So when the earth has drunk her fill, Parjanya is begged to hold back the rain and earn Men's gratitude once more.

It is not from utilitarian motives that Men praise and glorify the forest (RV X, 146) as the reservoir for earth and Men or as the ecological redresser of Men's excessive activism. The forest, which may simultaneously both frighten and allure Man, is regarded by him as an intimate part of his life and experience. The hymn portrays in a striking fashion the nightlife of the earth's densely wooded areas, when insects are humming, and that teeming wildlife is active which the poet describes as "creaking like a cart"; it depicts the lonely forest from which one can hear the sounds of Man in the distance, and the hospitable forest which is always scented and generous in its provision of food and restful hiding places. The hymn is dedicated to Araṇyānī, the Sprite of the Forest.

Lord of the Field

Kṣetrapati

RV IV, 57

19

1. We, with the Lord of the Field as our friend
and helper, obtain for our cattle and horses
food in plenty, that they may be sleek and well-fed.
May he graciously grant us his favor!

2. O Lord of the Field, like a cow yielding milk,
pour forth for us copious rivers of sweetness,
dripping honey like nectar and pure as pure ghee.
May the Lords of the Law grant us mercy!

3. Sweet be the plants for us, sweet be the heavens,
sweet be the waters and the air of the sky!
May the Lord of the Field show us honeylike sweetness,
May we follow his furrow unharmed!

4. In contentment may men and oxen both plough,
in contentment the plough cleave the furrow,
in contentment the yoke be securely attached
and the ploughman urge on his oxen!

5. Ploughshare and Plough, to our chant be propitious!
Take of the milk you have made in heaven
and let it fall here on this earth!

6. Auspicious Furrow, we venerate you.
We pray you, come near us to prosper and bless
and bring us abundant harvests.

7. May Indra draw the Furrow, may Pūṣan
guide well its course! May she yield us milk
in each succeeding year!

8. In contentment may the ploughshare turn up the sod,
in contentment the ploughman follow the oxen,
celestial Rain pour down honey and water.
Ploughshare and Plough, grant us joy!

1. Lord of the Field: *kṣetrapati,* God of the ploughshare and of happiness. Cf. AV III, 17, 5 (§ II 20) and Sāyaṇa's commentary.
2. Lords of the Law: *ṛtasya patayaḥ.*

3. Sweet: lit. rich in honey.
4. In contentment: lit. for (man's) happiness.
5. Ploughshare: *śunā*.
Plough: *sīra*.
6. Auspicious Furrow: *sītā*. Sītā is compared with the milk cow and is called Indrapatnī. In the Rāmāyana Sītā is said to have sprung from a furrow made by Janaka while he was ploughing the ground in preparation for a sacrifice for obtaining progeny. Cf. AV, III, 17, 4 (§ II 20) which repeats this verse.
7. Perhaps *śunā* and *sīra* are Indra (Rāma) and Pūṣan guiding and guarding *sītā* from every side. Cf. also TB II, 5, 9, 2.
8. Celestial Rain: Parjanya, the God of rain.

A Harvest Blessing

Kṛṣi

20

AV III, 17, 1-4; 8-9

1. Skillful men make ready the ploughs
and the yokes for the oxen; those who are wise
offer a prayer to the Gods for favor.

2. Harness the plough, then, yoke the stout oxen;
here in the furrow prepared sow the seed.
O Gods, may our ears of corn be abundant!
May the grain in due season fall before our sickles!

3. May the blade of the plough, the smooth-handled plough,
cleaving well the furrow, produce for our joy
much cattle and sheep, a horse for a chariot,
a handsome girl!

4. May Indra guide the Furrow, may Pūṣan guard it
on every side; may the Furrow, like a milch cow,
yield to us copiously year after year!

8. O blessed Furrow, we bring you our homage.
Turn your face to us; grant us your favor
and bear fruits for us abundantly.

9. The Furrow is steeped in ghee and honey.
She is blessed by all Gods. Channel hither, O Furrow,
your milky streams, rich in vigor and oil.

1. Skillful men: *kavayaḥ*, skillful artists. "Skilled artistry" is applicable to the practice of agriculture also.
4. Cf. RV IV, 57, 7 (§ II 19).
Furrow: *sītā*. There is a tendency to divinize the furrow in this hymn (vv. 8-9). All the actions of the farmer have a symbolic meaning. Cf. notes on preceding hymn.
5-8. Belong to RV IV, 57.
5. Cf. § II 19 (v. 8).
6. Cf. ibid. (v. 4).
7. Cf. ibid. (v. 5).
8. Cf. ibid (v. 6), the same text in a different translation.

As a Spring Gushes Forth in a Thousand Streams

Samṛddhiprāpti
AV III, 24

21

1. Brimful of sweetness is the grain,
brimful of sweetness are my words;
when everything is a thousand times sweet,
how can I not prosper?

2. I know one who is brimful of sweetness,
the one who has given abundant corn,
the God whose name is Reaper-God;
him we invoke with our song.
He dwells in the home of even the lowly
who are debarred from sacrifice.
The God whose name is Reaper-God,
him we invoke with our song.

3. Let the five directions and races of men
bring to our doors prosperity,
as after the rains (in a swollen flood)
a river carries down driftwood.

4. As a spring gushes forth in a hundred, a thousand,
streams, and yet stays inexhaustible,
so in a thousand streams may our corn
flow inexhaustibly!

5. Reap, you workers, one hundred hands,
garner, you workers, one thousand hands!
Gather in the bounteous corn that is cut
or still waits on the stalk.

6. Three measures I apportion to the Spirits,
four measures to the mistress of the house,
while you I touch with the amplest measure
(of all that the field has yielded).

7. Reaper and Garnerer are your two
distributors, O Lord of creation.
May they convey hither an ample store
of riches never decreasing!

1. Brimful of sweetness: lit. rich in milk.
2. The God whose name is Reaper-God: *sambhṛtvā nāma yo devaḥ*, the "collector."
Debarred from sacrifice: lit. who do not sacrifice: referring to the non-Brahmins, the working people.
5. Lit. hundred-handed and thousand-handed, as if referring to groups of fifty and five hundred workers.
6. Spirits: Gandharvas. Some have interpreted the mistress of the house as referring to the Apsarases, the female counterparts of the male Gandharvas.
7. Lord of creation: Prajāpati.

For a Bountiful Harvest

Bahur bhava, yava
AV VI, 142

22

1. Spring up, become fair, be distended, O barley,
   with your own increase!
   Burst all vessels designed to contain you!
   May lightning not smite you
   in that place where we make our appeal to you.

2. In response, divine barley, to our invocation,
   rise up there tall as the sky, inexhaustible
   as the boundless sea!

3. May those who tend you prove inexhaustible,
   inexhaustible their barns,
   inexhaustible those who offer you in sacrifice
   and those who consume you!

3. Inexhaustible: *akṣita,* undecaying, imperishable.

For Prosperity at Home

Saṁsphāna
AV VI, 79

23

1. May the Lord of the clouds protect our stores,
   piled high in our homes!

2. May the Lord of the clouds give us vitality in our homes,
   granting goods and riches!

3. O generous God, Lord of thousandfold Abundance
   impart to us now a share of Abundance;
   may we have a share in prosperity!

1. Lord of the clouds: *nabhaspati.*
Stores: *saṁsphāna,* nourishment, bread.
2. Vitality: *ūrjas,* vigor, sap, fatness, invigorating drink.
3. Abundance: *saṁsphāna,* growing fat, prosperity.

You Have Poured Down the Rain

Parjanya
RV V, 83

24

1. Invoke with this song the powerful God,
   renowned Parjanya; win him by your worship.

Like a bellowing bull with quickening streams
he deposits a seed of life in the plants.

2. He flattens the trees and smites the demons;
the whole world fears his powerful stroke.
Even the innocent flee from this God's strength,
when Parjanya thundering strikes the wicked.

3. Like a driver urging with a whip his horses
we see him driving his heralds of storm.
From afar is heard the roaring of the lion
when Parjanya makes the heavy rain clouds.

4. The winds burst forth, the lightnings flash,
the plants shoot up, the heavens stream,
the sap surges up in every stem,
when Parjanya quickens the earth with his seed.

5. You at whose bidding the earth bows low,
you at whose bidding the hoofed creatures scamper,
you at whose bidding flowers don various colors
and shapes, O Parjanya, grant us protection!

6. Gladden us, O Storm-Gods, with rain from heaven;
may the Stallion emit his life-producing flow!
Bring here your thundering, pour forth your rain floods.
You are Divine, our heavenly Father!

7. Thunder and roar! Release the seed.
Circle in your chariot heavy-laden with rain.
Tip downward your waterskin duly loosened.
Level the high places, fill in the hollows!

8. Draw the great vessel up, let it spill over,
let the floodwaters burst forth and flow far.
Saturate both heaven and earth with fatness;
give to the cattle fair thirst-quenching pools.

9. When, O Parjanya, roaring in fury
and thundering loudly you smite the wicked,
then the whole universe shouts for joy
and everything that is on earth rejoices.

10. You have poured down the rain; now withold it, we pray you!
You have made the deserts fit for travel.
To serve as food you have made the plants flourish.
Receive from us in return grateful praise!

4. Cf. AV XII, 1, 12 (§ I 19).
5. At whose bidding: *yasya vrate.*
6. Storm-Gods: Maruts.
Stallion: i.e., Parjanya, the rain.

Divine: Asura.
8. Vessel: *kośa,* i.e., for the storage of rain.
Fatness: *ghṛta,* symbol of fertility.
10. From us: lit. from the creatures.
Praise: *manīṣā,* thought, prayer.

Sprite of the Forest

Araṇyānī

25

RV X, 146

1. Sprite of the Forest, Sprite of the Forest,
   slipping so quietly away,
   how is it that you avoid people's dwellings?
   Have you no fear all alone?

2. When the cicada emits his shrill notes
   and the grasshopper is his accompanist,
   it's the Sprite of the Forest they hail with their praises,
   as with cymbals clashing in procession.

3. Cows seem to loom up yonder at pasture,
   what looks like a dwelling appears.
   Is that a cart with creaking wheels?
   The Sprite of the Forest passes!

4. Hark! there a man is calling a cow,
   another is felling a tree.
   At evening the guest of the Sprite of the woods
   fancies he hears someone scream!

5. The Sprite of the Forest never slays,
   unless one approaches in fury.
   One may eat at will of her luscious fruits
   and rest in her shade at one's pleasure.

6. Adorned with fragrant perfumes and balms,
   she needs not to toil for her food.
   Mother of untamed forest beasts,
   Sprite of the wood, I salute you!

1. Sprite of the Forest: *araṇyāṇī,* the "wife" of *araṇya* (the forest), overseer of the woods.
4. Guest of the Sprite of the woods: i.e., the forest dweller.

b) Human Work

Karman

A refreshing feature of the Vedic way of life, as we have already seen, is its healthy combination of the sacred and the secular. The intuitions underlying the concept of sacrifice demonstrate this to the full. Sacrifice is sacred, for it effects a breakthrough from the human plane to the divine and leads us to a new dimension of human existence; but it is also secular, for it requires human collaboration and engages the whole world in its performance. The three hymns we present in this subsection emphasize this idea and, though coming from differing backgrounds, all refer to sacrifice. The first one, RV X, 101, is a hymn addressed to the priests who offer the Soma-juice. It does not devote itself, as one might expect, to praise of the sacred office of the priest and to a detailed account of the various rites he must piously perform, but to a vivid and realistic description of the sacrifice in full swing with its atmosphere of busy activity, the various ritual acts being coordinated with careful precision.

At daybreak the sacred fire is lit and then, to use the accustomed phrase, the sacrifice is "set out," "stretched," just as threads may be set out on a loom. Sacrifice is next compared to a boat that transports the sacrificer to the opposite, that is, the heavenly, shore. Verses 3 and 4 compare sacrifice to ploughing. It is the priests who, being knowledgeable in the art of winning divine favor, yoke the ploughs. Verse 5 alludes in some detail to Soma, the "fount unfailing." Verse 7 goes on to compare sacrifice to a chariot and its ritual performance to a race course, while further mention is also made of the pressing stones which, under this new symbolism, become the chariot wheels. Verse 9 is a prayer that the divinity may be pleased to lend his ear, show himself favorable to the one who offers sacrifice, and shower abundant blessings upon him, "like milk from a bountiful cow."

The second hymn, which we have entitled "The Diverse Callings of Men," is dedicated to Soma and seems to be in a humorous vein. The third refers to the controversial *puruṣamedha* or human sacrifice, whether performed actually or symbolically. All three give a vivid picture of the highly organized Vedic society and the performance within it of a wide range of human activities.

There is no question here of presenting any human age of the past as a model for the present, nor of extolling the past to the detriment of the present. The importance lies in our observing how past ages have managed to deal with the human condition in the most variegated situations and to what extent a certain degree of specialization has enhanced or harmed human harmony and wholeness.

Work is not regarded in the Vedas as unworthy of Man or as the occupation of slaves alone; nor, on the other hand, is it the highest human activity. Of this these hymns are a proof. In the first everything is concentrated upon a higher action; in the second the poet is sufficiently far removed from the scene to view it with a humorous eye. In the third text the seer seems to be so convinced that the highest values lie on another level as to suggest that Man's proper course consists in the sacrifice of his activities, at least as a sincere token of total surrender.

In the third hymn, which is concerned with human sacrifice, we have inserted some explanations in square brackets, so as to make more specific the range of human activities under consideration. The rite of human sacrifice consists in binding representatives of all classes, professions, and types of men and women to the sacrificial stake and offering them symbolically to Prajāpati (v. 22). Collective humanity thus represents the one *puruṣa* and his primordial sacrifice. This rite was considered to be even more efficacious than the famous *aśvamedha*, horse sacrifice, Man being the most noble of all victims.[77] The irony, the relation among the different human trades, and the value each represents are obvious and require no commentary. It goes without saying that we are taking this hymn out of its context. We simply give it as an example of the many human activities of Vedic Man.[78]

Priestly Task

Ṛtvijaḥ

RV X, 101

26

1. Awake, my friends, united in heart.
   Kindle the fire, my numerous comrades.
   I call to your aid the attendants of God,
   the Fire, the Sun-Horse, the Goddess Dawn.

2. May your thoughts be harmonious; spin them out properly.
   Construct a rowboat to cross the broad waters.
   Do all things in order; make ready the implements.
   My friends, let the sacrifice now proceed.

3. Fix well the ploughshares, fasten the yokes.
   The furrows are ready, sow then the seed!
   If your word is received by attentive hearers,
   the richer the harvest will be for our sickles.

77. Cf. SB XIII, 6.
78. Cf. § III 23 for the problem of the human sacrifice.

4. The Seers prepare the ploughshares for ploughing;
they lay the yokes on either side.
These are they who, possessed of wisdom,
know how to win the favor of the Gods.

5. Arrange the buckets in their proper places
with ropes securely adjusted beneath.
We desire to draw from a copious fountain
where water flows freely, inexhaustible.

6. From the fountain whose bucket is well-prepared
with good strong ropes, where water flows freely—
from this copious fountain we draw, inexhaustible.

7. Refresh the horses and win the prize!
May your chariot become a vehicle of good fortune,
with press stones as wheels, its armor the sacred
vessels, its chassis the *soma*-vat!
From this I will draw the beverage of heroes.

8. Prepare a cowshed where your lords will drink.
Stitch a coat of armor strong and broad.
Make castles of iron unassailable.
Fix well your vessel. Let it not leak!

9. I bend to our cause at this solemn moment,
O Gods, your divine and holy attention.
May a thousand streams gush forth from this offering
like milk from a bountiful pasture-fed cow.

1. God: Indra.
Fire: Agni.
The Sun-Horse: *dadhikrā*, a divine figure of a horse, representing the rising sun.
Dawn: Uṣas.
2. A reference to spinning as the symbol of sacrifice, which "spins" the whole world.
Implements: lit. weapons, all the instruments for the ritual.
4. Seers: *kavayaḥ*, the skillful (or wise) sages, poets, the priest-poets. Cf. RV I, 76, 5; X, 63, 7, the sacrifice instituted by the first man and first poet.
5. Fountain: probably an allusion to Soma.
8. Cowshed: *vraja*, the place where *soma* is prepared (the idea common to both being the flowing of an invigorating drink). Soma also has the function of invigorating and protecting; hence the similes of the armor and the castle.
10-12. Omitted.

The Diverse Callings of Men

Vi vratāni janānām
RV IX, 112

27

1. We all have various thoughts and plans
and diverse are the callings of men.
The carpenter seeks out that which is cracked,

the physician the ailing, the priest the *soma*-press.
Flow, Soma-juice, for the sake of the Lord!

2. The smith with his store of seasoned plants,
with his feathers of birds and stones for the tips,
enkindles the flame to make arrows and then
seeks out a client bulging with gold.
Flow, Soma-juice, for the sake of the Lord!

3. I am a singer, my Dad's a physician,
my Mummy's task is to grind the corn.
Diverse are our callings but we all aim at wealth;
we run in its wake like a cowherd trailing cows.
Flow, Soma-juice, for the sake of the Lord!

4. A horse desires to draw a light cart,
gay hosts to evoke a laugh and a jest,
a male desires his mate's approach,
a frog a flood to plunge within.
Flow, Soma-juice, for the sake of the Lord!

The worshiper pours out the Soma-juice (*indu*) to the words of the refrain invoking Indra, the Lord.
4. The literal translation of line 3 is much more realistic: the phallus desires a hairy fissure.

The Sacrifice of Secular Man

Puruṣamedha

YV XXX

28

1. Inspire, O Vivifier God, the sacrifice, inspire
the lord of the sacrifice to take his share!
May the heavenly Angel, the purifier of the will, purify our wills!
May the Lord of the Word make pleasant our word!

4. We call upon the Lord, distributor of wonderful bounty,
the One who looks upon men.
[I bind to the stake in form of a token:]

[The Establishment]

5. for the priesthood — a priest

[The Guild of Entertainers]

6. for Song — a public dancer
for Duty — a courtier
for Laughter — a comedian

[The Guild of Construction Workers]

for Dexterity — a wainwright
for Firmness — a carpenter

[The Guild of Artificers]

7. for Trouble	a potter's son
for Invention	a craftsman
for Beauty	a jeweler

[Guild of Instrument Makers]

for Injury	a bowmaker
for Fate	a ropemaker

[Food Producers]

for Death	a hunter
8. for Rivers	a fisherman

[The under- and overemployed]

9. for Garrulity	an unemployed man
10. for Purification	a physician

[Professional inquirers]

for Insight	an astrologer
for Thirst of Knowledge	an inquisitive man
for Moral Law	a judge

[Animal Tenders]

11. for Eye Disease	a mahout
for Speed	a groom
for Nourishment	a cowherd

[Rural workers]

for Manliness	a shepherd
for Keenness	a goatherd
for Refreshment	a ploughman

[Business promoters]

for Sweet Beverage	a distiller
for Welfare	a watchman
for Ease	a wealthy man

[Workers skilled in transforming things]

12. for the Gods in heaven	a wood-carver
for Sacrifice	a laundress
for Delight	a woman skilled in dyeing

[Domestic employees]

13. for Strength	a servant
for Plenty	a courier
14. for Passion	an ironworker

[Miscellaneous workers]

for Form	a snob
for Virtue	a pharmacist
15. for Lakes	a fisherman

[Handlers of gold]

17. for Color	a goldsmith
for Balance	a shopkeeper
18. for the Dice King	a gambler

[The endowed or less endowed by Nature]

20. for Pastime	a prostitute
for Lust	a woman with a spotty skin
for Pleasure	a musician

22. Now he binds to the stake the following eight types of men:

one too tall	one too short
one too stout	one too thin
one too pale	one too dark
one too bald	one too hairy

—all to be offered to Prajāpati.

1. Vivifier God: *deva savitaḥ*.
Lord of the sacrifice: *yajñapati*, the one who organizes a sacrifice.
Heavenly Angel: *divyo gandharvaḥ*.
Lord of the Word: *vācaspati*.
2. The Gāyatrī mantra (RV III, 62, 10).
3. The same as RV V, 82, 5 (§ IV 8).
4. Lord: Savitṛ.
5. sq. The list is not complete: we have restricted it to the professions.

c) The Happy Life

Sukha

Desire for a good life has always and everywhere been a human aspiration. Many forms of religiousness, however, perhaps overzealous in defending the rights of the Gods, have tended to consider the human condition as essentially fallen and thus to accept suffering and dissatisfaction as the normal condition of mankind; they have expected thus to foster a desire for the other (eternal) life and also to exempt God from responsibility for the existence of suffering and evil in this world. Not so the Vedic

Revelation. It does not ignore evil or minimize suffering, but it stands unequivocally for the opposite viewpoint: happiness and joy are not abnormal situations nor is Man always under stress nor is he a constantly unsatisfied being. He is indeed frail and sometimes wretched, but not corrupt or evil. He asks the Gods for protection and blessings and knows that the Gods are free to bestow or withhold their graces, but he knows also that the order of the world and Man's role within it tend toward happiness and satisfaction as the normal accompaniments of the functioning of the universe. The human condition is not one of bondage or entanglement or of patient waiting for another really worthwhile form of existence. There is, certainly, another life; there is a fuller form of existence, but this temporal life is not a shadow, nor is it something so provisional as to be devoid of authenticity.

Vedic optimism is not anthropological but, on the whole, cosmological, or rather it is based on the cosmotheandric view of reality. It does not say that Man is good or bad, nor does it consider the world as good or bad, as provisional or definitive. It starts from a more holistic perspective which views Man and cosmos as a dynamic unity in which both are engaged in maintaining the very existence of the universe.[79] In other words, reality is as it is, and Vedic Man has no Platonic paradigm before his eyes telling him how the world should or could be. In later periods this does in fact occur, but the *śruti* is relatively free from such an ideal noetic world. The world of the Gods is as real, bountiful, and imperfect as that of Men.

The texts we select here are simple examples of a spirit pervading the whole of the Vedic Revelation. We have one almost ecstatic hymn as the poet contemplates the beauty of the sun, the symbol of life and light, and also the more ecstatic songs directed toward Man's desire for long life and freedom from all fears. We also have hymns directing our attention to the potentialities of different human activities for filling Man's life with joy and peace.

We close Part II with two hymns from the Atharva Veda and the Yajur Veda. They express for us within the compass of a few lines the deep desire for peace found in the Vedic era, for tranquillity and serenity, both in the world at large and in the hearts of Men. The Upaniṣads also make mention of peace but it is an internal and personal peace, the peace that characterizes the patient search

79. Cf. the concept of *lokasaṁgraha* in BG III, 20 (§ III 29).

for the One.[80] We may ponder without further comment the deep insight into the nature of happiness that the Chāndogya Upaniṣad reveals to us:

> When one obtains happiness then one proceeds to act.
> No one acts without first obtaining happiness.
> Only by obtaining happiness does one act.[81]

May I Attain the Span of a Hundred Winters *Rudra*

29 The optimism of Vedic Man is so deeply rooted in his world view that even when he is obliged to face the terrible aspect of the divinity, represented here in Rudra, the destroyer, the thunderer, the father of the Maruts or Storm-Gods, he is not taken aback and asks from this same God what his mercy can do. He approaches him with wily prudence, entreating him with due care so as to avoid arousing his anger. He enters boldly into his presence to request from him all the boons that, precisely, the terrible aspect of the divine can grant. The destructive and punishing God is always and also the benevolent and merciful one. This hymn in praise of Rudra is an expression of the varied emotions that this God simultaneously inspires.

It is difficult to decide whether or not there is a certain conscious diplomacy or strategy in this Vedic prayer. It gives the impression of being the sincere and genuine approach of a Man who does not question, though he cannot always understand, the power and whims of the divine. In any event, this masterpiece of entreaty requests happiness and converts the fear of God into another way of approaching the divine. It is Rudra to whom Man prays, whose destructive energy he desires to quiet. He begs him to be merciful, for he desires to escape his destructive might and to benefit from his healing power.

Rudra RV II, 33

1. O Father of Storms, may your favor flash upon us!
   Do not deprive us of the sight of the sun.
   May the hero mounted on his charger spare us!
   Grant us, O God, to live forth in our children.

80. Cf. SU IV, 11 (§ V 18) and 14; MahanarU 522.
81. CU VII, 22 (§ VI 3). The acting here has a sacrificial character.

2. Thanks to your wholesome remedies, O God,
may I attain the span of a hundred winters!
Drive far from us all hatreds and troubles;
scatter to the four winds every sort of sickness.

3. O thunder-wielding God, you of all beings
are most renowned and mightiest of the mighty.
Conduct us to the further shore of sorrows
in peace and frustrate all assaults of evil.

4. May we not anger you, O God, in our worship
by praise that is unworthy or by scanty tribute.
Restore our warriors with your medicaments.
I know, O mightiest, you are the best of healers.

5. With invocation and offering I approach him,
eager to appease this God with my praises.
May the God of mercy, of dark, handsome looks,
who is easy of entreaty, spare us his anger!

6. His Mightiness, escorted by the Storms, has brought me
strong comfort in distress. May I unharmed
find shelter with him as from glaring heat!
May I secure the goodwill of God!

7. How I long, O God, for the gracious touch
of your hand which heals and brings refreshment,
which softens all chastisements of the Gods.
Regard me, O Mighty One, with an indulgent eye.

8. To the great one, the brown and whitish Bull,
I offer a powerful hymn of praise.
Adore his splendor with adorations!
We glorify the mighty name of God.

9. This God of firm limbs, of many forms, the brown one,
the mighty, has decked himself with golden ornaments.
The power divine of this sovereign God,
the ruler of the universe, never dwindles.

10. Worthy are you of the bow and arrows,
worthy of the many-colored, noble insignia;
worthy are you to combat every horror,
for none, O God, is more powerful than you.

11. Praise to the youthful, far-famed God,
enthroned on high, who slays like a wild beast!
Have mercy on your singer when he sings your praises!
May your hosts spare us and cast down some other!

12. As a son salutes with reverence his father,
so I bow down, O God, at your approach.

I praise you, mighty Lord, giver of treasures.
Grant us your medicines when we extol you.

13. Your remedies so pure, O powerful Storms,
afford us relief and bring us joy.
Those which our father Manu chose
I beg from the Lord for my own well-being.

14. May God's missile be deflected from us,
may the anger of the blazing God o'ershoot us!
Relax your bow of wrath toward our well-wishers.
Have pity on our sons and on their children!

15. O mighty Power, the God who never slumbers,
be here attentive, O Lord; hear our cry.
Not for you, O God, to be angry or destroy!
May we speak, as men of valor, a strong word!

1. Storms: Maruts, the Storm-Gods.
Flash upon: *ā . . . etu,* come upon (us), erupt.
The word "God" is used for Rudra throughout this hymn. Cf. SU III, 1-6 (§§ V 18; I 28).
4. Mightiest: lit. bull.
6. His Mightiness, escorted by the Storms: lit. this bull, escorted by the Maruts.
7. Lit. where is your gracious hand which heals and refreshes?
Mighty One: lit. bull.
9. Power divine: *asurya.*
10. Many-colored: *viśva-rūpa,* or of all forms (cf. the same word in BG XI, 16, etc.).
Every horror: *viśvam abhvam* (about *abhva,* cf. § IV Introduction).
11. Have mercy: *mṛḷā,* cf. § IV B Introduction.
12. Lord: *satpati,* true master.
13. Powerful Storms: Maruts.
Manu: probably an allusion to the legend according to which Manu selected and saved certain herbs during the great flood (for the deluge cf. § V 17).
15. O mighty Power: lit. O brown-hued Bull.
Lord: Rudra.
A strong word: lit. in the assembly (*vidathe*).

The Cows Have Come — *Ā gāvo agman*

30 This hymn was later used as a blessing upon the cows returning to the stall; it expresses in a beautiful way the joy of the Man who lives in positive symbiosis with the animal world.

Whatever origin or value we may ascribe to the sanctity and worship of the cow in India, the fact remains that for a predominantly agricultural civilization the worth of the cow cannot easily be over estimated. Cows are not only the source of almost inexhaustible riches; they also symbolize dignity, strength, and endurance as well as work, maternity, and service.

The Vedic world often utilizes the cow as a symbol. Cows draw the car of Dawn and are also called its beams; reference is made to the rain cloud as a cow and even the Gods are sometimes said to be born of cows. For Men, cows represent riches and all the blessings of a happy earthly existence. In their honor the Ṛg Veda has a special blessing[82] and the Atharva Veda several magnificent hymns.[83]

Ā gāvo agman RV VI, 28

1. The Cows have come and have brought us good fortune.
   In our stalls, contented, may they stay!
   May they bring forth calves for us, many-colored,
   giving milk for Indra each day.

2. Indra seeks to help him who offers and gives,
   augmenting, not diminishing, his possessions.
   Evermore increasing his treasure, he places
   the pious in a realm inviolate.

3. These Cows shall not be lost, no robber shall harm them,
   no enemy dare to mislead them.
   With the man who sacrifices and offers to the Gods
   the lord of the Cows will long tarry.

4. The swift horse, raising the dust, does not catch them.
   Never do they go to the shambles.
   The Cows of the man who sacrifices roam
   on wide-extending pasture of fearlessness.

5. The Cows are Bhaga, the Cows are Indra,
   or a first-poured draught of Soma.
   Truly these Cows are Indra, my brothers,
   Indra for whom my soul yearns!

6. You make, O Cows, the thin man sleek;
   to the unlovely you bring beauty.
   Rejoice our homestead with pleasant lowing.
   In our assemblies we laud your vigor.

7. Abound in calves, graze on good pastures,
   drinking pure water at the springs.
   Owned neither by thief nor by wicked man,
   may you be spared the darts of Rudra!

8. May this potion, enhanced by the seed of the bull
   and by your power, O Indra,
   bring to these Cows fertility!

1. The same hymn is also found in AV IV, 21 (except that there is an eighth stanza in the RV).
2. Treasure: *rayi.*
The pious: *devayu,* the one who worships, reveres the Gods, the God-loving.

82. Cf. RV X, 169.
83. Cf., e.g., AV X, 9; X, 10.

Realm inviolate: *abhinna khilya,* lit. undivided realm. It may also refer simply to a field.
5. The cows are the embodiment of all human and divine virtues. Bhaga is the one who gives, the bestower (cf. RV III, 36, 5: Bhaga is Indra). Indra symbolizes power and Soma the strengthening factor.
8. This stanza seems to be a charm for fertility. It is not clear what kind of potion or mixture is referred to.

The Blessing of a House *Śālāpratiṣṭhā*

31 Man is an inhabitant of the earth, but his dwelling place is not simply what the earth offers; it is also the product of his hands and his skill. A happy human life is hardly understandable without a home, and a home has no meaning for man without its mistress, the woman of the house. Here is no "bourgeois" utopianism but an embodiment of man's desire for self-identity through recognition of his stable connection with the earth and all earthly values. A man without a house is like a man without a name, and in fact the name of a person is very often the name of his house. The house is to a man what roots are to a tree; the house is the first attribute of a free man, for even a slave has wife and children but has no house of his own. To evaluate a man by his status is a sign of a decadent culture, but to consider that there is such a thing as a man without status is a sign of a culture that is not yet mature.

The blessing of a house does not constitute the sanctioning of the principle of ownership in our modern sense. The house of the Vedic period does not "belong" to its "proprietor"; the house is part of the man, just as his body is. One can have plenty of cattle but one cannot have many houses, in the same way as one cannot have two bodies.

Another point, the stress laid on stability and firmness, is also noteworthy. Not only the language, but also the whole atmosphere of this hymn, praises the condition of being established and settled in life. The house is firmly rooted and stands firm as a rock against all assaults from outside. It is a symbol of man's strength and stability. To be a householder is a sacred duty for all those who aspire to be full citizens of the world. The others are either as yet too young or have already left the dimensions of geography and history.

Śālāpratiṣṭhā AV III, 12

1. Here do I fix my dwelling. May it stand firm,
flowing with melted butter!

May we approach you, O House, with all our people,
  sound in heart and limb.

2. Here do you stand, firm dwelling, rich in horses
  and cattle, pleasantly resounding,
wealthy in food abundant, ghee, and milk.
  Stand erect for great good fortune!

3. A refuge are you, O House, with broad roof
  and stores of good clean grain.
At evening may the calf and the young son enter
  your gates with a stream of cattle.

4. May Savitṛ and Vāyu, Indra and Bṛhaspati,
  protect this dwelling, the Maruts
besprinkle it with water and with ghee.
  May King Bhaga enrich its cornfields.

5. O Goddess made by the Gods in the beginning, the mistress
  of this dwelling, our shelter and joy,
be robed in grass. May you ever treat us graciously,
  giving us sons and wealth.

6. Stay firm on your post, O Pillar. May your righteousness shine far,
  driving away all foes!
Let your inmates not suffer any harm, may we
  and all men live a hundred autumns!

7. To this house, together with the calf and other beasts,
  has come the newborn boy;
to this house a jug filled full of foaming drink,
  together with bowls of curds.

8. Bring forward, woman, this full jar, a stream of ghee
  mingled with life's elixir.
Anoint those who drink with immortality. May our votive offerings
  ever protect this dwelling!

9. I bring this water free from all impurity.
  I bring this immortal Fire.
With these I set my foot within this dwelling
  and take possession of it.

1. Melted butter (ghee): *ghṛta,* always the symbol of abundance and an important ingredient of the sacrifice.
2. Pleasantly resounding: *sūnṛtāvatī,* full of exultation.
4. Bhaga: the God of fortune.
Cornfields: *kṛṣi,* agriculture.
5. Goddess: *devī,* the personification of the house; cf. AV IX, 3, 7 (§ II 32).
Shelter: *śaraṇa,* refuge.
The robe of grass of the Goddess of the house refers to the thatched roof.
Sons: *sahavīra,* lit. strong men.
6. Stay firm: *ṛtena,* lit. in the right order, which may also mean "according to the laws of stability."
7. Beasts: *jagat,* living creatures.

Foaming drink: *parisrut;* it may refer to Soma.

8. The lady of the House is requested to bring forward certain objects which are symbols of fullness and immortality (jar: *kumbha;* elixir: *amṛta*).

Votive offerings: *iṣṭāpūrta,* wish-fulfilling sacrifices.

9. Immortal Fire: *amṛtena sahāgnina,* lit. "along with the immortal Agni." The first things to be brought into the new house are Water and Fire, i.e., the fundamental human and divine elements, necessary for life and sacrifice.

This House is Built by Worship *Brahmaṇā śālāṁ nimitām*

32 The building of a house, or even any transaction concerning it, is not just a matter of masonry or of business. It is in both instances a liturgical act, in which human lives as well as the powers above and below are involved. A house is not real estate, but a human dwelling place, the prolongation, in a sense, of a Man's body; it is the first extension of man's real world. To take leave of one's house is to take leave of the world. The ascetic leaves the house and by the fact of so doing he leaves the world.

It is no wonder that even up to our own times the human habitat has been the last bastion to succumb to the desacralizing process. In almost all human traditions there have been innumerable blessings and spells, enchantments, and magic practices concerned with houses. The Atharva Veda is full of this kind of thing and special attention is paid to the purification of a house from all evil forces. A house is not only shelter for the body; it is shelter for the whole world also, for in the house sacrifice will often be performed. In fact the word *śālā* meant, first of all, the sacrificial building, and then came to signify a home, once sacrifice began to be performed regularly in people's homes. Because sacrifice is the center of the house and of Man's family life, the house is said to be built by *brahman,* liturgical action and sacred word, to be designed by the *kavi,* the poet or wise man, and to be the abode of *ṛta,* cosmic order.

Brahmaṇā śālāṁ nimitām AV IX, 3

1. O Pillars of this House of countless treasures,
O buttresses and crossbeams,
we loosen your bonds!

2. What is bound in you, who contain all riches,
those fetters and knots,
with a powerful word I unloose, like Bṛhaspati
breaking open the cavern.

3. [The sorcerer] stretched out the rope and tied it,
fixing firmly the knots.
Like a skillful butcher cleaving the joints,
with Indra's help we loosen them.

4. We unite the bonds of your beams and clasps,
of your thatch and your sides,
O House of all riches.

5. We loosen the bonds of the clamps and bundles,
of all that encircles
and binds the Lady of the House.

6. These hanging loops which are tied for enjoyment
within you, we loosen.
May the Lady of the House, when established within her,
be gracious toward us!

7. Receptacle of oblation and hall of Agni,
abode and domain of the wives are you.
You, Goddess House, are the seat of the Gods.

8. By Holy Word we unfasten the extended
thousand-eyed net
which rests upon the central beam,
well-placed and well-fastened.

9. May the one who receives you as a gift, O House,
queen among dwellings,
and the one who built you both enjoy long life
and reach ripe old age!

10. Here let her come to meet her owner.
Firmly fastened
and adorned are you, whose limbs and joints
we proceed to loosen!

11. The one who collected the trees, O House,
and built your walls,
the Highest Lord of creatures, has made you
for the increase of children.

12. To him be homage! Homage to the donor
and to the master of the House!
Homage to Agni and homage to the one
who performs his rites!

13. Homage to the cows and the horses, to all
that is born in this House!
O future scene of births and young life,
we loosen your bonds!

14. In your innermost heart, with both creatures and men,
you cherish God Agni.

O future scene of births and young life,
we loosen your bonds!

15. The expanse that lies between heaven and earth
I accept together with this your House.
The air it encloses I make a container
for wealth. I receive thus this House for her owner.

16. Abounding in food, abounding in milk,
with firm foundation set on the earth,
receptacle of every nourishing thing,
do no harm, O House, to those who receive you.

17. Covered with thatch and clothed in straw,
the House, like night, gives rest for her inmates,
she stands firm-fixed, her broad feet planted
on the earth like an elephant cow's.

18. I untie, remove, your covering of reed.
That which Varuṇa has tightly closed,
let Mitra open again in the morning!

19. This House is founded on Worship, designed
and built by the wise.
May Indra and Agni, the immortals, protect this House,
the abode of Soma.

20. One nest is placed upon a second, one container
laid upon another.
Within is born a mortal. From here
all things originate.

21. This House is constructed with two sides, with four,
with six, eight, or ten. In this Mistress dwelling
lies Agni like an unborn babe in the womb.

22. Facing thee, O House, who are facing me,
I approach thee peacefully:
sacred Fire and Water are within,
the main doors to Cosmic Order.

23. I bring here these waters free from disease,
destroyers of disease.
In this House, together with Fire immortal,
I take up my abode!

24. Do not bind us with fetters. May we find you a light,
not a weighty, burden!
Whithersoever we will, O House,
we lead you, like a bride.

25. From the eastern direction I summon a blessing
to the glory of this House.

Praise to the Gods, the praiseworthy,
forever and ever!

26-31. From the southern direction,
from the western direction,
from the northern direction,
from the depths below,
from the heights above,
I summon a blessing
to the glory of this House.
Praise to the Gods, the praiseworthy,
forever and ever!

1. Loosen your bonds: the spells that are "binding" the house are removed by this prayer.
2. Powerful word: *vāc,* spell.
Cavern: *bala (vala?).* Reference to the myth relating how Bṛhaspati broke open by a spell the rock that was retaining the waters. ·
5. Lady of the House: the personification of the house (cf. v. 7).
7. Goddess House: cf. AV III, 12, 5 (§ II 31).
8. Holy Word: *brahman.*
Net: *akṣu,* referring perhaps to a cloth covering the ceiling.
11. Highest Lord of creatures: *parameṣṭhi prajāpatiḥ.* He is the Lord of the House as far as progeny is concerned.
14. Lit. Agni is hidden in the center of the house.
15. This verse is recited for the acceptance of the house by the (new) owner. The house does not consist of walls but mainly of the space contained within it and above it.
18. Varuṇa is the night, Mitra the day.
19. Founded on Worship: *brahmaṇā śālāṁ nimitāṁ. Brahman* (prayer, sacred word, the sacred) is the true foundation of the house, and the wise, the inspired poets (*kavi*), are the real architects, i.e., those who know *ṛta,* cosmic order, and cosmic connections.
Indra and Agni: Indra protects from outside, Agni from within (possible interpretation).
20. Birth always takes place in an enclosed place and from there life is spread throughout the universe (*viśva*).
21. The image is that of the house as a woman (*patnī*) who bears in her womb Agni, who is as yet unborn, because the sacrificial fire has not yet been introduced (see v. 23).
22. Peacefully: *ahiṁsatīm.* This verse underlines the importance of a peaceful intention in the one who is about to occupy the house by using the word *ahiṁsā* to signify the resolve of the householder to keep all forms of violence far from his house.
Sacred Fire and Water: Agni and *āpas.*
Cosmic Order: *ṛta.*
Main doors: *prathamā dvāḥ,* lit. the first (and foremost) entrance. Here again the house is regarded as the abode of sacrifice, which maintains *ṛta,* holy order.
Cosmic Order: *ṛta.*
23. Disease: *yakṣma,* evil.
24. A house is often a burden. This prayer asks that the house may be of service to man (as a woman follows her husband) and not an encumbrance.

A Merchant's Prayer *Paṇyakāmaḥ vāṇijaḥ*

33 We have already on several occasions warned against katachronic interpretations, that is, against interpreting with our present-day categories situations that have emerged from and are understandable only within the framework of altogether different assumptions. We may remember that our previous text does not

extol the principle of property, as a superficial glance might suggest, nor does it uphold a model of bourgeois existence; similarly this present hymn is not advocating sheer egoism and antisocial attitudes. The fresh innocence and naiveté of this Merchant's Prayer bear witness not only to its authenticity but also to a world view altogether different from the modern one, in the context of which such a prayer would be less pure (though it is possible that more than one modern merchant might regret his inability to pray in these terms!).

However that may be, we have here a fine example of what could be called the way of familiarity with God, which is common in many religions and which gives rise to so many abuses. Nevertheless it is at its best another way of "religio," that is, of bridging the gap between an unapproachable Godhead and an abandoned Man. If God is to have any practical value (which idea one can contest, obviously—but then we have another problem altogether) he must be not only "available" but also approachable in our own "human" (and all too human) fashion. The following hymn is a fine specimen of this form of religiousness.

Another remark may be not inappropriate, expecially for those who, imbued with the idea of Man's sinfulness, may find such a prayer strange. Vedic Man does not consider that creation or the human order is basically wrong or radically sinful. There are certainly suffering and sin, but human life is not suffused with tears. It is not thought to be wrong to ask for one's own success and material wealth, and one does not feel the need of justifying such a prayer by adding that one will thus be enabled to help one's neighbor better or to perform a more valuable social task. Vedic Man is simpler than all this and most certainly no hypocrite.

Paṇyakāmaḥ vāṇijaḥ AV III, 15

1. First, now, I call upon the Lord,
   as merchant upon Merchant.
   May he come and be our example!
   May he drive away those that would harm us,
   the robber and the wild beast!
   May he, all-powerful, grant me riches!

2. Many are the paths of the Gods,
   winding heavenward.

May they stream for me with favors,
bringing me milk and butter!
  Thus in my business
may I succeed and accumulate treasure!

3. I offer this wood and this butter
  in your honor, O Lord,
with a prayer for energy and strength.
These sacred words I now chant
  with all my devotion,
to win by this hymn a hundredfold.

4. Please pardon, O Lord, our hardness,
  our long travels for gain.
May we purchase and sell with profit!
May the barter of goods make us prosperous!
  Good luck to our journeys!
Have regard, both Gods, to our offering.

5. My pile of gold for my trading,
  seeking wealth through wealth,
may it ever increase and not dwindle!
By this offering to the Gods, O Lord,
  check and frustrate
those who would spoil our profit.

6. The wealth which I use for trading,
  seeking, O Gods,
wealth to accrue to my wealth—
in this may Indra, Prajāpati,
  Savitṛ, Soma,
and Agni grant me renown!

7. To you, O Lord, the Priest
  Beloved of all men,
we bring our praise with reverence.
Keep watch over our children
  and ourselves, we pray.
Guard both our lives and our cattle.

8. Thus, steadfast and firm as a horse,
  we shall offer you praises,
Omniscient Lord, forever.
Replete with food and with riches,
  being close to you always,
may we never suffer reverses!

1. The dialogue and prayer are based on the idea of a certain give-and-take between kindred persons. Cf. RV III, 18, 1 (§ VII 37), "as friend to friend."
Lord: Indra.

3. Cf. RV III, 18, 3, which is identical, although given in § VII 37 in a different version.
Lord: Agni, also in vv. 4; 5; 7.
4. Cf. RV I, 31, 16, from which the beginning of this verse is taken.
The two Gods are Indra and Agni. The merchant asks Agni's forgiveness for failing to perform the *agnihotra* in foreign lands.
6. Renown: *ruci,* splendor, etc.
7. Beloved of all men: *vaiśvānara,* invocation to Agni.
8. Omniscient Lord: *jātavedas,* Agni.

Increase of Wealth *Rayisaṁvardhana*

34 After the merchant's prayer comes, quite naturally, the prayer for increase of wealth. This prayer is for everyone, both those who are engaged in trade and business and those who cultivate their fields. It is a morning prayer, appropriate for a time when men are looking forward to the new day, full of hope and confidence. When the first rays of the Sun appear and the hour of sacrifice approaches, what will men request from the Gods, if not the treasures of health, wealth and, offspring?[84] We should remember, however, that the word *rayi,* used several times in this hymn, does not refer exclusively to material wealth.[85] The innocence and candor that are found here, as well as in many other hymns of this type, derive precisely from the fact that human perfection and happiness are always viewed from an integrated perspective, which embraces both material and spiritual values in one indivisible and harmonious unity.

In this hymn all the Gods are addressed; all are considered to be present and accessible to the worshiper's petitions: Agni, Indra, Soma, Varuṇa, Sūrya, Savitṛ, Bṛhaspati, Tvaṣṭṛ, Vāyu, Vāta, Viṣṇu, Aryaman, Bhaga, even Sarasvatī and the Goddesses, are invoked in turn. The prayer starts with an address to Agni, the most friendly of the Gods, and concludes with an invocation to the Sun, the giver of life, who graciously grants the new day.

Not only are the Gods besought to give abundantly so that there may be a sufficiency, but they are also requested to give "over and above" so that the worshiper may share and pass on wealth in his turn (v. 5). The miser is not spared. He is urged not to resist the contagion of this liberal spirit, appropriate to both Gods and Men

84. Cf. AV IV, 39; VII, 17, etc., and § I 33.
85. Cf. §§ I 4; II 6; VII Introductions.

(v. 8) and exemplified even in the magnitude of the expanses of heaven (v. 9), but rather to give with a generous hand.

In its simple and realistic way this prayer expresses Man's search for plenitude and the infinite.

Rayisaṁvardhana AV III, 20

1. This is your appointed origin.
From here, once born, you shine.
Knowing this, O Agni, arise
and cause our wealth to increase!

2. Be present, O Agni. Speak!
Turn hither, benevolent.
Enrich us, Lord of peoples.
You are the source of our treasure.

3. May Aryaman enrich us,
Bhaga and Bṛhaspati!
May Grace and all the Goddesses
confer upon me riches!

4. With our songs we worship king Soma
and Agni. May they assist us!
Āditya, Viṣṇu, Sūrya
and the Brahman-priest Bṛhaspati.

5. With your fires, O Agni, you make strong
our sacrifice and prayer.
Inspire us, O God, to share
and grant us wealth to give.

6. We call here on Indra and Vāyu,
both of them easy of entreaty!
May the assembled people be friendly,
disposed to offer us gifts!

7. Indra, Aryaman, Bṛhaspati—
impel them to grant us gifts,
Vāta, Viṣṇu, Sarasvatī
and Savitṛ the powerful!

8. Now, by an access of that vigor
that dwells in all beings of this universe,
we have come truly to BE!
May the wise urge the stingy to give,
and may he bestow on us riches
and numerous men of valor!

9. May the five directions of space,
those wide realms, yield to capacity!
May I obtain all the desires
and hopes of my mind and heart!

10. May I speak a word that wins cows!
Soar above me in splendor.
May Vāyu surround us on all sides,
may Tvaṣṭṛ grant me abundance!

1. Origin: *yoni,* womb.
Wealth: *rayi.*
2. Treasure: *dhana.*
3. Grace: *sūnṛtā.*
Riches: *rayi* again.
4. Āditya: Varuṇa.
5. Prayer: *brahman.*
Share: *dātave,* to give.
6. Assembled people: lit. all people in the gathering; *saṁgati,* assembly, meeting.
8. By an access of that vigor: *vājasya prasave,* in the stirring of power.
The stingy: lit. the one who does not want to give.
9. Desires and hopes: *ākūtīḥ,* intentions. Cf. AV XIX, 4, 2 (§ VII B f, Antiphon).
10. Word that wins cows: *gosanim vācam,* i.e., a fruitful prayer, not a sterile utterance.
Splendor: *varcas.* The sun is addressed.

The Joy of Fearlessness *Abhaya*

35 Religion has often produced the fear of God as a kind of trump card to help Man overcome his fear of nature or his fear of his fellowman. Fear is nevertheless one of the congenital diseases of mankind. When the crude and primitive dread of nature is overcome, other forms of fear creep into the human mind and heart and, in spite of theological distinctions, the fear of God is still fear. Modern Man may no longer fear nature or God, but he is not easily rid of the fear of his fellows nor of that most insidious of all fears, the fear that is a mixture of fear of oneself and fear of nothingness.

Over against this background the following hymn may be considered a marvelous testimony as to how Man, being conscious of his human condition, tries to overcome all types of fear and even the very dread of fear which so often paralyzes the best intentions of mortal creatures. There is no happiness in fear, but there is no fearlessness without the courage to pray to be rid of any fear. In this hymn of the Atharva Veda there is already present an assurance that the prayer has been answered.

Abhaya

AV VI, 40

1. Breathe on us fearlessness, Heaven and Earth!
        By the Strength of God,
        by the Light of God,
    may we be free from fear!
   May the boundless atmosphere set us in fearlessness!
   May the offering of the seven Seers set us in fearlessness!

2. From the North and the South, the East and the West,
        let the Light of God
        direct on this village
    sustenance, welfare, and ease.
   May the Power of God grant us freedom from foes,
    removing all fear, deflecting all wrath.

3.   Below and above,
        behind and before,
   grant us freedom from enemies, O Power of God.

1. Strength of God: Soma.
Light of God: Savitṛ.
2. Light of God: Savitṛ.
Power of God: Indra.

Light, Fearlessness, and Blessing *Jyotirabhayaṁ svasti*

36 This hymn brings to a climax the prayer of the preceding one. There is fear of things, of the unknown, of nothingness, and there is also the fear of fear, about which modern psychology has much to say.

This prayer expresses the confidence that there is a wide world of light and grace where all the shadows of fear are banned, and that external obstacles in the way to happiness can be overcome by taking refuge in the strength of the Lord (v. 4). It is, further, by making friends with the world at large that fear is overcome, for, if all beings become our friends, fear simply cannot arise.

This stress upon fearlessness as a human value of capital importance and a sign of personal self-realization is maintained not only in the field of martial courage but also, and mainly, in the realm of human perfection. We read, for instance, in one Upaniṣad:

"Certainly, Janaka, you have achieved fearlessness"
—said Yājñavalkya.
"May fearlessness be with you, Sir!"
—replied Janaka of Videha,[86]

while in another we find the vivid metaphor: "the further shore of fearlessness."[87] That shore is heaven which we only attain when we practice and are surrounded by universal friendship. "In the heavenly world there is no fear."[88]

Jyotirabhayaṁ svasti AV XIX, 15

1. From that which we fear, O Lord, make us fearless.
O bounteous One, assist us with your aid.
Drive far the malevolent, the foeman.

2. Indra, the generous giver, we invoke.
May we please all creatures, both two-legged and four-legged!
Let not the armies of our foes overwhelm us!
Destroy all evil spirits!

3. Indra is the Savior who kills the Demon,
our longed-for protector, coming from afar.
May he defend us from the farthest point,
from the middle, from behind, and from before!

4. Lead us to a wide world, O wise one,
to heavenly light, fearlessness, and blessing.
Strong are your arms, O powerful Lord.
We resort to your infinite refuge.

5. May the atmosphere we breathe
breathe fearlessness into us:
fearlessness on earth
and fearlessness in heaven!
May fearlessness guard us
behind and before!
May fearlessness surround us
above and below!

6. May we be without fear
of friend and foe!
May we be without fear
of the known and the unknown!

86. BU IV 2, 4.
87. KathU II, 11: *abhayasya pāra*.
88. KathU I, 12 (§ V 27).

May we be without fear
by night and by day!
Let all the world be my friend!

1. From that which we fear . . . : *yata Indra bhayāmahe tato no abhayaṁ kṛdhi.*
Lord: Indra; also in v. 4.
2. Evil spirits: *druh.*
3. Demon: Vṛtra.
4. Blessing: *svasti,* grace, well-being.
Infinite refuge: *śaraṇa bṛhantā,* vast shelter.
6. Let all the world . . . : lit. may all the regions become my friends.

Prayer for Happiness *Svastyayana*

37 Here is a selection, taken from three of the Vedas, of certain short texts that articulate well in different ways the intense desire of Man for happiness, long life, wealth, prosperity, offspring, and good health. One is struck in all these prayers by their underlying confidence and overall conviction that happiness is the normal human condition and the duty and right of every man. The normal human situation is here portrayed as one of peace and happiness, and the abnormal as one of war and suffering. Man is not weary and yet he knows that without the favor of the Gods he cannot accomplish his task or overcome the many obstacles and perils of human existence. One of the texts (AV VII, 69) links up the entire universe with human happiness, requesting each element of the cosmos, wind, sun, and so on, to be a conveyor of happiness. Human joy is not the well-being of the "highest" part of our being, not "peace of the soul," but human "wholeness" which includes bodily health as well as psychic poise. The next prayer from the Atharva Veda (AV XIX, 60) expresses this feeling in the most concrete manner: physical wholeness is linked with spiritual beauty. The last passage, from the Yajur Veda, expresses the deep conviction that the source of every value lies originally not in Men, but in the divine world; and that the Gods are not jealous of their treasures, but are on the contrary ready to transmit to Men all that they possess. After all, they are *devas* and not *asuras* precisely because they are friends of Men and not their enemies.

Svastyayana

RV I, 89, 2; 5

i)

2. May the righteous Gods gladden our hearts
with the warmth of their love.

May the grace of the Gods encompass us;
  their friendship we seek.
May the Gods grant us life that we may live!

5. We invoke him, the Lord of what moves and what moves not,
the inspirer of our thoughts. May he come to our aid!
May this our divine Protector and Guard,
the unfailing one, cause our wealth to increase,
  that we may long flourish!

RV VI, 47, 11

ii)
  God the Rescuer,
  God the Savior,
almighty, whom always we joyfully adore,
  powerful God,
  invoked by all men,
may he, the bounteous, grant us his blessings!

RV VII, 100, 4

iii)
God bestrode the earth, being desirous
to give it to man for a home to dwell in.
In him the landless find their safety.
This great God has bequeathed them this whole wide world.

RV X, 4, 1

iv)
For you is my offering, to you I will pray,
to you who are worthy of homage and worship.
You, O God, are a spring in the desert
for the man who is thirsty for you, O everliving.

RV X, 25, 1

v)
Instill in us a wholesome, happy mind
with goodwill and understanding. Then shall we ever
delight in your friendship like cows who gladly rejoice
in meadows green. This is my joyful message.

AV I, 31, 4

vi)
Blessing and joy to our mother and father!
Joy to cattle, to beasts, and to men!
May all well-being and graces be ours!
  Long may we see the sun!

AV VII, 69

vii)
  May the wind blow us joy,
  may the sun shine down joy on us,

may our days pass with joy,
may the night be a gift
of joyful peace!
May the dawn bring us joy at its coming!

AV XIX, 60, 1-2

viii) May my voice remain strong,
my breath unfaltering,
my sight and my hearing acute!
May my hair not turn gray
nor my teeth become blackened,
may my arms not grow feeble and slack!
May my thighs remain sturdy,
my legs swift to go,
my feet neither stumble nor flag!
May my limbs remain whole,
each performing its function,
may my soul remain ever unconquered!

AV XIX, 67

ix) For a hundred autumns may we see,
for a hundred autumns may we live,
for a hundred autumns may we know,
for a hundred autumns may we rise,
for a hundred autumns may we flourish,
for a hundred autumns may we be,
for a hundred autumns may we become,
—and even more than a hundred autumns!

YV XIX, 9

x) You are Energy, give me energy;
you are Courage, give me courage;
you are Strength, give me strength;
you are Vigor, give me vigor;
you are Zeal, give me zeal;
you are Victory, give me victory.

YV XXI, 5

xi) Aditi, mighty Mother of just rulers
and queen of those who follow Eternal Order,
great ruler with a far-extending sway,
untouched by time, protectress, gracious guide,
to you we cry.

Texts i) - v) contain references to different Gods as follows:
■ i) 2. Viśvedevāḥ (All-Gods).

5. Pūṣan.
■ ii) Indra.
■ iii) Viṣṇu.
■ iv) Agni.
■ v) Soma (cf. RV X, 20, 1).
■ vi) Blessing and joy: *svasti*, happiness, prosperity.
Graces: *suvidatra*, good gifts.
■ vii) May the night be a gift: lit. may the night bring us joy, joyful peace, blessing (*śam*).
■ x) The concepts are: *tejas*, *vīrya*, *bala*, *urjas*, *manyu*, and *sahas*.

May Peace Bring Peace! *Śānti*

38 Man may possess everything: health, wealth, wife and children, knowledge and skill, power and glory; but still he can be the most miserable creature if he is lacking that gift of the Gods which does not depend on any other gift, and on which all other gifts depend if they are to be real blessings for Man: peace. Human fullness is incomplete without peace, whereas even the one who lacks everything else can still have peace within himself and peace with all beings, which in fact constitutes happiness. The Vedas were deeply aware of this and thus of the constant necessity to invoke peace with all the power of the mantra.

The *śānti* mantra or invocation of peace is an essential utterance at any beginning, and especially at the end of a sacred action or of the recitation of a sacred text. How can a holy word be uttered or heard unless there is peace in heaven, on earth, and in the human heart? The discord and dissonances in the universe and among Men have first to be pacified before any real, that is, sacred, act can take place. Here again we find a process of theanthropocosmic interaction. There can be no peace in the human heart if there is no peace on earth, but, conversely, there can be no earthly peace if there is discord in Man's inner being. The one affects the other and, at the same time, both interact with the world of the Gods in the same kind of double relationship.

Man is the powerful mediator, because he alone is capable of uttering this prayer for peace. He even dares (in our second short text) to wish peace to Brahman! God is not only in and through prayer—he *is* Prayer.

Peace—and the *śānti* mantra—must be at the beginning and end of everything. Nothing is achieved by external discord or internal unrest, and nothing is accomplished in the world or in human life unless it is grounded in peace. For this Man needs the collaboration of all the Gods: to establish peace in heaven, in the atmosphere and on earth. This is the meaning of the threefold wish: *śāntiḥ śāntiḥ śāntiḥ!*

Śānti

AV XIX, 9

i)

1. Peaceful be heaven, peaceful the earth,
   peaceful the broad space between.
   Peaceful for us be the running waters,
   peaceful the plants and herbs!
2. Peaceful to us be the signs of the future,
   peaceful what is done and undone,
   peaceful to us be what is and what will be.
   May all to us be gracious!
3. This supreme Goddess, Word, inspired by Brahman,
   by which the awe-inspiring is created,
   through her to us be peace!
4. This supreme Spirit, inspired by Brahman,
   by which the awe-inspiring is created,
   through it to us be peace!
5. These five sense organs, with the mind as the sixth,
   within my heart, inspired by Brahman,
   by which the awe-inspiring is created,
   through them to us be peace!
6. Gracious be Mitra, gracious Varuṇa,
   gracious Viṣṇu and Prajāpati,
   gracious to us be Indra and Bṛhaspati,
   gracious to us Aryaman.
7. Gracious be Mitra, gracious Varuṇa,
   gracious be Vivasvant and Death,
   gracious the calamities of earth and atmosphere,
   gracious the wandering planets.
8. Gracious to us be the trembling earth,
   when struck by the fiery meteor.
   Gracious be the cows yielding red milk,
   gracious be the earth receding.
9. Gracious be the constellations struck by the meteor,
   gracious incantations and all magic!
   Gracious to us be buried charms,
   the meteors and plagues that afflict us.

10. Gracious to us be the stars and the moon,
    gracious the sun and Rāhu,
    gracious be Death with his banner of smoke,
    gracious the powerful Rudras.

11. Gracious be the Rudras, gracious the Vasus,
    gracious the Ādityas and Agnis,
    gracious all the Gods and Bṛhaspati.

12. Brahman, Prajāpati, Dhātṛ, the worlds,
    the Vedas, the Seven Sages, and the fires,
    prepare for me a blessed path!
    May Indra be my refuge,
    may Brahman be my refuge,
    may all the Gods be my refuge!
    May the Gods united be my refuge!

13. May whatever appeasements there are in the world,
    known by the Seven Sages,
    may they all be gracious to me!
    May peace be with me!
    May fearlessness be with me!

14. Peace be to earth and to airy spaces!
    Peace be to heaven, peace to the waters,
    peace to the plants and peace to the trees!
    May all the Gods grant me peace!
    By this invocation of peace may peace be diffused!
    By this invocation of peace may peace bring peace!
    With this peace the dreadful I appease,
    with this peace the cruel I appease,
    with this peace all evil I appease,
    so that peace may prevail, happiness prevail!
    May everything for us be peaceful!

YV XXXVI, 17

ii) To the heavens be peace, to the sky and the earth,
to the waters be peace, to plants and all trees,
to the Gods be peace, to Brahman be peace,
to all men be peace, again and again
—peace also to me!

■ i) 1. Peaceful: *śānta.*
2. Signs of the future: *pūrvarūpāṇi,* tokens of things to come.
Gracious: *śam* (throughout).
3. Supreme Goddess, Word: *parameṣṭhinī vāgdevī.*
The awe-inspiring: *ghora,* the terrible.
4. Supreme Spirit: *parameṣṭinaṁ mano,* the highest mind.
5. Here *manas* is one of the *indriyas.*
7. Vivasvant is the father of Yama (death); cf § V 1 Introduction.

Death: *antaka,* lit. the ender.
Calamities: *utpātāḥ,* events. All the dangers of the universe are being appeased.
8. Red milk: *lohita kṣīrāḥ,* probably blood, referring to sick cows.
10. Rāhu is the demon who swallows the moon.
Rudras: the sons of Rudra, the Maruts (Storm-Gods).
12. Blessed path: *svastyayana,* happy way.
Refuge: *śarma,* protection.
13. Appeasements: *śāntāni.*
Happiness: *śiva,* grace, benevolence. The "dreadful" yields to peace (*śānta*), the "cruel" to *śiva.*
■ ii) Most of this same hymn YV XXXVI is given in § III 10.

PART III
BLOSSOMING AND FULLNESS

Śri

The awakening of human consciousness is not only the chief marvel of creation; it is also the most formidable adventure of Man and, as far as Man himself is capable of gathering, of God also, for the Lord is not a solitary Lord. Whatever Upaniṣadic or esoteric theology we may propound about him, it is only within this cosmic adventure that God appears and acts as God.

Part III unfolds a panorama of a marvelously broad horizon. In relation to the total Vedic world view it culminates in the lofty conception of sacrifice and finally presents, in the third section, the concept of renunciation, that most striking anticlimax of the human condition. The first section constitutes from start to finish an extraordinary hymn to Light, here no longer viewed as an exclusive possession of God or as something purely external which is the source of reflected light in Man, but as an all-embracing and all-penetrating quality that illumines the whole of reality from within and without. This Light is first and foremost a feature of the heavenly world, but this same cosmic splendor is to be found also, in an immediate fashion, in Man. In a word, Man discovers his own personal, divine, and, of course, human dignity.

Now, dignity involves responsibility and awareness. This is at the heart of Part III and it finds expression in the central section on sacrifice. Man discovers himself as Man, or rather as fully Man, as a center of the cosmos, fellow with the Gods, and partner of God himself. Between the two poles of reality Man discovers a link, an unbreakable relation, and the burden of this consciousness leads him to discover not only the laws of sacrifice, but also its nature. Man is going to lose his own life in the experiment, for the discovery that he too is God, that he may enter into the mystery of reality, not by an epistemic act of his mind, but by an existential and total involvement of his being, is going to consume him in the very fire of the sacrifice that he himself discovers and prepares. All he can do is to throw himself fully into this adventure and, heedless of all else, trust that the experiment will succeed. The one who emerges will not, of course, be the innocent individual of the beginning, but the risen person, the *puruṣottama,* a new being. This fullness is a plenitude that cannot be encompassed by human nature or by any individualistic embrace.

The third section brings us again to the realization of the exigencies and difficulties of the path. Many have not even tried, so difficult is any full experience of humanness; others have gone mad or gone astray and divinized themselves, ensnaring themselves inextricably in a net of their own ideas and falling ultimately and irretrievably into their own trap. Yet others have advanced a long way, and they beckon to us and to the whole human race. "The path is dark," in the words of the Ṛg Veda,[1] but it leads to the goal.

Part III gives us a balanced and mature picture of the world view disclosed in the Vedic Revelation. It is certainly optimistic and life-embracing. It is, without doubt, centered on Man and is thus, in a sense, humanistic; but this is only one facet of the whole. This sense of life and fullness is the complement and the result of the other facet, that of effort and asceticism. Moreover, the dynamism of the world does not proceed by way of uncritical progress or deterministic improvement. Freedom acquires a new seriousness, and liberation a dramatic aspect. *Ṛta,* the cosmic order that inspires the energy of the sacrificial act, is at the root of everything. This cosmic order, however, is not established once and for all. It grows by means of the very energy it accumulates; it formulates its own plan, as it were. Man, becoming aware of this, is then bound to create by his own freedom a more perfect freedom in the world.

1. Cf. RV I, 164, 47.

A. RADIANCE AND COSMIC REFULGENCE

Tejas

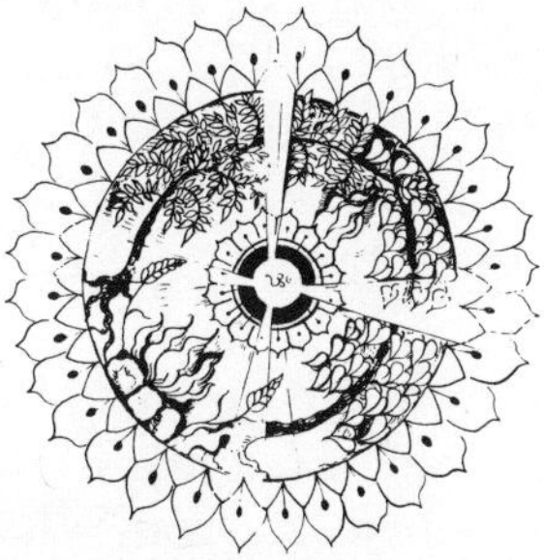

Diffusing glory with your rays,
you have scaled the shining realm of heaven.
By you are supported all things that are,
O God All-Creator, essence all-divine.

RV X, 170, 4

The texts of this section illustrate a basic insight of the whole Vedic Revelation: the "lightsome" character of reality, in all the meanings of that adjective—a concept that later speculations have developed by stressing here one point, there another. Reality is suffused with light; it is in fact light crystallized from the actual luminous source of light. It is for this reason that the light within recognizes and "sees" the light without, and vice versa. The light without is as it is because it comes from a luminous core which spills over, as it were, into certain beings.

Reality is lightsome, that is, radiant and beautiful. The world is not a mistake of the Gods or an error of the Creator. Nature is beautiful and human life is glorious. Its concrete details are stupendous in scope and the overall view is simply too enormous to be encompassed by Man. He stands in awe and admiration, infused with love and joy as he sees that the universe is so marvelous a reality, surpassing all dreams. Yet, even dreams are marvelous, though they portray only a pale image of reality. Dreams do not invent reality; they just mirror it, in a way that is fainter, obviously, than the original. It is understandable that the thirst to see the original is so vivid and lively throughout all the Vedas.

Reality is lightsome, that is, light and graceful. The earth, if truly viewed, is not a place for tragedy. Tragedy is only an invention of human pride when the individual takes himself and his position in the world too seriously. On the other hand, life might degenerate into comedy were it not for the fact that the suffering of Man is too intense to permit us to belittle it. The Vedic Revelation here brings us a message of poise and gracefulness. It tells us that reality is not ponderous, that it is *līlā*, a *play*, an adventure with no ulterior aims or goals outside the range of the game itself. Indeed, this game has many rules and not everybody knows them. In this game there are evil, suffering, and error, but all are part of the *play*. Moreover, the *play*, the lightsome character of reality, would be misunderstood if this dimension were to be severed from what really makes a play a play, namely, its feature of gratuity, of grace. Nothing is done from either obligation or necessity. There is this one advantage in the experience of contingency: the knowledge that all is contingent, including the rules of behavior of the contingent beings. To speak of contingency and then to shackle contingent beings with laws of necessity is disastrous, according to the Vedic Revelation. The world is lightsome, because it is grace, a product of grace and not of necessity.

Reality is lightsome, that is, lighthearted, gay, and nimble. Joy is not an exotic foreign plant. Colorfulness belongs to the very nature of things. Once we pierce the darkness of the surface we discover, as one text says, a sparkling like a wheel of fire, the color of the sun, full of vigor and power.[2] Light pervades everything and makes everything light and joyful. One has only to see.

Whatever one may say regarding the love of the mysterious shown by the Gods[3] or the attraction of the obscure to later Indian tradition, this section bears witness to the all-pervading luminosity of the Vedic Revelation. The metaphor of the eye and the symbol of light are here to the fore. Even subsequent elaborations will retain

2. Cf. MaitU VI, 24 (§ VI 12).
3. Cf. SB VI, 1, 1, 2; AB III, 33 (XIII, 9); VII, 30 (XXXV, 4); BU IV, 2, 2; AU I, 3, 14.

throughout metaphors of vision, and speak of *dṛṣṭi, darśana,* and the like. The Mediterranean luminosity of Greece and of the best of Western tradition is a luminosity of the sea; it is blue and green. The luminosity of the Vedic tradition is both an earthly luminosity of the mountains and plains with their colors of white and yellow, and a heavenly luminosity of the sky with its colors of light blue and gold.

Reality is lightsome; that is, it is like light, it contains light, but to the discerning eye it is not simply light, but also lightsome. Indeed, once suffused with light, one may no longer be able to distinguish whether the light that illumines the whole comes from without or from within. The effects are the same. A body is equally full of light whether the light is "received," like that of the moon, or whether the light is self-derived, like that of the sun. If the moon were to come sufficiently near to the sun, would it not become as bright as the sun? If the creature reaches the source of light, will it not become not only illumined, but light itself? If the whole cosmos returns to its source, it will not merely be like the moon but like a meteorite falling into the sun: it will no longer be distinguishable from the sun, but will be a part of it.

a) Divine Splendor

Śrī

Reality, as we have been saying, is wholly composed of light, and this statement should not be taken merely figuratively. Light shines everywhere, because everything that is is made of light. Light is being. Where there is darkness there is no light and there is no being. Furthermore, to make a distinction between light and things that are composed of light is an abstraction of the mind somewhat foreign to the Vedas. The modern cosmological concept of a light as being a physical body emitting beams that are radiant but do not themselves actually constitute "light" weakens the symbol of light as visualized by the Vedas. For the Vedas, wherever there is the light of the sun, there is the sun. The sun is not only in the sky "up there" nor is it only on the earth "down here." In other words, pure transcendence is a contradiction in terms, as also is pure immanence. Immanence and transcendence are intrinsically correlated and are possible only when held together in mutual tension. God is as little "up there" as he is just "down here."

The importance of light may be appreciated better when we reflect upon the fact that *śrī* has usually been translated as beauty when it really means brilliance, the implication being that anything radiant is beautiful. *Śrī,* in fact, may also be rendered as "prominent" or "important," inasmuch as it indicates the eye-catching quality of radiance. *Śrī* is glory and glory is the reciprocal exchange between Men and Gods.

When it is said that light is "the power of procreation"[4] or that Sūrya, the Sun, is "the living principle [*ātman*] of everything,"[5] the former statement should not be understood in a causal sense or the latter in a pantheistic sense. Both suggest that Light cannot be located or pinpointed as a "thing" but that it is rather the internal structure of reality itself.

The Vedas express these insights by simply extolling the splendor of the Gods, the glory of the divine. This is observable in all seven texts of this subsection: both in the hymns to Sūrya, Savitṛ, and Agni, who together constitute "the light of the Gods,"[6] and also in the less personified theology of Light as the inner Self and the power of Brahman. "The formless is the real; it is Brahman; it is Light," says one Upaniṣad,[7] and another affirms that it "is the same that shines within the person."[8] Furthermore, this light has no need of the cosmic luminaries in order to shine:[9]

> That splendor which is from the sun, which illumines
> this whole world,
> which is in the moon and in fire—know that splendor
> as also mine.[10]

This universal symbol of Light is surely one of the best symbols Man has found to express the delicate balance that almost all cultures have tried to maintain, with varying success, between a merely this-worldly or atheistic attitude and a totally otherworldly

4. TS VII, 1, 1, 1.
5. RV I, 115, 1.
6. TS VII, 1, 1, 1.
7. MaitU VI, 3. Cf. CU VIII, 3, 4 (§ VI 6).
8. CU III, 13, 7 (§ III 6); cf. CU VIII, 12, 3 (§ VI 6).
9. Cf. KathU V, 15 (§ V 5), MundU II, 2, 10 (§ III 6), and SU VI, 14, where the same insight is expressed.
10. BG XV, 12.

or transcendent attitude. There must be some link between the world of Men and the world of the Gods, between the material and the spiritual, the immanent and the transcendent. If this link is of a substantial nature, pantheism is unavoidable. If the link is exclusively epistemic, as Indian and many other scholasticisms tend to affirm, the reality of this world will ultimately vanish. The symbol of Light avoids these two pitfalls by allowing for a specific sharing in its nature by both worlds or even by the "three worlds."

This is the supreme light spoken of in the Ṛg Veda[11] and in the Brāhmaṇas[12]; it is mentioned also in the Chāndogya Upaniṣad[13] and in the well-known prayer of the Bṛhadāraṇyaka Upaniṣad: "Lead me from darkness to light!"[14] It is also the refulgent light of the golden vessel stationed in the dwelling place of the Divine: "The impregnable stronghold of the Gods has eight circles and nine gates. It contains a golden vessel, turned toward heaven and suffused with light."[15] This light is neither exclusively divine nor exclusively human, neither merely material nor merely spiritual, neither from this side only nor from the other. It is precisely this fact that "links the two shores." This light is cosmic as well as transcosmic.

The Joy of Every Single Eye — *Śaṁ no bhava cakṣasā*

1 If we conceive of Sūrya as a Galilean body or a Newtonian star (though Newton still believed that angels directed the movements of the heavenly bodies) we shall not understand this magnificent prayer for Light and to Light. This chant is uttered from two perspectives: that of distance from the cosmos, so that Man can take the initiative in asking for favors, and that of harmony wth and participation in the cosmos, for Man is aware that he himself fits harmoniously into the complex pattern of the universe. It is both a cosmic and a personal prayer because Sūrya is also both matter and spirit, physical and divine, the sun and the light, exterior and interior. Human happiness, the hymn suggests, is not exclusively psychological or exclusively physiological well-being; it is a matter neither of pure subjectivity nor of sheer objectivity. It is, rather, the result of a complete harmony in which the parts are not treated in

11. Cf. RV I, 50, 10 (§ III 2).
12. Cf. SB VII, 4, 2, 21; IX, 4, 2, 14.
13. Cf. CU III, 17, 7 (§ III 6).
14. BU I, 3, 28 (§ V 12).
15. AV X, 2, 31.

an egalitarian way, as if all sparks of being had the same ontological density. This prayer does not ask for miracles or for privileges; it asks for the realization, active and passive, of true universal harmony. It recognizes that there is such a thing as physical law, but that there are also other factors involved in the operation of the universe which are open to and even solicit human entreaty.

The whole hymn is pervaded by a parallelism between the spiritual and the material; it expresses both dimensions at the same time so that we discover their radical unity. Sūrya, the sun, dispels *tamas* (the forces of darkness, the inertia of matter) and *jyotis,* his light, banishes spiritual gloom, *anirā*. The sun's rays arouse the whole universe and are invoked particularly to remove sorrow and distress.

Sūrya is not only the sun; he is also light and warmth and life. He is time, for he measures all movement and all dynamism depends upon him.[16] Sūrya is called *viśvakarman,*[17] "all-creator," but he himself has been created: his father is Dyu, the heaven (v. 1). The Gods place him beyond the ocean,[18] while as a manifestation of Agni he stands in heaven.[19] He shines for Men and Gods alike.[20] He is the eye of the Gods.[21] All creatures depend on him.[22] He is one of the most powerful theandric symbols, for, though not the supreme godhead, he shares fully in both worlds and combines in himself all spheres of reality. Among the Gods he is the priest.[23]

Śaṁ no bhava cakṣasā RV X, 37

1. Homage to the Eye of Mitra and Varuṇa!
   To the mighty God offer this worship,
   to the farseeing emblem, born of the Gods.
   Sing praise to the Sun, the offspring of Heaven.

2. May this word of Truth guard me on all sides,
   while earth and heaven and days endure.
   To its rest goes all else that moves, but never
   do the waters cease flowing or the sun rising.

16. Cf. RV I, 50, 7 (§ III 2); VIII, 48, 7 (§ III 17).
17. Cf. RV X, 170, 4 (§ III A Antiphon).
18. Cf. RV X, 72, 7 (§ VII 2).
19. Cf. RV X, 88, 11.
20. Cf. RV I, 50, 5 (§ III 2).
21. Cf. RV VII, 63, 1 (§ VII 24).
22. Cf. RV I, 164, 14.
23. Cf. RV VIII, 101, 12 (*devānām . . . purohitaḥ*).

3. From ancient days no godless man
obstructs your path when you drive the winged sun-horse.
Your one dark side is turned eastward; with the other,
the light-filled side, you arise, O Sun.

4. By your light, O Sun, which scatters gloom,
by your rays which arouse the whole creation,
dispel from our hearts all languor, all neglect
of worship, all grief and evil dreams.

5. Sent forth as an envoy upon your course,
you superintend each creature's welfare,
rising with calm unvarying. May the Gods
grant us to achieve our goal today!

6. This prayer of ours may Heaven and Earth,
the Waters, Indra, and the Maruts heed!
May we never be deprived of the Sun's shining,
may we attain old age in happiness!

7. Keen of mind and keen of sight,
free from sickness, free from sin,
rich in children, may we see you rise
as a friend, O Sun, till a long life's end!

8. O farseeing Sun, the bearer of Light,
the joy of every single eye,
may we live to see your glorious radiance
flooding in as you ascend on high!

9. You shine, all living things emerge.
You disappear, they go to rest.
Recognizing our innocence, O golden-haired Sun,
arise; let each day be better than the last.

10. Bless us by your gaze, your brightness and shining.
Bless us in cold and in heat. O Sun,
grant us blessings at home and, when we are traveling,
bestow upon us your wonderful treasure.

11. Protect both our species, two-legged and four-legged.
Both food and water for their needs supply.
May they with us increase in stature and strength.
Save us from hurt all our days, O Powers!

12. Whatever grave offense we have committed against you,
by our tongue, O God, or by carelessness of mind,
lay the burden of this sin on the one who plans evil,
on him, O Vasus, who wishes us ill.

1. Worship: *ṛta*, sacrifice and also song, speech.
Emblem: *ketu*, sign, banner, often used for the sun.

2. Word of Truth: *satyokti*.
3. Godless man: *adeva*, "Ungott" (Geldner).
Obstructs: *ni-vās-*, obscure verb.
Sun-horse: Etaśa.
4. Light: *jyotis*.
Languor: *an-irā*, want of vigor, loss of spirit.
Neglect of worship: *an-āhuti*, nonsacrifice, i.e., lack of offerings, desecration.
5. With calm unvarying: *a-heḷayat*, without excitement, without causing anger; *svadhā anu*, spontaneously, willingly, according to wont.
7. Keen of mind and keen of sight: lit. good thinking and good seeing, *sumanas, sucakṣas*.
11. O Powers: *devāḥ*.

The Supreme Light *Jyotir uttamam*

2 There is no doubt that Sūrya means the sun, though the word is applied in the first place to the heavenly sphere described by the solar star and not to that solar star itself. But there is more doubt as to what "sun" really means. Whereas for the poets, for instance, Savitṛ appears to be connected with the sun but in no way identified with it, and whereas other minor solar deities, such as Bhaga, Aryaman, Pūṣan, and so on, represent certain of the functions of the sun, Sūrya undoubtedly refers to the whole complex reality that Vedic Man discerned in the sun.

> A red bird he now
> has entered the womb
> of the primeval Father.[24]

He appears in a chariot drawn by one or more steeds or bay mares. His rays are described as "seven horses"; his "mares" are called "the daughters of his chariot." He is omnipresent:

> Sūrya has pervaded air and earth and heaven.
> He is the soul of all that moves and moves not.[25]

His radiance is hymned tirelessly; his shining in the sky is worshiped as the apotheosis of Agni, the Sacred Fire.[26]

His appearance at dawn is majestic and the Rg Veda succeeds in conveying the solemnity in which Men, animals, plants, and the whole earth are enthralled. It is he who proclaims the hour of the ritual sacrifice and the resumption of human activity:

> All radiant from the bosom of the Morning,
> Sūrya, delight of singers, now ascends.

24. RV V, 47, 3, *pūrvasya yoniṁ pitur ā viveśa*.
25. RV I, 115, 1.
26. Cf. RV X, 3, 1-5; X, 88, 2-6; etc.

> Brilliant, farsighted, he rises in the heavens.
> His end is far, he hastens on, light-giving.
> Inspired by him, men go about their business,
> accomplishing their tasks whatever they may be.[27]

His light and warmth impart life to all beings:

> At all times may we be of daring courage
> and witness always the rising of the sun.[28]

Hymn I, 50 of the Ṛg Veda starts with a description of the progressive emergence of the Light "which knows all living things" (v. 1). At his approach the stars and night steal away like thieves (v. 2); rays of warm light shine upon mortal men (v. 3); then, having displayed the glory of his light (vv. 4 sq), he mounts in his chariot drawn by his seven bright mares (vv. 8 sq). The last stanza eulogizes Sūrya as the God of Gods and the expression of the Supreme Light.

We may pause here for a moment. Man until very recent times had only two sources of light: the heavenly bodies—the Sun and the Moon with the Stars—and Fire. Or should we not say rather that Light manifested itself in two different ways, a heavenly way and an earthly way? Without these two sources of light eternal darkness would cover the earth (and Man also). In the dark we may well be quiet and not moving; the static predominates, but without movement life would soon stifle. Now light was of two kinds: a cold one represented by the moon (the stars being negligible for, though they are certainly "visible," they do not permit vision; i.e., they do not enable men to see) and a hot one embodied in the two fundamental symbols of light: Sun and Fire. Man knew that Light was fundamentally Sun and Fire, but he had the blessed ignorance of not "understanding" sun and fire as merely a process of oxidization or a "loss of electrons" or as a simple combustion. He knew a great deal about the nature of light, even if he did not know that light manifests itself only in or as a certain wavelength. In any event, Vedic Man knew that light is one of those fundamental terms that are not exhausted by any rational or emotional, material or spiritual, approach. The word expresses many things simultaneously precisely because it does not stand for a "thing." One of the symbols of Light is the Sun or, in order to convey the Vedic

27. RV VII, 63, 3-4 (§ VII 24).
28. RV VI, 52, 5.

meaning of this expression, we could reverse it and say that one of the symbols of the Sun is Light. We may recall that by symbol we do not understand a merely epistemic sign, that is, a kind of arrow for our mind pointing toward something else, this latter being the "real" thing.[29] A symbol is the thing itself as it manifests itself; it is the proper appearance of the thing itself, not an artificial disguise but its proper ontic garb. The symbol is not a sign of another thing but is the very expression of the thing; the symbol always symbolizes itself as symbolized. In this sense Sun and Light are symbolically connected.

> Agni is Light; Light is the Sun. Praise.
> This is the Evening.
> The Sun is Light; Light is Agni. Praise.
> This is the Morning.[30]

A glimpse of this vision—unifying, though not confused—is given in the hymn.

Jyotir uttamam RV I, 50

1. His shining beams now introduce
   the God who knows all living things,
   that all may see the Sun.

2. Accompanying the somber Night,
   the stars, like thieves, now steal away
   at the all-seeing Sun's approach.

3. His herald rays are seen from far,
   shining on the homes of men like tongues
   of fire that burn and blaze.

4. Swift and beautiful are you,
   O Sun, maker of the Light, who illumine
   all the radiant sky.

5. You shine upon the host of Gods
   and likewise on the race of men, that all
   may see the heavenly Light.

6. With this your Eye, O pure Varuṇa,
   you keep strict watch upon the man
   who moves among the peoples.

7. You steer your path across the sky,
   O Sun, across the realms of space,

29. Cf. § I C Introduction.
30. TB II, 1, 2, 10. Praise: *svāhā*.

measuring the days by means of your shining,
observing all that comes to birth.

8. Seven bay mares drawing your chariot
conduct you, O far-seeing God,
Sūrya of the flaming hair.

9. The Sun has harnessed his seven mares,
the shining daughters of his chariot. He advances
driving his well-trained team.

10. Gazing beyond the dark we reach
the supreme Light and attain the Sun,
the God of Gods, the Light.

1. Sun: Sūrya.
4. Maker of the Light: *jyotiṣ-kṛt.*
7. Shining: *aktu,* can also mean night.
8. Seven bay mares: symbolizing the seven rays of the sun, sometimes the seven poetic meters.
10. Supreme Light: *jyotir uttamam,* highest Light. Cf. CU III, 17, 7 (§ III 6). Cf. also AV VII, 53, 7.
11-13. Omitted.

The Dispeller of Darkness *Tamase viprce*

3 Light and Darkness are correlated. Sūrya shines on both Men and Gods, as we have already seen.[31] He illumines the whole world,[32] and he sees what is happening in the entire universe.[33] Moreover, he performs the function of suffusing everything with light precisely because he dispels darkness.[34] He is, in fact, "the God who rolled up darkness like a skin,"[35] and he triumphs over "things unseen" and evil spirits.[36] His rays push down the darkness beneath the waters, as we are going to read.

In the following hymn this process is described in a magnificently simple way in the form of a morning song. Every morning the world reminds us that the light has power to overcome darkness in a way no less mysterious than the way in which the sun, though unsupported, does not fall down into the abyss—which is a marvel, even if we think we know the "laws" by which the heavenly bodies cohere.

An important point to stress here is the absence of any tendency

31. Cf. RV I, 50, 5 (§ III 2).
32. Cf. RV VII, 63, 1 (§ VII 24).
33. Cf. RV IV, 13, 3 (the hymn that follows).
34. Cf. RV X, 37, 4 (§ III 1).
35. RV VII, 63, 1 (§ VII 24).
36. Cf. RV I, 191, 8-10.

toward dualism. Light and Darkness are not on the same plane; they are not two forces of equal strength or two parallel principles governing the world. *Tamas* (i.e., darkness and the forces of evil) exists and is powerful enough to give us a realistic picture of the world's situation; but it is not to be compared with the radiance of Light, with the power of the Sun, with the healing forces of Sūrya.[37] To put it paradoxically but with rigorous logic: it is precisely by their *not* receiving the light that evil and darkness are vanquished. If they were to receive the light they would swallow it and convert it into darkness; their refusal is their defeat. The Dispeller of Darkness is stronger. Light is here not only the antagonist of Darkness; it is its other side. Let us not forget that Light is dark and that it becomes luminous only when it illumines (things, objects). What we see is only the outer or upper side. Light always shines *out of* Darkness; otherwise it would not shine.[38]

Tamase viprce RV IV, 13

1. Fire has gazed benignly
on the shining wealth-giving Dawn.
Come, Spirits, to your worshipers' dwellings.
The Sun rises in splendor!

2-3. The Sun-God extends far his radiance,
unfurling his flag in the sky,
like a strong man bent on spoil.
The higher Gods ply their course.
Masters of unchallenged domains,
they send forth the Sun on his way
with never-failing precision.
The Sun, dispeller of darkness,
whose eye contemplates all things,
is borne onward by seven shining mares.

4-5. His mighty steeds advance
inexorably, like a spider's web,
rending the night's dark robe.
The rays of the Sun, quivering,
push down beneath the waters
the darkness, like a heavy hide.
How strange the Sun! Untethered,
unsupported, he hangs in space.
Why does he never fall?

37. Cf. RV I, 191, 10; I, 50, 11 (§ III 2).
38. Cf. BU I, 3, 28 (§ V 12); CU VII, 26, 2 (§ VI 3); MundU II, 2, 6 (§ VI 5).

What inner power propels him?
Who can observe it? He guards
heaven's vault, the sky's pillar.

1. Fire: Agni.
Spirits: Aśvins.
Sun: Sūrya throughout.
2-3. Sun-God: Savitṛ.
The higher Gods: Varuṇa and Mitra.

The Mediator *Agniṁ īḷe purohitam*

4 Agni is, along with Indra, the God most frequently mentioned in the Ṛg Veda (over two hundred hymns are dedicated to him); he represents in fact one of the cornerstones of the Vedic world structure.[39] He is one of the most comprehensive symbols of the Reality that is all-encompassing, of the Divine, we might say, if by this word we understand not only an abstract Absolute but also a Relative, insofar as this latter is the Relative *of* and *to* the Absolute (which by this very fact ceases to be *ab-solutus,* i.e., unrelated). Agni represents, in point of fact, the theanthropocosmic transcendental dimension of all that is. No other symbol has this richness and this underlying unity.[40] No wonder that most of the theories about the Vedic theophanies are at a loss when they seek to compartmentalize Agni and to docket him in one of the neat and clear-cut divisions of the Vedic pantheon. Agni, like life-giving warmth, is spread everywhere.[41]

Agni is, first of all, a divine epiphany; he is leader of the Gods,[42] a kind of minister plenipotentiary of the Gods,[43] an envoy both among the Gods[44] and between them and Men;[45] he is the priest of the Gods,[46] their tongue,[47] and the spokesman to them on behalf of Men. Even more, he gives immortality to the Gods,[48] is superior

39. This is valid not only for the Vedas, but also for the Brāhmaṇas (cf. the curious etymology of Agni from *agre,* beginning, in SB II, 2, 4, 2 (§ I 6 notes) and for the Upaniṣads (cf. the central place of the *agnihotra,* e.g., in CU V, 24, 5; MaitU I, 1; KausU II, 5 (§ III 28); etc.)

40. Cf. what has been already said concerning Agni in § I 23, and cf. several hymns to Agni given in Part VII.

41. Cf. RV X, 80, 4 (§ III 16).

42. Cf. RV I, 188, 11.

43. Cf. RV III, 2, 8; X, 150, 4.

44. Cf. RV I, 161; III, 20, 4; V, 8, 6 (§ VII 38); V, 21, 3; V, 26, 6; VI, 7, 2; VIII, 23, 18; X, 110, 11; etc.

45. Cf. RV I, 27, 4; I, 36, 5-6; I, 71, 7; II, 6, 7; IV, 1, 2-3; V, 20, 1; VI, 2, 11; VIII, 16, 5; VIII, 19, 4; X, 4, 2; etc.

46. Cf. RV I, 58, 3; I, 128, 8; I, 148, 1; X, 110, 3; etc.

47. Cf. RV III, 54, 10; VI, 21, 11; VI, 50, 2 (§ IV 8); X, 65, 7; etc.

48. Cf. RV VI, 7, 4; etc.

in wisdom to the rest,[49] gives them strength,[50] and "encompasses" them.[51] Indeed, all the Gods worship him,[52] for he sets a watch over them[53] and commands them.[54] Nor is this all: he is the wise one among the Gods,[55] God among the Gods, first in rank,[56] the spirit of the Gods,[57] their Father and their son.[58] In one place he is actually called the "Father of his father."[59]

At the same time Agni's relationship with the Gods is ambivalent: the Gods beget him,[60] create him,[61] put him on earth among Men as their friend;[62] they appoint him as offerer[63] and make him strong.[64] He in his turn invites the Gods to the place of sacrifice and worships them,[65] intercedes for Men, and asks for the favor of the Gods,[66] whose good friend he is said to be.[67] In short, Agni is the divine priestly and sacrificial agent, bringing into existence the whole of reality.[68]

In the second place, Agni has a clearly terrestrial character. "We pay homage to Agni, who dwells in the earth," says one Upaniṣad.[69] He is a cosmic power. He is the Fire, he is earthly, "the navel of the earth,"[70] the "fruit of the womb of the world";[71] he makes the sun rise in the sky;[72] he is in fact the sun itself;[73] he is the seed of all,[74] the leader of the world,[75] the lord of the earth,[76] which he even eats,[77] fecundating everything.[78] He is at the same time the "king in

49. Cf. RV VII, 4, 5; etc.
50. Cf. RV I, 141, 9; VIII, 39, 4; etc.
51. Cf. RV V, 13, 6 (§ VII 49).
52. Cf. RV VI, 9, 5; 7 (§ III 5); etc.
53. Cf. RV III, 26, 3; etc.
54. Cf. RV VIII, 60, 15 (Pragātha).
55. Cf. RV I, 105, 14; etc.
56. Cf. RV IV, 11, 5 (§ VII 45).
57. Cf. RV III, 11, 6 (*kratur devānām*).
58. Cf. RV I, 69, 1.
59. Cf. RV VI, 16, 35; cf. RV I, 95, 4 for a similar paradox.
60. Cf. RV I, 59, 2; etc.
61. Cf. RV X, 88, 8-10.
62. Cf. RV II, 2, 3; II, 4, 3; etc.
63. Cf. RV I, 128, 8; etc.
64. Cf. RV X, 122, 7.
65. Cf. RV V, 13, 3 (§ VII 49); V, 21, 1; V, 26, 1; V, 28, 5; VI, 3, 7; VII, 17, 3-4; etc.
66. Cf. RV I, 36, 14; III, 16, 4; IV, 1, 10; V, 3, 10; VI, 48, 4; etc.
67. Cf. RV I, 31, 1; I, 36, 12; III, 4, 1; IV, 1, 1; 3; etc.
68. For the *agnihotra* cf. § III 16.
69. MaitU VI, 35 (§ VI 8).
70. RV I, 59, 2; cf. also I, 143, 4; III, 5, 9.
71. RV X, 45, 6.
72. Cf. RV X, 156, 4 (§ VII A a Antiphon).
73. Cf. RV III, 2, 7.
74. Cf. RV I, 70, 3-4.
75. Cf. RV VI, 7, 1.
76. Cf. RV I, 98, 1; VIII, 44, 16.
77. Cf. RV II, 4, 7.
78. Cf. RV III, 2, 10; etc.

the waters,"[79] and yet their child,[80] for it is said that the waters are his mothers.[81] Before his presence heaven and earth tremble,[82] though they follow his will[83] and are his wives.[84]

Third, he is the head of the heavens;[85] his light[86] and his strength are manifested in both heaven and earth.[87] He goes between heaven and earth,[88] sustains the sky,[89] and maintains the earth:[90]

> With fiery brightness, like a lover of Dawn,
> he has linked the two worlds with the light of heaven.[91]

We note, furthermore, that Agni is one of the most anthropomorphic symbols. He is not only born and even has many births[92] (he is the only one in the Ṛg Veda called *dvijanman*, "having two births"),[93] but he also grows[94] and develops,[95] eats,[96] and possesses human features such as head, mouth, teeth, body, and so on. Practically all creatures are on various occasions said to be his parents[97] and he also possesses more sublime parents such as *ṛta*,[98] Strength,[99] the supreme Father,[100] and so on. He is also the guest of every house and family,[101] the friend,[102] the closest friend.[103] He, the immortal, dwells among Men.[104]

Throughout, Agni has a markedly trinitarian structure. He is at one and the same time cosmic, human, and divine; he has a three-

79. Cf. RV X, 45, 5; etc.
80. Cf. RV I, 143, 1; III, 9, 1; etc.
81. Cf. RV III, 9, 2; etc.
82. Cf. RV I, 31, 3; I, 151, 1; etc.
83. Cf. RV III, 13, 2.
84. Cf. RV III, 1, 10.
85. Cf. RV I, 59, 2; III, 2, 14; VI, 7, 1.
86. Cf. RV VI, 1, 7; etc.
87. Cf. RV III, 22, 2; etc.
88. Cf. RV III, 3, 2; III, 6, 4; III, 55, 9; III, 58, 1; IV, 8, 4; etc.
89. Cf. RV III, 5, 10; etc.
90. Cf. RV I, 67, 5; etc.
91. RV I, 69, 1. Cf. VII, 12, 1; X, 45, 4; etc.
92. Cf. RV I, 95, 3; III, 1, 20; IV, 1, 7; X, 45, 1; etc.
93. Cf. RV I, 60, 1; I, 140, 2; I, 149, 4-5.
94. Cf. RV I, 1, 8 (the hymn that follows); II, 2, 4; etc.
95. Cf. RV II, 4, 7; etc.
96. Cf. RV I, 58, 2; VI, 15, 1; X, 16, 6 (§ V 16); etc.
97. E.g., Heaven and Earth (RV, I, 146, 1; III, 1, 3; III, 25, 1; etc.), the Dawn and the Night (RV V, 1, 4), Soma (RV IX, 96, 5), the woods (RV III, 1, 13), the trees, the plants, the waters, the stones (RV II, 1, 1), the heavens (RV VI, 49, 2), the priests (RV I, 31, 11; II, 5, 1).
98. Cf. RV X, 5, 7.
99. Cf. RV I, 26, 10; etc.
100. Cf. RV I, 141, 4; etc.
101. Cf. RV IV, 40, 5; V, 4, 5; VII, 42, 4; etc.
102. Cf. RV V, 24, 1 (§ VII 53); etc.
103. Cf. RV IV, 1, 3; 5; etc.
104. Cf. RV X, 45, 7; X, 79, 1; etc.

fold birth,[105] three heads,[106] and three bodies.[107] The Gods have made him threefold[108] and he dwells in the three places.[109] It is this character that makes him the mediator par excellence. Here perhaps it is appropriate to draw attention to the fundamental distinction between a mediator and an intermediary. The latter is only a broker, or at most an agent; he is not involved with either party, for he constitutes an external link; he is certainly a means of communication, but not of communion, for he separates as much as he unites; an intermediary functions as a middleman for purposes of exchange of material or spiritual goods. Not so the mediator. He is involved, because he himself belongs to both sides and has a stake in both camps; he is at home on the two shores and partakes in both spheres. This idea is developed further in the section dedicated to sacrifice: Agni is the triple sacrificial fire, he is the mediator rather than the intermediary, he is the priest of both worlds, that of the Gods and that of Men.[110]

> He, master and envoy, coming to both worlds,
> the herald well-established, great High Priest of men.[111]

Agni is the one who presents the sacrifice, renders it acceptable and pleasing, transforms and divinizes the gifts offered, and brings together the whole cosmos. Indeed, his ability to transform is total. His burning flame of sacrifice may also consume sins and wickedness, demons and foes.[112] Nothing can withstand him; everything must be burned, transmuted into light. Connected with this attribute is another aspect of Agni, infrequently mentioned but nonetheless important: the terrible corpse-consuming (*kravyād*) fire of the funeral pyre.[113] This flame, though impure by reason of its contact with the corpse, has power nevertheless to remove all stains and all traces of evil.

The following hymn is the first hymn of the Ṛg Veda. Addressed to Agni, it is a unique prayer in which praise, description, and a

105. Cf. RV I, 95, 3; IV, 1, 7—this in spite of being *dvijanman*, as quoted before.
106. Cf. RV I, 146, 1.
107. Cf. RV III, 20, 2.
108. Cf. RV X, 88, 10.
109. Cf. RV VIII, 39, 8, and VI, 8, 7, which refers also to three altars, situated in the sun, on the earth (fire), and in between (lightning).
110. Cf. RV IV, 3, 1.
111. RV III, 3, 2.
112. Cf. §§ IV 11; VII 41.
113. Cf. § V 16 and AV XII, 2.

whole theology of sacrifice are expressed with admirable simplicity and a high degree of poetic harmony.

Agniṁ īḷe purohitam RV I, 1

1. I magnify the Lord, the divine,
the Priest, minister of the sacrifice,
the offerer, supreme giver of treasure.

2. Worthy is the Lord to be praised
by living as by ancient seers.
He makes present for us the Gods.

3. The Lord brings us riches, food
in daily abundance, renown,
and hero sons to gladden our hearts.

4. Only that worship and sacrifice
that you, Lord, guard on every side
will reach the heavenly world of the Gods.

5. May the Lord, wise and true offerer,
approach, most marvelous in splendor,
encircled with his crown of Gods!

6. Whatever gift you may choose
to give, O Lord, to your worshiper,
that gift, refulgent One, is true.

7. To you, dispeller of the night,
we come with daily prayer
offering to you our reverence.

8. For you are Lord of sacrifice,
enlightener, shepherd of the world,
who wax mighty in your own abode.

9. So, like a father to his sons,
be to us easy of entreaty.
Stay with us, O Lord, for our joy.

1. Already given as the general Antiphon for the whole anthology.
Lord: Agni throughout. In this first hymn Agni is invoked three times as priest (sacrificer or offerer), viz., *purohita, ṛtvij, hotṛ*.
Giver of treasure: *ratnadhātama* (superlative).
2. Seers: *ṛṣis,* prophets.
Makes present: *vakṣati* is from the root *vah-*, i.e., lead, conduct.
The Gods: *devās,* may also mean powers.
3. Riches: *rayi*. Cf. §§ I 4; II 6; II 34; VII Introductions.
4. You guard on every side: lit. your presence filling every side.
Will reach . . . : lit. verily goes straight to the Gods.
5. Lit. may the God come (to us) with all the Gods (as his crown).

6. Worshiper: or servant from the root *dāś-*.
7. Night: *doṣā*.
Prayer: *dhī*, meditation, thought (cf. *dhyāna*, meditation).
8. Wax mighty in your own abode: reference to the receptacle on the altar holding the fire, but internal growth is also suggested. Cf. RV VI, 9, 4 (§ III 5).

The Universal Lord *Agni vaiśvānara*

5 Agni is well known in the Ṛg Veda under the title *vaiśvānara:* "he who belongs to all Men."[114] He belongs to all Men by virtue of his attribute of light, both external and internal. The hymn starts with the appearance of Agni the Universal, whose light scatters shadows. Then the sage, dazzled by the light, can no longer express what he senses to be behind it. He confesses his inability to grasp the mystery of reality by using a metaphor well known in olden times, the metaphor of weaving. The loom upon which the thread is stretched represents the sacrifice, not only with reference to its outward ritual performance in time but also to its timeless dimension. The thread that he does not find in the debating contest among the sages,[115] since he mistrusts all human discourse, is the link (the "religio") between Men and Gods. The sage acknowledges that the mystery is beyond him. It is Agni alone, the Shepherd of Immortality, who is able to find words to unravel the mystery; he knows the thread.[116] The poet is no better than his own father and master. There follows a magnificent paean of praise to Agni, cosmic light, the light of both fire and sun and also that immortal inner light, sole source of inspiration, which illumines the mind (mind being compared to the swiftest of all the birds of heaven). In verse 6 the poet, wholly absorbed in his contemplation, is rendered speechless by his own intuition, which transcends his faculties. Awed and overcome by the beauty and depth of his vision (before which even the Gods tremble, for it is a mystery both of darkness and light), the poet concludes with a final chant of praise to Agni, the universal, the immortal.

We have here a fine example of that meeting of opposites which is so characteristic of any theandric symbol. Agni is known and

114. The epithet is applied to Agni more than sixty times in the RV. Cf. § I 19 (note to v. 6).
115. Cf. RV II, 28, 5 (§ IV 17).
116. Cf. RV I, 142, 1.

unknown, far and near, bright and dark. One beautiful stanza puts it most poignantly:

> We know your three powers in three forms, O Agni,
> your forms diversified in many places.
> We know the supreme name you have in secret.
> We know the source from which you have proceeded.[117]

How can Agni have a secret name if we know it? We may say, with Indian scholasticism, that it is secret, that is, unknown to those who do not know the Vedas, and this could lead to magic and priestcraft. It is also possible to say that the secrecy of the name stands for the transcendence and inaccessibility of the Divine, and this, equally, could lead to religious hypocrisy. If we know that there *is* a transcendence, then, insofar as we know it, it is no longer transcendence: it enters into the domain of our knowledge. It is here that the Vedic Revelation, as on many other occasions, is shown to be bold and to possess a liberating power. It unveils without desecrating; it reveals without profaning. It declares that his name is veiled, and secret,[118] but declares nevertheless that we know it, that we know that his name is not noised abroad, is not this or that; that it is not to be expressed in any known name, because it is the most internal and hidden element of any name and may be concealed in any name. It is not a special name that nobody knows or that only specialists may discover. It is universal—and also ineffable: "What shall I utter, what my mind envisage?" The universal lordship of the Lord is so secret because it is everywhere revealed; it is so invisible because it does not conceal itself. It requires only an attentive and loving eye. It is an open secret—hidden in its infinite manifestations.

Agni vaiśvānara RV VI, 9

1. The day is dark and also bright. These two
   hemispheres, thanks to their own intelligence, revolve.
   Once born, the Universal Lord, the Monarch,
   thrust back by his own light the encroaching darkness.

2. I know not how to stretch the threads or weave
   or discern the pattern of those who weave in the contest.

117. RV X, 45, 2.
118. *Guhā*, lit. in a cave.

Whose son will be the one to speak so well
as to surpass, advancing from below, his father?

3. He who knows how to stretch the thread and weave
in their due time the proper words will speak.
He, the Shepherd of Immortality, knows it.
Though moving below he sees beyond any other.

4. Behold, then, the Priest, the first to perform the priestly function.
He is for mortal men the immortal Light.
He is born and is seated among us, not to be shaken,
the immortal, increasing constantly in his own body.

5. A steady light is set for men to gaze on,
of all the moving things the swiftest Mind!
All spirits divine with but one thought and intention
proceed unerring toward that unique Splendor.

6. My hearing fades away, my eyes grow dim.
The light that dwells within my heart grows brighter.
Far roams my mind, its confines overleaping.
What shall I utter, what my mind envisage?

7. In fear and trembling all the Gods hailed you,
O Lord, when you abode amidst the darkness.
O Universal Lord, accord us your grace.
May the Immortal now bestow his grace upon us!

1. Day and night rotate in ways intelligible to themselves or to their intelligence.
Once born: *jāyamāna,* as soon as risen, begotten, born (the triple metaphor running throughout).
The Universal Lord: Agni *vaiśvānara* (also in v. 7).
2. The sacrificial connotations of this text refer to the liturgical structure of the universe.
Advancing from below . . . : could also be translated as being younger (inferior) to his father.
3. Reference to transcendence and immanence: though living among men here below, he sees beyond and above.
Shepherd of Immortality: *amṛtasya gopā.*
4. Priest: *hotṛ.*
Increasing . . . : growing, developing, progressing in his own self, body, person.
5. Spirits divine: *devāḥ.*
6. The stanza describes an ecstatic form of consciousness. Cf. RV I, 164, 37 (§ I 11).
7. Lord: Agni.

The Inner Light — *Ātmajyotis*

6 We pass now from the texts that are centered on the mystery of light to the inner light which is the main subject of this group of Upaniṣadic texts but which we should not interpret in an exaggeratedly acosmic way. The process of interiorization which goes on in the Upaniṣads is not disconnected from the cosmological setting. Inner light it certainly is, but the Sun is still its best and

living symbol. Even when all the cosmological lights are transcended, as in the passages of the Bṛhadāraṇyaka and the Muṇḍaka Upaniṣads, explicit reference is made to all five cosmic sources of light: sun, moon, stars, lightning, and earthly fire. This Light of lights is none other than the Light that illumines all those other lights: it is the source of all the lights in the universe. It is the Bṛhadāraṇyaka Upaniṣad which, having said that God is "the Lord of what was and what shall be," adds that "Him the Gods revere as Light of lights."[119]

Within the cosmological representations of the time, the five cosmic lights present no underlying physical unity; Vedic Man does not imagine that all these lights can be seen as the same physico-chemical process. But he imagines, in a similar way, that there is a supreme light, transcendent and immanent, which is the source of all these other lights. The discoverer of the *ātman,* he who realizes the core of all things and the ultimate dimension of everything, must also discover this inner light. Even more, one could say that there is here a criterion for the authenticity of spiritual realization. The truly realized Man is a light to himself and is himself radiant for others. God is Light, the *ātman* is Light, and so the Man who has realized the *ātman* is self-luminous and radiant. In many traditions we can readily find examples of the luminosity of the saints, of the aura of the *jīvan-muktas.*

A text given later[120] tells us the dynamism by which we reach the inner light. It is described as a piercing, as by an arrow, of all intermediate stages, as an overcoming of darkness by penetrating it and going beyond, and as the discovery of reality as a wheel of fire and as the source of the light of both sun and moon, lightning and fire.[121]

Ātmajyotis

SuryU 71

i) Glory to God the shining.
  Protect me from death.
Glory to God the resplendent,
  the First Cause of all.

May the Sun in the East, may the Sun in the West,
may the Sun in the North, may the Sun in the South,
  may the Sun give perfect life,
  with long life endow us.

119. BU IV, 4, 15-16 (§ VI 11).
120. MaitU VI, 24 (§ VI 12).
121. Cf. MaitU VI, 3; CU III, 13, 7 (*v*).

PrasnU I, 6-7

ii) 6. The Sun, when rising, enters the eastern regions and gathers in his beams all the breath of life that is in the East. When he illumines the other regions, the South, the West, and the North, below, above, and in between, then he gathers in his beams the whole of the breath of life.

7. Thus arises the Sun as Fire, the universal Life-Breath which assumes every form.

BU IV, 3, 1-6

iii) 1. Yājñavalkya was going to visit Janaka, King of Videha. He thought to himself, "I will not say anything." Once, however, when Janaka, King of Videha, and Yājñavalkya were conversing together at an *agnihotra* sacrifice, Yājñavalkya granted the former a favor. The King chose to ask whatever question he wished and Yājñavalkya granted him this request. So the king proceeded to ask:

2. "Yājñavalkya, what serves as a light for man?"
"The sun, your Majesty," he replied. "For it is with the sun for a light that he sits, moves around, does his work, and returns again."
"Quite so, Yājñavalkya."

3. "But when the sun has set, Yājñavalkya, what then serves as a light for man?"
"Then the moon serves as his light," said he, "for it is with the moon for a light that he sits, moves around, does his work, and returns again."
"Quite so, Yājñavalkya."

4. "But when the sun has set, Yājñavalkya, and the moon has set, what then serves as a light for man?"
"Then fire serves as his light," said he, "for it is with fire for a light that he sits, moves around, does his work, and returns again."
"Quite so, Yājñavalkya."

5. "But when the sun has set and the moon has set and the fire has gone out, what then serves as a light for man?"
"Then speech serves as his light," said he, "for it is with speech as his light that he sits, moves around, does his work, and returns again. Therefore, O Majesty, when a man cannot see even his own hands, but a voice is uttered, then he goes straight toward it."
"Quite so, Yājñavalkya."

6. "But when the sun has set and the moon has set and the fire has gone out and speech is silenced, what then serves as a light for man?"
"Then the Self serves as his light," said he, "for it is with the Self as his light that he sits, moves around, does his work, and returns again."

CU III, 17, 7

iv) The early morning light we see
emerging from the primordial seed

and gleaming higher than the heaven.
And from the darkness that surrounds us,
gazing upon the highest heaven,
we attain to the Sun, the God of Gods,
the Highest Light, the Highest Light.

CU III, 13, 7

v) There is a Light that shines above this heaven, above all worlds, above everything that exists in the highest worlds beyond which there are no higher—this is the Light that shines within man.

SU V, 4

vi) Even as the radiance of the Sun
enlightens all regions, above, below,
and slantwise, so that only God,
glorious and worthy of worship, rules
over all his creation.

MundU II, 2, 10-11

vii) In the highest golden sheath is the Godhead,
unsullied, indivisible; pure is it,
the Light of lights. He who knows the Self knows it.
Neither sun nor moon nor stars shine there.
Neither lightning nor fire finds there a place.
With the radiance of that Light alone all things shine.
That radiance illumines all this world.

MahanarU 1-2; 152-156

viii)

1. In the boundless waters in the center of the universe,
on the back of the firmament, greater than the great,

2. having suffused with his splendor all the lights:
the Lord of beings stirs within the womb.

152. He who is the guardian in the center of the universe,

153. he who [bestows] the worlds to virtuous people,
and the golden glow of death,

154. that golden light established in heaven and on earth,

155. may he bestow on us that light!

156. The cosmic waters glow. I am Light!
The light glows. I am Brahman!

■ i) God: Mitra.
Sun: Savitṛ.
May the Sun give perfect life: provide all things, *suvatu sarvatātim,* from the root *su-,* to vivify, set in motion, to create, to bring forth, to yield; *sarvatāti:* totality, wholeness, perfect happiness, or prosperity.

■ ii) 3-5; 8. Cf. § II 6.
■ iii) 1. "I will not say anything": another variant reads, "I am going to speak with him" (*sam enena vadiṣya iti*).
Whatever question he wished: *kāmapraśna,* cf. SB XI, 6, 2, 10.
5. Speech: *vāc,* voice, sound.
6. The Self (*ātman*) is the "light within the heart" (*hṛdyantarjyotiḥ*), cf. BU IV, 3, 7.
■ iv) 1-6. Cf. § III 27.
From RV VIII, 6, 30. Cf. RV I, 50, 10 (AV VII, 53, 7; § III 2). The passage from death to life is homologized to a rebirth into light. The preceding passage of the same U explains that there are three thoughts upon which one must take firm hold at the moment of bodily death.
■ vii) 1-2. Cf. § VI 3.
3-4. Cf. § VI 12.
5-8. Cf. § VI 5.
9. Cf. § VI II.
The Light of lights: *jyotiṣāṁ jyotiḥ* the source of all other luminaries. Cf. KathU V, 15 (§ V 5); SU VI, 14 (practically the same text), and also BG XV, 6.
■ viii) 1. Waters: *ambhas,* the original fluid, also the heavenly water.
2. Lord of beings: Prajāpati.
Womb: *garbha,* cf. the *hiraṇyagarbha* myth. Prajāpati is also the "firstborn" from the cosmic womb.
3-4. Cf. § V 18.
153. Worlds to virtuous people: *puṇyakṛtān lokān,* i.e., the worlds (heaven) merited by good deeds.
Golden glow of death: cf. IsU 15 (§ VII 31) where the "golden vessel" covering the face of truth could be understood as death.
156. Cosmic waters: *ārdra,* the humidity of the original waters. One can observe four steps in this condensed text, starting from the cosmogonic up to the realization of Brahman.
157-158. Cf. § VI 9.

The Splendor of God *Brahmatejas*

7 Reality is luminous. The core of all things is the divine light dwelling in the heart of all. Light is within, but also without. Light shines in the innermost structure of things but is not imprisoned there. There is a divine splendor enwrapping everything but visible only when the inner and outer obstacles are removed. We do not see light, as we cannot see the seer or know the knower.[122] We see by means of and in light. The Bhagavad Gītā culminates in the luminous revelation of the Lord in the famous eleventh chapter: the Lord is transfigured, his splendor is seen to illuminate all things, and yet he regains his human form, "the body of a friend."[123]

The *śruti* does not enter into any scholastic controversy, whether the way of knowledge or that of love has the first rank among the paths toward realization. The Gītā is explicit in stating that this highest form of the Supreme "which even the Gods yearn to see"[124] can be known only (again *jñāna*!) in and through love, *bhakti,* devotion to Him.[125]

122. Cf. BU III, 4, 2 (§ VI 6).
123. BG XI, 50.
124. BG XI, 52.
125. Cf. BG XI, 54.

Brahmatejas

BG VII, 8-11

i) 8. The savor in the waters am I, the light
in the moon and the sun.
I am the Om in all Vedas, the sound
in space, in men vigor.

9. I am the sweet fragrance of earth
and of fire the brilliance.
I am the life within all beings,
the fervor in ascetics.

10. Know that I am the eternal seed
of every being.
I am the intelligence of the intelligent,
the glory of the glorious.

11. I am the strength of the strong, devoid
of desire and attachment.
I am the Love within all beings,
never contrary to Right.

XI, 12; 17

ii) 12. If suddenly the splendor of a thousand suns
shone forth in the sky,
such a shining might faintly resemble the glory
of that Supreme Self.

17. I dimly discern you, glory upon glory,
your crown, mace, and discus,
blazing on all sides, like fire, like the Sun,
incomprehensible.

XIII, 17

iii) He is the Light of all lights, averred
to be beyond darkness.
He dwells as Consciousness, its object and its goal,
in the hearts of all.

■ i) 8. Savor: *rasa,* taste, flavor, sapidity.
Space: *ākāśa,* the atmosphere that produces sound.
Vigor: *pauruṣa,* manhood.
10. Intelligence: *buddhi,* insight, intellect.
Glory: *tejas,* splendor, radiance, glow, energy, vital power, the tip of a flame (or the point of a knife), from a verb meaning to sharpen, etc.
11. Love: *kāma,* desire.
Right: *dharma,* duty.
■ iii) Cf. BU IV, 4, 16 and MundU II, 2, 10 (§ III 6).
Beyond darkness: cf. MundU II, 2, 6 (§ VI 5); SU III, 8 (§ VI 7); MaitU VI, 24 (§ VI 12); BG VIII, 9.
In the hearts of all: cf. SU III, 13 (§ VI 7); IV, 20.

b) Cosmic Splendor in Man

Yaśas

Modern Man tends to define himself as a bundle of needs and he asserts his right to the fulfillment of such needs. He needs food, clothing, shelter, "education," and work, and modern society is theoretically organized so as to provide for his needs. The Vedic view seems to be concerned less with organizing society and more with personal fulfillment. Instead of justice, glory seems to be the central value: a glorious Man and a glorious community.

Human glory seems here to be less an imitation of the divine glory than a participation in the universal and indeed divine splendor of creation. Man's glory is not a reflection of God's glory but a sharing in the very splendor of God by a full realization of the human function in the universal adventure of reality. In other words, the underlying pattern is not a dualistic one, with the lower instance striving to imitate and reach the higher one, but a pluralistic structure in which each being, including both the Gods and material things, has its own proper function.

Yet this pluralistic structure implies a unitarian basis. Each being can realize itself and reach its own plenitude because each plays its part in the one harmonious and perfect pattern that admits no final incompatibilities. It is the privilege of Man to discover this pattern and thus to be able to realize the ideal described in the Īśa Upaniṣad: to see all beings in his own self and his own self in all things.[126] This constitutes true human plenitude and an absence of delusion and sorrow.[127] The thirst for perfection, the striving for an even better human situation, are inherent in Man. All depends, however, upon one's notion of perfection. What is the perfect Man? What is the ideal or model for Man?

The texts of this subsection illustrate a certain fundamental trait of the Vedic tradition and at the same time show its evolution and pluralism. The fundamental trait is deliberately suggested by the title: *Cosmic Splendor in Man*. Human plenitude is not attained by isolation from the rest of the world, nor does it consist in the development of one part of the human being. Man integrates in

126. Cf. IsU 6 (§ VII 11).
127. Cf. IsU 7 (§ VII 16).

himself all the realms of the world and he radiates the splendor of the entire universe. Man is not the victim of blind cosmic forces nor is he a mere cog in the cosmic wheel; his situation is neither that of an absolute monarch nor of a slave cursed with the burden of responsibility. All such ideas are foreign and inappropriate here. The underlying idea is one of wholeness, of integration. The perfect Man is not he who merely possesses a pure mind or a healthy body, for perfection implies a certain integration of all existing human values. At the same time our texts show a variation in emphasis and even a wide pluralism in their understanding of this wholeness.

The first text, from the Atharva Veda (XIX, 51), sees human perfection as an undivided, integrated life not only embracing the entire human realm but also daring to embrace the divine.

The second hymn, taken from the Ṛg Veda (X, 158), evidences the same desire to embrace the whole of reality, but seems to be more concerned with encompassing the whole of the cosmic creation. Man does not want to be excommunicated from the world; he longs to embrace it by a single glance, both as a whole and in all its details. The happy life is here not to look at God, but to see the reality of the world face to face, in its entirety and in all its concrete particulars.

The following prayer, from the Yajur Veda (XXXVI), constitutes part of a ceremony and has a cultic character. The wholeness is here seen as harmony and peace, with Man having his own place in the framework of the universe. Disorder is the curse and the sin. Human perfection consists in being integrated in an orderly manner into the whole scheme of things.

The same atmosphere is breathed in another prayer, also from the Yajur Veda. It is addressed to Agni and asks for well-being of body, life, and mind and for whatever else may be needed for our perfection.

The two other excerpts from the Atharva Veda (III, 22; VI, 38) portray Man's longing to reach the summit of creation. Man cannot tolerate the thought of any splendor outside himself, that is to say, which he also may not possess. He wants the majesty of the elephant, the strength of the lion, the swiftness of the waters, the power of thunder, the might of the winds, and all the attributes of nature. He aspires even to the glory of the Gods and longs to be invested with it; he yearns to be king of the universe and thus candidly prays to the Gods to be endowed with unlimited power.

The Whole Man

Ayuto'haṁ sarvaḥ

AV XIX, 51

8

1. Unified am I, quite undivided,
   unified my soul.
   Unified my sight, unified my hearing,
   unified my breathing—both in and out—
   unified is my continuous breath.
   Unified, quite undivided am I.
   the whole of me.

2. Under the impulse of the divine Impeller,
   with the Powers for arms
   and the Spirit for hands,
   I, impelled, grasp hold of you!

1. Unified: *ayuta,* undisturbed, unrepelled, integrated, unbound. The exact meaning is uncertain.
In, out, continuous breath: *prāṇa, apāna, vyāna.*
2. Divine Impeller: Savitṛ.
Powers: Aśvins.
Spirit: Pūṣan.

Give Sight to Our Eyes

Cakṣurno dhehi

RV X, 158

9

1. May the Sun guard us
   in the highest heaven!
   May the breezes protect us
   in the airy spaces!
   May Fire be our guardian
   in earthly places!

2. May the Inspirer, whose glowing flame
   deserves a hundred
   sacrificial offerings,
   be pleased with us!
   From lightning flashes
   keep us safe.

3. May the God of light
   grant to us sight!
   May the heavenly peaks
   grant to us sight!
   May God the creator
   grant to us sight!

4. Give sight to our eyes
and sight to our bodies
that we may see.
May we see the world
at a single glance
and in all its details.

5. Thus, O Sun,
may we gaze on you,
most fair to behold!
May we see clearly,
with the eyes of Men!

1. Sun: Sūrya, the guardian of the sky (*div*).
Breezes: *vāta*, the ruler of the *antarikṣa*.
Fire: Agni, the protector of the earth.
2. Inspirer: Savitṛ.
Glowing flame: *haras*.
3. God of light: Savitṛ.
Heavenly peaks: *parvata*.
God the creator: Dhātṛ.
4. The world: *idam*, "this." Only the two different prefixes *sam-* (together) and *vi-* (apart) express the two ways of seeing, the unitarian and the analytical. The same occurs in v. 5.
Eyes of men: *nṛcakṣa*, human eye, or the eye of a hero. Cf. the *divya cakṣu* in BG XI, 8. To see the world requires a human eye, to see God a divine one.

Prayer for Well-Being

Balaprāpti

10

YV XXXVI, 1-2; 4; 6-7; 10-13; 18; 24

1. I take refuge in the Word as the Ṛg Veda,
in the Mind as the Yajur Veda,
in the Breath as the Sāma Veda.
I rely on sight and on hearing.
In me is the power of speech full of vigor.
I inhale and exhale deeply.

2. Whatever defect I have in my sight,
in my heart or mind,
may God amend!
May he, the Protector of the world, bless us!

4. What succor will he bring us, our wonderful Friend,
whoever prospers in his ventures?
With what most powerful aid will he support us?

6. You are the Protector of us who are your friends
and sing your praises.
Come to our help with a hundred aids.

7. O Strong One, what help are you going to bring us?
What do you give to those who sing your praise?

10. May the wind fan us with blissful breezes!
May the Sun warm us with delightful rays!
May the rain come to us with a pleasant roar!

11. May days come and go for us with blessings!
May nights approach us benignly!

12. May the celestial waters, our helpers, be sweet
to our taste and shower on us blessing!

13. May the earth also be pleasant to us,
our resting-place be free from thorns;
may it grant to us shelter far extending!
May light thrust far from us ill-fortune!

18. O earthen vessel, strengthen me.
May all beings regard me with friendly eyes!
May I look upon all creatures with friendly eyes!
With a friend's eye may we regard each other!

24. May we see your bright Eye, fixed by God,
rise again and again for a hundred autumns!
A hundred autumns may we live!

1. The anthropological triad is related to the three Vedas. Cf. BU I, 5, 5; etc.
I inhale and exhale deeply: lit. in me are in-breath and out-breath.
2. God (Protector of the world): Bṛhaspati.
4. Friend: Indra; cf. YV XXVII, 39; RV IV, 31, 1.
6. Protector: Indra; cf. YV XXVII, 41; RV IV, 31, 3.
7. Strong One: *vṛṣan,* Indra.
10. Rain: Parjanya.
13. Cf. YV XXXV, 21.
17. Cf. § II 38.
18. Earthen vessel: the vessel in which milk is heated for the sacrifice.
24. Cf. RV VII, 66, 16 (§ VII A d Antiphon). Reference to the sun.

Giver of Life

Āyurdā

11

YV III, 17-19; 29; 31-33; 37; 39-40

17. You, O Lord, are the body's protector.
My body protect.
You, O Lord, are the giver of life.
Grant life to me.
From you, O Lord, comes brilliance of mind.
Illumine my mind.
Whatever is lacking to my being, O Lord,
supply that to me.

18. Ourselves enkindled, we enkindle you, the shining one,
    through a hundred winters.
    Vigorous, we enkindle the giver of vigor;
    strong, the source of strength.
    Unharmed, we never have harmed you, O Lord,
    the harmer of our foes.
    O light-bedecked night, may I in safety
    reach your other shore!

19. You have won, O Lord, the splendor of the sun
    and the praises of poets.
    You have come, O God, to your own desired abode.
    So may I also
    attain length of days, splendor, and offspring,
    and a goodly store of riches!

29. May the Lord of the Word, the wealthy, the healer,
    the discoverer of treasure
    and increaser of well-being, swift to our aid,
    abide with us still!

31-33. We claim the powerful, invincible favor
    of the heavenly Three—
    Mitra, Aryaman, Varuṇa—over whom
    the malevolent foe
    wields no power, whether at home or on pathways
    beset with obstacles.
    For these sons of Infinity surround with light immortal
    mortal man, that he may live.

37. Earth, Space, and Sky! May I abound in children,
    in men, and in riches!
    O Friend of men, protect my children.
    O Adorable one,
    protect my cattle. O rapier of flame,
    protect my nourishment.

39-40. O Lord of the home, best finder of riches
    for our children are you.
    Grant to us splendor and strength,
    O Master of our home.
    A bounteous bestower of plenty is the God
    who is Master of our herds.
    Grant to us splendor and strength,
    O Lord and Master.

The nature of the YV obliges us to employ a certain license in the translation.
9; 11. Cf. § III 16.
17. Lord: Agni.
Brilliance of mind: *varcas,* splendor.
20-21; 25-26. Cf. § III 16.
29. Lord of the Word: Brahmaṇaspati of v. 28.

33. Infinity: Aditi, mother of the Gods.
37. Earth, Space, and Sky: *bhūḥ, bhuvaḥ, svaḥ,* the three ritual utterances (*vyāhṛti*).
38. Cf. § III 16.
39-40. Lord of the home: *agnir gṛhapatiḥ.*

Man's Glory — *Varcasprāpti*

12

AV III, 22

1. May the splendor of an elephant, the greatest of all creatures,
 may that great glory,
 which was born from the Boundless, now be diffused.
 The Gods together have bestowed it upon me.

2. On this splendor have all the powers of heaven
 concentrated their thought.
 May those Gods who nourish all life on earth
 anoint me with splendor!

3. That splendor that resides in an elephant, in a king
 among men, or within the waters,
 with which the Gods in the beginning came to godhood,
 with that same splendor make me splendid, O Lord.

4. O All-Knowing God, that powerful strength
 with which sacrifice endows you,
 the strength of the sun, the strength of the elephant,
 King among men—
 may the two Spirits, garlanded with lotus,
 vouchsafe that to me!

5. From the four directions, as far as the eye
 can direct its gaze,
 may that force, that elephant splendor, assemble
 and concentrate its virtue in me.

6. Behold the elephant, best of all creatures
 to mount and to ride!
 I anoint myself with his share of strength,
 with his elephant splendor!

1. Splendor of an elephant: *hastivarcasa.*
The Boundless: Aditi.
2. All the powers of heaven: lit. Mitra, Varuṇa, Indra, and Rudra.
3. Lord: Agni.
4. All-Knowing God: *jātavedas.*
Two Spirits: the Aśvins.
6. His share of strength: *bhaga,* also his fortune, his luck.

Human Splendor

Varcasya

13

AV VI, 38

1. With the splendor that resides in a lion, a tiger,
 an adder, the fire,
 Brahman, the sun,
may that blessed Goddess who gave birth to Indra
now come to us, endowed with splendor!

2. With the splendor that resides in an elephant, a leopard,
 in gold, in the waters,
 in cattle and in men,
may that blessed Goddess who gave birth to Indra
now come to us, endowed with splendor!

3. With the splendor that resides in a chariot, in dice,
 in a strong bull, in wind,
 in rain and in thunder,
may that blessed Goddess who gave birth to Indra
now come to us, endowed with splendor!

4. With the splendor that resides in a noble, a drumbeat,
 an arrow's flight, a man's shout,
 a mettlesome horse,
may that blessed Goddess who gave birth to Indra
now come to us, endowed with splendor!

1. Blessed Goddess: *devī subhagā*.
3. Rain: Parjanya, the Rain-God.
Thunder: lit. Varuṇa's vehemence.

B. SACRIFICE

Yajña

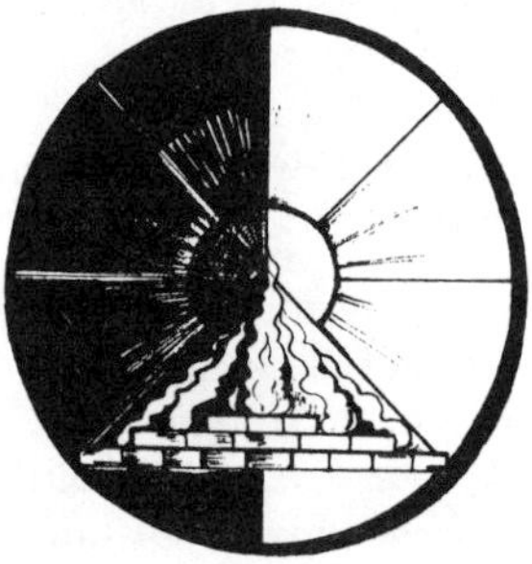

This sacrifice is the navel of the world.

RV I, 164, 35[128]

All power to our life through sacrifice!
All power to our lungs through sacrifice!
All power to our eyes through sacrifice!
All power to our ears through sacrifice!
All power to our backs through sacrifice!
All power to Sacrifice through sacrifice!

YV IX, 21

All this, whatever exists, is made to share in sacrifice.

SB III, 6, 2, 26

Sacrifice is a reliable ferry.

AB I, 13 (III, 2, 29)

The boat which father and son use for transport undergoes no damage. Now sacrifice is the boat of the Gods.

JaimB I, 165

One indeed is the sacrifice!

JaimB II, 70

128. *Ayaṁ yajño bhuvanasya nābhiḥ*. Cf. § I 11.

If one had to choose a single word to express the quintessence of the Vedic Revelation, the word *yajña,* sacrifice, would perhaps be the most adequate. Sacrifice is, in fact, an ancient, far-reaching, and pervasive intuition of the *śruti.* The conception of sacrifice, certainly, varied through the ages, and the term itself has received differing connotations, but the underlying intuition and its centrality have remained. The basic characteristic of *yajña* seems to be that of an action that reaches where it intends to reach, that really and truly offers something, that stretches out and extends itself. In other words, sacrifice seems to suggest an action that effectively "creates"; that is, it acts, is efficient, and produces what it intends. Or, again, sacrifice is the transitive act par excellence, the projecting act, the action that links directly the acting and its results in one and the same event. It is not something that, once done, remains suspended, as it were, independent from the act, but an action that forms part of the acting itself. The proper sphere of sacrifice is the sphere of communication, and communication constitutes the very structure of the universe. All this, of course, sounds inconveniently abstract, so it may become more intelligible if we proceed to describe the main themes related to sacrifice.

The conception of sacrifice found in the Vedas arises out of one of the two fundamental world views adopted by the human mind as it approaches the mystery of reality and seeks to discover therein the place of Man, that is, his human vocation. We could try to formulate this basic alternative in the following way. An early and universal human experience is the experience of the fact of change in the world or, in a word, that there is a becoming. Now, "becoming" can be understood in two ways: as a "coming from be(ing)" or as a "coming to be(ing)."

There is a trend within human thinking which leads to the assumption that nothing can come to be unless, somewhere and somehow, it already "is"; that nothing can be-come if it does not come from a Be, from a Being; that all that happens is potentially already there. This hypothesis assumes that there is a sort of infinite reservoir of possibilities, an infinite Being, a God, a Ground, ultimately responsible for all that is, for all change, for all becoming. The terms Immutability, Being, God, Creator, Ground, Origin, Substance, Essence, and a score of other notions convey this world view, and philosophies both inside and outside India have developed it to the highest degrees of subtlety and "depth." In the beginning was Fullness, and from this Fullness everything came, that is, be-came, and to it everything will return.

Another human option follows the second part of the alternative. Becoming is here not a coming-to-be *from* a *Be,* from a Being: change is not evolution, that is, a development or unfolding from what was already there, though undeveloped, folded, unstretched. On the contrary, becoming is a coming *into be,* into being. Being is simply such because it is be-ing, because it has come to be. Let us not hastily jump to the conclusion that here Nonbeing has the primacy,[129] but let us rather dwell particularly on the intuition here expressed that Nonbeing "is" *not* and thus cannot be handled as if it were negative Being. To affirm that there is nonbeing, that there *is* "not-is," is a contradiction in terms. The main reason for rejecting such an approach, however, arises from the notion of sacrifice as the primordial act, as Act, as *the* act that makes beings to be and is thus responsible for their becoming, without the assumption of a prior Being from which they come. In the beginning "was" Sacrifice.

In the beginning "was" neither Being nor Nonbeing,[130], neither Fullness nor Void. We cannot properly *say* that at the beginning there *was* Sacrifice, because neither *say* nor *was* has any meaning before there were Being and Word; and yet this would be the least inappropriate way of expressing this intuition. It is here that sacrifice finds its proper locus. It is the Prajāpati-sacrifice, in mythical terms, which gives birth to Being, as well as to beings, and which releases Being of the burden of having to be the origin and the cause of beings.[131]

At the origin of every being there is a sacrifice that has produced it. The texture of the universe is sacrifice, which is the act par excellence which produces all that is. Now this primordial act of sacrifice is a pure act devoid of any ontic or ontological attribute, positive or negative: it "is" neither being nor nonbeing. It "is" an act of which we can be aware only in the action itself and in connection with the "actor" or the "acted," though—as innumerable texts emphasize—we should distinguish, but not separate, four "moments": the *act,* the *action,* the *actor,* and the *acted (kriyā, karman, kartṛ, kārya).* The act is the sacrifice proper, the action is its inherent result, the actor is the agent (which is nothing other than

129. Cf. CU VI, 2, 1-2 (§ VI 2).
130. Cf. RV X, 129, 1 (§ I 1).
131. Cf. most of the texts of § I A.

the act acting), and the acted is another aspect of the action, namely, the concrete result of the act. We may distinguish, then, act (actor) and action (acted), but all is summed up in the single act, for the act as such includes everything else.

In the context of sacrifice this fundamental intuition is here not expressed in terms of being or nonbeing; it is not the dialectical approach that was developed in later periods. It is, however, the basis and the starting point of all Indo-European philosophizing. We may recall the two traditions that are to be found within most of the cultures of the world: the substantialist tradition and the functionalist, the one giving primacy to the stable and the other to the dynamic. It must be added that the Vedic intuition cannot be said to incline toward one and only one of these two philosophical views, for the paradoxical and enriching fact is that the dynamic or Heraclitean tone of the first Vedas is followed by the static or Parmenidean tone of the Upaniṣadic period. Or, to put it in a rather untraditional way, the first Vedas, prior to the Upaniṣadic interpretation of them, include the seed of both the classical Hindu and the classical Buddhist conceptions.

We must recall, once again, that the Vedic Revelation opens up reality not by means of concepts or, generally, by the telling of myths, but by means of symbols. We need to be aware of symbols in order to enter into communion with reality. A concept relates to logical intelligibility and is expressed in the different notes or attributes that define a word. A symbol, when expressed in words, stands for all that the word reveals over and above the conceptual intelligibility, though the latter is not necessarily excluded. Moreover, a symbol allows for a much wider range of interpretations than does a concept. For this reason the interpretation of Vedic words as concepts, which then have to be reinterpreted allegorically and metaphorically, has led to the discrediting of this ancient wisdom, as if it were only a collection of phantasmagoria. The Vedas are neither a metaphysical system nor a metaphorical or allegorical document, and that is why a special method of approach to them is required, for here Philosophy and Poetry, Speculation and Art, Theory and Praxis, are as yet unseparated.

Next we may note that Vedic sacrifice, as we shall read in the chapters of this section, is undergirded by an important symbol. This symbol, having received one particular name at the beginning, goes underground, as it were, in the subsequent periods, but remains none the less active and effective, even though under different names. This symbol is *ṛta*. As its etymology suggests[132] and as related words confirm,[133] *ṛta* stands for that nonontological but nevertheless real principle of order and of activity. *Ṛta* is the very energy of the sacrifice; it is what triggers the sacrifice. We may remember that ardor, truth, and *ṛta* share an intimate relationship.[134] Truth without *ṛta* would not be true.[135] All the powers of ardor, concentration, energy, and the like are connected with *ṛta*. Indeed, the whole order of the universe comes from and is maintained by the dynamism of *ṛta*.

Ṛta is generally translated by "Cosmic Order," which is a valid translation provided one bears in mind that cosmic order is not a fixed physical or mathematical law, but a "sacrificial" order. In the words of the Ṛg Veda itself: cosmic order is maintained by sacrificial order; that is, *ṛta* is upheld by *ṛta*.[136] It is through *ṛta* that Varuṇa governs the universe.[137] *Ṛta* is the ultimate foundation of everything; it is the "the supreme," although this is not to be understood in a static sense.[138] *Ṛta* points to an original and universal factor prior to the cosmic and human scission between the father and mother principles.[139] From *ṛta* comes the Firstborn (the Word?)[140] in the whole ordering of reality, while in another place it is affirmed that this Firstborn is no less than Prajāpati himself[141] or Agni[142] Agni is closely related to *ṛta*.[143] These and other utterances[144] are both bewildering and plainly contradictory, if *ṛta* is understood as a "substance" or a "thing," if *ṛta* can be "pinpointed," separated from and made independent of the "beings" it informs. *Ṛta* is rather the "law" or universal order embodied in sacrifice. It is the expression of the primordial dynamism that is inherent in every-

132. The root is *ṛ-*, *ar-*, to put in motion, to move; the Indo-European root *ar-* means to fit, to arrange (the spokes in the wheel), so that *ṛta* would be that which is well arranged, the established norm, "truth," order, etc., always with a dynamic connotation.

133. Cf. *ṛtu*, appropriate time, order, rule, season; *ṛju*, straight, upright, right; *arta* and *aśa* in Avestan, etc.

134. Cf. RV X, 190, 1 (§ I 2) and also AV XII, 1, 1 (§ I 19) where the six pillars of the earth are said to be truth, ardor, initiation, prayer, sacrifice, and *ṛta*.

135. A common word for untruth, falsity, is *anṛta*.

136. Cf. RV I, 23, 5 (§ IV B b); V, 68, 4.

137. Cf. RV V, 63, 1. Cf. § IV 8, where we shall see how Varuṇa punishes those who transgress *ṛta*.

138. Cf. TB I, 5, 5, 1: *ṛtam eva parameṣṭhī*. Cf. its relation with Soma.

139. Cf. RV I, 164, 8.

140. Cf. RV I, 164, 37 (cf. our motto and § I 11).

141. Cf. AV IV, 35, 1.

142. Cf. RV X, 5, 7.

143. Cf. RV V, 12, 1-3.

144. Cf. RV IV, 23, 8-10.

thing and also possesses its own internal coherence, a unifying force that could be said to be the very soul of sacrifice. This also explains why *ṛta* appears in the Ṛg Veda as being superior to and independent of the Gods, yet at the same time is their instrument. *Ṛta* is not a reservoir of energy upon which Gods or Men can draw for one purpose or another; *ṛta* as the principle of order is capable of growth, of expansion, of evolution out of itself: *ṛta,* in fact, can increase by means of *ṛta.*[145] The order of things, be they nature, Men, or Gods, is certainly a real order, but it is not an immutable and static one; the order of reality depends ultimately on reality itself.

The moment that *ṛta* is converted into a concept and is given a consistency in itself it is bound to appear as something rigid, immutable: a fixed cosmic order like a mathematical law which does not tolerate exceptions, a strict regulation which does not tolerate deviations, a stern ordinance which does not allow for freedom and improvization. It does not so appear, however, in the first Veda, where as an adjective, for instance, it means right, proper, holy, true, and the like, all words that denote flexible adaptation rather than rigid immutability.

This feature of *ṛta,* defying all that can properly be either objectified or substantivized, comes more clearly into view when we realize its intimate connection with sacrifice and all other cultic activites. *Ṛta* is, in point of fact, the actual functioning or rather the proper rhythm of the sacrifice, while sacrifice is that which causes things to be what they are. By sacrifice Gods and Men collaborate, not only among themselves but also for the maintenance and very existence of the universe. Reality subsists, thanks to sacrifice. But this truly primordial sacrifice is not left to the whim of either Men or Gods; it has an internal structure and mode of operation, namely, *ṛta.* Without *ṛta* the Vedic sacrifice would degenerate into a manipulation of the whole cosmic order by Gods or Men, and we would fall into a hideous world of magic, as Men are sometimes prone to do.

We would venture to describe this paradoxical intuition in this way: the self-subsistency of reality harbors its own absolute contingency. It is not necessary that beings or even Being exist; nothing prevents a total relapse into utter nothingness; nothing guarantees

145. Cf. RV I, 23, 5 (§ IV B b Introduction).

that time will endure forever, or that the world will not one day destroy itself. This Vedic vision awakens us from the illusion of ontological self-complacency: the whole of reality can collapse and disappear. Man can destroy himself, the world can have an end, existence is not indestructible, and even Being is not bound to be—as if it were obliged to be Being by a superior necessity. Nonbeing is not only a dialectical, but a real, possibility. The experience of nothingness, which implies the nothingness of the experience itself, is one of the deepest disclosures of the Vedic Revelation. The whole of reality "stands on its own feet"; that is, it does not lean on something or somebody else, but depends on, "hangs," from itself. It is, as it were, a divine contingency.

On the other hand, reality is not merely contingent: it does not simply depend on Another, that is, another reality, which in turn leans on something else. Nothing can destroy reality but itself. Nothing can challenge the existence of the universe, except the universe itself. There is no fear of any enemy, except the one that lurks inside us. In scholastic or theistic terms, God can destroy himself, if he so desires. In other words, the universe has the power to perpetuate itself, to be established in being, to exist, to overcome all threats and obstacles; but it has no eternal warrant. It has its own resources and from them it can pour forth eternal life. Moreover, this power is not a fiction; it is real and thus it can fail, it can be betrayed by reality itself.

Sacrifice is that which preserves the universe in existence, that which gives life and the hope of life. The universe in its totality does not repose on the shoulders of any extracosmic reality; if it did, it would not be the whole universe, but only an appendix to it. Reality has to include all that of which we can be aware. Neither God nor the Gods can be excluded from it. Now this universe is neither reposing on another Ground, nor reposing on itself, as if it were just a "mechanical" or "automatic" Being, as if freedom—and thus the freedom to cease to be—were not at the very core of reality. The universe does not repose on anything other than itself and its own structure. This ultimate structure is not to be regarded as "another" or "deeper" "thing" or substance; it is in fact sacrifice, which is, precisely, the internal dynamism of the universe, universal *ṛta*, cosmic order itself. This order, this sacrifice, obviously cannot be a static result of an already performed action. Sacrifice is the act that makes the universe. It does it, not through an external agent, but by the self-cooperation of the universe itself. Men alone cannot accomplish this, and the Gods left to themselves are equally impotent. The highest God, the supreme Being, is equally incapable of performing this act alone, for he is not God for himself but for the "creatures." In point of fact he is never alone; he is relational and belongs to reality, in spite of all the provisos and distinctions that a thinking philosophical and theological mind is bound to make in order not to fall into an oversimplified monism or an unsustainable dualism.

To perform the sacrifice is not to participate in a good act or to do good to the Gods, to mankind, or to oneself: it is to live, to "make" one's own survival and that of the whole universe. It is the act by which the universe itself continues in existence. An analysis of the different texts would help us to discover a double stage and a double team of agents in the unfolding of this sacrifice. The one stage is *ayaṁ lokaḥ*, this world of Men; the other is *asau lokaḥ*, the world beyond, the place of the heavenly beings. Moreover, of the two "teams," one consists of Men and the other of Gods and *asuras*. The cosmic liturgy that holds the world together and keeps it in existence is performed (1) by Men trying to ascend to the world of the Gods to celebrate the sacrifice there; (2) by the Gods responding to the call of Men and celebrating the sacrifice here on earth; (3) by Men performing it here also; and finally (4) by the Gods celebrating this life-giving sacrifice in heaven. A meditation on the texts will lead us to discover this fourfold conception.

If sacrifice is the ultimate and supreme principle, superior, thus, to the Gods and derived from God but not separable from either, it is understandable that some of the texts may sound magical to those who can accept only anthropomorphic world views. If the notion that God acts is not considered magic, the fact that sacrifice is efficacious cannot be said to be magical either. It would certainly be so if it did not constitute the ultimate structure of reality; but it is constantly taught in the Vedas down to the Upaniṣads, and it is repeated subsequently in philosophical works, that sacred science consists in the knowledge of sacrifice and that sacrifice is the ultimate principle. The deterioration of this world view begins when sacrifice is interpreted in a substantialized way, that is, when it is reified and thus permits the introduction of magical interpretations.

From this perspective of the primacy of sacrifice, the whole world appears new every moment and its path unpredictable. It will all depend on the sacrifice, on how the creative act is going to happen. This is a realm of true freedom, but it involves also the risk of misuse. That which allows for freedom may also allow for exploitation by those who understand the labyrinth of sacrifice. It is no wonder that the theory of *karman* appeared after a short time as an urgent corrective to a world view risking dependence only on whim and on the mere performance of rituals.

Before closing this introduction we should mention a general feature of sacrifice which appears in its post-Vedic development, whereby it is viewed under a more personalistic perspective. The proper name for this is perhaps *pūjā*, worship, rather than *yajña*, sacrifice.

Even when Man's worship has lost sight of the overall perspective just described, worship is still considered as a human activity by which Man attains the fulfillment of his being, not so much in the sense that our being is thereby enhanced or expanded as in the sense that it is only in worship that we fully *are*. Worship enables us to overcome the obstacles that obstruct the realization of being. Worship is not only a profoundly meaningful spiritual attitude; it is also an action in which Man's whole being is involved and through which Man realizes his "self."

In the performance of worship Man always endeavors to transcend time, to free himself from time. By this liberation he enters into the sphere of ultimate Reality. Liberation, *mokṣa*, is absolute freedom, it is an escape from subjection to time.[146] Worship permeates the whole of human life; it is both a means and an end, a means leading to final perfection, and an end, that is to say, perfection itself.

Creation is God's sacrifice, for not only does God bring it into existence, create it, but he also permits it to return to him again. He has in fact decreed its return. Now, to recognize an existence that restores itself by its own act is to invest it with immortality. Sacrifical acts, then, perform the function of finalizing this sort of exchange. Worship is the way to immortality.

Worship does not consist solely in prayer or feeling or knowledge; it is *action*, an action by which duality is transcended and dissimilarity banished. This act contains within itself, essentially, a

146. Cf. § VI C.

sacrificial aspect, a death and a becoming, a do-ing, *karman*. This word, which in the course of time will take on numerous other meanings, has here the significance of "action," understood as the act of worship and sacrifice. Action that does not include an element of making and remaking (creation and redemption) does not deserve the name. By worship salvation is rendered attainable and worship must needs entail sacrifice, for only sacrifice can produce the essential conversion. There is no other way to salvation except through sacrifice, for salvation is not attainable except by means of a break, a leap onto the other shore, or some sort of transference into a supranatural order. Man can be saved only by the performance of sacrificial worship; apart from such worship he is powerless, at the mercy of blind forces.

We must stress at this point the sacrificial element implied within the concept of *karman* and not load it with ideas of morality which it does not primarily contain.[147] The tendency to equate religion and morality, to see in *karman* a simple chalking-up of merits and demerits according to good or evil conduct, is secondary to authentic religiousness. For the Vedic Experience, religion is essentially worship and worship means a dynamic ontological two-way relationship of Man with the divine. *Karman* implies action, not only in its etymological but also in its intrinsic meaning, and, what is more, it implies an act of worship that is identified with sacrifice. *Karma-mārga* is a way of sacrifice and of worship.

Creation of Sacrifice *Yajñe jāte*

14 Cosmogony is liturgy and liturgy is cosmogony: thus we might sum up the main intuition of this text, which at the same time formulates one of the deepest convictions of the Vedic world view. The world owes its origin to a divine sacrifice and, thanks to the same sacrifice, it continues to be. If the first act is divine, the second is human. We have here a cosmotheandric action for which an appropriate symbol is the loom, connected with the human activity by which Man creates his own patterns and makes his own clothing.

In fact every liturgy has always been and still is a remaking of the world, a reenactment of the creative act by which the world

147. Cf. § V A Introduction.

comes into being. This "making of the world" can, however, be understood not only as a cosmological cosmogony but also as a historical or even a sociological one. Modern liturgy tends in fact to be the coming together of people in order to reshape the environment, social, cultural, political, ecological, and artistic.

Throughout the hymn there is an interplay between two ideas and sets of actions, weaving and sacrifice, the latter actions mirroring or rather reenacting the creational acts of the former. The meaning of this hymn becomes clearer when we remember parallel texts that speak of two maidens, symbolizing day and night, dancing in circles and endlessly weaving the stuff of the world, spreading all the colors of reality over the six regions of the universe.[148] This world-building action is not left, however, to cosmic forces alone; Men and the ancestors, or "Fathers," are also involved in the task of weaving the fabric and spinning the threads. The rituals are the threads, the hymns the shuttles, the weavers the ancestral sacrifices. As the cloth has its design, so the sacrificial texts have their meters. One Upaniṣad says[149] that the Gods were afraid of death and that each one covered himself with his respective meter for protection. The origin of this conception is to be found in the text given here, where each God has his own meter in which he is praised and which gives him strength. The power of poetry is such that the poets sometimes wonder whether it is the Gods who inspire their song or their poetry that gives life to the Gods. But the text also says (v. 5) that the human poets follow the already existing relationship, discovering divine power in every meter. A male figure, the *pumān,* which appears here is related to the *puruṣa,* the primordial Man, of our previous texts.[150]

Yajñe jāte RV X, 130

1. Sacrifice [resembles] a loom with threads extended
this way and that, composed of innumerable rituals.
Behold now the Fathers weaving the fabric; seated
on the outstretched loom. "Lengthwise! Crosswise!" they cry.

2. Behold now a Man who unwinds and sets the thread,
a Man who unwinds it right up to the vault of heaven.

148. Cf. AV X, 7, 42-43 (§ I 3) and also RV I, 113, 3 (§ I 30); I, 115, 4; II, 3, 6.
149. Cf. CU I, 4, 1-3 (§ VI 12).
150. Cf. §§ I 5 and I 6.

Here are the pegs; they are fastened to the place of worship.
The Sāman-hymns are used for weaving shuttles.

3. What was the model, the pattern, what the connection?
What was the ritual butter and the line of demarcation?
What was the meter, the hymn, the preliminary chant,
when all the deities sacrificed God in oblation?

4. The Gāyatrī meter became the yokefellow of Agni,
Savitṛ took as his companion the meter Uṣṇih,
Soma, the one who is praised by hymns, took Anuṣṭubh,
while the word of the Lord of Speech was strengthened by Bṛhatī.

5. The meter Virāj was reserved to Mitra and Varuna;
for Indra's day the meter allotted was Triṣṭubh.
The meter Jagatī had access to all the Gods.
To this arrangement the human poets conformed.

6. It was this same ritual the Seers, our Fathers, adopted
when in the beginning sacrifice was first created.
With the eyes of my mind I believe I can envisage
those who were first to offer this sacrifice.

7. The rituals, meters, and hymns were according to the rubrics,
even those of the Seven godlike Seers of old.
When the sages follow in the path traced by the ancestors
they take the reins in their hands like charioteers.

1. Innumerable: *ekaśatam*, lit. one hundred and one.
Rituals: *devakarman*, rite, act of worship.
Fathers: *pitaraḥ*, ancestral sacrificers as in v. 6.
2. A Man: *pumān*, the primordial man, i.e., *ādipuruṣa*, or the *puruṣa* of RV X, 90 (§ I 5). He is the sacrificer and the sacrifice at the same time: *yajñapuruṣa*. Cf. AV X, 7, 43 (§ I 3).
3. Correlation and analogy between model, pattern, and connection (*pramā, pratimā, nidāna*) and meter, preliminary chant, and hymn.
Ambivalent sentence: the deities offer to the unique God and also the deities offer God as sacrifice. Cf. RV X, 90, 6 (§ I 5).
All the deities sacrificed God: *yad devā devam ayajanta viśve*. Cf. the parallel idea in RV I, 164, 50. They offer the sacrifice of Man, the mediator of v. 2. These may be the ancestors, *pitaraḥ*, of v. 1 whose function is to "weave the hundred and one rituals."
4-5. Relate the Gods to their respective meters; cf. also AB VIII, 6, 3 (XXXVII, 2).
Lord of Speech: Bṛhaspati.

The Origin of Sacrifice *Brahmayajña*

15 We recall from the preceding hymn that sacrifice is envisaged as a universal fabric reaching everywhere; or rather, sacrifice is seen as the creative act of weaving that cosmic fabric in which everything has its place and receives its meaning. It is by means of this primordial act that the Gods are able to reenact that action

through which Reality is. The original *dharmas,* that is, the original structures of reality (or the primordial rites, statutes, ordinances) are thus prescribing what is mentioned in the first verse of the first hymn following and is repeated in several other places: a sacrifice to the Sacrifice by means of the sacrifice. To "offer" means to "stretch" and by this very fact to "reach" reality by means of performing the act by which reality is.

If we do not freeze reality into a form of static being, but consider it rather as the act acting, with the Gods as the first agents of the sacrifice, we may understand the stanzas of the hymn. The sacrifice is not a ready-made act, over and done with. It is, on the contrary, the act by which the world is, and thus this act comes to be, it becomes manifest, it is born and grows again and again. It becomes the ultimate criterion, the ruler, the highest instance: the overlord of even the Gods.

The third verse calls Men to partake in the divine banquet, in the feast of the Gods, in the authentic form of existence. The Gods are our forerunners and we pray that we may follow them and be allowed a place with them in the sphere of authentic existence: the *parama vyoman.* It is a place in which human life is unrestricted: we may experience this new and real dimension of our being while still continuing in our earthly life, while seeing the rising of the sun with our own personal eyes, now no longer limited, of course, to sensorial perception. In the *parama vyoman* human life is elevated to the life of the Gods. *Vyoman* is the realm of freedom from limitations. The rising of the sun corresponds also to the ascent of Man to that supreme stage.

The Gods have no existence of their own; they exist in, with, above, and also for Men. Their supreme sacrifice is Man, the primordial Man, whom we have already met in other hymns. It is overwhelming, this experience of being Man: Man is the most important and central creature in the universe but he is also the most miserable, the most suffering, and often even the most despicable. Human life is the most precious thing and at the same time the most lavishly wasted. Man is the sacrificer, but also the sacrificed; the Gods, in their role as the primal agents of sacrifice, offer their oblation with Man. Man is not only the cosmic priest; he is also the cosmic victim. Human history, we may venture to translate, is the most blatant example and confirmation of the truth that Man is both sacrificer and sacrifice. To say that the history of human existence on earth has a meaning amounts to declaring that the Gods performed their sacrifice with Man as their oblation. The last two verses, however, give us a glimpse of an intuition that the coming cosmic liturgy will no longer be the exploitation of Men by Men, or the religious sanction of it, but a new hymn, a new song, whose melody the Gods themselves will have to learn from Men, once the latter have invented it.[151]

The second text places the sacrifice in its true perspective: even if Brahman here is not the "absolute world ground" of the later philosophical sense, it is on the way to becoming so. The reciprocal definition of Brahman and sacrifice in the second verse illumines the meaning of both: Brahman *is* the sacrifice and all its elements precisely because it is the inner reality (or essence: *sattva*) of the sacrifice and also that ineffable power that makes the priests' sacrifice a real sacrifice. The text makes it quite clear that the different kinds of priests are merely instruments in the realization of the sacrifice and that as such they are praiseworthy. Yet a consciousness of the unity that exists among all the parts and elements of the sacrifice, and an awareness of the underlying reality of Brahman, are already beginning to pervade the performance and the understanding of the sacrifice itself.

Brahmayajña

AV VII, 5

i)

1. Through sacrifice the Gods sacrificed to the Sacrifice.
Those were the first established rites.
Their greatness enhanced, they ascended to heaven
where dwell the ancient Gods who must needs be appeased.

2. Thus originated sacrifice; it manifested itself.
It came to birth and then increased.
It became the Lord and Ruler of the Gods.
May sacrifice bestow upon us some treasure!

3. There where the Gods made an offering to the Gods,
where, immortal, they worshiped with heart immortal,
may we also revel, in highest heaven.
May we gaze on it in wonder at the rising of the sun!

4. Using the Man for their oblation,
the Gods performed the sacrifice.
But more powerful still than this oblation
was the offering they made with the Hymn's invocation.

151. Some holy men, says the BG, echoing this text, offer the sacrifice by the sacrifice. Cf. BG IV, 25 (§ III 29) (a text that, significantly enough, some modern exegetes find rather confusing).

AV XIX, 42, 1-2

ii)

1. Brahman is the priest, Brahman the sacrifice;
   by Brahman the posts are erected.
   From Brahman the officiating priest was born,
   in Brahman is concealed the oblation.

2. Brahman is the spoon dripping fatness;
   by Brahman the altar is established.
   Brahman is the essence of sacrifice;
   the priests prepare the oblation.
   To the minister, praise!

■ i) 1. Cf. RV I, 164, 50; X, 90, 16 (§ I 5) for the same stanza. Cf. also RV X, 130, 3 (§ III 14); SB X, 2, 2, 2.
3. In highest heaven: *parame vyoman*. Cf. RV I, 164, 34 (§ I 11).
4. The first two lines are the same as in RV X, 90, 6 (§ I 5).
Hymn: the hymn *vihavya*.
5. We have not given the last verse, which has many variant readings and is obscure.

■ ii) 1. Concealed: *antarhita*, placed within.
2. Essence of sacrifice: *yajñasya sattvam*.
Priests: *ṛtvijaḥ*.
Praise: *svāhā*.
3-4. These two last verses are omitted as they do not refer directly to the origin of the sacrifice.

The Fire Sacrifice — *Agnihotra*

16 Without light there is no life. We have already seen the central place and importance of light. But light is not an abstract reality; light is Sun and Fire. The Kauṣītaki Brāhmaṇa says that

> Light is Agni, Agni is light. The one who is light, he calls light. . . . Agni offers itself in sacrifice to the rising Sun and the setting Sun offers itself in sacrifice to Agni in the evening; Night sacrifices itself to the Day and Day sacrifices itself to the Night.[152]

The sacrifice is the *agnihotra*. Continuity is thus established, the circle is completed, harmony is preserved.

The Sunlight of the day not only gives way to the light of the night, the Fire, but in a sense gives birth to it, by reason of a certain cosmic solidarity in which Man too has his part to play. This is the function of the *agnihotra*. All other sacrifices and rites can be neglected, but not the *agnihotra*, for it is the quintessence of sacrifice[153] and through it one becomes immortal.[154] "The *agnihotra*

152. KausB II, 8. Cf. YV III in this chapter.
153. Cf. CU V, 24, 5.
154. Cf. KathU I, 13 (§ V 27); etc.

is the ultimate [*parama*] foundation of everything."[155] One can then understand the text of the Śatapatha Brāhmaṇa which says that if the priest did not perform the *agnihotra* in the morning, that day the sun would not rise.[156] This, as we see from the central thrust of the whole *śruti,* is certainly not owing to some mysterious magical connection between the *agnihotra* and the sun, but to the theanthropocosmic link that maintains the whole of reality in truth and order, for Man is not simply a spectator in the cosmic display or an outsider set there just to exploit the earth for his own benefit.

The *agnihotra* represents the simplest possible form of the whole Vedic conception of sacrifice. Any householder, provided he is properly initiated, may perform the sacrifice in the evening and morning of every day and recite the prayers, some of which are given here along with other texts on the same *agnihotra.* The two temporal moments, in which this sacrifice has to be performed, are important: they are *saṁdhyā,* the "holding together," the junction of Agni and Sūrya, the brief periods when the two lights meet, when one can distinguish no longer the one from the other, when Man can intervene as a part of the cosmos without disturbing the rhythm of the sun and the stars. In the morning the human heart is ready for life, while at sunset it is inclined to pour out its innermost feelings. Practically all religions of the world have considered these hours to be holy; these are the times even nowadays when the modern city dweller starts the new day with enthusiasm and hope, or longs at its decline for a friend, for love, for relaxation, for Soma.[157]

It is not necessary to describe the rite of the *agnihotra.* Suffice it to say that besides the sun, time, and the light—and thus also space—a minimum of three fires and three persons, some milk, and, when possible, the cow that has given the milk are required: a complete microcosm.

Agnihotra

RV V, 15, 1-2

i)

1. To the Lord, the far-renowned, the wise Ordainer,
ancient and glorious, I offer the tribute of a song.
Annointed with oil is he, the Lord, the powerful,
giver of bliss and guardian of noble riches.

155. MahanarU 527.
156. Cf. SB II, 3, 1, 5.
157. Cf. § VII Introduction.

2. On the power of sacrifice which is grounded in highest heaven
and by Cosmic Order in Cosmic Order established,
[our Fathers], though mortal, attained immortal seats
in those spheres above which firmly support the heavens.

RV X, 80, 4

ii) Agni extends the sacrifice to heaven:
his forms are scattered everywhere.

RV X, 100, 6

iii) Indra possesses power divine and glorious.
The singer in the house is Agni, the wise, the seer.
May our sacrifice be at hand and pleasing to the gathered people!
For freedom and for perfect bliss we pray!

YV III, 9; 11; 20-21; 25-26; 38

iv) 9. Fire is Light, Light is Fire. Glory!
Sun is Light, Light is Sun. Glory!
Fire is Splendor, Light is Splendor. Glory!
Sun is Splendor, Light is Splendor. Glory!
Light is Sun, Sun is Light. Glory!

11. Let us, proceeding to the sacrifice,
utter a prayer to the Lord,
who hears us even from afar.

20. You are sacred drink, may I enjoy your sacred drink!
You are greatness, may I share in your greatness!
You are power, may I partake in your power!
You are treasures, may I share in your treasures!

21. O shining ones, remain in this dwelling,
stay in this gathering, this place, this spot.
Remain right here and do not stir!

25. O Lord, be our closest friend, our savior
and gracious protection. O wonderful Lord
of glorious renown, come near us, we pray you,
and bestow upon us most splendid treasures.

26. To you, most brilliant and shining God,
we pray now for happiness for our friends.
Listen attentively to our call;
save us from every evil man.

38. Thus have we now approached the All-Knower,
the one who is the best procurer of good things.
Endow us, O Majesty, with strength and glory.

SB II, 3, 1, 13

v) And so they say: all other sacrifices have an end but the *agnihotra* does not come to an end. All that which lasts for twelve years is indeed limited; the *agnihotra* is nevertheless unlimited, for when a man has offered in the evening he looks forward with confidence to offering in the morning; and when he has offered in the morning he likewise looks forward with confidence to offering again in the evening. Thus the *agnihotra* is unlimited and, hence, from its unlimitedness, creatures also are born unlimited. Whosoever knows the unlimitedness of the *agnihotra* is himself unlimited in prosperity and offspring.

SB VII, 3, 1, 34

vi) You, O Agni, are the righteous, the truthful, the mighty, and most wonderful. You are indeed manifest to all: you, O Agni, are omnipresent. Men rank Agni highest for grace and joy, for grace and joy reside undoubtedly in sacrifice. You, who are heaven, the ruler and divine one, we human beings invoke with song.

■ i) 1. Lord: Agni.
Anointed with oil: *ghṛtaprasatta.*
Powerful: *asura,* lit. the benevolent Asura.
2. On the power: *śāke,* locative of *śāka,* might, power.
In highest heaven: *parame vyoman.*
By Cosmic Order in Cosmic Order established: *ṛtena ṛtaṁ dharunaṁ dhārayanta.*
Immortal seats: lit. unborn persons, probably the Gods. A difficult but important text.
ii) Extends: lit. stretches: *tatāna* from the root *tan-,* to stretch out. Cf. RV X, 130, 1 (§ III 14) and also RV I, 159, 4; X, 57, 2 for the same metaphor.
Cf. SB I, 4, 4, 1 (§ I 13) and what has been said about Agni in § III 4.
■ iv) 9. Cf. KausB II, 8 (quoted in the Introduction).
Fire: Agni.
Light: *jyotis.*
Sun: Sūrya.
11. The first approach to the sacrifice requires an invocation to Agni, the mediator.
17-19. Cf. § III 11.
20. Sacred drink: *andhas, soma* plant, invigorating life-giving food and drink.
Greatness: *mahas.*
Power: *bhakṣīya.*
Treasures: *rayi.*
21. Shining ones: *revatī,* which may refer to the cows, to the waters, and/or to holy speech.
Dwelling: *yoni,* womb, but also homely abode.
25. Saviour: *trātṛ,* protector.
Gracious: *śiva.*
Protection: *varūthya.*
Treasures: *rayi,* in a material as well as a spiritual sense.
26. Cf. RV V, 24, 3-4 (§ VII 53).
Most brilliant: *śociṣṭha.*
29; 31-33; 37. Cf. § III 11.
38. Majesty: *agni samrāj.* This prayer is uttered as the worshiper approaches the *āhavanīya* fire.
39-40. Cf. § III 11.
■ v) Have an end: are concluded, finished. There is a play here on the root *sthā-; saṁ-sthā:* to be concluded, to come to an end, and *an-upa-sthā-:* to be unfinished, not to come to an end. *Agnihotraṁ na saṁtiṣṭhate/anupasthitam agnihotram:* i.e., *agnihotra* is an everlasting, perennial sacrifice.
Unlimited in prosperity . . . : this may also refer to the spiritual effect of the perennial, creative sacrifice. Cf. SB II, 2, 4, 8 (§ III 23).
■ vi) A hymn of praise to Agni.

The Drop of Life *Soma pavamāna*

17 The sacrifice of the Soma-juice, to which all the Vedas so frequently allude, is one of the major Vedic sacrifices.

All the one hundred and fourteen hymns of Book IX of the Ṛg Veda are dedicated to Soma, as are also certain hymns of the other books.[158] The importance of Soma derives from the fact that its sacrifice is an act in which the divine and the human both take part. Soma is, properly speaking, the drink of the *soma*-plant which allows Men to feel that they are more than just conscious animals. Thus they are given the elixir of immortality and at the same time are permitted to share in some divine form of consciousness.

The *soma*-plant has been identified with a brown or reddish bush some three feet high.[159] The golden hue of its juice inspires poets to acclaim tirelessly the "radiance" of this divinity and his close connection with the Sun. He creates light and scatters darkness. Nevertheless the plant should also be understood in a concrete physiological way. The action of Soma has a stimulating and inspiring effect which is something more than comfort or strength, though less than intoxication or drunkenness.[160]

The process of extracting the juice from the *soma*-plant is described minutely with endless variations of ritual. The poets chant their hymns at that moment when Soma leaps forth from the press. The woolen strainer stands for heaven, the juice in liquid form is the rain; thus Soma is called Lord of the Rivers and son of Water. Elsewhere he is "a bull," and his descent into the milky water of the vat is likened to the insemination of a herd of cows. Thus the whole cosmos is involved in this very simple act of the extraction of the *soma*-juice.

The earthly origin of Soma is said to be in the mountains, on Mount Mūjavat,[161] but the mountains in general are also alleged to be his birthplace.[162] His true origin, however, is in heaven: "child of heaven,"[163] "milk of heaven."[164] He was brought to earth by an eagle who snatched him from the Castle of Brass where the Gan-

158. Cf. RV I, 91; VIII, 48 (the hymn that follows); VIII, 79; X, 25; etc.
159. *Ephedra intermedia?*
160. It has been remarked that *mad-*, the word denoting the effects of Soma, means something more than *begeistern* (arousing enthusiasm) and something less than *berauschen* (intoxicating) (Geldner).
161. Cf. RV X, 34, 1 (§ IV 12).
162. Cf. RV III, 48, 2; V, 43, 4; IX, 18, 1.
163. RV IX, 33, 5.
164. RV IX, 51, 2.

dharvas were guarding him.[165] In the Brāhmaṇas it is Gāyatrī (a name for Agni) who steals Soma. As the most important of all plants he is given the title of Lord of Plants.

Soma is the vehicle of immortality. Soma "is" immortality.[166] Immortality is acquired by the drinking of Soma and not by abstaining from the fruits of the earth. The way to immortality is not one of escape from the material world, but rather one of assimilating earthly realities. Soma has the power of rendering both Gods and Men immortal. "we have drunk Soma, we have become immortal, we have entered into light, we have known the Gods," says our text (v. 3). Immortality is not the birthright of any being; it has to be acquired, conquered, merited, given.

The most frequent epithet of Soma is *pavamāna,* the "flowing clear," which suggests both that the juice is purified in its elaborate processing and that it purifies by its effects.[167] Soma possesses healing powers: "The blind man sees, the cripple walks."[168] He also stimulates speech and evokes sublime thoughts. He is a poet, the "soul" of the sacrifice, a sage; his wisdom is often acclaimed and he is the giver of all blessings.

> The Sea are you, Seer, revealer of all things;
> under your sway are the World's five regions.
> You transcend both earth and heaven.
> Yours, O Purifier, are the Stars and the Sun.[169]

In several of the late hymns of the Ṛg Veda, as also in the Atharva Veda, Soma is identified with the moon. Soma is luminous, is magnified in water, and is termed a globule.[170]

Hymn VIII, 48, is a chant of praise to Soma, God of immortality. The poet prays for the divine strength that mortal Men are powerless to resist, for protection against all evil, for light and wealth, for a long life.

Soma is here, as in some other places, addressed as *indu,* "Drop," a word that came to be used also with reference to the moon, probably owing to its connection with Soma, a brilliant drop, a plant to be collected during full-moon night. We have already seen

165. Cf. RV IV, 26; IV, 27, 4.
166. Cf. SB IX, 5, 1, 8: *tad yat tad amṛtaṁ somaḥ sa.*
167. *Pavamāna,* purifying, comes from the root *pū-* to purify, cleanse, illumine (cf. *pavitra,* holy, pure, as further explained in § IV B c). Cf. §§ VII 5; 10; 15; 20; 25.
168. RV VIII, 79, 2.
169. RV IX, 86, 29.
170. Cf. RV VI, 44, 21.

that the waters are a symbol of life and that food is also a life-bringer. Now Soma, as a liquid, as a drop, is considered to be the drop of life, a drink that bestows health, both temporal and eternal. Without venturing any hypothesis regarding the actual Vedic use of Soma as a hallucinogenic potion, we may note the close connection between exciting material substances and religious life. Obviously there are negative factors in these practices, but there are also positive elements, for they demand an attitude that is life-affirming and accepts the importance of matter. Soma is praised, not as a way of escape from the normal human condition, but as a means of facing it more squarely. Second, the exciting effect of Soma tends to activate human potentialities, not to put them to sleep. Third, Soma, elevating the worshiper to a higher plane of human consciousness, claims to enhance his daily living and to help him to live with the awareness of a deeper dimension while he is carrying on his ordinary actions. These and similar ideas spring to mind as being involved in the old Vedic Soma sacrifice and its related rites in other cultures and religions, for the Soma sacrifice undoubtedly has connections with the *haoma* rites of Zoroastrianism and is viewed by some as having an inner relationship with the Eucharistic sacrifice.

The Soma spirituality (if we may use this expression) is an important characteristic of the Vedic Experience. We have already described it as being theandric. Both Men and Gods, that is, the human and the divine, are involved in the same adventure. Both must become immortal, both must coalesce. While the divinization of Men is a well-defined path, the humanization of the Gods is a mysterious process in which Soma is the link and sacrifice the means of attainment. The devinization of Man is not without repercussions on the Godhead, which in turn is humanized. Soma is the powerful symbol of this double and yet simple process.

This Soma spirituality is based on fullness and not on want. Many traditional religious forms seem to stress want, guilt, penance, asceticism, renunciation, and a flight from all corporal values and material pleasures—and rightly so when Man lives in conditions of hardship and strain, as he all too often does. But there is more to human life. Soma spirituality stresses the opposite facet: Soma bestows and celebrates strength, courage, loquacity, and eloquence; he unleashes our thoughts so that, once blessed by Soma, they flow without inhibition. It is not only immortality that we acquire when we drink Soma; it is also joy, purification, and protection from all evil influences. It is Soma who instills in us the proper mood that enables us to perform the sacrifice with dignity and to face life with confidence. Soma is invariably a sacred drink, though it is not always drunk with accompanying rituals—a significant fact in view of the later development of the *agniṣṭoma*, especially when it involved multitudinous and complicated rubrics.

An interesting corroboration of this positive Soma spirituality is the meaning and use that the word *somya* acquires from the Upaniṣads onward: the drinker of Soma, the one who is worthy to be offered Soma, he who is related to or that which belongs to Soma, has come to mean gentle, dear, kind, auspicious, and has become a form of address for respectable persons, such as Brahmins. A respectable and excellent man is not from this point of view the ascetic in rags, but the "moon-shining" man, who, being satiated with Soma, is therefore radiant and kind, gentle and loving.

Soma pavamāna RV VIII, 48

1. I have tasted, as one who knows its secret,
the honeyed drink that charms and relaxes,
the drink that all, both Gods and mortals,
seek to obtain, calling it nectar.

2. Once penetrated within my heart,
you become Aditi and appease the Gods' wrath.
O Drop, who enjoy Indra's friendship, convey
to us wealth, like a steed who is bridled, obedient.

3. We have drunk the Soma and become immortal!
We have attained the light, we have found the Gods!
What can the malice of mortal man
or his spite, O Immortal, do to us now?

4. Bless the heart, O Life-Drop, which has received you,
as a father his son, or a friend his friend.
Wise Soma, whose voice we hear from afar,
prolong our days that we may live.

5. These glorious drops are my health and salvation:
they strengthen my joints as thongs do a cart.
May these droplets guard my foot lest it stumble
and chase from my body all manner of ills.

6. Make me shine brightly like fire produced by friction.
Illumine us, make us ever more prosperous.

Enthused by you, Soma, I find myself rich!
Enter within us for our well-being.

7. With hearts inspired may we relish the Juice
like treasure inherited from our Fathers!
Lengthen our days, King Soma, as the sun
causes the shining days to grow longer.

8. Have mercy upon us, King Soma, and save us!
Do not forget that we are your disciples.
We are eager, O Drop, with zeal and dexterity!
Do not hand us over to our enemy's pleasure!

9. It is you, O Soma, who guard our bodies;
in each of our limbs you have made your abode,
O surveyor of men! if we have transgressed your statutes,
forgive us, O God, like a loving friend.

10. May I take him to myself like a well-disposed friend!
May this draught not harm us, O Lord of the bay horses—
this Soma now absorbed within me! For this
I pray to God to prolong my existence.

11. Our weariness and pains are now far removed;
the forces of darkness have fled in fear.
Soma has surged within us mightily.
We have reached our goal! Life is prolonged!

12. This drop that has penetrated our hearts, O Fathers,
this Soma, immortal deep within us mortals,
him would we honor with our oblations.
We long to abide in his grace and favor.

13. In an intimate union with the Fathers, O Soma,
you have extended yourself throughout Earth and Heaven.
You would we honor with our oblations,
desirous of becoming possessors of riches.

14. O guardian Gods, pronounce on us blessing!
Let sleep not overtake us nor useless talk.
May we forever be dear to Soma!
Having won the mastery, let us speak wisdom!

15. Imparter of strength, come, take full possession,
O Soma, light-finder, man's constant overseer.
Enlist your helpers, O Lord; place a guard
on our lives both in front and behind to protect us.

1. As one who knows its secret: *sumedhas* (a free translation), lit. having a good understanding, wise.
That charms and relaxes: *svādhyaḥ varivovittarasya,* that inspires and grants freedom, stirs and gives good thoughts.

2. You become Aditi: i.e., Aditi in her function of liberating from sin. When Soma is in the body he purifies and averts the anger of the Gods.

3. Cf. RV IX, 113, 7 (§ V 23).
4. Bless the heart: *śam naḥ bhava hṛde,* do good to our heart, be a blessing, a gift, blissful for us when drunk; *śaṁ hṛde:* refreshing the heart.
O Life-Drop: *indu,* drop (and also moon).
5. Glorious drops: *yaśas,* object of honor and veneration.
8. Save us: *svasti,* for our salvation, well-being.
Disciples: *vratyāḥ,* those who abide by your laws (*vrata*).
9. Surveyor of men: *nṛcakṣas.*
10. Lord of the bay horses: Indra.
God: Indra.
12. The Fathers, *pitaraḥ,* are here called to witness, as they also love Soma.
15. Lord: *indu.*

The Pressing Stones *Grāvastotra*

18 Among the objects used in the sacrifice and hence invested with sacredness are the stones between which the Soma stalks are pressed and crushed in order to extract the juice, the nectar of immortality. The pressing stones are made the subject of several hymns.[171] Here the stones hewn from the mountainside are personified: they are dancers, oxen, racehorses, speakers, and so on; they are godlike, immune to disease and fatigue and death. They play so integral a part in the sacrifice that the sacrificer even prays to them, offering them his reverence and homage, begging them to unloose the inspired tongue of the Soma presser. Finally, they are asked respectfully—or scornfully, according to some interpreters—to revert to their purely mineral state of being simply stones. The sacred character of a thing, we note, resides always in its function and not in its substance. For example, the *mūrtis,* the idols worshiped during popular festivals, are afterwards often immersed in the rivers or simply laid aside.

The whole world is called upon to contribute to the sacrifice; not only Gods, Men, animals, and plants, but also the earth and its elements. These stones are generally called *grāvā* and in Soma rituals the priest recites this Ṛg Veda hymn as part of the prescribed *stotra.*

Mention is made of these stones in many prayers so as to stress the sacramental, that is, the spiritual-material, aspect of this central and specifically human act:

> Fixing with careful attention the press stones
> of sacrifice, I invoke noble Heaven and Earth.

171. Cf. RV X, 76; X, 175, as well as the one given here.

Now, O Lord, raise your flames pure and beautiful,
bringing to men all manner of blessings.[172]

Grāvastotra

RV X, 94

1. Let them utter loud sounds! We too will utter!
Give tongue, one and all, to the Stones who give tongue,
when, O rocks, O mountains, swiftly clashing,
you bring to God's ears your rhythmic din.

2. These Stones, gnashing their green-tinted jaws,
emit sounds like a hundred, a thousand, voices.
Their task achieved, these Pressing Stones,
noble workers in a noble cause,
forestall the offerer in tasting the oblation.

3. They utter loud sounds as they find the sweet Soma.
Booming, they gnaw the pulp prepared.
These bulls, skillful pounders, bellow aloud
as they seize the branch of the reddish shrub.

4. Exalted and inebriated by Soma, they shout,
calling upon God through whom they have tasted
the ambrosial Soma. They skillfully dance
with the sisters, held in firm clasp together,
and make the earth resound with their stamping.

5. They have raised their voices to heaven, these eagles,
they have danced with vigor, these dark-colored hinds.
Now they sink toward the lower stone, find contact,
and effuse copious Soma-seed, brightly shining.

6. Like strong draught animals who draw a cart,
bulls who wear the yoke and are harnessed together,
the Stones emit bellows, panting and heaving.
Then the sound of their snorting is like that of horses.

7. Acclaim [the Stones] with their ten [workers],
ten belts, ten thongs, and tenfold harness,
with their ten reins, who, never growing old,
yoked ten times over, draw the ten yokes.

8. These Stones are like racehorses with ten sets of reins,
their bits well fixed within their jaws.
At the flowing of the Soma-juice they have been first
to taste the milky fluid of the first-crushed stalk.

9. These Soma-eaters kiss the bay steeds of Indra.
They are set for their stalk-crushing task on an oxhide.

172. RV III, 57, 4. Lord: Agni.

When Indra has drunk the sweet Soma they extract,
he increases in strength, waxes great, like a bull.

10. Your stalk is as strong as a bull. Naught will harm you!
You are ever full of juice, ever replete,
fair in glory, like the daughters of the rich
in whose sacrifice, O Stones, you take delight.

11. Smashing but never shattered, these Stones
are tireless; they know neither death nor cessation.
Exempt from sickness, old age, and suffering,
sleek-looking, free from thirst or craving.

12. Your fathers stand firm from age to age.
Enamored of repose, they stir not from their seat.
Untouched by age, of golden Soma never bereft,
they have forced heaven and earth to pay heed to their sound.

13. Thus speak the Stones at their release, when their journey
is over, as they clatter, like men drinking wine.
Like farmers sowing the seed, they decrease not,
but rather increase by their gulping this Soma.

14. They uplift their voices at the ritual pressing,
like children who playfully push at their mother.
Unshackle now the thoughts of the Soma-presser!
May they roll underneath, these stones till now revered!

1. God: Indra, throughout.
3. Sweet Soma: *mandu*.
Pulp prepared: the prepared juice is compared with cooked meat.
Reddish shrub: the *soma* plant.
4. Sisters: referring to the fingers of the priest pressing the *soma*.
5. Now they sink . . . : erotic comparison of the meeting between the upper and the lower stone.
Soma-seed: *retas*, semen.
7. The Stones: added for intelligibility.
Ten [workers]: the ten [fingers] engaged in pressing, which is here compared with the harnessing of a horse.
8. The ten reins are the ten fingers of the priest.
9. Bay steeds of Indra: as Indra himself drinks the Soma, his steeds are fed with the *soma*-herb.
Oxhide: the pressing of *soma* is compared with the milking of a cow, both actions being done while sitting on a skin.
11. Neither death nor cessation: *aśṛthitā amṛtyavaḥ*, neither interruption nor relaxation. Root *śrath-*, to loosen. The personification of the stones allows for a personified interpretation of the verse; otherwise we should translate: free from deterioration and erosion; or: active, effective.
Sleek-looking: oily, unctuous.
Free from thirst or craving: *atṛṣitā atṛṣṇajaḥ*.
12. Your fathers: the mountains from which the stones are taken.
Enamored of repose: *kṣemakāma*.
"They" in the last line refers again to the stones.
Sound: *rava*, again refers to the noise of pressing.
13. The stones are compared with horses released from their chariot.
Men drinking wine: *añjaspāḥ*; the meaning is doubtful. Does it refer to the horses "drinking at once"?
14. Roll underneath: *vivartantām*, from *vi- vṛt-*, to turn around or move hither and thither, i.e., to stop working.
Revered: *cāyamāna*, lit. considering themselves (the stones) to be something, i.e., sacred and important. The root *cāy-* means both to be afraid of and to respect.

The Sacred Tree *Vanaspati*

19 "With your apex you touch the heavens, with your middle portion you fill the air, with your foot you establish the earth," says one text of the Śatapatha Brāhmaṇa,[173] referring to the poles of sacrifice and likening them to the thunderbolt which is an emblem of world conquest.

Among all the creatures engaged in the sacrifice perhaps none is more important or more full of symbolic power than the cosmic tree, the tree of life, the lord of the forest, the poles of the sacrifice. The poles are stakes cut from a particular tall tree and used to form the cross on which the victim will be impaled and sacrificed. By unction the sacrificial tree becomes a mediator between Men and Gods and the bringer of every spiritual and material treasure. This tree is at the center of the world and at the summit of the earth. From it flows grace from heaven, the branch of the tree having itself been sacrificed and having acquired by this very fact a new life, a second birth.

None of this is new to any student of religion nor is it unknown to the conscious members of a number of religions. Even modern Man preserves a sense of sacredness for the forest whose reserves and parks are often nowadays called sanctuaries. Modern literature still considers the forest a sacred place, and contemporary ecology imparts a new sense of sacredness to the "green belts" in both country and town. Moreover, objects made of wood evoke an altogether different warmth of emotion than do those made of steel, plastic, or other material.

We have already alluded to the cosmic tree, sheltering the Gods in its branches,[174] "spreading on the surface of the earth,"[175] and providing lodging for the whole of reality, including Nonbeing.[176] There is a connection between the image of the world-encompassing cosmic tree and the sun, which also embraces the entire universe. For this reason, perhaps, in the Ṛg Veda the cosmic tree is an inverted tree, with branches below and roots above, because the sun directs his beams down toward the earth and keeps his roots up

173. SB III, 7, 1, 14.
174. Cf. AV X, 7, 38 (§ I 3).
175. AV II, 7, 3.
176. Cf. AV X, 7, 21 (§ I 3).

in heaven.[177] This tree in the Upaniṣads symbolizes Life,[178] God,[179] and the primordial Man;[180] its branches are space, wind, fire, water, earth, and so on—in fact, the whole of the universe.[181] As a tree in the forest, so is Man.[182] The Bhagavad Gītā sums it up again by combining all these motifs.[183]

Against this background the hymn we quote acquires a wider significance. It not only refers to the ritual of preparing the special branches for the performance of the sacrifice, that is, the blessing of them as utensils for the rite, but it also incorporates references to the cosmic sacrifice, the offering of the entire cosmos in order that it may have new life, be born again. The hymn seems to address itself sometimes to Vanaspati, the Lord of the forest, and sometimes to *yūpa*, the branches that form the poles of the sacrifice.

Vanaspati RV III, 8

1. At the time of sacrifice,
O Lord of the wood,
the worshipers smear you
with sacred oil.
When you stand upright
or when you repose
on Earth's bosom, you still
will grant us good fortune.

2. Set up to the East
of the sacred Fire,
you accept our prayer,
intense and unflagging.
Hold yourself high
to bring us prosperity.
Drive far away
dearth of inspiration.

3. Lord of the wood,
take now your stance
on this, the loftiest

177. Cf. RV I, 24, 7.
178. Cf. CU VI, 11 (§ VI 10).
179. Cf. KathU VI, 1 (§ V 5).
180. Cf. SU III, 9 (§ VI 7).
181. Cf. MaitU VI, 4.
182. Cf. BU III, 9, 28 (§ VI 3).
183. Cf. BG XV, 1-4.

spot of all earth.
Well-fixed and measured one,
give to the worshiper,
who brings a sacrifice,
honor and glory.

4. Girdled and adorned,
he displays youthful beauty,
yet is fairer by far
when brought to new birth.
With minds contemplative
and godward directed,
our sages of lofty
intelligence rear him.

5. Born anew, he is born
on a day most auspicious,
growing in wisdom
in the assembly of men.
Wise men and skillful
consecrate him with song.
Approaching the Gods,
the priest calls aloud.

6. O Lord of the wood,
whom god-fearing men
have firmly positioned,
and ax has fashioned,
be pleased to grant us,
O divine poles of sacrifice,
a precious treasure,
the gift of children.

7. May these posts which are felled
and fixed in the earth,
to which the sacrificial
ladle has been raised,
which fix the boundaries
of the sacred field,
gain for us from the Gods
what is meet to be chosen.

8. The Ādityas, the Rudras,
and the Vasus, directing
Earth and Heaven
and earth's airy spaces,
shall bless in concord
our worship and raise

our emblem of sacrifice
  high in the sky.

9. Like swans that fly
in a long-drawn-out line,
so these stakes have come to us
  brightly colored.
Raised aloft by the sages
and turned to the East,
they proceed as Gods
  to the Gods' habitations.

10. These posts, set in earth
and adorned with circles,
appear to my eye
  like the horns of horned creatures.
Unpraised by the priests
in supplication,
may they lend us their aid
  at the onset of battle!

11. O Lord of the wood,
whom this ax well-whetted
has set in our midst
  with resultant joy,
put forth branches
a hundred times over!
So may we also
  with thousands be blessed!

1. Lord of the wood: Vanaspati, applied here to the one particular tree out of which the *yūpa*, the sacrificial post, will be made.

Worshipers: *devayantaḥ*, those loving and serving God, the godly.

The tree is life-bringing, both when alive in the forest and when used as a pole of sacrifice.

2. Prayer: *brahman*.

Intense and unflagging: *ajaraṁ suvīram*, undecaying, unfading, and full of vitality (or "performed by the most eminent persons").

Dearth of inspiration: *amati*, lack of consciousness, of devotion, of awareness.

3. Loftiest spot: *varṣman*, the surface of the earth, the center of the world: the place of the altar. Cf. YV XXIII, 62.

4. Girdled: *parivīta*, lit. girt with a rope, i.e., the sacred cord (of grass) which is tied around the tree that is to be felled, so that it may become a *yūpa*, or pole of sacrifice. A symbol also of the second birth, which takes place through the sacrifice. This verse is used in the initiation ceremony, *upanayana*, according to some GS (cf. e.g., AGS I, 20, 9).

Brought to new birth: lit. being born, *jāyamāna*, present participle. The act of being raised is the tree's initiation, a new birth accompanied by prayer (cf. v. 5).

6. Precious treasure: *ratna*, jewel, pearl, treasure.

Gift of children: *prajāvat*, generative energy, offspring.

7. To which the sacrificial ladle: i.e., the ladle filled with sacred oil (cf. v. 1 and also RV IV, 6, 3) with which the posts are smeared.

Sacred field: *kṣetrasādhas*.

What is meet to be chosen: *vārya*, the most precious and valuable thing. Cf. *ratna* in v. 6.

8. Emblem of sacrifice: the *yūpa*.

9. Stakes: here probably the posts that mark the line of separation between the different sacrificial areas (dedicated to different Gods).

The Sacrificial Horse *Aśvamedha*

20 The horse sacrifice, or *aśvamedha,* is the "king of the rites"[184] and the rite of kings.[185] It is the royal sacrifice offered by a victorious king. It is the most solemn and impressive cultic celebration of the Vedas and at the same time it is one of the most secular and political. The priestly role is not here so prominent as in most of the other sacrifices. Though its actual duration is only three days, preparations for the rite take long months or even, according to the prescriptions, up to one year or sometimes two, with yet another year to conclude the ritual.

At the moment of sacrifice the royal court, including the queen who has an important role to play at a certain moment,[186] is assembled together with the entire population. At the start Somajuice is offered and then, after many ritual acts, the horse is immolated with solemnity. Numerous other animals are also led to the appointed spot and certain ones are offered in sacrifice. After the sacrifice of the horse has been performed the prescribed procedure demands the sacrifice of a number of cows, followed by the distribution of honoraria and other gifts to the priests.[187]

Today we are perhaps in a better position to understand the nature of this sacrifice, which has been the subject of much debate among scholars. Without taking part in the discussion we may see in this sacrifice the final, minutely detailed elaboration of a long process in which pre-Vedic elements, fertility rites, cosmogonic references, social motives, political factors, and priestly interests all play a part, together producing a highly elaborate and no doubt impressive ritual. In spite of its complicated, soon outmoded, and at times degraded ritual, the overall impression created by this rite, encompassing as it does the whole of the universe, is undeniably splendid. It is often called the Great Sacrifice, *mahākratu,* the great display of force and power. It blots out all sins, fulfills all wishes, answers prayers for a son, and also, at a deeper level, fulfills or perfects Prajāpati and identifies with him the one who is offering the sacrifice.

184. SB XIII, 2, 2, 1.
185. Cf. SB XIII, 1, 6, 3.
186. Cf. YV XIII, 18-19.
187. Cf. SB XIII, 1-5 and TB III, 8-9 for a detailed description of the *aśvamedha*. YV XXII to XXV contain the formulas of the ritual.

The Ṛg Veda has two hymns dedicated to the sacrifice of the horse. Whereas the hymn preceding our text has a more ritual character,[188] Ṛg Veda I, 163, does not set out to describe the *aśvamedha* rite; it is a cosmogonic hymn in which the horse of the *aśvamedha* is homologized in a grandiose fashion with the sun and with a primordial cosmic horse that represents the entire universe.[189] In this hymn are to be found both metaphorical and factual allusions, metaphorical with reference to the sun (e.g., this horse is a primordial horse) and factual with reference to the actual sacrifice. Thus verses 1 and 2 refer to the sun in the heavenly "ocean"; verse 5 speaks of a magnificent champion racehorse, while simultaneously referring to the perfect performance of the sacrificial rites over which the said horse presides. In verse 6 the horse in its earthly course is identified with the Sun in its heavenly course. Verse 8 brings us back to the *aśvamedha,* to that moment when the horse moves majestically onto the sacrificial parade ground.

Verse 9 describes certain features of the horse's appearance, while referring once again to the Sun. In verse 12 the horse arrives amidst due solemnity upon the place of sacrifice, followed by other animals, by poets, singers, and priests. The hymn concludes with a prayer uttered by the officiating priest to the horse which has now been offered in sacrifice.

Throughout the Indo-European world the horse has occupied a rather special position and has been considered a powerful symbol both of the human psyche and of the universe, the link between the two being perhaps the connection of the horse with the waters, and in the *aśvamedha,* significantly enough, the horse is immolated by suffocation. The Vedic contribution in this regard is to stress the horse's cosmic and universal character, in contrast with the particular features to which attention is drawn in Greece or central Europe, and also to stress its sacrificial role. The horse occupies so central a place precisely because it assumes in itself the whole universe and has a vicarious role to perform. It is significant that the chapters of the Śatapatha Brāhmaṇa where the *aśvamedha* is minutely described are followed by a chapter on the *puruṣamedha,* or human sacrifice,[190] which in turn is followed by a further chapter on the *sarvamedha,* or all-sacrifice.[191]

188. RV I, 162.
189. This idea of the primordial sacrificial horse is taken up again in BU I, 1.
190. SB XIII, 6.
191. Cf. SB XIII, 7 (§ I 6).

Our second text is from the Yajur Veda and is a prayer said by the officiating priest in the course of the *aśvamedha.*

Aśvamedha

RV I, 163

i) 1. How worthy of telling and how superb your birth,
O steed, when first you whinnied, on seeing the light,
as you rose from the ocean of sea or of space
with your eagle wings and limbs of swift gazelle.

2. This steed, the gift of Death, Trita has harnessed,
while Indra was the first of all to mount him,
the Gandharva first to grasp in his hands the reins.
From the substance of the Sun, O Gods, you fashioned this Steed.

3. You, O Steed, are Death, you the Sun;
you by a secret decree are Trita;
by only a little are you distinguished from Soma.
You have, they say, three connections in heaven.

4. In heaven, they say, you have three connections,
three in the waters and three within the ocean.
You resemble, O Steed, the Lord of the Waters,
for there, they say, is your highest birthplace.

5. Here, Racehorse, are your haunts for bathing;
here are the traces of your champion hooves.
Here I have seen the blessed reins that guide you,
which those who guard Cosmic Order cherish.

6. Your innermost self I have perceived in spirit,
a Bird from heaven who directs his course on high.
I have seen you rearing your winged head and advancing
by dust-free paths, fair and easy to travel.

7. There I have seen your exalted form seeking
to obtain food in the track of the Cow.
When mortal man approaches you for enjoyment,
the great devourer of plants has awakened.

8. Behind you, O Horse, come a chariot, the hero,
an offering of cows, and a troupe of fair maidens.
Desirous of your friendship, many follow.
With splendid courage the Gods have endowed you.

9. His horns are of gold, his feet of iron;
he is fleet as thought and swifter than Indra.
The Gods are gathered for this sacred meal, offered
to the one who first of all mounted this Stallion.

10. Like swans, the celestial coursers form a line
when they, the steeds, reach the heavenly arena,
the end of their lengthened row being motionless,
while those in the center still proceed.

11. Your body, O Steed, flies as with wings;
your spirit moves quickly like the wind.
Your horns are found in sundry places,
advancing in the forests with a jumping motion.

12. The fleet-footed Steed, his mind recollected
and thoughts directed godward, advances
to the place of sacrifice. A ram of his kindred
is led before; next come sages and minstrels.

13. The Steed has attained the abode supreme.
He has gone to the place of his Father and Mother.
May he find a warm welcome today among the Gods
and thus win good gifts for him who offers!

YV XXII, 22

ii) O Brahman, in this kingdom may priests be born who shine brightly with sacred knowledge! May here be born warriors of heroic stature, who are skillful shots, good marksmen, invincible chariot fighters! May cows in this kingdom yield milk in plenty, our oxen be tireless, our horses swift, our housewives skillful! To him who offers this sacrifice may a hero-son be born, a champion, a mighty warrior, a persuasive speaker!

May Heaven send us rain for our needs!
May our fruit-bearing plants ripen in season!
May joy and prosperity fall to our lot!

■ i) 1. Ocean . . . of space: *purīṣa,* a much-discussed word, meaning not earth, as was traditionally said, but originally source, flood, afterward fullness, and still later dirt. Here the word almost certainly denotes the primeval source, the primordial waters. Cf., e.g., RV III, 22, 4 and also SB VII, 1, 1, 24.

2. Death: Yama, the King or God of Death, but here perhaps referring to Agni.

Trita: a little-known divinity related to Indra.

3. Death: Yama.

Sun: Āditya.

Three connections: i.e., his relationships to the divinities mentioned above.

4. The horse's threefold origin in the waters and in the ocean is here a poetic parallel to the three "bonds" of Varuṇa. Cf. RV I, 24, 15, (§ IV 8).

Lord of the Waters: Varuṇa.

5. The homology with the Sun begins here. The Gods are the keepers of the reins and the guardians of *ṛta*.

6. Perceived in spirit: *manasā . . . ajānām*.

A Bird: the vital principle of the Steed is here identified with the Sunbird, i.e., the *ātman* of the Steed is the Bird.

Paths: i.e., paths leading to heaven.

7. Your exalted form: *te rūpam uttamam*.

Track of the Cow: either the firmament where the "trace" of the Cosmic Cow is found or, on earth, the racecourse where cows are won.

Devourer of plants: Agni.

8. An offering of cows . . . : lit. cows follow and the charm of virgins.
9. Horns . . . of gold: probably meaning hooves and referring to the rays of the sun. According to v. 2 it was Indra himself who first mounted the Steed.
10. The order is slightly modified to make it more intelligble. The idea is that the celestial, i.e., sun-horses, form a row of which the middle part is moving while the end stands still.
11. Spirit: *citta.*
Horns: perhaps referring to the hooves. Others see an allusion to quickly spreading forest fires.
■ ii) Priests: Brahmins.
Heaven: Parjanya.

The Struggle for Immortality *Daivāsura*

21 The quest for immortality is one of Man's deepest instincts. At the same time he is aware that immortality is not his "natural" lot; immortality belongs, if at all, to the Gods. Thus a yearning to become a God springs up spontaneously within Man. We have already heard the chant of victory:

> We have drunk the Soma and become immortal!
> We have attained the light, we have found the Gods![192]

Man can become immortal only if he is divinized or, rather, divinization amounts to immortality.

In connection with this theme the Vedic experience contributes two intuitions, the first of which is considered here and the second in the next text. The Brāhmaṇas tell us explicitly that not even the Gods were originally immortal, that immortality is not natural to the Gods, that they also had to struggle for it. Sacrifice is the way to immortality, because sacrifice is the one original and originating act, as we have already seen.

It would be merely a farce if the Gods were to achieve their immortality without a struggle, without the risk of not getting it—and so we have the scene set for the *asuras,* those beings that are usually referred to as demons, for lack of a better term. One should recall in this connection that angels and demons have the same origin and that their good and evil features are themselves the fruits of a struggle and a test.

The fact that the Gods are obliged to win their immortality has two important implications for Men. First, the Gods are real and inspiring examples, for they have gone through the same fundamental experience as Men: that of having to gain their real freedom.

192. RV VIII, 48, 3 (§ III 17).

To attain freedom means to become immortal, to be free from the clutches of time, for as long as one is tied to time one is not really free. The Gods are really Men's fellow travelers on the journey toward immortality. Men's relation with them is one of companionship, for Gods and Men share a common destiny in spite of their differing positions in an acknowledged hierarchy. The other implication, the recognition of which gives peace and serenity to Man, is that the Gods cannot be whimsical creatures, for there is a *ṛta,* an Order, whose dynamism is Sacrifice, which transcends both Men and Gods and which can in no way be manipulated or considered as being activated by an anthropomorphic will.

Let us now take a closer look at the tests themselves. Prajāpati, the Lord of all creatures, whose name is scarcely mentioned in the Ṛg Veda,[193] holds in the Brāhmaṇas a position of capital importance. According to a lengthy narrative in the Brāhmaṇas, Prajāpati is the primordial being before whom nothing whatever was in existence. The Śatapatha Brāhmaṇa tells us over and over again that "Prajāpati is sacrifice;" that is, Prajāpati performed an act of self-immolation, self-sacrifice, in order that creatures might come to be. Thus creation is regarded as the sacrifice of Prajāpati, as the ontological self-despoliation of the supreme principle in order to bring into existence the intermediate order of things which consists of the cosmos, which has come forth from the Father of all beings and is neither the Father nor sheer nothingness. This intermediate order, being neither stable nor self-existent, is by constitution transitory, or, in other words, dynamic. The creature is powerless in itself to sustain itself or to complete its full span of destiny, but must attempt by means of sacrifice to recover its true status, to return to its source, retrieve its unity, that is, to become immortal, divinized.

Prajāpati, we may remember, created two types of superior beings, the *devas* (Gods) and the *asuras* (demons). In the beginning neither the Gods nor the *asuras* were immortal. Both tried to become immortal and fought each other in order to achieve immortality. They discovered that only by means of sacrifice could they become immortal. Both performed sacrifice[194] and both strove to conquer the world.[195] The Śatapatha Brāhmaṇa abounds in anec-

193. Prajāpati is mentioned as God (excluding epithets) only four times, on each occasion in the late tenth Book: RV X, 85, 43 (§ II 15); X, 169, 4; X, 184, 1; and in the famous X, 121, 10 (§ I 4).
194. Cf. e.g., MaitS I, 9, 8; II, 5, 3.
195. Cf. e.g., AB I, 23 (IV, 6, 1).

dotes about this struggle for immortality, a struggle of a unique kind, a veritable ritual battle in which the combatants are priests and the weapons sacrifices. Sacrifice is the sole means by which the Gods may win the victory. Because the *devas* perform the sacrifice better than the *asuras* they win.[196] Before the final victory there are recurring conflicts and victories of a temporary nature, for the *asuras* try again and again to mount fresh assaults.

The rivalry between the Gods and the demons, the so-called *daivāsura* struggle, is the subject of one of the richest myths extant concerning the conflict constantly being waged between the two forces harbored in Man. The conflict here, however, is not ultimate. Both *devas* and *asuras* are offspring of the supreme God and it is not even certain which of the two are the firstborn.[197] The *asuras* are the enemies of the Gods but very seldom appear as enemies of Men. Both strive for immortality, but they also know that there is an incompatibility between them so that the victory can be won only by one side. The rituals of sacrifice, which is considered the sole total and all-inclusive act, constitute the rules of the game. The first instrument of sacrifice is the firstborn of Prajāpati, *vāc,* the word. They will have to fight with it and for it. But this primordial word is both right and wrong, true and untrue. The word is always ambivalent. The Śatapatha Brāhmaṇa goes on to say that truth took refuge among the Gods and untruth among the *asuras* and that for this reason the *devas* became feeble and poor, while the demons became rich; but in the long run he who abides in truth reaches fullness of existence, while he who remains in untruth loses everything. It is by means of this sacrifice to truth that the Gods finally attained victory.[198] The symbolism needs no further interpretation.

Daivāsura

SB I, 5, 2, 6

i) The Sacrifice ran away from the Gods. The Gods called out after it, "Listen to us! Come back here." It replied, "Let is be so," and went back to the Gods. Now with what had thus come back to them, with that the Gods worshiped, and by this worship they became the Gods that they are to this very day.

196. Cf. TS I, 6, 10, 2 (x).
197. Cf. MaitS IV, 2, 1; TB II, 3, 8, 1; etc.
198. Cf. SB IX, 5, 1, 12 sq.

SB I, 7, 3, 1

ii) It is through Sacrifice that the Gods proceeded to the heavenly realm.

SB II, 2, 2, 8-14

iii) 8. [Once upon a time] the Gods and the *asuras,* both of whom were offspring of Prajāpati, were striving between themselves. Both sides were destitute of spirit because they were mortal and he who is mortal has no spirit. Among these two groups of mortal beings one, Agni, was immortal and it was through him, the immortal, that they both had their being. Now, whichever of the Gods was slain by the *asuras* was in very truth slain irrevocably.

9. And so the Gods became inferior. They continued worshiping and practicing fervent concentration, however, in the hope of overcoming their enemies who were likewise mortal. Their gaze, then, fell upon the immortal sacred Agni.

10. "Come," they said, "let us establish this immortality in our inmost self! When we have placed that immortality in our inmost self and have become immortal and unconquerable, we shall defeat our enemies who are neither immortal nor unconquerable."

11. They said: "The Fire is with both of us; let us then speak openly with the *asuras.*"

12. They said: "Let us establish the two fires, but then what will you do?"

13. The *asuras* replied: "Then we shall set it in place, saying: eat grass here, eat wood here, cook rice here, cook meat here." The fire that the *asuras* set in place, it is by this that men eat [cooked food].

14. So the Gods established that Fire in their inmost self and, having established that immortality in their inmost self and become immortal and unconquerable, they defeated their mortal and conquerable enemies. And so he [the sacrificer] now establishes immortality in his inmost self, and though he has no hope of immortality, he attains a full lifetime. He becomes unconquerable, and when his enemy tries to overpower him, he is not overpowered. Therefore, when one who has established the Fire and one who has not are fighting, the one who has established the Fire overcomes. For by this [Fire] he becomes unconquerable, immortal.

SB II, 4, 2, 1-5

iv) 1. The beings came in a respectful manner to find Prajāpati; by "beings" is meant the creatures he had made.

"Arrange," they said to him, "how we are to live." First the Gods drew near, ritually invested with the sacred cord [of sacrifice] and bending the right knee.

He said to them: "Receive Sacrifice as your food, immortality as your life-force, and the Sun as your light-sphere."

2. Then drew near the ancestors, bearing over the right shoulder the cord of sacrifice and bending the left knee. To them he said: "Receive the funeral offerings of each month as your food, the *svadhā* libation as your mind-swiftness and the moon as your light-sphere."

3. Then drew near the race of men, clothed and bowing low. To them he said: "Night and morning shall you eat, your offspring shall be your death and fire your light-sphere."

4. Then drew near the animals. He allowed them to eat according to their fancy, saying: "Eat as chance allows, how, when, and where you will." And indeed they eat when and where they find something to eat.

5. Then, finally, drew near the *asuras*. To them he assigned darkness and power. The power of the *asuras* does indeed exist.

All those beings, it is true, have perished, but beings continue to live according to the ordinance Prajāpati has given them.

SB II, 4, 3, 3

v) It is by dint of sacrifice that the Gods have brought to completion all their proper undertakings, and the same did the sages also.

SB V, 1, 1, 1-2

vi) 1. The Gods and the *asuras*, both having Prajāpati as their origin, were rivals of each other. So the *asuras*, swollen with pride, said, "In what, pray, should we place our oblation?" And they proceeded to place their oblations in their own mouths.

2. The Gods then proceeded to place their oblations each in the mouth of one of his fellows. And Prajāpati gave himself over to them. In this way they became owners of sacrifice, for sacrifice is really the food of the Gods.

SB VIII, 4, 3, 2

vii) All that the Gods effect they effect by intoned recitation. Now intoned recitation is sacrifice; it is through sacrifice therefore that they do whatever they do.

SB X, 2, 2, 1

viii) And when he had emitted the creatures, he [Prajāpati] rose up on high and departed to that world where that [sun] shines; for up to then there existed no other that was worthy of sacrifice. The Gods began then to offer him in sacrifice.

SB XI, 1, 8, 2-4

ix) Prajāpati donated himself to the Gods. The sacrifice became verily theirs. Sacrifice is therefore the food of the Gods. When he donated himself to the Gods he emitted an image of himself, which is sacrifice. . . . By sacrifice he purchased himself back from the Gods.

TS I, 6, 10, 2

x) It was by the perfect accomplishment of the sacrifice that the Gods proceeded to the heavenly realm, and it was by reason of their defective performance of the same that the *asuras* were conquered.

■ i) Listen to us: *ā-śru-*.
Let it be so: *so' stu tathā iti.*
Sacrifice is the Gods' dynamic force.
■ ii) The verb *upa-ut-kram-* suggests an ascent by degrees.
■ iii) 8. Destitute of spirit: *anātman,* without *ātman,* seems here to have a personal meaning of "without a personal spirit." Cf. v. 10, where the Gods desire to insert this immortality, *idam amṛtam,* into their inmost self: *antarātman.*
9. The immortal sacred Agni: *etad amṛtam agnyādheyam.*
10. Established: *adadhata,* from the root *dhā-*, to establish. Immortality is always a second gift, the fruit of a second birth, the result of the sacrifice.
14. The sacrificer cannot attain immortality like the Gods, but he attains his own fullness as his complete *āyus* or lifetime.
One who has established the Fire: *āhitāgni,* the one who performs the *agnihotra* regularly. This sacrificial conclusion of a mythical text is typical of the B.
■ iv) Prajāpati gives sacrifice, immortality, and the sun to the *devas; māsi-śrāddha, svadhā-śrāddha* (cf. thought-swift: *manojavin*), and the moon to the ancestors (Fathers); alternation of day and night, offspring (*prajā*), and fire to men. To animals he gave no rite (and therefore no life-force) and no light, but only bodily sustenance; to the *asuras,* only darkness (*tamas*) and power (*māyā*). Some translate *māyā* as "illusion"; the power, however, is a shrewd and deceptive one, cunning might (Cf. § IV B b). Cf. SB XIII, 4, 3, 11, which again relates *māyā* to the *asuras* so that *asura-vidyā* becomes synonymous with *māyā,* probably connoting magic. Noteworthy also are the different ways of approach: the *devas* are ritually invested with the sacred cord (*yajñopavītin*) on the left; the *pitaraḥ* (Fathers) are *prācīnāvītin* (i.e., invested with the shoulder turned eastward, as for the *śrāddha* ceremony); men are clothed.
■ v) By sacrifice the Gods and the *ṛṣis* have accomplished everything that is proper for them to do, or have composed their rite.
Brought to completion: the root *kḷp-*, to make possible, to bring about, accomplish, perform, arrange, etc., is here used in the causative.
Proper undertakings: *kalpa,* fit; as a noun, rule, sacred ordinance.
■ vi) Cf. SB XI, 1, 8, 2 (ix).
■ vii) The Gods here are Prajāpati and the *prāṇas,* creating together by means of *stoma,* i.e., by intoned recitation, song of praise, chant.

Life-Giving Immolation *Haviryajña*

22 Our next texts, like those of the preceding section, all implicitly suggest that the human condition holds within it a deeper invisible dimension. This dimension Upaniṣadic spirituality seeks to develop (and sometimes to extricate) from the complexus of human reality in order to form out of it an autonomous body of

doctrine. This process runs the risk of becoming a discarnate or dematerialized spirituality. We are as yet far from this dichotomy, but already the emphasis is shifting more and more toward interiority.

Yet we should not forget the second and distinctive feature of Vedic spirituality mentioned in the preceding chapter. There exists in the Vedas a trend that is not directed toward immortality and takes no pleasure in the thought of it, but rather is repelled by the idea of "living forever." At this stage Man either seeks to interiorize and perfect the idea of immortality, or he prefers in his present human condition to renounce altogether such a dream of living forever. In a word, he craves either liberation, that is, escape from the given human condition, or its temporal reform, the latter desire finding its expression in the myth of rejuvenation. The Upaniṣads follow the former path, but we are still at this stage concerned with the latter, which, we may note, survives in popular religion until our own times. It is after all a constant desire of the human psyche: not to transcend time but to bring it to a halt.

There is a wonderful story in the Brāhmaṇas which may well be the origin of other similar legends.[199] It tells how a certain tribe was afflicted by dissensions and plagues as a punishment for their ill-treatment of the sage Cyavāna who was now passing through an abandoned old age in pain and decrepitude. Their chieftain, Saryāta, vexed to learn of this, went to the sage, paid him homage, and offered him in atonement his daughter Sukanyā. The Aśvins, coming on the scene, tried to seduce Sukanyā and sneered at her when she refused their advances, preferring to stay with the decrepit old man to whom her father had given her: "I will not abandon him as long as he lives," she said. The sage, aware of her promise (for indeed she told him), instructed her that if they came again she was to bring home to them their own incompleteness and imperfection, adding that he would not tell them in what respect they were incomplete and imperfect until they made him young again. The stratagem succeeded and the Aśvins made him young again by virtue of the waters of a certain pool. It is significant that what led them to make him young again was the desire they had to partake of Soma. Cyavāna then told them that they were imperfect

199. Cf. RV X, 59, 1 (§ V 8).

because they were excluded by the Gods from participation in a certain sacrifice they were performing in Kurukṣetra.[200]

Not only is the whole text concerned with sacrifice, but it also derives its meaningfulness from the obedience and fidelity of Sukanyā, who was ready to give her whole life in service to a ghostlike man rather than to disobey her father. This story supplies a vivid context for the more abstract quotations of this chapter.

Sacrifice consists of an immolation. We find here once again the thought that the sacrifice is "stretched out," just as thread is stretched on the loom to be woven. If it is a question of Soma-juice, then one presses it, extracts all its virtue, slays it; if it is fire, then it dwindles and dies. In the same way all sacrifice involves a dying. But this immolation is a dying-for-life, for the sacrifice in the very act of dying renews itself within the universe; it is thus a universal principle of life, everywhere in operation. All that is, the whole cosmos, comes to be through sacrifice. The highest act of God is that of Agni the sacrificer, the cosmic priest who constantly renews the life of every being. If it is unable to participate in the cosmic and universal sacrifice existence dwindles and is annihilated.

Haviryajña

SB II, 2, 2, 1

i) Verily, when this sacrifice is performed, it is slain; when one presses the *soma*-juice, one slays it; when one causes the victim to acquiesce and immolates it and thrusts a knife into it, one slays it. With the pestle and mortar or the two grindstones one slays the oblation.

SB III, 6, 2, 26

ii) Creatures who are not allowed to take part in sacrifice are reduced to nothingness. Therefore the sacrificer admits those who are not annihilated to take part in sacrifice, both men and beasts, Gods and birds, plants, trees, and everything that exists. Thus the entire universe takes part in sacrifice. Gods and men on the one hand and the Fathers on the other were wont in days gone by to drink together from the sacrifice. Sacrifice is their shared feast. In olden days they were to be seen as they came to this feast. Nowadays they are still present but remain invisible.

200. Cf. SB IV, 1, 5, 1 sq. We have introduced here some elements of the same story as told in the JaimB and reduced it to its bare essentials.

SB III, 9, 4, 23

iii) Now concerning why Soma is called sacrifice: when they press him, they slay him and when they stretch him out, they cause him to be born. He is born in being stretched out, he is born "going on": whence comes *yan-ja,* and *yañja,* they explain, is the same as *yajña.*

SB XIV, 3, 2, 1

iv) All that is, including all the Gods, has but one principle of life: sacrifice.

▪ i) Every sacrifice is an immolation.
Causes . . . to acquiesce: *saṁjñāpayanti,* causative of *saṁ-jñā-,* to agree, to consent. The sacrificial victim ought not to be led forcibly to its death, but made to accept it willingly.
Immolates: *viśasati,* from *vi-śas-,* to cut, to slaughter, thus to immolate.
▪ ii) Reduced to nothingness: *parābhūtā* (*parā-bhū-*), to perish, disappear, be lost, succumb, yield, to vanish, to sustain a loss. Ontological nothingness entails being excommunicated from the sacrifice. Cf. § III B Antiphon for one sentence of this text in a different version.
Sacrificer: i.e., Agni, probably in his function as priest.
Drink together: *saṁpibante,* i.e., the Soma, shared feast; *saṁpā,* from the same root *pā-,* to drink. Cf. SB I, 5, 2, 4; II, 3, 1, 20, which is the same text repeated (except for the last sentence).
▪ iii) Sacrifice: *yajña,* hence the play on words at the end of the passage; going on: *yan jāyate,* from which come the syllables that compose both *yañja* and *yajña.* The root *i-* suggests a cyclical conception.
He is born in being stretched out: *sa tāyamāno jāyate, sa yan jāyate,* with the idea of infinite extension and never-ending continuity.
▪ iv) Principle of life: *ātman.*

Sacrifice Is Man *Puruṣayajña*

23 Although Scripture says more than once that sacrifice is that through which the Gods acquired immortality, or that by means of which Man obtains both material benefits and immortality, it stresses equally that "sacrifice *is* Man."[201] It is Man who offers, it is through him that sacrifice is performed. Sacrifice corresponds to Man in stature and proportions. In certain passages of the Śatapatha Brāhmaṇa the different parts of the human body are compared to the different constituent elements of sacrifice and to the objects employed in it. If it is true that sacrifice *is* Man it can equally be said that Man is a sacrifice. Sacrifice involves both immolation and new life—and so it is with Man also. He is born, dies, and is reborn. The texts say that Man is born three times, once from his parents, a second time when he offers sacrifice, and a third time when, on dying, he is burned on the pyre. The second birth, that effected by sacrifice, is explained as follows: through the offering

201. Cf. SB I, 3, 2, 1 (i); III, 1, 4, 23.

that he makes the sacrificer communicates with the world of the Gods and there comes about a sort of exchange. Just as a snake sloughs off its dead skin, so he who offers sacrifice "sloughs off" his mortal body. He presents it to the Gods and receives in return an immortal body. There is a whole series of preliminary rites called *dīkṣā* leading up to the sacrifice proper. Through the *dīkṣā* the Man receives a second birth, this time a divine birth, and he becomes immortal. The sacrificer has thus two bodies and it is his mortal body that he offers to the Gods in sacrifice. Once he is assured of a divine body he descends to earth once more and purchases back from the Gods his sacrificed body.

Certain texts also speak of human life in terms of a constitutive debt; one is indebted to the Gods, indebted to the sages, indebted to the ancestors, and indebted to Men. Debt is perhaps an ambiguous word[202] owing to the sociological and judicial connotations it has acquired. *Ṛṇa* refers, certainly, to a kind of moral obligation or duty that Man is discharging when he sacrifices, but this is to be understood as an act that must be done because it entails the fulfilment of Man's own being. Man's life on earth is ontically linked with the whole of reality and it is only when he responds with openness, or, to put it another way, when he permits within himself the unhampered circulation of being, that Man can be said to possess real life. To recognize one's place in the world involves the acknowledgment of a fivefold link, a fivefold debt, not merely as a social obligation but as a constitutive bond of unity. We have come into existence by a "jumping outside," by a movement or "transgression" away from the undifferentiated whole, and it is specifically by sacrifice that we reintegrate ourselves into the total reality.[203]

The passage about the four debts may help us to understand the way in which the sacrifice reintegrates Man into the whole of reality. By sacrificing to the Gods he restores his unity with the heavenly world; by reciting the Vedas, he acquires wisdom, he rescues himself from isolation and banality; by having progeny he establishes his links with mankind, past and future; finally, by practicing hospitality he communes with his fellow beings in an actualized present. The four debts do not impoverish Man; on the

202. The term *ṛṇa*, duty, debt, seems to have an obscure etymology. *Ṛṇa-* connotes omission. *Ṛṇin*, *ṛṇika*, is a debtor, one who is indebted; the verb *ṛṇ-*, to go, to move, suggests in the word *ṛṇa* an element of transgression and guilt. Cf. Latin *reus*. Cf. § IV *Note on Sanskrit Terms*.

203. Cf. § III 21 Introduction.

contrary they enrich him by letting him partake in the totality of the universe.[204]

The last text in this group sums up all that has been said and foreshadows the teaching of the Upaniṣads. It reminds us in brief that the life of Man, Man's daily round, consists of a series of sacrifices. Here there is already an advance beyond ritualism, an advance beyond all desire for prosperity or this world's goods—a declaration that true sacrifice consists of sacred study. A development is now taking place which will transform the idea of sacrifice, interiorize it, and purify it until in its performance only true knowledge will count.

The more general and cosmic interpretation of sacrifice does not, however, take priority in these texts over the concrete and ritualistic one. It is not only the cosmic *puruṣa* who performs the sacrifice and not only the primordial Man who can be termed both sacrifice and sacrificer; the concrete human being also is said to be the sacrifice and it is by sacrifice that he lives, because sacrifice links him with the whole of existence and enables him to perform all his duties as Man.

The fulfillment of all "debts" would lead inexorably to the elimination of the individual, to the immolation of the little self, to the *puruṣamedha,* the human sacrifice. It is not a question here of the destruction of the whole *puruṣa,* which would amount to an annihilation of the whole of reality, but to the immolation of the little *puruṣa,* that is, the individualistic ego. This ego is understood as all that constitutes individuality. To this end elaborate rituals will furnish the victim with a borrowed body so that substitution forestalls the actual killing of any human being.[205] Yet Man is the first of the five victims[206] and so must be the first one to be sacrificed,[207] though (as other texts will say) the strength of one victim passes on to the next so that the horse is the substitute for Man, the bull for the horse, and so on,[208] until finally by the immolation of one victim all are adjudged to have been sacrificed.[209]

The human being is Man and Man is the sacrifice. This priestly identification of the individual with Man plays an important part in

204. Cf. SB I, 7, 2, 1-5 (ii); cf. also TS VI, 3, 10, 5.
205. Cf. AB II, 3 (VI, 3); II, 9 (VI, 9); SB III, 3, 4, 21, where the sacrificer redeems himself by this victim.
206. Cf. SB VI, 2, 1, 2 and passim. They are: man, horse, bull, ram, and goat.
207. Cf., e.g., SB VI, 2, 1, 18.
208. Cf. SB I, 2, 3, 6. Cf. also SB III, 1, 4, 22, for the dialectics of reducing the several sacrifices to a single one.
209. Cf. SB VI, 2, 2, 15.

the understanding of human sacrifice. There is a twofold rationale to be observed in human sacrifice (we are ignoring, of course, degraded forms of it which are also found). This rationale is concerned in the first place with the debts owed by the individual to the Gods, the ancestors, and so on, by virtue of his having come to individual existence at all. Only by the sacrifice of himself—as a separate ego—can Man redeem and rescue himself. The rationale includes also the idea of a sharing by the individual in the cosmic sacrifice of the *puruṣa*. If the whole world has come into being by the sacrifice of Man, the individual must reenact that creating and saving sacrifice by performing it himself. Man, in this sense, is priest for the whole cosmos and his priestly action must include the sacrifice of himself. From this perspective we can understand two main features of Man's self-sacrifice: the looking for substitutes, on the one hand, and the interiorization of the sacrifice, on the other

We may close this commentary on the human sacrifice by recalling the most ancient version of the story of Hariścandra as it is found in the Aitareya Brāhmaṇa[210] before its rich and variegated elaboration in the *itihāsas* and *purāṇas,* that is, in the epics and in popular literature. In spite of his hundred wives, King Hariścandra had no son and, having prayed to Varuṇa for an offspring, he promised at the same time that he would sacrifice any son born to him to the God. A son, Rohita, was born and his father by different excuses succeeded in postponing the sacrifice until the young man could bear his own arms. "My son," said the father to him, "it is Varuṇa who has given you to me. I must sacrifice you to him." Rohita escapes to the forest and wanders there for six years. He meets eventually a certain poor *ṛṣi,* who for a hundred cows consents to offer his second son Śunaḥśepa as a substitute for Rohita.[211] The king and the God agree. "A Brahmin is worth more than a Kṣatriya," says Varuṇa. For another hundred cows the same *ṛṣi* Ajīgarta binds his own son to the sacrificial post and for yet another hundred is ready to slay the boy himself, for nobody else is available to perform these actions, the four officiating priests having refused to bind the victim. At this Śunaḥśepa, realizing that he, a human being, is going to be sacrificed as if he were not a man, begins a mantra recitation to the Gods. His bonds loosen one by one as he recites this succession of verses in praise of Uṣas. At the final

210. Cf. AB VII, 13-18 (XXXIII, 1-6) and SSS XV, 17-27 which is practically the same.
211. Cf. RV I, 24, 12-13; V, 2, 7 (§ IV 8), which is the earliest reference to the Śunaḥśepa story.

verse the last knot is loosed and not only is Śunaḥśepa free but king Hariścandra also recovers from the dropsy with which he has been stricken. The famous sage Viśvāmitra, one of the four priests, receives Śunaḥśepa as his son and curses Ajīgarta.

Although this story is generally known as the *ākhyāna* (story) of Śunaḥśepa, we could consider also the figure of Rohita, Hariścandra's son, and call it "the myth of the human condition." Rohita represents Man in his basic human situation. He is born into life with a constitutive debt, the debt to the Gods. Rohita discovers the debt and escapes into the forest, but then recognizes his duty through his father's suffering (he has dropsy) and returns to face his destiny. Before returning he has to overcome, for the fifth time, the test (which comes not from a "bad" temptor, but from the God Indra himself) not to go back to his father and be sacrificed. It is only when he has set his heart and mind on the right way that he meets the poor Ajīgarta and his sons, and vicarious substitution becomes possible.

Here we have most of the motifs connected with sacrifice: life is a free gift which can be preserved and fully lived only by means of a gift given in return; there is a supreme order of things over which neither Men nor Gods have any power; the vicarious substitution, whatever its subjective motive may be, has an ontological justification, because ultimately human value does not reside in the individual but in the person and thus one person can take the place of, put on the mask of, another. Herein is the realm of human freedom and the mystery of love. Prayer has a power of its own and can reverse the order of things because it introduces an element of mercy which would otherwise be stifled by unmitigated justice. Human greed and the mysterious ways of the Gods are also vividly depicted in this myth.

One of the most human and universal conceptions of sacrifice is the so-called *pañcamahāyajña*, the five great sacrifices. Here the idea of sacrifice embraces all aspects of life and Man's relationship to all beings, from plants and animals up to Brahman. Man is related to all beings by means of sacrifice. Sacrifice is not his link exclusively with the Gods; even water offered to a guest has the same value and symbolic depth as a complicated ritual. The study of the Scriptures itself is the highest liturgical act, the sacrifice to Brahman. It is not water or ghee, but the student's intellect which is the substance of this sacrifice. Thus, even before the Upaniṣadic spiritualizing of sacrifice, this conception saves sacrifice from becoming a mere speciality of the priests and enables it to penetrate the whole of Man's life.

Puruṣayajña

SB I, 3, 2, 1

i) The sacrifice is man. It is man [who offers it] because it is man who spreads it out and because, in being spread out, it assumes exactly the same stature as man. For this reason, the sacrifice is man.

SB I, 7, 2, 1-5

ii)

1. When a man is born, whoever he may be, there is born simultaneously a debt to the Gods, to the sages, to the ancestors, and to men.
2. When he performs sacrifice it is the debt to the Gods which is concerned. It is on their behalf, therefore, that he is taking action when he sacrifices or makes an oblation.
3. And when he recites the Vedas it is the debt to the sages which is concerned. It is on their behalf, therefore, that he is taking action, for it is said of one who has recited the Vedas that he is the guardian of the treasure store of the sages.
4. And when he desires offspring it is the debt to the ancestors which is concerned. It is on their behalf, therefore, that he is taking action, so that their offspring may continue, without interruption.
5. And when he entertains guests, it is the debt to man which is concerned. It is on their behalf, therefore, that he is taking action if he entertains guests and gives them food and drink. The man who does all these things has performed a true work; he has obtained all, conquered all.

SB II, 2, 4, 8

iii) When a man dies, they place him on the pyre; then he is born out of the fire and the fire burns only his body. Even as he is born from his father and mother, so he is born from the fire. The man who does not offer the *agnihotra*, however, does not pass to new life at all. Therefore it is very necessary to offer the *agnihotra*.

SB III, 6, 2, 16

iv) Man, so soon as he is born, is to be regarded, his whole person, as a debt owed to death. When he performs sacrifice he is purchasing himself back from death.

SB XI, 2, 1, 1

v) Of a truth man is born three times over in the following way. First he is born from his mother and father. He is born a second time while performing the sacrifice that becomes his share. He is born a third time when he dies and they place him on the pyre and he proceeds to a new existence. Therefore they say: "Man is born three times."

SB XI, 2, 6, 13

vi) The question arises, "Which is the better, the man who sacrifices to the Self, or the man who sacrifices to the Gods?" "The man who sacrifices to the Self" must be the reply, for he who sacrifices to the Self is also the one who possesses the knowledge that through his sacrifice his body is brought to completion, through this sacrifice his body finds its proper place. Just as a snake rids itself of its dead skin, so the man who performs sacrifice rids himself of his mortal body, that is to say, of sin, and by dint of verses, formulas, Vedic melodies, and offerings takes possession of the heavenly realm.

SB XI, 5, 6, 1-3

vii) 1. There are five great sacrifices, namely, the great ritual services: the sacrifices to all beings, sacrifice to men, sacrifice to the ancestors, sacrifice to the Gods, sacrifice to Brahman.

2. Day by day a man offers sustenance to creatures; that is the sacrifice to beings. Day by day a man gives hospitality to guests, including a glass of water; that is the sacrifice to men. Day by day a man makes funerary offerings, including a glass of water; that is the sacrifice to the ancestors. Day by day a man makes offerings to the Gods, including wood for burning; that is the sacrifice to the Gods.

3. And the sacrifice to Brahman? The sacrifice to Brahman consists of sacred study.

▪ i) The sacrifice is Man: *puruṣo vai yajñaḥ*. Cf. CU III, 16, 1 (§ III 27). Man is of the same size as the altar. Cf. SB I, 2, 5, 14. And the altar is both the sacrifice and the center of the world. Cf. RV I, 164, 35 (§ I 11) repeated in YV XXIII, 62. The same idea is repeated in SB III, 1, 4, 23, which, in addition to the identification between sacrifice and the word two verses before, makes a connection (*mātrā*) between *yajña, puruṣa,* and *vāc*.
▪ ii) 1. The text could also have the contrary meaning: the Gods, etc., owing the debt. *Ṛṇam ha vai jāyate yo' sti*.
▪ iii) Cf. § III 16 concerning the *agnihotra*.
▪ iv) Debt: *ṛṇa*.
▪ v) Cf. § V A c for cremation rites and AV XII, 3 for cremation as a form of sacrifice.
▪ vii) The *pañcamahāyajña* ("five great sacrifices") constitute the central acts of worship. They are (in the order of this text) *bhūta, manuṣya-, pitṛ-, deva-,* and *brahmayajña* (cf. the list given by Manu III, 69-72). Cf. BU I, 4, 17 (§§ I 7 and III 26 Introduction).

The Desire of Heaven *Svargakāma*

24 *Svargakāmo yajeta,* "with the desire for heaven he sacrifices," is a traditional formula explicated in the post-Vedic period with the closest attention to detail. There is no point in expounding here the various sacrifices and the proliferation of sacrificial practices which took place. We may simply take note in passing that the power of sacrifice has been used and misused for satisfying human wishes of all kinds.

Tradition renders *svarga,* which literally means "heaven," as happiness,[212] and indeed the desire for heaven means the desire for happiness. Now happiness may be sought in different values: material riches, offspring, a wife, power, triumph, and the like. We detect here a peculiar process of secularization; sacrifice is being utilized for secular purposes, because in secular "values" Men see their relative or temporal heaven. One Upaniṣad, perhaps not without a certain irony, says that "one who desires heaven should offer the *agnihotra.*"[213]

There is no doubt that human religiousness has overdone the idea of heaven all too often, but on the other hand we should be on our guard against converting religion into so lofty and chemically pure a business that only the sophisticated and "pure" elites can be expected to understand and practice it. At one extreme is the idea that religion is only for the masses, while at the other is the belief that it is only for the elite. In the former instance the "enlightened" persons do not need religion. In the latter what the masses have is only superstition.

The desire of heaven under one image or another, that is, the longing for happiness along with the conviction that an endeavor toward such a goal is not totally hopeless, constitutes mankind's most constant and most powerful impetus since Man became Man. Its interpretation is quite another matter. Yet here the emphasis lies, as with most religious values, not on the orthodoxy but on the orthopraxy, that is, on the action a Man has to perform in order to attain the desired goal. Furthermore, today's practices probably illustrate yesterday's attitudes: many people perform the traditionally prescribed actions without being convinced of their meaning or concerning themselves with their possible interpretation.[214]

Svargakāma

SB IV, 2, 5, 10

i) Every sacrifice is a boat to heaven.

212. Cf. Mīmāṁsā Sūtra IV, 3, 15 and Commentaries.
213. MaitU VI, 36.
214. On heaven, cf. § V B c.

SB VIII, 6, 1, 10

ii) So great is the power of sacrifice that it is the Self of the Gods. When, out of the essence of sacrifice, the Gods had made their own Self, they took their seat in the world of heaven. Similarly, the one who sacrifices now, when out of the essence of sacrifice he has made his own Self, takes his seat in the world of heaven.

SB VIII, 7, 4, 6

iii) Sacrifice has only one sure foundation, only one abode, the heavenly realm.

SB IX, 2, 3, 27

iv) "Those journeying to heaven do not look back; they ascend the heaven, the two worlds;" that is, those who are en route to the heavenly world proceed straight on; they by no means look back. It is also said, "The sage performing the all-supporting sacrifice. . . ," because sacrifice is most certainly that by which the whole world is supported and those who perform it are the sages.

SB IX, 4, 4, 15

v) Daily the sacrifice is spread.
Daily the sacrifice is completed.
Daily it unites the sacrificer to heaven.
Daily by sacrifice to heaven he ascends.

AB IV, 27 (XIX, 5, 4)

vi) The hymns are arranged in groups. Just as one travels [here on earth] in different stages, changing each time the horses or the oxen for those who are less exhausted, in the same way one goes to heaven by reciting each time new hymns in meters that are not yet exhausted.

■ i) *Sarva eva yajño nauḥ svargyā.* Cf. JaimB I, 165 (§ III B Antiphon).
■ ii) Cf. SB XI, 2, 6, 13 (§ III 23) where another idea is expressed, namely, that the best sacrifice is the sacrifice to (or of) the Self (*ātman*), and that it is superior even to the sacrifice to the Gods, because it is more intimate and because it opens the way to the highest realm. Cf. § III 27.
World of heaven: *svargaloka.*
■ v) Daily by sacrifice . . . : *ahar ahar anena* (*yajñena*) *svargaṁ lokaṁ gacchati.* For this reason, the text goes on, yoking and unyoking of the fire altar has to be performed daily.
■ vi) An example of the concreteness of the rites leading to heaven; the liturgical ascension is taken realistically.
Hymns: *chandāṁsi,* meters.

Fidelity and Faith *Satyaṁ śraddhāyām*

25 The performance of sacrifice may become complicated and difficult, for any error or failure tends to be corrected by a new caution, which soon results in a proliferation of regulations. In

fact, "if the priest omits a syllable in the liturgy he is making a hole in the sacrifice,"[215] says one text, thus indicating the strict correspondence among word, action, and results. In the Śathapatha Brāhmaṇa we find frequent mention of "those who know," that is, the priests who are sure guides in this labyrinth of sacrifice. It is this knowledge on the part of priests which explains their importance (and hence that of Brahmins in general) and their superiority over the simple faithful. It explains also the strong tendency observable at the culmination of this process to consider them as Gods, as God-Men. In fact they have in their hands a formidable weapon, powerful both among Men and among Gods. No wonder, then, that before the performance of any important ritual priests must take an oath not to harm one another,[216] either intentionally[217] or by simple error.[218] It is not surprising that casteism and priestcraft have been among the most devastating abuses in all religions.

Those who perform sacrifice have to satisfy both the Gods above, to whom the sacrifice is offered, and the priests or Brahmins, to whom gifts must be presented. The presentation of gifts, which plays an important part in the ceremony, is called *dakṣiṇā;* the gifts may consist of gold, clothing, or cattle and horses. In the Atharva Veda we find stress laid upon these gifts to priests as "passports" to heaven.

Not only must sacrifice be flawlessly performed as regards the sequence of actions, but the prayers, verses, chants, and hymns must be impeccably pronounced. Just as the divine primordial sacrifice was accomplished through the medium of the word, so Man's sacrifice similarly employs words, which are for Man his sole instrument and indeed the inner soul-force of the sacrificial action without which no sacrifice could conceivably take place. Hence the extreme precision associated with the words of sacrifice. The primeval words are all cultic words.

This execution of sacrifice in as perfect a manner as possible does not demand merely the proper sequence of rites performed in a mechanical fashion. Sacrifice is valueless without a spirit of trust, without faith. Faith cannot be dissociated from precision, or fidelity to the rules. Moreover, there must be trust both in the sacrifice itself

215. AB III, 11 (XI, 11).

216. Cf. the so-called *tānūnapatra* ceremony, e.g., in AB I, 24 (IV, 7); SB III, 4, 2, 9.

217. Cf., e.g., AB II, 33 (X, 1); III, 3 (XI, 3).

218. Cf. SB I, 6, 3, 10 sq. for a famous example where a mistake in the pronunciation produced the opposite effect to the one intended.

and in the priests, since it is they who take the lead in the performance of the sacrificial action. This "trust" or "faith" appears also as a personified divinity.[219] The one who is faithful (*śraddhā-deva*) par excellence is Manu, the first priest, who accomplished the sacrifice so perfectly that he was thereafter frequently cited as a model to imitate.[220]

Even today in the Romance languages, though less in Anglo-Saxon idiom, one speaks of fidelity to observances and to rites, meaning both scrupulous observances and firm belief. There can be no fidelity without both elements: exactitude or precision, and faith or confidence. *Śraddhā* means both equally.

The word *śraddhā* has a fascinating origin. It is composed of *śrat* and the verbal root *dhā-*, to put (place, set, lay). If we recall that the Latin *credo,* to believe, and the Greek *kardía* (Latin, *cor*) are also related to *śrad* (or *śrat*), we have practically all the ingredients of the notion of faith: to put one's heart, to put one's whole being, to have one's trust and confidence in something.[221] *Śrat* has been related in the Indian tradition to *satya,* being, truth that here means not only truth but also truthfulness and exactitude.[222] *Śrat* means the fundamental trust that is based on nothing other than the very nature of our entire being—there where our whole being is based.[223] As already noted,[224] faith, truth, being, and cosmic order go together[225] It is on this ultimate level where the discourse on faith is meaningful and not on the epistemic level of discussion about different beliefs.

One passage of the Kauṣītaki Brāhmaṇa relates in a profound and simple fashion, by means of a story and a dialogue, the human longing for permanence and durable effects in connection with sacrifice. If sacrifice is real it cannot be merely a fleeting action but must be an act done once and for all with permanent results. Yet if it is not reenacted each time one feels the need, how can one enjoy its blessings, or how are we going to know that it is efficacious

219. Cf. § I 36.

220. On the subject of Manu cf. § V 17 where the story of Manu and Iḍā is given, Iḍā being in this text the personification of Trust in the effects of sacrifice. Cf. also SB XI, 2, 7, 20 (§ V B a Introduction).

221. Curiously enough, *śraddhā* can also mean the longing of a pregnant woman, her confidence that life will spring out of her.

222. Cf. "*Śraddhā* [faith] [*śrad-dhā*] is on account of being founded on *śrad* [truth]," *Nirukta* IX, 30.

223. It would be tempting to relate *śrad* to the verbal stem *śrath-*, to become loose, united, to relax, and say that faith is that ultimate rest of being where one can relax, be as one really is without pretending. Faith leads then to ultimate unconcern: absolute freedom, liberation.

224. Cf. § I E c.

225. Cf. RV IX, 113, 4.

for us? "What makes the sacrifice endure forever is faith; if one sacrifices with faith, the sacrifice is never lost."[226] Faith is the permanent and enduring element in sacrifice. "Certainly it is out of faith that the Gods fashioned the initiation (*dīkṣā*)."[227]

Faith also means truth and truth implies truthfulness, that is, the correct correspondence and right relationship among actions, words, meanings, and life. The external precision of the acts is only a symbol for the perfect correctness demanded from the sacrificer, for he does not perform the sacrifice through his own private capacity but enters into the ontological net of reality in order to maintain its cohesion and stability.

One text in this chapter (ii) leads us right up to the threshold of the Upaniṣadic world. Here the exactness of the rites is indeed essential, but still more essential is the spirit with which the ritual is performed. Imagine, the king says to Yājñavalkya, one of the most famous of sages, that the most elementary things are lacking for the performance of the *agnihotra*. What is to be used for the offering? The ontological interconnection of everything in the world permits Yājñavalkya to justify his substitution of one "thing" for another. When asked what would have to be done in the final extreme when nothing of the material world remains, he replies that one thing only remains: reality, truth (*satya*), and it is this that offers itself in faith; the sacrificer and the sacrifice coalesce when there is nothing else to offer.

It is the same Yājñavalkya who in the corresponding Upaniṣad of the later date[228] expresses the beautiful thought that the sacrifice depends on the offerings and the offerings depend on faith. "But on what," he is asked, "does faith depend?" "On the heart alone is faith based," he replies.[229]

There is an intimate relation not only between truth and exactitude and between both of these and faith, but also between both of these and sacrifice. Sacrifice is the connecting link. "He who has laid the sacrificial fires should not speak untruth," says another text; "he should rather not speak at all, but he should not speak untruth," and, finally and epigrammatically, "Truth alone is worship."[230]

226. KausB VII, 4. Never lost: *na kṣīyate*, not destroyed.
227. SB XII, 1, 2, 1.
228. BU belongs to the group of the SB.
229. BU III, 9, 21 (§ I 37). Cf. again the etymological meaning.
230. SB II, 2, 2, 20 *Satyam evopacāra iti* (cf. § VII Introduction).

Satyaṁ śraddhāyām

SB I, 5, 2, 15

i) If he who draws near the sacrifice were to make an improper utterance he would waste the sacrifice, just as he might waste water by spilling it from a full vessel. Where the priests perform sacrifice as described with perfect mutual understanding, however, there everything takes place properly and no trouble appears. Therefore it is in this fashion that sacrifice should be carefully cherished.

SB XI, 3, 1, 2-4

ii) Janaka of Videha once asked Yājñavalkya, "What is used for the *agnihotra,* Yājñavalkya? Can you tell me?"

"I can, O king," he replied.

"What is it, then?"

"Milk," he said.

"If there were no milk, what would you use for the offering?"

"Rice and barley."

"And if there were no rice and barley, what would you use?"

"Some other herbs."

"And if there were no other herbs, what would you use?"

"I would use wild herbs," he said.

"And if there were no wild herbs, what would you use?"

"Some fruit."

"And if there were no fruit, what would you use?"

"I would use water," he said.

"And if there were no water, what would you use?"

"Then indeed," he replied, "there would be nothing at all, and yet an offering could be made—truth with faith."

Janaka then said: "You know the *agnihotra,* Yājñavalkya; I give you a hundred cows."

SB XII, 2, 3, 12

iii) Such are the difficulties and dangers of sacrifice which take hundreds upon hundreds of days to negotiate; and if any man venture upon them without knowledge, then he is stricken by hunger and thirst, by wicked men or friends, just as friends might harass foolish persons wandering in a wild forest. But if those who know do so they proceed one step after another and from one safe place to another, just as one might pass from one stream to another, and they thus obtain happiness in the world of heaven.

AB I, 11, 4 (II, 5, 13-14)

iv) One must prevent the sacrifice from unloosing. Just as in everyday life one ties knots at the two ends of a rope to prevent its becoming loose, so one ties knots at both ends of the sacrifice to prevent its unloosing.

TS I, 6, 8, 1

v) Whoever offers a sacrifice without first taking firm hold on faith, that man's sacrifice inspires no confidence. . . . But if a man first takes firm hold on faith and then offers his sacrifice, then in that man's sacrifice both Gods and men place confidence.

■ i) Make an improper utterance: *apavyāharet*. As *vyāhṛti* is the effective and "proper" sacrificial utterance, its dangerous distortion is expressed by the prefix *apa-*.

Mutual understanding: *saṁvid*, which means also common knowledge.

■ ii) And yet an offering could be made—truth with faith: *athaitad āhūyataiva satyaṁ śraddhāyām*, then one could offer only truth with faith. Cf. The same text in JB I, 19 and also BU VI, 2, 9 (§ III 26), where it is said that the Gods offer faith. Cf. other texts mentioned above (§ III 23) on the human tendency to reduce everything to essentials. Cf. YV XIX, 30:

> By means of vows [*vrata*] one obtains consecration [*dīkṣā*],
> by consecration one obtains favor [*dakṣiṇā*, offering to the priest],
> by favor one obtains faith [*śraddhā*],
> by faith one obtains truth [*satya*].

■ iv) The knots at both ends of the sacrifice refer here to the introductory and concluding rites. If one of these rites were missing, the continuity and very existence of the sacrifice would be endangered. The metaphor of the loom is also in the background.

■ v) Takes firm hold: *ā-rabhya*, from the same root as *ārambha*, beginning, origin (taking firm grasp before undertaking anything). A play on words involving *śrad*, confidence, the verb *dhā-*, to put, and *śraddhā*.

The Anthropocosmic Sacrifice *Loko 'gniḥ*

26 The more ancient Upaniṣads make frequent mention of ritual sacrifice and seem to recognize the traditional ritual interpretations. Yet slowly there appears an interiorized and more anthropocentric notion of sacrifice, though its constituent parts remain the same. There is progress toward a more purely spiritual and interior concept.

One of the most important and ancient Upaniṣads belonging to the Śatapatha Brāhmaṇa is the Bṛhadāraṇyaka Upaniṣad. Its opening verses describe the sacrificial horse as symbol of the universal sacrifice: the head of the horse is the dawn, the eye the sun, the wind the breath, and so on.

We are still in the old order, but already the great leap has begun. Scripture is quoted as supporting the new ideas. Tradition has considered that meditation on the sacrifice is equivalent to the sacrifice itself, and a passage of the Śatapatha Brāhmaṇa is quoted which says, "either through knowledge or through work,"[231] and reference is made to another text that seems to equate the horse sacrifice with the knowledge of it.[232] Still another text says that the Self-offerer is better than the God-offerer,[233] which is understood to mean that to sacrifice to the Self is better than to sacrifice to the Gods. We are not interested in analyzing exegetical methods, but only in detecting a new trend leading to such interpretations. It was knowing this, the text of another Upaniṣad says, that is, realizing the power that faith possesses and recognizing the internal stream as the real one, that the ancients did not perform the sacrifice of the fire.[234]

It is possible to distinguish three phases in the Upaniṣadic treatment of sacrifice. There is, first, the transient phase in which the ancient-style sacrifices still predominate. It may be called the anthropocosmic sacrifice, because the place of Man is becoming central and his dispositions are considered to be of the utmost importance.

The second phase, which we may call the anthropocentric one, stresses less the traditional sacrifices but underlines the meaning of sacrifice for human life, almost identifying the two. Man becomes the center of the sacrificial act.

The third phase, which may be called the sacrifice of the mind, identifies the costly and difficult external sacrifice with the no less costly and difficult internal sacrifice of an undisturbed and perfect mind reenacting within itself the whole dynamism of the outer world, whose existence, if not always denied or doubted, is certainly minimized. We are present here at the birth of another ritual.

We consider these three phases in three separate chapters. In

231. SB X, 4, 3, 9 (§ V 3 Introduction). This interpretation of Śaṅkara BU Bhāṣya I, 1 (Introduction) is rather forced because the text explicitly adds: "the fire altar is the knowledge and the fire altar is the work."

232. Cf. TS V, 3, 12, 2. Again there is a certain violence in the interpretation of this text by Śaṅkara (*op. cit.*), which says literally, "he who knows it to be so," referring to the fact of knowing the power of the horse sacrifice to overcome or forgive all sins, even that of the killing of a brahmin (in this particular instance).

233. Cf. SB XI, 2, 6, 13 (§ III 23).

234. Cf. KausU II, 5 (§ III 28).

the first of the selected texts the cosmic symbolism of sacrifice is expressed in anthropocosmic terms, and we note here a first step toward the total interiorization of sacrifice. The text is given with very slight variations in the two most important Upaniṣads.[235] It has a colorful setting and deals with the so-called *pañcāgnividyā*, or doctrine of the five fires, which teaches the doctrine of the two ways after death: the so-called way of the Gods which leads to the world of Brahman with no return and the so-called way of the ancestors which leads to a return to this world.[236]

The setting is a delightful dialogue between different generations (father and son), between different castes (Brahmins and Kṣatriyas), and between different spiritualities (the sacred and the secular). The famous Śvetaketu, who has received full instruction from his father Gautama, does not know how to answer the questions of the king; nor does his father know anything about the two ways open to Men when they die, or about the reason why the other world is not filled to capacity, and so on. The old and famous father, great and rich Brahmin though he be, goes humbly to the Kṣatriya to be instructed. Our text reports part of the teaching of this member of the warrior class to the highly respected Brahmin, who declares that such a doctrine is unknown to the whole Brahmin brotherhood. Here is perhaps an indication that the Upaniṣadic trend toward interiorization and secularization of the ritual did not originate in the Brahmanical and priestly class, but in the secular class of ruling princes.

The answer represents a middle way between the ancient cosmic conception and the later purely interiorized and almost theoretical notion of Vedānta. The cosmos as a whole presents the traditional structure of a universal sacrifice, but the different parts of the cosmos are homologized with human destiny. There are five realities: the otherworld, the intermediate rain cloud, this terrestrial world, man, and woman. All of them are Agni, the sacrificial fire, and all of them have their own characteristic five elements for the sacrifice: fuel, smoke, flame, coals, and sparks. On each of the five fires the Gods offer the corresponding sacrifice which thus presents an interesting hierarchical structure, each of the five elements being based on its immediate predecessor. The completion of the circles

235. The version of the SB XIV, from which the BU is derived, seems to be the more ancient.
236. Cf. § V 4.

takes place in Man, who at the end of his life realizes the unity of the cosmic elements with the human. In the funeral pyre the fuel is no longer the sun, the year, the earth, the open mouth, the sexual organ, but simply fuel. The same is true of the other elements of the sacrifice. The circle is complete but the end can be twofold: a Man who has been transformed and has acquired the color of light may enter the eternal world of Brahman with no return to earth, or, failing to reach transformation, he may follow the way of the ancestors and come back to earth under a different form.

It is at the end of a similar homologization that another Upaniṣad clearly states:

> The Sacrifice is fivefold.
> An animal is fivefold.
> Man is fivefold.
> This entire universe,
> all that is, is fivefold.
> The man who knows this
> obtains this whole world.[237]

Sacrifice is the world. The three main fires of sacrifice are given an allegorical interpretation as the sacrificial piles which Prajāpati himself erected when he created the cosmos, namely, the earth, the intermediate space, and the sky. Fire is the ruling power in these three regions, that is, the year, the wind, and the sun, and it is by this power that the sacrificer is brought to the experience of Joy Supreme, that is, to the experience of Brahman. In other words, the sacrifice, embracing the three worlds, leads the sacrificer, once he knows the mystery of the person, once he discovers the personalistic structure of reality, toward the supreme Brahman and total plenitude. Prajāpati clearly performs here the role of a personal God, the Lord of Creation. The text suggests three lords of creation. In each of them the regeneration is effected by means of sacrifice.

Another text makes this homologization quite explicit. The universal Self, or the *vaiśvānara ātman,* is said to have the heaven as his head, the sun as his eye, the wind as his breath, the space as his body, the earth as his feet, and so on.[238]

The meaning of these and many other texts is immediately apparent. Man, who has ceased to be a spectator in the cosmic event, is

237. BU I, 4, 17 (§ I 7). Cf. the same idea, even further elaborated, in TU I, 7. Cf. also SB XI, 5, 6, 1-3 (§ III 23).
238. Cf. CU V, 18, 2.

deeply involved and ontologically committed: he is part and parcel of the cosmic sacrifice itself; he is not only a priest but a partner, not only a performer but a mediator. He is the yardstick by which everything is measured. Yet the anthropocosmic unity is maintained and Man's partnership is ultimately dependent on the objective superhuman order.

Loko 'gniḥ

BU VI, 2, 9-14

i) 9. Yonder world in truth is Fire, O Gautama; the sun is its fuel, the rays its smoke, the day its flame, the heavenly quarters its coals, the intermediate quarters its sparks. In this Fire the Gods offer faith as libation. From that offering arises king Soma.

10. The God of rain in truth is a sacrificial Fire, O Gautama; its fuel is the year, the clouds are its smoke, lightning is its flame, the thunderbolt its coals, thunder its sparks. In this Fire the Gods offer king Soma. From that offering arises rain.

11. This world in truth is Fire, O Gautama; its fuel is the earth, fire its smoke, night its flame, the moon its coals, the stars its sparks. In this Fire the Gods offer the rain cloud. From that offering arises food.

12. Man in truth is Fire, O Gautama; his open mouth is fuel, his breath the smoke, his speech the flame, his eyes the coals, his ears the sparks. In this Fire the Gods offer food. From that offering arises semen.

13-14. Woman in truth is Fire, O Gautama; the phallus is the fuel, the hairs the smoke, the vulva the flame, penetration the coals, the pleasure the sparks. In this Fire the Gods offer semen. From that offering arises a person. He lives as long as he lives. When he dies, they carry him to the fire. Here his fire becomes Fire, his fuel fuel, his smoke smoke, his flame flame, his coals coals, his sparks sparks. In this Fire the Gods offer a person. From that offering arises the person resplendent as light.

MaitU VI, 33

ii) Now, this sacrificial fire with its five bricks is the year. The bricks for this fire are these: spring, summer, the rainy season, autumn, winter. It has a head, two wings, a back, and a tail. This sacrificial fire is the earth for the one who knows the Person. It is Prajāpati's first sacrificial pile. Its strength lifts up the sacrificer to the middle world and offers him to the wind. The wind is indeed breath.

Now breath is sacrificial fire. Its bricks are the five different kinds of breath. It has a head, two wings, a back, and a tail. This sacrificial fire is the middle world for one who knows the Person. It is Prajāpati's second sacrificial pile. Its strength lifts the sacrificer up to the heavens and offers him to Indra. Indra is indeed the sun.

Now, the sun is sacrificial fire. Its bricks are the four Vedas, epic and legend. It has a head, two wings, a back, and a tail. This sacrificial fire is heaven for one who knows the Person. It is Prajāpati's third sacrificial pile. Its strength lifts the sacrificer up to the Knower of the Self. Then the Knower of the Self raises him up and offers him to Brahman. There he becomes full of bliss and joy.

■ i) Cf. CU V, 4, sq., a parallel passage.
1-8. Cf. § V 4.
9. Yonder world: the world beyond, as opposed to this world.
Fire: Agni, the sacrificial fire.
The Gods offer faith: *devāḥ śraddhāṁ juhvati.*
The whole cosmos presents the structure of a universal sacrifice and the different parts of the cosmos are homologized to the cosmic sacrifice.
10. The God of rain: Parjanya.
11. This world: *ayam* (*loka*) in contradistinction to *asau,* that world (of v. 9).
12. Man: *puruṣa,* used also in v. 13 in the sense of an embryo, and in v. 14 in the sense of a human person.
13-14. In this text "fire," as distinct from "Fire," refers to the funeral pyre.
Resplendent as light: *bhāsvara-varṇa,* having the color of light. Man has become all fire, passes into the flame.
15-16. Cf. § V 4.
■ ii) The sacrificial fires referred to are the three traditional fires of *gārhapatya, dakṣiṇa,* and *āhavanīya.*
Its strength: lit. hands.
Fire . . . for the one who knows the Person: *eṣo 'gniḥ puruṣavidaḥ.* This sentence has been also translated: "This Fire is like a man" (Gonda).
Middle world: *antarikṣa,* the atmosphere, the in-between (heaven and earth).
The five different kinds of breath: *prāṇa, vyāna, apāna, samāna,* and *udāna.*
Sun: *āditya.*
Four Vedas: *ṛg-yajuḥ-sāmātharvāṅgirasā.*
Cf. § III 28.
Epic and legend: *itihāsa-purāṇa.*
Knower of the Self: *ātma-vid,* referring here to Prajāpati.
There is a triple equation to be observed: time-sun-*brahman;* sun-*prāṇa*-fire; earth-*prāṇa*-sun.

The Anthropocentric Sacrifice *Śārīrayajña*

27 The "conscientization" brought about by the Upaniṣads does not end with the integration of Man into the framework of sacrifice; it centers sacrifice on Man. If Man performs the sacrifice without the necessary knowledge, if he is unconscious of its meaning, it will not be a true sacrifice. Man is an essential element in the sacrificial structure. Moreover, with the exclusion of possible magical interpretations we are led to recognize that sacrifice is not only—and one will soon be led to add, not even mainly—directed to the maintenance of the physical cosmos, but of the world of Man. A cosmic catastrophe may well occur if Man fails to perform

sacrifice, but defection in this regard is difficult to check. Moreover, there are so many Men on earth and the mechanism of the whole procedure is so complex that one cannot be absolutely sure of the function and importance of one particular thread. On the other hand, one thing is sure: that Man cannot lead an authentic human existence if he does not perform sacrifice. Sacrifice becomes more and more centered on Man. Human life is itself a sacrifice and there is an emphasis on both knowledge and Man.

The first text of this selection ends a long passage at the beginning of the Bṛhadāraṇyaka Upaniṣad which seems to indicate that all sacrifices culminate in the recognition that the all-embracing sacrifice is the sacrifice of, in, or to the Self, and that only by this kind of sacrifice is a worshiper saved from perishing. The dynamism of the whole text is worth pondering, for it gives another clue to this momentous Upaniṣadic mutation. This fourth *brāhmaṇa* gives a condensed explanation of the divine sacrifice by which the world came into being. It comes to the conclusion that all is the action of the *ātman*. If so, to worship the *ātman* is the way given to Man for collaborating in the world-making sacrifice. The text goes so far as to say that "one should worship the *ātman* alone as *loka*,"[239] that is, as "world," as the open space of which one can be aware, as the realm of one's own experience, as the world that opens up to a Man. For this reason it is also stated in the same place that "if a Man departs from this world without having seen his own world, that world, being unknown, will be of no avail to him, just as the Veda, if it is not recited, is of no avail."[240] It is then obvious that by meditating on such an *ātman* (in the active sense in which to meditate is to become what one meditates upon,[241] each worshiper obtains the object under which the *ātman* appears to him.[242] But this truth has to be known and discovered, otherwise the works are ineffectual.[243] Sacrifice is the human act par excellence, but it entails also the risk of its misuse for personal profit or greed.

The second text from the Chāndogya Upaniṣad takes up and develops the idea of human life as a sacrifice. All existent things are homologized to different sacrifices. By this means the full range of

239. BU I, 4, 15: *ātmānam eva lokam upāsīta*.
240. BU I, 4, 15.
241. Cf. AV X, 7, 24 (§ I 3); MundU III, 2, 9 (§ VI 11).
242. Cf. CU VIII, 2.
243. Cf. BU I, 4, 15.

Man's life on earth is sanctified, for everything corresponds to some facet of the life-giving and world-saving sacrifice. In this process of correlation stress is laid on the human element. It is affirmed, for example, that the *dakṣiṇā* or honorarium given to the priest at the time of sacrifice (which in ancient times was considerable and burdensome) cannot simply be reduced to *dāna* or almsgiving; it is not even specifically stated that the priests should be the beneficiaries. More important are the other four gifts mentioned: fervor, uprightness, harmlessness, sincerity.[244]

Another passage of the same Upaniṣad (iii) introduces an important act, which also demonstrates the man-centered character of sacrifice. The priest who knows the intricate cosmological origin of the different rites of sacrifice can undo certain mistakes that may have crept in, thus signifying the power Man has over the merely mechanical or blind forces of the sacrifice. The underlying idea is that of an ontological substitution by means of ritualistic identification. Prajāpati brooded over the worlds, and their "essences," their "juices," *rasāḥ,* were extracted. From the earth came forth its essence, fire, and from fire proceeded the Ṛg Veda. So any mistake in the Ṛg-Vedic recitation can be rectified by means of the corresponding fire sacrifice. Knowledge here is power.[245]

The importance of this new idea should not be overlooked. It is the beginning of Man's domination of the cosmic process, not for magical purposes, not for directing the forces of nature for or against other human beings, but for a restructuring of the same cosmos, for changing its course, as it were. The destiny of the world as cosmos begins to fall into human hands. Man emerges now as more than simply a partner in the cosmic process produced by sacrifice; he appears as the rectifying mind, as the spirit who by his knowledge can correct mistakes that false calculations may have allowed to creep in. One is tempted to say, extending the metaphor, that it resembles the course correction of a spaceship's orbit, needed when the utilization of the energy condensed in matter has not been properly calculated.

The Chāndogya Upaniṣad also contains a homologization between the life of a *brahmacārin,* that is, of a student of wisdom, and all the different sacrifices and stages of life (iv).

244. We use here terms deliberately different from those given in the text. The wealth of possible meaning is thus better conveyed.
245. Cf. CU IV, 17, 1-8.

The selection given here from the Mahānārāyaṇa (v) and Prāṇāgnihotra (vi) Upaniṣads elaborates further the same theme: the centrality of Man and his body to the whole concept of sacrifice. The body here is the microcosm, the mirror and representative of the whole universe; it is not, however, the body alone or the body independent of the mind which matters, but the whole Man. The *ātman,* the Self, is the sacrificer. Sacrifice is the integral human act and each act of life is a sacrificial act. Furthermore, in this connection the same Upaniṣad introduces the idea of death as the supreme purification, as the ultimate human sacrifice. A most significant verse closes this short Upaniṣad: liberation, *mokṣa,* can indeed be the fruit of a cosmological situation, like that of dying in the holy city of Vārāṇasī (and this Upaniṣad does not appear to deny the traditional belief), but the doctrine has as its main thrust the teaching that there is another way. Knowledge of the doctrine of the *prāṇāgnihotra,* the intellectual sacrifice, that is, the internal act and its self-knowledge, may also bring about *mokṣa.* The internal or inner *agnihotra* leads to the mental sacrifice, the sacrifice made by the mind, *mānasa yajña.* This text has been used in Yoga and Tantra to justify or explain the emphasis on the body and on body participation in the sacrifice.

The hymn of the Muṇḍaka Upaniṣad (vii) is a typical specimen of mature Upaniṣadic spirituality. It begins by extolling the practice of sacrifice and pondering over its benefits, but immediately adds that if sacrifice is regarded as an isolated entity, disconnected from everything else, that is, if we mistake the means for the end, then we are deluded; the hymn even takes a certain pleasure in using strong words to denounce mere ritualism. Moreover, the highest wisdom, which is the supreme stage, cannot be reached by sacrifice. One must go in a proper manner to a *guru* and discover from him the imperishable Man, the supreme reality.

The Scripture says "Sacrifice *is* Man," and this statement is eminently true. Sacrifice takes place within Man, through Man, so long as he is a Man of faith who believes, hopes, loves, and has made of his very existence an act of worship. His life is adoration, cooperation, prayer, activity, contemplation, action, and love of God and of all he has made. In worship Man is at one and the same time active and passive, helper and helped, actor and spectator. He forms part of the unique human-divine act that enables him to exist and to be.

Sacrifice in its universal significance is endowed with a twofold dynamism: a downward movement of the Divine toward the world, followed by an upward movement or restoration of the world toward the Divine. These two aspects are inseparable, the cosmic process being an exchange and in continual evolution. Eternity and Time blend in each instant. At each instant the universe is created and at each instant it returns whence it came. At each successive moment there is a new universe which in its turn does not tarry before declining. This new renewed world is the fruit of sacrifice.

Śārīrayajña

BU I, 4, 16

i) Now this is the Self, the world of all beings. If a man offers and sacrifices, he will attain the world of the Gods. If he recites [the Vedas], he will attain the world of the Seers. If he offers libations to the Forefathers and desires offspring, he will attain the world of the Forefathers. If he gives shelter and food to men, he will attain the human world. If he gives grass and water to animals, he will reach the animal world. If beasts and birds, [even] down to the ants, find a place in his house, he will reach their respective worlds. In the same way as a man wishes security for his own world, so all beings wish security to the one who knows thus. This is indeed known and investigated.

CU III, 16-17, 1-6

ii) 16, 1. Man, in truth, is himself a sacrifice. His first twenty-four years correspond to the morning libation. The Gāyatrī has twenty-four syllables and the morning libation is offered with the Gāyatrī. With this the Vasus are related. Now the vital breaths are the Vasus, because they cause everything to continue in existence.

2. If he should be afflicted by sickness at this period of life, he should say: "O vital breaths who are the Vasus, let my morning offering be extended till the midday offering. Let me, who am the sacrifice, not perish in the midst of the vital breaths, the Vasus!" and he gets up and becomes free from his sickness.

3. His next forty-four years correspond to the midday libation. The Triṣṭubh has forty-four syllables and the midday libation is offered with the Triṣṭubh. With this the Rudras are related. Now the vital breaths are the Rudras, because they cause everything to weep.

4. If he should be afflicted by sickness at this period of life, he should say: "O vital breaths who are the Rudras, let my midday offering be extended till the third offering. Let me, who am the sacrifice, not perish in the midst of the life breaths, the Rudras!" and he gets up and becomes free from his sickness.

5. His next forty-eight years correspond to the third libation. The Jagatī has forty-eight syllables and the third libation is offered with the Jagatī. To this the Ādityas are related. Now the vital breaths are the Ādityas, because they take everything to themselves.

6. If he should be afflicted by sickness at this period of life, he should say: "O vital breaths who are the Ādityas, let this my third libation be extended till my full life span is accomplished. Let me, who am the sacrifice, not perish in the midst of the vital breaths, the Ādityas!" and he gets up and becomes free from his sickness.

7. In truth, it was knowing this that Mahidāsa Aitareya used to say [to sickness]: "Why do you torment me like this, me who am not going to die by this affliction?" He lived for a hundred and sixteen years. The one who knows this will also live for a hundred and sixteen years.

17, 1. When a man feels hunger and thirst, when he does not rejoice, then he is undergoing his initiation rite.

2. When he eats and drinks and rejoices, then he is joining in the *upasada* rituals.

3. When he laughs and eats and has sexual intercourse, then he is taking part in chant and recitation.

4. Asceticism, almsgiving, moral integrity, nonviolence, truthfulness—these are his gifts for the priests.

5. Therefore one says [at the sacrifice]: "He will procreate, he has procreated," for this is his new birth. His death is the ablution after the ceremony.

6. Ghora Āṅgirasa, having told all this to Kṛṣṇa the son of Devakī, added: "When man is free from desire, in his last hour, he should take refuge in the three following [maxims]:

You are imperishable
You are immovable
You are firm in the breath of life."

CU V, 24, 1-4

iii) 1. If one were to offer the *agnihotra* without this knowledge, that would be just the same as removing the live coals and pouring the libation on ashes.

2. But if one offers the *agnihotra* with full knowledge one is offering it in all worlds, in all beings, in all selves.

3. Even as the tip of a reed, if laid upon a fire, would be burned up, so also are burned up all the sins of him who offers the *agnihotra* with full knowledge.

4. Therefore, if one who knows this offers the leftovers of his food to

an outcaste, he is offering it to the universal Self. On this point there is the following verse:

> As hungry children here below
> sit round about their mother,
> even so all beings expectantly
> sit round the *agnihotra*.

CU VIII, 5

iv) 1. Now what people call "sacrifice" is really the disciplined life of a student of sacred knowledge, for only by leading such a life does one who is a knower find the Brahman world. Now what people call "the sacrificial offering" is also really the disciplined life of a student of sacred knowledge, for only after sacrificing with the disciplined life of a student of sacred knowledge does a man find the Self.

2. Now what people call "a long course of sacrifice" is really the disciplined life of a student of sacred knowledge, for only by leading such a life does one find the protection of the true *ātman*.

Now what people call "the practice of silence" is really the disciplined life of a student of sacred knowledge, for only by leading such a life does one find the *ātman* and meditate.

3. Now what people call "the practice of fasting" is really the disciplined life of a student of sacred knowledge, for the *ātman* found by such a life does not decay.

Now what people call "the way of solitude" [*araṇya*] is really the disciplined life of a student of sacred knowledge. For *ara* and *ṇya* are the two oceans in the Brahman world in the third heaven. There is the lake Airammada and the sacred tree producing Soma; there is the city of Brahman, Aparājitā, and the golden hall constructed by the Lord.

4. Only those who, by the disciplined life of a student of sacred knowledge, attain the two oceans *ara* and *ṇya* in the Brahman world are free to move in all the worlds.

MahanarU 543-545

v) 543. At the sacrifice of one who knows this, the Self is the sacrificer, his wife is his faith, his body the fuel, his breast the altar, his hair the sacrificial grass, his hair tuft the sacrificial broom, his heart the sacrificial post, his love the melted butter, his anger the victim, his fervor the fire, his self-control which destroys [the passions] the priestly honoraria, his word the priest, his breath the singer, his eye the officiating priest, his mind the Brahman-priest, his ear the fire-kindling priest.

544. Henceforward, as long as he lives, his consecration lasts; whatever he eats is his oblation, whatever he drinks is his Soma-drinking, whatever he enjoys is his *upasada* celebration; when he moves about, sits down, gets up, this is his *pravargya* ceremony.

545. His mouth is the Āhavanīya fire, his utterance is the invocation, his understanding [of the procedure] is his offering. What he eats evening and morning is the fuel; what he [drinks] morning, noon, and evening are his three libations.

PranagnihU 22-23; 33-34; 37-38; 40; 44-50

vi)

22. Breath is the sacrificial Fire, the Supreme Self which is enveloped by the five winds. May he comfort all beings, may there be no fear for me!

23. You are the universe, you are common to all men, you assume all forms, all things that are born and carried by you. In you are offered all the offerings and they proceed there where you are the immortal Brahman.

33. Of this sacrifice of the body, performed with the sacrificial post and the girdle,

34. Who is the sacrificer? Who is his wife? Who are the priests? Who is the overseer? What are the sacrificial vessels? What are the oblations? What is the altar? What is the northern altar, what is the Soma vessel? What is the chariot? What is the victim?

37. In what consists the recitation of the hymns? In what consists the recitation of the sacred formula? In what consists nonviolence? What is the role of the sacrificer's wife? What is the sacrificial post? What is the girdle? What are the offerings? What is the priestly honorarium? What is the final purification?

38. Of this sacrifice of the body, performed with the sacrificial post and the girdle, the Self is the sacrificer, the intelligence is his wife, the Vedas are the priests, the ego is the subordinate priest and mind is the officiating priest.

40. The body is the main altar, the nose the northern altar, the skull is the vessel, the feet the chariot, the right hand the wooden ladle, the left hand the cauldron.

44. Memory, compassion, patience, and nonviolence comprise the role of the sacrificer's wife.

45. The sound OM is the sacrificial post, hope the girdle, the spirit is the chariot, desire the victim, the hair is the grass, the sense organs are the sacrificial vessels, the motor organs the oblations.

46. Nonviolence is all the offerings; renunciation is the priestly honorarium.

47. The final purification is death.

48. Thus all the divinities are established in this body.

49. Whether a man dies in Vārāṇasī or whether he recites this sacred text, he will attain liberation after one single life.

50. He will attain liberation. This is the Upaniṣad.

MundU I, 2

vii)

1. This is that truth: The rites of oblation, O lovers of truth, which the sages divined from the sacred verses, were variously expounded in the threefold Veda. Perform them with constant care. This is your path to the world of holy action.

2. When the fire, the purveyor of sacred offerings, is lit and the flame is flickering, then one should place his oblations with faith between the two portions of clarified butter.

3. The man who offers the *agnihotra* but fails to observe thereafter the rites of full or new moon or the seasonal rites or to offer the first fruits of harvest, who receives no guests and omits the general oblation, who offers in irregular manner or makes no offering—such a man will suffer the loss of all seven worlds.

4. The flickering flames of the sacred fire are seven: the black, the terrible, that which is swift as thought, the bright-red, the smoky, the sparkling, the well-shaped and shining.

5. The man who commences the rite while these flames are burning and receives the oblations at the proper time is conducted by these same oblations, now changed into rays of the sun, to the Lord of the Gods, to the one and only Abode.

6. "Come, come!" these radiant offerings invite the worshiper, conveying him thither on the rays of the sun, addressing him pleasantly with words of praise, "This world of Brahman is yours in its purity, gained by your own good works."

7. How frail, though, those rafts, the eighteeen forms of sacrifice, expressions of merely inferior types of action! Deluded men who acclaim this way as the best return again to old age and also to death.

8. They grope in darkest ignorance, those who believe themselves to be wise and learned; they do themselves violence, going round and round in a circle like senseless fools, like blind men led by one who himself is blind.

9. Straying through ignorance in many a diverse path they think in their folly, "Our goal is already achieved." Embroiled as they are in their actions and blinded by passion to actions' effect, they sink overwhelmed. Exhausted is the merit of all their worlds. They decline and fade.

10. Thinking, misguided souls, that almsgiving and oblations are to be perferred, they do not know anything better. Having had the reward of their piety in highest heaven, they reenter this world or even another lower!

11. But those who in penance and faith dwell in the forest, peaceful and wise, living a mendicant's life, free from passion depart through the door of the sun to the place of the immortal Person, the imperishable Self.

12. A Brahmin contemplating the worlds built up by ritual action may well despair. The uncreated will never emerge from that which itself is created. For the sake of this knowledge let him simply approach with fuel in hand to a master who is fully versed in the Scriptures and established in Brahman.

13. Let him approach him properly with mind and senses tranquil and peaceful. Then will this master disclose the essence of the knowledge of Brahman whereby may be known the imperishable Real, the Person.

■ i) Known and investigated: *viditaṁ mīmāṁsitam,* i.e., known both by experience or intuition and by reflection.

17. Cf. § I 7.

■ ii) 16, 1. Man in truth is himself a sacrifice: *puruṣo vāva yajñaḥ.* Cf. SB I, 3, 2, 1 (§ III 23).

The Gāyatrī, Triṣṭubh, and Jagatī are the three meters corresponding to morning, midday, and evening, each of them being connected with different deities. They cause everything to continue in existence: *sarvaṁ vāsayanti,* they make everything to dwell. The connection is "etymological," relating the Vasus with the root *vas-*, to dwell, live.

16, 2. The argument here and in succeeding stanzas is that life should not be cut short before its due completion, because every sacrifice has to be completed. Life, not death, is sacrifice.

16, 3. They cause everything to weep: *sarvaṁ rodayanti.* Again there is an "etymological" connection between Rudra and the root *rud-*, to howl, to weep.

16, 5. They take everything to themselves: *sarvaṁ ādadate,* the verb *ā-dā-* is related to Āditya.

16, 7. Mahidāsa Aitareya: cf. AA II, 1, 8; II, 3, 7. Sāyana narrates the story of Mahidāsa (the "servant of the earth") who was the son of a Brahmin and a *śūdra* woman. In spite of his low birth he attained to the same wisdom as the *ṛṣis.* The number 116 = 24 + 44 + 48 of the three periods mentioned.

17, 1. Initiation rite: *dīkṣā,* consecration.

17, 2. *Upasada:* a particular ceremony, involving the offering of milk and some feasting, which takes place before the Soma sacrifice and is characteristically joyful.

17, 3. Chant and recitation: *stuta-śastra.*

17, 4. Asceticism etc.: *tapas, dāna, ārjava, ahiṁsā, satya-vacana.*

17, 5. New birth: *punar-utpādanam,* the only occurrence of the world in Vedic literature.

Desire: *a-pipāsa,* without thirst: in the sense of appetite, eagerness. There are three possible syntactic placings of *a-pipāsa:* (*a*) it can be put at the end: he who receives or hears this message becomes free of desire; (*b*) it can be moved so as to be in opposition to Ghora: Ghora had become free of desire; (*c*) it can be taken as already in its proper place: this is our interpretation.

Imperishable: *akṣita,* unperishable, indestructible.

Immovable: *acyuta,* imperturbable, stolid.

Firm in the breath of life: *prāṇa-saṁśita.*

Some scholars find here the first reference to Śrī Kṛṣṇa.

The v. ends with "On this there are two Ṛg-Vedic stanzas."

17, 7. Cf. § III 6.

■ iii) 1. Without this knowledge: *idam avidvān,* without knowing this (what has just been described), i.e., the homology between the sacrifice and the five breaths: *prāṇa, vyāna, apāna, samāna,* and *udāna.*

4. Outcast: *caṇḍāla.*

Universal Self: *vaiśvānara ātman.*

■ iv) All the explanations of the different paths in terms of *brahmacarya* are of an "etymological" nature, which cannot be reproduced in the translation.

1. Sacrifice: *yajña.* A play of words on *yajña* and "one who is a knower": *yo jñātā.*

Sacrificial offering: *iṣṭa.*

After sacrificing (searching): *iṣṭvā.*
Self: *ātman.*
2. A long course of sacrifice: *sattrāyaṇa,* a sacrifice lasting several days.
The practice of silence: *mauna,* the vow of silence.
3. The practice of fasting: *anāśakāyana.* The text seeks to connect this word etymologically with *na naśyati,* does not decay.
The way of solitude: *araṇyāyana* lit. the way of the forest; the life of a hermit.
Brahman world: cf. the detailed description in KausU I, 3 (§ V 4).
4. Free to move in all the worlds: *kāmacāra,* complete freedom.
For the rest of CU VIII and all the ref. cf. § VI 6 (v) and notes.
■ v) We follow the notation given by J. Varenne.
540-541. Cf. § VI 12.
543. Who knows this: the one who knows OM, the Upanisad, and the mystery of the Gods; cf. 540-541 (§ VI 12).
Priest: *hotṛ.*
Singer: *udgātṛ.*
Officiating priest: *adhvaryu.*
Fire-kindling priest: *agnīdh.*
544. As long as he lives . . . : *yāvad dhriyate sā dīkṣā;* it can also mean: as long as he is in the womb, this is his initiation.
Whatever he eats . . . drinks . . . enjoys: eating, drinking, being joyful, are for him the oblation, the sacrifice, the celebration.
Upasada: a joyful offering.
Pravargya: the preparatory ceremony for the Soma sacrifice.
■ vi) 22. The Supreme Self which is enveloped by the five winds: a definition of the human body.
24-32. Contain prescriptions for ritual ablutions and a speculation on the four fires within man.
33. Sacrificial post: *yūpa,* stands for the stability of the sacrifice.
Girdle: *raśanā,* stands for the internal stability of the sacrificer.
35-36. Continue the queries of v. 34, asking about the various priests and the nature of the offerings.
37. Nonviolence: *ahiṁsā,* the respect for life, or, according to some interpreters who find this word here rather intriguing, respect or nonviolence to the text.
Cf. AB I, 30, 11 (V, 4); CU III, 17, 4; and here below v. 46.
38. Cf. MahanarU 543 sq. (v) for a more complex elaboration of the same correlations.
Intelligence: *buddhi.*
Ego: *ahaṁkāra.*
Subordinate priest: *adhvaryu.*
Mind: *citta.*
Officiating priest: *hotṛ.*
39. Contains the answer to the queries of v. 35.
40. The body is the main altar: *śarīraṁ vedir.* There follow further homologizations with the human body.
Skull: *mūrdhan,* head.
41-43. Contain the answers to the questions of v. 36, following the same order.
44. Memory, compassion, patience, and nonviolence: *smṛti, dayā, kṣānti, ahiṁsā.* These are all female virtues.
45. Desire the victim: *kāmaḥ paśuḥ.*
46. Renunciation is the priestly honorarium: *tyāgo dakṣiṇā.*
49. A later addition probably.
50. Concludes the U: This is the Upanisad: *iti upaniṣat,* this is the secret doctrine, this is the information, the correlation, the teaching.
■ vii) 1. This is that truth: *tad etat satyam.*
Expounded in the threefold Veda: *tretāyāṁ . . . santatāni,* which can also mean "which were extended in the three fires" (*gārhapatya, āhavanīya,* and *dakṣināgni*).
World of holy action: *sukṛtasya loka,* the domain of *dharma.*
3. One variant reading adds, after "in irregular manner," "without faith" (*aśraddhayā*); cf. *śraddhayā* "with faith" (v. 2).
4. Flames: lit. tongues.
The well-shaped and shining: or "all-formed divine," according to another reading.
5. The description of the flames in v. 4 is important in view of their identification with the rays of the sun which lead to the world beyond.
Lord of the Gods: *devānāṁ patiḥ.*
8. Cf. KathU II, 5; MaitU VII, 9.
10. Almsgiving and oblations: *iṣṭā* and *pūrta,* i.e., those pious and secular actions which are done for the sake of reward.
12. Fully versed . . . Brahman: *śrotriyaṁ brahma-niṣṭham,* the qualities of the *guru.*

The Sacrifice of the Mind *Mānasayajña*

28 We conclude Part VI of this anthology with a series of Upaniṣadic sayings concerning OM, but we might well have given them a place here. In these sayings, as also in certain other texts, sacrifice is interiorized to such an extent that external works are rendered irrelevant and ultimately disappear. We find here the third step that we have mentioned. Man is no longer the center of the sacrifice. If an excessive cosmological bias leads to sheer magic, an exaggerated anthropological emphasis leads to mere selfishness and to abuse of the sacrifice for petty human ambitions. The sacrifice has to be purified from the alloy of both cosmos and Man. What remains is then the pure sacrifice of the *ātman, ātman* referring in this instance not so much to a transcendent principle as to an immanent divine principle which not only performs the sacrifice but is also its recipient.

We may remember that we are at that critical moment in which Man discovers not only that he is an essential part in the sacrifice, but also that the real sacrifice happens within himself, for without his inner participation and faith the external act would be devoid both of sense and of reality. The real sacrifice is that which takes place within Man, the inner *agnihotra* as we have already seen. Now the mental sacrifice becomes not only the sacrifice imagined or thought, that is, performed by the mind, but the sacrifice of the mind itself. The *mānasayajña* of the preceding stage, which referred to the priestly function of the mind performing the sacrifice, now designates the mind as victim of the sacrifice. Now, finally, it is the mind itself which is immolated. What is cast into the fire is no longer either material things or the thought of them, but thinking itself and all that is contained in the cave of the heart,[246] in that hidden recess where all coalesces in a silence of mind and in an explosion of love.[247] We note that the mind and the heart are very often mentioned in close association in the Upanisads,[248] as also in Vedic tradition in general.[249]

The small human individualistic self disappears and the universal *ātman* now takes its place. But this *ātman* cannot be known be-

246. Cf. the typical Upaniṣadic reduction in CU III, 12, 7-9 (§ Gāyatrī). Cf. also TU I, 6, 1; II, 1 (§ VI 3); KathU II, 12 (§ V 5).
247. Cf. CU VIII, 1 (§ VI 6); etc.
248. Cf., e.g., AU I, 4 (§ I 7); III, 2 (§ VI 4); KathU VI, 9 (§ VI 11).
249. Cf., e.g., RV I, 61, 2; I, 171, 2.

cause it is the knower; it cannot be the object of any intentional act, because it is the doer of every act. Individual Man began as a spectator; by a progressive involvement he assumed the role, first, of fellow actor and afterward of sole agent, and now he is swallowed up in the process itself and ceases to be either a doer or a collaborator in the dynamism of reality. The sacrifice is not only perfect but also total; the holocaust leaves no residue.

Shortly after one of our passages given below (iii), the Kaṭha Upaniṣad uses an expressive metaphor:

> The Self-existent pierced holes outward.
> Therefore one looks outward and not inside oneself.
> Desiring immortality, a certain sage
> turned his eyes inward and saw the Self within,[250]

thus indicating that real internal vision consists not in "visualizing" within oneself external beings or actions but in visualizing vision itself, that is, in discovering no longer the "seen" but the Seer.

Herein lies the overcoming of every duality and the perfect sacrifice of the Self. "By what should one know the knower?" is a capital question of the Upaniṣads.[251] The perfect sacrifice is not that of sacrificing the known; it is not even the internal sacrifice in which the external object or the external action has been interiorized, but the sacrifice of the knower, who simply "knows," in an ecstatic attitude that defies description because it does not admit any reflective movement. The outcome is total ontological silence.

Therefore one grasps the meaning of that other Upaniṣad that stresses that *it* is known by those who do not know and not known by those who know.[252] This is not a paradox, but an immediate intuition: knowledge does not exhaust either being or consciousness. The object of consciousness, as such, can never be the subject of it. Those who know that they know, know certainly that they know, but this very knowledge is a shadow in their knowing which no longer purely "knows," but knows also its own knowing. Those who really do not know, do not pretend or dally with this knowledge which is ignorance.

We cannot then escape the conclusion of these reflections, namely, that the true sacrifice is the sacrifice *of* Brahman (in the double meaning of both subjective and objective genitive). The

250. KathU IV, 1 (cf. § VII 36).
251. Cf. BU II, 4, 14 (§ VI 4); IV, 5, 15 (i).
252. Cf. KenU II, 3 (§ VI 4).

sacrifice of Brahman is both performed by Reality in toto and that which Men offer to Brahman. Now, this latter conception may easily be misunderstood if we conceive of Brahman as the recipient of the sacrifice, that is, as that to "whom" we offer the sacrifice. It is here that the Upaniṣadic purification of the mind is required. Brahman is neither the object of the sacrifice nor an object of knowledge. He is the knower, the sacrificer, and not the known, the sacrificed. What is the place of Man here? There is no place for any spectator, or for any other agent. And yet the sacrifice takes place and Man is there, not to witness the sacrifice but to be it and thus to be Brahman. The price—if we want to continue this idiom—is the sacrifice of the mind, which is something not performed by the mind, but the offering of the mind itself in the fire of Brahman. The sacrifice is thus perfect. It has sacrificed itself by itself. Reality has become transparent.

The very evolution of the meaning of Brahman testifies to the central position of sacrifice. In a certain sense Brahman has throughout been the symbol that stands for the very center and ground of everything, but it has been variously understood. It is, thus, not so much that the word has changed its meaning, so as to mean first one "thing" and then another "thing," as the fact that the very "thing" Brahman has been interpreted in different ways. Brahman, in the first Vedic period, means prayer and even sacrifice; in the Upaniṣadic period it means absolute Being and Ground, precisely because the sacrifice was considered to be such a Ground. The formal meaning of Brahman has not changed; only the material contents of the concept have been differently "filled." In one instance Brahman was "sacrifice;" in the other, "being."[253] Needless to say, the process was a long and steady one, and the words "being" and "sacrifice" do not render with precision the notion of Brahman in either instance.

The last text, from the Maitrī Upaniṣad, is a passage of extraordinary depth and clarity. The psychological and ontological elements are here harmoniously blended. The ascetic has to burn, to consume, all his thoughts and to overcome all his desires, but not in order to reach a psychological state of stultifying vagueness or a subjective intoxication accompanied by a blank mind. It is because such an ascesis corresponds to the very structure of reality: the

253. Cf., e.g., CU III, 17 sq., where the discourse is on sacrifice and ends up with a speculation on the nature of Brahman.

sacrifice of the intellect reenacts the primordial sacrifice. This is not a neglect or a jettisoning of the mind and the rules by which it operates but, rather, it is the most serious effort to get to its root, to reach its source. But the roots are not the tree, nor is the source the river. There in the origin, in the primordial stage, the mind is not yet mind; no discrimination is yet needed because reality is not yet split. It is obvious that this existential way cannot be planned or even desired, for to do so would be to nullify it utterly and would be the worst sort of infatuation. For this reason many schools of spirituality speak of a calling, a being chosen, a passive and feminine attitude, and the like.[254] In connection with the attainment of Brahman neither perspective nor the distance afforded by reflection is possible; the pretension of the will is likewise unthinkable; neither lies nor conceit has here a place. To those who say that this is not possible there is no counterargument; to those who do not believe there is no answer. To those who believe there is no question. Does not any belief begin where questioning stops?

The sacrifice of the intellect is thus not done out of a particular will to perfection or an intellectual conviction that this is the ultimate act to be done. If any such thoughts or intentions were surreptitiously entertained they would make the whole enterprise futile, or even injurious. It all happens, as the texts say (using an image that is one of the primordial images of the whole East), just by a "consumption" of all the functions of thought and will. All is "consumed" in a consumption of the entire "material" of human structures: the thoughts are thought up to the very end, the intentions are pursued up to a final point, so that nothing remains to be thought and desired.[255] As long as there is some material to be thought or "willed" or desired, we are precluded from speaking of the sacrifice of the intellect; and those who do speak do so as if they were not speaking, acting, communicating anything. *Svāhā*![256]

Mānasayajña

BU IV, 5, 15

i) Where there is duality, there one sees another, one smells another, one tastes another, one speaks to another, one hears another, one knows

254. Cf., e.g., KathU II, 23 (§ VI 5).

255. Cf. the etymology of *nirvāṇa,* suggesting the exhaustion by consumption of all inflammable material, expiration.

256. *Svāhā* is the exclamation, or rather acclamation, which is used at the time of sacrifice and which calls down a blessing on the oblation offered. Here the same word is applied to the mental sacrifice.

another; but where everything has become one's own Self, with what should one see whom, with what should one smell whom, with what should one taste whom, with what should one speak to whom, with what should one hear whom, with what should one think of whom, with what should one touch whom, with what should one know whom? How can He be known by whom all this is made known? He, the Self, is not this, not this. He is ungraspable for He is not grasped. He is indestructible for He cannot be destroyed, He is unattached for He does not cling [to anything], He is unbound, He does not suffer nor is He injured. Indeed, by whom should the knower be known? By these words, Maitreyī, you have been instructed. Such, in truth, is immortality. Having spoken thus, Yājñavalkya departed.

KausU II, 5

ii) Now for the rule of self-restraint as enunciated by Pratardana, the inner-fire sacrifice, as it has been called. As long as a person is speaking, he is not able to breathe. Then he sacrifices breath to speech. Further, as long as a person is breathing, he is not able to speak. Then he sacrifices speech to breath. These two are infinite, immortal sacrifices: whether awake or asleep, one is sacrificing continuously. Now, other sacrifices have an end, for they are made of works. Knowing this, the ancients did not offer the fire sacrifice.

KathU III, 13

iii) The wise man should surrender his words to his mind;
and this he should surrender to the Knowing Self;
The Knowing Self he should surrender to the Great Self;
and that he should surrender to the Peaceful Self.

MaitU VI, 9-10b

iv) 9. Therefore, one who knows this has these two selves [i.e., breath and the sun] as his Self. He meditates only on the Self, he sacrifices only to the Self. This meditation, when the mind is absorbed in its practice, is praised by the wise. Then a man should purify the impurity of his mind with the verse: "What is defiled by leavings." He recites the verse:

Leavings and what has been defiled by leavings,
or by those who handled them, what has been given
by a sinful man or polluted by a stillbirth—
this may the rays of Fire and Sun
and the purification of the Vasus cleanse!
May they purify my food and all else that is sinful!

Then he proceeds to rinse [his mouth] with water [before eating]. With the five invocations: "Hail to the Breath! hail to the downward breath! hail to the diffused breath! hail to the distributary breath! hail to the upward breath!" he offers the oblation [the food]. Whatever remains, he eats, restraining his speech. Afterward he again rinses [his mouth] with water. Having rinsed it and having performed the sacrifice to the Self, he should meditate on the Self with these two [verses]: "Breath and Fire" and "You are the All":

> As Breath and Fire, as the five Winds,
> the Self supreme dwells within me.
> May he, pleased, please all, the enjoyer of all things!
>
> You are the All, you belong to all men.
> All that is born is supported by you.
> Into you may all the offerings enter!
> There where you are, All-immortal, are all beings.

He who eats according to this rule will not revert to the condition of food.

10b. Now there is still more to be known. There is a further modification of this sacrifice to the Self.

He who knows this is a renouncer and an ascetic, a Self-sacrificer. Just as one who does not touch a sensuous woman entering an empty house, so is he who does not touch the sense objects that have entered into him a renouncer, an ascetic, a Self-sacrificer.

MaitU VI, 34

v)

1. Just as fire without fuel is extinguished in its own source, so is the mind extinguished in its own source, when thoughts have ceased.
2. When the mind of a seeker after truth has become extinguished in its own source, he is no longer deluded by the sense objects, which are deceptive and are subservient to *karman*.
3. The mind indeed is this fleeting world; therefore it should be purified with great effort. One becomes like that which is in one's mind—this is the everlasting secret.
4. Only by a tranquil mind does one destroy all action, good or bad. Once the self is pacified, one abides in the Self and attains everlasting bliss.
5. If the mind becomes as firmly established in Brahman as it is usually attached to the sense objects, who, then, will not be released from bondage?
6. The mind has been declared to be of two kinds: pure and impure. It becomes impure when it is touched by desire, and pure when freed from desire.
7. When a man, having made his mind perfectly stable, free from attachment and confusion, enters upon the mindless state, then he attains the supreme abode.
8. Only so long must the mind be controlled, until it is annihilated in the heart: this truly is knowledge, this is liberation; the rest is nothing but pedantic superfluity.

9. The bliss that arises in the state of highest absorption, when the pure mind has come to rest in the Self, can never be expressed by words! One must experience it directly, one's own self, in one's inner being.

10. If a man's mind is merged in the Self, then he is completely released, just as water is not distinguishable in Water, or fire in Fire, or air in Air.

11. The mind alone is man's cause of bondage or release: it leads to bondage when attached to the sense objects, and to release when freed from them. Thus it is taught.

■ i) 1-3. Cf. § III 31.
Cf. BU II, 4, 14 (§ VI 4) for a similar passage.
Duality: *dvaita*.
He, the Self, is not this: *sa eṣa neti nety ātmā*.
The Knower: *vijñātṛ*.
Immortality: *amṛtatva*.
Departed: *vijahāra*, i.e., he renounced everything.
■ ii) Rule of self-restraint: *saṁyamana*.
The inner-fire sacrifice: *āntarāgnihotra*.
Breath: *prāṇa*.
Speech: *vāc*.
Made of works: *karma-maya*, i.e., the ritual actions.
■ iii) 10-11. Cf. § V 5.
12. Cf. § VI 5.
Many standard versions read also "words 'and' mind."
This: i.e., the mind or "words and mind."
Surrender: from the root *yam-*, which may also mean to restrain, support, raise, extend, establish, or even suppress. Here, however, it is not a question of a negative restraint, but of an ascent in consciousness. The three *ātman* are the knowing, the great, and the peaceful (*jñānātman, mahātman*, and *śāntātman*), representing the individual, the cosmic, and the absolute Self, i.e., the conscious, the universal, and the still and absolutely quiet self.
14-15. Cf. § V 5.
■ iv) 9. The purification of the Vasus: *vasoḥ pavitraṁ*, cf. YV I, 2.
Hail: *svāhā*.
"You are the All": *viśvo 'si*, addressed to Agni; cf. CU V, 24, 1-3 (§ III 27).
Condition of food: *annatva*.
10a. Cf. § II 11.
10b. We suggest here one possible interpretation of this difficult text. The emphasis here is on the correspondence and correlation between the self-sacrificer (*ātmayājin*), i.e., the performer of the self-sacrifice or sacrifice of the Self, and the renouncer (*saṁnyāsin*) or ascetic (*yogin*). In this case the self-sacrificer himself constitutes the sacrifice of the Self; therefore, ascetics and monks do not perform any external sacrifice. The other idea expressed is that the man who performs this self-sacrifice or renunciation is internally untouched by the sense objects (cf. the later idea of renunciation).
■ v) 33. Cf. § III 26.
34,1. This passage is IV, 3 of the Southern Version.
Extinguished: *upaśāmyati, upa-śam-* means to become quiet, tranquil, or to cease, to be extinguished. This it is appropriate both for the fuelless fire and for the tranquil mind. This cannot be rendered adequately in English.
Mind: *citta*.
In its own source: *svayonau*, in the place from which it has sprung forth.
2. Seeker after truth: *satya-kāma*, desirous of truth.
3. Fleeting world: *saṁsāra*.
4. Self: *ātman*, here used first in the sense of individual self and second for the universal, divine Self.
6. Mind: *manas*. If *citta* stands for the functioning mind, the thoughtful mind, *manas* is its underlying organ.
7. Mindless state: *amano-bhāva*, the state where there is no mind (because the mind ceases to exist, so to speak, when its functions are terminated), or the state-beyond-the-mind which no longer belongs to the realm of mind.
8. To be controlled: *niroddhavya*, to be suppressed. *Nirodha* is a term used in yoga. Cf. YS I, 2; I, 12; I, 51; III, 9.
Pedantic superfluity: *grantha-vistarāh*, bookish proliferation.

9. Bliss: *sukha.*
Absorption: *samādhi.*
Pure mind: *amala cetas.*
Inner being: *antaḥkaraṇa,* inner organ.
35. Cf. § VI 8.

The Integral Action *Karmayoga*

29 In any synthetic view we find the danger of eclecticism, that is, the arbitrary choice of such elements as are found to be common and the ignoring not only of peculiarities, but also of the depths and heights of any human conception. The Bhagavad Gītā may not have escaped the influence of its time, when the grandeur of the cosmic sacrifice had already declined, yet it offers an extraordinarily well-integrated conception of sacrifice. It maintains, though a little in the background, the ancient Vedic vision; it accepts the Upaniṣadic interiorization and it adds the element of love, of *bhakti,* of personal involvement. This last element, called the *bhakti-mārga* or the path of devotion, is the way of ardent devotion, love, and abandonment to the Lord who is the manifestation of Brahman to Man. The Śvetāśvatara Upaniṣad has already given an indication of this way but it is the Bhagavad Gītā that discloses it more fully. To be sure, it appears at first sight a little disconcerting. Lord Kṛṣṇa teaches his disciple that the way that is most perfect is one of action and knowledge combined, though hitherto the two have been opposed the one to the other. The dilemma, however, disappears when one realizes that, though worship here always means action, it does not mean external acting or intellectual activity. Worship, sacrifice, is above all an essentially loving activity, the loftiest activity in which Man can be engaged: that which employs his whole range of feeling powers, that personal love that makes of human existence a real sacrifice. The essential core of this sacrifice is detachment of spirit and availability; the offering of some material object is merely secondary. It is by his ardent devotion that Man is saved, a devotion, it is to be noted, that is also truth, and that is why it is called the sacrifice of the intellect.

Thus there is no dichotomy, but a harmonious synthesis in which are blended action, knowledge, and love. It is this blending that the Gītā calls the way supreme, superior both to the way of Vedic sacrifice and to that of the pure ontological knowledge of the

Upaniṣads. The new path does not reject tradition; it conserves, rather, its essential values while at the same time deepening and purifying them; it brings them within the grasp of the ordinary Man. The verses that follow are grouped in three sections according to the chapters to which they belong.

The performance of ritual sacrifice is the path of action (i). These verses mention the beginning of all things, Prajāpati, and the creation. They recall to mind that epoch when sacrifice was for Man the supreme, even the only, means of achieving his destiny.

The path of knowledge is described in Chapter IV (ii). Here sacrifice is still deemed to be action but it is action performed with detachment. Several sorts of sacrifice are mentioned, such as control of the self or the practice of austerities. Furthermore, certain ascetics may offer as a form of sacrifice their knowledge of the scriptures. However it may be performed and whatever may be the nature of the action offered, the Eternal Law of this world and of the world beyond is declared to be undergirded by sacrifice. Thus we arrive at the conclusion asserted so often by the Upaniṣads: that the highest sacrifice of all consists of wisdom, of real knowledge.

In the new path (iii), sacrifice consists in the offering of oneself to the Lord in love and self-surrender. All actions, even the most ordinary and insignificant ones, are to be offered to the Lord, who Himself will take care of the one whose life is a perpetual oblation and who will lead him to eternal joy.

There is now no longer need, as there was in the sacrifice of olden days, for large sums of money, the mediation of priests, or long and complicated ritual; nor is it any longer essential to retire into the forest or lead an ascetic life as taught in the Upaniṣads. This way is far less complicated and more compatible with human life, though it is by no means easy of achievement. The way of love, of abandonment of oneself and one's whole life to the Lord, without renunciation of action but with detachment from the fruits of this action, is the new path—a path that has attracted and continues to attract persons of all sorts and conditions of life.

We may recall at this point the three elements of the integral sacrifice—the cosmic, the anthropomorphic, and the theistic—by briefly analyzing three key terms used by the Gītā.

Action is a human necessity and also a divine need. Man cannot exist without some sort of action nor does the Lord cease for a moment to maintain the world and to sustain human life. Yet, for

Man, the real action is ritual action, the action that, in the words of the Gītā, contributes to the 'maintenance of the world': *loka-saṁgraha*. True liturgical action is that which has a cosmic as well as a social "reverberation," which is performed "having in view" (*saṁpaśyan*) the welfare and coherence of the world, as the etymology of the word suggests.[257] The cosmic repercussion of the sacrifice is affirmed; moreover, Man has to be conscious of this cosmic repercussion and indeed must specifically intend it if the sacrifice is to have any value. But the world does not consist only of the astronomic or geological cosmos; the world is also the *loka*, the human world, the open space that extends to the utmost limits of our vision, of our experience. This world is our human world and the man who *knows* performs his actions for the welfare of mankind. Sacrifice thus combines in one the cosmic and anthropocentric aspects, for according to this view those actions are truly human which tend to maintan the cohesion of the world (and here the background of the sacrifice as the threads of the cosmic loom is visible) and to preserve it as an open space, not closed in upon itself. A timely reminder to unbalanced secularisms!

If Men are to undertake so lofty an endeavor, these real human actions must be performed, as the verse immediately preceding emphasizes,[258] *a-sakta*, that is, with detachment.[259] A subtle but important distinction should be made here, so that we do not misunderstand the message of the Gītā. We may in this connection use different words in order to express two fundamentally different attitudes. The one word is nonattachment (unattached) or noncommitment (uncommitted); the other is detachment (detached, uninvolved). The former is not preached by the Gītā; the latter is not only strongly recommended, but affirmed to be a necessary condition for any valuable action. Lord Kṛṣṇa, in the Gītā, certainly does not preach abandonment and neglect of one's duties or the merely mechanical performance of one's actions. He does not preach that we should do things without enthusiasm, passion, and ideals. On the contrary, he permits no flinching or easygoing interpretation of each man's proper *dharma*. Nevertheless, he insists that all actions must be done with a pure heart and a detached mind, with the sovereign freedom that is the fruit of an uninvolved spirit and preserves the distance which is necessary for a proper perspective.

257. Cf. BG III, 20 (i) and the etymology of the word in the note.
258. Cf. BG III, 19 (i).
259. Cf. ibid. for the etymology.

Committed, not as a casual stranger, yet detached and uninvolved, not as a slave: this is how the Lord in the Gītā asks that we should perform all human actions.

Thus we have already arrived at the well-known maxim of the Gītā concerning the *naiṣkarmya,* the action that is performed with renunciation of the fruits that might accrue therefrom to the individual doer. Our emphasis here is not upon a particular aspect of moral philosophy, but upon the connection of this concept with sacrifice. In fact, any appropriation of the fruits of the action by the individual agent would damage the cosmic interrelationship among all the elements of the sacrifice; it would endanger the action itself, and indeed so pervert it as to excommunicate it from the cosmic web of real actions which sustain the world. Disinterested action is required not only for the sake of individual moral purity, but because the maintenance and welfare of the world cannot be realized otherwise. It is in this sense that we can easily understand the statement that sacrifice is born out of work[260] and also the nature of the relation between Brahman and sacrifice.[261]

Now, the surrender of all fruits of our work can be justified, practically and theoretically, only if there is a theistic Lord to receive the sacrifices,[262] with whom we enter into a relationship of love. The Gītā does not inculcate a slavish mentality by demanding from Men work but withholding their wages.[263] On the contrary, it spreads a message of participation and communion, which is the fruit of love. We "renounce" the fruits of "our" works, because we have realized that neither the fruit nor the work is ours. Without love the cosmos would cease to exist and human life would be meaningless and unbearable. To liberate us from the burden of selfishness the message of the Gītā combines in this harmonious unity the old and the new insights regarding the nature of sacrifice.

Karmayoga

BG III, 10-26

i) 10. Prajāpati, when he made both sacrifice and men,
said, "By this you shall multiply;
this shall be to you like a bounteous cow,
ever yielding your desires."

260. Cf. BG III, 14 (i).
261. Cf. BG III, 15 (i); IX, 16 (iii).
262. Cf. BG IX, 24 (iii).
263. Cf. BG XVIII, 5-6.

11. With sacrifice nourish the Gods; in return
    they will nourish you also.
    In partnership with them you will thus attain
    the highest good.

12. Nourished by your sacrifice, the Gods will grant you
    your heart's desires.
    What a thief is he who enjoys their gifts
    but gives nothing in return!

13. The good who consume the remains of the sacrifice
    are absolved from all guilt.
    But sinful are they, and sinful their food,
    who cook only for themselves.

14. From food beings come into being, while food
    is produced from rain;
    rain from sacrifice comes into being
    and sacrifice from works.

15. Know Brahman to be of all action the origin,
    itself sprung from the Imperishable.
    Thus Brahman the all-pervading is supported
    forever by sacrifice.

16. Whoso in this world fails to help turn
    the wheel thus moving
    is an evildoer, the senses his pleasure.
    His life is worthless.

17. But the man who delights and finds his satisfaction
    in the Self alone,
    in the Self his contentment—for him there is no work
    that needs to be done.

18. What interest has he in works done on earth
    or in works undone?
    Because he does not depend for gain
    on anything at all.

19. Therefore, always perform with detachment
    the work you must do;
    only by work performed with detachment
    does man reach the highest.

20. It was only by working that Janaka and others
    attained perfection.
    In the same way you in your turn should work
    for the maintenance of the world.

21. Whatever a great man does, that others
    will also do.

Whatever standard he sets, the same
  the world will follow.

22. In all three worlds there is no work whatever
  I needs must do,
 or anything left that I needs must obtain—
  yet in work I am engaged.

23. If ever I were to cease, O Arjuna,
  my tireless work,
 all men would straightway follow my example
  (and cease their own).

24. If I were to cease my work, these worlds
  would fall into ruin,
 and I would become a creator of chaos,
  destroying these creatures.

25. The ignorant act from attachment to work;
  the wise, however,
 should act, but in a spirit of detachment, with desire
  to maintain the world order.

26. The wise should not confuse the minds of the ignorant
  who are bound to action.
 Let him rather, himself both active and integrated,
  foster all works.

BG IV, 12; 23-25; 28; 31-33

ii)

12. Desiring success, they sacrifice to the Gods
  with ritual actions,
 for from such actions success comes quickly
  in the world of men.

23. Liberation achieved, attachments gone,
  with a mind fixed on knowledge,
 man's whole action becomes a sacrifice, his deeds
  melt entirely away.

24. Brahman is all: the act of offering,
  the offerer, and the fire!
 He who concentrates on Brahman in all his actions
  shall surely reach Brahman.

25. There are yogins who offer sacrifice to the Gods
  for the Gods' own sake,
 while others offer sacrifice by means of sacrifice
  in the fire of Brahman.

28. Some offer their wealth or austerities
  or the practice of yoga,

while others, men of control and strict vows,
  offer study and knowledge.

31. Consuming the immortal food remaining from the sacrifice,
  they reach the eternal Brahman;
but a loser is he who makes no oblation
  in this world or the next.

32. Many and varied are the sacrifices offered
  in the mouth of Brahman.
All these spring from work. If a man knows this,
  his deliverance is sure.

33. More precious by far than a sacrifice of wealth
  is the sacrifice of knowledge
For knowledge is surely the culmination
  of all ritual works.

BG IX, 15-16; 23-27

iii)

15. Others sacrifice with the sacrifice of knowledge,
  worshiping Me
as the one and also as the many, facing
  in all directions.

16. I am the ritual, I am the sacrifice,
  the oblation, and the herb.
I am the Prayer and the melted butter,
  the fire and its offering.

23. Even those who are devotees of other Gods,
  if they worship with faith,
are sacrificing to Me alone,
  though not adhering to the rule.

24. For I am Enjoyer and I am Lord
  of all sacrifices,
but men do not know Me in my true nature
  and therefore they fall.

25. Worshipers of the Gods will go to the Gods,
  of the ancestors to the ancestors.
Worshipers of the spirits will go to the spirits,
  but my worshipers to Me.

26. Whoever offers to me with devotion
  and purity of heart
leaf, flower, fruit, or water—that offering of love
  I accept with joy.

27. Whatever you do, whatever you eat,
whatever your offering,
whatever your alms or your penance, do all
as a sacrifice to Me.

■ i) 10. Bounteous cow, . . . : *kāmaduh,* the mythical cow yielding the milk of all (our) desires. Cf. BG X, 28.

11. Partnership: lit. nourishing each other. The verb used throughout is the causative of *bhū-*, to call to being, to vivify, nourish, sustain.

12. Nourished by your sacrifice: *yajña-bhāvita* sustained, made to be by the sacrifice.

13. Sinful their food: *bhuñjate te tv agham,* lit. they eat only sin (cf. Manu III, 118).

14. From food . . . : cf. § II 10 and 11 where we observe the relation of the texts there quoted to this doctrine of the BG, and also its integration into the total vision of sacrifice.

15. Imperishable: *akṣara,* which commentators consider to be the primal syllable OM.

16. The wheel thus moving: *pravartitaṁ cakram,* the wheel of sacrifice and of "creative" action in general.

His life is worthless: *mogham . . . sa jīvati,* he lives in vain.

17. Who delights . . . in the Self alone: *ātmarati,* cf. CU VII, 25, 2 (§ VI 8); MundU III, 1, 4.

19. With detachment: *a-sakta* detached, nonstop, or not intercepted, free from ties, independent, without obstacle or resistance. From the root *sañj-*, to cling or stick, adhere, be attached or engaged. Cf. BG IV, 14.

20. Janaka: the King of Mithilā, father of Sītā.

Maintenance of the world: *lokasaṅgraha,* from *loka,* open space, room, place, scope, free motion, world, wide space, the realm of the secular, *saeculum,* the temporal; and *saṁ-graha,* holding together, grasping, taking, gathering.

21. A great man: a superior man, the best. The actions of the best man have exemplary value.

Standard: *pramāṇa,* measure.

25. From attachment: *sakta.*

In a spirit of detachment: *asakta.* To be detached should be distinguished from an inhuman non-attachment.

Maintain the world order: *loka-saṁgraha,* to "hold the world together" (which otherwise would fall apart).

26. Confuse the minds: *buddhi-bheda* a term that could almost be translated as "schizophrenia."

Bound to action: *karma-saṅgin,* tied to works, attached, in bondage.

Integrated: *yukta,* the internal harmony created through yoga, the opposte of *buddhi-bheda.*

■ ii) 12. Ritual actions: *karman.*

Stanzas 14 to 23 speak of the "vanity" of work and the need to renounce its fruits, describing in 23 the perfect "mystique" of work.

23. Man's whole action . . . : i.e., all the actions of the man who works as if sacrificing.

24. He who concentrates . . . : he who realizes *brahman,* "sinking into" him.

Cf. § III 28 Introduction for the ultimate identity of the different elements of the sacrifice: the act of offering, the thing offered, the one who offers and, that in which the oblation is offered.

25. Sacrifice by means of sacrifice: *yajñaṁ yajñena.* Cf. § III 15 and RV I, 164, 50; X, 90, 16 (§ I 5). The "fire of Brahman," and indeed the whole verse, have been variously interpreted. Now follows a list of men's offerings: hearing, sounds, actions, breath, etc.

28. Offer their wealth . . . : *dravya-yajña, tapo-yajña, yoga-yajña.*

31. Eternal: *sanātana,* everlasting, primeval.

36-38. Cf. § IV 22.

39-40. Cf. § I 38.

■ iii) 15. Sacrifice with the sacrifice of knowledge: *jñāna-yajñena . . . yajantaḥ.* Cf. BG IV 33 (ii) for the sacrifice of the intellect as explained in § III 28.

One and . . . many: *ekatvena pṛthaktvena,* lit. by the oneness (and) by the manifoldness.

16. Herb: according to Śaṅkara, *auṣadha* stands here for the food of animals, but it may refer to medicinal herbs.

Prayer: mantra, the hymn, the sacred formula.

23. Not adhering to the rule: *a-vidhi-pūrvakam,* not in conformity with the Vedic injunctions.

24. Enjoyer: *bhoktṛ.* Cf. the correlation of food and sacrifice. The Lord is the receiver (enjoyer) of every sacrifice.

25. Spirits: *bhūtāni,* superior beings, intermediary between men and Gods.

C. BREAKING THE BOUNDARIES

Saṁnyāsa

To give up all acts that are prompted by desire
the wise call abandonment.
The surrender of the fruits of all works they aver
to be renunciation.

BG XVIII, 2

The price to be paid for the perfect performance of the sacrifice is nothing less than one's own life. The only fitting way of permitting the sacrifice to unfold itself fully and to realize all its potentialities is to remove all the obstacles that might hinder the eruption of the internal power residing in the sacrifice itself, obstacles that may come either from the object or from the subject. In order to accomplish the perfect sacrifice and thus to actualize the universe, Man has to offer his own individuality on the altar; he has to renounce everything and to transcend himself. Renunciation is the culmination of the sacrifice.

He who has realized that the true sacrifice is that of the Self in the Self to the Self or, in other words, of the Spirit in the Spirit to the Spirit, he who has discovered that ultimately the subject and the object of the sacrifice coincide, no longer desires to perform any sacrifice. Both external and internal actions of the sacrifice become meaningless for him, for he, his ego, and his individuality in society cease to exist. He not only renounces everything, he renounces his own self and even renunciation itself. For this reason the traditional *āśramas* indicate two stages of renunciation, while some saints and traditions even speak of a "stageless stage" beyond these two: *atyāśrama*.[264] Ultimately he really does not renounce anything, for *what* he renounces is nothing and he renounces only nothingness.

A total transparency is the ideal, but history and experience teach us that the way is long and that nobody can hope to short-cut all the twists and turns he has to negotiate before leaping into unlimited reality. There grows within us the intuition that the perfect renouncer has simply become the groundless consciousness in which the existence-giving sacrifice unfolds itself.

This is not true simply on the existential level of human life; it is equally so at the level of human thinking. Many misunderstandings and accusations regarding pantheism and monism would disappear if the texts that speak of the all-pervasiveness of God and the unity of the universe were viewed in their proper context, that is, in the context of an ultimate spiritual experience that has already eliminated the individual as spectator or subject. Sacrifice leads not only to the immolation of the victim, but also to the holocaust of the subject, even in his thinking capacity, as we have already seen.

It now becomes clear why we feel impelled to include the texts on renunciation precisely here, after the doctrine on sacrifice. The holy ascetic of Indian religiousness does not represent exclusively, and often not even mainly, an ideal of moral renunciation but rather that of an authentic, naked, and pure Life. His body is no longer the medium and container of (his) life, but he "exists" in the purity of the *ātman*, in the transparency of Brahman, in the baffling Presence, of which the witnesses of the life of a "saint" are aware, according to their own degrees of awakening.

Having said that the way is long and that the severest temptation of "holy men" is to practice the subtle idolatry of considering themselves as already realized persons, we now describe some of the features of the way.

There is a constitutive dissatisfaction in human life. Even if one has done one's best, other possible actions have remained undone. Disillusionment, is, according to Indian tradition, the beginning of

264. Cf. SU VI, 21.

philosophy.[265] It may also be said to initiate the process of transcending the human condition. The well-balanced *āśramic* system of India allows the husband and eventually the wife also to retire to the forest, once their obligation to society has been fulfilled, and to adopt a life of renunciation in search of the ultimate, for it seems that this ultimate is not reached in married life. There is a whole philosophy devoted to the so-called third *āśrama,* that of the *vānaprastha,* the forest dweller.[266]

There has, however, always been the option of a shortcut for the man who does not feel he must pass through the three earlier stages but who enters straightway into the life of the monk, the *saṁnyāsin,* the renouncer. His yearning is to merge into the One; he longs for total liberation from the temporal and spatial condition of human existence; he gives up his body, its care, and even all thought of it. A whole literature has flourished on this subject, which has been variously considered as a jewel and as a reproach to Indian culture. However this renunciatory aspect of Vedic spirituality may be viewed, we may take note of three of its features. They may be said to characterize the three main phases of the Scripture: the Vedic period, the Upaniṣadic intuition, and the interpretation of the Gītā.

The first feature is the relative absence of an ascetic spirituality, though asceticism was tolerated because it was already in existence and was considered a specialized human experience which some members of the community should be allowed to undertake. It would be completely wrong to characterize the Vedic Revelation as an ascetic spirituality. The present anthology is perhaps sufficient proof of this fact.

The second feature may be summarized in the famous saying of Yājñavalkya to his dear wife Maitreyī, before he enters upon the life of a *vānaprastha,* an anchorite or forest dweller, that the ultimate object of our desire and of our love is not the immediate object before our senses, but the *ātman,* the underlying Self present and effective everywhere: "It is rather for love of the Self that [all] beings are held so dear."[267] Thus renunciation is considered to be a means to an end, a way to reach the supreme goal, not by escapism or repression but by interiorization and overcoming. The husband,

265. Cf. § IV Introduction.
266. Cf. Manu VI, 2.
267. BU II, 4, 5 (§ VI 5).

the wife, and all other things are dearly loved and rightly so, but the underlying reason and the ultimate object of this love lie deeper than the outward appearance of things.

This position is further emphasized by the third feature, which could be said to form the cornerstone of asceticism as found in the Vedic Revelation. There are two ways of understanding renunciation: as a giving up of a positive value for the sake of a higher one, or as a giving up of that same value because you have discovered that for you that "value" is not a value at all, so that the renunciation only appears as such from the outside. For the *tyāgin,* the "renouncer," there is no renunciation; there is true renunciation only where it does not appear as such. As long as you desire something you should not renounce it. It is only when the desire has faded away that you may do so. This may explain the emphasis on right vision and the proper perspective in order to see things as they really are. Only "on knowing Him does one become an ascetic."[268] You truly renounce something only when you discover that for you this "something" was only a pseudo value, a would-be positive thing; otherwise you would do well not to incur the risk that such a repression would entail. Authentic renunciation renounces renouncement, the ultimate reason being not only the psychological fact that the desire of anything, even of renunciation, entangles you more and more, but the theological fact that the ultimate goal of Man is not to be attained by any "human" means because it is the result of a choice on the part of the absolute itself.[269] Moreover, some will say, there is also an ontological reason why the desire can only be overcome by letting the desire subside in its own source, and not by eliminating the object of the desire; that is because every desire is nothing but the projection outside of a "thirst" that is only within us.[270] You really become a *saṁnyāsin* the moment you discover that there is "no-thing" to renounce, not because there are no things "out there" but because you are "no-thing." Or, to quote the terse statement of one Upaniṣad:

> On the very day one is disillusioned,
> on the same day one becomes a renouncer.[271]

268. BU IV, 4, 22 (§ VI 6). This entire text should be considered as forming part of this chapter also.
269. Cf. MundU III, 2, 3 (§ VI 11); KathU II, 23 (§ VI 5).
270. Cf. BU III, 5, 1 (§§ IV 6; III 31).
271. JabU 4. (*yad ahar eva virajet, tad ahar eva pravrajet*) (§ III 31 in a slightly different version).

At Home in Both Seas, East and West *Muni*

30 It is probably an ascetic "clothed with the wind," as were the Jaina ascetics, who is described in this vidid hymn of the Ṛg. Veda. He has acquired powers of the highest order, though his way of life does not constitute one of the recognized stages or *āśramas*. His function is to collaborate directly with the Gods; he is their associate. His external appearance reveals his vocation and the sincerity of his way of life. He lives everywhere, his home is in both East and West, he is the universal Man. But the price he has to pay for this station is that he perhaps ceases to be a normal man. He, the *keśin*, the long-haired, is a *muni* or silent one.[272] He does not speak, not because he has many things to say yet forces himself into silence (which would be hypocrisy), but simply because he has nothing to say. He does not cut his hair; he is engrossed, rather, in "cutting" his thoughts and he intends also to cut the knot of time and space. Will he succeed?

Muni RV X, 136

1. Within him is fire, within him is drink,
   within him both earth and heaven.
   He is the Sun which views the whole world,
   he is indeed Light itself—
   the long-haired ascetic.

2. Girded with the wind, they have donned ocher mud
   for a garment. So soon as the Gods
   have entered within them, they follow the wings
   of the wind, these silent ascetics.

3. Intoxicated, they say, by our austerities,
   we have taken the winds for our steeds.
   You ordinary mortals here below
   see nothing except our bodies.

4. He flies through midair, the silent ascetic,
   beholding the forms of all things.
   To every God he has made himself
   a friend and collaborator.

5. Ridden by the wind, companion of its blowing,
   pushed along by the Gods,

272. *Muni* appears in RV VII, 56, 8, and VIII, 17, 14, with the meaning of one moved, inspired, or touched by impulse or eagerness, i.e., inward enthusiasm. Thus it comes to mean an ascetic, a saint, a monk, especially one who has taken the vow of silence. In AV VII, 74, 1, there is mention of a *muni-deva* with special healing powers. Cf. also AV VIII, 6, 17.

he is at home in both seas, the East
and the West—this silent ascetic.

6. He follows the track of all the spirits,
of nymphs and the deer of the forest.
Understanding their thoughts, bubbling with ecstasies,
their appealing friend is he—
the long-haired ascetic.

7. The wind has prepared and mixed him a drink;
it is pressed by Kunamnamā.
Together with Rudra he has drunk from the cup
of poison—the long-haired ascetic.

1. Fire: *agni.*
Drink: *viṣa,* poison, poisonous drink, or, as here, intoxicating liquor that burns inside like a fire (as is confirmed in v. 7). He "carries" earth and heaven, like Prajāpati to whom he approximates by divinization.
Long-haired ascetic: *keśin,* the wearer of loose long hair. Cf. the interesting explanation of SB V, 4, 1, 2 for long-haired man.
2. Silent ascetics: *munis.*
3. This stanza is put into the mouths of the *munis* themselves.
4. Beholding the forms of all things: here is a double meaning, a spatial one, owing to the association with the sun (seeing all things from above) and a more spiritual one (from a higher perspective).
5. The wind: *vāta.*
Companion of its blowing: *vāyu,* the divinity of the wind.
6. Spirits . . . nymphs: Gandharvas and Apsaras.
7. Wind: *vāyu.*
Kunamnamā: possibly a female spirit, connected with *vāyu.*
Cup of poison: *viṣasya pātra.* Cf. the later myth of Śiva drinking the poison.

Without Urge and without Identity *Vairāgya*

31 The process of interiorization set in motion by the Upaniṣads led subsequently to the resolute removal and abandonment of all the cloaks in which the real is shrouded. Two strands combine in the idea of the *saṁnyāsin,* the monk, the acosmic ascetic who has renounced everything.[273] First, the personal perfection of a Man who always speaks the truth, who has perfect control over all his passions and urges, who is full of compassion and love—indeed, whatever human ideal we may have in mind, the holy Man is its embodiment. Second, a total transcendence and overcoming of the human condition. The *sādhu,* the man who goes straight to the goal, is beyond all the limitations of human creatures, moral and social, physical and intellectual. He is no longer a citizen of this world but

273. Cf. Manu VI, 45-49 for a wonderful description of *saṁnyāsa.*

already lives on the other shore, bearing his witness not as a preacher but as a reminder to the rest of mankind who are still enmeshed in the clutches of *saṁsāra*, this phenomenal world. The balance has not always been kept, but in the Upaniṣads these two elements are strongly present.[274]

Perhaps one of the most striking expressions of this mature balance is the famous line of the Īśa Upaniṣad: "Find enjoyment by renunciation."[275] True asceticism is not narcissistic complacency, but the discovery that liberation from the bonds of desire allows us really to enjoy things, without being haunted by the fear of losing them or by the anxiety of not getting them. The ascetic is totally free.[276]

Vairāgya

BU III, 5b

i) The sages who have come to know this Self overcome the desire for sons, the desire for riches, the desire for worlds, and set forth on a mendicant's life. For desire for sons is desire for wealth, and desire for wealth is desire for worlds; both are nothing but desires. Therefore, let a sage go beyond learning and lead the life of a child. When he has gone beyond both childlike life and learning, then he becomes a silent sage. Only when he goes beyond asceticism and nonasceticism does he become truly a knower of Brahman. What makes him a true Brahmin, though? That through which he becomes such! All the rest is irrelevant.

BU IV, 5, 1-3

ii) 1. Now Yājñavalkya had two wives, Maitreyī and Kātyāyanī. Of these two, Maitreyī had understanding of Brahman, whereas Kātyāyanī possessed only the common knowledge of women. Now Yājñavalkya wished to prepare for another way of life.

2. "Listen, Maitreyī," said Yājñavalkya, "I am about to depart from this state. Come, let me make an arrangement between you and Kātyāyanī."

3. Maitreyī said to him: "My Lord, if even the whole earth filled with treasures were mine, would I become immortal by this, or not?"

"[Certainly] not," replied Yājñavalkya; "your life would be just like that of people possessing everything, but in riches there is no hope of immortality."

274. Cf. MundU I, 2, 11 (§ III 27); CU II, 23, 1.
275. IsU 1: *tena tyaktena bhuñjīthāḥ* (§ VII 6).
276. Cf. § VI C a.

MahanarU 505-517; 530-531; 537-538

iii) 505. Truth is the supreme, the supreme is truth. Through truth men never fall from the heavenly world, because truth belongs to the saints. Therefore they rejoice in truth.

506. Ardor, they say, [is the supreme], but there is no higher ardor than fasting, because the supreme ardor is difficult to attain. Therefore they rejoice in ardor.

507. Self-control [is the supreme], say the Brahman-students constantly. Therefore they rejoice in self-control.

508. Peace [is the supreme], say the silent monks in the forest. Therefore they rejoice in peace.

509. Almsgiving all beings praise. Nothing is more difficult than almsgiving. Therefore they rejoice in almsgiving.

510. Order [is the supreme], they say, for all this [universe] is encompassed by order. Nothing is more difficult than to abide by order. Therefore they rejoice in order.

511. Procreation [is the supreme], the majority [of people] think. Therefore a large number [of children] are born. Therefore most people rejoice in procreation.

512. The [three] fires [are the supreme], they say. Therefore the fires are to be established.

513. The *agnihotra* [is the supreme], they say. Therefore they rejoice in the *agnihotra*.

514. Sacrifice [is the supreme], they say, for by means of sacrifice the Gods have attained heaven. Therefore they rejoice in sacrifice.

515. The spiritual [is the supreme], so say the wise. Therefore the wise rejoice in the spiritual.

516-517. Renunciation [is the supreme], says Brahmā, for Brahmā is the supreme, the supreme is Brahmā. In truth, all these lower achievements are transcended by renunciation. [This is true for] him who knows this. This is the secret teaching.

530. The sages call Brahmā renunciation.

531. Brahmā is the universe, the supreme joy; he is self-existent; he is [what they call] "Prajāpati is the year."

537. Having realized [Brahman] with mind and heart, having become wise, you will no longer move on the path of death.

538. Therefore they call renunciation the ardor surpassing all others.

MaitU VI, 28

iv) There is still another saying: "Having passed beyond the elements, the senses, and their objects, and having next seized the bow whose string is the life of renunciation and whose stick is steadfastness, he pierces with the arrow of unselfishness through the door of Brahman, that obstructing defender who wears delusion as his crown, greed and envy as his earrings, whose staff consists of impurity and sin, and who, guided by self-conceit and wielding the bow whose string is anger and whose stick is lust, kills people with the arrow of desire. Having destroyed him, he crosses over in the boat of the sound OM to the other shore of the space within the heart and enters slowly, even as a miner in search of minerals, the inner space that is [thus] revealed. Thus he enters the hall of Brahman, thrusting away the fourfold sheath of Brahman, by the instruction of his master. Then he is pure, purified, empty, peaceful, breathless, selfless, infinite, indestructible, stable, eternal, unborn, free; he is established in his own glory. Having seen [the Self] who is established in his own glory, he looks upon the wheel of life as a wheel that rolls on." Thus it is said:

> If for six months a man practices yoga,
> eternally liberated he achieves the infinite,
> the highest, the mysterious, and the complete yoga.
> But a man who is full of passion and inertia,
> though he may be otherwise enlightened,
> and who is attached to son, wife, and family,
> can never achieve it, never at all!

JabU 4-6

v) 4. Janaka, King of Videha, once approached Yājñavalkya and said: "Reverend Sir, teach me, I pray, about renunciation."

Yājñavalkya replied: "After completing the life of a student, let a man become a householder. After completing the life of a householder, let him become a forest dweller, let him renounce all things. Or he may renounce all things directly from the student state or from the householder's state as well as from that of the forest dweller. Whether one has completed the vows or not, whether one is a student or not, even if one has not completed the rites, on the very day when one becomes indifferent [to the world], on the same day should one leave and become an ascetic. . . ."

5. Once Atri asked Yājñavalkya: "I ask you, Yājñavalkya, how can one who does not wear the sacred thread [as the sign of initiation] be a Brahmin?"

"Yājñavalkya replied: 'This alone is the sacred thread of him who observes the purification with water after eating. This rite is to be observed in order to leave the world and become an ascetic. One may die as a hero, or by fasting, or by entering water or fire, or by the great departure. Now the ascetic who wears discolored robes, whose head is shaved, who does not possess anything, who is pure and free from hatred, who lives on alms, he becomes absorbed in Brahman. If he is physically unfit, he may practice renunciation in spirit and word. This is the way found by Brahman, on which he moves. The ascetic becomes a knower of Brahman." Thus spoke the venerable Yājñavalkya.

6. The following are called *parama-haṁsas:* Saṁvartaka, Āruṇi, Śvetaketu, Durvāsa, Ṛbhu, Nidāgha, Jaḍa-Bharata, Dattātreya, Raivataka, and others. Their nature is unmanifest, their way of life is unmanifest; though they are not mad, they appear to behave as if they were. By saying, *bhū svāhā*! they renounce the trident, the begging bowl, the hair tuft, the sacred thread, throwing all into water, and then search for the *ātman* alone. Unencumbered as at birth, with no ties or possessions, they set foot resolutely on the path of Brahman. In purity of mind, in order to maintain life, they go out for alms at prescribed times with no other vessel than their stomachs, maintaining equanimity whether they get something or nothing. They may inhabit a deserted house, a temple, a bush, or an anthill, the root of a tree, a potter's hut, a fireplace, or a sandbank in a river, a hill, a cave, the hollow of a tree, a waterfall, or simply the ground without a home of any sort. Without regard for themselves, without urges and efforts, absorbed in contemplation and established in the higher Self, they endeavor to remove evil deeds and surrender their bodies by renunciation. Such is a *parama-haṁsa;* such indeed is a *parama-haṁsa*!

PaingU IV, 9

vi) With his mind purified, with his consciousness purified, with patience, thinking "I am He," and with patience when he has attained the consciousness of "I am He," he is established by wisdom in the supreme *ātman* who is to be known in the heart, and when his body has attained the state of peace, then the spirit with its light, the mind, becomes void. For what is the use of milk for one who is filled with nectar? What is the use of the study of the Vedas for one who has seen the Self? For the yogin who is filled with the nectar of knowledge there is nothing left to be achieved. If there still remains something, then he is not a man who has realized truth. He remains aloof, but not aloof, in the body, but not in the body; his inmost Self becomes the all-pervading. Having purified his heart and accomplished his perfect thinking, the yogin sees: I am the all, the highest bliss.

KaivU 2-6

vii) 2. Know this [Brahman] by the practice of faith, love, and concentration. Not through actions, not through offspring or wealth, but only by renunciation does one attain life eternal.

3. The ascetics enter into this shining [mystery] in the cave [of the heart] and beyond the heavens.

4. The ascetics who have well understood the end of the Vedas have become pure by the practice of renunciation. At the end of time they dwell

in the worlds of Brahman and, having overcome death, they are all liberated.

5. [Having reached] the last order of life, [one should sit] in a solitary place, in a relaxed posture, with pure heart, with head, neck, and body straight, controlling all the sense organs, having bowed with devotion to the master.

6. Meditating on the heart-lotus in the center, which is free from passion, pure, inconceivable, beyond sorrow, unthinkable, unmanifest, of eternal form, benevolent, peaceful, immortal, the source of Brahmā.

■ i) 5a. Cf. § IV 6. Cf. BU IV, 4, 22 (§ VI 6) where the same idea appears.
Sages: *brāhmaṇas.* Brahmins.
Desire for worlds: *lokaiṣaṇā,* ambition for superior states of being (in the realm of the sacred and also perhaps in that of the secular).
Go beyond: lit. overcome, do away with, put away, or despise.
A sage is neither a pandit nor a child: *bālyaṁ ca pāṇḍityaṁ ca nirvidya.*

■ ii) BU IV, 5 is identical with BU II, 4. Yājñavalkya is a classical example of one who renounces all and retires to the forest. The text shows that it was left to the wife to choose whether or not she would follow her husband on the path of renunciation. The element of choice is illustrated in the different attitudes of the two wives, whose decisions depended on whether their desire for immortality was stronger than worldly attachments.
1. Another way of life: *anyad vṛttam.*
2. Depart: *pra-vraj-,* the technical term for taking up the life of a wandering monk.
State: *sthāna.*
Cf. BU II, 4, 4-14 (§§ VI 5; VI 4).
15. Cf. § III 28.

■ iii) 505-517. The series of terms declared to be the highest (*para*) by different groups of people includes *satya, tapas, dama, śama, dāna, dharma, prajana, agnayaḥ, agnihotra, yajña, mānasa* (the spiritual or mental worship), and *nyāsa.*
518-530. The same ideas are repeated and expanded.
531. "Prajāpati is the year" is a formula for the totality (in the Brāhmaṇas). All the previously enumerated terms are different forms of *tapas,* the highest of which is renunciation (*nyāsa*).

■ iv) Life of renunciation: *pravrajya.*
Unselfishness: *an-abhimāna,* without self-conceit.
Door of Brahman: *brahma-dvāra,* probably referring to the yogic experience of the "opening" of the skull (*brahmarandhra*) as the last gate on the road to illumination.
That obstructing defender: referring to *ahaṁkāra,* the ego sense. The ego has to be killed before one can enter the "inner chamber" of the heart, which is the "hall of Brahman."
Space within the heart: *hṛdayākāśa.*
Hall of Brahman: *brahma-śālā,* the inner sanctuary.
The fourfold sheath of [i.e., covering] Brahman: *caturjālaṁ brahma-kośam.* Cf. the doctrine of the *kośas* or sheaths in which the Self is enveloped and which have to be removed gradually.
Master: *guru.*
Wheel of life: *sañcāra-cakra,* the wheel of transmigration, of which he becomes simply a spectator.
Eternally liberated: *nityamukta,* referring to the belief that bondage is not real and that therefore the object of yoga is simply to reveal again that state of liberation which is eternal.
Passion and inertia: *rajas* and *tamas,* those qualities (*guṇa*) of nature (*prakṛti*) which constitute an obstacle to the spiritual path.

■ v) 4. Renunciation: *saṁnyāsa.*
Life of a student: *brahmacarya.*
Vows: *vrata,* the Vedic injunctions.
Student: *snātaka.*
Cf. also MundU I, 2, 11 (§ III 27).
The rest of this passage deals with some other kinds of sacrifices.
5. Yājñavalkya here gives his interpretation of what it means to be a Brahmin, i.e., one who renounces everything. The different kinds of death or religious suicide mentioned here seem to identify renunciation with death.
Great departure: *mahāprasthāna,* perhaps meaning natural death.
Practice renunciation in spirit and word: *manasā vācā saṁnyaset,* i.e., he need not perform physical acts of asceticism.

This is the way . . .: *eṣa panthā brahmaṇā hānuvittas;* this phrase is not clear.
Knower of Brahman: *brahmavid;* i.e., the Brahmin mentioned by the questioner. Cf. BU IV, 4, 9.
6. *Parama-haṁsa:* lit. "highest swan," the category of a saint or a realized person.
For Śvetaketu cf. CU VI, 8 sq. (§ VI 10).
Unmanifest: *avyakta,* hidden.
Bhū svāhā: a sacrificial exclamation. Renunciation is again shown as the culmination of sacrifice.
Trident, etc.: the insignia of a religious man.

■ vi) "I am He": *so 'ham asmi,* cf. IsU 16 (§ VII 31); BU IV, 4, 12 (§ VI 9).
Void: *śūnya,* a Buddhist term. As is clear from the following sentence, *śūnya* is here equal to *pūrṇa,* fullness.
Filled with the nectar of knowledge: *jñānāmṛta-tṛpta.*

■ vii) 2. Not through actions: *na karmaṇā,* not by works or actions, or spiritual exercises and rituals, but through renunciation: *tyāgena. Karman* implies merit, which secures prosperity in the "worlds," whereas offspring and wealth are goods of this world. Cf. MundU III, 2, 3 sq (§ VI 11) for a theology of renunciation.
2b-3. Cf. MahanarU 227-228 for the same text.
Ascetics: *yatayaḥ; yati* is derived from the root *yat-,* to strive, to tend toward, to be eager, to persevere, to be watchful, to be prepared: all these are qualities of a seeker after truth, a renouncer.
4. Cf. SU VI, 22, for the end of the Veda (Vedānta). Cf. also PaingU IV, 9 (vi). This text, given in MundU III, 2, 6 (§ VI 11) and MahanarU 229-230, is always recited as an address of welcome when ocher-robed *saṁnyāsins* arrive.
Practice: *yoga.*
By the practice of renunciation: *saṁnyāsa-yogāt.* It may be understood that they dwell in the *brahmaloka* until the end of time when they will be completely liberated (*parimucyanti*).
6. Heart-lotus: *hṛt-puṇḍarīka.* Cf. CU VIII, 1 (§ VI 6).
Source of Brahmā: *brahma-yoni.* The pure center is even the origin of the creator.
7-10. Cf. § VI 11.
11. Cf. § VI 12.

The True Yogin *Yukta vimukta*

32 We shall not discuss the polarity and tension between action and contemplation, works and renunciation, engagement and withdrawal, which occupy the attention of post-Vedic spirituality. As early as the Gītā, however, all the elements of this fundamental human problem are in a fairly developed stage. The Bhagavad Gītā tries to put forward a synthesis by saying that pure inaction is not possible,[277] that action without the core or soul of contemplation is useless,[278] that, therefore, acts should be performed as a sacrifice[279] and even the acts of the spirit as intellectual sacrifices.[280]

The true yogin is not the Man who does not act but the Man who acts with detachment, that is, without hankering for the results of his actions, not only on a moral but also on an ontological plane.[281] The true ascetic not only has perfect control over himself[282] and

277. Cf. BG III, 8.
278. Cf. BG III, 27.
279. Cf. BG III, 9; IV, 23 (§ III 29).
280. Cf. BG IV, 33 (§ III 29).
281. Cf. BG II, 47; III, 4; III, 17 (§ III 29); IV, 20.
282. Cf. BG VI, 8 (ii).

total equanimity,[283] but he is also liberated from all desires,[284] sees the Lord everywhere and everything in the Lord,[285] and is ready for action when it is required and seen as his duty.[286]

The message of the Bhagavad Gītā is still fundamentally the same as that of the Upaniṣads and yet it introduces fresh melodies. The Gītā restores the balance by readjusting lopsided interpretations. The authentic yogin, the truly integrated Man, is not the acosmic monk striving for an altogether impossible ideal of inaction and unattachment. The Gītā certainly preaches total "detachment" from the works done and from their fruits,[287] but this detachment should not be confused with unattachment, either ontological, as if values could exist in isolation, or psychological, as if commitment were evil in itself. The Gītā recognizes that there are actions that have to be done and that not to perform them would be wrong. The integrated Man is both *yukta,* yoked to the whole of reality, involved in the net of relationships, and *vimukta,* free, liberated. He is committed but not concerned, he is detached but not unattached, he is involved but not entangled. Hence derives his "holy indifference," his serenity, his peace, which is not one of having taken refuge in an ivory tower or an inaccessible aerie but is the result of being situated in the very heart of reality.

Yukta vimukta

BG V, 2-3

i)

2. Both renunciation of works and also their practice
 lead to the Supreme.
 But of these to act rather than to renounce
 is the better path.

3. The heart of the man of true renunciation
 neither hates nor desires.
 He is easily released from bondage, being free
 from all dualities.

BG VI, 1-16; 18-23

ii)

1. He who acts as he should, yet is unconcerned
 for the fruits of his action,

283. Cf. BG VI, 9 (ii).
284. Cf. BG VI, 18 (ii).
285. Cf. BG VI, 30.
286. Cf. BG III, 20 (§ III 29); XVIII, 73.
287. Cf., e.g., the concept of the detached man (*a-sakta*), found in BG III, 19 (§ III 29 and Introduction).

is a true renouncer, true yogin, not the riteless
man who does not worship.

2. Know, Arjuna, that what men call renunciation
is the authentic yoga;
for without renouncing all desire
no man becomes a yogin.

3. The silent sage climbing toward yoga
uses work as a means.
Quiescence and serenity are the proper course
for one who has attained.

4. When a man does not cling to the objects of sense
or to his own achievements,
but surrenders his will, then he scales, it is said,
the heights of yoga.

5. Let a man lift himself by the Self and not allow
himself to sink down,
For the Self alone is self's friend and the Self
may be also self's foe.

6. To him who has conquered his self by the Self
the Self is a friend,
but to him who has no such mastery the Self
becomes hostile, like a foe.

7. In the one who has conquered his self and is peaceful,
the Supreme Self,
in heat or cold, joy or pain, honor or disgrace,
abides in serenity.

8. He who is full of wisdom and understanding,
calm and controlled,
to whom a clod, a stone, and gold are the same,
is in truth a yogin.

9. He whose heart is impartial to foes, friends, companions,
to the indifferent and neutral,
to hateful people, relatives, saints and sinners,
has indeed succeeded.

10. The yogin shall abide in secret and solitude,
united to the Self,
his thoughts, his whole self, well-controlled, free from striving,
stripped of possessions.

11. Let him set a firm seat in a place wholly pure,
not too high or too low,

and cover it with sacred grass, with a deerskin,
and, finally, with a cloth.

12. Let him, seated thereon, make his mind one-pointed,
controlling his thought
and his senses. Thus let him concentrate on yoga
to purify his being.

13. Motionless, holding his body erect,
his head and his neck,
let him fix his gaze on the tip of his nose,
his eyes held steady.

14. Tranquil and fearless, steadfast in chastity,
with mind controlled,
let him sit, his thought on Me, absorbed in Me,
integrated within.

15. Ever keeping himself in discipline and harmony,
his mind controlled,
the yogin reaches peace and the Goal Supreme
abiding in Me.

16. Yoga is not for the one who overeats
or who eats too little;
nor is it for the one who sleeps too much
or for him who is too wakeful.

18. When thought, disciplined, is focused on the Self
and on the Self alone,
free from the assault of longings, he is said
to be integrated.

19. To a lamp in a windless place, unflickering,
is likened in a simile
the yogin whose thought is controlled, who practices
integration of the Self.

20. That in which thought, mastered by the practice
of yoga, is at rest,
that in which one sees the self in the Self
and finds peace and content.

21. When he knows with his mind the joy supreme
beyond the reach of the senses,
then, perceiving, he stands still, adhering
firmly to Reality.

22. Having laid hold on Reality he avers it
        a matchless prize.
    Established therein, he is unmoved even by
        the direst sorrow.

23. Let that be known as true yoga.

■ i) 2. Renunciation: *saṁnyāsa.*
Practice [of works]: *karmayoga,* way of action.
3. The man of true renunciation: *nityasaṁnyāsin,* true renouncer, eternal renouncer.
Free from all dualities: *nirdvandva. Dvandva:* pair of opposites, dualities.

■ ii) 1. Renouncer: *saṁnyāsin.*
The "fruit" of the action, *karma-phala,* should not be confused with the "intrinsic goal" of the action.
Does not worship: lit. does not light the fire (of sacrifice).
2. Yoga: practice, performance of the prescribed works, disciplined action.
Desires: *saṁkalpa,* intention, will, resolution. *Asaṁnyastasamkalpa:* one who has not renounced all purposes, selfish desires, preplanned "wishful" thinking.
3. Quiescence and serenity: *śama,* equanimity, sameness, "holy indifference."
Who has attained: *yogārūḍhasya,* of one who has attained yoga, union, integration.
4. His own achievements: *karmasu,* his deeds, works.
Surrenders his will: *saṁkalpa-saṁnyāsī,* renounces his ideas and ambitions.
5. Self's friend: *ātmano bandhur.*
6. Who has no such mastery [of the self]: *anātman,* who is left without a self, whose self is unconquered. This "self" may be either the material or the spiritual self.
7. Supreme Self: *paramātman.*
Serenity: *samāhita* concentrated, quietened, steadfast.
9. Impartial: *sama-buddhi,* equal-minded, one whose mind is even, calm, serene, and endowed with "holy indifference."
10. His thoughts, his whole self (taken as two separate terms): *cittātmā,* conscious Self.
Stripped of possessions: *aparigraha* Cf. IsU 1 (§ VII 6).
12. Mind one-pointed: *ekāgram manaḥ;* single-pointedness is one of the elements of yoga (cf. YS II, 41).
To purify his being: *ātma-viśuddhaye,* for the purification of his soul.
13. His eyes held steady: lit. not looking around.
15. Goal Supeme: *nirvāṇaparama,* which culminates in *nirvāṇa.*
16. The middle path.
17. Cf. § IV 7.
18. Integrated: *yukta,* one who has bound together in himself all human qualities; yoked, joined, united, from the verb *yuj-,* to yoke.
19. Lamp in a windless place: a classic simile for a peaceful mind. Integration of the Self: *yuñjato yogam ātmanaḥ,* or union with the Self.
20. Sees the self in the Self: *ātmanātmānaṁ paśyann ātmani tuṣyati,* seeing the self by means of the self (he) is satisfied in the self. Two interpretations are possible: self-reflection or reflecting oneself in the Self. Cf. BU IV, 4, 23 (§ VI 6) for the same idea.
21. Adhering firmly to Reality: lit. not moving from Reality (*tattvataḥ*), cleaving to it. Cf. the idea of "no return" of the one who has become realized.
22. A matchless prize: lit. there is no other gain.
23. Cf. § IV 7.

PART IV
FALL AND DECAY

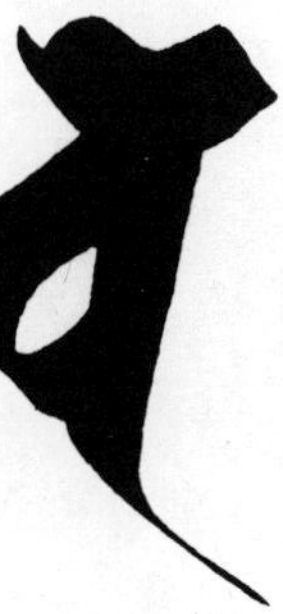

Varuṇa

The last subsection of Part III describes a phenomenon, a state of existence, which in its plenitude is accessible only to a very few and, indeed, represents an anticlimax in Man's experience. Yet this phenomenon expresses, in a sometimes lopsided and often exaggerated way, something that is inherent in the human condition as such: Man's personal experience of his own limitation in all spheres of reality and thus his yearning to break the boundaries of his humanness. The human individual is not infinite like God; he cannot even compare himself with the immortal Gods. He begins now to discover that he is not even Man, but just one member of the species and often at variance with his fellow Men. Even more, he discovers that within himself also there is a lack of harmony or, in the words of the Gītā, that there is something obstructing his own will and compelling him to sin.[1] Man experiences failure not only because he suffers from his own limitations, but also because he is often ill-treated by God, spurned by the Gods, and attacked by his fellow beings, who exploit, betray, and even kill him. Worst of all, Man is defeated by circumstances which he could have avoided but which in point of fact he did not. In a word, Man is betrayed by his own self. No wonder that he will start searching for the Self. Man experiences his own impotence and he suffers disillusionment not only with others but also with himself. He fails to do what he wants and even feels that he cannot really want what he would like to want. Moreover, he senses the contingency of his own existence, he discovers that there are things and states that are irreparable. Until very recent times, to give a somewhat banal example, an adult could not replace his or, worse, her teeth if they were broken or lost in an accident of some kind. There are dreams that cannot be fulfilled and desires that have to be abandoned. There is nothing abnormal in this situation. To grow to maturity means to learn to accept the real human predicament. This acceptance of the human predicament is a common human experience and one that may be witnessed also in the development of Vedic Man's consciousness. By human predicament we understand not so much the objective human condition as Man's actual awareness of that condition. Thus Man's consciousness of his condition is also part of the human predicament.

In other words, the ecstatic attitude described in previous parts

1. Cf. BG III, 36 (§ IV 22).

is here diminished. Interiorization is no longer the privilege of select souls but the common lot of every Man entering this world, for no one escapes the experience of pain and suffering or the temptation to frustration and even despair. Man looks inward, not, first of all, to make the lofty discovery of a new and untarnished world, but to solve the riddle of his own self; he is a suffering being, trying to understand what has gone wrong with him, for the results are not what he expected or desired.

Man cannot grow indefinitely; blossoming cannot go on forever; to halt and remain in the optimum situation is not a real possibility. Man faces fall and decay. As we shall soon see, Vedic Man makes a clear distinction between long life and old age. The former is a blessing, the latter a curse; the former is a desideratum not of a single individual will but of the entire theanthropocosmic situation, the latter—except when something still worse, an untimely death, intervenes—an unavoidable destiny; the former is a sign of growth and maturity, the latter the unmistakable sign of fall and decay.

We should be very careful at this juncture not to use words that connote already developed theories or relate to other world views. We do not say, for example, that the *śruti* does not know the problem of evil or that it does not consider the fact of human sin. We simply point out that these two words, "evil" and "sin," are in serious danger of being misunderstood if they are not kept directly related to the primordial attitude reflected in the Vedic Scriptures.

In the first place, anything that we say about sin and evil has to be understood against a backdrop formed by the concepts of *ṛta,*[2] *satya,*[3] *dharma,*[4] and *karma.*[5] We may notice in passing that it is not legitimate to personify these four notions; Man's attitude toward them is not as if he were facing a personal God. Neither, however, do they fit into a scheme of merely impersonal values, as if Man were caught in an imposed, inflexible, and faceless framework with no possibility of dialogue or freedom. Perhaps the personal-impersonal dilemma is less universal than it may appear to be, so

2. Cf. §§ III B Introduction and IV B b.

3. *Satya* is closely connected with *ṛta;* it sustains the world. Cf. RV X, 85, 1 (§ II 16 Introduction), repeated in AV XIV, 1, 1. Frequent reference is made to *satya* in the RV, where the adjectives *satya-dharman, satya-karman, satya-mantra,* and *satya-vāc* also appear. Cf. also the compound *satyānṛta* in RV VII, 49, 3 (§ I 16) with the meaning truthfulness and lie, as in MundU III, 1, 6.

4. Cf. Numerous references in this anthology, the glossary, and the following passages: RV I, 22, 18; I, 164, 43; 50; III, 3, 1; III, 17, 1; III, 60, 6; V, 26, 6; V, 63, 7; V, 72, 2, and also AV XI, 7, 17; XII, 5, 7; TS III, 5, 2, 2.

5. Cf. § V A Introduction.

long as the concept of person is not disentangled from its anthropomorphic connotations. On the one hand, these four terms express a supremely personal relation, for only in a personal universe do these terms have any intelligible meaning. On the other hand, they certainly do not represent individuals; they are not personifiable. They are transpersonal.

Furthermore, we may recall that the Vedic mentality takes it almost for granted that Man is not alone in the universe, that spirits of all kind, *devas* and *asuras*, are struggling not only among themselves, but also with Man, and that any abnormal interference may cause pain, suffering, and distress. In the final analysis there are no neutral values, no indifferent or irrelevant actions; everything is regarded as either good or bad in the most simple and pragmatic way.

A further point may be noted. As already mentioned in the preceding section, in the post-Vedic philosophical tradition disillusionment is often considered the beginning of philosophical reflection. The mind turns to philosophical inquiry once it has been disillusioned or, in other words, once it discovers the illusory character of the given appearances and tries to pierce through them to the real "thing." In contrast with this attitude, other traditions affirm a sense of wonder to be the beginning of philosophizing. Amazement and wonder, we are told, direct the attention to what the eye does not actually see and thus the mind embarks upon philosophical speculation.

Both attitudes stem from one assumption: there exists more than meets the eye; there is a sense of discrepancy between the immediate data and what these data really are (or are pointing out, revealing, concealing, and the like). In both instances there is the conviction that the real is not immediately given or at least not immediately recognized. Here the human spirit responds in one of two directions: one Man is disillusioned because he expects more, that is, he expects the world to be more—nicer, truer, deeper, fuller—than it appears to be. There is an underlying optimism here which is disappointed when Man's expectations are not met. A second Man, on the other hand, is astounded when he starts by not expecting so much and discovers the world to be less ugly, less shallow, and less disappointing than it appears. There is an underlying pessimism here that feels amazement when Man's expectations are excelled. One is disillusioned because things are not the "real thing." The other is amazed because things are "really the thing." Obviously the two attitudes can be interpreted both ways, that is, as considering that the data are disappointing or amazing because they are or are not the "real thing."

Our texts here speak of the great disillusion and abysmal disappointment, because Man is not as he should and could be or because Man is as he is, namely, mere Man. The first part of this alternative is illustrated by the spirit of the Vedas proper, the second one by the Upaniṣadic spirituality.

The first section deals with Man's primordial unhappy experience: the bare and unavoidable fact of suffering and sorrow. We divide it into two subsections, one dedicated to the Vedic insight and the other to the Upaniṣadic vision.

The second section deals with a human experience that is no less primordial, concentrating on its more reflective, often sophisticated, or simply spiritual aspect: the experience of sin and mercy. The three subsections present an internal logic, easily detectable. There is a gradation from (*a*) disgust with oneself and a sense of guilt, that is, from the internal movement of regret and fear, to (*b*) the external encounter with a power, an agency, a God, ready to forgive and open to entreaty, and thence to (*c*) a third step in which the internal movement and the external one meet in the sacramental, that is, the theandric action, by means of which Man gets rid of his stain and obtains the longed-for forgiveness in a way that is neither exclusively wrought by himself nor merely granted freely by an external power, but comes to pass by means of an intimate and ultimately mysterious collaboration between the two. This is, in the last instance, the meaning of every living ritual.

The key words of this part are extraordinarily rich in meaning and, inevitably, the English words commonly used to translate them have very different connotations. We have therefore added the following note in order to clarify the meaning of those universal factors of human existence which in English we call evil, sin, suffering, and sorrow.

NOTE ON SANSKRIT TERMS

Enas, n., crime, sin, misfortune, mischief, offense, fault, and thence also evil, unhappiness, blame.[6] It is one of the words most

6. Related to the Avestan *aênô* and to the Greek *ainos*, terribl

frequently used in the Ṛg Veda for evil in general, though its original meaning was more specifically some kind of violent act.[7] The adj. *enasvat*, guilty, sinful, is also commonly used. "Do not let us suffer for the sins of others";[8] or, "Indra is our savior, even from grave offense."[9]

Āgas, n., transgression, offense, injury, sin, fault.[10] It also appears quite frequently in the Ṛg Veda[11] with the meaning of sin against both Gods and Men. In the hymn VII, 86[12] the words *āgas*, *enas*, and *anṛta* are closely related, as are the words *enas* and *abhidroha* (transgression) in Ṛg Veda VII, 89, 5.[13]

Drugdha and *abhidroha*[14] derive from the same root *druh-* with the original meaning "to afflict or harm somebody," whence *druh* as an adjective, which means harmful, afflicting, and refers frequently to a demon. The participle *drugdha* when used as a masculine noun means the transgressor, the evildoer, while as a neuter noun it means transgression, evil deed.

Aṁhas, n., anxiety, trouble, oppression. It occurs both as verb and noun in the Ṛg Veda with the idea of pressure, coercion, compulsion (from foes, situations, and the like).[15]

Agha, bad, afflicting and, as a neuter noun, evil, mishap; later on it acquires the meaning of sin, impurity.[16] *Aghaśaṁsa* is the one who is planning evil, the evil-wisher, the wicked man.[17]

Kilbiṣa, n., probably had the original meaning of stain, dirt; from the Ṛg Veda onward it means sin, guilt, fault, offense,[18] and *kilbiṣaspṛt* means the removal or avoidance of sins.[19]

A series of words formed with the prefix *dus-*, connoting badness, evil, difficulty, are frequently used. The most common term among them is:

7. Cf. RV II, 28, 7 (§ IV 17), and also I, 24, 9 (§ IV 8); I, 125, 7; I, 189, 1 (§ VII 9); II, 12, 10 (§ II 4); X, 128, 4; etc.
8. RV VI, 51, 7 (§ IV 8).
9. RV VII, 20, 1.
10. Cf. the Greek *ágos*, which with its meaning of "consecration" is used in a pejorative sense to denote malediction and curse.
11. Cf. RV II, 28, 5 (§ IV 17); VII, 86, 4 (§ IV 18); cf. also RV I, 179, 5; I, 185, 8 (§ IV 10); II, 27, 14; IV, 12, 4 (§ IV 8); V, 3, 7; V, 85, 7 (§ IV B Antiphon).
12. § IV 18.
13. § IV 19.
14. With the prefix *abhi-* the verb *druh-* means to inflict suffering or to do injustice to somebody, to offend (mostly the Gods). *Abhidroha* is an offense against the Gods.
15. Cf. RV I, 42, 1; I, 63, 7; II, 23, 4; IV, 20, 9; VI, 44, 16; VIII, 19, 6; X, 63, 6; etc.
16. Cf. RV I, 42, 2 (§ VII 4); VI, 62, 8; VII, 104, 2; etc.
17. Cf. RV I, 129, 6; etc. Interestingly enough, in later usage the *aghaśaṁsin* is the one who confesses his sin.
18. Cf. RV V, 34, 4.
19. Cf. RV X, 71, 10 (§ I 9).

Duḥkha, m., from *duḥ-* (*dus-*) and *kha* (aperture, hole, cavern; axle hole), that is, having a bad axle hole, and hence uneasiness, pain, dissatisfaction, sorrow, trouble, distress, as opposed to *sukha*, happiness, ease, and so on.[20]

We also find:

Durita, n., "bad course," difficulty, danger, discomfort, on the one hand, and evil, sin, injustice, on the other.[21]

Duṣkṛt, part., "doing evil," used also as a masculine noun meaning evildoer, sinful man;[22] and *duṣkṛta*, n., sin, lit. the evil done, wrong accomplished.[23]

Duḥśaṁsa, evil-speaking, cursing, and hence evil, impious, or blasphemous.[24]

Dūḍhī, evil-minded, of evil intention,[25] and a few minor words of similar formation.[26]

Abhva, n., from the root *bhū-* with negative prefix, lit. non-existence, means in both Ṛg Veda and Atharva Veda a horror, monstrosity, something terrible and frightening.[27]

Anṛta, what is opposed to *ṛta*, truth, order, that is, falsity, untruth, injustice, lawlessness, unrighteousness, lie.[28]

Adharma, n., used at a later date for *anṛta* with a very similar meaning: whatever is opposed to *dharma*, order, law, religion, that is, irreligiosity, unrighteousness, demerit, guilt.[29]

Tamas, n., from the root *tam-*, to be stunned, stupefied, exhausted, suffocated, means not only external darkness but also, from the Ṛg Veda onward, evil, confusion, error, blindness, and so on.[30]

Nirṛti, f. noun from *nir-r-*, to go out or off, be deprived or dissolved. In the Ṛg Veda *nirṛti* is the personification of dissolution, destruction, calamity, corruption, death, and also the abysmal

20. Cf. § IV 6.
21. From *dus-* and the root *i-*, to go. Cf. also perhaps *duṣṭa*, bad wrong, wicked, inimical, etc. and *duṣṭi*, corruption, depravity. *Duṣṭa* as a neuter noun means also sin, guilt, crime, and is a very commonly used word for an evildoer or wicked man up to the present day. Cf. RV I, 23, 22 (§ IV 8); I, 185, 10 (§ IV 10).
22. Cf. RV VI, 16, 32; VII, 104, 7 (§ V 20), etc.
23. Cf. RV VIII, 47, 13; X, 164, 3 (§ IV 8); etc.
24. Cf. RV I, 23, 9, etc.
25. Cf. RV I, 190, 5; VIII, 19, 15; IX, 53, 3, etc.
26. E.g., *duḥśāsus*, of evil will, bad (RV X, 33, 1); *duḥśeva*, evil-minded, fatal (RV I, 42, 2, § VII 4); *duṣprāvī*, unkind, hardhearted, stingy (RV IV, 25, 6).
27. Cf. RV I, 24, 6; I, 39, 8; I, 185, 2 (§ IV 10).
28. Cf. RV I, 105, 5; I, 152, 3; VII, 49, 3 (§ I 16); X, 124, 3; etc.
29. Cf. CU VII, 2, 1 (§ I 14); KathU II, 14 (§ V 5); BG, I, 40-47; IV, 7; etc.
30. Cf. RV I, 32, 10; I, 46, 6; I, 54, 10; etc.

abode of dissolution.[31] It has also been personified as the Goddess of destruction.

Pāpa, bad, evil, vicious, sinful;[32] used as a neuter noun in the Brāhmaṇas, Upaniṣads, and Smṛtis, where it means guilt, sin, crime (with *puṇya*, merit, virtue, as its opposite).

Pāpman, m., evil, misfortune, calamity, crime, sin, used from the Atharva Veda onward. It is also personified Evil, the devil or demon.

Pīḍā, f., from the root *pīḍ-*, to be squeezed or pressed out,[33] then to oppress, hurt, harm, injure; means pain, suffering, injury, affliction, and so on, always with the connotation of pressure or restriction, limitation.

Śoka, m., from the root *śuc-*, to burn, to shine, to suffer heat, to be afflicted, to grieve, means sorrow, affliction, pain, grief, anguish. In the Ṛg Veda it means almost exclusively heat, light, flame.[34]

Cintā, f., originally thought, is used for anxiety, care, worry (anxiety as an effect of thought, from within). It does not occur in the Ṛg Veda, but only in Smṛti literature.

Aparādha, m., from *apa-rādh-*, to miss, to offend, to sin, means sin, offense, fault, mistake. It does not occur in the Ṛg Veda.

Asādhu means simply the negation of goodness (*sādhu*), wicked, bad, evil, disgrace, and so on.

Ṛṇa, n., means from the Ṛg Veda onward sinful, guilty, guilt, sin, transgression in the sense of something missing, due, lacking; hence debt, duty, obligation. Traditionally any *dvija* ("twice-born") has a lifelong obligation toward the *ṛṣis*, the Gods and the Forefathers.[35]

Anutāpa, m., from *anu-tap-*, lit. to heat, then to repent, to suffer the consequences of one's deeds, means repentance, penitence. It is an important concept in the Dharmaśāstras. "If after committing a sin a man feels repentance for having done it, he becomes free from that sin. He becomes purified only by the resolution 'I shall not act thus again.'"[36]

31. Cf. RV I, 38, 6; X, 59 (§ V 8); etc.
32. Cf. RV I, 129, 11; X, 108, 6; X, 164, 5 (§ IV 8); AV XI, 8, 19.
33. As Soma; in the RV the nominal forms do not occur.
34. Cf. RV I, 125, 7 for the latter meaning.
35. Cf. § III 23 Introduction.
36. Manu XI, 231.

Pātaka, n., from the causative of the root *pat-*, to fall, means that which causes the fall, that is, sin, crime. In the Dharmaśāstras it is as frequently used for sin as *pāpa*. From the root *pat-* are also formed *patana*, fall, sinfulness, and *patita*, the fallen one, the sinner.[37] *Patanīya* is synonymous with *pātaka*.

Doṣa, m., from the root *duṣ-* (to become bad, corrupted, impure, to sin), means fault, vice, deficiency, sinfulness, offense, guilt; it occurs in the Upaniṣads and Smṛtis (but not in the Ṛg Veda).

Kleśa, m., from the root *kliś-*, to torment, trouble, afflict, to suffer, means pain, affliction, distress.[38] In the Yoga Sūtras five *kleśas* are given as the basic causes of affliction.[39]

37. These terms occur frequently up to the medieval *bhakti* literature.

38. Cf. SU I, 11 (§ IV 21); BG XII, 5; XVIII, 8; etc.

39. I.e., *avidyā* (ignorance), *asmitā* (egoism), *rāga* (passion), *dveṣa* (aversion), *abhiniveśa* (desire to live). Cf. YS II, 3.

A. SORROW AND SUFFERING

Śoka

Only when men shall roll up space
as if it were a simple skin,
only then will there be an end of sorrow
without acknowledging God.

SU VI, 20[40]

This difficult and ambivalent verse, which is found at the very end of a late Upaniṣad and thus at the end of the whole *śruti*, sums up Vedic reflection on the problem of sorrow. The text may be understood as saying either that to roll up the sky like a skin[41] is a sheer impossibility and so also is the suppression of sorrow without the realization of God; or, that it is indeed possible to overcome the spatial fallacy, the *māyā* character of space, and that it is certainly possible to transcend time; then you may succeed in putting an end to sorrow, even without having to postulate the existence of God, though not necessarily denying him. In the former instance there is a definite axiom which is more in keeping with the rest of this particular Upaniṣad, whereas in the latter there is a different and

40. Space: *ākāśa*. End of sorrow: *duḥkhasyānta*. Without acknowledging God: *devam avijñāya*, without discerning *Śiva*.
41. Or, as some translators have rendered it, "to wrap yourself with the sky as with a skin."

uncompromising attitude which assumes that it is possible without any hypothesis about God to overcome the human condition and thus reach the desired goal of eliminating sorrow. In the one case we have the theological reduction (with God as the clue) and in the other the cosmological one (cosmic reality offering the key). In the one case God—a real God and not an idol capable of manipulation by human hands, mind, or heart—is the ultimate refuge and the solution to the human riddle; God is the end of suffering and Man's deliverer from distress. In the other case the cosmoanthropological picture is that of a reality with two faces, as it were: an outer visible face, which is that of time-space, body-matter, and, obviously, sorrow and suffering; and an inner invisible face for which we possess no category, though consciousness is the favorite philosophical term and Brahman the religious one. This Brahman is utterly real and is not an idealistic background or an extrapolation of any human structure, mental or spiritual. Brahman or pure consciousness is here total bliss and realization.

We are touching here one of the central problems of Man's experience, the mystery of human sorrow, of which, indeed, the Vedas make more than one attempt at explanation. These attempts are made in depth and not on a merely sociological plane in which the pair of opposites, pessimism-optimism, might be appropriately employed. There are two clearly distinct periods in the Vedic Revelation, the Vedic and the Upaniṣadic, and they seem to take two contrasting and extreme positions: the one minimizes sorrow to such an extent that one finds it difficult to select pertinent texts at all, whereas the other radicalizes the nature of sorrow to such a degree that the only resort is total escape into another form of existence.

One common trait, however, connects these two conceptions of the sorrowful: namely, both consider sorrow to be an awakening to the transcendent. Suffering brings Man to the point of "rupturing" his humanness and thus to the threshold of transcendence. Man experiences his own suffering as something foreign to him, something outside himself, as if it came from the unknown, from another world, so to speak. This suffering is either the scorpion sting of some evil power or the very means through which he discovers his true nature beyond all the entanglements of the human condition. The first myth is represented by the Vedic period, and the second is typically Upaniṣadic and Vedāntic, though in fact a too clear-cut distinction would be wrong. In the one case sorrow is that which disturbs the physical as well as the psychic harmony; it is abnormal and external and thus can be overcome only if the causes are properly known and the appropriate remedies applied. In the second case sorrow is the very factor that enables Man to rupture the bonds of his human predicament; it is normal and intrinsic and thus it can be transcended only if the human situation is properly understood and the discipline leading to such a realization is seriously undertaken. It is against this double background that the texts of the next two subsections should be considered.

One type of reflection is conspicuously absent from the whole of the Vedic experience: that is the question, later on so agonizing, of *why*. The fact of suffering, the reality of human distress, is taken as given, as a real datum, as something that has to be dealt with, whether by regaining the lost poise and happiness or by transcending totally the sorrowful human predicament. Vedic speculation, however, does not take the path of inquiring about the why.

It is certainly true that speculation of a later date quotes scriptural texts to support different philosophical doctrines; the *śruti* itself, however, does not seem concerned with explaining the essence of sorrow but only with explaining away its existence. Once again we discover the existential character of the Vedic experience. Furthermore, the question of the *why* seems to be thematically avoided, as if speculation concerning it would result in an utterly false perspective. To ask ultimate questions about the why of evil implies two very grave assumptions: (*a*) that there is something or somebody responsible for it, and (*b*) that evil belongs to the realm of intelligibility. The Vedas do not make either of these assumptions.

a) If sorrow, evil, distress, and the like have an independent ultimate cause we cannot avoid dualism, for ultimate evil is then postulated as an irreducible principle. It amounts, in the final analysis, to a tragic conception of reality, because life, survival, goodness, and beauty are possible only by dint of subduing and forever repressing the other half of reality. Even without defining the ultimate consequences of this attitude, to presuppose that evil has an independent and substantial why enables us to transfer onto this moral or ontological scapegoat all the evil we resist acknowledging in ourselves. It implies that we simply repudiate the problem and heap on another that which we eliminate from ourselves. In modern terms we could apply ecological categories: the purification of one part of the environment by polluting another. It would be rewarding to examine more closely the dualistic mentality underlying ecological problems. It is a distinctive feature of the Vedas that responsibility for the existence of human suffering is not transferred to a Prince of Darkness in one form or another; rather, evil is taken to originate in a malfunctioning of the given structures of reality, owing to a clash or conflict of interests. Evil is situational, we may say, and not ontological.

b) Evil, suffering, and sorrow have no why, because if we could really know the why of them—and not only the how—we would explain them away. They are precisely negative "values" because we cannot give any why, any rational explanation. The dark side of reality (the nocturnal aspect of Man) is dark precisely because light (or the diurnal aspect) has not reached it. If light reaches darkness, darkness automatically ceases to be what it is. Is it not a fact of common experience that evil of whatever kind denotes a certain situation that is precisely as it is because there is no reason to account for it, no satisfactory explanation, no justification whatsoever? If a why could be given to the nature of suffering and evil the whole problem would be shifted to the nature of that why; that is, we revert to the question of the preceding paragraph. Here also tradition has extracted the ultimate and logical consequences of this attitude: the denial of reality to evil and suffering. The seeds of this denial are to be observed in many texts of the Upaniṣads and Gītā.

a) Physical Ailments

Roga

In the hymns of the Ṛg Veda scarcely any explicit mention is made of suffering as such. The poets, however, frequently beseech the divinity to grant protection against sundry ills, against enemies and evil spirits, and we find them constantly praying for a long and happy life and for freedom from suffering. Suffering is a human invariant that cannot easily be explained away.

Now, the most immediate experience in regard to the origin of suffering is the pain inflicted by wrong functioning of the human organism, which we call illness. Man discovers, further, that illness is generally caused by an external agent encroaching on the human body or affecting the whole person. Sometimes the agent is obvious and visible; at other times it is hidden and invisible. On most occasions Man infers that the cause of the malady is both visible and invisible, both material and spiritual, and this conjecture is followed by first steps for a praxis against ailments; the visible and invisible cause must be discovered and conjured away.

A considerable number of hymns of the Atharva Veda are prayers for the healing of ailments. These hymns are addressed either to the illness personified or to the demons or spirits who are assumed to be at the root of such ills and sicknesses. Other hymns, such as Atharva Veda IV, 17,[42] are addressed to the plant that is the cure for a particular sickness. Others are addressed to Water[43] or to Fire,[44] both of which have the power to chase away demons.

Among the selected texts certain verses are addressed to "Fever" or, to be more precise, to Takman, the evil spirit personifying fever. Yet others are addressed to "Worms," reckoned to be the cause of many malaises, or to physical ailments and bodily infirmities in general. The last hymn invokes a plant that has the power of freeing from ills.[45]

These various passages reveal the mental agony and the fear aroused in Man by bodily ailments; they depict also his longing to be delivered from such ills, both by natural methods and, above all, through the intervention of the divinity, under whatever guise, obscure or less obscure, he may be invoked.

The origin of most evils is external, certainly, but is not always to be sought in either the world above or the world below. It can also come from Man himself, from his neighbors, and, more particularly, from his enemies. Many texts tell us that Man has not only the unknown forces of evil to fear, but also the all too well-known power of his foes. Life on earth is not merely a struggle against superhuman powers. It is, and often much more so, a real combat with one's fellowmen, not necessarily one's enemies; sometimes they are only competitors. And so we hear also the prayer of the man who fears "defeat in games of dice and chance."[46] These texts from the Atharva Veda depict a hardy race of Men, struggling

42. Cf. AV V, 4 and 5 for two other examples of prayers addressed to healing plants.
43. Cf. § I 17.
44. Cf. § IV 11.
45. Cf. AV II, 4; III, 9, for prayers against rheumatism.
46. AV IV, 17, 7 (§ IV 4).

against physical suffering and human rivals with both courage and optimism, refusing to succumb.

A word should be said here regarding so-called magic practices. To say a prayer before eating is not, as such, magic, though it could be if one believed that unless the prayer was said the food would not perform its biochemical function in the organism. To utter a blessing on a medicinal plant or to pray before using a certain herb is not necessarily magic, unless one is prepared to overlook the intermediary order of things and attribute direct and exclusive efficacy to what is only a concomitant factor. A certain confidence in medical treatment, which includes both the physician and the medicines, is an indispensable factor in its efficacy.

The texts that follow are all taken from the same source, the Atharva Veda, which has all too often been considered a book of mere incantations and charms. We need to understand that any ritual seen only from the outside is bound to appear strange, weird, and often magical. In making this statement we neither deny the existence of magic and magical practices nor enter into a discussion regarding the nature of magic and its connection with religion.[47]

Vedic Man has a holistic idea of fever and not a specialized theory of quickened molecular movement caused by the extra work imposed on the cellular region concerned. Knowing that fever is, rather, a symptom with alarming effects, he wants to do away with it, though he is often puzzled by its recurrent character and its tenacity. He both prays and applies medicines, as two moments of one and the same human act of fighting disease. He knows that the medicine by itself will not work and that mere words will not suffice. Each human act has the theandric nature of a sacrament.

The prayers that follow are more than simple aspirations; they are more than impotent cries or mere wishes. They are action as well as utterances; they are expressions of the human fight against disease. These prayers are not speculative hymns or theoretical treatises. They are totally involved in the suffering condition and make one feel that one is facing the suffering Man speaking and acting. Human malady is not a trifling matter and here there is no room for lofty considerations nor is there a way of escape. Man is totally engaged in his existential struggle for well-being and he is facing the dire reality of a power that seems to rob him of his health

47. Cf. § I D Introduction on the same subject.

and even of his life. Yet he is determined to face the menace, to struggle, and in the end to win. He has in his hand a medicinal herb, on his lips a sacred mantra, in his heart a burning hope, and in his mind an unflinching faith. He is well aware of the complex web of relations which crisscrosses the whole of reality and he intends to intervene in order to restore the lost harmony and balance.

Acute or chronic diseases, however, are not the only ailments that undermine Man's health and constitution; some persons are hardly affected by such illnesses. Nevertheless there is one kind of physical condition that every one has to face: *jarā*, decrease and old age.

Length of days is something to which Vedic Man aspires as the completion and fulfillment of his own life and as part of a natural process in which life, when it starts diminishing in the father, nevertheless goes on in the children and the children's children with unbroken continuity. Although few texts specifically describe the process of decay in old age, the fear of it lurks beneath many passages.[48] Old age as a diminishment of all the powers in Man, both physical and mental, is regarded as unavoidable and, unlike sickness, as incurable. Therefore the desire to be free from old age accompanies the desire to be free from death,[49] and Man prays for *ajarā* (agelessness), *nijarā* (freedom from old age), and *amṛta* (deathlessness) almost as synonyms.[50] Precisely because it is unavoidable, old age is also a constant reminder to Man that he cannot maintain indefinitely a healthy and unimpaired physique.

On this subject also the Upaniṣadic experience opens up different perspectives, discovering that evil does not in reality consist so much in this or that sickness or danger as in the very fact that Man is destined to become old and decrepit and ultimately to die. There is none of the optimism of the Saṁhitās, but an acute awareness of decay as the unavoidable factor in man's expectations which cannot be cured or prayed away. Even if an old Man happens to be restored to health, he knows only too well that it is a temporary reprieve and not a definitive return to life.

The first two texts describe the process of diminution: a Man

48. For *jarā* cf. RV I, 89, 9; I, 140, 8; II, 34, 10; V, 41, 17; AV XII, 2, 24; BU III, 5, 1 (§§ IV 6; III 31); IV, 3, 36 (§ IV 5).
49. Cf. § V, passim.
50. Cf. CU VIII, 1, 5 (§ VI 6); SU II, 12; KausU I, 3 (§ V 4).

when old is burdened under the *ātman*, as if he were bent under a heavy load. He is gradually reduced to skin and bones, and all his organs, which were so prompt to serve him when he was young, now quit his service, as the simile of the arrival and departure of a king in a village colorfully suggests. The organs merge into one another and the Man, bereft of both speech and mind, is no longer able to recognize his dear ones. There is no way back, no escape, for even *prāṇa*, the life breath, his last attendant, is getting heavy and is about to abandon the body.

That the decay of the body is one of the main reasons for total disillusionment is shown in the beautiful story of Indra and Prajāpati, from which we quote only the pertinent passage. Prajāpati declares that the only thing worthy to be sought is the unaging, deathless *ātman*.[51] The *devas* and the *asuras*, both desiring to receive instruction about the *ātman*, send their representative to learn from Prajāpati. Indra among the *devas* and Virocana among the *asuras* approach the Father of beings in the humble manner of disciples in search of truth. They are requested to live thirty-two years of apprenticeship with their master, who thereby tests the sincerity and constancy of their search. He then imparts to them his first instruction, telling them that the *ātman* is nothing else but the person, our self as we see it in another's eyes or as we perceive it if we look into a pan of water as if into a mirror. Virocana is satisfied with this theory and he goes away to inform the *asuras* that the bodily self, and it alone, needs to be made happy.[52]. Not so Indra. On his way back to the Gods he is overcome by doubts as to whether the body that can be affected by injury and decay can conceivably be the permanent *ātman*. He returns to Prajāpati and humbly dwells with him for another thirty-two years, after which Prajāpati imparts to him the next instruction, in which the *ātman* is identified with the soul in the dream state. Twice more Indra returns to his master, each time discovering defects in these various theories regarding the *ātman*. Only when he is thus prepared for the highest teaching does Prajāpati declare that the body is not the *ātman*, because the body is mortal whereas the *ātman* is immortal.[53] Disillusionment had led Indra to the ultimate truth. The desire for the unaging state, free from decay, is nothing other than the search for the *ātman*, the unaging and deathless in Man.[54]

51. Cf. CU VIII, 7, 1 (§ VI 6).
52. Cf. CU VIII, 8, 4-5 (§ VI 6).
53. Cf. CU VIII, 12, 1 (§ VI 6).
54. Cf. CU VIII, 1, 4-5 (§ VI 6).

Spare Us, O Burning Fever

Takmanāśana

1

AV, V, 22, 1-2; 4; 6; 10-13

1. May Fever flee hence,
exorcised by Agni,
exorcised by Soma
and the Pressing Stone,
by Varuṇa, sheer Mind,
the altar, the grass
of sacrifice,
and the blazing logs!
May all harmful things scatter!

2. How yellow the victims
you consume as with fire
and devour with your heat,
O Fever; but now
your power will all vanish!
Take yourself off
to the regions infernal,
the regions below!

4. To the depths I dispatch,
though with cautious politeness,
this promoter of dysentery!
Let her now return
to the place where she belongs!

6. O Fever all gray
with an arsenic tinge,
accompanied by pains
and covered with blotches,
go seek a new victim
to strike with your plague!

10. Now cold, now burning,
you rack with a cough.
Terrible are your features,
O Fever. Pray spare us
the sight of your face!

11. Do not bring in your train
either languor or cough
or rasping of breath.
Return never more
to the place you have quit.

12. Go away, Fever,
and take along with you
your brother Consumption,

your sister Cough,
and your cousin Herpes.
Into strangers depart!

13. I adjure you, O Fevers
of every sort,
whether rife in the autumn
or monsoon or summer,
intermittent or continuous,
shivering or burning,
depart and vanish!

1. Grass of sacrifice: *barhis*, the *kuśa*-grass.
2. How yellow: probably a reference to jaundice.
4. Cautious politeness: *namaḥ kṛtvā*, having paid homage.
Place where she belongs: lit. to the Mahāvṛṣā, probably a people of northwest India.
6. Various words in this stanza have a double meaning.
12. Consumption: *balāsa*.
Cough: *kāsikā*.
Herpes: *pāman*.
13. Intermittent: i.e., the fever that returns every third day or two days out of three (e.g., malarial).
Vv. 3, 5, 7-9, and 14 describe the (geographical) places from where fever comes and where it is to be returned by the spell.

Away, and Come No More! *Krimijambhana*

2

AV II, 31

1. With Indra's great millstone,
of all worms the crusher,
I mince up these worms
like grains on a grinder!

2. Visible and invisible—
both have I crushed,
not sparing Kurūru,
Algaṇḍus or Śalunas!
We destroy all these worms with our spell!

3. With a powerful weapon
I destroy the Algaṇḍus;
charred or uncharred,
they are drained of life sap!
Present or absent,
with my spell I subdue them!
Let no single worm stay alive!

4. The worm in the entrails,
the worm in the head,

the worm in the ribs,
we crush with this spell!

5. Whether worms in the hills,
or worms in the woods,
whether worms in the plants or the waters,
whether worms that reside
within cattle or men—
this whole breed of worms I exterminate!

Both this hymn and the following one (AV II, 32) are directed against all types of worms and parasites.

2. Kurūru, Algaṇḍu, and Śaluna are different kinds of worms.
Spell: *vacas,* powerful word.
3. Drained of life sap: *arasa.*

Sickness . . . Keep Off! *Yakṣmanivāraṇa*

3

AV IX, 8

1. Headache, head pain, earache, inflammations,
all that now afflicts the head
expel we by our prayer.

2. From your ears, each part thereof,
the earache and the throbbing pain,
all that now afflicts the head,
expel we by our prayer.

3. So that consumption may recede
from your ears and from your mouth,
all that now afflicts the head,
expel we by our prayer.

4. Whatever makes man dumb or blind,
all that now afflicts the head,
expel we by our prayer.

5. Limb-splitting, limb-destroying pain,
the ache that throbs in every part,
all that now afflicts the head,
expel we by our prayer.

6. The fever that assails man each autumn,
whose fearful aspect makes man tremble,
expel we by our prayer.

7. The deadly disease that invades the thighs
and reaches also to the groin,

disease that spreads from the inner parts,
  expel we by our prayer.

8. If the disease was caused by love
or hatred, by the heart's affections,
this too from the heart and limbs
  expel we by our prayer.

9. The yellow jaundice from your limbs,
the colic lodged in your intestines,
the disease that plagues your inner self,
  expel we by our prayer.

10. May this throbbing turn to ashes!
May it become infected urine!
The poison of every wasting disease
  from you I exorcise!

11. Forth from the orifice let it come,
the rumbling sound from your intestines!
The poison of every wasting disease
  from you I exorcise!

12. From your stomach and your lungs,
from the navel and the heart,
the poison of every wasting disease
  from you I exorcise!

13. Those piercing pains that cleave asunder
the crown and skull and penetrate further,
let them go forth at the orifice,
  without ill effect, harmless!

14. The pangs that stab the heart and pass
along the spine from top to bottom,
let them go forth at the orifice,
  without ill effect, harmless!

15. The stabbing pains that pierce the sides
and penetrate along the ribs,
let them go forth at the orifice,
  without ill effect, harmless!

16. The shooting pains that dart crosswise
and penetrate within the stomach,
let them go forth at the orifice,
  without ill effect, harmless!

17. The pains that creep along the intestines,
confounding all within the entrails,
let them go forth at the orifice,
without ill effect, harmless!

18. The pains that suck the marrow out
and cleave and rend the bones asunder,
let them go forth at the orifice,
without ill effect, harmless!

19. The wasting diseases that numb the limbs,
racking the frame with colic pains,
the poison of every wasting disease
from you I exorcise!

20. Erupting spots and abscesses,
rheumatic pains and eye disease,
the poison of every wasting disease
from you I exorcise!

21. From your feet, your knees, your hips,
from your buttocks and your spine,
from your neck and from your head,
I have expelled all sickness!

22. Sound are the bones of your skull. Your heart
once more beats soundly. Arising, O Sun,
you have chased far away with your rays the headache
and stilled the racking pain!

1. Inflammations: *vilohita,* an inflammatory disease, perhaps erysipelas. *Lohita* is a particular disease of the eyelids.
Expel we by our prayer: *nir-mantrayāmahe,* a compound word composed of *mantra* (prayer) with prefix *nir-*, lit. "we pray it away," we exorcise.
2. Part thereof: conjectural for *kaṅkūṣa,* an obscure word.
Throbbing pain: *visalyaka,* the name of a disease causing throbbing pains (another reading has *visalpaka*).
3. Consumption: *yakṣma.*
4. Dumb: or perhaps deaf and dumb.
6. Fever: *takman,* probably malaria.
7. Deadly disease: *yakṣma.*
8. Love: *kāma,* desire.
Hatred: *apakāma,* aversion.
9. That plagues your inner self: lit. from your inner self (*antarātmanaḥ*), which may refer to mental disease, through *ātman* may also be translated "body."
10. I exorcise: *niravocam aham,* from *nir-vac-*, to drive away, expel, by word.
13. Harmless: *ahiṁsantīḥ,* not injuring.
19. Numb: *madayanti,* intoxicate, make senseless.
20. Erupting spots: *visalpa.*
Abscesses: *vidradha.*
Rheumatic pains: *vātīkāra.*
Eye disease: *alaji.*
21. Expelled all sickness: *rogam anīnaśam.*
22. Sun: Āditya.

Deliver Us from All Afflictions

Apāmārga

4

AV IV, 17

1. I take you, Plant, of cures the Queen,
conqueror of ills. For all our needs
I impart to you energizing force,
for every man a thousandfold.

2. O truly conquering, curse-averting
powerful Plant, backward turned,
you and all plants have I invoked:
"Save us from this!" I prayed.

3. She who has cursed us with a curse,
she who is wholly rooted in sin,
who has seized a child to take his blood—
let her devour her own offspring!

4. Whatever ill they intend for you
in a dish unbaked or of blue-red hue,
whatever prepared in uncooked flesh,
with that same subdue the sorcerers!

5. Evil dreaming, evil living,
demons, monsters, hags, and witches,
all of ill-repute or fame,
these we now destroy.

6. Death by hunger, death by thirst,
lack of cattle, lack of children,
by your aid, Plant that expels,
we now expel these maladies.

7. Death by thirst, death by hunger,
defeat in games of dice and chance,
by your aid, Plant that expels,
we now expel these maladies.

8. The Plant that expels is sole controller
of all the herbs. By its aid we now expel
all harm that has befallen you.
Depart, free from disease!

1. I impart to you: I am endowing you with—so as to emphasize the power of the human spell.
2. Truly conquering, etc.: names of plants (*oṣadhīḥ*) that have the power to prevent evil.
3. This v. is found also in AV I, 28, 3, and refers to sorceresses.
Wholly rooted in sin: *āghaṁ mūram ādadhe,* has taken evil as her root.
4. Dish unbaked, etc.: all objects for witchcraft, which are here used by reversion against the sorcerers themselves. Cf. AV V, 31, 1.
5. Destroy: efface, expel, remove, always in the causative form, *vāśayati* (from *vaś-*), cause to disappear.
6. Plant that expels: *apāmārga,* a medicinal plant, commonly considered "magical," the *achyranthes aspera,* still used against stings of scorpions, etc. Etymologically its name means "cleansing," "expelling" (disease).

Decrease and Old Age *Jarā*

5

BU IV, 3, 35-38

i) 35. Just as an overloaded cart lumbers along creaking, in the same way the self in this body, loaded by the Self of wisdom, lumbers along creaking when its breath is getting heavy.

36. When he becomes reduced, whether by old age or by disease, then, just as a mango fruit or a fig or a pipal fruit [detaches itself from its stem], so this person, being released from his limbs, returns to Life, to the place whence he has come.

37. Just as, when a king is arriving, the guards, the officers, the drivers, and the village elders await him with food, drink, and a place for his dwelling, saying, "Here he comes, here he comes!" even so all beings await him who knows this [saying]: "Here comes Brahman, here he comes!"

38. Just as the guards, the officers, the drivers, and the village elders gather around the king at his departure, even so all the powers of life gather around this self at the end of his time, when his breath is getting heavy.

CU VI, 15, 1-2

ii) 1. When a man, my dear, is stricken with disease, his relatives come near to him, asking: "Do you recognize me? Do you recognize me?" As long as his speech has not merged in his mind, his mind in his breath, his breath in light, and the light in the supreme Godhead, so long does he recognize them.

2. But when his speech has merged in his mind, his mind in his breath, his breath in light, and the light in the supreme Godhead, then he does not recognize them any longer.

CU VIII, 9

iii) 1. Now, Indra, before reaching the Gods, became aware of this fear: "[if the Self is the body] then when the body is decorated, the self too is decorated, when the body is well dressed, the self is well dressed, when the body is adorned, the self is adorned; in the same way, if the body is becoming blind, the self also will be blind, if the body is maimed, the self also will be maimed, if the body is mutilated, the self also will be mutilated, if the body is destroyed, the self also will be destroyed along with it. In this I do not find any consolation."

2. With fuel in his hand he came back again, and Prajāpati said to him: "O Maghavan, with your heart at peace, you left together with Virocana. Desiring what have you returned?" He said: "When the body is decorated, the self too is decorated, when the body is well dressed, the self is well dressed, when the body is adorned, the self is adorned; in the same way, if the body is becoming blind, the self also will be blind, if the body is maimed, the self also will be maimed, if the body is mutilated, the self

also will be mutilated, if the body is destroyed, the self also will be destroyed along with it. In this I do not find any consolation."

3. "Even so is it, O Maghavan," he said. "However, this I will further explain to you. Live with me for a further thirty-two years!" Then he lived with him for a further thirty-two years. Then he [Prajāpati] said to him [Indra]:

■ i) 35. Loaded by the Self of Wisdom: *prājñenātmanānvārūḍhaḥ*, implying that when the great, intelligent Self takes possession of a man, he cannot bear its weight for a long time; his body is weighed down by the spirit like a cart under a heavy load.

When its breath is getting heavy: *ūrdhva ucchvāsī bhavati*, i.e., when he is about to expire.

36. Reduced: *aṇiman*, thinness.

Life: *prāṇa*.

Place whence he has come: *yoni*, womb.

37. Referring to the birth of a person.

38. At the end of his time: *antakāle*, at the time of death. Vv. 37 and 38 are similes referring to the behavior of the *prāṇas* in relation to the person when he is born or dies.

■ ii) 8-14. Cf. §VI 10.

15, 1. Stricken with disease: approaching death.

Speech: *vāc*, voice, word.

Light: *tejas*, also heat, the energy that remains when the breath leaves the body.

Supreme Godhead: *parā devatā*.

The order of "return to the source" is: *vāc, manas, prāṇa, tejas, parā devatā*. This series implies a whole Upaniṣadic anthropology. Cf. BU IV, 4, 2 (§ V 12).

There follows in v. 3 the famous instruction to Śvetaketu, in which it is explained that what "remains" at the end of the whole process, the most subtle thing, is the *ātman*. Cf. CU VI, 14, 3 (§ VI 10).

16. Cf. § VI 10.

■ iii) Consolation: *bhogya*, something useful or enjoyable. Indra finds "no fun" in the understanding that the *ātman* is identical with the perishable body (*śarīra*).

For the continuation of the dialogue, see the rest of CU VIII and the references in § VI 6 (v) notes.

b) The Obstruction on the Way

Duḥkha

Wherever there are Men there is also a cry of suffering and pain accompanying the human condition. This is true not only at times of big calamities or during onslaughts of personal sickness. It is equally true of human reality as such in its most normal condition. The setting of one of the Upaniṣadic texts we have given puts it very clearly:

There was a king called Bṛhadratha who, when he had enthroned his eldest son, turned to the forest in search of the eternal. After a thousand days of most severe penance he was approached by the sage Śākāyanya, an *ātma-vid*, knower of the Self, who offered him a boon. The king asked to know the nature of *ātman*, but the sage refused to elaborate upon it, saying that it was too difficult a question. The king then burst forth into the litany of our text in which the talk is not about unusual catastrophies but about ordinary human miseries. The text finishes with the sincere cry:

> I am like a frog in a dry well.
> Lord, you alone are our refuge,
> you alone are our refuge.[55]

If "all is suffering," as has been proclaimed by Buddhism[56] and by yoga,[57] there is little use in tackling minor ailments here and there and in applying mere palliatives. One has to transcend sorrow totally and the only medicament is to realize fully the human predicament and by this very fact to transcend it, "rolling up the skies,"[58] going to the other shore of sorrow, as another Upaniṣad tells us.[59] There is hardly any other moment in human history in which so gigantic an effort has been made to explain suffering by explaining it away, as in the period of post-Upaniṣadic spirituality.

Thus suffering and pain are not seen here as biological or psychological facts. Medicine and psychiatry would not suffice for Upaniṣadic culture, nor would common sense and insistence on joy in the little things of everyday life. There is no point in soft-pedaling the situation or in ignoring the fact of ontological distress, which now begins to be called by a neologism: *duḥkha*.

The first period of the Vedas describes the human condition in terms of a well-oiled axle hole of a cart which proceeds smoothly toward its destination through the protection of the Gods and the collaboration of human industry. *Sukha*[60] is the word for this, which in the Ṛg Veda is still used in a literal sense.[61] No doubt there is suffering and there are obstructions, but the sundry obstacles that Man encounters on his pilgrimage are all external and nearly always surmountable. No doubt Man is fearful of the unknown and dreads his enemies, he is afraid of disease and death is lurking everywhere; yet nothing seems to be irreparable and even death is not so dreadful, for life continues on the several planes of a multistory universe.

55. MaitU I, 4 (§ V 18).
56. Cf. the Sermon of Vārāṇasī on the Four Noble Truths as reported in Saṁyutta-nikāya, V, 420, for instance.
57. Cf. YS II, 15, and the commentaries on it.
58. SU VI, 20 (§ IV A Antiphon).
59. Cf. CU VII, 1, 3 (§§ IV 6; VI 3).
60. From *su-* (prefix denoting a positive value: goodness, beauty, happiness, etc.) and *kha* (see above, *duḥkha*): agreeable, gentle, comfortable, and later, pleasant, joyful, etc. Cf. RV VIII, 77, 3; VIII, 91, 7; X, 156, 3, for *kha* as the hole in the nave of the wheel in which the axle is inserted.
61. Cf. RV I, 20, 3; I, 49, 2; I, 120, 11; III, 35, 4; V, 63, 5.

With the Jaina and Buddhist upheaval, both paralleled and confirmed by the Upaniṣads, the picture radically changes. The human condition is no longer *sukha* and the pain is no longer accidental. The human condition is not said to be *asukha,* a word that does not appear until much later, but *duḥka*: the cart axle now functions badly; there is an intrinsic defect which does not allow the smooth functioning of Man. There is not only physical pain and psychological suffering, but there is also a constitutive distress comprising a stricture and an anguish which convince Man that his present predicament is neither right nor definitive. The defect must be radically overcome, not merely markedly improved. *Duḥkha* is more than just sorrow or pain, more than simple suffering or grief, more than mild stiffness in all our joints so that we cannot run our course unhampered. It is an internal blockage in our own movement, an injury that affects our deepest nerves, so that we can no longer regard our performance here on earth as the real way in which we are intended to run in order to reach the Real itself, the authentic goal of human existence. Thus the very distress of our existence is at the same time the starting point for transcending our human condition altogether.

One can easily detect, however, an element of continuity between the first and second periods, the already mentioned process of interiorization. Evil is external, but the interiorization of evil is due not only to a deepening within the consciousness but also to the ritual itself. Many texts emphasize that the rituals carry with them the risk of a rebound against the very performers who should be their beneficiaries. Errors may creep in, interferences from other rituals may occur, wrong use of the ritual may cause effects diametrically opposed to those intended, and so on. In all these instances the evil result comes from the ritual itself; that is, it becomes endogenous and is interiorized. There is only one way *out,* and that is the way *in,* that is, into the experience of all the potentialities of Man and of the cosmic repercussions of his actions. In order to achieve liberation Man has to freely acknowledge his own situation and respond fully to the exigencies of such knowledge. The notion that freedom is not only freedom for, but freedom from, begins to take shape.

It is against this background that the texts that follow can be properly evaluated. One may agree or disagree, but first of all one has to understand what they intend to convey: the uncompromising attitude of the sage who has discovered that human distress must be overcome by transcending completely the human predicament:

> There a father is no longer a father, . . .
> nor are the Gods any longer Gods, . . .
> [only then] will man pass beyond
> all the sorrows of the heart.[62]

No longer is reform of one's life indicated, a betterment of the human condition or a continuation of it on a heavenly plane, but a total rupture and absolute change. Only then is Man "untainted by the distress of the outside world."[63] So the Bhagavad Gītā proclaims in the most unambiguous way: "You should not be distressed"[64] in spite of all the miseries you see in the world. All are pangs of a new birth, which is the more joyful as you realize that, properly speaking, it is not another birth because the real being was already there.

The Gītā, as usual, adds its own touch of practicality. The distress of the human predicament can be overcome and sorrow can be eliminated. The process is, precisely, the true yoga. It consists not only in adjusting to the inevitable or in acquiring a sense of proportion, as one is tempted to say; it is more than an ascetic detachment. It is the positive and disciplined act of cutting the knot that connects our existence with all that is perishable. *Sukha* and *duḥkha* are not primordially ethical and much less eudaemonistic categories, as if everything were on the level of pleasure and pain. It is rather a question of being or not being, of salvation, of realization.

Later traditions, like all scholasticisms intent on analysis, have distinguished several states of liberated souls. Significantly, the criteria are usually the reaction to pain and the attitude toward suffering. There are, for instance, three degrees of enlightened persons, according to one classical division: first, those liberated souls who, in spite of having realized the Self, continue to feel the pain and suffering of life like ordinary Men; second, those who still go through the human distresses of life, but do so as if in a dream

62. BU IV, 3, 22 (§ IV 6).
63. KathU V, 11 (§ VI 2, where we give a slightly different and more contextual meaning of the text. The outside world is not opposed to an inside world but to the *ātman*).
64. BG II, 25, sq. (§ IV 7).

and thus remain unconcerned; and, third, those who are unperturbed and untouched by the sufferings themselves, remaining in perfect bliss.

Another idea also must be kept in mind in order to understand the radical utterances of these and similar texts. We could call it the concentric, or rather the pyramidal, conception of reality. The sage who overcomes sorrow and pain is not, when he is loyal to his vicarious and representative vocation, an escapist or a selfish individual insensitive to the *Weltschmerz*, as the Kaṭha Upaniṣad puts it.[65] Nor are the sufferings of the world denied, as some schools claim from their interpretation of the texts. The sufferings are said, rather, not to "smear" the *ātman*,[66] not to reach the depth of the soul, not to have an ultimate ontological consistency, so that the enlightened person transcends the mental and physical planes and thus does not suffer. But there is still more. It seems as if the underlying assumption is that each great soul, *mahātman*, by eliminating sorrow in himself, helps to eliminate the sorrow of the world. Such elimination is possible because a great soul is not just an individual who has overcome his own troubles, but a condensed part of the whole of reality, an image of the whole, containing in a mysterious way the totality of the world. A state of total and unvarying unselfishness is imperative, therefore, for such an enterprise, and it is no wonder that there is almost unanimous agreement that this state is reached by only very few.

Beyond Sorrow and Suffering *Vītaśoka*

6

BU III, 5a

i) "Yājñavalkya," said he, "explain to me the Brahman that is perceptible clearly and not obscurely, the *ātman* that dwells within all things."

"The *ātman* in you is that which indwells all things."

"Tell me, Yājñavalkya, about this *ātman* that indwells all things."

"It is that which transcends hunger and thirst, sorrow and delusion, old age and death."

BU IV, 3, 22

ii) There a father is no longer a father and a mother no longer a mother; the worlds are no longer worlds, the Gods are no longer Gods, and the Vedas

65. *Loka-duḥkha;* KathU V, 11 (§ VI 2).

66. The root used is *lip-*, to stick to, to adhere, to smear. Cf. e.g., IsU 2 (§ VII 6).

are no longer Vedas. There a thief is no longer a thief, a murderer is no longer a murderer, and an outcaste is no longer an outcaste; a lowly born man is no longer lowly born, a monk is no longer a monk, an ascetic is no longer an ascetic; [for there] he is untouched by merit and untouched by sin; then he will have passed beyond all the sorrows of the heart.

BU IV, 4, 13-14

iii) 13. He who has found and awakened to the *ātman*
which has entered the otherwise impenetrable body,
he is the maker of the universe, of all things.
The world is his! The world itself is he!

14. This we may know, indeed, while here on earth.
If we do not know it, great is the destruction.
But those who know it become immortal.
The others attain only distress.

CU VII, 1, 3a

iv) "I am one, sir, who knows, to be sure, the sacred prayers but not the *ātman*. I have heard from masters like you that he who knows the *ātman* transcends sorrow. And I am suffering, sir. Help me, sir, to cross over to the other shore of sorrow."

MaitU I, 3

v) "Sir, how is it possible to enjoy one's desires in this body [of ours], which is ill-smelling, unsubstantial, a heap of bone, skin, muscle, marrow, flesh, semen, blood, mucus, tears, rheum, feces, urine, wind, bile, and phlegm? How is it possible to enjoy one's desires in this body, afflicted as it is with desire, anger, greed, delusion, fear, frustration, envy, separation from what one longs for and association with what one abhors, hunger, thirst, old age, death, disease, sorrow, and similar things?"

■ i) Perceptible clearly and not obscurely: *sākṣād aparokṣād*, i.e., that which stands before the eyes and that which is not hidden, sometimes translated as "immanent and nontranscendent."
Dwells within all things; (*ātmā*) *sarvāntaraḥ*, repeated three times.
Sorrow: *śoka*.
5b. Cf. § III 31.

■ ii) 19-21. Cf. § VI 8.
There: a description of the state of the Self in the state of deep sleep.
Worlds: *lokāḥ*.
Note the conciseness of the language throughout: *pitā 'pitā, mātā 'mātā, devā 'devāḥ*, and *vedā 'vedāḥ*, etc.
Murderer: lit. one who produces an abortion or kills an embryo.
Outcaste: *cāṇḍāla*, the son of a Śūdra from a Brahmin woman.
Lowly born: *paulkasa*, the son of a Śūdra from a Kṣatriya woman.
Monk: *śramaṇa*.
Ascetic: *tāpasa*.
Merit . . . sin: *puṇya . . . pāpa*, which can also have the meaning here of good and evil.
Sorrows: *śoka*.
Cf. the same idea in KathU I, 12 (§V 27) and also in MundU III, 2, 9 (§ VI 11).

■ iii) 13. Awakened: *pratibuddha*.

The otherwise impenetrable body: *asmin saṁdehye gahane,* i.e., the body as a place that is difficult to penetrate, like an inaccessible and perilous cavern.
14. Distress: *duḥkha.* It is said to be the first time that this word appears (Hauer). Cf. YS II, 15.
15-21. Cf. § VI 11.
22-25. Cf. § VI 6.
■ iv) 1, 1-2. Cf. § VI 3.
One . . . who knows . . .: sacred prayers: *mantra-vid,* as against *ātma-vid.*
Transcends: lit. to cross (to the other side of the ocean of) sorrow. The Buddhist flavor is very noticeable in this test.
Sorrow: *śoka.*
1, 3b. Cf. § VI 3. For the rest of CU VII and all the ref. cf. § VI 3 (v) and notes.
■ v) Again note the Buddhist flavor of this passage.
How is it possible to enjoy one's desires: *kiṃ kāmopabhogaiḥ*: what is the use of the enjoyment of desires.
Sorrow: *śoka.*
4. Cf. § V 18.

You Should Not Be Distressed — *Duḥkha-saṁyoga-viyoga*

7

BG II, 24-26; 28; 30

i) 24. Invulnerable is he to the sword and to fire,
to water and wind,
eternal, all-pervading, fixed, immovable,
the same forever.

25. Unmanifest, unthinkable and never changing
is he averred to be.
Therefore, recognizing him as such,
you should not be distressed.

26. Even if you think he is constantly born
and constantly dying,
even then, O Arjuna, mighty in war,
you should not be distressed.

28. Invisible in its beginning is every being,
at its end invisible.
It is visible only in the middle state.
What cause for lament?

30. The Dweller in the body of each is eternal
and cannot be slain.
Therefore for no being whatever
should you be distressed.

BG V, 22

ii) For the pleasures that come from external contacts
are mere sources of distress.
They come and they go; it is not upon these
that the wise man sets store.

BG VI, 17; 23

iii) 17. He who is moderate in eating and resting,
in sleeping and waking,
who is always controlled—that man's yoga
eliminates distress.

23. The disconnection of the connection with distress
he should know as right connection.
This yoga should be practiced with firm resolve
and a courageous heart.

[True Knowledge]

BG XIII, 8

iv) Aversion to the objects of the senses,
absence of the ego,
perception of the evils of birth and death,
age, sickness, and pain.

BG XIV, 16

v) Of work well done the fruit, so they say,
is goodness unalloyed,
while the fruit of passion is pain, and ignorance
is the fruit of dullness.

■ i) 25. You should not be distressed: *na śocitum arhasi,* you should not grieve, mourn, pain, feel sorrow.
27. Cf. § V 6.
30. Dweller in the body: *dehin,* the *ātman.*

■ ii) Sources of distress: *duḥkha-yoni,* womb (origin) of pain, suffering.
24-25. Cf. § V 28.

■ iii) 1-16. Cf. § III 32.

17. Is moderate: *yukta* (past passive participle of the root *yuj-,* to join, unite, integrate), suggesting discipline, moderation, the mature Man. The thrice-mentioned *yukta* leads to the *yoga* of the elimination of distress: *duḥkha-han.*

18-22. Cf. § III 32.

23. Disconnection of the connection with distress: *duḥkha-saṁyoga-viyoga,* the unlinking of the link with pain. This is the "right connection," *yoga.* Cf. § III 32 for the context.

■ iv) Aversion: *vairāgya.* renunciation, indifference. Cf. § III 31.
Absence of the ego: *an-ahaṁkāra.*
Evils: *doṣa,* defect, worthlessness.
Pain: *duḥkha.*

■ v) The theory of the three *guṇas* or fundamental human attributes is the background of this verse.
The fruit of passion is pain: *rajasas tu phalaṁ duḥkham.*

B. SIN AND MERCY

Pāpa-Mṛḍīka

If we have sinned against the man who loves us,
have wronged a brother, a dear friend, or a comrade,
the neighbor of long standing or a stranger,
remove from us this stain, O King Varuṇa.

RV V, 85, 7

The seers of the Vedic period possessed a peculiar awareness of sin and guilt. A brief study of the terms used in the Vedas for sin and evil leads us to discover three basic insights which, like three seeds, may later develop into complete theories.

We discover, first, a series of words indicating an external cause for all sorts of violence, harming, hurting, and afflicting.[67] Here the cause of evil comes from the outside; it encroaches upon us and hinders the happy and smooth development of our being. The evil is transcendent.

Another set of words seem to denote an internal source. These words speak of anxiety, narrowness, lack of expansion, a feeling of imprisonment within oneself.[68] Here the cause is within and seems to be inherent in our own nature. We cannot blame others but only

67. Cf. *enas, āgas, drugdha, pīḍā.*
68. Cf. *aṁhas, tamas.*

ourselves. We would like to be different and yet we are not. Evil is here immanent.

A third set of words, most of them compounds,[69] seem to suggest that evil springs from maladjustment and malfunctioning of a system that otherwise is far from being bad. These words postulate a kind of factual ambivalence in almost any human value, which can turn out to be either negative and mischievous or positive and beneficial. Evil here depends on the direction events and values take, on the use we or others make of the data.

We thus realize that sin is here conceived of as more than simply a pollution, and that it would be inappropriate to reduce the Vedic theology of evil to a cosmological theory. The distinction between the cosmic and the ethical should not, however, make of them two separate realities. Man, in fact, is not seen as a cosmic anomaly, but as part and parcel of the total reality.

The words used for evil and sin reinforce the impression that there is a close connection between these two notions. They are two sides of one and the same reality. Sin is not the cause of evil or of suffering, nor can evil be said to be the cause of sin. Unlike other traditions that seem to recognize sin as the one single source of evil and put the blame on the free will either of Man or of another being, the *śruti* seems to find a close relationship between the two, though not a casual one, because they are not considered to be two really different things. It is not sin that is first and foremost responsible for suffering, nor does any kind of human distress lead inevitably to sin.[70] The dichotomy between an ethical and a cosmic order is foreign to Vedic thinking, not because the ethical order is ignored but because the really existential order is anthropocosmic and thus includes both the ethical and the cosmic in one.

When we consider Varuṇa in the second subsection we shall see that there is also room for compassion and mercy. One feature that will be noticed immediately is the noncapricious character of the readiness to forgive and the sober character of compassion. There is place for both mercy and compassion, but not as the result of an almighty Will operating outside order or reason. Mercy and compassion have their place in the framework of the universe; they too,

69. Cf. *duḥkha, durita,* etc., and *anṛta, adharma,* etc.

70. As we shall see in the subsection on Varuṇa, however, more than once a prayer is addressed to him for relief from a disease caused by sin; cf. AV I, 25, 3; VII, 112, 2; VIII, 7, 3. Nevertheless, the disease seems not to be an automatic consequence of sin but to have been sent by Varuṇa or the Gods as a punishment.

we might say, have their own laws. Here the peculiar character of *ṛta* and *dharma* should be taken into account. There is no place for an automatic or mechanical ordering of the universe, or for a mathematical one, or for a certain type of physical determinism, so that miracles must be viewed as exceptions, mercy as a break of justice, or compassion as a sentimental weakness. The situation is different because the pattern of the universe is not physicomathematical. Mercy can come about only as the fruit of a relationship, but the relationship is not exceptional nor does it militate against existing regulations; it is a part of the overall order of *ṛta*. Neither *ṛta* in the first period nor *karman* as it slowly begins to emerge in the pre-Upaniṣadic period is an automatic, merely mechanical force: both *ṛta* and *karman* are always functional and they function according to a set of relational factors, one of which is the human will along with its sentiments and feelings.[71]

Before the three already mentioned subsections we offer a selection consisting of verses mostly from the Ṛg Veda and covering a wide variety of experiences regarding sin and mercy.

The Vedas employ a term for grace which, unlike later words of common use, implies forgiveness pure and simple. The Gods are requested to forgive Man's real sins and also his constitutional shortcomings. Man is never worthy of grace from the divine.[72] *Mṛḍīka,* though occurring only nine times in the Ṛg Veda,[73] denotes the grace that elevates Man and wipes away all his stains.[74] We have here a forgiveness that comes, unpredictably and undeservedly, from the divine.

It would overstep the limits of this anthology to analyze all the passages referred to in the footnotes. Nevertheless, we may remark that this concept rests on a personalistic world view and on an approach to the Gods much more like the approach to an earthly monarch than to a cosmic power.

Among these hymns, one prayer to Agni is a religious composition almost around the word *mṛḷīka.*[75] Each stanza ends on the same theme: ". . . with your mercy come to us!" (v. 1); "We mortals

71. For the concept of *karman* cf. § V A Introduction.

72. Cf. RV I, 17, 1; I, 36, 12; I, 94, 12; I, 114, 2; 9; II, 27, 14; II, 33, 11; 14 (§ II 29); IV, 43, 2; VII, 93, 7; VIII, 48, 9 (§ III 17); X, 25, 3; X, 34, 14 (§ IV 12); X, 64, 1-2.

73. Cf. RV I, 25, 3; 5 (§ I 26); IV, 1, 3; 5; VI, 33, 5; VI, 48, 12; VI, 50, 1; VII, 86, 2 (§ IV 18); VIII, 48, 12 (§ III 17); X, 150, 1-5 (quoted here).

74. The root *mṛḍ-*, Ṛg-Vedic *mṛḷ-*, means first of all to forgive, and then to be merciful, gracious, to bestow favor (cf. § IV 19).

75. RV X, 150 to Agni. *mṛḷīka* is also the name of the *ṛṣi* of this hymn.

invoke you, fiery God, for mercy we are craving" (v. 2); "Show your grace to us who love your laws" (v. 3); "At the great contest we cry for your grace, for victory!" (v. 4); "The priest calls upon mercy" (v. 5). None of the other terms has this implication. *Kṣamā*[76] means the patience and forbearance of the Gods with us mortals, and hence comes to mean mercy, compassion. *Dayā* is mercy that is prompted by a sense of compassion and sympathy. The later words for grace, *anugraha* and *prasāda,* have altogether different implications.

> As a charioteer, O Varuṇa, tethers his horses,
> so with our songs may we bend your heart toward mercy.[77]

Break the Chains That Bind Us *Pāśaṁ śrathāya*

8 Varuṇa scrutinizes Men's deeds, good and bad alike. His piercing eye sees everything, and he, the all-powerful ruler of the universe who combines justice and mercy, knows how to punish the recalcitrant and forgive the penitent. Yet Varuṇa is by no means the only one to whom Men open their hearts and look for justice, compassion, and forgiveness. This selection is composed of verses taken from many different hymns and addressed to different deities: the Waters, Varuṇa, Mother Aditi, Indra, Uṣas, Savitṛ, Viśvedevāḥ, Rudra, Agni, Sūrya, the Vasus, Soma, Bṛhaspati, Heaven, and Earth.[78]

Sin is a stain which the Waters are begged to wash away, a chain which Varuṇa will break, the infringment of a divine law which merits wrath and destruction (i-iv). Sin is so interwoven in human life that Men can well foresee their daily weaknesses and implore Varuna in advance not to get angry (iii). We have here a whole range of feelings: awareness of sin, guilt, anguish, fear, repentance, longing for pardon, hope of purification (vi; xiv-xx). Underlying the complexities of the human heart and mind there are always the need for justification, the protestation of innocence and ignorance, the humble recognition of a constitutive weakness, and a sense of solidarity with other Men (v; vii-viii; xii; xiv). And what could be more expressive than the prayer to Soma-Rudra (xiii) which in-

76. From the root *kṣam-*, to be patient, merciful; cf. *kṣamā*, the earth.
77. RV I, 25, 3 (§ I 26).
78. For practical reasons we have arranged the verses according to the books of the RV to which they belong, though we could equally well have arranged them according to the different Gods they address, or according to the kinds of feelings they express.

cludes everything, bodies and souls, diseases and sins? Rudra, "the God who never slumbers," is asked to be attentive to our cry,[79] for we sometimes sin out of utter carelessness.[80] Man is asking for forgiveness because to do so belongs to his existential condition.[81]

Pāśaṁ śrathāya

RV I, 23, 22

i)

Whatever sin is found in me,
whatever evil I have done,
if I have lied or falsely sworn,
Waters, remove this stain from me!

RV I, 24, 9; 15

ii)

9. Yours, O King, are solaces a hundred, a thousand!
Great and far-reaching be also your favors!
Drive far away from us baneful Destruction.
Remove from us whatever sin we have committed.

15. Loosen the bonds, O Varuna; which bind us.
which crush us, cramping our every movement.
Make us sinless in respect to your Holy Law,
unbound for Boundlessness, O son of Aditi.

RV I, 25, 1-2

iii)

Whatever law of yours, O God Varuṇa,
we, being mortal men, may violate
day after day, do not consign us, we beg,
as prey to death or to your own fierce anger,
to be destroyed by reason of your displeasure.

RV I, 104, 6

iv)

Give us, Lord, a share of sunlight, of waters,
freedom from sin and communion with the living.
Do not tarnish the joy of our hearts
for we have put our trust in your name.

RV I, 123, 3

v)

When you present before the Lord this day,
O Dawn of noble birth, the race of men,

79. Cf. RV II, 33, 15 (§ II 29).
80. Cf. RV X, 37, 12 (§ III 1).
81. We could equally well have quoted from the AV prayers for obtaining pardon (AV VI, 51; VI, 96) and for freedom from sin (AV VI, 97, 2; VI, 121; VII, 77, 3; VII, 83; VII, 89, 3; VII, 112, 2).

may Savitṛ the God, friend of the homestead,
bear witness to the Sun that we are innocent.

RV II, 29, 5

vi) It is I alone, who against you have sinned many times.
You have punished me as a father punishes his gambler son.
My offense, O Gods, remove far; then remove far your snares.
Do not pounce upon me like a bird swooping down on her offspring.

RV IV, 12, 4

vii) God ever youthful, whatever sin unwitting
we have committed, as men are prone to do,
cleanse us, we pray, in the sight of Mother Aditi.
Entirely remove, O Agni, our every sin.

RV IV, 54, 3

viii) If we weak men have sinned against the Gods
through thoughtlessness and frailty or through pride,
absolve us from this fault, O Savitṛ,
and make us clean from sin before Gods and men.

RV V, 2, 7

ix) You set free Śunaḥśepa from a thousand stakes,
when he was already set for the sacrifice.
So Agni, wise Priest, come and take your place
and liberate us from the bonds that bind us.

RV V, 82, 5-6

x) All that is harmful, Savitṛ, God,
drive far away from us, we pray.
Send to us only what is good!

May we be sinless in the sight of Aditi
through the gracious help of the God Savitṛ.
May we obtain all excellent things!

RV VI, 50, 2

xi) Come near to prove us free from sin,
O Sūrya, Lord of mighty power.

RV VI, 51, 7

xii) Do not let us suffer for the sin of others
or ourselves do the deeds you punish, O Gods.

RV VI, 74, 3

xiii) Soma and Rudra, provide for our bodies
all needful medicines. Loosen and withdraw
from within us whatever sin we have committed,
which still adheres within our persons.

RV VII, 88, 6

xiv) If your true friend has sinned against you, O Varuṇa,
he yet remains your friend, the one you love.
Not as sinners, O Living One, may we come before you!
Grant protection to him who hymns you, as to a sage!

RV VIII, 1, 14

xv) We were slow and weak, O Powerful One.
Once again we desire to receive a share
in your bounty, O Hero, and find again
joy in your praise.

RV VIII, 45, 34

xvi) Not for one sin, or two, or three,
slay me, O Mighty One, nor yet for many!

RV X, 35, 3

xvii) Today may that great pair, Heaven and Earth,
preserve us in peace and happiness, free from evil!
May Morning, sending forth her light, drive sin afar!
We pray to Agni, now kindled, to bring us joy.

RV X, 164, 3-5

xviii) 3. If we have sinned, awake, asleep,
knowing, unknowing, through evil nature,
may Agni banish far from us
all such hateful wicked deeds!

4. O Indra and Brahmaṇaspati, hear us!
If we have gone the evil way,
may the farsighted son of heaven
protect us from suppression at the hand of our foes!

5. Victorious now, we are free from sin!
May evil dreams and bad intentions
be directed to those who wish us ill
and those whom we ourselves detest!

AV VI, 45, 1-2

xix) 1. Sin of the mind, depart far away!
Why do you utter improper suggestions?
Depart from this place! I do not want you!
Go to the trees and the forests! My mind
will remain here along with our homes and our cattle.

2. Whatever wrong we have committed, O Agni,
waking or sleeping, by ill will or hatred
or cursing, remove it from us, whatever
displeases you. Thrust it afar!

AV VI, 96, 3

xx) In whatever way we have sinned with our eyes
or our minds or words, awake or asleep,
may Soma by his own pure nature cleanse us!

AV VI, 121, 4

xxi) Open yourself, create free space;
release the bound one from his bonds!
Like a newborn child, freed from the womb,
be free to move on every path!

■ i) Cf. RV X, 9 (§ I 17).
■ ii) 9. King: Varuṇa.
Destruction: *nirṛti*.
15. Cramping our every movement: lit. above, around, and beneath.
Holy Law: *vrata*.
Boundlessness: Aditi. Cf. SU I, 11 (§ IV 21).
■ iii) Law: *vrata*, ordinance. Cf. § IV B b for its synonyms.
3-21. Cf. § I 26.
■ iv) Lord: Indra.
Communion with the living: *jīvaśaṁse*, lit. with the praise (or speech) of the living (beings).
Name: lit. your Indra name.
■ vi) O Gods: Viśvedevāḥ.
■ ix) For the Śunaḥśepa story cf. §III 23 Introduction. Another version, referring to this same story, would read: bound for a thousand cows. In this instance the thousand cows are the price paid in order that Śunaḥśepa may be bound to the sacrificial post.
Priest: *hotṛ*.
■ xii) Sin: *enas*.
Gods: Vasus.
■ xv) O Powerful One: Vṛtra-slayer, i.e., Indra.
■ xvi) O Mighty One: *śūra*, hero, Indra.
■ xvii) Morning: Uṣas.
■ xviii) 4. The evil way: *abhidroha*.
Son of heaven: Aṅgirasa, here an epithet for Agni or Bṛhaspati.
Suppression: *aṁhas*.
5. The last part of stanza 5 has several readings.
■ xix) Sin of the mind: *manaspāpa*.
■ xxi) Open yourself: does it refer to *amṛta*, immortality, of v. 3?
Create free space: *lokaṁ kṛṇu*.
The last two lines are addressed to the person who is freed by this prayer.

a) Evil and Fear

Abhva

The first three hymns of this subsection, given after the Upaniṣadic myth, come from the inexhaustible Ṛg Veda, but they differ widely except in one respect: all evidence Man's deep instinct for survival and his heartfelt cry for delivery from doom. In the first hymn Man uplifts his voice before the overwhelming grandeur of the heavens and the earth, their marvelous harmony and beauty, while at the same time he feels his own smallness and contingency. Man's life here on earth continues to be possible only if the universe in all its complexity runs smoothly. Man prays to be spared the terror of the infinite. The second example is typically "religious," or ritualistic. Here Man does not face the universe but himself and, discovering his creatureliness and sin, sends up a prayer to Agni, the Lord. In the third hymn the feeling is neither cosmic nor anthropological. It is neither the sublimity of the cosmos nor the depravity of Man which gives rise to these deep and authentic human sentiments, but the experience of personal failure, of one's own misery and sinfulness. Here Man does not face himself in an abstract way but is confronted with his own present wretched life which he has failed to master.

The three following hymns are taken from a group of psalms of the Atharva Veda, all of them with striking simplicity asking for forgiveness and mercy. After a psalm requesting pardon for the many faults the priests may commit in performing the sacrifice,[82] we have the simple prayer of a sinner asking to be cleansed and purified, as butter is cleansed after passing through the strainer. Man is a debtor on earth, for he feels himself to be a debtor to God as well as to his fellowmen.[83]

All too often, there is fear in Man's life, but there is also an unlimited confidence that all his shortcomings can be overcome, not so much by looking back to the past as by looking forward toward the future.

We may note that repentance, regarded as an ethical virtue, presupposes certain cosmological assumptions, one of which is a

82. Cf. AV VI, 114.
83. Cf. §§ IV 14; 15.

particular relation with time and, more specifically, with the past. Repentance means to break with the past in one way or another in order to come back to the sinless state, to the original starting point, to start anew. It is the means to recovery of the lost paradise. Now, to make it possible for Man to recover the sinless state, time (more specifically the past) has to be of such a nature as to permit him to start anew. Perhaps this is one of the reasons that explain both the peculiarity of the Vedic conception and the character of the later Vedāntic speculation. Leaving the latter aside, we may briefly consider certain traits of the former.

The word "repentance" does not generally mean merely to feel sorrow for an action one has committed; it connotes also to "turn back," to "recover," to start again, to "reinstall," and the like, all of these being operations connected with the past. It is assumed, moreover, that such reversions are meaningful and possible. This conception of repentance is hardly possible, or rather understandable, given the notion of time which has prevailed and still prevails in the Indian subcontinent. According to that notion, what has happened has happened and no power on earth or in heaven can undo what has been done. The past cannot be canceled. What Man can do, however, is to handle the future so as to modify it and get rid of the impact of the past; it is still in his power to prevent the actions of the past from conditioning by their repercussions the actions of the present.

The English word "rue," probably connected with the Sanskrit *karuṇa*,[84] may convey, perhaps in a less alien manner than "repentance," the meaning of Vedic sorrow for sins committed. "Rue" in a Vedic context does not look back into the past in order to "redeem" it. It looks rather into the future in order to avoid a repetition of the same mistake and also the possible bad results or punishment for the mistake in question. Looking ahead is so deeply built into this world view that later on the idea of rebirth came to have a direct connection with it. The past is neither blotted out nor exempt from the reckoning; it will yield its fruits in the future and it is in view of the menacing future that Man, especially in later times, will feel rueful. Rue then will not expect to abolish the past by regretting it or need the almighty power of God to bring about forgiveness, but

84. Rue comes from the Old English *hrēow*, compassion (cf. also Old Norse *hryggja, hryggva*, distress, grief). *Karuṇa*, n., comes from the root *kṛ-* (*kṛṇoti*), with the meaning of sacred work, holy action (RV I, 100, 7).

will contain a thrust toward the future. Thus the aim of a sacrifice or any expiatory rite is not that of undoing what cannot be undone, but of avoiding the destructive consequences of the past action.[85] The subjective factor is here paramount. An ontic structure has been damaged or broken and rue aims at repairing it insofar as its effects in the future are concerned.

The subjective factor here is not repentance or sorrow, that is, the feeling of having done something intrinsically wrong, of having betrayed the confidence of the Gods or broken a human pact; it is rather fear, fear of incurring punishment, fear of having set in motion a negative movement in the world, of having to go on living with a broken piece or a defective element.

The objective factor, however, is also present. A bad action is certainly bad and is to be deprecated, but the very fact that one has done it means that it could be done and thus that it was in the range of the possible and therefore that it was not absolutely evil. Absolute evil cannot be done. Evil is destructive of goodness. Absolute evil would destroy itself and its own action. What is done, therefore, cannot be ultimately and totally regretted, but only accidentally. This does not mean a wholly selfish or self-centered attitude, but rather a conviction of the objectivity and autonomy of the world of actions. It implies both a sober and realistic attitude to evil actions and a settled belief that the important thing is not to brood over the past, but to prepare for the future. Yet the Lord can burn away our sins.[86] *Ṛta* is more flexible than *karman*. The two conceptions coexist for quite some time. Is any synthesis possible?

The Origin of Evil *Pāpasaṁbhava*

9 If we try to trace the origin of evil in the world, we will find ourselves returning to the origin of the world itself or, in Vedic-Upaniṣadic terms, to the beginning of duality. The Vedas do not provide a clear myth of a fall of Man or of the origin of evil. We shall see later how Yama does not succumb to the temptation presented to him by Yamī and thus becomes, not the first fallen Man, but the first immortal, the first to transcend death.[87] Nevertheless,

85. Cf. AV I, 10, a rite by which a sinner who has offended Varuṇa is forgiven. Cf. SB XIII, 5, 4, 1, the performance of the horse sacrifice for expiatory reasons.
86. Cf. § IV 11.
87. Cf. § V 1.

although it is nowhere explicitly stated that Prajāpati's desire for a second contained within itself the germ of evil and suffering, we cannot escape the fact that dissension and disobedience started precisely with the "second." The Prajāpati myth describes not the original Sin, but the originating Fall. Prajāpati, being alone and "desirous of a second," dismembered himself in order to produce his own offspring, in order to create. Once the world of multiplicity is there, the struggle begins. It is not the fall of Man or the fall of the creature, but the fall of God, if we want to continue to use that idiom. We have seen in the context of sacrifice[88] that Prajāpati "corrected" his initial "mistake" by means of the sacrifice, retrieving thus his original wholeness. Many texts from the Brāhmaṇas describe this process, as also the constant struggle between good and evil powers, the *devas* and the *asuras*, which takes place at all levels of divine, cosmic, and human life.

One of the numerous accounts of the *devāsura* fight, given in the Bṛhadāraṇyaka Upaniṣad, provides a further clue to the origin of evil. The *asuras* are always intent on disturbing any sacred act and any good intention. The *devas*, who are the good powers, are mostly weak, unable to resist the attacks of their opponents. Yet both are the descendants of Prajāpati, Lord of all creatures, and thus they are not two absolute principles, opposed to each other, but inimical brothers, the one assuming the role of good, the other of evil.[89] Even in later periods, the most famous enmities and struggles in Indian myth and history are those that take place among brothers or relatives. The enemy is not a principle of absolute evil, not something totally external to us, but our own brother, a part of ourselves. Evil is here neither substantialized nor isolated in an absolute way.

The *devas*, to continue with our text, want to use the most sacred and powerful means they can find to overcome their enemies. This weapon is the holy chant, the Udgītha. All the human organs—divinities—take part in the chant, but they are not sufficiently strong in themselves and as a result they succumb to the wicked *asuras*. Thus not only do all the organs perform holy actions, pronounce holy words, and think pure thoughts, but they also perform evil deeds, speak evil words, and think evil thoughts. They are

88. Cf. §§ I 6; III 21.

89. Cf. BU I, 3, 7 (in this chapter), where the word used for "enemy" means at the same time the cousin-brother, *bhrātṛvya*.

subject to duality, being torn between good and evil. No human organ is totally pure, without a tinge of evil and sin.

The only "divinity" that is not overcome by the powers of evil is the principle of life, the central life breath, *prāṇa*, which is frequently identified with the *ātman*.[90] Here again we have the strong conviction that life itself is invincible, that the Self is untainted and untouched by evil. Only the external organs, only the nonessential part of reality, and not the very core of life, the *ātman*, can be overpowered by evil or fall victim to the *asuras*. Sin affects Man only in his manifestations, not ultimately in his very Being, unless, of course, he is an *ātmahan*, as the Īśa Upaniṣad says, that is, one who slays his own Self.[91] Thus it is only this selfsame core of our existance which will ultimately overcome evil.

Even when it is overcome, evil is not totally annihilated. In the language of this Upaniṣad, it is only expelled or sent to the very ends of the earth (or, historically speaking, to the limits of one's own "civilized" world); hence it is dangerous to go beyond certain limits, even geographically, because one may be affected by evil. Evil and death are encountered at the limit,[92] and any transgression of the set limits exposes us to their influence. The conquest of evil brings with it the conquest of death.

Pāpasaṁbhava BU I, 3, 1-11

1. The offspring of Prajāpati were of two kinds: Gods and demons. Of these the Gods were the younger and the demons the older. They were disputing the possession of these worlds. The Gods said: "Well, let us overpower the demons at the sacrifice with the Udgītha chant."
2. They said to speech: "Chant for us!" "Very well," she said. So speech chanted for them the Udgītha. Whatever delight is in speech, that she chanted for the Gods; whatever she speaks well, that is for herself. The demons knew: "By this singer they will overpower us." They attacked her and pierced her with evil. The evil that makes one speak what is improper, that is that evil.
3. Then they said to the breath: "Chant for us!" "Very well," he said. So the breath chanted for them the Udgītha. Whatever delight there is in breath, that he chanted for the Gods; whatever fragrance he smells, that is for himself. The demons knew: "By this singer they will overpower us." They attacked him and pierced him with evil. The evil that makes one smell what is improper, that is that evil.

90. For *prāṇa* cf. § II 6.
91. Cf. IsU 3 (§ VII 6).
92. Cf. SB XI, 6, 1 sq. (§ V 21).

4. Then they said to the eye: "Chant for us!" "Very well," he said. So the eye chanted for them the Udgītha. Whatever delight there is in the eye, that he chanted for the Gods; whatever beautiful he sees, that is for himself. The demons knew: "By this singer they will overpower us." They attacked him and pierced him with evil. The evil that makes one see what is improper, that is that evil.

5. Then they said to the ear: "Chant for us!" "Very well," he said. So the ear chanted for them the Udgītha. Whatever delight there is in the ear, that he chanted for the Gods; whatever he hears well, that is for himself. The demons knew: "By this singer they will overpower us." They attacked him and pierced him with evil. The evil that makes one hear what is improper, that is that evil.

6. Then they said to the mind: "Chant for us!" "Very well," he said. So the mind chanted for them the Udgītha. Whatever delight there is in the mind, that he chanted for the Gods; whatever he thinks well, that is for himself. The demons knew: "By this singer they will overpower us." They attacked him and pierced him with evil. The evil that makes one think what is improper, that is that evil. Thus they afflicted these divinities with evil; they pierced them with evil.

7. Then they said to the Life Breath in the mouth: "Chant for us!" "Very well," he said. So the Breath chanted for them. The demons knew: "By this singer they will overpower us." They attacked him and wanted to pierce him with evil. But just as a lump of earth is scattered when it strikes on a stone, in the same way they were scattered in all directions and perished. Therefore the Gods increased and the demons diminished. He who knows this increases in himself and his enemies diminish.

8. Then they said: "What has become of him who thus took care of us? He is within the mouth; he is called Ayāsya Āṅgirasa, for he is "the essence of the limbs."

9. Assuredly, the name of this divinity is Dūr, for death remains far from him. From him who knows this, death is far off.

10. Moreover, this divinity, having warded off evil and death from those other divinities, made them go to the farthest limits of the four regions; there he placed the evils. Therefore one should not go to those people; one should not go to those limits, lest one go to evil and death.

11. As that divinity had warded off evil and death from those other divinities, it led them beyond death.

Cf. the parallel passage CU I, 2, 1 sq.

1. Gods: *devas*.

Demons: *asuras*, devils.

Younger: *kānīyas*, which can also mean inferior, and *jyāyas*, superior.

Udgītha is the chanting of the Sāma Veda. Here the (musical) recitation which involves all the sense organs is a powerful instrument in the struggle between *devas* and *asuras*.

2. Speech: *vāc*.

Delight: *bhoga*, enjoyment or usefulness.

The merit of a proper pronunciation goes to *vāc* herself, whereas the "fruit" of the recitation goes to the *devas*.

Evil: *pāpman*.
Improper: *apratirūpa*, incorrect and also unpleasant.
3. Breath: *prāṇa*, here referring to the organ of smell, not to the Life Breath.
6. Divinities: *devatāḥ*, sense organs.
7. Life Breath in the mouth: *āsanya prāṇa*, the vital Breath.
The Gods increased: *devā abhavan*, lit. they became (powerful).
Increases in himself: *bhavaty ātmanā*, lit. becomes (established) in himself. Cf. TS II, 4, 3, 3.
8. Ayāsya Āṅgirasa: a *ṛṣi* who is identified with the Life Breath, his name being explained as meaning "essence of the limbs": *aṅgānāṁ rasaḥ*, life sap of the body.
9. Pun with Dūr as a name and *dūra*, far.
10. Limits: *anta*, the ends of the known world. Cf. the story of Bhṛgu who is sent to the "ends of the regions" to meet with evil (SB XI, 6, 1 sq., § V 21).
11. Led them beyond: *atyavahat*, carried over.
In vv. 12-16 there follows the description of how the different divinities (*devatā*), i.e., sense organs, are led beyond death. The new life is not a disincarnated one!

Heaven and Earth Deliver Us from Evil *Dyāvā-pṛthivyau*

10 *Dyāvā-pṛthivī*, Heaven and Earth, form a pair indissolubly linked. In not a single hymn of the Ṛg Veda is Heaven mentioned alone, while Earth is addressed alone only in one short hymn.

Another hymn says explicitly that Heaven was created from the head and Earth from the feet of the *puruṣa*.[93] Here the question of the first stanza seems to be somewhat rhetorical, for the poet does not go on to answer the query *how*, but states that between them Heaven and Earth support all other beings and that their tension is relational so that the one cannot be without the other. There is no earth without a heaven and heaven would be devoid of meaning if it were not populated by the dwellers on earth. Heaven and Earth encompass human life and even the life of the Gods. They are the parents of Men and Gods alike. We are all embarked on the same adventure. It would be misleading to speak of "nature-mysticism" in this connection. This hymn is describing rather the all-encompassing reality that shelters the divine-human drama. It is precisely the awareness of this reality which evokes on the lips of the poet and in the heart of his hearers an urgent cry for deliverance from the horrors and evils of the cosmos. This prayer for protection is addressed, not to another power mightier than the one that threatens, but to the power that, like a mother whose child runs back to her after a scolding, both menaces and shelters us.

93. Cf. RV X, 90, 14 (§ I 5).

Dyāvā-pṛthivyau

RV I, 185

1. Which of these two came earlier, which came later?
How did they come to birth? Who, O Seers, can discern it?
They contain within them all that has a name,
while days and nights revolve as on a wheel.

2. You two, though motionless and footless, nurture
a varied offspring having feet and movement.
Like parents clasping children to their bosoms,
O Heaven and Earth, deliver us from evil!

3. I crave from the Infinite a matchless favor,
generous, irresistible, resplendent, inviolable, awesome.
O you two worlds, procure it for this worshiper!
O Heaven and Earth, deliver us from evil!

4. Close to them may we stay—they know no suffering,
these parents of the Gods who grant men favors.
Both are divine, with days and nights alternate.
O Heaven and Earth, deliver us from evil!

5. These twin maidens, like two friendly sisters
nestled close together, rest in their parents' bosom
and kiss together the center of the world.
O Heaven and Earth, deliver us from evil!

6. These wide and lofty realms, the parents of the Gods,
I invoke with reverence, their favor asking;
they bring us life, showing us kindly faces.
O Heaven and Earth, deliver us from evil!

7. This far-flung Pair, variegated and vast,
I at this sacrifice address with awe.
Quick to our aid, they set us in a state of bliss.
O Heaven and Earth, deliver us from evil!

8. Such sin as we at any time committed
against the Gods, a friend, or a family chief,
of this may our prayerful musing be expiation!
O Heaven and Earth, deliver us from evil!

9. May Heaven and Earth, twin objects of men's praises,
bless and attend me with their help and favor,
to the liberal God-fearer grant greater riches!
May we be strong, O Gods, nourished on plenty!

10. With wisdom have I now uttered this truth,
calling, for all to hear, on Earth and Heaven.
Guard us from every fault and erring course;
like father and mother succor and protect us.

11. Fulfill, O Heaven and Earth, this my prayer,
with which, O Father and Mother, I now address you.
Be of all Gods the nearest with your favors,
in order that we may savor your quickening food.

This hymn, like many others, is susceptible of a wide variety of interpretations. There is throughout a reference to the problem of time.

1. All that has a name: *yad dha nāma,* all existing things.
2. Having feet and movement: i.e., space and time. Heaven and Earth are beyond space and time and thus are said to generate them.

Evil: *a-bhva,* immense power, horror, etc.

3. The Infinite: Aditi.

The six adjectives, each difficult to translate by a single term, are *anehas, dātra, anarva, svarvat, avadha, namasvat,* all related to Aditi with a genitive. For a reference to Aditi as the light of life, cf. RV II, 27, 14; IV, 25, 3; VII, 82, 10; X, 185, 3.

You two worlds: *rodasī,* twin firmaments (in voc. dual).

4. They know no suffering: *atapyamāne,* they are not (painfully) heated.
5. Twin maidens: day and night.

Center of the world: lit. the navel (*nābhi*), probably referring to the altar of sacrifice.

6. With reverence: *ṛtena,* sincerely, or according to the true order, rite.

Life: *amṛta,* immortality.

They bring us life . . .: lit. they bear immortality, having their benevolent faces turned toward us.

9. May we be strong, . . . nourished on plenty: *iṣā madanta iṣayema. Iṣ* means a draught, refreshment, refreshing waters of heaven, strength, food, sap, libation.
10. Truth: *ṛta. Ṛta* can be truth as well as the truly or duly performed act (action, sacrifice). Fault: *durita.*
11. Fulfill: lit. let this become true (*idaṁ satyam astu*). The idea is that all gifts come to us from Heaven and Earth—a reference to libation, sap, and the Soma-juice.

Savor your quickening food: *iṣam vṛjanaṁ jīradānum,* the life sap that strengthens and gives life.

May the Lord Burn Away Our Sin! *Śucir agniḥ*

11 In this heartful prayer, the human, divine, and cosmic elements are all present. Agni is the material fire, but he is also God and the fire within us. He shines in all directions, purifying all he touches; he kindles our own interior fire and imparts to all fires their power and strength. He illumines us and thus rescues us from darkness.

This hymn affirms clearly that there is a fire that has power to burn away all impurities and sins. Unlike other creatures, Man has the privilege and the responsibility of praying for the cleansing of his stains; or, to express it in stronger and more appropriate terms, for the cauterizing of his evil. The message of this psalm is that such an operation is still possible and needful: Agni may still burn away our sin.

Śucir agniḥ RV I, 97

1. Shine brightly, Agni, and chase away
our sin; beam down upon us grace.
May the Lord burn away our sin!

2. We make our offering to you
for fruitful fields and pleasant homes.
May the Lord burn away our sin!

3. May he and our elders who worship surpass
all others who sing your praises!
May the Lord burn away our sin!

4. May high priests spring from you, O Lord!
May we also be born again in you!
May the Lord burn away our sin!

5. The Lord's all-conquering beams go far;
his face shines bright on every side.
May the Lord burn away our sin!

6. Your face is turned toward every side.
Everywhere you pass, the all-protecting.
May the Lord burn away our sin!

7. O God, whose face shines every side,
convey us safely as in a boat.
May the Lord burn away our sin!

8. Rescue us safely, as in a boat,
across the stream, from dark to light.
May the Lord burn away our sin!

1. May the Lord burn away our sin: *apa naḥ śośucad agham,* lit. consumes away every evil, *agha* being the antithesis of *rayi,* spiritual and material wealth, grace, mercy, blessing, welfare. For *rayi* cf. §§ I 4; II 6; II 34; VII Introductions.

The Lord: Agni, throughout. For Agni cf. §§ I 22; III 2; 3; 4, and the several hymns to Agni in § VII.

2. Fruitful fields . . . : lit. desiring the possession of good fields (*sukṣetriyā*), of spiritual welfare (*sugātuyā*), and of prosperity (*vasūyā*). Cf. the symbolism of the field (*kṣetra*). Cf. § II C a.

4. There is, however, another possible interpretation: Your faithful worshipers are we. Give to us the blessings of children.

Born again: *pra jāyemahi,* from *pra-jan-* to be born or produced, to become an embryo, to be begotten; here, to be reckoned as your children.

8. Rescue us: *parṣā,* from the root *pṛ-* which means to protect, bring over, deliver from, rescue.

Lament of a Rueful Gambler

Akṣāḥ

12 Among the hymns of the Ṛg Veda the lament of the unlucky gambler is certainly one of the most vivid and realistic. It is a dialogue of the gambler with his conscience (represented by two "witnesses," the poet himself and the God Savitṛ) when passion for the gaming board has destroyed his happiness.

The first verses describe in a graphic fashion how, carried away by the lure of the dice, he has been the downfall of his family. He would like to renounce gambling but is incapable of doing so (v. 5). The irresistible attraction of the fatal dice is described both realistically and poetically (vv. 7, 9). Once again he is overwhelmed by remorse and by the misery of being gripped so inextricably by his craving. Suddenly, however, he makes a decision to start a new life, to abandon the dice board, make his wife happy, and cultivate his fields. It is the God Savitṛ who bids him rebuild his life and who encourages and inspires him to the task.

The Indian reader will here remember one of the climaxes of the Mahābhārata. Yudhiṣṭhira, the living symbol of righteousness, the embodiment of *dharma,* the real hero of the whole epic, had a weakness for dice. He fell under their spell, and in the presence of King Dhṛtarāṣṭra and all the Pāṇḍavas as well as of Duryodhana and all his retinue, played and gambled away all that he had, he himself and even Draupadī, the virtuous wife of all the five brothers. Having regained all that he had lost because of the presense of mind of Draupadī, who challenged the validity of Yudhiṣṭhira's wagering her, when he had already lost his own freedom, he yet returned to the fatidic game and lost. As a result he and his brothers were forced to spend the famous twelve years in the forest and a thirteenth year in hiding before the great battle. Against this background the hymn surpasses its moral character and attains epic grandeur. The greatest Man is not perfect and yet his weakness reveals the power of *dharma* the more forcefully.

Akṣāḥ

RV X, 34

[The Gambler:]

1. These nuts that once tossed on tall trees in the wind
but now smartly roll over the board, how I love them!
As alluring as a draught of Soma on the mountain,
the lively dice have captured my heart.

2. My faithful wife never quarreled with me
or got angry; to me and my boon companions
she was always kind, yet I've driven her away
for the sake of the ill-fated throw of a die.

[The Chorus or the Poet:]

3. His wife's mother loathes him, his wife rejects him;
he implores people's aid but nowhere finds pity.
A luckless gambler is no more good
than an aged hack to be sold on the market.

4. Other men make free with the wife of a man
whose money and goods the eager dice have stolen.
His father and mother and brothers all say:
"He is nothing to us. Bind him, put him in jail!"

[The Gambler:]

5. I make a resolve that I will not go gaming.
So my friends depart and leave me behind.
But as soon as the brown nuts are rattled and thrown,
to meet them I run, like an amorous girl.

[The Chorus or the Poet:]

6. To the meeting place the gambler hastens.
Shall I win? he asks himself, hoping and trembling.
But the throws of the dice ruin his hopes,
giving the highest scores to his opponent.

7. Dice, believe me, are barbed: they prick and they trip,
they hurt and torment and cause grievous harm.
To the gambler they are like children's gifts, sweet as honey,
but they turn on the winner in rage and destroy him.

8. Fifty-three strong, this band jumps playfully,
like Savitṛ, the God whose statutes are true.
They pay no heed to the anger of the powerful;
the king himself pays heed to them.

9. Downward they roll, then jump in the air!
Though handless themselves, they can keep the upper hand
over those who have! On the board, like magic coals,
they consume, though cold, the player's heart to ashes.

10. Abandoned, the wife of the gambler grieves.
Grieved, too, is his mother as he wanders vaguely.
Afraid and in debt, ever greedy for money,
he steals in the night to the home of another.

11. He is seized by remorse when he sees his wife's lot,
beside that of her neighbor with well-ordered home.
In the morning, however, he yokes the brown steeds
and at evening falls stupid before the cold embers.

12. To the mighty chieftain of your whole band,
the one who has become the king of your troop,
to him I show my ten fingers extended.
No wealth do I withhold! I swear I speak truth!

[The God Savitṛ:]

13. Steer clear of dice. Till well your own field.
Rejoice in your portion and value it highly.
See there, O Gambler, your cattle, your wife.
This is the counsel of noble Savitṛ.

[The Chorus or the Poet:]

14. Grant us your friendship, have mercy upon us!
Do not overwhelm us with your fierce attack!
May your anger and evil intention be assuaged!
Let the brown dice proceed to ensnare another!

The Sanskrit indicates by means of direct and indirect discourse those who participate in this hymn. In our version we introduce the speakers at the beginning of the respective stanzas.

1. On the mountain: Mūjavat, name of a mountain and also of a *soma*-plant growing on that mountain. Dice: Vibhīdaka, name of a tree (*Terminalia bellerica*) whose nuts were used as dice.

7. Like children's gifts: *kumāra-deṣṇāḥ*, gifts that children give but then ask to have returned.

8. Fifty-three: or 150, i.e., three times 50.
Like Savitṛ, the God whose statutes are true: *deva iva savitā satyadharmā*, ordaining man's fates.

12. Addressed to the dice, as is also v. 14.

Cleanse Me from My Sins *Pāpamocana*

13 In this prayer addressed to all the Gods, the psalmist prays that he may be set free from all possible sins, committed willingly or unwillingly, in the waking state or asleep, in the past or in the future. The comparisons that the poet uses here remind us of different sacrificial acts. He feels that his guilty conscience ties him to a state of sin just as a victim is tied to the sacrificial stake, and he begs for release from sin in the same way as a victim is freed from the stake. Again, he wants to be as completely pure from the defilement of guilt as a man who is pure after a cleansing bath, or to be as transparent and free from impurities as sacrificial butter that has been carefully strained.

These comparisons are just faint expressions of a deep and strong yearning to get rid for all time of all guilt, wickednesses, and impurities—to be wholly purified. However, this yearning can never be fulfilled once and for all, and the poet, knowing human frailty only too well, prays in advance to be set free from future sin.

Pāpamocana

AV VI, 115

1. Any sin we have committed,
consciously or unconsciously,
deliver us from it,
O Gods one and all!

2. From whatever sin
I, a sinner, committed
awake or asleep,
may both past and future
set me free,
as if from a stake
to which I was fastened!

3. May I be set free
as if loosed from a pillar
or loosed from the dirt
after taking a bath!
May all the Gods
cleanse me from sin,
as butter is pure
after passing through the strainer!

1. Sin: *enas,* throughout.
Consciously or unconsciously . . . : cf. RV X, 164, 3 (§ IV 8).
Gods: *viśvedevāḥ.*
2. Stake: *drupada,* wooden pillar, a post (to which captives are tied), any pillar or column.

Forgive Us Our Debts *Ānṛṇāḥ syāma*

14 This hymn is addressed to Agni who, like Varuṇa, unlooses all bonds. Man is preoccupied with the debt he owes to the "other world." Whether it is the prayer of a man who in old age thinks of his imminent departure to the beyond and who wants to be cleared from any debt to Yama and to the Gods, or whether it is simply the routine prayer of a man engaged in the daily sacrifice, the same sentiment is apparent: "Man, so soon as he is born, is to be regarded, his whole person, as a debt owed to death."[94] It is through sacrifice that he purchases himself back from death. Throughout his lifetime he is preoccupied with freeing himself from

94. SB III, 6, 2, 16 (§ III 23).

his existential debt to his fellowmen, to the sages, to the ancestors, and to the Gods,[95] who form a link between this world and the other. Furthermore there are precise regulations regarding the special offering due to Yama.[96] One hymn of the Atharva Veda says that when the deceased reaches Yama's realm he has to pay one sixteenth of his "wish-fulfilling sacrifices" but that he may discharge this debt in advance in his earthly life by offering a ram in sacrifice.[97]

Ānṛṇāḥ syāma AV VI, 117

1. The food that I eat
   and the debt that I owe
   and my offering to Yama
   which ever sustains me—
   O Agni, make me
   free from these debts,
   you who know
   how to loosen all bonds.

2. Standing before you,
   we restore this gift.
   I restore it, O Agni,
   the grain I have eaten,
   the living for the living,
   so that I may become
   free from guilt and debt.

3. Free from guilt and debt,
   in this world and the higher,
   free from guilt and debt
   in the third world also;
   in the world of the Gods
   and in those of the Fathers,
   on all our paths,
   may we ever remain
   free from guilt and debt!

1. Free from . . . debts: *anṛṇa.*

2. The living for the living: *jīvā jīvebhyo;* i.e., grain, as a living seed, is offered on behalf of living persons.

Free from guilt and debt: *anṛṇa,* i.e., without *ṛṇa,* which includes both what we owe to the Gods because of our guilt and to men because of our debts. Cf. what has already been said on *ṛṇa* (§§ III 23; IV Introductions).

95. Cf. SB I, 7, 2, 1-5 (§ III 23 and Introduction).
96. Cf. AV VI, 116, 1.
97. Cf. AV III, 29.

Free Us from Our Creditors *Ānṛṇya*

15 Gambling, as is well recognized, was one of the favorite pastimes of Vedic Man. As we have already seen,[98] this pastime led to the ruin of the gambler and of his family and aroused in him strong remorse for the money wasted, the life spoiled, and the debts contracted. The present hymn, another supplication of a remorseful gambler, begs for forgiveness for cheating at the gaming table. As in the preceding psalm the man who utters the prayer may or may not be on the point of death. He is worried at the thought that the man he has wronged may get him tied up in the land of Yama; that is, he may have to pay there a heavy debt for his cheating.

This prayer, which is addressed, it seems, to two Apsarases (who like Varuṇa scrutinize Men's deeds) and to all the Gods, expresses sincere regret and the fear of well-deserved punishment. It is a cry for mercy and compassion.

Ānṛṇya AV VI, 118

1. For the various ways we have sinned with our hands,
desiring to possess the reward of the dice,
forgive us this day our guilt and our debt,
you frightening and all-conquering spirits.

2. Forgive the transgressions we committed while gambling,
you terrifying ones, who scrutinize men.
May we not be compelled to pay the debt
in the world of Yama, tied with a rope!

3. Let not my creditor or his wife whom I approach
or the man to whom I go begging, O Gods,
raise their voices against me overwhelmingly,
O you divine spirits, companions of the Gods!

1. Guilt and . . . debt: *ṛṇa*.
Frightening and all-conquering spirits: allusion to two Apsarases.
2. Transgressions: *kilbiṣāṇi*.
Who scrutinize men: *rāṣṭrabhṛt*, lit. scrutinizer of the people; he who looks after the order of the country.
3. Divine spirits: Apsarases.
Companions of the Gods: *patnī*, wives of the Gandharvas.

98. Cf. § IV 12.

b) The Merciful Lord

Varuṇa

Varuṇa, the Universal Ruler, the mightly Lord who establishes, controls, and surveys both the operation of cosmic law and the deeds and activities of Men, is along with Indra the most prominent of the Vedic symbols for the Divine.[99] It is not simply that he combines in himself several attributes or functions; rather, he embodies in himself various completely contrasted features. The result of accumulating in the divine so many attributes, however, in no way diminishes his vitality, concreteness, and thus his effective power.

There is an intriguing continuity in the religious history of mankind. Any living faith, any popular feast, any sacred place, and effective God, even any doctrine prevalent at a given time, is invariably older than its official formulation. Certainly there are changes and there is evolution, but there are no radical creations in the religious world. Varuṇa is probably of pre-Vedic origin, adopted and transformed by the Aryans on their arrival. He has predecessors as well as successors. In fact he passes on his lordship to Prajāpati in the later Vedic period and his name then continues as only a Water-God.

He is the God of justice to whose scrutiny the life of Man lies completely exposed. In him resides power to inflict punishment or to free Men from their sins, to produce in them a sense of fear and humility, admission of guilt, and regret. The hymns addressed to Varuṇa are unrivaled for the sincerity of their expression, for the depth of their contrition, and for their strong confidence in the mercy of God.

Before presenting the texts concerning sin and pardon we must acquaint ourselves with Varuṇa and the part he plays in Vedic religiousness. First of all, Varuṇa is a Sky-God and seems to come into prominence once the luster of Dyu, the personification of the sky, is on the wane.[100] Varuṇa is the "encompassing one," accord-

99. Though he is quantitatively not prominent in the RV (10 hymns to him alone, 23 to him and Mitra, and 9 to him and Indra), Varuṇa occupies one of the first places—if not the first—in the Vedic pantheon. Scattered references are to be found throughout the RV (35 times in the tenth *maṇḍala*, for instance).

100. Dyu (cf. the greek Zeus) is the actual sky, occurring about 500 times in the RV alone. He is also called *dyaus pitā*, "Father heaven" (RV I, 164, 33; I, 191, 6; VI, 51, 5).

ing to the most probable etymological reading.[101] His eye with which he sees everything[102] is the sun.[103] He is "farsighted,"[104] and he has around him his own watchmen,[105] his messengers,[106] and his wise helpers.[107]

No wonder that this master of the sky is represented as sovereign Lord over Men and Gods and holds sway over all natural phenomena: no bird can fly, no river can run, no human heart can beat, nothing in the three heavens or on the three earths can "do its own thing" without his knowledge and his permission.[108] Varuṇa is King, *rājan*,[109] king of the universe, *samrāj*,[110] and king of Men and Gods alike.[111] He rules over all that exists.[112] He has set firm the earth and the sky: "The all-wise Asura propped up the heavens and measured out the broad earth's expanse. All worlds does the great King hold in his sway."[113] "He has put intelligence in hearts, fire in the waters, the sun in the sky, and the *soma*-plant on the hills."[114] The stars and the waters obey his decrees.[115]

Varuṇa is, next, a Water-God. He is the Lord of the waters[116] and rivers and, with Mitra, the dispenser of rain:[117]

> Hither descend, O mighty kings and princes,
> protectors of cosmic order, lords of rivers.
> O Mitra and Varuṇa, generous givers of bounty,
> send to us rain, the bringer of every blessing![118]

101. From the root *vṛ-*, to cover, to encompass. Cf. Varana in the Avesta as the "all-encompassing sky," though there is a learned controversy regarding the origin and nature of this God (cf. also the greek Uranos). Cf. also the Armenian word *garuna*, sky. Other etymologists derive Varuṇa from *vāri*, water (*vār* in Avestan is connected with *varṣa* in Sanskrit, i.e., rain), and cite as their justification the close relation of Varuṇa with the waters. Others adduce the root *uer*, to bind (cf. the Palaeo-Asiatic root *baru*; the Sanskrit *varaka*, strap; the Lithuanian *weru*, to thread, to embroider, etc.), stressing the ethical character of Varuṇa, the looser of bonds. Finally, others prefer the root *ver-*, to speak, and consider Varuṇa, along with the inseparable Mitra and Aryaman, the true speaker.

102. Cf. RV VII, 34, 10; AV IV, 16 passim (§ IV 16).

103. Cf. RV I, 50, 6 (§ III 2).

104. Cf. RV I, 25, 5; 16 (§ I 26); VIII, 90, 2.

105. Cf. RV I, 25, 13 (§ I 26). Watchmen, *spaśa*, are also mentioned now and again in connection with other Gods, such as Agni and Soma, but in a coincidental manner and not, as is Varuṇa, as their inseparable satellites.

106. Cf. AV IV, 16, 4 (§ IV 16).

107. Cf. RV VI, 67, 5.

108. Cf. RV I, 24, 6; I, 25 passim (§ I 26); VII, 87, 5; VIII, 41, 1; 7; etc.

109. Cf. RV VII, 34, 11. The *rājasūya* sacrifice is offered specifically to him: SB V, 4, 3, 1.

110. Cf. RV I, 136, 1; VIII, 42, 1 (quoted here).

111. Cf. RV II, 27, 10; X, 132, 4. The Brāhmaṇas call him frequently "King of the Gods." Cf., e.g., MaitS II, 2, 1; TB II, 5, 7, 6.

112. Cf. RV V, 85, 3; VII, 87, 6.

113. RV VIII, 42, 1.

114. RV V, 85, 2.

115. Cf. RV I, 24, 10 (§ VI B b Antiphon).

116. Cf. AV V, 24, 4-5 (§ VII 55).

117. Cf. RV V, 63 passim, etc.

118. RV VII, 64, 2.

Or, as we are going to read, he makes "the rivers flow,"[119] It is this role that he retains after his eclipse. He remains God of the seas.[120]

Third, we turn our attention to the source of Varuṇa's might, that is, to his power, for which one of the most *powerful* and *elusive* terms of Indian *wisdom*,[121] *māyā*,[122] is often used. Varuṇa is the great *māyin* among the Gods.[123] It is by *māyā* that Varuṇa establishes the earth. As the poet says:

> I will speak of the mysterious deed of Varuṇa renowned,
> the Lord Immortal,
> who, standing in the firmament, has measured out the earth,
> as it were, with a yardstick.[124]

Through *māyā* Mitra and Varuṇa send the rain and through *māyā* they keep a watch on their law;[125] through *māyā* the sunbird is garlanded.[126]

The *māyā* of Varuṇa[127] or of Mitra and Varuṇa[128] is good, but there can also be bad *māyā*, as in the word *durmāyu*, user of bad craft.[129] It has been said that the English word "craft" denotes fairly well the ambivalence of *māyā*, a power that, being derived from a certain uncommon knowledge, can be used either for good or for bad purposes; thus it is an intelligent power or a cunning shrewdness.[130] This power appears to be detachable from the one to whom

119. RV II, 28, 4 (§ IV 17).

120. This function begins to appear clearly in the AV, e.g., IV, 15, 12; VII, 83, 1. In the Brāhmaṇas it is already stated that "Varuṇa is in the waters" (TB I, 6, 5, 6). Hence arises his connection with snakes, the *nāgas* in the MB, where we also read that the Gods made Varuṇa the Lord of waters (MB IX, 46). Cf. also XII, 122, where Śiva makes him Lord of waters, and MahanarU 160: " . . . Varuṇa, King of the primordial waters, he who purifies from every sin; it is through him that we are delivered from evil." Thus the "supernatural" cleansing power of the waters.

121. The three italicized words give some idea of the meaning of the word *māyā*: power, elusiveness (deceit), wisdom.

122. The most obvious etymology, put forward by the first generation of Orientalists, is today once again considered to be the most likely, i.e., the root *mā-*, to measure, to build, to construct. There is a connection here with the Greek *mētis*, insight, shrewdness, cunning, advice, craft. It has also been related to the Greek *mimos*, imitator, and the Latin *mirus*, wonderful. In Avestan there is a word *māyu*, skillful, clever, and there are cognate Indo-European words meaning to nod, to indicate by a sign, to deceive, swindle, lie, enchant. Another proposed etymology is from the root *man-*, to think, while yet other translations give "change," "creative act."

123. Cf. RV VI, 48, 14; VII, 28, 4; X, 99, 10; X, 147, 5.

124. RV V, 85, 5. Mysterious deed: *māyā*. Note the relation here between *māyā* and *māna*, measure, both from the root *mā-*, to measure.

125. Cf. RV V, 63, 3; 7.

126. Cf. RV X, 177, 1.

127. Cf. RV V, 85, 5-6; VIII, 41, 3.

128. Cf. RV I, 151, 9; III, 61, 7.

129. Cf. RV III, 30, 15. Note also that we sometimes find the word *sumāyā* indicating the good use of this power. Cf. RV I, 88, 1; I, 167, 2.

130. Indra defeats by his own *māyā* the *māyā* of the demons (cf. RV I, 11, 7; V, 31, 7), but sorcerers also use *māyā* (RV VII, 104, 24 [§ V 20]), and men of evil power are called *māyin* (RV I, 39, 2). Indra is *purumāya*, having much *māyā* (RV VI, 18, 12). The Maruts (RV V, 63, 6), Agni (RV, III, 27, 7; V, 2, 9), and Soma (RV IX, 83, 3) all use *māyā*.

it belongs, so that it may be used for different purposes, both good and bad. It has indeed both a personal and cosmic character. No wonder that, since power tends to corrupt, even this greatest power of the Gods is corrupted not only in its usage by them but also in the very conception of its meaning, so that later on *māyā* came to mean the power of deception and delusion.

In Upaniṣadic documents the word appears for the first time in the Śvetāśvatara Upaniṣad, where it still has the same basic meaning as in the Vedas and an undeniable ambivalence, which gives rise to the post-Upaniṣadic meaning of *māyā* as illusion, trick, error, or veil of ignorance:[131] "Know that *māyā* is Nature and the *māyin* the mighty Lord."[132]

Fourth, we need to connect Varuṇa with another of the pivotal concepts of the whole Vedic world view: the notion of *ṛta*.[133] Varuṇa and Mitra are the guardians of *ṛta*:

> Those Lords of *ṛta*, of light, I invoke
> who uphold *ṛta* by means of *ṛta*,
> Mitra and Varuṇa.[134]

Through Varuṇa's *ṛta* order is established in the universe.[135] It is Varuṇa's *ṛta* that keeps the rivers in their beds,[136] for he is the fountainhead of *ṛta*[137] to such a degree that when Agni is striving for *ṛta* he is called Varuṇa.[138] "According to Eternal Law you govern the whole world."[139] It is by *ṛta* also that Men are saved from their iniquities, for this concept does not refer only to cosmic order; it includes also the ethical sphere which is not separate and autonomous but is ontonomically linked with the state of the cosmos.

The fifth and most distinctive character of Varuṇa, the ethical God, as he has sometimes been called, though this expression is somewhat alien, is that he is a forgiving and merciful God. He does not merely go about his own business in splendid isolation or even devote himself to the protection of mankind. He liberates, he is merciful, he forgives; his justice is more than impersonal. *Ṛta*, in fact, when in the "hands" of Varuṇa, acquires personal features, or,

131. In fact, the current translations range from "creative power" to "illusion." Cf. SU IV, 9.
132. *māyāṁ tu prakṛtiṁ viddhi, māyinaṁ tu maheśvaram*. SU IV, 10. *Prakṛti*, nature, is *māyā* as much as *māyā* is *prakṛti*.
133. Cf. § III B Introduction, on *ṛta* in connection with Sacrifice.
134. RV I, 23, 5. Cf. also V, 63, 1.
135. Cf. RV V, 62, 1.
136. Cf. RV II, 28, 4 (§ IV 17).
137. Ibid.
138. Cf. RV X, 8, 5.
139. RV V, 63, 7.

if we prefer, relational character, or, in the words of the Ṛg Veda, a pure and beautiful face.[140] *Ṛta* in his hands becomes more than a legalistic system. *Ṛta* is righteousness and *anṛta* simply a lie,[141] and it is Varuṇa who discerns the one from the other.[142]

Varuṇa's ordinances are firm.[143] Curiously enough, what does vary are the names given to Varuṇa's injunctions: *vrata*,[144] observance; *dharma*,[145] law; *dhāma*,[146] decree; *kratu*,[147] will; *dakṣa*,[148] power.

As we have already seen, moral order and cosmic order are not two separate things. It would not be proper, however, to say that there is no moral order and that all is cosmic. It would be equally improper to affirm that there is no cosmic order and that all is subsumed into a moral world view. The fact is that this division does not apply and that the real order of the world is, if we still want to employ these terms, both moral and cosmic. Sin, therefore, is neither simply a moral concern of the individual or of the group, nor merely the cosmic catastrophe of a natural stain.

Varuṇa undoubtedly manifests anger [149] and punishes falsity, *anṛta*;[150] his well-known watchmen inspect Men's lives[151] and keep an account of their sins.[152] Yet these and similar attributes do not overshadow the fact that in almost every hymn to Varuṇa there is a prayer for the gracious forgiveness of sins and the removal of guilt, in a way that is not employed for any of the other Vedic deities. Significantly, no anecdotes are told about Varuṇa.

The two hymns given below, Ṛg Veda VII, 86, and VII, 89, are two masterpieces illustrating a rather uncommon feature in Vedic spirituality.[153] Man is not aware of his sin and yet is conscious that Varuṇa is angry with him. Recognizing that there must have been a break in the fellowship with God, he declares himself to be sinful and from the bottom of his heart asks for personal forgiveness, not

140. Cf. RV VI, 51, 1.
141. Cf. RV IV, 5, 5 (§ V 20); V, 12, 4; VII, 60, 5, plus references given in § IV Introduction.
142. Cf. *satyānṛte janānām*, RV VII, 49, 3 (§ I 16).
143. The recurrent term is *dhṛtavrata*. Cf. RV I, 25, 8; 10 (§ I 26).
144. Cf. RV I, 25, 1 (§ IV 8); II, 28, 8 (§ IV 17).
145. Cf. RV VII, 89, 5 (§ IV 19).
146. Cf. RV IV, 5, 4; VI, 67, 9.
147. Cf. RV IV, 42, 1-2.
148. Cf. RV VII, 65, 1.
149. Cf. RV VII, 62, 4.
150. Cf. RV VII, 60, 5; VII, 61, 5.
151. Cf. RV VII, 61, 3.
152. Cf. RV VII, 60 passim; VII, 65, 3.
153. Most of the hymns that express confession of sin, prayers for forgiveness, and resolutions to be more obedient belong to one particular group of hymns connected with the priestly Vasiṣṭha family.

only for the reparation of a rupture in cosmic order. Varuṇa is a merciful and gracious God who not only chastises the sinner[154] but at the same time provides innumerable remedies.[155] Sin is here the transgression of Varuṇa's law,[156] which, indeed, is often quite explicit: not to curse or kill,[157] not to deceive,[158] not to gamble,[159] not to cheat when playing.[160] What Varuṇa punishes severely is untruthfulness, which is the worst transgression Man can commit and for which Man ceaselessly begs for mercy. It is in truth that Varuṇa's unrivaled sovereignty is grounded:

> This great God rules over all Gods,
> for the precepts of Varuṇa, the King, are true.[161]

He Counts the Blinks of Every Eye *Satyānṛta-samīkṣaka*

16 This hymn, which, though not centered on forgiveness, is one of the most complete descriptions of Varuṇa, is given here as an introduction to his theology. It is extremely well composed, harmoniously blending general aspects with concrete instances. The first stanzas describe the omnipresent Varuṇa. Among all the Gods Varuṇa is the one who knows perfectly all that Men are doing wherever they are, be it openly or secretly. He penetrates into the inmost recesses of the human heart; he cannot be deceived. If the human heart and mind are the special objects of his love and concern, he is nonetheless involved in the cosmos also: he is both great and small; the sky is his abode and yet he is equally present in a drop of water. Stanzas 6 and 7, though related to his omnipresence, contain a strong and realistic imprecation. The poet, in righteous (or unrighteous) indignation, makes an appeal to Varuṇa the just, the one God who leaves no sinner unpunished, especially the liar who, it is said, receives just retribution for his lies, while the truthful man goes on his way in peace. Here, undoubtedly, is a strong sense of right and wrong, as well as a powerful desire for retribution which demands that the wicked of this world be justly punished.

154. Cf. RV II, 28, 7 (§ IV 17).
155. Cf. RV I, 24, 9 (§ IV 8).
156. Cf. RV I, 25, 1-2 (§ IV 8); VII, 86 (§ IV 18).
157. Cf. RV I, 41, 8.
158. Cf. RV II, 27, 16; VII, 65, 3.
159. Cf. RV II, 29, 5 (§ IV 8).
160. Cf. RV V, 85, 8.
161. AV I, 10, 1.

The eighth stanza is a kind of doxology. We may give a free version:

God is the point of convergence of all things.
He is the point of divergence of all.
God belongs to us; he belongs to the others.
God is divine; he is also human.

Satyānṛta-samīkṣaka AV IV, 16

1. The mighty overseer on high
espies our deeds, as if he were
quite close at hand.
The Gods through him know all men do,
though often men contrive to act
all stealthily.

2. A man may stand quite still, or walk,
or run, or flee, or hide himself,
as he thinks, secretly;
two men may hatch a plot together;
Varuṇa knows it all, being present
as the third one.

3. This earth is his; to him belongs
the lofty boundless sky above.
Varuṇa contains
within his body both the oceans,
and yet he also is contained
within one droplet.

4. Whoever would climb up to heaven
and even beyond would not elude
the Lord Varuṇa.
His watchmen with a thousand eyes,
descending from heaven, sweep the earth
with all-seeing glance.

5. Whatever exists in heaven and earth,
whatever lies beyond—all this
Varuṇa scans.
He counts the blinks of every eye
and reckons, like a skillful dicer, his throw
in the cosmic game.

6. May the seven times seven threads of net
stretched out three times—a fatal trap
to catch the unwary—
ensnare the man who tells a lie,

but let the man pass safely by
who speaks the truth.

7. Seize and bind with a hundred cords,
O Varuṇa, the one who utters falsehood.
Let him not pass!
Let the rogue be, his belly distended,
like a bursting barrel whose bands are cut
and contents spilling!

8. Varuṇa is the warp of the loom,
Varuṇa is the woof of the loom
of this universe.
Varuṇa is of us, Varuṇa is foreign,
Varuṇa is divine, he is also human,
Varuṇa the King.

9. I bind you, so-and-so, son of so-and-so,
with all these bonds,
all these I assign to you!

4. Watchmen: *spaśaḥ*, spies.
5. Like a skillful dicer . . . : like a gambler with his dice, so he settles all these (things, people).
8. Warp and woof of the cosmic loom renders the idea of the *samāmya* and *vyāmya*, i.e., extending in length (vertically) and extending under (horizontally).
9. This stanza is perhaps a later addition, the oldest part of the hymn being vv. 1-5. The personal and family names of the person to be secured by fetters are to be inserted, a fact suggesting that this hymn was used ritually.

Let the Thread of My Song Not Be Snapped While I Sing *Mā tantuś chedi vayato dhiyaṁ me*

17 Ṛg Veda Hymn II, 28, to which we have already made several references, is addressed to Varuṇa and combines in a harmonious and poetic fashion both depth of feeling and beauty of expression. It starts with an address of praise to the divinity who is light and goodness (v. 1). The poet alludes in verse 2 to Agni and then proceeds to implore divine pardon and favor. He compares the stream of his life with that of a river never weary of flowing, and from his heart springs spontaneously this prayer (v. 5):

> Loose me from my sin as from a bond that binds me.
> May my life swell the stream of your river of Right.

He prays that Varuṇa, the Lord omnipotent, without whom he is powerless even to open his eyes, may deliver him from all fear and from the "dreadful weapons that strike the sinner" (v. 7). He praises the God Supreme, whose laws are as unchangeable as the mountains, and humbly begs for pardon in a spirit of hope and assurance that is renewed with each dawn (vv. 8, 9). Finally he expresses to King Varuṇa his longing for protection and prosperity. This psalm, like most of those that extol Varuṇa, conveys an impression of peace, harmony, and order in all spheres of life.

Mā tantuś chedi vayato dhiyaṁ me RV II, 28

1. I hymn the self-luminous wise Lord
to be praised and glorified above all forever,
Varuṇa the mighty! I beg him for renown,
the God who shows love to all those who adore him.

2. With reverence and care we sing your praises.
Happy we feel in your service, O Varuṇa!
We hymn you like the fire that arises each dawn
to usher in the day with its promise of riches.

3. O Leader of heroes, whose words reach far,
may we ever abide in your shelter, O King!
O sons of the Infinite, Gods ever faithful,
forgive us our sins; grant us your friendship.

4. The God Varuṇa made the rivers to flow.
At his Order they run and he sustains them.
They cease not flowing and never feel weary.
They move with swiftness like birds in full flight.

5. Loose me from my sin as from a bond that binds me.
May my life swell the stream of your river of Right!
Let the thread of my song not be snapped while I sing
or my work be cut short before its completion!

6. Drive far, O Varuṇa, all perils. Receive me
graciously, O King. Like a calf from its cords,
undo me from the troubles that bind me. Without you
I am powerless even to open my eyes.

7. Spare us, O Varuṇa, those dreadful weapons
that strike the sinner when you utter the word.
Let us not pass from light into darkness.
Disperse, for our comfort, all that would harm us.

8. We will sing your praises, O God almighty,
now and forever, even as of old.
On yourself, O Immutable, are fixed our resolves,
firmly established as if upon a mountain.

9. Remove far from me the sins I have committed.
Let me not suffer for the guilt of others!
Many dawns shall yet arise to shine upon us.
Let us partake of them so long as we live!

10. The man, O King, be he workmate or friend,
who has scared me in a dream, enhancing my fears,
and the thief and the wolf who plan to harm us—
from these, O Varuṇa, protect us, we pray!

11. May I never be deprived of my donor beloved,
of my generous friend, O Varuṇa! Never
may I lack, O King, well-appointed resources!
May we speak, as men of valor, a strong word in the assembly!

1. Lord: *āditya,* here referring to Varuṇa.
3. The Infinite: Aditi.
4. Order: *ṛta,* with the double connotation of order and command.
5. River of Right: spring of *ṛta,* order, ordinance.
6. Perils: *bhiyas,* fear.
Troubles: *aṁhas,* oppression.
8. Resolves: *vratāni,* laws, vows, ordinance.
9. The guilt of others: *anyakṛta,* what is done by others; may I not have to bear the consequences of others' deeds. Cf. RV VI, 51, 7 (§ IV 8).

I Question Myself on My Sin *Pṛche tad enaḥ*

18 As already noted, this hymn along with a few others strikes an original note in Vedic literature: the *ṛṣi* addresses a sincere petition for forgiveness to God. He surrenders himself, humbly acknowledging his own guilt, with the hope that the mercy of the Lord—and that alone—will bring him justification. Tradition, followed and enlarged by the Purāṇas, has built upon these hymns a whole story. The key to the anguish of Vasiṣṭha is to be found in hymn 104 of the same book (VII). Vasiṣṭha has fallen out of favor with his king Sudā and, he feels, with the God Varuṇa also. Finding himelf the target of the accusations of his enemy Viśvāmitra, the proud Brahmin priest humbles himself before God. Here is a typical example of the way in which in religious literature the concrete story and the particular events of a single person acquire a paradigmatic and thus quasi-universal value applicable to any Man in a similar situation.

Pṛche tad enaḥ . RV VII, 86

1. The peoples are wise through the greatness of him
who has fixed in their stations the heaven and the earth,
who has thrust up on high the vast dome of the sky
and the stars and has spread out the earth down below.

2. I muse in my heart and I ponder this question:
When shall I again be at one with Varuṇa?
Will he accept without rancor my offering?
When, reassured, shall I taste of his mercy?

3. I question myself on my sin, O Varuṇa,
desirous to know it. I seek out the wise
to ask them; the sages all give me this answer:
"The God, great Varuṇa, is angry with you."

4. What, then, O God, is my greatest transgression
for which you would ruin your singer, your friend?
Tell me, O God who knows all and lacks nothing,
so that, quickly prostrating, I may sinless crave pardon.

5. Loose us from the yoke of the sins of our Fathers
and also of those we ourselves have committed.
Release your servant, as a thief is set free
from his crime or as a calf is loosed from its cord.

6. The evil, Varuṇa, was not done on purpose;
it was wine, dice, or anger that led us astray,
or thoughtlessness, sometimes the elder a younger.
Even in sleep evildoing is not wholly banished.

7. I am eager to serve you as a slave serves his master,
you, God, all-watchful, I free from sin!
This most wise God gives knowledge to the simple
and spurs to achievement the clever and the discreet.

8. O God, whose power is self-subsisting,
may these praises now reach you and lodge in your heart!
Well may it go with us in peace and in warfare!
Ever protect us, O Gods, with your blessings!

2. When shall I again . . . : *kadā nv antarvaruṇe bhuvāni.*
3. Sin: *enas.*
4. Transgression: *āgas.*
Would ruin: *jighāṁsasi,* desiderative form of *han-,* to strike, put to death, to wish to kill or ruin. Who knows all and lacks nothing: *dūḷabha svadhāvo,* lit. who cannot be deceived and is self-supporting.
5. Cf. TB III, 7, 12, 3 for the idea of being freed from the sins of one's ancestors.
Servant: Vasiṣṭha, one of the seven *ṛṣis* and supposedly author of the seventh *maṇḍala* of the RV and chief priest of King Sudā. Here is a reference to the story of the quarrel between Vasiṣṭha and Viśvāmitra, author of the third *maṇḍala*. Vasiṣṭha sees himself as a thief who has performed penance for his theft. The author of BrDev, a work enumerating the deities of the RV, explains (VI, 11 sq.) how Vasiṣṭha had entered

Varuṇa's abode by night in a dream (cf. V. 6) in order to steal because he was hungry, a mystical (and psychological) theme.

7. Spurs to achievement: *rāye junāti* . . . .

The clever and the discreet: *gṛtsam*.

8. Whose power is self-subsisting: *svadhāvaḥ*, from *sva-dhā*, self-position, self-power, self-supporting (same word as in stanza 4).

In peace and in warfare: *kṣeme* . . . *yoge*, with reference both to spiritual states and also to rest and labor.

Forgive, Lord, Have Mercy! *Mṛḷā sukṣatra mṛḷaya*

19 This simple heartfelt prayer is addressed to Varuṇa by a sufferer who recognizes his guilt and implores the Lord for forgiveness. The man who utters this intensely human cry does not specify the character of the suffering he is experiencing or of the sin that incurred it. The intricate feelings of the human heart are expressed in all sincerity. Varuṇa appears to Men as being simultaneously the wielder of thunder, the watcher of Men's deeds who punishes by suffering and death, and the gracious God who forgives. Man, though a sinner, still craves life and finds all possible excuses to explain his shortcomings and sins: ill chance, slowness of intellect, thoughtlessness. Verse 4 remains enigmatic: Does it allude to the thirst caused by dropsy, with which Varuṇa is known to strike evildoers, or to the thirst of avarice in the midst of abundant wealth? Either way it expresses in a profound and poetic manner the concrete existential situation of the Man who is starving from lack of the very thing that is most abundant around him, who looks for friendship when he is living among friends, craves solitariness when he could easily withdraw, desires happiness when all that could make him happy is at hand, thirsts for water when he is surrounded by it on every side. The truth comes home to us in the refrain that sums up the whole hymn: forgive, Lord, have mercy!

Mṛḷā sukṣatra mṛḷaya RV VII, 89

1. Let me not pass to the house of clay,
   King Varuṇa, as yet.
      Forgive, Lord, have mercy!

2. If I totter along, O wielder of thunder,
   like a puffed-up wineskin,
      forgive, Lord, have mercy!

3. If by ill chance in the dullness of my wits
   I went straying, O Holy One,
      forgive, Lord, have mercy!

4. Thirst is plaguing your worshiper, even when he stands
   surrounded by waters,
      forgive, Lord, have mercy!

5. If we men commit, O Varuṇa, an offense
   against the heavenly ones,
   or in thoughtlessness transgress your laws,
      oh punish us not!

1. House of clay: urn or vessel used for storing the ashes of the dead: metaphor for death. Cf. AV V, 30, 14 (§ V 9).

Forgive, Lord, have mercy: *mṛlā sukṣatra mṛlaya*. The verbal stem *mṛl-* or *mṛd-* means to be gracious or favorable, to pardon, to spare.

Lord: *sukṣatra*, good master, one who rules well, has power.

2. O wielder of thunder: *adrivaḥ*, O you who are armed with stones or thunderbolts. *Adri*, a stone, referring especially to the stone used for grinding *soma* (cf. § III 18), but the master of the grinding stones is properly Indra and not Varuṇa.

Some interpreters see here the prayer of a man suffering from dropsy, whose body is swollen by the disease (cf. also v. 4).

3. The first three stanzas are dominated by three vocatives: *rājan:* O King!; *adrivah* (as above); *śuce:* O Holy One!

5. Thoughtlessness: *acitti*.

Laws: *dharma*.

c) Purification

Pavitratā

Life would be unbearable if Man had to carry inexorably, with no hope of riddance, all the burden of his past and all the anxiety of his future. Man can survive only if he unloads the weight of his sins and if he sees at least some bright spots on the horizon of his future.

The three subsections given below cover a wide range. They all illustrate the sacramental order, the order in which the spiritual and the material, the immanent and the transcendent, the human and the divine, collaborate in order to help Man to reach his goal, to fulfill his mission, to realize himself. We may sum up these widely different texts as follows: the Brāhmaṇas tell us to perform a complete bathing ritual in order to acquire the desired purification. The water is more than "water," but without the water there is no real forgiveness. The Upaniṣads try to convince us that ultimately the stain is not a stain on our real self, that sin has no ultimate ontological status, and that therefore the prime necessity is to discover the nonultimate character of all our defilements. This conviction cannot be induced or feigned, but the one who reaches such a conviction by doing so gets rid of his sins, which by virtue of this knowledge cease to be real sins. The Gītā, along with some Upaniṣads, elaborates on a kindred theme: that real knowledge purifies and that true wisdom performs a catharsis of the soul. He who really knows is freed from every stain.

A reference to the most common Sanskrit word for holiness, that is, the state of purity and sinlessness, will help us to understand the underlying connection linking the three above-mentioned perspectives. *Pavitra* is basically a "means of purification," that which cleanses. It comes from the root *pū-* to purify, to cleanse, to brighten, from which *pavītṛ* (also *pavana*), the purifier, and often the God of wind as purifying breeze, air, and so on, and other words are derived.[162] The idea of dirt, sin, guilt, stain, and the like changes according to varied understandings of what constitutes the proper means of purification. In the Ṛg Veda, *pavitra* is the strainer that clarifies and thus purifies the *soma* so that it becomes the pure par excellence. In the Brāhmaṇas it is the cleansing bath that washes away transgressions committed against the ritual order. In the Upaniṣads it is wisdom that purifies Man from bad tendencies and accumulated *karman*. In each instance, however, the sacred or holy or saintly is essentially that which is pure, purified, and purifying. And, as tradition later on is fond of stressing, the very presence of a saint has the purifying effect of all conceivable cleansing baths or purifying rites.

It must be added that, especially in the Brāhmaṇic period, rituals and ceremonies of purification begin to proliferate and the beginnings of an exuberant casuistry are already visible. Without either hiding such practices or denying that a process of degeneration often does take place, we may observe that such rituals do not contain the same interest for all times. Nevertheless, we give some examples, taken (perhaps surprisingly) from among the Upaniṣads, without entering into the minutiae of the Brāhmaṇas.

162. Cf. the etymology of *pavamāna* in § III 17.

The Cleansing Bath *Snāna*

20 Although the Yajur Veda gives some importance to the performance of expiatory rites,[163] the Brāhmaṇas frequently evidence consciousness of guilt and longing for purification. In this period religious acts follow prescribed patterns and formulas; the spontaneity and poetic verve of the Ṛg Veda are to some degree subdued.

Of the three texts that follow, the first two, taken from the Yajur Veda and the Śatapatha Brāhmaṇa, speak of the ritual bath that constitutes a complete purification, if taken in strict accordance with the rules. We should not fail to note, however, that the man who sets out to perform each ritual act (such as a bath, a sacrifice, etc.) must as a preliminary, in company with his wife, observe a fast, follow the directions of the officiating priest, and make certain offerings. There is no doubt that all this preparation is not a mere outward observance but is undertaken with a view to achieving the more important inner purification. The third text, from the Taittirīya Āraṇyaka, is the well-known "sin-effacing" mantra, which may be recited at the time of the morning bath.

At a later date the code of Manu reiterates in its own fashion the ideas of the Ṛg Veda regarding guilt and confession, repentance and pardon, but now they appear in the form of minute regulations to be followed and practices to be observed if expiation of sin and purification are to follow. The longing for expiation and for a means of atonement (*prāyaścitta*) leads to a meticulous, often rigidly prescribed, ritual ceremony where so much stress is laid on the perfect fulfillment of each penitential observance that little opportunity remains for sincere emotion or real contrition of the heart.

Snāna

YV III, 48

i) O swiftly moving purifying Bath, you flow gently down. With the help of the Gods may my sins against the Gods be removed and with the help of mortals may my sins against mortals be washed away.

Protect us from harm and from the loudly speaking [enemy].

SB IV, 4, 5, 22-23

ii) 22. O cleansing Bath, cleansing as you flow, may I wipe out with the help

163. Cf. YV III, 45; VI, 17; VIII, 13; 14; XX, 14-20.

of the Gods such sin as I have committed against the Gods and with the help of men such sin as I have committed against my fellowmen. . . .

23. Having put on fresh clothing, they step out of the old. Even as a snake sloughs off its skin, so does the penitent slough off his sin; there is not in him even as much sin as there is in a newborn child.

TA X, 1, 12-13

iii) I seek the Lord of the Waters of golden appearance.
May he hear our entreaty and grant us a place of ablution!
Whatever food I have taken in the house of the wicked,
whatever gift I have received at the hands of the crafty,
whatever sin of thought or word or deed
I have committed, from this may Indra, Varuṇa,
Bṛhaspati, and Sūrya cleanse me again and again!
If I have eaten or drunk to excess, or consorted
with people of violent ways, may King Varuṇa
wipe it all away! Thus, rid of impurity and evil
and free from my sin, may I find liberation and pass
to the world of the Lord of creation!

▪ i) The sacrificer and his wife are performing the ritual ablution (*avabhṛtha*). It is important to note that sins can be expiated only in the same realm in which they have been committed.
▪ ii) For the metaphor of the serpent's skin, cf. PrasnU V, 5 (§ VI 12) and the comments in § IV 21 Introduction.

Purifying Knowledge *Jñānaśuddhi*

21 The Upaniṣads do not dismiss ritual purification altogether, but they are more interested in finding out the source of all purification, the hidden power of the cleansing waters. Gradually this source becomes the only real means of purification. The Upaniṣadic discovery is *jñāna,* saving and purifying knowledge.

The order in which we offer the texts is intended to indicate the process of this discovery. We see how from a merely ritualistic conception we pass to an intensive coexistence of *karmakāṇḍins* and *jñānins,* or ritual and gnostic trends, and how finally the latter seem to eliminate the former, substituting for ritual action an ultimate insight into the nature of evil. Evil is regarded more and more as a constitutive part of the world itself, which consequently becomes more and more estranged from the *ātman,* which is itself untouched by darkness, sin, or evil in any form.

The Upaniṣads are quite aware of human weakness[164] and of the necessity of daily purification (i). They take into consideration both the cosmic aspect of impurity and purification (iii) and the human dimension of guilt and forgiveness (iv). It is the whole Man, represented by the triad *manas* (mind), *vāc* (speech), and *śarīra* or *prāṇa* (body or life, which corresponds to *karman*, physical action), who commits sin and it is the whole Man who has to be released from the guilt of sin committed on these three levels (i). Even the ritually orientated text of the Mahānārāyaṇa Upaniṣad ends with the intuition that only the discovery of the light core in Man is capable of purifying him completely (vii). Again, it is the actual knowledge of the meaning of the rite which has the same power to "burn" sins as Agni has on the altar (x). The Kauṣītaki Upaniṣad refers to the procedure for purification of sin at the three important moments of the day (*saṁdhyā*). Here, too, we have a ritual text, known as the "daily adoration of the Sun for the removal of sin."

The development of the doctrine of *karman*[165] shows that sin and purification are more than individual processes: all actions in the universe are interrelated in a web of inextricable causes and effects. *Karman* transcends individuality, for the consequences of good or evil deeds reach the very limits of the world and their sum total constitutes the whole circle of *saṁsāra*.[166] Thus the ultimate aim of purification is to rid oneself of the chains of *saṁsāra*; to this end the Upaniṣads undertake an ardent and unwearying search and an almost superhuman effort to purify the self, to disengage it from the vicissitudes of human life and the cycle of rebirth in order that it may gain liberation. There is a significant shift from the passage about the snake sloughing off its skin as reported in the Śatapatha Brāhmaṇa[167] to the same idea as expressed in one Upaniṣad.[168] Here the text emphasizes that purification is effected not by a purifying bath or any other sacred action, but by meditating on the *puruṣa* (the primordial person) as the fruit of *jñāna*, gnosis.

Several texts warn us not to disconnect this saving knowledge from our daily life and from the normal code of conduct. Other texts powerfully emphasize that knowledge is saving by itself and that to the really freed and enlightened soul there is no sin and no possibility of committing sin, even if he should perform the externals of

164. Cf. the description of the individual (*bhūtātman*) in MaitU III, 1-5.
165. For *karman* cf. § V A Introduction.
166. For *saṁsāra* cf. § V 6.
167. Cf. § IV 20.
168. Cf. PrasnU V, 5 (§ VI 12).

the most hideous crimes. Just as water neither pollutes nor even wets the lotus leaf, so sin does not touch the man who knows. He does not even blush, says one very daring text, adducing the example of Indra. The only condition is to "know him," and thus, as other texts on *ātman* and *brahman* would add, "to be him [or it]." The state of a *jñānin*, a knower of the Self, has always been considered to be "beyond good and evil," precisely because he is beyond *karman* and its laws (x, xv). Let us remember that to do evil necessarily means that one is not beyond it. Whatever this state of being beyond good and evil may be, by definition, it cannot be immoral. If to be beyond good and evil is an evil state, then it is not beyond good and evil. Just as there is undeniable intellectual evidence (once I am convinced through intrinsic evidence of a certain truth I cannot undo that conviction unless it is replaced by another one), there is also a means of moral evidence (conscience) which no one can overrule, unless that conscience itself yields to a better light. What the Upaniṣads are telling us is that the enlightenment of our conscience is also possible. They affirm, further, that an enlightened conscience, piercing as it does all appearances, cannot be the source of an act that is morally wrong, even if sometimes that act when observed from the outside may seem to be otherwise. To act in perfect conscience implies that one has reached perfect consciousness. Meanwhile we are only on the way.

A remarkable text, which we give later on, stresses the greatness of the authentic Brahmin.[169] It says, first, that the core of reality does not increase by good works or decrease by bad ones. The inner space dwelling in the depths of the heart is untouched by works, even if they are sacred actions. The text adds that such a knower of Brahman is not haunted by scruples about works that he has done or left undone, or performed well or badly. He is not attached to them and thus he is free. He knows that all that has happened has a meaning and a purpose and he thus accepts the real as it realizes itself. His knowledge has purified him.

Jñānaśuddhi

MahanarU 132-133

i) If I have done wrong in thought, word, or deed,
may Indra, Varuṇa, Bṛhaspati, and Savitṛ
purify me again and again!

169. Cf. BU IV, 4, 22-23 (§ VI 6).

MahanarU 138

ii) Free from my sins, I shall be liberated,
freed from guilt, without spot or stain!

MahanarU 317-318

iii) May the Waters purify the Earth,
may this Earth so purified purify me!
May the Lord of the Holy Word purify me,
may [Earth], purified by Brahman, purify me!

MahanarU 321-323

iv) May Agni, the zealous, and the lords of wrath
guard me from sins committed in anger!
The sin that I this day committed
in thought, in words, with my hands or my feet,
by my stomach or by my generative organ—
may this day efface it!
And this evil within me I offer in sacrifice,
together with myself, in the womb of the Immortal,
in the Truth, in the Light. *Svāhā*!

MahanarU 325-326

v) The sin that I this night committed
in thought, in words, with my hands or my feet,
by my stomach or by my generative organ—
may this night efface it!
And this evil within me I offer in sacrifice,
together with myself, in the womb of the Immortal,
in the Truth, in the Light, *Svāhā*!

MahanarU 414-416

vi) You are the expiation for the sin of the Gods. *Svāhā*!
You are the expiation for the sin of men. *Svāhā*!
You are the expiation for the sin of the Ancestors. *Svāhā*!
You are the expiation for the sin of myself. *Svāhā*!
You are the expiation for the sin of another. *Svāhā*!
You are the expiation for the sin of all. *Svāhā*!

MahanarU 441

vii) May the word, the mind, the eye, the ear,
the tongue, the nose, the semen, the intelligence,
the intention, and the will be purified in me!
I am light! May I be purified from all stain and sin!

BU I, 5, 20

viii) Whatever sufferings creatures undergo remain with them. Only good deeds reach God, for no sin reaches the Gods.

BU V, 7

ix) It is said that Brahman is lightning. It is called lightning because it cleaves. He who knows that lightning is Brahman cleaves sin, for Brahman is lightning.

BU V, 14, 8

x) It is Agni who is its mouth. Whatever quantity of fuel they lay on a fire, it burns it all. Similarly he who knows this, even if he commits very much sin, burns it all and becomes clean and pure, ageless and immortal.

CU IV, 14, 3

xi) As water does not adhere to a lotus leaf, so evil deeds do not adhere to the man who knows this.

CU VIII, 13, 1

xii) From the dark I go to the colored, from the colored to the dark. Shaking off sin as a horse shakes off dust from its hair, freeing myself from the body as the moon frees itself from the mouth of Rāhu, I enter into the unmade world of Brahman with a fulfilled *ātman*. I enter into the world of Brahman.

KausU II, 7

xiii) Next come the three adorations of the invincible Kauṣītaki: . . .

> At the rising of the sun he would say:
> "O Deliverer, deliver me from my sin."

Likewise, when the sun was midway in heaven he would say:

> "O Deliverer, risen to the heights, raise me to
> the heights and deliver me from my sin."

Likewise, when the sun was setting he would say:

> "O Deliverer who can deliver completely,
> deliver me completely from my sin."

And he delivers him from whatever sin he has committed in the day or at night.

KausU III, 1

xiv) Pratardana, son of Divodāsa, reached the well-loved abode of Indra by means of struggle and effort. Indra thus spoke to him:

"Pratardana, choose a boon!"

Pratardana said: "You yourself choose it for me, the boon that you consider most beneficial for mankind."

Indra said to him: "A greater, to be sure, does not choose a boon for a lesser. You yourself choose!"

"That is no boon at all for me," said Pratardana.

Then Indra did not desist from truth, for Indra himself is truth.

Indra said: "Know me. The most useful enterprise for men is to know me.

"I slew the three-headed son of Tvaṣṭṛ; I delivered the Arunmukhas and the ascetics to the wild dogs; I have transgressed many agreements; I killed the Prahlādas in the sky, the Paulomas in the space between, and the Kālakañjas on earth, and not a single hair of mine was hurt.

"So the world of the man who knows me does not deteriorate by any action he may do, whether he steals or procures an abortion or kills his mother or his father. Whatever sin he commits, he remains unabashed."

SU 1, 11

xv) When a man knows God all fetters are loosed.
Sorrows are no more; birth and death cease.
By meditation on him, at the body's dissolution,
there comes the third state, that of supreme mastery.
His desires are fulfilled; he is absolutely free.

▪ i) The following mantras are recited as a confession before the ritual bath.
▪ ii) The idea of freedom from sins and guilt is repeated time and again throughout the U.
▪ iv) The zealous: *manyu,* the spirit of zeal which later means the incarnation of wrath. There is a pun on *manyu:* the "lords of wrath" may be those who have overcome anger.
Evil: *durita.*
In the womb of the Immortal: *amṛtayonau,* which could also be translated as "in the bosom of the eternal Father." The self-oblation is made to the three aspects of the Absolute: *amṛta, satya,* and *jyotis.*
▪ vi) The text proceeds with a litany of sins repeating the same refrain.
Sin: *enas.*
▪ vii) The text goes on to enumerate other parts of the human being, repeating the same theme.
▪ viii) Sufferings: *śocanti,* they grieve.
Good deeds: *puṇya,* merit, etc.
God: lit. him, i.e., the godhead, Prajāpati, mentioned a few lines before.
Sin: *pāpa,* which may also be translated as "evil."
Suffering is proper to men, goodness is proper to God. When man goes to God only good accompanies him. Meanwhile he carries the burden of his creatureliness.
▪ ix) 6. Cf. § VI 7. A Sanskrit pun. Lightning: *vidyut;* cleaves: *vidyati,* destroys, divides (all) evil; *pāpa,* sin.

- x) 6-7. Cf. Gāyatrī Introduction.
- xi) A recurring idea. Cf. KausU 1, 4 (§ V 4); BG V, 10.
- xii) Sin: *pāpa*.

Unmade world of Brahman with a fulfilled *ātman: akṛtaṁ kṛtātmā brahma-lokam* . . . : with a disciplined, completed, perfected soul I reach union with the uncreated Brahman world. For the rest of CU VIII and all the ref. cf. § VI 6 (v) and notes.

- xiii) Sin: *pāpa*. In a more literal version: You are one who gathers; twist off my sin when the sun is at the zenith. You are one who tears; root up my sin by the setting sun. You are one who seizes; take hold of my sin.
- xiv) Boon: *vara*.

Most beneficial for mankind: *manuṣyāya hitataman*, the most favorable for humanity.

A greater . . . : one cannot choose for another.

Indra himself is truth: *satyaṁ hīndraḥ*.

Know me: *mām eva vijāni*, understand myself.

Son of Tvaṣṭṛ: Viśvarūpa, whose conflict with Indra is referred to in TS II, 5, 1 sq.; SB I, 6, 3, 1-2. Cf. also RV X, 8, 8-9.

Wild dogs: the episode is described in AB VII, 28 (XXXV, 2).

Prahlādas: Prahlāda was a famous *asura*.

Paulomas: demons.

Kālakañjas: demons of another kind.

2-3. Cf. § II 6.

- xv) 6-10. Cf. § VI 11.

11. Absolutely free: *kevala*, unconditioned, isolated.

12. Cf. § VI 11.

15-16. Cf. § VI 5.

The Fire of Wisdom *Jñānāgni*

22 Our selection from the Bhagavad Gītā starts with a rather remarkable *śloka* (III, 36) describing an inner tension in Man which leads him to sin against his will. The inertia of inherited *karmans* may be a partial answer to the question posed, but the problem remains. Furthermore, we have here a highly particularized query in the sense that it is not an abstract question about sin or evil, but the burning and agonizing question of the human heart after profound introspection: something in me, which is equally "me," offers resistance to the well-being of my existence.[170] This is not an interrogation concerning the nature of evil so much as an inquiry about human weakness. After the speculation of the Upaniṣads the Gītā sounds once again a human note.

The following verse speaks of wrong action, of sin. These terms are used with the connotation already noted in connection with "purifying knowledge." The Man who, by the grace of the Lord, has renounced all things, in whom there is complete harmony, to whom true wisdom and true *jñāna* (knowledge) have been re-

170. Cf. what was said about *duḥkha* in IV A b Introduction.

vealed, whose being is united with the Lord—that Man is no longer affected by any action whatever or by any sin; he has attained the supreme bliss of Brahman. Furthermore, even the Man who is not yet altogether detached, to whom wisdom has not yet been fully imparted, who is still living an imperfect, even evil, life—he too, if he adores the Lord with all his being and with sincere intention, will be purified and will come to know wisdom and that peace in the Lord which will last forever.

The overall picture of the *śruti* brings out in strong colors the sorrow and suffering of Man and does not conceal his sinfulness or ignore his evil, but it does not stop there. It is equally full of traits depicting mercy, purification, and forgiveness. There is fear on earth and in Man, but there is also a message of fearlessness. And yet the last test has still to come.

Jñānāgni

BG III, 36

i)

Impelled by what power is a man driven
against his resolve
to commit sin, as if he were constrained
by some outward force?

BG IV, 36-38

ii)

36. Even if you should be the worst
among all sinners,
you will cross, by the boat of wisdom alone,
the sea of evil.

37. As a blazing fire reduces the wood
to ashes, O Arjuna,
so does the fire of knowledge reduce
all activity to ashes.

38. There is nothing on earth which possesses such power
to cleanse as wisdom.
The perfect yogin finds this knowledge in himself
by himself in due time.

BG IX, 1

iii)

To you who have faith I will tell a deep mystery
that holds within itself
both vision and knowledge. By knowing this mystery
you will be freed from all evil.

BG XVIII, 58

iv) Concentrating on Me, you shall overcome
by my grace all dangers;
but if from self-conceit you will not listen,
you will surely perish.

- i) Sin: *pāpa.*
- ii) 36. The worst among all sinners: *pāpebhyaḥ sarvebhyaḥ pāpakṛttamaḥ.*
  Wisdom: *jñāna.*
  The sea of evil: *sarvam . . . vṛjinam,* lit. all falsity, inauthenticity, evil.
  38. Power to cleanse: *pavitra,* lit. purifying, holy, pure, sanctified.
  39-40. Cf. § I 38.
- iii) Evil: *aśubha,* lit. shamefulness, badness.
- iv) Grace: *prasāda.*
  Self-conceit: *ahaṁkāra,* selfishness, self-centeredness, egotism.

PART V
DEATH AND DISSOLUTION

Yama

It is only seemingly a paradox to affirm that a strong will to live entails an equally strong will to die. If the will to live is a realistic will to live a real life and not a whimsical desire for an imaginary life, we must recognize that inasmuch as real life is lived under the existential condition of death, death itself has to be taken into account and equally willed. To desire to live and not to desire the same degree of death that life may contain is not a realistic desire to live but a mere product of our imagination, which seeks to grasp at an illusory "life." Fear of death, by the same token, is of the same nature as fear of life. To wish for an X without wishing for all that the X contains is not really to wish for it, but to wish for an idealized and altogether different X.

We do not find so explicit an argument in the Vedas, but their all-pervading mood seems to correspond very closely to what we have just been saying. The Vedic attitude, which is strongly life-affirming, has as its corollary the acceptance of death. But we cannot reduce life and much less death to neat rational schemes. There are equally real human attitudes to life and death which are not rational and, further, we have to ask what kind of life we really love and what kind of death we really fear.

One thing that is clear is the integration between life and death in the *śruti.* That integration is examined in this part, whose connection with the preceding part requires no further comment.

To extricate the Vedic experience of death from its cosmological background, with which it is almost inseparably interwoven, is particularly difficult. In order to interpret correctly the human experience of death which permeates the Vedas, we must take into account the evidence provided by the history of religions for the periods that precede and follow the Vedic age, but we cannot include here such a preface to our study. We try to present only the results that a particular method produces. This method is based on involvement and distance: involvement in Vedic culture, so as to see it as far as possible through the eyes of Vedic Man, and distance from it, looking at it from without with critical awareness.

The difficulty here is compounded because, unlike other fields of human experience, the actual subject of this chapter is not empirical Man but rather *man* living in another realm outside this perceptible universe. Thus the cosmological model in which this "otherworld" is situated has to be understood first. Yet the cosmological model not only affects but also conditions that very insight into the eschatological problem.

We would like, then, to extricate, insofar as possible, the anthropological experience of Vedic wisdom regarding the central problem of death from the cosmological world view of that time. We are not assuming that there are two separable experiences, the cosmological and the anthropological. What we are saying is that the anthropological experience, that is, the subjective conviction (in this instance regarding death), can be expressed independently of the particular cosmological substructure. We certainly do not want to suggest that a pure demythologization is possible; rather, we are trying as it were to wrap the Vedic experience in another myth, the present-day one, so that through such a "transmythization" we may try to understand, or even reenact, the experience disclosed in the *śruti*.

Modern Man wonders about death and weaves innumerable theories about it; he seems to be sure about only one thing: its factual reality and thus its inevitability. In spite of startling news produced now and then by the scientific shamans of our age, contemporary Man seems at a loss when he is confronted with one of the most ancient myths of mankind: the possibility of avoiding death. Because death is seen to be inevitable, modern society tends to wipe out from the memory of the living all dealings with the dying and the dead. The fundamental Vedic attitude is almost the opposite: it does not reckon with death's inevitability and it does not try to smuggle death away from everyday life.

According to this vision, which is common to other cultures as well, death is not inevitable; it is only accidental. You die if your life is snatched away before you reach maturity, or before you marry, or if something unexpected happens to you which prevents you from achieving what you yourself or society was expecting of your life. Death is limited to this rupture, this misfortune, this accident. Thus it is always an unnatural event, and it is always *akāla mṛtyu*, untimely death.

On the other hand the old Man, "the Man of long life," as the Vedas call him, the one who has lived his life, who has fulfilled his life span, his *āyus*,[1] does not die; he does not experience a break

1. *Āyus* means vital power, life in its temporal, changing, and fluctuating manifestation. The term appears often in the RV in many forms. Cf., e.g., RV I, 10, 11 (§ V A Antiphon); I, 24, 11; I, 34, 11; I, 37, 15; etc.

and, thus, a trauma; he has simply consumed the torch and exhausted the fuel. The flame of his life goes on and it burns in his sons, his daughters, his children's children, his friends, his work, and in his ideas which are scattered to the four winds. Even his body, with its own energy, has already enriched the earth on which he has walked, the rivers in which he has bathed, and the living beings with whom he has been in communication and communion. Only the last gifts of his body and breath still remain to be given away. The old Man does not die; he simply finishes his commerce with life and achieves the transmission of all that he himself has received, as the Upaniṣads describe.[2] He cancels the constitutive *ṝṇa,* the debt of gratitude for the gift of his existence.[3] The natural extinction of one particular carrier of life or the completion of one's own life is not death.

Indeed, not every Man who is old in years reaches long life, maturity, and thus immortality. It is not a question of mere number of years but of growth, for which the passing of years—the hundred autumns—is certainly required but of which it is not the only condition. Time, in fact, is more than its measurement by the passing of days and seasons; it is the qualitative coefficient of human growth itself. To disentangle the immortal from the mortal, to liberate himself from the claws of death, is the task of every Man. On the one hand there is the *asu* or life-principle, the power of life or vital strength, which is assimilated in some traditions to the *ahaṁkāra,* the selfish ego of unfulfilled desires and unachieved projects. This ego is not pure, later periods will say, inasmuch as it consists of unburnt *karmas;* it is this ego that is afraid of death, because it must certainly die. There is, on the other hand, the personal *ātman,* that spark of the *paramātman,* which does not die. *Jīva,* in spite of the variety of meanings given by different schools, could also be another word for immortal Man.

The notion that the old Man who has reached the end of his life span and finished the task entrusted to him does not die is more convincing for Vedic Man than for modern Man because of the deeper sense of collective consciousness which the former enjoys in comparison with contemporary Man.[4] The Vedic Covenant is

2. Cf. KausU II, 15 (§ V 12).
3. Cf. § III 23 Introduction.
4. We do not speak here of the "collective unconscious" but of a collective consciousness which is that real consciousness whose subject or support is not the individual but the community.

directed not to Men but to Man, not to disconnected individuals but to the rich web of personhood, which is, as we shall see, neither singular nor plural. Because the coefficient of individuality is very low, individual death presents a very small problem for the old Man whose vitality, or rather whose body, just fades away. Against this background we may perhaps acquire an adequate perspective that will enable us to envisage this central human problem as experienced in the beginnings of Indo-European civilization; we may also perhaps learn something of our own attainable immortality.

It would not be proper to reduce the rich range of the Vedic experience to only a few features. It contains, moreover, a double complexity: horizontal and vertical. The complexity is horizontal insofar as the millennium of human experience concentrated in the *śruti*—without of course considering the prehistory from which it originated—is far too wide to allow oversimplifications. We have, for instance, already stressed the tension between the self-understanding of Man in the Saṁhitās and in the Upaniṣads. What may be valid for one may be contested by the other and the eschatological ideas of one period may not tally with those of the other. By saying that the complexity is also vertical we want to indicate the fascinating fact that the Vedic Revelation discloses itself at very widely differing levels of human experience, ranging from the most simple, primitive, and literal understanding of an afterlife as a copy or rather an idealization of this one, to a sophisticated and highly refined vision of forms of survival which transcend imagination and even thought.

The hymns and texts that follow may give some idea of this experience. We divide this part into two sections; one describes the phenomenon of death, the break, the departure. It contains three subsections which should be easily understandable. The first one contains myths dealing with the mystery of the beyond. The second one has an immediate existential flavor. It mostly consists of prayers dealing with the concrete struggle with death; these prayers represent the everlasting tension between the living and the dying as well as between living and dying. The third one deals with the moment immediately after death. It is a moment for effective action, not one of theoretical reflection. It is the last of the human rites and the *antyeṣṭi* completes the triangle composed of birth (with initiation, which is the spiritual birth), marriage, and death. For this reason we include the rite here as we have done in other instances.

The second section is limited to basic texts that describe the state of mind of Man when confronted with the idea of another world. We adduce only those eschatological representations directly connected with death and dissolution, without entering into other types of cosmographies. The first subsection has a particular interest as it describes the anthropological and theological settings of the end of the world, represented respectively by the myth of the deluge in the Śatapatha Brāhmaṇa and the assertion of the Gītā that God is both the origin and the dissolution of the world. The two remaining subsections deal with conceptions of hell and heaven.

A. THE GREAT DEPARTURE

Mahāprasthāna

O Indra, prolong our life once more!
RV I, 10, 11[5]

Just as a cucumber is removed from its stalk,
so from Death's bonds may I be removed
but not from Immortality!
RV VII, 59, 12

Desireless, wise, immortal, self-existent,
full of bliss, lacking in nothing,
is the one who knows the wise, unaging,
youthful ātman: *he fears not death!*
AV X, 8, 44[6]

The three verses chosen as antiphons for this section express the gist of the many texts concerning what the Kaṭha Upaniṣad calls the "Great Departure."[7]

The first one stresses what we are going to hear time and again: the "afterlife" and the "otherworld" may be very attractive prospects, but nothing is so dear and desirable as our human, concrete,

5. Cf. RV X, 59, 1 (§ V 8).
6. Cf. § VII 27, where we give another version of the same text.
7. Cf. KathU I, 29 (§ V 5).

bodily life here on earth and under the sun, with fellow human beings, animals, and objects surrounding us. If later on certain Upaniṣadic sages and, more so, some of their followers despise life here below and all human values, the Vedic *ṛṣis* are still in love with this world.

The poet of the second verse knows only too well that Death does not wait for the fruit to fall from the tree by itself through its own impulse. He uses the metaphor of the plucked fruit and asks to be saved from the embrace of Death and handed over to Immortality. The cucumber dies when plucked; Man enters immortality.

The third antiphon comes from the always astonishing Atharva Veda. Composed long before the Upaniṣads, it introduces us to the conception of *ātman*, the discovery of which is the one means of overcoming both death and the fear of death. The concept was to be minutely developed in a later period. This existential discovery, which is much more than mere abstract knowledge, makes life glow with self-confidence. It is the secret of happiness and of the conquest of death, for it cannot be touched by the change and the decay caused by the passage of years.[8]

This text is similar to others found elsewhere, for instance, in the Śatapatha Brāhmaṇa, speaking of either Brahman[9] or of *ātman*.[10] It already foreshadows the trend of later speculation about death and also about life.[11] These sayings tell us that the secret of immortality and happiness is hidden neither on inaccessible peaks of heroic deeds nor in the equally unapproachable depths of universal knowledge, but is simply concealed in any human heart just "alongside" oneself.

Something similar must be said about another important insight, which represents perhaps the most common feature of the great majority of Eastern spiritualities: the notion of *karman*. Not only is the idea of *ātman* foreshadowed in the Vedas but there is also discernible the seed of the conception of *karman*, though not the idea of rebirth. The term *karman* occurs almost forty times in the Ṛg Veda, but never in the sense of the later theories on transmigration. It means simply works, deeds, and, especially, sacred actions. *Karman* is directly related to the central idea of sacrifice. What

8. Some of the adjectives qualifying the *vidvas*, the knower, are *akāma* (desireless), *dhīra* (wise), *amṛta* (immortal), *svayambhū* (self-existent), *rasena tṛptaḥ* (full of sap).
9. Cf. SB X, 3, 5, 10-11 (§ VI 3).
10. Cf. SB X, 6, 3, 1-2 (§ VI 5).
11. Cf. also AV X, 2, 32; X, 8, 43 (§ VII 27), as hints in the same direction, foreshadowing the Upaniṣads.

appears clearly, mainly in the Brāhmaṇas, is the idea of a superhuman justice which entails true belief in retribution.[12] All human deeds have good or bad effects according to their nature, that is, to their moral value.

The conception of *karman* emerges later as the connecting link between the two ideas of immortality and retribution. If not everything disappears at death, and if justice is to be accomplished, there will have to be a continuity. *Karman* stands here for this continuity, that is, for all the elements gathered around a personal core, which can be shared by others and thus also transmitted from one person to another. The *karmans* are not only the good or bad dispositions, but the very causes of such dispositions; they are the links in the chain of cosmic solidarity, a kind of crystallization of Man's deeds on earth, which do not disappear with individual death.

The only Ṛg-Vedic text that has been traditionally interpreted as supporting the *karman* theory refers only to the anthropocosmic unity of reality, so that the eye goes back to the sun, the spirit to the wind, and so on. As noted earlier, it also refers to the cosmoethical harmony of the universe;[13] thus the merits and demerits of the person have cosmic repercussions because they belong to the same world.[14] Other texts from the Ṛg Veda,[15] Atharva Veda,[16] Upaniṣads,[17] and Gītā[18] may also be considered in this connection.

Summing up the many threads of this tradition, we may detect three operative ideas: *karman* as the saving sacrificial action, mainly stressed in the Saṁhitās; *karman* as the subtle structure of temporal reality, as that which all existing things have in common and in which they share, disclosed mainly in the Upaniṣads and developed in later times; *karman* as the path of action, of good works, and thus also as a way to salvation, emphasized in the Bhagavad Gītā. We could even add that the theory of *karman* is probably the fruit of a process of secularization away from the Vedic Brāhmaṇic conception of the sacrifice to the general conception of life itself as a

12. Cf. SB VI, 2, 2, 27; XI 2, 7, 23 (§ V 3).
13. Cf. § IV B.
14. Cf. RV X, 16, 3 (§ V 16). It is noteworthy that the word *karman* does not occur here; instead, the term *dharma* is used.
15. Cf. RV I, 22, 19; II, 21, 1; III, 33, 7; VI, 37, 2; VIII, 21, 2; IX, 46, 3; X, 28, 7.
16. Cf. AV IV, 2; V, 23, 3; XI, 8, 6.
17. Cf. BU III, 2, 13 (§ VI 12); IV, 4, 5 (§ VI 11).
18. The idea of *karman* permeates the whole of the Gītā. Cf., e.g., BG II, 42-43; II, 47-57; III, 4-9; IV, 14-24; V, 1-14; XVIII, 2-25; and III, 14-15; 19-20; 22-25; IV, 32-33, all in § III 29.

sacrifice, maintained no longer by a specific *yajña* but by the karmic action of Men. Be that as it may, what the *śruti* discloses is not a theory of *karman* but an attitude in the face of the problem of death. A few features may be noted.

First, there is the belief that the temporal world is not everything, that human life is not exhausted in space and time on earth, and that the person is not totally dissolved into his constituent elements. There is "another world."

Second, there is the belief that this otherworld is intimately connected with this world and for this reason not only does human life on earth condition the otherworld, but also the last rites, the blessings for the journey, and the climactic moment of death are of capital importance. They condition the new form of human existence. They open up the gates of the otherworld. It is for this reason that the various rituals are so important. Man cannot live without rituals, nor can he die without them. They are needed not only for corporate human life but also for the great departure.

Third, there is a peculiar continuity and discontinuity between these two worlds, which is differently interpreted in the Vedas and the Upaniṣads. According to the Vedas the rupture between this world and the otherworld is an anthropological break (i.e., Man is certainly transformed, but it is Man who is still living at the other side); in the Upaniṣads the chasm is ontological (and *ātman* is the bridge). The Ṛg Veda foreshadows what becomes clear in the Upaniṣadic period: the deceased goes either the way of the Fathers, *pitṛyāna,* or the way of the Gods, *devayāna.*[19] Later, with the theory of rebirth or *punar-janman,* there is a lively traffic behind the three worlds. According to the more radical doctrine of the Upaniṣads, all three belong to this side of the shore, all three are still under the law of *karman* and subjected to cause and effect. The other way, the Upaniṣads say, because it leads "no-where," does not even need to be a way. This is, properly speaking, liberation.

According to the Vedas, moreover, the great departure is to "another world." This otherworld has its own structure, but it seems to be still conditioned by time and space, though in a peculiar way. The Upaniṣads are not satisfied with a spatiotemporal conception. The great departure is not to another parallel, superior, or inferior world, but a radical departure from the human condition

19. Cf. BU VI, 2, 2; 15-16 (§ V 4); CU IV, 15, 5; V, 3, 2; V, 10, 1; KausU I, 2-3 (§ V 4).

itself. This idea forms the background of the doctrine about the *ātman*, as we shall see in several chapters of this part and the next.

If the idea is valid, the very metaphor of departure will be contested, because, although we certainly depart from this human condition, we neither reach another realm nor are we annihilated. We throw off the spatiotemporal wrapping and jump, stripped of any contingency or creatureliness, to the other shore, though here the word "shore" is also inappropriate, for it suggests the existence of another realm. *Brahma-nirvāṇa* has no shores.[20] They are visible, as a mirage, only from the other (this) side.

a) The Mystery of the Beyond

Paraṁ rahasyam

It would be preposterous to claim that the Vedic Revelation has so clearly disclosed the mystery of the beyond that the only remaining requirement is to listen to it. It would also be out of place to pretend that the Vedas have given the answer for which mankind is constantly searching. No answer to any existential question can be given once and for all, nor can we find solutions by proxy to personal issues. We may immediately add that any intellectual answer to the problem of death is methodologically weak, for human reason would then leap outside the area in which it is competent.

What we can learn from the *śruti* is not an intellectual elucidation or a theoretical answer to the problem of death, but rather an attitude and a disposition. We may even realize new dimensions of the problem of death which may help to enlighten our own confrontation with the darkness of the beyond. Anything we say or think about death is bound to be unsatisfying. Death is precisely such because it is a state where "all words recoil," to quote a Upaniṣad speaking about the bliss of Brahman.[21] We may in a way speak more properly about deathlessness than about death, because if we belong to the living we can more congruently deal with life than with what is not life.

20. Cf. BG V, 24-26 (§ V 28).
21. TU II, 4 (§ VI 7).

The documents in this subsection do not talk much, in point of fact, about death. They speak about Yama, Naciketas, Immortality, this temporal world (*saṁsāra*), and the two ways leading from this world. They bear witness to an attitude of hope, of joy, of faith; they depict a human situation which is neither overwhelmed nor excessively worried by death; they seem to describe an existential attitude that takes cognizance of the phenomenon of death but denies to it any character of ultimacy, either psychological or metaphysical. It is by integrating the fact of death into life, by reabsorbing, as it were, death into life, by not losing ground, or rather by finding a ground that is common to both death and life, that we can find the proper Vedic perspective.

The six chapters of this subsection, reinforced by scores of other texts, including many of those that follow in subsequent subsections, all present the same characteristic feature: they do not overstress the rupture and the discontinuity at the price of losing sight of the harmony and the continuity between life and death. Life and death are not on the same level, as it were. There is not a principle of life on the one hand and a principle of death on the other. Life and death are intertwined and death is almost inbuilt into life. Moreover, life, although this seems at first sight to be contradicted by the Upaniṣads, is this earthly human life, though seen in a deeper perspective than the merely empirical one. The Atharva Veda unambiguously declares: "this world is the most beloved."[22]

The next subsection offers striking examples of this attitude. Even the Upaniṣads, at a second reading—and they have certainly been read many times—do not place the "otherworld" outside this life. They stress so much the radical difference between real life, that is, the liberated life, on the one hand, and the unauthentic existence of the life of the senses or of the body on the other, that the former can be almost perfectly immanent in the latter. The *ātman* is so different from and so superior to the body that it does not rest on or depend upon the body, as later periods forcefully affirm with expressions like "the world is the great illusion," "Brahman is the ultimate subject of *avidyā*," "*saṁsāra* is Brahman," "*nirvāṇa* is *saṁsāra*," "*saṁsāra* is *nirvāṇa*," and the like.

Be that as it may, we could almost say without being too paradoxical that a feature of the Vedic experience is that it treats the

22. AV V, 30, 17 (§ V 9).

problem of death as a noneschatological question. Death does not belong to the *eschata,* to the last things, but is an accident in the life of the individual and an incident in the life of society. The beyond is the unfathomable ocean which makes the beaches on this side worth walking on and playing on. The texts, however, tell us more than further comment could.

The Twin of Gods and Men *Yama-Yamī*

1 Among the many figures of the Vedas only a few have successfully passed through the fine metaphysical strainer of the Upaniṣads and the even finer sieve of time. Most of them have become lumber of the past or have been transformed into other deities or notions which conserve a certain continuity in the memory of the specialists but very little in the minds of ordinary people or in the events of everyday life. Among those few survivors we have the fascinating and intriguing figure of Yama. We shall try to expound this fundamental myth shorn of its many later additions and contradictions.[23] We may perhaps in this way find an explanation of the fact that Yama has for so long remained in the realm of the mythical and has not been downgraded to the mythological. We do not give a complete interpretation of the figure of Yama down the ages. In point of fact we have in Yama a commingling of many motifs. We have a whole gamut of factors concurring in Yama, from fertility rites to Egyptian and Iranian myths, so that it would be a mistake to reduce them to an artificial unity. Instead, we select some of the most salient features of Yama and submit what we think constitutes the core of the Yama myth: Yama, the primordial historical Man, reached immortality and thus a divine state by overcoming the double temptation that springs from selfishness and from the fear of death. He overcame this temptation by his fidelity to *ṛta,* truth, and through his loyalty to the Gods.

Although Yama's name is found some fifty times in the Ṛg Veda, only three hymns are dedicated to him. The main reason that he has survived most of the other deities may be precisely that he is not, properly speaking, a God, but a Man; he is not just an animal called Man, but a full Man, that is, a divinized or immortal Man, actually

23. The contradictions not only add to the charm of the myth but also represent the fact that Yaı fundamentaly an embodiment of contradictory human nature.

the first Man to cross to the realm of the beyond.[24] Although later periods like to portray him as a judge, with Citragupta as his scribe, and stress the role of his two dogs as his messengers, he is not in Vedic times a figure who punishes, but a hero who runs before us and shares with us both the human condition and the divine calling.[25] He is the first Man to become immortal, the first one to attain his destiny. He is the Forerunner, as we shall see,[26] or, as the Atharva Veda puts it in a paraphrase of the same Ṛg-Vedic hymn:

> Yama was the first to die among the mortals,
> the first to go forth to that world before us.[27]

Yama stands for the personified link between the two worlds. He does not come from the otherworld to ours but, on the contrary, he goes from our world to the other realm. Yama is the bridge to immortality, constructed from our side. But, unlike other bridges, Yama is a person; the bridge is personified.

Furthermore, Yama touches one of the deepest human realities: the fact of death. Yama is the king of the dead[28] and death is his path.[29] In point of fact he is a king of the human realm that is the kingdom of the dead.[30] He is really the "gatherer of people."[31] All Men at one moment or another are gathered by him. He gives them a resting place.[32] He is more the hero of the dead than the God of death. People pray to him in order to be released from their bondage.[33] We shall have occasion to meet Yama yet again in connection with death.[34]

The story in our particular hymn is clear and well known. Yamī, the twin sister of Yama, not only loves him but is convinced that the law of nature, which she certainly represents, demands that man and woman procreate and love each other. Moreover, as twins, Yama and Yamī have already been lying together in their mother's womb. But their first responsibility is toward future generations: if

24. Cf. RV X, 14, 1-2 (§ V 7).
25. The name Yama has a double etymology. Whereas for the first period he can be said to be the "twin" (not only of Yamī but of men and Gods), in the second period his name is interpreted as meaning "the restrainer."
26. Cf. RV X, 14 (§ V 7).
27. AV XVIII, 3, 13. Probably the "mortals" do not include the Gods here, though, as we have already seen, (§ III 21), they were not originally immortals. Yama belongs to Man's history.
28. Cf. RV X, 16, 9 (§ V 16).
29. Cf. RV I, 38, 5.
30. Cf. RV IX, 113, 8 (§ V 23); X, 14 throughout (§ V 7).
31. Cf. RV X, 14, 1 (ibid).
32. Cf. RV X, 14, 9 (ibid); X, 18, 13 (§ V 15).
33. Cf. RV X, 97, 16.
34. Cf. §§ V 2; V 5; V 7.

they do not overcome the taboo of incest, mankind will perish forever and the race of Men will be extinguished. All the arguments are in favor of Yamī.

Yama, however, does not yield. He retorts that evil times will certainly come later, in which unlawful actions will be done, but that he is not prepared to do such a deed. Earth, Heaven, Mitra, Varuṇa, and all the Gods will disapprove of it. He is unmoved by dialectical arguments and unconcerned with pragmatic reasoning, for he the primordial man is truthful to his vocation. We have, however, already suggested the main reason for Yama's refusal: his loyalty to *ṛta,* his rejection of *anṛta:*

> Shall I utter truth aloud and murmur untruth secretly? Shall I be a hypocrite and only keep up appearances? Shall I act according to somebody else's caprice, or even follow my own likings, disregarding the true cosmic order of things? Shall I, in short, not be truthful?[35]

Fidelity to truthfulness seems to be the pivot of the whole story.

Although they are supposed to be alone, Yama with an extremely refined psychological device simply directs the imagination of Yamī to embrace another. There is an indication here that the gratifying of the sexual urge does not stand in the foreground.

The act of incest is not committed and yet mankind subsists. Men are mortal and yet they became immortal. Here lies the power of this myth. We may indicate some of the leading threads.

Yama is a brother to the Gods. His father Vivasvat[36] is certainly a solar deity, perhaps the sun itself. Saraṇyu, his mother, is none other than the daughter of the God Tvaṣṭṛ. But Yama is also a brother to Men. Though he is offered the Soma and is thus accorded a privilege of the Gods, he is never explicitly called a God.[37] He is a real Man and the whole story of his temptation proves that he has had to work out his own salvation. By nature, that is, by birth, Yama is twin to Gods and Men. But by grace, that is, by conquest, merit, deeds, and by his fidelity to his life, he has overcome death, has become immortal, and divinized, he has become the father of all Men once they are on the other side of time and space. He is the King of the dead.

35. This passage is a paraphrase of RV X, 10, 4 (§ V 1).

36. Vivasvat, the brillant one, the shining forth (from *vi-vas-*), is the father of the Aśvins as well (RV X, 17, 2 [§ V 14]) and also of Manu (who is constantly called by the patronymic *vaivasvata*) with whom Yama is identified, as we shall see later.

37. Cf. RV X, 135, 1 (§ V 2).

Later legends tell of the death of Yama and of the inconsolable grief and sorrow of his sister Yamī, which gives rise to the beautifully human explanation of the cosmic rhythm of day and night. It banishes the grief of a devoted sister. The Gods, seeing the sadness of Yamī who was unable to forget the death of Yama, created the night:

> Yama had died. The Gods tried to persuade Yamī to forget him. Whenever they implored her to do so, she said: "But it is only today that he died." Then the Gods said: "Like this she will certainly never forget him; we will create night." So the Gods created night and thus there arose a morrow; thereupon she forgot him. Therefore people say: "Without doubt day and night together let sorrow be forgotten."[38]

Often the myth of Yama and Yamī is called difficult and strange; it is regarded as a mere ballad, a nice but incongruous narrative, and so on. If we do not look for what is not to be found there we may perhaps understand its message. The silence of the myth also has to be incorporated into the interpretation and the silence about the incest is total. The fact that mankind was not extinguished and that offspring came out of the first pair does not justify speaking of a hidden or later incest as if only a Fall could be at the origin of the human race. It would perhaps be more accurate to speak of a Miracle, of a double one indeed, that of generation and that of immortality. Both things go together. Procreation is immortality. Yama's loyalty has effected both, and thus he became both the first immortal Man and the father of Men.[39] It is interesting to note the similarity between Yama and Manu, who is also said to be our father[40] and the first sacrificer, the first to present offerings to the Gods.[41]

The hymn about Yama is more than a recital of a moral or edifying story about our Forefathers. It is important to understand the overcoming of the temptation by which Yama conquered death and reached immortality, as clearly expressed in the third stanza of the hymn:

> It is this that the immortals wish from you:
> an offspring from the unique mortal.

If Yama does not yield, death will reign over the whole earth and he

38. MaitS I, 5, 12.
39. Cf. RV X, 135, 1 (§ V 2).
40. Cf. RV II, 33, 13 (§ II 29).
41. Cf. RV X, 63, 7.

himself will die without offspring, most miserable destiny.[42] He could hardly suffer a stronger temptation, and we can understand here incidentally that if the ethical sphere were autonomous and unrelated to the cosmic one, there is no reason on earth (and Indian culture, too, knows casuistry) why the merely moral taboo should in this instance not be broken and overcome. Yet Yama does not yield because he does not understand the problem in terms of individual casuistry or of the merely ethical grounds of autonomous morals. It is the victory over death which brings him immortality and we can understand why. He has really passed beyond death, has despised it, has not yielded, has not been frightened of dying, of remaining without offspring, and thus of leaving the whole world unpeopled. The temptation is not in Yamī, the dear sister, but in what she says, in her reasons.

The myth tells us that Yama has conquered immortality. It does not need to tell us that he has conquered life also, for human life goes on here in this world, without the perpetration of the incest. At the origin of the human race there is a miracle, a miracle both of life and of immortality.

On the basis of the vast Vedic tradition we may suggest another reason that the act of incest was not perpetrated. The true incest that perpetuates the human race is not merely a human act of procreation between brother and sister, but the theandric action of the divine Father of creatures uniting himself with his daughter; this stresses the fact that man is not only an animal but also a divine offspring.[43] The origin of mankind cannot be traced to an act of human weakness but to a divine one, if weakness it really is.[44] It is God who has pity on his creation and unites himself with his own offspring.[45] If Yama had wanted to, he could have usurped the place of God, but he could not commit such a cosmic crime.

Yama is not simply a Vedic deity; he is neither a God nor just a mortal man. He is man, the Man, but he is not the cosmic *puruṣa* or the metaphysical *ātman*. He is the concrete historical and transhistorical Man; he is mortal and yet he has an immortal life before him which he has to win by conquest, by overcoming the temptation to break the order of the universe for the sake of his own concupiscence or for the sake of complying with others or of

42. Cf. RV V, 4, 10, where it is said that through our children we can become immortal.
43. Cf. the enigmatic RV X, 61.
44. The desire of Prajāpati for a "second"; cf. BU I, 4, 3 (§ I 7); CU VI, 2, 3 (§ VI 2).
45. Cf. RV X, 61, 5-7; TMB VIII, 2, 10; JaimB III, 2, 61 sq.; TB II, 3, 10 sq.; etc.

following the arguments of his own mind. Yama overcomes all attempts to make him the supreme criterion of truth and righteousness. Let the world remain empty of mortals[46]—yet he will not yield.

If we overlook later legendary accretions which made of Yama a terrible God of death and hell, we may conclude that the core of the myth is as follows. Yama is the symbol of Man, of an achieved and fulfilled Man, who has thus already transcended his earthly condition yet preserves his full identity as Man. He is the "master of the house," yet he fails to keep the rules of hospitality, so that he has to apologize by dispensing his favors.[47] He has a fully human identity and yet is no longer subject to the limitation of this spatio-temporal world. He is the risen Man. The origin of the human race and the historical existence of mankind go back to the fidelity of the Primal Man to truth. No wonder the children of Man have a divine destiny.

Yama-Yamī RV X, 10

[Yamī:]

1. May I entice my friend toward friendship,
far though he has gone beyond the oceans!
The sage shall produce a grandchild for his fathers,
considering what will happen here on earth.

[Yama:]

2. Your friend repudiates such a friendship
as will make of his sister a woman unrelated.
The heroes, sons of the mighty Asura,
sustainers of the heaven, view all from afar.

[Yamī:]

3. Do not the immortals require of you that
from the sole existing mortal issue an offspring?
Let your heart and mine be fused together.
Enter now as husband the body of your wife!

[Yama:]

4. Shall we do now what has hitherto been spurned?
Shall we who speak truth now countenance wrong?

46. Although stanza 10 speaks of later ages it does not invalidate this point, any more than the other husband and another wife of stanzas 10 and 12-14 invalidate the fact that Yama and Yamī are supposed to be the first human pair.

47. Cf. § V 5.

The Merman and the Nymph within the waters—
these are our origin, our intimate kinship.

[Yamī:]

5. Even in the womb God, the Ordainer
and Vivifier, the molder of forms, made us consorts.
No one transgresses his Holy Laws;
to this both Heaven and Earth bear witness.

[Yama:]

6. Who knows about the first day? Who has seen it?
Who can of that day produce firm proof?
Great is the decree of Mitra and Varuṇa,
What, temptress, will you say to men to seduce them?

[Yamī:]

7. Desire for Yama overwhelms me, Yamī,
to lie with him on a common bed.
As a woman to her husband I would yield my body.
Like chariot wheels let us move to and fro!

[Yama:]

8. They do not rest or close their eyes,
these watchmen of the Gods who pace around us.
Go, temptress, with another, not with me!
With him move like chariot wheels to and fro!

[Yamī:]

9. By day and by night would Yamī cherish you.
For a moment the eye of the Sun would vanish!
Twins unite in a bond like that of Earth and Heaven.
The blame for the incest of Yama will be Yamī's.

[Yama:]

10. It may well be that in later generations
brother and sister will act against the law.
Look for another than myself, O fair one,
and offer your arm to another lover.

[Yamī:]

11. What brother is he who protects not his sister?
Does she count as a sister when destruction is at hand?
Swept along by love, I whisper again:
unite your body with this body of mine!

[Yama:]

12. Never will I unite my body with yours.
Sin it is called to approach one's sister.
Not with me—with another find your delight!
Your brother, O fair one, does not desire it.

[Yamī:]

13. O miserable coward! In you, O Yama,
I do not find either soul or heart.
Very well; let another entwine herself around you
as a girdle, as a creeper encircles a tree!

[Yama:]

14. Entwine yourself also, O Yamī, around another.
Let another embrace you as the creeper a tree!
Seek to win his heart and let him win yours
and form with him a blessed union!

2. Sister: *salakṣmā*, she who has the same features, is of the same parentage.
Sons of the mighty Asura: the Aṅgirases who perform the role of moral overseers in the same way as the divine watchmen in stanza 8.
3. The sole existing mortal: a frequent designation of Yama.
Heart: *manas*.
4. Truth: *ṛta*.
Wrong: *anṛta*, unrighteousness. Cf. RV III, 4, 7, which may shed some light on more than one aspect: truth-untruth, the connection with Sacrifice, with Manu, etc.
Merman: Gandharva.
Nymph: Apsaras, here understood to be the parents of Yama and Yamī.
Origin: *nābhi*, lit. navel.
Kinship: *jāmi*, blood relation, sister.
5. Ordainer: Tvaṣṭṛ.
Vivifier: Savitṛ.
Holy Laws: *vratāni*.
6. Temptress: *āhanas*, lascivious woman.
7. Bed: *yoni*, lit. womb.
8. Watchmen of the Gods: *devānāṁ spaśaḥ*.
Temptress: *āhanas*.
9. Bond like that of Earth and Heaven: cf. stanza 5; a reference to the myth of Heaven and Earth who are called sisters in RV I, 159, 4, and yet are the parents of the universe.
Incest: *ajāmi*, "what is not proper for brother and sister," lawless act. Without the sun there is night and then the God would not see.
10. Act against the law: *ajāmi*.
Lover: lit. bull.
11. Destruction: *nirṛti*.
14. Blessed union: *saṁvidaṁ subhadrām*.

Drinking Soma With the Gods *Devaiḥ saṁpibate*

2 This intriguing hymn contains three parts which present three aspects of the mystery of death. The first and the last verses constitute a frame, describing the realm of Yama, who was the first among mortals to reach the otherworld and who is Death personified. There is nothing fearful about the "seat of death;" rather, it inspires a lofty idea of a paradise where the dead join Yama and the Gods in a heavenly feast, drinking Soma and hearing the flute and songs of praise.

The second part of the drama of death (vv. 1-2) is more down to earth and shows the grief of a son for his departed father. It seems to be only the son, representing the surviving family, who grieves; the father, on the contrary, desires to join his predecessors, those who have gone before him to the heavenly world. The beauty and the simplicity of the heavenly and human sides of death are strikingly clear. The third part (vv. 3-6) adds an enigmatic story which leaves us in perplexity.

Verses 3-6 have been variously interpreted. Some have understood that a boy—the son (or a person whose name is Kumāra)—dies and is addressed either by his father or by death himself. It seems as if, seeing the death of his father, the boy does not want to go on living, and so he mounts the symbolical chariot for the journey to Yama's realm. The chariot, like the boat (v.4), is the Vedic symbol for the sacrifice by which the dead person ascends to the heavenly realm. The dead man leaves behind the priests who proceed to celebrate the funeral rites, and thus the Sāman chant still follows him on his journey. Verse 5 puts a series of questions about the boy's origin, about the way ("chariot") by which the boy reached Yama's kingdom, and, third, about the obscure *anudeyī*, "that which is given after." It probably means the funeral gifts, or it may perhaps refer to the bride, asking why the youth died before being married. Other interpreters have understood the ascent of the boy to the seat of Yama not as real but as an imaginative or ecstatic movement. A hint of this meaning can be found in the expression that the chariot is "made by the mind" of the boy (*manasākṛṇoḥ*) because he only mentally follows his departed father. The questions in verse 5 would then cast doubt on the reality of the boy's "journey."

Indian tradition[48] has seen in these difficult stanzas a first version and a foreshadowing of the well-known story of Naciketas.[49] Whichever interpretation we may make our own, in each of the three instances—whether the youth dies, whether he ascends to Yama in imagination or in reality—we can see in verse 5 the exclamations and questions that arise when Man is faced with the overwhelming fact of death. They are concerned with the origin of the youth (even in a cosmogonic sense), the "whence," with his departure from this world (the "wheelless chariot") and with that third obscure "thing" given to him either as the "nourishment," the

48. Cf. Sāyaṇa *hoc loco*.
49. Cf. § V 5.

"equipment," or the "funeral gift" of the dead. It is this last "gift" that becomes the measure, we may say, of life. Verse 6 adds to the obscurity and leaves room for almost any temporal, spatial, existential, or ritual interpretation. If we read an existential meaning into it, we might venture to say: according to the measure "given" to a man (*anudeyī*)—later periods would say according to his *karman*—such is his origin (*agra*). First the ground (or depth) of life is extended, spreads forth, and then, when his span is over, a passage or exit is made and Man leaves the place of his earthly existence. The *idam* with which the next stanza (7) opens, referring to the seat of Yama, may confirm this interpretation: at this exit from life we reach the abode of the Gods, the heavenly realm, and we hear the sound of Yama's flute whose music no mortal can resist.

Devaiḥ saṁpibate RV X, 135

[The Son]

1. Near the fair-leafed tree where Yama drinks
   in the company of the Gods,
   our father, master of our house, is seeking
   the fellowship of the ancients.

2. I gazed with reluctance upon him as he
   trod the evil path,
   seeking the fellowship of the ancients; and I longed
   to see him again.

[The Father]

3. Without seeing it you mounted, young man, the new chariot
   constructed by your mind;
   wheelless it is, with only one pole,
   yet it moves in all directions.

4. The chariot, young man, which you made to roll forward,
   taking leave of the priests,
   was followed by a chant, conveyed on a boat
   from here to there.

5. Who was father of the youth? Who caused the chariot
   to proceed on its way?
   Who can tell us today the nature
   of the viaticum's gift?

6. According to the nature of the gift
   arose the beginning.
   First was the base extended; later
   was contrived an exit.

7. Such is the seat of Yama, called also
   the home of the Gods;
there the God plays on his flute, there he dwells,
   glorified by songs.

1. Seeks the fellowship: *anu-ven-*, looks for, desires to see.
The ancients: *purāṇāḥ*, the ancestors, his predecessors.
2. The evil path: death, which is regarded by the son as an evil way.
I longed to see him: the root *spṛh-* may also mean to envy; both meanings could fit into the hymn, because the following vv. show the desire of the boy to follow his father.
3. Constructed by your mind: *manasākṛṇoḥ*, imagined?
4. Priests: *viprāḥ*, the wise, the speakers, but here referring to the priests performing the funeral rite.
Chant: *sāman*, funeral hymn.
5. The nature of the . . . gift: lit. how was the gift, *anudeyī*, an obscure word probably meaning funeral gift (or equipment for the journey to death?): viaticum.
6. Beginning: *agra*, could also mean top (of the chariot), and then the translation would be in spatial instead of temporal terms (i.e., "in front" instead of "first," "behind" instead of "later").
Exit: *nirayaṇa*, also result.
7. This very poetic stanza corresponds to the description of Yama's world in the first two lines of stanza 1.
Glorified: *pariṣkṛta*, lit. adorned.

Within Death There Is Immortality — *Antaraṁ mṛtyor amṛtam*

3 We know by now how startling the Brāhmaṇas are. The two texts that follow undoubtedly have an immediate cultic context. The first has to do with the ritual of the fire altar; the second reflects the existence of an ordeal. But both texts point beyond their immediate background, for, according to the Brāhmaṇas themselves, everything has a specular character and thus reflects something of the yonder and more real world.

In this sense we can interpret the first passage as disclosing that death and nondeath are not so opposite to and separate from each other as we might be tempted to assume. Two paradoxical statements put it in a striking way: death does not die and thus within Death itself there is immortality. Here is something more than what we learn from the Upaniṣads, that "life does not die."[50] We are not satisfied with discovering a *jīva*, a soul resistant to the bite of death; we hear that death itself belongs to immortality, that death is not the "end" of life, not something on the frontier of and, eventually, frightening to life, but a constitutive element of life itself.

50. Cf. CU VI, 11, 3 (§ VI 10). This famous passage suggests that the *jīva* is immortal because the *ātman* is its life.

Death is not at the limit of life, but in the middle of it. One has to be born thrice, in fact, in order to be immortal.[51]

The very universality of death makes Man give it a superhuman character, and thus it acquires a quasi-divine status. What does it mean to say that the Gods have the privilege of immortality? It means not merely that after death comes immortality, as the text has sometimes been understood to say, but that it is only through death that immortality is reached, and thus that death itself already contains the seed of immortality. Another passage in the same Brāhmaṇa illustrates the same point. The setting, obviously sacrificial, deals with immortality which some sacrifices may afford. We are in the period in which the Gods were still working out their destiny; they performed the proper sacrifice and thus became immortal:

> Death then spoke to the Gods: "If this is so, then surely all men will become immortal. What will then be my fate?" The Gods said: "From now on no one will become immortal with the body. After you have taken the body as your portion, then only shall whoever is going to become immortal, either by wisdom or works, become immortal, that is, after having laid down the body."[52]

For the human race, therefore, immortality is reached only through death; death becomes the gate to immortality.

In the same vein we may add that only mortal things are immortal. Immortality is not sheer deathlessness, the mere continuation of a given earthly and temporal condition; it is rather the overcoming of death, the passing through it and reaching the other shore, a shore that can exist only because the river of death lies between it and life. A stone, even in an unscientific cosmology, is not immortal. We have here a profound and extraordinary intuition, which yielded fruit in many schools of thought and spirituality. Death is the very token of its contrary, immortality. Here death is not the sequel of evil or of sin but the very condition of authentic life. Death is thus not even bad; it is the door to the realm where Man can fully be what he ultimately is. "Death is suffused in light," says our text; death clothes itself in brightness.

The second Brāhmaṇa connects the two worlds in a forceful way and gives us the hope of being eternally victorious in the yonder

51. Cf. SB XI, 2, 1, 1 (§ III 23).

52. SB X, 4, 3, 9. The same word, *bhāga,* is used for both "fate" and "share." Wisdom and works are *vidyā* and *karman*. This text is one of those Vedānta cites to sustain its theory of knowledge being homologized to the sacrifice, viz., *vidyā* to *karman,* though the text goes on to say that both *vidyā* and *karman* are the fire altar. Cf. also the paragraph that immediately follows for the coming into life again of those who know.

world if we succeed in being triumphant in this one. The pair of scales is the symbol of justice in this world and in the other—a a metaphor that is almost universal. Another interesting feature is the inverse relation between the two worlds. It is the right weighing here which will spare an unfavorable judgment there. Whatever is done on earth has repercussions in heaven.[53]

Antaraṁ mṛtyor amṛtam

SB X, 5, 2, 3-4

i) 3. He verily is Death, that Person in the yonder orb. That orb's blazing ray is the immortal; thus Death cannot die either, for he is enclosed within the immortal; thus Death cannot be seen, for he is enclosed within the immortal.

4. On this point there is a verse: "Within Death there is immortality," for after Death comes immortality. "On Death is based immortality," for it is within immortality that the Person established in yonder orb shines. "Death clothes itself in Light," for Light, to be sure, is yonder Sun, because this light changes day and night, and so Death clothes itself in Light and is surrounded on all sides by Light. "The Self of Death is in the Light," for the Self of that Person is assuredly in that orb. Thus says the verse.

SB XI, 2, 7, 33

ii) Now, regarding the balance of the right side of the altar: whatever good a man does, that is placed upon the altar; whatever evil a man does, that is placed outside the altar. Therefore he should sit down, touching the right side of the altar, for he will be placed on the balance in the otherworld. He must follow the path of the raised balance, whether for good or for evil. He who knows this places himself on the balance even in this world and is thus released from the balance of the other world, for his good deeds raise the balance, not his evil deeds.

■ i) 3. Death: *mṛtyu*.
Orb: *maṇḍala*, the disk of "yonder Sun."
Blazing ray: *arcis*, the glowing light, radiance (of the sun).
Within the immortal: *amṛte . . . antaḥ*.
4. Within death there is immortality: *antaraṁ mṛtyor amṛtam*.
After death: could also be translated as "near death" (*avara*).
On death is based immortality: *mṛtyāv amṛtam āhitam*.
Light: *vivasvat*, the radiant one, the brilliant one, a name of the sun. Yama is said to be the son of Vivasvat; cf. § V 1. There is here a pun on the verb *vi-vas-*, meaning both to shine forth and also to change, to depart, and the verb *vas-*, to clothe.
■ ii) Balance: *tulā*.
Altar: *vedi*, the place of the sacrifice.
Good: *sādhu*.
Evil: *asādhu*.

53. Cf. the same idea of retribution in SB XII, 9, 1, 1.

Two Ways Are Given to Mortals *Pitṛyāna-devayāna*

4 The Ṛg Veda speaks of a way leading to the Gods. The same way, moreover, is used by the Gods themselves when they come down to the sacrifice,[54] so that it carries a two-way traffic, Men ascending and Gods descending.[55] In one place Death is requested to move on a road far distant from the one that leads to the Gods, so as not to disturb those who tread there.[56] The Upaniṣads systematize the whole subject of the different paths on which the departed proceed to the otherworld. From the dialogue between Śvetaketu and Pravāhaṇa it appears that this field of enquiry is new,[57] as new as the belief in transmigration. The questions are posed: Who is to proceed on which path after death? Who is to return to earth? The Upaniṣads leave no doubt that "the one who knows," the one who has realized the truth and leads the austere life of a *vānaprastha,* a forest dweller, will proceed on the way of the Gods.[58] Here the sacrificial, cosmological, and *jñānic* or gnostic ways are combined in an organic whole without break or contradiction. In this instance, the dead passes into the flame of the funeral pyre; he goes along the auspicious temporal path, which is the bright half month (*śuklapakṣa*) and the northern way of the sun (*uttarāyaṇa*), passes into the sun, and is finally led to the *brahma-loka* from which there is no return. Those who have not yet attained so high a state, who are still on the level of performing rituals and good works (probably the householders [*gṛhastha*]), go along the inauspicious temporal path, during the dark half month (*kṛṣṇapakṣa*) and the southern way of the sun (*dakṣiṇāyana*), whence they proceed to the moon. In the moon these spirits become food for the Gods and must once more pass through the cosmological elements and return to earth in order to be reborn.

The second text (ii) shows in a striking manner how even those who go along the way of the Fathers (*pitṛyāna*)[59] and are reborn can be released if they know who they are. What is important with

54. Cf. RV I, 183, 6; III, 58, 5; IV, 37, 1; X, 51, 2; etc.
55. Cf. RV I, 162, 4; V, 43, 6; VII, 38, 8; VII, 76, 2; X, 51, 5; X, 98, 11; X, 181, 3; TS IV, 7, 13, 4.
56. Cf. RV X, 18, 1 (§ V 15).
57. Cf. BU VI, 2, 2 (§ V 4); KausU I, 1.
58. Cf. MundU I, 2, 11 (§ III 27).
59. *Pitṛyāna* occurs only once in the RV (X, 2, 7) where Agni is said to know the path of the Fathers. Cf. also AV XVIII, 4, 1.

regard to both these ways is to know them and to know what is to be done in order to attain them. He who really knows will not return again.

We may discover from these and similar texts a twofold insight: universal cosmic solidarity and the hierarchical world-building power of knowledge. We may give some idea of the first insight by saying that death is considered from two angles. It is the end of a temporal and spatial earthly road and also the gateway to the temporal and spatial road outside this earth. In fact, the whole universe forms a unity, for we live our lives together with our ancestors and between us we populate the entire universe. The world of Men is coextensive with both the physical and the spiritual universe. There are no empty stars and no time devoid of temporal beings.

Everybody, according to our second text, which is known as *paryaṅkavidyā* ("science of the couch"),[60] goes to the moon and there his destiny is decided according to the wish he expresses; a wish that depends upon his knowledge or nonknowledge of who he is. "Who are you?" is the crucial question of each man's cross-examination. Here the vital insight is that Man collaborates in the building of the universe. Everybody is invited to contribute to the (re)construction of the world. You may like to share your lot once again with Men or to fly to the heavenly world of the Gods, where other tasks will await you, but you can do so only if you put your whole self behind your affirmation of what you are and what you want to be. This is the meaning of the cryptic identification formulas that keep cropping up in these texts.

Pitṛyāna-devayāna

BU VI, 2, 1-8; 13-16

i) 1. Then Śvetaketu Āruṇeya went to the Council of the Pañcālas. He went to Jaivali Pravāhaṇa who was being attended by his servants. When the latter saw him, he said to him: "Young man!" "Yes, [sir]!" he answered. He then said: "Have you been instructed by your father?" "Yes," said he.

2. "Do you know how people here, when they have departed from this life, proceed on different paths?" "No," he said. "Do you know how they return again to this world?" "No," he said again. "Do you know how it is that the otherworld is not filled completely with the many who ceaselessly ascend to it?" "No," he said again. "Do you know after the offering of

60. With reference to the couch upon which Brahman is sitting. Cf. KausU I, 5 (ii).

which oblation it is that the waters acquire a human voice and, arising, speak?" "No," he said again. "Do you know the means of access to the path of the Gods or to the path of the Fathers, and what is to be done to proceed either on the path of the Gods or on the path of the Fathers? And have you not heard the word of the sage:

> Two ways, I hear, are given to mortals:
> the path of the Fathers and the path of the Gods.
> Upon these two all things proceed together,
> whatever moves between the Father and the Mother."

"No, I know nothing whatever of all this," he said.

3. Then he [the king] invited him to stay, but refusing to stay the boy ran away. He went to his father and said to him: "Sir, before you have called me well learned." "How is that, O wise one?" "The man of royal lineage asked me five questions of which I did not know the answer of even one." "What questions?" "The following," he said, repeating them.

4. The father said: "My son, you should know me as I am, that whatever I myself know, I have told to you. But let us go there and live in purity and the study of Brahman." "Sir, you may go alone," said [the son]. So Gautama went to the place where Pravāhaṇa Jaivali lived. There the king brought him a seat and had water brought for him. He gave him respectful hospitality. Then he said to him: "I shall grant a boon to the venerable Gautama."

5. Gautama replied: "You have promised me this boon. Please tell me, then, the words you spoke in the presence of my son."

6. He said: "This boon belongs to the divine boons; ask rather for a human one."

7. Gautama said: "It is well known that I have abundance of gold, cows, horses, female attendants, objects to fulfill my wishes, and garments. Do not deprive me of that which is of great value, eternal and boundless." "This, O Gautama, you will have to request in the proper way." "I approach you, sir, as a disciple." For with these words the ancient ones used to approach their master. Having declared himself as a disciple, he [Gautama] stayed [with the king].

8. The king said to him: "Neither you nor your Forefathers should take offense at this. This knowledge has from of old never remained with any brahmin. But I will declare it to you. For it is not proper to refuse it to you who speak like this."

13. . . . Out of this oblation a person comes to be. He lives as long as his life lasts. When he dies

14. they carry him to the [funeral] fire. . . .

15. Those who know this and those also who in the forest realize that faith is truth, they pass into the flame, from the flame into the day, from the day

into the bright fortnight, from the bright fortnight into the six months when the sun goes northward, from these months into the sun, from the sun into lightning. When they have reached the region of lightning, a spiritual person leads them into the worlds of Brahman. In these worlds of Brahman they dwell in the highest of the highest. For them there is no return.

16. But those who win the worlds by means of sacrifice, gifts, and austerity, they pass into smoke, from smoke into the night, from night into the dark fortnight, from the dark fortnight into the six months when the sun goes southward, from these months into the world of the Fathers, from the world of the Fathers into the moon. When they have reached the moon, they become food. There the Gods, in the same way as they say to King Soma, "Increase, decrease!" and partake of him, so also do they consume them. When that has taken place, they enter into this space, from space into the wind, from wind into rain, from rain into the earth. Having reached the earth, they become food; again they are offered into the fire of a man, whence they are born in the fire of a woman, and, arising in the worlds, again move in the circle. But those who do not know these two paths, they become crawling and flying and biting beasts.

KausU I, 2-6

ii) 2. He said: those, in truth, who leave this world all go to the moon. In the bright half the moon grows large because of these beings and in the dark half it causes them to be born [again]. The moon, assuredly, is the gate to the heavenly world. Those who answer the moon [properly] are released, but those who do not answer [properly] become rain and rain down [on earth], where they will be born again in different conditions of life, according to their works and according to their knowledge, either as an insect, or as a bird, or as a fish, or as a big bird, or as a lion, or as a bear, or as a snake, or as a tiger, or as a man, or as some other being. When he reaches there, a man is asked "Who are you?" He should reply:

> From the radiant one, O seasons, the seed was collected,
> from the fifteenfold, from the world of the Fathers.
> Place me in man as an agent, and thence,
> with the man as an agent, place me in a mother.

[Or he should say:]

> So was I born, brought forth in the twelfth
> or thirteenth month, sired by a father
> who is twelve- or thirteenfold by nature.
> Knowing this, I understand; knowing this, I am.
> By this Truth, O seasons, by this Ardor make me deathless!
> I am season, a son of the seasons.

"Who are you?" [asks the moon.] "I am you!" [he replies.] Then he releases him.

3. When he proceeds on the path leading to the Gods, he reaches the world of Agni, then the world of Vāyu, the world of Varuṇa, the world of Indra, the world of Prajāpati, the world of Brahman. This world contains the lake Āra, the hours Yeṣṭiha, the river Vijarā, the tree Ilya, the city Sālajya, the palace Aparājita, the doorkeepers Indra and Prajāpati, the hall Vibhu, the throne Vicakṣaṇa, the couch Amitaujas, the beloved "Mind" and her counterpart "Vision" who, taking flowers, weave the worlds, and also the mothers, the nurses, the nymphs, and the rivers. To this world he who knows this comes. To him Brahman speaks: "Go toward him! for it is my glory that made him reach this undecaying stream, and assuredly he will not decay."

4. Then five hundred Apsarases approach him, a hundred with fruits in their hands, a hundred with ointments in their hands, a hundred with garlands in their hands, a hundred with garments in their hands, a hundred with perfumes in their hands. They adorn him with the ornament of Brahman. When he is adorned with the ornament of Brahman, he, the knower of Brahman, goes to Brahman. Then he reaches the lake Āra; he crosses over it by the mind. Those who approach it, knowing only the present, are drowned. Then he reaches the hours Yeṣṭiha, which run away from him. Then he reaches the river Vijarā which he crosses over by the mind alone.

   Then he shakes off his good and evil actions. Those who are dear to him take over his good actions, and those who are not dear to him, his bad actions. Just as a chariot driver looks down on the two chariot wheels, he too looks down upon day and night, upon good and evil actions, and upon all pairs of opposites. Thus he is free from good and evil, a knower of Brahman, and he goes to Brahman.

5. He comes to the tree Ilya and the fragrance of Brahman enters into him. He comes to the city Sālajya and the essence of Brahman enters into him. He comes to the palace Aparājita and the splendor of Brahman enters into him. He comes to the doorkeepers Indra and Prajāpati who run away from him. He comes to the hall Vibhu and the glory of Brahman enters into him. He comes to the throne Vicakṣaṇa whose front feet are the Sāman chants Bṛhad and Rathantara, whose hind feet are Śyaita and Naudhasa, whose bars stretching lengthwise consists of Vairūpa and Vairāja, whose bars stretching crosswise are Śākvara and Raivata. It is wisdom, for by wisdom one sees.

   Then he comes to the couch Amitaujas which is the Breath of life and whose front feet are past and future, whose hind feet are beauty and comfort, whose head parts are [the chants] Bhadra and Yajñāyajñīya, whose bars stretching lengthwise consist of Bṛhad and Rathantara, whose lengthwise cords are the Ṛg Veda hymns and the Sāman chants, whose crosswise cords are the Yajus formulas. The Soma-fibers are the mattress, the Udgītha chant is the cover, beauty is the cushion. He comes to the couch

Amitaujas which is Life. . . . On this couch Brahman is seated. He who knows this ascends to it with one foot only. Brahman asks him: "who are you?" He shall respond:

6. "I am season; I am son of the seasons. From space as origin I am born as seed of a woman, as the splendor of the year, as the self of every being. What you are, that I am." He asks him: "Who am I?" "Reality," he replied. "What is this reality?" "Whatever is different from the Gods and from the vital breaths, that is 'real,' but the Gods and the vital breaths are '-ity.' Therefore it is expressed by the word 'reality,' which comprises all that is. You are all that is." Thus he speaks.

■ i) This passage is similar to CU V, 3-10.

2. The Father and the Mother: i.e., Heaven and Earth.

4. In purity and the study of Brahman: *brahmacaryam.*

6. Belongs to the divine boons: *daiveṣu . . . vareṣu.* Cf. KathU I, 20-27 (§ V 5) where in the same way Yama tries to avoid the spiritual questions by tempting Naciketas with material wishes.

7. In the proper way: *tīrthena,* in the traditional manner, i.e., according to the ritual (consisting here of a short formula).

8. Offense: *aparādha.*

This instance is one of many in the U where a Kṣatriya is teaching the highest wisdom to a brahmin.

9-14. Cf. § III 26.

15. Realize that faith is truth: *śraddhāṁ satyam upāsate,* worship faith in truth, or meditate with faith on truth.

Spiritual person: *puruṣo mānasaḥ,* a person consisting of *manas* (mind, spirit).

Highest of the highest: *parāḥ parāvataḥ,* or, for long periods, immeasurable length.

■ ii) 2. Beings: *prāṇāḥ,* spirits, breath souls.

Released: *ati-sṛj-,* i.e., they proceed on the way of the Gods, *devayāna.*

Fifteenfold: i.e., the moon, which in the Hindu calendar is reckoned in units of fifteen days (the half month).

Or he should say: another type of answer for the candidate for the *devayāna.*

Twelfth or thirteenth month: i.e., within the span of a year.

Knowing this . . . : the *idam* may refer to the *devayāna* and *pitṛyāna,* respectively.

Truth: *satya.*

Ardor: *tapas.*

I am season: the individual soul depends upon the moon and time and hence is identified with "time," with the seasons.

3. Vijarā: lit. unaging, translated below as the "undecaying stream."

Aparājita: lit. unconquered. Cf. CU VIII, 5, 3 (§ III 27).

The beloved "Mind": *priyā ca mānasī.*

"Vision": *cākṣuṣī.* These are two female attendants of the throne of Brahman, representing two ways of knowledge: by understanding (*manas*) and by direct vision (*cakṣus*).

The image of weaving the worlds is again present.

4. Ornament of Brahman: *brahmālaṅkāra.*

Mind: *manas.*

Knowing only the present: *sampratividaḥ,* those who know only what is in front of them, and nothing beyond, cannot cross over to the "other shore."

The hours Yeṣṭiha . . . : because the knower of Brahman has already transcended time, even the mythical "time" of the Brahma world evaporates in front of him.

Good and evil actions: *sukṛta-duṣkṛta.* By the law of solidarity and interrelatedness, the merit derived from a man's good deeds goes to his dear ones (*priya*) and the fruit of his evil deeds, to his enemies (*apriya*).

Pairs of opposites: *dvandvāni.* Cf. BG IV, 22.

5. Doorkeepers: Indra and Prajāpati can reach no farther than the threshold of the world of Brahman, whereas the released person enters within.

Wisdom: *prajñā.*

Breath of life: *prāṇa.*

The throne and the couch of Brahman are made of the components of sacrifice, and mainly of the Sāman chant. This mythical description reveals the process by which Brahman becomes the Absolute, that is, by means of the sacrifice and the sacred chant.

6. The reply to the ultimate existential question refers both to the temporal self and to the ultimate Self of a person.

Sons of the seasons: *ārtava*, related to the season, i.e., temporal; derived from *ṛtu*, season.

From space as origin: *ākāśād yoneḥ; ākāśa* is the cosmic womb.

Reality: *satyam*. We have tried to reproduce the Sanskrit pun which splits the word into *sat* and *tyam*, by a similar device: "real-ity." Cf. also BU II, 3, 1 (§ VI 7); V, 5, 1; CU VIII, 3, 5 (§ VI 6).

You are all that is: *idaṁ sarvam asīti*. It is interesting that in this ultimate dialogue, man is a "you," *tvam*. Cf. § VI 10.

The Last Journey *Sāmparāya*

5 The Upaniṣads take us straight to the heart of the metaphysical problem connected with death. By means of lively dialogue the Kaṭha Upaniṣad brings us step by step to the disclosure of the mystery of death. The dialogue is between Yama and a young Brahmin, Naciketas by name. The parable of Naciketas belongs to an already highly developed stage in human consciousness. It combines the symbolism of Yama with elements of the earlier story of the Taittirīya Brāhmaṇa, thus weaving together in one artistic fabric the different threads of the Vedic tradition. The Kaṭha Upaniṣad presents to us one facet of the human experience of the universal phenomenon of death.

Yama is depicted both with human features (he was not at home when Naciketas went to him, he feels sorry, and apologizes) and with divine knowledge (he imparts the highest wisdom to the young man). Naciketas represents Man at his noblest, longing for enlightenment and realization, haunted by the problem of death and capable of overcoming the allurements and temptations to which Yama subjects him when attempting to avoid compliance with his request. He is not satisfied with individual comforts or concerned with individual problems. To discover the real meaning of death is the one thing that will satisfy him and he chooses the boon that will allow him to penetrate the mystery. The theme of temptation, which later on assumes considerable importance, is here only discreetly mentioned.

It is instructive to notice the divergencies between the story of the Brāhmaṇa and that of the Upaniṣad. Whereas the former is steeped in ritual and, by playing on words, elaborates the doctrine of the Naciketas fire through which one becomes imperishable, the latter, though acknowledging the value of rituals and repeating the first two boons, converts the third one into a spiritual realization which involves saving knowledge as well as ritual practices.

In the Taittirīya Brāhmaṇa[61] the third gift aims at the conquest of "death again" or "repeated death" (*punar-mṛtyu*).[62] The Upaniṣad, on the other hand, insists upon the necessity of knowing the mystery of the great departure and the teaching is imparted accordingly.

Out of desire for reward, Vājaśrava gave away all his wealth in order to perform a sacrifice. His son Naciketas, either because according to the customary ritual he himself is to be given away as part of the sacrifice or because "faith enters into him" offers himself also as oblation (*dakṣiṇā*) for the sacrifice and asks his father three times over to whom he has to go. "Go to hell!" is the impatient rejoinder of the father and there the boy goes, to the kingdom of death. Because of the absence for three days of King Yama, however, Naciketas does not receive the customary attention demanded by hospitality. To atone for the lapse Yama offers three favors or boons to Naciketas. The boy proceeds to ask, first, that the wrath of his father may be appeased and, next, that Yama may give him instruction concerning the fire of sacrifice which gains entry to heaven for a man. These two favors are granted.[63] As his third favor the young man begs to be enlightened on the crucial question: "Does Man—the life principle in a Man—continue to exist or not after death?" Or, more tersely and more vividly: "Is he or is he not?"[64]

KathU I, 20-21

i) [Naciketas:]

20. The doubt that exists about a man when he is dead—
for some say "he is" and others, "he is not"—
about that I would clearly know, instructed by you.
This is my third and final favor.

[Yama:]

21. Even the Gods were once in doubt about this question.
To know is not easy, so subtle is the problem.
Choose, Naciketas, another favor.
About this do not press me! Let it be!

Yama tries to dissuade him by offering him more tempting and

61. Cf. TB, III, 11, 8.
62. Not to be confused with *punar-janman,* rebirth or transmigration.
63. Cf. KathU I, 1-19 (cf. §§ I 37; V 27).
64. *Astīti; nāstīti.* The crucial question is put in two different ways in I, 20 (i) and I, 29 (ii).

solid favors, which Naciketas rejects. Yama finds the young man ripe for instruction and indeed better prepared than himself, for Naciketas is ready to give up all material and spiritual wealth in order to know the ultimate mystery.[65] There is a fundamental difference between the second favor, which is to know *svarga-loka,* the "world of heaven,"[66] and the way leading to *ananta-loka,* the infinite world,[67] and the third one, which is concrete existential knowledge of existence or nonexistence.

KathU I, 29

ii) [Naciketas:]

Tell us, I pray, of the great Departure
about which doubt exists, O Death.
The boon that will elucidate this mystery—
it is that and none other that Naciketas chooses.

Then Yama, judging him to be worthy of receiving Brahma knowledge, discloses to him the profound secret of *ātman-brahman.*

KathU II, 12-14

iii) 12. The hard-to-perceive and wrapped in mystery,
set in the cave and hidden in the depth—
he who, wise indeed, realizes this as God,
by means of an awareness centered on the Self,
leaves far behind both joy and sorrow.

The question about the Great Beyond is taken in an absolute way by Naciketas. It is not mere curiosity about afterdeath but an all-encompassing query about total transcendence.

13. The man who has understood and grasped this well,
who, stripping off all else, has plumbed this mystery,
will rejoice, having obtained what merits rejoicing.
For you, I think, the house is wide open, Naciketas!

[Naciketas:]

14. Declare to me then what you deem to be
beyond what is righteous and what is unrighteous,
beyond what is done and what is undone,
beyond what was and what shall be.

Yama's answer consists of an explanation of OM.[68] He then goes on to say that this mystery is beyond any observable appearance and is apparent only by its own grace.

65. In the TB the temptation in connection with the boon of *punar-mṛtyu* does not occur.
66. KathU I, 12 (§ V 27).
67. KathU I, 14 (§ V 27).
68. Cf. the texts on OM (§ VI C b).

KathU II, 18

iv) The Inspired Self is not born nor does he die;
he springs from nothing and becomes nothing.
Unborn, permanent, unchanging, primordial,
he is not destroyed when the body is destroyed.

KathU II, 20

v) Smaller than the small, greater than the great,
the *ātman* is hidden in the core of every creature.
One free from desire and thus free from grief
sees the greatness of the *ātman* by grace of the Ordainer.

Then follows a description of the *ātman* and the dispositions of the heart necessary for its realization. Next comes the famous metaphor of the chariot in which the *ātman* is the lord, the chariot is the body, the driver is the intellect (*buddhi*), the reins are the mind (*manas*), and the horses are the senses (*indriyāṇi*). Through yoga, affirms Yama, one begins to overcome death, and he proceeds to extol in a great crescendo the realization of the *ātman* as a means of overcoming death.

KathU III, 10-11

vi)

10. Beyond the senses are their objects,
beyond the objects is the mind,
beyond the mind is the intellect,
beyond the intellect is the great *ātman*.

11. Beyond the Great is the Unmanifest,
beyond the Unmanifest is the Person,
beyond the Person there is nothing:
it is the end, the highest state.

Yama now declares to Naciketas that he must set out on the difficult path of liberation from death.

KathU III, 14-15

vii)

14. Arise! Awake! Seek to understand
the favors you have won. The sharpened edge
of a razor is hard to cross—thus the sages
declare the intricacies of the path.

15. When one has realized that which is soundless,
intangible, formless, unchanging, tasteless,
odorless, unwavering, beginningless, and endless,
that which is infinite and perfectly stable,
then one is freed from the jaws of death.

Two stanzas bring to a close the story of Naciketas, but this question (I, 20) still haunts Man, and the Upaniṣad, in what is probably a later addition, continues its reflection. Chapter IV attempts to define the identity, the complete oneness, of *ātman* and Brahman by the expression "this is that," declaring that those who do not understand this essential unity pass from death to death, that is to say, from rebirth to rebirth, never transcending the world of space and time. The whole chapter is an injunction to turn inward and to discover the inner vision that will lead to immortality.[69] Chapter V reverts to the theme of the identity of *ātman-brahman* and, stressing the immanence-transcendence of the *ātman*, declares the supeme joy that results from the knowledge of this truth. It is this *ātman*, the *antarātman* or inner soul, which frees a man from death. We still hear echoes of the teaching of Yama to Naciketas:

KathU V, 6-7

viii)

6. Now I will teach you concerning
this mysterious everlasting Brahman
and also what becomes of the *ātman*
when death arrives, O Gautama.

7. Some go into a womb
to receive once again a body;
others enter inert things
according to their works and knowledge.

KathU V, 14-15

ix)

14. "This is that"—thus they recognize
the supreme ineffable happiness.
How will I then discern "it"?
Does it shine or does it reflect light?

15. There the sun does not shine, or moon or stars,
lightnings do not shine there, much less this fire.
All things shine as reflections of his shining
and this whole world is bright with his light.

The Upaniṣad concludes, in Chapter VI, with a vision of the world as an everlasting tree with its life, or roots, firmly fixed above, in Brahman, the immortal, and with its branches directed downward. The powerful breath of Brahman fills the universe with

69. For the whole of KathU IV cf. §§ VII 36; 40; 44; 48; 52; 56.

so much energy that fear seizes all things. Because of this fear the fire burns and the sun gives heat; because of this fear, also, Indra, Vāyu (the wind), and Death speed on their ways. He who is freed from all desires becomes immortal. It is this immortality that is bestowed upon Naciketas when he is purified and becomes one with Brahman.

KathU VI, 1-3

x)

1. This everlasting fig tree, whose roots are on high
and whose branches are below, is the Pure, is Brahman,
what is called the Immortal. In that all worlds
are established and nothing passes beyond.
This in truth is that!

2. This whole world—whatever exists—
both springs from that and moves by his breath.
Herein is great fear as in a brandished thunderbolt.
Those who know that become immortal.

3. From fear of that burns the Fire,
from fear of that blazes the Sun,
from fear of that both Indra and Vāyu
and Death, to name a fifth, speed on their ways.

KathU VI, 14-18

xi)

14. Once freed of all desires that lie in the heart,
then a mortal man becomes immortal.
Even in this life he attains to Brahman.

15. Once all the knots of the heart are cut,
then a mortal man becomes immortal.
This is the end of the instruction.

16. A hundred and one are the channels of the heart;
one of them leads to the crown of the head.
By this channel, proceeding upward, one goes to immortality.
The rest serve for movement in various directions.

17. The Person of a thumb's size, the *ātman* within,
ever dwells in the heart of beings.
One should draw him out of one's body with care
just as an inner stem is drawn from its sheath.
Him you should know, the Pure, the Immortal;
him you should know, the Pure, the Immortal.

18. Then Naciketas, instructed by Death,
having embraced this knowledge and the whole yoga discipline,
passed over to Brahman and became free from stain

and exempt from death; and so too is he
who possesses this knowledge of the Self within him.[70]

If Yama is the risen Man, the Man who has transcended his earthly condition, Naciketas is the Man on pilgrimage, the *homo viator,* the symbol of mankind's itinerant condition. He is the perpetual seeker, the Man of faith, driven by his desire to know, which leads him to ignore all other pursuits. He is a young man, a student, on the way.[71] He breaks with his father and even enrages him. He is the generous youngster, according to another interpretation, who reminds his father that he has not yet given up everything, as his son still remains to be offered as an oblation. Yama discovers that he will not be content with rituals and, perplexed by this obduracy, tries to convince the young man that he should be amply satisfied that the sacrificial fire will henceforth be called by his name. Rebuffed, he next tries to allure Naciketas with all sorts of earthly temptations.

After so graphic a buildup one would expect some spectacular disclosure regarding the meaning of death. We have here, certainly, one of the deepest revelations concerning the mystery of the beyond, but its hallmark of authenticity lies in its simplicity and universality. There is nothing spectacular here. The realm of the beyond is neither beyond nor far away; it is neither inaccessible to the majority nor reserved for the superhuman. Naciketas is the common Man who finds residing within his own self that for which he is searching. He is equipped simply with the desire to know, with a thirst for knowledge. Yet his thirst is not only intellectual; it is not an epistemological curiosity that drives him, but a gnostic-existential thrust, if we are allowed to phrase it this way: it is the desire to know salvation, to decipher not objective problems but the mystery of human existence, to master the riddle that consists of himself. Naciketas is Man desiring to know whether he is or is not, because in this knowledge is contained all his being. It was later called *mumukṣutva* or existential desire for liberation.[72] Some may see in Naciketas a sage, others a philosopher. He is in any event the searcher aspiring to reach fullness of life by discovering the mystery

70. Thus ends this U, which is followed by the *śānti-mantra* that we give at the end of this chapter.
71. Tradition has sometimes understood the name *na-ciketas* as "the one who does not know" (root *cit-*), hence the seeker.
72. Cf., e.g., Śaṅkara, BS *Bhāṣya* I, 1, 1.

of being itself. Here the problem of death is bound up with the question of being or not being, and Naciketas is the symbol of Man intent on this supreme quest.

The answer is immortalized in the simple words, "*this* is *that*," that is, that which you see and smell and think and will, that which comes within the range of your human experience, *this* is that, *this* is what you are looking for, *this* is that which transcends everything, that which is really beyond, that which is imperishable and absolute—except that you must really know the *this* and the *that*. You must know, furthermore, that the *this* is *that* and yet not confuse them, for the *that* certainly does not appear except in the form of *this* but if you mistake the *this* for the *that*, then you are deluded. Naciketas, know the *this* and know the *that*, know that *this* is *that* and yet do not mix or confuse them, do not blur the *this* and the *that*, precisely because *this* is *that*.

The Upaniṣad ends with the same invocation with which it started and which occurs also in other texts. Although it does not belong to the Upaniṣad proper, it acquires here a profound meaning:

May He help both of us,[73]
may He be pleased with both of us,
may we act together in a vigorous way,[74]
may our study be successful,
may we never hate each other.
Om! Peace, peace, peace.

■ i) 20. He is, he is not: *asti, nāsti,* with double reference to the immediate context and to the wider one of the *āstikas* and *nāstikas,* or orthodox and heterodox views on religion and reality.

21. Problem: *dharma,* doctrine, truth, state of affairs.

■ ii) Of the great Departure: *sāmparāye mahati.*

Mystery: *gūḍha,* covered, hidden, concealed, invisible, secret.

■ iii) 12. Set in the cave: *guhāhitam,* i.e., in the heart.

Wise: *dhīra,* i.e., the one who is firm in meditation, wise as a result of his realization of God.

Awareness centered on the Self: *ādhyātma yoga,* yoga relating to the deepest Self, spiritual yoga or spiritual communion or concentration. This phrase appears in the Upaniṣads only here.

13. Mystery: *dharmyam,* that which possesses *dharma.*

14. Beyond: *anyatra,* an adverb that can also mean other than, different, independent from.

Righteous, unrighteous: *dharma, adharma:* good and evil, merit and demerit, duty and nonduty, etc.

Done, undone: *kṛta, akṛta.*

What was and what shall be: *bhūta, bhavya,* past and future.

■ iv) Inspired Self: *vipaścit,* a name for the *ātman,* i.e., aware (*cit*) of *vipas* (inward vibration, internal stirring), hence, inspiration. The root *vip-* means to quiver, to tremble. Cf. BG II, 20, where this text is the substance of Kṛṣṇa's argument for engaging Arjuna in battle against his kin but on behalf of *dharma.*

■ v) Core: *guhā,* the cave, the heart, the secret place, the hidden spot.

Free from desire: *akratu,* without will, without craving.

By grace of the Ordainer: *dhātuḥ prasādāt.* If one adopts the variant *dhātu-prasādāt,* the text would read "through tranquillity of spirit [mind, senses, faculties]."

73. Teacher and student.

74. In a vigorous way: *saha vīryam,* with manly power, courage.

■ vi) 10. Senses: *indriyāṇi.*
Objects: *arthāḥ.*
Mind: *manas.*
Intellect: *buddhi.*
Cf. KathU VI, 7-8 (§ VI 11), where a similar progression is given and where the concept of *aliṅga puruṣa* is expressed: the bodiless, signless, attributeless person.
11. Unmanifest: *avyakta.*
Person: *puruṣa,* which here could perhaps be better rendered as Spirit.
Highest state: *parā gatiḥ,* the highest path, the supreme way, the final goal.
Parā is the word constantly used: beyond this or higher than this.
■ vii) 12. Cf. § VI 5.
14. Intricacies of the path: *durgaṁ pathas,* a way difficult to go.
■ viii) 6. Mysterious everlasting Brahman: *guhyaṁ brahma sanātanam.*
Gautama: *Gautama-kumāra* (young Gautama), says the TB and it is generally understood that Gautama refers to the clan (*gotra*).
7. According to their . . . knowledge: *yathāśrutam,* according to the tradition they received (what has been heard, learned), is the same as *yathāvidyām* in KausU I, 2 (§ V 4): according to knowledge. Cf. for a similar idea § V 12.
8. Cf. § VI 7.
9-13. Cf. § VI 2.
■ ix) 14. "This is that": *tad etad.*
Ineffable happiness: *paramaṁ sukham.*
Does it shine or does it reflect light: Many interpreters make a distinction bettwen *bhāti,* shining by its own light, and *vibhāti,* reflecting the light of another. Another reading has, "does it shine or does it not," *na bhāti vā* instead of *u bhāti vibhāti vā.* Ultimately the two readings come to the same, for in both the question is whether it shines or whether it reflects (i.e., does not shine of itself).
15. Reflections: here the same verb, *bhāti,* is used (as in v. 14) with the prefix *anu-;* thus *anu-bhāti,* shines after.
■ x) 1. Cf. the hymn to *skambha* (§ I 3). Cf. also RV I, 24, 7, and BG XV, 1, where again the *arbor inversa,* the inverted cosmic tree, is said to be immortal.
2. Breath: *prāṇa;* the universe originated from and develops owing to life.
Great fear: *mahad bhayam, mysterium tremendum!*
3. Cf. TU II, 8, 1, a similar stanza.
Indra and Vāyu here symbolize not only storms and winds but also all the cosmic powers: Agni, Sūrya, Indra, Vāyu, and Mṛtyu. The TB substitutes the moon for Indra.
■ xi) 4-11. Cf. § VI 11.
12-13. Cf. § VI 9.
14. This stanza is given also in BU IV, 4, 7 (§ VI 11).
15. It seems that this was the final verse of the second enlarged version of the Upaniṣad.
16. Channels of the heart: *hṛdayasya nāḍyaḥ,* the arteries. Cf. CU VIII, 6, 6; PrasnU III, 6 (§ II 6).
Crown of the head: *mūrdhan,* referring to the conception of *brahmarandra,* the opening of the skull which the soul passes through at the time of death.
17. Cf. MaitU VI, 38.
Ever dwells in the heart of beings: *sadā janānāṁ hṛdaye sanniviṣṭaḥ.*
To draw out with care the *puruṣa* from one's body is the supreme yoga discipline (*yogavidhi,* v. 18) and cannot be only a *mṛtyuproktā vidyā,* a teaching imparted by death.
18. Passed over to Brahman: *brahmaprāpta,* having attained or realized *brahman.*
Self within: *adhyātman,* relating to the Self.

The Breaking of the Death Cycle *Mṛtyu-saṁsāra*

6 The word *saṁsāra* was first coined in Upaniṣadic times. It is unknown in the Vedas but occurs in the Gītā. Later it was widely used in literature and in everyday language.[75] It means literally a going or wandering through, a course or passage through a succes-

75. For the Śāstric period cf. Manu I, 117, and the whole of Manu XII.

sion of states or stages.[76] Then it came to be used directly to mean the passing through a succession of existences, that is, of births and deaths, or, in a word, the cycle of life.[77] The meaning of the word was then extended so that it came to denote the totality of transitory things, that is, this fleeting world.

The Bhagavad Gītā uses *saṁsāra* to denote rather the cycle of death, for it is through and by death as the gate that living beings pass through and wander from one stage to another.[78] Death, therefore, is not seen as an end, but rather as a gate. One could almost call it a sluice through which the different elements of this world go as they move from one stage to another in the cosmic evolution of all empirical "reality."

Saṁsāra is not the cosmos but the world in its dynamic and evolutionary aspect; it is the world's movement, implying both change and continuity; it is the cyclical process of all the elements of this world. In terms of the present-day cosmological world view we could say that *saṁsāra* stands for cosmic transformation, and thus transmission, in all its manifestations, including that of matter. *Saṁsāra* is the universal circulation of the entire world traffic.

Together with the idea of *karman,* the notion of *saṁsāra* suggests the contingency and the caducity of all things, their mutual interrelatedness, and the dynamic nature of all the elements of the empirical world. It also points to the fact that there is a transempirical reality which Man is called upon to enter once he breaks through the cycle of *saṁsāra,* once he realizes (this word implies more than a merely epistemic act) the true nature of reality, that is, once he discovers his true and real *ātman*.

Therefore it is not difficult to understand the other affirmation in the mouth of the Lord Kṛṣṇa, that he, Kṛṣṇa, is not only deathlessness but also death, for he is both appearance and reality. The appearance could not be such if it were not the appearance of the real, and in this world of *saṁsāra* the real can be manifested only as appearance. Wisdom does not consist in denying the appearances but in recognizing them as such. This can be done, the Gītā says (and here it represents a new emphasis), only if our mind and heart are totally and sincerely surrendered to the Lord.

76. The word comes from *saṁ-sṛ-,* to flow together, to wander through, etc.
77. Cf. MaitU I, 4 (§ V 18); SU VI, 16 (§ I 28).
78. Cf. BG IX, 3 (§ I 38).

The immediate implication is that death also belongs to *saṁsāra,* that is, that death appertains to this side of the shore, that it is the very expression of contingency. If so, a change will be noticeable: death is no longer the gate through which Man reaches immortality. Death is only the condition for change within the world itself. Immortality does not depend on death: immortality is primordial, original, and not the result of a process of death and new life. All that rises again to life was certainly not immortal. Resurrection was only a figure of speech. You *are* risen!

Slowly the two conceptions sharpen their positions. On the one hand is the primeval Vedic notion of death as the gate to immortality, which makes possible the idea of a real resurrection to a new life. On the other hand, there is the later notion of death as an internal, this-worldly, *saṁsāric* process having nothing to do with true immortality. According to this view Man is constitutively immortal and so he does not need to die in order to live forever. The *ātman* "is" because it already "was" Brahman. Is there any middle way between these two views? This question is the concern of Part VI. Meanwhile, we shall meditate on the mortal condition.

Mṛtyu-saṁsāra

BG II, 27

i)

Death is certain for all that is born
and birth for all that dies.
Therefore for what is unavoidable
you should not be distressed.

BG VIII, 5-6; 10

ii)

5. And whoever at the end of his span of life,
when leaving the body,
remembers Me alone, he attains my own being;
of this there is no doubt.

6. Whatever state of being he recalls when at the end
he abandons his body,
to that state he attains, being ever assumed
into that condition.

10. If at death with steady mind, disciplined in love
and the power of yoga,
he locates his vital strength between the eyebrows,
he will reach the supreme Person.

BG IX, 19

iii) I am the producer of heat. I withhold
and send forth the rain.
I am deathlessness and also death,
being and nonbeing.

BG X, 34

iv) I am death, the devourer of all,
yet the source of things to be.

BG XII, 7

v) Those whose thoughts are set on Me
I shall deliver—
and that quite soon—from the ocean, O Arjuna,
of ever-recurring death.

BG XIV, 20

vi) Transcending the three attributes of nature
which give the body its existence,
man, freed from birth, death, old age, and pain,
attains immortality.

▪ i) Cf. § IV 7.
▪ ii) 5. At the end of his span of life: *antakāle,* lit. at the end of time or the last moment.
My own being: *mad-bhāva,* my state of being, my nature.
6. State of being: *bhāva,* nature.
Being ever assumed into that condition: *tad-bhāva-bhāvita,* lit. made to become in the state of that; i.e., he reaches that particular state of being in which he remains.
10. At death: *prayāṇa-kāle,* time of passing away.
Disciplined in love: *bhaktyā yuktaḥ.*
Power of yoga: *yoga-bala,* power of discipline.
Supreme Person: *paraṁ puruṣam . . . divyam,* the highest divine being.
▪ iii) 18. Cf. § I 29.
19. Producer of heat: *tapāmi,* lit. I heat.
21. Cf. § V 28.
▪ v) Ocean . . . of ever-recurring death: *mṛtyu-saṁsāra-sāgara.*
▪ vi) Attributes of nature: *guṇa.* Cf. BG XIV, 5: goodness (*sattva*), passion, greed (*rajas*), dullness, negligence (*tamas*).
Man: *dehin,* lit. the embodied one, having a body, the corporeal (man); hence, the soul as being in a body. *Deha,* the body, is often one of the components of the anthropological triad (*deha, manas, vāc*). *Dehin* is the soul in bondage to the body, the incarnate soul. Once the Self is realized, man passes beyond that state. Hence Janaka, the great *jīvanmukta* is called *videhin,* freed from the embodied state.
Cf. the Buddhist view about the sufferings of birth, death, and old age.

b) The Blessings for the Journey

Mṛtyusaṁjīvanī

The Vedic attitude to death steers a course between two extremes: on the one hand it avoids a tragic and almost obsessive attitude, while on the other it does not trivialize or ignore the place of death in human life. The group of texts presented here give ample evidence of this middle way.

Again there is a certain free association of ideas in the different themes dealt with in this subsection. Life is a great value; indeed, if properly understood, it is the highest value. It seems to be the task of death to help us realize the value of life, to enhance it, and to give earthly existence all the value it deserves. Man should not leave this earth too early, before his time. Indeed, if by accident he has already had to abandon his earthly mansion, one should even try to let him come back. The blessings for the journey are not last-minute consolations. They are blessings that are offered in order to call us back or to delay the time of departure. They are final blessings in the sense that they are directed to what is going on at the moment of dying. Let the dead depart in peace, in the hope that life has been a good thing and that it is still the highest blessing.

The first part of one of the oldest Upaniṣads ends with a cryptic sentence referring to the structure of reality as being threefold: name, form, and act (*karman*). It says that "immortality is veiled by reality,"[79] meaning that truth or the real is what veils immortality. It does not say that the world of names and forms is unreal and that only the underlying *ātman* is real. It explicitly affirms that immortality is covered by reality, that the real is the veil of deathlessness, or in other words that truth is the outer shell of an everlasting core.

The core is not covered by an illusory veil, by an unreal fiction, but by truth itself. Truth is the very cover that conceals and at the same time reveals the immortal core hidden in all things. But what is that core without its real manifestation? Man cannot consider death as something irrelevant, as the sloughing off of a skin. The attainment of deathlessness is achieved at the price of leaving reality behind. This feeling is encountered in many texts of this subsection.

The Forerunner *Yama*

7 This is the first of the traditional funeral hymns of the Ṛg Veda. Like many other texts dealing with the subject of death it has certain striking features: there is no sign of grief; the whole hymn is markedly sober in tone; and it is pervaded by a spirit of subdued

79. *Amṛtaṁ satyena channam*, BU, I, 6, 3.

joy: "O King, rejoice in this oblation."[80] Neither bereavement nor regret is visible here. On the contrary, the dead Man is going to be gloriously united with Yama and the Fathers. Death is seen here from the viewpoint of the dead man himself and not from that of those he leaves behind him. The center of life lies not in the temporal span of our earthly years but in the other world. The dead Man is going to the resting place prepared for him by Yama the forerunner of men, who has gone before us to prepare a place for us and to show us the way, who was not originally a God but a Man, who has endured, as we have, the entire burden of the human condition and who has overcome the ordeal of the great departure.

We may now concentrate our attention on an interesting point, which proves once more that the importance of a text does not lie in what it says but mainly in what one reads out of it and in the overall interpretation that each epoch has given to it. The truth lies in the interpretation. We refer to stanza 8 where the deceased is addressed as follows:

> Come home again, leaving your stains;
> assume a body bright with glory.

A similar idea is found in another funerary hymn:

> Putting on new life, let him approach the remaining ones,
> let him reunite with a body, All-Knowing One!"[81]

Life in the otherworld is not discarnate; it is life with a new body, a body of glory. This idea is considered almost obvious, not only by later tradition but also by the Atharva Veda, when speaking about life beyond. Here is another example of the holistic view of the Vedic Revelation.

The title suggests the exemplary role of Yama, a role that might almost be called teleological. He goes before, he calls, he attracts. Thus he will have the right of knowing who is coming to his house, that is, of judging them. Yama establishes true fellowship between Men and Gods; in his home or realm, Men and Gods feast together and the cosmic dichotomy is overcome. But Men without their bodies would not be Men. And it is with their bodies that they share Soma with the Gods. Yama is certainly the forerunner. He is the one who has found the trail leading to immortality, the path to the

80. RV X, 14, 4 (the hymn that follows).
81. RV X, 16, 5 (§ V 16).

Gods, the way to total humanness. If religion is considered to be the way to salvation, we can call Yama a religious founder par excellence, a truly religious man who follows to the very end the way that he himself has discovered.

Yama RV X, 14

[The chronicler]

1. The one who has climbed the mighty steeps,
   thus blazing a trail for many to follow,
   the son of Vivasvat, the gatherer of men,
   Yama, the King, we worship with offerings.

2. Yama was the first to find us a way,
   the pastures that no one shall steal from us.
   The path that our ancient Fathers took
   all mortals, once born, must tread for themselves.

3. Mātalī is there, united with the ancient
   poets and Yama, with the priests of old
   and Bṛhaspati, praise of the singers, both those
   who extol the Gods and those the Gods extol.
   Some rejoice in lip praise; others, in the oblation.

[Invocation of Yama]

4. Take your seat, O Yama, on the sacred grass,
   together with the priests of old and with the Fathers.
   May the prayers of the sages bring you hither!
   O King, rejoice in this oblation!

5. Come, O Yama, with the holy priests of old!
   Here, together with the Vairūpas, rejoice!
   Seated on the sacred sacrificial grass,
   I summon also Vivasvat your father.

6. May the priests of old, our Fathers, the Navagvas,
   the Atharvans and Bhṛgus, all worthy of Soma,
   regard us with kindliness—deserving, they, of worship—
   and keep us ever in their grace and favor!

[The last blessings (to the dead)]

7. Proceed, proceed along the ancient pathways
   whereon our Forefathers have passed before us.
   There you shall see God Varuṇa and Yama,
   the two kings, rejoicing in the offerings.

8. Meet Yama and the Fathers in the highest heaven
   along with your offerings and praiseworthy deeds.

Rid of imperfection, seek again your dwelling
and assume a body, bright with glory.

[To the evil spirits]

9. Off with you, spirits! Flee, rampage elsewhere!
For him the Fathers have prepared this place.
Yama will grant him a place of relaxation,
where days and nights rotate and waters flow.

[To the deceased]

10. Speed on your happy pathway, outstripping
the two brindled dogs, each with four eyes,
sons of Indra's messenger. Then approach the kindly
Fathers who rejoice in the fellowship of Yama.

[To Yama]

11. Put him, O King, under the protection
of your two dogs, each with four eyes, the guardians
and keepers of the way, who gaze upon men.
Bestow on him happiness and well-being.

12. May the broad-nosed dark-hued pair, the life stealers,
the messengers of Yama who run in men's wake,
restore to us today a life of happiness,
that we may live to see the sun!

[To the priests]

13. For Yama press the Soma-juice,
To Yama offer the sacrifice.
Toward Yama it mounts, a perfect offering,
with Agni as herald going before.

14. Present to Yama an offering rich
in ghee; come forward and take your places.
May he conduct us to the Gods,
so that in their midst we may live forever!

15. The offering steeped most richly in honey
present now to the royal Yama.
We offer homage to the Seers of old,
to the pioneers who discovered the way.

1. Steeps: *pravataḥ*, the distant and steep ways leading to the limits of the earth and to the region where Yama now lives. Cf. AV XVIII, 3, 13.

3. Mātalī: a celestial being; or, the charioteer of Indra.

Ancient poets: *kavyas*, a group of manes.

Priests of old: Aṅgirases (also in vv. 4-6), a group or house of priests in days of old.

Lip praise: *svāhā*, the sacrificial exclamation, standing for the sacrifice itself.

Oblation: *svadhā*, the offering to the dead.

4. Prayers: mantras, sacred hymns.

5. Vairūpas: they belong to the family of the Aṅgiras.

6. Navagvas: a priestly clan or class of *ṛṣis* (as also the Atharvans and Bhṛgus).
Kindliness: *sumati,* benevolence, favor.
Grace and favor: *bhadre saumanase,* in their gracious goodwill, benevolence.
7. Both Yama and Varuṇa are called kings, but only Varuṇa is said to be a God.
Offerings: *svadhā,* the offerings to the dead.
8. Offerings and praiseworthy deeds: *iṣṭā-pūrta,* the sacred and secular works that earn merit in the world beyond. This is the only occurrence of this term in the RV.
Seek again your dwelling: i.e., at the time of ancestor worship.
9. Where days and nights . . . : lit. distinguished by waters, days, and nights.
10. Sons of Indra's messenger: *sārameyau,* i.e., the two dogs, sons of Saramā, Indra's hound; (cf. § V 13 iv).
12. Dark-hued: *udumbalau,* doubtful word.
Life stealers: *asutṛpāh,* taking away the life of others.
15. Who discovered the way: *pathikṛt,* those who prepared the path.
16. There is a last stanza, which may have been added at a later date.

Let Him Come Back Again *Tat ta ā vartayāmasi*

8 The hymns that follow illustrate an interesting and original feature of the Vedic experience of death, namely, the refusal to consider it to be a final or irreversible fact. No wonder, then, that Vedic Man tries to rescue his fellowmen from the clutches of death or even to recover them once they have actually died.

These two hymns belong to the same group of the Gaupāyana hymns. In a continuous narrative they describe the efforts made to bring back the priest Subandhu from death. He had been deprived of life by the incantations of two other priests. His three brothers, who are also priests, pray a blessing[82] followed by a ritual injunction in order to get his life back (i). They also entreat several Gods, especially the Goddess Nirṛti, to preserve the life of their brother (ii). The last hymn of the group is a thanksgiving offered to king Asamāti[83] in spite of the fact that it was he who had appointed the two other priests in place of the four brothers.[84]

Hymn X, 58, enumerates all the possible places where a dead man may have gone. Yet the return to earth is considered the greatest blessing. One can hardly conceive of an attitude that is more secular, and yet at the same time it is sacred. We may recall what we said on the subject of premature death and on the extinguishing of one's life as being its own fulfillment. Here Subandhu was violently

82. Cf. RV X, 57.
83. Cf. RV X, 60.
84. Cf. JaimB III, 168-170, and also BrDev VII, 85-102, for the whole legend, which seems to come originally from the Ṛg Veda.

snatched from the realm of the living and he is conjured back to it.[85] Interestingly enough, the last verse, without any special sense of paradox, says that among the many places to which he might have gone are the past and the future. From past and future time he may also come back to the real present.

Hymn X, 59, is an impassioned appeal for the dead man's return, for the prolongation of his human life so that he may still be allowed to share in its blessings. Life triumphs over death. There is one particular theme we must not allow to pass unnoticed, though we have already mentioned it in the context of the sacrifice;[86] that is the theme of rejuvenation. In this hymn the desire is expressed that the risen Subandhu may have a renewed life, and the name of Cyavāna is cited as an example of such renewal.[87]

Since the story is already familiar, we shall simply point out some of the details in the actual process of rejuvenation. Cyavāna was made young again by the act of peeling off his skin like a garment. As a result he not only became acceptable to his young wife but was also made "husband of maidens."[88] He was made young again, [89] given another form, [90] freed from old age, [91] and renewed like a chariot so that he could run again.[92] We do not discuss here the later additions to the story.[93] It is important to note that there is no question of Cyavāna remaining eternally young; he regains his lost youth by means of an appropriate bodily change. Nor does he become immortal; he is given back his youth after having lived a long and healthy life. Last, there is also no question of his being born again in a young body.

Tat ta ā vartayāmasi

RV X, 58

i)

1. Your spirit which has gone afar
   to Yama, son of Vivasvat,
may it return to you again
   that it may live and dwell here.

85. The name of Subandhu is not mentioned in the hymn, perhaps because it is a name of a living person, and thus is no longer valid for him when departed. Subandhu is mentioned in X, 59, 8 (i), when he is supposed to have been recovered from the otherworld.
86. Cf. § III 22.
87. Cf. RV X, 59, 1 (ii).
88. Cf. RV I, 116, 10.
89. Cf. RV I, 117, 13; I, 118, 6.
90. Cf. RV VII, 68, 6.
91. Cf. RV VII, 71, 5.
92. Cf. RV X, 39, 4.
93. Cf. e.g., MB III, 121, 1 sq.

2. Your spirit which has gone afar
   to heaven and earth,
   may it return to you again
   that it may live and dwell here.

3. Your spirit which has gone afar
   to the four corners of the earth,
   may it return to you again
   that it may live and dwell here.

4. Your spirit which has gone afar
   to the four directions of space,
   may it return to you again
   that it may live and dwell here.

5. Your spirit which has gone afar
   to the waves of the ocean,
   may it return to you again
   that it may live and dwell here.

6. Your spirit which has gone afar
   to the shining light rays,
   may it return to you again
   that it may live and dwell here.

7. Your spirit which has gone afar
   to the waters and the plants,
   may it return to you again
   that it may live and dwell here.

8. Your spirit which has gone afar
   to the Sun and Dawn,
   may it return to you again
   that it may live and dwell here.

9. Your spirit which has gone afar
   to the highest mountains,
   may it return to you again
   that it may live and dwell here.

10. Your spirit which has gone afar
    to the whole world,
    may it return to you again
    that it may live and dwell here.

11. Your spirit which has gone afar
    to the farthest realms,
    may it return to you again
    that it may live and dwell here.

12. Your spirit which has gone afar
    to the past and the future,
may it return to you again
    that it may live and dwell here.

RV X, 59

ii)

1. Now may his life be renewed and further extended,
as by two skilled charioteers, pursuing their course!
May he, like Cyavāna, attain the goal!
May Goddess Destruction move to distant places!

2. This is a song for wealth, for food in plenty.
Let us do many noble deeds to win glory!
Now may the singer rejoice in all our doings!
May Goddess Destruction move to distant places!

3. May we surpass our foes by deeds of valor,
as heaven surpasses earth and mountains surpass the plains.
All these our deeds the singer has acclaimed.
May Goddess Destruction move to distant places!

4. Do not deliver us over to Death, O Soma!
Still may our eyes behold the rising of the sun!
May the full life span determined by the Gods be ours!
May Goddess Destruction move to distant places!

5. O guide of the spirits, retain our heart within us.
Prolong for us the life span yet to be lived!
Allow us still to enjoy the vision of the sunlight!
Strengthen your body by means of the fat we bring you!

6. O guide of the spirits, restore to us our sight,
give us again our life breath and powers of enjoyment.
Long may our eyes behold the rising of the sun!
O gracious Goddess, grant us your favor and bless us.

7. May Earth restore to us our breath of life,
may Goddess Heaven and the aery space return it!
May Soma give us once again a body
and Pūṣan show us again the way of salvation!

8. May both the worlds accord to Subandhu a blessing,
they who are youthful mothers of cosmic Order.
May heaven and earth remove all evil and shame!
May you be troubled neither by sin nor by pain!

9. The healing remedies descend from heaven
in twos and threes, or singly roam the earth.
May Heaven and Earth conspire to dispatch the evil
into the ground! May sorrow no more affect you!

10. Restore, O Indra, the ox that brought to this place
the chariot bearing the wife of Uśīnara.
May Heaven and Earth conspire to dispatch the evil
into the ground! May sorrow no more affect you!

■ i) Spirit: *manas* throughout.
12. The past and the future: *bhūta* and *bhavya*.
■ ii) 1. Just as Cyavāna was once restored and rejuvenated (cf. RV I, 116, 10), so may Subandhu, the *ṛṣi* of this hymn, experience the same.
Goddess Destruction: *nirṛti*. A dark Goddess frequently associated with Yama and death.
2. Song: *sāman*.
Singer: *jaritā*, as also in v. 3 Subandhu himself.
4. Determined by the Gods: *dyubhir hitaḥ*, fixed by the heavenly ones or else "with the passing of days." For our translation cf. RV I, 89, 8, where we read: *devahitaṁ yad āyuḥ*.
5. Guide of the spirits: *asunīti*.
6. Gracious Goddess: Anumati. Cf. § VII 32.
8. Mothers of cosmic Order: *ṛtasya mātarā*, i.e., heaven and earth (even heaven is sometimes conceived of as a mother).
10. The wife of Uśīnara: Uśīnarāṇī. Sāyaṇa takes it to mean a healing herb; others see in her the wife of Subandhu (also called Uśīnara after his country). The chariot may be understood symbolically (cf. v. 1).

Deliverance and Freedom

Unmocana-pramocana

9 This hymn from the Atharva Veda is a form of conjuration to ward off death. We see here a heartfelt and impassioned striving, a supreme effort to keep the dying man in the land of the living, to snatch him from destruction:

> Remain here! Go not hence nor follow the Fathers!
> I firmly bind your breath of life. (v. 1)

This vivid and detailed description starts by enumerating the causes that may have brought the dying man to the brink of death. Has he been bewitched? Has he laid violent hands on someone? Is he undergoing the consequences of some sin of his parents? Doubt remains, and yet at the same time the sure conviction grows that the sick man is going to be delivered from death and is going to recover his life. "Do not fear! You will not die" (v. 8).

The priest, who seems here to have also a prophetic role, now resolutely exhorts the living, first the two sages, the Watcher and the Waker, the ever watchful guardians of the breath, then Agni the Savior, Light, the one who scatters the shadows of Death. Next as a token of respect he renders homage to Yama, Death, and to the Fathers. Then, fully confident of Agni's powers, the poet begs the vital forces "invigorated by Agni" (v. 14) to bring fresh life to the breath, the mind, the eye, the breathing (both in and out), the tongue, and the whole body. He also invokes the Sun whose rays at early dawn infuse energy into the life of the world.

The last verse praises human existence and bids the dying man live once more. In this hymn the human and the divine, the spiritual and the physical, darkness and light, death and life, confront each other in a powerful and evenly matched contest of strength. Light and Life win the day, thanks to the divine omnipotence of Agni and Sūrya.[94]

We have here a typical expression of a fundamental trait of Vedic spirituality. Vedic Man has sometimes been described as a hedonistic- and eudemonistic-minded being, with an exclusive concern for material life. It is not necessary to point out the falsity of this assumption at this juncture. We simply want to draw attention to the healthy attitude that considers that death can be conjured away, that it is an evil whose reality no eschatological picture can deny, and that the completing of one's days in old age is not properly death. This is not the attitude of an unbeliever, but the realistic posture of a man who, precisely because he believes in the "otherworld," believes equally strongly in the present one, which he is not prepared to neglect or despise or abandon because of a rosy picture of the other one. For the time being—and one might say for the being in time—this world is more important and more real than the other one. This is the human perspective of which Vedic Man is not ashamed and which he does not attempt to camouflage.

Unmocana-pramocana AV V, 30

1. May near things stay near to you and far things also!
   Remain here! Go not hence nor follow the Fathers!
   I firmly tie up your breath of life.

2. If one has bewitched you—a man of your people
   or perchance a stranger—I proclaim by my voice
   these two things to you: deliverance, freedom.

3. If you have done violence or, heedless, have maligned
   a man or a woman—I proclaim by my voice
   these two things to you: deliverance, freedom.

94. If this prayer is successful in restoring the man to life he should, according to the Śāstras, offer a "Soma sacrifice or an animal or an ordinary sacrifice and take his dwelling again in the village" (AGS IV, 1, 4), though he may also do so "without such a sacrifice" (ibid. 5).

4. If you lie there prone owing to sin of your mother
or sin of your father—I proclaim by my voice
these two things to you: deliverance, freedom.

5. Accept the healing remedy your mother and your father bring
together with your sister and your brother.
I make you one who reaches ripe old age.

6. Live on, O man, with your spirit unimpaired.
Do not follow the messengers sent by Yama!
Remember the cities where the living dwell!

7. Come back hither in response to our calls,
you who know the path that lies ahead,
the way and the ascent of every living person!

8. Do not fear! You will not die. I shall bring you at the last
to a ripe old age. I have exorcised
from your limbs the consumption and burning fever.

9. The limb-splitting fever and the burning pain,
the disease of the heart and all consumption,
have fled far away like a falcon by the power of my word.

10. May those two Sages, the Watcher and the Waker,
the sleepless and the vigilant, guardians of your breath,
be alert for your safety by night and by day!

11. All hail to Agni whom with reverence we approach!
May the Sun continue to rise here for you!
Arouse yourself from the pit of Death,
from the shadows, however dark they may be!

12. Homage to Yama, homage to Death,
homage to the Fathers and those who conduct you!
I set forth Agni, who is able to save,
before the eyes of this man, that he languish no longer.

13. Come breath, come mind, come eye, come strength!
Let the body resume and integrate its power!
Let it stand firm and steady on its feet!

14. Reunite him to his breath, O Agni, to his sight!
set his whole body and its powers in motion!
You know the secret of deathlessness.
May he stay, not depart to a house of clay!

15. May your out-breath not falter, your in-breath remain
quite unobstructed! May the sovereign Sun
snatch you from death by the power of his rays!

16. Trembling and halting, the tongue in his mouth
utters words. From her I have exorcised
the consumption, the hundred symptoms of fever.

17. Best loved is this world of ours: to the Gods
let us leave the unconquered world. O man,
whatever be the death assigned to you from birth,
we recall you hither till old age comes!

1. May near things etc.: i.e., may your eyesight not fail at the onset of death.
Breath of life: *asu.*
2. Deliverance, freedom: *unmocana-pramocana;* unfastening and loosening, i.e., complete release.
3. Done violence: *dudrohitha.*
5. Healing remedy: *bheṣaja.*
6. With your spirit unimpaired: *sarveṇa manasā saha,* with all your mind, possessing fully your mind.
Yama's messengers, the two dogs, envoys of the God of death. Cf. RV X, 14, 11 (§ V 7).
7. The different terms for path, etc., are: *ayana, patha, ārohaṇa, ākramaṇa.*
8. I have exorcised: *niravocam aham.*
9. Consumption: *yakṣma.*
By the power of my word: *vācā.*
10. Two Sages: *bodha-pratibodha,* names of the two *prāṇas.*
11. Death: *mṛtyu.*
12. I set forth Agni: the verb *puro-dhā-* means also to appoint for a priestly function (to place at the head), or to place foremost, to honor.
14. Deathlessness: *amṛta.*
To a house of clay: be one whose housing is the earth, i.e., be a dead man; cf. RV VII, 89, 1 (§ IV 19). Some scholars see here the practice of burial instead of cremation.
17. Best loved is this world of ours: *ayaṁ lokaḥ priyatamaḥ.*
Unconquered (world): *aparājita,* a reference to heaven.
We recall you hither: i.e., do not die before (old age).

Prayer for the Fulfillment of Life *Dīrghāyuṣprāpti*

10 For two reasons we are justified in including in this subsection the two prayers from the eighth book of the Atharva Veda. They are undoubtedly concerned with death and on certain occasions they were the prayers said for a dying man, in spite of the fact that they are precisely prayers for life and for the blessings of human and terrestrial life: "May the sun warm you with blessing."[95] The second reason, which is related to the first, is that the presence of death is felt throughout these hymns as it is felt throughout human life on earth. Death is not something that comes only at the last moment of life; it permeates every human act. It is the fact of death which gives uniqueness to our separate acts, making them unrepeatable and different from one another. In this sense these two hymns are also blessings for the journey, because the journey toward death begins with birth and we can meet death at any moment.

The first hymn (Atharva Veda VIII, 1) is most impressive. It has

95. AV VIII, 1, 5 (the hymn that follows); lit. I warm your body.

sometimes been considered a simple incantation to prolong the life of a dying person. A closer examination of the text, the fact that the hymn is used in the *upanayana* ceremony, the startling salutation to death with which it begins—all suggest that its main emphasis lies in recovering life for a man when he has not yet fully lived it and in bringing him to a new hope of life when he has given up hope because of sickness or for some other reason. It is in a certain sense a hymn of resurrection, about overcoming death by not allowing it to come before its proper and duly appointed time. It is a prayer for good health and a benediction to conjure away death. *Dīrghāyus* is a term used in the Vedas to express the life of a man lived until it has yielded all it had to give.[96]

This hymn is a prayer to scatter away melancholy and recreate the will to live. It plainly contradicts what is said elsewhere,[97] for it emphasizes that for this particular man it is in the yonder world that there is fear, while here on earth there is confidence and no dread: "Beyond there is fear, on this side fearlessness."[98]

The hymn says plainly that it is morbid to dwell upon the ancestors, or perhaps upon the recent death of a dear one which tempts us to follow in their footsteps, abandoning those who still love us and are grasping our hands. It is a kind of pact with Death, putting the man again under the protection of all the cosmic powers so that he may live his full *āyus,* his "whole lifetime," *sarvam āyus.* To live the whole life span allotted to us, to exhaust all the possibilities and seize all the opportunities that life presents to us, to squeeze out the elixir of life to the last drop, before we become light—this is the Vedic ideal and an injunction of the Vedic Revelation to modern Man.

Dīrghāyuṣprāpti AV VIII, 1

1. Homage to Death, the end of life!
   Here rest your breath, both inward and outward!
   May the life of this man be maintained in the realm
   of the Sun, in the world of deathlessness!

96. From *dīrgha,* long in space as in time, and *āyus,* vital power, life, with a reference to the temporal factor. Cf. RV IV, 15, 9-10; X, 85, 39 (§ II 15); also *dīrghāyutva,* RV X, 62, 2; etc. The term is more frequent in the AV than in the RV.
97. Cf. KathU I, 12 (§ V 27).
98. AV VIII, 1, 10 (the hymn that follows).

2. The power of God has raised him up,
the heavenly Drink has raised him up,
the powers of the Storm, of Heaven and of Fire,
have raised him up to well-being.

3. Here be your life—its full span—your breath
and your mind! We save you from the bonds of Perdition
by means of the divine Word.

4. Rise up from this place, O man, do not fall down,
but cast off the fetters of Death which now hold you.
Do not cut yourself off from this world of men,
from the sight of the Fire and the Sun.

5. May the great Wind breathe purification upon you,
May the Waters rain immortality upon you,
may the Sun warm your body with blessing, may Death
show you mercy! Do not perish!

6. I charge you to rise, O man, not to fall.
Long life I impart to you and skill for living.
Mount safe and sound on this chariot of deathlessness.
You shall speak in old age, full of wisdom!

7. Let not your mind stray away and be lost.
Do not spurn the living and follow the Fathers!
May All-Gods protect you right here!

8. Do not give thought to the departed ones
who lead men away to a far-off land.
Arise out of darkness! Come to the light!
Come, we grasp your two hands!

9. From Yama's two watchdogs sent forth on the path,
the black and the spotted, may you stay safe!
Come, do not waver! Do not stand there
with your mind deflected from here.

10. Do not proceed on that dread-filled path,
not yet trodden by you—I give you good warning!
To that darkness, O man, do not descend.
There is fear, here fearlessness.

11. May the sparks that dwell in the Waters protect you,
may the Fire that the sons of men kindle protect you,
may the Universal Lord, the All-Knowing, protect you,
heavenly fire and lightning not consume you!

12. Let not the funeral pyre consume you!
Elude the Destroyer! May Heaven and Earth,
the Sun and the Moon, protect you! May space
protect you from the stroke of the Gods!

13. Let the Wise and the Knower both protect you,
let the Dreamless and the Sleepless both protect you,
let the Guardian and the Wakeful both protect you!

14. Let them protect you, let them guard you!
To them be homage, to them be "all hail"!

15. May the Lord of the Wind, the Sky, the Creator,
the saving Sun, restore you to communion with the living!
Let not your breath or your strength forsake you!
It is for your sake that we call back your life!

16. Let not the fiend of the snapping jaws
find you, or darkness, or the tongue of the demon!
Shall you be subject to Death? No, never!
May all the powers raise you up, may the Lord
of the sky and of Fire raise you up to well-being!

17. Heaven and Earth and the Lord of creation
have raised you up! The plants and the herbs,
with the heavenly Drink, have saved you from Death!

18. Here let this man dwell, O Gods, not yonder!
We rescue him from Death with a thousandfold charm!

19. Lo, I have now released you from Death!
May life-giving breaths breathe in concert!
Let not the wild-haired women
nor the dismal howlers howl at you!

20. I have brought you back, I have found you again.
You have come back renewed, all your members complete,
your sight unimpaired, your whole life span intact!

21. Life has breathed on you! Light has come!
Far away from you has darkness retreated.
Far from you are Death and Perdition and Decay.

1. Homage to Death, the end of life: *antakāya mṛtyave namaḥ.*
Life: *asu.*
2. Power of God: Bhaga.
Heavenly Drink: lit. the stalky Soma.
Powers of the Storm: Maruts.
Of Heaven and of Fire: Indra and Agni.
3. Life (*asu*), breath (*prāṇa*), life span (*āyus*), and mind (*manas*) are the essentials of human life. The Upaniṣads reduce the first three to *prāṇa* only.
Perdition: *nirṛti.*
By means of the divine Word: *daivyā vācā,* the saving aspect of *vāc.*
5. Great Wind: Mātariśvan.
6. Long life: *jīvatātu.*
Skill for living: *dakṣatāti,* ability.
8. Do not give thought to . . .: *mā . . . ā dīdhīthāḥ,* do not regard, etc., for the very thought of the dead leads a sick man far away.
Darkness: *tamas.*
Light: *jyoti.* Cf. the famous prayer of BU I, 3, 28 (§ V 12).
9. Mind deflected: *parāṅmanaḥ,* the mind turned back.

10. There is fear . . . : *bhayaṁ parastād abhayaṁ te arvāk,* lit. beyond is fear, on this side fearlessness.
11. The kindly and dangerous aspects of Agni are invoked.
Universal Lord: *vaiśvānara.*
All-Knowing: *jātavedas.*
12. Funeral pyre: *kravyād* (Agni).
Destroyer: *saṁkasuka,* another destructive aspect of Agni.
13. Cf. AV V, 30, 10 (§ V 9). According to the commentator these are the names of six *ṛṣis.*
15. Lord of the Wind: Vāyu.
Sky: Indra.
Creator: Dhātṛ.
Saving Sun: *savitā trāyamāṇaḥ.*
16. All the powers: The Ādityas and the Vasus.
Lord of the Sky: Indra.
Fire: Agni.
17. Lord of creation: Prajāpati.
Heavenly Drink: Soma, the king.
18. Thousandfold charm: lit. power.
19. May life-giving breaths . . .: or, may the givers of strength melt you together.
Howl at you: probably a reference to ritual mourners. (Even today women with loosened hair mourn the dead with a ritual lamentation.)
20. Whole life span: *sarvam āyus,* lit. I have found your whole sight and your whole life span.
21. Decay: *yakṣma,* a particularly deadly disease.

Go Forth into the Light of the Living *Jīvatāṁ jyotir abhyehi*

11 Like the peceding hymn, this one is used both at the beginning and the end of life. It is often recited at the ceremony of the name giving (*nāma-karaṇa*), and it is also used when death threatens to come before its proper time. The danger of death threatens Man from his earliest childhood. This prayer attempts to summon the four elements of the universe from which man is created and with their aid to protect their creature who was made by the expenditure of such prodigious energy. From the wind came his breath, from the sun his sight: O Death, do not strike this Man! Let him first live a hundred years and enjoy the gift of life. Do not deceive him with metaphysical theories or high-flown doctrines; give time to time and let him first have his share of immortal life here on earth.

This hymn seems to be almost a salute to life rather than a prayer to death. For example, the opening phrase of the second stanza, "Go forth . . . into the light of the living," is another felicitous formula of Vedic spirituality. From our point of view the interesting point to note is that this phrase does not mean to go into "eternal" or "everlasting" life, but to enter into the earthly life of the living. We are the living, we are building up the universe, we are performing the life-giving sacrifice, we are struggling in order to be, and we enjoy the supreme joy and gift of life. That is the affirmation of this prayer, and it is speaking of our human terrestrial condition.

Jīvatāṁ jyotir abhyehi AV VIII, 2

1. Guard well, O Man, your share of immortality,
that you may reach old age without mishap.
Spirit and life I now impart to you!
Do not vanish into shadow and darkness! Do not perish!

2. Go forth, I adjure you, into the light of the living.
I draw you toward a life of a hundred autumns.
Releasing you from the bonds of death and malediction
I stretch forth your life thread into the distant future.

3. From the Wind I have taken your breath, from the Sun your eyesight.
I strengthen your heart in you, consolidate your limbs.
I adjure you to speak with tongue free from stammering.

4. With the breath that dwells in creatures of two legs or four,
I blow upon you as one blows on a fire just kindled.
To you, O Death, to your sight and your breath, I pay homage!

5. Let him live, not die! This man we now revive.
I bring him healing. O Death, do not strike this man!

6. A life-possessing, life-bestowing plant,
powerful, salvific, potent, I here invoke,
to bring this man once more to health and strength!

7. Speak in his favor! Seize him not, but release him,
yours though he be. Let him stay here with all his strength!
Have mercy upon him, O powers of destruction, protect him!
Grant to him fullness of days, removing all evil!

8. Bless this man, O Death, have mercy upon him!
Let him rise and depart, safe and sound, with unimpaired hearing!
May he reach a hundred years and enjoy life's blessings!

9. May the missile of the Gods be deflected from you! I make you
emerge from the realm of darkness; from Death I have saved you!
Far have I removed the Fire of the funeral pyre.
I place a protective wall for your life's preservation.

10. We rescue him, Death, from your murky path which admits
of no return, and, protecting him from the descent,
we make a shield to guard him—this our prayer.

11. To you I now impart in-breath and out-breath,
a ripe old age, death at its close, well-being!

All the messengers of Death who prowl around—
I send them far away!

12. I drive to a distant place Malignity, Destruction,
the Demon who grabs and ghosts who feast upon corpses.
All demons and evil powers—like darkness I destroy them!

13. From Agni, the deathless One, the living and All-Knowing,
I snatch back your breath, so that you may be unharmed,
immortal in union with him. I perform this rite
on your behalf, that you may reach perfection.

14. May Heaven and Earth be gracious unto you,
may those two splendors set you free from suffering!
May the Sun warm you with blessings! May the Wind
waft its propitious breezes to your heart!
May the heavenly Streams, rich in milk, flow within you auspiciously!

15. May the herbs of the earth be to you a propitious aid!
I have raised you up from the lower realm to the higher.
There may the Sun and Moon, the Boundless Ones, guard you!

16. The cloth that is covering you, encircling your waist,
that we make soft to the touch, a caress to your body.

17. When, by means of a fine and sharpened razor,
you shave like a barber our hair and beards, let our faces
shine bright, but our length of days be uncurtailed!

18. May rice and barley bring to you good fortune!
Never may they produce in you sickness or wasting!
Let them, rather, serve to release you from anguish!

19. Whatever you eat or drink, the grain of the field
or milk, food of all kinds, edible, inedible—
all these I make for you devoid of poison.

20. We now entrust you to both, the Day and the Night.
Protect him from the clutches of the demon who seeks to devour men.

21. We grant you a hundred, ten thousand years,
two, three, or four generations.
May Indra and Agni and all the Gods
  grant you this boon without anger!

22. To Autumn, Winter, Spring, and Summer
we now entrust you. May the Rainy Season,
  which makes the plants grow, console you!

23. Over all creatures of two feet or four
Death holds dominion, but you I rescue
  from his clutches! Do not fear.

24. Do not fear, you will be safe!
You shall not die, you shall not die!
At that point men do not die
or go to the lowest darkness!

25. At that point all creatures live,
the cow, the horse, and human beings—
here where this holy word is uttered,
true protection for life!

26. May it protect you from your peers, from evil
incantations, from the wiles of your relatives!
May you be deathless, long-lived, immortal,
may your breath not abandon your body!

27. From the hundred and one kinds of death,
and the powers of destruction that must be combated,
may the Gods deliver you—by the power
of Agni, Universal Lord!

28. You are the body of Agni, ready to save;
you are a slayer of demons and of foes.
You, expeller of sickness, the healing herb,
Pūtudru by name.

1. Guard well: may also be translated as trust in, hold on to.
Without mishap: without break or interruption.
Spirit: *asu,* soul, breath, life.
Life: *āyus,* vital power.
2. Light of the living: *jīvatāṁ jyotiḥ.*
Malediction: *aśasti.*
3. Heart: *manas,* mind.
5. Healing: *bheṣaja,* remedy.
7. Powers of destruction: Bhava and Śarva, minor deities related to Rudra.
8. Enjoy life's blessings: *ātmanā bhujam aśnutām,* let him obtain enjoyment for himself.
9. Fire of the funeral pyre: lit. *agni kravyād,* the corpse-consuming fire.
10. Murky path which admits of no return: *niyānaṁ rajasaṁ . . . anavadharṣyam,* your dark (or misty) path which is to be shunned.
12. Malignity, Destruction: *arāti, nirṛti.*
Like darkness: *tama iva,* or into darkness, as it were.
13. Breath: *prāṇa.*
14. Gracious: *śiva,* benevolent, auspicious.
15. The Boundless Ones: Ādityas, applied here to Sun and Moon.
17. This refers to the custom of shaving hair and beard on the death of a relative.
20. Demon: *arāyas.*
22. A prayer against the evil influences of the climate.
23. I rescue from his clutches: lit. from the Lord Death (*mṛtyor gopateḥ*). *Gopati,* the herdsman, is a positive term suggesting his care for his flock.
24. Safe: *ariṣṭa,* whole, unhurt.
25. Holy word: *brahman,* rite.
Uttered: *kriyate,* performed.
26. From the wiles of your relatives: *sabandhubhyaḥ,* or from your friends!
27. By . . . Agni: *agner vaiśvānarāt,* or from Agni *vaiśvānara*?
28. Pūtudru: either a kind of acacia, or else the deodar tree (common in the Himalayas).

The Last Surrender *Antakāla*

12 The four Upaniṣadic extracts that follow are very different in nature and yet they belong together, for they illumine from three different angles the same mystery of death and immortality. All four are concerned with what in death does not die, and we find a crescendo in the four queries.

The first text, which has a more ancient and rather more philosophical counterpart in another Upaniṣad,[99] deals with the so-called *saṁpradāna* or *saṁpratti,* that is, "transmission" or "tradition."[100] Immortality is here conceived of as being, as it were, on a strictly horizontal plane. It is something handed over by a dying father to his son. By his own birth and by the birth of his son the father has contracted a debt with life. In this moving "transmission" ceremony he repays this debt. He does so by passing on to his son all that he has, the prayers, the sacrifice, and the portion of the world which he is. The son receives what his father gives, and thus the continuity between the generations is established and the immortality of the father secured. Herein lies the reason for one of the final injunctions, namely, that if the father does not die after all he will have to be subjected to his son, to whom he has handed over everything. If he dies, the funeral rites will terminate his mission on earth. In a real sense, in passing away in this manner there is no death.

Here again there is a blending together of the cosmic, anthropological, and sociological factors. The father is the steward of spiritual, moral, biological, and material values. All are given back and deposited in their right place. The son is entrusted with all that is still left to the father. The "tradition" is then complete and the father can leave this world. The *lokya,* "he who has world," will from now on be the *putra,* the son, "he who protects [his father]" or "he who fills the hollows left from the father."[101] But all the father's gifts that the son cannot keep will return to the elements from which they came. Nothing is lost.

The second excerpt is about *karman,* and it has been considered to be the first authoritative document on the matter. The sage

99. Cf. BU I, 5, 17 (§ VI 8).
100. From *saṁ-pra-dā-,* to give completely up, to surrender, to hand over, to grant, etc. *Sampradāya* is the living tradition handed over from master to disciple, hence the word is usually translated by "sect," i.e., any particular tradition.
101. Cf. BU I, 5, 17 (§ VI 8).

Yājñavalkya answers five questions put by Jāratkārava Ārtabhāga. The first one relates to the number of Man's organs of apprehension. The second concerns our problem: it asks about the death of death, about the end of all perishable things. It takes the concrete form of asking which is the deity for whom death is food, for we know that everything is food for death. The answer is Agni, the triumphant God of the second death, the *punar-mṛtyu*. Later tradition interprets this text as saying that the knowledge of the *ātman* is the water that puts out the fire and overcomes death.[102] The third question asks to know something that transcends the individual; the answer is his vital breath, his *prāṇa*. It survives the death of the individual, for it makes his body swell, so that in a way we can "see" the *prāṇa* after its owner has died. The fourth question asks what is the immortal core of Man, that which does not leave him. "When a person dies, what is it that does not leave him?" (v. 12). The answer is not sociological, for it is not his fame or prestige, that is, his name which does not leave him. The answer is theological, for the name is Brahman.[103] The climax is obviously the fifth and last question: "What becomes of the person?" When the elements of the dead person have all gone to their proper places where they belong, is there nothing left? Is death the absolute end of everything? And they spoke, but not openly, on *karman*. This is the locus of *karman*. Is there in the individual something more than the sum of all his constituent parts? In this passage immortality transcends not only the individual but also the order of the elements and visible things; immortality is not simply retransmitted on a horizontal line from the father to the son or from the individual to the imperishable elements composing him, but it belongs to a higher sphere, to the human and cosmic solidarity not of the elements but of the actions and their fruits. The immortal here seems to be a cosmic solidarity, the whole universe, the world of actions and reactions, the spiritual world.

The third text represents a third step. It is expressed in an enigmatic form susceptible to many interpretations. Here the movement is, significantly enough, the opposite to that of the preceding texts. The discourse is not about giving up, distributing, passing on, and transmitting, but about saving "the tip of the heart," "taking into himself the sparks of light" and concentrating them in the

102. Cf. BU I, 2, 7, interpreted in this light.
103. Cf. CU VII, 1, 5 (§ VI 3).

heart. The whole text is more than just a biological description of the last moments. It describes a process of unification and not of dispersion.

The phrase *ekī-bhavati* is the recurrent theme of the text. If we follow the whole course of the passage we can well understand this phrase in its literal meaning of "becoming one," without having to force the translation.[104] Man, at the hour of his death, certainly becomes one; that is, he simplifies his life, he discards what is merely accidental, and in particular he concentrates and condenses his whole being so that what he leaves behind or passes on to others is the very core of his being, the kernel of his person, the *ātman*, which will not fade away. The text puts the expression in the mouth of the people, as if popular wisdom could here grasp the truth on two planes. On the plane of appearances the dying man gathers together his faculties and becomes more and more united, while on the plane of underlying reality he is ontologically becoming one, he is reaching the unity that gathers together all that he still has: his intelligence, his experience, his wisdom. Thus death is here the supreme act. Until that moment one is dispersed, not yet unified. Now, people say, "he is becoming one." The pilgrimage toward unity, toward oneness, is the mortal path of Man.

The fourth text has been unceasingly repeated and chanted until our own time; it is in truth a liturgical prayer, a fact that should not be overlooked. It homologizes *asat* (nonbeing, nothingness, unreality) and *tamas* (darkness, blindness, gloom) with death and prays to be guided to immortality, which is also understood as the real, being, existence, and as light, vision, insight. Therefore deathlessness is not the mere absence of death; it is reality and light. It is not the mere continuation of a life in which the authentic and the unauthentic, brightness and obscurity, are mixed; it is living in pure being and spotless light. We are dealing here with a prayer of purification, a prayer to purify our earthly existence from any shadow of unreality and darkness. We know from empirical evidence that unless we become light itself there will always be shadows, and that unless we live in the realm of total truthfulness and authenticity there will always be errors and lies in our lives. This cannot be avoided unless we become the very source of light and of being itself. The prayer seeks to set in motion the dynamic

104. Cf. also BU I, 2, 7 where "becoming one" refers to union with the "divinities."

movement toward that identification. It is thus a prayer for the living: it asks a blessing for our journey through the world, and it asks for the gift of immortality, by which it means far more than a mere "afterlife."

Antakāla

KausU II, 15

i) Next comes the Father-and-son ceremony or the Transmission, as it is called.

A father, when he is about to die, summons his son. He first spreads new grass on the floor of the house and lays the fire; then, after placing near the fire a jar of water together with a dish of rice, he lies down, covers himself with a fresh garment, and remains thus. The son comes and extends himself on his father, touching his hands, feet, and so on with his own corresponding organs, or the father may perform the act of transmission while the son sits before him. Then he bestows his powers upon the son, [saying]:

The father: Let me impart my word to you.
The son: Your word within me I receive.
The father: Let me impart my life breath to you.
The son: Your life breath within me I receive.
The father: Let me impart my eyesight to you.
The son: Your eyesight within me I receive.
The father: Let me impart my hearing to you.
The son: Your hearing within me I receive.
The father: Let me impart my tastes to you.
The son: Your tastes within me I receive.
The father: Let me impart my works to you.
The son: Your works within me I receive.
The father: Let me impart my pleasure and pain to you.
The son: Your pleasure and pain within me I receive.
The father: Let me impart my joy and delight and my power of begetting to you.
The son: Your joy and delight and your power of begetting within me I receive.
The father: Let me impart my movement to you.
The son: Your movement within me I receive.
The father: Let me impart my mind to you.
The son: Your mind within me I receive.
The father: Let me impart my wisdom to you.
The son: Your wisdom within me I receive.

If, however, he is unable to speak much the father may use this comprehensive statement: "Let me impart my life breath to you," and the son may reply: "Your life breath within me I receive." Then, turning to the right, the son goes out toward the East. The father calls after him: "May honor, spiritual brilliance, and fame be well pleased in you!" Then the son looks over his left shoulder, covering his face with his hand or with the edge of his garment, and says: "May you attain the heavenly worlds and all your desires!"

If the father becomes well he should nevertheless remain under the authority of his son or wander about as an ascetic. If, however, he dies, let it be accomplished [with funeral rites], as is right and proper, as it should be accomplished.

BU III, 2, 10-13

ii) 10. "Yājñavalkya," he [Jāratkārava Ārtabhāga] said, "all this [universe] is food for death. Now, which is the divinity of which death is the food?" "Fire, most certainly, is death and fire is the food of water. Thus he who knows this wins over repeated death."

11. "Yājñavalkya," he said, "when this [holy] person dies, do his life breaths arise out of him or not?" "No," said Yājñvalkya, "they are all collected in him. He gets swollen, he is inflated, and, thus inflated, he lies dead."

12. "Yājñavalkya," he said, "when this person dies, what does not depart from him?" "Name," he replied, "for name is eternal, all the Gods are eternal, and he wins an eternal world."

13. "Yājñavalkya," he said, "when the voice of this dead person enters into fire, his life breath into wind, his eye into the sun, his mind into the moon, his ear into the regions, his body into the earth, his self (*ātman*) into space, when his blood and his semen are placed in the waters, what, then, happens to this person?" "Take my hand, Ārtabhāga, my friend. We two alone shall know about this. It is not for us to disclose it in public." Away they went together and together they spoke with each other. What they were discussing was *karman* and what they were praising was *karman*. By good action, indeed, one becomes good and by sinful action sinful. Then Jāratkārava Ārtabhāga kept silent.

BU IV, 4, 1-2

iii) 1. When this *ātman* becomes weak and unconscious, then all the life-powers collect around him. Then he gathers to himself all the particles of light and descends into the heart. When the person in the eye withdraws from him, he no longer recognizes forms.

2. "He is becoming one," they say, "he does not see."
"He is becoming one," they say, "he does not smell."
"He is becoming one," they say, "he does not taste."
"He is becoming one," they say, "he does not speak."
"He is becoming one," they say, "he does not hear."

"He is becoming one," they say, "he does not think."
"He is becoming one," they say, "he does not feel."
"He is becoming one," they say, "he does not understand."

The tip of his heart gets illumined and, being illumined, the *ātman* departs through the eye or the head or some other part of the body. As he departs, the breath of life departs after him; and when the breath of life departs, all other breaths follow. He then is reunited with consciousness and departs together with consciousness. His knowledge and his works and his past experience [alone] accompany him.

BU I, 3, 28

iv) And now comes the ceremony of the purificatory rites.

The singing priest sings the chant. While he is singing, let [the sacrificer] recite in subdued tones:

From unreality lead me to reality;
from darkness lead me to light;
from death lead me to immortality.

When he says: "from unreality lead me to reality," the "unreality" means death, of course, and "reality" means immortality; that is, "from death lead me to immortality; make me immortal." This is what he means.

"From darkness lead me to light"—darkness means death, of course, and light immortality; that is, "from death lead me to immortality; make me immortal." This is what he means.

"From death lead me to immortaity"—there is nothing obscure in this.

■ i) Word: *vāc,* which may also mean speech here or, more simply, voice.
Life breath: *prāṇa.*
Works: *karman,* deeds.
Honor: *yaśas,* glory.
Spiritual brilliance: *brahmavarcas,* divine splendor, sacred luster.
Fame: *kīrti.*
Let it be accomplished: *samāpayitavya,* referring to the funeral rites that conclude the existence of the individual as such.

■ ii) 10. Thus . . . he wins . . . : according to the Upaniṣadic conception, "he who knows this." In this reply everything depends upon what the questioner understands by "water"—obviously not the physical element but water symbolizing a means for overcoming death.

11. The reply seems to refer to a holy man, because when the death of an ordinary person occurs it is said that the *prāṇas* depart from the body (cf. v. 13).

12. The name (*nāman*) is eternal (*ananta*). Cf. CU VII, 1, 5, (§ VI 3).

13. All the human organs enter the elements, including the *ātman* which goes into the *ākāśa.* Of the person only his *karman* remains.
Together they spoke . . . : *mantrayāṁ cakrāte.*
Good: *puṇya,* virtuous, meritorious.
Sinful: *pāpa.*
Kept silent: *upararāma,* he was contented, he held his peace.

■ iii) 1. Unconcious: *sammoha,* confusion, etc. Lit. "goes to weakness and unconsciousness."
Life-powers: *prāṇāḥ.*
Particles of light: *tejomātrāḥ,* the life-sparks.

Person in the eye: *cākṣuṣaḥ puruṣaḥ*, the individual principle that sees and is seen. When it is about to disappear, individual identity dissolves.

2. Becoming one: *ekībhavati*, he goes back to primordial unity.

Tip of his heart: *hṛdayasyāgre*, the fine point of the heart; it can also mean "center", orifice.

Consciousness: *vijñāna*, intelligence.

Knowledge: *vidyā*.

Works: *karmāṇi*.

Past experience: *pūrva-prajñā*, knowledge of the past, remembrance, memory (of previous lives?). The fate of the departed will be decided by the balance of these three factors.

3-7. Cf. § VI 11.

8. Cf. § V 27.

■ iv) Purificatory rites: *pavamāna*.

The singing priest sings the chant: *prastotā sāma prastauti*.

From unreality . . . :

asato mā sad gamaya,
tamaso mā jyotir gamaya,
mṛtyor māmṛtaṁ gamaya.

c) Liturgy for the Dead

Antyakarma

At the dawn of his life a man was blessed and welcomed as an infant by his parents and relatives, and by the Waters, Fire, Savitṛ, Earth, and Sarasvatī. He was not yet conscious of the human, cosmic, and divine realities, but Men, the cosmos, and the Gods received him. He lacked nothing. The Gods, the Sages, the Fathers, and sacrifice were all invoked to ensure him a long life; even the wisdom of the Vedas was "instilled" into him.[105] Later, having become a youth, he was initiated according to the rites by his *guru*[106] and united to a bride[107] with whom he settled in his home where he himself offered the daily sacrifice and prayed to the Gods. He enjoyed a long span of life.

Gradually he grows old, until one day he no longer possesses human vitality and strength; the flame of his earthly life is consumed and he is no more conscious of his surroundings or of what is going on around him. Now once again, as at the time of his birth, his relatives, the cosmos, and the Gods are going to bless him and take care of him. In his infancy it was his father who had presented him to the Gods, but now it is his own son who is going to perform the funeral and the subsequent rites. Each of those rites aims at

105. Cf. *Jātakarman* § I 35.
106. Cf. *Upanayana* § II 14.
107. Cf. *Vivāha* § II 17.

purifying him from his earthly stains so that he may reach the Fathers' realm. In the last rites (*antyeṣṭi*),[108] as in the first rites (*jātakarman*), the relatives, the cosmos, and the Gods attend him: the Waters, Fire, Savitṛ, Earth and Sarasvatī are present once more.

Opinions differ as to the way in which Vedic Man disposed of his dead. It is generally accepted that cremation was the normal way, though burial was also practiced.[109] The cremation rites are a continuation of the daily sacrifice. The dead person who can no longer offer the sacrifice is himself offered in sacrifice so that all his impurities may be burned away before he reaches the heavenly world.[110] This explains why the innocent child who had not reached the age of two was not cremated, but buried.[111] It is probably for the same reason that ascetics were buried, a custom that still prevails today. By embracing the wandering life of an ascetic, the holy man has renounced everything, including the offering of the daily sacrifice, because he has interiorized this offering and as it were exhausted the sacred Fire. Hence cremation would be superfluous: all his impurities have already been burned away.

There is a precise and detailed description of the funeral rites in the Śrauta Sūtras and some of the Gṛhya Sūtras. These two *sūtras* differ in several details of the ceremony; nevertheless in each of them the rites are derived from some hymns of the Ṛg Veda[112] whose inspiration they follow, incorporating some of the verses at important moments of the ceremony. Though in the course of time several alterations to the original texts of the Gṛhya Sūtras have occurred, even today the bulk of the funeral rites still have their source in those *sūtras*.

In order to present a vivid description of the ceremony, we give a paraphrase of each of the rites as it is set out in the Āśvalāyana Gṛhya Sūtra. Hymn RV X, 17, which follows, though not incorporated in the Gṛhya Sūtras, is sometimes considered to be a funeral hymn. Next come the hymns of the Ṛg Veda on which the Gṛhya Sūtra texts are based.

The funeral rites for all twice-born[113] persons are the same ex-

108. *Antyeṣṭi:* from *antya* (last) and *iṣṭi* (sacrifice, oblation).

109. Some texts suggest that burial too was practiced in Vedic times, though the actual evidence is slight. Cf. RV VII, 89, 1 (§ IV 19); X, 15, 14; AV V, 30, 14 (§ V 9); XVIII, 2, 25; XVIII, 2, 34.

110. "Leaving your stains," as is said in RV X, 14, 8 (§ V 7).

111. Cf. PGS III, 10, 5.

112. Cf. RV X, 14; X, 16; X, 18 (§§ V 7; 16; 15).

113. Cf. § II 14 for the *upanayana* rites.

cept for the number of fires used. The cremation of an *āhitāgni*[114] is performed with the three sacrificial fires; someone who has kept only the *smārta*[115] or *aupāsana*[116] fire is cremated with that fire alone; and someone who has not kept any fire is burned with ordinary fire.[117] The description of the funeral rites according to the Āśvalāyana Sūtra that follows is for an *āhitāgni*.

Let us now look at the text of the three hymns, and in particular at those aspects not contained in the Gṛhya Sūtras.

In Ṛg Veda X, 17, Pūṣan, who knows the roads and the highways,[118] who is the protector of travelers and of the comings and goings of cattle, escorts and protects the dead man on his way to his new abode. With Pūṣan the deceased is in perfect safety, for he has a perfect knowledge of the roads between heaven and earth. The departed is never uncared for, never left alone in the unknown; while Pūṣan protects him, Savitṛ conducts him and Agni ushers him into the company of the Gods (vv. 3-6). The following verses deal with the living who are engaged in the offering of the sacrifice. These verses are addressed to Sarasvatī who comes in a chariot with the Fathers and sits on the sacrificial grass. Although these verses seem somewhat unrelated to the preceding ones, they are to be found in the cremation rites of the Kauśika Sūtra.[119] It is possible that waters from the rivers were used in earlier versions of the funeral rite, and that these waters were identified with Sarasvatī, the holy river. Sarasvatī is asked to protect the worshipers against sickness, and the Waters, who are addressed as Mothers, are asked to wash away every kind of stain.[120]

Hymn X, 18, is often described as a funeral hymn. It may not have originally been intended for use at a funeral ceremony, but later *sūtras* made use of some of its verses, though a different order of events is often followed in the ceremony itself. The hymn is addressed in turn to death, to the dead man, and to his survivors, with whom in fact it is primarily concerned. The hymn's train of thought does not correspond exactly to the order of the rite.

114. *Āhitāgni:* one who has consecrated the *śrauta* fires.

115. *Smārta* fire: the "traditional" fire (acc. of Smṛti). The *smārtas* follow the Vedic prescriptions but they introduce also new forms of worship of the Gods in temples. They are considered less purely Vedic than the *śrautas*.

116. *Aupāsana* fire: the domestic fire.

117. Cf. SB XIII, 8, 4, 11.

118. For Pūṣan cf. § II Introduction.

119. KausS LXXXI, 39; cf. AV XVIII, 1, 41-43, for similar verses.

120. Cf. § IV 20 for the cleansing power of the waters.

The first stanza, though addressed to death and urging it to depart, is really concerned with the living. The next four stanzas are addressed to the relatives of the deceased when they return to their home after the funeral. In these verses the glory of life is extolled in contrast with the void caused by death. The "barrier" or "mound" in stanza 4 probably refers to a stone that was symbolically placed as a boundary mark between the dead and the living. This use of a boundary testifies, once again, to the desire to keep death at a distance and to the human craving for a long and prosperous life. Stanza 5, which is also addressed to the relatives, probably alludes to the place assigned to them in the funeral procession, in which the elders come first and the younger follow. The order of precedence corresponds to that which prevails in the cosmos and which is itself determined by the divine Ordainer. Stanzas 7 and 8 allude to the widow, but in a more elaborate way than in the Āśvalāyana Gṛhya Sūtra. Here the beauty, grace, and vitality of the young womenfolk of the household are stressed. Next we are told of the burial of the ashes as in the Āśvalāyana Gṛhya Sūtra, in which verses 10 and 13 are repeated. If one takes verse 11 out of its context without referring to the rest of the rite, one might conclude, as certain commentators have done, that the corpse is buried, since interment was practiced in Vedic times. The post or "pillar" mentioned in stanza 13 was probably a kind of pedestal or support for the urn to rest upon. In the last verse the poet seems to pray for himself: he wants to sever all ties and connections with the dead man and with death, just as a feather is loosed from an arrow. The hymn as a whole shows a strong will for life and deep solicitude toward the dead man.

If we were to follow the traditional funeral rites, hymn X, 16, should be interpolated between X, 18, stanzas 9 and 10, as it deals with the funeral fire. It is a hymn addressed to Agni, who is besought not to consume the dead man entirely, not to destroy his spirit, but to introduce him to the Fathers. Stanza 3 mentions the different elements of his body which will continue to exist in other realms of the world. In stanza 4 Agni is fervently asked to preserve the corpse and to burn the goat instead;[121] it is the goat that, after passing through thick darkness, announces to the Fathers the deceased's arrival.[122] Stanza 5 alludes to the new and heavenly life

121. Cf. § V 13 for the sacrifice of the goat or the she-animal.
122. Cf. AV IX, 5, 1; 3.

where the deceased will have a new and perfect body. Agni and Soma are asked (stanza 6) to heal any wounds or bites inflicted on the dead man's body by crows, ants, snakes, or wild beasts. In a very realistic way (stanza 7) the deceased is asked to protect himself with the fat of the cow (or goat) so that the Fire may not devour him. In stanza 9 a clear distinction is made between Agni the "body-consuming,"[123] who removes all stains from the departed, and Agni the "All-Knowing,"[124] who brings the offerings to the Gods.

Agni was invoked at the ceremony after the birth of the child, was with him again as a young man (especially at his initiation), witnessed the blessing of his marriage, and was always both host and friend in the man's home. Now, faithful to this friendship, Agni accompanies the deceased to his last abode where he, Varuṇa, and the other Gods will remain with him forever, enjoying both happiness and one another's company. The following stanza admirably summarizes the unique role of Agni among the living and the dead.

> Prolong, O Agni, life's span for the living.
> May the dead proceed to the world of the Fathers!
> True guardian of the home, consume all evil.
> For this man may each sunrise be fairer than the last![125]

The Rites *Antyeṣṭi*

13

i) *Leaving Home for the Cremation Ground*

[AGS IV, 1, 1-19; 2, 1-9]

If the sick man has not been restored to life and dies, a suitable plot of ground facing the South or the Southwest should be selected by the relatives and well dug.[126] It should be covered with grass and the thorns pulled out; moreover, it should not be a damp spot. When the dead body has been shaved, bathed, and properly dressed, large quantities of sacrificial grass and clarified butter are prepared. The butter mingled with curd becomes the "sprinkled butter," which is also used for the offering to the Fathers.[127]

Then from the home of the deceased the funeral procession starts. The relatives carry the sacred fire and the sacrificial vessels of the dead man. As many people as

123. Body-consuming: *kravyād*, flesh-eating. For further description of Agni *kravyād* cf. AV XII, 2.
124. All-Knowing: *jātavedas*. For further description of Agni cf. § III 4.
125. AV XII, 2, 45.
126. The cremation ground is called *śmaśāna;* the same word designates the place where bones of the dead body are collected and buried. Cf. SB XIII, 8, 1, where rules for the selection of the ground are given.
127. The offering to the Fathers is *pṛṣadājya*.

possible follow, men and women in two different groups; the body is carried by those walking at the back or, according to some, is drawn by two oxen. A cow or a she-goat is taken to be sacrificed.[128] Among the relatives the elders come first, then the young men; they all wear the sacrificial cord around their waists and unloose their hair.

ii) *The Funeral Fire Is Prepared*

[AGS IV, 2, 10-22]

When the relatives and friends have reached the spot, the one who is to perform the rite[129] walks three times around the place and with a branch of *śamī*[130] sprinkles water on the body to chase away the evil spirits.[131] Then he places the *āhavanīya* fire in the Southeast, the *gārhapatya* fire in the Northwest, and the *dakṣiṇa* fire in the Southwest. When the funeral pyre has been prepared some sacrificial grass and a black antelope skin are spread out on it to receive the dead body. The wife of the deceased then lies on the north side of the body. Her brother-in-law or a student of her late husband or an elderly servant beseeches her to rise: "Arise, O wife, to the world of the living!"[132] If the deceased is a Kṣatriya, instead of his wife his bow is placed by his side and then quickly taken away and broken into pieces.[133]

iii) *He Will No More Offer the Agnihotra*

[AGS IV, 3, 1-19]

Next, according to a strict order, the sacrificial utensils [for the *agnihotra*] which have belonged to the deceased are in turn touched against his different limbs. Those utensils that have a hollow are filled up with the melted butter previously prepared. The son of the dead person keeps for himself the millstones and the utensils made of copper, iron, and terra-cotta.

iv) *A Goat or Cow Is Offered as a Sacrificial Victim*

[AGS IV, 3, 20-27]

The goat or the cow is offered in sacrifice, its viscera extracted and put on the head and the mouth of the deceased, while a prayer is said asking that he should be protected against Agni the corpse-eater.[134]

The two kidneys [right and left] of the animal are put into the right and left hands of the deceased, who is warned to avoid the two dogs of Saramā, the keepers of the road going to hell; instead, he is told to follow the right path leading to Yama's

128. The goat, *ajā*, offered as oblation is caled *anustaraṇī*. For the sacrificial goat cf. AV IX, 5.
129. The one who performs the rite is the *antyakarmādhikārin;* he it is who also performs the *śrāddha*. The task of performing the funeral ceremony belongs by right to the dead man's son, but in his absence other members of the family in order of precedence may replace him.
130. *Śamī:* a tree with very hard wood.
131. Cf. RV X, 14, 9 (§ V 7).
132. RV X 18, 8 (§ V 15). The meaning of this verse is uncertain and it has given rise to much controversy. Some commentators want to see in it a reference to *satī*, the custom that demanded that a widow should be burned alive on the pyre at the side of her dead husband; but that is not very probable. Cf. AV XVIII, 3, 1-2, where the reference to an "ancient custom" probably means that *satī* was performed in early times.
133. Cf. RV X, 18, 9 (§ V 15).
134. Cf. RV X, 16, 7 (§ V 16).

kingdom where the Fathers rejoice.[135] The heart of the animal is put on the heart of the dead man. The different limbs of the victim are placed on the corresponding limbs of the corpse and then are covered with the animal's skin.

While the sacrificial waters [*praṇīta*] are brought Agni is asked not to upset the cup from which the Gods drink.[136] The officiating priest pours four oblations into the *dakṣiṇa* fire, saying:

To Agni *svāhā*!
To Kāma *svāhā*!
To the World *svāhā*!
To Anumati *svāhā*![137]

He then makes a last oblation on the chest of the deceased, saying:

In truth you have been born from this one.
May he now be born out of you, N. N.!
To the world of Heaven, *svāhā*![138]

v) *May Agni Send Him to the Fathers: Cremation*

[AGS IV, 4, 1-8]

Now the performer of the rites gives the order to kindle the three fires.[139] It is said that, according to which fire reaches the body first, the dead person will first reach either heaven, the space world, or the world of the Fathers. If the three fires reach the body at the same moment it is an extremely auspicious sign and it means that the deceased will enjoy great happiness.

Then the body is consumed by the flames, while the deceased is told to follow the path of the elders which will take him to the kings Yama and Varuṇa.[140] It is believed that the smoke conveys the dead man to heaven.

vi) *The Purification of the Living*

[AGS IV, 4, 9-17]

When the cremation is finished the relatives, who are now ready to return home, are addressed in an exhortation that glorifies life and wishes them a long span of days. . . .[141] They turn around from right to left and leave the cremation ground without looking back. When they reach a bathing place they bathe in it once and take some water into their hands, pronouncing the clan [*gotra*] and name of the dead man;[142] they put on fresh clothes and remain at the bathing place until the

135. Cf. RV X, 14, 10 (§ V 7).
136. Cf. RV X, 16, 8 (§ V 16). All the sacrificial vessels that lie on the corpses are to be burned with it, but the priest asks that the cup be spared so the deceased may use it in the Fathers' world.
137. Anumati: here the Goddess of favor, assent, or grace; the entire hymn AV VII, 20, is addressed to her (§ VII 32).
138. The invocation is addressed to Agni, born out of the dead body. Cf. SB II, 3, 3, 5; XII, 5, 2, 15.
139. Cf. RV X, 16, 4 (§ V 16) and AV XVIII, 2, 8-10, which are also about cremation.
140. Cf. RV X, 14, 7 (§ V 7). The AGS says that here the same texts as those indicated in the Śrauta Sūtra should be recited, i.e., verses taken from RV X, 14; X, 16; X, 17; X, 18; X, 154 (§§ V 7; 16; 14; 15; 24).
141. Cf. RV X, 18, 3 (§ V 15).
142. By doing so they are offering water to the dead (*udaka-karma*).

stars appear in the sky. Then they return home in a procession in which the younger lead and the older follow. When they reach the house they touch a stone, the fire, cow dung, fried barley, sesame seeds, and water. On that night no food should be cooked; the meal has to be bought, or else it can be prepared before the rite takes place.

For three days the relatives must take no salt. If the deceased was a father, a mother, or a teacher, they may neither give alms nor study the Vedas.[143]

vii) *The Last Embrace of Mother Earth*

[AGS IV, 5, 1-10]

On the eleventh, thirteenth, or fifteenth day of the dark fortnight[144] after the cremation, the relatives return to the cremation ground. The one who performs the rites walks around the ground [which should be dry] and with a *śamī* branch sprinkles it with water, asking the plant "full of coolness" to fill Agni with gladness.[145]

When the bones have been purified and gathered and placed in an urn, a hole is dug in the earth and the urn is placed in it. Mother Earth is earnestly beseeched to keep the deceased safe from the womb of Nothingness.[146] While a last prayer is addressed to the Fathers and Yama,[147] a lid is placed on the urn and the hole is filled up with earth. Then the relatives leave the place without looking back and take a bath. After some time they perform the *śrāddha*[148] ceremony for the dead man.

Escorted by the Gods — *Pūṣā tvā pātu prapathe*

14

RV X, 17, 1-10

1. Tvaṣṭṛ prepares his daughter for her marriage.
On hearing the tidings the whole world assembles.
The mother of Yama, wife of great Vivasvat,
vanished while being conveyed to her dwelling.

2. From mortal man this immortal woman
was hidden by the Gods. Fashioning another
in her likeness, they gave this second to Vivasvat.

143. Cf. also PGS III, 10, 16-43.
144. The moon decreases in the dark fortnight.
145. Cf. RV X 16, 13-14; here there is probably an allusion to the water sprinkled upon the ashes of the corpse after cremation.
146. Cf. RV X, 18, 10 (§ V 15).
147. Cf. RV X, 18, 13 (ibid.).
148. The *śrāddha* ceremony performed a short time after the funeral rites of a relative is called *ekoddiṣṭa*, as it is performed only for a person who has recently died (cf. AGS IV, 7, 1). It is said that *antyeṣṭi* and *ekoddiṣṭa* are extremely beneficial to the deceased, as he is believed to be a wandering spirit with no real body. It is only after the first *śrāddha* rite has been performed that he can dwell among the Fathers. The *śrāddha* ceremony is observed at fixed times as an act of respect and veneration to deceased relatives. It consists of a water oblation; on some occasions *piṇḍas* or balls of rice are offered with the intention of sustaining the deceased who, after the funeral rites and the first *śrāddha* rite have been performed for him, has assumed an ethereal body.

She, Saraṇyū, bore the two Aśvins
and then abandoned both sets of twins.

3. May the all-knowing Pūṣan, guardian of the earth,
whose cattle do not perish, dispatch you hence!
May Pūṣan consign you to the Fathers' keeping,
may Agni escort you to the Gods who know you!

4. Life universal shall guard and surround you.
May Pūṣan protect and precede you on the way!
May Savitṛ the God to that place lead you
where go and dwell the doers of good deeds!

5. May Pūṣan who knows all these regions conduce us
by ways that are freest from fear and danger,
preceding us, the shining one, giver of blessings,
wise and unerring, escort of all heroes!

6. On distant pathways Pūṣan is born,
on a road that stretches far from earth and from heaven.
He passes on his way, with perfect knowledge,
to both the realms that men hold most dear.

7. During the sacrifice the worshipers call
on Sarasvatī. Sarasvatī they worship.
May Sarasvatī grant bliss to the giver—
Sarasvatī, revered by pious works!

8. O Goddess Sarasvatī, accompanier of the Fathers,
who joins them in rejoicing at our offerings, be seated
with joy on this sacred grass. Give food
that strengthens and ward off all sorts of sickness.

9. O Sarasvatī, the one whom the Fathers invoke,
they who, coming from the right, approach the sacrifice,
grant to those who now sacrifice all good things,
a portion worth as much as a thousand of the offering!

10. These Mother Waters, which cleanse the holy oil,
with this selfsame oil shall cleanse all our stains.
Their divinity washes off all defilement.
I rise up from them purified and brightened.

This hymn is directed to many deities and has no internal unity. Many of the stanzas are to be found in AV XVIII, 1, a hymn for funeral use. We omit the last four verses which deal with the drops of Soma which may have fallen to the ground during the sacrifice (vv. 11-13) and with the singers' aspirations (v. 14).

1-2. These verses give in condensed form the story of Yama's parents, Saraṇyū and Vivasvat. According to this account, the Gods abduct Vivasvat's wife (or she escapes with their help) and put another in her place. Saraṇyū is the mother of both sets of twins, the Aśvins and Yama and Yamī (cf. RV X, 10; § V 1); according to another interpretation the "real" Saraṇyū, who is immortal and the daughter of the Ordainer, Tvaṣṭṛ, is the mother of Yama and Yamī, whereas her "duplicate" is the mother of the Aśvins.

3. Pūṣan is invoked as *anaṣṭapaśu,* one whose herd does not perish, and as *bhuvanasya gopā,* lit. shepherd of the earth.

Hence: from this world to the next.
Gods who know you: lit. the Gods who are easily accessible or easy to find or into whose presence it is easy to enter.
4. Life universal: *āyu,* life personified in a divine being, giver of life. *Āyur viśvāyuḥ* refers to Pūṣan. Some read *vāyu.*
7-9. These verses are very similar to AV XVIII, 1, 41-43, and are used in the KausS LXXXI,39, for the cremation. Cf. RV VI, 61, and VII, 95, addressed to Sarasvatī.
9. All good things: *rāyaspoṣa,* increase of riches.

Effacing the Traces of Death

Mṛtyoḥ padaṁ yopayantaḥ

15

RV X, 18

1. Pursue, O Death, the distant path,
the path that is yours, not trodden by the Gods.
I charge you, who can both see and hear:
do not harm our children or our comrades.

2. When, effacing the traces of Death,
you return to prolong your span of days,
may you, enhanced with offspring and riches,
live lives pure and bright, bringing honor to the Gods!

3. Separated from the dead are these, the living.
Our appeal to the Gods has been vouchsafed.
We now repair to dancing and laughter,
returning to prolong our span of days.

4. I fix a barrier around the living,
so that none of them this boundary may pass.
May they live a span of a hundred years,
penning in Death beneath this mound!

5. As days follow days in orderly succession,
as seasons faithfully succeed one another,
so shape the lives of these, O Supporter,
that the younger may not forsake his elder.

6. Attain your prime; then welcome old age,
striving by turns in the contest of life.
May the Ordainer, maker of good things,
be pleased to grant you length of days!

7. The women with husbands still living and strong
advance, annointed with fragrant balm,
tearless and free from sorrow. They mount first,
adorned with their jewels, to the resting place.

8. Arise, O lady! To the world of the living
return! He is dead by whose side you are lying.

Your marriage is over to this your husband
who held your hand and ardently wooed you.

9. I take from the hand of the dead this bow.
It will bring us valor and prestige and power.
You depart, we remain and are eager, as heroes,
to frustrate all the snares and assaults of our foes.

10. Subside into the lap of Earth, your mother,
this Earth wide-spreading, this kind and gracious maiden
who is soft as wool to the generous giver!
From the womb of Nothingness may she preserve you!

11. Make a vault, O Earth; do not press down upon him!
Grant him easy access. Afford him shelter.
Cover him up with the skirt of your robe,
just as a mother envelops a child.

12. May Earth, arched over him like a vault,
lie lightly, propped by a thousand pillars.
May this be a home for him dripping with fatness,
a place of refuge to him forever.

13. I prop up around you the earth in a mound.
May I ever myself be free from harm!
May the Fathers support firmly this pillar!
May Yama grant this to be your dwelling!

14. In days to come they will affix me
like a feather on an arrow. I, however,
restrain my speech, as the rein does a horse.

1-7. These stanzas are said after the cremation, corresponding to the *śāntikarman* (the rite of appeasement).

1. The distant path: or "the other path." Death is sent away, far from the living.

2. The survivors are addressed. The traces of the funeral procession are effaced with a branch. Bringing honor to the Gods: *yajñiya,* eager in worship, devoted to sacrifice, hence pious, holy.

3. Vouchsafed: *bhadra,* lit. auspicious.

5. Supporter: Dhātṛ, establisher, creator, ordainer.

Younger: *apara,* lit. later one.

Elder: *pūrva,* lit. earlier, previous one.

6. The Ordainer, maker of good things: *tvaṣṭā sujanimā,* lit. the Fashioner, giving good origin (good birth).

Be pleased: *sajoṣas,* agree, be in unity, be like-minded with you.

7. Women with husbands . . . : *avidhavāḥ,* lit. the unwidowed.

Resting place: *yoni,* usually interpreted as referring to the funeral couch, but it may refer also to the marriage couch. The stress is on the return to normal life.

9. Bow: distinctive sign of the Kṣatriya, whose power is now transferred to the living.

10. To the generous giver: *dakṣiṇāvate,* the one who offers the priestly honorarium, the one of generous gifts.

Nothingness: *nirṛti,* destruction, perdition (personified as a Goddess).

12. Refuge: *śaraṇa.*

14. Obscure verse susceptible of various interpretations. It is the prayer of the poet who wants to avoid the evil consequences of his contact with death.

Putting on a New Life

Āyurvasāna

16

RV X, 16, 1-9

1. Do not burn him or utterly consume him,
O Agni. Do not scatter his limbs and his skin!
Perfect him, O you who survey men's deeds,
and send him on to the abode of the Fathers.

2. When you have prepared him, O All-Knowing One,
then deliver him up to the Fathers.
When he arrives in the realm of the spirits
he will become a controller of the Gods.

3. The Sun receive your eye, the Wind your spirit!
Go, as is your merit, to earth or heaven,
or, if that be your lot, to the waters,
with your body diffused in the plants of the field.

4. Your share is the goat—burn him with your heat!
May your blazing light and flame consume him!
By these your auspicious forms, All-Knowing One,
convey this man to the world of the saints.

5. Release him again, O Agni, to the Fathers.
The one offered to you now proceeds to his destiny.
Putting on new life, let him approach the surviving,
let him reunite with a body, All-Knowing One!

6. Whatever wound the black bird has inflicted
upon you, or the ant, the snake, or the jackal,
may Agni, the all-consuming, make it whole,
and Soma, who has entered within the priests.

7. Shield yourself from Agni with the parts of the cow
and smear your body with fat and oil,
so that the daring Agni, eager to devour you,
may not embrace you with his fiery blaze.

8. O Agni, do not overturn this chalice,
dear to the Gods and to those deserving Soma.
From this chalice the Gods quench their thirst;
in it the immortals find delight.

9. The body-consuming Fire I send far away!
Removing all dross, let him go to Yama's realm!
But may the other, the All-Knowing, the skillful,
convey this offering direct to the Gods!

2. All-Knowing One: *jātavedas* throughout.
Realm of the spirits: *asunīti,* the life of the deceased in the world of spirits. Cf. *asu* in AV VIII, 2, 1 (§ V 11).

Controller of the Gods: *devānāṁ vaśanīḥ*. Here *deva* refers to the powers given to man which he must seek to master.

4. Your share is the goat: Agni's share is the sacrificial goat.

Heat: *tapas,* ardor.

Auspicious forms: *śivās tanvaḥ,* gracious bodies.

Saints: *sukṛtāḥ,* those who have done good deeds, the pious, etc.

5. Destiny: *svadhā,* own nature, own will, determination, etc. Later it means the sacrificial drink.

The surviving: *śeṣa,* referring either to the bones left after the cremation or to the survivors of the deceased.

6. Black bird: crow.

8. Chalice: *camasa,* the cup from which the Gods drink (made of wood).

Those deserving Soma: *somyānām.* Cf. note on *somya* in § III 17 Introduction.

Immortals find delight: *devā amṛtā mādayante,* the Gods are inebriated, rejoice, etc.

9. Body-consuming Fire: *kravyādam agnim,* the flesh-eating Agni; Agni in his terrible aspect at the funeral pyre.

All-Knowing: *jātavedas* is the less fearful aspect of Agni.

The skillful: lit. knowing well.

10-14. The four following stanzas repeat the main thrust of the hymn.

B. THE OTHER WORLD

Asau lokaḥ

In truth there are two states of this person: the state of being in this world and the state of being in the other world. There is a third twilight state of being: that of sleep. In the twilight state of being he sees the other two: that of this world and that of the otherworld. When entering into this third state of being, since it constitutes an approach to the state of being of the other world, he sees both, that is to say, the evils and the joys. When he falls asleep, taking with him all the elements composing this state of being, he takes them apart and reconstructs them as he likes, dreaming by means of his own radiance, his own light. Then this person becomes his own light.

BU IV, 3, 9

The text given as antiphon of this subsection tells us of two states or conditions of Men, the state of existence in this world and the state of existence in the other or higher one: the *para-loka-sthāna*. There is, however, an intermediary state also, the state of sleep.[148] There we are in contact, the text says, with both the other worlds.[149] In sleep we begin to overcome the temporal and spatial differentiation between the two worlds and no longer imagine the "other" world to be "after" or "above" this world. Here cosmology

148. Cf. also BS III, 2, 1.
149. Cf. § VII Introduction where the connection between this third stage and prayer is underscored.

is reabsorbed in anthropology, but this will constitute the last, the unique, step of the Upaniṣads.

There is a certain autonomous conception of Man which seems to see human destiny at variance with the destiny of the world. Man dies. He may enter another plane of existence, he may rise again, or a part of him may be immortal, but he still has to go through the gates of death regardless of whether, once the threshold is crossed, there is fullness, emptiness, or a renewal of the whole process of life. The world, on the other hand, does not seem to have to die and certainly nobody has ever seen the death of the cosmos or even of a substantial part of it. Perhaps it is the fact of his own inevitable death, in contrast with the world's continuing existence, which has led Man to differentiate himself from the surrounding cosmos: only what is alive may cease to live.

The Vedic view seems to take exception to that conception. We have already looked at some different understandings of the relationship between Man and the world, and we have seen how the Vedic experience tends toward a nondualistic understanding of this relationship. Man is not an undifferentiated part of the world, nor, however, is he a foreigner. He is not even a temporary resident or guest on this planet, for the world is his home, just as his body is, and body and world are linked together in a common destiny. Just as Man, in one way or another, has to face death, so the whole world too, in one way or another, will have to confront the problem of death. Thus the destiny of the world is not different from human destiny, which is not to say that Man shares in the specific caducity of the cosmos, for that would suggest that the cosmos is predominant; nor is it to affirm that the cosmos shares in the peculiar mortality of Man, for that would be to err in the opposite direction and confer predominance on Man. Man and cosmos are both involved in one and the same venture and both undergo the same process, though each in its own way. The cosmos, like Man, dies and is also immortal.

Modern psychology may speak of a process of transference, as if Man could transfer onto the world what he experiences within himself. Indian thinking may retort that transference is possible precisely because Man and cosmos are united both in their being and in their destiny. Vedic experience embraces the cosmos as well as Man.

We have already mentioned the existence of the three worlds, the earth, the sky, and the in-between,[150] as well as the worlds of the *ṛṣis*, the *pitṛs*, and the *devas*.[151] We have seen that according to the Vedas the life of Man is not limited to the confines of this world alone; his existence is not solitary or isolated. Here we see that the existence of the world itself is neither solitary nor isolated, and for exactly the same reason: the Vedic experience abhors the idea of an absolute beginning or an absolute end. Such ideas are felt to be impossible, to be stifling of all life and even of all thought. If the universe is all that exists, then the idea that the universe should have an absolute limit is impossible, for absoluteness is the negation of all limitations.

Cosmological infinity as viewed in the Vedic experience offers an alternative both to the closed world view of many traditional cosmologies and to the purely scientific infinity of an ever-expanding universe. Vedic cosmological infinity is not a rival to the infinity of God, at least not to that of a supreme personal God, for these two infinities belong to different orders. Nor does it contradict a merely scientific infinity. It is rather, as it were, the spatiotemporal infinity of the Godhead. The world had no beginning and will have no end, for beginning and end are themselves intraworldly categories and thus fall within this side of the whole picture. If we were to undertake a journey across the world in time and space, or with the mind alone, and try to reach the beginning or the end, we could never do so, even supposing such a journey was possible. The end of any path, temporal, spatial, or even spiritual, would be the end of the world and of its observer as well.

The Vedic cosmological experience is not mainly temporal or spatial, as if Man were thrown into a limitless temporal or spatial sea, he himself being of different material and capable of witnessing what was happening. It is a prolongation of the experience of Man himself. The worlds are not empty places devoid of Men: they are Man's great body, the real theater where his existence unfolds. To think of worlds with no relation to Man whatsoever is as much an abstraction as thinking of Man without a world. To substantiate what we have been saying we may recall the meaning of the word

150. Cf. §§ Gāyatrī Introduction; II B and below V B c; VII Introduction.
151. Cf. § V 4.

loka as open space, as the place of our experience and the horizon of our knowledge.[152]

Significantly enough, the silence of the Vedas on the ages of the world, their destruction and succession, is going to be more than counterbalanced by the profusion of Purāṇic and epic literature on the subject. The Vedas say hardly anything about cosmological eschatology.[153] They concentrate primarily on Man. The three subsections that follow clearly illustrate this emphasis. The first one contains two of the infrequent mentions of cosmic dissolution, for the idea of *pralaya,* the destruction of the world, or any other idea of cosmic disintegration is very rare in the *śruti.* Only a few Upaniṣadic texts provide the link with later periods. We offer the texts according to a certain internal order. The other two subsections are devoted to the main utterances about heaven and hell, for these are the other two places where Man's life continues unfolding.

a) Cosmic Disintegration

Pralaya

Both Man and nature are subject to the canker of decay, but deep within both is also to be found the seed of immortality. The pattern of Day and Night is not only a terrestrial phenomenon; it occurs also in the heavens year after year. Moreover, we have known that Prajāpati is the year[154] and that this word means simply time, which amounts to saying that day and night are the expression of the cosmic rhythm of the entire universe. Each day the world reaches an end, just as each day a Man's life is completed and expended, so that the one who reserves himself for the morrow is living an unauthentic life. Furthermore, the same day-night rhythm operates also in every day of Brahmā or every *yuga.* The reason for this, the Gītā says, is that behind all the dynamism the Lord is present, effecting both the destruction and the reconstruction of the world.

152. Cf. §§ III 27 Introduction and III 29 on the concept of *loka* and *loka-saṁgraha.*

153. The passage of AB VII, 15 (XXXIII, 3), about *kali, dvāpara, tretā,* and *kṛta,* the traditional four ages of the world, does not need to be interpreted in this way (so A.B. Keith against Max Müller and Weber, for instance). Cf. also Manu IX, 302.

154. Cf. SB XI, 1, 6, 1 sq. (§ I 6); AB II, 17 (VII, 7, 2); MahanarU 531 (§ III 31).

The same homology is to be found in the first of the given texts. It seems as if the emphasis on the destruction of mankind is intended to highlight and emphasize its reconstruction. We shall not here analyze this account, the only one in the whole *śruti,* of what in other cultures is a very common myth: the myth of the flood and the periodic purification of the cosmos by the waters. The description is so closely interwoven with the doctrine of sacrifice and so intimately connected with its ritual that any foreign origin is highly questionable. We have here not so much a description of a cosmic event or of a metahistorical fact as a new emphasis on sacrifice and on the cosmoanthropocentric aspect of the doctrine concerning sacrifice. Each sacrifice is a sacrifice of the whole of mankind and effects the regeneration of mankind. Each sacrifice is a salvation from the flood and is relevant for the fate of the whole human race.

Furthermore, "Iḍā is faith," as is affirmed in the same Brāhmaṇa in order to stress that confidence or trust, as the sine qua non of authentic sacrifice, is an essential element of human life: "Iḍā is faith. He who knows that Iḍā is faith himself acquires faith and all that one can obtain through faith. He certainly obtains all this."[155] Iḍā has a complex history. On the one hand "it" is the fivefold offering that is eaten in common by all the participants after the sacrifice. On the other hand "she" is the daughter of Manu and thus the instrument for the divine incest which is to be the origin of the human race: the creatures, produced by God, their Father, are incapable of fulfilling their destiny alone and require a second coming down of God, a second initiative—the divine incest—in order to achieve their own existences.[156]

This passage illumines in an original manner the character of Vedic eschatology. The story does not tell us the cause of the Flood nor does it describe the destruction of all things by the waters, but it narrates the tale of Manu, the one man who, thanks to the good offices of a fish, was saved and was destined, after the waters had subsided, to receive the blessing of offspring and riches in response to his offering of oblations.

We should keep in mind the whole context of this Indian myth and not try to center it on any historical flood. Nor has it any

155. SB XI, 2, 7, 20
156. Cf., e.g., RV X, 61; SB I, 7, 4, 1-4; VI, 1, 2, 1 sq; BU I, 4, 3 sq. (§ I 7).

covenantal overtones. The world is not here destroyed because it was wicked, nor is there any promise or pact not to destroy it again. The context of the myth, as the many commentaries confirm, is the cultic climate of the Brāhmaṇas. Even when in later versions the cyclic character of temporal events in the cosmos is stressed, the fact remains that the emphasis lies in the power of the sacrifice in regenerating the whole world, the power of the sacrifice to produce Iḍā again by virtue of which the entire universe is remade.

At a later date, that of the Mahābhārata and the Purāṇas, the idea began to gain ground that in ancient times there dwelt upon earth an ideal race of Men, perfect in all respects; it was the age of the great sages. Then, little by little, there comes a progressive deterioration of morale and a degeneration in bodily physique until the era is brought to a climax of dissolution by a great flood, which in its turn is followed by a new creation when all once again is perfect. At the time of each flood it is the water, preexisting before each act of creation, which dissolves and purifies all things and then ushers in a new humanity, regenerate and revitalized.

The next two groups of texts, after an introductory passage from the Maitrī Upaniṣad, which stresses the process of decay observable in the whole universe, direct our attention above and beyond the world and claim to have found the fulcrum on which depends the turning of the universe. All things can dissolve and come again into being because there is a point, the One, which is outside this dynamism. It is indeed this One that brings about the circular movement of the universe.[157]

An early Upaniṣad makes this function so integral to the concept of the absolute that it defines Brahman precisely as

> That from which beings are born,
> that by which, once born, they live,
> that into which, once dead, they enter,[158]

as if to say that the central point around which everything revolves is at the same time the foundation or ground into which everything dissolves. The world is contingent and decaying because there exists something outside the flux, something into which the world can lapse, as the Bhagavad Gītā declares with its beautiful parable

157. Cf. MundU II, 1, 1 (§ VI 7).
158. TU III, 1 (§ II 11).

of the day and the night, symbolic of the cosmic rhythm of the whole universe.[159]

The Deluge *Samplava*

17

SB I, 8, 1, 1-10

1. One morning they brought to Manu water for his ablutions, just as now also they bring water for washing the hands. When he was washing himself, a fish came into his hands.

2. [The fish] thus spoke to him:

   "Tend me carefully and I will save you!"

   "From what will you save me?" [Manu enquired.]

   "A flood will wash away all these living beings. I will save you from that!"

   "How can I tend you carefully?"

3. [The fish] said:

   "As long as we are small, there is great danger of our destruction, because fish devour fish. You should first keep me in a jar. When I outgrow that, you will dig a pond and keep me in it. When I outgrow that, you will take me to the sea, for then I shall have overcome the danger of destruction."

4. It soon became *jhaṣa* [a large fish], for this is the fish that grows largest. The fish said further: "In such and such a year that flood will come and you should build a ship and be near me. When the flood comes you should enter into the ship, and I will save you from it [the flood]."

5. After he had tended it in this way, he took it to the sea. And in the same year predicted by the fish, he built a ship and remained near the fish. When the flood had come, he entered into the ship. The fish then swam toward him, and he tied the rope of the ship to its horn and by that means he reached the northern mountain.

6. Then the fish said to him: "I have saved you. Fasten the ship to a tree, but do not let the water wash you away while you are on the mountain. You may gradually descend as the waters subside!" And, in fact, he gradually descended, and thus it came about that the slope of the northern mountain is called "Manu's descent." Now the flood had swept away all living beings and Manu alone remained here.

7. He took to worship and austerities, because he was desirous of bringing forth living beings. He then performed also a *pāka*-sacrifice: he offered in the waters clarified butter, sour milk, curds, and whey. After a year a woman was

159. Cf. also BG IX, 18 (§ I 29).

produced from all that. She emerged, taking solid form, clarified butter still remaining in her footprints. Then Mitra and Varuṇa met her.

8. They asked her, "Who are you?"

"I am Manu's daughter," she answered.

"Say you are ours," they said.

"No," she said, "I belong to the one who has begotten me."

They wanted to have a share in her. She neither agreed nor disagreed, but slipped straight past them. She came to Manu.

9. Manu asked her, "Who are you?"

"I am your daughter," she answered.

"How, [blessed] one, are you my daughter?"

"With those offerings of clarified butter, sour milk, curds, and whey, made in the waters, you have begotten me. I am Blessing: make use of me at the sacrifice! If you will make use of me at the sacrifice, you will have many offspring and cattle. Whatever blessing you invoke through me shall be fully granted to you!"

He then made use of her in the middle of the sacrifice, for the middle of the sacrifice is intermediate between the first and the last offerings.

10. So with her he took to worship and austerities, because he was desirous of offspring. Through her he begot this race, which is humanity; and whatever blessing he invoked through her, that was fully granted to him.

7. *Pāka*-sacrifice: lit. cooked sacrifice (*yajña*), a simple sacrifice with the fire of the hearth. Manu, eager to escape from his loneliness and acquire children, practices austerity and offers an oblation of milk and butter. From this oblation is born his daughter. Iḍā is the personification of offering and in this passage her father Manu unites with her to be assured of an offspring.

10. Humanity: lit. the race of Manu.

In Whom All Things Dissolve *Saṁhāra*

18

MaitU I, 4

i) We see that all this [universe] is perishable: these flies, for example, mosquitoes, and so forth, the grass and the trees which grow and decay.

But what of all these? There are even other beings, superior to them: great warriors; world rulers like Sudyumna, Bhūridyumna, Indradyumna, Kuvalayāśva, Yauvanāśva, Vadhryaśva, Aśvapati, Śaśabindu, Hariścandra, Ambarīṣa, Nanaktu, Saryāti, Yayāti, Anaraṇya, Ukṣasena, and the rest; and also kings like Marutta, Bharata, and others—all of whom have abandoned their great glory in the sight of their friends and relatives and have departed to the other world.

But what of them? We even see the destruction of other beings, superior to them, like Gandharvas, demons, sprites, ogres, ghosts, troops of genii, goblins, serpent-demons, vampires, and the like. But what of them? We even see worse things: the drying up of big oceans, the downfall of mountain peaks, the displacing of the polestar, the tearing of the wind cords, the submergence of the earth, the fall of the Gods from their throne. How is it possible to enjoy one's desires in such a world? For we see that men, having tasted them, return again to the world from which they have come. Deliver me, I pray, Sir, for in this cycle of existence I am like a frog in a dry well. Lord, you alone are our refuge, you alone are our refuge.

SU III, 2

ii) One alone is God; there cannot be a second.
It is he alone who governs these worlds with his powers.
He stands facing beings. He, the herdsman of all worlds,
after bringing them forth, reabsorbs them at the end of time.

SU IV, 1; 11

iii) 1. May he who is one, who though colorless bestows countless colors
with mysterious purpose and multiple practice of his power,
the God into whom at the end all is dissolved
as in the beginning, endow us with purity of mind!

11. The One who holds dominion over every source,
in whom all things unite and dissolve again,
the Lord who grants men favors—when a man beholds him,
the God who is ever to be worshiped, he forever finds peace.

SU V, 3

iv) That God who in this terrestrial field spreads out nets,
one after another in various ways, then withdraws them—
he the great Self, creating the lords afresh,
rules once again as Lord over all these things.

MahanarU 3-4

v) 3. That in which all things are gathered together
and scattered again,
that in which all the Gods had their seat—

4. it is That which was and which shall be.
That dwells in the imperishable highest heaven.

■ i) 3. Cf. § IV 6.
Demons: *asuras*.
Sprites: *yakṣas*.
Ogres: *rākṣasas*.
Ghosts: *bhūtas*.

Troops of genii: *gaṇas.*
Goblins: *piśācas.*
Vampires: *grahas.*
Tearing of the wind cords: cf. the conception that the stars are held by wind cords.
Dry: *andha,* waterless, without issue, lit. blind.
Refuge: *gati,* which can mean also way and goal, i.e., way of salvation, place of refuge; cf. § I 29 notes. You alone are our way.

■ ii) God: Rudra, the Terrible, "the awe-inspiring," is here the personification of the supreme reality.
There cannot be a second: *na dvitīyāya tasthuḥ,* lit. they (those who know) do not stand for a second.
There is here a parallelism *īśata īśanībhiḥ,* lit. rules with ruling powers.
The herdsman: *gopā,* the watcher, the surveyor to whom is assigned the function of keeping an eye on something, the protector.
3-4. Cf. § I 28.

■ iii) 1. Colorless: *avarṇa* without distinctions, determining features, in opposition to *varṇa.* The first meaning of *varṇa* is the external painting or dye, i.e., the color (luster, splendor, glory) by which a form becomes visible; hence race, character, "caste." In the context of the SU the sociological dimension vanishes before the metaphysical symbolism of the manifold which does not endanger oneness.
With mysterious purpose: *nihitārtha,* of hidden aim, inscrutable design, with no extrinsic motivation.
Practice of his power: *śakti-yoga.*
God: *deva.*
With purity of mind: *buddhyā śubhayā,* with good understanding.
11. Source: *yoni.*
Unite and dissolve: *saṁ ca vi caiti,* meet and separate.
Lord: *īśāna.*
God: *deva.*

■ iv) Field: *kṣetra.*
Withdraws: *saṁharati,* reabsorbs, collects.
4. Cf. § III 6.

■ v) 1-2. Cf. § III 6.
3. Gathered together and scattered: *saṁ ca vi caiti,* are united and divided.
4. In the imperishable highest heaven: *akṣare parame vyoman,* or, in the imperishable, in the highest firmament.

The Nightfall of the World — *Jagadrātrī*

19

BG VII, 6

i) I am the origin and also the dissolution
of this whole world.

BG VIII, 18-19

ii) 18. At the dawn of day all manifest things
issue forth from the unmanifest.
At nightfall once more they dissolve into the same,
what is called the unmanifest.

19. These same myriad beings, emerging one by one,
ineluctably dissolve
at nightfall, O Arjuna, and emerge again
into existence at daybreak.

BG XIV, 2

iii) When they have acquired this knowledge, their nature resembles my own:
they are not born at the world's creation nor troubled at its dissolution.

- i) Origin: *prabhava,* source.
  Dissolution: *pralaya.*
  8-11. Cf. § III 7.
- ii) 18. Manifest: *vyakta.*
  Unmanifest: *avyakta,* i.e., the primal matter, *pradhāna,* of the Sāṁkhya system.
- iii) My own [nature]: *mama sādharmya.*
  World's creation: *sarga.*
  Dissolution: *pralaya.*

b) Hell

Naraka

In a world suffused with the radiance of the Sun, where all aspirations tend toward the realm of Light, where Dawn brings new hopes each day, where Earth provides Men with good things in plenty and the daily sacrifice to Agni leads them toward Heaven—in that world is there no shadow of darkness, no realm of dreadful obscurity? Texts on this subject are rather scarce. Nevertheless, all is not bright: sin, wickedness, injustice, enemies, untruthfulness, crimes, also exist.[160] Punishment as a means of reestablishing justice and the right order of things certainly has a place, but is the punishment temporary or will it continue after this life and last forever? Where and how will the punishment be administered? Here and there we find texts that express, albeit imprecisely and with a certain characteristic restraint, the idea of what a later and less reticent tradition, taking a somewhat sardonic pleasure in describing its tortures, named *naraka-loka,* hell, the infernal world. Yet hell, before assuming the allegorical features developed later on in the rich imagery of the Purāṇic world view, is first of all experienced as negation. For the Vedic *ṛṣi* it is the realm of *asat,* of nonbeing, of absence of structured reality, which is the most

160. Cf. § IV B on sin.

frightful. Indeed, as the famous Upaniṣadic prayer concisely states, nonbeing (*asat*), darkness (*tamas*), and death (*mṛtyu*) are the characteristics of the sphere that we would call "hell."[161]

In the present selection it is interesting to note that the stanzas from the Ṛg Veda are addressed to Agni, Indra, and Soma, who are the dispellers of darkness in all its aspects. It is known that the combinations Agni-Indra, Agni-Soma, and Indra-Soma are allies in the fight against demons, evil spirits, and fiends, and against the impudent rascal who dares to desecrate the sacrifice. Under the name of whatever spirit evil operates, the two Gods of light together with Soma the purifier strike at its root, whether in Man or in demon. Here there is no room for Varuṇa's mercy;[162] sinners are thrown into an abyss, a deep pit, an underground place, where they will "see no more the rising of the sun." It is the burning flame of Agni which utterly destroys, consuming both miscreants and liars. There is no remission. Let them be burned!

The Atharva Veda is no less adamant. It gives more details about the person of the miscreant; here he is a vile man who has insulted a Brahmin, there one who has not offered the gift of a cow to the priests.

The Yajur Veda adds: "Hell is either for the homicide or for the man who is no longer worthy to have the sacrificial fire."[163]

Most of the texts are concerned with preserving the sacredness of the sacrifice. Whatever sullies that sacredness must be punished with extreme measures, whether by Agni's flames or in an abysmal region of utter darkness.

There follows a rather extraordinary dialogue from the Śatapatha Brāhmaṇa, between a young man Bhṛgu and people in hell. The text is usually acknowledged to be a traditional description of the torments of hell, as imagined by the common folk of the time, though it is a document concerned specifically with the sacrifice of the *agnihotra.*

The young Bhṛgu, who is puffed up with vanity, is sent by his father Varuṇa to the four regions, East, West, South, and North, in order to see and know what is happening there. With dismay and horror the boy sees only "men dismembering one another, cutting off each of their limbs." As they have been treating others they are

161. Cf. BU I, 3, 28 (§ V 12).
162. § IV B b on Varuṇa.
163. YV XXX, 5; cf. § II 28 for rest of the hymn.

themselves treated now, that is, with the utmost cruelty. Evil engenders evil; it calls for evil, for wrath. Gripped with repugnance, Bhṛgu asks if there is really no way to expiate and to avoid such terrible crimes. The miserable creatures answer that there is a way out and that only Varuṇa knows it. The rest of the passage is the explanation Varuṇa gives to his now less arrogant son: the *agnihotra* has the power to master even this wrath. The meaning is allegorical, explains Varuṇa: the men in the East are the trees; the men in the South are the cattle; the men in the West are the herbs; the men in the North are the waters; the two women Bhṛgu met later, one beautiful, the other ugly, are belief and unbelief; the black man with yellow eyes is wrath. One by one all these elements belonging to the offering of the *agnihotra* are mastered; by offering the daily sacrifice to Agni one subdues everything. Thus once more, even if we are taken a little far from our subject, the importance of sacrifice is emphasized. As for the hell Bhṛgu visited, except for the torments, we do not learn much about it, nor is it clear whether this type of torment is going to last forever.

The Upaniṣadic period that follows seems not to be much concerned about hell.[164] Some commentators have suggested that the Kaṭha Upaniṣad may be pointing to it when it says that "to the childish and the careless, deluded by the glamor of wealth, there is no departure for the beyond,"[165] but no further description is given.

The Gītā is far more outspoken. It does not waste time in describing hell or its torments; it specifies, rather, those for whom this *naraka-loka* is destined: those who have no regard for family laws and break them and those who are entangled in their own desires, blinded by the veil of delusion. In fact, the gate giving entrance to hell has, so to speak, a triple porch: desire, anger, and greed. Those vices ruin the *ātman* in Man and lead to perdition. The Gītā adds that these are gates of darkness and that the man who has avoided them is on the way to salvation.[166] Even if the doctrine is more elaborated and if Man's consciousness has gone a long way since the Ṛg Veda, the basic intuition is the same: human life is a texture of darkness and light; Man shuns gloom and darkness and craves light. True brightness is as described by the Kaṭha Upaniṣad:

164. Cf., however, IsU 3 (§ VII 6); here the word is not *naraka* but *asuryā*.
165. KathU II, 6. Cf. also BU IV, 4, 10-11, and IsU 9 (§ VII 16).
166. Cf. BG XVI, 22.

it is the brightness of the Brahma-world where one sees reality, that is, shadow and light.[167] Once the shadows and the dark spots of hell are discovered, they must, if life is not to become a hell, be removed. Hell, like Heaven, can be everywhere—including the here and now.

The Bottomless Abyss *Padaṁ gabhīram*

20

RV II, 29, 6

i)

Incline toward us today, O Holy Ones.
With awe I approach you to win your hearts.
Protect us, O Gods, from the devouring wolf.
Save us from falling into the pit, O you Holy Ones!

RV IV, 5, 5

ii)

Hardened sinners are these, like obtrusive young women
of evil conduct who deceive their husbands.
In their hearts no truth or faithfulness is found.
It is they who have produced this abysmal region.

RV VII, 104, 3; 7; 11; 24

iii)

3. Into the abyss, Indra and Soma, plunge
the wicked! Into bottomless darkness fling them,
so that not one of them may ever return!
May your fierce power prevail and subdue them!

7. Be attentive to our prayer. Slay swiftly the wicked!
Destroy the evil and treacherous demons!
O Indra and Soma, may the wicked not prosper,
whoever persecutes us with cunning power!

11. May he be lost, himself and his children!
Let him be consigned beneath the three earths!
May the fair name of him who day and night
seeks to harm us, O Gods, be totally blighted!

24. Slay, O Indra, the male magician
and also the witch who boasts of her magic.
May idolaters perish with broken necks!
No more for them the rising of the sun!

RV IX, 73, 8

iv)

The Guardian of Order, most wise, is not mocked.
In his heart are three means of purification.

167. Cf. KathU VI, 5 (§ VI 11).

He who knows espies all living beings.
The ruthless transgressor he throws into the pit.

RV X, 87, 14; 20

v) 14. Destroy with your heat the workers of magic;
destroy with your power the evil spirits;
destroy with your flames idolatrous persons;
burn to nothingness murderous scoundrels!

20. From above and from below, from behind and before,
protect us, O Agni!
With their glowing coals your flames, ever blazing,
will wholly consume the untruthful man.

RV X, 152, 2; 4.

vi) 2. Giver of salvation, Lord of the people,
destroyer of the demon,
overpowerer of enemies,
O powerful Lord, enjoyer of Soma,
go before us,
calming our fear.

4. Scatter our foes, O Indra, subdue
those who attack us.
Send them down to nethermost darkness
who seek to destroy us.

AV II, 14, 3

vii) There may the evil ghosts dwell—
in the house infernal!
There may Decay and every witch
find an abode!

AV V, 19, 3

viii) Those who have spat or dribbled mucus
on a holy man
sit in a stream flowing with blood,
devouring hair.

AV XII, 4, 36

ix) In Yama's realm the cow grants all desires
to him who has offered her.
But hell, so they say, is the lot of the one
who is asked, but refuses.

YV I, 25

x) At earth's remotest end, Savitṛ,
bind him with a hundred cords, as also
those who hate us and whom we hate.
Thence never release him!

■ i) To Viśvedevāḥ.
■ ii) To Agni.
Cf. the four terms used: *dureva, pāpu, anṛta, asatya.*
Abysmal region: *padaṁ gabhīraṁ,* which could also be rendered as mysterious or obscure sentence, word (of the enemy in the disputation).
■ iii) To Indra-Soma (the same hymn is given in AV VIII, 4).
3. Fierce power: *sahase manyum,* the might of your wrath.
7. Demons: *rakṣasaḥ.*
Cunning power: *druh,* also evil, etc.
11. Himself: lit. his body.
Three earths: *pṛthivīḥ,* which correspond to the "three heavens" and indicate the lowest possible place.
Fair name: *yaśas,* also glory, honor.
24. Magician: *yātudhāna.*
Idolaters: *mūradevāḥ,* worshipers of demons or a clan of demons. Cf. RV IV, 4 (§ VII 41).
■ iv) To Soma.
Order: *ṛta.*
Means of purification: *pavitrāḥ,* used usually with reference to the three strainers of Soma, here symbolically.
Transgressor: *avrata,* the one who does not keep the holy law, who does not serve the Gods, etc.
Pit: *karta,* abyss.
■ v) To Agni.
14. Workers of magic: *yātudhānāḥ.*
Evil spirits: *rakṣas.*
Idolatrous persons: *mūradevāḥ* (or *mūladeva* according to some commentators).
■ vi) To Indra.
2. Salvation: *svasti,* blessing, well-being, happiness.
Powerful Lord: lit. bull Indra.
Calming our fear: *abhayaṁkara,* giving us peace.
■ vii) Against evil creatures.
Evil ghosts: *arāyaḥ,* evil spirits, hags, witches. Cf. RV X, 155, 1, and AV I, 28, 4.
Decay: *sedi;* the commentator says *nirṛti.*
Witches: *yātudhānyaḥ,* sorceresses.
■ viii) Against those who insult Brahmins.
Holy man: Brahmin.
■ ix) Against the man who refuses to give a cow to the Brahmin.
Reference to the wish-fulfilling cow (*kāmadhenu*) which is obtained only by those in heaven who have been generous on earth.
Hell: *naraka loka.*
■ x) Only part of stanza 25 addressed to Earth is given here. The whole hymn contains the prayers for the New and Full Moon sacrifices.

Men Dismembering Each Other

Bhīṣma loka

21

SB XI, 6, 1-13

1. Bhṛgu, son of Varuṇa, considered himself superior to his father in wisdom. Varuṇa had noticed that he considered himself superior in wisdom.

2. He spoke to him: "My son, go to the East, and having seen what is to be seen

there, go to the South, and having seen what is to be seen there, go to the West, and having seen what is to be seen there, go to the North, and having seen what is to be seen there, go to the Northeast, and whatever you shall see there, tell it to me.

3. So he went from there to the East. There men were dismembering one another, cutting off each of their limbs, saying: "this to you, this to me!" He said: "Oh, horrible! Men are here dismembering one another, cutting off each of their limbs!" They replied: "In this way they have treated us in the other world, and in the same way we now treat them in return." He asked: "Is there no expiation for this?" "Yes, there is." "What is it?" "Your father knows it."

4. So he went from there to the South. There men were dismembering one another, cutting into pieces each of their limbs, saying: "this to you, this to me!" He said: "Oh, horrible! Men are here dismembering one another, cutting into pieces each of their limbs!" They replied: "In this way they have treated us in the other world, and in the same way we now treat them in return." He asked: "Is there no expiation for this?" "Yes, there is." "What is it?" "Your father knows it."

5. So he went from there to the West. There men sitting in silence were devoured by men sitting in silence. He said: "Oh, horrible! Men sitting in silence are here devouring one another!" They replied: "In this way they have treated us in the other world, and in the same way we now treat them in return." He asked: "Is there no expiation for this?" "Yes, there is." "What is it?" "Your father knows it."

6. So he went from there to the North. There men crying loudly were devoured by men crying loudly. He said: "Oh, horrible! Men crying loudly are here devouring one another!" They replied: "In this way they have treated us in the other world, and in the same way we now treat them in return." He asked: "Is there no expiation for this?" "Yes, there is." "What is it?" "Your father knows it."

7. So he went from there to the Northeast. There were two women, one beautiful and one ugly, and a black man with yellow eyes and a stick in his hand stood between them. Having seen him, he was seized with fear, and he returned and entered his house. His father told him: "Study your holy scripture. Why don't you study it?" He said: "What shall I study? There is nothing at all." Then Varuṇa knew: "He has really seen it."

8. He said: "Those men whom you have seen in the East dismembering one another and cutting off each of their limbs, saying: "This to you, this to me," they were trees. When one puts the wood as fuel, one conquers the trees and wins the world of trees.

9. And those men whom you have seen in the South, dismembering one another and cutting into pieces each of their limbs, saying, "This to you, this to me," they were cattle. When one offers milk in sacrifice, one conquers the cattle and wins the world of cattle.

10. And those men whom you have seen in the West, sitting in silence and being devoured by men sitting in silence, they were herbs. When one lights the fire with grass [straw], one conquers the herbs and wins the world of herbs.

11. And those men whom you have seen in the North, crying loudly and being devoured by men crying loudly, they were the waters. When one pours water [in the milk], one conquers the waters and wins the world of the waters.

12. And those two women whom you have seen, one beautiful and one ugly—the beautiful one is faith. When one offers the first libation, one conquers faith and wins faith. The ugly one is nonfaith. When one offers the second libation, one overcomes nonfaith and wins nonfaith.

13. And the black man with yellow eyes and a stick in his hand, standing between them, is wrath. Assuredly he who, knowing this, performs the *agnihotra,* wins all and conquers all.

1. Bhṛgu: In the RV the name usually appears in the plural. The Bhṛgus are mythical beings, whose role is the kindling of the sacrificial fire on earth. In some passages, however, the name designates a clan of ancient sacrificers. In later time Bhṛgu is a sage (cf. AV V, 19, 1; AB II, 20, 7 (VIII, 2)) who is adopted by Varuṇa and is even, as in the present passage, called his son.
3. Expiation: *prāyaścitti,* atonement, the only way of avoiding the retribution of evil deeds.
7. Ugly: *atikalyāṇā,* or extremely beautiful.
Holy scripture: *svādhyāya,* the daily lesson or reading of the Veda.
8. Trees: *vanaspatayaḥ.*
9. Cattle: *paśu.*
10. Herbs: *oṣadhayaḥ.*
12. Faith: *śraddhā.*
Nonfaith: *aśraddhā.*
13. Wrath: *krodha.*
He . . . wins all: *sarvaṁ jayati.*

The Triple Gate of Hell — *Narakadvāra*

22

BG I, 44

i)

For men who have destroyed, O Janārdana,
their families' laws,
there is ordained most surely an abode in hell—
thus we have heard.

BG XVI, 4; 16; 21

ii)

4. Hypocrisy, arrogance, and self-conceit,
anger and harshness,
as well as ignorance, characterize the man
who is born demonic.

16. Seduced by many a fancy, entangled
in a net of delusion,

enslaved to the indulgence of desires, they fall
into loathsome hell.

21. Triple is the gate of hell which leads
to the ruin of the *ātman:*
desire, anger, and greed. These three
one should therefore abandon.

- i) Janārdana: i.e., Kṛṣṇa.
  Hell: *naraka.*
- ii) 4. Demonic: *āsurī,* belonging to the *asuras.*
  21. Desire: *kāma.*
  Anger: *krodha.*
  Greed: *lobha;* cf. BG II, 62-63.

c) Heaven

Svarga

The typology of heaven in the Vedic insight regarding the final station of the human pilgrimage seems to be conceived of on three planes: the cosmological, the ontological, and the mystical. Heaven, viewed from the cosmological perspective, varies according to whether it is based on the primacy of space or of time. If space has primacy, heaven is a place of bliss and reward, a region where Man can finally enjoy life and make up for all the limitations, anguishes, and anxieties of earth. If the primacy of time is stressed, heaven is a "moment" of infinite time, in which Man will enjoy a never-ending existence with no relapse into sorrow and suffering. Not only the Vedic tradition but also subsequent world views have understood heaven mostly in the cosmological sense, because the ontological and mystical goals of the human pilgrimage transcend ordinary imaginings concerning a heavenly world.

In the Vedas there is no doubt that above our human world and above the open space there is a "third world" full of light and radiance, where "the sun does not set." *Svar* is the heavenly light[168] and *svarga* the going to or being in that light, hence the world of light, heaven. Earth also has no doubt been experienced as full of light but not light invariable and unimpeded, not light that is invulnerable to darkness. The enjoyment of earthly light is ac-

168. Cf. the three worlds as contained in the three sacrificial utterances *bhūḥ* (earth), *bhuvaḥ* (mid-space), *svaḥ* (heaven).

companied always by the fear of losing it, the fear that darkness may overcome it, whereas in heaven there is "no trace of fear"[169] because "light unfailing ever shines."[170] We do not find many descriptions of the beauties of that world beyond, because the supreme image remains that of light which encompasses all other glories. This heavenly realm is inhabited by radiant beings, the celestials, the Gods, and also by the sages, seers, and saints who have attained immortality. It is a world abounding in celestial waters—of which our earthly waters are but an image—flowing with milk and honey, and certainly filled with Soma, the juice of immortality and delight. It is a place of rest and happiness, and even a place of loving communion which Men long to join. The ways by which Men ascend to this realm seem to be manifold, just as their callings are diverse; sacrifice, the means par excellence of reaching heaven, does not seem to be the only means, for ascetics attain it by fervor (*tapas*), warriors by their bravery, the fathers by their fidelity to cosmic order (*ṛta*), and the poets by their songs.[171] The fact that sacrifice is the real "boat to heaven"[172] does not exclude the possibility of a man's reaching heaven by an act of "grace" on the part of the divine. The hymns are real prayers expressing the sincere longing for a world of wholeness, immortality, goodness, freedom, and joy, which can never be the automatic outcome of a mechanical performance but which has to be the fruit of striving (*tapas*), of faithfulness (to *ṛta*), of daring, and of generosity:

> He who gives liberally goes straight to the Gods;
> on the high ridge of heaven he stands exalted.[173]

One could even say that heaven by definition is the fulfillment of all desires, though in a certain hierarchical order.[174] The Atharva Veda specifies more precisely that heaven is a place where one will possess a healthy body and enjoy the company of his beloved ones on earth in a more perfect way.[175] Heaven is a perfect mirror of earth—or earth is an imperfect reflection of heaven. Just as on earth there are different degrees, so also in heaven, thus allowing for higher and higher ascents.

169. KathU I, 12 (§ V 27).
170. RV IX, 113, 7 (§ V 23).
171. Cf. RV X, 154 (§ V 24).
172. SB IV, 2, 5, 10 (§ III 24).
173. RV I, 125, 5; cf. also RV X, 154 (§ V 24).
174. Cf. RV IX, 113, 11 (§ V 23); AU IV, 6.
175. Cf. AV XII, 3, 17 (§ V 26), etc.

A foretaste of—and not only a means to—heaven is given in the sacrifice itself, particularly in the sharing of Soma.[176] The bliss (*ānanda*) and immortality (*amṛta*) contained in Soma constitute a heavenly joy which may be experienced even on earth; it is this same experience that the Upaniṣads deepen and dissociate from its ritual setting, locating the real source of joy in the heart of Man himself. The experience of joy is composed of many intertwining threads, and it would be wrong to attempt to disentangle them and to speak of a purely ritualistic or a purely spiritualized experience, for one can hardly be imagined without the other. Heaven would be an empty word if here on earth one had caught no spark of the experience of Soma and *ānanda*.[177] One of the characteristics of the heavenly existence is the freedom to move at will in all worlds, to be present everywhere, which means not to be limited by time and space.

However the heavenly world is imagined, the fact did not escape the penetrating eye of the Upaniṣadic sage that it is still a world, a *loka,* another kind of world, perhaps, in a different dimension, but nevertheless a world. Heaven, *svarga,* is part of the *triloka* scheme; it is simply the culmination of the this-worldly reality on another plane. *Loka* belongs to the realm of the seen and not, as the Upaniṣads would put it, of the seer, much less of the unseen. It is thus not an ultimate state. In psychological terms, heaven is still a projection of the mind which may have its own degree of reality but is not ultimate.

Later traditions belonging to the *jñāna-mārga*[178] say that "the worlds" are attained by sacrifice and action (*karman*) and that the state beyond is attained by knowledge (*jñāna*). For them the attainment of heaven is by no means ultimate. Treading on that path, we reach the realm of the spirit, the metaphysical model of heaven.

On the ontological plane heaven no longer has to do with space or time. It is a state in which not only spatiotemporal bonds are broken but also all ontic limitations are overcome. It is the state in which the different beings have merged into Being and reached their fullness. Pure Being, the Upaniṣadic *ātman,* is the supreme state, the real heaven.

We may leave aside the question whether the idea of pure trans-

176. Cf. RV IX, 113, 6 (§ V 23).
177. Cf. § III 17.
178. Cf., in particular, Vedānta.

cendence is originally Buddhist or is to be found independently in Upaniṣads. The fact remains not only that the expression *brahma-nirvāṇa* appears in the Gītā but also that the intuition that underlies it lurks, as it were, everywhere in the Upaniṣads. This type of heaven is no longer a place in time or space, nor is it even being or Being, but it transcends every category in order to plunge into the infinite state of what the later Buddhist tradition calls total and absolute emptiness: *śūnyatā*.

Mokṣa or liberation is here so total that it is considered not only as deliverance from all bonds and limitations but also as liberation from Being itself. The mystical conception of heaven entails the liberation from the concept of Being and even of any shade of "reality" we may be tempted to give to that "Being." *Mokṣa* is here more than the freedom of Being; it is the liberation from it. The silence then reaches an unsurpassable ontological depth. There is nothing to say, because there *is* nothing.

Where Light Unfailing Ever Shines — *Yatra jyotir ajasram*

23

RV IX, 113, 6-11

6. Where the priest, reciting the metrical word
and handling the pressing stone, exults in Soma,
through Soma creating, O Purifier, bliss,
flow, Soma-juice, for Indra's sake!

7. Where light unfailing ever shines,
where dwells the Sun, in that deathless world
place me, O Purifier, beyond harm's reach.
Flow, Soma-juice, for Indra's sake!

8. Where the Son of Vivasvat holds sway,
the shrine of heaven where the waters flow
ever young and fresh, there make me immortal.
Flow, Soma-juice, for Indra's sake!

9. Where Men move at will, in the threefold sphere,
in the third heaven of heavens, where are realms full of light,
in that radiant world make me immortal.
Flow, Soma-juice, for Indra's sake!

10. In the place of vows and eager longings,
the realm of the golden Sun, of libations
and fullness of joy, there make me immortal.
Flow, Soma-juice, for Indra's sake!

11. Where happiness and joy abound,
 pleasures and delights, where all desires
 find their fulfillment, make me immortal.
  Flow, Soma-juice, for Indra's sake!

1-5. Omitted because they do not relate to heaven but to different mythological stories connected with Soma.

6. Metrical word: *chāndasyāṁ vācam,* the sacred hymns in measured rhythm.

Purifier: *pavamāna,* Soma.

Bliss: *ānanda,* delight.

7. Beyond harm's reach: *akṣita* undecaying.

8. Son of Vivasvat: Yama the King.

Shrine: *avarodhana,* lit. enclosed place, paradise.

Make me immortal: *mām amṛtaṁ kṛdhi.*

9. Move at will: *anukāmaṁ caraṇam;* cf. *kāmacāra* in CU VII, 25, 2; VIII, 1, 6 (§§ VI 8; VI 6).

10. Vows and eager longings: *kāma nikāmā,* corresponding to "libations and fullness of joy" (*svadhā* and *tṛpti*).

11. Where all desires find their fulfillment: *yatrāptāḥ kāmāḥ.* Cf. the Upaniṣadic conception of the realized Man whose desires are all fulfilled (*āptakāma*); cf. BU IV, 3, 21; IV, 4, 6; SU I, 11 (§§ VI 8; VI 11; IV 21); MundU III, 1, 6.

The Community of Saints

Bhāvavṛtta

24

RV X, 154

1. To the company of those
 for whom Soma is purified,
 who relish melted butter,
 for whom honey flows freely—
  to them let him go!

2. To the company of those
 who through Fervor are invincible,
 through Fervor have reached heaven,
 who make Fervor their glory—
  to them let him go!

3. To the company of heroes
 who contend for war's spoils,
 who fling away their lives,
 who make a thousand gifts—
  to them let him go!

4. To the company of the Fathers
 who first followed Truth,
 who were faithful to Truth,
 who were strong in their Fervor—
  to them, Yama, send him!

5. To the company of the poets,
who know a thousand skills,
who stand guard over the Sun,
fervent Sages born of Fervor—
to them, Yama, send him!

The poet of this hymn is Yamī (woman *ṛṣi*), sister of Yama, who invokes her brother (vv. 4-5).
1. According to SB XI, 5, 7, 6 sq. Soma-juice, ghee, and honey were offered, respectively, to the ancestors of those who studied the Sāma Veda, Yajur Veda, and Atharva Veda.
2. Fervor: *tapas,* ardor, sanctity, as also in vv. 4 and 5.
3. Gifts: *dakṣiṇā,* priestly honoraria.
4. Truth: *ṛta,* here a sacrificial term: faithful to the sacrifice and thus to cosmic order.
5. Skills: *nīthā,* ways, songs.
Sages: the *ṛṣis* are qualified by the word *tapojān* (acc. plur.): reborn through *tapas,* born anew. Cf. RV X, 183, 1 (§ I 33).

The World of Goodness — *Sukṛtasya loka*

25

AV VI, 120

1. If we have injured space, the earth, or heaven,
or if we have offended mother or father,
from that may Agni, fire of the house, absolve us
and guide us safely to the world of goodness.

2. May Earth our mother, Boundlessness our origin,
and Space our brother save us from damnation!
May father Heaven make peace for us with our Fathers!
Having reached the world of our kindred, may we never be ejected!

3. Where Men of goodwill and good deeds rejoice,
their bodies now made free from all disease,
their limbs made whole from lameness or defect—
in that heaven may we behold our parents and our sons!

This hymn is used liturgically as an expiatory rite, e.g., after eating certain kinds of food, when canceling debts to a deceased, when somebody's master dies, etc.
1. Fire of the house: *gārhapatya,* the homely aspect of Agni.
World of goodness: *sukṛtasya loka,* heaven.
2. Boundlessness: Aditi, i.e., the "boundless" deity, Infinity. Hence we might also translate it as "Freedom."
Damnation: *abhiśasti,* curse, etc.
Make peace for us with our Fathers: . . .*pitryācchaṁ bhavāti,* perhaps a request to be released from paternal guilt.
Having reached, etc.: lit. having gone to our kindred, may we not fall from that world!

3. Of goodwill: *suhārda,* of good heart.
Disease: *roga.*
Heaven: *svarga.*

Paradise *Svargaloka*

26

AV IV, 34, 5-6

i)

5. By means of rice offering, this widespread oblation,
the best of all sacrifices, he enters heaven,
where every kind of lotus abounds.
May all these streams reach you
in honey-filled heaven!
May ponds full of lotus await you!

6. May lakes of melted butter abound,
banks of honey, streams of milk and water and curds,
and draughts of wine, free-flowing like water!
May all these streams reach you
in honey-filled heaven!
May ponds full of lotus await you!

AV XII, 3, 17

ii)

Guide us to the world of the supreme heaven.
May we there find again our husband, wife, sons.
I take your hand. May Destruction not prevail
nor adversity pursue us close at heel!

AV XVIII, 3, 4

iii)

You know, O inviolable, the world of the living
and follow the pathway of the Gods to heaven.
This is your lord; be favorable to him
and let him ascend to the heavenly realm.

■ i) This description of heaven is set within the sacrificial context of preparation of the Viṣṭārin offering, which contains rice and several juices.

5. Rice offering: *viṣṭārin,* a rice preparation cooked in the manner of gruel; lit. the outstrewn, expanded.

Every kind of lotus: free version for an enumeration of unidentifiable water plants: *bisa, śālūka, śaphaka, mulālī.*

6. Wine: *surā,* strong, inebriating drink.

■ ii) Destruction: *nirṛti.*

Adversity: *arāti.*

■ iii) Inviolable: *aghnyā,* the cow used in the funeral rite.

Lord: *gopati,* lit. herdsman; it probably refers to the deceased husband (cf. vv. 1-2 of the same hymn).

The Everlasting World *Anantaloka*

27

BU III, 1, 6

i) "Yājñavalkya," said he [Janaka], "since the atmosphere appears to be without a foundation, by what means of ascent does the sacrificer climb up to the heavenly world?" "By the Brahman-priest, by the mind, through the moon, for the mind is the priest of the sacrifice, and that which is here the mind is the yonder moon. This is Brahman. This is liberation; this is complete liberation. So much concerning Liberation." Now follows the accomplishment.

BU IV, 4, 8

ii) On this subject there are the following verses:

The ancient, narrow path that stretches afar
has been attained by me, has been realized by me.
In this way the wise, the knowers of Brahman,
ascend, liberated, to the world of heaven.

CU VIII, 4

iii) 1. Now this *ātman* is the bridge and the boundary separating these worlds. Day and night do not cross over this bridge, or old age, or death, or sorrow, or good works or bad works; all evils turn back from it, for this world of Brahman is free from evil.

2. Thus, after crossing that bridge, the blind man sees, the wounded one is healed, the sufferer is freed from suffering. Therefore, for the one who has crossed that bridge, even the night is transformed into day, for the world of Brahman is ever illumined.

3. But the world of Brahman belongs only to those who find it by the practice of chastity and the study of Brahman. For them there is freedom in all the worlds.

KausU IV, 8; 16

iv) 8. Bālāki said: "The Person who is in space—he it is upon whom I meditate."

Ajātaśatru said to him: "You need not make me converse on him; I meditate on him as the full, nonactive Brahman. The one who mediates on him in this way will be increased with offspring, cattle, glory, divine splendor, and the heavenly world. He will complete his full life span."

16. Bālāki said: "The Person who is in the body—he it is upon whom I meditate."

Ajātaśatru said to him: "You need not make me converse on him. I meditate on him as Prajāpati. The one who meditates on him in this way will be increased with offspring, cattle, glory, divine splendor, and the heavenly world. He will complete his full life span."

KathU I, 12-14; 19

[Naciketas:]

v) 12. In the world of heaven there is no trace of fear.
You, Death, are not there. There one dreads not old age.
Thirst and hunger transcended and sorrow overpassed,
a man rejoices in the world of heaven.

13. You know, O Death, the fire that leads to heaven.
Declare it to me who am full of faith:
how do dwellers in heaven partake of deathlessness?
This I choose as my second boon.

[Yama:]

14. To you I will declare it. Hear me with attention,
for I know well that fire that leads to heaven.
That fire by which one gains the Infinite, O Naciketas,
is the Ground of all, hidden in the secret cave.

19. This, O Naciketas, is your fire that leads to heaven,
which you have chosen as your second boon.
Men to come will call this fire by your name.
Now, Naciketas, you may choose your third boon.

■ i) Atmosphere: *antarikṣa*.
Brahman-priest: mind (*manas*) and moon (*candramas*) are related inasmuch as the Brahman-priest is the "mind" of the sacrifice and the moon is the cosmic correlation of *manas*.
Liberation: *mukti*.
Liberation: *mokṣa*.
Accomplishment: *sampadaḥ*, i.e., achievements, results of the sacrifice.

■ ii) 1-2. Cf. § V 12.
3-7. Cf. § VI 11.
Attained: *spṛṣṭa*, lit. touched.
Wise: *dhīrāḥ*.
Liberated: *vimukta*, completely freed.

■ iii) 1. Bridge: *setu*, at the same time the demarcation line between the temporal world of suffering and the unconditioned *brahma-loka*. For the bridge of immortality cf. MundU II, 2, 5 (§ VI 5).
3. The practice of chastity and the study of Brahman: *brahmacarya*.
Freedom: *kāmacāra*, freedom to move at will.
For the rest of CU VIII and all the ref. cf. § VI 6 (v) and notes.

■ iv) Person . . . in space: *ākāśe puruṣaḥ*.
Converse: *sam-vad-* in caus. talk, discuss.
Full: *pūrṇa*.
Nonactive: *apravṛtti*, not involved in activity.
Glory: *yaśas*.
Divine splendor: *brahma-varcas*.

■ v) 14. The Infinite: *ananta loka*, eternal, endless world.
Ground: *pratiṣṭhā*.
Hidden in the secret cave: *nihitaṁ guhāyām*, referring to the heart.
20-21; 29. Cf. § V 5.

The Gates of Heaven *Svargadvāra*

28

BG II, 32; 37; 72

i) Happy are the warriors to whom the occasion
of fighting such a battle
comes by itself. The gates of heaven
for them are flung wide.

37. Slain, you will go to heaven; victorious,
you will enjoy the earth.
Therefore stand up, O son of Kuntī,
and resolve to fight!

72. This attained, the eternal state of Brahman,
one is no more confused.
One established therein at the hour of death
reaches *brahma-nirvāṇa.*

BG V, 24-25

ii) 24. He who finds his happiness, his joy, and his light
solely within,
that yogin attains *brahma-nirvāṇa*
and becomes himself Brahman.

25. *Brahma-nirvāṇa* is attained by those seers
whose sins are no more.
Doubts gone, minds steady, they rejoice in the welfare
of every being.

BG IX, 21

iii) Having enjoyed heaven's vast realm, they return to men's world,
their merit exhausted;
Those who follow the three Laws, desirous of enjoyments,
win only the changeable.

- i) 32. Warriors: Kṣatriyas.
Gates of Heaven: *svarga-dvāra.*
72. Hour of death: *anta-kāla,* last time.
- ii) 22. Cf. § IV 7.
24. Becomes himself Brahman: *brahma-bhūta;* for *brahma-bhavati,* cf. BU IV, 4, 25 (§ VI 6); MundU III, 2, 9 (§ VI 11).
Verse 26 also describes *brahma-nirvāṇa.*
- iii) Heaven's . . . realm: *svarga-loka.*
Three Laws: *dharmas,* the injunctions of the three Vedas.
Desirous of enjoyments: *kāma-kāma,* desiring desires.
22. Cf. § I 29.
23-27. Cf. § III 29.
31-32; 34. Cf. § I 29.

PART VI

NEW LIFE AND FREEDOM

Jñāna

Only what is alive can cease to live, we have said. But what sort of life is meant?* Real life does not die.[1] How could it? It would cease to be life; the most one could say of it would be that it appeared to be life. Anything that can die is mortal, and therefore mortal life, that is, a life that will die, amounts to a nonliving life, which is a contradiction in terms. There is no such thing as mere temporal life, or life dragging on only for a time, for the mortal element it contains is only a passing guest, a parasite that will obviously die when it ceases to suck the life sap from life itself. There may be mortal beings, beings that have life only for a time, but life itself is immortal. To live life involves, then, transcending the temporal order. But does life exist at all apart from its living parasites? Is it merely a question of keeping "alive" a chain of living beings caught in a temporal-spatial succession? Is life only a miserable and tragic joke? What is real immortal life? Or rather, is not life always and constantly new? Is not life itself this incessant renewal and permanent newness? Immortality cannot be the clinging to a continuation of mortal life. It cannot be "life" artificially kept "alive" as in a modern hospital. True immortal life, therefore, implies not only the transformation of the object ("life") but also the transformation of the "living" subject as well. This radical metamorphosis is liberation (*mokṣa*).

These are topics which Man has always pondered, and Upaniṣadic Man did so in a very special way. What is a full and authentic life and how may we reach it?

The Vedic experience is not one of death and resurrection as two dialectical moments of a process. The concepts of death and resurrection, if introduced at all, should not be understood as belonging on the same plane. The Vedic experience contains no idea of a temporal link connecting the two, as if resurrection were coming after death in a temporal sequence. In fact it is this great fallacy which the Upaniṣads are striving to overcome. What Upaniṣadic Man is interested in is not a return to the old familiar life, not a "new" old life; not a resurrection, but a "surrection," an ascent to the heights of real and everlasting life. A mere reversion to "life" is precisely the danger and the dread. It is *saṁsāra,* that is to say, the clinging to the spatiotemporal world of intranscendent

*This part is a revised version of my Teape Lectures delivered at Cambridge University in 1965.

1. Cf. CU VI, 11, 3 (§ VI 10); *na jīvo mriyate!*

events, slavery to history, entanglement in the chain of *karman* which confines us to this world until we have exhausted our "epiontic" obligations, or even our cosmic duties, our *ṛṇa*.[2]

The Upaniṣads do not teach a death experience, but an experience of life. Ultimately there is no experience of death and the death experiment is, in the last analysis, unreal because the "subject" who died was not real. The supreme Upaniṣadic experience is discovered precisely by realizing that the experiment of death is only a psychological experience, made by the immortal *ātman*.

The Vedic experience is one of liberation, of freedom from everything. It thus includes freedom or liberation from time. What both fascinates and haunts Upaniṣadic Man is not anything that comes after, but that which has no after. As long as we are entrammeled in the net of mere temporal existence, we are in the clutches of death, even if we postpone death by a sequence of successive existences. An afterlife is as inauthentic a life as a prelife. The piercing of the skin of time as with a needle, without either hurting or destroying the spatiotemporal epidermis and yet transcending it, is what liberation is all about.

Part VI needs a word of explanation. We have followed the course of the human and cosmic cycles as mirrored in the Vedas. Now, the end is not death and dissolution, nor is it an indefinite and horizontal repetition of one and the same circle. One of the discoveries of the Vedic wisdom is precisely that, whereas time is circular, Man is not, so that for him it is not a question of beginning all over again. On the contrary, it is imperative that he escape the enclosure of the circle. The circularity of time indicates its ontic finitude, whereas Man is infinite. Man has to break the circularity of time in order to reach the ontological fullness of his being. To enter into this other nontemporal, but no less real, sphere is to attain realization, to reach liberation from the encirclement of time and freedom from temporal chains. It is a truly new life, not in the sense of a "recycled" life but in the sense of a new type, a new kind of life, indeed, the only real and authentic life.

There is a misleading semantic ambiguity in what we have just been saying. We said "Man" where it might perhaps have been better to write "person," or that "core of the human being" which transcends temporality and thus is capable of speaking and under-

2. Cf. § III 23 Introduction and § IV Note on Sanskrit Terms.

standing this kind of language. Man, however, does not consist only of that core; there is also something temporal in him. We may like to call it individuality or another similar name. Yet, and here is our point, the temporal and the "eternal" (for we have to name it in one way or another) are not two elements, not two separable parts of the one Man. If Man ceases to be temporal, then he succumbs as Man, for Man consists of temporality; if he remains only temporal, then he is not yet born as Man, for Man consists also of transtemporality. The temporal and the transtemporal, however, are not on the same plane; they are not homogeneous and, for this reason, cannot be considered as two elements of his nature.

The Vedic Revelation, in accordance with the sayings of the Upaniṣads which seem to recognize a theological,[3] a cosmic,[4] and an eschatological[5] trinity, or as it is summed up in the affirmation of the Mahābhārata that "everything proceeds in a triple manner,"[6] could be said to convey a threefold experience. The preservation of the harmony of this experience—which could be described as the New Life—is one of the most precious contributions of the Vedas to Man's maturity.

The first feature of this experience is that it embraces life in all its fullness in the most immediate and material way. To live a full life means to prosper in the world, in love, in one's family, in the community, and in other affairs. There is no full human life without this dimension. The Vedic Revelation is a constant reminder of the generosity of the world, of its self-offering to Man, like that of the young bride who presents her charms and the allurement of all her finery to her husband. Life is emphatically earthly, and Vedic Man has no qualms about enjoying it. Without indulging in any psychological or psychoanalytic theory, the *śruti* rejects every kind of repression and every form of renunciation of positive values, even if such renunciation is for the sake of objectively—but not existentially—higher values.

The second feature of this experience does not negate the first one; rather it goes through it, pierces it, as it were. If the first feature is crystallized in the first three *puruṣārthas* or human values of the Indian tradition—*kāma, artha, dharma*; love, riches (or the power

3. Cf. BU I, 2, 3.
4. Cf. BU I, 6, 1.
5. Cf. CU III, 17, 6 (§ III 27).
6. MB XIV, 39, 21.

imparted by riches), virtue—the second feature corresponds to the fourth *puruṣārtha,* namely, *mokṣa,* liberation. Furthermore, there is a correspondence within the traditional *āśramas* or stages of life. It is only after the first stage of discipleship (*brahmacarya*) and the subsequent period of life as a full-fledged citizen and householder (*gṛhastha*) that a man can enter upon the third stage of hermit or forest dweller (*vānaprastha*) and eventually the fourth stage, namely that of a renouncer (*saṁnyāsa*).

The second feature is embedded in the first one. It could be said to arise from a certain disillusionment at not finding the desired fullness or joy in human values; or it could be said to stem from the discovery of the hidden dimension of all those worldly experiences. In either event it is the experience of supraspatial and transtemporal reality, the discovery of the mystery concealed in the cave of the heart, of which the texts so often speak. A post-Upaniṣadic tradition turned this idea into the exclusive center of life and existence and developed out of it the well-known ascetic and world-denying attitude of certain Indian spiritualities. Such an attitude can be a powerful and welcome corrective to an extreme this-worldly one, but the radical acosmism of such schools cannot be said to represent the spirit of the Vedas.

It is the third feature that synthesizes the other two. We would like to stress this feature particularly, not only because we consider it to be at the center of an adult human spirituality but also because it represents the core of the Vedic experience. In point of fact it is stressed again and again that the message of the Vedas is without internal contradiction, that it is harmonious and also one. Now, this oneness is not the oneness of a discarnate quintessence, which for the sake of passing beyond everything leaves reality behind, but a total cosmotheandric or Advaitic intuition, as we may now proceed to call it. This third feature combines the first two and sets them in a proper perspective. Without it the other two insights are incompatible and even doctrinally contradictory.

This third experience-within-an-experience is all-encompassing and thus proceeds neither by accumulation (like the first one) nor by elimination (like the second one), but by integration; it is, however, a peculiar integration which may often present itself as an oversimplification to the eyes of those who view it from without. It is a special and unique kind of simplification which does not reject anything, but condenses and concentrates everything until the highest simplicity is reached. It is not without reason that words like *yoga, yukta, tantra,* and many others suggest a *via positiva* rather than a *via negativa*. The Laws of Manu rightly summarize the injunctions of tradition in their declaration that "in agreement with *śruti* and *smṛti,* the householder is said to be superior to all [the other *āśramas* or states of life], for he supports all three," adding that "just as all rivers, big and small, go to their rest in the sea, so men of all stages of life find their rest in the householders."[7]

Indeed, viewed from the outside, the accumulation of material or intellectual values may resemble a cancerous proliferation, but it is precisely this third trend that prevents possible exaggerations in the other two. It is easy enough to adduce examples of "material" repression or "spiritual" indigestion. The middle way of the Buddha is, we submit, a genuine understanding of the Vedic experience. However this may be, this Vedic insight is far from being a compromise or a reduction of the rigors of a healthy asceticism. It is certainly not an attitude that is merely this-worldly, a spirituality confined to the construction of the human city or the proper arrangement of the sociological needs of a human kingdom. The city of Brahman is not a city of politics, just as the real temple of the divine is not the house built of wood or stone. This attitude consists neither in total involvement in nor in absolute withdrawal from the city of Man; nor, again, is it a timid refusal to engage oneself fully in the pursuit of total human perfection, the word "human" signifying all the ambiguity contained in different anthropologies and different world views.

This basic attitude is neither a compromise to reduce the needs of Man to a minimum, as if he were a pure soul dwelling in a borrowed body, nor an ideal synthesis between opposites such as may afford a way of escape from the human condition. It is rather a harmonizing of polarities and an inclusion of both poles without eliminating either and without sublimating them in such a way that they become no longer recognizable. It is, thus, not a *via negativa* of enduring the tensions in constant expectancy of a constantly postponed solution; it is, on the contrary, a positive affirmation of the other two dimensions together with the discovery of their ontonomic relationship. This discovery renders unnecessary any drastic emasculation of life, which appears unavoidable only when

7. Manu VI, 89-90.

we lose that all-suffering and all-transforming active patience of which sages speak.

This spirituality does not maintain a separation between the sacred and the profane, the religious and the secular, the cultic and the political. There is not here a diplomatic coexistence of two independent domains. That would be a misleading "katachronistic" interpretation. On the contrary, all is integrated into one insight which allows for the tension and struggles of the human condition and incorporates them, like so many threads of a loom, into the structure of the weaving so that together they constitute the total theanthropocosmic sacrifice.

This insight, then, would seem to be the loftiest peak of Vedic wisdom. No wonder that few have reached it and that the way is steep and difficult. No wonder also that for one who has arrived there the temptation invariably arises to remain on the peak, although it is so sharp that it permits only a prayerful standing posture. Since this breakthrough occurs in the Upaniṣads, we limit ourselves entirely to the Upaniṣadic witness, with the exception only of a few pioneering texts from other parts of the *śruti*. Because we do not give here any text of the Bhagavad Gītā we may make a brief reference to the synthesis offered by the Gītā. In point of fact the Bhagavad Gītā puts before us this experience in unmistakable terms. On the one hand, it does not preach flight from the world or recoil from one's secular duties. It does not point toward a nontemporal and everlasting kingdom in the caves of the earth or the depths of the heart. On the other hand, neither an earthly kingdom nor a political victory is to be sought. No hopes are pinned on the triumph of the Pāṇḍavas, or on a just and happy temporal society on the plains of this world; nor does the Gītā feel impelled by a kind of ethical monism to defend nonviolence at any price, nor does it defend a theory of just war or justify the temporal gains and rights of the righteous. The Gītā invariably takes a third path and offers advice that does not cease to challenge us, a counsel that becomes fatal the moment that we do not have the purity of mind and heart which is required on all occasions. The Gītā does not admit casuistry, nor can it be turned into a piece of legislation. It does not belong to the mere sociopolitical world, nor is it otherworldly or merely a "spiritual document." "It is not a battle that is going to be fought but a great sacrifice that is going to be celebrated, with Kṛṣṇa as the high priest," says Karṇa the half brother of the

Pāṇḍavas in a moment of insight. "Let us die in the sacred field of Kurukṣetra," he adds, knowing well that he is going to lose. You cannot, if you are a man, refuse to participate in the cosmic sacrifice! Arjuna is told to fight, to win, to care, but with so much intensity, with so much insight, that he pierces the appearances and reaches reality. But he meets reality as he goes to encounter it, not flying from it or denying it. He is told, not that all he sees before him is unreal and that therefore he must flee toward the only real, but that the real core of all things resides in those very things themselves and that only by mastering them will he attain true deliverance. Exactly the same point is made to Arjuna's elder brother, the righteous king Yudhiṣṭhira, by Kṛṣṇa himself when he proposes to retire to the forest, after his total victory over the Kurus, instead of remaining as king. No, he must act as king that he is, renounce any sense of possession, but perform nevertheless his earthly duty.[8]

The eternal is not outside but within the temporal; the world is not an illusion, if it is seen for what it really is. The illusion is to mistake it for what it is not; the mistake, in other words, is to have an unreal notion of reality and thus to mistake as real that which is only the veil of the real. The veil is certainly real, but it is no less certainly a veil. The one error is to mistake it for that which it veils, while the other error, so the Gītā constantly warns us, is to think that we can see things without a veil, that we can discard or remove the veil altogether, as if behind the veil were a naked reality. This is sheer concupiscence. There is nothing behind the veil, because it reveals precisely by concealing. This is the symbolic character of reality, to which we have already often referred. Perhaps one of the most stringent formulations of this insight is the one that derives from a later but not unrelated tradition and perhaps brings it to its greatest depth: *nirvāṇa* is *saṁsāra* and *saṁsāra* is *nirvāṇa*. This does not mean that these two concepts express two sides of the same coin, but rather that we have two viewpoints from which to look at reality, which itself is not independent of our vision of it.

The way to the New Life is a long and elaborate one. In Part VI we seek to expound some of the stepping-stones on the way. In its three sections we attempt to trace the unfolding of this experience mainly as it is recounted in the Upaniṣads, which deal almost exclusively with this theme from all imaginable angles. The purport of

8. Cf. MB XIV, 12-13.

the *śruti,* and in particular of the Upaniṣads, is, according to a practically unanimous and exceedingly ancient tradition, *mokṣa* or liberation. Yet when we read the Upaniṣads we do not do so from the exclusive position of any single school, but in the light of the whole *śruti.* We seek to extract from them what they really seem to be saying within that context.

Mindful of the fact that our introductions are not commentaries on the texts, but simply presentations of them in such a way as to avoid obtruding between them and the reader, we concentrate our attention on detecting the internal dynamism of the Vedic Revelation, leaving the rest to personal meditation. If the reader is wise he will take the advice of living masters, not only because to swim in the waters of realization is an arduous internal adventure, but also because there are many external crocodiles infesting the rivers that flow to the ocean of release.

Our exposition profits from traditional wisdom and takes as signposts on our path toward the goal the four great Upaniṣadic dogmas or Sayings, classically known as *mahāvākyas.* While resisting the scholastic temptation of justifying our choice by some more or less artificial device according to which a fifth *mahāvākya* corresponds to a fifth Veda, we would like, without swerving from the tradition of four *mahāvākyas,* to place them between two other no less great Utterances, thus presenting a total of six Utterances as the supreme embodiment of Indian wisdom.[9]

An orthodox view may take exception to our extension of the title of *mahāvākya* beyond the hallowed number of four. Yet all will agree that our first utterance is not only in harmony with the four classical *mahāvākyas* but even centers them. *Om,* our last utterance, could be taken as the *paramavākya* in the sense of an elliptical sentence; it is certainly a *vāc,* a word that in the simplest way "speaks" all reality and thus Brahman. It will be recalled that the purport of the great utterances, according to tradition, is to disclose Brahman. Our two additional sentences do not have any other purport. Be that as it may, we present the four *mahāvākyas* enframed by our first and sixth utterances.

9. According to tradition the second to the fifth *mahāvakya* (in our order) correspond to the RV, AV, SV, and YV respectively. Traditionally the *purāṇas* and *itihāsas* are considered to be the fifth Veda. Cf. CU VII, 1, 2 (§ VI 3) and also MB III, 55, 8. We could enlarge the list and, reckoning the *darśanas* as the sixth Veda, make our first utterance correspond to the *darśanas* and our last to the fifth Veda, thus making six *mahāvakyas.*

We divide this part into three sections, each containing two subsections. Each subsection has as its title the corresponding *mahāvākya* and presents the relevant texts of each of the six Utterances, together with related texts. Needless to say, although we have emphasized the different kairological moments in the sections and subsections, they should not be considered as independent insights. They are simply different dimensions of one and the same Advaitic intuition.

A. THE ASCENDING WAY

Brahmajñāna

That is Fullness, this is Fullness,
from Fullness comes Fullness.
When Fullness is taken from Fullness,
Fullness remains.

BU V, 1[10]

"Man is on pilgrimage to his *ātman*," says the Prince of the Advaitins. In this pilgrimage Man sets out to find the underlying oneness of all things and discovers, as it proceeds, the tool by which such a search is undertaken: consciousness. Oneness and consciousness are the two landmarks on the ascending way.

On the upward path Man does not cast a backward look. Like Arjuna, when put to the test by Droṇa, he does not even notice what is at his side; his eyes are fixed on the goal ahead.

The double title of this section is intended to encompass the first steps of this pilgrimage. The English title could be rendered by the traditional *brahmajijñāsā*,[11] the desire to know Brahman, the thrust toward realization, the ascending way, or again in traditional terms

10. *Pūrṇam adaḥ pūrṇam idam, / pūrṇāt pūrṇam udacyate. / Pūrṇasya pūrṇam ādāya, / pūrnam evāvaśiṣyate.* Cf. IsU (§ VII 6) and also AV X, 8, 29 (§ VII 27) for a similar stanza, referring probably to the moon.

11. Cf. BS I, 1, 1: *athāto brahmajijñāsā*, "now therefore the desire of [the inquiry into and query about] knowing Brahman."

mumukṣutva, the state of existentially tending toward, wholeheartedly desiring to reach *mukti*, liberation, salvation.[12] This state is the necessary precondition and we may assume that this seed, this dynamism, is constitutive of our factual existence.

The Sanskrit title expresses the result of this search, the goal of the pilgrimage, *brahmajñāna*, the knowledge of Brahman.[13] Knowledge here is obviously not a merely epistemic or abstract cognizance of a certain state of affairs, but the total *jñāna*, the perfect and conscious realization of what Brahman is: the real, the truth, the One.

a) Toward the One

Ekam evādvitīyam
One without a second

We take the saying of the Chāndogya Upaniṣad as our first Utterance, for it is in its light that we find the true perspective for viewing all the others. Likewise, in the Decalogue of the Bible, the opening sentence, "I am Yahweh your God," though not incorporated into any of the Ten Commandments, constitutes the background that makes them meaningful. Similarly, in the Indian context, the ten commandments or tenfold law of Manu, "Firmness, forgiveness, self-control, not stealing, inner and outer purity, sense mastery, insight, wisdom, truthfulness, and meekness,"[14] must all be understood as being both the manifestation of *dharma* and its fulfillment. Thus the four *mahāvākyas* of the Upaniṣads make sense only if viewed against the background of this first Utterance, which affirms the uncompromising primacy of the One. Nothing short of the One can be ultimate truth. No kind of dualism or plurality can be the lasting and final foundation of all.

We may try to understand this insight by recalling its most striking formulation in one of the oldest Upaniṣads. This Upaniṣad, significantly enough, also contains the *mahāvākya* which is considered the zenith of Upaniṣadic teaching. Furthermore, both these

12. Cf. Śaṅkara's commentary on BS I, 1, 1, putting this "intense desire to be free" as the fourth and last condition for the search for Brahman.

13. Though the word *brahmajñāna* does not occur in the principal U, its components are their main theme. We have avoided *brahmavidyā* here because of its later scholastic connotations.

14. Manu VI, 92.

teachings are imparted to Śvetaketu by his own father Uddālaka Aruṇi, teacher of the famous Yājñavalkya.

The setting is delightful.[15] The young Śvetaketu, following the best Brahmanical tradition that Brahminhood is not just a privilege of birth, goes away for twelve long years to study the Vedas. Coming back puffed up with pride, after spending half of his total sum of years in academia, he is cross-examined by his father who asks him whether he knows how that which has not been heard becomes heard, that which has not been thought becomes thought, that which has not been understood becomes understood. The learned young man knows nothing of any such teaching.

This is an elegant way of saying that a new doctrine is about to be imparted, a doctrine unknown to the most famous Brahmanical school of the time. And yet it is the fundamental question of the human spirit in search of the infinite. In a period when information has reached its saturation point, when it is practically impossible to know and understand all the details of the constantly proliferating sciences and discoveries, when people begin to question the efficacy and even the possibility of a way out, of a comprehensive world view, then the Upaniṣadic "way in" of sitting quietly and trying to reach the roots of all things appears again in all its effectiveness. We cannot know and experience everything and yet we have a universal urge to do so. If there is any answer to such a quest it can come only from an attitude like that of the Upaniṣads.

But is there any means whereby we may hear, think, and know what is actually unheard, unthought, and unknown?[16] Is there an enlightenment that makes it possible to share in the light of things without actually having access to the things so illumined? Just as knowledge of clay, copper, or iron entails knowledge of everything that is made of clay, copper, and iron, all the rest being only accidental modifications, so by knowing the Ultimate, this teaching implies, we shall know all that is made out of it.

The three examples given to elaborate the answer, which some have seen as expressing the three constituents of matter (fire, water, and food), refer to clay, copper, and iron as the *satya*, truth or reality of all things made of clay, copper, or iron, all the rest being mere names and verbal distinctions. These three examples, of

15. Cf. CU VI, 1, 1 sq. (§ VI 2).
16. Cf. the Sanskrit text in the corresponding note below. Cf. the use of similar words in KenU II, 3 (§ VI 4).

course, are intended only to point our minds in the right direction in order to find the right answer. They are intended to make us aware of the "material" cause as the most fundamental cause and of the "formal" cause as the secondary one. Or, following the metaphors of Yājñavalkya's teaching to his wife Maitreyī, the sounds of a drum or a conch or the music of a lute are none of them really mastered until we take hold of the instrument and of the player.[17] Only in this way can we grasp the ungraspable, because we seize it before it is grasped, see in the uncarved block all its potentialities, seize all music at its root before it is played. It is undoubtedly going to be a silent music, an invisible statue. In other words, the Upaniṣadic seer leads us to consider the identity of things and not their diversity. It is a way of thinking based on the primacy of the principle of identity over against other ways of thinking based on the primacy of the principle of noncontradiction. We cannot stop at clay, copper, or iron but must go deeper and ask for that thing by knowing which all that is made of those three elements is also known. In this way we may eventually reach the One, whose nature still remains to be investigated.

After this introduction comes the central instruction regarding the *one only without a second*. There are, the text says, two opinions: one says that at the beginning this world was Being, one only without a second, and the other affirms, on the contrary, that at the beginning there was just Nonbeing, one only without a second. By closer examination, however, we discover that there is no contradiction in saying that Being on the one hand and Nonbeing on the other are one without a second, because the subject of both sentences is not Being or Nonbeing but *idam, this,* the nominative singular neuter of the demonstrative pronoun. We have already met this *idam*[18] and discovered its existential character: it refers to whatever may come within the range of our actual or possible experience. *This,* that is, anything about which we may be able to think, *this,* which may constitute the goal of all our intentionality, *this,* says the text, is one only without a second. *This,* moreover, applies in all cases, even in the most disparate ones that can be conceived, such as the extremes of Being or Nonbeing at the beginning of all things. *Idam,* not being a concept, includes everything of which we can be aware. The phrases *idaṁ sarvam asi, you are all*

17. Cf. BU II, 4, 7-9 (§ VI 4).
18. Cf. § I A Introduction.

this,[19] and *idaṁ sarvam, all this,*[20] do not need to be interpreted in a pantheistic vein. The *idam* to which Man is capable of pointing has already entered into relationship with him, which implies a certain epistemological communication and ontological communion.

This, the *idam,* whether you consider it to be at the beginning Being or Nonbeing, is one. Anything to which you can say *this, idam,* is, by this very fact, one. If anybody were to object that the *idam* is not one, the Upaniṣadic seers would reply that the *pūrva-pakṣa,* the opponent, says so precisely because he has mistaken the *idam* for a particular idea of it. Because he has identified the *idam* with his particular conception of it, it is no longer an *idam* that can be applied to everything and to every person who is capable of uttering *idam* sensibly. *Idam* is anything that can fall within the range of any possible human experience. There cannot be two *idams* in actual fact. The "second" one would be a mental object only and not that which stands at the "end" of our experience.

The ultimate object of any human experience is one, says our text, and adds immediately another essential point. This One, this *ekam,* is qualified in a very special way. It is in fact the qualifying word, *advitīya,* which renders the affirmation of oneness fruitful and rescues it from being a barren tautology.

The word *advitīya* or nondual has sometimes been considered to stem from a monistic world view, but this is not necessarily so. Even grammatically the word is painstakingly chosen to denote, not *ekatva, kaivalya, ekātma,* and the like, but *a-dvaita,* that is, negation of all duality. It is also appropriate that the word should be a negative qualification, for only in this way is it possible to qualify the *eka* without destroying its internal unity. Nothing positive is added to the One; it is only negatively qualified. The *eka* of this Utterance is indubitably without a second. This is a unique oneness, that oneness which has no second, which has no other one at its side, and most important, which in itself, in its very interior, is nondual. This is fundamental affirmation.

It affirms, to begin with, that no dualism can ever satisfy the human mind or the human heart. It cannot satisfy the mind, for a reduction to unity is in fact the condition of intelligibility. It cannot satisfy any genuine experience of love, for love by its very nature tends to transcend any kind of separation.

19. KausU I, 6 (§ V 4).
20. Cf. RV VIII, 58, 2 (Vālakhilya X, 2; § VI 1); X, 129, 3 (§ I 1); etc.

It affirms, second, that it is not only our intellect and our will that tend toward the transcending of duality; in addition, our whole being cannot really be until it has reached unity with Being. The very acceptance of a plurality of beings implies a certain implicit postulation of Being. If there is to be a real distinction between beings, what is to make this distinction if not another being? Thus there would be a process ad infinitum, unless there is a Being in which beings, in one way or another, participate. We may remark in passing that we are postulating the essence and not the existence of such a Being.

It affirms, third, that the very negation of the duality of the One is what makes beings to be and to exist. This very negation creates the existential tension that gives, precisely, existence to beings. God and the world, to take a traditional example, cannot be two. We would ask immediately: "Two what?" The "being" embracing the two would be greater, better, and more comprehensive than God. Either we conclude that the concept of God is self-contradictory or that God and the world cannot be said to be two "anything."

No monism can be true either; no monistic explanation of reality can ever be convincing, because in pure monism there is no place whatever for any explanation, no room for any kind of unfolding, metaphysical or even epistemological. No amount of subtlety can dispense with conceding some degree of reality to the "appearance," to *avidyā*, ignorance, to the *vyāvahārika*, the phenomenal level, and the like. In other words, the fact that the One can appear as many, even if the appearance itself is declared an illusion, or that the appearance can be mistaken for reality, or that appearance has to be declared unreal, and thus error also nonexistent—this fact makes the monolithic block of an unqualified monism philosophically inconsistent.

The first Utterance represents the genuine middle way between monism and dualism. It posits the primacy of the One in an incontrovertible manner, so that *advaita* stands for a full and uncompromising Oneness. To call it a middle way may be misleading, if that is understood as a compromise. It is rather the only path between the Scylla of an absolute subject and the Charybdis of absolute objects. At the same time *advaita* makes room for pluralism, not as a competitor of the One, but as enhancement of effective oneness. It allows for a free interplay among all the tensions of existence, and yet does not dissolve the polarity of the real into irreconciliable parties with no interconnecting bridge. It says that reality is neither a monistic block nor a metaphysical apartheid leading to chaotic anarchy. It discovers a dynamism in the very heart of the One, which itself longs to be many and is desirous of offspring. Here we have the old coincidence of the divine with the cosmic and the human. We witness three moments of one and the same ultimate process: the *divine* giving himself up so as to be able to produce the world out of himself; the *cosmos* coming and exploding into beings once the procession from Nonbeing and Being is triggered off; *man* discovering the all-encompassing One and finding at the same time a place for himself in the *advitīya* of the oneness.

The cosmotheandric reality is neither a product of the mind (it would then be pure monism and would deny the reality of the "outer" world) nor a raw material independent of the mind (it would then be sheer atomistic plurality with no possible connecting links whatsoever), but the only one reality. This oneness is of a nondualistic nature; it is an Advaitic oneness, which here amounts to saying that it is real oneness and not imagined or merely "thought." The Advaitic character of reality does not permit ultimate dichotomies between matter and spirit, thinker and thought, creator and created, and the like. Nor does it blur distinctions. On the contrary, it underlines them: the three worlds of the divine, the cosmic, and the human are differentiated, but not separated; they are three real dimensions of the one and the same reality, and it is precisely this three-dimensionality, as it were, which makes reality one.

Another of the given texts may provide the proper background for understanding the problem as it is seen and solved by the Upaniṣadic *ṛṣis*.[21] The text, which comes at the very end of a long passage on the origins of everything, sums up the relation of Man with the rest of the world. Man is here seen not as a mere spectator of the universe, or even as a part of it in more or less mystical or mythical participation, but as an image, a mirror, an expression of the whole of the universe, as the whole reality not exactly in miniature (microcosm) but in reflection. Man is incomplete, says the text, until he realizes that the mind scattered everywhere, the wife desired outside, the people populating the earth, the sounds of the universe, and all the activity of the cosmos are *his* mind, speech,

21. Cf. BU I, 4, 17 (§ I 7).

breath, eye, ear, body, and so on. "His" does not mean here private property but real belonging. We could speak of correspondence, of homologization, of reflecting, and the like, provided these items are rightly understood in the Upaniṣadic perspective. It is not that the body of Man is the whole universe or that the individual "contains" the whole, but that the whole of reality is present in every conscious and free, that is, personal, beam of it. The specular conception of reality does not make of Man the center of the universe; it makes of him an image, a reflection, of the entire reality.

The process of *realization*, of discovering the whole of reality and finding in it the role of Man, has four acts, the four acts of the theanthropocosmic drama. The four classical *mahāvākyas* represent these four acts. Finally, the falling of the curtain, the resumption of all into the One, though not as it was "before" the Prelude, is represented by our sixth and final Utterance.

The drama is not only a display of the One, but also its "play" in order that the many may become and may realize oneness. All this is expressed in the *ekam evādvitīyam*. The nature of the nonduality that accomplishes the One without diminishing its oneness is the topic of our next question.

The One *Tad ekam*

1 Many texts of the Ṛg Veda and Atharva Veda point toward the mysterious "One," *eka*, which underlies and makes possible all multiplicity. We have seen them in Part I, in the context of the Origins, where the One is that which exists "before" any beginning and also that which comes to be.[22] Other hymns describe the One as symbolized in the cosmic Pillar.[23] In fact, the sages name in various ways that which is One (i; v).

We find in these texts two ways of speaking about the One: either we have a question, expressing a search and query (i); or we have an affirmation arising from a mystical experience (ii). Only he who "has seen" can properly speak about the One:

> Vena has seen the Supreme, hidden in the cave,
> wherein all things assume one single form.[24]

22. Cf. RV X, 129, 2-3 (§ I 1).
23. Cf. AV X, 7; X, 8 (§§ I 3; VII 27).
24. AV II, 1, 1 (cf. also the rest of the hymn).

After this experience, everything is perceived in its oneness (iv), and all numbers used to describe things are reduced to (the) one (vii), which with its dynamic immortality supports all things (iii). And yet this One, which other texts simply call "that" (viii), is not an abstract principle, not only a distant God, but the "guest of Men" (vi) and their guide (ix). Men are thus requested to offer hospitality to the One and to follow him (or it) on their path.

Tad ekam

RV I, 164, 6; 46

i)

6. Not understanding, and yet desirous to do so,
I ask the wise who know, myself not knowing:
who may he be, the One in the form of the Unborn,
who props in their place the six universal regions?

46. They call him Indra, Mitra, Varuna,
Agni or the heavenly sunbird Garutmat.
The seers call in many ways that which is One;
they speak of Agni, Yama, Mātariśvan.

RV III, 54, 8-9

ii)

8. All beings they unite and separate.
They support the mighty Gods, but do not tremble.
The One is lord over all things, fixed or moving,
walking or flying—this whole multiform creation.

9. From afar I perceive the Ancient One, the Father
of mighty power, the Generator, our connection,
singing the praise of whom the Gods, stationed
on their own broad pathway, go about their business.

RV III, 56, 2ab

iii)

The One, without moving, supports six burdens.
The cows have gone to him, the highest Instance.

RV VIII, 58, 2

iv)

Only One is the Fire, enkindled in numerous ways;
only One is the Sun, pervading this whole universe;
only One is the Dawn, illuminating all things.
In very truth, the One has become the whole world!

RV X, 114, 5ab

v)

By their words the inspired sages impart
manifold forms to that Bird which is the One.

AV VII, 21

vi) Assemble all, with prayer to the Lord of heaven,
He is the One, the all-pervading, the guest of men.
He, the ancient of days, abides in the present.
Him, the One, the many follow on their path.

AV XIII, 4, 12-21

vii)

12. Power entered within him.
He is the One, the Onefold, the only One.
13. In him all the Gods become unified.
14. Fame and glory, fruitfulness and fertility,
Brahman splendor, food and nourishment,
15. belong to him who knows this God as One only.
16. Not second or third or fourth is he called—
he who knows this God as One only.
17. Not fifth or sixth or seventh is he called—
he who knows this God as One only.
18. Not eighth or ninth or tenth is he called—
he who knows this God as One only.
19. He watches over all existent beings,
those that breathe and those that breathe not.
20. Power entered within him.
He is the One, the Onefold, the only One.
21. In him all the Gods become unified.

YV XXXII, 1-3

viii)

1. That, verily, is Agni.
The Sun is that,
the Wind is that,
the Moon is that.

That is the Light,
that is Brahman,
that is the Waters,
Prajāpati is he.

2. All moments originated
from the Person like lightning,
no one has comprehended him,
above, across, or in the center.
3. There is no image of him
whose name is Great Glory.

TA III, 11, 1

ix) He who lives in us as our guide, who is one, and yet appears in many forms, in whom the hundred lights of heaven are one, in whom the Vedas are one, in whom the priests are one—he is the spiritual *ātman* within the person.

■ i) 6. Form of the Unborn: *ajasya rūpa,* rather, "under the symbol of the unborn."
Six universal regions: i.e., three heavens and three earths. Cf. RV III, 56, 2 (iii).
46. The seers call . . . : *ekaṁ sad viprā bahudhā vadanti.*
■ ii) 8. They: i.e., Heaven and Earth.
Multiform creation: *viṣuṇaṁ vi jātam.*
9. Connection: *jāmi,* paternal bond, the kinship with the universal Father.
■ iii) Six burdens: three earths and three heavens, or, acc. to Sāyaṇa, the six seasons (double months) of the year.
Cows: in later terms the *śaktis* or powers of the One, symbolized by cows in the RV.
Instance: *ṛta,* truth, order.
The second half is somewhat obscure.
■ iv) This hymn is Vālakhilya 10 (v. 2).
All things: *idaṁ sarvam,* this all.
■ v) Cf. also RV VIII, 11, 8.
Inspired sages: *viprāḥ kavayaḥ,* the singing poets.
Impart manifold forms: *bahudhā kalpayanti,* express in many ways.
Bird: *suparṇa,* the Sun, symbol of the One.
■ vi) This short hymn is addressed to the *ātman* as deity, but tradition has also attributed it either to the Sun or to Yama.
Prayer: *vacas.*
Lord of heaven: *patiṁ divaḥ.*
The second half is rather obscure.
■ vii) Cf. AV X, 8, 11; 25; 43-44 (§ VII 27).
12. Power: *sahas.*
13. Unified: *ekavṛt,* simple, single, onefold.
14. Fruitfulness: *ambhas.*
Fertility: *nabhas,* lit cloud, the humidity necessary for fertility.
■ viii) 1. All the Gods are simply that One, *tat.*
2. Moments: *nimeṣāḥ,* also twinklings (of the eye).
Person like lightning: *vidyutaḥ puruṣa.*
3. Image: *pratimā,* symbol, idol, icon.
Great Glory: *mahad yaśaḥ.*
■ ix) Spiritual: *mānasī,* consisting of *manas,* mind, spirit.

The One Only *Ekam eva*

2 One of the questioners of the great Yājñavalkya, the "clever" Vidagdha, does not know the danger of asking questions without realizing their implications. And yet we owe to his searching spirit one of the most striking "reductions" of the multiplicity of Gods (i). He will not stop at anything before the One, the only One to which all powers, all Gods, can be ultimately reduced, which is both known (as *prāṇa,* the breath of life) and unknown (as *tyad,* that). But, as if he had to demonstrate by his life that these questions are far from being rhetorical, his ignorance of the true Upani-

ṣadic *puruṣa* costs him his head.[25] The warning that Yājāvalkya had given to Gārgī for her unrestrained questioning has here come true.[26] Vidagdha dies, probably because he did not understand that the *ātman* is not another but the One only.

We have already introduced the central message of the Chāndogya Upaniṣad (ii). The Kaṭha Upaniṣad (iii), stating the oneness of *ātman* in all beings, immanent and yet beyond, affirms also that it is only the realization of the One in oneself which can give joy and peace. This One is not an abstract principle but the very core of our experience, the *ātman*.[27]

The Śvetāśvatara Upaniṣad (iv) adds to this understanding of the One only one Word: God (*deva*), giving thus a theistic face to the transcendent Absolute.

The Muṇḍaka Upaniṣad (v) gives an indication of how the undivided, imperceptible One can be perceived: by a purified mind, by grace, and by contemplation. That the One, which was in the beginning everything, is also that inner power in the cosmos and in the heart of Man, as well as in fire, is shown in the Maitrī Upaniṣad (vi). In this as also in the following text (vii), it is a matter of personal discovery, of attaining the state where there is no "second," but only the nonduality of the One.

Ekam eva

BU III, 9, 1-9

i) 1. Then Vidagdha Śākalya asked him: "How many Gods are there, Yājñavalkya?"

He replied according to the Nivid, quoting the number mentioned in the Nivid of the All-Gods: "Three hundred and three and three thousand and three."

"Yes," he said, "but how many Gods are there really, Yājñavalkya?"

"Thirty-three."

"Yes," he said, "but how many Gods are there really, Yājñavalkya?"

"Six."

"Yes," he said, "but how many Gods are there really, Yājñavalkya?"

"Three."

25. Cf. BU III, 9, 26 (§ VI 5).
26. Cf. BU III, 6, 1.
27. Cf. the other vv.: KathU V, 6-7; 14-15 (§ V 5).

"Yes," he said, "but how many Gods are there really, Yājñavalkya?"

"Two."

"Yes," he said, "but how many Gods are there really, Yājñavalkya?"

"One and a half."

"Yes," he said, "but how many Gods are there really, Yājñavalkya?"

"One."

"Yes," he said, "but which are those three hundred and three and three thousand and three?"

2. Yājñavalkya replied: "These are but their powers; there are only thirty-three Gods."

"Which are these thirty-three?"

"The eight Vasus, eleven Rudras, and twelve Ādityas make thirty-one; thus with Indra and Prajāpati there are thirty-three all told."

3. "Which are the Vasus?"

"Fire, the earth, wind, space, the sun, the sky, the moon, and the stars—these are the Vasus. In them is stored all treasure; hence they are called Vasus."

4. "Which are the Rudras?"

"The ten breaths that are in man, and the *ātman* is the eleventh. When they leave the mortal body, they cause men to weep. Because they cause men to weep, they are Rudras."

5. "Which are the Ādityas?"

"The twelve months of the year, these are the Ādityas. They move onward, carrying along all that is; hence they are called Ādityas."

6. "Who is Indra? Who is Prajāpati?"

"The thunder is Indra, the Sacrifice is Prajāpati."

"What is thunder?"

"Lightning."

"What is sacrifice?"

"The victim."

7. "Which are the six?"

"Fire, the earth, the wind, space, the sun, and the sky—these are the six, for these six are all."

8. "Which are the three Gods?"

"The three Gods are the three worlds, for in them all those Gods exist."

"Which are the two Gods?"

"Food and Life Breath."

Which is the one and a half?"

"The one who blows."

9. "About this God they say: as the one who blows [the air] is one only, why speak of one and a half? Because in him all this has developed, hence it is called one and a half."

"Which is the one God?"

"Life Breath; he is Brahman, which they call 'that' [*tyad*]."

CU VI, 1, 1-7; 2, 1-3

ii) 1, 1. Once there was Śvetaketu Āruṇeya. His father spoke to him:

"Śvetaketu, live a life of chastity and search for Brahman. For truly, no one in our family who is not learned should be called a Brahmin merely because of blood-relationship."

2. So he left at the age of twelve [to study with a master]. He returned at twenty-four, having studied all the Vedas, arrogant, thinking that his learning had made him knowledgeable.

His father spoke to him:

3. "Śvetaketu, my dear, now that you are arrogant, thinking that your learning has made you knowledgeable, did you also ask for that instruction by which the unheard becomes heard, the unthought becomes thought, the unknown becomes known?"

"What, sir, is this instruction?"

4. "My dear, just as by one lump of clay all that is made of clay is known, the modification being only a name based on speech, the reality being nothing but clay;

5. "just as, my dear, by one vessel of copper all that is made of copper is known, the modification being only a name based on speech, the reality being nothing but copper;

6. "just as, my dear, by one pair of nail-scissors all that is made of iron is known, the modification being only a name based on speech, the reality being nothing but iron; this, my dear, is the instruction."

7. "Certainly, my revered masters did not know this. For had they known it, how could they not have told me? But, sir, please tell it to me."

"Well, my dear," he said.

2, 1. "In the beginning, my dear, this was Being alone—*one only, without a second.* Some say, it is true, that in the beginning only Nonbeing was, *one only, without a second;* and that from that Nonbeing Being was born.

2. "But, my dear, how could it be this?" said he. "How could Being be born from Nonbeing? On the contrary, my dear, it was Being alone that was this in the beginning, *one only, without a second.*

3. "It thought: 'Would that I might be many! Would that I might procreate!' It sent forth fire. This fire also thought: 'Would that I might be many! Would that I might procreate!' "

KathU V, 9-13

iii) 9. As fire which is one, on entering creation,
conforms its own form to the form of each being,
so also the One, the *ātman* within all beings,
assumes all forms, yet exists outside.

10. As the wind, which is one, on entering creation,
conforms its own form to the form of each being,
so also the One, the *ātman* within all beings,
assumes all forms, yet exists outside.

11. As the sun, the eye of the whole world, is not touched
by external blemishes seen by the eye,
so the One, the *ātman* within all beings, is not touched
by the sufferings of the world. He remains apart.

12. The One, the Controller, the *ātman* within all beings,
the One who makes his own form manifold—
the wise who perceive him established in themselves
attain—and no others—everlasting joy.

13. Permanent among the impermanent, conscious among the conscious,
the One among the many, fulfiller of desires—
the wise who perceive him established in themselves
attain—and no others—everlasting peace.

SU VI, 10-13

iv) 10. May the One God who, in accordance with his nature,
covers himself like a spider with threads
spun out of matter, grant us union with Brahman!

11. The One God, hidden in all beings, all-pervading,
the *ātman* existent within every being,
the surveyor of all actions, dwelling in all creatures,
the witness, the spirit, the unique, free from attributes.

12. The One, Controller of a passive multitude,
makes his one seed manifold.

The wise who perceive him within their own selves,
they, and they alone, have eternal joy.

13. Eternal among the eternal, conscious among the conscious,
the One among the many, fulfiller of desires,
the Cause discovered through inquiry and discipline—
having realized God, one is freed from all chains.

MundU III, 1, 8

v) Eye cannot see him, nor words reveal him;
by the senses, austerity, or works he is not known.
When the mind is cleansed by the grace of wisdom,
he is seen by contemplation—the One without parts.

MaitU VI, 17

vi) In the beginning this was Brahman, One and infinite, infinite in the East, infinite in the South, infinite in the West, infinite in the North, infinite above and below, infinite in every direction. For him there are, of course, no directions such as the East and so on, no across, no above, and no below.

Inconceivable in this supreme *ātman*, immeasurable, unborn, inscrutable, unthinkable, he whose Self is [infinite] space. He alone remains awake when the universe is dissolved, and out of this space he awakens [again] the world consisting of thought. By him alone is all this thought [into being] and in him it dissolves again. His shining form is that which burns in the sun; it is the multiform light that shines in the smokeless fire and it is that which digests the food in the body. For thus it has been said:

He who dwells in the fire,
he who dwells in the heart,
he who dwells in the sun,
he is One.
The man who knows this,
he verily attains
the Oneness of the One.

KaivU 23

vii) For me there is no earth, no water, and no fire.
For me there is neither wind nor ether.
The one who has discovered the supreme *ātman*
dwelling in the heart, without parts, without a second,
the universal witness, neither being nor nonbeing,
attains the pure form of the supreme *ātman*.

■ i) This text belongs to the series where Yājñavalkya is questioned by different seekers. Cf. Bu III, 7-8 (§§ VI 5; VI 3).

1. Nivid of the All-Gods: a text in praise of the Viśvedevas.

Yes: *aum*. Cf. § VI 12.

2. Powers: *mahimānaḥ*, manifestations of their power.
3. Treasure: *vasu*, which is essential for intelligibility, is omitted in some manuscripts. The sentence reads: *idaṁ sarvaṁ vasu hitam*. *Vasu* meaning also "good treasure," this can be a plausible "etymology," parallel to those of vv. 4 and 5.
4. They cause men to weep: *rodayanti*. Caus. of the root *rud-* with which the name Rudra is traditionally connected. Cf. § II 29 on Rudra.
5. They move onward, carrying . . . : again a popular etymology of Āditya with the roots *ā-dā-* and *i- (yanti)*.
6. Victim: *paśu*, animal.
8. Food and Life Breath: *anna* and *prāṇa*, the two powers sustaining life. Cf. §§ II 5, 6; 11.
The one who blows: or who purifies: *pavate* (the wind).
9. Developed . . . : *adhyārdhnot*, again a pun with *adhyardha* (one and a half).
'That': *tyad*, that, the transcendent.
10-17. Cf. § VI 7.
21. Cf. § I 37.
24-25. Cf. § I 14.
26. Cf. § VI 5.
28. Cf. § VI 3.

■ ii) 1, 1. Life of chastity and search for Brahman: *brahmacarya*.
Brahmin . . . because of blood-relationship: *brahma-bandhu*, used here in an ironical sense.
1, 3. By which the unheard . . . : *yenāśrutaṁ śrutaṁ bhavati, amataṁ matam, avijñātaṁ vijñātam iti*.
1, 4. The modification being only a name based on speech: *vācārambhaṇaṁ vikāro nāmadheyam*. This sentence is frequently discussed.
2, 1. Being: *sat*.
Nonbeing: *asat*.
One only, without a second: *ekam evādvitīyam*, the famous fundamental sentence of the whole of the Upaniṣads.
2, 2. How can Nonbeing be the cause, the origin, or whatever, of anything and thus of Being? The question is not only fair but places Nonbeing in its proper perspective: one cannot deal with Nonbeing as if it were a being and apply to it the same rules of thinking. *Sat* and *asat* are not on the same level.
2, 3. The "many" desired by the One is not the multiplication of its oneness but its enhancement by growth and development.

■ iii) 6-7. Cf. § V 5.
8. Cf. § VI 7.
9. Fire: Agni, assuming all the forms of the objects it burns (wood, stone, etc.).
Conforms its own form . . . : *rūpaṁ rūpaṁ pratirūpo babhūva*. Cf. RV VI, 47, 18 (§ II 4 Introduction) where the same expression is used for Indra, who assumes various forms.
Ātman within all beings: *sarva-bhūtāntar-ātman*, the inner *ātman* in all beings.
11. Is not touched: *na lipyate*, untainted, not stained. Cf. BU IV, 4, 23 (§ VI 6); IsU 2 (§ VII 6).
Sufferings of the world: *loka-duḥkha*, "Weltschmerz."
Apart: *bāhya*, lit. outside (as in previous vv).
12. Cf. SU VI, 12 (iv).
Form: *rūpa*. Another version reads *bīja*, seed.
Established in themselves: *ātmastha*. If taken, as traditionally is done, in the singular: standing in the self, or in the body, or also self-subsistent. It refers then to the *eka* and not to the wise.
13. Cf. SU VI, 13 (iv).
Permanent: *nitya*, eternal.
Conscious: *cetana*.
14-15. Cf. § V 5.

■ iv) Cf. KathU V, 10-13 (iii).
7-9. Cf. § I 28.
10. Matter: *pradhāna*, primal nature (*prakṛti*).
Union with Brahman: *brahmāpyaya*, "entrance into Brahman."
11. The unique: *kevala*, the alone, the only one, the absolute, the transcendent.
12. Passive multitude: *niṣkriyāṇāṁ bahūnām*, lit. of many inactive ones, he being the sole inspirer of activity in all beings.
13. Inquiry and discipline: *sāṁkhya-yoga*.
Having realized God: *jñātvā devam*.
Cf. § VI C and also SU I, 8; II, 15 (§ VI 11); IV, 16; V 13 (§ I 28), leitmotiv of this U.
16-19. Cf. § I 28.

■ v) By the grace of wisdom: *jñāna-prasādena*, by calmness of knowledge, by clearness of intuition.
One without parts: *niṣkala*.

■ vi) Whose Self is [infinite] space: *ākāśātmā*; cf. CU III, 14, 2 (§ VI 6).
World consisting of thought: *idaṁ cetāmātram*.

Is . . . thought: *dhyāyate,* or in him alone is all this contemplated.

■ vii) Universal witness: *samasta-sākṣi.*

Pure form of the supreme *ātman: śuddhaṁ paramātma-rūpam,* pure existence or nature of the *paramātman.*

b) Transcendental Consciousness

Prajñānam brahma
Consciousness is Brahman

How is it possible to discover the nonduality in the *eka*? How do we make room for the *advitīya*? This question amounts to asking: What is the nature of reality itself, or how is the One itself constituted so that there is a place for pluralism without destroying the unity? Is there anything that allows for movement, distinctions, life, without endangering the One? What kind of plurality can coexist with oneness? We can put the same question in a reflective manner and ask: What induces in Man this uncompromising longing for unity? What makes Man cling with such conviction to the *ekam evādvitīyam*? What is the nature of such nonduality?

The *mahāvākyas* emerge out of and reflect the most fascinating search for the *advitīyam*, for that reflection of the One, for its manifestation, for its companion, a companion who, like an Indian wife, is not an independent partner but part and parcel of the husband, his prolongation and expression. Is there such a thing as *ekam evādvitīyam*? For it could well be that all this is a kind of transcendental fallacy of our mind alone.

The answer of the *mahāvākya* is clear: consciousness and consciousness alone is able to assume multiplicity without endangering oneness. In the world of human experience, in point of fact, consciousness is the only power that embraces the manifold without losing its identity and unity. A multiplicity of thoughts as well as the many objects and contents of consciousness do not disrupt but rather reinforce the unity of consciousness. Consciousness is both one and also a unifying force. The overwhelming plurality of the world of our experience reverts to a unity in the recesses of our consciousness. Furthermore, consciousness itself is one and is not affected by a plurality of objects. Consciousness can be aware of the many without being split into multiplicity.

This process constitutes one of the most profound and revolutionary human experiences. It is perhaps this experience that makes Man really Man, not the awareness of things (which animals also possess) but the awareness of his own consciousness, in the first place, and of consciousness as such, at the end of the process. This process constitutes the history of this particular *mahāvākya*. Herein is the discovery of a light in Man, of a power of synthesis, of the ultimate character of himself and of all things. Apart from consciousness, not only would Man have no knowledge whatsoever, but also things themselves would not be as they actually are. Irrespective of whether things are "outside" consciousness or whether to be is to be known (knowable), one fact is certain: only things that are known are as they actually are, for the knowledge of things modifies and transforms the things so known. Irrespective, again, of whether we postulate an identity or a difference between being and thought, the realm of consciousness is unquestionably the ultimate and more extensive one. Being over and above consciousness is a contradiction in terms, for by the very fact that we define "being" as the reality that transcends consciousness, we are including it in our consciousness of being; and this is true even if we call Nonbeing that pure transcendence. Any verbalization belongs to the realm of consciousness.

The important text containing this *mahāvākya* offers a long list of terms, some of which are compounds of the central verbal root *jñā-*, to know. It ends by saying that all these forms of knowing in one way or another are different names for consciousness, for ultimately everything is rooted in consciousness.[28]

The discovery of pure consciousness represents a radical departure from the first natural movement of our being, mind, heart, senses, and so on. That is, it implies the reversion of the natural movement toward the object, toward the other, and it entails a direction toward the subject, toward the knower. Where there is duality, there you understand another, you think of and think the other; but by what do you understand the understander or think the thinker?[29] For you cannot see the seer, you cannot understand the understander and know the knower.[30] This is indeed a radical impossibility, for if by hypothesis you know the knower, it would cease by this very fact to be the knower and would have been

28. Cf. AU III, 1-4 (§ VI 4).
29. Cf. BU II, 4, 14 (§ VI 4).
30. Cf. BU III, 4, 2 (§ VI 6).

converted into the known. Is there any way out of this impasse? The Upaniṣads tell us that there is a way out, although they prefer to call it a way in. But we must first learn the lesson of this *mahāvākya*.

In the search for pure consciousness we have to eliminate any possible object. Schools of thought and of spirituality are founded with this aim in view. To reflect upon an object may indirectly give us a glimpse of how our consciousness operates, but it will not disclose to us the nature of consciousness. Pure consciousness is not reflective consciousness; it is thus not self-consciousness; it cannot be consciousness of consciousness. Where one sees nothing, understand nothing, there is the infinite. Pure consciousness is established in its own greatness or even not in it.[31] It has no support; it is self-illuminating and self-illumined. Nothing can be its object.

The texts are emphatic. Though one does not understand—how can you understand the understander?—it is by understanding that you understand that you do not understand.[32] The Upaniṣads are thoroughly consistent. There is no rhetoric here. These are sober statements:

> It is not understood by those who understand.
> It is understood by those who do not understand.[33]

This Upaniṣad or instruction is to be taken literally, that is, as meaning what it says.[34] Our nonunderstanding is real, and is certainly a nonunderstanding of *it*, Brahman, but nevertheless it is already a certain understanding, it is an understanding that we do not understand and thus it is included in the sum total of our imperfect understanding: "not understood by those who understand." But there is still more. Those who say that they know, certainly know, but they know only what they do know, which is very little. They truly know, but what they know is always the known, not the knower. The understanding of our ignorance is not the same thing as either infinite ignorance or blessed ignorance, which does not understand itself. They are doubly ignorant, for in addition they are conceited, thinking that their not-knowing is a superior form of knowledge. The Upaniṣads dismiss them altogether. In this realm there can be no pretense. The next point also is

31. Cf. CU VII, 24, 1 (§ VI 3).
32. Cf. BU IV, 3, 30.
33. KenU II, 3 (§ VI 4).
34. Cf. § III 28 Introduction.

to be taken literally. "It is understood by those who do not understand," not by those who understand that they do not understand it. These latter are the truly ignorant (knowers of their own ignorance). It is understood, on the contrary, by those who really do not understand in such a way that they do not even understand that they do not understand, much less think that they understand. To understand one's own nonunderstanding is not true understanding; not to understand that one understands, that is, the nonunderstanding of the understander, is the true understanding. Innocence cannot be forged or feigned.

It is with the discovery that pure consciousness is not self-consciousness that the discourse on Brahman starts. Brahman is not the object of consciousness, or even the subject. Brahman is pure consciousness. Our *mahāvākya* can be rendered by simply saying that "consciousness *is*" or by affirming "there is consciousness." It is not said that consciousness is being or that being is consciousness. Pure consciousness has no support. Brahman is this nonsupport; Brahman is not a substance. Thus the understanding of Brahman does not allow for reflection, that is, for a second understanding of the understanding. If you really understand Brahman, you do not understand that you understand it (this would be a second awareness and by this very fact would furnish the proof that the first understanding of Brahman was not exhaustive). If you understand that you understand, then you do not understand Brahman, but only your own understanding (of it). Finally, if you do not understand (not if you pretend that you do not understand, but if you really do not understand), because there is nothing, no-thing to understand, then you really understand (Brahman). Needless to say, this is only absolutely true of Brahman. In any other instance we are no longer dealing with pure consciousness. Consciousness, then, is not a substance, but an action, an act. Brahman *has* no consciousness, and thus no self-consciousness. Brahman *is* consciousness.

This is the point to which this Great Saying leads us. From the bringing together of the epistemic and ontic questions effected by this *mahāvākya*, there emerges a total vision of the universe. This *mahāvākya* could be called the onto-epistemic principle.

We may attempt to explain this in another less technical way. Men *have* consciousness, they are conscious beings, but they are not (yet?) consciousness and much less pure consciousness. The sole consciousness that exists is an all-encompassing consciousness; it is Brahman whom Men do not need either to fear or even to love or care about, because that ontic or meta-ontic realm is simply there, or rather it is to such a degree pure reality that our acceptance or rejection of it is already included in it and is of no effect whatever. In the words of one Upaniṣad, which we already know,[35]

> That from which beings are born,
> that by which, when born, they live,
> that into which, when dying, they enter,
> that you should desire to know:
> that is Brahman.

This Brahman, source and end of everything, is not a separated "being," is not merely at the beginning and end of the ontic pilgrimage: Brahman is consciousness. All beings are nothing but the reflections, the shadows, the thoughts, the objects, the creatures, of that pure consciousness. We are insofar as we are in and from Brahman. He is the ultimate Oneness of reality.

The Absolute *Brahman*

3 Brahman[36] is the culmination and the goal of the entire Vedic world, of its prayers, hymns, sacrifices, and of the aspirations contained in them.[37] Its superiority is foreshadowed in the Ṛg Veda[38] and the Atharva Veda[39] and affirmed in the Śatapatha Brāhmana.[40] Nothing is prior to or beyond Brahman (i). It is Brahman that attracts the attention of all the truth seekers of the Upaniṣads and inspires their meditation and dialogue. Discussions about Brahman (*brahmodya*) are no longer part of sacrifice but become essential for the search after the Ultimate, the Imperishable, the Ground and Goal of everything (ii). The search for truth finds its fulfillment in Brahman, and hence truth is identified with Brahman and Brahman with truth (iv, vi). But Brahman is far more than a principle satisfying intellectual inquiry. It is the subtle center of our existence, that is, consciousness (*cit*), and also the ultimate joy and bliss (*ānanda*) (iii). The later Vedāntic definition of Brahman as *sat*

35. TU III, 1 (§ II 11); cf. also KaivU 19 (§ VI 9).
36. Brahman, n., accented on the first syllable, against *brahman*, m., accented on the last, meaning the priest, the knower of Brahman. Cf. also BU I, 4, 10 (§ VI 9).
37. Cf. also §§ I 12; I 14, and III 28 (Introductions).
38. Cf. RV I, 164, 35 (§ I 11); etc.
39. Cf. AV IV, 1, 1 (§ I 12); etc.
40. Cf. SB XI, 2, 3, and our text (i).

(being), *cit* (consciousness), and *ānanda* (bliss) is foreshadowed in the Upaniṣads in various ways (vi). But the stress is always on "knowing," that is, on realizing the unknowable as it is hidden in one's own heart, for to know it is to become it. And the goal of Upaniṣadic knowledge is nothing less than the attainment of this state of being which is the being of Brahman itself.[41]

The Chāndogya Upaniṣad describes the ascent of knowledge identifying Brahman step by step with different realities (v). Although the original order of terms may have been upset at places, there is a whole order of human values (not to speak of the ever-recurring cosmic terms) which serve as stepping-stones in the ascent and are discarded only by the recognition of something greater transcending them. But even at lower degrees of wisdom the knower attains states of freedom or fulfillment of desires corresponding to his understanding of Brahman. Brahman does not fall from the sky as some incomprehensible revelation; it is discovered by going through the whole range of human realms of freedom. One stopping place in this list seems to be life itself (*prāṇa*), but the ultimate freedom is found only in the infinite, in fullness. Brahman is neither this nor that; it is only the unlimited.

The quest for Brahman can never be the quest for an object (of knowledge); rather, it is the quest for the origin of the questioner himself (vii), for the "mind of his mind." The Kena Upaniṣad averts all possible errors in the search for Brahman, keeping it apart from all possible objects of vision, speech, thought, or worship. That by which the mind is thought cannot possibly be thought by the mind.

The Muṇḍaka Upaniṣad (viii) is more affirmative and calls Brahman the spiritual center of all the world, that toward which all beings strive as their very life.

Brahman

SB X, 3, 5, 10-11

i)

10. That is the greatest Brahman, for there is nothing greater than this. He who knows this becomes greatest and best among his own people.

11. Nothing is prior to this Brahman and nothing is beyond it. He who knows this Brahman as having nothing prior to it and nothing beyond it will be second to none among his own people.

41. Cf. the frequent formula: *ya eva veda sa eva bhavati*.

BU III, 8

ii)

1. Then Vācaknavī said: "Revered Brahmins, I am going to ask him [Yājñavalkya] two questions. If he replies to me, none of you will ever be able to defeat him in debates about Brahman." "Ask, O Gārgī!"

2. She said: "As a warrior of the land of the Kāśis or Videhas strings his loosened bow and takes in his hands two arrows, sharpened to pierce his enemies, likewise, O Yājñavalkya, I stand up before you with two questions. Tell me their answers." "Ask, O Gārgī!"

3. She said: "That, O Yājñavalkya, which is beyond the heaven, which is below the earth, which is between heaven and earth, which is called past, present, and future—in what is it interwoven? In what is its warp and woof?"

4. He replied: "That, O Gārgī, which is beyond the heaven, which is below the earth, which is between heaven and earth, which is called past, present, and future—all this is interwoven in space as its warp and woof."

5. She said: "Hail to you, O Yājñavalkya, who have answered my first question. Be prepared for the second one." "Ask, O Gārgī!"

6. She said: "That, O Yājñavalkya, which is beyond the heaven, which is below the earth, which is between heaven and earth, which is called past, present, and future—in what is it interwoven? In what is its warp and woof?"

7. He replied: "That, O Gārgī, which is beyond the heaven, which is below the earth, which is between heaven and earth, which is called past, present, and future—all this is interwoven in space as its warp and woof." "But in what is space interwoven? In what is its warp and woof?"

8. He replied: "That, O Gārgī, the knowers of Brahman declare to be the Imperishable. It is neither gross nor subtle, neither short nor long, neither fire nor liquid, neither shade nor darkness, neither wind nor space. It is unattached, without taste or smell, without eyes or ears, wind nor space. It is unattached, without taste or smell, without eyes or ears, without speech or mind, without heat, without breath, without face, without any measure, without inside or outside. It neither eats nor is it eaten.

9. "In truth, O Gārgī, it is by order of that Imperishable that the sun and the moon are fixed in their positions; it is by the order of that Imperishable, O Gārgī, that heaven and earth are fixed in their positions; it is by the order of the Imperishable, O Gārgī, that the seconds, the hours, the days and nights, the half months, the full

months, the seasons, and the years are fixed in their positions; it is by order of that Imperishable, O Gārgī, that the rivers flow, some in the East, others in the West from the white mountains, in their respective directions. It is by order of that Imperishable, O Gārgī, that men praise almsgiving, the Gods the sacrificer, and the Forefathers the offering to the dead.

10. "He who, O Gārgī, in this world offers sacrifice or practices asceticism for many, even for a thousand years, and yet does not know that Imperishable—all his efforts will be in vain. And he, O Gārgī, who departs from this world without having known it is wretched. But he, O Gārgī, who departs from this world having known that Imperishable is a knower of Brahman.

11. "It is in truth that Imperishable, O Gārgī, who is not seen but is the seer, who is not heard but is the hearer, who is not thought but is the thinker, who is not known but is the knower. There is no other seer but him, no other hearer but him, no other thinker but him, no other knower but him. And it is that Imperishable which is the warp and the woof of space."

12. She said: "Revered Brahmins, if you can avoid an argument with him at the price of paying him homage, then count yourself happy, for none of you can defeat him in debates about Brahman." Thereupon Vācaknavī kept silent.

BU III, 9, 28

iii) Brahman is consciousness and joy,
the highest reward of the offerer of gifts
and of the one who stands still and knows.

BU V, 4, 1

iv) This, in truth, is that; this, indeed, was that, namely truth. He who knows that great, wonderful genius, the firstborn, as Brahman, the truth, overcomes these worlds and thus may overcome nonbeing also, he who knows that great, wonderful genius, the firstborn, as Brahman, the truth. For truth alone is Brahman.

CU VII, 1; 2, 2; 3-8; 10-18; 21-24; 26

v) 1, 1. "Instruct me, Sir." Thus Nārada approached Sanatkumāra. The latter said: "Let me know what you know and I will tell you what is beyond that."

1, 2. [Nārada said]: "I know, sir, the Ṛg Veda, the Yajur Veda, the Sāma Veda, the Atharva Veda as the fourth; as the fifth [Veda], the Ancient Stories. [I know further] the Veda of Vedas, the ritual for ancestors, calculus, augural sciences, the knowledge of the signs of the times, dialectics, ethics and political sciences, sacred knowledge, theology, knowledge of the spirits, military science, astrology, the science of snakes and of celestial beings. This, sir, is what I know."

1, 3b [Sanatkumāra] then said to him: "All that you have been saying is nothing but name.

1, 4. "Certainly, a name is the Ṛg Veda, the Yajur Veda, the Sāma Veda, the Atharva Veda as the fourth, [as well as] the Ancient Stories as the fifth, [and also] the Veda of Vedas, the ritual for ancestors, calculus, augural sciences, the knowledge of the signs of the times, dialectics, ethics and political sciences, sacred knowledge, theology, knowledge of the spirits, military science, astrology, the science of snakes and of celestial beings. All this is mere name. Meditate on the name.

1, 5. "He who meditates on name as Brahman, his freedom will extend to the limits of the realm of name, he who meditates on name as Brahman."

"But, sir, is there anything greater than name?"

"Yes, there is something greater than name."

"Then please, sir, tell me about it!"

2, 2. "He who meditates on the word as Brahman, his freedom will extend to the limits of the realm of the word, he who meditates on the word as Brahman."

"But, sir, is there anything greater than the word?"

"Yes, there is something greater than the word."

"Then please, sir, tell me about it!"

3, 1. "Mind, verily, is greater than word. In the same way as the human fist can grasp two fruits of *āmalaka* or of *kola* or of *akṣa,* so the mind grasps both word and name. When one by his mind puts into his mind: 'I want to study the sacred hymns,' then he studies them, or, 'I want to perform sacred actions,' then he performs them, or, 'I want sons and cattle,' then he wants them, or, 'I want this world and the other world,' then he wants them. Mind is verily the *ātman*. Mind is verily the world. Mind is certainly Brahman. Meditate on Mind.

3, 2. "He who meditates on mind as Brahman, his freedom will extend to the limits of the realm of the mind, he who meditates on mind as Brahman."

"But, sir, is there anything greater than mind?"

"Yes, there is something greater than mind."

"Then please, sir, tell me about it!"

4, 1. "Purpose, verily, is greater than mind. When a man purposes something then he has it in mind and he says a word and gives it a name. It is in name that the sacred hymns become one as well as the sacred actions in the sacred hymns.

4, 2. "All these find their union in purpose, they have purpose as their self and are grounded in purpose. Heaven and earth came to be by purpose, wind and space came to be by purpose, water and fire came to be by purpose. Because these came into being, rain came into being. Because rain came into being, food came into being. Because food came into being, the vital breaths [of living creatures] came into being. Because the vital breaths came into being, the sacred hymns came into being. Because the sacred hymns came into being, sacred actions came into being. Because sacred actions came into being, the world came into being. Because the world came into being, everything comes into being. This is purpose. Meditate on purpose.

4, 3. "He who meditates on purpose as Brahman, he attains the worlds that he has willed; being stable he obtains stable worlds, being well established he obtains well-established ones, being unwavering he obtains unwavering ones. His freedom will extend to the limits of the realm of purpose, he who meditates on purpose as Brahman."

"But, sir, is there anything greater than purpose?"

"Yes, there is something greater than purpose."

"Then please, sir, tell me about it!"

5, 1. "Thought, verily, is greater than purpose, for when a man thinks then he purposes and has it in mind and he says a word and gives it a name. It is in name that the sacred hymns become one as well as the sacred actions in the sacred hymns.

5, 2. "All these find their union in thought, they have thought as their self and are grounded in thought. Therefore, if even a man who knows much does not think, they say of him that he is nobody, whatever he may know. For if he really knew, he would not be without thought. And even if a man who knows little thinks, people want to listen to him. For thought is verily the union of all these, the self and the ground of all these. Meditate on thought.

5, 3. "He who meditates on thought as Brahman, he attains the world he has thought; being stable he obtains stable worlds, being well established he obtains well-established ones, being unwavering he obtains unwavering ones. His freedom will extend to the limits of the realm of thought, he who meditates on thought as Brahman."

"But, sir, is there anything greater than thought?"

"Yes, there is something greater than thought."

"Then please, sir, tell me about it!"

6, 1. "Contemplation, verily, is greater than thought. For the earth, as it were, contemplates; the atmosphere, as it were, contemplates; heaven, as it were, contemplates; water, as it were, contemplates; the mountains, as it were, contemplate; Gods and men, as it were, contemplate. Therefore the one who attains greatness among men has, so to say, a share in contemplation. Small-minded people are quarrelsome, wicked, and slanderous, whereas the excellent have, so to say, a share in contemplation. Meditate on contemplation.

6, 2. "He who meditates on contemplation as Brahman, his freedom will extend to the limits of the realm of contemplation, he who meditates on contemplation as Brahman."

"But, sir, is there anything greater than contemplation?"

"Yes, there is something greater than contemplation."

"Then please, sir, tell me about it!"

7, 1. "Wisdom, verily, is greater than contemplation. For by wisdom one knows the Ṛg Veda, the Yajur Veda, the Sāma Veda, the Atharva Veda as the fourth, the Ancient Stories as the fifth, the Veda of Vedas, the ritual for ancestors, calculus, augural sciences, the knowledge of the signs of the times, dialectics, ethics and political sciences, sacred knowledge, theology, knowledge of the spirits, military science, astrology, the science of snakes and of celestial beings; heaven and earth, air and atmosphere, water and fire, Gods and men, animals and birds, grass and trees, wild beasts, worms, flies and ants, right and wrong, true and false, good and bad, pleasant and unpleasant, food and drink, this world and the other—all these are known by wisdom. Meditate on wisdom.

7, 2. "He who meditates on wisdom as Brahman, he attains the worlds of wisdom and of knowledge. His freedom will extend to the limits of the realm of wisdom, he who meditates on wisdom as Brahman."

"But, sir, is there anything greater than wisdom?"

"Yes, there is something greater than wisdom."

"Then please, sir, tell me about it?"

8, 1. "Energy, verily, is greater than wisdom. For an energetic man makes a hundred wise men tremble. When a man is full of energy, he arises, and arising he serves [others], and while serving he worships. By worshiping he becomes a seer, a hearer, a thinker, an enlightened one, a doer, an understander. By energy is the earth established, by energy the atmosphere, by energy heaven, by energy the mountains, by energy are Gods and men established, by energy animals and birds, grass and trees, wild beasts, worms, flies and ants, by energy are the worlds established. Meditate on energy.

8, 2. "He who meditates on energy as Brahman, his freedom will extend to the limits of the realm of energy, he who meditates on energy as Brahman."

"But, sir, is there anything greater than energy?"

"Yes, there is something greater than energy."

"Then please, sir, tell me about it!"

10, 1. "Water, verily, is greater than food. Therefore, when there are no good rains, the living beings are afraid that food will be scarce. But when there are good rains, the living beings are happy [thinking], there will be much food. It is water in its different forms which is the earth, the atmosphere, heaven, the mountains, Gods and men, animals and birds, grass and trees, wild beasts, worms, flies and ants. All these forms are only water. Meditate on water.

10, 2. "He who meditates on water as Brahman, he obtains all desires and becomes fulfilled. His freedom will extend to the limits of the realm of water, he who meditates on water as Brahman."

"But, sir, is there anything greater than water?"

"Yes, there is something greater than water."

"Then please, sir, tell me about it!"

11, 1. "Radiance, verily, is greater than water. Therefore it seizes the air and heats the atmosphere. People say: it is hot, it is burning, it will rain. When the radiance has shown this first, the water is poured out. Then thunder rolls with lightning above and across [the sky]. Therefore they say: lightning flashes, it is thundering, it will rain. When the radiance has shown this first, the water is poured out. Meditate on radiance.

11, 2. "He who meditates on radiance as Brahman becomes radiant and attains radiant worlds, overcoming darkness. His freedom will extend to the limits of the realm of radiance, he who meditates on radiance as Brahman."

"But, sir, is there anything greater than radiance?"

"Yes, there is something greater than radiance."

"Then please, sir, tell me about it!"

12, 1. "Space, verily, is greater than radiance. For in space are the sun and the moon, lightning, the stars and fire. Through space one calls, through space one hears, through space one replies. In space one delights or one does not delight. In space one is born and onto space one is born. Meditate on space.

12, 2. "He who meditates on space as Brahman, he attains the worlds of space and light, unimpeded and far-reaching. His freedom will extend to the limits of the realm of space, he who meditates on space as Brahman."

"But, sir, is there anything greater than space?"

"Yes, there is something greater than space."

"Then please, sir, tell me about it!"

13, 1. "Memory, verily, is greater than space. For even if many people were to gather but had no memory, they would not hear anything or think or understand. But if they remember, then they would hear and think and understand. Through memory one recognizes one's sons and one's cattle. Meditate on memory.

13, 2. "He who meditates on memory as Brahman, his freedom will extend to the limits of the realm of memory, he who meditates on memory as Brahman."

"But, sir, is there anything greater than memory?"

"Yes, there is something greater than memory."

"Then please, sir, tell me about it!"

14, 1. "Hope, verily, is greater than memory. For with hope enkindled, memory learns the sacred hymns and performs sacred actions, desires sons and cattle, this world and the other. Meditate on hope.

14, 2. "He who meditates on hope as Brahman, all his desires will be fulfilled through hope, his prayers will not be in vain. His freedom will extend to the limits of the realm of hope, he who meditates on hope as Brahman."

"But, sir, is there anything greater than hope?"

"Yes, there is something greater than hope."

"Then please, sir, tell me about it!"

15, 1. "Life, assuredly, is greater than hope. For just as the spokes are fixed in the hub, so everything is fixed in life. Life is sustained by the life breath, the life breath gives life, it gives life to life. Life is the father, life is the mother, life is the brother, life is the sister, life is the teacher, life is the knower of Brahman.

15, 2. "If one answers harshly to one's father, mother, brother, sister, teacher, or to a Brahmin, people say: shame on you, you are killing your father, mother, brother, sister, teacher, you are a killer of a Brahmin.

15, 3. "But if life has departed from them and one gathers their bones with a stake and burns them completely, then people will not say, he is killing his father, mother, brother, sister, teacher, or he is a killer of a Brahmin.

15, 4. "All these [beings] are only life. He who sees, thinks, and understands it thus, he is a great speaker. If people tell him, 'You are a great speaker,' he should say, 'I am a great speaker.' He should not deny it.

16. "But only the one who speaks the truth speaks better than others."

"Let me, then, sir, speak the truth."

"First you must desire to comprehend truth."

"Sir, I do indeed desire to comprehend truth."

17. "Only if one understands can one speak truth. Without understanding one cannot speak the truth, for only after having understood can one speak the truth. But one should desire to comprehend knowledge."

"Sir, I do indeed desire to comprehend knowledge."

18. "Only if one thinks can one understand. Without thinking one cannot understand, for only after having thought does one understand. But one should desire to comprehend thought."

"Sir, I do indeed desire to comprehend thought."

21. "Only if one performs sacred actions does one persevere. Without sacred actions one cannot persevere, for only by sacred actions does one persevere. But one should desire to comprehend sacred actions."

"Sir, I do indeed desire to comprehend sacred actions."

22. "Only if one attains happiness does one perform sacred actions. One does not perform sacred actions if one is unhappy, for only having attained happiness does one perform sacred actions. But one should desire to comprehend happiness."

"Sir, I do indeed desire to comprehend happiness."

23. "Fullness, indeed, is happiness. In something limited there is no happiness; only in fullness is there happiness. One should desire to comprehend fullness."

"Sir, I do indeed desire to comprehend fullness."

24, 1. "Where one does not see another, or hear another, or know another—that is fullness. But where one sees another, hears another, knows another—that is limitation. That which is fullness is immortal, but that which is limited is mortal."

"In what, sir, is fullness established?"

"In its own greatness, or not even in greatness."

24, 2. "What is called greatness on earth consists of cows and horses, elephants and gold, servants and wives, fields and houses. I do not speak of this," he said, "for there one thing is depending upon another."

26, 1. The man who sees in this way, who thinks in this way, who knows in this way—from his *ātman* proceeds life, from his *ātman* hope, from his *ātman* memory, from his *ātman* space, from his *ātman* radiance, from his *ātman* water, from his *ātman* proceed the manifestation and disappearance [of the world], from his *ātman* proceeds food, from his *ātman* energy, from his *ātman* wisdom, from his *ātman* contemplation, from his *ātman* thought, from his *ātman* purpose, from his *ātman* mind, from his *ātman* the word, from his *ātman* name, from his *ātman* prayer, from his *ātman* sacred actions, from his *ātman* comes all this.

26, 2. On this there is a verse:

He who sees this does not see death;
he sees neither illness nor suffering.
He who sees this sees all that is,
he attains everything everywhere.

He is onefold, threefold, fivefold,
sevenfold, ninefold he becomes.
He is told to be elevenfold,
a hundred and elevenfold
and even twenty thousandfold.

The purity of food will procure the purity of the entire being. In purity of being will the whole tradition become firm. Tradition will liberate from all bondage.

To such a one [Nārada] purified from all impurities, the blessed Sanatkumāra shows the farther shore of darkness. He is called *skanda*, yes, he is called *skanda*.

TU II, 1

vi) *Om*. He who knows Brahman attains the Supreme. About this it has been said:

Brahman is truth, knowledge, and infinity,

hidden in the heart and in the highest heaven;
who thus knows Brahman obtains all desires,
he also obtains Brahman the wise.

From this *ātman* originated space, from space, air, from air, fire, from fire, water, from water, the earth, from the earth, the plants, from the plants, food, and from food, the person. This truly is the person that consists of the essence of food; this is his head, this, his right side, this, his left side; this is his self, this is his lower support.

KenU I, 1-9

vii)

1. Impelled by whom does the mind dart forth?
Directed by whom does life start on its way?
Incited by whom is the word we speak?
Who is the God who directs eye and ear?

2. The ear of the ear, the mind of the mind,
the word of the word and the breath of breath,
the eye of the eye—the wise, once liberated,
depart from this world and become immortal.

3-4. Thither the eye does not reach, or speech or mind. We do not know or understand how this can be taught. It is other than the known and beyond the unknown. Thus we have learnt from the sages of old who explained it to us.

5. That which cannot be expressed by words
but that by which the word is expressed—
this is Brahman, understand well,
and not what is worshiped here as such.

6. That which cannot be thought by the mind,
but that by which, they say, the mind is thought—
this is Brahman, understand well,
and not what is worshiped here as such.

7. That which cannot be seen by the eye,
but that by which the eyes have sight—
this is Brahman, understand well,
and not what is worshiped here as such.

8. That which cannot be heard by the ear
but that by which the ear has hearing—
this is Brahman, understand well,
and not what is worshiped here as such.

9. That which cannot be breathed by breath,
but that by which the breath can breathe—
this is Brahman, understand well,
and not what is worshiped here as such.

MundU II, 2, 1-2

viii) 1. Revealed and yet dwelling hidden in the cave
is that which is called the great Abode.
Whatever moves and breathes and blinks
is fixed therein. Know this as being
and also nonbeing, the desire of all hearts,
transcending knowledge, best beloved of every creature.

2. Burning as a flame and subtlest of the subtle,
in which are firmly fixed the worlds and all their peoples—
that is the imperishable Brahman. That is life
and word and spirit, the true, the immortal!
That, my friend, is to be known—know that!

▪ i) Nothing is prior to: *apūrva,* unprecedented, unparalleled, incomparable.
Nothing is beyond: *a-para,* rather than *apara,* having something after it.

▪ ii) This Upaniṣad appears to be another, more elaborate version of the story told in BU III, 6, which ended with Yājñavalkya's warning to Gārgī not to question beyond the limit (*atipraśna*), otherwise her head would fall off. Cf. BU III, 9, 26 (§ VI 5).

1. Vācaknavī is the patronymic of Gārgī.
Debates about Brahman: *brahmodya*; the Vedic *brahmodya* consists of riddles which have to be solved, the intellectual part of sacrifice, as it were. In the Upaniṣadic period these riddles developed into proper theological discussions.

2. Gārgī's attitude is more aggressive than searching. There are two kinds of dialogue in the U: the challenge by a partner who does not feel himself inferior to the questioned person, and the humble quest of a disciple at the feet of his master.

3. Warp and woof: *tad otaṁ ca protaṁ ca,* again the ancient image of weaving, referring to the texture of the universe.

4. Space: *ākāśa,* empty atmosphere as the state of everything.

8. Imperishable: *akṣara.* What follows seems to be a description of *nirguṇa brahman* in Vedāntic terms.

9. The Gods the sacrificer: *yajamānaṁ devāḥ*; the order seems to be reversed, but actually it reveals the interdependence of *yajamāna* and *devaḥ*.
Offering to the dead: *darvī.*

10. His efforts will be in vain: *antavad evāsya tad bhavati,* lit. his efforts will have an end, they will not be fruitful.
Wretched: *kṛpaṇa,* miserable, pitiable.

11. Cf. BU III, 7, 23 (§ VI 5).

12. At the price of paying him homage: *namaskāreṇa,* by bowing to him (without any further discussion).

▪ iii) Consciousness: *vijñāna,* knowledge.
Joy: *ānanda,* bliss.
Brahman is the goal of both the active and the contemplative lives.

▪ iv) Truth: *satya,* reality.
Wonderful genius: *yakṣa.*

▪ v) The concepts identified with Brahman are: *nāman, vāc, manas, saṁkalpa, citta, dhyāna, vijñāna, bala, anna, āpaḥ, tejas, ākāśa, smara, āśā, prāṇa, satya, mati, śraddhā, niṣṭhā, kṛti, sukha, bhūman, ātman.*

1, 2. Ancient Stories: *itihāsa-purāṇa,* epic and ancient lore.
Veda of Vedas: *vedānāṁ veda,* i.e., grammar.
Ritual for ancestors: *pitrya,* rites for the dead, the manes.
Calculus: *rāśi,* mathematics, arithmetic, science of numbers.
Augural sciences: *daiva,* divination, sciences of portents, of divine exploits, mantics.
The knowledge of the signs of the times: *nidhi,* chronology, the science of time.
Dialectics: *vākovākya,* logic.
Ethics and political sciences: *ekāyana,* politics, rules for behavior, worldly wisdom.
Sacred knowledge: *deva-vidyā,* etymology and philology.
Theology: *brahma-vidyā,* sacred wisdom, knowledge of the sacred texts, spirituality, and contemplation.
Knowledge of the spirits: *bhūta-vidyā,* science of ghosts, demonology.
Military science: *kṣatra-vidyā,* knowledge of archery, of war, of rulership.
Astrology: *nakṣatra-vidyā,* astronomy, science of the stars.

Science of snakes and celestial beings: *sarpa-devajana-vidyā,* the knowledge of serpents and half-gods or muses, man-gods (*jana-deva*).

According to commentators, all these are fine arts. A similar but shorter list appears in BU II, 4, 10 (§ VI 4); IV, 1, 2; IV, 5, 11. Most of the translations of these words rely on Śaṅkara's commentary.

1, 3a. Cf. § IV 6.

1, 4. Meditate on the name: *nāma upāssva.* Some translators prefer to explain the sentence in relation to the immediately following *sa yo nāma brahma iti upāste,* i.e., "he who meditates [or considers] name [or the names] as Brahman." In that case it would mean to take the right attitude or proper vision regarding the value of names. "Reverence or revere the name" is also a common translation.

1, 5. Freedom: *kāmacāra,* "movement at will."

2, 1. Cf. § I 14.

3, 1. When one by his mind puts into his mind: *sa yadā manasā manasyati,* if one by his mind has a mind to . . .

Sacred hymns: mantras.

Sacred actions: *karmāṇi,* sacrifices, rituals.

Mind is verily the *ātman.* This sentence and the two following ones break the flow of the progressive teaching and may well be an interpolation.

4, 1. Purpose: *saṁkalpa,* conception, will, thought.

Become one: *ekaṁ bhavanti,* i.e., the mantras (sacred hymns) are included in name as the *karmāṇi* (sacred actions) in the mantras.

4, 2. Union: *ekāyanāni,* merge into, find their focal point, are centered (in purpose). Cf. BU II, 4, 11 (§ VI 4).

Heaven and earth . . .: *samakḷpatāṁ dyāvāpṛthivī;* the phrase is repeated using the verb *sam-kḷp-* in its different forms.

5, 1. Thought: *citta,* intelligence, reflection.

5, 2. Want to listen: *śuśrūṣante,* suggesting obedience and following.

6, 1. Contemplation: *dhyāna.*

The earth, as it were, contemplates . . .: *dhyāyatīva pṛthivī;* the *iva* could be understood as "unconsciously, by nature," i.e., by the restful being of all things. *Dhyāna* would then be the ecstatic, unreflective, unselfconscious attitude, while *vijñāna* (7, 1) is the conscious understanding.

A share in contemplation: *aṁśa.* Human greatness is nothing but participation in the cosmic act of contemplation.

7, 1. Wisdom: *vijñāna,* understanding, discernment.

Right and wrong: *dharma, adharma.*

8, 1. Energy: *bala,* strength, power, force.

Worships: *upa- sad-,* whence *upaniṣad,* to approach (a *guru*), to sit near, hence to revere, to worship. It is by sitting near the *guru,* after having served him, that a disciple becomes wise. He becomes a pupil, a man near to and familiar with wisdom.

9, 1-2. Cf. § II 11.

11, 1. Radiance: *tejas,* the brilliance or heat of the sun, fire. Cf § III A.

12, 1. Space: *ākāśa,* the atmosphere or ether. *Ākāśa* is the medium of sound.

13, 1. Memory: *smara.*

14, 1. Hope: *āśā,* the driving force of religious and secular actions.

15, 1. Life: *prāṇa.*

Life is the father . . .: these identifications obviously illustrate that all these people are sustained by *prāṇa.*

15, 2. This and the following verse seem to say that life (*prāṇa*) is not the body of a person but his soul. To speak harshly to one's own people is to kill them, rather than the act of burning their dead bodies (v. 3).

15, 4. A great speaker: *ativādin,* a master of speech, a dialectician, a sophist. The word also has a pejorative meaning as in MundU III, 1, 4.

This passage is unlike all the previous ones in that Nārada does not ask further, and yet the teaching proceeds deeper and deeper.

19-20. Cf. § I 37.

21. Sacred actions: *karoti, kṛtvā, kṛti,* all forms of the verb *kṛ-,* to do, to act. The action is here not just any act, but the liturgical act, the sacrifice.

22. Happiness: *sukha,* bliss, pleasure, here more the internal joy of man when in harmony with the entire universe.

23. Fullness: *bhūman,* infinity, plenitude of being.

Limited: *alpa,* lit. small.

24, 1. Where one does not see another: *yatra nānyat paśyati,* where one does not see anything else. Cf. BU IV, 3, 31; IV, 5, 15 (§ III 28).

25, 1-2. Cf. § VI 8.

26, 1. Prayer: *mantrāḥ,* sacred hymns.

26, 2. Cf. MaitU V, 2, for the analogous idea of the manifold development of the *ātman.*

Purity of food: *āhāra-śuddhi.*
Purity of the entire being: *sattva-śuddhi.*
The whole tradition . . .: *dhruvā smṛtiḥ.* One could also translate *smṛti* as memory.
All bondage: *sarva-granthīnām,* all knots (of the heart, of doubts, of bondage).
Skanda: lit. he who jumps (to the farther shore). Cf. MundU II, 2, 6 for the same sentence about the shore (§ VI 5).

▪ vi) Truth: *satya.*
Knowledge: *jñāna,* intelligence corresponding to the *cit* of the later formulation *sac-cid-ānanda.*
Infinity: *ananta,* which later was transformed into *ānanda,* bliss.
Hidden in the heart: *nihitaṁ guhāyām*: cf. also KathU I, 14, (§ V 27); II, 20 (§ V 5); III, 1; IV, 6-7 (§§ VII 40; 44); MundU II, 1, 10 (§ VI 7); III, 1, 7.
The wise: *vipaścit,* intelligent.
Person . . . of the essence of food: *puruṣo anna-rasa-mayaḥ,* the lowest, material layer of the person. The text ends announcing: On this there is a *śloka.*
2. Cf. § II 11.
3-5. Cf. § VI 7.
6-7. Cf. § I 7.
8-9. Cf. § VI 7.

▪ vii) 1. The interrogative pronoun *kena* ("by whom?") has been adopted as the name of this U.
Life: *prāṇa,* the first (*prathama*) among all organs; cf. CU I, 2, 7 etc.
Word: *vāc*; cf. AV X, 8, 33 (§ VII 27); AB II, 5 (VI, 5).
2. Wise: *dhīrāḥ,* i.e., those who know the replies to the questions of v. 1.
Once liberated: *atimucya,* once freed from the mere appearances furnished by the ear, mind, etc.
3. Cf. KathU VI, 12 (§ VI 9); TU II, 9 (§ VI 7).
4. Cf.IsU 10; 13 (§§ VII 21; 26).

▪ viii) 1. Cf. AV X, 8, 6 (§ VII 27).
Revealed: *āviḥ,* manifest.
Abode: *pada,* a word with many meanings: step, place, support, word, symbol, etc. Here the conception of the "third step of Viṣṇu" comes to mind, which, from the RV onward, means heaven or the supreme state (cf. § I 27).
Desire of all hearts: *vareṇya* (cf. the Gāyatrī mantra). Best beloved: *variṣṭha,* the highest. (Or, if one relates *prajānām* to *paraṁ vijñānāt,* it would read: "beyond the knowledge of people, the highest.")
2. Life and word and spirit: *prāṇa, vāc, manas,* the triad representing Man.
3-4. Cf. § VI 12.
5-8. Cf. § VI 5.
9. Cf. § VI 11.
10-11. Cf. § III 6.

Consciousness *Prajñāna*

4 The long discourse of the proud Brahmin Dṛpta Bālāki on Brahman (i) shows a trend of thought in the Upaniṣads whereby Brahman is supposed to be reached by identifying it with different cosmic and human manifestations of the *puruṣa.* As Ajātaśatru, king of Kāśī, confirms, to meditate on these various identifications is not just barren speculation. But none of these meditations is able to make Brahman known, and here ends the wisdom of the Brahmin. It is the Kṣatriya who now has to teach the Brahmin, by taking his hand and showing him a sleeping man. Only direct experience can convey the ultimate message. The message is that consciousness does not depend on Man's state of waking but that it is ever present in him, in whatever state he may be. For only out of consciousness

arise vital breaths and with them the worlds and the Gods, and consciousness that is Brahman leads us to the discovery of the *ātman*.

To grasp consciousness means to grasp the player of the instrument, and not its sounds, and yet consciousness remains ungraspable because it penetrates everything like salt in water (ii). Yājñavalkya's instruction remains paradoxical for his wife Maitreyī, and it is only in a paradoxical way that this truth is understood.

The following texts describe the direction we have to take in order to discover pure consciousness: we must seek not to understand the objects, but the subject, the speaker, the hearer, the thinker (iv). This subject cannot be treated as an object. Thus we arrive at the fundamental paradox of consciousness: its purity is destroyed by self-consciousness (v). Pure consciousness cannot be dualistic, but Advaitic knowledge is really ineffable (vi). Consciousness is not *vāc*, the word, but that which permits the word to be.

Prajñāna

BU II, 1

i) 1. Dṛpta Bālāki was a learned man of the Gārgya family. He said to Ajātaśatru of Kāśī: "Let me expound Brahman to you."

Ajātaśatru said to him: "For such a speech I will give you a thousand [cows]. For people come running [to me], shouting, 'Janaka, Janaka!' "

2. Then Gārgya said: "The Person who is there in the sun, on him do I meditate as Brahman."

Ajātaśatru said: "Oh, please do not tell me about him! I meditate on him as the all-surpassing, the head and the king of all beings. He who meditates on him thus becomes himself all-surpassing, the head and the king of all beings."

3. Then Gārgya said: "The Person who is there in the moon, on him do I meditate as Brahman."

Ajātaśatru said: "Oh, please do not tell me about him! I meditate on him as the great, white-robed king Soma. He who meditates on him thus, for him the Soma is daily poured out and poured forth. His food will not come to an end."

4. Then Gārgya said: "The Person who is there in lightning, on him do I meditate as Brahman."

Ajātaśatru said: "Oh, please do not tell me about him! I meditate on him as the one full of radiance. He who meditates on him thus will become radiant and his offspring also will be radiant."

5. Then Gārgya said: "The Person who is there in space, on him do I meditate as Brahman."

   Ajātaśatru said: "Oh, please do not tell me about him! I meditate on him as the full and the immutable. He who meditates on him thus will attain fullness of offspring and cattle, and his people will not vanish from this world."

6. Then Gārgya said: "The Person who is in the mind, on him do I meditate as Brahman."

   Ajātaśatru said: "Oh, please do not tell me about him! I meditate on him as Indra Vaikuṇṭha whose army is invincible. He who meditates on him thus will be victorious, invincible, and an overpowerer of his enemies."

7. Then Gārgya said: "The Person who is in the fire, on him do I meditate as Brahman."

   Ajātaśatru said: "Oh, please do not tell me about him! I meditate on him as the resistant one. He who meditates on him thus will become resistant, and his people too will become resistant."

8. Then Gārgya said: "The Person who is in the water, on him do I meditate as Brahman."

   Ajātaśatru said: "Oh, please do not tell me about him! I meditate on him as the beautiful one. He who meditates on him thus as the beautiful, will be approached only by what is beautiful, not by the ugly, and from him only the beautiful will be born."

9. Then Gārgya said: "The Person who is here in the mirror, on him do I meditate as Brahman."

   Ajātaśatru said: "Oh, please do not tell me about him! I meditate on him as the shining one. He who meditates on him thus becomes himself shining and his offspring will be shining. He will be more shining than those who approach him."

10. Then Gārgya said: "The sound that follows someone when he walks, on him do I meditate as Brahman."

    Ajātaśatru said: "Oh, please do not tell me about him! I meditate on him as life. He who meditates on him thus will attain his full life span in this world and he will not meet an untimely death."

11. Then Gārgya said: "The Person who is in the regions of space, on him do I meditate as Brahman."

    Ajātaśatru said: "Oh, please do not tell me about him! I meditate on him as the inseparable companion. He who meditates on him thus will have a companion and his company will not be separated from him."

12. Then Gārgya said: "The Person who consists of shadow, on him do I meditate as Brahman."

Ajātaśatru said: "Oh, please do not tell me about him! I meditate on him as death. He who meditates on him thus will attain his full life span in this world and he will not meet an untimely death."

13. Then Gārgya said: "The Person who is here in the body [*ātman*], on him do I meditate as Brahman."

Ajātaśatru said: "Do not tell me about him! I meditate on him as one who is endowed with a body [*ātman*]. He who meditates on him thus will be endowed with a body and his offspring also will be endowed with a body." After this Gārgya kept silent.

14. Then Ajātaśatru said: "Is this all?" "This is all," replied Gārgya. "With merely this much [Brahman] is not known," observed Ajātaśatru. Then Gārgya said: "Let me come to you as a disciple."

15. Ajātaśatru said: "This is the wrong order of things that a Brahmin should approach a Kṣatriya as a disciple, to learn about Brahman. Yet I desire to instruct you."

He took his hand and they both got up. They approached a man who was asleep. Ajātaśatru addressed him by the name: great, white-robed king Soma, but he did not get up. He woke him up with his hand and he got up.

16. Then Ajātaśatru said: "When this man was asleep, where was his conscious spirit, whence did it return?" And Gārgya did not know.

17. Then Ajātaśatru said: "When this man was asleep, his conscious spirit, having assumed into himself by his consciousness the consciousness of all the life powers [*prāṇāḥ*], was dwelling in the inner space within the heart. When he holds these [life powers], then a person is said to be asleep. When his breath is withheld, his speech is withheld, his eye is withheld, his ear is withheld, his mind is withheld.

18. "When he moves about in a dream, these are his worlds. There he becomes like a king or a great brahmin; he enters, so to say, on conditions high or low. And just as a king, taking his people, moves in his country as he wishes, so also this [person], taking his life powers, moves in his own body as he wishes.

19. "Now when he is in a state of deep sleep, when he does not know anything, then the seventy-two thousand arteries called *hitāḥ* move from the heart to the pericardium. Entering into them, he rests in the pericardium. Just as a young man or a king or a great brahmin might rest, when experiencing extreme joy, so does he rest.

20. "As a spider, advancing, produces thread and as small sparks spring forth from fire, so from this *ātman* spring forth all sense powers, all

worlds, all Gods, all beings. This secret doctrine is the truth of the real. The vital breaths are the real; the *ātman* is their truth."

BU II, 4, 7-14

ii) 7. "Just as when a drum is beaten one cannot take hold of the external sounds, but when one takes hold of the drum or of the drum beater, one takes hold of the sounds also.

8. "Just as when a conch is blown one cannot take hold of the external sounds, but when one takes hold of the conch or of the conch blower, one takes hold of the sounds also.

9. "Just as when a lute is played one cannot take hold of the external sounds, but when one takes hold of the lute or of the lute player, one takes hold of the sounds also.

10. "As when a fire is lit with damp fuel, different clouds of smoke come forth, in the same way from this great Being are breathed forth the Ṛg Veda, Yajur Veda, Sāma Veda, Atharva Veda, the epics and the Purāṇas, the sciences and the Upaniṣads, the verses, the aphorisms, the explanations and the commentaries. From this all these are breathed out.

11. "And just as the ocean is the one meeting place of all the waters, so the skin is the one meeting place of all kinds of touch, the nose is the one meeting place of all the smells, the tongue is the one meeting place of all the tastes, the eye is the one meeting place of all the forms, the ear is the one meeting place of all the sounds, the mind is the one meeting place of all the thoughts, the heart is the one meeting place of all knowledge, the hands are the one meeting place of all actions, the generative organ is the one meeting place of all delights, the anus is the one meeting place of all excretions, the feet are the one meeting place of all movements, the Word is the one meeting place of all the Vedas.

12. "Just as a lump of salt thrown into water dissolves and there is no means of taking hold of it, but from wherever one may take water, it is altogether salty, so, in truth, this great, infinite, unlimited Being is a compact mass of wisdom. [At death] one rises up from these elements [composing the body] and dissolves into them again, for after death there is no consciousness. This, my dear, is what I have to tell you."

Thus spoke Yājñavalkya.

13. Maitreyī said to him: "With this you have confused me, saying that after death there is no consciousness."

He replied: "I have not said anything confusing; what I say is for your instruction."

14. "Where there seems to be a duality, there one smells another, one sees another, one hears another, one talks to another, one thinks of another, one knows another. But when all has become the *ātman* alone, then by

what and whom should one smell, by what and whom should one see, by what and whom should one hear, by what and to whom should one talk, by what and of whom should one think, by what and whom should one know? By what could one know that by which all this is known? By what is it possible to know the Knower?"

AU III

iii) 1. "Who is the one on whom we meditate as the *ātman*? Which one is the *ātman*?"

"He is that by which one sees, that by which one hears, that by which one smells scents, that by which one utters a word, that by which one distinguishes sweet from bitter.

2. "That which is the heart, moreover, is spirit, it is comprehension, perception, discrimination, knowledge, wisdom, intuition, stability, thought, intelligence, impulse, memory, imagination, purpose, life, desire, will—all these are different names of consciousness.

3. "He is Brahman, he is Indra, he is Prajāpati and all these Gods. He is the five elements, earth, wind, space, water, light; he is all things that are combinations, as it were, of subtle elements, and all things that are born from a seed or from an egg or from a womb, from sweat or from a seedling; horses, cattle, men, elephants, whatever breathes on earth, whatever moves or flies or stands still—all these are guided by wisdom and founded on consciousness. The world is guided by wisdom, it has its foundation in wisdom. *Consciousness is Brahman.*"

4. By means of this conscious *ātman* [the sage] arose from this world. Then, having fulfilled all his desires in the heavenly world, he became immortal; yes, immortal he became.

KausU III, 8

iv) It is not speech that one should seek to understand; one should know the speaker.

It is not scent that one should seek to understand; one should know the one who smells.

It is not the appearance [of things] that one should seek to understand; one should know the one who sees.

It is not sound that one should seek to understand; one should know the one who hears.

It is not the taste of food that one should seek to understand; one should know the one who tastes the food.

It is not action that one should seek to understand; one should know the one who acts.

It is not joy and suffering that one should seek to understand; one should know the one who experiences joy and suffering.

It is not bliss, delight, and procreative power that one should seek to understand; one should know the one who experiences bliss, delight, and procreative power.

It is not movement that one should seek to understand; one should know the one who moves.

It is not the mind that one should seek to understand; one should know the one who thinks.

For all these ten degrees of existence depend upon consciousness, and the ten degrees of consciousness depend upon existence. Indeed, if there were no degrees of existence, there would be no degrees of consciousness, and if there were no degrees of consciousness, there would be no degrees of existence, for nothing whatever originates out of the one without the other.

In this there is no plurality. For just as the rim of a chariot wheel is fixed onto the spokes and the spokes are fixed onto the hub, so the degrees of existence are established on the degrees of consciousness, and the degrees of consciousness are established on life. This life is the conscious *ātman*, blissful, ageless, immortal.

KenU II, 1-3

v)

1. If you think that you know it well,
you know very little—just a form of Brahman,
the form that is in you or in the Gods.
Investigate, then, what you do not know.

2. I do not think that I know it well,
nor do I think that I know it not.
The one of us who knows it, knows;
he knows not that he does not know.

3. He by whom it is not conceived, by him it is conceived.
He by whom it is conceived, he does not know!
It is not understood by those who understand;
it is understood by those who do not understand!

MaitU VI, 7

vi) Thus it has been declared:

When there is a dualistic consciousness, the *ātman* hears, sees, smells, tastes, and touches all things and is conscious of it. When there is a nondualistic consciousness, it [the *ātman*] is free from effect, cause, and action; it is unutterable, unique, indescribable. What is it? It is ineffable!

■ i) Cf. KausU IV, 1-20 (§§ V 27; VI 5).

1. Kāśī: today's Vārāṇasī (Benares).

Janaka, Janaka: King Ajātaśatru may be compared with the illustrious king Janaka because of his generosity and his knowledge, by which he surpasses the Brahmin although he is a Kṣatriya (v. 15).

2. Person . . . in the sun: *asāv āditye puruṣaḥ*, the cosmological definition of the *puruṣa* or Brahman.

Do not tell me about him: the verb *sam-vad-* (to converse) is used with the locative (*etasmin*).

All-surpassing: *atiṣṭhāḥ*.

3. White-robed king Soma: *pāṇḍara-vāsāḥ somo rājā*, one of the manifestations of the *puruṣa* as light (cf. BU II, 3, 6 (§ VI 7). The personification of the moon.

6. Indra Vaikuṇṭha: cf. RV X, 47-50, where the name refers either to Indra or to a *ṛṣi*. In RV X, 48, 11, Indra is also called *aparājita* (invincible).

7. Fire: Agni.

Resistant: *viṣāsahi*; cf. RV X, 166, 1.

8. Beautiful: *pratirūpa*, reflection (in the water).

10. Life: *asu*, vital life.

12. Person who consists of shadow: *chāyāmayaḥ puruṣaḥ*.

13. In this instance *ātman* clearly refers to the body.

15. The teaching of the Brahmin is only theoretical, whereas that of the Kṣatriya is practical.

Great, white-robed king Soma: a name of the *puruṣa* (cf. v. 3).

16. Conscious spirit: *vijñānamayaḥ puruṣaḥ*, lit. the Person consisting of consciousness.

19. State of deep sleep: *suṣuptaḥ*. Cf. MandU 5.

20. Cf. MundU I, 1, 7 (§ I 7).

Secret doctrine: *upaniṣad*.

Vital breaths: *prāṇāḥ*, sense powers.

The truth of the real: *satyasya satyam*. This translation points out the difference between the two *satyas*.

■ ii) Cf. § III 31 for BU IV, 5, 1-3 (similar to BU II, 4, 1-3).

4-6. Cf. § VI 5.

The similes of vv. 7-9 suggest that the *ātman* is the instrument or its player, and the whole world is the sound or music (for the background cf. YV XXX, 19 [§ II 28]).

9. Lute: *vīṇā*.

10. From this great Being: *mahato bhūtasya*; cf. v. 12. Here not only the four Vedas but also all categories of contemporary literature are included in the direct "revelation."

11. One meeting place: *ekāyana*, one goal, resting place, etc.; cf. CU VII, 4, 2 (§ VI 3). Although it is not explicitly stated, the conclusion of this series is that the *ātman* is the one goal of all the senses (*indriyas*). Cf. BU I, 4, 7; CU VIII, 12, 4 (§ VI 6); etc.

12. Cf. BU IV, 5, 13; CU VI, 13 (§ VI 10).

Compact mass of wisdom: *vijñānaghana*, "mass of knowledge," i.e., wisdom through and through. Cf. *prajñānaghana* in BU IV, 5, 13.

Consciousness: *saṁjñā*.

13. Cf. BU IV, 5, 14, where Yājñavalkya adds that the *ātman* is indestructible.

14. Cf. BU III, 4, 2 (§ VI 6); IV, 3, 7; IV, 4, 19 (§ VI 11).

Duality: *dvaitam iva*.

The *ātman* is the subject and not the object of knowledge. Cf. BU IV, 5, 15 (§ III 28) for a parallel passage.

■ iii) 1. For the inquiry about the *ātman*, cf. CU V, 11, 1, etc.

2. Heart: *hṛdaya*.

Spirit: *manas*, mind.

The series of terms that follow are all forms of consciousness (*prajñāna*): *saṁjñāna, ājñāna, vijñāna, prajñāna, medhā, dṛṣṭi, mati, manīṣā, jūti, smṛti, saṁkalpa, kratu, asu, kāma, vāśa*.

3. Combinations . . . of subtle elements: *kṣudra-miśrāṇi*.

Guided by wisdom: *prajñā-netram*.

Founded on consciousness: *prajñāne pratiṣṭhitam*. The terms *prajñā* and *prajñāna* suggest the meanings of consciousness, intelligence, and wisdom.

Consciousness is Brahman: *prajñānaṁ brahma*, the *mahāvākya*. Cf. TU II, 5 (§ VI 7).

4. The sage: Vāmadeva, mentioned in AU II, 1, 5 (§ I 34),

■ iv) Speech: *vāc*.

Appearance [of things]: *rūpa*, form, shape.

Joy and suffering: *sukha-duḥkha*.

Degrees of existence: *bhūta-mātrāḥ*, elements of being.
Consciousness: *prajñā*.
The text stresses the interdependence of sense organs and their conscious agent.
No plurality: lit. not many.
Life: *prāṇa*, breath of life.
Conscious *ātman*: *prajñātman*.

■ v) 1. Form of Brahman: *brahmaṇo rūpam*.

That is in you . . .: *yad asya tvaṁ yad asya deveṣu; tvam* stands for *tvayi*. The pupil knows only the manifestation of Brahman in himself and in the Gods whom he worships.

What you do not know: another version reads *manye viditam* (the student adding), "I think that I know it."

2. *nāhaṁ manye suvedeti*
no na vedeti veda ca
yo nas tad veda tad veda
no na vedeti veda ca.

3. *yasyāmataṁ tasya mataṁ*
mataṁ yasya na veda saḥ
avijñātaṁ vijānatāṁ
vijñātam avijānatām.

Cf. § VI A b.
4-5. Cf. § VI 11.

■ vi) Cf. BU II, 4, 14 (ii).
Is conscious of it: knows it.
Cf. the Gāyatrī (Introduction) for the beginning of this text.
Nondualistic consciousness: *(a)dvaitībhūtaṁ vijñānam* (wisdom, knowledge).
Free from effect, cause, and action: *kārya-kāraṇa-karma-nirmuktam*.
Unutterable: *nirvacana*, wordless, unpronounceable.
Unique: *anaupamya*, incomparable, unparalleled.
Ineffable: *avācya*, inexpressible, unspeakable.
Advaitic knowledge is ultimate and thus has no further point of reference; it is Brahman.

B. THE INTERNAL WAY

Puruṣo 'ntarātmā

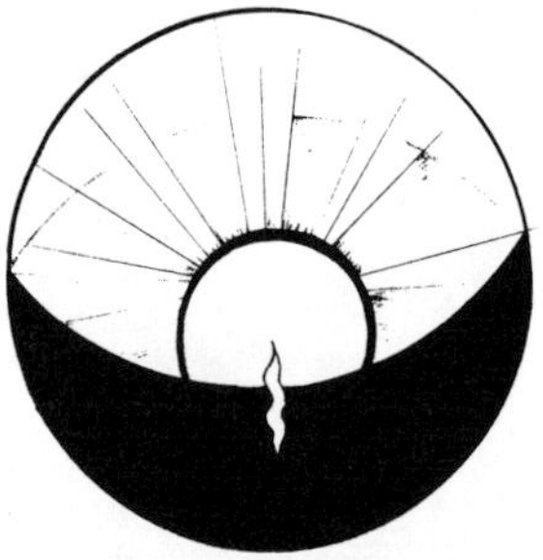

Who am I?

AU I, 3, 11

Consciousness cannot always be ecstatic, that is, it cannot be constantly without a support, a substance, a thinking subject. It is all very well to denounce the subject-object dichotomy, to undermine the two pillars and let them both (subject and object) collapse and disappear. You may then discover pure consciousness, without an object and without a subject. But can we really cast off the ladder that has helped us to ascend to such heights? Even if it is possible, once you have climbed the highest peaks you will be obliged to descend, though probably not by the same path you took when marching toward the unknown. The valley also belongs to reality.

We descend by a sort of interior path. We discover, as we proceed, the only two possible subjects to that utterly simple consciousness which still maintains unpolluted the clarity of the One: the *ātman* and the *aham*, the third person and the first. Brahman: He is—and I am saying it (inasmuch as the *ātman* says it). This descent is the path we now follow.

Here also, as in the first section, the double title is intended to express the dynamism of this second movement. It is an internal path, a way of interiorization. The Kaṭha Upaniṣad from which the Sanskrit title is taken[42] has another passage in which the *antarātman* is also mentioned. This passage suggests that the movement of the *svayaṁbhū* or Self-existent is toward the exterior, whereas the dynamism of the seeker who desires immortality is inward.[43] This *antarātman* or inner soul of everything[44] is a *puruṣa,* a person. That is what we are going to see in this descent into the depths.

a) The Discovery of the Ground

Ātman brahman

Speculation about the One may sound very abstract and the considerations about Brahman may seem utterly remote from life. It does not need to be that way, except when, for the sake of brevity, all is said, as it were, in code. This *mahāvākya* does not permit us to view it from any distant or abstract vantage point, because it intimately concerns each one of us and confronts us with an inescapable existential challenge. From now on the meditation has a markedly personalistic character. Indeed, whereas the discovery of consciousness may be an impersonal truth, the following *mahāvākyas* could be said to constitute the unfolding of the mystery of the person in all its dimensions.

We are not concerned here with studying the evolution of the concepts of *brahman* and *ātman,* how the one from one end of the spectrum of Man's experience and the other from the opposite one, after an extraordinary adventure that touches the shores of almost the whole of reality, come to a meeting point.[45] *Ātman,* alone in the Upaniṣads, means the body,[46] the vital divine breath,[47] awareness,[48] the subject of all sensations[49] and of everything,[50] the inde-

42. Cf. KathU VI, 17 (§ V 5).
43. Cf. KathU IV, 1 (§ VII 36).
44. Cf. KathU V, 9 (§ VI 2).
45. Most of the texts are given in this part. The following footnotes serve only as an orientation.
46. Cf. BU I, 4, 17 (§ I 7); I, 6, 3 (§ V A b Introduction); II, 1, 13 (§ VI 4); CU VIII, 8, 1 (§ VI 6); TU II, 1 (§ VI 3); etc.
47. Cf. BU I, 5, 20 (§ IV 21); KausU III, 2 (§ II 6); etc.
48. Cf. KausU IV, 20 (§ VI 5); etc.
49. Cf. BU I, 4, 7; III, 4, 1 sq. (§ VI 6); KausU III, 8 (§ VI 4); etc.
50. Cf. BU III, 7, 3 sq. (§ VI 5); etc.

pendent active subject,[51] the real self in and of Man,[52] the self of the world,[53] the subject of all spiritual actions as well as the subject of cosmic consciousness,[54] and finally Brahman.[55] It begins by meaning the immediate subject or self in a concrete empirical way and it ends by meaning the ultimate subject or self of the whole of reality. *Brahman,* on the other hand, starts its intriguing career as a concept meaning prayer and from there goes on to mean the basic hymns of the *śruti*[56] as well as the *śruti* in its entirety,[57] ritual, and thence an immanent cosmic force,[58] the all-present,[59] spiritual,[60] creator of the world,[61] the entire universe[62] and its ultimate ground,[63] until as the culmination of this whole process the *ātman-brahman* identity is disclosed. It begins by meaning the most concrete form of sacred utterance and it ends by meaning the most general and ultimate source of everything.

To understand the equation *ātman-brahman* we must transcend both mathematical or pure logical thinking and physical or pure empirical thinking. Logically and empirically speaking, if *ātman* stands for something and Brahman is not just a synonym for it the two cannot be equated. But human forms of awareness are not exhausted by dialectical or empirical thinking. It has been said either that *ātman-brahman* is a logical monstrosity only possible in an unmitigated monism or that it is a barren tautology. We would like to show that neither of these views represents the truth.

It is, in fact, a qualified tautology, as every ultimate principle is bound to be. If it were not a tautology it could not be an independent principle. It would require some other ground on which to depend. If "S is P" were not self-illuminating or self-evident it would demand another principle as its basis, and so on ad infinitum. But the tautology has to be qualified if it is to be more than a

51. Cf. BU IV, 3, 7; CU VIII, 3, 3 (§ VI 6); AU I, 3, 11 (§ VI B Antiphon); etc.
52. Cf. BU III, 7, 3 sq. (§ VI 5); etc.
53. Cf. BU I, 4, 7; 16 (§ III 27); II, 1, 20 (§ VI 4); II, 4, 5-6 (§ VI 5); etc.
54. Cf. BU III, 4, 1 (§ VI 6); III, 7, 23 (§ VI 5); II, 8, 11; IV, 3, 7; CU VIII, 12, 4 sq. (§ VI 6); etc.
55. Cf. CU III, 14, 4 (§ VI 6); etc.
56. Cf. Limiting ourselves to the Upaniṣads; cf. CU I, 7, 5; etc.
57. Cf. BU I, 5, 17 (§ VI 8); CU III, 5, 2; etc.
58. Cf. BU II, 5, 1 (§ VI 6); CU III, 19, 1; etc.
59. Cf. BU V, 3, 1; CU III, 14, 1 (§ VI 6); etc.
60. Cf. BU II, 5, 19 (§ VI 6); III, 9, 28 (§ VI 3); TU II, 5, 1 (§ VI 7); KathU V, 6 (§ V 5).
61. Cf. CU VI, 2, 1 sq. (§ VI 2); VI, 3, 2; TU II, 6 (§ I 7); etc.
62. Cf. BU I, 4, 5 (§ I 7); II, 3, 1 sq. (§ VI 7); etc.
63. Cf. TU III, 1 (§ II 11); etc.

barren identity. It needs a certain dynamism, a certain tension within the principle itself, so as to make it a real principle, that is, productive, really saying something, bringing a message. It is precisely this saying, this *vāc,* which converts the tautology into a principle, which performs the passage from myth into Logos, from something instinctively or unconsciously taken for granted to a reflective knowledge and a critical intuition. Any principle or anything that is irreducible to anything else and thus rests upon itself has to express an identity, but the very expression of it is already a breaking of that identity. The affirmation of the identity is based on the qualified identity which is such insofar as it "breaks," thus expressing itself.

The equation *ātman-brahman* can be understood only as a qualified identity, that is, as a qualified tautology. What is this "qualification" that allows us to intuit the identity? We may try to "qualify" it a little more, hoping for the insight to "break." We shall limit ourselves to describing the internal dynamism that leads from the nondualistic conception of reality and the discovery that the ultimate ground of everything is consciousness to the insight that this consciousness, which is Brahman, needs an ultimate subject, which is *ātman.*

We are already acquainted with the question concerning the desire to see the seer of seeing and to think the thinker of thinking. No weight of logic can suppress or stifle Man's desire in this regard. You certainly cannot know the knower, but you can do more than just know the "known"; you can know along with the knower, you can become the knower, so that you no longer need to know the knower because you have become the knower himself. This movement of the human spirit leads from the impersonal to the personal, from the theological to the existential. This movement triggers off the search for the *ātman,* for the ultimate subject. One passage we have quoted makes it quite explicit: He is never thought, but he is the thinker. He is the inner controller; he is your *ātman.*[64]

We have already indicated the thrust of the Upaniṣadic search. It is attracted not so much by the object as by the subject of knowledge, the knower. The knower is not my senses, or even my reason, for you also have a reason and we observe that we both seem to

64. Cf. BU III, 7, 23 (§ VI 5).

obey certain dialectical laws, so that neither my reason nor yours can be the ultimate subject, the real knower. This leads to the emergence of the concept of *ātman* as the ultimate subject, as the ultimate knower.

The problem remains—and is given different answers by different philosophical systems—with regard to the relation between the ultimate *ātman* as the subject of everything and the *ahaṁkāra,* the *jīvātman,* the psychological ego, the individual soul. Indeed, several texts affirm clearly that there are, as it were, two selves. Yet both are *ātman.* They are distinct but the separation should not be overdone if we want to remain within the domain of Upaniṣadic intuition.

The personal discovery of the *ātman* requires us to follow a particular way. It is the spiritual way indicated in texts already quoted. It consists in looking beyond the *nāma-rūpa,* the name and form, which appears to constitute the core of my own self, and in being attentive to the factual material constituent of my being.[65] The salt dissolved in the pond of water[66] has not ceased to be salt because it has lost its form and perhaps also its name as a separate entity called salt. It becomes more truly itself in fulfilling its mission of making things salty than it would if it had remained as a mere lump. The salt in the ocean is, in a way, more truly salt than the isolated lump, just as money is more truly money when fruitfully circulating than when frozen in a private safe. Reality is not the universe decomposed into its elements, just as the essence of water is not its three independent elements or the essence of a molecule merely its atoms. A molecule is rather the unity of its atoms in a particular form so that, in a sense, the atoms of a molecule are more themselves, have a greater degree of reality, when they form a higher complex than when they are isolated. The whole universe is the real entity and more real than the sum of its parts. The lump of salt is only an empirical segregation, an individualization. It is the entire universe that has the whole reality.

In order to understand the true qualification of the final formula *ātman-brahman* we may adduce another example, classical in more than one culture: the drops of water which, merging into the river as the river also merges into the ocean, are symbols of our individual destiny:

65. Cf., eg., CU VI, 1, 4 (§ VI 2).
66. Cf. BU II, 4, 12 (§ VI 4); CU VI, 13 (§ VI 10).

> Just as rivers flowing to the ocean
> merge in it, losing their name and form,
> so the wise Man, freed from name and form,
> attains the supreme, divine Person.[67]

All things, including human beings in a specialized manner, can be said to be drops of water, participants in or reflections of the single One, beings of the Being. They are all water, but they are all separated, individualized, multiplied, dispersed into multiplicity, wrapped, so to speak, in finitude. This finitude is the superficial tension that distinguishes and separates them, forming their different individualities.

What is the drop of water? Is it the drop of the water or the water of the drop? Is it the container, the form, or the contents, the matter? Is it the surface tension, the peculiar individualized form it possesses, or is it the water that form contains? In the former instance, when the drop merges into the ocean it disappears as a drop of water. In the latter instance, it remains as the water of that particular drop and is also merged into the ocean, so that it has lost nothing except its limitations. Indeed it has fulfilled and enhanced all its potentialities as water. If we accept that the individuality is the surface tension and the personality the water of the particular drop, we may agree in saying that when the human being dies, his individuality disappears while his personality remains and is even enhanced. For what until then were only external relations across the barriers of finiteness have now become internal relationships.

Can we not have it both ways? Can the drop of water not be both the drop of the water and the water of the drop? Certainly it can be and in fact it is. But this admission does not solve the problem, because it arises again the moment we consider a second drop of water, or when an increase (in the volume) of water in the drop destroys the drop.

When in search of the objects of consciousness, we may well stop at the drops, at the forms and names of things; but when in search of the subject of consciousness, we have to look for something more permanent, more universal. What happens when change comes, when the drop dies? What remains, the "drop" (of the water) or the water (of the "drop")? Undoubtedly, the water.

67. MundU III, 2, 8 (§ VI 11). Cf. also PrasnU VI, 5, and also, for further reflection, KathU IV, 15 (§ VII 56); CU VI, 10 (§ VI 10), and Manu VI, 90.

This is the direction followed by the Upaniṣadic trend of thought when it looks for the underlying reality that is resistant to all changes. This is what the many texts tell us.

Now, the *ātman-brahman* equation stands for this insight into the nature of reality. It wants to make us realize that we are water and not merely separate drops. The equation says that the "substance" below equals the "being" above, that divine transcendence corresponds to divine immanence, and that the one implies the other. And yet it does not identify them in an indiscriminate manner. *Ātman* is *brahman,* but it is not said that *brahman* is *ātman,* if we allow the verbal form *is* (*bhavati*) to carry the dynamism of the process of identification.[68] It is saying that the realization of the *ātman* leads us to discover its identity with *brahman,* that to discover its ultimate immanence leads to its recognition as the absolute transcendence. But it does not allow us to speculate on *brahman* with our categories, much less is it saying that *brahman* is my *ātman.* This *ātman* is the supreme Person, *uttama puruṣa,* as one of our texts affirms.[69] The (water contained in the) drop is the ocean once it has reached the ocean, but the ocean is not the drop.

When it is affirmed that *ātman* is *brahman* we have to keep in mind that the primacy of the principle of identity, which governs Indian thinking, allows us to consider the *ātman* as the essence of a being. We understand by essence that which that thing *is.* Now, this type of thinking understands what a thing *is* as that which that particular being "is," that is, has in common with other beings. This communality is its *being,* because *nāmarūpa* is not considered "essential" to a being. In a type of thinking governed by the principle of noncontradiction, on the other hand, what a being is, is understood as expressing what that being has—"is"—in contradistinction to other beings. What being *is,* is here precisely what other beings are not. We do not need here to decide which is the better way, but only to take into consideration the two different perspectives.

It is certainly true that the *ātman-brahman* intuition represents the discovery of the equivalence between the macrocosm and the microcosm, but this *māhāvākya* intends to do more than simply enunciate a speculative homology; it intends to convey a saving message. The *ātman* must be realized and its identity with *brahman*

68. "S is P" does not imply that P (qua S) is S (qua P), but only that P (qua P) is S (qua S); so that "S is P" but not vice versa without Subject and Predicate becoming meaningless.
69. Cf. CU VIII, 12, 3 (§ VI 6).

discovered, an injunction that is repeated again and again. It means that it is not a self-evident truth placarded before our eyes; it is not given as an immediate datum within the range of our common experience. It is not a question of finding an objectified *ātman*. The *ātman* that has to be realized is something that emerges in the very process of discovery, in the very process of unveiling the veil of *māyā* by recognizing it to be a veil. Indeed, once the intuition dawns upon us, we will be inclined to say that it was already there, only we did not know it. In other words, the *ātman* is definitely not our creation. Yet even this should not be interpreted in a static way, as if we were simply to discover something that was already there, for it is precisely by this very discovery that we have come to be. We have realized ourselves by the realization of the *ātman*. We have become the revealed reality.

The qualification required for recognizing the *ātman-brahman* equation amounts to the discovery of the overall span under which the whole of reality is inscribed. It means realizing that transcendence has no real meaning except in relation to immanence, that the ultimate reality of everything is not different from ultimate reality as such, precisely because the arch *ātman-brahman* overspans the whole of reality and expresses its unity.

One of the greatest obstacles to understanding this powerful intuition consists in assuming an implicit "is" and then interpreting this "is" in a mere essentialistic way: *ātman* "is" *brahman* and thus all that *ātman* "is" would also apply to *brahman*. Indeed, it is true that *ātman* is *brahman*, but the meaning of the verb *is* here is built into the *ātman* which *is brahman* and expresses only the ultimate identity between them.

For example, when we say "John *is* good," or "water *is* liquid," or "God *is*," or "five *is* more than three," in each instance the verbal form *is* depends on the subject and the predicate it unites, for each time it expresses a different relation. To consider the word *is* independently from the things it links would be to misunderstand it. John *is* not good in the same sense that five *is* more than three. John can cease to be good; he is good now but not necessarily always; John's *is* depends on his very being. On the other hand, five would cease to be what it is if it could cease to be more than three; the five's *is* also depends on the nature of the five. The *is* of "God *is*" depends on the very nature of God and thus cannot be compared with any other thing that "is." The *is* of the *ātman* that is *brahman* is again sui generis and depends on the specific nature of *ātman*. It is not a logical, but an *ātman*, identity.

The *ātman-brahman* equation, understood in this way and realized along the interior personal path, leads toward the discovery of the underlying unity of all things without destroying their diversity. Yet there is on this path a pitfall, and history bears abundant witness that it is not always avoided. We refer to the danger of monism into which one may fall when the *ātman* is regarded merely as substance. This *mahāvākya* needs an urgent corrective. Within this context the Buddha offered one possible corrective: the *anātmavāda* or doctrine of the unsubstantiality of the *ātman*. The Upaniṣads offer another solution, though it is not always clearly understood: the *puruṣa-vidyā*, or the intuition of the structure of reality as personhood. This is what we shall try to discover after our perusal of the texts that follow.

The Self *Ātman*

5 Meditation on Brahman leads to pure ecstasy, for one is lost in the groundless object of the infinite, while meditation on *ātman* leads to pure "enstasis," for it is the meditator this time who is lost in the ultimate ground that seems to have engulfed him. This seems to be the gist of the injunction of the Śatapatha Brāhmaṇa (i). Therefore Brahman is never an object of love. The only real object of love in all other objects is the *ātman*, as Yājñavalkya teaches his wife Maitreyī who is about to renounce the love of her husband for love of the *ātman* (ii). To love a person or a thing without transcending it in the very act of love, that is, without loving the *ātman* in it, would be idolatry, and ultimately it cannot satisfy either the lover or the beloved. Only love that is transparent—to the *ātman*—can be the means of ascent, the way to liberation and immortality.[70]

The revelation of the *ātman* as the thread holding all things together, without which they would fall apart, and as the *antaryāmin*, the inner guide of all beings, starts from the extraordinary question of the Gandharva possessing the wife of Patañcala Kāpya, teacher of sacrifice. The great Yājñavalkya knows this teaching by his own experience, and he expounds it (iii). Yet the *ātman* remains ungraspable, because it is neither "this" nor "that," *na iti, na iti* (iv).

70. Cf. BU II, 4, 2, or BU IV, 5, 3 (§ III 31).

The *ātman* is that which holds the human person together in unity and guides the individual selves as their Lord (v).

The Kaṭha Upaniṣad reveals the paradoxical nature of the *ātman* (vi)[71] which cannot be grasped by an intellectual approach, but only by an act of grace, by a choice on the part of the *ātman*. But to receive this grace requires purity of life and mind, concentration and internal peace (v. 24). Only with this grace can the seers perceive the invisible (vii).[72]

The Śvetāśvatara Upaniṣad (viii) adds that the *ātman* is not discovered without effort but that it is the product of effort. For just as butter is not produced automatically by milk or cream, but by a definite effort on the part of someone, so also the *ātman* has to be gained from the individual self by effort, truthfulness, and fervor.[73] The overarching nature of *ātman*, its cosmic character and spiritual reality, are again stressed in the Muṇḍaka Upaniṣad (ix).

Ātman

SB X, 6, 3, 1-2

i) 1. One should meditate on Brahman, the truth. Now, man possesses insight and, on departing from this world, he will attain the world beyond in accordance with his degree of insight.

2. One should meditate on the *ātman* which consists of spirit, whose embodiment is life, whose form is light, whose essence is space, which changes its form at will, swift as thought, of true resolve and true stability; which contains all odors, all tastes, pervades all regions and encompasses the whole world, speechless and indifferent.

Like a grain of rice or barley or millet, like a tiny grain of millet, so is the golden Person within the *ātman*. Like smokeless flame, greater than heaven, greater than the atmosphere, greater than the earth, greater than all beings, he is the *ātman* of life, my own *ātman*. On departing [from this world] I shall become that *ātman*. He who has this confidence, he shall not waver. This was spoken by Śāṇḍilya and it is truly so.

BU II, 4, 4-6

ii) 4. Yājñavalkya spoke to Maitreyī: "Being dear to me you speak dear words. Come, sit down, I will explain to you, and while I explain you should meditate on it."

71. Cf. also IsU 4-5 (§ VII 11).
72. Cf. also SU III 20 (§ VI 7).
73. For other texts on *ātman*, cf. § I 7.

5. Yājñavalkya said: "It is not for love of a husband that a husband is loved, but rather for love of the *ātman*.

"Nor is it for love of a wife that a wife is loved but rather for love of the *ātman*.

"Nor is it for love of sons that sons are loved but rather for love of the *ātman*.

"Nor is it for love of wealth that wealth is loved but rather for love of the *ātman*.

"Nor is it for love of the priesthood that the priesthood is loved but rather for love of the *ātman*.

"Nor is it for love of power that power is loved but rather for love of the *ātman*.

"Nor is it for love of the worlds that the worlds are loved but rather for love of the *ātman*.

"Nor is it for love of the Gods that the Gods are loved but rather for love of the *ātman*.

"Nor is it for love of creatures that creatures are loved but rather for love of the *ātman*.

"Nor is it for love of all that all is loved but rather for love of the *ātman*.

"Then, O Maitreyī, it is the *ātman* that should be seen, heard, thought about, and deeply pondered. It is only by seeing, hearing, thinking about, and deeply pondering the *ātman* that all this is known."

6. The Brahmin refuses one who knows him to be different from the *ātman*. The warrior refuses one who knows him to be different from the *ātman*. The worlds refuse one who knows them to be different from the *ātman*. The Gods refuse one who knows them to be different from the *ātman*. The beings refuse one who knows them to be different from the *ātman*. Everything refuses one who knows it to be different from the *ātman*. This Brahmin, this warrior, these worlds, these Gods, these beings—all these are the *ātman*.

BU III, 7, 1-16; 18-23

iii) 1. Now Uddālaka Āruṇi asked him:

"Yājñavalkya," he said, "we stayed among the Madras, in the house of Patañcala Kāpya, studying sacrifice. He had a wife who was possessed by a spirit. We asked the spirit, 'Who are you?' "

He said, "I am Kabandha, descendant of Atharvan."

He said to Patañcala Kāpya and to the students of sacrifice: "Do you know, O Kāpya, that thread, with which this world, the world beyond, and all beings are bound together?"

And Patañcala Kāpya said, "No, I do not, sir."

He said to Patañcala Kāpya and to the students of sacrifice: "Do you know, O Kāpya, that Inner Controller, who directs this world, the world beyond, and all beings from within?"

And Patañcala Kāpya said: "No, I do not, sir."

He said to Patañcala Kāpya and to the students of sacrifice: "He who knows that thread and that Inner Controller, he knows Brahman, he knows the world, he knows the Gods, he knows the Vedas, he knows all beings, he knows the *ātman*, he knows all."

Thus he explained to them, and hence I know it. "If you, Yājñavalkya, do not know that thread and that Inner Controller and yet take away the cows which belong only to the knowers of Brahman, you will lose your head."

"But I know, O Gautama, that thread and that Inner Controller."

"Anyone might say, 'I know it, I know it.' If you really know it, tell us about it."

2. He said: "The Wind, O Gautama, is that thread. For with the wind as with a thread this world, the world beyond, and all beings are bound together. Therefore, O Gautama, they say of a man who died that his limbs are unloosed, for with the wind as with a thread they are bound together."

"Very well, O Yājñavalkya. Now tell us about the Inner Controller!"

3. "He who dwells in the earth, yet is other than the earth, whom the earth does not know, whose body is the earth, who controls the earth from within—he is the *ātman* within you, the Inner Controller, the immortal.

4. "He who dwells in the waters, yet is other than the waters, whom the waters do not know, whose body is the waters, who controls the waters from within—he is the *ātman* within you, the Inner Controller, the immortal.

5. "He who dwells in the fire, yet is other than the fire, whom the fire does not know, whose body is the fire, who controls the fire from within—he is the *ātman* within you, the Inner Controller, the immortal.

6. "He who dwells in the space, yet is other than the space, whom the space does not know, whose body is the space, who controls the space from within—he is the *ātman* within you, the Inner Controller, the immortal.

7. "He who dwells in the wind, yet is other than the wind, whom the wind does not know, whose body is the wind, who controls the wind from within—he is the *ātman* within you, the Inner Controller, the immortal.

8. "He who dwells in the sky, yet is other than the sky, whom the sky does

not know, whose body is the sky, who controls the sky from within—he is the *ātman* within you, the Inner Controller, the immortal.

9. "He who dwells in the sun, yet is other than the sun, whom the sun does not know, whose body is the sun, who controls the sun from within—he is the *ātman* within you, the Inner Controller, the immortal.

10. "He who dwells in the regions of space, yet is other than the regions of space, whom the regions of space do not know, whose body is the regions of space, who controls the regions of space from within—he is the *ātman* within you, the Inner Controller, the immortal.

11. "He who dwells in the moon and the stars, yet is other than the moon and the stars, whom the moon and the stars do not know, whose body is the moon and stars, who controls the moon and the stars from within—he is the *ātman* within you, the Inner Controller, the immortal.

12. "He who dwells in the atmosphere, yet is other than the atmosphere, whom the atmosphere does not know, whose body is the atmosphere, who controls the atmosphere from within—he is *ātman* within you, the Inner Controller, the immortal.

13. "He who dwells in the darkness, yet is other than the darkness, whom the darkness does not know, whose body is the darkness, who controls the darkness from within—he is the *ātman* within you, the Inner Controller, the immortal.

14. "He who dwells in the light, yet is other than the light, whom the light does not know, whose body is the light, who controls the light from within—he is the *ātman* within you, the Inner Controller, the immortal.

"So far with reference to the divinities. Now with reference to beings.

15. "He who dwells in all beings, yet is other than all beings, whom all beings do not know, whose body is all beings, who controls all beings from within—he is the *ātman* within you, the Inner Controller, the immortal.

"So far with reference to beings. Now with reference to the body.

16. "He who dwells in the life breath, yet is other than the life breath, whom the life breath does not know, whose body is the life breath, who controls the life breath from within—he is the *ātman* within you, the Inner Controller, the immortal.

18. "He who dwells in the eye, yet is other than the eye, whom the eye does not know, whose body is the eye, who controls the eye from within—he is the *ātman* within you, the Inner Controller, the immortal.

19. "He who dwells in the ear, yet is other than the ear, whom the ear does not know, whose body is the ear, who controls the ear from within—he is the *ātman* within you, the Inner Controller, the immortal.

20. "He who dwells in the mind, yet is other than the mind, whom the mind does not know, whose body is the mind, who controls the mind from within—he is the *ātman* within you, the Inner Controller, the immortal.

21. "He who dwells in the skin, yet is other than the skin, whom the skin does not know, whose body is the skin, who controls the skin from within—he is the *ātman* within you, the Inner Controller, the immortal.

22. "He who dwells in the understanding, yet is other than the understanding, whom the understanding does not know, whose body is the understanding, who controls the understanding from within—he is the *ātman* within you, the Inner Controller, the immortal.

23. "He who dwells in semen, yet is other than semen, whom the semen does not know, whose body is semen, who controls semen from within—he is the *ātman* within you, the Inner Controller, the immortal.

"He is the unseen seer, the unheard hearer, the unthought thinker, the unknown knower. There is no other seer than he, no other hearer than he, no other thinker than he, no other knower than he. He is your *ātman*, the Inner Controller, the immortal.

"Anything else is the cause of suffering."

Then Uddālaka Āruṇi was silent.

BU III, 9, 26

iv) On what are you and your *ātman* established?
On the breath of life.
— And on what is breath of life established?
— On exhalation.
— And on what is exhalation established?
— On the circulating breath.
— And on what is the circulating breath established?
— On the up-breath.
— And on what is the up-breath established?
— On the central breath.

That *ātman*, however, is not this, not this. It is ungraspable, for it cannot be grasped. It is indestructible, for it cannot be destroyed. It is untouched, for it cannot be touched. It is unfettered, it does not suffer, it does not decay.

KausU IV, 20

v) Now it is in this breath of life alone that he [in sleep] is integrated into one. Speech together with all names is absorbed into it. The eye together with all forms is absorbed into it. The ear together with all sounds is absorbed into it. The mind together with all thoughts is absorbed into it.

And when he awakes, just as from a blazing fire sparks leap forth in all directions, in the same way from this *ātman*, the sense powers leap forth to their respective stations: from the sense powers the senses and from the senses the sense objects.

This is the breath of life, the conscious *ātman* which has entered into this physical self, even up to the hairs and the nails. Just as a blade is hidden in a sheath or fire in a brazier, in the same way this conscious *ātman* has entered into this physical self, even up to the hairs and the nails. On this *ātman* the other selves depend just as men depend upon their chief. Just as the chief flourishes together with his men and his men flourish together with their chief, in the same way this conscious *ātman* flourishes together with the other selves and the other selves flourish together with the *ātman*. As long as Indra did not know this *ātman*, the *asuras* prevailed over him. But when he knew this *ātman*, then he smote the *asuras* and was victorious. He attained supremacy, freedom, and lordship over all the Gods and all beings. In the same way, he who knows this will attain supremacy, freedom, and lordship over all beings—he who knows this, yes, he who knows this!

KathU II, 21-25

vi)

21. He sits, and yet he wanders far;
he is lying, and yet goes everywhere.
Who then but me is able to know
the God who exults and does not exult?

22. Bodiless among bodies, stable among the unstable,
the great and all-pervading *ātman*—
recognizing him thus, the wise do not grieve.

23. This *ātman* is not attained by instruction
or by intelligence or by learning.
By him whom he chooses is the *ātman* attained.
To him the *ātman* reveals his own being.

24. The one who has not turned away from wickedness,
who has no peace, who is not concentrated,
whose mind is restless—he cannot realize
the *ātman*, who is known by wisdom.

25. He for whom priest and noble are both
a mere dish of rice with death as a sauce—
that one, who knows in truth where he is?

KathU III, 12

vii)

Hidden in all beings, the *ātman* does not shine forth,
but he can be perceived by those subtle seers
by means of their fine and subtle intelligence.

SU I, 15-16

viii) 15. As oil in sesame seed, as butter in cream,
as water in hidden springs, as fire in fire sticks,
so is the *ātman* grasped in one's own self
when one searches for him in truth and with fervor.

16. The *ātman* pervades all, like butter hidden in milk;
he is the source of Self-knowledge and ascetic fervor.
This is the Brahman-teaching, the highest goal!
This is the Brahman-teaching, the highest goal!

MundU II, 2, 5-8

ix) 5. In him are woven the sky, the earth,
airy space, mind, and all sense powers.
Dismissing all else, know him as the one
true *ātman*, the bridge to deathlessness.

6. Where the arteries merge like spokes in the hub
of a wheel, there the *ātman* moves within
in manifold forms. By the saying of "OM"
meditate upon the *ātman*. May you succeed
in crossing to the farther shore of darkness!

7. All-knowing is he, all-wise; his glory
expands through all the earth. He is established
as the *ātman* in the city divine of Brahman,
in the space of the heart.

8. He consists of spirit; he guides the life powers
and dwells within the heart, being based upon food.
Him do the wise perceive by means of wisdom,
the immortal, the radiant, whose nature is bliss.

▪ i) 1. Insight: *kratu*, will.
2. Spirit: *manas*.
Embodiment: *śarīra*, body.
Life: *prāṇa*.
Essence: *ātman*, soul or Self.
Thought: *manas*.
Stability: *dhṛti*, firmness, resolution.
Golden Person: *puruṣo hiraṇmayaḥ*. Cf. BU IV, 3, 11, etc.
Flame: lit. light.
▪ ii) 1-3. Cf. § III 31.
4. Meditate: *nididhyāsasva*.
5. Priesthood: *brahman*, Brahminhood.
Power: *kṣatra*, state of Kṣatriya or warrior.
All: *sarva*.
6. Brahmin: or Brahman(?) or the religious order.
Refuses: *parādāt*, abandons, leaves, deserts.
Warrior: *kṣatra*, the princely ("worldly") power.
7-14. Cf. § VI 4.
▪ iii) Another version of the same story is told in BU III, 3.

1. Spirit: Gandharva. It is not by chance that this Gandharva is related to Atharvan, for the AV is concerned with supernormal powers as well as with the knowledge of Brahman.

Thread: *sūtra*. The verb can suggest either the image of a flower bouquet bound together, or the thread holding together the beads of a necklace (*mālā*).

Inner Controller: *antaryāmin*.

2. Wind: *vāyu*.

3. Other than the earth: *pṛthivyā antaraḥ*, which can also mean "who is within the earth." And the like with all the following homologizations.

6. Space: *antarikṣa*.

12. Atmosphere: *ākāśa*.

13. Darkness: *tamas*.

14. Light: *tejas*.

With reference to the divinities: *adhidaivata*.

With reference to beings: *adhibhūta*.

15. With reference to the body: *adhyātma*, with reference to the self (*ātman* means here the undivided person, as the following terms show).

17. Cf. § I 14.

22. Understanding: *vijñāna*.

23. Cf. BU II, 4, 14 (§ VI 4); III, 4, 1-2 (§ VI 6); III, 8, 11 (§ VI 3).

Anything else is the cause of suffering: *ato 'nyad ārtam*; or, more freely, "all the rest is improper, inauthentic," i.e., whatever is different from the *ātman* is painful, evil. *Ārta*, from the verb *ār-* (*ā-ṛ-*), to insert, inflict, etc., means oppressed, disturbed, afflicted; suffering, thus evil. No idea of moral evil is here implied.

▪ iv) 1-9. Cf. § VI 2.

10-17. Cf. § VI 7.

21. Cf. § I 37.

24-25. Cf. § I 14.

26. Breath of life: *prāṇa*. The names of the other four *prāṇas* are *apāna, vyāna, udāna, samāna*.

Not this, not this: *neti neti*.

The text continues with a discussion and with the falling of the head of Vidagdha Śākalya, the questioner of Yājñavalkya.

28. Cf. § VI 3.

▪ v) This is the last verse of this Upaniṣad (vv. 18-19, according to another version).

Breath of life: *prāṇa*.

Integrated into one: *ekadhā bhavati*; in sleep, cf. BU II, 1, 19 (§ VI 4).

Sense powers: *prāṇāḥ*, the vital breaths as the dynamic powers behind the senses. Cf. BU II, 1, 20 (§ VI 4).

Senses: *devāḥ*, divinities, in this context the functioning sense organs.

Sense objects: *lokāḥ*, the worlds, here in relation to the senses.

Hairs and nails: cf. BU I, 4, 7.

Conscious *ātman*: *prajñātman*.

Physical self: *śarīram ātmānam*.

Freedom: *svārājya*.

▪ vi) 20. Cf. § V 5.

21. God: *deva*.

Exults and does not exult: *madāmada*; it could be rendered as *sobria ebrietas*, "mad soberness" or "sober madness": *coincidentia oppositorum*. It could be read also as an intensive form: ever exulting. The root *mad-* means to exhilarate, to be exhilarated.

23. Cf. MundU III, 2, 3 (§ VI 11).

By learning: *śrutena*, by what is heard, secondary knowledge, or by merely hearing the Vedas (*śruti*). There is here a pun on the verbs *vṛ-*, to choose, and *vi-vṛ-* to reveal, manifest.

Own being: *tanūṁ svām*, own forms or bodies, own nature, own person.

24. Wickedness: *duścarita*, evil way.

Who has no peace: *aśānta*.

Who is not concentrated: *asamāhita*, not recollected (cf. *samādhi*, the state of concentration).

By wisdom: *prajñānena*.

25. Priest: *brahman*, priesthood.

Noble: *kṣatram*, nobility, warrior caste.

▪ vii) 10-11. Cf. § V 5.

12. Does not shine forth: *na prakāśate*.

Intelligence: *buddhi*.

13. Cf. § III 28.

▪ viii) 15. In truth and with fervor: *satyena . . . tapasā*.

16. Self-knowledge: *ātma-vidyā*.

Brahman-teaching: *brahmopaniṣad*.

■ ix) 1-2. Cf. VI 3.
3-4. Cf. VI 12.
5. Airy space: *antarikṣa,* interspace between heaven and earth. Cf. BU III, 8, 7 (§ VI 3).
Sense powers: *prāṇāḥ,* vital breaths.
Dismissing all else: *anyā vāco vimuñcatha,* lit. give up other words, any other name, "word" standing here for everything else.
For the bridge to immortality, cf. SU VI, 19 (§ I 28); CU VIII, 4, 1 (§ V 27); BU IV, 4, 22 (§ VI 6); KathU III, 2.
6. May you succeed: *svasti vaḥ,* for your happiness, well-being, salvation.
Farther shore of darkness: cf. CU VII, 26, 2 (§ VI 3), SU III, 8 (§ VI 7).
7. All-knowing . . . all-wise: *sarvajña, sarvavid.*
Space of the heart: *vyoman,* the inner atmosphere.
8. He consists of spirit: *manomayaḥ.*
Life powers: *prāṇa-śarīra,* either a compound ("the body consisting of breath") or "breath and body."
By means of wisdom: *vijñānena,* by their discrimination.
9. Cf. § VI 11.
10-11. Cf. § III 6.

The Absolute Self *Paramātman*

6 The so-called *madhu-vidyā* ("honey-wisdom") of the Bṛhadāraṇyaka Upaniṣad (i) is the doctrine of the interdependence of all things (like honey and bees). The same final refrain is constantly repeated: the *puruṣa* in the cosmos and the *puruṣa* in Man are said to be the *ātman,* the immortal Brahman, the whole universe (*idaṁ sarvam*). The list of macro-microcosmic correlations contains: earth-body, water-seed, fire-speech, wind-breath, sun-eye, regions-hearing, moon-wind, lightning-inner light, thundercloud-sound, space—space within the heart, holy order—obedience to holy order, truth-truthfulness, humanity-humanness, and finally the cosmic and personal *ātman.* Thus Brahman and *ātman* are included in the all-embracing power of the *puruṣa.*

Uṣasta Cākrāyaṇa, one of the questioners of the sage Yājñavalkya, goes straight to the heart of the matter (ii). He is not satisfied with the common explanation of the *ātman* as the "breath of the breath" which seems to him to be an objective description like that of a cow or a horse, but not of Brahman. When Yājñavalkya is thus pressed to speak, he can only state the unknowability of the Knower who is the very *ātman* of the questioner. He therefore cannot but keep silent.

The third text chosen from the Bṛhadāraṇyaka Upaniṣad, part of the great dialogue between Janaka and Yājñavalkya, shows already a high development of the doctrine of *ātman-brahman.* The one who has realized this equation is emphatically declared to be beyond good and evil, beyond—not behind or beside—the level of morality, because he has transcended all desires, finding his whole world in the *ātman*. The *ātman* is neither a desire nor an object of desire; it is beyond all that. *Ātman* is Brahman—this realization frees one from all fear. The Chāndogya Upaniṣad (iv) again stresses that the teaching concerning *ātman-brahman* is a matter of experience. While meditating on the light of the *ātman* one may have visions, or while listening to the inner voice one may hear some kind of sound.[74] But the ultimate experience which, as this text affirms, is happening at the time of death is beyond everything, being at the same time the most universal and the most intimate. Only the search within, the going deeper and deeper into the recesses of one's own heart, will reveal that indestructible center which is the *ātman* (v). It is like a hidden treasure which one passes without noticing it, though it is always present within us.

The message of the *ātman,* proclaimed by Prajāpati, reaches the Gods and demons who are eager to learn it because the effect of this knowledge is full of reward.[75] It is Indra's dissatisfaction with any reply that is not ultimate which enables him to receive the highest instruction and to realize the *ātman* within. This discovery reveals the freedom of the *puruṣa,* the peaceful, liberated person whose existence is described as a play (v. 12, 3).

With striking simplicity the Māṇḍūkya Upaniṣad sums it all up (vi). It affirms a radical apophatism, striking the Buddhist note of double negation and avoiding thus any kind of psychological or epistemological "hold" on the *ātman:* it is neither the conscious nor the unconscious; it is simply beyond all our categories, and yet *sa vijñeyaḥ,* it is to be "known," "realized," in spite of the betrayal of all the words.

Paramātman

BU II, 5, 1-15; 19

i)

1. The earth is the honey of all beings, and all beings are honey for the the earth. He who is the resplendent, immortal Person in the earth and who, with reference to oneself, is the resplendent, immortal Person in the body, he indeed is that which is the *ātman,* the immortal, Brahman, the all.

2. Water is the honey of all beings, and all beings are honey for the water. He who is the resplendent, immortal Person in the water and

74. Cf. also MaitU VI, 22 (§ VI 12).
75. Cf. CU VIII, 7 sq. The story of Indra and Prajāpati has been introduced in § IV 5.

who, with reference to oneself, is the resplendent, immortal Person consisting of seed, he indeed is that which is the *ātman*, the immortal, Brahman, the all.

3. Fire is the honey of all beings, and all beings are honey for fire. He who is the resplendent, immortal Person in fire and who, with reference to oneself, is the resplendent, immortal Person consisting of speech, he indeed is that which is the *ātman*, the immortal, Brahman, the all.

4. Wind is the honey of all beings, and all beings are honey for the wind. He who is the resplendent, immortal Person in the wind and who, with reference to oneself, is the resplendent, immortal Person consisting of breath, he indeed is that which is the *ātman*, the immortal, Brahman, the all.

5. The sun is the honey of all beings, and all beings are honey for the sun. He who is the resplendent, immortal Person in the sun and who, with reference to oneself, is the resplendent, immortal Person consisting of sight, he indeed is that which is the *ātman*, the immortal, Brahman, the all.

6. The regions are the honey of all beings, and all beings are honey for the regions. He who is the resplendent, immortal Person in the regions and who, with reference to oneself, is the resplendent, immortal Person consisting of hearing and resounding, he indeed is that which is the *ātman*, the immortal, Brahman, the all.

7. The moon is the honey of all beings, and all beings are honey for the the moon. He who is the resplendent, immortal Person in the moon and who, with reference to oneself, is the resplendent, immortal Person consisting of mind, he indeed is that which is the *ātman* the immortal, Brahman, the all.

8. Lightning is the honey of all beings and all beings are honey for lightning. He who is the resplendent, immortal Person in the lightning and who, with reference to oneself, is the resplendent, immortal Person consisting of light, he indeed is that which is the *ātman*, the immortal, Brahman, the all.

9. The thundercloud is the honey of all beings, and all beings are honey for the thundercloud. He who is the resplendent, immortal Person in the thundercloud and who, with reference to oneself, is the resplendent, immortal Person consisting of sound and tone, he indeed is that which is *ātman*, the immortal, Brahman, the all.

10. Space is the honey of all beings, and all beings are honey for space. He who is the resplendent, immortal Person in space and who, with reference to oneself, is the resplendent, immortal Person within the the space of the heart, he indeed is that which is the *ātman*, the immortal, Brahman, the all.

11. Righteousness is the honey of all beings, and all beings are honey for righteousness. He who is the resplendent, immortal Person in righteousness and who, with reference to oneself, is the resplendent, immortal Person consisting of obedience to righteousness, he indeed is that which is the *ātman,* the immortal, Brahman, the all.

12. Truth is the honey of all beings, and all beings are honey for truth. He who is the resplendent, immortal Person in truth and who, with reference to oneself, is the resplendent, immortal Person who is truthful, he indeed is that which is the *ātman,* the immortal, Brahman, the all.

13. Humanity is the honey of all beings, and all beings are honey for humanity. He who is the resplendent, immortal Person in humanity and who, with reference to oneself, is the resplendent, immortal Person who is human, he indeed is that which is the *ātman,* the immortal, Brahman, the all.

14. The *ātman* is the honey of all beings, and all beings are honey for the *ātman.* He who is the resplendent, immortal Person in the *ātman* and who, with reference to oneself, is the resplendent, immortal Person who is the *ātman,* he indeed is that which is the *ātman,* the immortal, Brahman, the all.

15. This *ātman* is the Lord of all beings, the King of all beings. Just as the spokes are fixed in the hub and the rim of a chariot wheel, in the same way all these beings, all the Gods, all the worlds, all life breaths, all these selves, are fixed in the *ātman.*

19. Brahman has not an earlier or a later, has neither inside nor outside. Brahman is the *ātman,* the all-experiencing. This is the instruction.

BU III, 4, 1-2

ii) 1. Then Uṣasta Cākrāyaṇa asked him:

"Yājñavalkya," he said, "explain to me that Brahman which is manifest and not concealed, that which is the *ātman* within everything."

"That is your *ātman,* which is within everything."

"How is it within everything, Yājñavalkya?"

"That which breathes with your breath, that is your *ātman* which is within everything. That which exhales with your exhalation, that is your *ātman* which is within everything. That which breathes diffusedly with your diffused breath, that is your *ātman* which is within everything. That which breathes up with your up-breath, that is your *ātman* which is within everything. This, in truth, is your *ātman* which is within everything."

2. Then Uṣasta Cākrāyaṇa said:

"You have explained this to me as if one says: 'This is a cow, this is a horse.' Now explain to me that Brahman which is manifest and not concealed, that which is the *ātman* within everything."

"That is your *ātman* which is within everything."

"How is it within everything, Yājñavalkya?"

"You cannot see the seer of seeing, you cannot hear the hearer of hearing, you cannot know the knower of knowing. This *ātman* which is within everything is your very own *ātman*. Anything else is the cause of suffering."

After this Uṣasta Cākrāyaṇa was silent.

BU IV, 4, 22-25

iii) 22. In truth, this is the great, unborn *ātman* who is the spiritual element among the life powers. He dwells in that space within the heart, the Ordainer of all, the Lord of all, the Ruler of all. He does not become greater by good works or less great by bad works. He is the Lord of all, the Ruler of all beings, the Protector of all beings. He is the bridge that holds these worlds apart. It is he whom Brahmins desire to know through study of the Veda, through sacrifice and almsgiving, through ascetic fervor and fasting.

The man who has found him becomes a silent monk. Desiring him alone as their world, ascetics leave their homes and wander about. Knowing this the men of old did not desire progeny. "What shall we do with progeny," they thought, "we whose whole world is the *ātman*?" Having transcended the desire for sons, the desire for wealth, the desire for worlds, they go about as mendicants. For the desire for sons is the desire for wealth, and the desire for wealth is the desire for worlds; all these are nothing but desires. He, the *ātman*, is not this, not this. He is ungraspable for he is not grasped, he is indestructible for he is not destroyed, he is free from attachment for he does not attach himself [to anything]; he is unfettered, he does not waver, he is not injured.

The one who knows this is not assailed by these two thoughts, "In this I did wrong" and "In this I did right." He has passed beyond such thoughts. What he has done and what he has not done do not affect him.

23. This has been said in the verse:

The eternal greatness of a knower of Brahman
is neither enhanced by works nor diminished.

All that matters is to know the nature of Brahman.
One who knows is untainted by evil action.

Therefore, he who knows this, having become peaceful, controlled, detached, patient, and concentrated, sees the *ātman* in himself and sees all in the *ātman*. Evil does not overcome him, but he overcomes all evil; evil does not consume him, but he consumes all evil. Free from evil, free from passion, free from doubt, he becomes a knower of Brahman. "This is the world of Brahman, your majesty, and you have attained it," said Yājñavalkya. "I give you my people and myself, venerable sir, to serve you," said Janaka, king of Videha.

24. This is the great, unborn *ātman*, the eater of food, the giver of treasure, and he who knows this surely finds a treasure.

25. This is the great, unborn *ātman*, which never ages and never dies, which is immortal and free from fear: this is Brahman. Brahman, indeed, is fearlessness, and he who knows this becomes [himself] the fearless Brahman.

CU III, 14

iv) 14, 1. Indeed, all this is Brahman. One should meditate on it in silence as "that in which everything is, breathes and dissolves." Now man, in truth, is made of insight. According to the insight a man gains in this world, so he becomes on leaving it. Therefore, let him gain insight!

2. He who consists of mind, whose body is the breath of life, whose form is light, whose thoughts are truth, whose *ātman* is space, who contains all works, all desires, all perfumes and all tastes, who encompasses this whole universe, beyond speech and beyond desires—

3. he is my *ātman* within the heart, smaller than a grain of rice or a grain of barley, smaller than a grain of mustard or a grain of millet. He is my *ātman* within the heart, greater than the earth, greater than the sky, greater than heaven itself, greater than all these worlds.

4. He contains all works, all desires, all perfumes, and all tastes. He encompasses the whole universe; he is beyond speech and beyond desires. He is my *ātman* within my heart, he is Brahman. On departing from here I shall merge with him. He who thus says has no doubt indeed. Thus said Śāṇḍilya, Śāṇḍilya.

CU VIII, 1; 3; 7-8; 10-12

v) 1, 1. Hari OM. In this city of Brahman there is a dwelling in the form of a lotus flower, and within it there is an inner space. One should search for that which is within that inner space; it is that which should be sought, it is that which one should desire to know.

2. If anyone asks, "Please tell me concerning this dwelling within the city of Brahman and the lotus flower and the space that is within it:

What is there that we should seek? What is there that we should desire to know?" Then he should say:

3. "As far, indeed, as the vast space outside extends the space within the heart. Within it, indeed, are contained both heaven and earth, fire and wind, sun and moon, lightning and the stars, both what one possesses here and what one does not possess—all is contained within it."

4. If anyone asks, "If within this city of Brahman there is contained all this—all beings and all desires—then what is left of it when old age comes upon it or when it perishes?" Then he should say:

5. It does not grow old when the body grows old
or perish when the body perishes. This
is the true city of Brahman. In this
are contained all desires.

It is the *ātman,* free from evil, free from old age and death, free from sorrow, free from hunger and thirst: this is the *ātman,* whose desires are truth, whose purpose is truth. Just as people here on earth act in accordance with command, living in the country or on the piece of land of their choice.

6. Just as here [in this life] the world earned by work fades away, likewise the world beyond earned by meritorious deeds fades away also. He who departs from this world without having found the *ātman* and true desires will lack freedom in every world. But he who departs from this world, having found the *ātman* and true desires, will enjoy freedom in every world.

3, 1. These real desires are veiled by the unreal. Though they are real, they are covered with the veil of the unreal. When anyone departs from this world, he can no longer be seen here.

2. But all his fellows, whether living or dead, and all his unfulfilled desires—all these he finds by going within. It is there that all these real desires exist which are veiled by the unreal. People who do not know the field in which a treasure of gold is buried pass over it many times without finding it. Likewise all beings go on day after day without finding the world of Brahman within because they are enveloped by unreality.

3. The *ātman* dwells within the heart. Its etymology is explained in this way: "It dwells within the heart, therefore it is called heart." He who knows this proceeds daily to the world of heaven.

4. Now that peaceful [Person], when he arises out of the body, attains the supreme light and is manifest in his own form. He is the *ātman,* immortal and fearless; this is Brahman. The name of that Brahman is Truth.

5. The word "truth" contains three syllables: *sat-ti-yam. Sat* [being] is immortality, *ti* is the mortal, and *yam* is that which binds the two together, and because it binds the two together [*yacchati*], it is called by its root *yam*. He who knows this proceeds daily to the world of heaven.

7, 1. "That *ātman* which is free from evil, free from old age and death, free from sorrow, free from hunger and thirst, whose desires are truth, whose purpose is truth—this a man should seek, this a man should desire to know. He who has found and recognized that *ātman,* he attains all worlds and all desires."

Thus spoke Prajāpati.

2. Both the Gods and the demons learned this and said: "Let us seek that *ātman,* by searching for which one attains all worlds and all desires." Indra went out from among the Gods, and Virocana from among the demons. They both came without speaking to each other into the presence of Prajāpati, with fuel in their hands [as a sign of discipleship].

3. For thirty-two years they both lived a life of chastity and religious study. Then Prajāpati spoke to them: "Desiring what have you been living here?"

They both said: "That *ātman* which is free from evil, free from old age and death, free from sorrow, free from hunger and thirst, whose desires are truth, whose purpose is truth—this a man should seek, this a man should desire to know. He who has found and recognized that *ātman,* he attains all worlds and all desires." This they proclaim as your word. "Desiring this we have been living here."

4. Prajāpati said to both of them: "the person who is seen in the eye, he is the *ātman,*" he said. "This is the immortal, the fearless, this is Brahman."

"But, Lord, who is the one who is perceived in water or in a mirror?"

"It is he himself who is perceived in all these," he said.

8, 1. "Look at yourself in a jar of water, and tell me, what of yourself [the *ātman*] you do not understand."

They both looked in a jar of water. Prajāpati asked both of them, "What do you see?"

They replied: "We both see ourselves, a complete reflection right down to the hairs and nails."

2. Then Prajāpati told them: "Array yourselves well, putting on beautiful clothes and adorning yourselves, and look into a jar of water."

They both arrayed themselves well, putting on beautiful clothes and adorning themselves, then they looked into the jar of water.

Prajāpati asked them: "What do you see?"

3. They both said: "As we are ourselves, Lord, well arrayed, with beautiful clothes and adorned, so we see [the reflections] well arrayed, with beautiful clothes and adorned."

"That is the *ātman,*" he said, "the immortal, the fearless, this is Brahman."

They both went away with their hearts at peace.

4. Seeing them, Prajāpati said [to himself]: "They go away without having attained or known the *ātman*. Whoever will believe such a teaching, they will be lost, whether they are Gods or demons."

Virocana returned to the demons with his heart at peace, and he proclaimed that teaching to them: "One should make oneself happy, one should serve oneself. By making one's own self happy and serving one's own self, one obtains both the worlds, this world and the other world."

5. Therefore they call him a demon who is not a giver, who has no faith, who does not offer sacrifice, because this is the teaching of the demons. They decorate the body of a deceased person with objects which they have begged, with clothes and ornaments, thinking that in this way they will win the other world.

10, 1. "The one who moves about happy in dream, this is the *ātman,*" Prajāpati said. "This is the immortal, the fearless, this is Brahman."

Indra went away with his heart at peace. But before he even reached the Gods he perceived this danger: "Though the *ātman* [in dream] does not become blind when the body is blind, or lame when the body is lame, nor does it suffer of the defects of the body,

2. though it is not killed when the body is killed, nor does it become lame when the body is lame. But yet [the self in dream] is, as it were, killed and exposed and experiences unpleasant things, as if weeping. I do not see any joy in this."

3. He came back with fuel in his hands. Prajāpati said to him: "O Maghavan, you have left with your heart at peace. Desiring what have you come back?"

"Though [the self in dream] does not become blind when the body becomes blind or lame when the body becomes lame, nor suffers from the defects of the body,

4. though it is not killed when the body is killed nor does it become lame when the body becomes lame. But yet it is, as it were, killed and exposed and experiences unpleasant things, as if weeping. I do not see any joy in this."

"So is it, O Maghavan," Prajāpati said; "this I will further explain to you. Live with me for another thirty-two years."

Then he lived with him for another thirty-two years. Then Prajāpati said to Indra:

11, 1. "When one is fast asleep, calm and serene, and not dreaming, this is the *ātman*," said Prajāpati. "This is the immortal, fearless Brahman."

Indra departed with his heart at peace. But before he even reached the Gods he perceived this danger: "Truly this [*ātman*] does not know his own self. He does not know who he is, nor does he know other beings. He has, so to speak, disappeared. I do not see any joy in this."

2. He returned with a stick of fuel in his hand. Prajāpati spoke to him: "O Maghavan, you left with your heart at peace. Desiring what have you come back?"

He replied: "Sir, this [*ātman*] does not know his own self, who he is, nor does he know other beings. He has, so to speak, disappeared. I do not see any joy in this."

3. "So it is, O Maghavan," said Prajāpati, "but I will further explain to you, on the condition that you live with me for another five years." He lived with him for another five years. Thus they were together for a hundred and one years. Therefore people say: Indra lived for a hundred and one years with Prajāpati in chastity and religious study. Then Prajāpati said to Indra:

12, 1. "O Maghavan, mortal, indeed, is this body and under the sway of death. Yet it is the seat of the deathless and incorporeal *ātman*. But the one who is in the body is gripped by pleasure and pain. As long as one is in the body, one is gripped by pleasure and pain. Only when one is free from the body is one untouched by pleasure and pain.

2. "Bodiless is the air, bodiless are the clouds, lightning, and thunder. And as these, when they arise out of yonder atmosphere, attain the supreme light and appear in their own respective forms,

3. "so this peaceful [Person], when he arises out of the body, attains the supreme light and appears in his own form. He is the supreme Person. There he moves about, laughing, playing, taking delight with women or chariots or friends, without remembering the burden of this body. For as an animal is yoked to a cart, so is the breath of life yoked to this body.

4. "When the eye is directed to space, then it is the Person in the eye who sees; the eye serves [only] for seeing. Now when a man is aware of

smelling, it is the *ātman* who is aware of smelling; the nose serves [only] for smelling. When a man is aware of speaking, it is the *ātman* who is aware of speaking; speech serves [only] for speaking. When a man is aware of hearing, it is the *ātman* who is aware of hearing; the ear serves [only] for hearing.

5. "When a man is aware of thinking, it is the *ātman* who is aware of thinking, the mind is its divine eye. Seeing these heavenly joys with his divine eye of the mind, the *ātman* rejoices.

6. "Assuredly, the Gods in the world of Brahman meditate upon the *ātman*. Therefore they attain all worlds and all desires. He too, who knows and who has discovered the *ātman*, attains all worlds and all desires." Thus spoke Prajāpati, thus spoke Prajāpati.

MandU 2; 7

vi) 2. Yes, in very truth, all this is Brahman,
this *ātman is Brahman.*
This *ātman* has four stages.

7. That which is neither internal consciousness nor external consciousness nor both together, which does not consist solely in compact consciousness, which is neither conscious nor unconscious, which is invisible, unapproachable, impalpable, indefinable, unthinkable, unnameable, whose very essence consists of the experience of its own self, which absorbs all diversity, is tranquil and benign, without a second, which is what they call the fourth state—that is the *ātman*. This it is which should be known.

■ i) Honey: *madhu*, regarded as the most nourishing and delicious substance and used here as a symbol for the interdependence of the cosmos and all beings. V. 16, which follows our text, quotes RV I, 116, 12 as one of the sources for the *madhu-vidyā*, "honey-wisdom," which seems to have more connection with the AV. Cf. also RV VI, 70, 5, etc. Honey is connected not only with anything pleasant (sweet), referring to love (cf. AV I, 34) and unity, but also with the heavenly joys. Viṣṇu's "third step," i.e., heaven, is filled with honey, and honey overflows in the heavenly world (cf. AV IV, 34, 6; § V 26). In their unique way, the U make honey the symbol of the knowledge (*vidyā*) of the interconnection of all things, the knowledge of the immanence of the *puruṣa* and of his identity with *ātman-brahman*.

9. Thundercloud: *stanayitnu*.

Consisting of sound and tone: *śābdaḥ sauvaraḥ*, derived from *śabda* and *svara*.

11. Righteousness: *dharma*, religiousness, holy order, justice, law.

Obedience to righteousness: *dhārma*, consisting of *dharma*, penetrated by *dharma*.

13. Humanity: *mānuṣa*.

14. Here both, the individual *ātman* and the universal *ātman*, are brought together.

19. Not an earlier . . .: *a-pūrva, an-apara, an-antara, a-bāhya*.

All-experiencing: *sarvānubhū*.

■ ii) 1. Manifest and not concealed: *sākṣād aparokṣāt*, that (Brahman) which can be apprehended only by direct and immediate vision.

The five vital breaths: *prāṇa, apāna, vyāna, udāna,* and *samāna* (not mentioned here). Cf. BU III, 9, 26 (§ VI 5).

That is your *ātman* . . . : *eṣa ta ātmā sarvāntaraḥ*, the *ātma* with universal interiority, within all (beings).

2. This is a cow: allusion perhaps to the meaning of *ātman* as breath (cf. German *atmen*) and thus saying a mere redundance. Anything else is the cause of suffering. Cf. § VI 5 iii, note 23.

■ iii) Cf. § IV 21 Introduction.

15-21. Cf. § VI 11.

22. Spiritual element among the life powers: *vijñānamayaḥ prāṇeṣu*, consisting of consciousness, made of intelligence, within the life breaths.

Bridge: *setu,* also dyke, dam. Cf. CU VIII, 4, 1-3 (§ V 27); KathU III, 2; MundU II, 2, 5 (§ VI 5). This *setu* unites and separates.

The man who has found him: *etam eva viditvā,* or known him.

Silent monk: *muni.*

World: *loka,* as their proper place, as the proper locus of liberation. Cf. the improper "worlds" of liberation just below. Cf. BU IV, 3, 20 (§ VI 8).

Not this, not this: *neti neti.* Cf. BU IV, 5, 15 (§ III 28).

Affect: *tapataḥ,* burn, consume, also meaning that he does not repent or worry. Cf. TU II, 9 (§ VI 7).

23. Untainted: *na lipyate,* not stained, defiled, untouched. Cf. KathU V, 11 (§ VI 2).

Evil: *pāpman.*

24. Unborn: *a-ja* also without origin, beginningless, uncreated.

25. Never ages . . .: *ajaro 'maro 'mṛto 'bhayo brahma.*

■ iv) 14, 1. That in which everything is, breathes and dissolves: *tajjalān,* one of the purposely enigmatic Upaniṣadic expressions (cf. *tadvanam,* KenU IV, 6) which are understood only by the initiated. This translation conveys the traditional meaning attached to it.

Insight: *kratu,* will, and also ritual act; a human action including intellect and will.

14, 2. Cf. SB X, 6, 3, 2 (§ VI 5).

Beyond speech and beyond desires: *avāky anādaraḥ.*

■ v) 1, 1. Cf. § VII Introduction.

City of Brahman: *brahmapura* the body, or the heart.

1, 3. Space within the heart: *antar-hṛdayākāśaḥ.*

Both what one possesses here and what one does not possess: *yac cāsyehāsti yac ca nāsti,* or its presence and absence.

1, 5. Whose desires are truth: *satya-kāma,* of true desires.

Whose purpose is truth: *satya-saṁkalpa,* will, conception.

These lines are repeated below in CU VIII, 7, 1, in a slightly different translation. The last sentence seems to be incomplete.

1, 6. Meritorious deeds: *puṇya.*

Freedom: *kāmacāra.*

3, 1. Real desires veiled by the unreal: *satyāḥ kāmāḥ anṛtāpidhānāḥ.* Cf. *satyānṛta* in RV VII, 49, 3 (§ I 16), etc.

3, 2. People who do not know the field: *akṣetrajñaḥ.* For *kṣetrajña* cf. SB XIII, 2, 3, 2; cf. also RV IX, 70, 9 (*kṣetravid*); RV X, 32, 7 etc. Later the term becomes of philosophical significance (the body or nature is the field, the conscious *ātman* or *puruṣa* is the knower of the field). Cf. SU VI, 16 (§ I 28); BG XIII, 1-2; 26; 34.

3, 3. Etymology: *nirukta* Cf. BU V, 3.

Pun: within the heart: *hṛdy ayam;* heart: *hṛdayam.*

3, 4. Cf. BU II, 1, 18-19 (§ VI 4); IV, 3, 7.

Peaceful: *saṁprasāda,* calm, serene.

Truth: *satya.*

4, 1-3. Cf. § V 27.

5, 1-4. Cf. § III 27.

6, 5. Cf. § VI 12.

7, 1. Free from evil: *apahata-pāpmā.*

7, 3. Life of chastity and religious study: *brahmacarya.*

7, 4. Person who is seen in the eye: *akṣiṇi puruṣah;* cf. BU II. 3, 5 (§ VI 7); V, 5, 2; CU I, 7, 5; IV, 15, 1. Prajāpati's teaching is truly Upaniṣadic; it becomes misleading only because of the low level of understanding of his two disciples.

8, 1. What of yourself you do not understand: *yad ātmano na vijānīthas . . .;* it could also be rendered: whether you do not recognize yourself (or: the *ātman*). As *ātman* can be used in the simple reflexive meaning, the double meaning cannot be rendered by one translation.

8, 4. Teaching: *upaniṣad.*

They will be lost: *parābhaviṣyanti,* they will perish.

Oneself: *ātmānam,* here clearly in the simple reflexive sense.

8, 5. Demon: *asura.*

Teaching of the demons: *asurāṇāṁ hy eṣa upaniṣat.*

9, 1-3. Cf. § IV 5.

11, 1. Who he is: *ayam aham asmi,* "I am this one."

12, 1. Free from the body: *aśarīra.*

12, 2. Bodiless: *aśarīna.*

12, 3. Cf. MaitU II, 2.

Peaceful [Person]: *saṁprasāda* [*puruṣa*].

Own form: *svena rūpeṇa;* cf. BU IV, 4, 4 (§ VI 11).

The Supreme freedom of the *jīvanmukta.*

12, 4. Cf. BU I, 4, 7, etc.

Person in the eye: *cākṣuṣaḥ puruṣaḥ.*
Aware of . . . : lit. when he knows I am smelling, etc.
12, 5. Heavenly joys: cf. v. 3.
12, 6. Cf. BU I, 4, 10 (§ VI 9).
13, 1. Cf. § IV 21.
■ vi) 1. Cf. VI 12.
2. The Upaniṣadic equation *sarvam = brahman, ātman = brahman.*
Sarvaṁ hy etad brahma, ayam ātmā brahma: the last three words are the traditional *mahāvākya.*
Four stages: *catuṣ-pāt,* four feet, i.e., the states of the *ātman* in waking, dreaming, deep sleep, and beyond (*caturtha*). Cf. BU V, 14, 3-4; 6-7 and also MaitU VI, 19; VII, 11, 7 (here called *turīya*).
6. Cf. § I 28.
7. Internal consciousness: *antaḥ-prajña.*
External consciousness: *bahiḥ-prajña.*
Consist solely in compact consciousness: *prajñāna-ghana,* a heap of consciousness; cf. BU IV, 5, 13.
Unthinkable: *a-cintya.*
Whose very essence . . . : *ekātmapratyayasāra,* the oneness of the Self.
Absorbs all diversity: *prapañcopaśama,* the quieting or extinction of the world of objects.
Tranquil and benign: *śāntaṁ śivam;* cf. AV XIX, 9, 1 (§ II 38).
Fourth state: *caturtha,* the transcendent state beyond the three "visible or audible quarters of reality."

b) The Disclosure of the Subject

Aham brahman

I am Brahman

The discovery of the *ātman* is in the last analysis the discovery of the third person. In spite of all provisos and cautions not to reify the insight of the preceding Great Utterance, the *ātman* appears always in front of us as substance, and as such it lacks the immediacy and the fluidity of the I; it is not yet the revelation of the first person. We can understand and even say that *ātman* is Brahman, and yet keep a certain distance and remain detached in the saying. The discovery of the *ātman* is the fruit of a predominantly objectified investigation, whereas the disclosure of the I is the result of a subjective introspection in which not only the object but also the subject as a substance evaporates. The passage from the *ātman-brahman* to the *aham-brahman* is a capital one. The ground is Brahman, but it is the person passing from *ātman* to *aham* who crosses over to the other shore. The Sanskrit saying makes the same point in a striking way: "He who knows that Brahman exists—his is an indirect knowledge; he who knows 'I am Brahman'—this is a direct knowledge."[76]

The first question was: What is *this*? Our first Utterance replied:

76. *Asti brahman iti ced veda parokṣaṁ jñānam eva tat; aham brahman iti ced veda pratyakṣaṁ jñānam eva tat.* The polarity *parokṣa-pratyakṣa* is fundamental in Indian thinking.

This, whether it is Being or Nonbeing, is One only without a second. The next Utterance added: This One can only be consciousness, for nothing else can fulfill the strict demands of oneness. Consciousness has to "land" somewhere. Even after the elimination of any possible object as a limitation of consciousness it still has to find a subject, a support. This was the purport of the last saying of our preceding subsection. But how are we going to realize this subject if we ourselves remain outside the picture, as it were, if we do not shift from the third person to the first? This is the purport of this present *mahāvākya.*

We can hear a kind of crescendo in the orchestration of this insight. It all begins with the apprehension that "He is," as one text explicitly affirms.[77] This "He" is the *ātman,* the realization of which is the realization of the mystery of existence. This realization is not apprehended by the word or by the spirit; it dawns only as "naked" existence, as the wonder that "He is!" The word and the spirit may be his supreme manifestations, but they are not the source.

In the Bṛhadāraṇyaka Upaniṣad there is a passage that portrays the two states of sleep and dreamless sleep and uses them to expound the transition from the *ātman* to the *aham.* The passage describes how, when we are tired and the sense of the ego fades slowly away, we tend to identify ourselves with the subject of our dreams and put ourselves forward: "I am all this." Duality disappears and yet within the dream there is smelling, tasting, thinking, knowing. This dream state occurs only when there is no desire, when desire and the *ātman* are undifferentiated. In this state we have achieved something that is otherwise beyond our power; we have taken a second step, we have succeeded in performing all the acts of the waking state but without duality, for smelling, tasting, knowing, and the like all happen within ourselves. In this "enlargement" or second step we have identified ourselves with the whole world; thus we are in the highest bliss.[78]

All this happens in a dream, but when we awake, recognizing it as a dream, we destroy that identity and we cannot, in our right mind at least, conceive any longer that we are the whole world. Yet the way has been opened up before us. Can we in any way reasonably realize that "I am this whole world," that I am *all this* of which I can conceivably be aware?[79]

77. KathU VI, 13 (§ VI 9).
78. Cf. BU IV, 3, 19-34.
79. Cf. BU IV, 3, 20 (§ VI 8).

The third step may be discovered in another saying, repeated in different contexts, which affirms: "I am He." Significantly enough, one text contains this insight in connection with dreams and the awakening from the dream state,[80] another text has a markedly cosmic frame of reference,[81] while a third specifically refers to the realization of the *ātman*.[82] Considering these and similar sayings together, we may extract from them an account of the experience of identification, when the mind and heart together find reality: I am the beloved, I am the thing sought, I am the understood truth, I am He. We are close here to realizing the identification of the I with the He.

A fourth step may be found in the realization that this I is beginning to differentiate itself more and more from the ego. There now dawns the realization of the mystery character of the I, the revelation, in other words, of the Upaniṣadic structure of the I, that is, that it is a secret name.[83] We begin to be less sure that our individuality is identical with the I. The real personality is emerging.

We are thus prepared for the fifth step: the immediate realization, not that I am He, which always implies a third element, a spectator, and a remnant of objectification, but that "I am you," and this can be true only in authentic dialogue, in an existential situation, when not "speaking about," but actually "speaking to" and having the experience. "I am *you*" is meaningful only in the vocative, in an encounter, in prayer, in concrete situations like that described in one of the texts: "Who are you?" "I am you" is the immediate answer, and the Upaniṣad continues: "Then he releases him.[84] The question about one's own identity is here put at the most important moment in life, namely, at the moment of death, or rather at the vital moment of decision regarding one's future destiny.[85] Without this identity no salvation is possible. Without this identity there is only excommunication, segregation, or rejection. If I cannot truthfully say "I am you," how can I be united with you?

But we are not yet at the end of this internal journey. The "you" can be a petty you; the identification with the beloved may be merely an act of throwing ourselves into the arms of some idol. In

80. Cf. CU VIII, 11, 1-2 (§ VI 6).
81. Cf. IsU 16 (§ VII 31).
82. Cf. BU IV, 4, 12 (§ VI 9).
83. Cf. BU V, 5, 4 (§ VI 8).
84. Cf. KausU I, 2 (§ V 4).
85. Cf. SB I, 8, 1, 9 (§ V 17) for another beautiful reply to this same question: "I am your daughter."

other words, not every "you" is a saviour. Thus there is need for a sixth step. The *you* cannot be conditioned by our whims; the *you* has to be utterly unconditioned.

At this point the transforming power of love becomes evident and the great conversion takes place. The *you* cannot be my projection, my creation, my creature. That would be idolatry. The relation must be reversed. The *you* begins to dawn as the authentic I. Whatever you are, whoever you are, and wherever you are, this also I am and there also I am. This is what another group of passages tells us. You are this world, you are all this. Whoever that person may be, that also am I.[86] When this surrender has been achieved, when the conversion is taking place, we are in a position to understand this *mahāvākya,* which is the revelation of the I, the eternal I, the I that is Brahman: *aham brahman.*

The question "What *is* the *ātman*?" is a predominantly intellectual question. Even assuming that one discovers oneself to be the *ātman,* this *ātman* will always remain the predicate of the sentence expressing it—"I am the *ātman*"—and thus one will never be able to bridge the gulf between the subject and the predicate. The authentic and personal question about the subject has then to take the form, not of asking what, or even who, is the *ātman,* but what or rather *who am I*? It is here that *neti, neti* enters upon the scene: not this, not that.[87] Nothing answers the question adequately. I am not my body (only), I am not my mind (alone), I am not (exclusively) what I am today or was yesterday or shall be tomorrow. We are not asking what the I *is,* but searching out who I *am,* who I am in the deepest recesses of my being, who I am in the last analysis, who I ultimately am as mover and lover and knower and being or whatever. It is obvious that this ultimate I can in no way be identified with a psychological ego.

It is here that the *aham brahman* dawns, when the real *aham* that is Brahman is able to reenact in and through me the true statement of the *mahāvākya.* The I that can say this is in truth the real I and the only real and true I. Only the realized Man can say in truth *aham-brahman.* All the rest is secondhand knowledge and superimposed wisdom, mere hearsay. The intuition of the I as the I and the only unique I represents the highest wisdom. From this point of view to call God the Other or, even worse, the totally Other is perhaps

86. Cf. KausU I, 6 (§ V 4); BU V, 15, 2 (IsU 16 (§ VII 31)).
87. Cf. BU II, 3, 6 (§ VI 7); III, 9, 26 (§ VI 5); IV, 2, 4 (§ II 36 Introduction); IV, 4 22 (§§ VI 6; IV 21).

sheer blasphemy and blatant anthropocentrism. He who worships the divinity as another, says one Upaniṣad, and thinks that he is one thing and God another, does not know.[88] God in this sense is not the Other but the I, the absolute I, the ultimate I of every act. We should not assume the role of the first person if we are not it-He: the I. This *mahāvākya* does not tell me that my ego is Brahman. Quite the reverse. If put in nonexistential terms it says that Brahman is I, the I; put in proper experiential terms it affirms: I am Brahman. The one who is capable to say I, may say this. Only the I can say truly: *aham brahman.* This is what, in various different ways, the texts that follow tell us.

The Person *Puruṣa*

7 We have already met the *puruṣa,* the primordial Man,[89] the cosmic Man, the supreme Person.[90] What is fascinating in the Upaniṣads is the bringing together of the two trends of thought: the cosmic Man and the inner Man. Both are forms of Brahman (i). The passage chosen from the Bṛhadāraṇyaka Upaniṣad (ii) gives us one of the many cosmotheandric relations that serve to foster an understanding of the whole of reality, in which the underlying unity does not disturb the manifold diversity. The *puruṣa* is based each time on a different support, has a different realm, and corresponds to a different divinity. A whole new science internally linking the three realms of reality, all centered in the *puruṣa,* is here discernible.[91] The person, for the Upaniṣads, is not phenomenal, but either universal Man or the interior, spiritual Man. Ultimately, it is the inner Man who is also the Lord of all (iii).

The Taittirīya Upaniṣad (iv) describes in a crescendo the personal structure of the ultimate experience.[92] The five layers of the person are food, breath of life, mind, consciousness, and bliss. A whole anthropology is here reflected: each of these layers has itself a personal structure, a human form, and the higher form each time "fills" the lower form, that is, completes it and sublimates it. And all these layers are integrated in the ultimate experience (v. 8), which can only be a personal experience; in it the cosmic *puruṣa* in

88. Cf. BU I, 4, 10 (§ VI 9).
89. Cf. § I 5.
90. Cf. also CU VIII, 12, 3 (§ VI 6).
91. Cf. also CU III, 12, 2-9 (§ The Gāyatrī).
92. Cf. also TU II, 2 (§ II 11); II, 6-7 (§ I 7).

the sun and the spirit in Man merge. The inner Man is ever wakeful, ever active, and ever pure (v).

The Śvetāśvatara Upaniṣad (vi) succeeds in a unique way in combining intuitions about the *puruṣa,* about Brahman and *ātman,* with its conception of God. The personal God here emerges from the Vedic *puruṣa,* assuming both his cosmic-transcendent and his hidden-immanent aspects. Similarly, the Muṇḍaka Upaniṣad summarizes once more the conception of the primordial Man from whom everything originated. But unless he is realized in this "cave of the heart," the knot of ignorance will not be cut.

Puruṣa

BU II, 3, 1-6

i) 1. There are two forms of Brahman: the embodied and the bodiless, the mortal and the immortal, the stable and the moving, the tangible and the intangible.

2. The embodied is different from the air and from space; it is the mortal, the stable, and the tangible. The essence of this embodied, mortal, stable, tangible one is that [sun] which gives heat, for it is the essence of the tangible.

3. The bodiless is air and space; it is the immortal, the moving, the intangible. The essence of this bodiless, immortal, moving, intangible one is the Person in the sphere of yonder sun, for he is the essence of the intangible. This is with relation to the cosmic powers.

4. Now with relation to the *ātman:* The embodied one is what is different from the life breath and from the inner space within the heart. The mortal, the stable, the tangible one is the eye, for it is the essence of the tangible.

5. Now the bodiless is the life breath and the inner space within the heart. It is the immortal, the moving, the intangible. The essence of this bodiless, immortal, moving, intangible one is the Person in the right eye, for he is the essence of the intangible.

6. The form of this Person is like a saffron-colored robe, like white wool, like a firefly, like a white lotus, like a sudden lightning flash. He who knows this in very truth—his glory will shine like a sudden lightning flash. This, then, is the instruction: not this, not this, for there is nothing superior to this instruction, that he is not this. This is called the truth of the real. The life powers are the real, but he is their truth.

BU III, 9, 10-17

ii) 10. "He who knows that Person whose support is the earth, whose world is fire, whose light is the mind, the ultimate resort of the self of all, he is truly a knower, Yājñavalkya."

"But I know that Person, the ultimate resort of the self of all, about whom you speak. He is this embodied person. Tell me, Śākalya, who is his God?"

"The immortal," he said.

11. "He who knows that Person whose support is pleasure, whose world is the heart, whose light is the mind, the ultimate resort of the self of all—he is truly a knower, Yājñavalkya."

"But I know that Person, the ultimate resort of the self of all, about whom you speak. He is this person consisting of pleasure. Tell me, Śākalya, who is his God?"

"Women," he said.

12. "He who knows that Person whose support are the forms, whose world is the eye, whose light is the mind, the ultimate resort of the self of all—he is truly a knower, Yājñavalkya."

"But I know that Person who is the ultimate resort of the self of all, about whom you speak. He is the Person in the sun. Tell me, Śākalya, who is his God?"

"Truth," he said.

13. "He who knows that Person whose support is the atmosphere, whose world is the ear, whose light is the mind, the ultimate resort of the self of all—he is truly a knower, Yājñavalkya."

"But I know that Person who is the ultimate resort of the self of all, about whom you speak. He is the Person in hearing and in the echo. Tell me, Śākalya, who is his God?"

"The regions of space," he said.

14. "He who knows that Person whose support is darkness, whose world is the heart, whose light is the mind, the ultimate resort of the self of all—he is truly a knower, Yājñavalkya."

"But I know that Person who is the ultimate resort of the self of all, about whom you speak. He is the person consisting of shadow. Tell me, Śākalya, who is his God?"

"Death," he said.

15. "He who knows that Person whose support are the forms, whose world is the eye, whose light is the mind, the ultimate resort of the self of all—he is truly a knower, Yājñavalkya."

"But I know that Person who is the ultimate resort of the self of all, about whom you speak. He is the person seen in the mirror. Tell me, Śākalya, who is his God?"

"Life," he said.

16. "He who knows that Person whose support is water, whose world is the heart, whose light is the mind, the ultimate resort of the self of all—he is truly a knower, Yājñavalkya."

"But I know that Person who is the ultimate resort of the self of all, about whom you speak. He is the person in the water. Tell me, Śākalya, who is his God?"

"Varuṇa," he said.

17. "He who knows that Person whose support is in the seed, whose world is the heart, whose light is the mind, the ultimate resort of the self of all—he is truly a knower, Yājñavalkya."

"But I know that Person who is the ultimate resort of the self of all, about whom you speak. He is that person in the form of a son. Tell me, Śākalya, who is his God?"

"Prajāpati," he said.

BU V, 6

iii) This Person consisting of spirit is of the reality of light, within the heart; [he is as small] as a grain of rice or of barley. He is the Lord of all, the controller of all, he rules over all this [world], whatever there is.

TU II, 3-5; 8-9

iv) 3.

The Gods breathe with the life breath,
so, too, do men and animals.
Breath is the life of beings,
hence it is called the life of all.
Those who meditate on Brahman as life
attain a full life span,
for breath is the life of beings.
Hence it is called the life of all.

This dwells in the same corporal *ātman* as the preceding one. Different from and interior to the *ātman* consisting of breath is the *ātman* consisting of mind; by that is this filled. This has the form of a person. Because of its likeness to the *puruṣa* it has also a personal form. His head consists of sacrificial formulas, his right side of hymns, his left side of songs, his self of the word of authority; his lower support consists of prayers and incantations. About this there is a verse:

4.

Whence words recoil, together with the mind,
unable to reach it—whoso knows
that bliss of Brahman has no fear.

This dwells in the same corporal *ātman* as the preceding one. Different from and interior to the *ātman* consisting of mind is the *ātman* consisting of consciousness; by that is this filled. This has the form of a person; the other also has the form of a person. His head consists of faith, his right side of holy order, his left side of truth, his self of union with the divine; his lower support consists of power. About this there is a verse:

5. By consciousness is spread out sacrifice;
it also spreads out the worlds.
All the Gods meditate on Brahman
as the foremost wisdom.
He who knows Brahman as wisdom
and is not neglectful, who has destroyed
sin in his body—that man attains
all his desires.

This dwells in the same corporal *ātman* as the preceding one. Different from and interior to the *ātman* consisting of consciousness is the *ātman* consisting of bliss; by that is this filled. Now this has the form of a person, and because it has the form of a person, the other also has the form of a person. His head consists of love, his right side of delight, his left side of extreme delight, his self is bliss; his lower support is Brahman.

8. . . . The one who is here in the person and who is yonder in the sun—he is one. He who knows this, on leaving this world, proceeds to the *ātman* consisting of food, the *ātman* consisting of life breath, the *ātman* consisting of mind, the *ātman* consisting of consciousness, the *ātman* consisting of bliss. About this there is a verse:

9. Whence words recoil, together with the mind,
unable to reach it—whoso knows
that bliss of Brahman has no fear.

He is not tormented at the thought: Have I done good, have I committed a sin? For he who knows is himself released from both good and evil; truly he who knows is himself released from both. This is the teaching.

KathU V, 8

v) That person who remains awake within the sleepers
fashioning all desires;
he is called the pure, Brahman, the immortal;
on him all worlds repose. None can transcend him.
This, in truth, is that!

SU III, 7-21

vi) 7. Still higher is Brahman, the supreme, the great,
hidden in the bodies of all these beings,
the One, encompassing the All, the Lord—
having realized him, men become immortal.

8. I have come to know that mighty Person,
golden like the sun, beyond all darkness.
By knowing him a man transcends death;
there is no other path for reaching that goal.

9. Higher than him is nothing whatever;
than him nothing smaller, than him nothing greater.
He stands like a tree rooted in heaven,
the One, the Person, filling this whole world.

10. That which is exalted high above this world—
an absence of form, an absence of suffering—
those who know this become immortal.
The others merely enter upon sorrow.

11. Dwelling in the face, head, and neck of all,
hidden in the heart of every being,
all-pervading, the Lord is he.
Hence he is called the omnipresent, the Auspicious.

12. This Person indeed is the mighty Lord;
it is he who impels all that there is, inspiring
to the purest attainment. He is Master
and Light unchanging.

13. A Person of a thumb's size is the inner *ātman,*
ever dwelling in the heart of beings.
He acts by and through the heart, mind, and spirit.
Those who know that become immortal.

14. A thousand-headed is the Man
with a thousand eyes, a thousand feet;
encompassing the earth on all sides,
he exceeded it by ten fingers' breadth.

15. The Person, in truth, is all this world,
what has been and what yet shall be.
He is the Lord of immortality, the ruler
of every creature that is nourished by food.

16. On every side are his hands and feet,
on every side his eyes, his head,
and his face, on every side his hearing.
He stands encompassing all in the world.

17. Reflecting the qualities of all the senses,
yet himself devoid of all the senses,
he is the Lord and God of all;
he is the universal refuge.

18. The soul, embodied in the nine-doored city,
playfully sports to and fro outside it.

Controller is he of all the world,
of all that moves and of all that moves not.

19. Without hands, he grasps; without feet, he runs;
without eyes, he sees; without ears, he hears.
What is knowable he knows, but none knows him!
They call him the great primeval Person.

20. Subtlest of the subtle, greatest of the great,
the *ātman* is hidden in the cave of the heart
of all beings. He who, free from all urges,
beholds him, overcomes sorrow, seeing
by grace of the creator, the Lord and his glory.

21. Him do I know, the unaging primeval
ātman who pervades all with penetrating power.
Birth, they say—it stops for the one
who knows him whom the Brahman-knowers call Eternal.

MundU II, 1, 1-10

vii) This is the truth:

1. As a thousand sparks from a fire well blazing
spring forth, each one like the rest,
so from the Imperishable all kinds of beings
come forth, my dear, and to him return.

2. Divine and formless is the Person;
he is inside and outside, he is not begotten,
is not breath or mind; utterly pure,
farther than the farthest Imperishable.

3. From him springs forth the breath of life,
the power of thought and all the senses,
space, wind, light, and water,
and earth, the great supporter of all.

4. Fire is his head, the sun and moon
his eyes, the compass points his ears.
The revealed Vedas are his word.
The wind is his breath, his heart is the all.
From his feet proceeded the earth. In truth,
he is the inner *ātman* of all beings.

5. From him comes fire with its fuel, the sun;
from the moon comes rain, thence plants on the earth.
The male pours seed into the female;
thus from the Person creatures are born.

6. From him come hymns, songs, and sacrificial formulas,
initiations, sacrifices, rites, and all offerings.

From him come the year, the sacrificer, and the worlds
in which the moon shines forth, and the sun.

7. From him take their origin the numerous Gods,
the heavenly beings, men, beasts, and birds,
the in-breath and the out-breath, rice and barley,
ascetic fervor, faith, truth, purity, and law.

8. From him take their origin the seven breaths,
the seven flames, their fuel, the seven oblations;
from him these seven worlds in which the breaths are moving,
each time seven and hidden in secret.

9. From him come the oceans, from him the mountains,
from him come all plants together with their juices—
with all beings he abides as their inmost *ātman*.

10. The Person is all this—work, ascetic fervor,
Brahman, supreme immortality. Who knows
that which is hidden in the [heart's] secret cave,
he cuts here and now, my dear, the knot of ignorance.

■ i) 1. Cf. MaitU VI, 3 (§ III A a Introduction).
Embodied: *mūrta,* formed, shaped.
Bodiless: *amūrta,* unformed.
Tangible and intangible: pun with *sat* and *tyam,* which form *satyam,* truth, reality. *Sat* can also be translated as the existent, as being, *tyam* as the transcendent.
2. Essence of the tangible: *sato hy eṣa rasaḥ.*
3. Person: *puruṣa.*
With relation to the cosmic powers: *adhidaivata* or *adhi-devata.*
4. The two aspects of the person (*ātman*) are shown: the embodied one whose essence is the eye, and the spiritual one in v. 5. The embodied person is "stable" (*sthita*), whereas the spiritual person is "moving" (*yat*).
5. Inner space within the heart: *antar-ātmann-ākāśaḥ.* Here *ātman* refers to the heart.
Person in the right eye: the microcosmic correspondence to the cosmic *puruṣa* who is located in the sun.
6. All the metaphors stress the surprising and shining form of the "inner man."
Not this: *na iti,* or no, no.
Truth of the real: *satyasya satyam.*
Life powers: *prāṇāḥ.*
■ ii) The Mādhyandina recension of the BU has certain differences (e.g., the "Gods" in vv. 10-15 are *striyaḥ, cakṣu, prāṇa, manas, vāc, mṛtyu*), which shows that various versions of these correspondences existed.
The Kāṇva recension (our text) has the following system of correlations: in most of the examples the "support" (*āyatana*) is an element and, with the exception of *kāma,* pleasure or love (v. 11), the cosmological aspect of the *puruṣa.*The world or realm (*loka*) is the organ or center in the person (with the exception of fire in v. 10 which has to be understood as the metabolic fire in man). The heart is the dominating realm of the person. The only invariable factor in all the aspects of the *puruṣa* is the mind as his light or, one might say, the spirit as the illuminating principle.
Then follow the designations of the different types of "person," or rather, different manifestations of the same *puruṣa,* from the cosmic *puruṣa* in the sun down to the child (v. 17). The "god" (*devatā*) of each of these *puruṣas* can be understood as their goal (e.g., v. 10), their object (v. 11), their ultimate principle (v. 12), or their supervising deity (vv. 16-17).
1-9. Cf. § VI 2.
10. Ultimate resort: *parāyaṇa,* highest goal (throughout).
12. About the relation of the *puruṣa* in the sun and truth (*satya*), cf. also IsU 15 (§ VII 31).
13. About the correspondence between the ear and regions of space, cf. RV X, 90, 14 (§ I 5); MundU II, 1, 4 (vii).
14. Darkness: *tamas,* the element of death.
15. Life: *asu.*

17. Seed: *retas,* semen.
Prajāpati is the Lord of procreation.
For other ref. to BU III, 9 cf. § VI 5 (iv notes).

■ iii) Cf. SB X, 6, 3, 2 (§ VI 5).
Consisting of spirit: *manomaya.* Cf. TU II, 3 (iv).
Reality of light: *bhāḥ satyaḥ.*
Lord of all: *sarvasyeśānaḥ.*
7. Cf. § IV 21.

■ iv) 1. Cf. § VI 3.
2. Cf. § II 11.
3. Life: *āyu.*
Ātman consisting of breath: *prāṇamaya;* cf. v. 2.
Ātman consisting of mind: *manomaya.*
Sacrificial formulas: *yajus* (Veda).
Hymns: *ṛc* (Veda).
Songs: *sāman* (Veda).
Word of authority: *ādeśa,* the guidance of the master by which the disciple finds the truth; or it means the U.
Prayers and incantations: *atharvāṅgirasaḥ,* the AV.
The "body" of the spiritual person consists of the scriptures (the Veda), while his soul is constituted by the personal word of the *guru.* Or else, the four Vedas are the parts of the body, the U the *ātman.*
4. Whence words recoil: *yato vāco nivartante,* i.e., speech returns without having attained the goal; cf. v. 9.
R. Tagore translated: "From Him come back baffled both words and mind. But he who realizes the joy of Brahma is free from fear."
Here *ātman* refers to the body. The five layers of the subtle body consist of food (*annamaya,* cf. TU II, 2; § II 11), breath (*prāṇamaya*), mind (*manomaya*), consciousness (*vijñānamaya*), and bliss (*ānandamaya*). Cf. also the conception of the *kośa.* All the inner layers of man are personal (*puruṣavidha*).
Faith: *śraddhā.*
Holy order: *ṛta.*
Truth: *satya.*
Union with the divine: *yoga ātmā,* his soul is yoga.
5. By consciousness is spread out sacrifice: *vijñānaṁ yajñam tanute,* lit. wisdom extends the sacrifice.
Love: *priya.*
Delight: *moda.*
Bliss: *ānanda.*
We have translated in a slightly different way the same obscure sentence in the middle of *anuvākas* 3, 4, and 5.
This paragraph ends by saying: "about this there is a verse," which introduces the following stanzas.
6-7. Cf. § I 7.
8. The omitted passage contains a long dissertation on bliss (*ānandasya mīmāṁsā*). Cf. also BU IV, 3, 33.
9. Teaching: *upaniṣad.* Cf. BU IV, 4, 22 (§ VI 6).

■ v) 6-7. Cf. § V 5.
8. Fashioning all desires: *kāmaṁ kāmam* (desire after desire) . . . *nirmimāṇaḥ,* i.e., he is the origin and end of all desires of the heart. Cf. BU IV, 3, 9 sq. (§ V B Antiphon).
9-13. Cf. § VI 2.

■ vi) 7. Lord: *īśa.*
8. Cf. YV XXXI, 18 (§ VI 11).
No other path . . .: *nānyaḥ panthā vidyate 'yanāya,* no other way leads to salvation.
9. Tree rooted in heaven: cf. TA X, 10, 3; KathU VI, 1 (§ V 5).
10. Cf. BU IV, 4, 14 (§ IV 6).
Sorrow: *duḥkha.*
11. Cf. RV X, 81, 3 (§ VII 7); X, 90, 1 (§ I 5).
Auspicious: *śiva.*
12. Mighty Lord: *mahān prabhuḥ.*
All that there is: *sattva,* or the pure aspect of being which he promotes (*pravartaka*). Cf. KathU VI, 7 (§ VI 11).
Attainment: *prāpti,* happening, event.
13. Person of a thumb's size: *aṅguṣṭhamātraḥ puruṣaḥ,* cf. KathU IV, 12-13 (§ VII 52). Cf. also KathU VI, 9; 17 (§§ VI 11; V 5).
14. Verse identical with RV X, 90, 1 (§ I 5).
15. Cf. RV X, 90, 2 (§ I 5); AV XIX, 6, 4 (§ I D Antiphon).
16. Cf. BG XIII, 13.
17. Cf. BG XIII, 14.
Universal refuge: *sarvasya śaraṇam bṛhat.*

18. Soul: *haṁsa,* swan.
Nine-doored city: the body with the senses.
Playfully sports: *līlāyati* (or *lelayati*), the freedom of a bird.
20. By grace of the creator: *dhātu-prasādāt.* Cf. KathU II, 20 (§ V 5).
Lord: *īśa,* where KathU has *ātman.*
21. Birth . . . it stops: *janma-nirodham,* cessation, stoppage, elimination of, exemption from birth.
Eternal: *nitya.*
▪ vii) 1. Cf. also § V 18. Cf. BU II, 1, 20 (§ VI 4); MaitU VI, 26; 31; MundU I, 1, 7 (§ I 7).
All kinds: *bhāvāḥ,* types, modes of being.
2. Cf. BU II, 3, 5 (§ VI 7), III, 8, 8 (§ VI 3), etc., for the traditional epithets.
Formless: *amūrta* also bodiless, incorporeal.
Imperishable: *akṣara.*
3. Power of thought: *manas.*
4. The revealed Vedas are his word: *vāg-vivṛtāś ca vedāḥ,* from the verb *vi-vṛ-,* to uncover, to open up; to manifest, to illumine, etc.
His heart is the all: *hṛdayaṁ viśvam,* his heart is all-pervading, the whole universe, the world.
5. Cf. CU V, 4, 1; V, 5, 2; V, 8, 2.
6. Hymns, songs, and sacrificial formulas: *ṛcaḥ sāma yajūṁsi;* cf. RV X, 90, 9 (§ I 5).
Initiations: *dīkṣāḥ.*
Moon shines forth: *somo . . . pavate,* with the double meaning of Soma (the root *pu-* is always used in this connection) and the moon. The whole stanza uses sacrificial terms.
7. Purity, and law: *brahmacaryaṁ vidhiś ca.*
8. The seven breaths (*prāṇāḥ*) are sometimes related to the seven *ṛṣis;* here the sense organs are meant.
Seven flames: cf. PrasnU III, 5; MundU I, 2, 4 (§ III 27).
The functions of the sense organs are compared to a sacrifice; the seven worlds are the sense objects.
9. Cf. BU III, 8, 9 (§ VI 3).
10. Cf. RV X, 90, 2 (§ I 5).
Knot of ignorance: *avidyā-granthi.* Cf. CU VII, 26, 2 (§ VI 3).

I *Aham*

8 The first awakening of consciousness finds its spontaneous expression in the words "I am" *aham asmi.*[93] *Aham,* I, is thus the first word, the first name, as the same Upaniṣad tells us, not only of the primordial *ātman* but of every Man. But it is also Man's last word. This "secret name of the *puruṣa*" (iii) is the innermost identity of the person. In one of the ceremonies of transmission from the dying father to the son, what the father passes on or transfers is his very identity (i). And the identity of his "I" is, within the Vedic universe, Brahman (the goal), sacrifice (the way), the world (this shore). The "I" is all this. Only then, having reached the I, does Man attain immortality and thus depart from this earth. It is the full consciousness of the "I" (which is the opposite of egoistic self-centeredness) which frees a Man from all fears (ii). Only the full consciousness of the "I" is real freedom, *svarāj,* because one does not depend on others (iv).

If in the beginning there was the "I am," the pure awareness of

93. BU I, 4, 1 (§ I 7).

the "I," this same "I" will also be at the end of the human pilgrimage. There is but one basic difference. It is the dying Man who discovers his ultimate identity with the *puruṣa,* with the *aham.*[94] Making the discovery is what constitutes human life on earth, the real process of human growth. The Maitrī Upaniṣad (v) again expands the thought that the oneness with and of the One, Brahman, is realized only by the realization of the "I." The *aham* is the principle of unity even in the Absolute.[95]

Aham

BU I, 5, 17

i) Now follows the transmission [from father to son]. When a man thinks that he is going to leave [this world], he speaks thus to his son:

"You are Brahman, you are sacrifice, you are the world."

And the son replies: "I am Brahman, I am sacrifice, I am the world." For in truth, whatever has been learned, all this is gathered up in Brahman. And whatever sacrifices have been offered, they are all gathered up in [the one] Sacrifice. And whatever worlds are there, they are all gathered up in [the one] World. So great is this all. As he is all, let him fulfill it. Therefore they call a son who is learned "experienced in the world," and thus they instruct him. Therefore, when one who knows this departs from this world, he enters into his son with his vital breaths. Whatever wrong he has done, the son frees him from all that and therefore he is called "son." It is by his son that the father is established in the world. Then the divine, immortal breaths enter into him.

BU IV, 3, 19-21

ii) 19. As an eagle or another bird becomes tired after flying about, closes its wings, and speeds to its nest, so is the person hasting to this state where he neither feels any desires nor sees any dream.

20. There are his arteries called *hitā* which are as minute as a hair split in a thousand parts and filled with white, blue, yellow, green, and red [particles]. Now when [in dream] he is killed, as it were, or subdued, as it were, or persecuted by an elephant, as it were, or falls into a well, as it were—whatever fear he experiences in the waking state, he [now] imagines because of his ignorance. But when he thinks like a God or a king, "I am this, I am all!" that is his supreme state.

21. This is his manifestation which is beyond craving, beyond evil and fear. Just as a man embraced by his beloved wife does not know what is out-

94. Cf. IsU 16 (BU V, 15, 2) (§ VII 31).

95. *Aham* is etymologically connected with Greek *egô,* Latin *ego,* German *ich.* A popular etymology of *a-ham* analyzes it as consisting of the first and last letter of the Sanskrit alphabet (*a—ha*), plus a final nasalization. Thus *aham* would be alpha and omega, the first and the last.

side and what is inside, likewise the person, when he is embraced by the conscious *ātman,* does not know what is outside and what is inside. This is his manifestation where his desires are fulfilled; his only desire is the *ātman* and [hence] he is free from desires. There his sorrow ceases.

BU V, 5, 4

iii) Concerning this Person who is in the right eye: his head is the syllable *bhūḥ,* for his head is one and the syllable also is one. His arms are *bhuvaḥ,* for he has two arms and there are two syllables. His feet are *svaḥ,* for he has two feet and there are two syllables. His secret name is "I." He who knows this destroys evil and passes beyond it.

CU VII, 25, 1-2

iv) 1. That [fullness] is below; it is above, it is behind, it is before, it is in the South, it is in the North. That indeed is all that is.

Now regarding the teaching about the I-sense: I am below, I am above, I am behind, I am before, I am in the South, I am in the North, I indeed am all that is.

2. Now the teaching concerning the *ātman:* the *ātman* is below, it is above, it is behind, it is before, it is in the South, it is in the North. The *ātman* indeed is all that is. He who sees, reflects, and knows this — he has joy in the *ātman,* he plays with the *ātman,* he unites with the *ātman,* his is the bliss of the *ātman*. He becomes free and is free to move in all the worlds. But those who think otherwise are ruled by others and their worlds are perishable. They are unfree in all the worlds.

MaitU VI, 35

v) Praise to Fire who dwells on earth and protects the world, give this world to the sacrificer!

Praise to Air, who dwells in the atmosphere and protects the world, give this world to the sacrificer!

Praise to the Sun, who dwells in the sky and protects the world, give this world to the sacrificer!

Praise to Brahman who dwells in all and protects all, give all to the sacrificer!

The face of truth is covered over
by a golden vessel. Uncover it, O Pūṣan,
for Viṣṇu, whose order is truth.
He who is that Person in the sun, I am He!

He is the one whose order is truth, that which is the sunhood of the sun, which is the pure, the personal, the uncharacterized. But that is only one part of the Energy which pervades the atmosphere, that which is, as it were, in the center of the sun, in the eye, and in fire, that is Brahman, that is the immortal, that is splendor, that is the one whose order is truth. That is only one part of the Energy which pervades the atmosphere, which is the immortal in the center of the sun, of which the moon and living beings are but an offshoot, that is Brahman, that is the immortal, that is splendor, that is the one whose order is truth. That is only one part of the Energy which penetrates the atmosphere, which is in the center of the sun, where the *yajus* shines:

It is OM,
it is the waters,
it is the essence of light, the immortal Brahman.
Bhūḥ bhuvaḥ svaḥ OM.

The eight-footed, the pure, the swan,
with three threads, the infinitesimal, immutable,
blind to good and evil, kindled with energy:
one who sees Him sees all.

That is only one part of the Energy which pervades the atmosphere, which is in the center of the sun; having risen it becomes two rays. That is the knower, the one whose order is truth, that is the *yajus*, that is heat, fire, wind, life, water, moon.

That is the pure, the immortal, the realm of Brahman. That is the ocean of radiance, in which the worshipers dissolve like a lump of salt. That is oneness with Brahman, in which all desires are contained. On this there is a saying:

As a lamp twinkles, stirred by a slight breeze,
so too does he who has entered within the Gods.
He who knows this, becomes a knower
of the One and of duality, he who has attained
to the oneness of the One, to the selfsame nature.

Like drops springing up perpetually,
like lightning, lights playing in the clouds
in the highest firmament—these lights
are supported by the power of Glory,
appearing like the flame crests of fire.

■ i) Cf. the transmission ceremony in KausU II, 15 (§ V 12).

Transmission: *saṁpratti*. Whatever the father has realized in his life, he passes on to his son. Sacrifice is the link between the two spheres. Life is not complete without knowing the three.

As he is all let him fulfill it: *sarvaṁ sann ayamito bhunajad*, referring probably to the father's thought. As the son has become all (through this ceremony), he can save his father.

Experienced in the world: *lokya*, or possessing, obtaining the world (for his father).

Therefore he is called "son": although the popular etymology does not actually occur here (the verb is *muñcati*, frees, and not *trāyate*, saves, as would be required for the explanation of *pu-tra*), it is referred to. *Putra* (son) is explained as the one who saves his father from hell (cf. GopB I, 1, 2; Manu IX, 128).

■ ii) 19. Person: *puruṣa*, man.

State: *anta*, goal, end, i.e., the state of rest, deep sleep (*suṣupti*), which comes closest to the state of liberation.

20. There: i.e., in his heart, into which he "retreats," so to speak, in sleep. Cf. BU IV, 2, 3; KausU IV, 19.
I am this . . .: *aham evedam sarvo 'smi.*
Supreme state: *paramo lokaḥ,* highest world. Cf. BU IV, 4, 22 (§ VI 6) for the use of *loka.*
21. Manifestation: *rūpa,* form or state.
Embraced . . .: cf. BU I, 4, 3 (§ I 7).
Conscious *ātman: prājñenātmanā,* by the Spirit.
His desires are fulfilled . . . : the three steps are *āptakāma, ātmakāma, akāma,* which correspond to a transformation and gradual simplification of the desires.
22. Cf. § IV 6.

■ iii) The *puruṣa* in the cosmos is sometimes conceived as inverted: his head is *bhūḥ,* the earth; his arms are *bhuvaḥ,* the atmosphere; and his feet are *svaḥ,* heaven.
His secret name is "I": *tasyopaniṣad aham iti. Aham* is for the person what the Upaniṣad is for the Veda (its inner meaning).

■ iv) 1. Fullness: taken from CU VII, 23 1 (*bhūman*) (§ VI 3).
I-sense: *ahaṁkāra,* here not in the later sense of egoism, but as the ultimate and therefore universal "I."
2. He has joy in the *ātman . . . : ātma-rati, ātma-krīḍa, ātma-mithuna, ātmānanda.* The terms that refer otherwise to the erotic experience apply here to the *ātman.* Cf. also BU II, 4, 5 (§ VI 5).
Free: *svarāj,* self-ruled.
Free to move: *kāmacāra,* moving at will.

■ v) 34. Cf. § III 28.
Fire: Agni.
Air: Vāyu.
Sun: Aditya.
Protects the world: most of the readings have *lokasmṛte,* remembers the world, but the correct version is *lokaspṛte,* bestows or protects the world.
The face of truth . . .: cf. BU V, 15, 1 and IsU 15 (§ VII 31) with the change of only one word (*viṣṇave* for *dṛṣṭaye*).
Whose order is truth: *satyadharma,* of true reality.
Personal: *puruṣa.*
Uncharacterized: *aliṅga,* or sexless. Some versions drop "personal" and "uncharacterized."
Energy: *tejas,* brilliance, heat. The text here is full of repetitions and interpolations.
Splendor: *bhargas.*
The *yajus* shines: refers either to the next verse (starting with "it is OM") or to the *puruṣa* consisting of the four Vedas. Cf. TU II, 3 (§ VI 7).
Blind to good and evil: *dvidharmo 'ndham,* lit. blind to the two realities (attributes).
Having risen: *uditvā,* or *ud ity eva,* i.e., "it is [the syllable] *ud*" (of Udgītha, cf. CU I, 5, 1).
Heat: *tapas.*
Life: *prāṇaḥ.*
Realm of Brahman: *brahma-viṣaya.*
Knower of the One and of duality: *sa savit sa dvaitavit; sa* is here understood to refer to the One.
Glory: *yaśas.*

I Am Brahman Without a Second — *Brahma advayam asmi*

9 The *ātman* is the most precious thing. But who loves it? Obviously it can only be the *aham,* the I. But again, whose *aham?* Certainly not my private petty ego. What is that I then that can love the *ātman*? "What am I?" asks one text (iv). Only Brahman can correspond to the *ātman.* But has Brahman an *aham*? Here is the new step taken by this *mahāvākya.* An *aham* that is closed in itself would be a pure mental abstraction. The *aham* is in fact such because it is open. But only the infinity of Brahman will not close the I. *Aham* is radical openness.

This is what is said in our first text (i). In the beginning Brahman was alone, but the moment "He" realized his aloneness "He" opened up his own existence, as it were. "He" cried as in wonder, *I am Brahman*! and in this consciousness he opened up the possibility of existence for the entire universe. Communication was made possible; communion appeared; the relation was installed and with it the existence of reality. That is why the ignorant Man is he who ignores that ultimate and constitutive relation and thinks, "I am one and he is another" (i). Between *brahman* and *aham-brahman* lies the entire temporal universe.

The only possible utterance of the *aham* is Brahman. Any other word either is not ultimate or else is a lie. I *am* neither body (alone) nor mind (only) nor creature (exclusively) nor God (uniquely)—*I am* certainly all this as well as much more: *aham brahman*. For this reason the only spontaneous attitude of the Man to whom his revelation dawns is to cry *māṁ juhomi:*[96] "I offer myself in oblation" (iv).

It is the tremendous discovery both of *I am He* (ii) and *He is* (iii) which leads to the full realization of the *jīvanmukta* or the liberated person, who can then speak the language of Brahman (iv). There is no longer a duologue but a real dialogue, a piercing through—and by—the logos into the *brahma-advayam asmy aham*.

Brahma advayam asmi

BU I, 4, 8-10

i) 8. Dearer than a son, dearer than wealth, dearer than all else, the innermost of all, is the *ātman*. If one were to say about someone who considers something else dearer than the *ātman*, "He will lose what is dear to him," most assuredly that would happen. One should meditate only on the *ātman* as dear. He who meditates on the *ātman* alone as dear, what is dear to him will not perish.

9. Thus they said: men think that by knowing Brahman they will become the All. What, then, did Brahman know by means of which it became the All?

10. In truth, in the beginning this was Brahman alone. It knew itself only as *I am Brahman*. Hence it became the all. And as the Gods one by one awakened [to this], they too became that, and likewise the seers, and likewise men.

Realizing this, the sage Vāmadeva discovered, "I was the father of humanity and I was the sun!" Even nowadays he who knows *I am*

96. This cultic verb means to pour butter into the fire, to offer. It is an almost exclusively technical term for sacrificial ceremonies. The root *hu-*, usually translated as sacrifice, has the active meaning of sprinkling, presenting an oblation, worship (to eat, etc.).

Brahman becomes this all. The Gods themselves are not able to prevent this, for he becomes their *ātman*.

Now then, he who worships another God, [thinking] "He is one and I am another," he is ignorant. In relation to the Gods he is like a [domestic] animal, for just as many animals serve men, so each man serves the Gods. If even a single animal is removed it causes displeasure. What if many are removed? Therefore the Gods are not pleased that men should know this.

BU IV, 4, 12

ii)

The man who realizes the *ātman*
knowing: "I am He"—
what craving or what urge could cause
him to cling to the body?

KathU VI, 12-13

iii)

12. Neither by the word nor by the mind
nor by sight can he ever be reached.
How, then, can he be realized
except by exclaiming, "He is"?

13. One must realize him first as "He is"
and then also his existential nature.
When realized as the "He is,"
then he shows forth his existential nature.

MahanarU 157-158

iv)

What am I: *I am Brahman!*
Yes, *I am Brahman,* I am!
I verily offer myself in oblation!
Svāhā!

KaivU 19

v)

In me alone originates the All,
in me the All is established,
in me all things come to rest.
I am that Brahman without a second!

▪ i) 1-5. Cf. § I 7.
8. Cf. BU II, 4, 5 (§ VI 5).
9. By knowing Brahman: *brahma-vidyayā*.
10. We have the following equations: *idam* = *aham; aham* = *brahman; tad* = *brahman; brahman* = *sarvam*. Hence it became: *tasmāt*, i.e., because of its self-consciousness, not because of its simple existence. At this stage *brahman, ātman* and *aham* are identical, but they start to be differentiated by the very act of self-reflection.
Vāmadeva is a famous Ṛg Vedic *ṛṣi* with a markedly philosophical outlook. Cf. the entire Book IV of the RV.

Father of humanity: Manu. Cf. RV IV, 26, 1, where this line occurs.

The Gods are jealous of the realized Man because he is no longer different from them and because by reason of his realization he gives up any worship of the Gods as "other." To worship God as another (*anya*) is not different from the service of a domestic animal.

He who worships another God: *atha yo 'nyāṁ devatām upāste,* or he who worships (considers) God as another.

He is one . . .: *anyo 'sau, ayo 'ham asmīti.*

He is ignorant: *na sa veda,* he does not know.

16. Cf. § III 27.

17. Cf. § I 7.

▪ iii) 1-3. Cf. § V 5.

4-11. Cf. § VI 11.

12. Realize: *upa-labh-,* to apprehend, perceive, conceive, receive, attain.

13. Then also: lit. in both ways; grasping the *asti* as well as the *tattva-bhāva.*

Existential nature: *tattva-bhāva,* the "state of being of that-ness," the state of identity.

Shows forth: *prasīdati,* becomes clear or manifest; reveals.

14-18. Cf. § V 5.

▪ iv) 152-156. Cf. § III 6.

157. *Yo 'ham asmi brahmāham asmi, aham asmi brahmāham asmi.*

▪ v) The last line reads: *tad brahma advayam asmy aham.*

C. THE ENCOUNTER

Yoga

Having realized "I am Brahman,"
one is released from all bondage.

KaivU 17[97]

We climbed in search of the absolute object only to find that the very concept is contradictory, but we were not disappointed because we discovered pure consciousness, which is not an object. We descended by another way, the interior path, looking for the absolute subject, and when we thought we had found it, it eluded us, for we certainly are not the absolute subject. It is only the same absolute subject that can say "I am." But where are we? Is there any place at all for what we definitively, or at least provisionally, are? It is too cold on the peak. It is too hot on the plains. Going up the way of transcendence we lost trace of Man. Coming down the path of interiorization we did not find any upward track. Is there any crossing, any encounter? Then only in these terms can we speak of salvation. A salvation that saves nobody is not truly salvation; it is a mockery. To install us as little monarchs in the realm within, and to try to convince us that the realm without is only an illusion, appears

97. Cf. the theistic emphasis of SU VI, 13 (§ VI 2): "Having realized God, one is freed from all chains": *jñātvā devam* [*tad brahmāham iti*] *mucyate* [*pramucyate*] *sarva-pāśaiḥ* [*bandhaiḥ*]. The words found in the text of KaivU are given in brackets.

too much of an alienation and is in any event a lie. We spoke of a middle way and of an integrating experience. The traditional term for integration is *yoga,* the union of all polarities. *Yoga* leads to liberation. This is the moment to see whether *mokṣa* means freedom or flight, liberation or escapism.

a) The Fulfillment of the Person

Tat tvam asi

That art thou

We are still searching for the full meaning of *advitīya*. We have already seen that the nonduality of the One can be safeguarded only if the nature of the One is pure consciousness; thus we were introduced to the universal character of reality. But reality is not only universal; it is also concrete. The *puruṣa* or personal character of reality, that is, its polarity and interrelatedness, represents its concrete aspect. Concreteness, unlike particularity, is not incompatible with universality, but only with abstraction and generality. This personal or relational aspect of reality has already emerged. We have seen in fact how the third person and then the first person appeared on the horizon. This provided the only possible way to maintain empirical multiplicity without endangering metaphysical oneness. No wonder the personal character of reality is stressed in an Advaitic world view. In point of fact, what is the person if not pure relationship devoid of unrelated opaque points? Is personhood not pecisely communion within polarities? Personality or personhood is pure Advaita. A real person is neither one nor two. It is not one, because an isolated, individualized "person" is a contradiction in terms. An I is only such if there is a thou, and the thou can only be such if there is a he/she/it giving scope to the utterance of the I to the thou and to the latter's response. On the other hand, a real person is not two either. The thou is totaly dependent on the I, of and from which it is the thou that it is. The I, furthermore, is not if the thou does not "make" it, does not allow it to be the I (of the thou) that it is. One canot really isolate two "things" in the person.

The real person is beyond the singular and the plural. The

person is never in the singular or properly in the plural. A plurality of "persons" is only a plurality of personified objects, a collectivity of individuals, not of real persons. Plurality can be posited only of the nonpersonal aspects of individuals. A plurality is always somewhat homogeneous qua plurality, and thus it is interchangeable. Personal relationships are not interchangeable. They are unique. In a word, the person does not belong to the realm of quantity.[98]

Everything in the person is interrelated. Person is a net of relationships. An individualized person is an abstraction made for practical purposes. Any single person is a knot in that net of relationships. As a knot, it is unique and that concrete crossing of threads is irreducible to anything else. But the knot is made of threads. The threads—personal relationships—are not accidental relationships between two things or individuals; they constitute the person. Any other type of relations, that is, those that do not touch the knot, are precisely nonpersonal. What we call personal relationships are constitutive of the person in such a way that apart from them there is no other independent nucleus of relationships. Person is really one without a second. Each person is unique and has no second, no equivalent; it is a "moment" in this particular crossing within the cosmic web of reality. What is unique in each person is precisely the different—irreducible—situation and function of each one. Each knot is unique because it is that particular crossing of threads which constitutes precisely that knot and not another. It is not unique because it has a peculiar "substance" of its own but because the threads of reality cross in that particular point and not elsewhere. The knot is not just the threads, but it is nothing besides that particular crossing of threads. The Vedic metaphor of the loom is a valid contemporary symbol for the *puruṣa* character of the entire universe.

The clue to the mystery of the person is the thou. Without thou there is no I, but only a monolithic and lifeless block in a solipsistic pit. There is only an I when he is capable of uttering, discovering, creating, a thou. We have tried to catch this cry of the I from the beginning of this anthology.[99] But, again, the thou in order to be such is not a passive and lifeless receiver of the emanation of the I, but a living response, an answer, even at times a resistance. A thou

98. Cf. BU IV, 4, 19 (§ VI 11).
99. Cf. § I A Introduction.

is only such if there is room for his reaction, that is, if there is an empty space between the I and the thou. This empty space is the guarantee of personal itimacy and of freedom. In other words, only the existence of a common he/she/it discovered by both, or rather made possible by the very relationship between the I and the thou, makes this relationship possible, personal, and free. The I and the thou encounter each other in the he/she/it of the third person. If the response of the thou to the I could not go its own way, if it were obliged to return on the same track on which it came as an invitation and a challenge, there would be no freedom but simply an automatic reaction. It is the third person that permits a free response from the thou (which can then create its own way back) and itself is constituted by that very act. To discover oneself as a thou does not imply that one recognizes oneself as a mere puppet or imitation of the I. It does imply that one is aware of the many free responses the thou can give. This gift of the thou is the third person, the other, the world, the interval in which my being reaches its fulfillment responding to the I. The third person is the gift; there is here not a dialectical but a free dialogical relationship.

Now this is what the most important of all *mahāvākyas*, according to tradition, is going to disclose to us. Because Brahman is the I, there is place for the thou: *that art thou,* the thou of the I, the thou of Brahman. This is what you are, a thou, nothing more and nothing less; nothing more, so that without the I you are sheer negative nothingness and have no consistency or existence of your own and do not belong to yourself, to your ego; but also nothing less, so that you are Brahman, of Brahman, equal to Brahman and have infinite value and are like Braman, *sat cit* and *ānanda* being, spirit, and glory.[100] That is what this Great Utterance affirms.

Brahman is the absolute, the One without a second. There is really no second, but there is an *aham* and also an *ayam,* a *sa,* a *tad,* a he. Significantly enough, the place for the thou is discovered only when the *aham-brahman* is realized in its proper way as an existential statement and not as a mere mental construct.

Before coming to the main text we may note that if this *mahāvākya* were telling us only that we are Brahman, that is, "thou art that," it would not be telling us anything new or different from the other *mahāvākyas* we have already studied. We would not understand why tradition has accorded such immense importance to this

100. Cf. TU II, 1 (§ VI 3) for Brahman as *satya*, *jñāna*, and *ananta*.

particular one and has linked salvation with the realization of it. This *mahāvākya,* however, has undoubtedly something very special to reveal: that we are the thou of Brahman, his partners, his offspring, his relation and relationship, and that we are the thou of the I.

We are not attempting at this point to elaborate a philosophical theory, to trace its outworkings in the different schools, or to discuss the many problems that arise from it. Our saying does not rule out the philosophical approach, but we are not concerned with that approach here. For instance, we are not obliged to agree with the much discussed doctrine of the one-sidedness of the relation "Brahman-world," though one could defend that doctrine without contradicting the present interpretation. In other words, we do not present this *mahāvākya* in a polemic way but simply try to convey an intuition.

This intuition entails the great conversion that the *mahāvākya* is demanding from us, namely, that we should completely reverse the apparent order of things in order to acquire the true vision of reality. It requires from us a change of heart, just as it also demands the change of object into subject and vice versa, the overcoming of egocentrism, and the recovery of the true thou-character of the creature. It represents a radical change of perspective: we are a thou and the thou has meaning only for the I and existence only from the I. The thou is only "be-ing," that is, a response, thanksgiving, and love. This response, moreover, is completely free; otherwise it would not be a response at all, but simply a mechanical echo. According to this intuition, our proper relationship with the Supreme—or the supreme relationship, for that matter—is not one of *I-thou* but, just the opposite, one of *thou-I.* The Absolute or Brahman or God (or any other term we may prefer) is not the thou (to whom we may pray or about whom we may think) but the I, and we are his thou. This personal aspect makes room for the total development of my being and my person.

We have already met Śvetaketu and his father, who has been instructing his son for a long time. We have now arrived back at the same chapter of the same Upaniṣad, perhaps accidentally. The culmination of this particular instruction starts, as did our previous text, with a reference to sleep within a context that stresses *sat,* being, as *mūla,* the root, of everything. When a person sleeps, the text affirms, it is said that he has been unified with *sat*.[101] In a word, "All creatures, my friend, have *sat* as their root, have *sat* as their abode, have *sat* as their support [ground, *pratiṣṭhā*]."[102] And now nine times in succession the great teaching is imparted, each time preceded by an analogy and concluded by the same sentence: "That which [is] this ultimate element, all this [world] has as its self, that is reality, that is *ātman, that art thou,* Śvetaketu."[103] There is a significant change of person from the original elliptic third person of the verb "to be" to the second person in the last part of the sentence—from the *asti* to the *asi*.

The tenor of all the examples is to reduce an empirical reality to its elements, to the ultimate *aṇiman* or minutest element, the subtlest part, the atom.[104] Then the text proceeds to say that this simplest constituent part of that empirical reality is the same in the whole universe, in the *idaṁ sarvam,* which we have often met. This is the *ātman* of all, and it is through this *ātman* that all that is, is. This is *satyam,* truth, reality, and this is also the *ātman*. Up to this point we have been given the already familiar Upaniṣadic instruction: this is the *ātman,* which is also *brahman*. Now comes something new. The subject of the sentence is the same and each time is explicitly repeated, *tat,* that. But the person of the verb changes; it becomes the second person and the discourse is now directed to Śvetaketu: "that are you," "that art thou," *tat tvam asi*. Literally, we may note, the text does not say "thou [subject] art that," but just the reverse: "that [subject] art thou [predicate]" and rightly so, for if *that* refers to Brahman it can never be the predicate of anything.

That is *ātman,* that is Brahman, that is reality. Now, that which you are, which is in you, the *aṇiman* residing in you, that is, namely, *tvam,* a thou, the thou. It is not a different thing, it is not another "that," it is your thou. You are, Śvetaketu, not an undiscriminated part of the universe, you are not just a thing among things; you are neither a faceless and amorphous atom lost among the myriad particles populating the universe, nor are you a totally different

101. Cf. CU VI, 8, 1 (§ VI 10).

102. CU VI, 8, 4; 6. (§ VI 10).

103. *Sa ya eṣo 'ṇimaitad ātmyam* [or *ātmakam*] *idaṁ sarvam: tat satyam, sa ātmā. tat tvam asi, Śvetaketo, iti:* this which (is) the *aṇimā* all this (world) (has) as its self [that which (is) the *aṇimā* belongs to the nature of all this (world)]. That is *satyam*. This is *ātman*. That you are; Śvetaketu.

104. *Aṇiman* means fineness, minuteness, the smallest particle. Cf. *aṇu,* meaning the smallest part (of time, matter, space), i.e., an atom.

thing; you are not apart, you are not of another class, you do not belong to a second category of beings; there is no second in the *ekam evādvitīyam*. You are the thou of all this, you are the partner of Brahman, not different from him and much less separated, but you are his thou, his other pole, his tension, his "person," as we might cautiously add. We say his person because, properly speaking, in the personal structure of being what is properly a person, in our common use of that word, is always the thou, the respondent, the beloved, the known. The I can be called a person only in what is for us a secondary way, while it is the thou that presents all the features of a personal existence. The human being is a person because he is a thou and he emerges as a person, not when he begins to feel or to know objects but when he realizes that he is being loved, known, watched, sought, and cared for, or, on the contrary, neglected or despised. Personhood arises with thou-awareness.

Śvetaketu, you are a person, a human person, a thou; you are inasmuch as you are loved, known, produced, by the I, inasmuch as you respond to this call, to this act of the I. You are not the I, Śvetaketu, there is only one I, only one I capable of saying in truth I am, *aham-asmi,* I am Brahman, *aham-brahman.* This is the *paramātman,* the ultimate *ātman*. It resides in you, is you, and is you in such a way that only by realizing it can you become and are you, your-self. *Tat tvam asi: Tat,* Brahman, is a *tvam,* a thou in you. Brahman! you are a thou in Śvetaketu. This is possible, Śvetaketu, precisely because *ātman-brahman,* that is, because that *he,* which you have discovered as being the I, that *ātman,* which has been disclosed, revealed to you as *brahman,* is, has a thou in you—otherwise you would not be. But you are, you are a thou, the bridge between the *ātman* and *brahman,* the link that unites and identifies them. It is this discovery of pure consciousness of *prajñānam brahman* which makes this possible, because neither are you without the I nor is He without you. And it is this realization of yours which makes you emerge as a *tvam,* a thou which is not *dvandva,* not duality, but the very expression of the *advitīyam,* of the nonduality of the *ekam,* of the One.

The whole of reality subsists in this relational or personal structure. Braman, the nature of which is pure *consciousness,* is the unique and ultimate *I* which exists precisely because it has a *thou,* which responds to its own constitutive calling by responding via the *he,* the *ātman,* without splitting the pure *oneness* of all. This stretching of the Nonduality, this tension and polarity within the One, making it really Nondual but without breaking its oneness, is precisely the mystery of life disclosed in the Upaniṣads, whose climax is found in the experience of *tat tvam asi*.

No wonder that Śvetaketu asks his father for nine different explanations until he finally understands. It is significant that the last example is no longer of a material but of a moral kind. The fact that the innocent man is not burned in the ordeal, that is, that the truth, "this is the that which is the whole world, reality, the *ātman*," is self-authenticating—this is what brings Śvetaketu to the realization that he is a thou: *tat tvam asi*.

The many texts expounding the thou help us to grasp this notion better, and once we have discovered it experientially it will bring us to all the peace and bliss of Brahman.

You *Tvam*

10 We have already seen many texts that stress the importance of *idam, this,* and of *tat, that.* They are intended to sharpen our awareness of all that there *is*. They lead us to pierce the veil of appearances and discover the *satyasya satyam,* the truth of the real.

The following texts no longer stress ecstatic consciousness, but emphasize the *tvam,* the thou. They intend to make us aware of the unique position of the thou, of the person, of the nonobjectifiable in ourselves. We recover what had seemed lost in the pure awareness of the I.

Tvam

CU VI, 8-14; 16

i) 8, 1. Uddālaka Aruṇi spoke to his son Śvetaketu:

"Learn from me, my son, concerning the state of [deep] sleep. When a person here sleeps, my dear, then he has attained Being; because he has entered into himself, therefore they say 'he sleeps,' for he has entered into himself.

2. "Just as a bird, tied to a string, after flying about in different directions and not finding any other resting place, finally finds a perch in the place of its captivity, so also the mind, my dear, after flying about in different directions and not finding any other resting place finally finds a support in the breath of life, for the mind, my dear, is tied to the breath of life.

3. "Learn from me, my son, concerning hunger and thirst. When a person here is hungry, it is water that carries off his food. Just as people speak of a carrier-off of cows, a carrier-off of horses, a carrier-off of men, so also water is called the carrier-off of food.

So, you must know, my dear, that this [body] is an offshoot, for there nothing will be without a root.

4. "What else could be [the body's] root but food? Likewise, my dear, if we regard food as an offshoot, we must look for water as its root, if we regard water as an offshoot, we must look for heat as its root, and if we regard heat as an offshoot, we must look for Being as its root.

"All these living beings, my dear, have their root in Being, have their resting place in Being, have their support in Being.

5. "When a person here is thirsty, it is heat that carries off his drink. As they speak of a carrier-off of cows, a carrier-off of horses, a carrier-off of men, so also heat is called a carrier-off of water."

"So you must know, my dear, that this is an offshoot for there nothing will be without a root.

6. "Now, what else could be [the body's] root but water? Likewise, my son, if we regard water as an offshoot we must look for heat as its root, and if we regard heat as an offshoot, we must look for Being as its root."

"For, my dear, all these living beings have Being as their root, have their resting place in Being, have their support in Being.

"Now my dear, it has already been explained how these three divinities, having entered the realm of the human, each become threefold.

"When a person, my dear, departs from here his speech is absorbed in his mind, his mind is absorbed in his breath of life, his breath of life in heat, and heat in the highest divinity.

7. "That which is this finest element, the whole world has for its self:

"That is truth; that is the *ātman*; *that are you,* Śvetaketu!"

"Let me learn even more, sir!"

"Very well, my dear," he said.

9, 1. "Just as, my dear, the bees prepare honey, collecting the juices from different trees and making one juice out of them,

2. "and just as these juices cannot distinguish anymore that 'I am the juice of this particular tree, I am the juice of that particular tree,' likewise, my dear, all these living beings, once they have been united with Being, do not know that they have been united with Being.

3. "Whatever they are here, either a tiger or a lion or a wolf or a bear or a bird or an insect or a mosquito, they become that.

4. "That which is this finest element, the whole world has for its self: That is truth; that is the *ātman; that are you,* Śvetaketu!

"Let me learn even more, sir!"

"Very well, my dear," he said.

10, 1. "The rivers, my dear, flow, those in the East toward the East and those in the West toward the West. They flow from ocean to ocean and they become the ocean. Just as these rivers do not know any longer that 'I am this one, I am that one,'

2. "likewise, my dear, all these living beings, having attained Being, do not know that " we have reached Being;" whatever they are here, either a tiger or a lion or a wolf or a bear or a worm or a bird or an insect or a mosquito, that they become [again].

3. "That which is this finest element, the whole world has for its self:

That is truth; that is the *ātman; that are you,* Śvetaketu!"

"Let me learn even more, sir!"

"Very well, my dear," he said.

11, 1. "If my dear, someone were to cut this mighty tree at its root, its sap would flow because it is alive. If someone were to cut it in the middle, its sap would flow because it is alive. If someone were to cut it at its top, its sap would flow because it is alive. Thus it stands, pervaded by the living *ātman,* rejoicing and full of sap.

2. "If life abandons one of its branches, that branch dries up. If it abandons a second branch, that too dries up. So too if it abandons a third, it dries up. If it abandons the whole tree, the whole tree dries up. In the same way, my dear, you should know!" Thus he said,

3. "This body dies when deprived of life, but life does not die. That which is this finest element the whole world has for its self. That is truth; that is the *ātman; that are you,* Śvetaketu!"

"Let me learn even more, sir!"

"Very well, my dear," he said.

12, 1. "Bring me a fruit of the fig tree!"

"Here it is, sir."

"Break it open!"

"There it is, sir!"

"What do you see?"

"These fine seeds, like tiny particles."

"Break one open!"

"There it is, sir."

"What do you see?"

"Nothing at all, sir!"

2. He said to him: "Believe me, my dear! This finest element, which you cannot perceive—out of this finest element, my dear, comes this big fig tree!

3. "That which is this finest element, the whole world has for its self: That is truth; that is the *ātman; that are you,* Śvetaketu!"

"Let me learn even more, sir!"

"Very well, my dear," he said.

13, 1. "Put this salt in the water and come to me again tomorrow morning." He did so. Then he said to him: "Bring the salt that you put in the water last evening!"

When he searched for it, he could not find it, for it was all dissolved.

2. "Taste the water on this side! How does it taste?"

"Salty."

"Taste from the middle; how does it taste?"

"Salty."

"Taste from that side; how does it taste?"

"Salty."

"Taste once more and come to me!"

He did so, [saying] "it is always the same."

Then his father said to him: "In the same way you do not perceive Being here, although it is always present."

3. "That which is this finest element, the whole world has for its self: That is truth; that is the *ātman; that are you,* Śvetaketu!"

"Let me learn even more, sir!"

"Very well, my dear," he said.

14, 1. "Imagine, my dear, that a person is led away blindfold from the land of the Gāndhāras and abandoned in the wilderness. This man would stray toward the East or the North or the West or the South, for he has been abandoned blindfold.

2. "But if someone were to undo his bandage and tell him, 'In this direction is the land of the Gāndhāras, go in this direction,' the man, if he were intelligent and wise, by asking his way from village to village, would reach the land of the Gāndhāras. In the same way a person who has found a master knows, 'I shall remain here as long as I am not liberated and after that I shall attain the goal.'

3. "That which is this finest element, the whole world has for its self: That is truth: that is the *ātman; that are you,* Śvetaketu!"

"Let me learn even more, sir!"

"Very well, my dear," he said.

16, 1. "Imagine, my dear, that people bring a man handcuffed [to the ordeal], asserting: 'He has stolen, he has committed a theft! Heat the ax for him [to test him]!' If he is the culprit then his untruth will be demonstrated. By telling untruth he tries to protect himself with untruth and, touching the heated ax, he is burned, and then he is killed.

2. "But if he is not guilty, his truth will be demonstrated. By telling the truth he protects himself with truth and, touching the heated ax, he is not burned, and then he is released.

3. "That [truth] on account of which he is not burned, is of the same nature as all this. That is truth; that is the *átman; that are you,* Śvetaketu!" Thereupon he realized, yes, he realized.

TU I, 1

ii) Hari OM.
May Mitra give us peace,
may Varuṇa give us peace,
may Aryaman give us peace,
may Indra and Bṛhaspati give us peace,
may Viṣṇu, the far-striding, give us peace!
Adoration be to Brahman!
Adoration be to Vāyu!

You are in truth the visible Brahman.
I will proclaim you as the visible Brahman.
I will speak the right, I will speak the truth.
May this protect me, may it protect my teacher!
May this protect me, may it protect my teacher!
OM peace, peace, peace!

KaivU 16

iii) That which is the supreme Brahman
the *ātman* of all, the great foundation
of this whole universe, more subtle

than the subtle, eternal—that are you!
You are that!

■ i) 8, 1. State of [deep] sleep: *svapnānta,* lit. end of the dream.
Attained Being: *satā . . . sampanno bhavati;* may be meant as another popular etymology.
The text connects the root *svap-* (to sleep or dream) with *sva,* self (cf. SB X, 5, 2, 14; BU II, 1, 17; § VI 4; etc): He sleeps (*svapiti*).
He has entered into himself: *svaṁ hy apīto bhavati.*
8, 2. Cf. SB X, 3, 3, 6. Mind: *manas.*
Breath of life: *prāṇa.*
8, 3. Uddālaka teaches his son to search for the root of every phenomenon (vv. 3-6), which leads ultimately to the discovery of the ultimate indivisible particle (*aṇiman*), the *ātman* (v. 7). Another play on words: *nāya,* carrier, leader; *aśanāyā,* hunger; *aśa-nāyā,* carrier-off, (leader) of food. The verbal root *aś-* means, in fact, to eat, but there is no word *aśa* for food. The underlying biological conception is that water washes away food, thus producing hunger.
Offshoot: *śuṅga* the sheath or calyx of a bud; here in the figurative sense of result, effect.
Without a root: *amūla,* without a cause.
8, 4. Being: *sat.*
8, 6. See CU VI, 5, 1-4, where food (*anna*) is related to mind (*manas*), water (*āpaḥ*) to life breath (*prāṇa*), and heat (*tejas*) to speech (*vāc*).
Divinities: *devatāḥ,* potencies, realms, principles (*tejas, āpaḥ, anna*). The next sentence of this pragraph undoubtedly belongs to the following one, and it has been shifted accordingly.
8, 7. Finest element: *aṇiman,* from *aṇu* (atom), minuteness, atomic nature. Cf. the ordinary use of this word above (CU VI, 6, 1): "When churned the finest element of the milk becomes butter."
That are you: *tat tvam asi* (*mahāvākya*).
9, 1. Juices: *rasāḥ,* nectar. Cf. MaitU VI, 22 (§ VI 12) for the same metaphor of honey.
9, 3. They become that: *tad ābhavanti,* controversial sentence which may indicate that particular things remain particular—also in their self-consciousness or identity—insofar as they remain "individualized."
10, 2. Having attained Being . . . or having come forth from Being: they don't know that they have attained or come forth from Being.
11, 1. In the example of the tree (*vṛkṣa*), *ātman* is identical with life (*jīva*).
11, 3. Life does not die: *na jīvo mriyata iti.*
12, 1. Fig tree: *nyagrodha,* banyan tree.
14. Salvation is a return home from exile, and the way is shown both by a guide (*ācārya*) and by one's own intelligence. Cf. KathU II, 8.
15, 1-2. Cf. § IV 5.
15, 3. The same refrain as in 14, 3.
16, 1. The simile of the ordeal shows the power of truth, in the sense of "truthfulness" (*satya*).
16, 3. Realized: *vijajñau,* he knew or understood.
■ ii) This is the invocation (*śānti-mantra*) of the TU.
You: *tvam,* probably referring to Vāyu, the divinity invoked by the student, but we may understand it in a broader sense. The "you" (any "you") is the visible, perceptible (*pratyakṣa*) aspect of Brahman: *tvam eva pratyakṣaṁ brahmāsi.*
■ iii) 16. That are you . . .: *tat tvam eva, tvam eva tat.*
17b. Cf. § VI C Antiphon.

Liberation *Mokṣa*

11 The entire purport of the *śruti* is liberation or freedom. Freedom may be interpreted in many ways. It is Brahman, it is *ātman,* it is *nirvāṇa.* Or it can be said to consist in Being, in Happiness, in Release from all bondage. More numerous still are the ways supposed to lead to it. Right action, true knowledge, and real love are the classical ways.

Our selection stresses only some features of *mokṣa*. The thrust of most of the texts is true to the basic meaning of the word, from the root *muc-* or *mokṣ-*, to loose, to free, release, let loose, let go, and thus also to spare, to let live, to allow to depart, to dispatch, to dismiss, and even to relax, to spend, bestow, give away, to open. There is a climate of simplification, of elimination, of utter freedom and even unconcern, which forms one of the fundamental features of the entire Vedic experience. Not by accumulation and increased concern, but by simplification and unconcern, will Man reach his final destination. The consequences of this attitude are a whole life-style.

Moksa

YV XXXI, 18

i) I know that Primordial Man, golden as the sun,
beyond darkness. Knowing him a man even now
becomes immortal. This is the way
to attain him; there is no other.

BU IV, 4, 3-7; 15-21

ii) 3. Just as a caterpillar, having reached the end of a blade of grass and approaching another one, collects itself [for making the transition], even so this *ātman*, having discarded the body and overcome ignorance, approaching another one collects itself [for making the transition].

4. Just as a goldsmith, taking an object of gold, fashions it afresh into another new and more beautiful form, so the *ātman*, discarding this body and dispersing its ignorance, makes for itself another new and more beautiful form: that of the Fathers, the spirits, the Gods, Prajāpati, Brahman, or of other beings.

5. This *ātman* is in truth Brahman, consisting of consciousness, mind, life, eye, ear, earth, water, air, atmosphere, light and no light, of desire and desirelessness, of anger and freedom from anger, of righteousness and unrighteousness, consisting of all that. Hence it is said: it consists of this, it consists of that. According to one's deeds, according to one's behavior, so one becomes. The one who does good becomes good, the one who does evil becomes evil. One becomes virtuous by virtuous action and evil by evil action. But others say: Man consists of desire; as is his desire, so is his intention, and as is his intention, so is his action. And whatever action he does, that he obtains.

6. On this there is a verse:

That to which the heart is attached,
toward this the subtle body moves

together with its action which still adheres.
Attaining the goal of whatever actions
he performed here on earth, he goes once more
from that world to this world of action.

This refers to the man of desire.

The man free from desire, the one who is without desire, released from desire, whose desires are fulfilled, whose only desire is the *ātman*—his life does not depart. Being just Brahman, he goes to Brahman.

7. On this there is a verse:

When he is released from all the desires
that bind the heart, then mortal man
even here becomes immortal and realizes Brahman.

Just as the cast-off skin of a snake lies on an anthill, dead, discarded, even so does this body lie. This disembodied immortal life is in truth Brahman, it is indeed Light; O king!

"I give you a thousand [cows]," said Janaka, [the lord] of Videha.

15. If one sees God face to face as the *ātman*,
as Lord of what has been and what shall be,
one shrinks not from him.

16. That in the wake of which the year
revolves together with its days—
that the Gods worship as Light of lights,
as life immortal.

17. On whom are established the five times five
beings, and space—him I believe
to be the *ātman*, knowing him, the deathless,
as the deathless Brahman.

18. Those who know the breath of breath,
the eye of the eye, the ear of the ear,
and the mind of the mind—they have realized
Brahman, ancient and primeval.

19. Only by the mind is it to be seen.
In it there is no plurality. The man
who perceives what seems to be plurality here
proceeds from death to death.

20. Only in oneness is it to be seen,
the stable *ātman*, immeasurable.
Free from blemish is it, beyond space,
unborn, great, unwavering.

21. Let the wise, the knowers of Brahman, realizing Him,

practice their wisdom. Let them not ponder
many words, for in speech is mere weariness.

KenU II, 4-5

iii) 4. [Brahman] is grasped in a flash of awakening.
Then it is thought that one attains immortality.
By the *ātman* one achieves spiritual strength,
and by wisdom is found immortality.

5. Wherever he is known, there is truth;
wherever not known, ruination.
Discerning him in every being,
the wise, departing from this world, become immortal.

KathU VI, 4-11

iv) 4. If here and now one knows him before
the decay of the body, then one is prepared
to receive a body in the worlds of creation.

5. In the *ātman* one sees as it were in a mirror,
in the world of the Fathers one sees as in a dream,
in the world of the spirits, as reflection in water,
in the world of Brahman, as light and shade.

6. When the wise man knows the sense perceptions—
their rising and their setting, each one in separation—
and the origin of each, then he grieves no more.

7. Beyond the senses is the mind,
beyond the mind, pure intellect,
beyond the intellect, the great *ātman,*
beyond the great, the Unmanifest.

8. Beyond the unmanifest, moreover, is the Person,
all-pervading, uncharacterized.
When a man knows him, he attains liberation
and proceeds to immortality.

9. His form is not in the field of vision.
No one is able to see him with the eye.
Apprehending him by heart, by thought, and by mind,
those who know him thus become immortal.

10. When the five organs of perception are still,
together with the mind, when the reason does not function—
this they aver to be the highest state.

11. This they deem to be yoga—the steady

concentration of the senses. Man then becomes
pure attention, for yoga is both
origin and extinction.

SU I, 6-10; 12

v) 6. In this great wheel of Brahman, the life
and foundation of all, the soul wanders like a swan,
thinking himself and the Inspirer to be separate.
When grace comes from Him, he attains immortality.

7. This has been praised as the supreme Brahman
in which the threefold reality is established,
and the imperishable. Those who know Brahman within,
realizing Brahman and absorbed in Brahman,
are released from birth.

8. The Lord encompasses this all, composed
of things perishable and imperishable, formed and unformed.
The self, a mere enjoyer, suffers without a Lord,
but he who knows God is freed from all fetters.

9. Two are unborn, the knower and the ignorant;
the Lord and the not-Lord. The one, an enjoyer,
is chained to enjoyments; the other, the *ātman*,
is infinite, of universal form, nonactive.
By knowing the threefold, one also knows Brahman.

10. Perishable is matter; immortal, imperishable
the Lord, who, the One, controls the perishable
and also the soul. Meditating on him,
uniting with him, becoming more and more like him,
one is freed at the last from the world's illusion.

12. The Eternal which resides in the *ātman* should be known.
Beyond this there is nothing that needs to be known.
The enjoyer, the object of enjoyment, the Inspirer—
this has been declared to be the All, the threefold Brahman.

SU II, 14-15

vi) 14. As a mirror covered with dust, when cleaned,
shines with fresh brightness, so the embodied self
is unified on seeing the *ātman*'s true nature,
attains its goal and is released from sorrow.

15. He who with the truth of the *ātman*, unified,
perceives the truth of Brahman, as with a lamp,
who knows God, the unborn, the stable, the One free
from all forms of being, is released from all fetters.

MundU II, 2, 9

vii) When the knot of the heart is loosened, then
all doubts are dispelled and all works abolished
of the one who has seen the highest and the lowest.

MundU III, 2, 1-9

viii) 1. He knows the supreme abode of Brahman,
established in which the universe shines brightly.
Free from desires, the wise worship the Person,
and thus transcend the state of impurity.

2. He who is full of desires and hankerings
is reborn here and there, owing to his desires.
But he whose desires are fulfilled, whose self is perfected—
the desires of that man disappear here on earth.

4. The *ātman* is not reached by the man devoid of strength,
or by the careless one, or by vain practice of austerity.
But if one who knows strives by these means,
his self enters the abode of Brahman.

5. Attaining him, the seers, replete with knowledge,
perfected, free from all passion, tranquil,
pass into him who pervades all things everywhere
and enter the All with wisdom and steadiness.

6. Those who have mastered Vedāntic wisdom
and purified their natures by sustained renunciation,
are all liberated completely and dwell, immortal,
at the end of time in the world of Brahman.

7. The fifteen parts return to their origin,
and all the powers, to their respective divinities.
One's deeds, united with the wise *ātman*,
merge in the supreme, immutable Being.

8. Just as rivers flowing to the ocean
merge in it, losing their name and form,
so the wise man, freed from name and form,
attains the supreme, divine Person.

9. Who knows the supreme Brahman himself becomes Brahman.
Among his people no one ignorant of Brahman will be born.
He overcomes sorrow and sin; released
from the secret, interior knots he becomes truly immortal.

KaivU 7-10

ix) 7. Contemplating him who has neither beginning,

middle, nor end, the One, the all-pervading,
who is intellect and bliss, the formless, the wonderful,
whose consort is Umā, the highest Lord, the ruler,
having three eyes and a blue throat, the peaceful—
the silent sage reaches the source of Being,
the universal witness, on the other shore of darkness.

8. He is Brahmā, he is Śiva, he is Indra,
he is the Imperishable, the supreme Majesty.
He is Viṣṇu, he is life, he is time,
he is fire, and also the moon.

9. He is all, what has been and what shall be, eternal.
Having realized him, one overcomes death.
No other path leads to liberation.

10. When he sees the *ātman* dwelling in all beings
and all beings within the *ātman*, he departs
to the supreme Brahman. There is no other way.

■ i) This verse has been integrated in SU III, 8 (§ VI 7, with a slightly different translation).
Primordial Man: *puruṣa*.
■ ii) 1-2. Cf. § V 12.
3. Collects itself: *ātmānam upasaṁharati*, also meaning to withdraw, to absorb, hence the double meaning (physical in the example of the caterpillar, spiritual in the case of the *ātman*).
ātman: the Mādhyandina recension has *puruṣa*, i.e., here the sense of person is implied in *ātman*.
4. More beautiful form: *kalyāṇataraṁ rūpam*. Cf. IsU 16 (§ VII 31).
Spirits: Gandharvas.
5. Consisting of consciousness: *vijñānamaya;* cf. BU II, I, 16 (§ VI 4), etc.
Righteousness: *dharmamaya*.
According to one's deeds: *yathākārin*, i.e., *karman*.
Behavior: *yathācārin*, i.e., *carita*, "way of life." There is a distinction between actions and behavior; cf. TU I, 11, 2.
Consists of desire: *kāmamaya*.
Intention: *kratu*, will.
Action: *karman*.
6. Heart: *manas*, the mind, the spirit.
Subtle body: *liṅga*.
Man of desire: *kāmayamāna*.
Whose only desire is the *ātman: ātma-kāma*.
Life: *prāṇa*.
7. Cf. KathU VI, 14 (§ V 5).
Realizes: *samaśnute*, attains, reaches, unites with Brahman.
Disembodied immortal life: *a-śarīro 'mṛtaḥ prāṇaḥ*.
Light: *tejas*.
8. Cf. § V 27.
12. Cf. § VI 9.
13-14. Cf. § IV 6.
15. God: *deva*.
Face to face: *añjasā*, straight, direct, immediate, clear.
Lord: *īśa*.
Cf. KathU IV, 12 (§ VII 52).
16. Life immortal: *āyur . . . amṛtam;* life span, time, world, . . . immortal.
17. Five times five beings: according to the commentator, the Gandharvas, the Fathers, Gods, *asuras* and *rakṣas* (cf. AB III, 31). The expression can also refer to the sense organs, or to five groups of people. Cf. also SU I, 5.
Space: *ākāśa*.
19. Plurality: *nāna*, variety, diversity.
20. Immeasurable: *aprameya*, or indemonstrable.

21. Practice . . . wisdom: *prajñāṁ kurvīta;* it can mean that spiritual practices should be continued as well as that the wisdom should not remain theoretical but be put into practice.

In speech is mere weariness: *vāco viglāpanaṁ hi tat,* to reflect on words leads to weariness; words lose their original strength.

22-25. Cf. § VI 6.

■ iii) 1-3. Cf. § VI 4.

4. Flash of awakening: *pratibodha,* illumination; cf. BU IV, 4, 13 (§ IV 6).

Spiritual strength: *vīrya,* energy.

Wisdom: *vidyā;* cf. IsU 11 (§ VII 21).

5. He: or it, Brahman, or also the *ātman.* Cf. BU IV, 4, 14 (§ IV 6).

Ruination: *mahatī vinaṣṭiḥ,* great loss or destruction.

■ iv) 1-3. Cf. V 5.

4. This difficult text has received many interpretations and also readings. Either it says that the knowledge of Brahman is not enough to liberate man from bondage to the body (against tradition), or the embodiment does not seem to be the imprisonment of the *ātman.*

5. The different modes of vision in the different states. Cf. BU IV, 4, 4 (§ VI 11).

Spirits: Gandharvas, beings dwelling in the airs. Cf. BU IV, 3, 33 for the different worlds.

As light and shade: lit. as shade and heat, i.e., with clear distinction.

6. Sense perceptions: *indriyas,* senses. Observing the process of sense perception is a yogic exercise.

7. Mind: *manas.*

Pure intellect: *sattva.*

Unmanifest: *avyaktam uttamam,* lit. the supreme unmanifest (*ātman*).

8. Unmanifest: *avyakta.*

Person: *puruṣa.*

9. Cf. SU IV, 20.

In the field of vision: *saṁdṛśe.*

By heart, by thought, and by mind: *hṛdā maīṣā manasā.* Cf. RV X, 129, 4 (§ I 1).

10. Organs of perception: *jñānāni,* i.e., *indriyāṇi.*

Reason: *buddhi,* the highest mental organ.

Highest state: *paramāṁ gatim,* supreme attainment.

11. Concentration: *dhāraṇā,* the "holding fast," a discipline of yoga. (Cf. YS II, 29; III, 1).

Pure attention: *apramatta,* lit. vigilant, attentive.

Origin and extinction: *prabhava-apyayau.* Another interpretation says that yoga is coming and going and that, as it can be lost, one has to be attentive to maintain one's concentration.

12-13. Cf. § VI 9.

14-18. Cf. § V 5. These *ślokas* should also be considered here.

■ v) 6. Wheel of Brahman: *brahma-cakra,* the *saṁsāra.*

The soul wanders like a swan: *haṁso bhrāmyate.*

Inspirer: *preritṛ,* from the verb *pra-īr-,* to move, to impel, hence the impeller, the mover, the inciter. Cf. also KenU I, 1 (§ VI 3), (*keneṣitam . . .*).

7. Threefold reality: the world, the Self, and the Lord; or nature, the soul, and God. Cf. vv. 6; 9.

Imperishable: *akṣara.*

Who know Brahman within: *antaraṁ brahmavidaḥ,* or the Brahman-knowers, discerning that which is within it.

Released from birth: *yoni-muktāḥ,* freed from the womb.

8. Formed and unformed: *vyaktāvyakta,* manifest and unmanifest.

Lord: *īśa.* Cf. KathU III, 4.

God: *deva.*

9. Unborn: *aja;* both the Lord and the individual soul are unborn.

Threefold: cf. v. 7. Brahman is the reality underlying the three and is thus realized when the three are known.

10. Matter: *pradhāna,* primary nature.

Lord: *hara,* the remover, the destroyer, i.e., Śiva.

The One: *deva ekaḥ,* the unique God.

Becoming more and more like him: *tattva-bhāvād bhūyaḥ,* becoming more and more of his being, essence, nature. Cf. KathU VI, 13 (§ VI 9).

Freed . . . from the world's illusion: *viśva-māyā-nivṛttiḥ,* cessation of the universal ignorance, released from the power of this world.

11. Cf. § IV 21.

12. Eternal: *nitya.*

Enjoyer: *bhoktṛ,* the soul.

Object of enjoyment: *bhogya,* the "food" of the soul, the world.

Inspirer: *preritṛ,* the Lord.

Threefold Brahman: *trividham brahman,* i.e., Brahman in its threefold manifestation as *bhoktṛ, bhogya,* and *preritṛ.*

▪ vi) 14. Mirror: *bimba;* the only occurrence in the Veda.
Unified: *ekaḥ . . . bhavate.*
True nature: *ātma-tattvam.*
Released from sorrow: *vīta-śoka,* transcended sorrow.
15. Truth of the *ātman: ātma-tattva,* reality, "thatness" of the *ātman* (and of Brahman).
Unified: *yukta* (cf. yoga).
Who knows God: *jñātvā devam.*

▪ vii) Cf. CU VII, 26, 2 (§ VI 3); KathU VI, 15 (§ V 5).
The highest and the lowest: *parāvare;* the ultimate vision includes also the lower realms of reality (cf. also the later Vedāntic conception of Brahman as *para* and *apara*).

▪ viii) 1. Supreme abode of Brahman: *paramam brahma dhāma.*
Worship the Person: *upāsate puruṣam,* meditate on the *puruṣa.* Cf. MaitU VI, 24 (§ VI 12).
Transcend the state of impurity: *aśukram . . . ativartanti;* the common variant reading is *śukram,* in which case it would mean: transcend the seed (or semen); i.e., do not procreate.
2. Self is perfected: *kṛtātmanaḥ.*
Cf. KathU II, 23 (§ VI 5), the same stanza.
4. By the man devoid of strength: *bala-hīnena;* both physical and psychic strength are prerequisites for the spiritual path.
Vain practice of austerity: *tapaso vāpy aliṅgāt,* i.e., asceticism without understanding, proper direction, and proper attitude.
5. Perfected: *kṛtātmanaḥ,* cf. CU VIII, 13 (§ IV 21), corresponding to *yuktātmanaḥ* in 1. 4 (" with concentrated, controlled Self").
Free from all passion: *vīta-rāgāḥ,* beyond attachment (an important concept in Jaina spirituality).
6. Mastered Vedāntic wisdom: *vedānta-vijñāna-suniścitārthāḥ,* who have understood the meaning of Vedāntic knowledge, the wisdom of the Veda's end.
By sustained renunciation: *saṁnyāsa-yogāt,* lit. by the yoga (practice) of *saṁnyāsa.*
7. Fifteen parts: the constituent parts of the person; cf. PrasnU VI, 2-5.
Powers: *devāḥ;* i.e., the sense organs dissolve into their respective elements.
One's deeds, united with the wise *ātman: karmāṇi vijñānamayaś cātmā,* the two aspects of the person, the material and the spiritual.
8. Cf. VI B a Introduction. Cf. PrasnU VI, 5.
Freed from name and form: *nāma-rūpād vimuktaḥ,* released from the phenomenal world.
Supreme: *parāt param,* higher than the high, the highest.
Divine Person: *puruṣam . . . divyam.*
9. Overcomes sorrow and sin: *tarati śokam tarati pāpmānam.* Cf. CU VII, 1, 3; 26, 2 (§§ IV 6; VI 3).
Secret, interior knots: *guhā-granthibhyaḥ,* the knots of the (hidden) cave, the heart.
10. Cf. § I 37.

▪ ix) 2-6. Cf. § III 31.
7. Formless: *arūpa.*
Wonderful: *adbhuta,* surprising.
Whose consort is Umā: i.e., Śiva, whose description follows (*trilocana* and *nīlakaṇṭha* are classical epithets of Śiva).
Highest Lord: *parameśvara.*
Source of Being: *bhūta-yoni.*
8. Supreme Majesty: *paramaḥ svarāt.*
Life: *prāṇa.*
Time: *kāla,* a great power extolled in AV XIX, 53; 54 to which this U belongs (§§ II 7; 8).
9. Cf. YV XXXI, 18 (i).
10. No other way: *nānyena hetunā,* lit. by no other cause.
11. Cf. § VI 12.

b) The Absolute Simplicity

OM

Deep down in the most profound recesses of Man's being there is a longing, even a need, for the simplification of his entire life, not only in words but also in deeds. After a period of almost unquenchable thirst for experience and knowledge there comes a period of saturation which leads to maturity, provided Man is wise enough to check at the right time the continuing intake of information and stimuli through which he tries to elaborate his personal and unique synthesis, his own world view, his wisdom. He then becomes conscious of the littleness of both his knowledge and his ignorance. He has, at this stage, two ways open to him: either to begin all over again and increase and broaden the flow of information, or to begin to simplify, to condense, to concentrate, so that all once again becomes simple, more transparent, as if he were recovering his lost innocence, though in a higher degree and a deeper sense. This may happen because he has attained enlightenment, though it may also occur when a Man, realizing that he will never master the whole domain of knowledge and human experience, makes a virtue of necessity and acts accordingly. Man is beginning to grow old and wise. He is no longer so quick and alert as he was; he does not even know as much as the next generation which has profited almost painlessly from the efforts of his own. He is now simplifying things, both outwardly and inwardly; more and more he finds that he prefers *sūtras* to lengthy treatises; indeed, he is becoming a *sūtra* himself. In an unsurpassable way one Upaniṣad puts it: "Just as all the leaves of a sprig are held together by its stem, so all words [*sarvā vāk*] are held together by the sound OM."[105] This *om* is not mere reductionism of the bountiful reality: "The *oṁkāra* is *idaṁ sarvam,* all this, the entire universe."[106] Simplification does not mean amputating reality; it has, certainly, the danger of degenerating into reductionism, just as a false sublimation becomes sheer repression, but authentic simplification does not chop away the real. Simplicity is the power of concentrating the real in bringing it to the full human scale, to the unity and dimensions of the *puruṣa.*

By virtue of the anthropocosmic homology peculiar to the śrautic wisdom, the process we have just described as affecting Man is not regarded as a mere sign of psychological maturity but is also interpreted in all its cosmic and divine implications. It is not only Man who feels the need to simplify; the cosmos also strives toward unification and God himself desires, as it were, to regain the pure

105. CU II, 23, 3 (or 4, according to another notation).
106. Cf. ibid.

source from which the whole creation has come about; or, in the words of one Upaniṣad,[107] the threefold offspring of Prajāpati, *devas*, Men, and *asuras*, listening to the teachings of their Father, all alike said: *om*, yes.[108]

The first function or meaning of *om* is to condense and simplify without jettisoning anything of value. The second function is to be a response to Man's need for affirmation, for acceptance, for saying yes (or *amen*, which some earlier scholars would have liked to connect with *om*). *Om* is yes, fulfillment, or, as the Chāndogya Upaniṣad puts it, "truly this syllable is assent—and this is indeed fulfillment."[109] It is not so much, as a hurried reading of some texts might induce us to believe, that the mere pronounciation of *om* fulfills all desires and forgives all sins, but the other way around, that he who has fulfilled and is fulfilling his desires is led to exclaim and to chant the imperishable *om*.[110]

This anthology of hymns, prayers, and meditations starts with the Gāyatrī mantra and concludes with *om*. The first is the most important of all mantras; the second is the best known of all syllables throughout the centuries, the most used day by day. Though differing in origin and import, both express in different ways the Ultimate Reality.

The sacred syllable *om* is extremely simple. It is formed of three elements, A and U, which combine to make the sound O, and M, which prolongs the O in a nasal resonance. It is thus composed of three letters in a single sound. The syllable *om* is not found in the Ṛg Veda or the Atharva Veda. We find its first veiled appearance in the Taittirīya Saṁhitā of the Black Yajurveda,[111] and it is frequently used in the Brāhmaṇas where it is generally the response of the priest, who presents the offerings (the *adhvaryu*), to versicles of the Ṛg Veda pronounced by the officiating priest (the *hotṛ*). It appears that in that period this sound expressed acquiescence in the action that was taking place or in the formulas that were being uttered: "So be it!" In the Aitareya Brāhmaṇa, however, a deeper significance is attached to *om*. It now signifies the "essence" both of the

107. Cf. BU V, 2, 1-3.
108. Cf. also SB I, 4, 1, 30; X, 6, 1, 4; XI, 6, 3, 4 sq. for *om* as pure affirmation, as yes.
109. CU I, 1, 8 (i).
110. As we shall observe in the texts, *akṣara* means both "syllable" and "imperishable"; cf. CU I, 1, 5 (i). Sometimes the texts suggest both meanings, as in CU I, 1, 6 (i), for instance, which is one of the texts under consideration. Is not the syllable the imperishable sound?
111. Cf. TS III, 2, 9, 6, where the *praṇava* indicates the sound made by the priest at the end of the offertory verse. Cf. also YV II, 13.

Vedas and of the whole cosmos. The Upaniṣads, pursuing this meaning further, not only saw in this syllable an expression of Brahman but also identified *om* with Brahman, that is, with *brahman* as manifested by the sound of *om*.

Several Upaniṣads endeavor in various ways to describe and explain more fully the syllable *om*. In the Kaṭha Upaniṣad, when Naciketas requests Yama to give him instruction concerning eternal reality, the latter replies that the whole revelation of the Vedas and the aim of all ascetic practice and holy living has no meaning apart from Brahman, which the syllable *om* alone is capable of expressing: "This syllable indeed is eternal Brahman."[112] One can only say, perhaps, that the sound *om*, so simple, so inarticulate, passing as it does into complete silence, constitutes the last possible support upon which a Man may lean before returning into the silence of the Absolute, of Brahman. It is in fact the word "support" that verse 17 of this same chapter uses to define *om*, the final, supreme support; once one has comprehended its nature one has already passed to the other side, into Brahman. This implies that *om* is indeed *for* Man, although in the process of disappearance into the One and at that ontological level one may equally say that *om is* Brahman. Each time that *om* is uttered there is a progressively deeper penetration into the One, proportionate to the recollection, detachment, and degree of awareness with which it is pronounced. It is pronounced at the beginning and/or the end of readings or chantings of the Scriptures, before the performance of actions that are considered holy and as a salutation of those to whom reverence is due. It is the utterance par excellence of ascetics, some of whom repeat it tirelessly and without ceasing.

The processes and techniques by which verbal prayers are interiorized (*japa*) are known in many traditional cultures. *Om* is an example. By constant repetition the name, as it were, reenters the place from which it emerged and thus assists in the reintegration of Man. *Om* is extreme and it can be said to represent the acme of a religious path. Unlike may other prayers, *om* has no specific content or peculiar meaning. Thus it does not need interpretation; any exegetical device weakens its power. *Om* is, further, not predominantly psychological or even anthropological but rather theanthropocosmic. *Om* is not the prayer of Man uttering the name of God in

112. KathU II, 16 (v).

order to absorb it and thus effect his reunion with God; it is not the human communion with the divine; it is rather the very cry of the whole of reality, the very pulse of the human being as the priest, the sacrificer of all that there is.

The tale of Śunaḥśepa[113] ends with a cultic explanation for the use of these prayers in the royal sacrifice, the *rājasūya,* and also for those who desire a son. There, after the injunction to answer *om* to a *ṛc*-verse and *yes* to a *gāthā* or epic verse, it is said: "*Om* is divine and *yes* is human,"[114] as if stressing the sacramental or cosmotheandric purport of *om*. It is not a mere affirmation, not mere passive acceptance, but it entails effective commitment and active involvement in the action thus performed. Whereas in the human field a fictitious yes, that is, a lie, is possible; in the divine realm a false *om* is radically impossible, since it lacks the underlying basis on which the simulation could rest.

Strength, courage, and concentration are absolutely necessary for the practice of the art of the archer. Keeping in mind Gāṇḍīva, Arjuna's famous bow, and many legends of the Mahābhārata and the Purāṇas, we may readily understand the Upaniṣadic metaphor that speaks of hitting Brahman, the target, with the arrow of one's *ātman* and the bow of *om*.[115] The arrow has to be sharpened by concentration and meditation.[116] The bow has to be bent by the study of the wisdom of the Vedas, by courageous living, and by the strength of the faith that, like the *om* which accompanies all cultic recitation, is the very soul of any real and fully human act.[117]

The need for simplification is the outcome of a desire for affirmation, but this is not all. It also answers the ultimate longing to transcend everything, not by negation but by acceptance and affirmation. To say nothing, to think nothing, to express nothing, does not constitute liberation until one realizes that there is no-thing, not-a-thing, to say and that it is possible to say, to express, to affirm all, but in a way that is devoid of particular content which would weaken the power of expression and affirmation. The sphere of *om* is the self-affirmation of Brahman: *śabda-brahman*.

As already noted, we do not call *om* a *mahāvākya* because it is properly not a *vākya,* a sentence. The implicit statement, "*Om* is

113. Cf. § III 23.
114. AB VII, 18 (XXXIII, 6). Yes: *tathā*.
115. Cf. MundU II, 2, 3-4 (vi).
116. For this reason another Upaniṣad prefers to say that "the arrow is *om*." Cf. MaitU VI, 24 (ix).
117. Cf. YS I, 27, where it is said that the *praṇava* (*om*) is the mystic syllable expressing Him (*īśvara*).

Brahman, *om* is all this [world],"[118] even assuming an elliptical verb,[119] cannot be said to be identical with *om,* the pure sound alone, with no explicit meaning and no interpretation. *Om* is *vāc,* pure word, the simple word of the beginning.[120] In this sense it is not even a Great Word, but Word as such. For this reason the next step is the utter silence from which the word has sounded. That is why the Maitrī Upaniṣad says that at the beginning *this,* all this, the *idam,* this world, was unuttered,[121] although, recognizing that it is by sound alone that the soundless Brahman is revealed,[122] it can affirm without hesitation that "*Om* is both the higher and the lower Brahman."[123] *Śabda-brahman* is certainly not the higher soundless Brahman, yet it is the one and only revelation of it. The sound *om,* the imperishable syllable *om,* is truly imperishable, is *śabda-brahman.* But *om* is not only the sound. It is also the silence following the utterance of *om.* This is the fourth state described in the Māṇḍūkya Upaniṣad, the *turīya:*[124] the silence achieved by having spoken out all sound, all thought (meaning and content), and even all being (cf. the *śūnyatā* of the Buddhist tradition). And yet this ontic silence is still connected with the word, for this is that empty, soundless *om* which is the highest Brahman, the ultimate wisdom, the groundless ground, the absolute mystery.

The Māṇḍūkya Upaniṣad consists of a brief, condensed exposition of the identity of the syllable *om* and the Supreme Reality. Man passes through successive stages of awareness before merging into the supreme silence, a silence that is "soundless unmanifest Brahman."[125] It is to this silence and this alone that the hymns of the Ṛg Veda and the Atharva Veda, the sacred rites of the Brāhmaṇas and the Gṛhya-Sūtras, and the verses of the Upaniṣads and the Bhagavad Gītā have led us. All these praises, prayers, rites, speculations, and fervent devotions reveal to us above all else the fascination of Man with the divine, along with his agony, disquiet, and yearning for final salvation, his longing to attain plenitude of being and realization in the One. Scripture teaches us that to arrive at true knowledge and self-realization a Man must hold himself in

118. TU I, 8 (iv).
119. *Om iti brahma, om iti idaṁ sarvam.* In point of fact equational sentences do not need a verb.
120. Cf. § I B.
121. Cf. MaitU VI, 6.
122. Cf. MaitU VI, 22 (ix).
123. MaitU VI, 5.
124. Cf. MandU 12.
125. MaitU VI, 22 (ix).

silence—no elation, no sacrifice, no ritual, no speculation, no desire of any sort whatever, but silence. True worship springs from silence and loses itself completely in utter, eternal Silence.

Om is the first Word, the first symbol of the entire universe, the first manifestation, the concentrated reality made word, that is, sound, content, form, matter, spirit. It is the Word before the world, it is Word according to which the world is formed. It does not say any thing; it simply says. It is the saying of all that can be said, of the whole world. It has no meaning of its own, because it stands at the root of all meanings and gives meaning to everything. It is the primordial word. It is the symbol of the whole, it expresses all that is real and true in every word, in everything that is said: *Om tat sat.*

The Sacred Syllable *Praṇava*

12

CU I, 1, 1-9

i) 1. OM. One should meditate on this syllable as the Udgītha chant, for every chant starts with OM. Of this the explanation is as follows:

2. The essence of all beings is the earth;
the essence of the earth is water;
the essence of water is plants;
the essence of plants if man;
the essence of man is speech;
the essence of speech is the Ṛg Veda;
the essence of the Ṛg Veda is the Sāmaveda,
and the essence of the Sāmaveda is the Udgītha chant.

3. The Udgītha chant is the most essential of all essences, the supreme, the highest, being the eighth [in the series].

4. Which is the Ṛg Veda? Which is the Sāmaveda? Which is the Udgītha chant? This is to be considered.

5. Speech is the Ṛg Veda, breath is the Sāmaveda, the syllable OM is the Udgītha. Now, these [two] form a union, speech with breath and the Ṛg Veda with the Sāmaveda.

6. Their union consists in OM; it is in this syllable that they are united. Whenever they come together and unite, they fulfill each other's desire.

7. He who knows this and meditates on this syllable as the Udgītha chant—he himself becomes a fulfiller of desires.

8. This is the syllable of assent, for when one agrees with something, one says: OM, "yes." That [prayer] to which assent is made will be fulfilled. He who, knowing this, meditates upon the Udgītha chant as the syllable OM will have all his desires fulfilled.

9. In it moves the threefold wisdom [the Vedas]. With OM they recite, with OM they offer praise, with OM they sing, paying reverence to the greatness and essence of this syllable.

CU I, 4, 1-5

ii) 1. OM. One should meditate on this syllable as the Udgītha chant, for every chant starts with OM. Of this the explanation is as follows:

2. When the Gods feared death, they took refuge in the threefold knowledge [the Veda]; they covered themselves with meters. Because they covered themselves [*acchādayan*] with them, these are called meters [*chandas*].

3. Death perceived them as one sees a fish in water. He saw them [hidden with-]in the hymns [Ṛgveda], the chants [Sāmaveda], and the sacrificial formulas [Yajurveda]. When they discovered this, they arose out of the hymns [Ṛgveda], chants [Sāmaveda], and sacrificial formulas [Yajurveda] and took refuge in sound alone.

4. When one recites a hymn or a chant or a sacrificial formula, one ends with OM. This sound is that imperishable syllable, that immortal and fearless one. When the Gods took their refuge in it, they became immortal and fearless.

5. He who knows this and makes this syllable resound takes refuge in this syllable, in the immortal and fearless sound; having taken refuge he becomes immortal like the Gods.

CU VIII, 6, 5

iii) When he leaves the body, he proceeds upward on the rays [of the sun], or he arises by saying OM, as quickly as his mind can think. From there he goes to the sun. This is the door of the world by which those who know enter, while those who do not know are barred.

TU I, 8

iv) OM is Brahman.

OM is this whole [world].

OM is a response, for at the bidding, "Recite," he recites.

With OM they sing the *sāman*-chant, with OM *śom* they praise and pray, with OM the officiating priest gives his reply, with OM the Brahman-priest starts the invocation, with OM [the sacrificer] gives his assent at the fire sacrifice. With OM the brahmin begins his recitation, adding, "May I attain Brahman," and with this petition he attains Brahman.

KathU II, 15-17

v) 15. The word which all the Vedas extol,
toward which all asceticisms point,
in quest of which men live disciplined lives,
that will I tell you: that is OM.

16. This syllable, indeed, is imperishable Brahman;
this syllable, indeed, is the End supreme.
The one who knows this selfsame syllable
will surely obtain whatever he desires.

17. This is the best support of all
and the highest. The man who knows
this support is deemed great in the world of Brahman.

MundU II, 2, 3-4

vi) 3. A mighty weapon, the Upaniṣad! Take it as a bow.
Affix an arrow, sharpened by devotion.
Bend the bow by a thought concentrated on That.
Hit the target, my dear—the Imperishable!

4. OM is the bow, the *ātman* is the arrow;
Brahman, they say, is the target, to be pierced
by concentration; thus one becomes
united with Brahman as an arrow with the target.

MahanarU 540-541

vii) By the saying of OM let the *ātman* be unified!
This in truth is the great teaching,
the mystery of the Gods. He who knows this
attains the greatness of Brahman!

PrasnU V, 1-7

viii) 1. Then Satyakāma Śaibya asked Pippalāda: "Sir, which world does he win at the end of his life who, among men, meditates upon the sound OM?"

2. He replied to him: "The sound OM in truth is both the higher and the lower Brahman. Therefore the one who knows, if he takes this as his support, attains the one or the other.

3. "If he meditates on one element, A, he will be enlightened even by that and he will quickly return to life. The hymns lead him to the world of men. There he experiences greatness by the practice of ascetic fervor, chastity, and faith.

4. If he meditates in his mind on two elements, A and U, he will be led by sacrificial formulas to the atmosphere, to the world of the moon. Having experienced glory in the world of the moon, he again returns [to this world].

5. But if he meditates on the Supreme Person with the three elements, A, U, and M, of that syllable OM, he attains to the light, to the Sun. As a snake is freed from its skin, so he will be liberated from evil. He will be led by the chants to the world of Brahman. Then he sees the Person dwelling in the city of the body who is higher than the highest existence. On this there are two verses:

6. If the three elements are used singly,
they lead to death, but if properly combined,
in outward, inward, or intermediate actions,
then the knower does not tremble.

7. By means of the hymns [one attains] this world,
by the sacrificial formulas the space inbetween,
by holy chant the world revealed by the Sages.
With the syllable OM as his sole support
the wise man attains *that* which is peaceful,
unaging, deathless, fearless, the Supreme.

MaitU VI, 22-25

ix) 22. Now this has been said elsewhere: There are two Brahmans to be contemplated: Brahman as sound and the soundless Brahman. Now it is by sound that the soundless is revealed. The sound here is OM. By the sound OM one proceeds upward and attains rest in the soundless. This is the goal, this is immortality, this is union, this is happiness. Just as a spider that climbs up its own thread reaches free space, so also one who meditates rises up by saying OM and reaches ultimate freedom. But those who believe in [Brahman as] sound proceed differently. They listen to the sound within the space of the heart by placing the thumb on the ear. This is compared to seven things: a river, bells ringing, a copper vessel being struck, the creaking of a wheel, frogs, rain, speaking in a quiet place. Having transcended all characterization, [these sounds] merge into the supreme, soundless, unmanifest Brahman. There they are free from individualizing characters and differentiations, just as different sorts of nectar having blended into honey have lost their individualizing characters. Thus it has been said:

Two Brahmans there are to be known: one as sound
and the other Brahman supreme. Having known
Brahman as sound one reaches Brahman supreme.

23. Now this too has been said elsewhere: [Brahman as] sound is the syllable OM. Its culmination is tranquil, soundless, free from fear and sorrow, full of sheer joy, lacking in nothing, steadfast, motionless,

immortal, unfailing, enduring forever. Its name is Viṣṇu the omnipresent. One should meditate on both to attain the supreme state. For thus it has been said:

> The God who is both higher and lower,
> who is called by the name of OM, is soundless
> and devoid of being. Therefore a man
> should concentrate on the highest place.

24. Now it has been said elsewhere: The body is the bow, the syllable OM is the arrow, the mind is its tip, darkness is the goal. Piercing darkness one reaches that which is not wrapped in darkness. Piercing that which is wrapped in darkness one beholds Brahman—as it were a sparkling wheel of fire, of the color of the sun, powerful, beyond darkness, the Brahman that shines in yonder sun, in the moon, in fire, and in lightning. Having seen him one enters upon immortality. Thus it is said:

> Inward-directed contemplation on the Highest
> is often deflected to outside objects.
> Unqualified understanding thus becomes qualified.
> But the happiness obtained when the mind is absorbed
> has only the *ātman* as witness.
> That is Brahman, the pure, the immortal,
> that is the goal, that certainly is the world!

25. Now this too has been said elsewhere: If a man has the senses withdrawn as in sleep and a perfectly pure heart, he sees as if in a dream in the emptiness of the senses the *praṇava* [OM], the leader whose form is light, who is beyond sleep, old age, death, and sorrow. Then he himself becomes the one who is called *praṇava*, the leader whose form is light, who is beyond sleep, old age, death, and sorrow. Thus it is said:

> When the yogin unites his breath with OM
> or is united with the all in manifold ways,
> it is called yoga.
> This oneness of breath, mind, and senses,
> the renunciation of all existence—
> this is termed yoga.

KaivU 11

x)

> Taking his *ātman* for one firestick
> and the syllable OM as the second one,
> a knower, by a vigorous kindling of knowledge,
> burns away the bonds [of ignorance].

MandU 1

xi) OM, this indefectible word, is the whole universe, and this is advanced in explanation of it:

What was, what is, and what shall be—
all this is OM.
Whatever else is beyond the bounds of threefold time—
that also is only OM.

■ i) 1. Syllable: *akṣara.*
Udgītha chant: cf. BU I, 3, 1 sq. (§ IV 9).
2. Essence: *rasa.*
Speech: *vāc,* used both as the organ of speech in Man and as the revealed word, the Veda. Cf. § I B.
5. Union: *mithuna,* a couple. Cf. also BU VI, 4, 20, where the husband says to his wife: "I am Sāman, you are Ṛc."
7. Fulfiller of desires: *āpayita ha vai kāmānām.*
8. Assent: *anujñā,* agreement.
Fulfilled: *samṛddhi.*
Desires fulfilled: or, he becomes a fulfiller of desires (for others); cf. v. 6.
9. Threefold wisdom: *trayī vidyā,* the three Vedas. Recitation, praise, and song of the YV, RV, and SV, respectively.
Essence: *rasa.*
10. Cf. § I 37.
■ ii) 1. Cf. CU I, 1, 1 (i).
2. Threefold knowledge: *trayī vidyā,* of the RV, YV, and SV.
They covered themselves with meters: *chandobhir acchādayan,* a play with words. Because the meters are the form of the Veda, they serve as a "covering" for the Gods.
3. As one sees a fish in water: *yathā matsyam udake . . . ;* i.e., the Vedas are transparent like water.
Sound: *svara,* i.e., OM (v. 4), the ultimate substratum of all the Vedas. Cf. also CU I, 3, 2.
4. Hymn: *ṛc.*
Chant: *sāman.*
Sacrificial formulas: *yajus.*
Ends: *atisvarati,* sounds out.
■ iii) In the utterance of OM at the time of death, one crosses to the world beyond (on the *devayāna*). Cf. § V 4. There are several variations and suggested readings of this text.
For CU VIII and ref., cf. § VI 6 (v) and notes.
■ iv) Response: *anukṛti,* or assent. No sacred action can be performed without OM. Cf. YV II, 13.
For the syllable *śom,* cf. AB III, 12, 1. It has been suggested that *śom* is a contraction of *śam* and *om.*
Brahman here is Prayer, the Sacred Word (cf. one of the possible etymologies).
■ v) 12-14. Cf. § V 5.
15. Word: *pada,* or goal; also way, place.
Asceticisms: *tapāṁsi,* austerities, spiritual exercises.
Disciplined lives: *brahmacarya,* chaste lives or study of Brahman. Cf. BG VIII, 11.
16. Cf. MaitU VI, 4.
17. Support: *ālambana.*
World of Brahman: *brahma-loka.* Cf. § V 4.
18. Cf. § V 5.
■ vi) 3. Devotion: *upāsa,* or meditation.
Though concentrated on That: *tadbhāva-gatena cetasā.*
Imperishable: *akṣara,* also the syllable OM.
4. OM: *praṇava.*
By concentration: *a-pramattena,* without distraction.
One becomes united: *tanmayo bhavet.* Cf. KathU VI, 11 (§ VI 11).
For reference to MandU II, 2, cf. § VI 3 (vi notes).
■ vii) Unified: *yuñjīta,* yoked, concentrated.
Great teaching: *mahopaniṣad.*
Mystery of the Gods: *devānāṁ guhyam.*
■ viii) 2. The higher and the lower Brahman: *paraṁ cāparaṁ ca brahma.* Cf. MundU I, 1, 4; MaitU VI, 22 sq. (below). In later Vedāntic interpretation, these are the unqualified (*nirguṇa*) Brahman and *īśvara,* the Lord (*saguṇa brahman*).
Support: *āyatana.*

3. Element: *mātra.*
Enlightened: *saṁvedita.*
Hymns: *ṛcaḥ.*
World of men: *manuṣya-loka.*
Ascetic fervor, chastity, and faith: *tapas, brahmacarya, śraddhā.* i.e. he who is thus reborn, will become a holy man.
4. Sacrificial formulas: *yajus.*
Atmosphere: *antarikṣa.*
World of the moon: *soma-loka,* the world of the Fathers (Cf. § V 4).
Glory: *vibhūti.*
5. Supreme Person: *paraṁ puruṣam.*
Liberated from evil: *pāpmanā vinirmuktaḥ.*
Chants: *sāman.*
Person dwelling in the city of the body: *puriśayaṁ puruṣam* (a play on words).
Higher than the highest existence: *jīvaghanāt parāt param.*
6. The three *mātras* of AUM have to be meditated upon in all situations, in order to lead one beyond death.
7. By means of the hymns: *ṛgbhiḥ,* corresponding to the earth.
By the sacrificial formulas: *yajurbhiḥ,* corresponding to *antarikṣa,* the space in between.
By holy chant: *sāmabhiḥ,* leading to heaven.
Wise man: *vidvān.*

■ ix) 22. Sound: *śabda,* word.
Soundless: *aśabda,* nonword.
Proceeds upward . . . : cf. the yogic practice of letting the sound OM ascend to the crown of the head, but here the context is cosmic.
Goal: *gati,* also way.
Union: *sāyujyatva,* the state of unification.
Happiness: *nivṛtatva,* cessation.
Ultimate freedom: *svātantryam,* independence.
Those who believe in . . . sound: *śabdavādinaḥ;* suggests the school of thought for which *śabda* is the highest reality. Their practices are here described.
Having transcended all characterization: *taṁ pṛthag-lakṣaṇam atītya,* after experiencing the subtle, internal sounds.
Cf. CU VI, 9, 1-2 (§ VI 10) for the metaphor of honey.
Brahman as sound: *śabda-brahman,* Brahman as logos.
23. God . . . higher and lower: *parāparo devaḥ.*
Soundless: *niḥśabda.*
Devoid of being: *śūnya-bhūta.*
Highest place: the head or the heart in anthropomorphic interpretations.
24. Bow: cf. MundU II, 2, 3-4 (vi).
OM is the arrow: cf. KathU II, 17 (v).
Sparkling wheel of fire: *alātacakra,* famous simile developed by Gauḍapāda in MandKar IV, 47-52.
Unqualified understanding: *aviśeṣa-vijñāna.*
Pure: *śukra,* radiant, the semen (of the whole world). Cf. MundU III, 2, 1 (§ VI 11).
25. Perfectly pure heart: *śuddhitamayā dhiyā.*
Beyond sleep . . . : *vigata-nidra, vijara, vimṛtyu, viśoka.*
United: *yunakti,* from the same root *yuj-* from which yoga is derived.
Renunciation of all existence: *sarva-bhāva-parityāga.* Yoga is both unification of body and mind and abandonment of "becoming" (*bhāva*).

■ x) Illumination is compared with the kindling of fire.
Bonds [of ignorance]: *pāśa,* fetter.
Cf. SU I, 14, and mark the difference (here it is said that one may see God).
For ref. to KaivU, cf. § VI 11 (ix notes).

■ xi) Indefectible word: *akṣara;* both meanings—syllable and imperishable—are here combined.
2. Cf. § VI 6.

PART VII
TWILIGHT

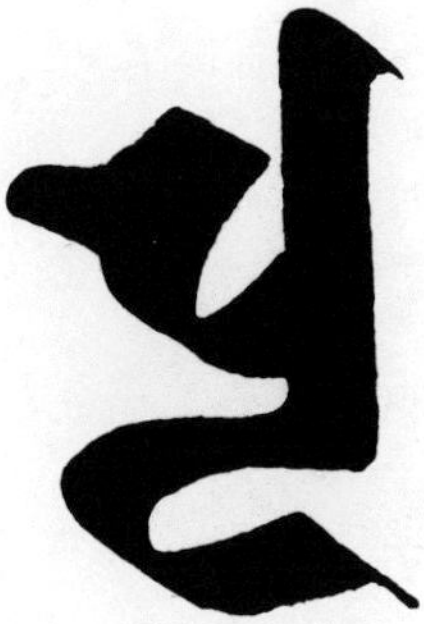

Pṛthivī

The whole universe proceeds on its way and we have tried to describe the theanthropocosmic cycle according to the Vedas. The whole of our personal existence also follows its own path and describes a similar cycle, following and reenacting the divine and the cosmic ones. There is a correspondence between the celestial and terrestrial spheres. Between these two—the sphere of the Gods or the divine reality and the sphere of the earthly or cosmic existence—there is yet a third and intermediate sphere: the *antarikṣa*,[1] the region between *dyu* (heaven) and *pṛthivī* (earth).[2] The third sphere is the realm of Man, the mediator between the two. In other words, the *ātman* is the connecting link between this *loka* and the *brahma-loka*.[3]

Within the intermediate sphere there is an "inner shrine; it is this that we should seek";[4] it is from here that we contemplate both our own existence and the destiny of the entire reality. It is the sphere of prayer, meditation, contemplation, or simply of personal consciousness. We cannot encompass in one single act our own life, much less the whole of reality. Both have to go their way. But they are unfolding before our very eyes; we can be aware of this process, we can become aware of the state of affairs in which the universe and our own selves are involved. Nor is this all. We can be conscious of the overall movement of reality in a way that is not a merely passive *re*flection but an active *in*flection in the process itself.

The third sphere is not just an intermediate one; it is rather a mediator between the two. Consciousness does more than simply reflect that which is. It modifies, to say the least, the thing that it "reflects." Man's conscious existence is not a mere copy or a simple mirroring of that which is, but a constitutive factor of reality itself. This is the life of the spirit or the life of prayer. It is not a state of mere passivity, nor is it a disconnected activity. It is the marriage, the union, the *maithuna*, between the two.

We use the traditional name of prayer, because, from time immemorial, when Man was led to pray, there was in the depths of

1. Cf. BU II, 3, 2-3 (§ VI 7); III, 1, 6 (§ V 27).
2. We have often seen these three worlds. Cf. also BU I, 1, 1; V, 14, 1; CU I, 3, 7; III, 15, 5; etc.
3. Cf. BU III, 7, 6 (§ VI 5); CU VIII, 4, 1 (§ V 27).
4. CU VIII, 1, 1 (§ VI 6); cf. also CU III, 14, 3 (§ VI 6).

his being, besides immediate motives such as fear, doubt, joy, and gratitude, a still more powerful drive to hold his own life together and to hold it so together with the existence of the entire universe. Prayer can take many forms and we may pray for many immediate reasons, yet the common underlying assumption or implicit belief—though it may be worded variously according to different world views—is that in the act of prayer Man is sharing in the central dynamism of reality and penetrating into the heart of the world. Prayer is truly Brahman.

We have already taken note of the first meaning of Brahman as holy word, sacred utterance, sacrificial formula.[5] This meaning persists as an invisible thread running through the many meanings of the word and providing a connection, the *bandhu* of which we have also heard,[6] between the opposite extremes of reality.

Another "connection" has also since olden times been symbolized in Indian spirituality by the significant word, *saṁdhyā*. Literally it means a holding together, union, junction, or juncture, and it comes from a prefix *saṁ-*, denoting cumulation, synthesis, reunion,[7] and a root *dhā-*, to put, to place; hence *saṁ* and *dhā* together denote to unite, combine, reconcile, mend, put together, and similar notions.

We have already seen that *saṁdhyā* sometimes refers to the intermediate state between this world and the other, the "state of sleep,"[8] but it has come to mean almost exclusively the meeting together, the union, the conjunction, of the three divisions of the day: morning, noon, evening. It symbolizes the union and reconciliation of the three times, past, present, future, expressed in the three juncture moments of every day and thus of every life as well as of every time span, for the day is merely an abbreviation of the whole life span and the unifying element of real human temporal life. In a more restricted sense, perhaps because the strains and stresses of active life were already known to ancient times and permitted little noontime leisure, it came to mean the meeting of the two lights at evening and morning, the conjuncture of the two moments not only of time but of all pairs of opposites and conflicting tendencies which constitute human and cosmic real-

5. Cf. § I 12.
6. Cf. AV IV, 1, 3 (ibid.).
7. Like the Greek *syn-* and the Latin *cum-*.
8. Cf. BU IV, 3, 9 (§ V B Antiphon), where it is said that we can "see" the other two worlds from this *svapna-sthāna*. Cf. BS III, 2, 1.

ities, of all *dvandvas:* old and young, man and woman, sun and moon, day and night, good and evil, God and creature, light and darkness. *Saṁdhyā* refers to the two privileged moments of sunrise, when everything can still become everything, and of sunset, when all has been said and done and there is nothing else to do; or of dawn, when Man can still hope because the whole day lies in front of him, and of dusk, when he can, simply, love because the day is already over and nothing else remains to be done. *Saṁdhyā* represents that third sphere which encompasses our whole life and destiny as well as the life of the universe. This is the meaning of prayer: it is that human or rather total cosmotheandric act by which Man transcends both time and space and discovers that within his own human heart at least a part of the destiny of the whole universe is being played out and reenacted. No wonder that calmness, attention, and silence are needed. *Saṁdhyā* is the meeting of the lights, of the morning light, that form of consciousness which like the brilliance of the dawn is shed on things from a heavenly and invisible source, and of the evening light, that form of consciousness which springs from the brightness of earthly things when they have been bathed all day long in the beams of the king of the sky.

Saṁdhyā is a theanthropocosmic twilight; it suffuses the three worlds. It expresses the peculiar dual polarity residing in the very heart of the great *ātman*. An astounding distich finishes one of the major Upaniṣads:

> In order to enjoy what is true and what is false
> the great *ātman* has a dual nature;
> yes, the *mahātman* has a twofold essence![9]

Truth and falsity are here *satya* and *anṛta,* being and disorder, existence and chaos. All is for the sake of experiencing, enjoying, tasting, the polarity of things. This polarity is real, but it is a constitutive tension of reality itself which does not destroy the ultimate nonduality of all that there is. It is this dual nature that finds its cosmic expression in *saṁdhyā,* in the twilight of the cosmos, and is reflected and overcome in the meditation of Gods and Men during the crossing of the lights.

In other words, *saṁdhyā* stands for the meeting of the objective and subjective forms of knowledge, the encounter between human

9. MaitU VII, 11, 8. Dual nature: *dvaitī-bhāva*. The repeated sentence in Sanskrit is identical with the preceding one.

and divine ways of dealing with reality. Anything known by revelation, by hearsay, by external illumination, and by the light of reasoning is as one-sided as merely subjective, private, and experiential knowledge. Only when both meet, when the external and internal revelations coalesce, when the language of things and our own language speak the same idiom, are we beginning to reach the shores of truth where speaking and listening converge. We speak the word we hear only because we have learned to listen to the not yet spoken word.

Saṁdhyā is both the time of prayer and the prayer of time. It is the early morning time of prayer, the first act of all which will expand into all other human activities; it is also the early evening prayer time when the experience of our limitation is fresh and yet the desire for perfection and for the infinite has not yet subsided. In these two moments Man represents the whole universe; the Gods are with him and the material world is gathered around him. It is the time of prayer, the time of meditation, of concentrating in himself the whole stuff of the world and of condensing in himself all the desires and dynamisms of the entire universe. It is the time of stretching up to the very ends of the world, not by a mere effort of imagination but by the power of the Spirit permeating everywhere, even to the four corners of reality. Were it not for these moments Man would not be Man, but only a moving machine, doing many things but not becoming anything, not condensing in himself the whole of reality, not discovering his unique place and thus the uniqueness of his own mysterious being.

Saṁdhyā is, equally, the prayer of time. When he is at prayer, Man is not performing a private individual act. He is performing a priestly action in the name of the whole of reality; he is the mediator between all possible extremes, the conductor line between all existing and conceivable tensions. Into and through Man at prayer pass the sun, the moon, and the stars; in his heart the Gods have their meeting place and the Spirit is present, inspiring, instilling into the world all the force and energy it needs in order to go on existing. *Saṁdhyā* is the prayer of time, for the world could not subsist if it were only a series of temporal successions. How would it pass from one instant to the next if there was no link between the two? This link is the Spirit, the spirit of prayer that unfolds in the mind and heart of the enlightened person, of the one who is rejuvenated by the waters and reborn by the rites of a second birth.

To be a Man, then, is not only to be a part of the world but to be the universe itself, as we have already heard: "the world is his; the world itself is he!"[10]

The same message may be transposed into the following terms: To build a bridge or to dig a well is a real act, a fully human act, only if we are building a bridge on which human beings are moving about on their business, are encountering others, exchanging goods and ideas, and thus enhancing life. We dig a well only if it quenches thirst, gives life to plants, allows a more human life, facilitates human conversation and social justice. To build a bridge that nobody would use and that would profit nobody would not be a human act; it would lack its "core," the spiritual dimension, its soul, the accompanying prayer, which is not necessarily a mantra; it can equally well be a desire to contribute to the welfare of our neighbors and the happiness of our fellow beings, or an ideal to enhance the quality of human life around us. When the spirit of prayer does not permeate an action, that act degenerates to the subontic level.

The pages that follow serve as an introduction to that life of prayer which has nurtured for millennia a considerable part of mankind in its quest for happiness and in its search for the ultimate meaning of life.

Two practices should be recommended at this point. The one is utter silence and quiet, emptiness and void, an active removal of all obstacles in order to let the Spirit act unhampered; this is the way of absolute freedom which implies even freedom from being. Here no word is allowed. It would deform the experience and, if formulated, would be objectionable. Here "all words recoil"[11] or, as one Upaniṣad, now lost (and how could it be otherwise?), said, "*ātman* is silence."[12] The other practice is the traditional prayer of morning and evening, built of praise and springing from mingled fear and hope, contemplation and thrust toward action. This prayer is human and concrete. It integrates into itself all aspects of human life on earth. God is a partner of Man, not an aloof, mighty power. God is an accomplice, one could almost say; he is asked to collaborate with Man in all human undertakings, good and, even, less good. It is here that the so-called incantations and charms have

10. BU IV, 4, 13 (§ IV 6).
11. TU II, 4 (§ VI 7).
12. *Upaśānto 'yam ātmā,* apud Śaṅkara's BS Bhāṣya III, 2, 17.

their place and also all efforts at assuring the support of the Gods in battles public or private.

In order to offer an organic scheme of prayer we have chosen a simple and easily discernible pattern.

The first division is according to the seasons. The seasons constitute one of the marriages between space (or earth) and time (or "heaven"); they have a meaning and a message:[13]

> Where do the half months and the months together
> proceed in consultation with the year?
> Where do the seasons go, in groups or singly?[14]

They are related to Men:

> Your circling seasons, years, nights succeeding days,
> your summer, O Earth, your splashing rains, your autumn,
> your winter and frosty season yielding to spring—
> may each and all produce for us their milk![15]

They are also related to the sun:

> But the sun also reflects all the seasons. When he arises, then it is spring. When the cows are driven homeward, then it is summer. When it is noon, then it is the rainy season. When the day declines, then it is autumn and when the sun sets, then winter has come.[16]

Every season is a new beginning; it brings with it a radical change and thus also a new hope. Yet it also recalls to us, or rather reenacts for us, the mystery of death and new life:

> The year, assuredly, is equal to Death; it is he [Prajāpati or time] who by means of daytime and night destroys the life of mortal creatures so that they die. So the year is, assuredly, equal to Death; and so he who recognizes the year as Death will not destroy his life, by daytime or at night, before he reaches his full life span at old age.[17]

Moreover, the cosmic and theological meanings of the seasons are emphasized time and again:

> At the end of a year the Father of creatures essayed an utterance: *bhūḥ*. This word became the earth, *bhuvaḥ* became the air, and *svaḥ* became yonder sky. . . . From the five syllables that compose these three words he made the five seasons; hence they arose.[18]

13. On the seasons cf. RV I, 25, 8 (§ I 26); VII, 66, 11; X, 90, 6 (§ I 5); AV X, 8, 4 (§ VII 27).
14. AV X, 7, 5 (§ I 3).
15. AV XII, 1, 36 (§ I 19).
16. SB II, 2, 3, 9.
17. SB X, 4, 3, 1.
18. SB XI, 1, 6, 3; 5.

Another text says forcefully, "I am season; I am son of the seasons,"[19] which means that I am, insofar as I am in harmony with cosmic order, *ṛta,* that is, I am *ṛtu,* season. I am, insofar as I embody that part of the cosmos entrusted to me which makes my own "me." If on this ultimate level excommunication were possible, it would mean total annihilation. We are, insofar as we share in the total process of the world and insofar as, being conscious of this fact, we participate willingly in its dynamism and unfolding.

Man is time, this text is saying, but not an empty time or a mere flow of the elements of his being. Man is temporal, "seasonal" (*ārtava*), inasmuch as he is a part of the cosmic order (*ṛta*) that is manifested in the annual cycle of the seasons (*ṛtu*). Man is "seasonal" inasmuch as he is not only waxing and waning like the moon, or being cold and warm, dry and humid, like the seasons, or passing through day and night like the earth, but has his own special rhythms, his peculiar seasonal forms, which belong to the overall dynamism of the universe. Mere reason fails to discover this cosmic connection, but it is here that prayer, rightly understood, performs its proper function.

Agni, the mediator, the God who transforms human gifts into offerings fit for the Gods, the priestly God, is addressed as "Lord of seasons, knower of seasons,"[20] and he is asked "to sanctify the seasons."[21]

One entire hymn of the Ṛg Veda is dedicated to *ṛtu,* the season, here considered as a deity.[22] Its message is clear, despite difficulties of exegesis: time and worship belong together, the seasons and the activity of the Gods are also connected, time is not an abstract value or an empty concept. Liturgy is nothing other than Man's participation in the temporal unfolding of the universe. Just as we can have "portions" of the world according to spatial divisions, so we can have "portions" of the universe according to temporal intervals. But this "temporal" portion is real only insofar as we do not exclude from it the Gods, Men, animals—all that is and is alive "there." The recognition of all this is the prayer of time.

The other great division is that of the three moments of the day: morning, noon, evening. We have already mentioned them and given some idea of their meaning.

19. KausU I, 2 (§ V 4).
20. RV X, 2, 1.
21. RV X, 11, 1.
22. Cf. RV I, 15.

In the arrangement of the texts for each season and also for morning and evening we have tried to follow a certain pattern. Three or four main texts from the Vedas, stressing the fundamental mood of both Man and cosmos according to the particular hour and season, are followed by an Upaniṣadic text for meditation and contemplation, all being preceded by an antiphon or mantra that gives the tone, as it were, of the whole *hour*. The twilights of morning and evening, as the prayerful hours of day, embrace the whole of the day and the whole of the night: they bring us a moment of awareness when we reenact the full range of human activity that takes place during both halves of the daily circle; or, as the texts themselves beautifully express it, "from ancient time round heaven and earth they travel, Night with her dark limbs, Dawn so fair and radiant."[23] Or again, "Praise we both Night and Dawn who visit us smiling, but differing in the color of their appearance."[24] The Brāhmaṇas emphasize also the connection with Man, going so far as to say, "The Day is my father and the Night my mother."[25]

The seasons in their totality, together with morning and evening, build time, the year, the whole universe, Prajāpati, the Lord of all creatures. We may tend, of course, to transcend time, but we can do so only in and through time itself. All this has little to do with either "nature-mysticism" or "pantheistic" trends, which spring out of another quite different fundamental intuition. The word "nature" cannot be used with reference to this attitude because in this context there is no background of the "supernatural" nor is there any separation from the "personal." To superimpose the pair "nature-supernature" or "nature-person" may be interesting from a polemical point of view, but it will not help toward an understanding from within. The same applies to the term "pantheism." Pantheism is an alien conception that cannot be applied without distorting and doing violence to the world view of the Vedic experience.

We are dealing here with one of the fundamental options of mankind: *advaita*. The use of words is, of course, all the more dangerous because it is unavoidable and in fact we can understand only by incurring the risk of misunderstanding. By referring here to the Advaitic insight in differentiation from any other monistic,

23. RV I, 62, 8.
24. RV III, 4, 6; cf. also AV X, 8, 23 (§ VII 27).
25. JaimB I, 50, 1.

dualistic, or pluralistic world view, we do not imply the developed philosophical doctrine of later Indian periods, but rather the incipient awareness, on the one hand, of the inadequacy of any monistic or dualistic vision of reality and the realization, on the other, that it is only by transcending—not denying—the reasoning reason that Man can encompass reality. This approach to reality proceeds neither exclusively from the outside (which would lead to dualism) nor exclusively from the inside (which would lead to monism) but from an atypical awareness that embraces at the same time both the inside and the outside, that is, both the identity and the difference as mirrored in Man's consciousness.[26]

However we may prefer to state this in philosophical terms, we have here the experience of a life of prayer which expresses something that transcends dialectical assumptions and starts from a dialogical attitude. We are not belittling dialectics; we may be allowed, however, to point out that in addition to and not in opposition to dialectics (otherwise we would already be in the dialectical field) there is the dialogical attitude, which we find foreshadowed in the Vedic experience. In this experience the deity is not "over there," representing a dialectical opposition or a dialectical absolute. The rules of divine-human intercourse are not dialectical; there are no rules of "yes" and "no," whereby each follows his own nature and simply discovers some possible "synthesis" in their antinomic relationships. On the contrary, the Man-God relation is dialogical in character; neither party is bound by a dialectical law or required to be "consistent" in itself; both sides can regret, retract, and even contradict themselves. God is not the "other" or the "self," but the I, an I that postulates a thou and could not exist without it, so that the mutual existence of thou and I is intrinsically related, though the independence of neither is in jeopardy. In other words, Vedic prayer is a constant dialogical—not a dialectical—dialogue with the superior powers. This dialogue is considered to be part of life itself, so that it is not an irrelevant peccadillo to omit to ask a favor from the Gods or to abstain from making a particular sacrifice on the "excuse" that the Gods already "know" what we deserve and, being good, will grant it to us. The Vedic Gods are not philosophical constructions; nor is Vedic prayer philosophical speculation.

Prayer is a real dialogue in which I may succeed in convincing

26. Cf. § VI A a.

the other, in which the other is really open to me and open to being convinced and won over to my side because he is not fixed or committed to his own nature, that is, to another law outside the dialogical dialogue in which we are engaged. In the same way I may be defeated in prayer and the world is going to be different according to how I fare in this highest human act in which, in and through me, the whole universe is engaged.

This explains also the immediacy and boldness of many Vedic prayers. It would be incorrect to say that they stress only the material and temporal aspects of reality, for the distinction between "material" and "spiritual" is not so well defined as to postulate two independent and separate domains. We have already seen, for instance, the complex meaning of the word *rayi,* so difficult to translate because it refers to material welfare and temporal values as well as to spiritual gifts and intemporal realities.[27] The "treasures," "gifts," "riches," and "graces" with which we have translated *rayi* are always both material and spiritual, although we tend to divide the single rich and "harmonic" notion of the word into two different elements, whereas in truth *rayi* is always a holistic value. It is thus not simply the desire for cattle for the sake of cattle or good grain for the sake of grain which constitutes the kernel of Vedic prayer but rather the desire for that life without which both cattle and good grain are no longer meaningful.

Another word may also be relevant here. Much has been written about Vedic polytheism, henotheism (kathenotheism), monotheism, deism, and even atheism. We will refrain from comment upon this list, but we should perhaps say a word regarding the traditional concept of *iṣṭa-devatā,* the deity one chooses for one's own worship and devotional practices. Although this phrase is of later origin, it expresses the original Vedic intuition and formulates in a practical way the existential attitude of the worshiper. We should not make the mistake of interpreting this notion as a whimsical and private choice, as if it were just a matter of subjective and individual taste.[28] Anthropology would say that the choice is already conditioned by *karman,* family, caste, and the particular inspiration of the deity itself, but we must also keep in mind that the notion of

27. Cf. §§ I 4; II 6; II 34 Introductions.

28. The translation one finds sometimes of "favorite deity" is misleading. *Iṣṭa* means, certainly, wished, desired, beloved, respected, but comes from *iṣ-,* to seek, to desire, with anthropocosmic rather than psychological overtones.

iṣṭa-devatā is not a kind of sociological compromise designed to further the cause of peace and tolerance or a psychological device to keep everybody happy with his or her own mascot. The notion springs rather from the insight that the act of worship, in spite of being nonfinite as the divine act that it is, is at the same time a concrete human act performed by a finite being in a finite time and in a particular state of mind. The worshiper cannot embrace the whole of the Godhead nor can he insert the whole of his own life into one single act of worship. The first statement is obvious; the second is equally evident, for if we could really make an act of perfect worship, we would not need to perform it over and over again.[29] Any repetition would then prove that we have not in truth "perfected" the "perfect adoration" of the previous act of worship; indeed we would need to worship for the second time with a certain sense of guilt, for the very act of repeating and renewing denies the validity of our first declarations.

The notion of *iṣṭa-devatā* takes care of all this, redeems us from any sense of guilt, gives us the right human perspective, and clothes the infinite Godhead in a finite congruent manifestation. It recognizes that a perfect act of worship can be made only if it takes into account our own constitutive limitations, in space and time, of imagination, mood, and intellect. Furthermore, it is in accordance with the truth that a perfect and total disclosure of the infinite is impossible except in the womb of the infinite itself.

The underlying assumption of the *iṣṭa-devatā* is, therefore, that in order to worship the Godhead I have to be concentrated both in my desire and in the representation I make of the Godhead. The Godhead has to take some form for me, even if I think of it as a formless "form." It has to have a name, even if it be "nameless." It has to take place somewhere, even if it is in the cave of the heart. It has to take place within a particular time, even if it touches the eternal. The *iṣṭa-devatā* concretizes without pinning us down.

We have avoided overemphasizing the names of the different Vedic symbols for the divine, just as we have refrained from subscribing to any particular theory regarding the nature of the Vedic Gods. Yet, human prayer is not a mere type of spiritual gymnastics, rational or irrational, nor is it an abstract enterprise. It is all concrete and thus given color, form, name, place, and time. Furthermore, in

29. A certain Advaita-Vedānta spirituality would claim this to be the case.

each sincere and profound act of worship the whole of the human being is involved, to the greatest extent possible in the particular circumstance. In another moment or for another person the act may be different. The *iṣṭa-devatā* allows for this difference. Agni, Indra, Varuṇa, Soma, Uṣas, Vāyu, the Aśvins, and other Vedic deities may no longer be our *iṣṭa-devatās*, yet they may still be windows opening up regions of our own all too closed souls to the refreshing winds that blow from the mountains and the plains of other realms.

We are not concerned here with the many regulations regarding the recitation of the Vedas[30] or the no less colorful prohibitions cited as obstacles to their recitation.[31] We may, instead, try to discover their spirit beneath and beyond the particularities of one culture and the accretions of later periods. We may discover them to be forms of prayer still relevant to our situation.

The sense of awe is not predominant, nor is the sense of submission to superhuman powers. It has been said that a spirit of almost legalistic relationships of do ut des is a characteristic of Vedic spirituality. Such an attitude does sometimes seem to prevail, but we affirm that it is not the most genuine or the deepest attitude of the Vedic prayers. They at times sound legalistic precisely because intercourse with the divine is not governed by a dualistically conditioned type of spirituality. The Vedic dialogue with the divine is not one of a totally deprived and powerless creature bowing before an almighty and unconditioned Creator, but rather that of a partner playing his part in the supreme mystery of reality, where indeed there is a hierarchical order but nevertheless a unitarian, or rather a nondualistic, structure.

Let us consider, for instance, the following psalm, commentary upon which would require many pages. Here we find neither anthropomorphism nor a total abyss between the human and the divine. Here we have neither a succumbing to atheism nor an attitude of indifference vis-à-vis an ineffective God, but rather a consciousness of the different roles to be played and the exciting possibility of an interchange:

O Agni,
Son of strength,
bright Friend
whom we adore,

30. Cf. Ṛgprātiśākhya, XV, 1 sq.
31. Cf. Vasiṣṭha Dharma Sūtra, XIII, 8-40.

if you were the mortal
and I the immortal,
I would not deliver you
to evil tongues,
O good One, or to calumnies,
O trustful One.
My devotee would not be
in distress, O Agni,
or in sin or be hated![32]

Yet on another occasion the poet can explode: "I the mortal cry unto you the immortal!"[33]

We all belong together; things, animals, Men, and Gods form together the family of reality, not indeed a democratic assembly, but nevertheless a real community. We are all called upon to drink the Soma. Man is not alone, because he is not "man" alone. Indeed, to be "man" is only a mental abstraction, since "man," truly viewed, is just a "cut" in the complex web of reality. Each being has its own identity, but this is possible precisely because the identity is seen and experienced against the background of a hierarchical differentiation. This is the revelation of the *puruṣa*.

When Man rises at morning and proceeds to pray, or when he utters some prayers before retiring at night, he does so not out of a sense of duty or because he is impelled by an urgent love, but for the same "reason" that the waters flow, the sun shines, and the Gods keep the world together—certainly, out of no mechanical compulsion, but out of the deepest performance of his humanness. The *śruti* puts it in one short sentence, "Truth alone is worship,"[34] and to be true to ourselves means also to be truthful to the shaping of the universe just by being, that is, by becoming, what we really are called upon to be.

I hope that the prayers that follow may combine the concreteness of the single tradition with a universality that may enable them to be recited and prayed by people from outside the Vedic phylum. When we have retained proper names for the Vedic Gods, the reader may readily understand them as symbols of the superhuman rather than as particular personages linked exclusively with a single orthodoxy. Perhaps the advantage for today of the Vedic prayers is

32. RV VIII, 19, 25-26.
33. RV V, 4, 10.
34. SB II, 2, 2, 20; cf. § III 25 Introduction.

that, just because most of them have already died, they are ready to rise again in a more universal way. Modern Man may sometimes find difficulty in reading these texts as prayers. We should not consider here the rightness or wrongness of such an attitude, but limit ourselves to observing that these hymns can also be read in a less pietistic frame of mind, as manifestations of the Spirit, as our own internal dialogue, or as the crystallization of a human experience of which we are the heirs.

In Part VII we do not intend to distract the reader with Indological notes or to burden him unnecessarily with difficult versions. This is the justification for the absence of the former and for a less literal rendering of the latter.

A. AT SUNRISE

Sūryodaya

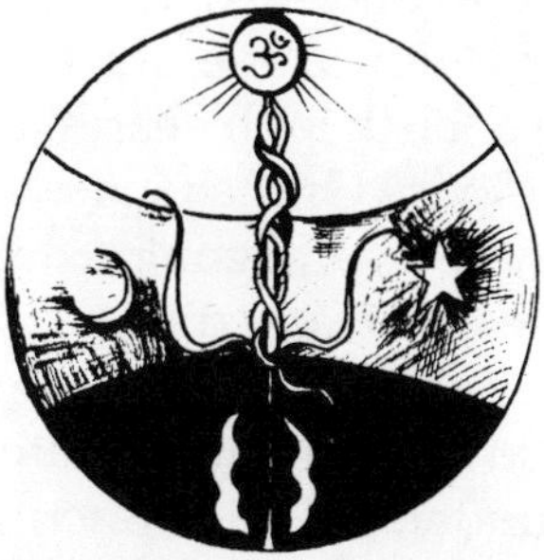

All that has been said about worship is meant to help us have the proper attitude of heart and mind as we approach the selected texts which, in their turn, are not an end in themselves, but simply companions on the road toward the final station of Man. The texts gathered here for prayer at sunrise follow a simple and natural pattern. Each season of the year presents five texts that contain certain underlying ideas: (1) The Mystery of the Origins; (2) The Awakening to Life and Light; (3) The Shining of the Sun: Prayers for Protection and for the Offering of the Sacrifice; (4) Praise to the Sacred Drink; and (5) The Discovery of the One.

Before we enter into the experience of prayer we wish to summon an invisible guide who will faithfully direct us; it is Gracious Disposition, *śivasaṁkalpa*. Without the grace of the Spirit—however we may envisage it—nothing can be properly thought, nothing can be properly done, no correct bearings can be taken, no real prayer can be uttered.

1. THE MYSTERY OF THE ORIGINS

It is still dark, just before the appearance of dawn. Man would like to pierce the obscurity, to understand what it is that overcomes and overwhelms him, to find an answer to the questions that haunt his mind about the beginning of everything, the mystery of beings and of Being. How did Men, the cosmos, come to be, come to life? What, who, is behind the scenes? Groping in the dark, hesitant, never sure which aspect of the reality they are trying to approach, the Vedic seers have made an attempt to describe some insights into these perennial questions. They do not expound metaphysical theories; they only whisper in a poetic murmur something of the mystery of the world.[35]

Could it be a divine Artificer—here Brahmaṇaspati the Lord of the Holy Word—who fashioned the universe?[36] Or Aditi, the Universal Mother, who gave birth to the earth and then herself came to birth, followed by the Gods? Or the Gods, who produced the earth while dancing? All these cosmogonic conjectures remain hypothetical, while the one clear assertion is that from nonexistence comes existence, or, stated more simply, existence is.

Later on we are told of a divine Architect, *viśvakarman*.[37] Here the whole process is understood as a sacrifice, in which the sacrificer, the priest, is also the victim.[38] The universe is declared to be the work of a person, a poet, a seer,[39] a sculptor, a smith, a carpenter. What was the primal matter, the substance? The query remains unanswered. Nevertheless behind everything that is visible or tangible, behind any work of craftmanship, is invariably the One, who knows everything and who gave the Gods their names.

In one hymn of the Atharva Veda the "mighty mystery" to be known is that Heaven and Earth are the universal Father and Mother.[40] In another it is the Sun, the vivifier and generator, who brings to birth both Heaven and Earth.[41]

It seems as if all the searchings, speculations, and yearnings of preceding ages are packed into the long, enigmatic, and at times obscure hymn to the Support of the Universe, *skambha*.[42] The main trends of thought here seem to be centered (*a*) on the Support itself, which holds everything, knows everything, and is the repository of all living beings; (*b*) on the solar Support, that is, the Sun, which alone remains stable while the generations of Men are destroyed

35. For a general introduction to this subject and further texts see § I A.
36. Cf. § VII 2.
37. Cf. § VII 7.
38. For the same idea RV X, 90 (§ I 5).
39. Cf. § VII 12.
40. Cf. § VII 17.
41. Cf. § VII 22.
42. Cf. § VII 27; cf. also § I 3 for the other hymn to *skambha*.

and consumed by Time, the maker of seasons, months, and days, and which marks the time of sacrifice; (*c*) on the One, Brahman, which is frequently identified with the Sun and which in the compass of one stanza is identified, in rapid succession, with Fire, and with the threefold Swan (v. 17)—the One that embraces all things and yet is finer than a single hair (v. 25). He is fullness (v. 29), he is near and far, he does not die, he never grows old (v. 32), he is the Unborn (v. 41). The hymn ends on a clear note: the revelation of the *ātman,* wise, immortal, ever young, self-existent (v. 44).

2. THE AWAKENING TO LIFE AND LIGHT

And it is Dawn! The exquisitely graceful and smiling Goddess awakens sleeping mortals to life and joy, for work or worship.[43] She is ever radiant, clothed in light, the light that announces a new day and restores vigor, courage, and hope to Men. As soon as Dawn appears, she prompts the worshiper to prayer, to the offering of the sacrifice. Then, having diffused her radiance, she disappears, youthful and immortal, before the splendor and warmth of the Sun.

3. THE SHINING OF THE SUN: PRAYERS FOR PROTECTION AND FOR THE OFFERING OF THE SACRIFICE

At the rising of the Sun a new day starts and Man is caught up in all kinds of activities.[44] He has to face once more the unknown, the struggles, difficulties, and evils that await him; he has to take care of his land, his cattle and horses, his goods, his relatives, his varied tasks—and himself. It is Pūṣan, divine Providence,[45] whom he spontaneously implores for protection against the wicked, against robbers, even against the untimely heat. It is to him that he addresses his prayers for green pastures, smooth paths, food in plenty, and spiritual energy.

Now the time has come to sacrifice to Agni, the bringer of peace, the priest who conveys Men's offerings to the Gods in order to renew each day Man's commerce with the divine.[46] It is he, pure light, from whom Men implore protection from evil and disease, for he is truly a tower in which all can take refuge and feel secure.

43. Cf. §§ VII 3; 8; 13; 18; 23; 28.
44. Cf. §§ VII 4; 9; 14; 19; 24; 29.
45. For Pūṣan cf. § II Introduction.
46. For *agnihotra* cf. § III 16; for Agni cf. § I 23 and §§ III 4; 5.

4. PRAISE TO THE SACRED DRINK

The preparation of the Sacred Drink Soma is not, like the *agnihotra,* a regular ritual; it is not of daily occurrence. It is an offering of the wealthy, the privilege of the rich and noble, an oblation for special occasions. Its sacred character makes it the supreme sacrifice of the Ṛg Veda with a highly elaborated ritual performance. Though the *soma*-juice may be prepared three times a day, we confine ourselves to hymns sung in praise of Soma during its purificatory rite. It seemed appropriate to include them in the selection for morning prayers.[47] The six hymns given, like all those belonging to the Book IX of the Ṛg Veda, are addressed to *pavamāna,* the self-purifying. They deal with the self-purification of the *soma*-juice as it passes through the woolen sieve, the most solemn act in the making of the sacred drink. These hymns therefore are extolling the highest qualities of the liquor, its cleansing power. Again and again its purity, clarity, and luminosity are praised. Soma, like Agni, chases away evil, sorrow, darkness, and impurity. He is all-powerful, the life-quickener who imbues his worshipers with vitality, health of mind and body, and noble thoughts. He is the sage par excellence who bestows wisdom and brings with him peace and joy, ecstasy and illumination. He leads to immortality.

Here we are already in a purely spiritual sphere. The early morning praise of the sacred drink awakens in the heart and mind of Man a desire for purity, wholeness, and wisdom; it brings to his awareness the stream of vitality and vigor which flows within him. Soma inspires in him a consciousness also of the immortal within him. It should be added that so sacred is this drink that in Vedic times only Gods and priests were allowed to partake of it. If we include these hymns in a daily prayer, it is because we are bold enough to mix Soma in our everyday bread.

5. THE DISCOVERY OF THE ONE

What is astounding about the Īśa Upaniṣad is that within the compass of only eighteen verses it sets forth a series of intuitions, the more profound for their simplicity, which disclose the mystery underlying all these prayers, praises, and speculations of the Ṛg Veda and the Atharva Veda given in the sunrise selection.[48]

47. Cf. §§ VII 5; 10; 15; 20; 25; 30; for Soma cf. § III 17.
48. Cf. §§ VII 6; 11; 16; 21; 26; 31.

The Īśa Upaniṣad reveals the One in his transcendence and immanence, the One who is everywhere and nowhere. The path to him, it declares, is the path of nonduality, of oneness, through which one reaches true liberty, joy, and wisdom. Here is to be found immortality; here is to be found liberation. It is important to stress that the message of this Upaniṣad is not reserved for hermits, sages, recluses of the forests, monks, and the like. It may not be addressed to the masses, but it is in no way confined to those who have "left the world." It is an error to think that the attitude of nonpossession, first step toward a unity of being, presupposes that one must abandon one's earthly belongings and retire to a lonely spot. Nonpossession is an attitude of heart and mind where the ego, the little self, exists no more. It is complete unselfishness in everything, which makes one lightsome and free as a bird. It is the first existential step, and unless one resolutely enters upon that path, one will never grasp the wisdom revealed by this Upaniṣad.

The last four verses seem to have no direct link with the rest of the Upaniṣad. According to tradition they are a prayer for a dying person, followed by prayers to Agni, to the Sun, and to Pūṣan.

Gracious Disposition — *Śivasaṁkalpa*

1

YV XXXIV, 1-6

1. That Divine which soars aloft when Man awakes
and returns to its same place when he is sleeping,
the one Light of lights which travels afar—
  may that spirit be graciously disposed toward me!

2. That through which the wise are active in sacrifice,
the understanding perform their duty in assemblies,
that incomparable spirit, interior to all beings—
  may that spirit be graciously disposed toward me!

3. That which is wisdom, consciousness, and firmness,
that Light immortal interior to all beings,
without whose will we perform no action—
  may that spirit be graciously disposed toward me!

4. That immortal by which this universe is encompassed,
all that was and is and is yet to be,
by which with seven priests the sacrifice is extended—
  may that spirit be graciously disposed toward me!

5. That in which the prayers, the songs, and the formulas
are fixed firm like spokes in the hub of a cartwheel,

in which are interwoven the hearts of all beings—
may that spirit be graciously disposed toward me!

6. That which guides Men as a charioteer
drives his powerful horses with the reins,
which dwells within the heart, swiftly moving—
may that spirit be graciously disposed toward me!

a) Spring

Vasanta

The Light of Man

Agni

O shining One, cause now the Sun,
that unaging star, to climb the sky,
imparting light to men.

You, O Lord, are mankind's bright sign,
best, most beloved of the people. Awake!
Give strength to the singer!

RV X, 156, 4-5

To the Divine Craftsman

Viśvedevāḥ

2

RV X, 72

1. With all the pleasing skill we may,
the birth of Gods we now proclaim
in chanted hymns, that Men to come
may know the truth of what befell.

2. The Lord of the Holy Word, like a smith,
blasted and smelted them together.

In erstwhile ages of the Gods
from nonexistence existence came.

3. In earlier ages of the Gods
from nonexistence existence came.
Then came to birth the cardinal points
from within the upward-moving Power.

4. And from the upward-moving Power
sprang earth, from earth the cardinal points.
Dakṣa was from Aditi born,
from Dakṣa's bosom Aditi.

5. Then did Aditi issue into being,
she who, O Dakṣa, was your daughter.
After her the Gods, the blessed ones,
Sharers of immortal life, were born.

6. When at that time you were found in the waters,
O Gods, pressed together, close-clasping one another,
a storm of dust arose from your feet
as from the stamping feet of dancers.

7. When, O Gods, like wonder-workers,
you inflated the worlds and all that is,
you restored to the realm of day the Sun,
who was lying hidden beneath the sea.

8. Eight in number are the sons of Aditi,
who from her body sprang to life.
With seven she joined the ranks of the Gods;
the eighth, the Sun, she thrust to one side.

9. So with her seven sons Aditi
advanced upon the earlier age.
She brought the Sun to earth that he
might bring things to life and then pass to his death.

You Who Shine Forth, Bring Blessings to Men *Uṣas*

3

RV I, 92

1. Now the Dawns have made their bright appearance,
unfurling their splendor in the eastern firmament.
Like strong men preparing their weapons, these mothers,
the reddish morning clouds, arise.

2. The rosy morning rays have arisen unhindered,
hitching to their chariot the willing red clouds.
Restoring to all things their erstwhile clarity;
the red-hued Dawns have assumed brilliant splendor.

3. They chant a hymn like women active in worship,
united on the same path, coming from afar.
They convey refreshment to the liberal giver
and bestow all good things on the preparer of oblation.

4. Dawn like a dancer puts on her ornaments;
as a cow yields her udder, so she bares her bosom.
She creates light for all living beings, flinging wide
the gates of darkness, as cows their enclosure.

5. We have beheld the radiance of her shining.
Advancing, she drives away the horror of the night.
Like a colored post, anointed at the sacrificial feast,
so the Dawn, Heaven's daughter, is adorned with wondrous splendor.

6. Now we have crossed to the other shore of darkness.
Dawn, shining forth, brings a limpid clarity.
She smiles like an enchantress, shining in glory.
Her beautiful countenance awakens us for joy.

7. The singing priests have praised radiant Dawn,
the daughter of Heaven, the bringer of graces.
You, O Dawn, strengthen us with offspring and Men;
you make us rich in horses and cattle.

8. O Dawn, grant us renown, stalwart sons and servants,
ample treasure and possession of horses.
You who shine forth in glory and splendor,
impelled by your own powers, bring blessings to Men.

9. Gazing out over all the world
and spreading her light rays westward, Dawn shines.
She wakens to motion all living creatures
and heeds the voice of every worshiper.

10. This ancient of days is continually reborn,
adorning herself with similar colors.
As a bird catcher holds in his power flying creatures,
so this Goddess diminishes the life of mortals.

11. Now she discloses heaven's farthest horizons,
chasing far away her sister the Night.
She reflects the splendor of the Sun, her lover,
and makes the score of days of all creatures to dwindle.

12. Bright Dawn, the blessed One, spreads forth her rays
like grazing cattle or expanding floodwaters;
never infringing divine precepts, she appears
with escorting sunbeams, visible to all.

13. Ample, O Dawn, is your store of treasure.
Grant us your wondrous boons that we
may nourish our children and our children's sons.

14. Your shining evokes sweet sounds of life.
    Grant us your favor this day that we
    may abound in herds of cattle and in horses.

15. O Dawn, made more splendid by holy worship,
    yoke to your car your reddish steeds
    and bring to us all felicity.

16. O powerful Spirits, with one mind and will
    direct your chariot toward our home
    and make it rich in cattle and gold.

17. You who brought down from heaven sweet song,
    a light that enlightens the race of Men,
    grant to us now, O Spirits, strength.

18. May those who wake at dawn bring hither the Gods,
    the givers of refreshment and doers of marvels,
    on paths of gold that they may drink Soma.

Lead Us to Pastures Green, O God

Pūṣan

4

RV I, 42

1. Shorten our path, O God, remove
   all stumbling blocks, Deliverer.
   Be at hand to guide.

2. Scare from our road the wicked wolf,
   the ill-intentioned one who lies
   in wait to harm.

3. The robber lurking round our path,
   who cunningly contrives our hurt,
   chase far away.

4. Trample beneath your feet the burning
   brand of the wicked, whoever he be,
   the double-tongued.

5. From you, wise wonder-working God,
   we claim today that selfsame aid
   you gave our Fathers.

6. So, Giver of favors, you who wield
   the golden sword, grant to us riches
   easily won.

7. Help us elude pursuers, O God,
   and make our path both smooth and fair.
   Show us your might.

8. Lead us to pastures green, O God.
   Protect us from untimely heat.
      Show us your might.

9. Be gracious to us, fill us wholly,
   impart to us food and spiritual vigor.
      Show us your might.

10. All that God does shall win our praise.
    We magnify his name with hymns,
       seeking boons from the Mighty.

O Cleansing Drink, Make Us Perfect

Soma

5

RV IX, 4

1. O cleansing sacred Drink,
   conqueror of high renown,
      make us perfect.

2. Bring us to light, the light
   celestial, and all pure joys,
      make us perfect.

3. Enhance our skills and powers
   of mind; drive far all foes;
      make us perfect.

4. O purifier, prepare
   this Drink, a draught for the Lord.
      Make us perfect.

5. Give us a share in the Sun
   by your wisdom and favor.
      Make us perfect.

6. Sustained and helped by you,
   long may we see the Sun!
      Make us perfect.

7. Almight God, upon us pour
   a double portion of your grace.
      Make us perfect.

8. O King ever victorious,
   impart to us your wealth.
      Make us perfect.

9. Strengthened by Man's worship,
   O purifier, you grant gifts.
      Make us perfect.

10. Grant us, O God, Life-quickener,
    all that this world affords;
    make us perfect.

All Is Enveloped by the Lord *Īśāvāsyam*

6

Benediction

That is Fullness, this is Fullness,
from Fullness comes Fullness.
When Fullness is taken from Fullness,
Fullness remains.
Om, peace, peace, peace.

IsU 1-3

1. This whole universe, all that lives
   and moves on earth, is enveloped by the Lord.
   Therefore find joy in abandoning the transient.
   Do not hanker for another Man's lot.
2. When he performs all actions with integrity,
   a Man may desire to live a hundred years.
   For you also there is no other way.
   A Man's deeds do not cling to him.
3. Infernal are some worlds called, enwrapped
   in deepest darkness. Thither at death
   go those who try to slay the *ātman*.

b) Summer

Grīṣma

Source of Light and Joy

Sūrya

Across the expanse of the whole horizon
the seven bay mares draw the Sun on his chariot,
the Lord of each single thing, moving and inert,
to bring us joy.

RV VII, 66, 15

The Divine Architect

Viśvakarman

7

RV X, 81

1. The Seer, our father, once offered all these worlds in oblation,
assuming a priestly role, and sought to gain riches
by the power of prayer; he himself entered later creations,
while shrouding in mystery the first creative moment.

2. What was the primal matter, what the substance?
How could it be discerned, how was it made?
From which the Designer of all things, beholding all,
fashioned the Earth and shaped the glory of the Heavens?

3. A myriad eyes are his, a myriad faces,
a myriad arms and feet, turning each way!
When he, sole God, creates the Earth and Heavens,
he welds them together with whirring of arms and wings.

4. What was the timber and what the tree from which
the Heavens and also the Earth were chiseled!
Ponder, O wise Men. Question in your hearts.
On what did he rely when he formed these worlds?

5. The haunts where you dwell, O Designer ever true to your laws,
on high, in the depths, and in every region between,
disclose to your friends at the hour of oblation. Willingly
offer your body in sacrifice, thus enhancing its vigor.

6. O Designer of all, who enhance your own vigor through oblation,
offer as sacrifice for yourself the Earth and the Sky!
Let others around us wander hither and thither!
May we find a generous patron to offer his bounty!

7. Let us now invoke for our aid the Lord of Speech,
the Designer of all things that are, the inspirer of wisdom!
May he, the ever kindly, be well disposed to our summons,
and may he, whose work is goodness, grant us his blessing!

Dawn Spurns None, Whether Lowly or Mighty *Uṣas*

8

RV I, 124

1. Dawn shines forth at the kindling of the fire.
When the Sun rises, light is spread.
The Inspirer God now sends us forth,
both two-and four-legged, each to its own task.

2. Never transgressing the heavenly laws,
marking the passing of human generations,
Dawn shines forth—the last of endless
mornings and the first of dawns to follow.

3. This Daughter of Heaven has revealed herself
in the eastern region, all clothed in light.
Faithfully she follows the path of Cosmic Order;
well understanding, she measures out the regions.

4. Like a wondrous bird she reveals her breast.
She discloses delights like a singer of songs.
She awakens sleeping mortals like a fly,
ever returning, a most faithful apparition.

5. In the eastern half of the sky's firmament
the mother of the cloud-cows has set up her banner.

She goes on diffusing her light far and wide
until she fills the expanse of earth and heaven.

6. The first among many is she to be seen,
debarring from her light neither kinsman nor stranger.
She radiates, proud of her pure appearance,
spurning none, whether great or lowly.

7. As a girl without a brother seeking for men,
ascending the stage as if in search of treasures,
Dawn, like a loving wife for her husband,
fair-robed and smiling, unveils her bosom.

8. Departing like one who will return, sister Night
relinquishes her place to her elder sister,
who, beaming forth with the rays of the Sun,
is adorned, like maidens going to a festival.

9. In the sequence of sisters, in the course of days,
each later one goes behind a former.
May these Dawns radiate abundance as before,
may they now herald for us a good day!

10. Awaken, O Dawn, the generous giver;
let the stingy miser sleep on in his bed!
Shine brightly, O bounteous teller of our days,
on those who now worship and sing their praise.

11. The maiden from the East has shone upon us,
harnessing her team of red-hued oxen.
She shines; the light floods in to rouse us.
May the Fire be present in every dwelling!

12. As birds fly forth from their roosting places,
so men rise at your summons to replenish their store.
Even to the sacrificer who remains in his home
your daily arrival brings much gain.

13. May my prayer confer praise on you, the praiseworthy!
The procession of Dawns has increased our riches.
By your good favor may we be endowed
with riches a hundred, a thousandfold!

Most Loving God, Guard Us from Evil

Agni

9

RV I, 189

1. By the right path, O Lord, lead us to plenitude;
lead us, O Lord. You know every path.
Deliver us from the sin that would lead us astray.
We desire to hymn you in myriad ways.

2. By your favors granted enable us, O Lord,
once again to leap over the pitfalls that face us.
Be a high tower, powerful and broad, for both us
and our children. To our people bring well-being and peace.

3. Spare us, O Lord, from all diseases.
Let them strike at those who are bereft of your aid!
May this earth afford us a gracious transit,
thanks to you, O Adorable, and all the immortals!

4. Protect us, O Lord, with your perpetual aid,
so that, now that you shine in your well-loved abode,
O Deity youthful, panic may not strike
your songster either today or tomorrow.

5. Abandon us not, O Lord, to the wicked,
the destroyer, the liar, the hapless wretch.
Do not hand us over to the demon who gnashes
or the toothless one or the man who may despoil us!

6. A God like you, O Lord, born of truth,
will furnish with armor the man who extols him,
preserving him from those who would harm or slander,
for you, O Lord, are the deliverer from ambush.

7. You alone can discern both the opposites.
Before the sacrifice you seize on Man
but during the sacrifice Man seizes you!
Like a racehorse, you let yourself be reined by the priests!

8. To propitiate this God we have uttered these phrases.
I, son of Man, have hailed Agni the strong.
May we, by the help of innumerable seers,
be surrounded on all sides by superabundance!

Lord, We Desire Your Friendship *Soma*

10 RV IX, 31

1. Forth flows the Soma-juice,
pure, beneficent,
producing visible fullness.

2. Increase for us splendor
from earth and heaven.
Be the Lord of all might!

3. For you the winds blow,
full of love; for you
the rivers flow.
They enhance, O Soma, your greatness.

4. Surge, O Soma!
May potent strength
gather from all sides within you!
Be the central point of all power!

5. For you, o brown-hued Soma,
the cows have yielded
on the highest summit
imperishable milk and fatness.

6. O Lord of all,
we desire your friendship,
O Drop, powerful defender.

He Moves and He Moves Not

Ejati tan naijati

11

IsU 4-6

4. Unmoving, the One is swifter than the mind.
No power can reach him as he speeds on before.
Standing still, he outstrips those who run.
From him life-power thrills through all things.

5. He moves and he moves not; he is far, yet is near;
he is within all that is, yet is also outside.

6. The Man who sees all beings in the Self
and the Self in all beings is free from all fear.

c) Rainy Season

Varṣa

Joyful Streams of Praise

Bṛhaspati

Like the cry of watchful birds swimming in water,
like the loud claps of thundering rain clouds,
like joyful streams gushing from the mountain,
so have our hymns sounded forth to the Lord.

RV X, 68, 1

The Divine Creator *Viśvakarman*

12

RV X, 82

1. The Father of vision, the wise in spirit, created
   in the manner of ritual oil both these worlds that bow before him.
   As soon as the eastern ends were firmly secured,
   the Sky and the Earth were in their turn extended.

2. Exceedingly wise, exceedingly strong is the Designer.
   He is Creator, Disposer, Epiphany supreme.
   Mortal Men rejoice that their votive offerings are heeded
   there where they say the One is, beyond the Seven Seers.

3. He is our Father who begat us, he the Disposer
who knows all situations, every creature.
It was he alone who gave to the Gods their names;
to him come questioning all the other creatures.

4. To him the seers of old offered their substance
in sacrifice, as did also the multitude of singers
who fashioned this whole universe when first the spheres,
both the shadowy realm and the bright, were set in their places.

5. That which the Waters first received, beyond the heavens,
beyond the earth, beyond both Gods and demons—
say, what was that, the first primeval germ,
when all the assembled Gods, and they alone, were watching?

6. He was the primal germ borne by the Waters,
wherein all the Gods were coalesced together;
at the navel of the Nonborn the One and Only is set,
he upon whom depend all created beings.

7. You have no knowledge of him who created these worlds;
some other thing has interposed between you.
The reciters of hymns who ravish life in their ritual
proceed with their muttering, enwrapped in confusion and ignorance.

Dawn, Emblem of the Immortal

Uṣas

13

RV III, 61

1. O Dawn, whose enterprises never fail
and who understands all things, accept our songs.
O ancient yet ever-youthful Goddess, you proceed
in accordance with Law, endowed with wealth and fullness.

2. O immortal Goddess, beam forth your rays.
Let your shining chariot, loaded with gifts,
bring you hither in the company of your docile steeds,
your powerful steeds, O golden Lady!

3. Arising, you turn your face toward all creatures.
You, O Dawn, are the emblem of the Immortal.
You who each day proceed to the same goal,
direct toward us, O Maiden, your chariot.

4. Spinner of light, beautiful Dawn,
you proceed on your way to your wonted haunts.
You bring light to birth, O generous One,
and encompass the confines of Heaven and Earth.

5. I hail you, Goddess, Dawn of light!
To her let us offer the homage of our songs!

She imparts to us sweetness, she steadies the Heaven
and lavishes abroad her radiant splendor.

6. Our songs have awakened this Daughter of Heaven.
Equitable, generous, she has scaled the two worlds.
Toward Dawn, O Fire, when she comes in her brightness,
you advance, eager to share her fair treasures.

7. The Mighty One, firm-based on Order, speeds after
each dawn and makes his debut in the worlds.
Great are the powers of Mitra and Varuṇa.
Dawn in all directions diffuses her splendor!

The Divine Inspirer Arises *Agni-Sūrya*

14

RV IV, 14

1. At many a dawn of shining splendor
has the Lord presided.
Come on your chariots, far-ranging Spirits,
come to our sacrifice.

2. Suffusing light for every creature,
the Inspirer God rises.
The Sun has filled heaven and earth with his radiance,
disclosing his presence.

3. Rosy Dawn advances, adorned with the brightness
of many a beam.
She pursues her way on her well-equipped chariot,
arousing Men to joy.

4. Come, O twin Spirits, at break of day
on your powerful chariots.
We offer in sacrifice this honey-sweet draught
for your delectation.

5. How is it that, though united and unsupported,
he does not fall down!
By what inner power moves he? Who has seen? A firm pillar,
he protects heaven's vault.

Inspire Us to Skill of Mind and Hand *Soma*

15

RV IX, 36

1. Like a chariot horse
he speeds through the sieve
and spurts into the cup.
The winner of the race has reached the goal.

2. Become pure, O Soma,
as you flow with due care,
calling on the Gods,
passing through the sieve to the honey-dripping bowl.

3. Foremost Purifier,
let your lights
shine on us now,
inspiring us to skill of mind and hand.

4. His beauty enhanced
by the hands of those faithful
to Sacred Order,
he is purified, as he flows, in the woolen strainer.

5. May Soma bestow
on the offerer all treasures,
both earthly and heavenly,
and those that pertain to the airy spaces!

6. To the height of heaven
you ascend, O Soma,
O Lord of Power,
in search of horses and cattle and heroes!

In Him Dwells All Wisdom

Kavir manīṣī

16

IsU 7-9

7. When, to a Man who knows, all beings
have become one with his own self,
when furthermore he perceives this oneness,
how then can sorrow or delusion touch him?

8. He is radiant, encompassing all,
incorporeal, devoid of scar or sinew,
invulnerable, pure, unpierced by evil.
He is seer, sage, omnipresent, self-existent.
To everything he has assigned its due place
through ages and ages unending.

9. Into blinding darkness enter those Men
who revere ignorance; into blinder still
go those who pride themselves on knowledge.

d) Autumn

Śarad

The Eye of Light

Mitra-Varuṇa

The Eye of Light, established by the Gods,
may we see at his rising for a hundred autumns!
Yes, may we live for a hundred autumns!

RV VII, 66, 16

Know, O People, a Mighty Mystery

Mahadbrahma

17

AV I, 32

1. Know, O people, a mighty mystery,
   about to be proclaimed—
   that which is not found on earth or in heaven,
   that by which the plants breathe.
2. In space is their stay, like a platform for the wearied,
   the place of support
   for all that is. This the wise know—
   or perhaps they do not?
3. That which the trembling worlds and the earth
   together created
   is now in perpetual movement, like the streams
   of the mighty ocean.

4. The one has encompassed all; it is established
 upon the other.
 To Heaven and to Earth, which possesses all things,
 I have offered my worship.

Light Up Our Path . . . Lead Us to Worship *Uṣas*

18

RV VII, 75

1. From her birthplace in heaven
 rosy Dawn is revealed
 as ordained by Cosmic Law—
 the presage of glory!
 She has chased away fiends
 and hateful darkness;
 she lights up the paths—
 most noble of the noble!

2. Arouse us today
 to success and good fortune.
 To loftier joys
 promote us, O Dawn!
 Grant to us wealth
 of every kind,
 O Goddess renowned,
 friend of Man!

3. Look! The fair splendors
 of Morning approach us,
 everlasting, bedecked
 with every color.
 Filling the region
 between earth and heaven,
 they mount on high,
 eliciting worship.

4. This Daughter of Heaven,
 Queen of the world,
 yokes her chariot
 and goes far away.
 She visits all the lands
 where the five peoples dwell,
 surveying the deeds
 and the hearts of mortals.

5. Rich in treasure
 beyond all telling,
 this bride of the Sun
 controls all wealth.

Our youthfulness she steals,
yet the seers extol her!
The priests sing the praises
of radiant Dawn.

6. Here come her steeds
of varying hues,
the red steeds drawing
resplendent Morning.
On her beautiful car
the fair Goddess advances,
bringing much wealth
for her faithful servant.

7. True with the true,
mighty with the mighty,
divine with the divine,
holy with the holy—
she flung down all barriers
and released the sunrays,
who greeted Morning
with shouts of joy!

8. O Dawn, grant us riches
to rejoice our hearts,
cattle and horses
and men of true valor.
Protect from trampling feet
our sacred grass.
Preserve us, O Gods,
evermore with your blessings!

The Priest of All Joy *Agn*

19

RV VII, 1

1. Agni the golden, lover of the Dawn, spreads forth
his far-extending radiance. Brightly he shines,
refulgent, within a halo of pure light.
He has aroused and inspired our eager thoughts.

2. He shines forth at dawn like the sunlight, deploying the sacrifice
in the manner of priests unfolding their prayerful thoughts.
Agni, the God who knows well all the generations,
visits the Gods as a messenger, most efficacious.

3. To Agni are directed our songs and aspirations,
seeking the God and petitioning bounteous favors—
to the pleasant to behold, the handsome one, the mighty,
the mediator, conveyor of Men's oblations.

4. O Agni, bring to us Indra, together with the Vasus,
bring hither the powerful Rudra with all his followers,
Aditi, kindly to all Men, together with her sons,
and longed-for Bṛhaspati with the singers!

5. At sacrifice the prayerful congregation worships Agni,
the priest of all joy, the ever-youthful deity.
It is he who holds dominion over all treasures,
unwearied envoy to the Gods at the hour of oblation.

Pure and Ever More Pure

Soma

20

RV IX, 59

1. O Soma, be pure
and ever more pure!
Win cattle and horses and the treasure of children
—all that brings joy!

2. Be pure for the waters,
be pure for the plants,
be pure for the sacrifice and ever more pure,
O you the inviolable!

3. O Soma, be pure
and ever more pure!
Surmounting all dangers you sit as a sage
on the sacrificial straw!

4. Attain, O Purifier,
the heavenly light!
Once born you wax great, O sacred Drop,
surpassing all!

Passing over Death

Mṛtyuṁ tīrtvā

21

IsU 10-12

10. To one result leads knowledge, they say,
to another ignorance. Thus we have heard
from the wise who explained it to us.

11. The Man who understands both knowledge and ignorance,
holding the two in tension together,
by ignorance passes over death
and by knowledge attains immortal life.

12. Into blind darkness enter those Men
who revere the permanent, into blinder still
go those who in the impermanent exult.

e) Winter

Hemanta

Imparter of Vigor

Śyena

Across the wastes,
across the waters,
the solar Falcon, observer of Men, has cleft
an unerring path
to his haven desired.
Transcending all
the lower regions,
may he wing his way hither as harbinger of blessings,
accompanied by Indra!

May this heavenly eagle,
observer of Men,
this thousand-footed Falcon with progeny a hundredfold,
imparter of vigor,
restore to us the treasure that was stolen from us!
May he grant us ample
means of libation,
as he did to our Fathers in days of old!

AV VII, 41

Grant to Us Life, Power, and Riches

Savitṛ

22

AV VII, 14

1. I offer a song to this God, Inspirer
   of heaven and earth, surpassingly wise,
   possessed of real energy, giver of treasure,
   dear to all hearts!

2. His splendor extends far and wide, his light
   shines brightly in creation. He traverses the sky,
   golden-handed, measuring the heaven by his appearance,
   full of wisdom!

3. It was you, God, who inspired our father of old,
   granting him space above and on all sides.
   May we too enjoy day by day your blessings
   and life abundant!

4. This Inspirer God, the Friend whom we adore,
   has bestowed on our Fathers life, power, and riches.
   Let him drink Soma, rejoicing in our offerings.
   In his Law walks the pilgrim!

O Dawn, Convey to Us Joy

Uṣas

23

RV VII, 78

1. The first rays of Dawn have appeared once again!
   Her splendors diffuse their radiance on high.
   O Dawn, giver of Light, who draw near
   on your lofty chariot, convey to us joy!

2. The well-kindled Fire lifts up its voice loudly;
   the singers greet her with hymns of praise.
   Goddess Dawn approaches with her light,
   driving away all darkness and danger.

3. There in the East the day is appearing;
   the lights of morning, increasing, shine brightly,
   bringing forth the Sun, Sacrifice, and Fire,
   while evil darkness withdraws in the West.

4. Heaven's bounteous Daughter has come once again,
   and all eyes behold the Dawn in her shining.
   She has mounted her chariot, empowered by its own impulse
   and drawn by its team of well-yoked horses.

5. Awaking, we greet you with confident minds,
we and our nobles who furnish the oblations.
Show yourselves favorable, O Dawns, as you arise
and protect us forever with your blessings!

The Inspirer of All Men, Heart's Delight

Mitra-Varuṇa

24

RV VII, 63

1. Here comes the Sun beneficent! His gaze
rests upon all Men, on all Men his blessing.
The God, the eye of Mitra and Varuṇa,
has rolled up darkness like a scroll of parchment.

2. The Inspirer of all Men advances, the Sun,
displaying his mighty shimmering banner.
Now he will turn again the chariot wheel
which, harnessed to the shaft, the sun-horse pulls.

3. Emerging resplendent from the bosom of the mornings,
he ascends, heart's delight of all the singers.
This is the God I hail as Vivifier!
He never infringes the Order's harmony.

4. This bright jewel of the sky rises—limitless his vision!
Far is his goal; he hastens on resplendent.
Now, animated by the Sun, earth's people
can go about their business and perform their tasks.

5. He follows, like an eagle with flight unswerving,
the course designed for him by the Immortals.
Directly the sun rises, Mitra and Varuṇa,
we are eager to serve you with worship and oblations.

6. May Mitra, Varuṇa, Aryaman, grant us freedom
and space enough for us and for our children!
May we find pleasant pathways, good to travel!
Preserve us evermore, O Gods, with blessings!

Born for Glory, Come Forth for Glory!

Soma

25

RV IX, 94

1. Like ornaments vying for the neck of a winner,
like the cries of men contending for light,
so our songs strive for Soma who, in accordance with his choice,
is purified by waters as a sage. His wisdom
is like an enclosure for the rearing of cattle.

2. It is he who has revealed the abode of immortality.
All worlds have expanded for him who found the Light.
Our songs, increasing like cows in the pasture,
hail aloud the sacred Drop with deep devotion.

3. Encompassing wisdom on all sides, the Seer,
the Hero, moves through all worlds like a chariot,
preparing for mortals glory among the Gods, rewards
for the skillful, new things among the Gods at their appearing.

4. Born for glory, he has come forth for glory.
He endows the singers with glory and strength.
Robed in glory, they have gone to immortality.
He, measuring his course, is successful in the encounter.

5. Stream for us nourishment, horses, and cattle!
Shed light abroad, give delight to the Gods!
All this for you is easy of achievement,
for you, Soma Purifier, repel all enemies.

Immortality

Amṛta

26

IsU 13-14

13. To one result leads the impermanent, they say,
to another the permanent. Thus we have heard
from the wise who explained it to us.

14. The Man who understands both the impermanent and the permanent
holding the two in tension together,
by the impermanent passes over death
and by the permanent attains immortal life.

f) Frosty Season

Śiśira

The Divine Friend

Mitra

He who is called Divine Friend brings Men together.
The Divine Friend supports both earth and heaven,
watching over the peoples, never closing an eye.
To the Divine Friend offer an oblation of fatness!

RV III, 59, 1

In Whom Dwells All That Lives and Breathes *Skambha*

27

AV X, 8

1. Homage to him who presides over all things,
that which was and that which shall be;
to whom alone belongs the heaven,
to that all-powerful Brahman be homage!

2. It is thanks to Skambha that Heaven
and Earth remain each fixed in place.
In him dwells all that lives and breathes
and all that opens and shuts the eye.

3. Three generations are past already;
   others have followed in the relay of praise.
   On high is positioned the measurer of space.
   The Golden One has entered the green-gold plants.

4. One is the wheel; the bands are twelve;
   three are the hubs—who can understand it?
   Three hundred spokes and sixty in addition
   have been hammered therein and firmly riveted.

5. Take heed, O Savitṛ. Six are twins;
   one is born singly. The twins desire
   to unite themselves with the one that is born alone.

6. Though manifest, it is yet hidden, secret,
   its name the Ancient, a mighty mode of being;
   in Skambha is established this whole world;
   therein is set fast all that moves and breathes.

7. Advancing in the East, withdrawing in the West,
   it turns on one wheel, one rim, a thousand elements.
   With a half of itself it begat all creation.
   What has become of the half that remained?

8. The five-horsed chariot draws onward all creatures
   with fleet-footed side horses pulling from the rear.
   One sees of it the not yet vanished portion, not the vanished.
   The Beyond appears nearer, the Before more distant.

9. A bowl there is with aperture at side and base upturned;
   within it is accumulated every form of glory.
   Upon it on their seven thrones are set the Seven Sages,
   appointed as protectors of this whole vast sphere.

10. The verse hitched in front and the verse hitched behind,
    the verse hitched to each and to every portion,
    the verse through which the sacrifice proceeds to consummation—
    which is it, I ask you, of all the verses?

11. What moves, what flies, what stands quite still,
    what breathes, what breathes not, blinks the eye—
    this, concentrated into a single One,
    though multiple its forms, sustains the earth.

12. The infinite extends in many places,
    the infinite and finite having a common border;
    the guardian of the firmament alone can trace
    that line, he who knows what has been and shall be.

13. The Lord of creatures stirs within the womb;
    unseen himself, he comes to diverse births.

With half of himself he brought forth the whole world.
Of the other half what is the special sign?

14. Like a woman carrying water in a pitcher,
so he conveys the water on high.
All creatures behold him with their eyes,
but all do not know him with the spirit.

15. He dwells far away with that which is full.
Far away is he, free from deficiencies,
a great marvel in the center of the universe.
To him do sovereign rulers bring tribute.

16. That from which the Sun arises,
that into which the Sun subsides—
that I believe to be the Supreme.
There is nothing whatever that goes beyond.

17. Those who know or of old or in times between
refer by word of mouth to the knower of the Veda,
they speak one and all of the Sun in first place,
next, of Fire and of the threefold Bird.

18. The Sun, the Bird who soars in the sky,
spreading his wings on a thousand-day flight,
pursues his course, gathering all the Gods
in his bosom, surveying all the worlds.

19. By Truth he blazes forth on high,
by Sacred Word he surveys below,
by Breath he breathes across these worlds—
the one in whom resides the Supreme.

20. The Man who knows the two fire sticks
from which by friction wealth is obtained—
it is he whom they call a knower of the Supreme,
it is he who knows the mighty Brahman.

21. In the beginning he came into being, footless.
In the beginning he bore the heavenly light.
Four-footed now, he has become the abode
of delightfulness, assuming [in himself] all delights.

22. In the same way whosoever reveres
the everlasting God who reigns Supreme,
will himself become the abode of delights,
will himself receive food in abundance.

23. Men say that he is everlasting,
and yet he is renewed today.
Day and night with different forms
by turns give birth to each other.

24. A hundred, a thousand, tens of thousands, millions—
innumerable are the forms of the Self entered in him.
They are destroyed; he gazes [imperturbable]!
Thus shines this God; thus is he!

25. The One is finer than a single hair;
the One is utterly invisible;
and yet this Deity, to me so dear,
is vaster than the whole wide universe.

26. Dwelling immortal in the house of mortals
is a fair maiden, never growing old.
The one for whom she was created lies prone
and he who made her has himself grown old.

27. You are woman, you are man,
you are boy and young girl, too.
You are the old man leaning on his staff.
When born, you everywhere reveal your face.

28. He is their father and no less their son,
at once the eldest brother and the youngest.
The One God penetrates within the mind,
the Firstborn—yet even now within the womb.

29. From fullness he pours forth the full;
the full spreads, merging with the full.
We eagerly would know from whence
he thus replenishes himself?

30. She is of ancient days, born in long ages past;
she the primeval has traversed creation.
The great Goddess Dawn, the shining One,
looks out from each being that blinks the eye.

31. The Deity whose name is "Helpful" dwells
encompassed by Cosmic Order.
It is by reason of her color that these trees
are green, and green their garlands of flowers.

32. Behold the marvelous mystery of God.
Near though he is, one cannot leave him!
Near though he is, one cannot see him!
He does not die, nor does he grow old.

33. Words uttered by the One who existed
before all else convey things as they are;
the place to which they go, reverberating,
is called by men great Brahman, the Ultimate.

34. That base on which both Gods and Men
are founded, like spokes set firmly in a hub,

in which the waters' flower by supernatural means
made its appearance—who or what is he?

35. The Gods who set the wind a-blowing,
who hold in relation the five compass points,
who deem themselves to be superior to offerings—
these guides of the Waters, who are they?

36. One among them is clothed with the earth;
another encompasses the airy spaces;
one, the Disposer, holds firm the heaven,
while others protect all the four quarters.

37. Who knows the fine-drawn thread on which
the creatures that we see are spun,
who knows the thread of that same thread—
he also knows Brahman, the Ultimate.

38. I know the fine-drawn thread on which
the creatures that we see are spun;
I, even I, the thread know of the thread
and, consequently, Brahman, the Ultimate.

39. When, betwixt heaven and earth, the Fire
sped onward, consuming all things, there
where the wives of a single husband stood afar—
then where was Mātariśvan to be found?

40. Mātariśvan then had entered the Waters;
the Gods also had passed beneath the waves.
On high was the Sun, the measurer of space.
Soma, purified, had entered the golden flames.

41. Loftier even than the lofty Gāyatrī,
strode he forth toward the Immortal.
Where, I ask, is the Unborn visible?
The knowers of song after song alone know it.

42. He who sends creatures to their rest,
who amasses great wealth, whose laws are as true
as the God Savitṛ—that One stands firm,
as firm as Indra, in the struggle for riches.

43. Behold now the lotus with nine gates, encircled
by the three strands; within is a great marvel
consisting in the Self. This it is
of which the knowers of Brahman have knowledge.

44. Who knows the Self, wise, youthful, never aging,
will have no fear of death, being free from desire—
immortal, wise, in his own Self resourceful
full of fresh sap, in nothing falling short.

Dawn Has Arisen, Our Welfare Is Assured

Uṣas

28

RV VII, 79

1. Arousing the lands where dwell the five peoples,
Dawn has made visible the pathways of Men.
The beautiful dawn clouds convey her radiance.
The light of the Sun has disclosed earth and heaven.

2. The Dawns advance like clans arrayed for battle,
their bright rays tingeing the sky's distant bounds.
The Sun extends his arms; the rose-colored dawn clouds,
imprisoning the darkness, beam forth their luster.

3. Goddess Dawn has arisen, endowed with great wealth,
eliciting homage—our welfare is assured!
Noblest of the noble, this Daughter of Heaven
grants to her worshipers varied treasures.

4. Give to us, Dawn, that copious bounty
with which you have rewarded those who sang your praises!
Loudly they acclaimed you, like the strong bulls that bellowed
as you unbarred the doors of the firm-set mountain.

5. Prevail on each God to give us his bounty!
Now at your appearing impart to us the charm
of pleasant voices and thoughts for our uplift.
Preserve us evermore, O Gods, with your blessings!

May He Who Knows Lead the Way!

Pūṣan

29

AV VII, 9

1. On distant pathways is the birthplace of the Lord,
remote from Heaven, remote from Earth.
To the two abodes that are dear to his heart
he comes, then departs, knowing each path.

2. He knows and traverses each heavenly realm.
May he guide us in ways that are wholly secure!
Undertaking our welfare, shielding from all harm—
may he who knows lead the way with vigilance!

3. We take up our stance, Lord, beneath your law.
May we, who now praise you, incur no harm!

4. May the Lord interpose his right hand to protect us;
may he retrieve for us that which we have lost!
Yes, may we recover that which is lost!

Drive Far All Sorrow!

Soma

30

RV IX, 104

1. Be seated, O friends;
your songs uplift
for him who is undergoing
purification.
Array him like a child
in festive attire!
Bring him an offering!

2. Unite him to his worshipers
as a calf to its herd—
this bringer of prosperity,
producer of bliss
which delight the Gods,
doubly potent!

3. Purify him
who gives us power—
a banquet, he,
[most blessed One!],
for our Friend and our Protector
and all their attendants!

4. Our songs have followed you
like lowing cows,
O procurer of treasure!
We add to your flow
a stream of milk,
cream-hued to tawny.

5. You, sacred Drop,
are the master of ecstasies,
favorite drink
of the immortal Gods.
Show us the path,
O guide supreme!

6. Drive far away
the rapacious demon,
whoever he may be!
Drive far the godless,
the Man who is false.
Drive far all sorrow!

Unveil Your Face That I May See the Truth!

Satyadharmāya dṛṣṭaye

31

IsU 15-18

15. The face of Truth is covered over
by a golden vessel. Uncover it, O Lord,
that I who love the truth may see.

16. O Lord, sole Seer, Controller, Sun,
son of the Father of beings, shine forth.
Concentrate your splendor that I may behold
your most glorious form. He who is yonder—
the Man yonder—I myself am he!

17. Go, my breath, to the immortal breath.
Then may this body end in ashes!
Remember, O my mind, the deeds of the past,
remember the deeds, remember the deeds!

18. O Lord, lead us along the right path
to prosperity. O God, you know all our deeds.
Take from us our deceitful sin.
To you, then, we shall offer our prayers.

B. AT SUNSET

Sūryāsta

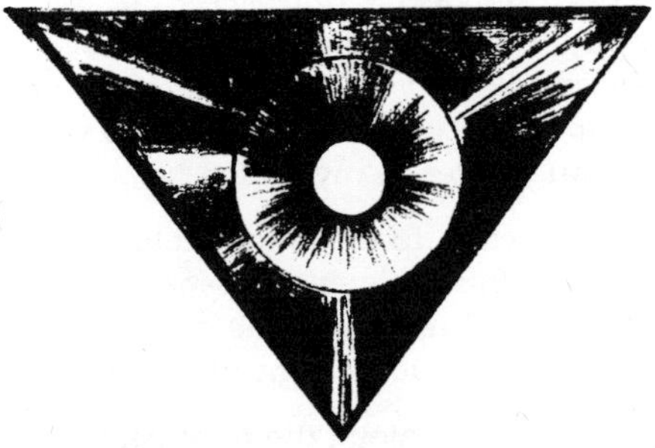

When the sun steals away, and the dim light of dusk precedes night, when the tasks of a busy day are over, Man comes back home from his varied tasks. He longs for peace, rest, friendship, intimacy, protection, and he turns to the sacred, to the less banal. In order to enter this other sphere or, in other words, to lift himself above the trivial, indeed to pray, he invokes Divine Grace, Anumati,[49] through whose good offices he hopes that the Gods will lend an ear to his prayer and be disposed to grant him all the gifts, both material and spiritual, for which he prays. Once the Gods have heard his call, sacrifice, prayer, and meditation will follow.

The selections for sunset, like those for sunrise, follow a simple and natural pattern: (1) Gathering around the Light; (2) The Longing for Friendship; (3) Blessed Night Has Come; and (4) The Pure Water of Knowledge.

1. GATHERING AROUND THE LIGHT

Agni, the sacred fire, the priest, mediator between earth and heaven, between this world and the world of the Gods, the brother and friend, is now blazing and shining in the home, radiating

49. Cf. § VII 32.

warmth and good cheer. Now that the time of quiet has come, Man, as at sunrise, feels the need for protection, for security.[50] Pūṣan, we may remember, was implored to secure the safety of cattle and roads; the prayer addressed to Agni, pure light, is deeper and more interiorized. Evil exists in all spheres of life; sin, injustice, and evil intentions are only too well known; they resemble stains and blotches, the evidence of a dreadful and contagious disease that Light cannot endure. Therefore Man, hurt, perhaps, in mind or body during the course of the day, bursts into strong imprecations against evil, malice, enmity, and sin. May Agni the strong, the blazing, mercilessly burn away all kinds of evil! May he, the faithful guardian, direct his bow against the malevolent and the wayward! May he drive them away and reduce them to ashes!

If Agni is the guardian of righteousness, he is also the inspirer of poetic wisdom, stirring to life Man's noblest faculty. His flame enkindles in Man the poetic inspiration that, going beyond the level of appearances, penetrates to the very core of reality.

2. THE LONGING FOR FRIENDSHIP

A true friend is always welcome in the home; he is one who shares in the joys and sorrows of the family. What, then, of Agni, who is not merely an occasional guest or even a close friend, but one who constantly dwells in the family hearth? It is not surprising that he has been called "closest kinsman and friend."[51]

The warmth that Agni diffuses calls for warm human relationships, for a unity of hearts and minds.[52] In the many hymns of the Ṛg Veda addressed to Agni, the divine friend, we also come across a few texts that express in a very vivid manner the beauty of liberality, of sharing with others, especially with the needy, the urge to extend the circle of friendliness and unity outside the limited family group.[53]

In the evening, when the business of the day has come to an end, when activities have ceased, a few moments of leisure are

50. Cf. §§ VII 33; 37; 41; 45; 49; 53.
51. RV VII, 15, 1 (§ VII 42).
52. Cf. §§ VII 34; 38; 42; 46; 50; 56.
53. Cf. §§ VII 46; 56; cf. also AV IX, 6, where hospitality offered to a guest is highly praised and is considered as important as the offering of sacrifice, each act of hospitality being shown to correspond to one of the sacrificial acts.

given to Man to ponder about the day that is past and to contemplate the morrow, which may renew and increase the friendly contacts of today. Thus he too may be a burning and shining flame which, like Agni, will warm and rejoice the hearts of all.

3. BLESSED NIGHT HAS COME

So fervent have been the Ṛg-vedic songs and hymns in honor of the Sun and Light, so numerous the hymns to Dawn, so poetic the descriptions and of such exquisite delicacy and detail—for it is Uṣas who brings Men hope and joy and the courage to live—that it would appear by comparison that Night has been almost entirely neglected. Just one hymn in the Ṛg Veda is addressed to her, and four in the Atharva Veda.[54] One is struck by the fact that Night is acclaimed at all only because she too is luminous, "full of eyes," lit by the stars. She is addressed as a passing traveler, as the herald of light, and as the sister of Dawn. Men salute her as marking the end of their daily toil, the hour of repose. She, the immortal, will bless their sleep.

Man's constant aspiration toward the light arises out of the dread, the insecurity, and the fear associated with shadows and darkness. Men utter fervent prayers for protection. Such prayers spring both from metaphysical anguish, for Man is not destined for the dark, and also from practical feelings of alarm, at least in the Atharva Veda. The poets enumerate all the dangers of the night: demons who may assault the soul, robbers who may carry off cattle and horses, the wolf that may slaughter the sheep, and the snake that is well known for its nocturnal visitations. Thus prayer is offered for deliverance from all ills, and coupled with it are hope and a yearning toward happiness, prosperity, and peace.

As there are only five hymns to Night, we have added a hymn from the Atharva Veda, the prayer of a priest asking for the right accomplishment of his priestly task and protection from all the Gods.[55] In this simple litany we meet again the familiar names encountered all through this anthology. Each God is invoked according to his own special attributes. Even Yama, the Forefathers, and the Fathers are included. As always, this prayer is a sacrificial prayer. In it and in the following *ślokas* from the Kaṭha Upaniṣad is

54. Cf. §§ VII 35; 39; 43; 47; 51. For the creation of the Night in a later tradition, cf. MaitS I, 5, 12 (§ V 1 Introduction).
55. Cf. § VII 55.

concentrated the entire message of the Vedic experience, if we have succeeded in discerning behind each name of the long litany those aspects of the divine Reality which the Vedic seers are eager to convey.

4. THE PURE WATER OF KNOWLEDGE

The last meditation, the final thoughts before going to sleep, are all oriented toward a further discovery of the One. Chapter IV of the Kaṭha Upaniṣad sums up the essential core of the Upaniṣadic message: the identity, the oneness, of *ātman-brahman,* Advaita, the non-duality of the One and of all that is.[56] This identity is acclaimed in a paean of praise as the seer eulogizes the whole cosmos, both the macrocosm of visible things and the microcosm of Man's interior being; he recalls the origin of all things, the prelude, Agni, the Sun. Each "binding" ends with the refrain "This is that," meaning "there is no distinction, no duality;" all that exists exists through and in Him who *is* and He is nothing of that which is. He is the Spirit, a burning yet smokeless flame. He is from all eternity.

Evil, or sin, the cause of suffering and of nonrealization, is to place oneself outside, in separation from the Spirit, to live in isolation, in a state of duality, to confine oneself to the surface of people and things, to be bound and hampered by a conglomeration of external psychological and emotional factors, to miss the brightness and purity of the inner glance. The way leading to complete and absolute oneness is that which transcends all duality, and the chapter ends with a meaningful verse:

> But as pure water poured into pure
> becomes the selfsame—wholly pure—
> so too becomes the self of the silent sage,
> of the one, O Gautama, who has understanding.[57]

Divine Grace *Anumati*

32

AV VII, 20

1. Render, O Grace, our sacrifice today
   acceptable to the Gods.
   May Agni convey the oblation of my worship!

56. Cf. §§ VII 36; 40; 44; 48; 52; 56.
57. KathU IV, 15 (§ VII 56).

2. Regard us with favor, O Grace, and bless us.
        Accept, O Goddess,
    this proffered oblation and grant to us offspring.

3. Approving, may he accord us wealth inexhaustible
        together with offspring!
    Void of anger, may he keep us in his mercy and favor!

4. Approachable, O Grace, best of guides, is your name,
        pleasant and bountiful!
    For your own name's sake fulfill our sacrifice,
        O source of all riches,
    and grant us, O Blessed One, treasures and heroes.

5. Grace, in response to our well-performed oblation,
        draws night to impart
    fair lands and brave heroes. Her providence is kindly.
        Guided by the Gods,
    may she enhance still further the sacrifice we offer!

6. Grace has become this All—whatever stands,
        whatever walks and moves.
    Accept us, O Goddess! Grant us your favor!

a) Spring

Vasanta

May the Wind Blow Sweetness!

Viśvedevāḥ

May the wind blow sweetness,
the rivers flow sweetness,
the herbs grow sweetness,
for the Man of Truth!

Sweet be the night,
sweet the dawn,
sweet be earth's fragrance,
sweet Father Heaven!

May the tree afford us sweetness,
the sun shine sweetness,
our cows yield sweetness—
milk in plenty!

RV I, 90, 6-8

You Are of All Men the Brother

Agni

33

RV I, 75

1. Accept our praise resounding,
the food beloved by the Gods,
opening your mouth to consume our oblations!

2. O Lord, noblest of the noble,
wisest and best mediator,
may we utter an acceptable prayer, efficacious!

3. Who among men is your brother?
Who offers you holy worship?
Who are you, Lord? On whom dependent?

4. You are of all Men the brother
and dear companion, O Lord,
the Friend whose name we may invoke for our friends!

5. Sacrifice to Mitra and Varuṇa
in our name. Honor the Gods
according to Holy Law upon your own hearth!

We Praise You in Our Home

Agni

34

RV II, 8

1. Even as a charioteer in the race
acclaims his own chariot, so now acclaim
the harnessing of Agni the glorious, the bountiful,
[to the chariot of sacrifice]—

2. The one who leads his worshiper aright,
who, himself undiminished, diminishes the wicked,
the God of cheerful countenance,
the recipient of worship—

3. The one who is magnified in our homes,
whose beauty is extolled at evening and at dawn,
whose law is inviolate—

4. The radiant one who beams forth his light
as the Sun does his splendor, whose flames are undying,
who glistens with fatness.

5. Our hymns have lent strength to Agni the Devourer
wherever he holds away. He has now assumed
to himself all comeliness.

6. With the help of Agni, Indra and Soma,
yes, of all the Gods, may we dwell unharmed,
overcoming our foes!

Night Immortal, Bless Our Rest

Rātrī

35

RV X, 127

1. Here comes the Night; with her twinkling eyes
   the Goddess has lit many places,
   adorned once again with all her beauty.

2. The immortal Goddess enwraps the world,
   its valleys and lofty peaks.
   By the shining of her light she repels all darkness.

3. Advancing quietly, the Goddess has restored
   once again her sister the Dawn.
   The shadows will now also steal away.

4. Be gracious this night! At your approach
   we now repair to our homes,
   like birds seeking their roosting places.

5. The villagers likewise and all that walks
   or flies have gone to their rest.
   Even the hungry hawks are still.

6. Ward off wild beasts, the wolf and his mate
   or the robber, O Night undulating.
   May your passage bring us safely to the other side!

7. The shades of night enfold me now,
   arrayed in black apparel.
   Banish them, Dawn, like haunting debts!

8. O Daughter of Heaven, to you I direct
   my hymn like a precious offering.
   Accept it, O Night, as a paean of praise.

The Search Within

Āvṛtta cakṣuḥ

36

KathU IV, 1-2

1. The Self-existent pierced sense openings outward;
   therefore a Man looks out, not in.
   But a certain wise Man, in search of immortality,
   turned his gaze inward and saw the Self within.

2. The foolish go after outward pleasures
   and walk into the snare of all-embracing death.
   The wise, however, discerning immortality,
   do not seek the permanent among things impermanent.

b) Summer

Grīṣma

The Moon Keeps Watch

Varuṇa

The stars fixed on high appear at night.
By day they depart, we know not whither.
Varuṇa's laws are faithful. The moon
sails on at night with a watchful eye.

RV I, 24, 10

Liberal Lord, Grant Us Your Treasure

Agni

37

RV III, 18

1. Be gracious, O Lord, to our approach,
   kindly as a friend or a father or a mother.
   Man oppresses his brother man.
   Consume all evil that plots against us.

2. Consume the neighbor full of malice
   and hostile curses from impious lips.
   Consume, O all-seeing One, the foolish;
   surround yourself with undying flames.

3. This wood and sacred oil, O Lord,
I eagerly present to enhance your powers,
with sacred words worshiping, as far as in me lies.
By this hymn divine I crave a hundred blessings.

4. O Son of strength, impart by your warmth
to those who now praise you and toil in your service
vitality and power, to the seers well-being.
We anoint your body again and again.

5. Grant us your treasure, O liberal Lord,
rich as you are when brightly enkindled.
With your shining arms and flickering shapes
convey it to the home of your blessed singer.

The One Who Brings Comfort to All Men

Agni

38

RV V, 8

1. It was you, O Agni most ancient, whom the ancients of old,
observers of Cosmic Law, enkindled for their aid,
O God created by life-power, the shining, the adorable,
the one who brings comfort to all Men, worthy of worship,
God of the hearth and home.

2. It was you, O Agni of the flaming hair, whom the peoples
enthroned as their foremost guest, the master of their households,
O God of the lofty ensign, of manifold shapes,
the winner of stakes, our kindly protector and helper,
devourer of ancient forests.

3. It is you, O Agni, whom the races of mankind acclaim
as connoisseur of sacrifice, Discerner, incomparable donor
of treasures, visible to all yet dwelling in secret,
O God most blessed, loud-sounding, skilled in worship,
glorified by the oil of sacrifice.

4. It is you, O Agni ever true to yourself, whom we mortals
have ever approached with reverence, singing your praises.
Wherefore, O God most noble, esteem well our sacrifice
and burst into glorious flames, your Godhead enkindled
by the hand of mortal Man.

5. It is you, O Agni of manifold shapes, who impart
life-power to each race of Men, as in days of old,
O God highly praised! By means of this your life-power
you control all sorts of food. That light of yours,
when you shine forth, blazes indomitable.

6. It is you, O Agni most youthful, whom, once enkindled,
the Gods have chosen as messenger, conveyer of oblations.
You, O God of vast range, situated in oil
and nourished by offerings, the Gods have made their bright Eye,
the inspirer of thought and fancy.

7. It is you, O Agni, whom Men through the ages have sought
with sacred oil and with fuel easy to kindle.
Thus, imbued with strength, your size increased by the plants,
you spread over all the world.

Keep Watch, O Night, We Pray

Rātrī

39

AV XIX, 47

1. O Night, you have filled this entire earth with your presence
in accordance with the Father's command.
Outstretching your arms you reach to the highest heavens;
the twinkling darkness draws near.

2. One cannot descry the opposite bank of her stream
nor yet what lies in between.
In her bosom reposes all that lives and stirs.
Grant, O wide darksome Night,
that we may safely attain your farther shore,
attain, pray, your farther shore!

3. Ninety and nine are your Scrutinizers, O Night,
who gaze on mortal Men.
Eighty and eight or seventy and seven are they.

4. Sixty and six, O opulent One, are they,
fifty and five, O Happy One.
Forty and four and thirty and three are they,
O Night, you who are powerful.

5. Twenty and two are your Scrutinizers, O Night,
eleven and fewer still.
With these protectors guard us well today,
O Night, Daughter of the Sky.

6. May no demon, no speaker of evil, hold power against us,
no baleful person malign us!
This night may no thief hold power against our cattle
and no wolf against our sheep!

7. O beauteous Night, may no robber approach our horses
and no witch cast spells on our men!
Let the thief and the marauder take flight by the farthest paths!

8. May he perish afar, that cord with the teeth that bite,
   that miscreant serpent, O Night!
   Blind him, stifle him, chop off his head, crush his jaws
   of the wolf! Trap the thief in a gin!

9. We make our dwelling in you. Our hearts crave sleep.
   Keep watch, then, O Night, we pray.
   Grant your protection to our cows, our horses, our households.

The Self Within *Antarātman*

40

KathU IV, 3-6

3. That by which one perceives form and taste,
   perfumes, sounds, and loving caresses,
   by that selfsame one knows. What else remains?
   This, I now declare, is that!

4. By knowing as the great all-pervading Self
   that by which one is conscious of both
   the dream state and also the state of wakefulness,
   the wise remain exempt from sorrow!

5. The one who knows that Self within,
   who enjoys like a bee the honey of the spirit,
   Lord of what was and what is to be,
   will never shrink away from Him.
   This, I now declare, is that!

6. He who was born of old from austerity,
   the one who was born of old from the waters,
   who enters the cave [of the heart] and dwells there,
   This, I now declare, is that!

c) Rainy Season

Varṣa

The Giver of Growth

Parjanya

May God, the giver of growth to plants,
who holds sway over the waters and all moving creatures,
grant us threefold protection to guard us
and threefold light to aid and befriend us!

RV VII, 101, 2

Rise, Lord, Direct Your Bow at Our Foes

Agni

41

RV IV, 4

1. From your body, O Lord, fashion a fast net.
Advance like a powerful monarch with his escort.
Entangle the demons in your net, O Archer;
transfix them with your burning fiery arrows.

2. Pursue the demons with your whirling flames.
Clasp them closely, O bright-shining Lord.
Firebrands are darting like birds from all quarters,
shot by your tongue. You are bound by no fetter!

3. Swiftly send out your scouts to explore!
Be for our people a guardian never failing.
Let not the one who, from far or from near,
is bent on our ruin venture to cross you!

4. Rise, Lord, direct your bow at our foes
and reduce them to ashes, O you with sharp darts!
May the fire we kindle consume like dry stubble
those who have thought to work us ill!

5. Rise, Lord, drive them far away from us!
Show us, O Lord, your powers divine.
Make slack the bows of the Evil One's henchmen.
Shatter them, whether they be kinsmen or strangers!

6. In your good graces, O God ever young,
is the man who has marked out his path of devotion.
Shine, O Lord! Fling wide for him the doors
to prosperity, riches and unequaled splendor!

7. Yes, may the man who within his home
pleases you all his days with songs and with offerings
receive a rich reward, be loaded with your gifts!
To him be happiness! This is our prayer.

8. I sing now your bounty. Listen, turn your face!
May my words awake you like a lover's serenade!
We desire to embellish you with chariots and horses
that you may forever uphold our dominion.

9. We seek to serve you, who lighten us by night
and who shine, O Lord, each hour of the day.
We rejoice with happy hearts; we give you our homage.
By your aid we surpass all others in glory.

10. To the man who possesses gold and fine horses
and comes on a chariot laden with treasure,
you afford, O Lord, both protection and favor.
He enjoys thereafter your gracious welcome.

11. By the power I inherit from my father Gotama,
I your kinsman destroy by these words the enemy.
Heed this my speech which I dedicate to you,
O youthful Offerer, God of the hearth!

12. May your guardian hosts, Lord, eager and vigilant,
persistent and kindly, friendly and unwearied,
gather in his place on our behalf,
for our help and protection, O Lord unfailing!

13. Your guardian rays in olden times,
preserved from affliction, blind Māmateya.

In their turn the gracious All-Knowing one guarded them.
Evil men bent on damage could do no harm.

14. Together with you, aided by you,
and guided by you, we shall win the day.
May both our praises win acceptance, we pray!
Act as you choose, God of truth and boldness!

15. Accept for your service our fuel and our hymns,
O you who are great as Mitra is great!
Reduce now to ashes all infamous demons
and guard us from evil, from reproach, and from shame.

Our Closest Kinsman and Friend *Agni*

42

RV VII, 15

1. Pour in his mouth an oblation,
the God who is worthy of reverence,
our closest kinsman and friend!

2. The God who has fixed his abode
in each home of every people—
the seer, the proprietor, the youthful.

3. May this Agni keep watch on every side
on our homes and all they contain!
May he keep distress at bay!

4. I will bring forth a new song
of praise for Agni, the falcon.
He will surely impart to us riches.

5. How fair, how desirable, his glories,
as he glows at the place of sacrifice,
like a man possessed of noble sons!

6. May Agni be pleased with our call,
may our songs find favor with him,
best worshiper, best mediator!

7. You who are worthy of Men's prayers,
our leader, our God, rich in heroes—
may we install you glowing and glistening!

8. Shine forth at night and at morn!
Your favor has kindled our hearths!
By your favor we shall be great!

9. Our nobles, seeking their reward,
come forward, our singers with their hymns
and Speech with her thousand syllables.

10. Agni, the shining, the pure,
the purifier, worthy of worship,
drives far the powers of evil.

11. Wherefore, young son of strength,
convey us—you are able!—many blessings!
May Bhaga grant us what is good!

12. It is you, O Agni, who invest us
with the glory of heroes. The Gods
are the givers of all good gifts.

13. O Agni, guard us from distress!
Consume with your burning flames,
O unaging, the Man who seeks our harm!

14. Be now for us a strong fortress
of iron, made secure a hundredfold,
O you the unconquerable!

15. O God, brightener of the night,
infallible, protect us from distress,
from the wicked, by day and by night!

O Kindly One, Guard Us as We Sleep

Rātrī

43

AV XIX, 48

1. All our stores, O Night,
we entrust to you—
all that our treasure chest holds.

2. Take charge of us till Dawn,
O Night our Mother!
May Dawn escort us safely
to the brink of day
and from day to you once more,
O shining One!

3. From all that flies,
from all that crawls,
from all that prowls on the mountain,
may you, O Night, protect us!

4. Behind, in front,
above, below,
do you, O Night, defend us!
Behold us singing your praises!

5. The Escorts of Night
who keep watch and ward

on the living and guard our cattle—
they protect our lives and our herds.

6. Most certainly, O Night,
   I know your name.
You are the "cream of bounty,"
   O kindly One!
Guard, as we sleep, ourselves
   and all our goods.

The Cave of the Heart *Guhā*

44

KathU IV, 7-9

7. She who comes into being through the breath of life,
from whom the Gods all took their birth,
the Boundless Goddess of Infinity,
who enters the cave [of the heart] and dwells there—
   This, I now declare, is that!

8. Fire the All-Knowing, hidden within the fire sticks
like the seed of life cherished by pregnant women,
worthy of worship daily offered
by reverent men bringing their oblations—
   This, I now declare, is that!

9. That from which the sun arises,
into which it sinks to rest,
that in which all the Gods are fixed
and beyond whose reach no one can go—
   This, I now declare, is that!

d) Autumn

Śarad

A Loving Friend

Soma

O God, be happy in our hearts to dwell,
as cows in milk rejoice in grassy meadows,
or as a bridegroom rejoices in his own house!
When in your friendship a mortal finds delight,
then, mighty Sage, you grant him your favor.
Save us, O Lord, from distress and damnation.
Come to us, Lord, as a loving friend!

RV I, 91, 13-15

From You Springs Inspiration

Agni

45

RV IV, 11

1. Your auspicious face, O mighty Agni,
beams brightly even when the sun is nigh.
Visible even at night is its shining.
The sight of him reveals the soft food he consumes.

2. In response to our praise, O God of strength,
open for your singer who trembles with fervor
a channel of inspiration, a powerful thought
such as you, O honorable, and all the Gods approve.

3. From you, O Agni, spring poetic wisdom,
inspiration, and hymns most efficacious.
From you comes wealth adorned with heroes
to the worshiper whose thought is properly attuned!

4. From you springs the horse who wins the prize,
of incomparable size and strength and spirit;
from you, O Agni, god-sent wealth for our joy,
from you the swift charger, ranging afar.

5. It is you, O sweet-spoken Agni, the immortal,
whom the god-loving seek first to win with their prayers—
o you who remove far all hostility,
unerring friend and master of the home!

6. Remove, as our helper, all poorness of thought;
drive far all sorrow, all evil intention.
Deal kindly, O Agni, son of strength, at evening
with him whose salvation, as God, you provide!

In Praise of a Generous Giver *Dhanānnadānam*

46

RV X, 117

1. Say not, "This poor man's hunger is a heaven-sent doom."
To the well-fed, too, comes death in many forms.
Yet the wealth of the generous giver never dwindles,
while he who refuses to give will evoke no pity.

2. The man with food stored up who hardens his heart
against the poor man, once his benefactor,
who now comes hungry and sick to beg for bread—
that man, I say, will himself find no pity!

3. The liberal man is he who gives to the beggar
who wanders in search of food, lean and forlorn;
the one who helps the passerby, when asked,
makes of this same a friend for days to come.

4. He who shares not his food with a friend,
the comrade at his side, is no true friend!
From such a one withdraw—no real home his!
Stranger though he be, receive from another!

5. The powerful man should give to one in straits;
let him consider the road that lies ahead!

Riches revolve just like a chariot's wheels,
coming to one man now, then to another.

6. In vain the foolish man accumulates food.
I tell you truly, it will be his downfall!
He gathers to himself neither friend nor comrade.
Alone he eats; alone he sits in sin.

7. The ploughshare cleaving the soil helps satisfy hunger;
the traveler, using his legs, achieves his goal;
the priest who speaks surpasses the one who is silent;
the friend who gives is better than the miser.

8. The sun with one foot outruns man with two!
The man with two overtakes the hoary with three!
Four-footed creatures come when the two-footed summon
and stand [as watchdogs] near the herd, observing.

9. The hands are alike but in their work they differ;
so also two cows, offspring of a single mother,
may yet give differing yields of milk; even twins
are not the same in strength, or kinsmen in bounty.

You Have Come, Blessed Night

Rātrī

47

AV XIX, 49

1. That lively maiden, young friend of our homes,
all-encompassing Night, dear to Savitṛ and Bhava,
easy of entreaty and adorned with glory,
has filled with her greatness both earth and heaven.

2. Night profound has risen above all things.
She has scaled—most splendid!—the loftiest heights.
She lovingly extends her auspicious presence
like that of a friend who moves at will.

3. You have come, blessed Night, gentle-born, the object
of our hymns and longings. Be favorable! Abide!
Guard us, ourselves and all our possessions,
all the prosperity that resides in cattle!

4. Benevolent Night has assumed to herself
the splendor of a lion, a leopard, a tiger,
the neighing of a horse and the call of a man.
The shining maiden takes many a form.

5. May Night, succeeding the Sun, be auspicious!
May this mother of frost be attentive to our cry!
Turn your ear, O blessed, to this song of praise
with which I worship you on every side!

6. As a king in his stately splendor, you enjoy,
O radiant Night, our hymn of praise.
May we, as one Dawn succeeds another,
possess many heroes, be filled with all wealth!

7. Lovely is the name that you have assumed.
Those who have evil designs against my wealth,
destroy them, O Night! Let no thief be found!
I say it again, let no thief be found!

8. You are fair, O Night, like a well-shaped chalice!
You possess the grace of a youthful maiden!
Full of eyes, you lovingly reveal your forms,
adorning yourself with the stars of heaven.

9. Whatever thief may come this night
or mortal foe who plots our harm—
let Night, advancing, encounter him!
Let her sever his head and his neck from his body!

10. Let her sever his feet that he walk no more,
his hands that he harm not! Whoever he be,
let him go to his place vanquished and maimed,
depart far away, depart to the desert!

Only by the Spirit . . . *Manasaiva*

48

KathU IV, 10-11

10. Whatever is here, the same is there;
whatever is there, the same is here.
Whoever perceives just separateness
passes from death to death without cease.

11. Only by the spirit can this intuition be grasped:
in this world there is nothing whatever separate.
Whoever thinks he perceives separateness
passes from death to death without cease.

e) Winter

Hemanta

The Joy of All Hearts

Agni

O blazing splendor, purifying flame,
joy of all hearts, with cheerful songs
we venerate you, the cheerful one!

RV VIII, 43, 31

May the Lord Find Pleasure in Our Praises

Agni

49

RV V, 13

1. All set for the kindling of the sacred fire,
   we hymn you, O Lord, with our verses, invoking
   your powerful grace.

2. In your praise, O Lord, who reach highest heaven,
   we compose our song, eager to obtain
   your treasure divine!

3. May the Lord find pleasure in our song of praise!
   Priest among Men, may he offer due homage
   to the heavenly beings!

4. Great, O Lord, is your renown.
   Through you, O blessed one, worthy mediator,
   may we complete the sacrifice!

5. The poets exalt you with their hymns—
   you whose undertakings are ever successful.
   Grant us great vigor!

6. As the spokes are bound by encircling iron,
   so you encompass the Gods, O Lord.
   I yearn for your bounty!

Your Minds Be of One Accord! *Agni*

50

RV X, 191

1. O Lord almighty, enkindled on the altar,
   confer upon us your treasures—
   you who gather all things into one,
   even what comes from the stranger!

2. Gather together, converse together!
   Your minds be of one accord,
   just as in harmony the Gods of old
   took their ritual shares of oblation!

3. United be your counsel, united your assembly,
   united your spirit and thoughts!
   A single plan do I lay before you;
   a single oblation do I offer!

4. United your resolve, united your hearts,
   may your spirits be at one,
   that you may long together dwell
   in unity and concord!

Sinless, O Night, Lead Us to Dawn *Rātrī*

51

AV XIX, 50

1. O Night, [for our safety]
   make the snake blind,
   scorch him, behead him!
   Gouge out the eyes
   of the wolf and entrap
   the thief in a snare!

2. With your sturdy oxen,
sharp-horned and swift,
transport us safely
over every danger!

3. May our passage each night
be performed without hindrance,
while the mean, lacking boats,
fail to cross the stream!

4. As a millet seed, blown,
is scattered beyond trace,
so blow him, O Night,
who wishes us ill!

5. Keep far from us the thief
and the stealer of cattle
and him who would stealthily
lead off our horses!

6. When you come with your favors,
O Night, well proportioned,
give us our due share.
Do not pass us by!

7. O resplendent Night,
may you lead us sinless
to Dawn, from Dawn to day,
and from day back to you!

He Who Was and Ever Shall Be — *Īśāno bhūta-bhavyasya*

52

KathU IV, 12-13

12. The Person of the size of a thumb resides
within oneself; he is the Lord
of that which was and that which shall be.
One will never shrink away from him.
This, I now declare, is that!

13. The Person of the size of a thumb resides
within like a steady smokeless flame—
Lord of that which was and that which shall be,
the same both today and tomorrow.
This, I now declare, is that!

f) Frosty Season

Śiśira

Right Purpose

Ākūti

Blessed divine Intention I place steadily before me.
May she, the Mother of the mind, be ever accessible.
May whatever hope I cherish be wholly realized.
May I see that hope well settled in my mind.

AV XIX, 4, 2

Be Present, O Lord *Agni*

53

RV V, 24

1. Draw near in friendship.
   Save us and help us.
   Show yourself gracious, O Lord!

2. Be present, O Lord,
   wonderful, adorned.
   Shower on us treasure most precious!

3. Hear now our cry.
Lend us your ear.
Shield us from sin's contagion!

4. To you, radiant God,
we bring this prayer.
Shine on our friends in blessing!

Like Spokes around a Hub

Sāṁmanasyam

54

AV III, 30

1. Of one heart and one mind I make you,
devoid of hate.
Love one another, as a cow
loves the calf she has borne.

2. Let the son be courteous to his father,
of one mind with his mother.
Let the wife speak words that are gentle
and sweet to her husband.

3. Never may brother hate brother
or sister hurt sister.
United in heart and in purpose,
commune sweetly together.

4. I will utter a prayer for such concord
among family members
as binds together the Gods,
among whom is no hatred.

5. Be courteous, planning and working
in harness together.
Approach, conversing pleasantly,
like-minded, united.

6. Have your eating and drinking in common.
I bind you together.
Assemble for worship of the Lord,
like spokes around a hub.

7. Of one mind and one purpose I make you,
following one leader.
Be like the Gods, ever deathless!
Never stop loving!

We Call on the Gods, Again and Again

Brahmakarma

55

AV V, 24

1. O Lord of all that furthers Men's designs,
O Savitṛ, protect me
in this my prayer,
in this my act,
in this my priestly duty,
in this my performance,
in this my thought,
in this my purpose and desire,
in this my calling on the Gods! All Hail!

2. May Agni, Lord of the forest, protect me
in this my prayer,
in this my act,
in this my priestly duty,
in this my performance,
in this my thought,
in this my purpose and desire,
in this my calling on the Gods! All Hail!

3. May Heaven and Earth, Sovereigns of bounty, save me
in this my prayer,
in this my act,
in this my priestly duty,
in this my performance,
in this my thought,
in this my purpose and desire,
in this my calling on the Gods! All Hail!

4. May Varuṇa, Lord of the waters, save me
in this my prayer,
in this my act,
in this my priestly duty,
in this my performance,
in this my thought,
in this my purpose and desire,
in this my calling on the Gods! All Hail!

5. May Mitra-Varuṇa, Lords of rain, preserve me
in this my prayer,
in this my act,
in this my priestly duty,
in this my performance,
in this my thought,
in this my purpose and desire,
in this my calling on the Gods! All Hail!

6. May the Maruts, Lords of the mountains, protect me
in this my prayer,
in this my act,
in this my priestly duty,
in this my performance,
in this my thought,
in this my purpose and desire,
in this my calling on the Gods! All Hail!

7. May Soma, Lord of plants and herbs, protect me
in this my prayer,
in this my act,
in this my priestly duty,
in this my performance,
in this my thought,
in this my purpose and desire,
in this my calling on the Gods! All Hail!

8. May the Wind, Lord of the middle air, protect me
in this my prayer,
in this my act,
in this my priestly duty,
in this my performance,
in this my thought,
in this my purpose and desire,
in this my calling on the Gods! All Hail!

9. May the Sun, Lord of every eye, protect me
in this my prayer,
in this my act,
in this my priestly duty,
in this my performance,
in this my thought,
in this my purpose and desire,
in this my calling on the Gods! All Hail!

10. May the Moon, Lord of constellations, save me
in this my prayer,
in this my act,
in this my priestly duty,
in this my performance,
in this my thought,
in this my purpose and desire,
in this my calling on the Gods! All Hail!

11. May Indra, the Lord of the Gods, protect me
in this my prayer,
in this my act,
in this my priestly duty,
in this my performance,

in this my thought,
in this my purpose and desire,
in this my calling on the Gods! All Hail!

12. May the Father of the Winds, Lord of cattle, save me
in this my prayer,
in this my act,
in this my priestly duty,
in this my performance,
in this my thought,
in this my purpose and desire,
in this my calling on the Gods! All Hail!

13. May Death, Lord of living creatures, save me
in this my prayer,
in this my act,
in this my priestly duty,
in this my performance,
in this my thought,
in this my purpose and desire,
in this my calling on the Gods! All Hail!

14. May Yama, Ruler of the Fathers, save me
in this my prayer,
in this my act,
in this my priestly duty,
in this my performance,
in this my thought,
in this my purpose and desire,
in this my calling on the Gods! All Hail!

15. May the Forefathers of ancient days protect me
in this my prayer,
in this my act,
in this my priestly duty,
in this my performance,
in this my thought,
in this my purpose and desire,
in this my calling on the Gods! All Hail!

16. May the Fathers of succeeding ages save me
in this my prayer,
in this my act,
in this my priestly duty,
in this my performance,
in this my thought,
in this my purpose and desire,
in this my calling on the Gods! All Hail!

17. Next may the Fathers of our fathers save me
        in this my prayer,
        in this my act,
    in this my priestly duty,
        in this my performance,
        in this my thought,
    in this my purpose and desire,
  in this my calling on the Gods! All Hail!

The Pure Water of Understanding

Yathodakaṁ śuddham

56

KathU IV, 14-15

14. As water descending on mountain crags
    wastes its energies among the gullies,
    so he who views things as separate
    wastes his energies in their pursuit.

15. But as pure water poured into pure
    becomes the selfsame—wholly pure,
    so too becomes the self of the silent sage,
    of the one, O Gautama, who has understanding.

LAST MANTRA

The Ṛg Veda is not the whole *śruti,* but it enunciates the most central part of it and lays the foundations for all the rest. It is befitting, then, to conclude this anthology with the final mantra of the Ṛg Veda, just as we opened it with the invocation of the first. Having traversed the long road of praise, exaltation, meditation, and sacrifice, having traveled through the upper realms of the Gods and the underworld of the demons, having reached the loftiest peaks of mystical speculation and touched the lowest depths of the human soul, having gazed, as far as we could, upon the cosmos and upon the divine, we arrive at this last stanza, which is dedicated to the human world and is a prayer for harmony and peace among Men by means of the protection of Agni and all the Gods, but ultimately through the acceptance by Men of their human calling. The last mantra knows only Man's ordinary language and Man's own cherished ideas; it comes back to the simplicity of the fact of being human: a union of hearts and a oneness of spirit, the overcoming of isolating individualisms by harmonious living together, because Man as person is always society and yet not plural. He is a unity with so many strings that they incur the risk of wars and strife, but also offer the possibility of a marvelous harmony and concord.

Last Mantra

RV X, 191, 4

samānī va ākūtiḥ
samānā hṛdayāni vaḥ
samānam astu vo mano
yathā vaḥ susahāsati

United your resolve, united your hearts,
may your spirits be at one,
that you may long together dwell
in unity and concord!

SANSKRIT GLOSSARY

Vaiśravaṇa

ABHAYA	Fearlessness, freedom from anguish, safety.
ABHVA	Monstruosity, horror, terrifying; a monster. From *a-bhū*, lit. nonbeing, nonexisting.
ĀCĀRYA	Teacher of the Vedas, spiritual guide who performs initiation. The word occurs earlier than *guru*.
ĀDHIBHAUTIKA	"Relating to the beings" (*bhūta*). One of the three levels on which Vedic texts can be interpreted: the cosmological dimension (cf. *ādhidaivika, ādhyātmika*).
ĀDHIDAIVIKA	"Relating to the Gods." One of the three ways of interpreting Vedic texts: the theological dimension (cf. *ādhibhautika, ādhyātmika*).
ADHIPATI	Overlord, master (both human and divine).
ĀDHYĀTMIKA	"Relating to the Self" (*ātman*). The way of interpreting Vedic texts centered on the real (Man as) *ātman;* the anthropological or spiritual dimension. The only interpretation recognized by Vedānta (cf. *ādhidaivika, ādhibhautika*).
ADHVARYU	One of the four main officiating priests in the sacrifice. He is in charge of the ritual actions and recites the *yajus* formulas.
ADITI	Adj.: free, unbound; f. noun: boundlessness (of heaven), infinity, freedom. Personified as mother of the Gods called Ādityas. Aditi is the symbol of unbound, divine freedom and generosity, of inexhaustible fullness.
ĀDITYA	Lit. son of Aditi, in sg. the solar deity, in pl. class of Gods (cf. Rudras, Vasus). The most important Ādityas and Varuṇa, Mitra, Aryaman, Vivasvat, Bhaga, sometimes Indra and later Viṣṇu.
ADVAITA	Nondualism (*a-dvaita*). Spiritual insight which sees ultimate reality as being neither monistic nor dualistic. It is the recognition that the merely quantitative problem of the one and many of dialectical reason does not apply to the realm of ultimate reality. This latter presents polarities that do not split into disconnected multiplicity.
ADVITĪYAM	Lit. "not having a second." Cf. *advaita, eka*.
AGNI	The fire of sacrifice and the divine Fire, one of the most important Gods or divine manifestations, the mediator or priest to Men and Gods.

AGNIHOTRA	Daily fire sacrifice which was performed morning and evening in every household of the higher castes, consisting in an oblation of milk sprinkled on the fire.
AGNIṢṬOMA	Soma sacrifice, lasting for several (usually five) days; one of the most important Vedic sacrifices (cf. Soma).
AGRE	Loc. of *agra,* that which precedes, top, beginning, origin. "In the beginning": usually the first word of cosmogonic texts.
AHAM	"I," the first person. *Aham brahman:* "I am Brahman," one of the *mahāvākyas. Aham* as an ontological principle is usually distinguished from *ahaṁkāra* as a psychological principle.
AHAṀKĀRA	The ego sense (cf. *aham*), principle of individuality and egoistic limitations.
ĀHAVANĪYA	One of the three main fireplaces for the sacrifice, square in shape and situated at the east end of the *śālā.* The *āhavanīya* fire (lit. "that which is to be offered") is lit with the fire of *gārhapatya.*
AHIṀSĀ	"Nonviolence," respect for life, nonkilling and nonhurting, no desire to do violence to reality. Moral and philosophical principle based on an ultimate harmony in the universe. The root *hiṁs-* from *han-* means to hurt, to kill. Not a Vedic notion properly; appears only a few times in the U, has had its development in Jainism and Buddhism.
ĀHITĀGNI	He who has "placed" the sacred fire (on the altar), i.e., a twice-born who constantly maintains the sacred fire in his house (and who, at his death, is burned in the same fire).
AKĀLA MṚTYU	"Untimely death," death before the proper time (*kāla*).
ĀKĀŚA	Air, sky, space, ether, vacuity (emptiness), atmosphere, the fifth of the primordial elements (cf. *mahābhūtāni*) which is the element of sound. It is all-penetrating and infinite, hence frequently identified with Brahman.
ĀKHYĀNA	The telling of a story, ancient legend, or myth.
AKṢĀḤ	The dice; an important game in ancient India.
AKṢARA	Adj.: imperishable, undecaying, inexhaustible (*a-kṣara*); n. noun: syllable, smallest part of speech, hence "word" in general. Refers mainly to the "imperishable syllable" OM, also to Brahman.

ĀMNĀYAMAÑJARĪ — *Mañjarī*, f., bouquet, of *āmnāya*, m., holy tradition, sacred texts, traditional handing down of a religious message, that which is to be remembered (by heart) and studied. Traditional instruction.

AMṚTA — Adj.: "immortal, imperishable" (*a-mṛta*); referring mainly to the Gods; n. noun: immortality, deathlessness, and the nectar of immortality, Soma, the sacred drink (ambrosia).

ĀNANDA — Joy, bliss (cf. *sukha*), the delight of love, and especially the highest spiritual bliss. One of the three "qualifications" of Brahman (cf. *sat, cit*).

ANANTALOKA — The infinite world or realm, heaven (cf. also *svargaloka*).

ANĀTMAVĀDA — The predominantly Buddhist doctrine of the unsubstantiality of the *ātman* or Self. *Nairātmyavāda*.

AṄGIRAS — Name of a *ṛṣi* to whom many hymns of the RV are attributed, forefather of the Aṅgirases, class of semidivine beings (cf. Gk. *angelos*), related to Agni (who is sometimes called an Aṅgirasa), mediators between the world of Men and the Gods. Associated with the descendants of Atharvan and supposedly coauthor of the AV.

AṆIMAN — Derived from *aṇu*, atom; fineness, minuteness, "atomicity."

ANIRA — "Without strength," lacking vigor, weak.

ANNA — N.: food, the material, nourishing aspect of reality, substance. It came to be identified with Brahman.

ANNAPRĀŚANA — A ceremony in which a child is fed with solid food for the first time (usually at the age of six months).

ĀNṚṆYA — N.: freedom from debt or guilt.

ANṚTA — "What is opposed to *ṛta*, absence of *ṛta*," i.e., untruth, lie, chaos, lack of rectitude, and disorder.

ANTARA — Within, interior, intimate, near, and also different from.

ANTARĀTMAN — The "inner Self," spiritual center of Man (whereas *paramātman* is the supreme Self).

ANTARIKṢA — The "in-between," the airy space between heaven and earth, atmosphere, midspace (cf. *dyu* and *pṛthivī* as the two other terms of the *triloka*).

ANTARYĀMIN — The "inner Controller" (*antar-yam-*); in the U the *ātman* conceived of as the inner presence and internal guide of every being.

ANTYEṢṬI — Funeral rites, last oblations to the dead.

ANUBHAVA — Direct experience, knowledge derived from immediate spiritual insight.

ANUGRAHA — Divine grace (not Vedic).

ANUMATI — Lit. "assent, agreement"; also grace, benevolence. Personified as a Goddess of love and goodness (RV, AV).

ĀPAḤ — F. pl.: the waters, both earthly and heavenly, the first cosmogonic element which has a purifying, healing, and vivifying power. Female in gender and character, they are called "Goddesses" (*devīḥ*).

APĀṂ NAPĀT — "Offspring of the waters," spirit of the waters (cf. *āpaḥ*), of Indo-Iranian origin, principle of fertility, also considered to be an aspect of Agni, the "water-born."

APĀNA — One of the five breaths (vital airs, cf. *prāṇa*), inhaling and also excreting.

APAURUṢEYA — "Not of human origin" (cf. *puruṣa*). The traditional view of Vedic interpretation is that the Veda is not composed by human authors but is the manifestation or revelation of the "eternal Word" (cf. *vāc*), although the inspired *ṛṣis* are instruments of revelation.

APSARASES — Female spirits or nymphs, connected with trees, water, and air. Their male counterparts are the Gandharvas. Beautiful celestial maidens of ambivalent character, whose peculiar art is dance.

ARAṆYĀNĪ — Female genius of the forest, sprite of the forest, wife of *araṇya*, the forest.

ARDHANĀRĪŚVARA — "Half woman and half man," "the Lord being half woman," the androgynous nature of the Godhead (Śiva). A term indicating the transcendent nature of the Godhead which contains in an eminent way the characteristic of all the pairs of opposites (*dvandva*).

ARJUNA — The third of the five Pāṇḍava brothers and a famous warrior. To him Kṛṣṇa revealed the BG.

ĀRTAVA — Derived from *ṛtu*, season: belonging to the seasons, related to time.

ARTHA — Wealth, value, possession, and power, i.e., the objects of worldly activity. One of the four *puruṣārthas* or human goals (cf. *dharma, kāma,* and *mokṣa*).

ARYAMAN — Vedic deity belonging to the class of the Ādityas. He personifies hospitality and is a giver of goods or gifts and a protector. He is also intimately connected with the household and with the domestic fire.

ASAKTA — "Detached, free"; said of the saint or *yogin* (in the BG), as opposed to *sakta.*

ASAT — "Nonbeing" as opposed to *sat,* being.

ASAU LOKAḤ — "That world," "the world beyond," heaven, as opposed to *ayaṁ lokaḥ.*

ĀŚRAMA — Stage of life, the four traditional periods in the life of a "twice-born": student (*brahmacārin*), householder (*gṛhastha*), forest dweller (*vānaprastha*), and wandering ascetic (*saṁnyāsin*). Also the hermitage of a monk and thus the title of an ascetic.

ASU — M.: life, vitality, both physical and spiritual.

ASURA — Adj.: spiritual, incorporeal, divine. In the RV the highest spirit, God (from *asu,* life, spiritual life). Varuṇa is said to be an *asura.* Later the meaning changes entirely and *asura* (now analyzed as *a-sura,* i.e., "not God") means a demon or an evil spirit constantly opposed to the *devas* (B).

AŚVAMEDHA — The horse sacrifice performed by a king, one of the most important and complicated sacrifices in the Veda.

AŚVIN — "Possessing horses"; name of twin Gods riding a golden horse chariot; bringers of light, they are described as handsome youths of luminous nature. They are invoked for help in danger and sickness, as they represent the divine healing power.

ATHARVAN — Fire priest; name of an ancient sage who was the first fire priest. Mythical author of the fourth Veda (AV), associated with Aṅgiras.

ĀTMAHAN — "Killing the Self [one-self]," destroying the *ātman;* a term that occurs in the IsU.

ĀTMAN — The principle of life, breath, the body, the Self. It refers to the full, undivided person and also to the

	inmost center in Man, his undecaying core, which in the U is discovered to be identical with Brahman. The Self or inner essence of the universe and of Man.
ĀTMAVID	Knower of the Self (*ātman*), one who has realized his innermost being.
ATYĀŚRAMA	The stage beyond the traditional four stages in the spiritual development of a Man (cf. *āśrama*), trancending them in complete spiritual freedom.
AUM	Cf. OM.
AUPANIṢADIC	The adjectival form of Upaniṣad (also Upaniṣadic).
AUPĀSANA	(Agni), the fire used in domestic worship, upon which the offerings are cooked.
AVĀCYA	Not expressible in words, unutterable, unspeakable; the last word of the U about Brahman.
AVATĀRA	The "descent" of the divine (from *ava-tṝ-*, to come down), the "incarnations" of Viṣṇu in different animal and human forms. Traditionally there are ten such *avatāras: matsya* (the fish), *kūrma* (the tortoise), *varāha* (the bear), *narasiṁha* (the man-lion), *vāmana* (the dwarf), Paraśurāma (Rāma with the ax), Rāma, Kṛṣṇa, Buddha, and Kalkī at the end of times.
AVIDYĀ	Ignorance, absence of the true and liberating knowledge, often identified with *māyā* and cause of illusion and delusion.
AYAṀ LOKAḤ	"This world," the known universe, as opposed to *asau lokaḥ*.
ĀYUS	Vital strength, vitality, life, temporal existence, the life span allotted to Man. Cf. Gk. *aiôn,* the eons.
BANDHU	Bond, connection, relation, friendship, friend.
BARHIS	The sacrificial grass on which the Gods are seated during the sacrifice and on which the offerings are spread.
BHAGA	Prosperity, happiness, love, share (cf. the root *bhaj-*, to share). Name of an Āditya who is the personification of happiness, the giver of gifts and blessings.
BHAGAVAT	"Blessed, adorable, glorious, venerable, Lord," a term used for holy persons as well as for God.
BHAKTA	Worshiper, devotee, one who follows the path of love of God and has totally surrendered himself to the divine (cf. *bhakti*).

BHAKTI	Devotion, surrender, love of God, personal relationship with God, mysticism of love.
BHAKTI-MĀRGA	The path of love and devotion, one of the three classical spiritual paths (cf. *karma-mārga, jñāna-mārga*).
BHĀṢYA	Commentary.
BHĀṢYAKĀRA	Commentator.
BHṚGU	An ancient *ṛṣi* and in the pl. a class of semidivine beings, related to the Aṅgiras; in the B and U we find Bhṛgu, son of Varuṇa.
BHŪḤ	One of the three original utterances (*vyāhṛti*) by which the earth was created (cf. also *bhuvaḥ, svaḥ*). A cultic interjection.
BHŪMI	The earth; cf. *pṛthivī*.
BHUVAḤ	One of the three original utterances by which the midspace, the atmosphere, was created (cf. *bhūḥ, svaḥ*). A cultic interjection.
BĪJA	Seed, germ, semen, seed corn, grain, and thus also origin, support, and truth. Some letters (syllables) expressing the essence of a particular deity: a mystical syllable.
BĪJA-MANTRA	The core of the mystical syllable of a mantra, that which expresses the essence of the mantra of any deity.
BINDU	Lit. drop, dot, spot; an important concept in the philosophy of language and Tantrism: the subtlest element of the word and the cause of the unfolding of the universe. It is related to *nāda*.
BRAHMĀ	M., the creator God (cf. the later "trinity" Brahmā, Viṣṇu, Śiva). He is not important in the Veda but later inherits many of the features of Prajāpati.
BRAHMACĀRIN	A student of Brahman, i.e., of the Veda, novice, who lives a life of chastity and purity. One passing through the first of the four *āśramas*.
BRAHMACARYA	The life of a student of Brahman, hence also chastity and search for Brahman. The first of the four *āśramas* (cf. *gṛhastha, vānaprastha, saṁnyāsa*).
BRAHMAJIJÑĀSA	Desiderative of the root *jña-*, to know (cf. *jñāna*): the desire to know Brahman, the longing for realization of Brahman.
BRAHMAJÑĀNA	The knowledge or realization of Brahman.

BRAHMALOKA	The world of Brahman, heaven.
BRAHMAN	N.: prayer, sacrifice, the power inherent in sacrifice; the Absolute, the ultimate Ground underlying everything; in the U the immanent Self (*ātman*) is identified with it. M.: one of the four priests performing the sacrifice (cf. also *hotṛ, udgātṛ, adhvaryu*), or the priesthood in general.
BRĀHMAṆA	Priest, brahmin, member of the priestly class. Also a body of texts following the Saṁhitās and containing ritual and mythical matters (cf. Note on Vedic Literature).
BRAHMAṆASPATI	Divine artisan, Lord of the Holy Word (cf. Bṛhaspati).
BRAHMA-NIRVĀṆA	"Extinction in Brahman," i.e., ultimate freedom, liberation, bliss. The concept occurs in the BG.
BRAHMAVIDYĀ	F.: the wisdom or knowledge of Brahman, sacred science, theology.
BRAHMODYA	Discussion about Brahman, theological or philosophical debate, sometimes in the form of a riddle.
BṚHASPATI	Also called Brahmaṇaspati: "Lord of the Holy Word" (from the root *bṛh-* and *pati*, Lord). The inspirer of prayer and the divine prototype of the priest, the priest of the Gods. He is closely related to Indra as his house priest (*purohita*) and is sometimes identified with Agni in his priestly function. Later on he is identified with an ancient *ṛṣi*, belonging to the family of the Aṅgiras. As regent of the planet Jupiter he became identified with the planet itself.
BUDDHI	The highest faculty of intelligence, also understanding, thought, meditation.
CAKRAVĀKA	A kind of bird famous for his longing for his mate and the image of conjugal love and loyalty.
CAṆḌĀLA	An outcaste, one who does not belong to the four great divisions of society.
CIT	From the root *cit-*, to perceive, understand, etc.: consciousness, intelligence. One of the three "characteristics" of Brahman (cf. *sat, ānanda*).
CITTA	The mind as the organ of thought, the functioning mind (cf. also *manas*).
CŪḌĀKARAṆA	The ceremony of a child's first haircut, usually performed at the age of three or later. Until then the hair is allowed to grow.

CYAVĀNA	Name of a *ṛṣi* rejuvenated by the Aśvins.
DADHIKRĀ	A celestial sun-horse, related to the morning sun.
DAIVĀSURA	Relating to the *devas* and *asuras,* chiefly in connection with their mutual struggle for superiority, mainly in the B.
DAKṢA	Lit. dexterity, ability, skill, power, wisdom. Name of one of the Ādityas, God of creative power. In the RV at the same time son and father of Aditi, in the B he is one of Prajāpati's sons or identified with Prajāpati himself. In later myths he assumes different forms.
DAKṢIṆĀ	The honorarium or fee of the priests, gifts for the sacrifice, consisting of cows and other goods.
DAKṢIṆĀGNI	The "southern" fire, one of the three main fireplaces for the sacrifice (cf. *āhavanīya, gārhapatya*); it has the form of a half circle or an arch.
DAKṢIṆĀYANA	The southern way of the sun; the six months during which the sun moves southward (cf. *uttarāyana*).
DAṀPATĪ	Dual: the lords of the house, i.e., husband and wife, the pair of householders.
DĀNA	Gift, almsgiving; one of the religious injunctions, mainly the duty of the householder.
DARŚANA	From the root *dṛś-*, to see, to observe, hence vision, view; philosophy, Weltanschauung. In the religious context it means the sight of a saint or God, therefore also meeting, audience, visit.
DAYĀ	Mercy, compassion; both that which is to be practiced by Men and, later, in the sense of God's mercy.
DEṢṬRĪ	F.: lit. the guide, personified as a Goddess: she who indicates the way.
DEVA	From *div,* heaven, light (cf. Lat. *divus, deus*), celestial, divine; m.: God, deity, celestial being, cosmic power. The *devas* are not on the same level as the one God (sometimes also called *deva,* in the sg., or *īśvara*) or the Absolute (Brahman). They are powers performing different functions in the cosmos. Later the human sense faculties are also termed *devas* in the U.
DEVAYAJÑA	Sacrifice of the Gods, or to the Gods. From *deva,* God, deity, and *yajña,* sacrifice, worship.
DEVAYĀNA	"Leading to the Gods," the path on which, after death, Man proceeds to the world of the Gods (cf. also *pitṛ-yāna*).

DEVĪ — Goddess, female counterpart of *deva*.

DHĀMAN — Abode, realm (of the Gods); also ordinance, holy law.

DHARMA — Cosmic order, right, duty, religious law, social and religious observances handed down by tradition; "religion" regarded as a set of practices and laws. That which holds the world together. One of the four "human goals" (*puruṣārtha*). Cf. *artha, kāma,* and *mokṣa*.

DHĪ — F.: prayer, though, vision, mystical insight, the intuition with which the seers or *ṛṣis* are preeminently endowed.

DHYĀNA — Meditation, contemplation.

DĪKṢĀ — Initiation; the preliminary rites; consecration of the sacrificer at the beginning of a Soma sacrifice, which amounts to a "new birth." Outside the sacrificial context *dīkṣā* is the initiation of the disciple by the *guru* into *saṁnyāsa,* the life of a wandering monk.

DĪRGHĀYUS — Long life.

DIV — Cf. *dyu*.

DROṆA — The *guru* of the Kurus and Pāṇḍavas (MB).

DṚṢṬI — View, vision, hence opinion, point of view (cf. *darśana*). Also dogma.

DUḤKHA — Pain, sorrow, suffering, distress (lit. "with a bad axle hole," i.e., not moving smoothly), a basic concept in Buddhism. The opposite of *sukha*.

DURMĀYU — Witchcraft, evil power.

DVANDVA — Pair of opposites, such as heat and cold, pleasure and pain.

DVĀPARA — Originally the side of the die with two dots; the name of the third of the four cosmic periods (*yuga*).

DVIJA — "Twice-born," an initiated member of one of the three higher castes.

DYAUS — The sky, Heaven, personified as divine Father (cf. *pṛthivī*). Cf. *div* and *dyu* for the Ṛg Vedic forms.

DYĀVĀ-PṚTHIVĪ — Heaven and Earth, the divine pair, parents of the universe.

DYU — The sky, heaven; generally opposed to *bhūmi, pṛthivī* (earth). Also light, day.

EKA	One; frequently *tad ekam* (n.), the One as the origin of everything, later identified with Brahman.
EKATVA	Oneness.
ETAŚA	The sun-horse.
GANDHARVA	M.: celestial being or class of beings of uncertain origin. The Gandharva (sg.) is closely related to the sun; he proclaims divine mysteries. The Gandharvas (pl.) are the male counterparts of the Apsaras and they play an important role as genii of fertility and conception. They possess the girl before marriage, and are sometimes of ambivalent character. Later they assume the role of heavenly musicians and patrons of music.
GĀRGĪ	Vācaknavī, a famous woman philosopher in the U.
GĀRHAPATYA	The fire of the householder, one of the three main fires of the sacrifice, from which the other fires are lit. It is circular in shape and is used for cooking the offering (*havis*). It is used in the *saṁskāras* (e.g., *upanayana, vivāha,* etc.) because it is related to the life of the family.
GARUTMAT	Mythical sunbird (cf. later Garuḍa, the vehicle of Viṣṇu).
GĀYATRĪ	General meaning: song, hymn. A Ṛg Vedic meter of twenty-four syllables (three times eight); the most sacred mantra of the Veda (RV III, 62, 10).
GOTRA	Brahminical clan or family.
GRĀVAN	Stone, especially the stones used for pressing the Soma.
GṚHASTHA	The state of householder, the married man, the second in order of the four *āśramas*.
GRĪṢMA	Summer, the hot season.
GUṆA	Quality, property, etc. In the Sāṁkhya system the three "qualities" or fundamental constituents of *prakṛti* (nature), viz., *sattva, rajas, tamas*.
GURU	Lit. "heavy," Master, spiritual guide, and preceptor, also teacher (cf. *ācārya*).
HARIŚCANDRA	A king of the solar dynasty, later famous in the Purāṇas. Cf. the story of Śunaḥśepa (AB).
HEMANTA	Winter.

HIRAṆYAGARBHA	"The golden germ," the primordial egg or seed, born from the waters, out of which Brahmā, the creator, originated. An important concept in Vedic cosmogony.
HIRAṆYAVARṆA	Golden-colored.
HOTṚ	Priest (in general), or one of the four officiating priests whose task is the recitation of Ṛg Vedic mantras.
HṚDAYA	The heart, spiritual center in Man.
IḌĀ	The part of the sacrificial oblation which is divided, distributed, and eaten together by all participants. Iḍā is also personified as the daughter of Manu.
IDAM	"This," nominative singular n. of the demonstrative pronoun. It usually stands for "this [universe]." *Idaṁ sarvam*: all this, "this all," the visible universe. *Idam* is "this" end of all intentionality and experience, as distinct from *tat* as the "other," transcendent end.
INDRA	The great divine warrior who wins all battles in favor of his worshipers, either against the resisting clans (Dasyus or Dāsas) or against demons like Vṛtra and Vala. His manly power is irresistible, and it is Soma who provides him with energy for his mighty exploits. He is the liberator from obstructive forces; he sets free the waters and light. His weapon is *vajra*, the thunderbolt.
INDRIYA(S)	Sense organs. As they are presided over by deities, they are also called *deva*. There are different lists of senses, usually five organs of action (*karmendriya*) and five organs of knowledge (*jñānendriya*).
INDU	"Drop," referring to the sacred Drop, Soma, and later also to the moon.
IṢṬADEVATĀ	The deity proper to a person or a group for worship and meditation; the chosen or proper deity.
IṢṬĀPŪRTA	Religious and secular pious works and the merit accumulated by the rites and good works performed on earth.
ĪŚA, ĪŚVARA	The Lord, from the root *īś-*, to be master, to rule, to possess. Although a general term for Lord, in the later religious systems it is more often used for Śiva than for Viṣṇu. In Vedānta, *īśvara* is the manifest, the qualified (*saguṇa*) aspect of Brahman.

ITIHĀSA — Lit. "so it was" (*iti ha āsa*). History, story, the "historical tradition," the epic (cf. the two great epics, MB and R).

JAGANNĀTHA — The Protector and Lord of the world, mostly applied to Viṣṇu-Kṛṣṇa.

JAGATĪ — Vedic meter consisting of four feet (*pāda*) with twelve syllables each.

JANAKA — Great king of Videha, known in the U for his generosity and his wisdom. In the R he is the father of Sītā.

JANMAN — Birth, origin. Also related to caste and rebirth.

JAPA — Silent or muttered repetition of sacred formulae (mantra) or of the names of God as a spiritual exercise. The prayer is usually performed with the help of a rosary (*mālā*).

JARĀ — Old age, decay of physical life.

JĀTAKARMAN — Ceremony after birth, the first *saṁskāra* or sacrament.

JĀTAVEDAS — "Knowing [*vedas*] the beings [*jāta*]," hence "all-knowing, omniscient"; an important epithet of Agni.

JĪVA — Living being (from *jīv-*, to live); the soul in its individuality, as distinct from the *ātman*, the universal soul. There are as many *jīvas* as individual living beings.

JĪVANMUKTA — "Liberated while alive," the highest category of saint or realized person who has reached the goal in this life and thus in the human body.

JÑĀNA — Knowledge (from the root *jña-*, to know), intuition, wisdom; frequently the highest intuitive understanding, the realization of *ātman* or *brahman*. *Jñāna* is the outcome of meditation or revelation. Cf. *jñāna-mārga*.

JÑĀNĀGNI — The fire of knowledge or wisdom. Agni is among the Gods what *jñāna* is within Man.

JÑĀNA-MĀRGA — The path of knowledge, contemplation, and intuitive insight; one of the three classical ways of spiritual experience, generally considered to be superior to *karma* and *bhakti*, though many *bhaktas* regard *jñāna* as simply a form of *bhakti*.

JÑĀNĪ — Sage, wise Man, follower of the path of knowledge, wisdom, contemplation (*jñāna-mārga*).

JYOTIS	Light, in all its aspects, external (e.g., the stars) and internal (the eye); the inner light of the *ātman* overcoming darkness.
KA	Interrogative pronoun *who;* one of the names of Prajāpati.
KAIVALYA	Isolation, solitude, detachment; a spiritual state of supreme freedom (YS).
KĀLA	Time, right time, fate, death. In the AV and MB it is celebrated as a great power that determines everything, hence its meaning of fate and even death (*mahākāla*).
KALI	The side of the die with one dot. The last and most degenerate of the four cosmic periods (*yuga*). We are now living in the *kaliyuga.*
KĀMA	The creative power of desire, personified as the God of love; one of the *puruṣāsthas.*
KĀMADHENU (or KĀMADUGHĀ)	The mythical heavenly cow that fulfills all wishes.
KARMAKĀṆḌA	The part of *śruti* relating to works, rituals, or sacrifice (*jñānakāṇḍa* being the part relating to knowledge).
KARMAKĀṆḌIC	According to the ritualistic interpretation of the Veda.
KARMAKĀṆḌIN	A ritualist.
KARMA-MĀRGA	The path of action; one of the three classical ways of spirituality (cf. *bhakti, jñāna*). In the Vedas it refers to sacrificial actions regarded as the way to salvation; later it includes moral deeds, or rather, all actions which are performed in the spirit of sacrifice.
KARMAN	"Work, action," originally the sacred action, sacrifice, then also moral deeds. The results of all deeds and actions issue in the law of *karman* which governs actions and their results in the universe. Later on related to rebirth.
KARUṆĀ	Compassion; important concept in Buddhism.
KAŚYAPA	A mythical sage, sometimes said to be the husband of Aditi.
KAUṢĪTAKI	A master in the Ṛg Vedic branch of the Kauṣītakins (or Śaṅkhāyanas), after whom one U of the RV is named.

KAVI	Poet, wise Man, sage, seer, prophet; often used of the Gods and also of men. Cf. also *ṛṣi*.
KEŚIN	"Having long hair [*keśa*]," the long-haired, the ascetic, monk.
KRATU	Strength, capacity, both physical and spiritual; understanding, insight, will (also divine will).
KṚṢI	Agriculture.
KṚṢṆA	*Avatāra* of Viṣṇu (lit. "the black one") and one of the most popular of the Gods. He does not occur in the Veda, but it is he who reveals the BG. He is the divine child and the cowherd God in Vṛndāvana, the incarnation of love and the playful God par excellence.
KṚṢṆAPAKṢA	The dark half of the month; the fifteen days ending with the new moon.
KṚTA	The side of the die with four dots. The first of the four *yugas*, also called *satya*, the golden age.
KṢAMĀ	F.: patience, forbearance; mercy, compassion, grace.
KṢATRIYA	A member of the second caste, comprising kings, warriors, and nobility.
KṢETRA	"Field," in both the literal and the metaphoric sense.
KṢETRAPATI	"Lord of the field," protector of the field, or simply "farmer."
KUMBHA	Jar, vessel; a symbol of fullness.
KURUKṢETRA	The battlefield on which the war of the MB took place and where Kṛṣṇa revealed the BG to Arjuna.
KUŚA	Also called *darbha*, a special grass used for sacrificial purposes. It is spread on the *barhis*.
LĪLĀ	Divine play, the world, viewed as God's sport. The conception is not Vedic but Purāṇic.
LOKA	"World," open space, place, realm. Cf. *triloka*.
LOKASAṀGRAHA	"The holding together, the maintenance of, the world" by the wise Man or the saint in the liturgical or sacred action (conception of the BG).
MADHU-VIDYĀ	"Honey-wisdom," a teaching of the BU.
MAHĀBHŪTĀNI	The great (primordial) elements, i.e., earth, water, fire, air, ether.

MAHĀKRATU	"Great sacrifice."
MAHĀTMĀ	"Great soul"; title of a sage or a saint.
MAHĀVĀKYA	The (traditionally four) Great Utterances of the Upaniṣads concerning *ātman* and *brahman*. Plural: *mahāvākyāni* simplified to *mahāvākyas*.
MAITHUNA	Coupling, copulation, union, in both the sexual and the metaphoric sense.
MAITREYĪ	Wife of the sage Yājñavalkya. She was said to be a "knower of Brahman" (cf. BU).
MANAS	Mind in the widest sense, heart, intellect, the inner organ as the seat of thinking, understanding, feeling, imagination, and will. In Upaniṣadic anthropology *manas* is one of the three main constituents of Man (cf. *vāc, prāṇa*).
MĀNASA YAJÑA	"Mental sacrifice" or spiritual sacrifice, substituted for the external action.
MAṆḌALA	Lit. a circle; a book of the RV (a "circle" of hymns). The RV consists of ten *maṇḍalas*. A mystic picture of the entire reality; a pictorial representation of the homology between the microcosm (Man) and the macrocosm (the Universe).
MAṄGALA	Auspiciousness, happiness, fortune, prosperity in the spiritual and material sense, blessing, benediction. It is one of the concepts denoting a state of completeness where external conditions are only an expression of an inner wholeness and harmony (not Vedic).
MAÑJARĪ	Flower or cluster of blossoms.
MANOVĀK	The word of the spirit, of the mind, the interior word. From *manas*, mind, spirit, and *vāc*, word.
MANTRA	Prayer, sacred formula (from the root *man-*, to think), holy word, a Vedic text or verse. Usually only the Saṁhitā portion of the Veda is termed *mantra*. Being a powerful word, it can also have the meaning of spell or incantation.
MANU	The father of humanity, the Man par excellence; also the first priest who established the sacrifices.
MANUṢYA	Man (cf. also *puruṣa*).
MANYU	Anger, the personification of wrath.

MARUT(S) — Storm-Gods (always in plural), associated with Rudra and Indra.

MĀTARIŚVAN — An aspect of Agni; also a divine being bringing the fire from heaven down to earth (especially to the Bhṛgus). Later connected with the wind (Vāyu), an aspect of the wind.

MĀYĀ — F.: the mysterious power, wisdom, or skill of the Gods, hence the power of deceit, illusion. In Vedānta it is used as a synonym for ignorance and also to signify the cosmic "illusion" veiling the absolute Brahman.

MĀYIN — "Possessed of *māyā*" (said of Indra, etc.); i.e., either the powerful, mysterious aspect of the Gods or their deceptive side.

MĪMĀṀSĀ — One of the six classical systems of Indian philosophy dealing mainly with the foundations of and the rules for interpreting Vedic texts. From the root *man-*, to think. The two main schools are the Pūrvamīmaṁsā which is concerned with the ritual interpretation of the Veda (cf. *karmakāṇḍa*), and the Uttaramīmaṁsā or Vedānta which gives a philosophical and spiritual interpretation (cf. *jñānakāṇḍa*).

MITRA — The God of contract and friendship. Closely related to Varuṇa, he too belongs to the class of the Ādityas. Originally he must have been the divinized personification of the contract and the (divine) Friend. He is friend and lover of Men.

MOKṢA — Liberation, absolute freedom, release from *saṁsāra*, the cycle of birth and death.

MṚḌĪKA — Grace, mercy, from the Vedic root *mṛḍ-*, to forgive, to be merciful, to grace.

MŪJAVAT — Name of the mountain on which the *soma*-plant is found; hence also a designation for Soma.

MŪLA — Root, origin, cause.

MUMUKṢUTVA — Desiderative from the root *muc-* (cf. *mokṣa*): the desire for salvation, striving and longing for liberation, the necessary precondition for entering upon the path to liberation.

MUNI — A silent monk, ascetic; an ecstatic. One who practices *mauna*, silence.

MŪRTI — Solid form, body, hence embodiment, person, figure, statue, image. Mostly used for holy images of Gods. The Veda does not contain any image worship (*pūjā*), which is a later development in Hinduism.

NACIKETAS — Name of a young brahmin who descends to the realm of Yama and converses with him on the ultimate questions (in the KathU). Some have interpreted his name as meaning "he who does not know," i.e., the novice, the seeker.

NĀDA — Sound, original vibration in the emanation of the word; an important concept in Tantric cosmogony (cf. also *bindu*).

NAIṢKARMYA — Inactivity, abandonment of actions (*karman*). In the BG it is combined with the concept of *karmaphalatyāga*, the work that is done while renouncing the fruits of the action (and thus avoiding its binding effects).

NĀMA-DHEYA — The ceremony of name-giving for a child, also called *nāma-karaṇa.*

NĀMA-JAPA — The prayer of the name (of God); repetition of the divine name (cf. *japa*).

NĀMA-RŪPA — "Name and form," the phenomenal world which constitutes the *saṁsāra.*

NARAKA — Hell, the infernal world. The conception of abysmal regions meant for the punishment of the wicked, hardly hinted at in the Vedas, is developed in the Purāṇas.

NĀRĀYAṆA — The "son of Man" (*nara*), i.e., of the original *puruṣa;* a name for God in the form of Viṣṇu or Kṛṣṇa.

NĀSADĪYA SŪKTA — The name of the hymn (*sukta*) RV X, 129, of which the original title is *bhāvavṛttam* (ontological or metaphysical statement). The name is taken from the first words of the hymn: *nāsadāsīnno sadāsīt* . . . ("neither Nonbeing nor Being . . .").

NĀSTIKA — A person of heterodox opinions, an atheist or unbeliever; derived from *na asti,* "it is not," the negation of faith in the *śruti* (opposite to *āstika,* believer, the one who affirms).

NETI NETI — "Not this, not this" (*na iti*), i.e., the denial of any characterization of the *ātman* or *brahman* in the U; pure apophatism.

NIRGUṆA BRAHMAN	Brahman without qualities, the unqualified, transcendent Absolute.
NIRṚTI	Dissolution, destruction, personified as a Goddess; the embodiment of evil and chaos.
NIRVĀṆA	Extinction, lit. "the blowing out [of the flame]," final extinction, consumption of all thinkable limitations, including time, space, and being. Liberation, the ultimate goal (mainly in Jainism and Buddhism).
NITYĀNITYA-VASTU-VIVEKA	"The discrimination between the real [eternal] and the unreal [temporal]" (Śaṅkara): philosophical term not found in the Veda—a condition for wisdom or realization (*jñāna*).
OM	The sacred syllable, consisting of the three letters A-U-M. It means also "yes," "so be it" (cf. *amen*). It is used at the beginning and end of any recitation of sacred texts and is supposed to have a mystical meaning.
PĀDA	Foot; one fourth of a stanza or *ṛk*.
PAÑCĀGNI-VIDYĀ	"The doctrine of the five fires," a teaching in the BU about the process of the cosmos, life, and death.
PĀṆḌAVAS	The five sons of Pāṇḍu who, in the MB, were fighting the war against the Kurus (or Kauravas). The BG was revealed by Kṛṣṇa to Arjuna, one of the brothers.
PĀPA	Evil, sin, wickedness, crime (cf. *puṇya* as its opposite).
PARAMAHAṀSA	Lit. "highest swan," i.e., supreme soul, a liberated person who enjoys complete freedom, a class of ascetics.
PARAMĀTMAN	The supreme *ātman*, God; the term used to distinguish the universal from the individual *ātman*.
PARAMA VYOMAN	"Highest heaven," ultimate realm of freedom; also the "place" where the mystery is hidden.
PARAMEṢṬHIN	The highest, the most exalted One, the sovereign: signifies both a cosmic principle and a personified God; used as an epithet of Prajāpati.
PARJANYA	God of rain and of the thunderstorm; bringer of fertility to the earth.
PARYAṄKAVIDYĀ	Lit. "science of the couch [of Brahman]," the eschatological teaching of the KausU about the Brahmaloka.
PATHASPATI	"Lord of the path," an epithet of Pūṣan.
PATI	Lord, master; applied to God and also to husbands.

PATIDEVA — The husband regarded as a God for his wife.

PAVAMĀNA — Epithet of Soma: "flowing clear, being purified, and purifying," thus holy and sanctifying.

PAVITRA — Originally "means of purification," filter; hence what is pure, purified, holy.

PIPPALĀDA — Great master in the Atharvanic tradition; teacher of the PrasnU.

PITṚ (PITARAḤ) — Father, the forefathers, ancestors. A special worship is performed for them (cf. *pitṛyajña, śrāddha*).

PITṚYĀNA — The way of the fathers; one of the two ways on which Men proceed after death (cf. *devayāna*). The deceased pass through the moon and reach the world of the forefathers, whence they have to return to the earth. This conception is first expounded in the U.

PRABHU — Lit. "being before," i.e., superior: the Lord, Master.

PRAJĀPATI — "The Lord of creatures," the primordial God, Father of the Gods and of all beings. His position is central in the B.

PRAJÑĀNA — N.: consciousness, wisdom, intelligence, understanding. One of the four *mahāvākyāni* says that Brahman is consciousness.

PRAKṚTI — F.: nature, primary matter; in Sāṁkhya one of the two fundamental principles of the universe (cf. *puruṣa*).

PRALAYA — Cosmic destruction or disintegration (occurring periodically).

PRAMOCANA — Liberating, setting free, derived from the root *muc-*, to release, liberate (cf. *mokṣa*).

PRĀṆA — The vital breath, life, the breath of life, the life-force holding the body together. In the U one of the three main constituents of the human being (cf. *vāc, manas*). It is divided into five kinds of breath (*prāṇa, apāna, vyāna, samāna, udāna*). The cosmic correspondent of *prāṇa* is Vāyu, air, wind.

PRĀṆĀGNIHOTRA — A spiritual practice of breath control, substituted for the *agnihotra*.

PRAṆAVA — Name of the sacred syllable *Om* or *oṁkāra*; from the verb *pra- ṇu-*, to sound.

PRASĀDA — Divine grace, benevolence, serenity (not Vedic).

PRAŚNA	Question, query, inquiry. One U is named thus because it consists of the disciples' questions and the *guru's* answers.
PRATIṢṬHĀ	F.: support, basis, foundation.
PRĀYAŚCITTA	Expiation or means of atonement for a mistake in ritual and for any committed sin.
PṚTHIVĪ	Earth; in the Veda generally mentioned together with *dyaus,* heaven. She is revered as the mother of living beings.
PŪJĀ	Worship, reverence, adoration. The concept is more related to the *bhakti* cult than to Vedic worship.
PUMĀN	M.: weak stem *puṁs:* Man, but mostly the male; also in the sense of hero. Cf. also *puruṣa.*
PUNAR-JANMA	Rebirth, transmigration (cf. *karman, saṁsāra*).
PUNAR-MṚTYU	Repeated death.
PUṆYA	Religious merit, reward of acts of worship, virtue (cf. its opposite, *pāpa*).
PURĀṆA	Ancient tale, story, myth; class of literature incorporating Hindu mythology.
PURANDHI	Personification of happiness and generosity.
PUROHITA	Lit. "placed ahead, set before" ("precedent"); priest appointed by a family or by a king for domestic worship.
PURUṢA	The Person, spirit, Man. Both the primordial Man of cosmic dimensions (RV) and also the "inner Man," the spiritual person in Man (U). In Sāṁkhya the spiritual principle of reality (cf. *prakṛti*).
PURUṢAMEDHA	"Human sacrifice." Man is considered to be the highest victim of the sacrifice, whether materialistically or metaphorically is not clear. The sacrifice of Man in both senses.
PURUṢĀRTHA	The aim or goal of human life. Indian tradition speaks of four such values: *kāma, artha, dharma, mokṣa,* but the ultimate aim is *mokṣa.*
PURUṢA-VIDYĀ	The personal knowledge, wisdom of the supreme Person, insight into the personal structure of reality.
PURUṢOTTAMA	"The highest, the best, of Men," also the supreme being; epithet applied to Viṣṇu and Kṛṣṇa.

PŪRVAPAKṢA	The opponent's view in the text of a philosophical discussion, always used dialectically with the *uttara-pakṣa* to establish the *siddhānta* the final or correct view.
PŪṢAN	Vedic deity closely related to the Sun, he is the divine herdsman, the protector and guide on the roads, the "nourisher" (related to the root *puṣ-*, to nourish). He guides the bride in marriage and leads the dead across to the "other shore" (cf. IsU). All his aspects are summarized in the idea that he is the God of Providence. He is often mentioned together with Indra, Soma, and Bhaga.
PUTRA	Son.
RĀHU	A demon who is said to swallow up the sun, respectively, the moon, at the time of eclipse; also one of the nine planets.
RĀJĀS	Atmosphere, dust, impurity; one of the qualities of nature.
RĀJASŪYA	Elaborate Vedic rite for the consecration of a king.
RĀMA	*Avatāra* of Viṣṇu and one of the most popular Hindu Gods, the model of righteousness. As son of Daśaratha and husband of Sītā he is the great hero of the Rāmāyaṇa.
RASA	Liquid, sap, essence, nourishing drink (applied to Soma); later, taste, savor, and aesthetic taste, the essence of the aesthetic experience.
RĀTRĪ	F.: the night; also personified as a Goddess.
RAUHIṆA	Name of a demon who was conquered by Indra.
RAYI	Wealth, treasure, riches, both spiritual and material.
RETAS	Semen, seed, also the embryo produced from it. Rain regarded as the fertilizing element is called the semen of heaven.
ṚK	One stanza (verse) of a Ṛg Vedic hymn; one Rg Vedic mantra.
ṚṆA	Debt, duty, obligation toward the Gods, ancestors, and fellow beings.
ROGA	Sickness, disease.
ROHITA	Lit. red, a name of the sun, a proper name, king Hariścandra's son, for instance.
ṚṢI	Seer, sage, wise Man; the poet-sages to whom the Veda was revealed (cf. also *kavi*). They are conceived

ceived of as a special class of beings, superior to Men and inferior to the Gods. There is a tradition that there were seven *ṛṣis*, probably the same as the seven priests with whom Manu performed the first sacrifice and the seven poets who are judges in the assembly. Their identification with names of ancient seers and with the stars of the Great Bear is of later origin (B).

ṚTA — Cosmic and sacred order, sacrifice as a universal law, also truth, the ultimate dynamic and harmonic structure of reality.

ṚTU — Fixed time (for worship), order, season of the year. Etymologically related to *ṛta*.

ṚTVIJ — He who sacrifices in due season (*ṛtu*); the officiating priest. The four main priests (*mahārtvij*) of the sacrifice are *brāhman, hotṛ, udgātṛ*, and *adhvaryu*.

RUDRA — Vedic God whose name is derived either from *rud-*, to cry, howl, or from *ruc-*, to shine. He is the terrible God of storms, father of the Rudras as a class of Gods, and of the Maruts. He is closely related to Indra and Agni. Later he becomes one of the manifestations of Śiva.

ŚABDA — Sound, word. One aspect of Brahman as the revealed, manifested one (cf. *śabda-brahman*).

ŚABDA-BRAHMAN — The Brahman-sound, the revealed aspect of Brahman.

SĀDHU — Straight, leading right to the goal, good, right. A good person, a renouncer, a monk, or an ascetic.

SĀDHYAS — A group of ancient Gods who are classified as minor deities, personified prayers; "those who are to be attained, propitiated."

SAGUṆA BRAHMAN — Brahman with qualities; in Vedānta the equivalent of *īśvara*, the Lord (cf. *nirguṇa*).

ŚAKTI — Power, energy; the female, active power of a God (usually Śiva), personified as a Goddess who assumes the creative function.

ŚĀLĀ — Hall (for the sacrifice), house, temple.

SAMĀDHI — State of deep concentration or absorption; the last of the yogic spiritual stages; also the tomb of a holy person.

SAMANVAYA — Harmony, unity, agreement, association.

ŚAMBARA — Name of a demon conquered by Indra.

SAṀDHYĀ	The meeting of the lights at morning (dawn), noon, and evening (dusk), which are sacred times for worship and meditation.
SAṀHĀRA	M.: lit. collection, accumulation; the destruction of the universe at the end of a cosmic period (*kalpa*).
SAṀHITĀ	That which is put together, collection, the first part of the Vedas. Cf. Note on Vedic Literature.
ŚAMĪ	A tree whose branches are used in different rituals.
SĀṀKHYA	Lit. "enumeration, numbering," i.e., of the philosophical principles. One of the six traditional philosophical schools (*darśanas*), the ontology underlying the Yoga system.
SAṀNYĀSA	Renunciation, the fourth stage of life spent as a wandering monk (from *sam- nyas-*, to put down together, to give up, to abandon).
SAṀNYĀSIN	Renouncer, wandering monk, and ascetic belonging to the fourth stage of life (*āśrama*).
SĀMPARĀYA	The passage from this world to the otherworld; relating to the otherworld.
SAMPLAVA	Flood, deluge.
SAMPRATTI (or SAMPRADĀNA)	Transmission, usually from father to son at the time of death. Tradition as the handing over, passing on, of knowledge and experience.
SAṀRĀJĀ	Sovereign, supreme monarch, ruler.
SAṀSĀRA	The phenomenal world, the cycle of temporal existences, state of bondage.
SAṀSKĀRA	"Sacrament," a rite marking the different important events in the life of Man (cf. *jātakarman, upanayana, vivāha,* etc.). Also karmic residues, psychic impressions left by previous lives and influencing to some extent a person's individual existence.
SANĀTANA DHARMA	The everlasting, eternal law, order, or religion; the self-understanding of the traditional religiousness in India.
ŚĀNTI	F.: peace, tranquillity, quiescence. Final mantra to many prayers and oblations.
ŚĀNTI-MANTRA	Invocation or introductory prayer of an U which is usually common to all the U of the same Veda. It is

recited at the beginning and usually at the end of an Upaniṣadic reading, though actually it does not belong to the text.

ŚARAD — Autumn.

SARAMĀ — Female dog, messenger of Indra.

SARASVATĪ — Name of a sacred river; later the Goddess of knowledge, learning, holy speech, and music.

ŚARĪRA — Body; the U speak of three or five "bodies" of the person: *annamaya* (the material body consisting of food), *prāṇamaya* (the body made of breath), *manomaya* (the mental layer), *vijñānamaya* (the body of consciousness), and *ānandamaya* (the inner, psychic layer consisting of bliss).

SARVAMEDHA — "All-sacrifice, universal offering," a *soma*-sacrifice lasting for ten days.

SARVEŚVARA — "The Lord of all."

ŚĀSTRA — Precept, command, instruction, rule, authoritative teaching; a body of authoritative texts, or any text containing religious injunctions (*śruti* or *smṛti*).

SAT — Being (present part. of *as*-, to be), existence, the real. Ultimately only Brahman is *sat* as the pure Being and Ground of all existence. In Vedānta one of the three "qualifications" of Brahman (cf. *cit, ānanda*).

SATĪ — The faithful wife, ideal of the wife who follows her husband even to death; hence the widow who is voluntarily burned with her dead husband in the last sacrament.

SATTVA — Essence, reality ("being-ness"); one of the three fundamental qualities of nature (*prakṛti*) in Sāṁkhya: goodness, purity (cf. also *rajas, tamas*).

SATYA — Truth, truthfulness, reality, "that which is," objectively and subjectively.

SAVITṚ — Lit. the vivifier, the impeller, the inspirer (from the root *su*-). Vedic divinity related to the sun as its impelling, stimulating force, sometimes identified with the sun. It is he who is invoked in the Gāyatrī mantra, hence also called Sāvitrī.

SĀVITRĪ — F., the Ṛg Vedic stanza related to Savitṛ; the Gāyatrī mantra (RV III, 62, 10).

ŚIŚIRA — The frosty season, the passage from winter (*hemanta*) to spring (*vasanta*).

ŚIṢYA — Disciple (cf. *guru*).

SĪTĀ — Lit. "the furrow." In the Rāmāyaṇa the daughter of King Janaka and wife of Rāma.

ŚIVA — As an adj., auspicious, gracious, kind, benevolent. The Auspicious One; in the Veda it is Rudra who, since the SU, is known as Śiva, one of the most important Gods of the Hindu tradition. He is the destroyer of the universe (cf. also Brahmā, Viṣṇu). Śiva is also the great yogi and model of ascetics. His consort is Pārvatī or Umā.

SKAMBHA — The cosmic pillar, understood to be the stable center of the universe (*axis mundi*) and its hidden support.

ŚLOKA — Stanza, verse, usually Anuṣṭubh (four times eight syllables), epic meter. Generally used for a stanza, but not for vedic mantras.

SMĀRTA — According to or following tradition (*smṛti*); cf. *śrauta*. A *smārta* follows not only the *śruti* (Veda) in his sacrificial and religious practices, but also the *smṛti*, which means that he also worships Gods of the later Hindu cults.

ŚMAŚĀNA — Cremation ground.

SMṚTI — Lit. remembrance, memory. Tradition; the scriptures coming after the *śruti*, such as epics (*itihāsa*), lawbooks (*dharma-śāstra*), etc., and having less authority than the *śruti* itself, on which they are based.

SNĀNA — Ritual bath for external and internal purification.

ŚOKA — Heat, burning, hence pain, affliction, sorrow, grief.

SOMA — The sacrificial plant from which the *soma*-juice is extracted with elaborated rituals, hence the sap or drink of immortality (*amṛta* is another name for Soma); a deity ("Soma the king"). Soma was used ritually to enter into a higher state of consciousness. Later it also came to signify the moon.

SOMYA — "The one who is worthy of Soma, the drinker of Soma"; also used as a form of address to respected persons, "dear one," "kind one," etc.

SPHOṬA — Lit. bursting and the sound created by it (from the root *sphuṭ*-). In grammar and philosophy of language the eternal, indivisible element of the word and its creative power, the carrier of meaning.

ŚRADDHĀ — F.: faith, the active confidence (in the Gods or in the rite itself) required in any act of worship. In RV (X, 151) *śraddhā* is invoked almost as a deity.

ŚRĀDDHA — Rite of homage to deceased relatives; offering to the ancestors which is generally performed by the son of the deceased and repeated on certain occasions. It consists of food oblations to the forefathers and a meal for relatives and priests.

ŚRAMAṆA — Monk, ascetic, renouncer; from the root *śram-*, to make an effort, to strive, to get exhausted. A term for "monk" in Jainism.

ŚRAUTA — According to, following, the *śruti*, i.e., the pure Vedic tradition, not mixed with later elements (cf. *smārta*). A *śrauta* sacrifice is performed in accordance with Vedic injunctions. The adjectival form is *śrautic*.

ŚRĪ — Splendor, brilliance, glory, beauty, prominence; used as a title for Gods, saints, and respected persons; the consort of Viṣṇu.

ŚRUTI — "That which is heard," the Vedic Revelation, the whole body of the Veda which was transmitted orally.

STOMA — Chant, song of praise, way of recitation of a *stotra*.

STOTRA — Hymn of praise, cantata, song, chant of a Ṛg Vedic text, the music of the SV. Later hymn of praise to the Gods.

ŚŪDRA — A member of the fourth caste whose lot is to serve the other three castes (*brahman, kṣatriya, vaiśya*). He is then usually a servant. According to the *puruṣa-sūkta*, he is born from the feet of the *puruṣa*.

SUKHA — Happiness, joy, bliss, pleasure (as opposed to *duḥkha*).

ŚUKLAPAKṢA — The bright half of the month, the fifteen days before the full moon.

SŪKTA — Lit. the "well-uttered," "beautiful, good word"; a song of praise, a Vedic hymn.

ŚUNAḤŚEPA — Son of Ajīgarta, said to be the poet of the hymns RV I, 24-30, and IX, 3. His famous story represents one of the myths of the human condition (cf. AB).

ŚŪNYA, ŚŪNYATĀ — Adj. and noun: Void, absolute emptiness as the ultimate reality in Buddhism (cf. *nirvāṇa*).

SŪRYA — M.: the sun, the sun-God.

SŪRYĀ — Daughter of Sūrya, the sun. The marriage of Sūryā with Soma is the exemplar of every human marriage.

SŪRYĀSTA — Sunset.

SŪRYODAYA — Sunrise.

SŪTRA — Lit. thread; an aphoristic text that usually cannot be understood without a commentary (*bhāṣya*). The Sūtra literature belongs to the *smṛti* and is meant for easy memorizing.

SVADHĀ — Sacrificial exclamation in the ancestor sacrifice; also the oblation to the forefathers, the benediction in the *śrāddha* ceremony.

SVĀHĀ — Sacrificial exclamation at the end of the recitation accompanying the offering of the oblation in the fire. It could be translated by "hail" or "amen."

SVAR — Light, realm of light, sky, heaven (cf. *svarga*); one of the three "utterances" (*vyāhṛti*) by which heaven was created (cf. *bhūḥ, bhuvaḥ*), repeated at the sacrifice.

SVARĀJ — Freedom, independence; lit. "self-ruling." A characteristic of the liberated person.

SVARGA — Lit. "leading to the light"; world of light, heaven, the highest of the three worlds (*triloka*), the dwelling of the Gods.

SVARGAKĀMA — The "desire for heaven" which, according to the Mīmāṁsā, is the main purpose in performing any rite or sacrifice.

SVASTI — "Well-being" in its most complete sense, embracing material welfare, physical health, and spiritual blessing or salvation.

ŚVETAKETU (or ĀRUṆEYA) — Son of Gautama, a famous disciple of Uddālaka in the CU to whom the highest teaching (*tattvamasi*) is imparted. Also called Āruṇeya.

TAD — Demonstrative pronoun: that. Contrary to *idam* (this), it refers to Brahman. When occurring alone, it points to the ultimate reality without naming it. *Tad ekam:* the One, that One.

TAMAS — The forces of darkness, the inertia of matter; in Sāṁkhya one of the three *guṇas* of *prakṛti* (cf. *sattva, rajas*).

TANTRA — Lit. texture, weaving, loom; religious system that is not based on the Veda, consisting of secret doctrines and practices which give access to hidden powers. Tantric tradition has permeated practically the entire spiritual tradition of Asia. The basic assumption of all Tantric practices is the interrelation of body and spirit, of matter and soul, *bhukti* (enjoyment) and *mukti* (liberation).

TAPAS — Lit. heat; hence inner energy, spiritual fervor or ardor; austerity, asceticism, penance. One of the forms of the primoridial energy, along with *kāma*.

TATTVA — Lit. "that-ness," i.e., essence, true nature, reality; philosophical principle.

TAT TVAM ASI — "That you are": one of the four great utterances (*mahāvākyāni*) of the U which was taught to Śvetaketu.

TEJAS — Heat, light, brightness, splendor, energy.

TRETĀ — The side of the die with three dots. The second of the four ages (*yuga*).

TRILOKA — The "three-world," totality of the universe, consisting of three realms: earth, atmosphere, and heaven, or earth, heaven, and the regions below (later hell); the inhabitants of the three worlds are Gods, Men, and demons.

TRIṢṬUBH — Common Vedic meter consisting of four feet (*pada*) of eleven syllables each.

TRITA — Ancient, pre-Vedic deity, conqueror of demons and connected with water; he was probably replaced by Indra who took over his functions.

TVAM — Personal pronoun, second person sg.: you.

TVAṢṬṚ — Creator God, divine artisan, and bestower of forms, also connected with fertility.

TYĀGIN — One who abandons all possessions and attachments, renouncer, ascetic. Cf. also *saṁnyāsin, yati, keśin, śramaṇa, sādhu, muni.*

UDGĀTṚ — The singer, one of the four main celebrants of the sacrifice, who is in charge of chanting the *sāman* (SV).

UDGĪTHA — An important part of the *sāman* chant.

UPADEŚA — Spiritual instruction or direction, precept, given by the *guru*.

UPANAYANA — from *upa- nī*, to lead near; *saṁskāra*, ceremony of initiation and investing the sacred thread, rite of introduction to the *guru*. Only boys of the three higher castes receive it. Initiation corresponds to a second birth, hence they are called "twice-born" (*dvija*).

UPASADA — A preliminary rite connected with the Soma-sacrifice, it consists of an offering of milk and ghee and is performed morning and evening (after the *dīkṣā*).

UṢAS — The Goddess Dawn, invoked in the most poetic hymns of the RV. Later she loses importance.

UTTAMA PURUṢA — The supreme Person (cf. *puruṣa, puruṣottama*).

UTTARĀYANA — The northern way of the sun, the six months during which the sun moves northward (cf. *dakṣiṇāyana*).

VĀC — Word; the sacred, primeval, and creative Word; sound; also speech, language, the organ of speech, voice. Sometimes the RV only, sometimes the whole Veda, is referred to as *vāc*.

VĀGVISARGA — From *vāc*, word, and *visarga*, sending forth, emission, creation (from *vi-sṛj*). The emitting of the word, the breaking of silence.

VAIRĀGYA — "Dispassion," indifference, renunciation; one of the requirements of the spiritual path.

VAIŚVĀNARA — An epithet of Agni meaning "he who belongs to all Men"; refers also to the fire of digestion.

VAISVADEVA — "Belonging to All-Gods," name of a sacrifice directed toward the Viśvedevas.

VAIŚYA — A member of the third caste, a peasant-merchant. The *vaiśya* is related to the soil; agriculture and trade are his professions. Cf. also *brāhmana, ksatriya, śūdra*.

VAJRA — The mythical weapon of Indra, the thunderbolt, lightning.

VĀKYA — Sentence; cf. *mahāvākya*.

VALA — "That which covers or closes," enclosure, cave. Name of a demon who obstructs the cows (the waters) and who is conquered by Indra or Bṛhaspati.

VĀMADEVA — A Ṛg Vedic seer, poet of the hymns of Book IV.

VĀNAPRASTHA — Forest dweller, hermit; the third stage of life or *āśrama* when the householder retires into solitude after having performed his worldly duties with or without his wife.

VANASPATI	"Lord of the wood," forest tree; also the sacrificial post.
VARCAS	Brilliance, energy, power to illuminate, luster, in the cosmos as well as in Man.
VARṆA	Lit. color, dye; hence, from the color of the skin: race, caste, class of people (in the Veda these were originally only two: the Aryans of fair complexion and the dark *dāsas*). Later applied to the four castes or subdivisions of society (*brāhmāṇa, kṣatriya, vaiśya, śūdra*).
VARṢA	Rain; the rainy season, monsoon; hence also year.
VARUṆA	One of the greatest Gods in the Veda, he is king, ruler, and surveyor of the moral conduct of Men. He is the Lord of *ṛta*, cosmic and moral order. He is frequently invoked together with Mitra. His close relationship with the waters makes him later on only a water God, the Lord of the ocean.
VASANTA	Spring.
VASIṢṬHA	Lit. the brightest, most excellent. Name of a famous Vedic *ṛṣi*, author of Book VII of the RV. According to later tradition he belongs to the group of the seven *ṛṣis*.
VASU	Lit. good, beneficent. Name of a class of Vedic Gods whose leader is Indra, usually eight in number.
VĀTA	Wind, air, personified as a God; sometimes identical with Vāyu.
VĀYU	Wind, air, personified as a God in the Veda (cf. Vāta, Marut); also the wind in the body (cf. *prāṇa*).
VEDA	Lit. knowledge (from the root *vid-*, to know); the sacred knowledge incorporated in the Veda as the whole body of "Sacred Scriptures" (although originally transmitted only orally). In the narrow sense "Veda" refers only to the Saṁhitās (RV, YV, SV, AV); in the broader sense B, A, and U are included. In the plural it refers to the four Vedas.
VEDĀNTA	Lit. "end of the Veda," i.e., the U as the culmination of Vedic wisdom. In the sense of Uttaramīmāṁsā or Vedāntavāda, one system of Indian philosophy (advaita Vedānta, dvaita Vedānta etc.) based on the U and teaching a spiritual interpretation of the Vedas.
VEDI	The proper ground for the sacrifice, altar, the sacrificial bed strewn with sacred grass between the

three fires; as *mahāvedi* the elevated altar made of earth as seat of the fire.

VENA — The Seer, the vigilant one, also the longing or loving one (from *ven-*, to see, to be attentive, to long for); sometimes called a *ṛṣi*, he is a mysterious being who has the ultimate vision of things (cf. AV II, 1); sometimes identified with the sun in the middle region. He seems to be between a sage and a God, the prototype of a seer.

VIDYĀ — Knowledge, wisdom, also branch of knowledge; a section of an Upaniṣadic text.

VIJIJÑĀSA — Desiderative form of the root *jña-*, to know: the desire to know, the longing for wisdom, which is the necessary condition for attaining *jñāna*, wisdom.

VIMUKTA — "Totally liberated," from the same root *muc-*, to liberate, set free, release, as *mokṣa* and *mukti*.

VIRĀJ — Lit. ruling widely, sovereign, excellent; an all-penetrating power (cf. *śakti*), sometimes considered as masculine, sometimes feminine, from which the *puruṣa* was born. As a feminine cosmogonic principle, closely related to *vāc*, the Word. Also the name of a Vedic meter (with *pādas* of ten syllables each).

VIROCANA — Name of an *asura* (father of Bali); also the sun.

VIṢṆU — Important God in Hinduism, already occurring in the Veda; his name means something like "the all-penetrating." He is known for the three wide steps with which he measures out the three worlds. He is related to the sun. Later he becomes the second of the *trimūrti*, the preserver, and he is mainly worshiped in his *avatāras* (cf. Kṛṣṇa, Rāma).

VIŚVAKARMAN — "The all-maker," the divine architect of the universe.

VIŚVĀMITRA — Name of a *ṛṣi* ("the friend of all") to whom most hymns of Book III of the RV are attributed; also the family of the *ṛṣi*.

VIŚVĀVASU — Lit. "possessing all goodness"; name of a Gandharva.

VIŚVEDEVĀḤ — All the Gods, or the All-Gods as a class of celestial beings.

VIVĀHA — Lit. the "leading away" of the bride from her father's house to her new home; marriage, wedding ceremony; one of the *saṁskāras* or sacraments of the Indian tradition.

VIVASVAT — A solar deity, father of Yama.

VRATA — Resolve, vow, divine ordinance or divine will, religious observance.

VRATYA — An old, probably Iranian, institution of communities with special *vrata,* vow. A man belonging to a particular *vrāta,* group, which has made that particular vow.

VṚTRA — Etymologically the name means "obstruction" or "resistance," and in the pl. also "enemies," "adverse powers." Name of a demon who retained the waters and who was slain by Indra in a famous exploit. (Indra is therefore called *vṛtrahan.*) Vṛtra is also called *ahi,* serpent, dragon (cf. *vala*).

VYĀNA — The diffused breath, one of the five breaths in the body (cf. *prāṇa*).

VYĀVAHĀRIKA — "Relating to worldly matters, to common life," i.e., the worldly way of viewing reality, the practical perspective; in Vedānta opposed to *pāramārthika,* the ultimate (and only valid) perspective.

VYOMAN — Heaven, atmosphere, aerial space. Cf. *parama vyoman.*

YAJÑA — Sacrifice, worship, praise (from the root *yaj-,* to offer). Central concept and practice in the Veda. Its three elements are the sacrificial substance (*dravya*), the divinity to whom it is addressed (*devatā*), and the act of abandoning or renouncing (*tyāga*). The persons involved are the sacrificer (*yajamāna*) and his wife and the four main priests (*ṛtvij*).

YĀJÑAVALKYA — Great Upaniṣadic sage (cf. BU).

YAJUS — Sacrificial formula, mantra of the YV which is the collection of sacrificial utterances.

YAMA — The "twin" of Yamī, the first man and the first to pass through death and to reach immortality, hence the forerunner for Men on the path of death and the ruler in the realm of the dead. Later he becomes the personification of Death and Lord of the infernal regions.

YAMĪ — Twin sister of Yama with whom she forms the first pair of humans on earth. Although she tempts her brother to commit incest with her, he does not yield to her temptation, according to some texts.

YAŚAS — N.: glory, splendor, grace, salvation, well-being, bestowed by the Gods on human beings.

YATI — Renouncer, ascetic.

YOGA — From the root *yuj-*, to yoke, to join, to unite, to prepare, to fix, to concentrate: union; method of physical, mental, and spiritual unification, concentration, and contemplation, using among other means bodily postures (*āsana*), breath control (*prāṇāyāma*), and spiritual techniques. Yoga appears to be a very ancient Indian practice which was developed into a system by Patañjali (YS) and made to correspond with the Sāṁkhya system of philosophy. Yoga as a method has become a basic factor in practically all religions of Indian origin.

YOGIN — The ascetic, the man of self-control, follower of the path of Yoga.

YONI — Female organ of generation, womb, hence also dwelling place, resting place; also the support or inner part of anything.

YUGA — Generation, one of the four cosmic ages that are repeated in the same order: Kṛta (or Satya), the golden age, Tretā, Dvāpara, and Kali (the present, degenerated age). They represent a gradual decay in human life and morals.

YUKTA — "Integrated," "joined," "united," from the root *yuj-*, to yoke, unite, etc.; *yoga* is also derived from this root.

YŪPA — The sacrificial post or pole to which the victim was bound.

ॐ

TABLE OF QUOTED SCRIPTURES

Note: This table gives titles of quoted literature in the order they appear in the Index of Texts and References (the Upaniṣads in the Anthology follow a conjectural chronological order). The square brackets of the Saṁhitās refer to the different sakhas (branches), versions, or recensions of the same texts. The parentheses indicate synonymous titles. The few other Vedic texts that do not appear in this Anthology do not figure in the table.

	Vedas				Kalpa Sūtras			Other Texts
	Saṁhitā	Brāhmaṇa	Āraṇyaka	Upaniṣad	Śrauta Sūtra	Gṛhya Sūtra	Dharma Sūtra	
Ṛg Veda	Ṛg Veda [Śakala] [Bāskala]	Aitareya Kausītaki (Śāṅkhāyana)	Aitareya	Aitareya Kauṣītalo (Kauṣītaki Brāhmaṇa)		Āśvalāyana Śāṅkhāyana		Ṛg Veda Prātiśākhya
Atharva Veda	Atharva Veda [Śaunaka] [Paippilāda]	Gopatha		Muṇḍaka Praśna Māṇḍūkya Kaivalya		Kauśika Sūtra		Bhagavad Gītā Brahma Sūtra Yoga Sūtra
Sāma Veda	Sāma Veda [*Kauthama*] [*Rāṇayanīya*] [*Jaiminīya*]	Jaiminīya Taṇḍya Mahā (Pañcaviṁsa)	Jaiminīya Upaniṣad Brāhmaṇa (Talavakāra)	Chāndogya Kena (Talavakāra)			Gautama Vasiṣṭha	Mīmāṁsa Sūtra Nirukta Māṇḍūkya Kārika Bṛhad Devāta Mahābhārata
Yajur Veda: Kṛṣṇa YV (black)	Taittirīya (Apastambīya) Maitrāyani	Taittirīya	Taittirīya	Taittirīya Kaṭha Śvetāśvatara Mahānārāyana Maitrī Prāṇāgnihotra	Āpastambīya Sāṅkhāyana	Baudhāyana Hiraṇyakeśi	Manu Smṛti Baudhāyana	Bhagavata Purāṇa Bṛhadāraṇyaka Upaniṣad Bhāṣya
Yajur Veda: Śukla YV (white)	Vājasaneyi [*Kāṇva*] [*Mādhyamdina*]	Śatapatha		Bṛhadāraṇyaka Īśa Jābāla Paiṅgala Sūrya		Pāraskara		Brahma Sūtra Bhaṣya Saṁyutta-nikāya

INDEXES

INDEX OF TEXTS AND REFERENCES

Boldface type indicates a fully translated text. Roman type preceded by an asterisk indicates that some nonsubstantial parts of the text have been omitted. For typographical and aesthetical reasons no other sign has been given in the book, so that the Index is often the only way to detect whether there are untranslated portions under the same rubric.

Italic type indicates texts only referred to in the Anthology. Cross-references of and to translated texts, some minor references, as well as recurrent and parallel passages, have been omitted. The index facilitates a continuous reading of texts.

Ṛg Veda

I

Atharva Veda

Aitareya Āraṇyaka

Jaiminīya Upaniṣad Brāhmaṇa

Taittirīya Araṇyaka

Aitareya Upaniṣad

GENERAL INDEX

The Vedic Experience resists being split into artificially (alphabetically) disconnected words. The value of this index may lie in giving a global vision (like the Vedadīpa given at the beginning of the book) of the main concerns of the *śruti*. For this reason the index refers to the translated texts only and not to the Introductions and is limited to the English vocabulary in a nonexhaustive way.

Bold type indicates that a chapter, subsection, or section deals with the subject.

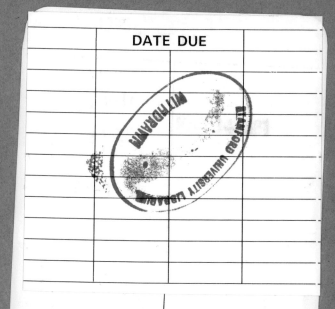